AF608033

# The Warsaw Ghetto
## Oyneg Shabes–Ringelblum Archive

This book was made possible by a gift
from Esther Cohen of Encino, California,
in dedication to her grandchildren, and
in the cause of remembrance.

# The Warsaw Ghetto
## Oyneg Shabes–Ringelblum Archive
### Catalog and Guide


Edited by
Robert Moses Shapiro and Tadeusz Epsztein

Translated by Robert Moses Shapiro

Introduction by Samuel D. Kassow



*Published in association with the*

United States Holocaust Memorial Museum,
Washington, D.C.

*and the*

Jewish Historical Institute,
Warsaw, Poland

Indiana University Press
Bloomington and Indianapolis

This book is a publication of

Indiana University Press
601 North Morton Street
Bloomington, IN 47404-3797 USA

www.iupress.indiana.edu

*Telephone orders* 800-842-6796
*Fax orders* 812-855-7931
*Orders by e-mail* iuporder@indiana.edu



In 2009, the Jewish Historical Institute, Warsaw, was renamed the Emanuel Ringelblum Jewish Historical Institute. To ensure timely publication, the previous name has been used throughout this book.



The paper used in this publication meets the minimum requirements of American National Standard for Information Sciences—Permanence of Paper for Printed Library Materials, ANSI Z39.48-1984.

Manufactured in the United States of America

Library of Congress Cataloging-in-Publication Data

Ringelblum-Archiv.
The Warsaw ghetto Oyneg Shabes–Ringelblum Archive : catalog and guide / edited by Robert Moses Shapiro and Tadeusz Epsztein ; translated by Robert Moses Shapiro ; introduction by Samuel D. Kassow. — English-language ed.
p. cm.
Includes bibliographical references and index.
ISBN 978-0-253-35327-6 (cloth : alk. paper) 1. Ringelblum-Archiv—Catalogs. 2. Oyneg Shabes (Group)—Catalogs. 3. Jews—Persecutions—Poland—Warsaw—Sources. 4. Holocaust, Jewish (1939–1945)—Poland—Warsaw—Sources. 5. World War, 1939–1945—Jews—Poland—Sources. 6. Warsaw (Poland)—Ethnic relations—History—20th century—Sources. I. Shapiro, Robert Moses. II. Epsztein, Tadeusz. III. Title.
DS134.64.R56 2009
025.06'94053185384l—dc22
2009013962

1 2 3 4 5 14 13 12 11 10 09

The assertions, arguments, and conclusions contained herein are those of the volume editors or other contributors. They do not necessarily reflect the opinions of the United States Holocaust Memorial Museum.

Dedicated to the men and women of the Oyneg Shabes and all who persevere in preserving and understanding the Jewish past and the Jewish present as foundations for the Jewish future

I want my little daughter to be remembered. Margalit is 20 months old today. She has fully mastered the Yiddish language and speaks it perfectly. At nine months she began to speak Yiddish clearly. In intelligence she equals children of 3 or 4 years. I don't boast. People who witness it and tell me so are the staff teaching at the school at 68 Nowolipki Street. . . . I don't lament my own life or that of my wife. I pity only this little nice and talented girl. She too deserves to be remembered.

— Izrael Lichtensztajn, July 31, 1942, 11th day of the Great Deportation from the Warsaw Ghetto

What we were unable to cry and shriek out to the world we buried in the ground. . . . I would love to see the moment in which the great treasure will be dug up and scream the truth at the world. So the world may know all. So the ones who did not live through it may be glad, and we may feel like veterans with medals on our chest. We would be the fathers, the teachers and educators of the future. . . . But no, we shall certainly not live to see it, and therefore I write my last will. May the treasure fall into good hands, may it last into better times, may it alarm and alert the world to what happened . . . in the twentieth century. . . . We may now die in peace. We fulfilled our mission. May history attest for us.

—Dawid Graber, age 19, 2 August 1942, Warsaw Ghetto

. . . I don't know what's going to happen to me.
*Remember, my name is Nachum Grzywacz.*

—Nachum Grzywacz, age 18, 30 July 1942, Warsaw Ghetto

# Contents

# Foreword

Beneath the ruins of a Jewish school at 68 Nowolipki Street in what had been the Warsaw Ghetto, ten metal boxes containing clandestine Warsaw Ghetto documents, underground press, photographs, memoirs, and letters lay buried from August 1942 until September 1946. The successful effort to recover this buried treasure owed much to Hersz Wasser, the former secretary and one of the few survivors of Oyneg Shabes, a team of Jewish scholars, intellectuals, and other activists, led by Dr. Emanuel Ringelblum, who set out to preserve a record of Jewish life in the Warsaw Ghetto during the Holocaust. A second part of what has come to be known as the Ringelblum Archive, imperfectly preserved in two milk cans, was unearthed in December 1950. A third portion never has been recovered despite repeated attempts to locate it.

Ringelblum, a Jewish historian of particular perception who came of age during the decades between the two world wars, realized that the German invasion of Poland represented an ominous new departure in Nazi policy toward Jews. In a singular act of resistance, he determined to document and analyze the occupiers' design and the responses of the Jews who were their targets. The materials that Oyneg Shabes assembled depicted developments throughout occupied Poland, with special focus, of course, on the situation in the Warsaw Ghetto, where they were all confined.

The members of Oyneg Shabes secured and hid away their precious documentation when they realized that the Germans intended to murder the Jews of Warsaw and that the ghetto would soon be liquidated. They wanted to ensure that the world would learn of the fate of Poland's Jews, to pass on the stories of the people who had lived and died in the ghetto, or had been transported to their deaths from the infamous *Umschlagplatz*. A note from nineteen-year-old Dawid Graber, who helped bury the materials, was included in the archive: "What we were unable to cry and shriek out to the world we buried in the ground. . . . I would love to see the moment in which the great treasure will be dug up. . . ."

More than half a century later, in 1999, UNESCO placed the Oyneg Shabes Archive on its "Memory of the World" Register of uniquely valuable archival collections—collections of powerful educational potential that enable mankind better to understand the human condition. The archive has unique memorial and educational significance. The diversity and volume of the documentation, its unquestionable authenticity, the courage of those who assembled it, the very survival of the collection, and the powerful reminder it provides that systematic annihilation was to be the fate not only of Poland's Jews but of the entirety of European and world Jewry as well—all speak to the Ringelblum Archive's lasting importance.

Recognizing that the full potential of the archive could never be achieved in the absence of a systematic descriptive catalog of its contents, the Jewish Historical Institute (JHI) and the United States Holocaust Memorial Museum (USHMM) joined forces to prepare and publish the present work. The project was more complex than originally contemplated. Its completion was made possible only through the extraordinary generosity and remarkable patience and understanding of Mrs. Esther Cohen of Encino, California, to whom both JHI and the USHMM owe special thanks. Through her support of this project, Mrs. Cohen wanted to make a special gift to her grandchildren. In fact she has made a very special contribution to the cause of Holocaust research and remembrance and provided a gift to the children and grandchildren of all people of goodwill in this and future generations.

There are more than 35,000 pages of documentation in the archive and, despite the passage of several decades, many of them had never been adequately described or analyzed. The materials were partially organized in the mid-1950s, with an attempt to group related documents, but it was not possible in the partially handwritten, partially typed inventory created at that time to develop an organizational framework that might reflect the plan or intent of Emanuel Ringelblum and his Oyneg Shabes colleagues. Research done in the intervening five decades, mainly at JHI, the development of close and highly productive working relationships between the archival and research staffs of the USHMM and JHI, and the availability of modern computer technology provided essential foundation stones for this new catalog. Every stage of the preparation of the catalog required careful consideration to ensure respect for the history of the archive and at the same time to make certain that researchers and others interested in using the archive could evaluate the importance of its documentation for their particular projects and locate the materials of interest easily and efficiently. While the project proceeded, the Jewish Historical Institute and the USHMM completed work on the conservation of the original documents, which are in the JHI Archive. Work also was completed, first on microfilm, and then on digital copies of all of the documents in the collection, which now can be consulted in the Archives of the USHMM as well as in Warsaw.

The result of several years of effort, *The Warsaw Ghetto Oyneg Shabes–Ringelblum Archive: Catalog and Guide* presents for the first time a comprehensive description of the contents of the Oyneg Shabes Archive, reorganized in logical fashion, category by category, and document by document. Special appreciation is due to the many individuals who dedicated their intellectual energy, historical knowledge, and archival and linguistic expertise to this achievement. By enhancing access to this unique archival treasure, they have given voice to the internees of the Warsaw Ghetto and, through them, to all of the victims of the Nazis, making it easier to understand the details of their daily lives, struggles, and sufferings. Life continued amid terrible conditions of hunger, abuse, and disease, and despite the constant fear of violence, deportation, and death.

*The Warsaw Ghetto Oyneg Shabes–Ringelblum Archive: Catalog and Guide* will enrich our knowledge of a crucial time and place in the history of the Holocaust. It is dedicated to the memory of the people who suffered the worst there yet still managed to pass on the precious legacy of this documentation to our own and all future generations.

PAUL A. SHAPIRO
DIRECTOR
CENTER FOR ADVANCED HOLOCAUST STUDIES

ELEONORA BERGMAN
DIRECTOR
JEWISH HISTORICAL INSTITUTE, WARSAW

FELIKS TYCH
DIRECTOR EMERITUS
JEWISH HISTORICAL INSTITUTE, WARSAWV

# Translator's Preface

## Robert Moses Shapiro

This English translation of the Polish catalog of the Ringelblum Archive at the Jewish Historical Institute in Warsaw is intended to facilitate research by scholars who are not fluent in Polish. The original Polish sequence of data in each catalog entry has been retained, although corrections in descriptions have been made where appropriate.

The various documents of the Ringelblum Archive are mainly in Yiddish, Polish, German, and Hebrew, and occasionally in Russian, French, Italian, English, Romanian, and Ukrainian. The present translation is based on the manuscript of the new Polish catalog that was completed by a team of scholars under the leadership of Dr. Tadeusz Epsztein in 2003, with corrections and additions to the Polish text provided by Professor Epsztein in 2007 and 2008. The English translation has been prepared by Robert Moses Shapiro of the Judaic Studies Department at Brooklyn College of the City University of New York. Valuable early assistance was provided by Rochelle Uffman and USHMM archivist Aleksandra Borecka, who prepared a draft translation of Dr. Epsztein's essay on the "Structure and Organization of the Ringelblum Archive and Its Catalog."

The present translation has been edited in collaboration with Dr. Epsztein and with the very substantial assistance of Dr. Claire Rosenson, Assistant Editor of Academic Publications, as well as of Aleksandra Borecka, Teresa Pollin, and Alina Skibińska of the USHMM. Gary Floam of Baltimore contributed valuable assistance in dealing with several computer programming problems connected with editing a very large and complex manuscript.

Spelling of personal and place names is a complicated problem when dealing with sources created by Polish Jews who were fluent in and used a variety of languages. While an attempt has been made to be consistent in spelling, the goal has been to preserve the utility and accuracy of the catalog as a tool for English-reading scholars. Thus, transcriptions of Yiddish have been adapted to the standard YIVO system. Yet, there is the conundrum of how to spell the names of the man who concealed the Oyneg Shabes Archive: Izrael Lichtensztajn, Israel Lichtenstein, Yisroel Likhtnshtayn, reflecting Polish, English, and Yiddish usage. Anyone using this catalog must be aware of the potentials for transcription of names and places. It is hoped that a general electronic index will be compiled that includes cross-references between conventional English spellings and transcriptions and their Polish equivalents.

The existing indexes to names and geographic locations reflect the Polish spelling used by the Jewish Historical Institute team headed by Tadeusz Epsztein, although alternate Yiddish or German spellings may have been used in the original documents. An attempt has been made to include different conventional English spellings of some names (e.g., Vladimir Jabotinsky in addition to Włodzimierz Żabotyński). Dates are indicated in the European fashion: e.g., 02.01.03 for 2 January 1903.

It should be noted that the word *transcript* is here used to designate a copy made from an original document. *Transcript* is used to translate the Polish *odpis*, normally rendered "copy," in order to avoid confusion with translation of the Polish *egzemplarz* that also means copy, as in "multiple copies of a transcript."

I want to thank Benton Arnovitz, Director of Academic Publications, and Paul Shapiro, Director of the Center for Advanced Holocaust Studies at the United States Holocaust Memorial Museum, for entrusting me with the task of helping to make the treasures of the Oyneg Shabes–Ringelblum Archive of the Warsaw Ghetto more accessible to present and future generations.

Work on the present translation commenced in July 2004 and went through six drafts by March 2007. Copyediting of the book coincided with the year of mourning for my late father, Sender ben Moyshe ve-Blime Szpira, who died on 20 January 2008. Born in Sosnowiec, Poland, on Purim 1923, he completed elementary school and helped his family by working as a cap maker. During the German occupation, he continued to work and was forced into the local ghetto at Środula, from which he was deported to Auschwitz and its satellite forced labor camp, Blechhammer. During the death march of prisoners in January–February 1945, he escaped and was eventually liberated by Soviet troops. Upon witnessing the murder of an acquaintance in Katowice, Poland, he fled to Munich, Germany, where I was born. My father's Yiddish, Polish, and German, and his experiences contributed materially to the completion of this book.

# Introduction

Samuel D. Kassow[1]

Just six days before the Gestapo discovered his crowded underground hideout in Warsaw, Emanuel Ringelblum wrote a coded letter in early March 1944 to his longtime friend and party comrade, Adolph Berman. Perhaps he had a premonition. What if the Germans catch us, he asked in the letter, and what if none of us survive the war? What will happen to our underground archive, the Oyneg Shabes?[2] He had good reason to worry. By the time Warsaw was liberated, of the dozens of people who worked with him in the archive only three would survive—Hersh Wasser, Wasser's wife Bluma, and Rachel Auerbach. Wasser, who would help lead the search for the archive after the war, survived by the slimmest of margins. Once he jumped from a train going to Treblinka. A year later, in 1944, his bunker was surrounded by SS and most of his comrades were killed.

After the war Wasser helped organize what can only be called an archeological expedition to dig underneath the ruins of the ghetto. He knew that the archive had been buried under the former Borochov school at 68 Nowolipki Street. But nothing was left, neither of the Jews nor the ghetto, just acres of rubble. Taking bearings from the spires of a church, surveyors and engineers guided searchers toward the spot and on 18 September 1946 a team from the Jewish Historical Institute found the first cache of the archive—thousands of documents packed in ten tin boxes. The Wassers and Auerbach were both elated and frustrated. The tin boxes had not been hermetically sealed and water had seeped in and destroyed many of the documents and photographs. They were also certain that the ten tin boxes were only a fraction of the archive. Digging continued, but the searchers found nothing else. But in December 1950, Polish construction workers in the same area stumbled upon a second cache buried in two milk cans. These documents, which covered the period from August 1942 to late January 1943, were in much better condition. There was yet a third cache, with important materials on the Jewish fighting organization, hidden under 34 Świętojerska, the present site of the Chinese embassy in Warsaw. But that was never found. All in all, about 25,000 documents have surfaced. Perhaps as many were lost. Still, the Oyneg Shabes had better luck saving documents than in saving its own people.

The Oyneg Shabes did not appear in a vacuum; it was a direct outgrowth of one of the important movements in prewar East European Jewish cultural history—*zamling*, the collection of documents with the aim of fixing the writing and reading of history as a new pillar of Jewish consciousness.

About fifty years separated a beginning and an end. In 1891 the Jewish historian Simon Dubnow issued his famous appeal to East European Jews to collect documents and study their history. In 1940 Emanuel Ringelblum and a group of associates in the Warsaw Ghetto organized the Oyneg Shabes Archive to document the ordeal of Polish Jewry under the Nazi occupation. During the half-century that separated the Dubnow appeal from the Oyneg Shabes, East European Jewish historians—with no support from governments, state archives, or universities—turned the collection of sources and documents into a mass movement and the writing of history into a national mission for the Jewish people.

The simple translation of the Yiddish word *zaml* is "to collect." But over time, in Eastern Europe *zamling* acquired a new meaning: a common effort to create archives, save documents, and serve notice that Jews would not only make their own history but also write it. *Zamlers* collected not only community records and chronicles but also folklore, proverbs, jokes—the oral traditions of the common people. The task brought together scholars and ordinary Jews. It signaled a new respect for the Jewish masses, their way of life, their past, and their once-despised language, Yiddish. Historians and scholars would no longer study only the Jewish "Sabbath": rabbis, elites, religious scholarship. In the words of the Polish Jewish historian Isaac Schiper, they would also turn their attention to the "weekday"—the world of work, the culture of the common people and economic history.

Dubnow, who had compared the state of East European Jewish history to an uncharted continent, tasked future Jewish historians to pursue two goals that were not necessarily congruent. The first was to write the objective history of the Jewish people. The second was to use history to craft a modern, secular Jewish identity and bolster national self-confidence. Historians would seek the truth—and at the same time they would teach and console their people. This creative tension between objective scholarship and scholarship as a national mission would characterize Jewish historical research in Eastern Europe—and imbue the Oyneg Shabes with its fervent determination to prove that truth and justice were ultimately two sides of the same coin.

Other Jewish intellectuals picked up Dubnow's message and began to zaml. In 1912 Shloyme Zanvil Rappoport (better known as S. Ansky) organized an ethnographic expedition through Ukraine that became a landmark expression of the

1. For elaboration of the points in this essay, see Samuel D. Kassow, *Who Will Write Our History? Emanuel Ringelblum, the Warsaw Ghetto, and the Oyneg Shabes Archive* (Bloomington and Indianapolis: Indiana University Press, 2007).

2. Oyneg Shabes was the code name for the secret archive. Oyneg Shabes, or the Pleasure of the Sabbath, was used because the staff of the archive would meet on Saturday afternoons.

Jewish intelligentsia's new interest in folk culture. In 1915 the important Yiddish writer Yitzhak Leibush Peretz called on Jews in war-ravaged Eastern Europe to gather documents and write their own history. If they did not, their enemies certainly would. A people that did not write its own history, Peretz warned, could not help itself, protect itself, or convince outsiders that it merited respect and self-determination. After the Ukrainian pogroms of 1918–1921 another Jewish historian, Eliyahu Cherikover, organized a large archive to document the Jewish losses—and to call for justice. Cherikover's documents helped defend Shalom Schwartzbard, who assassinated Ukrainian leader Simon Petlyura in 1926.

The founding of the YIVO (Yiddish Scientific Institute–Yidisher Visnshaftlekher Institut) in Vilna in 1925 was a milestone in the cultural history of East European Jewry. Dedicated to interdisciplinary study of the Jewish people and to research in Yiddish, YIVO brought together a diverse group of scholars who did not let political differences interfere with their shared dedication to zamling and to engaged scholarship. Eliyahu Cherikover assumed the leadership of YIVO's historical section, and Simon Dubnow served on its board. One of the first letters Cherikover received in 1925 was from an eager young history student in Warsaw, Emanuel Ringelblum. Ringelblum, not yet twenty-five, asked to become a member of YIVO and pledged to help the fledgling organization in any way he could. He became one of its most important scholars.

The roots of the Oyneg Shabes were embedded in many of the same cultural processes that were transforming interwar Polish Jewry. Emanuel Ringelblum was deeply involved in three major spheres of Polish Jewish life: historical scholarship, mutual aid, and radical politics. By the 1930s he was the de facto leader of YIVO's history section in Poland. He worked for the Joint Distribution Committee as the editor of its monthly journal *Folkshilf* and as the organizer of the heroic relief effort to help Polish Jews expelled from Germany in 1938. For his whole adult life, he was also a dedicated member of the radical Left Poalei Tsiyon (Left Labor Zionists) and helped lead its major cultural and educational arm, the Ovnt kursn far arbeter (Evening Courses for Workers). This interplay of history, politics and self-help is essential to understanding Ringelblum's development and the genesis of the Oyneg Shabes.

Like most important Jewish historians in interwar Poland, Ringelblum was a native of Galicia, born in Buczacz in 1900 and related on his mother's side to then twelve-year-old Shmuel Agnon who in another sixty-six years would win the Nobel Prize for Literature. The Russian invasion of Galicia in 1914 forced Ringelblum and his family to flee to Sanz (Nowy Sącz) in West Galicia. The years in Sanz—between 1914 and 1919—turned out to be a formative intellectual experience. Saul Amsterdam, who later became a prominent leader of the Polish Communist Party under the name Henrykowski, recruited Ringelblum into the Poalei Tsiyon party and kindled in him a deep interest in Yiddish literature. In the closely knit youth group of the Sanz Poalei Tsiyon, Ringelblum made two other lifelong friends: Raphael Mahler and Artur Eisenbach. Both would become eminent Jewish historians.

The week that he turned seventeen—in early November 1917—brought news of two momentous events in modern Jewish history: Britain's promise of a Jewish National Home in Palestine and the Bolshevik Revolution. While many Jews saw Zionism and communism as competing ideologies, Ringelblum made a lifelong commitment to a movement that tried to combine both. When the Poalei Tsiyon split in 1920, he stayed with the left faction, which argued that the road to Jerusalem led through Moscow. Soviet-led world revolution, not British promises, would pave the way for Jewish liberation, in a binational socialist Palestine.

The Left Poalei Tsiyon was not a large party and during the 1930s it steadily lost influence and numbers. All the more telling, therefore, was the devotion of those who stayed. And Ringelblum stayed to the very end. The party marked him in many ways. It instilled a fervent commitment to the study of Jewish history, a love of Yiddish, a devotion to the Jewish masses, and a deep sense of moral pathos that shaped Ringelblum's development as a historian and communal leader. The party embraced Yiddish not only because the Jewish working class in Poland spoke it but also because it believed that only a labor Zionism based on Yiddish rather than Hebrew could avoid a corrosive estrangement between the Jewish masses in the Diaspora and the new Jewish working class in Palestine.

The party's founder, Ber Borochov (1881–1917), left another legacy to his disciples: the conviction that Yiddish scholarship—a worthy end in itself—had to be a collective enterprise. Ringelblum always took this to heart. In the early 1930s when extreme leftists in his party called for a boycott of YIVO, Ringelblum rushed to its defense. His radicalism was real but so was his readiness to reach out to ideological opponents in a common effort to further Yiddish culture and Jewish history. So too did the Oyneg Shabes Archive bring together rabbis and communists, Zionists and anti-Zionists in a common cause.

In 1919 Ringelblum left Sanz for Warsaw University where, after some hesitation, he decided to become a historian. In Warsaw he met Professor Marceli Handelsman, his official thesis supervisor, and Dr. Isaac Schiper, who guided his development as a Polish Jewish historian. Schiper and Handelsman were not only great scholars; they were also public intellectuals and, as such, role models for the young Ringelblum (this, despite the fact that Handelsman, of Jewish descent, had converted to Catholicism and Schiper had already left the Poalei Tsiyon). Handelsman, who later became a leader of the tiny Polish Democratic Party, helped Ringelblum publish his first book and linked him to the wider world of Polish historians. He also allowed Ringelblum to organize a Jewish section at the International Historical Congress in Warsaw in 1933.

Schiper helped set Ringelblum's agenda as a Jewish historian: to see Jewish history not in isolation but in the context of constant interaction with the non-Jewish world, to understand the importance of economic history and class conflict, and to explore the early roots of popular Yiddish culture. Ringelblum's relationship with Schiper would have its ups and downs but the intellectual impact was critical.

Ringelblum came to Warsaw at a time of growing interest in both Polish and Polish Jewish history. Now that Jews once again found themselves under Polish sovereignty, their history took on new relevance and urgency as a factor that would define the new relationship between Poles and Jews. Polish antisemites used historical arguments to label Jews as alien parasites and interlopers and to demand that they leave the country. In turn, as Ringelblum stressed in a 1926 article, Jewish historians had to defend their people and show that the Jews lived in Poland by right and not on sufferance. They had to record Jewish participation in Polish wars of independence and show how Jewish toil and sweat built Poland. Jewish historians were to use the history of Jewish artisans and workers to refute Polish charges that Jews were congenital hucksters and speculators who had never farmed or worked with their hands.

Jewish historians also threw themselves into the sharp internecine battles that marked the politics of interwar Polish Jewry: religion vs. secularism, Yiddish vs. Hebrew, Zionism vs. Diaspora nationalism, and worker vs. middle class. Arcane historical controversies became acutely relevant. Were the Jewish communal bodies of the sixteenth and seventeenth centuries guardians of Jewish unity or organs of class exploitation? Could religion take the credit for Jewish survival over the centuries or should one look to economic factors? Were Yiddish literature and theater recent creations of modern political radicalism or were they deeply rooted in a centuries-old popular culture? History also became a major theme of interwar Jewish popular culture. Many Yiddish historical novels became best-sellers. Popular articles by Jewish historians became regular features of the Yiddish- and Polish-language Jewish daily press.

Young Jewish historians such as Ringelblum therefore saw themselves as fighters as well as scholars. As Jews, they had no hope of a conventional academic career in interwar Poland. (For many years Ringelblum would support himself by teaching in a girls' high school and would grab a few hours in the late afternoon to do his historical research.) Nonetheless they regarded scholarship as a national mission and came together to create a community of historians. In 1923 Ringelblum and Mahler organized the Yunger Historiker Krayz (Young Historians Circle) of Jewish historians at Warsaw University. The *krayz* ran a monthly seminar, attracted more than forty regular participants, and met regularly until 1939. (Some veterans who survived the war included Joseph Kermish, Isaiah Trunk, and Artur Eisenbach—all important Jewish historians.) The *krayz* became the backbone of YIVO's historical section in Poland. It would issue two journals, *Yunger historiker* which appeared in 1926 and 1929, and *Bleter far geshikhte*, which appeared in 1934 and 1938.

In a 1955 essay, a former member of the *krayz*, Meir Korzen, noted that before the war Ringelblum had been known more as an organizer than as an original thinker and historian. Korzen was not entirely wrong, but he ignored the sociocultural context of interwar Polish Jewish historiography. Without university or government support Jewish historians needed good organizers. Less concerned with academic fame than with encouraging the writing of Polish Jewish history, Ringelblum saw himself as a facilitator as well as a scholar. It is good that he did so. A Meyer Balaban or an Isaac Schiper, the most famous and accomplished Jewish historians in prewar Poland, would not have organized a collective undertaking like the Oyneg Shabes. Ringelblum did.

To be sure, Korzen underestimated Ringelblum, who compiled a respectable record as a historian—all the more remarkable for the fact that his many jobs left him little time to work in archives. He published the first academic history of early Warsaw Jewry, landmark articles on Polish-Jewish relations in the eighteenth century, an important monograph on the Jewish role in the Kościuszko Uprising, a splendid investigation of the Jewish book trade, many articles on the history of Jewish medicine in Poland, and an excellent study of discussions of the economic restructuring of Polish Jews in the eighteenth century. He did so with practically no financial help and little time. And after all, he was not yet thirty-nine when the war broke out.

Two basic themes defined Ringelblum's prewar historical research. The first was the story of the Jewish masses. As Jacob Shatzky pointed out, Ringelblum helped to "democratize" the subject matter of Polish Jewish historiography. He felt a particular responsibility toward the forgotten Jews of the past: women, apprentices, beggars. Jewish historians, Ringelblum believed, had paid too much attention to elites—rabbis, scholars, wealthy businessmen—and had forgotten the people. In a tribute to obscure eighteenth-century Jewish jesters, he wrote, "These jesters can be seen as the ancestors of Jewish actors, who in hard times did what they could to amuse the Jewish masses. At the same time they enriched and disseminated popular culture (*folksshafung*). Therefore let us mention their names so that they will be remembered (*lezikhroyn oylem*). . . ." This sense of obligation to the forgotten masses stayed with him right into the war. Through Oyneg Shabes he tried to ensure that their voices would be heard and remembered, long after they perished in Treblinka.

The second basic theme in Ringelblum's research—which also carried over into the war—was the story of Polish-Jewish relations. Ringelblum tried to counter two starkly different perceptions of these interactions. The first was the perception of Poland as a liberal haven where Jews could find refuge. The second saw Poland as a country marked by eternal and endemic antisemitism, with Polish-Jewish relations rooted in a history of unbridgeable antagonism and mutual alienation. The truth, Ringelblum believed, was more complicated. Polish-Jewish relations reflected a constant interplay of rivalry and cooperation, religious alienation and close personal ties, economic tension and mutual collaboration. But historians, he believed, could help the two peoples understand each other and cut through the barriers of prejudice and ignorance. Poles would come to see Jews as real people, not as an abstract "other," while Jews could realize that their Polish neighbors were not born enemies. The two peoples had lived side by side for centuries and, as Ringelblum argued in his first book, on the history of Warsaw Jewry until 1527, no "Chinese Wall" separated them. When the Second World War began, amid a brief interlude of Polish-Jewish cooperation, Ringelblum began to chronicle the history of the occupation in the hope that he would be serving not only future scholarship but also future understanding between the two peoples.

This conviction of Polish-Jewish interconnectedness never left Ringelblum. Hersh Wasser, a secretary of the Oyneg Shabes, recalled that Ringelblum once said that "I do not regard the archive as a separate project, as a matter only of Jews, for Jews and by Jews. My whole being revolts against that concept. As a Jew, as a historian, and as a socialist I can't agree with such an approach. In the whole complexity of social processes, where everything is interdependent, it is impossible to shut ourselves off in our narrow world. Jewish pain and Jewish liberation is part of a . . . [wider story]."

Ringelblum the historian looked behind and beyond the formal sources. Official laws and edicts told only half the story, and one reason to zaml was to reveal what official documents could not. In a youth journal of the Left Poalei Tsiyon, *Fraye yugnt*, Ringelblum emphasized that excessive reliance on legal documents and charters had led nineteenth-century Jewish assimilationist historians such as Hilary Nussbaum and Alexander Kraushar to exaggerate the liberalism and tolerance of the old Polish Commonwealth. But the same process worked in reverse. The impact of antisemitic legislation was often softened by self-interest and economic needs, factors that historians could locate only by looking behind the formal record. In his wartime writings Ringelblum repeatedly cited Polish-Jewish economic collaboration, especially smuggling, as an example of how real life (*eyts khayim*, he called it) thwarted the German plan to strangle the Jews economically. With the Oyneg Shabes Archive, Ringelblum made a conscious effort to ensure that future historians would construct an image of Polish Jewry and of its struggle to survive that would be based on Jewish and not just on German or Polish sources.

Ringelblum wanted historians to leave their ivory tower to work with the people. History was not only scholarship; it was also community-building, a process to bring together scholars and ordinary Jews. Ringelblum wanted historians to encourage amateur historical societies to write local histories, gather old chronicles, study tombstones, and photograph synagogue architecture. Oral history fascinated him, and he wrote long and detailed questionnaires to encourage local history buffs to study their towns. He also headed the Landkentenish (Study of the Land) Society, a group that encouraged educational tourism for Polish Jews.

Ringelblum was particularly encouraged by the 1931 publication of the local history of the small town of Pruzhany (Prużany), collected and written by a local group of teachers and students at the Yiddish school there. This collective effort by amateurs gleaned information about architecture, economics, and politics. Unlike earlier Jewish local histories it also investigated the non-Jewish population and their ties to local Jews. In the *Literarishe bleter* Ringelblum noted that the Jews of Pruzhany "don't feel that they're guests in Pruzhany. Rather they regard themselves as long-established veterans who have put down deep roots in the local area thanks to their work and toil." The Pruzhany project, he hoped, would signal a new wave of local histories.

Although he saw history as a national mission, Ringelblum worried that it must retain scholarly integrity and not elide into propaganda and simplistic nationalism. Just before the outbreak of the Second World War, in a review of Philip Friedman's *History of the Jews of Lodz from the Earliest Settlement until 1863*,[3] Ringelblum expressed some worries about the dilemmas faced by Jewish historians in Poland. Involved as they were in the tough battle to protect Jewish honor and to fight for Jewish rights, how could they walk the fine line between engaged scholarship and abject apologetics? How could they write about their people without succumbing to the temptation to answer antisemitic attacks with pompous Jewish nationalism? Ringelblum declared that the Jewish historian had to navigate, in his words, a narrow course between the Scylla of apologetics and the Charybdis of Jewish nationalist megalomania. Only a history based on high professional standards and solid sources could ultimately stand the test of time. The best way for the Jewish historian to serve the Jewish people was to write good history based on facts, to reveal the negative along with the positive, and to let the chips fall where they may.

This was a rule that Ringelblum would remember in the Oyneg Shabes. Right after the war Doctor Mark Dvorzhetsky, a survivor of the Vilna ghetto and German concentration camps, wrote an article, "Whether We Should Tell the Whole Truth?" and asked the following question: Should Jews write about Jewish police who turned their brothers over to the Germans? Should they reveal details of the corruption and the demoralization in the ghettos? For Ringelblum and the rest of the Oyneg Shabes, there could be only one answer: yes. The archive collected an enormous amount of negative material. But in the process it implicitly underscored the quiet heroism of those who did not lose their moral bearings: the organizers of the house committees in the ghetto, the selfless women who fed poor children, the caregivers and teachers who worked in desperate conditions, ordinary Jews who tried to feed their families and at the same time hold on to their moral dignity.

A turning point in Ringelblum's prewar career was his involvement with the Joint Distribution Committee, the major American Jewish aid organization in Poland. In the early 1930s thanks to his mentor, Joint director Yitzhak Giterman, Ringelblum had taken a part-time job as the editor of the *Folkshilf*, the monthly newspaper of the extensive network of free-loan credit societies (*Gmiles khesed kasses*) inspired by the Joint Distribution Committee. Many Polish Jews were reeling from the effects of economic antisemitism, boycotts, and, in the late 1930s, pogroms. These societies, or *kasses*, gave interest-free loans, organized occupational retraining, and helped Jewish artisans pass licensing exams. Based on a fifty-fifty partnership between small-town Jews and the Joint, the *kasses* encouraged self-reliance, not begging. Ringelblum measured their success not so much by the money they lent as by the moral message they sent: the small-town Jews were not alone, they were not abandoned, they could rely on each other. It was a lesson he took into the Warsaw Ghetto.

Each issue of the *Folkshilf* was full of poignant and stirring accounts of how Polish Jews fought back against economic

3. Filip Friedman, *Dzieje Żydów w Łodzi od początków osadnictwa do roku 1863* (Łódź, 1935).

antisemitism. These accounts—vignettes and reportages from dozens of towns—were written by ordinary Jews and contained first-rate material for historians, economists, and even ethnographers. Many reports even had literary merit. Without a doubt they bolstered Ringelblum's conviction that the Jewish intelligentsia had to seek out and develop "hidden talents" among the ordinary people, a pursuit that paid obvious dividends in the Oyneg Shabes Archive.

Like YIVO, *Folkshilf* provided Ringelblum with an important counterpoint to the political divisiveness and ideological infighting that were undermining the defense efforts of Polish Jewry. Here were institutions where people tried to forget political differences and worked together for the good of a common cause. The whole political spectrum of Polish Jewry, from the religious Aguda to the socialist Bund (with reservations) supported them. In many cases, he noted, the *kasses* had more political legitimacy than the *kehilles*, the legal Jewish communal boards.

At the end of October 1938, Nazi Germany expelled thousands of Polish Jews by literally pushing them across the Polish border. Since the Polish authorities at first refused to allow most of the victims into Poland, a desperate situation arose on the border. At Zbąszyń, a major crossing point between Germany and Poland, about 6,000 hapless refugees, hungry and cold, found themselves stranded. Giterman immediately sent Ringelblum to organize a relief effort. Without a doubt, this was the greatest challenge he had faced up to that time and his finest hour. Ringelblum showed himself to be a brilliant organizer. Slowly but surely, he was moving out of the shadow of others and gaining confidence in his own abilities. Applying the lessons he had learned in the *Folkshilf*, he was careful to treat the refugees with dignity rather than as abject and passive charity cases. He led a team effort that encouraged them to take over many of the duties in the camp: a postal service, a housing department, a legal bureau, and the like. Characteristically he also fostered the use of Yiddish. He sensed that many of these unfortunate Jews, some of whom had spent decades in Germany, were ready to reestablish contact with the rich folk culture of East European Jewry. Predictably, Ringelblum did not forget his duties as a historian. He encouraged the refugees to write down their experiences and hoped to use the material for future research. Zbąszyń was the first harbinger of Nazi brutality, quickly followed by Kristallnacht. Ringelblum keenly felt the suffering of the deportees: in letters to Raphael Mahler and Eliyahu Cherikover he confessed to frequent bouts of mental anguish and emotional torment. In a letter to Cherikover sent in December 1938, Ringelblum wrote that "we worked 18 to 20 hours a day. I came back from there mentally and physically shattered. I am still not myself. It will take me a long time yet before I become a normal person again." But characteristically he also saw the positive: the fervor of the youth in the camp, the interest in culture, the willingness to maintain "discipline" under trying circumstances.

When the war began, Ringelblum had just returned to Warsaw from Switzerland, where he had been a Left Poalei Tsiyon delegate to the Twenty-First Zionist Congress. Within days the Polish defenses crumbled and many key Jewish leaders fled the Polish capital. Artur Eisenbach, Ringelblum's brother-in-law, begged Ringelblum to leave but he refused. During the siege of Warsaw he discovered, as did many other ordinary Warsaw citizens, that he was capable of physical courage. He stood his civil defense watches under heavy fire and carried a wounded woman to a hospital in the middle of an air raid. And every day, Ringelblum made the long journey to his office in the headquarters of the Joint Distribution Committee where he helped organize emergency relief and refugee aid.

With the coming of the war, two major strands of his prewar activity, history and social welfare, now came together. He became a major leader of the principal Jewish mutual aid organization in Warsaw, the Aleynhilf, and helped coordinate aid to refugees and soup kitchens. He also helped organize an extensive network of house committees and tried to make them into the social base of the Aleynhilf. He and others consciously used the Aleynhilf to create posts for the Jewish intelligentsia—teachers, writers, scholars, and others who might otherwise be doomed to starvation in the ghetto. As time went on Ringelblum began to see the Aleynhilf as a counterpoint to the Judenrat, a symbol of a "democratic" as opposed to a "bureaucratic" Jewish institution. In turn this consciousness of representing the *real* community permeated the self-perception of the Oyneg Shabes collective.

The Oyneg Shabes Archive was organized by Ringelblum but was embedded in the networks of the Aleynhilf at refugee points, soup kitchens, house committees, and clandestine schools. These networks would provide information, documents, and testimonies for the archive. More than ever, Ringelblum saw social self-help and zamling as two sides of the same coin. They were interdependent and both strove to remind Jews that they were still a proud people and not a mob of passive, demoralized victims.

Ringelblum's major role in the Aleynhilf ensured that many refugees arriving in the Warsaw Ghetto would seek him out for aid. Out of these new contacts Ringelblum recruited much of the nucleus of the Oyneg Shabes Archive. He brought in key people such as Hersh Wasser, Eliyahu Gutkowski, and David Chołodenko from Łódź and Rabbi Shimon Huberband from Piotrków. In a 22 November 1940 meeting at his Leszno Street apartment, shortly after the ghetto was established, Ringelblum and six close associates met to lay down the basic framework of the project. Ringelblum also recruited heavily from his trusted friends in the prewar YIVO and the Joint: Yitzhak Giterman, Shmuel Winter, Shie Rabinowitz, Menakhem Linder, Abraham Lewin, and Rachel Auerbach.

In the summer of 1943, in the Majdanek concentration camp, Isaac Schiper told a fellow inmate that

> Everything depends on who transmits our testament to future generations, on who writes the history of this period. History is usually written by the victor. What we know about murdered peoples is only what their murderers vaingloriously cared to say about them. Should our murderers be victorious, should *they* write the history of this war, our destruction will be presented as one of the most beautiful pages of world history, and future generations will pay tribute to them as dauntless

> crusaders. Their every word will be taken as gospel. Or they may wipe out our memory altogether, as if we had never existed, as if there had never been a Polish Jewry, a ghetto in Warsaw, a Majdanek. Not even a dog will howl for us.
>
> But if we write the history of this period of blood and tears—and I firmly believe we will—who will believe us? Nobody will want to believe us, because our disaster is the disaster of the entire civilized world. . . . We'll have the thankless job of proving to a reluctant world that we are Abel, the murdered brother.[4]

Unlike Schiper, Ringelblum had no doubt that the world would indeed believe what had happened—as long as it had the proper evidence. He set out to amass a record whose thoroughness, objectivity, and sheer scope would force those "future generations" to look the truth in the face.

What emerged from the milk cans and tin boxes in 1946 and 1950 was a record of extraordinary cultural resistance and dedication. For three years a small group—a dedicated brotherhood, Ringelblum called them—of men and women, rabbis and Marxists, prominent leaders and obscure volunteers systematically documented with questionnaires, surveys, interviews, and essay contests the entire social history of the Warsaw Ghetto.

There were archives and chronicles in other ghettos: Łódź, Białystok, and Vilna, for instance. But in many ways the Oyneg Shabes, a collective enterprise, was unique. It was far larger, far more ambitious in its agendas. Unlike with the other archives, there were almost no links, official or unofficial, between Oyneg Shabes and the Judenrat. Certainly the conditions of the Warsaw Ghetto made it easier for Oyneg Shabes to function and to preserve secrecy. Compared to the Łódź ghetto, the Warsaw Ghetto was much less isolated and regimented. The network of relatively autonomous self-help organizations in Warsaw made it easier to maintain secrecy and distance from informers and unreliable elements. The house committees created a "social space" for a counter-community and for the dissemination of information. Jews knew that on the other side of the ghetto walls, the "Aryan Side," was a Polish community that thoroughly detested the occupier. This too created clandestine links, mainly but not only economic, that facilitated the work of the archive. And the sheer size of the Warsaw Ghetto presented both a challenge and an opportunity for the Oyneg Shabes staff. Jewish Warsaw had been a sprawling mosaic of different Jewish worlds, a nodal point where before the war many of the tensions and contradictions of East European Jewry had come together. Now Warsaw, which had absorbed more than 100,000 refugees, was Europe's largest ghetto. It presented a daunting array of research agendas that required careful conceptualization and organization. Of course the Oyneg Shabes did not limit its activities to Warsaw. Thanks to its close links to refugee organizations in the ghetto (*landsmanshaftn*), it made a concerted effort to get materials from other localities: Łódź, small towns in Congress Poland, and the Soviet occupation zone.

The Oyneg Shabes established an effective division of labor. At the center was an executive committee that raised money and charted strategy and agendas. There were also frequent writers and occasional contributors, as well as a group of copiers and transcribers. The archive tried to make multiple copies of all materials, in order to ensure that at least something would survive. There was also a "technical group" led by the teacher and writer Israel Lichtenstein, who had physical possession of the materials and who waited for orders to bury them.

The workers of the archive faced constant danger. To interview refugees in the filthy and overcrowded refugee centers exposed the members of the archive to the risk of contracting typhus. There was also the ever-present danger of Gestapo agents. One of Ringelblum's greatest achievements was that the Germans never stumbled upon the secret.

The archival staff was cohesive enough to ensure secrecy and diverse enough to secure access to a varied array of information. Although as a rule the archive avoided close contacts with the Judenrat for security reasons, one of its key members, Shmuel Winter, a former YIVO leader, played a major role in the Provisioning Authority and in the Judenrat. Winter helped the Oyneg Shabes in many ways: with money, food, and critical information. After September 1942, when movement in the decimated ghetto became very difficult, it was Winter who gave surviving Oyneg Shabes members "cover" to move around, as well as access to a telephone for conversations with the "Aryan" side. Menakhem Kon, a wealthy merchant before the war, was the archive's treasurer. Kon would disburse money for paper and writing supplies, hand out small stipends to the archive staff, and handle emergencies: medicines for archive members who had typhus or the money to send a key informant on the Chełmno death camp out of the Warsaw Ghetto. Yitzhak Giterman and Daniel Guzik linked the archive to the Joint Distribution Committee. Alexander Landau and Shie Rabinowitz, relatively wealthy prewar businessmen, also helped raise money. Gustawa Jarecka and Marcel Ranicki-Reich, who worked in the Judenrat, made copies of Judenrat documents and its correspondence with the German authorities.

The two secretaries of the archive, Hersh Wasser and Eliyahu Gutkowski, also played critical roles; along with Ringelblum, they kept track of the archive's daily activities, checked ongoing projects and made sure that writers completed their assignments. Wasser, a member of the Left Poalei Tsiyon, and Gutkowski, of the Right Poalei Tsiyon, were also active in the underground press, feeding it with information from the Oyneg Shabes. Wasser ran the *landsmanshaft* department of the Aleynhilf and thus became the key link between the archive and the refugees, who in turn provided information about events in the provinces. The archive established links with the two major Zionist youth organizations in the ghetto, Dror-Frayhayt and Hashomer Hatsair. Gutkowski was the key contact with Dror, while Ringelblum enjoyed a close friendship with the leadership of Hashomer Hatsair, including Mordecai Anielewicz,

4. Alexander Donat, *The Holocaust Kingdom* (New York: Holt Rinehart and Winston, 1965), p. 211, quoted in Alvin Rosenfeld, *A Double Dying* (Bloomington: Indiana University Press, 1980), pp. 37–38

who would later become the commander of the Jewish Fighting Organization. Two other leaders of Hashomer, Shmuel Bresław and Joseph Kaplan, also served on the executive committee of the Oyneg Shabes. In this way the archive was in a position to follow the establishment of a resistance movement in the ghetto.

Other members of the archive provided an important array of skills and contacts. Rabbi Shimon Huberband was a key link to the Orthodox community. Nehemia Tytelman specialized in collecting street songs and ghetto folklore, while Yehuda Feld, a member of the underground Communist Party, furnished information about children and refugees as well as well-crafted stories about ghetto life. Peretz Opoczyński left a series of brilliant reportages; Rachel Auerbach a diary and an important essay about the soup kitchen that she ran at Leszno 40. And there were many others.

Ringelblum's agenda was sweeping and ambitious. Over time, this agenda came to embrace the collection of artifacts and documents, the study of Jewish society, the gathering of individual testimony, the documentation of German crimes, and alerting the outside world to the German mass murder. These goals were not mutually exclusive and the archive would pursue them simultaneously.

The Oyneg Shabes Archive collected an enormous range of material: the underground press, documents, drawings, candy wrappers, tram tickets, ration cards, and theater posters. It filed away invitations to concerts and lectures and took copies of the convoluted doorbell codes for apartments that often contained dozens of tenants. There were restaurant menus that advertised roast goose and fine wines and a terse account about a starving mother who had eaten her dead child. Carefully filed away were hundreds of postcards from Jews in the provinces, individuals about to be deported to an "unknown destination." The Oyneg Shabes preserved the poetry of Władysław Szlengel, Yitzhak Katzenelson, Kalman Lis, and Joseph Kirman. It preserved the entire script of a popular ghetto comedy, *Love Looks for an Apartment*, and long essays on the ghetto theaters and cafés. The first cache of the archive also contained many photographs, seventy-six of which more or less survived.

The Oyneg Shabes filed away hectographed readers used in the ghetto schools and the reports that nurses wrote in the ghetto orphanages. After 22 July 1942, the archive collected the German posters that announced the Great Deportation, and those that promised anyone voluntarily reporting for deportation 3 kilograms of bread and a kilogram of marmalade. Crammed into the milk cans of the second cache were penciled notes whose shaky handwriting betrayed the desperation of their authors. These pieces of paper, smuggled out of the Umschlagplatz, were frantic appeals for a last-minute rescue from the waiting death trains. Among the last documents buried in the second cache were posters calling for armed resistance.

The Oyneg Shabes commitment to comprehensive documentation went hand in hand with another important commitment: to postwar justice. It was this quest to gather evidence that explained why the archive collected enormous amounts of material on events in as many localities as possible. At first glance, much of this material is repetitious. But it did fix, town by town and village by village, what exactly the Germans did, when they did it, who gave the orders, and who helped them. If the Oyneg Shabes did not do this, then who would?

As time went on, the Oyneg Shabes, unlike most of the other archives, would also acquire a new role as a center of "civil resistance."[5] When German plans for the Jews became clearer, the Oyneg Shabes began to issue its own bulletin and worked closely with the ŻOB, the Jewish Fighting Organization in the Warsaw Ghetto.

The relative prominence of the various tasks and agendas of the Oyneg Shabes constantly shifted to reflect changing circumstances. Broadly speaking, the Oyneg Shabes went through different periods. From the outbreak of the war until the establishment of the ghetto, Ringelblum kept his notes, gathered information, and scouted out potential collaborators. This was a difficult time to collect material because constant German searches made Jews afraid to write and to keep written material. One can surmise from Ringelblum's notes that during this period he encountered many frustrations. Many people he had hoped could help him failed to meet his expectations, and he believed that apart from himself, few Jews were writing or collecting documentation.

A second period began with the establishment of the ghetto in the fall of 1940. Paradoxically the establishment of the ghetto made the work of the archive easier. Fear of German searches eased and Jews sensed that while the Nazis intensely followed the activities of the Polish underground, they had little interest in what Jews said or wrote. Thus in addition to the "social space" created by the house committees and the Aleynhilf, a new kind of "cultural space" emerged in the ghetto, making it easier for Ringelblum to develop the archive.

One sign of this "cultural space" was the expansion of a large and varied underground press published by political parties and youth groups.[6] The archive made the collection of these newspapers a major priority. Had it not been for the Oyneg Shabes, very few of these newspapers and pamphlets would have survived to provide a priceless source of information about life in the ghetto, political debates, Polish-Jewish relations, and how Jews followed the military situation.

Over time a complementary relationship developed between this underground press and the Oyneg Shabes. Many re-

5. The idea of the Oyneg Shabes as a center of civil resistance has been discussed by Ruta Sakowska in "Opór cywilny getta warszawskiego," BŻIH, 86–87, 1973, pp. 79–81.

6. There are several good treatments of the Jewish underground press in the Warsaw Ghetto. See Joseph Kermish, ed., *Itonut ha-Mahteret ha-Yehudit be-Varsha*, "Introduction," Volume 1 (Tel Aviv, 1979), pp. xxvii–lxxxi; Daniel Blatman, "Itonut mahteret ve-hevra," in Daniel Blatman, ed., *Geto varsha, sipur itonai* (Jerusalem, 2002), pp. 7–87; Israel Gutman, *The Jews of Warsaw, 1939–1943: Ghetto, Underground, Revolt* (Bloomington: Indiana University Press, 1982), pp. 146–154.

ports that flowed into the archive were published in edited form in the underground newspapers. Several members of the executive committee of the Oyneg Shabes, including Wasser, Gutkowski, and Bresław, also edited underground newspapers. The underground press and the archive covered many of the same themes: daily life in the ghetto, complaints about the Judenrat and police corruption, escalating mortality from hunger and disease, problems in the labor camps, events in the provinces, the plight of children and refugees, street humor, and ghetto folklore. In October 1941, the underground press began to publish the first accounts of mass executions. By the spring of 1942 the Oyneg Shabes would publish an underground bulletin of its own, full of information about the oncoming Final Solution.

While the archive itself had to remain secret, it indirectly benefited from the ability of the underground press to disseminate information, remind their readers of prewar values and moral codes, and foster a comradely counter-community. The flow of information disseminated by the underground newspapers helped create an awareness of the need to record what was happening, while their moral and political exhortations bolstered a determination to use this testimony to bring to justice not only Nazi perpetrators but also Jews who had failed the moral tests of national solidarity and honesty. The underground press, through its articles on the military situation, became the major source of information about the war. Even when things looked bleakest, such as during the fall of France, the underground press furnished commentaries that kept hopes alive.

This period also saw massive expulsions of refugees into the Warsaw Ghetto and, with it, a major effort by Oyneg Shabes to collect refugee testimonies, a task made much easier by Wasser's control of the *landsmanshaft* department of the Aleynhilf. As more and more Jews were hauled off to labor camps in the spring of 1941, the archive also made it a priority systematically to document these camps. In a short time the Oyneg Shabes succeeded in documenting almost every important labor camp and in collecting information from hundreds of refugees. After Germany attacked the Soviet Union in June 1941, many Jews began to return to the Warsaw Ghetto from the eastern territories. The archive eagerly sought their testimony in order to document Jewish life under Soviet occupation.

If Ringelblum had seen history as a powerful tool to shape national consciousness and affect political agendas before the war, he would have even more reason to think so after the war began. Until German designs became clear, he and the rest of the Oyneg Shabes could hope that there would be a Polish Jewry after the war. Couldn't the archive, therefore, help shape a "usable past" that could affect the future?

Through a careful reading of his diary one can infer that in the very first years of the war Ringelblum saw great opportunities for the engaged historian: to reverse the debilitating linguistic assimilation of the prewar years, to discredit the Jewish bourgeoisie and expose those elites who failed to meet the test of wartime leadership, to document the resilience and vital force of the Jewish masses, to demonstrate that in a moment of trial Jews had once again proven their loyalty to Poland, to use history and sociology to create a meaningful base for Jewish secular culture, and to continue a work in progress—a new iconography of the Jewish urban experience—that would take its place alongside the iconography of the shtetl.

One of Ringelblum's major concerns was the question of Jewish honor. How would future historians view the behavior of various segments of the Jewish population? The war had caused widespread corruption and demoralization within the Jewish community. In his diary Ringelblum railed against the Judenrat and its unfair tax policy. He lambasted the Jewish Police and bitterly noted how it was the poorest Jews that they dragged off to deadly labor camps. He pointed to other Jews who had acted badly: porters, doctors who took bribes to exempt buildings from the dreaded disinfection (*parówki*), well-to-do Jews who walked over the bodies of dead children to enter expensive restaurants. Some intellectuals in the ghetto, such as Aaron Einhorn who was the former editor of the important prewar Yiddish daily *Haynt*, went further and argued that corruption reflected deep-seated national pathologies. What the ghetto had exposed, Einhorn believed, was a festering rot that had attacked Polish Jewry long before the war had begun.

It was on this crucial point, on the broader significance of the pathologies of ghetto life, that Ringelblum parted company with Einhorn. No, Ringelblum countered after much inner turmoil, the Jewish people acted no worse than anyone else, but rather even better. Given the nature of the ghetto, given the necessity to break the law in order to survive, then what happened in the ghetto was no worse than what might have occurred with another people. In the Oyneg Shabes project there was an underlying tension between the imperatives of objective fact-gathering and a natural determination to protect the good name of the Jewish masses. But one might say that this concern for national honor was in many ways a direct continuation of the prewar YIVO tradition with its tension between the imperatives of national self-defense and objective scholarship.

Perhaps the clearest sign of this YIVO heritage was the major study project, "Two and a Half Years." Projected to run to 1,600 pages, the project planned to research and study dozens of different subjects: intellectuals, economics, women, children, corruption, Jews under Soviet occupation, German-Jewish relations, Polish-Jewish relations. Ringelblum and the rest of the Oyneg Shabes staff wrote long and detailed questionnaires to set the research agendas, guide the interviewers, and ensure objectivity. Even on the touchy issue of German-Jewish relations, the Oyneg Shabes developed guidelines that stressed the need to avoid blanket generalizations about German character and German behavior.

No sooner did the Oyneg Shabes begin this project than news began to arrive about Nazi massacres, first in the eastern territories, then in Chełmno, and then in the provinces surrounding Warsaw. Racing against time to complete the "Two and a Half Years" project, Ringelblum and the staff now began to work on a new challenge: to gather and disseminate information about Nazi killing. At first Ringelblum, like many others, could not believe that the Nazis intended to kill all Jews, even after he had heard reports of massacres in Vilna, Słonim, and other cities in eastern Poland. But in early 1942 "Szlamek," an escapee from the Chełmno death camp, arrived in the Warsaw Ghetto. Hersh Wasser interviewed him for the Oyneg Shabes. Soon the archive processed a flood of information about mass killings in other parts of Poland. The noose was drawing tighter. In the spring of 1942 the Oyneg Shabes began to publish an information bulletin that alerted Warsaw Jewry to the growing danger. It also, along with the Bund, used the channels of the Polish underground to get the information on the Final Solution to Britain.

But even as late as June 1942 Ringelblum still clung to some shreds of optimism. In June 1942, the BBC had just broadcast news of German killings of Jews in Poland, relying on a report based on Oyneg Shabes materials. When Ringelblum heard the BBC report, he had a sudden surge of hope. Our work has not been in vain, he wrote. Now that the German people knew about the mass murder they would force Hitler to stop the killings. Hitler was so concerned about keeping the genocide secret because he feared what the German people would say if they knew. Like many Marxists, Ringelblum believed in what later came to be called "generic fascism." Thus mass murder was ultimately caused by crisis-ridden elites rather than by the allegedly antisemitic masses. Just as Ringelblum loved the Jewish masses, so did he keep hoping for the innate humanity of the German masses.

Just one month later, the SS began the liquidation of the Warsaw Ghetto. By September, more than 300,000 Jews had been sent to the gas chambers of Treblinka or killed in the ghetto. Among the dead were many key members of the Oyneg Shabes—Rabbi Huberband, Cecylia Słapakowa, and many others. But with the temporary lull that began in September, Ringelblum went back to work. The members of the Oyneg Shabes now worked under inhuman psychological pressure and under much worse conditions than before 22 July 1942, the start of the Great Deportation. They had seen their close comrades and friends disappear. Some, like Abraham Lewin, Yechiel Górny, and Shmuel Winter, had suffered the agony of losing wives and children. After the first phase of the Great Deportation ended in September 1942, the ghetto was divided into isolated enclaves, with movement forbidden without special passes. Yet the Oyneg Shabes went on.

In the fall of 1942 Ringelblum asked the leftist Polish Jewish writer Gustawa Jarecka to write a report on the Great Deportation. Jarecka managed to finish only the introduction before the Germans deported her and her two children in January 1943. In December 1950 Jarecka's introduction surfaced in the two milk cans discovered by Polish construction workers:

> The record must be hurled like a stone under history's wheel in order to stop it. . . . One can lose all hopes except the one—that the suffering and destruction of this war will make sense when they are looked at from a distant, historical perspective. From sufferings, unparalleled in history, from bloody tears and bloody sweat, a chronicle of days of hell is being composed, in order that one may understand the historical reasons that shaped the human mind in this fashion and created government systems which made possible the events in our time through which we passed.[7]

In her introduction, Jarecka set down many reasons to write in the face of death. Through the written word one could confront the terrible present with dignity of the past and recapture the themes and symbols of prewar culture. In the face of horror, language could simultaneously frustrate and console. To write was to assert precious individuality even at the brink of death. To write was to resist, if only to bring the killers to justice. To write was to complete the defeat of the killers by ensuring that future historians would use the victims' cries to change the world.

Like Jarecka, Ringelblum also wanted to cast a "stone under history's wheel." He was absolutely convinced that the story of Jewish suffering, no matter how terrible, was a universal, not just a Jewish story. And evil, no matter how great, could not be placed outside history. The archive could still become a weapon in the struggle for a better future. Even though he now knew that most Polish Jews would not survive, he still continued the Oyneg Shabes—with new agendas. The Oyneg Shabes now collected all official documents and placards that recorded the mass murder, eyewitness accounts of Treblinka, studies of the rump ghetto and workshops, reports to be sent abroad. One of his most important goals was to explain for future historians the behavior of the "Jewish masses" during the war, to shield them against future charges of cowardice and fecklessness.

Ringelblum, Wasser, and Gutkowski also began to put out a Polish-language bulletin, *Wiadomości*, that gave a sober, unadorned account of the ongoing mass murder. They thereby sought to dispel any remaining illusions that Jews might still have concerning German intentions. *Wiadomości* also bluntly told Poles that they would ultimately share the same fate as the Jews. Through *Wiadomości* the Oyneg Shabes sent the message that there was only one course open to the surviving Jews: resistance. In one of his most important contributions, Ringelblum recorded and described the psychological transformation of the ghetto survivors from terrorized passivity to a grim determination to fight back. The few who had weapons prepared to use them; most who did not feverishly began to build bunkers and hiding places.

The second cache of the archive was closed and buried in February 1943. By that time, some key surviving members of the Oyneg Shabes, including Ringelblum and Wasser, had already gone into hiding on the "Aryan Side." But they both made frequent visits to the ghetto to bring in money and to try to find hideouts for friends and leading cultural figures on the Aryan Side. They were still politically active. Ringelblum was also on a committee to raise money to buy weapons for the Jewish Fighting Organization.

When the Warsaw Ghetto uprising broke out in April 1943, Ringelblum was trapped in the fighting ghetto, caught by the Germans and sent to the labor camp of Trawniki. There

7. See catalog entry Ring. II, no. 272, on p. 377 ("Last stage of resettlement is death"). Reprinted in Joseph Kermish, ed., *To Live with Honor and Die with Honor: Selected Documents from the Warsaw Ghetto Underground Archives "O.S." ("Oneg Shabbath")* (Jerusalem: Yad Vashem, 1986), p. 704.

he and others in a camp resistance organization managed to establish clandestine contact with the underground Jewish National Committee. In August 1943 his party comrade Adolph Berman sent two intrepid couriers, Tadeusz Pajewski and Emilka Kossover, to Trawniki to rescue Ringelblum and bring him back to Warsaw, where he rejoined his wife Yehudis and his fourteen-year-old son Uri in a crowded underground bunker at Grójecka 81.

In those last months of his life, in terrible conditions, Ringelblum sat and wrote. In a kind of *apologia pro vita sua*, Ringelblum memorialized the progressive Jewish intelligentsia, and especially the murdered leaders who had done the most to shape him as a historian and as a public figure: Isaac Schiper, Shakhne Zagan, and Yitzhak Giterman. Ringelblum rarely wrote about himself, but in these essays he came closest to leaving his final testament. In his essay on Mordecai Anielewicz, Ringelblum paid a poignant tribute to the young commander of the Jewish Fighting Organization, who was killed in May 1943.

Ringelblum capped a long scholarly career with his best historical work, a passionate and powerful essay on Polish-Jewish relations during the Second World War. The essay was a unique synthesis of the immediacy of contemporaneous testimony with the analytic perspective of retrospective historical analysis. The book reflected the tension between the imperative of historical objectivity and shock of the enormous crimes that he witnessed not as a bystander but as a direct victim. Detached historians could make necessary distinctions between perpetrators and bystanders, between Polish and German antisemitism, between active complicity and indifference. For a member of a victimized people to do so required a major effort of intellectual discipline.

To the very last, as his essay showed, Ringelblum remained an engaged historian who was convinced that scholarship could also serve important national and political agendas. Even in the face of death, Ringelblum hoped that "Polish-Jewish Relations" might contribute to a better Poland after the war, with improved ethnic relations in the future.

On 7 March 1944, a Polish informer betrayed the hideout to the Gestapo. The Germans took all the Jews to the Pawiak prison. Ringelblum and his son Uri sat in a separate cell with the other men. The late Yekhiel Hirschaut was a prisoner in Pawiak and wrote in his memoirs that as soon as the other Jewish prisoners learned that Ringelblum was in the death cell, they looked for ways to rescue him. They hatched a plan to attach Ringelblum to a work detail in the prison. Hirschaut sought out Ringelblum. Ringelblum told him how the Gestapo had just tried to torture information out of him. Ringelblum was covered in black and blue marks, his son Uri sitting on his lap. Hirschaut outlined his plan: we can try to get you out of here. And what about my wife and child? Ringelblum asked. There was a long silence: Ringelblum understood and said, "I can't leave my family." And he pointed to his son: "*Vos iz er shuldik, der kleyner—tsulib im veytigt mir shtark dos harts*" ("What is this little fellow guilty of? I'm so heartsick on his account"). Hirschaut never saw Ringelblum again. The Germans shot all the Jews they caught in the bunker as well as two of the Poles who helped them.

When searchers opened the first tin boxes of the archive that were retrieved in 1946 they found a testament written by Izrael Lichtensztajn, who had supervised their burial in 1942. Lichtenstein concluded his stirring testimony with the following words: "We are the redeeming sacrifice for the Jewish People. I believe that the nation will survive. We the Jews of Eastern Europe are the redeemers of the People of Israel. . . ." At the very end of his life he reaffirmed his belief in the future of the Jewish people. And he reminded us that they were not just victims: they were people and proud members of a living and resilient nation. This is the important legacy of the Oyneg Shabes Archive.

# THE WARSAW GHETTO
## OYNEG SHABES–RINGELBLUM ARCHIVE

# Structure and Organization of the Ringelblum Archive and Its Catalog

TADEUSZ EPSZTEIN

The Ringelblum Archive (RA),[1] the Underground Archive of the Warsaw Ghetto, has enormous significance as a documentary collection for the history of the annihilation of Jews on Polish territory during the Second World War. In 1999, UNESCO placed it on the list of the most precious archives in the world. Much of the material assembled in the RA has no equivalent in any other archival collection worldwide. Among its unique sources are, for example, the collections of personal accounts and testimonies, letters sent into the Warsaw Ghetto, monographs prepared by the Oyneg Shabes[2] team, underground publications from the Warsaw Ghetto, texts of literary works created there, documents of private origin (from donations), and so forth. On the other hand, certain segments of the RA include materials that were also preserved in other archival collections. To this category belong some of the official documents relating to the Warsaw Ghetto or the Łódź ghetto, German documents and documents of the Jewish councils, documents of the Jewish Social Self-Help (ŻSS), official press organs, and other printed matter.[3] The Polish underground press is also to be found in many libraries and archives. Nevertheless, this does not reduce the importance of the RA. On the contrary, its diversity and richness indicate the range of interests and possibilities of its creators. The Ghetto Archive's organizers shaped not only the themes of the documentation, but also its character and structure. The Ringelblum Archive was intended to be and in part became a reservoir of materials serving research and scholarly publications, for preparation of materials for the contemporaneous underground press, and for informing the world about the situation of the Jewish population.

## THE RINGELBLUM ARCHIVE'S REPOSITORY AND DESCRIPTION OF THE RA

The RA is housed in the collections of the Jewish Historical Institute in Warsaw. The legal owner of the collection is the Jewish Historical Institute in Poland Association (Stowarzyszenie Żydowskiego Instytutu Historycznego w Polsce). The archive consists of two parts: Ringelblum I and Ringelblum II. Ring. I contains about 20,740 sheets and 25,540 pages, while Ring. II consists of some 7,906 sheets and 9,829 pages; altogether, the documents total more than 35,000 pages. Prior to the recent rearrangement, Ring. I was composed of items numbered 1–1219, and Ring. II of items numbered 1–493. Even before work commenced on the new catalog, some archival units were superseded in both segments and the materials consolidated. It is not always known where specific documents were transferred, nor which materials or their fragments were consolidated.[4]

1. Trans. note: The abbreviation RA (for Ringelblum Archive) is used in this translation, although the abbreviation ARG, for the Polish *Archiwum Getta* or Ghetto Archive, was also employed on documents collected by the Oyneg Shabes group (see Ring. II/338). *Note*: All catalog numbers cited in this overview are old catalog numbers listed in the appended concordances of old/new catalog numbers.

2. Oyneg Shabes is the Hebrew-Yiddish code name for the efforts of the team of men and women engaged by Dr. Emanuel Ringelblum in clandestinely gathering and preserving documentation of the catastrophic and day-to-day experiences of the Jews confined within the Warsaw Ghetto and elsewhere in occupied Poland. In modern Hebrew, the term is transliterated Oneg Shabat, meaning "Sabbath's pleasure," used to refer to friendly gatherings on the Sabbath.

3. E.g., among the materials relating to the Warsaw Ghetto should be mentioned such collections in the holdings of the Archiwum Państwowe m.st. Warszawy (State Archive of Warsaw): Amt des Gouverneurs des Distrikts Warschau (Office of the Governor of the Warsaw District), Der Kommissar für den Jüdischen Wohnbezirk (The Commissioner for the Jewish Residential District), Transferstelle Warschau [Warsaw Transfer Station], Der Obmann des Judenrates in Warschau (The Head of the Jewish Council in Warsaw). Documents concerning the Łódź ghetto preserved in the Archiwum Państwowe w Łodzi (State Archive in Łódź) include collections from the German ghetto administration (Gettoverwaltung) and the Jewish ghetto administration (Der Älteste der Juden in Getto Litzmannstadt), the so-called Rumkowski Archive. Materials concerning the Piotrków ghetto are located in the collections Akta m. Piotrkowa (Piotrków Records) and Stadtkommissar von Petrikau (Piotrków City Commissioner) in the State Archive in Piotrków Trybunalski (Archiwum Państwowe w Piotrkowie Trybunalskim). Among documents preserved in the Archive of the Jewish Historical Institute (JHI = Polish ŻIH) in Warsaw are materials from the ŻSS (Jewish Social Self-Help), Centos (Central Jewish Orphan Care Society), and the Joint (American Jewish Joint Distribution Committee), as well as various occupation-period publications scattered among various collections. Documents of ŻSS were also preserved in the State Archive in Kraków (Archiwum Państwowe w Krakowie) in the collection Akta poniemieckie (German Documents), as well as in the Jagiellonian University Library.

4. A list of superseded Ring. I and Ring. II archival units appears at p. 465.

## CHRONOLOGY

Materials collected in both parts of the RA date to the years 1902–1943; a majority was created during the years 1939–1943. The older items are exclusively papers donated to the RA, including, for example, some fragments of the literary legacies of Itzik Manger (see the Papers of Rachela Auerbach) and Mojżesz Kaufman. In Ring. I, the last dated documents added to the collection were the handwritten statements by Dawid Graber and Nachum Grzywacz, dated 3.08.1942 (Ring. I/432 and I/1018). Dating from the end of July or beginning of August 1942 are Gela Seksztajn's will (Ring. I/1196) and the personal statement by her husband, Izrael Lichtensztajn (Ring. I/1190).[5] There is a letter dated 27.07.1942 to Hersz Wasser with a request for help (Ring. I/586/4). In Ring. II, the latest document bears the date 1.02.1943 and is a special issue of the *Biuletyn Informacyjny Żagiew* (Torch Information Bulletin; Ring. II/316/1).[6]

## LANGUAGE

There are also significant linguistic differences between Ring. I and II. In Ring. I, Yiddish and Polish dominate. Yiddish appears in ca. 930 documents, while Polish appears in ca. 900. German appears in ca. 230, while Hebrew appears in ca. 45. In Ring. II, ca. 570 documents are in Polish, ca. 190 are in Yiddish, ca. 140 in German, and more than 35 in Hebrew.[7] Other languages appear in the RA sporadically, chiefly in printed items, representing English, French, Russian, Romanian, Ukrainian, and Italian. Frequency of appearance of individual languages is dependent on the character of the documentation. Yiddish predominates in materials of private origin, principally in personal accounts, reports, and literary works. Polish and German occur in official documents of the German and Jewish authorities, in ŻSS documents, and also in private correspondence.

## STATE OF PRESERVATION

Differences between Ring. I and II are also apparent in the technical state of the materials contained in both parts of the archive.[8] The first segment of the materials of the RA was buried in boxes made of zinc sheets. The boxes were not welded shut, nor were they in any other manner protected. Therefore, the materials found in them were exposed to the effects of water and other external factors. When Ring. I was unearthed in 1946, most of the containers had to be cut open in order to extract the damp papers.[9] Some documents were completely destroyed, while others were preserved in fragments or are barely legible. Metal clips and fasteners, corroding in the soil, caused much damage to the documents they held together. Traces of the effect of water are apparent on most of the materials. Relatively well preserved are handwritten manuscript transcripts[10] made with pencil on carbon paper in several copies. Some texts written with ink underwent significant damage, since the dye was washed out due to the effect of humidity.[11] The second portion of the RA was preserved in very good condition even though it had remained in the earth several years longer (until 1950), because the metal milk canisters that had concealed Ring. II effectively protected the documents from the effect of atmospheric conditions.

Immediately after exhumation, the RA's materials (especially those in Ring. I) were subjected to conservation efforts that continued in subsequent years. However, due to limited

5. Trans. note: Lichtensztajn was in charge of concealment of the Oyneg Shabes archive.

6. After the excavation of Ring. II, two much later underground publications were erroneously included in the collection: *Głos Warszawy* [Voice of Warsaw], no. 24 (33), dated 8.05.1943 (Ring. II/319); and *Ucz się po niemiecku! Najszybciej opanujesz język niemiecki, jeśli nauczysz się następujących wyrazów i zwrotów, niezbędnych dla każdego Polaka* [Learn German! You'll very quickly master the German language if you learn the following expressions and phrases, essential for every Pole], Warsaw, 1944 (Ring. II/344).

7. The figures presented here should be considered approximate, since they apply not only to the language of the document, but also to some data appearing in it. The real number of documents is fewer. At the same time, it should be taken into account that several languages often appear simultaneously in a single document.

8. I restrict the present observations to basic information on the topic of the technical state of the documentation of the RA, and I would direct those interested in more detail to the report compiled at the Conservation Laboratory of ŻIH at the request of the United States Holocaust Memorial Museum in Washington: Zofia Goliszewska and Anna Michaś, "Raport o stanie zachowania oraz konserwacji (za lata 1946–1999) dokumentów z podziemnego Archiwum Getta Warszawskiego (Archiwum Ringelbluma część I i II)" [Report on the State of Preservation and Conservation (1946–1999) of the Documents from the Underground Archive of the Warsaw Ghetto (Ringelblum Archive, parts I and II)], Warsaw, 2000 (typescript).

9. Michał Borwicz, one of the witnesses to the digging up of the archive, recalls: "The organizers did not manage to solder the containers shut before burial. The faithful soil defended the collections against German fury, but in the course of four years of underground lethargy—water filled the interior of the boxes, saturating the materials concealed in them. Dangerous fungus sprouted repeatedly. Bundles of valuable papers increased in volume—due to moisture and swelling. Moreover, they were lying tightly packed and adhering very tightly to the metal walls. As a result—it was apparent at the first glance that a wet and elastic mass filled the box. In order not to damage it during removal, the metal container was taken apart." See: *Pieśń ujdzie cało. Antologia wierszy o Żydach pod okupacją niemiecką* [The Song survives: anthology of poetry about Jews under German occupation], ed. M. Borwicz (Warsaw-Łódź-Kraków, 1947), p. 43.

10. Trans. note: "Transcript" designates a copy made from an original document. The word *transcript* is used to translate the Polish *odpis*, normally rendered "copy," in order to avoid confusion with translation of the Polish *egzemplarz* that also means copy, as in "multiple copies of a transcript."

11. The oldest fragments of the manuscripts of Ringelblum's *Kronika getta* or Chronicle of the Ghetto (chiefly from 1939) have such damage; see Ring. I/507/1.

resources, the extent of these efforts was initially minimal, and by the end of the 1980s only a portion of the RA's materials had been subjected to conservation. Systematic attempts to preserve the RA commenced only during the years 1987–1990, and after a short interval were renewed in 1992 in the Jewish Historical Institute's own conservation workshop. Due to these efforts, a significant portion of the documents have now been treated for preservation. Initiation of the Preservation Workshop of JHI (1991) and continuation of the preservation efforts on documents in the ghetto archive were possible thanks to the aid of the United States Holocaust Memorial Museum in Washington (USHMM). Funds from the USHMM enabled special fireproof cabinets to be acquired for the safekeeping of the documents.

## THE OYNEG SHABES ARCHIVE IN THE WARSAW GHETTO

Emanuel Ringelblum considered the notes for his *Chronicle*, collected from the first days of September 1939, as the first items for the later ghetto archive collection. As early as May 1940, Ringelblum began to give his documentation work organizational structure, including his circle of friends and acquaintances in it.[12] In a fragment of Ringelblum's *Chronicle* dating to early 1943 and included in Ring. II,[13] we find general information about the first resources of the archive. Comparing the account by the founder of Oyneg Shabes with documents preserved in Ring. I, we note that Ringelblum quite accurately recalled the individual authors and their texts that entered the collection. Unfortunately, his description is fragmentary and speaks more about the program, goals, and work plans of the Oyneg Shabes team than about concrete and realized aims. The author mentions only examples of papers and reports written with the participation of selected collaborators in Oyneg Shabes, among them Eliasz Gutkowski, Szymon Huberband, Perec Opoczyński, Abraham Lewin, Daniel Fligelman, Nechemiasz Tytelman, and Jerzy Winkler. Many of the materials mentioned in Ringelblum's Chronicle survived and are now in Ring. I, but Ringelblum also mentions documents that are missing. This information additionally confirms that the collections of Oyneg Shabes were not completely preserved. It is impossible to estimate the extent of losses on the basis of such a haphazard description.

## COLLECTION AND ORGANIZATION OF DOCUMENTS BY OYNEG SHABES

It seems that the initial organizational work aimed chiefly to safeguard the documents from destruction. The best solution was to copy collected items and hide individual copies in different places. It appears that the compilers intended to send sets of the copied materials to different public collections in Poland and abroad.[14] In the first stage, the collectors worked at copying the materials, using originals or transcripts. However, with official documents, it is obvious that only a few originals could reach the collections of Oyneg Shabes. German documents and those of the Jewish councils (aside from official publications) were chiefly gathered as copies. Ringelblum's team had trusted coworkers at the Jewish Council in Warsaw for this process.[15] In the changed circumstances after the first liquidation action in summer 1942, the ghetto archive's workers seized the opportunity to take small fragments of the original documentation of the Jewish Social Self-Help, and even papers of the Jewish Council. These materials went into the second part of the archive (Ring. II). Deportees from provincial communities brought in official documents. Originals or copies of material of private origin, including personal accounts, testimonies, reports, and correspondence, were also acquired directly from residents of the ghetto.

Many reports were written by members of Oyneg Shabes who had interviewed various people or who transcribed comments of people who had conversationally been invited to share their experiences at general meetings of the Oyneg Shabes

12. Ringelblum himself gave such information (see *Kronika getta*, p. 472). According to Hersz Wasser, the founding meeting of the Oyneg Shabes group took place only on 22.11.1940 in Emanuel Ringelblum's home at ul. Leszno 18, apt. 31. Menachem Mendel Kon, Szmul Lehman, Jehoszua Rabinowicz, Lejzer Lipa Bloch, B. Sukiennik, and Hersz Wasser attended, in addition to Ringelblum. See H. Wasser, "The Ghetto Archives—The Enterprise of Dr. Emanuel Ringelblum," in *A Commemorative Symposium in Honour of Dr. Emanuel Ringelblum and His "Oyneg Shabes" Underground Archives* (Jerusalem 1983), p. 35. In contrast, the Oyneg Shabes account ledger (Ring. II/212) suggests that the founding meeting took place on 5.10.1940, before the sealing of the ghetto.

13. Ring. II/233, see *Kronika getta*, pp. 470–494. We find general information about the Oyneg Shabes staff in numerous monographs published after the war, among others: A. Eisenbach, "O pracach naukowo-badawczych w getcie warszawskim," BŻIH, 1951, no. 1, pp. 27–48; M. Szulkin, "Emanuel Ringelblum—historyk i organizator podziemnego archiwum getta warszawskiego," BŻIH, 1973, no. 86–87, pp. 111–125; *Archiwum Ringelbluma*, "Introduction," pp. 5–30; *A Commemorative Symposium in Honour of Dr. Emanuel Ringelblum and his "Oyneg Shabes" Underground Archives* (Jerusalem 1983); Joseph Kermish, ed., *To Live with Honor and Die with Honor: Selected Documents from the Warsaw Ghetto Underground Archives "O.S." ("Oneg Shabbath")* (Jerusalem: Yad Vashem, 1986), "Introduction," pp. xiii–xxxv; I. Gutman, "Emanuel Ringelblum, the Chronicler of the Warsaw Ghetto," *POLIN*, vol. 3 (1988), pp. 5–16; R. Sakowska, "Archiwum Ringelbluma—ogniwem konspiracji warszawskiego getta," parts I–III, BŻIH, no. 152 (1989), pp. 91–102, no. 153 (1990), pp. 79–95, no. 155–156 (1990), pp. 153–160; *Listy o Zagładzie*, "Introduction," pp. xi–xxix (for further literature, see ibid., pp. 342–349).

14. Abraham Lewin's account indicates (see below) that the YIVO Institute for Jewish Research in New York was certainly an intended recipient, while Dawid Graber expressed the wish during the burial of Ring. I that the ghetto archive's materials be placed after the war in the Borochow Museum in Palestine: see Ring. I/432.

15. Gustawa Jarecka worked in the chancellory of the Jewish Council in Warsaw, as did Marcel Reich-Ranicki, who provided copies of documents to the collections of the ghetto archive. See M. Reich-Ranicki, *Moje życie* (Warsaw 2000), pp. 130, 136–137; *Kronika getta*, pp. 579–580.

staff.[16] Abraham Lewin described both forms of meetings in his diary, mentioning an Oyneg Shabes gathering held on Saturday, 30 May 1942, at which "a certain attorney from Lwów" spoke about the "entire Gehenna" of the Jewish population of Lwów and eastern Galicia. On the same occasion, Lewin heard the report of Rywa Ruda of Dobrzyń.[17] On Friday, 28 August 1942, during the first liquidation action in the Warsaw Ghetto, the compilers of the ghetto archive, including Lewin, conducted an interview with Dawid Nowodworski, a fugitive from Treblinka. The notes of that report are preserved in the archive's collections (Ring. II/296).[18] This document shows us how difficult it was to transcribe a spoken text accurately, without deletions and corrections. Eliasz Gutkowski, who most probably wrote the record of that meeting, began the text in Yiddish and carefully recorded the first sentences, but after a short time he shifted to Polish and wrote the balance of the account in that language, in writing that was simplified and barely legible since he could not keep up with the speaker. It appears also that it was easier for him to write rapidly in Polish than in Yiddish, even though he knew both languages very well. In this case we might conclude that notes taken during interviews required further editing if they were to become a text designated for preparing a clean copy. We do not have either the working notes or rough drafts; these were either destroyed after transcripts were made from them or were concealed separately.[19] The originals of these accounts, from which copies were made in Oyneg Shabes, were not preserved in the ghetto archive. We might ask if they were collected by Oyneg Shabes and concealed elsewhere and then destroyed, or we might speculate that they were returned to the authors after a copy was made.[20] We have more original texts of testimonies in Ring. II, since after July 1942 the Oyneg Shabes team no longer had the opportunity to record and copy accounts on the same scale as formerly. In autumn 1942, the emphasis was on collecting texts that had already been prepared. However, this does not mean that the process of copying documents and recording oral reports was entirely abandoned.[21]

Based on the various preserved versions of the same documents in the RA's collections, we can attempt to follow the sequence of the typical projects conducted by Oyneg Shabes's workers as they gathered materials in the Warsaw Ghetto. Some documents were received in original forms (author's manuscripts that we designate with the letter A), and some of those originals were preserved in the collection, including the statements of Marian Liberman (Ring. I/422) or the manuscript of an unknown woman signed with the initials "H.S.L." (Ring. I/1071). A selected ghetto archive worker made a copy (we designate copies by the letters B and C). In the case of documents from Ring. I/422 and I/1071, we have both A and B versions, both the original manuscript and the copy made by Oyneg Shabes. For Ring. I/422, a detailed outline of the sequential stages of work on the document was simple to produce:

| A | → | B |
|---|---|---|
| (manuscript written by author Marian Liberman, given to Hersz Wasser, on 16.07.1941) | | (manuscript copy made after 16.07.1941 by copyist Jechiel Górny of Oyneg Shabes) |

In Ring. I/153, not only version A survived, but two copies, B and C, exist as well. For the most part we not only do not have the autograph originals of statements, but we do not know if they even existed. In numerous cases, the first written version of a given statement could be the notes (designated by the letter W) of the person who listened to the recollections. We also are not certain whether the person recording version W was also the author of the next version of this document, the B copy. In the present state of research, we are often unable to decide ultimately if there was a version A or a W. Therefore, for many documents we must conditionally take both versions into account; for example, with Zygmunt Millet's statement (Ring. I/480), the dependence among the various versions could have been as follows:[22]

| A or W | → | B | → | C |
|---|---|---|---|---|
| Author's manuscript or notes from the conducted interview (did not survive) | | Manuscript. Transcript of the author's original or a clean copy of the account heard prepared by an Oyneg Shabes member (E*). | | Manuscript. Copy of document B prepared by copyist CA* from Oyneg Shabes. |

16. *Kronika getta*, pp. 477–478, 480–481.

17. A. Lewin, *Dziennik z getta warszawskiego*, serialized in BŻIH, no. 19–20 (1956), pp. 196–197, 198–199. Neither account could be identified.

18. A. Lewin, *Dziennik z getta warszawskiego*, BŻIH, no. 22 (1957), p. 95. Lewin not only describes the meeting with Nowodworski, but also notes: "On the basis of his account, we wrote down the testimony which is so horrible and shocking that there is no way to express it with human language." According to Lewin, the talk with Nowodworski took place on 28.08.1942; an analogous date is in the documents of Ring. II/296. Abraham Lewin, in a later part of his diary, mentions subsequent escapees from Treblinka, who submitted their testimonies to, inter alia, Jakub Rabinowicz (see Ring. I/298): see Lewin, Dziennik, BŻIH, no. 22 (1957), pp. 104–105; *Kronika getta*, p. 416.

19. Several documents survived that could be characterized as rough drafts, materials intended for recopying cleanly, e.g., Jechiel Górny's notes with the texts of his account (see Ring. I/255 and I/1219), and Eliasz Gutkowski's notes in Ring. II/296 (see above). The numerous notes of Hersz Wasser may have a similar character, containing fragments of testimonies.

20. E.g., Ringelblum writes about the making of a copy of Chaim Aron Kapłan's diary, borrowed by Oyneg Shabes from the author (*Kronika getta*, p. 491).

21. Aside from the aforementioned account by Nowodworski, recollections of other escapees from Treblinka were also written down, e.g., Jakub Krzepicki (see Ring. II/299). See also Ring. II/295, II/298.

22. A similar diagram could be made for documents in Ring. I/57, I/104, I/123, I/475, I/487, I/851, I/873, I/938, and I/1047.

We also often find the following structure:

| A or W | → | B |
|---|---|---|
| (not preserved) | | Manuscript or typescript (copy of document A or W made by RA's copyist) |

An atypical situation took place in Ring. I/956/a; this document includes statements by former prisoners of the camp in Pomiechówek:

| W | → | A | → | B |
|---|---|---|---|---|
| Manuscript. Notes of the oral statement prepared by Salomea Ostrowska of Oyneg Shabes (not preserved) | | Manuscript. Clean copy prepared by Salomea Ostrowska, including the texts of the oral statements, and signed by the authors of the recollections | | Typescript. Copy of A made at Oyneg Shabes. |

In this case, Ostrowska's clean copy is accepted as the original because it was certified by the persons submitting the statement. At the same time, we have no doubt here that the author of the clean copy was also responsible for conducting the interview. However, we can ascertain this fact in only a small portion of the surviving statements in the RA; these are found in several texts recorded by Daniel Fligelman, Szymon Huberband, Hersz Wasser, and others.[23]

Copies of various documents created by the members of Oyneg Shabes may be categorized into two groups. The first contains items prepared in a single copy from which additional copies were made, in accordance with the RA's accepted principles for dealing with original documents. The second group consists of transcripts prepared at one time in several copies, mostly in two through four copies prepared manually or on a typewriter. Carbon paper was generally employed for handwritten copies;[24] the sheets (A4 in size) were folded in half, with a pencil carbon situated between the sheets. As a rule, copies of each document were made separately, with their own pagination. A certain exception was the copybook in which were recorded some of the so-called "Płock letters," as well as Józef Piotrkowski's testimony (Ring. I/838). The handwritten manuscript was prepared by an anonymous copyist (TT*)[25] in four copies, with pencil on carbon paper, giving it continuous pagination; pages 2–74 have survived.[26]

In general, the process of making several copies of a document concluded its duplication, although the workers occasionally made several additional copies. This may have happened independently, as various persons from the ghetto archive's staff had access to the same materials; it is also possible that particularly interesting documents were selected for more assured preservation in this manner.[27]

The question of censorship also arises. As we compared different versions of surviving documents, we ascertained that in these cases exact copies were made of the entire contents. The occasional minor changes did not significantly alter the contents of the document.[28] Of course, we cannot make such statements with regard to texts for which we do not possess original documents. In those cases, we must wonder about the degree to which some of the archive's transcribers interfered with the contents of the statements.[29]

The preparation of copies was an enormous undertaking, but was only one domain in which the Oyneg Shabes group was occupied. Some documents had to be translated, most often into Yiddish; others were recorded exclusively in the Hebrew alphabet. Hersz Wasser, in a postwar note, underscored that writing with "Hebrew letters" was done for "security" (see Ring. I/288).[30] Occasionally, Yiddish documents were also translated into Polish.[31]

Because many of the documents were anonymously written, it was difficult to differentiate them at first glance. Very often, then, a different sort of marking system was adopted, probably to facilitate the possible identification of specific copies of a document.[32] This system was useful for mixing manuscripts

23. To differentiate this type of text from other copies, I describe them in the catalog as originals with a suitable designation: "oryg.(o)"; notes from conducted interviews receive a similar qualification—W.

24. It is worth noting that most transcripts made in several copies (handwritten and typed) were made on good-quality writing paper, of uniform characteristics. Perhaps the Oyneg Shabes team assembled it in large quantity or had access to some other regular supply of such paper.

25. A list of the abbreviations designating a document's characteristics is appended to this essay.

26. It seems that the copybook was initially considered one document, buried as such in 1942 (nos. 735–736), but only after the war was it broken up into separate documents with different call numbers: Ring. I/534 (pp. 2–11), I/541 (pp. 12–13), I/539 (pp. 14–17), I/533/b (pp. 18–26), I/533/c (pp. 27–35), I/537 (pp. 36–40), I/536/d (pp. 41–42), I/536/f (pp. 43–44), I/536/i (pp. 45–47), I/838 (pp. 48–74).

27. For example, both Jerzy Winkler and Eliasz Gutkowski made copies of a document from Ring. I/272.

28. This general rule was sometimes ignored. We find a distinct trace of censorship of a text by the Oyneg Shabes's copyist in Ring. I/809. Bluma Wasser, who prepared the copy of this statement, omitted original fragments that critically discussed the attitude of several social activists in the Warsaw Ghetto (among others, at the Joint) in regard to refugees from Góra Kalwaria. One can wonder at the effectiveness of such censorship when both examples of the statement were preserved together. It seems, however, that the original of this statement, like others, was supposed to be kept separately or returned to the author.

29. A document in Ring. I/846 may be an example of a faithfully recorded statement that preserves the original, quite awkward language of the recollections' author. Also see E.R.'s observations (*Kronika getta*, p. 483).

30. Ring. I/276, I/880, I/1129, I/1161, I/1188.

31. Ring. I/549/a, b, c.

32. Significantly less often, similar markings were placed on originals, e.g., many of them can be seen on the manuscripts of Emanuel Ringelblum's *Ghetto Chronicle* (e.g., Ring. I/507).

within the conspiratorial conditions required for preserving materials, their movement, and their concealment. No key has been found in the archive's materials that might reveal the meaning of particular markings; hence our determinations are hypothetical. The markings or symbols were of some utility during the preparation of the new catalog of the ghetto archive.

The copyists themselves produced some of the markings, while others were introduced later. Mostly, one document was marked in a uniform fashion, but this was not always the case with its copies. Sometimes only selected copies were marked. For example, in the copybook of the so-called "Płock letters," by an anonymous copyist (TT*), markings were placed on the first and fourth copies of the document (e.g., Ring. I/536/d). This procedure might indicate that these copies were intended to be kept apart from the rest.

Markings made by the copyists or other persons connected with the Oyneg Shabes group may be divided into letter markings using the Hebrew, Latin, or Greek alphabet. There are also symbolic markings that take the form of geometric figures such as triangles, rectangles, circles, lines, and parallel lines, as well as other symbols.[33] Symbols also include little crosses ("+") drawn with red pencil; these often appear alongside other markings and were likely utilized by one person. Perhaps this was a sign after the entry of the document into a register unknown to us or a confirmation of other record-keeping activities.[34] Individual markings are indicated in the catalog in technical descriptions of documents.

The materials were also inventoried. A precise list was made of part of the correspondence known as the "Kalisz letters," including items by various persons sent to Kalisz and to people from Kalisz who were in the Warsaw Ghetto. There are also copies of letters from German POW camps for officers. We do not know whether the compilers intended to create similar lists for the rest of the correspondence. The Kalisz collection is a particularly valuable example of the organizational efforts conducted in the Oyneg Shabes collections, since not only its inventory, written in the hand of Jechiel Górny, has survived (Ring. I/542),[35] but a large selection of the letters themselves was saved as well (Ring. I/595, I/599). The cataloging efforts initially embraced a much larger collection of correspondence (more than 290 letters), which for unknown reasons was later restricted to just 146 items. All the letters were numbered and individually described in an appended list (noting sender, addressee, and the date the letter was written). Originals were gathered in this collection, as well as a large collection of copies (i.e., correspondence from POW camps).

Other lists of the Oyneg Shabes collections were created. Ring. I/1176 preserves fragments of a list containing descriptions of several dozen documents with information on contents (or title), authors (copyists), and numbers of pages. Lists of other texts made presumably for financial purposes assembled information about individual documents; most likely, these marked details about the payment of honoraria to authors for carrying out concrete projects, recording statements, and so on.[36] This data was also reflected in documents on which Hersz Wasser placed a special code, showing matches in general lists.[37] These activities facilitated compilation of general reports (statistics) and enable establishing with certainty the extent of the collected materials relating to individual thematic groups. Wasser compiled this kind of general statistical summary, including information on a theme such as the number of described cities (appended to a list of those cities), the number of papers written, or the number of pages.[38] Working papers on acquisitions were also included in the ghetto archive's collections. It is difficult to say how systematically this type of records was kept, since preserved fragments originated exclusively from the spring and summer of 1942 (Ring. I/1147/b).

It is still not clear what Hersz Wasser intended to show with the records known as "transports." Possibly the term indicates preparation for division and concealment of the collected material. Descriptions of three "transports" have survived from January 1942: 107, 108, and 109.[39] The first included exclusively printed items: underground periodicals, second and third copies of different documents, statements, correspondence, and

33. Various markings appear particularly often in the manuscripts of some copyists, e.g., on documents prepared by Bluma Wasser, Mordechaj Szwarcbard, and the anonymous AA* and TT*.

34. See Ring. I/533/a, I/865, I/869/a, I/897/a, I/892, I/902/a, I/902/b, I/910, I/912, I/987, I/1005, I/1028, and I/1040/13. The majority of these are manuscripts produced by Mordechaj Szwarcbard and Bluma Wasser.

35. Presumably, Jechiel Górny, who originated from Kalisz, not only made a list of the entire collection, but also assembled and organized it. All the copies of letters from POW camps in the collection were also prepared by his hand.

36. We find this type of fragmentary Oyneg Shabes financial record in Ring. I/1176.

37. The code consists of three parts: number, the abbreviation in Yiddish "st" and the Yiddish word "zayt" [page], e.g., "4,5 st—zayt." Presumably the letters "st" are an abbreviation of the word "standard" (in Yiddish), so that the entire entry can indicate how many "standard" pages comprise the given document. [Trans. note: The Yiddish word "shtandard" begins with the letters shin-tes, or sh and t; perhaps Wasser's abbreviation "st" reflects German spelling that approximated the Yiddish pronunciation.] It is not entirely clear what parameters that standard page had, according to which the volume of texts in the ghetto archive was reckoned. Registers in Ring. I/1176 present a sum of the number of "standard" pages of various documents. Parallel to these lists of numbers of pages, in a second column Wasser recorded other lists of figures that he also added up. It is worth noting that this second column adds up to only about 6.2 percent of the first figures. We also do not know the purpose of this last operation.

38. In Ring. I/1176 we find several such balance sheets illustrating Oyneg Shabes's documentational activity, e.g., 1,529 pages of reports were collected on 116 towns, as well as 121 photographs, and 117 periodicals. There were 57 reports on 270 pages about Łódź; and 114 different documents on 684 pages about 57 camps.

39. See Ring. I/1176.

reports. In addition to the list of materials going into the "transport's" makeup, certain markings were made on the documents (exclusively from "transports" 108 and 109).[40] Wasser inserted these on the top of the first pages, in a visible place. In the case of several copies of the same documents, the number of the "transport" was usually recorded on the second copy.[41] Thanks to Wasser's records, we know that other "transports" also existed, for which separate lists did not survive, but we find their traces in the materials of the ghetto archive; for example, several documents are included in "transport" 104 of 1941.[42] Among others, the collection included documents relating to forced labor and labor camps for Jews. Wasser inserted additional notations on these: "Labor Department—Materials" or only "Department" (Ring. I/6, I/28, I/372). Texts prepared by Bernard Kampelmacher were found in "transport" no. 105 (Ring. I/10, I/71, I/658).[43]

The aforementioned lists contain documents about which there are larger or smaller traces in the ghetto archive, and there is a list of printed leaflets that are missing among the rescued materials. That collection, numbering 707 items (see Ring. I/1147), may have undergone destruction before the burial of Ring. I, or could be concealed in another, unknown place.

Smaller traces of record-keeping are still encountered on many documents of Ring. I, including on the Oyneg Shabes bulletins. Materials collected by Oyneg Shabes also were used in bulletins issued by the underground press in the ghetto and beyond its borders. These documents were prepared by Gutkowski and Wasser. It is possible that traces of such a collective bulletin with common pagination have been preserved in fragments among the Oyneg Shabes bulletins in Ring I/261 (formerly Ring. II/486), I/469, I/471, and I/473.[44] Another attempt to catalog selected manuscripts is present in numbers 1–6, and 9–11; they appear on certain documents prepared by Mordechaj Szwarcbard.[45]

The purpose of registering the collected materials was also to divide them into thematic groups in accordance with the general program of the Oyneg Shabes group. Information qualifying a given study for a concrete thematic group was inserted by the authors or the copyists themselves. The form of the inscription on different documents was similar; it started with the words "from the series . . ." or "from the cycle, . . ." after which followed the name of the series, including "2½ [years] (Ring. I/1220/31), "Białystok and others . . ." (Ring. I/1220/31), "Courtyard singers . . ." (Ring. I/172), "Jewish wages in the ghetto" (Ring. I/226), "Jewish earnings" (Ring. I/250), "Places of entertainment in the ghetto" (Ring. I/186), "Friends of Jews" (Ring. I/165), or "Jews in the Polish Army. . . ."[46]

Cataloging the ghetto archive included not only preparation of finding aids and the marking of documents, but also gathering and preservation of them in the prescribed manner. As a good amount of the material of Ring. I was kept in binders, we must ask if there was no fear about keeping the Oyneg Shabes collections in a visible place; these items were possibly even for a certain time in the office cabinets of the ŻSS at Tłomackie 5.[47] At the start of the occupation, the situation was different. People feared searches and destroyed a great number of valuable manuscript and printed materials. However, the succeeding months showed that the Germans were not interested in the written and printed words kept in a Jewish home. As was true of others, Emanuel Ringelblum did not intend initially to reveal his work as a chronicler. Therefore, during the first months of the occupation he backdated his entries, inserting dates preceding 1 September 1939. He also made the documents look like letters and recorded individual fragments on loose sheets, so that in the event of a search, the Chronicle would look more like a collection of correspondence than a systematically kept diary.[48]

It is more difficult to trace the arrangement of the materials in Ring. II. For example, the collection of press clippings in Ring. II/345 was numbered in one and the same handwriting, in the manner of clandestinely printed other matter of Ring. II.[49]

40. The same description contained the following items, e.g., "108–1942/1 January."

41. See Ring. I/478–479. It seems that this number was consistently entered on the second copy of the transcripts, but at this moment we cannot always ascertain it due to missing pages and other damage to many documents.

42. Ring. I/6, I/28, I/663, I/1220 (see Ring. I/198).

43. Data about other "transports" are lacking.

44. See Ring. I/469 (pp. 1–2), Ring. I/471 (pp. 3–5), Ring. I/261 (formerly Ring. II/486) (p. 6), Ring. I/473 (pp. 7–8).

45. Not only the uniform character of Mordechaj Szwarcbard's writing links all of these documents, but also the fact that they were buried in one box (no. 3).

46. Document from the ghetto archive not preserved in the collections of the Jewish Historical Institute; see *Selected Documents*, pp. 226–227.

47. Significantly, more than two hundred documents from Ring. I were kept in binders.

48. See Ring. I/507/1. Ringelblum recalls that "the Germans did not care what a Jew did while at home. So the Jew took to writing. Everybody wrote: journalists, literary men, teachers, social activists, youths, even children. . . . The creation of the ghetto, the closure of Jews behind the walls, established more favorable conditions for archival work. . . . The Gestapo's Jewish agents were busy searching out rich Jews, warehouses with goods, ferreting out smuggling, and so forth. Politics did not interest them. It reached the point that illegal publications of all the trends appeared nearly openly. They were read almost openly in coffee houses, press funds were collected, people argued with opponents' publications. In a word, people acted not a little like before the war. Not strange that in conditions of such 'freedom' prevailing among the ghetto's slaves, Oyneg Shabes had favorable conditions for development. At that time its activity blossomed." See *Kronika getta*, pp. 471, 473.

49. On the basis of numbers made with red pencil (nos. 1, 5, 9–10, 17, 19–28a survived), we are able to reconstitute a fragment of the collection of underground printed matter, now scattered among the files Ring. II/317, II/324, II/328, II/329, II/330, II/332, II/334, and II/341.

This collection presumably belonged to one person (Eliasz Gutkowski?) and was arranged by that person. The collection of clandestinely printed matter was arranged and described no earlier than the start of January 1943, or a few weeks before the second part of the ghetto archive was hidden.

## HIDING OF THE GHETTO ARCHIVE

The beginning of the first liquidation action in the Warsaw Ghetto on 22 July 1942 interrupted the cataloging work of the ghetto archive. There was no time to divide the collected material and bury it in various locations.[50] The tragic development of the situation in the ghetto compelled the workers of Oyneg Shabes to adopt a flash decision for saving the collections. We do not ultimately know how and where the group initially planned to bury the archive materials: Was transfer of the archive or part of it "to the Aryan side" considered? Were safe places only sought within the ghetto's terrain? Perhaps the first solution seemed too risky, as in the event of failure the collections would be threatened with destruction.[51] The leaders finally decided to conceal the archive within the ghetto itself. Teacher Izrael Lichtensztajn, one of the collectors, together with his pupils Dawid Graber and Nachum Grzywacz, prepared the materials for concealment on the night of 2–3 August 1942, in the cellar of the school building at ul. Nowolipki 68. They themselves probably buried the ten metal boxes on the afternoon of 3 August.[52] We know about these events from written statements by Grzywacz and Graber, completed on that day (3.08.1942) and placed in the boxes with the materials of the ghetto archive. Hersz Wasser also knew the archive's burial place.[53]

We do not know whether the materials were kept in one location or in different places within the ghetto before their burial. Were they assembled in the school at ul. Nowolipki 68 shortly before the final concealment? Or had they been kept there previously as well? Thanks to a list made in 1946, we do know the form in which Ring. I was hidden. It appears that most of the materials were packed into the boxes in a haphazard fashion, and that sometimes individual copies of the same documents were separated. For example, the original and three copies of the statement "Recollections from the Pawiak, told by a Jew, a citizen of the USSR" were secreted in different places (Ring. I/198, I/668, and I/1220). Two copies found their way into box no. 6, and a third into box no. 7. While we do not know where the original was placed, it was rejoined with the scattered items after being dug out (Ring. I/1220). Scattered to an even greater degree was the Yiddish statement of Józef Piotrowski, "History and War Experience of Kutno" (Ring. I/838). Its individual copies and fragments were discovered in boxes nos. 3, 5, 8, and 10 (No. 312, 735, 1208, and 1672).[54]

There are several exceptions, however, among which must be counted the effects of Izrael Lichtensztajn and his wife Gela Seksztajn. Their papers were placed almost entirely in box no. 4.[55] Also, part of the printed matter was distributed in larger batches into the same boxes; among these, the collections of proclamations from Piotrków, Łódź, and Warsaw were found in box 5. Ignoring these exceptions, the arrangement of the collection after packing shows that the archive was hidden in great haste and that the workers did not have time to separate individual documents.

The second part of the ghetto archive's materials was hidden most probably in February 1943, also within the terrain of the building at ul. Nowolipki 68, in two large metal milk canisters.[56] In contrast to Ring. I, the exact date and circumstances connected with the burial of Ring. II are unknown.

50. It is not certain whether or not the plan to divide the ghetto archive was in part realized. First, it appears that in many instances of copies made with pencil and carbon paper, the fourth copy is missing; it could have been detached and hidden earlier or in another place together with the remaining materials. Second, some materials included in Ring. II were collected before August 1942, but for reasons unknown to us they were not hidden with Ring. I (e.g., Ring. II/301, II/303, II/305, II/310). Perhaps they were concealed in another place within the ghetto and were not added in time to the rest of the archive located at the start of August in the school at Nowolipki 68.

51. Preparations for securing and hiding the materials of Oyneg Shabes commenced before the liquidation action, for these matters were discussed at a meeting on 18 July 1942. See H. Wasser, *The Ghetto Archives*, op. cit., p. 43. However, we have no certainty about whether small fragments of the collection were earlier placed on the other side of the ghetto wall. After 22 July 1942, the issue of hiding the collection was a matter of high priority at successive meetings of Oyneg Shabes. The fact of the packing of materials into uniform metal boxes (see below) also bears witness that the coworkers of Oyneg Shabes had a little time to prepare for hiding the archive. See A. Lewin, *A Cup of Tears: A Diary of the Warsaw Ghetto*, edited by Antony Polonsky, Oxford 1988, p. 141.

52. The boxes were identically made of zinc sheet metal (dimensions ca. 495×300×147 mm).

53. According to Michał Borwicz, Hersz Wasser participated in the burial of the ghetto archive. See *Pieśń ujdzie cało. Antologia wierszy o Żydach pod okupacją niemiecką*, ed. M. Borwicz (Warsaw-Łódź-Kraków, 1947), p. 42.

54. Less frequently, documents themselves were broken up. In Ring. I/388, p. 15 (transcript in 3 copies) was buried apart from the rest of the pages of that document; after the war, it was not restored and was included among the fragments (Ring. I/1220). Two copies of a letter from Ring. I/540 were buried together and preserved in very good condition, while the third copy of this document was placed elsewhere and suffered serious damage; after the war it was added to the fragments (Ring. I/1220).

55. Taking into account that Izrael Lichtensztajn could not only participate in the concealment of the ghetto archive, but also in packing it into boxes, the arrangement of his own papers together with his wife's effects seems quite logical.

56. Currently, one of the two milk canisters is displayed at the United States Holocaust Memorial Museum in Washington, while the other is at the Jewish Historical Institute in Warsaw. The canister displayed in Warsaw is ca. 630 mm high, while the diameter of its bottom is ca. 320 mm; on the rim at the neck is an impressed inscription: "Kraszewo."

## RING. III

The materials hidden in 1942 and 1943 did not include the entire Oyneg Shabes collection.[57] After the concealment of Ring. II, further fragments of the ghetto archive and documents collected later were buried in the building at ul. Świętojerska 34. In November and December 1949, at the request of the Central Committee of Jews in Poland, Jan Michalik's construction firm carried out demolition and excavation work in the first outbuilding (*oficyna*)[58] of the real estate parcel at ul. Świętojerska 34. The cellars were to be cleared of rubble and excavated to a depth of 1.5 meters. However, no trace of papers was found during the search.[59] At the end of March 2003, another attempt was undertaken to find the third part of the ghetto archive; this occurred when excavations were begun on the site of the former Świętojerska 34, now occupied by the embassy of China. The effort ended without success.

## HISTORY AND ARRANGEMENT OF THE RINGELBLUM ARCHIVE AFTER THE WAR

The materials of Ring. I were retrieved on 18 September 1946 with the participation of Hersz Wasser.[60] The second part of the collection could not be found at the time but was stumbled upon by accident on 1 December 1950, during construction work on the site of ul. Nowolipki 68.

The first attempt to register the rescued fragments of the archive was undertaken immediately after its excavation. On 23 September 1946, the first two boxes were opened by the Historical Commission, and a list of documents was compiled ("Catalog of Dr. Emanuel Ringelblum's Archive").[61] Documents from successive boxes were listed separately. The work lasted, with interruptions, until 25 November 1946, when the review of the documents found in the tenth and final box was concluded.[62]

Nevertheless, not all of the materials were cataloged then. For example, the collection of damaged documents was only generally described: "3 files of loose pages and shreds, [sheets] 172, 137, 163";[63] and after 25 November 1946, collections of papers including texts by Itzik Manger were added, but with no indication of the specific boxes in which they were found. The "Catalog of Dr. Emanuel Ringelblum's Archive" was written by Dr. Laura Eichhorn. Others who participated with her included Dora Elbirt, Józef Lejman, Abraham Penzak, Józef Sandel, Mojżesz Sztajn, Bluma Wasser, Hersz Wasser, Rachela Auerbach, Józef Wulf, and Nachman (Natan) Blumental.[64] Following the start of the cataloging work in the 1950s, new document

57. Even after the final liquidation of the Warsaw Ghetto, a few Oyneg Shabes coworkers, who survived subsequent liquidation actions and managed to escape to the "Aryan side," continued their documentary efforts, e.g., Emanuel Ringelblum, Rachela Auerbach, and Hersz Wasser. As in the ghetto, Wasser prepared reports that were intended to be sent abroad. However, there were no longer conditions for conducting broader activity and so they were limited chiefly to individual creativity. Materials developed at that time were not collected in one place and only a small part of them survived to the war's end. Among others, manuscripts of Emanuel Ringelblum and Rachela Auerbach were preserved. See R. Auerbach, *Baym letstn veg. In geto varshe un oyf der arisher zayt*, Tel Aviv, 1977, pp. 279–280, 302; *Żydzi Warszawy*, p. 223; W. Bartoszewski, Z. Lewinówna, *Ten jest z ojczyzny mojej. Polacy z pomocą Żydom* 1939–1945 (Kraków, 1969), p. 999.

58. Trans. note: Most Warsaw residential buildings were constructed in the form of a compound with a gate on the street leading to a courtyard around which were rear buildings with their own entrances from the courtyard. Such outbuildings are called *oficyna* in Polish.

59. Information on the topic of the third part of the ghetto archive is in, among others, B. Mark, "Ruch oporu i geneza powstania w getcie warszawskim," BŻIH, no. 1/1951, p. 4; documents discussing the searches in 1949 are preserved in the ŻIH Archive (Wydział Techniczno-Budowlany Centralnego Komitetu Żydów w Polsce [Technical-Construction Department of the Central Committee of Jews in Poland]).

60. That unusual moment is recalled by a participant in the searches for the ghetto archive:

> Calculations began on the basis of testimonies and guesses as well as trial removal of debris under the direction of the engineer Pliszczyński. Finally—to the underground terrain at the former Nowolipki Street, where the building designated with the number 68 at one time stood. They broke through a sort of chimney, reached by removal of a bank of bricks. Accessible underground were only two chambers, whose ceiling somehow held; the rest was totally covered. Where was the archive buried? Wasser had been present when the boxes were concealed. However, at that time the place was entered differently, which frustrated orientation. After shoring up the ceiling, excavation commenced. We knew that the sought-after archive might be found a meter beneath the surface. Shovels tossed out one decimeter of earth after the other. We workers of the Historical Commission—Wulf, Blumental, and I—stood, looking at each other, reading in each other's eyes the same thought: Is there something after all . . . ? Suddenly, a shovel strikes something hard. After a certain time, the first metal box appears. After that, by layers: eight. In the second chimney—two more . . .

See *Pieśń ujdzie cało. Antologia wierszy o Żydach pod okupacją niemiecką*, ed. M. Borwicz (Warsaw-Łódź–Kraków, 1947), pp. 42–43 (here also are included photographs illustrating the work during the excavation and cataloging of Ring. I in September 1946; also see the photograph after p. 48).

61. The initial catalog ("Katalog Archiwum dr Emanuela Ringelbluma" [Catalog of the Archive of Dr. Emanuel Ringelblum]) was written by hand in three school notebooks (handwritten in ink in Polish, 148×208 mm, sewn). The description was divided into the following items: ordinal reference number (notebook 1 [Lb. 1–756], notebook 2 [Lb. 757–1442], notebook 3 [Lb. 1443–1737] ), author, title, date, language, number of pages, handwritten, typed, printed, ink, pencil, format, condition of the document, remarks.

62. Individual boxes contained the following documents (date of opening given in parentheses): Boxes 1 and 2 (23.09.1946): nos. 1–302; Box 3 (8.10.1946): nos. 303–669; Box 4 (14.10.1946): nos. 670–677; Box 5 (15.10.1946): nos. 678–838; Box 6 (23.10.1946): nos. 839–998; Box 7 (24.10.1946): nos. 998 [sic]–1148; Box 8 (no date): nos. 1149–1467; Box 9 (7.11.1946): nos. 1468–1548; Box 10 (15–25.11.1946): nos. 1549–1720.

63. Subsequently, two units were created out of these materials: Ring. I/599 and Ring. I/1220 (the so-called *rozsyp* of fragmentary documents), that were finally arranged only during the work on the new inventory during 2001–2002.

64. H. Wasser, "Archiwum dra Emanuela Ringelbluma," *Przełom*, 1946, no. 3 (October), p. 7; N. Blumental, "Di arbet iber Ringelblums ksavyadn," *Yediyes. Biuletin fun Yidishn Historishn Institut*, 1949, November, pp. 3–6.

call numbers were added. The old call numbers have been preserved on the jackets of some documents (e.g., "no. 1715").

Entries in the "Catalog" were made when the documents were first viewed, so their content is limited to general information that is not always accurate. Descriptions of the contents were limited to one- or two-word designations and it is difficult to determine their actual content. The technical descriptions are also not always accurate. Often omitted is information about the total number of copies and the number of pages that survived in several copies. Under these circumstances, there could be no talk of full verification of the contents of individual manuscripts, or of comparing them with other previously described ones. Despite these gaps, the "Catalog" does provide basic data on Ring. I. It permits partial verification of descriptions, reconstruction of the original arrangement of the materials, and gathering of data on losses and missing materials. However, no list of the Ring. II materials found in 1950 has been preserved. The first documentation of the second part of the ghetto archive that we possess was the inventory of 1955.

## HERSZ WASSER'S CATALOGING WORK

Hersz Wasser not only participated in the unearthing of Ring. I and its registration in 1946, but also took part in the first cataloging efforts. First and foremost, he conducted the initial verification and description of the documents found. He did this on loose pages attached to individual documents. At the moment, we do not know whether he covered the entire collection or only a selected portion, because most of Wasser's notes were scattered and lost. Sometimes the only traces of the lost notes are entries in the inventory of 1955, into which part of the information passed on by Wasser was entered.

Wasser's explanations are an irreplaceable source of information. Without them, our knowledge about the archive would be very limited. Wasser provided us with diverse data, often presenting even trivial information on subjects such as the contents of a manuscript, never going beyond an elementary description of the document. However, in many cases, he added essential details about a document's authorship, origins, or date. Many of these data had tremendous significance for properly identifying the ghetto archive's materials, including information on authors and provenance of texts preserved in the collection. Sometimes, an item of information helped to determine the question of authorship.

Nevertheless, analysis of Wasser's entries at times revealed that he did not always accurately reconstruct the history of the preserved manuscripts; sometimes it seems that he unwittingly diverged from the truth. He ascribed the same texts to different authors, did not recognize the handwritings of Oyneg Shabes's regular collaborators, and made statements that contradicted his own notes from the occupation period. We find in Ring. I/375 and I/389 a particularly telling example of contradictory data, included in two of Wasser's notes attached to the same testimony.[65] Under those call numbers were preserved two different copies of a statement about the labor camp in Mordy. The document from Ring. I/375 was prepared by Daniel Fligelman from an anonymous testimony. Three typed copies were produced from the original manuscript in the ghetto archive, and are now in Ring. I/389. While preparing his notes after the war, Wasser did not have both copies simultaneously before his eyes, so he described one first, and the other later. He recognized Fligelman's handwritten original without difficulty, since the latter's handwriting is very idiosyncratic. When describing the typescript from Ring. I/389, Wasser ascribed the preparation of the statement to himself, but named as its author Abram Erlich, about whom he had forgotten with relation to Ring. I/375. We cannot be certain if Erlich was actually the statement's author as ascribed by Wasser, or if Wasser confused Ring. I/389 with another text that he prepared for the ghetto archive.

Similar ambiguities are evoked by information transmitted by Wasser on various copies of the statement by [Michał] Suryc, a Warsaw attorney. The statement's text has been preserved in a damaged and illegible copy by Fligelman (Ring. I/1220), to which Wasser presumably did not append notes, because in 1946 the document was placed among the fragments *(rozsyp)*. There also exists a version produced from Fligelman's manuscript by an anonymous copyist (BTT*) in three copies (two in Ring. I/198 and the third in Ring. I/668). Before the ghetto archive was hidden, Wasser wrote on the third copy (Ring. I/668) that the document was prepared by "Kon" or Natan (?) Koniński. However, Wasser's note attached to Ring. I/198[66] suggests that the statement was not recorded by ghetto archive workers, but was submitted in the original by B. Rotenberg of Żyrardów. The recollections could have been borrowed in the original or in the copy produced by a third person, while a copy was made in the ghetto archive and the original text was returned. Koniński could have made the initial copy, and perhaps Fligelman copied Koniński's transcript or independently made a second copy from the original. So far as can be seen, we cannot ultimately reconstruct the history of the aforementioned document on the basis of the conflicting data provided by Wasser.[67] Though the information deposited before the conceal-

65. Ring. I/375, appended note by H.W.: "Labor camp in Marki [*sic*] near Warsaw. Deposition recorded by Daniel Fligelman." Ring. I/389, appended note by H.W.: "Labor camp in Mordy near Siedlce 1941 (Judenlager Mordy). Fragment of a testimony given by Abram Erlich, written down by H. Wasser."

66. Ring. I/198, appended note by H.W.: "Recollections from Pawiak, told by citiz[ens] of USSR of Jewish nation[ality]. 2 copies, cit[izen] B. Rotenberg of Żyrardów (Zionist activist) forwarded this deposition to cit[izen] Suryc. 1941."

67. Another example of conflicting information is provided by the notations attached to the anonymous statement relating to the Warsaw Ghetto: Ring. I/212—appended note by H.W.: "Submitted by Aron Koniński"; Ring. I/239—appended note H.W.: "Submitted by Szymon Wyszewiański (J.H.K.)." In Ring. I/930 Wasser wrote in his notation that Nechemiasz Tytelman recorded the statement, while only a copy handwritten by an anonymous copyist TT* has been preserved; to Ring. I/1166 Wasser attached a note stating that it is Nechemiasz Tytelman's manuscript, while the anonymous copyist MA* actually wrote the document. However, a notation made by H.W. before burial of the documents declared that the text's author is Glater, about whom nothing is said in the postwar note.

ment of the ghetto archive may be more reliable, we cannot be certain as to whether we are correctly reading its content. This also applies to postwar notes placed on texts.

To the statement "Legal Position of Refugees" (Ring. I/474), Wasser appended a note saying that the document had been forwarded to the ghetto archive by Abraham Lewin. From that information we can draw entirely diverse conclusions: that Lewin recorded the statement, or another person wrote it and Lewin delivered it to the ghetto archive. Both conclusions are possible. The statement's text was preserved in a copy by an anonymous copyist (CC*), but could have been made on the basis of notes, though not preserved, by Lewin, who conducted the interview with the author of the statement. Somewhat different problems arose in the course of preparing a document from Ring. I/934. Those recollections by an anonymous female author were preserved in a copy prepared by Jechiel Górny. In a postwar note, Wasser confirmed the authorship of this transcript, but in the list in Ring. I/1176, next to the document in question, he wrote the cryptonym of Natan Koniński ("Kon"). This meant that Koniński presumably transcribed the statement and Górny only copied it, a factor that Wasser must have forgotten.

We encounter yet another situation in the description of Ring. I/420. Wasser described the document in the following manner: "Deposition of Helena Kagan, forwarded by Dr. Emanuel Ringelblum." Two versions of this statement were preserved: a copy handwritten by Salomea Ostrowska and a typescript. Both documents lack notations indicating their connection with the person who created Oyneg Shabes. Moreover, we know of no document—other than the author's own texts—prepared by Ringelblum. Did Wasser err in this case as well or did Salomea Ostrowska make her own copy from the original that Ringelblum supplied or lent her from the author?[68]

While composing his postwar notes, Wasser did not include any document call numbers. If the contents of notations do not permit identification with the given manuscript, we are not always sure if Wasser's surviving postwar descriptions are in the right place. Only in recent years have the call numbers of the documents to which they apply been added.[69]

## THE FIRST INVENTORY OF THE RINGELBLUM ARCHIVE

Work on the first archival inventory of the entire collection commenced only in early 1955 under the direction of Arno Otto Zahler, an employee of the Jewish Historical Institute's Archive.[70] The 1955 inventory included most of the materials of the ghetto archive (Ring. I and II). With the collection, but outside the cataloging records, remained the fragments *(rozsyp)*, that only during the preparation of the present inventory were finally catalogued (ca. 300 sheets) and assigned the call number Ring. I/1220. The collection of photographs was entirely removed from Ring. I and transferred to the Jewish Historical Institute's iconographic collections, where the contents were dispersed.[71] Also removed were the works of Gela Seksztajn; after being described, they became a separate collection in the Jewish Historical Institute's Museum.[72] A portion of the printed matter was also isolated; these included the majority of the preserved issues of the *Gazeta Żydowska*.[73]

The inventory prepared in 1955 is more of a general list of documents than a real archival inventory. Many of the descriptions were compiled without properly recognizing the contents of the described units and individual documents. The general description provided little data about the real condition of the contents.[74] To a large extent, the first part of the collection was prepared on the basis of Hersz Wasser's notations. Laconic descriptions of the contents of documents say little about the actual contents of the records; for example, the valuable collection of correspondence (in the so-called "Kalisz letters") and other documents, numbering more than 100 items, was described as "various fragments of letters." Very often, the author did not include even existing titles of documents, nor did he differentiate between the text of the source and his own. While transcribing Wasser's notes, the author did not inform the reader about the source of the data. The technical description also contains numerous gaps. For Ring. I, the 1955 inventory's author did not make use of some information contained in the list of 1946. Despite these omissions, the inventory of 1955 served readers of

68. Wasser also had difficulties with identification of the author in the instance of the statement from Ring. I/397. In one place, he declares Stefan Cukierman as its author, but in another place Izrael Bursztyn. Presumably the author was Cukierman, since his name appeared before the ghetto archive was hidden.

69. This work was done in large degree by Dr. Ruta Sakowska.

70. "Podziemne Archiwum Getta Warszawskiego (założone przez Emanuela Ringelbluma) [Inwentarz]" [Underground Archive of the Warsaw Ghetto (founded by Emanuel Ringelblum) [Inventory] ], part. I and part II, Warsaw [1955], manuscript, notebooks 1–2, ŻIH Archive in Warsaw.

71. I described the collection of photographs in the inventory under call number Ring. I/1222.

72. I placed the description of the collection of works of Gela Seksztajn into the inventory under the call number Ring. I/1221.

73. According to the list of 1946 (no. 1530–1532), 8 numbers of *Gazeta Żydowska* from 1940 were dug out, 57 from 1941, 34 from 1942. However, only no. 2 of 4 Jan. 1942 has been preserved in the ghetto archive (see Ring. I/702), while the remainder were included in the library collections of ŻIH. Currently, the Library of the Jewish Historical Institute has the following issues of *Gazeta Żydowska* (call no. D.11L), that presumably originate from the RA: Year 1940, nos. 1–2, 36, 41–42, 44, 46; Year 1941, nos. 1–4, 6–7, 10–11, 15, 17–28, 30–37, 39–40, 42–43, 45–48, 58, 60–73, 75–76, 78–82, 84, 90, 97; Year 1942, nos. 2–4, 6–8, 10–21, 24–25, 28, 30–34, 36–44, and 46.

74. The description of the contents of Ring. I/758 is an example of erroneous identification of documents. According to the 1955 inventory, it contains a German newspaper, *Das Generalgouvernement*. In fact, there are fragments of the *Krakauer Zeitung* [Kraków Newspaper] in which one of the sections bears the title, "Das Generalgouvernement." An example of incomplete description is the characterization of the contents of Ring. I/1040: "Journal notes of life of ghettos—Warsaw and the provinces. By M. Szwarcbard." In fact, there are eighteen different texts in this unit, concerning many localities and matters.

the ghetto archive for nearly half a century. After 1955, indexes and subject guides for Ring. I and II were prepared in the Jewish Historical Institute Archive. These finding aides considerably eased usage of the collection's documents, but for the most part did not introduce new details about individual units. Also undertaken was an effort to make typed copies of all the documents. This work was not completed, but a large part of the materials was indeed typed up. At the same time, microfilming of the ghetto archive was begun and finally completed in 2001, thanks to the assistance of the United States Holocaust Memorial Museum in Washington.

Since 1955, the arrangement and contents of the ghetto archive have undergone various minor changes. The cataloging work continued, particularly consolidation of fragmented documents scattered among various call numbers. Descriptions in the inventory and on the file jackets were completed and corrected.[75] Gradually, some documents from the fragments also began to be included in the inventory. Also included was a copy of Emanuel Ringelblum's *Stosunki polsko-żydowskie w czasie drugiej wojny światowej* (Polish-Jewish Relations during the Second World War), that had never been a part of the Archive (not to be confused with notes concerning the subject, which were written down by Ringelblum while he was in the Warsaw Ghetto), as well as the original of this study written after Ringelblum's departure from the ghetto. After 1955, several other documents were also inappropriately inserted into the archive. In the course of preparing the new inventory, these materials were removed and placed into other collections of the JHI Archive.

On the other hand, during the last half-century more than a dozen losses have been noted in the collection. The decisive majority went missing before 1970, when the Jewish Historical Institute did not yet have suitable conditions for preserving the collection and making it accessible.[76] In 1995, forty-three documents that had been preserved in the Ringelblum Archive in several identical copies were transferred to Yad Vashem in Jerusalem.[77]

## AUTHORS AND COPYISTS IN THE RINGELBLUM ARCHIVE

A very important problem that arose during the cataloging of the collection was the question of the authorship of texts found in the collection. It was then necessary to differentiate authors from copyists.[78] Studies deposited into the collections of the ghetto archive were mostly anonymous, as were the texts and copies prepared by Oyneg Shabes workers. This was a general principle applied from considerations of security. Sporadically, pseudonyms were used or people signed with initials; for example, Nechemiasz Tytelman sometimes signed his own manuscripts "N.R." or "N. Rocheles," from his own first name and his mother's first name (Rachela).[79] Eliasz Gutkowski once used the pseudonym "A. Ben-Jakub" (Ring. I/61). We do not know the name of the person who signed her papers with the initials, "H.S.L." (Ring. I/176, I/1071), while Emanuel Ringelblum at times signed his notes with the name "Fajwel"or "Fajwisz."[80] Texts of Kalman Huberband can be identified by the signature, "K.H. Band" (Ring. I/218 and Ring. II/309). While Hersz Was-

75. Dr. Ruta Sakowska has done much work in consolidation of documents and completion of descriptions during the last twenty years.

76. Missing in the ghetto archive are the following units: Ring. I/33, I/106, I/149, I/207, I/242, I/323, I/369, I/430, I/455, I/561, I/981, I/1044, I/1127, and I/1140; Ring. II/120, II/446, II/447, II/448, II/449, II/450, II/451, and II/473. Most of these losses were confirmed on the basis of an audit conducted in 1970. The absence of Ring. I/369 was confirmed in 1999.

77. The call numbers of the documents transferred to the collections of Yad Vashem: Ring. I/38, I/39, I/47, I/54, I/58, /73, I/100, I/104, I/108, I/115, I/116, I/126, I/142, I/145, I/147, I/148, I/150, I/168, I/171, I/176, I/189, I/202, I/203, I/215, I/253, I/254, I/269, I/291, I/337, I/413, I/428, I/431, I/464, I/474, I/480, I/536, I/537, I/538, I/539, I/541, I/566, I/573, and I/663.

78. Differentiation of authors from copyists has not been consistent in many monographs and editions of sources concerning the ghetto archive. This occurred for many reasons. Often lacking were proper recognition of many documents and introduction of a uniform method of describing materials in accord with the general principles of processing archival and library manuscripts. Lack of consistency in ascribing authorship of texts occurs in the monographs of Ruta Sakowska. For example, when discussing texts recorded by Daniel Fligelman, she deals with both his own recollections and statements of other persons which he wrote down or only copied. See R. Sakowska, "Relacje Daniela Fligelmana—członka 'Oneg Szabat' [Testimonies of Daniel Fliegelman, a member of Oyneg Shabes]," BŻIH, no. 137–138 (1986), p. 167 and n.; the very title of this article suggests that Daniel Fligelman's statements are its exclusive theme, and not various texts written down by Fligelman. Sakowska applied a different description for Ring. I/989, where the copyist, Bluma Wasser, was omitted, but only the presumed author was mentioned. See *Dzieci*, p. 130. In Ring. II/296 and II/1196, the authors of the testimonies were also recognized as authors of the preserved manuscripts; see *Archiwum Ringelbluma*, pp. 106, 110. The latter example shows that it is difficult properly to describe a manuscript if we do not identify the character of the handwriting. For example, in *Archiwum Ringelbluma* manuscripts by Eliasz Gutkowski were erroneously ascribed to Emanuel Ringelblum; see ibid., pp. 57, 261. Similar problems appear in other publications, e.g., in Shimon Huberband, *Kiddush Hashem: Jewish Religious and Cultural Life in Poland during the Holocaust*, ed. J. S. Gurock and R. S. Hirt (New York, 1987), where other persons' testimonies that were only written down by him are treated as authored by Huberband (e.g.. Ring. I/185, I/379, I/450).

79. Ring. I/172.

80. According to not entirely confirmed information, the author of the statement from Ring. I/176 and I/1071 was supposedly Helena Syrkus; see T. Epsztein, "Nowy inwentarz Podziemnego Archiwum Getta Warszawskiego (Archiwum Ringelbluma)," *BŻIH*, no. 213/2005, pp. 89–91. However, that should be rejected on the basis of the latest research and analysis of the handwriting of manuscripts of the RA and autographs of Helena Syrkus. (The latter was communicated to me inter alia by Ms. Marta Ciesielska of Warsaw.) For examples of signatures of Emanuel Ringelblum, see Ring. I/507/1.

ser cataloged and described materials of Oyneg Shabes in the Warsaw Ghetto, he rarely placed the full name of the author or copyist on a document (e.g., "Berliner,"[81] "Tykociński,"[82] "Lebensold"[83]). Much more often he employed only pseudonyms, an abbreviated form of a name, initials or other markings, such as "Bliml" (in Yiddish: "Little Flower" for Emanuel Ringelblum);[84] "Razirn" (in Yiddish: "Shave," for Mordechaj Szwarcbard);[85] "Fligar," "Flig" (Daniel Fligelman);[86] "Kampel" (Bernard Kampelmacher);[87] "Kon," "Kohn" (Aron or Natan Koniński?);[88] "I. Ber." (Icchak Berensztein).[89] For texts of the author who signed herself with the initials "H.S.L.," Wasser used the abbreviation, "Vel," while for Bencjon Chilinowicz he used only the letters: "Ch."[90] It has not been possible to identify some cryptonyms: "Hober,"[91] "Kler,"[92] "Lew (Lev),"[93] "Zylber,"[94] "Lomer" (in Yiddish: "Lame"),[95] "Tilem"[96] (in Yiddish: "Psalms"), "Guter,"[97] "Wink,"[98] "Goldfarb," "Iliard," "Cuczel" (Tsutshl ?), and "An."[99]

Wasser also avoided citing full personal data in the lists of the Oyneg Shabes collections that he himself compiled. Instead, he used abbreviated forms for the surnames discussed above, including "Kampel," "Fligar," "Flig," "Vel," "Hober," and "Kler." Other abbreviations include "Szajner" (Szajnkinder), "Ichiel" (Jechiel Górny), and "Mordechaj" (Mordechaj Szwarcbard). Still another method of encoding personal data appears in several of his lists. Instead of using the surname of the text's author or copyist, he states the names of streets where the given person resided, such as "Zamenhof" (Szymon Huberband), "Nowolipie" (Abraham Lewin), "Nowolipki" (Eliasz Gutkowski), "Orla" (Szajnkinder), and "Wołyńska" (Perec Opoczyński) (Ring. I/1176).

Some collaborators included brief profiles of the persons depositing testimonies, since they were unable to give their personal data. Very often, details of this type appeared at the start of a text, before the actual testimony, and referred chiefly to age, occupation, and origins of the author of the recollections. Daniel Fligelman, among others, preferred to provide such information.[100]

Rules about not revealing personal data were not followed with regard to original personal documents such as personal records and correspondence. Nevertheless, in individual instances personal information was erased in the originals (see Ring. I/1135). Decisions to suppress personal data could occur even after a document's completion or during its creation; for example, the person recording the statement in Ring. I/1117 ini-

81. Ring. I/216, I/226.

82. Ring. I/104, also see Ring. I/57.

83. Ring. I/835 and I/873.

84. Emanuel Ringelblum's pseudonym appears in many documents, most of all on various transcripts of his *Kronika getta*; see Ring. I/504, I/505.

85. Ring. I/1039, I/1040/2–3.

86. Ring. I/94, I/499 ("Flig."), I/789, I/839, I/844, I/864, I/940. It is worth noting that only in one case (Ring. I/789) did Wasser designate a manuscript by Fligelman by the abbreviation "Fligar" or "Flig" and in the remaining cases, the handwritten manuscripts and typescripts were ascribed to other persons.

87. Ring. I/9, I/10, I/15, I/71, I/658, I/914, I/941, I/1072.

88. Ring. I/188, I/212, and I/282; I separately discuss the problem of distinguishing between Aron and Natan Koniński. See note 110 below.

89. Ring. I/1138.

90. Ring. I/215, I/322.

91. Ring. I/253, I/868, I/896, I/920.

92. Ring. I/371.

93. Ring. I/256.

94. Ring. I/854.

95. Ring. I/968.

96. According to Józef Kermisz (*Selected Documents*, p. 143), Nechemiasz Tytelman; see Ring. I/361.

97. This cryptonym appears on the copy (TT*) of the statement (Ring. I/424), whose author was discovered. In a postwar note, Wasser affirms the authorship of this text, but at the same time adds that Eliasz Gutkowski wrote down the deposition, meaning that Gutkowski could also be hidden under the pseudonym "Guter" designating the copyist. Of help to us in clarifying this matter is another copy of Kaufman's statement, preserved in HWC (call no. 53/1) and probably prepared by Gutkowski; in other words, this coworker of Ringelblum may be concealed under the pseudonym "Guter."

98. This abbreviation is not a cryptonym for Jerzy Winkler, a coworker of Oyneg Shabes, whose numerous exclusively Polish manuscripts were preserved in the ghetto archive, while "Wink" appears only on documents in Yiddish (Ring. I/818, Ring. I/187, I/797, and manuscripts described in the lists in Ring. I/1176). This may have been the cryptonym of Izrael Winnik; see Ring. I/1152/2.

99. The last three cryptonyms are found exclusively in lists inserted in Ring. I/1176. Could "Iliard" have a connection with Hersz Iliard, whose name is found in Wasser's notes in Ring. I/1152/1?

100. See also Ring. I/932. Rarely, descriptions of authors were added later. One such instance took place in the account in Ring. I/930, where Hersz Wasser characterizes the author as "a 20-year-old girl of little intelligence."

tially wrote down the author's surname, but later crossed it out. In the next typed copy of that statement, this information completely vanished, aside from the first letter of the surname inside the text, which was perhaps inadvertently included. There is also no trace of the author's surname in a copy of the statement by Marian Liberman, although it did appear in the original conveyed to the ghetto archive (Ring. I/422). The copyist of Hanna Lewkowicz's statement acted similarly, removing the names of various Jewish activists figuring in the original text of recollections (see Ring. I/479).

The additional markings on the documents and other records of Oyneg Shabes do not generally provide all the data needed for establishing authorship and full identification of texts. A further step to correct this was a detailed analysis of the handwritings appearing in ghetto archive manuscripts in combination with Wasser's notations.[101] This led to isolation of groups of documents, both originals and copies, written by persons known by name and surname. Thanks to analysis of the handwriting, it was also possible to isolate a group of anonymous authors and copyists whose service to the Oyneg Shabes group became better known. One can hope that in time further research will allow the identification of a greater number of authors.

Difficulties in determining authorship arise also from the fact that persons connected with Oyneg Shabes often appear in the archive's materials both as authors of their own texts and as copyists of documents who wrote down the statements of third persons. It was often very difficult, even bluntly impossible, to separate the functions of author and copyist. Additionally problematic were the at times contradictory data concerning authorship conveyed by Hersz Wasser and the nature of the script in which a given manuscript was prepared. Some documents were preserved in two copies, produced by different copyists, while the actual author of the text was a third person.

Analysis of handwriting styles made it possible in large measure to recognize Oyneg Shabes's regular collaborators. Even though we have lists of the group's members,[102] we can now also appreciate the individual contribution of some specific persons whom we have managed to identify. Mordechaj Szwarcbard made the greatest contribution in copying various documents of the ghetto archive. His handwriting appears in nearly 170[103] documents of the collection and was often identified by Hersz Wasser.[104] Szwarcbard chiefly produced texts in Yiddish, but he also supplied a few in Polish, copying testimonies and official documents. In transcribing some documents in Polish or German, he employed the Hebrew alphabet. He transcribed many copies of Ringelblum's notes. Szwarcbard most often wrote with copy-pencil, making one copy through carbon paper. His manuscripts were marked with various letters and identification symbols, whose meaning has not been ultimately clarified. Szwarcbard came from Łódź and authorship of many of the texts concerning that city is ascribed to him. Emanuel Ringelblum left behind many manuscripts (as many as 127), but they are exclusively texts written by him (notes and monographs); no copies of other texts in his handwriting have been preserved.[105]

Eliasz Gutkowski was also a very valuable copyist of the Oyneg Shabes group (ca. 100 documents). He wrote in Yiddish and Polish, and sporadically in German, copying other people's texts but also leaving his own. Wasser recognized Gutkoswki's handwriting several times.[106] Jechiel Górny also invested much labor in making copies, recording and editing statements, and copying correspondence and other documents. He is also the author of diaries whose fragments were scattered within Ring I. He left behind more than seventy documents in Polish and Yiddish.[107]

Hersz Wasser's wife, Bluma, was occupied in the Oyneg Shabes group chiefly with making copies; about sixty documents transcribed by her in Yiddish have survived. It has not been possible to identify her manuscripts in Polish.[108] Hersz Wasser copied relatively few texts, but did leave his journals and numerous notes (together some 55 documents). Traces of his very characteristic, slanted handwriting are apparent in many documents, because Wasser, as secretary of the Oyneg Shabes group, dealt with the archive's records. A large part of the notations with data regarding identification and the initial cataloging of the archive is in his handwriting.

Several persons produced between twenty and thirty manuscripts found in the ghetto archive: Szymon Huberband (perhaps 29 documents), Natan Koniński (27), Daniel Fligelman (23), Jerzy Winkler (21), Nechemiasz Tytelman (19). In this group are also such anonymous authors and copyists as AA* (ca. 21), TT* (ca. 21), and BTT* (ca. 18).

Rabbi Szymon Huberband's manuscripts were identified on many occasions by Hersz Wasser. Huberband's journals and recollections survived in the ghetto archive, along with various monographs concerning the current situation of the Jewish population, as well as historical sketches. Huberband also recorded other people's accounts. Although he did not

101. Roma Avishai of Jerusalem assisted me greatly in this work.

102. Lists of the ghetto archive's coworkers are located, inter alia, in Ring. I/1152/2, II/212.

103. The figures stated by me exclusively concern handwritten manuscripts or typescripts supplemented with handwritten notes; the actual number of preserved texts of a given person could be larger.

104. E.g., Ring. I/288, I/965, I/967, I/967, I/1004, I/1079.

105. This fact vividly shows the division of tasks in Oyneg Shabes. Ringelblum was involved with organizational matters, while the on-going collection and copying of documentation was in the hands of other members of the group.

106. Texts in Yiddish were best identified; e.g., Ring. I/61, I/166/1, I/167, I/318, I/979, I/1033. Occasionally, texts in the Latin alphabet are accompanied by notes in Yiddish, which also allowed identification of documents written exclusively in Polish and German by Gutkowski.

107. We find Hersz Wasser's identification of Górny's manuscripts in Ring. I/29, I/187, I/646 (texts in Yiddish); Ring. I/22, I/268, I/934 (in Polish).

108. We find identification of Bluma Wasser's manuscripts in Ring. I/235, I/407, I/409, I/972.

leave many texts, in regard to volume and scope of problems touched upon, his literary estate occupies an unusually important place in the ghetto archive. Huberband's preserved handwritten manuscripts and typescripts are exclusively in Yiddish and Hebrew.

Nusen (Natan) Koniński was active as well. He presumably originated from Kalisz and is the author of extensive memoirs touching on events from the first months of the war and occupation in 1939. The text of his account, consisting of five parts, was divided among various call numbers in the old inventory.[109] Koniński prepared many other texts, some of which he himself wrote, but others were exclusively copies. It was possible to identify only his texts written in Polish and German; we do not know if he also used Yiddish. It is assumed that Aron Koniński, an educator and director of the boarding school at ul. Mylna 18, also collaborated with Oyneg Shabes. However, we do not know whether he left behind any texts in the ghetto archive. It is also unclear why after the war Hersz Wasser ascribed to Aron part of the documents probably produced by Natan Koniński.[110]

Manuscripts by Daniel Fligelman can be easily distinguished from the rest, as they were written in ink, with a careful, even script of characteristically ornately shaped letters in Polish.[111] He mostly noted down statements, supplementing them sometimes with short introductions and notes, in which he inserted various clarifications, data about the authors, and his own commentary. However, he carefully separated editorial observations from the statements themselves, inserting quotation marks for the latter.[112] He had the habit of giving his own title to the recorded statements, which like the handsome script of those texts clearly testified to Fligelman's education and interests. In addition to other people's recollections, he also wrote his own, titled "From Aleksandrów [Kujawski] to Warsaw (Aleksandrów-Łowicz)" (Ring. I/789), as well as a journal, whose fragment is in Ring. I/263.[113] Daniel Fligelman's manuscripts were also preserved in Ring. II (Ring. II/301, II/303, II/305, and II/310). However, the latter are texts written down before the first liquidation action in the Warsaw Ghetto, but for unclear reasons were not included in the materials of Ring. I buried at the start of August 1942.

Jerzy Winkler copied many official documents, primarily the records of the Jewish Council, particularly correspondence with German authorities. He was also interested in economic affairs. We only know his texts in Polish and German, written in ink in a characteristic but not always legible script.[114]

Nechemiasz (Nechemia) Tytelman was among the few members of Oyneg Shabes who often signed or initialed their work (see above), thanks to which his manuscripts are more easily identified than those of other authors and copyists. Tytelman wrote in Yiddish with ink, prepared copies, and also worked on his own texts. He was interested, inter alia, in folklore and the daily street life of the Warsaw Ghetto.[115]

Considerably fewer texts were left behind by Stanisław Różycki (10), Sz. Szajnkinder (7), Samuel Bresław (Brasław?) (7), Salomea Ostrowska (7), Chaskiel Wilczyński (6),[116] as well as the anonymous authors and copyists CA* (ca. 13), CC* (ca. 13), and RR* (9).

Only some of the authors and copyists known to us from the first part of the ghetto archive also appear in the second part. The largest numbers of manuscripts preserved here are by Chaskiel Wilczyński (ca. 27),[117] among which predominate the texts of his own historical works. Numerous documents were also produced by Eliasz Gutkowski (16), Emanuel Ringelblum (14), Hersz Wasser (11), Perec Opoczyński (11), and Rachela Auerbach (8).

Typewritten documents create even greater problems than handwritten documents for identifying authors. Aside from a few instances, it has not been possible to establish the origin of individual copies produced on typewriters. To those exceptions must be counted those typescripts on which the authors

109. Ring. I/476, I/825, I/826, I/830. Hersz Wasser identified Koniński's handwriting in Ring. I/476, I/483, I/484.

110. See Ring. I/188, I/212. Under the influence of Hersz Wasser's contradictory information, sometimes both Konińskis are merged into one Aron Nusen (Natan) Koniński in the historical literature on the subject. See *Selected Documents*, pp. 48, 370–371, 783; Abraham Lewin, *A Cup of Tears: A Diary of the Warsaw Ghetto*, edited by Antony Polonsky (Oxford, 1988), p. 279; *Przewodnik*, p. 624; *Scream the Truth at the World*, p. 44; *Oneg Schabbat*, p. 48; *Relacje z Kresów*, p. 3. Also R.S. in her latest work (*Dzieci*, p. 358) writes: "Nusen Koniński is surely identical with Aron Koniński, Ringelblum's brother-in-law, a well-known educator. . . ." R.S. (ibid.) attributed to Aron Koniński the work "Oblicze dziecka żydowskiego" ("The Face of the Jewish Child") (Ring. I/47 = new catalog no. Ring. I/593), which is one of the few studies in the ghetto archive that is signed with the name and surname of the author: Nusen Koniński. The manuscript of that work was written in a hand that Hersz Wasser identified as that of N. [Natan] Koniński (see above). Natan Koniński is also mentioned in the list of Oyneg Shabes coworkers, on which Aron Koniński does not appear; see Ring. I/1152/2.

111. Manuscripts and typescripts of Daniel Fligelman's texts were carefully identified by Wasser while in the Warsaw Ghetto and his postwar notes confirmed these identifications (see Ring. I/94, I/487, I/789, I/839, I/44, I/940).

112. Deserving of special attention is Fligelman's commentary on the author of the statement, appended to the memoirs of Neuman, "Koło (Z opowiadań młodego Żyda)" (Koło: from the stories of a young Jew); see Ring. II/303 [new catalog no. Ring. II/347].

113. Ruta Sakowska wrote more broadly on some of the statements recorded by Daniel Fligelman: "Relacje Daniela Fligelmana—członka 'Oneg Szabat'," BŻIH, no. 137–138 (1986), pp. 167–171; but she omitted the texts recorded by Fligelman and located in Ring. II.

114. Hersz Wasser often identified the handwriting of Jerzy Winkler; see Ring. I/179, I/292, I/296, I/575/2, I/664. A certain disquiet may be caused by the fact that Wasser also identifies as being in Winkler's handwriting documents clearly written in a different script in Ring. I/53, I/62, and I/284.

115. See Ring. I/111, I/145, I/172, I/236, I/875, I/973, I/1220/31.

116. These six documents by Wilczyński were created as part of the documentary projects of Oyneg Shabes, unlike Wilczyński's other private documents located in Ring. II.

117. See preceding note.

inserted handwritten supplements. In this manner, it was possible to identify as originals some of the texts of Bernard Kampelmacher, or Szajnkinder's typescript from Ring. I. In the first part of the ghetto archive, typed copies were produced on several machines, whose characteristic typefaces can be identified, but it is not known to whom these machines belonged, nor has it been established who made those copies. It is possible that many typed copies of the Warsaw Jewish Council correspondence were the work of Gustawa Jarecka, who collaborated with Oyneg Shabes.[118]

In the case of texts preserved only in the form of typescripts and lacking Wasser's notes, not only do we have difficulty in establishing who prepared the typed copy, but we usually do not know the author or copyist. However, in a few cases we are able to glean from other sources facts necessary for the identification of those documents.[119]

## GHETTO ARCHIVE MATERIALS OUTSIDE THE COLLECTIONS OF THE JEWISH HISTORICAL INSTITUTE IN WARSAW

Warsaw ghetto archive materials are found in other collections around the world. The largest fragment of the archive is at YIVO in New York in the Hersh Wasser Collection (HWC). It includes approximately 170 different documents, among which only some 40 have been identified as duplicates in the collections of the Jewish Historical Institute in Warsaw.[120] Among materials not having duplicates in Ring. I are the notes of Emanuel Ringelblum's *Chronicle of the Ghetto* (scores of sheets),[121] Nechemiasz Tytelman's manuscript (70 sheets),[122] fragments of Abraham Lewin's journal,[123] and a large collection of underground printed items.[124] We do not know the circumstances behind their removal from the RA collection. No information about them is found in the 1946 list, a factor suggesting that they were not in the excavated boxes. Yet, damage characteristic of the materials of Ring. I is also visible on many documents of HWC. One wonders whether the documents in the YIVO collection were for reasons unknown to us not described after the excavation of the RA in September 1946. Alternatively, one might ask if the YIVO materials were hidden elsewhere and dug up under other circumstances? We cannot yet answer these questions. However, we do know that several months after discovery of the Ringelblum Archive, materials that later entered the HWC were dispatched in letters from Poland to various addressees in the West. It is difficult to say whether all the documents sent out from Poland in this manner ultimately reached the YIVO collections. What role might Hersz Wasser have played in this undertaking? If he was the initiator of the transfer of this collection to YIVO, then for understandable reasons he strove to preserve total anonymity. Therefore, there were a variety of return addresses on the letters containing Oyneg Shabes documents, and the envelopes were mostly addressed in typescript.[125]

In addition to the YIVO Archive, scores of documents (duplicates) from Ring. I have also been at Yad Vashem in Jerusalem since 1995, as mentioned above.

Separate scrutiny is required for materials produced by the Oyneg Shabes team and transferred for informational purposes to Polish underground organizations. Copies of some reports and information service bulletins prepared by Ringelblum's coworkers were preserved in places such as the archive of the Delegatura Rządu Rzeczypospolitej Polskiej na Kraj [Home Delegacy of the Government of the Polish Republic] (Archiwum Akt Nowych in Warsaw).[126]

118. E.g., documents from Ring. I/274, I/276, I/278, I/300, I/310, I/656, I/1105. On Gustawa Jarecka, also see above.

119. For instance, on the basis of *Kronika getta* (pp. 473, 484), it is possible to describe the account about the camp in Kampinos (Ring. I/379); thanks to the recollections of Bluma Wasser (*"Likht in der nakht,"* in *Pinkas Hrubieszów*, Tel Aviv, 1962, pp. 705–707), we know that she transcribed the statement of Szlamek, preserved in the ghetto archive in the form of a typescript; see Ring. I/412.

120. Among documents duplicated in the collections of ŻIH and YIVO is, inter alia, Kalman Huberband's account, entitled "Der marsh in mikve arayn, onhoyb yor tsh'a" (Yiddish: March to the ritual bath, start of 5701 [fall 1940 in the Jewish calendar]) (Ring. I/218), that initially consisted of two different transcripts, each preserved in two copies. But one copy of transcript (a) contained three pages, while transcript (b) had four pages. The person distributing this document mistakenly took the second copy of transcript (a) and page 4 of transcript (b) and that copy finally reached YIVO's collections, while there were preserved in Ring. I/218 at ŻIH: 1 copy of transcript (a) and two copies of transcript (b), but missing from the second copy of transcript (b) is p. 4, which is at YIVO!

121. HWC, 31/12. Part of Ringelblum's texts housed at YIVO are typed transcripts of which there are sometimes duplicates in the ŻIH collections; see HWC, 31/6–8.

122. HWC, 38/2.

123. HWC, 31/11; 32/2, 4, 6.

124. HWC, 60.

125. Trans. note: A new finding aide and catalog for the Hersh Wasser Collection at the YIVO Archives has been prepared by Robert Moses Shapiro and YIVO archivists, in conjunction with new microfilming and digitization of the HWC. It is clear from examination of the HWC documents that Wasser acted to transfer Oyneg Shabes materials to YIVO. His motives presumably included fear for the fate of the precious documents in an increasingly Communist-dominated Poland, as well as his knowledge that on 26 July 1942, the executive committee of Oyneg Shabes "resolved to send the archive to YIVO in New York after the war" (Samuel Kassow, *Who Will Write Our History?* p. 333).

126. For example, the copy of the report "Gehenna Żydów polskich pod okupacją hitlerowską" [Polish Jews' hell under Nazi occupation] (Archiwum Akt Nowych [AAN], call no. 202/II-30). This report was preserved in four copies made on a typewriter with carbon paper. Two are in ŻIH (Ring. I/44), one in HWC, and the fourth in the AAN. Nevertheless, it is important to emphasize that the typescript at AAN varies from the others by handwritten corrections and additions made by Hersz Wasser.

## RING. I AND RING. II—TWO SEPARATE PARTS OF ONE ARCHIVE

We do not know the precise criteria used for preparing the materials for burial, neither for the first part of the ghetto archive, nor for the second. In designing the new inventory of the ghetto archive, the following question had to be raised: Should the two preserved parts of the collection remain divided or be combined? It is possible to present arguments supporting both decisions. The history of the Oyneg Shabes group spoke in favor of combining the two parts. Its first stage of work was interrupted by the first liquidation action in July 1942 and climaxed with burial of part of the collected material. But the group's activity continued. Ring. II contains materials that could not be hidden in August 1942, but also documents collected during and after the first action in the Warsaw Ghetto. Collections of the same press titles appear in both parts. Thus, many of the documents in Ring. I and Ring. II share features and are the product of work by similar groups of people.

At the same time, many arguments speak against combining both parts of the archive. Foremost is the fact that the materials were collected and buried as two separate wholes in different historical circumstances. An important segment of Ring. I consists of materials collected and processed by members of the Oyneg Shabes group, above all a large collection of testimonies written down and then duplicated in several copies. This collection of transcripts is not matched by a clear equivalent in Ring. II. Furthermore, Ring. II contains none of the many handwritten carbon copies made with pencil that are characteristic of Ring. I. The transcripts preserved in Ring. II were in the majority made in one copy. The multiple copies in Ring. I well illustrate the work methods applied in the first period of the Oyneg Shabes group's activity. The changed circumstances in the ghetto after the start of the first liquidation action in July 1942 are also reflected in the character of the ghetto archive's documentation found in Ring. II. More frequently in the later phase, original documents reached the ghetto archive, as opposed to materials created by the innermost collaborators of Oyneg Shabes. In the later phase there arose the possibility of acquiring parts of the archival material of institutions that operated openly within the ghetto, but whose activity had suffered total or partial collapse, including the ŻSS or the Jewish Council.[127] The general situation also fostered transfer of private documents to the ghetto archive's collections. Though this phenomenon had occurred during the first phase of the ghetto archive, in Ring. II its extent significantly increased. Materials that ended up in the collection included, for example, personal documents and works of Emanuel Ringelblum, Eliasz Gutkowski, Hersz Wasser, Rachela Auerbach, Chaskiel Wilczyński, Izrael Lichtensztajn, and Icchak Giterman.

An important argument for keeping the parts separate is the fact that for more than half a century they have functioned independently in the scientific literature and are powerfully fixed in this way in the researchers' consciousness. Taking into account the arguments pro and con, the decision was made to preserve the division of the collection into Ring. I and II, for this arrangement better documents different aspects of the history of this archival collection against the background of events in the Warsaw Ghetto and the fates of individual workers of Oyneg Shabes. The attempt to combine the materials into a single collection could lead to obliteration of those characteristic differences.

## ARRANGEMENT OF THE DOCUMENTS IN THE INVENTORY

During the initial work to prepare the new inventory of the ghetto archive, the question arose about whether to preserve the existing arrangement of documents within Ring. I and II or to arrange them according to a new pattern. The decisive argument for constructing a new arrangement lay in the imperfection of the status quo. The existing arrangement after the excavation of the collection was developed in a haphazard fashion and did not take into account the nature of the collection and the character of individual files. Due to a lack of full identification of many documents, their placement was faulty, to such a degree that transcripts of the same statements were placed under different call numbers in different parts of the archive. Smaller or larger fragments of these same documents of homogeneous character were located in different units and in separate parts of the collection. After the original excavation of Ring. I, a substantial collection of so-called fragments (the *rozsyp*) from unidentified documents included numerous portions of documents that were already described in the former inventory. In the course of processing the units, it became necessary to consolidate materials, a process that had an impact on the initial arrangement of the collection.

A new arrangement had to fulfill several fundamental conditions. First, it had to refer to the specifics of both parts of the collection—their character and fate—to consider the chief directions of the interests of the Oyneg Shabes group, and to exhibit the methods and effects of the actions of the group and the archive's creators.[128] In adhering to these conditions, the new arrangement aimed to ease access for the reader to materials of interest. Processing a collection like the ghetto archive, which includes documents of very diverse character and provenance, demanded great care and many compromises. It was not possible to preserve uniform principles of cataloging for every document. Serious difficulties arose in the classification of individual documents; in many instances exact criteria of selection were

127. We do not know under what circumstances both collections came to be in the ghetto archive's possession. We can more easily reconstruct the fate of the ŻSS documents since many of the Oyneg Shabes coworkers, led by Ringelblum, were connected with this institution; on the other hand, a fragment of the Jewish Council's archive could have reached the ghetto archive's collections in various circumstances, e.g., during the move of the Jewish Council's headquarters in August 1942.

128. Emanuel Ringelblum provided us with information on this subject in his *Kronika* (p. 474ff.); the major groups of materials in the ghetto archive have been isolated based on this.

lacking. The differences between Ring. I and II presented an additional problem. The new arrangement could not satisfy all the demands, and certainly there are within it some omissions and inconsistencies, yet it seems to generally fulfill the most important tasks mentioned above.[129]

*The first group* of materials differentiated from the entire collection includes documents about the history of the Oyneg Shabes group and its archive. It contains lists of workers, fragments of lists of materials in the ghetto archive, and financial documentation connected with the activity of Oyneg Shabes.

*The second group* holds general studies about the fate of the Jewish population. The materials were arranged factually: first, plans and drafts of projects, questionnaires prepared for collecting testimonies and various data; and then the Oyneg Shabes bulletins (found only in Ring. I; these served as an information service on the topic of resettlement and liquidation actions in various ghettos on Polish territories), studies, scientific papers, statements, articles, reports, summaries, and notes. Materials were arranged thematically (including general situation, martyrology of the Jewish population, social conditions, situations of different groups of the population, economic life, and culture). Two separate collections of correspondence, the so-called "Kalisz letters" and "Płock letters," were attached as an addendum to the second group (only in Ring. I).[130]

*The third group* includes materials connected with the fate of the Jewish community in Warsaw and in the Warsaw Ghetto between 1939 and 1943. Within this group, the materials were divided into the following sections:

1. Official documents (organizational documents, minutes, reports, correspondence of the German authorities and institutions, public Jewish authorities such as the Jewish Council and Jewish Social Self-Help, as well as other open and clandestine institutions and organizations). The documents were arranged in an alphabetical and factual order according to individual offices and their organizational cells and agendas. An exception was made for ŻSS materials in Ring. II, which kept their original chronological order.

2. Reports (journals, chronicles, testimonies, and memoirs) arranged alphabetically by author, with anonymous entries placed at the end in chronological order;

3. Correspondence, including letters sent within the Warsaw Ghetto as well as sent out from Warsaw (in copies), arranged alphabetically by author;

4. Written works (plans and surveys of work, scientific papers, charts, tables, notes), arranged analogously to the material in the second group;

5. Materials concerning Jewish schools (general studies, school reports, and children's compositions), but only for Ring. I;

6. Photographs of the Warsaw Ghetto; again only for Ring. I. The collection of photographs was described on the basis of what appeared in the 1946 list, but the photographs have not been retained in the archive's collections. Individual photographs from this collection are part of another department of the Jewish Historical Institute in Warsaw.

*The fourth group* holds documents about the situation of the Jewish population in various localities (ghettos) within Polish territories (outside Warsaw) and in other countries. The materials have been arranged alphabetically by locality;[131] however, within the framework of individual ghettos' documents they are divided in the same manner as the third group.

*The fifth group* (only in Ring. I) includes a collection of accounts about the September Campaign in Poland in 1939 and about POW camps. Descriptions of September 1939 appear in many documents in the ghetto archive, but in the fifth group are included only texts dealing exclusively with that topic. Gathered here are recollections of soldiers who took part in the war, with accounts describing battles and the organization of defense. Finally, there are reports about the situation of Jewish soldiers of the Polish army in German prisoner-of-war camps. These are organized alphabetically by author, with anonymous reports at the end.

*The sixth group* (the fifth group in Ring. II) contains materials about labor camps, transit camps, and extermination centers. Documents are arranged alphabetically by location. Documents relevant to individual camps are arranged in the same way as in the third group. Songs from different camps have been placed at the end.

*The seventh group* (the sixth group in Ring. II) consists of literary compositions (stories, poetry, plays, etc.). The documents are arranged in alphabetical order by author, with anonymous texts placed at the end. In Ring. II, religious texts were also found here, including sermons of Rabbi Kalonimus Szapiro and texts of prayers.

*The eighth group* (the seventh group in Ring. II) is composed of periodicals and other ephemeral one-time printed matter, as well as leaflets and press clippings. These include openly published and clandestine materials, as well as books and pamphlets. Prewar printed items form a separate group. The periodicals and legally printed matter are separated into Polish, German, and Yiddish sources. Underground publications are divided into those published by Jewish groups and appearing in the Warsaw Ghetto, and those published by Polish groups and issued on the so-called "Aryan side."

*The ninth group* (the eighth group in Ring. II) includes archival bequests from both parts of the ghetto archive. These were conveyed in the form of donations or deposits. Deposited documents are materials accepted for temporary safekeeping and are not the property of the archive or other institutions. We do not know exactly which documents could have been placed into the ghetto archive's collections in such form. Most people whose papers were in the ghetto archive did not live to see the end of the war and could not seek the return of their materials.

129. For an overview of the contents of the inventory of Ring. I and II, see below.

130. Both collections have been preserved in the arrangement introduced by the creators of the collection (see above).

131. The materials were placed according to the first locality named in the title or description of the unit.

Of those who survived, only Rachela Auerbach wanted to retrieve her personal documents from the ghetto archive.[132] Hersz Wasser could also have sought return of his materials, but it is not evident that he did so. We do not know when the preserved bequests were added to the ghetto archive collections. In some instances, these collections took form gradually, as was the case with the materials of Hersz Wasser or Ringelblum, especially in Ring. I. There is no information on the provenance of the materials of Mojżesz Kaufman (in Ring. I), Henryk Piórnik, Wacław Kączkowski, and Cwi Prylucki (in Ring. II). Full identification of these materials encounters obstacles, particularly regarding bequests of persons who were part of the narrow circle of collaborators of Oyneg Shabes (e.g., Wasser, Gutkowski, Auerbach, and Lichtensztajn). Prewar and wartime materials are mixed together. Some bequests even contain other bequests (e.g., Itzik Manger's materials within Rachela Auerbach's bequest).

*The tenth* and final group (the ninth group in Ring. II) contains miscellaneous loose materials, mainly of prewar origin. It is likely that most of these were conveyed to the collections together with other documents within certain bequests, but they currently cannot be identified as associated with any of the other groups.

Dividing the ghetto archive materials into thematic and topical groups eases access to individual documents, but does not solve all the problems connected with locating materials about specific individuals, offices, locations, or subjects. It should be recalled that many significant materials on topics within the various thematic groups are also hidden in the bequests. Classifications of many documents must have been quite mechanical. For example, descriptions of the Warsaw Ghetto are often in accounts placed in group 4, dealing mainly with provincial ghettos. However, a person interested in Lwów will also find pertinent material in memoirs placed in the section on Kalisz. We encounter similar problems with monographs whose topics go significantly beyond the subject group in which they were placed. Arrangement and classification of materials of official origin raise the least difficulties, but here we must recall the complex structure of the authorities and organizations that functioned both overtly and covertly within the ghetto. Many of the institutions functioning in the Warsaw Ghetto were formally dependent on the Jewish Social Self-Help; among these were apartment house committees, children's homes, and shelters for displaced persons. At the same time, they were sometimes used for conspiratorial work; for example, the Sponsor's Committee [Patronat] for Jewish Cultural Activity was the legally operating front for the clandestine YIKOR (Jewish Culture Organization).

To avoid missing important documents, it is necessary to review the major sections of the inventory. Researchers will find additional help in the indexes placed at the end.

## DIAGRAM OF THE DESCRIPTION OF A DOCUMENT (ARCHIVAL UNIT) IN THE INVENTORY

A uniform structure for description of documents has been adopted, including the following items in sequence:

1. Consecutive number (new call number)
2. Old call number
3. Microfilm number in the collections of JHI and USHMM
4. Date and place of the document's creation
5. Name of the document
6. Abstract
7. Technical description
8. Additional information

For items 1–3: If a new unit comprised documents from several old units, all call numbers are provided. This applies exclusively to units consolidated during the work connected with preparing the present new inventory. Most changes to the structure of Ring. I and Ring. II before the start of the new inventory have not been described in detail because it was not possible to reconstruct previous locations of many documents and the fragments.[133] In the case of Ring. I, next to the old call numbers are also call numbers that were valid before the creation of the first inventory in 1955. These oldest call numbers were placed in parentheses immediately after the currently valid call numbers: for example, Ring. I/1146 (1465). Also added in the case of Ring. I is the number of the document according to the list of documents in Ring. I of 1946 ("Katalog Archiwum dr Emanuela Ringelbluma"). These numbers are preceded with the Polish abbreviation "Lb." (consecutive number) placed in parentheses after the call numbers. Here is a sample description of the call numbers of a selected unit:

769. Ring. I/826 (1145). (Lb. 842); I/825 (1144). (Lb. 842). Mf. ŻIH—826; USHMM—38. Ring. I/476. Mf. ŻIH—786; USHMM—17. Ring. I/830 (1149). (Lb. 866). Mf. ŻIH—827; USHMM—39.[134]

132. It can be assumed that Rachela Auerbach sought only the return of materials belonging to Itzik Manger, and therefore they were separately listed on the 1946 list (no. 1721–1736). The issue of the return to Rachela Auerbach of materials from the ghetto archive was considered by the Presidium of the Central Committee of Polish Jews and on 4.10.1946 the following decision was adopted: "After consideration of Citizen Auerbach's application in the matter of issuing to her documents comprising her property and located in Dr. Ringelblum's unearthed archive, it has been decided to postpone the matter until the motion is filed by the commission for arrangement of the Dr. Ringelblum Archive, with an opinion by the Department of Culture and Propaganda." See ŻIH Archive, doc. 303/3, k. 165. Ultimately, no documents were returned to Auerbach; see R. Auerbach, *Baym letsn veg*, pp. 168–169.

133. A concordance also provides a list of the call numbers superseded as a result of consolidations prior to the start of preparation of the present inventory.

134. The oldest call numbers and call numbers from the 1946 list were mostly placed in the descriptions of those documents on which markings have been preserved (directly on the document or on postwar archival file jackets).

In the case of documents lost after the war, the notation "original missing" has been added after the call numbers.

For item 4: Precise dating of documents in the ghetto archive is difficult to determine, particularly in descriptions of numerous copies of documents, mostly personal statements.[135] Many (mostly at the end) were assigned unsure dates because it was not always possible to indicate the day of the interview, nor to determine the time of preparation of the elementary record of the statement heard, nor of the final editing of the text and the creation of copies. It seems, however, that they rather indicate the date of the interview.[136] There were more minor problems with designations of the place where a document originated, since most of the transcripts must have been made in Warsaw or within the Warsaw Ghetto after 15.11.1940; therefore, a uniform designation of "Warsaw" or "Warsaw Ghetto" was adopted.

For item 5: "Name of the document" provides information about the document's creator (e.g., author, office, institution, or organization); about the character of the document (e.g., statement, study, letter, notice, or literary work); about the document's title or lack of a title; and about its general contents (e.g., "Study on the Old Synagogue in Łódź"). Original titles of documents are given in quotation marks,[137] and titles of printed items are in italics. Titles of printed items in Polish have been parenthetically translated into English. Titles in Yiddish and Hebrew are given in two ways: in English transliteration and in English translation.[138]

If the date of preparation is on the given document, that fact is also placed in the description. It must be remembered that this date does not always coincide with the date at which the document (archival item) was created. This situation occurs in the case of originals, and much more rarely in copies (mostly of official documents). In cases of correspondence and official publications, the date is placed after the document's name. For instance, "Letter of 15.08.1941 . . ." or "Notice of 22.07.1942. . . ." With other documents, the date is stated in parentheses after the main description; for example, "(25.09.1941)."

For item 6: The abstract contains a short summary of the contents of the document, including information about the author drawn from the document and about attachments.[139] For units containing homogeneous documents of similar character—for example, collections of announcements or collections of literary works—instead of an abstract there is a full description of the documents. No abstract was provided in the case of units in which item 5 exhausted all information about the document.

For item 7: The specific character of the materials in the ghetto archive required introduction into the technical description of a clear differentiation between original documents and copies made within the framework of Oyneg Shabes. Counted among originals are texts physically written or typed by their authors, original official documents (including office copies made within the given office's or organization's framework of activities), press items, books, and pamphlets. All handwritten and typed transcripts of documents (except for authors' autograph texts) are counted as copies. Here it must be explained that to be accepted as an author's autograph text, the document had to be handwritten or a typescript with handwritten supplements. Such author's autograph texts include studies, memoirs, letters, or literary works whose author was the person who composed the given document. A separate identification ("original [o]") was assigned to rough drafts and clean copies (handwritten) of statements heard and written down (edited) by the workers of Oyneg Shabes. A requirement to qualify for this group was verification that the same person conducted the interview and prepared the written text of the verbal account. It must be underscored that all copies, like original documents, became an integral part of the ghetto archive's collections and came into being before their concealment in 1942 (Ring. I) and 1943 (Ring. II). In many instances, final classification of a document was not possible, so the designation "original or transcript" was applied. In the collection there are currently more than a dozen copies made after 1946 of documents that had disappeared. To differentiate them from original transcripts prepared during the occupation, these copies were designated "postwar transcript."[140] Next to the designation "original or transcript" is added information about the number of copies of the given document. On the basis of the manner in which the documents were produced, they were divided into handwritten, typed, multiple typed, or hectographic copies *(mps powielane)*, printed items, or photographs. Information is added about handwriting

135. Very rarely are there transcripts whose dating does not evoke doubts. For instance, the account from Ring. I/932 (transcript a) was written down in several stages and the interviewer separately dated each stage, thanks to which we can exactly tell when the text was created, but transcript (b) of that document had to be dated only indicating the initial date.

136. This fact is not yet certain. For instance, in Ring. I/809 was preserved the original or a transcript of the statement from which Bluma Wasser made a copy, placing at its end the date "19.08.1941." That date is not on the original or the transcript, which means that it has no connection with its creation. In this case, the date may mark when the copy was made and not when the statement was originally written down. Similarly, on the transcript of the account from Ring. I/1046 (we do not have the original) also made by Bluma Wasser is the date: "15.07.1941." H.W., in a postwar note, distinctly indicated that the document "was copied 15.07.1941."

137. Trans. note: In the present English translation, Polish titles have generally been rendered in English, while titles in German have generally not been translated.

138. Trans. note: In the Polish original of the inventory, the entry also provides a Polish transliteration and Polish translation of the Yiddish or Hebrew title.

139. Trans. note: "Attachments" refers to cover letter and other items attached to or enclosed with another described document.

140. See Ring. I/33, I/106, I/149, I/242, I/323, I/430, I/455, I/981, I/1044. Trans. note: Foregoing catalog numbers refer to the old catalog; see the appended concordance of old/new catalog numbers.

script, alphabetic symbols (a list of these abbreviations follows), and the number of different handwritings. Placed here also is information about whether the given manuscript was written in a notebook. Handwritten documents are divided into those written with ink or with pencil. The description also contains information about mixed writing techniques of document production; for example, some typescripts are supplemented with handwritten notations in ink or pencil.

Data is also provided in this part of the entry on the subject of traces of seals or stamps affixed to the document. Additional information on this (e.g., the content of a seal or stamp) is placed under the technical description (see below regarding item 8). Information about the stamp of the Jewish Historical Institute Archive with which the documents of the ghetto archive were marked after the war has been omitted.

Next are data on the language (or languages) in which the document was written. Then the dimensions of the document are listed. When individual parts of documents are of different dimensions, only the extreme dimensions are in the description. Sometimes, in order to more accurately describe several fragments of a given document—for instance, the original and transcript or other copies—they are individualized and given separate technical descriptions. For example,

Description: transcript (a) (handwritten by RR*, in ink, 155×200 mm; transcript (b) (handwritten by JG*, pencil, 145×218 mm), Yiddish, sheets 18, pp. 23.[141]

In units comprised of materials from different previous call numbers, separate technical descriptions have been included for the individual parts. For example,

Description: Ring. I/1002—original, handwritten, ink, Yiddish, 219×353 mm, minor damage and losses of text, ca. 1, 2 pp.; Ring. I/990—transcript, handwritten by MS*, pencil, Yiddish, 148×208 mm, sheets 1, p. 1.[142]

Also included in the technical description is selected information about the state of preservation of the documents and the legibility or impairment of the text. The basic part of the technical description concludes with information on the number of sheets and pages comprising the document. All sheets are counted; on the other hand, only pages with writing (with the exception of bound and printed items for which all the pages are given).

For item 8, supplemental information depends on the character of the document. For example, there may be additional data about the document's contents (e.g., a list of chapter titles), descriptions of stamp imprints, descriptions of "foreign" notations on the document (excluding notations and archival markings made after the war), description of the document on the reverse of which the given item was written, and a description of Hersz Wasser's postwar identifying notations and information attached to the document. If the information in Wasser's notations complements the data included in the document, longer or shorter quotations from Wasser's remarks are included. Cross-references are given separately, and refer to other Ring. documents and to other manuscript collections containing material from the ghetto archive. Lastly, there are bibliographic information and data about publication of the described documents. The published materials surveyed included only the larger collections of documents and some scholarly journals.[143] Only the latest editions and those containing entire documents or larger fragments of them were included. A more detailed description is included for the entries of Ringelblum's ghetto chronicle (*Kronika getta*) in view of the significance and character of those texts (see Ring. I/503, I/504, I/505, I/506, and I/507).[144] A review

141. "Opis: odpis (a) (rkps—RR*, atrament, 155×200 mm), odpis (b) (rkps—JG*, ołówek, 145×218 mm), j.żyd., k. 18, s. 23."

142. "Opis: Ring. I/1002—oryg., rkps, atrament, j.żyd., 219×353 mm, drobne uszkodzenia i ubytki tekstu, k. 1, s. 2; Ring. I/990—odpis, rkps (MS*), ołówek, j.żyd., 148×208 mm, k. 1, s. 1."

143. Among others, *Tsvishn lebn un toyt*, ed. B. Mark (Warsaw, 1955) (German edition: *Ghetto. Berichte aus dem Warschauer Ghetto 1939–1945* [Berlin, 1966]); *Eksterminacja Żydów na ziemiach polskich w okresie okupacji hitlerowskiej. Zbiór dokumentów*, ed. T. Berenstein, A. Eisenbach, A. Rutkowski (Warsaw, 1957); *Archiwum Ringelbluma; Antologia poezji żydowskiej*, ed. S. Łastik, A. Łucki (Warsaw, 1983); *The Jewish Underground Press in Warsaw* [in Hebrew], 6 vols., ed. Joseph Kermish and Israel Shaham (Jerusalem: Yad Vashem, 1979–1997); *Dwa etapy* (German edition: *Die zweite Etappe ist der Tod* [Berlin, 1993]); *Selected Documents; Kiddush Hashem; Listy o Zagładzie; Relacje z Kresów; Przewodnik; Dzieci.* Foremost among the scholarly journals surveyed are the titles published by the Jewish Historical Institute: *Bleter far geshikhte* (Warsaw, 1948–1993) and *Biuletyn Żydowskiego Instytutu Historycznego w Polsce* (Warsaw). Although an anthology of texts from the Ringelblum Archive appeared in *Karta* (Warsaw, nr 39/2003, pp. 4–58), I omit it in the text of the inventory, since it contains chiefly smaller or larger fragments of selected documents.

144. Ringelblum's Yiddish entries were compared with the Polish translation, *Kronika getta* (Warsaw, 1983, 2nd ed., 1988). There are several editions of Ringelblum's *Ghetto Chronicle*. The first appeared in *BFG* (v. 1/1948, pp. 5–54; v. 4/1951, no. 1, pp. 82–85; v. 5/1953, no. 3, pp. 32–52; v. 11/1958, pp. 3–58; v. 12/1959, pp. 3–49; v. 15/1962–1963, pp. 93–169). A selection of the entries appeared in book form in Warsaw 1952 (*Notitsn fun varshever geto*). All of the material from the period of the occupation preserved at ŻIH appeared in two volumes in Yiddish (*Ksovim fun geto*, ed. T. Berenstein, A. Eisenbach, B. Mark, and A. Rutkowski [Warsaw, 1961–1963]); and in Polish translation in BŻIH no. 2/1951, no. 3, pp. 81–207; no. 3/1952, pp. 46–82; no. 11–12/1954, pp. 122–166; no. 13–14/1955, pp. 211–267; no. 15–16/1955, pp. 245–290; and no. 25/1958, pp. 3–30. On the basis of the Polish editions there appeared an English translation, *Notes from the Warsaw Ghetto: The Journal of Emanuel Ringelblum* (New York, 1958), prepared by Jacob Sloan, but including significant omissions (e.g., complete lack of entries from 1939). This American edition became the basis for subsequent editions: French *Chronique du ghetto de Varsovie* (Paris, 1959) (2nd ed., 1978); Italian *Sepolti a Varsovia. Appunti dal Ghetto* (1962); and Japanese (1980). The Yiddish edition (*Ksovim fun geto*, Tel Aviv 1985), the Polish translation of 1983, and the Hebrew translation of 1992 were based on the two-volume edition of 1961–1963. The most complete edition is the Hebrew translation (*Yoman u-reshimot mi-tekufat ha-milhamah: Geto Varshah, September 1939–Detsember 1942*), ed. Y. Gutman, Y. Kermish, and Y. Shaham [Jerusalem, 1992]), which includes fragments omitted in previous editions.

of the contents of previous publications, including texts from the ghetto archive, has been omitted because it would have required significant extension of many of the inventory descriptions. For materials already published, the descriptions in the inventory include certain differentiations relating to authorship, technical description, and dating, as well as corrections of mistakes arising from erroneous reading of sources.[145]

Some of the units were provided with separate indexes of names ("Index") that include concise data about persons described in the given document but not mentioned in the inventory description. In addition to name and surname, other biographical information arising in the text appears. For technical reasons, these indexes do not include all the persons mentioned in the materials of the ghetto archive. Special attention is devoted to murdered victims, oppressed persons, officials, social activists, and the like.

Doubtful information is marked with a question mark in brackets ("[?]"). A question mark alone or one in parentheses ["(?)"] was transferred from the original text.[146] Brackets were also used for other supplementary information.[147]

An attempt was made in the inventory to preserve uniform terminology, relating to the formal description of individual documents, as well as the characteristics of their contents.

## CONCLUSION

Preparatory work on the new Polish-language inventory was started in 2000. The first full archival descriptions of the documents of Ring. I were entered into a digital document in spring 2001. In June 2002, the description of Ring. II was completed and editorial work begun. In November 2002, the new archival arrangement was applied to the collection (in an electronic version). In May 2003, the proofreading and indexing, as well as work on the archival introduction to the inventory, were completed.[148]

After completion of the cataloging work, the ghetto archive collection numbers 1,487 units in the first part (Ring. I) and 558 units in the second (Ring. II).

***

In closing, I would like to acknowledge those persons and institutions without which the creation of the new inventory of the Ringelblum Archive would not have been possible. The plan to produce a new inventory arose thanks to the cooperation of the Jewish Historical Institute in Warsaw with the United States Holocaust Memorial Museum in Washington. The overall project was supervised by a team from the Jewish Historical Institute that included Dr. Feliks Tych, Dr. Ruta Sakowska, Dr. Eleonora Bergman, and Agnieszka Jarzębowska, and from the United States Holocaust Memorial Museum (Warsaw) Jerzy Halbersztadt, Alina Skibińska, and Dr. Tadeusz Epsztein (Institute of History of the Polish Academy of Sciences).

In preparing the inventory, I was aided by employees of the Jewish Historical Institute's Archive, foremost by Agnieszka Jarzębowska, who provided me with constant assistance from the moment that work began on the archive. Inter alia, she prepared the introductory description of the units of Ring. I/599–I/1220, as well as of Ring. II; she compiled the list of the preserved works of Gela Seksztajn and participated in the audit of Ring. I and II. I could also always count on the help and advice of the director of the Jewish Historical Institute's Archive, Marek Jóźwik. Magdalena Tarnowska of the Museum at the JHI provided information about Gela Seksztajn's works and drawings that were saved in the Ringelblum Archive. Urszula Kobiałka-Fuks of the JHI identified, for the requirements of the new inventory, the collection of photographs from the Warsaw Ghetto unearthed in Box no. 8 of the ghetto archive in 1946. Jan Jagielski helped locate other photographs from the Oyneg Shabes collection that were preserved in originals or copies in the collections of the JHI. Tremendous work was done by Sara Arm, who for two years translated and prepared summaries of Yiddish documents. She also assisted in the audit of the archive by identifying manuscripts in Yiddish. Joanna Nalewajko-Kulikov and her husband Gennady Kulikov helped with the Hebrew texts. I received much valuable information and advice from Dr. Ruta Sakowska, who was a regular participant at meetings of the program team supervising this research project. Roma Avishai of Jerusalem carried out graphological identification of selected ghetto archive handwritten manuscripts. I heartily thank them all for their help and collaboration.

145. For example, in *Selected Documents* (p. 474) in a document from Ring. I/204, two of three addresses given in the title of the document contain distortions: ul. Nowolipki 39 instead of 68, ul. Krochmalna 96 instead of 36. In many foreign publications, there is no mention of where the originals of the published documents are kept, nor of the correct call numbers in Ring. I and II; see, for example, *Selected Documents* and *The Jewish Underground Press*. Information relating to other publications of sources is also included above.

146. This notation does not concern personal and geographic indexes.

147. Trans. note: Translator's doubt regarding information is indicated by "[?]."

148. Trans. note: Preparation of the draft English translation of the Polish inventory commenced in July 2004 and was completed in April 2007.

# Contents of the Inventory

## RINGELBLUM II

# Abbreviations

This list includes the Polish abbreviations employed in the Polish version of the inventory, together with English translations to facilitate use by non-Polish readers. Abbreviated references to published works are also included here, as well as selected English abbreviations.

**AAN** Archiwum Akt Nowych w Warszawie [Central Archives of Modern Records in Warsaw]

***Archiwum Ringelbluma*** *Archiwum Ringelbluma. Getto warszawskie lipiec 1942-styczeń 1943*, ed. R. Sakowska, Warsaw, 1980 [The Ringelblum Archive. Warsaw Ghetto, July 1942–January 1943]

**AJDC** American Jewish Joint Distribution Committee

***Antologia*** *Antologia poezji żydowskiej*, eds. S. Łastik, A. Łucki, Warsaw, 1983. [Anthology of Yiddish Poetry]

**APP** Akcja Pomocy Przesiedleńcom (getto warszawskie) [Campaign to Aid Those Resettled (Warsaw ghetto)]

**ARG** Podziemne Archiwum Getta Warszawskiego (Archiwum Ringelbluma) [Underground Archive of the Warsaw Ghetto (Ringelblum Archive)]

**b.** były, była [former, late]

**b.d.** brak daty [no date, date unknown]

**BFG** *Bleter far Geshikhte* (ŻIH, Warsaw, 1948–1993)

***Bibliografia druków*** W. Chojnacki, *Bibliografia zwartych druków konspiracyjnych wydanych pod okupacją hitlerowską w latach 1939–1945*, Warsaw 1970 [Bibliography of Underground Publications Issued during the Nazi Occupation in the Years 1939–1945]

**b.m.** brak miejsca powstania dokumentu [place unknown; no data on place where the document was created]

**b.nr** brak numeru [not numbered]

**BŻIH** *Biuletyn Żydowskiego Instytutu Historycznego w Polsce* (Warsaw) [Bulletin of the Jewish Historical Institute in Poland]

**b.r.** brak roku [no year, year unknown]

**Centos** Związek Towarzystw Opieki nad Dziećmi i Sierotami Żydowskimi "Centos" [Association of Societies for Care of Jewish Children and Orphans]

***Centralny catalog*** *Centralny katalog polskiej prasy konspiracyjnej 1939–1945*, ed. L. Dobroszycki, Warsaw 1962 [Central Catalog of the Polish Underground Press 1939–1945]

**CKL** Centralna Komisja Lokalowa [Central Location Commission]

**CKP** Centralna Komisja Patronatów (ŻTOS) [Central Commission of Patronates (Jewish Association for Social Welfare)]

**CKPP** Centralna Komisja Popierania Pracy w Szopach przy Wydziale Niesienia Pomocy RŻ w Warszawie [Central Commission for Support of Labor in the Workshops at the Department for Providing Aid of the Jewish Council in Warsaw]

**CKU** Centralna Komisja Uchodźców [Central Commission of Refugees]

**CSS** Centralny Sektor Społeczny [Central Social Sector]

**Cukierman** I. Cukierman, "Antek," *Nadmiar pamięci (Siedem owych lat). Wspomnienia 1939–1946*, ed. M. Turski, Warsaw, 2000 [Surplus of Memory (Seven of Those Years). Memoirs 1939–1946]

***Czerniaków*** *Adama Czerniakowa dziennik getta warszawskiego 6 IX 1939—23 VII 1942*, ed. M. Fuks, Warsaw 1983 [Adam Czerniaków's Diary of the Warsaw Ghetto, 6 IX 1939—23 VII 1942]

**Destrukt (plural: destrukty)** A severely damaged document or documents; from the Latin *destructio.*

**doc.** document

**dok.** document [document]

**d.st.** data stempla pocztowego [postmark date]

***Dwa etapy*** R. Sakowska, *Dwa etapy. Hitlerowska polityka eksterminacji Żydów w oczach ofiar. Szkic historyczny i dokumenty*, Wrocław 1986 [Two Stages. The Nazi Policy of Extermination of Jews in the Eyes of the Victims. Historical Sketch and Documents]

**dyr.** dyrektor [director]

***Dzieci*** *Archiwum Ringelbluma. Konspiracyjne Archiwum Getta Warszawy*, t. 2, *Dzieci—tajne nauczanie w getcie warszawskim*, ed. R. Sakowska, Warsaw 2000 [2002] [Ringelblum Archive. Underground Archive of the Warsaw Ghetto, vol. 2: Children—Clandestine Teaching in the Warsaw Ghetto]

***Eksterminacja Żydów*** *Eksterminacja Żydów na ziemiach polskich w okresie okupacji hitlerowskiej. Zbiór dokumentów*, eds. T. Berenstein, A. Eisenbach, A. Rutkowski, Warsaw 1957 [The Extermination of Jews on Polish Territories during the Nazi Occupation. A Collection of Documents]

**E.R.** Emanuel Ringelblum

**fot.** fotografia [photograph]

**franc.** francuski [French]

**GŻ** Gmina Żydowska [Jewish Community]

**hebr.** hebrajski [Hebrew]

**H.W.** Hersz Wasser

**HWC** Wasser Collection (YIVO Institute for Jewish Research, New York City)

**inf.** informacja [information or data]

**inv. = inw.** Inwentarz Archiwum Ringelbluma, rkps, Archiwum ŻIH. [Inventory of the Ringelblum Archive, manuscript, Jewish Historical Institute Archive]

**j.** język [language]

**J.H.K.** Jüdische Hilfskomitee (see ŻKOM) [Jewish Relief Committee]

**JHI** Jewish Historical Institute in Warsaw (see ŻIH)

**JIKOR (YIKOR)** Yidishe Kulturorganizatsye [Yiddish Culture Organization]

**JIWO (YIVO)** Yidisher visnshaftlekher institut (w 1940 r. przeniesiony do Nowego Jorku) [Jewish Scientific Institute, in Wilno until 1940 when it was transferred to New York as the YIVO Institute for Jewish Research.]

**J.J.** Jan Jagielski

**J.K.** Józef Kermisz [= Joseph Kermish]

**JSS** Jüdische Soziale Selbsthilfe, see ŻSS [Jewish Social Self-Help]

**j.w.** jak wyżej [as above]

**k.** koło [circa, about], in the vicinity of; kartka [sheet, card, folio].

**kanc.** kancelaryjny [office]

***Kiddush Hashem*** S. Huberband, *Kiddush Hashem. Jewish Religious and Cultural Life in Poland During the Holocaust*, eds. J. S. Gurock and R. S. Hirt, trans. David Fishman, New York 1987.

**KK** Komisja Koordynacyjna (see KKOSiP) [Coordinating Commission]

**K.K.L.** Jewish National Fund (Hebrew: Keren Kayemet Le-Israel)

**KKO** Komunalna Kasa Oszczędności [Communal Savings Bank]

**KKOSiO** Komisja Koordynacyjna Organizacji Społecznych i Opiekuńczych "TOZ" i "Centos" przy SKSS w Warszawie (ul. Leszno 13) [Coordinating Commission of the Social and Welfare Organizations TOZ and Centos at the Capital Committee for Social Self-Help in Warsaw, 13 Leszno Street]

**KOM** Komitet Opiekuńczy Miejski, see ŻKOM [Municipal Guardian Committee]

**KOP** Komitet Opiekuńczy Powiatowy [County Guardian Committee]

**kpr.** kapral [corporal]

***Kronika getta*** E. Ringelblum, *Kronika getta warszawskiego*, Warsaw 1983

**l.** luźne, lata, list [loose, years, letter]

**Lb.** liczba kolejna wg spisu z 1946 r. dokumentów Ring. I ("Katalog Archiwum dr Emanuela Ringelbluma"), rkps, Archiwum ŻIH [Sequential document number according to the 1946 list of documents of Ring. I ("Catalog of Dr. Emanuel Ringelblum's Archive"), manuscript, Jewish Historical Institute Archive].

***Listy o Zagładzie*** *Archiwum Ringelbluma. Konspiracyjne Archiwum Getta Warszawy*, t. 1, *Listy o Zagładzie*, ed. R. Sakowska, Warsaw 1997. [Ringelblum Archive. The Underground Archive of the Warsaw Ghetto, vol. 1, Letters on Extermination]

**LOP** *See* LOPP

**LOPP** Liga Obrony Powietrznej i Przeciwgazowej [Air and Anti-Gas Defense League]

***Ludzie*** R. Sakowska, *Ludzie z dzielnicy zamkniętej. Żydzi w Warszawie w okresie hitlerowskiej okupacji—październik 1939–marzec 1943*, Warsaw 1975 [People of the Closed District. Jews in Warsaw during the Nazi Occupation—October 1939–March 1943]

**m.** mieszkanie (apartment)

**mf.** microfilm

**min.** minister

**mps** maszynopis [typed, typescript]

**niem.** niemiecki [German]

**NN.** anonymous, no name

**NSV** National-Sozialistische Volkswohlfahrt (Warsaw) [National Socialist Public Welfare]

***Obozy*** *Obozy hitlerowskie na ziemiach polskich 1939–1945. Informator encyklopedyczny*, Warsaw 1979 [Nazi Camps on Polish Territories 1939–1945. Encyclopedic Guidebook]

**OBW** Ostdeutsche Bautischlerei Werkstätte [East German Construction Carpentry Workshops]

***Ocalone z*** Exhibition Catalog: *Ocalone z warszawskiego getta—Archiwum Ringelbluma, Muzeum Żydowskiego Instytutu Historycznego w Polsce, Warszawa 15 IV–30 V 1993 r.* [Warsaw 1993] [Saved from the Warsaw Ghetto—The Ringelblum Archive, Museum of the Jewish Historical Institute in Poland, Warsaw 15 April–30 May 1993]

**odpis** Transcript or copy of an original document [Term used in the technical descriptions of items in the inventory to designate transcripts (copies) of original documents collected by the Oyneg Shabes group. Such transcripts in turn were often copied one or more times by the Oyneg Shabes staff.]

**ok.** około [circa, approximately]

***Oneg Schabbat*** [Catalog of the exhibit] *Oneg Schabbat. Das Untergrundarchiv des Warschauer Ghettos-Ringel-*

*blum-Archiv, 28 September 2000–21 Januar 2001, Börnegalerie im Museum Judengasse*, Warsaw 2000 [Oyneg Shabes. The Underground Archive of the Warsaw Ghetto—Ringelblum Archive, 28 September 2000–21 January 2001, Börnegalerie in the Judengasse Museum]

**OPL** Obrona przeciwlotnicza [anti-aircraft defense]

**oprac.** opracowanie [monograph, paper, study]

**oryg.** oryginał [original]

**oryg.(o)** brudnopis lub czystopis relacji wysłuchanej i spisanej przez współpracownika "Oneg Szabat" [rough draft or clean copy of an oral account heard and written down by a coworker of Oyneg Shabes]

**O.S.** Oyneg Shabes

**O.Sh.** Oneg Shabbat (modern Hebrew), Oyneg Shabes (Yiddish)

**OSz.** "Oneg Szabat"—konspiracyjna nazwa zespołu E. Ringelbluma. [Oyneg Shabes: the conspiratorial name of E. Ringelblum's team]

**Oyneg Shabes** Yiddish transcription of Oyneg Shabes, the code name used by the clandestine organization of the underground archive in the Warsaw ghetto

**p.** pułk [regiment]

**PCK** Polski Czerwony Krzyż [Polish Red Cross]

**pocz.** początek [beginning]

**pol.** polski [Polish]

**poł.** połowa [half]

**por.** porównaj [compare]

**poszyt** dokument szyty [sewn document]

**p.p.** pułk piechoty [infantry regiment]

**PP** Policja Państwowa [State Police]

**ppor.** podporucznik [second lieutenant]

**prof.** profesor [professor]

***Przewodnik*** B. Engelking and J. Leociak, *Getto warszawskie. Przewodnik po nieistniejącym mieście*, Warsaw 2001. [Warsaw Ghetto. Guide through a Non-Existent City]

**ps.** pseudonim [pseudonym]

**PSB** *Polski słownik biograficzny*, Kraków 1934–2003 [Polish Biographical Dictionary]

***Relacje z Kresów*** *Archiwum Ringelbluma. Konspiracyjne Archiwum Getta Warszawy*, vol. 3, *Relacje z Kresów*, ed. A. Żbikowski, Warsaw 2000 [Ringelblum Archive. Underground Archive of the Warsaw Ghetto, vol. 3: Accounts from the Eastern Borderlands]

**RA** Ringelblum Archive at the Jewish Historical Institute in Warsaw.

**regest, regesty** A summary of contents of a document or documents under the date and place of issue, as well localities and family names occurring in the document.

**RGO** Rada Główna Opiekuńcza [Central Guardian Council]

**Ring. I** first part of the Ringelblum Archive, unearthed in 1946.

**Ring. II** second part of the Ringelblum Archive, unearthed in 1950.

**Rkps** rękopis [handwritten, handwritten manuscript]

**ros.** rosyjski [Russian]

**rozdz.** rozdział [chapter]

**R.S.** Ruta Sakowska

**RSt.** Rada Starszych Gminy Żydowskiej [Council of Elders of the Jewish Community]

**rum.** rumuński [Romanian]

**[s]** [*sic*]

***Scream the Truth*** *Scream the Truth at the World: Emanuel Ringelblum and the Hidden Archives of the Warsaw Ghetto*, Museum of Jewish Heritage, November 7, 2001–February 18, 2002 [Exhibition catalog]

***Selected Documents*** *To Live With Honor and Die With Honor: Selected Documents from the Warsaw Ghetto Underground Archives "O.S."* ["Oneg Shabbath"], editor J. Kermish [=Kermisz], Jerusalem 1986

**SKSS** Stołeczny Komitet Samopomocy Społecznej (Warsaw) [Capital Committee for Social Self-Help]

***Służba Porządkowa*** A. Podolska, *Służba Porządkowa w Getcie Warszawskim w latach 1940–1943*, Warsaw 1996 [Order Service in the Warsaw Ghetto in the Years 1940–1943]

**SP** Służba Porządkowa [Order Service = Jewish ghetto police force]

**SPS** Sekcja Pracy Społecznej (przy ŻSS) [Social Work Section at the Jewish Social Self-Help]

**ss.** sheets

**Temkin-Berman** B. Temkin-Bermanowa, *Dziennik z podziemia*, Warsaw, 2000 [Journal from the Underground]

***The Jewish Underground Press*** *Itonut ha-mahteret ha-yehudit be-Varsha*, ed. Joseph Kermish and Israel Shaham 6 vols., Jerusalem, 1979–1997 [The Jewish Underground Press in Warsaw (Hebrew)]

**tłum.** tłumaczenie [translation]

**Toporol** Towarzystwo Popierania Rolnictwa [Society for the Support of Agriculture]

**TOZ** Towarzystwo Ochrony Zdrowia Ludności Żydowskiej w Polsce [Society for the Protection of the Health of the Jewish Population in Poland]

**"trzynastka (13)"** "Urząd do walki z lichwą i spekulacją" (ul. Leszno 13) [Office to Combat Usury and Speculation, known colloquially as "The Thirteen" after the group's address, 13 Leszno Street]

**Transcript** A careful copy, handwritten or typed, of an original document; additional copies were often made from a transcript.

**ukr.** ukraiński [Ukrainian]

**ul.** ulica [street]

**Umgekumene** B. Mark, *Umgekumene shrayber fun di getos un lagern,* Warsaw 1954 [Murdered Writers of the Ghettos and Camps]

**USHMM** United States Holocaust Memorial Museum, Washington, D.C.

**uzup.** uzupełnienie [supplemental information]

**włos.** włoski [Italian]

**WP** Wojsko Polskie [Polish Army]

**WZO** Wydział Zbiórki Odzieżowej (ŻSS-KOM. SPS) [Department for Clothing Collections (Jewish Social Self-Help—Municipal Guardian Committee Social Work Section]

**YIKOR** Yiddish Culture Organization (Polish: JIKOR)

**YIVO** *See* JIWO

**zach.** zachowane [saved, preserved]

**z.** zeszyt [notebook, fascicle, issue]

**zm.** zmarł, zmarła [deceased]

**ZOM** Zakład Oczyszczania Miasta (Warsaw) [City Cleaning Unit]

**ZWZ-AK** Związek Walki Zbrojnej—Armia Krajowa [Association for Armed Combat—Home Army]

**ZZ** Zakład Zaopatrywania przy RŻ w Warszawie [Provisioning Unit at the Jewish Council in Warsaw]

**ŻIH** Żydowski Instytut Historyczny w Warszawie [Jewish Historical Institute in Warsaw; see JHI]

**ŻKOM** Żydowski Komitet Opiekuńczy Miejski (in Warsaw from 17 Oct. 1940.) [Municipal Jewish Guardian Committee]

**ŻOS** Żydowska Opieka Społeczna [Jewish Social Welfare]

**ŻS** Żydowska Samopomoc (ŻSS) [Jewish Self-Help]

**ŻSS** Żydowska Samopomoc Społeczna (Jüdische Soziale Selbsthilfe—JSS) (from Oct. 1940 ŻTOS Żydowskie Towarzystwo Opieki Społecznej) [Jewish Social Self-Help; from Oct. 1940 Jewish Society for Social Welfare]

**ŻTOS** Żydowskie Towarzystwo Opieki Społecznej [Jewish Society for Social Welfare]

**żyd.** żydowski [Jewish or Yiddish]

***Żydzi Warszawy*** I. Gutman, *Żydzi Warszawy* 1939–1943, Warsaw 1993 [The Jews of Warsaw, 1939–1943]

# Abbreviations for Identifying Handwriting in the Inventory of the Ringelblum Archive

| | |
|---|---|
| **AA*** | NN. |
| **AP*** | Abram Prowalski |
| **BB*** | NN. |
| **BG*** | Bronka Górna |
| **BTT*** | NN. |
| **BW*** | Bluma Wasser |
| **CA*** | NN. |
| **CC*** | NN. |
| **ChW*** | Chaskiel Wilczyński |
| **CK*** | Cwi Klejnman [Tsvi Kleinman] |
| **D*** | Stefa Szereszewska [?] |
| **DD*** | Lebensold [?]. |
| **E*** | Natan Koniński [?] |
| **ER*** | Dr. Emanuel Ringelblum |
| **F*** | NN. |
| **FLIG*** | Daniel Fligelman |
| **GG*** | NN. |
| **H*** | Eliasz Gutkowski [Elijahu Gutkowski] |
| **HL*** | Hanna Lewkowicz |
| **Hub.*** | Szymon Huberband, rabbi [Shimon Huberband] |
| **H.W.*** | Hersz Wasser [Hersh Wasser] |
| **I*** | Józef Honig [?] |
| **IK*** | Icchak Kacenelson [= Yitshak Katzenelson] |
| **IL*** | Izrael Lichtensztajn [Israel Lichtenstein] |
| **IM*** | Itzik Manger [Icyk Manger] |
| **JG*** | Jechiel Górny (see U*) |
| **JP*** | Jehoszua Perle |
| **JW*** | NN. |
| **KK*** | Salomea Ostrowska |
| **LEG*** | Eliasz Gutkowski (see H*) |
| **LP*** | NN. |
| **Ł*** | Nechemiasz Tytelman [Nehemiah Tytelman] |
| **MA*** | NN. |
| **MK*** | Menachem Mendel Kohn [Menahem Mendel Kon] |
| **MM*** | Marian Małowist |
| **MS*** | Mordechaj Szwarcbard [Mordekhai Shvartsbard] |
| **NG*** | NN. From Gąbin (author of letters to Tauba Różana (Warsaw, ul. Dzielna 1[..?]) |
| **Np.*** | Mordechaj Szwarcbard [See MS*] |
| **NN*** | NN. |
| **OO*** | Stanisław Różycki [?] (see SR*) |
| **OP*** | Perec Opoczyński [Peretz Opoczyński] |
| **POM*** | NN. (author who helped Hersz Wasser to write down the statements of former prisoners of the camp in Pomiechówek) |
| **RA*** | Rachela Auerbach [Rachel Auerbach, Rokhl Oyerbakh] |
| **RR*** | NN. |
| **SB*** | Samuel Bresław (Brasław) [?] |
| **SJ*** | K.M.[?] Band |
| **SR*** | Stanisław Różycki (see OO*) |
| **Sz.*** | S. Szajnkinder |
| **Szaj.*** | Simcha Bunim Szajewicz |
| **Ś*** | Abraham Lewin |
| **TA*** | NN. |
| **Tr*** | NN. |
| **TT*** | NN. |
| **TW*** | NN. |
| **U*** | Jechiel Górny |
| **WINK*** | Possibly Izrael Winnik |
| **Z*** | NN. |
| **Ż*** | Dawid Berliner |

# Catalog of Ringelblum I

The order of each entry: Serial number of each entry; new call number (old pre-1955 call number), (1946 catalog number with Lb. prefix), ŻIH microfilm no., USHMM microfilm no. The entry then lists the date and place of the document's creation; author's name, if known; the name of the document; an abstract; technical description; and additional information.

To avoid errors, all dates are rendered in the European and military fashion (day.month.year). Since the actual documents use that format, readers should be aware of the European style of dates.

Abbreviation ss. = sheets, so ss. 1 means that a document consists of a single sheet, while pp. 1 means that it consists of a single page with writing. Thus, the notation for a document consisting of a single sheet with writing on both sides would be "ss. 1, pp. 2."

## I. Oyneg Shabes Records: Ring. I

### 1. RING. I/1152/2 (1471). Mf. ŻIH–833; USHMM–45

- Date unknown, Warsaw Ghetto
- Hersz Wasser], Address list of 37 persons (coworkers of Oyneg Shabes)
  - Szymon Huberband (ul. Zamenhofa 19),
  - Rajde [?] Zylbersztajn,
  - Majer Najman (ul. Nowolipie 36),
  - Liba Majeranc (ul. Nowolipki 19),
  - Wolf Zysman (ul. Nowolipie 57),
  - Ruchla Zylberberg (ul. Nowolipki 66),
  - Calel Zylberberg (ul. Nowolipki 66),
  - Natan Koniński (ul. Ogrodowa 5),
  - Salomea Ostrowska (ul. Ogrodowa 27),
  - Izrael Winnik (ul. Miła 27),
  - Eliasz Gutkowski (ul. Nowolipki 31),
  - Bluma Kirszenfeld (ul. Muranowska 6),
  - Daniel Fligelman (ul. Śliska 24),
  - Abram Lewin (ul. Nowolipie 1),
  - Luba Gutkowska (ul. Muranowska 7),
  - Perec Opoczyński (ul. Wołyńska 21),
  - Nechemia Tytelman (ul. Muranowska 31),
  - Mojżesz Węgrowiec (ul. Nowolipie 66),
  - Lejb Pluskałowski (ul. Leszno 42),
  - Jakub Zylberberg (ul. Nowolipie 21),
  - Fela Herclich (ul. Leszno 3),
  - Lejb Goldin (ul. Prosta 17),
  - Maurycy Landau (ul. Nowolipie 49),
  - Rebek[a?] Wasserman (ul. Nowolipie 49),
  - Samuel Bresław (ul. Dzielna 9),
  - Chaim Adler (ul. Franciszkańska 25),
  - Chil Górny (ul. Miła 69),
  - Pinkus Goldberg (ul. Leszno 68),
  - Icchak Szafur [Szafir?] (ul. Dzielna 4),
  - Hersz Klajman (Pl. Parysowski 15),
  - Salomon Tytelman (ul. Gęsia 10),
  - Chana Uszer (ul. Dzielna 4),
  - Rywen Heller (ul. Pawia 31),
  - Małka Hornowicz (ul. Ogrodowa 26),
  - Rywka Gotlib (ul. Nowolipie 21),
  - Eliasz Tytelman (ul. Pawia 5),
  - Izrael Lichtensztajn (ul. Dzielna 93).
- ***Description:*** original, handwritten manuscript (H.W.*), ink, Polish, 144×190 mm, ss. 1, pp. 1.
  - On the reverse, notation by H.W. in Yiddish: "Chapter about a Jewish camp."
  - Doc. is on a sheet torn from a notebook described in Ring. I/1151.
  - Attached note by H.W.

### 2. RING. I/1176 (1495). Mf. ŻIH–834; USHMM–46. RING. I/675. Mf. ŻIH–816; USHMM–28. RING. I/1088 (1407). (Lb. 1540). Mf. ŻIH–833; USHMM–45

**a) Ring. I/675, I/1088, I/1176**

- 06–07. 1942, Warsaw Ghetto
- [Hersz Wasser], Lists of archival materials of Oyneg Shabes (fragments)
- Printed matter, reports, studies. Information about authors (cryptonyms), volume (number of pages) and authors' honoraria.
- ***Description:*** Ring. I/1176—original, handwritten manuscript (H.W.*), ink, Polish, Yiddish, 155×196, 216×285 mm, minor damage and losses of text, ss. 4, pp. 4; Ring. I/1088, original, handwritten manuscript (H.W.*), ink, Polish, 190×158 mm, serious damage and losses of text (fragment of sheet), ss. 1, pp. 1; Ring. I/675—original, handwritten manuscript (H.W.*), ink, Polish, Yiddish, 215×285 mm, extensive minor damage and losses of text, ss. 1, pp. 2.
  - Doc. is a fragment of one or more lists; preserved pages are: 3–4, 8–[9], [10?–11] and fragment of

a sheet, as well as one sheet of another format, which could belong to another manuscript.

b) **Ring. I/1176**
- 1942, Warsaw Ghetto
- [Hersz Wasser], Lists of archival materials of Oyneg Shabes (fragments)
- Printed matter, reports, studies. Information about authors, volume (number of pages).
- ***Description:*** original, handwritten manuscript (H.W.*), ink, pencil, Polish, Yiddish, 105×174, 160×204 mm, damage and losses of text, ss. 8, pp. 12.

Attached note by H.W. in Yiddish
See Ring. I/1147.

**3. RING. I/1147 (1466). Mf. ŻIH–833; USHMM–45**

a)
- Date unknown, Warsaw Ghetto
- NN., "List of printed matter"
- List of archival materials of Oyneg Shabes (mainly printed matter, contains 707 items).
- ***Description:*** original or transcript, handwritten manuscript (JG*), pencil, Polish, 103×295, 109×245 mm, minor damage and losses of text, ss. 25, pp. 25.

b)
- 06–07.1942, Warsaw Ghetto
- Lists of continual publications and other materials included in the collections of Oyneg Shabes (19.06., 26.06., after 29.06.1942).
- ***Description:*** original or transcript, handwritten manuscript (H*, LEG*), pencil, ink, Polish, Yiddish, 110×142, 160×219 mm, minor damage and losses of text, ss. 4, pp. 4.

c)
- After 1940, Warsaw Ghetto
- Lists of archival materials of Oyneg Shabes.
- ***Description:*** original, handwritten manuscript (BW* [?]), ink,Yiddish, 146×209, 154×199 mm, ss. 2, pp. 3.

Notation in Yiddish: "Undescribed materials."
Attached notes (3) by H.W. in Yiddish.

**4. RING. I/674/6. (Lb. 1688). Mf. ŻIH–816; USHMM–28**
- Date unknown, Warsaw Ghetto
- [Hersz Wasser], Notations concerning the work of the Oyneg Shabes team
- List of various texts (subjects [?]), lists of authors, etc.
- ***Description:*** original, manuscript (H.W.*), pencil, ink, Yiddish, 158×179 mm, ss. 1, pp. 2.

Index: Huberband, Bliml (Little Flower) [ER], Kohn, Halbosz [?], Reinberg, Zylberberg, Melech, Furmański, Szentl[?], Natanblut, Lewin, Witelzon [Witelson], Kapłan, Kluger, Rozenbojm, Herclich, nurse, Mirmelczyk [?]

## II. General Studies on the Situation of the Jewish Population during the War. Drafts and Overviews of Work, Questionnaires

**5. RING. I/105. Mf. ŻIH–776; USHMM–7**
- Early 1942, Warsaw Ghetto
- NN., Collection of materials entitled "Tsvey un a halb yor milkhome" (Two and a Half Years of War)
- Surveys, questionnaires, overviews, prepared for the composition of a dissertation on the life of the Jewish population before the start of the war and during the war and occupation (1939–1941).
  a) A survey for writers (prosaists, poets, playwrights, diarists, reporters); questions concerning: family life, housing conditions, sources of income, literary plans, completed works in hand, lost works, the relation of Jewish charitable institutions to authors, to the literary contributions of deceased authors, etc. Attached list of authors selected to take part in the survey.
  b) Survey concerning Yiddish theater and places of amusement; questions concerning: the life of Jewish artists writing in Yiddish, Polish, and Hebrew, the repertoire of the theaters, the current situation of the Yiddish theater, repertoire, amateur troupes, the material condition of theaters, the audience, language, and so forth.
  c) Survey for Jewish youth (aged 14 to 21) in Warsaw; questions concerning: personal life of respondents, their families, wartime wanderings, environment, labor, education, etc.
  d) Outline of a study concerning life of cities, the economic situation of different social segments and relations between Jews and Poles, Germans and Poles before the war and after outbreak of war.
  e) Outline of a study on corruption and thievery in different Jewish institutions during the war.
- ***Description:*** original and transcript (some in several copies), typescript (from a manuscript corrected in ink, pencil), Yiddish, 114×205, 207×292 mm, serious damage and losses of text, ss. 60, pp. 60.

Published: *Selected Documents*, pp. 29–31, 452–453 (fragments).

**6. RING. I/117. (Lb. 1043). Mf. ŻIH–777; USHMM–8**
- Date unknown, Warsaw Ghetto
- [Emanuel Ringelblum?], "Survey" designated for gathering materials about the fate of Jewish population centers (small towns) on Poland's territory before the war and during the Nazi occupation.

- *Description:* original or transcript, typescript, Yiddish, 200×295 mm, ss. 4, pp. 4.
  Inventory and list of 1946: "E. Ringelblum is the author."
  Published: *Selected Documents*, pp. 24–26.

7. **RING. I/134. (Lb. 1086). Mf. ŻIH—777; USHMM—8**
   - After 22.01.1942, Warsaw Ghetto
   - "Klolim fun faktografishn konkurs oyf oysgevaylte temes fun yidishn lebn in der milkhome-tsayt" [Rules of the Factographic Contest on Selected Topics from Jewish Life in Wartime] adopted at the session of 22.01.1942 (fragment).
   - Contest opened by Oyneg Shabes. Includes 15 topics, among others, a study of the Jewish population, Polish–Jewish relations, children, education, smuggling, the police, important moments in the life of Jews. Fourteen monetary prizes were foreseen (from 100 to 1000 zł.). Jury consisting of: D. [Dawid] Guzik, I. [Icchak] Giterman, Sz. [Szmul] Winter, M. [Menachem] Linder, D. [Dawid] Chołodenko, M. [Menachem] M. Kon, Dr. E. [Emanuel] Ringelblum.
   - *Description:* original or transcript (3 copies in fragments), typescript (handwritten manuscript additions, ink),Yiddish, 207×220, 207×130 mm, significant damage and losses of text, ss. 5, pp. 5.
     Published: *Selected Documents*, pp. 27–28.

8. **RING. I/142. (Lb. 1598). Mf. ŻIH—778; USHMM—9**
   - After 1939, Warsaw Ghetto
   - NN., Questionnaire: "Bialistok un andere mizrekh-shtet in di ershte teg fun september 1939" [Białystok and other eastern cities in the first days of September 1939] for conducting interviews with new arrivals from the territories of Poland occupied by the USSR in 1939.
   - The situation on the German–Soviet border, aid to refugees, the housing problem, the situation of Jews, economic life, migrations of Jewish population, Jews in the Communist Party, Jewish schools, interethnic relations, cultural and religious life.
   - *Description:* Transcript (a) (handwritten manuscript—U*—7 copies, pencil, 205×290 mm, extensive minor damage and losses of text);
     Transcript (b) (typescript, 205×283, 205×80 mm, extensive damage and loss of text); Yiddish, ss. 35, pp. 35.
     Published: *Relacje z Kresów*, pp. 39–47.

9. **RING. I/640. (Lb. 667). Mf. ŻIH—815; USHMM—27**
   - Date unknown, Warsaw Ghetto
   - NN., study entitled "Badingungen un tezn fun yugnt-konkurs" [Conditions and thesis of the youth contest]
   - Information about the rules of preparation of text in the form of: a study, memoirs, diary, literary work, report or letter, registering the experience of young people during the war (September 1939) and occupation.
   - *Description:* transcript, typescript, Yiddish, 208×296 mm, minor damage and loss of text, ss. 3, pp. 3.

10. **RING. I/127. Mf. ŻIH—777; USHMM—8**
    - Date unknown, Warsaw Ghetto
    - NN., Survey for collection of materials on the living situation and attitudes of Jewish youth
    - Education, attitude to family, religion, housing situation, employment and earnings, free time, emigration, attitude toward (membership in) trade unions and political organizations.
    - *Description:* original or transcript, handwritten manuscript, Yiddish, 177×175 mm, significant damage and loss of text, ss. 12, pp. 12.
      Manuscript written on the back of forms (printed, Yiddish): Order form of the Joint's office in Warsaw for books, printed materials, etc. (e.g., financial ledgers).

11. **RING. I/507/4. Mf. ŻIH—789; USHMM—20**
    - After 28.08.1941, Warsaw Ghetto
    - [Emanuel Ringelblum], Outline of a study concerning the Jewish woman (fragment)
    - Women's role in various spheres of life during the war
    - *Description:* original, handwritten manuscript (ER*), ink, Yiddish, 110×148 mm, 95–135, ss. 2, pp. 4.
      For writing, 2 ss. were used from a fragment of a document of ŻSS-KOM of 28.08.1941 to NN. (regarding a meeting with Chairman Szereszewski).

12. **RING. I/155. Mf. ŻIH—778; USHMM—9**
    - Beginning of 1942 [?], Warsaw Ghetto
    - General topics for preparing a study on Jewish population centers (small towns) during the occupation
    - Life and appearance of the Jewish small town before 1939; outbreak of war and the situation of the population after entry of the Germans; social and economic life of the population during the occupation; German repressive measures (deportation, liquidation of ghettos, etc.).
    - *Description:* transcript (2 copies), typescript,Yiddish, 216×347 mm, minor damage and loss of text (in the second copy), ss. 4, pp. 4.

13. **RING. I/45. Mf. ŻIH—773; USHMM—4**
    - 1942, Warsaw Ghetto
    - NN., study entitled "2.5 yor milkhome in lebn fun der yugnt (iberblik)" [2.5 years of war in the life of the youth (overview)] (lacking conclusion)
    - The situation of Jewish youth during the war and occupation (participation in 1939 defense of Warsaw, flight to the east, situation in the USSR, forced labor

in labor camps, youth comprised 80% of camp participants, situation in the ghetto, attempts to aid the youth, organization of schooling).
- ***Description:*** original or transcript, handwritten manuscript (Ś*), ink, Yiddish, 148×223 mm, ss. 10, pp. 10.

14. RING. I/507/3. Mf. ŻIH–789; USHMM–20
- Date unknown, Warsaw Ghetto
- [Emanuel Ringelblum], Outline of a study concerning Jewish youth (fragment)
- Division of youth into various groups. Information about authors of individual chapters: e.g., Gutkowski (school youth).
- ***Description:*** original, handwritten manuscript (ER*), ink, Yiddish, 150×115 mm, ss. 1, pp. 2.

15. RING. I/126. (Lb.1564). Mf. ŻIH–777; USHMM–8
- Date unknown, Warsaw Ghetto
- NN., Outline for a study entitled "Fun religyezn lebn" [Of religious life]
- Religion in the life of Jewish society.
- ***Description:*** transcript (3 copies), typescript, Yiddish, 203×287 mm, damage and losses of text, ss. 3, pp. 3.

At bottom (first copy) supplement, handwritten manuscript (ink).

Published: *Selected Documents*, 412–413.

16. RING. I/131. Mf. ŻIH–777; USHMM–8
- Date unknown, Warsaw Ghetto
- NN., "Thesis for paper on Jewish handicrafts"
- Outline of a study on the situation of Jewish handicrafts before the war and during the war (also about handicrafts in the Warsaw Ghetto).
- ***Description:*** original or transcript, handwritten manuscript, ink, Polish, 155×196 mm, ss. 2, pp. 3.

17. RING. I/132. Mf. ŻIH–777; USHMM–8
- Date unknown, Warsaw Ghetto
- NN., "Handicrafts and Light Industry (Theses)"
- Outline of a study on Jewish handicrafts and light industry during the war.
- ***Description:*** original or transcript, handwritten manuscript (H*), pencil, Polish, 205×290 mm, minor damage and losses of text, ss. 2, pp. 3.

18. RING. I/42. (Lb. 271). Mf. ŻIH–773; USHMM–4
- Date unknown, Warsaw Ghetto
- NN., "Plan for a paper on nominal and real wages of a Jewish craftsman, cottage worker and laborer"
- Outline of a scientific study.
- ***Description:*** original, typescript (with handwritten manuscript supplements, pencil), Polish, 205×296 mm, ss. 1, pp. 1.

19. RING. I/141. (Lb. 113, 113A). Mf. ŻIH–778; USHMM–9
- Beginning of 1942, Warsaw Ghetto
- NN., "German–Jewish Relations (Theses)"
- Outline of a study concerning the Third Reich's policy in relation to Jews in Polish lands.
- ***Description:*** original or transcript (2 copies), handwritten manuscript, pencil, Polish, 220×350 mm, minor damage and losses of text, ss. 2, pp. 4.

20. RING. I/339. Mf. ŻIH–781; USHMM–12
- Date unknown, Warsaw Ghetto
- NN., Theses of a study on Jewish–German relations.
- ***Description:*** original or transcript, handwritten manuscript (LEG*), pencil, Yiddish, 220×335 mm, ss. 1, pp. 1.

At top left the names: "Landau, Wasser and Milejkowski."

21. RING. I/137/3. Mf. ŻIH–777; USHMM–8
- After 03.1940, place unknown
- NN., Notes concerning chronology of German orders directed against Jews in the Generalgouvernement (Nov. 1939–March 1940).
- ***Description:*** original, handwritten manuscript, pencil, Polish, 205×330 mm, ss. 1, pp. 1.

22. RING. I/492. (Lb. 80, 298). Mf. ŻIH–788; USHMM–19

a)
- Date unknown, Warsaw Ghetto
- [Emanuel Ringelblum], Outline of a study entitled "Stosunki polsko-żydowskie" (Polish–Jewish Relations).
- ***Description:*** original, handwritten manuscript (ER*), ink, Polish, 110×256, 110×195 mm, ss. 4, pp. 8.

On p. 1 notation (crossed out) in Yiddish: "Polish–Jewish Relations"

Inventory: "Manuscript of Dr. E. Ringelblum."

b)
- Date unknown, Warsaw Ghetto
- NN., Outline for a study entitled "Stosunki polsko–żydowskie" (Polish–Jewish Relations). (lacking conclusion)
- Supplemented and expanded text from manuscript (a).
- ***Description:*** original or transcript, handwritten manuscript (H*), pencil, Polish, 200×297 mm, ss. 2, pp. 4.

c)
- Date unknown, Warsaw Ghetto
- NN., Outline for a study entitled "Stosunki polsko-żydowskie" (Polish–Jewish Relations)
- Supplemented and expanded text from manuscript (a) and (b).
- ***Description:*** original or transcript (2 copies), typescript (with handwritten manuscript supple-

ments—ER* on first copy, H* [?] on second copy), Polish, 220×350 mm, minor damage and losses of text, ss. 2, pp. 4.

## *OYNEG SHABES BULLETINS*

### 23. RING. I/259. (Lb. 1289). Mf. ŻIH—780; USHMM—11

- After 27.03.1942, Warsaw Ghetto
- Bulletin of Oyneg Shabes: "Mitaylungen" [News Reports], no. 1. "Di yidishe bafelkerung untern tseykhn fun fizisher oysrotung" [The Jewish Population under the Sign of Physical Annihilation]
- Description of the total or partial liquidation of Jewish population centers in the following localities: Lublin, Izbica Lubelska, Rawa Ruska, Biłgoraj, Wąwolnica, Mielec, Lwów, Okuniew, Wawer, Miłosna. Gives dates, balance sheets concerning persons deported, those left in place and those executed. Information about the extermination camp in Bełżec and those shot (see Ring. I/262).
- ***Description:*** original, handwritten manuscript (LEG*), pencil, Yiddish, 208×293 mm, ss. 4, pp. 4.

Bulletin contains information elaborated in Ring. I/262.

See HWC, 60/7 (another version of this document in form of duplicated typescript, ss. 3).

### 24. RING. I/262. (Lb. 1198). Mf. ŻIH—780; USHMM—11

- 04.1942, Warsaw Ghetto
- Bulletin of Oyneg Shabes containing information on the situation of Jews in various localities on the territory of the Polish Republic during March–April 1942 (3.04.1942)
- Description of the total or partial liquidation of the Jewish population centers in the following localities: Lublin, Izbica Lubelska, Rawa Ruska, Biłgoraj, Wąwolnica, Mielec, Lwów, Okuniew, Wawer, Miłosna. Gives dates, balance sheets concerning people deported, those left in the place, and those who perished. Information about the extermination camp at Bełżec; about the shooting of the following persons: Budnik (from Kalisz), Matys Powsinoga, Szyja Zysman, Dawid Stanisławski, Fajga Stanisławska, Szlama Bursztyn, Łaja Rotstein, Dwojra Rubin, Jakub Oszer Rzetelny from Miłosna, Szymon Zylberman.
- ***Description:*** original (2 copies), handwritten manuscript (H*), pencil, Polish, 165×86, 205×148, 206×294 mm, very significant damage and losses of text (second copy), ss. 8, pp. 8.

### 25. RING. I/473. (Lb. 273, 560). Mf. ŻIH—786; USHMM—17. RING. I/937 (1256). Mf. ŻIH—830; USHMM—42

- 04.1942, Warsaw Ghetto
- Bulletin of Oyneg Shabes entitled "Wypadki chełmińskie" [Chełmno Events]
- Description of the mass extermination of Jews in the camp at Chełmno nad Nerem.
- ***Description:*** Ring. I/473—original or transcript (a) (typescript, 195×290 mm, extensive minor damage and losses of text); original or transcript (b) (typescript, 205×270 mm, serious damage and losses of text, lacking beginning); Polish, ss. 3, pp. 3; Ring. I/937—original or transcript (2 copies), typescript, 195×275 mm, extensive damage and losses of text, ss. 4, pp. 4.

Ring. I/473: Docs. a and b include the same text. In transcript (a) pagination preserved (ink): "7" (p. 1) and "8" (p. 2); both ss. were paginated and hidden together with p. 1 (first copy—Ring. II/486), on which the pagination has been preserved (ink): "6"; see Ring. I/261. Transcript (b) was presumably part of the bulletin from Ring. I/469 (second copy), judging by the identical format and destruction of the two documents.

Ring. I/937: Doc. was hidden together with a report concerning Wilno and other localities (see Ring. I/937).

Attached note by H.W.: "1942. Chełmno Events. Within the framework of the Underground Press Service Department, H. Wasser, MA, prepared a condensed description of Chełmno."

### 26. RING. I/665. Mf. ŻIH—816; USHMM—28

- 04.1942, Warsaw Ghetto
- Bulletin of Oyneg Shabes [?], Letter to NN
- Description of extermination of Jews in the camp in Chełmno nad Nerem.
- ***Description:*** transcript, typescript, Polish, 207×290 mm, ss. 2, pp. 2

Document includes a text similar (aside from the heading) to one in Ring. I/473.

Attached note by H.W. in Yiddish: "On 02.03.1942 in the Warsaw Ghetto with the aid of Oyneg Shabes it was decided to send out a report about the tragedy in Chełmno; H.W. prepared materials."

Published: *Dwa etapy*, pp. 133–136; *Selected Documents*, pp. 683–686.

### 27. RING. I/469. Mf. ŻIH—786; USHMM—17. RING. I/937 (1256). Mf. ŻIH—830; USHMM—42

- 04.1942, Warsaw Ghetto
- Bulletin of Oyneg Shabes. Report on the extermination of Jews in Polish territories, entitled "Drugi etap" (Second Stage)
- Information about liquidation actions in the following localities: Wilno, Słonim, Krośniewice, Żychlin, Hancewicze near Baranowicze, Równe-Sosenki, Lublin.
- ***Description:***

(a) Ring. I/469—original or transcript (2 copies,

typescript, in the first copy handwritten corrections—H.W.*, ink), Polish, 205×295 mm, minor damage and losses of text, serious damage and losses of text (second copy), ss. 8, pp. 8;

(b) Ring. I/937—original (2 copies), typescript, Polish, 195×287 mm, significant damage and losses of text, ss. 8, pp. 8.

In doc. (a) pp. 1–2 (first copy) have an old pagination (ink): "1" and "2" and were paginated and hidden together with p. 1 of the bulletin of 25.06.1942 (first copy—Ring. II/486); see Ring. I/261 and the bulletin from Ring. I/471 as well as Ring. I/473.

Docs. a and b contain the same text written on different typewriters.

Published: BŻIH, no. 194/2002, pp. 253–256.

## 28. RING. I/1217. Mf. ŻIH—835; USHMM—47

- 12.04.1942, Warsaw Ghetto
- Bulletin of Oyneg Shabes. Report about the extermination of Jews in Polish territories [12.04.1942] (fragment)
- Information about liquidation actions in the following localities: Równe (Sosenki) (execution of 17,000 Jews in 11.1941) and Opole Lubelskie (26.03.[1942]).
- ***Description:*** original, handwritten manuscript (LEG*), pencil, Yiddish, 170×110 mm, serious damage and losses of text, ss. 2, pp. 2.

Information concerning execution in Sosenki near Równe also appears in Ring. I/469.

One of the copies of this bulletin survived in its entirety (original, handwritten, LEG*, pencil, Yiddish, ss. 6, pp. 6) in AAN, no. 202/II-29, pp. 26–32 (collection of the Delegatura Rządu RP na Kraj).

## 29. RING. I/1062/1 (1381). Mf. ŻIH—832; USHMM—44

- After 05.1942, Warsaw Ghetto
- Bulletin of Oyneg Shabes of 29.05.1942 containing information on the situation of Jews in various localities on the territory of the Polish Republic in the period Feb.–May 1942. Title of the bulletin: "Di megile fun payn un oysrotung" [The Scroll of Suffering and Annihilation]
- Description of the total or partial liquidation of Jewish population centers in the following localities: Otwock, Tłuszcz, Włodawa (information about the shooting in the second half of May 1942 of about 100 people), Dęblin (Irena labor camp), Ryki, Końskowola, Międzyrzec Podlaski, Kraśnik, Chodel, Sielce, Wojsławice, Wólka Leszczańska, Kumów.
- ***Description:*** original (2 incomplete copies), handwritten manuscript (LEG*), pencil, Yiddish, 206×292 mm, minor damage and losses of text, missing first page (in second copy), ss. 7, pp. 7.

See HWC, 2/2 (third copy, handwritten manuscript, pencil, ss. 4).

Index: Lajner, rabbi of Radzyń, killed in Włodawa in May 1942; Markinsztern, rabbi, killed in Włodawa in May 1942

## 30. RING. I/1062/2 (1381). Mf. ŻIH—832; USHMM—44

- 11.06.1942, Warsaw Ghetto
- Bulletin of Oyneg Shabes of 11.06.1942, containing information on the situation of Jews in various localities on the territory of the Polish Republic in May 1942
- Description of total or partial liquidation of Jewish population centers in the following localities: Łęczyca, Brzeziny, Włodawa.
- ***Description:*** original, handwritten manuscript (LEG*), pencil, Yiddish, 147×206 mm, ss. 1, pp. 1.

## 31. RING. I/1062/3 (1381). Mf. ŻIH—832; USHMM—44

- 13.06.1942, Warsaw Ghetto
- Bulletin of Oyneg Shabes of 13.06.1942 containing information on the situation of Jews in various parts of Europe
- Notation concerning the Jewish population in occupied Holland and France, as well as the fate of refugees in Switzerland.
- ***Description:*** original, handwritten manuscript (LEG*), pencil, Yiddish, 206×292 mm, ss. 1, pp. 1.

## 32. RING. I/813 (1132). Mf. ŻIH—826; USHMM—38

- 06.1942, Warsaw Ghetto
- Bulletin of Oyneg Shabes containing information on the situation of Jews in various localities on the territory of the Polish Republic in April–May 1942. (20.05.1942)
- Descriptions of total or partial liquidation of Jewish population centers in the following localities: Hrubieszów, Pabianice (liquidation action of 16.05.1942—5,000 people), Łask, Brzeziny, Koluszki (40 Jews murdered).
- ***Description:*** original (2 copies), handwritten manuscript (LEG*), pencil, Yiddish, 150×195 mm, minor damage and losses of text, ss. 10, pp. 10.

Date in the second copy: "22.05.42."

On p. 1 (first copy) notation by H.W. in Yiddish (ink): "2 st[andard] pages."

Index: Finkelsztajn (age 38), died 1.05.1942 in Hrubieszów; Blonder (age 37), died 1.05.1942 in Hrubieszów; Sztern, died 1.05.1942 in Hrubieszów

## 33. RING. I/261. Mf. ŻIH—780; USHMM—11. RING. II/486. Mf. ŻIH—809; USHMM—64

- 06.1942, Warsaw Ghetto
- Bulletin of Oyneg Shabes containing information on the situation of Jews in various localities in the territory of the Polish Republic in April–June 1942 (24.06., 25.06., 30.06.1942)

- Descriptions of total or partial liquidation of Jewish population centers in the following localities: Kraków, Tarnów, Włodawa, Końskowola, Kraśnik, Turobin, Zamość, Chełm Lubelski, Hrubieszów, Grabowiec, Dubienka, Tyszowce, Trawniki, Komarów, Zawiercie, Tłuszcz. Provides dates, numerical lists regarding people deported, those left in place, and those who perished. Also information on the deportation of Poles from Grabowo (Warthegau).
- *Description:* original (1 p. in 3 copies), typescript, Polish, 208x284, 218x284 mm, minor damage and losses of text, ss. 5, pp. 5.
  On p. 2 date "24.[06.1942]"; on p. 1 (first copy—Ring. II/486) date: "25.06.42" and pagination (ink): "6," this sheet was paginated and hidden (buried) together with pages of the bulletin ("Chełmno Events") from Ring. I/471 and bulletins from Ring. I/473; on p. 1 (second and third copy) date: "30.06.42" inscribed with one handwriting (LEG*), pencil. On pp. 2 and 3 is the numeral: "I" (pencil), on p. 1 (third copy) is the numeral: "II" (pencil) (handwritten manuscript LEG* [?]).
  Page 1 (first copy—Ring. II/486) was concealed in a different place than pp. 2–3 (other damage, including water damage).
  Ring. II/486—doc. Included by mistake into Ring. II.

## 34. RING. I/317. (Lb. 470). Mf. ŻIH—781; USHMM—12

- 06.1942, Warsaw Ghetto
- Bulletins of Oyneg Shabes containing information on the situation of Jews in various localities on the territory of the Polish Republic during March–June 1942 (5.05–8.06.1942)
- Descriptions of total or partial liquidations of Jewish population centers in the following localities: Wąwolnica, Rejowiec, Szczebrzeszyn, Międzyrzec Podlaski, Wisłowice [?] near Lublin, Kraśnik, Dubienka, Solec nad Wisłą, Mielec, Grodzisk Mazowiecki, Piotrków, Tomaszów Mazowiecki [?], Sosnowiec, Zawiercie, Kraków. Dates, balance sheets regarding people deported, those left in place, and those who perished (e.g., killed: attorney [Szmul Józef] Szternfeld of Tomaszów and the Markiewiczes).
- *Description:* original, handwritten manuscript (LEG*), pencil, Yiddish, 205x288 mm, ss. 8, pp. 8.
  Published: *Selected Documents*, pp. 116–120 (fragment, bulletin of 5.05.1942).
  See HWC, 2/6 (second copy of bulletin of 5.05.1942, handwritten manuscript, pencil, ss. 6).

## 35. RING. I/472. Mf. ŻIH—786; USHMM—17. RING. I/1063 (1382). Mf. ŻIH—832; USHMM—44. RING. II/487. Mf. ŻIH—809; USHMM—64

- 06–07.1942, Warsaw Ghetto
- Bulletins of Oyneg Shabes containing information on the situation of Jews in various localities on the territory of the Polish Republic during Feb.–July 1942. (18.06., 3.07. and 18.07.1942) (fragments [?])
- Descriptions of total or partial liquidations of Jewish population centers in the following localities: Warsaw, Treblinka, Tłuszcz, Otwock, Kołomyja, Brzeżany, Biała Podlaska, Będzin, Sosnowiec, Łęczyca, Kraków, Tarnów, Włodawa, Końskowola, Chełm, Kraśnik, Chodel, Turobin, Zamość, Hrubieszów, Grabowiec, Dubienka, Uhanie, Bełz, Rzeszów, Radom, Olkusz, Zelów, Jaworzno (Małopolska Wschodnia), Jawornik near Rzeszów, Kock, Ozorków, Chmielnik Kielecki, Skarżysko-Kamienna, Ostrowiec Kielecki, Bełżec, Lwów, Janów Podlaski, Kowel, Łomża. Also information about the Jewish population in Kiev as well as about repressive actions against Poles (e.g., in Ostrowiec on 21–22.06. and in Włoszczowa on 29.06).
- *Description:* original (bulletin of 18.07.1942 in 2 copies, first copy from Ring. I/1063), handwritten manuscript (various handwritings, inter alia: H.W.*), ink, pencil, Polish, 220x353 mm, damage and losses of text, ss. 10, pp. 11.
  pp. 2 (bulletin of 18.06.1942) from Ring. II/487.
  Bulletins of 18.06.1942 and of 3.07.1942 were paginated together (ink): "1–6" (pagination was entered in the same hand on the ss. of various bulletins; see Ring. II/486 [Ring. I/261], Ring. I/471, I/473).
  Ring. I/472—Attached note by H.W.: "Press Service, bulletins of 18.06.1942, 3.07.1942, 18.07.1942."
  Ring. I/1063—Attached note by H.W. in Yiddish: "Ring. Arch. A press service was created for the Jewish and Polish underground press. The press department was run by E. Gutkowski, MA and H. Wasser, MA. This is one of those weekly bulletins."
  Some information is repeated in subsequent bulletins.
  Published: *Selected Documents*, pp. 31–33 (bulletin of 18.07.1942).
  See HWC, 6/1 (preserved one sheet with information concerning Ostrowiec, lack data about whether the doc. is handwritten or typescript).[1]

1. Trans. Note: The document in YIVO Archives RG 225 Hersh Wasser Collection, folder 6.1, is a Yiddish testimony, headed "Ostrowiec (near Kielce)," dated July 1942, and consisting of a single page. The unidentified informant characterizes life in the Ostrowiec ghetto as relatively normal.

### 36. RING. I/471. (Lb. 273). Mf. ŻIH—786; USHMM—17

- After 8.07.1942, Warsaw Ghetto
- Bulletins of Oyneg Shabes containing information on the situation of Jews in various localities on the territory of the Polish Republic, April–July 1942 (2.07. and 8.07.1942) (fragments [?])
- Descriptions of total or partial liquidation of Jewish population centers and other repressive actions against Jews in the following localities: Warsaw, Treblinka, Kołomyja, Brzeżany, Rawa Mazowiecka, Łęczyca, Grabowiec, Uhanie, Bełz, Rzeszów, Zelów, Jaworzno (Małopolska Wschodnia), Ostrowiec Kielecki. Also information about repressive actions against Poles (e.g., in Ostrowiec on 21–22.06. and in Włoszczowa on 29.06).
- ***Description:*** original (bulletin of 8.07.1942 in 2 copies), typescript, Polish, 206×270, 206×290 mm, minor damage and losses of text, ss. 3, pp. 3.

  Dates: "8 VII 42" and "2 VII 42" (handwritten manuscript—H*, ink, pencil). The ss. have old pagination (ink): "3" (8.07.1942), "4" (no date), "5" (2.07.1942) and were paginated and concealed (buried) together with p. 1 (first copy—Ring. II/486), see Ring. I/261, and with the bulletin of Ring. I/473.

  Attached note by H.W.: "Press Service. The archive directed E. Gutkowski, MA and H. Wasser, MA to prepare and publish press bulletins for the Jewish and Polish underground press. 3 bulletins: 25.06.1942 [this sheet is now in Ring. II/486], 2.07.1942, 8.07.1942.—4 pages"

  Text includes information very similar to Ring. I/472.

### 37. RING. I/1220/38. Mf. ŻIH—835; USHMM—47

- 07.1942, Warsaw Ghetto
- Bulletin of Oyneg Shabes containing information on the situation of Jews in various localities on the territory of the Polish Republic, March–July 1942. Descriptions of total or partial liquidation of Jewish population centers and other repressive actions toward Jews in the following localities: (fragment)
- Descriptions of total or partial liquidation of Jewish population centers and other repressive actions against Jews in the following localities: Lublin, liquidation action in an unknown small town 23–24.03.1942, Hancewicze near Baranowicze.
- ***Description:*** original, handwritten manuscript (LEG*), pencil, Yiddish, 189×134 mm, very serious damage and losses of text, ss. 4, pp. 4.

### 38. RING. I/1220/39. Mf. ŻIH—835; USHMM—47

- 12.04.1942, Warsaw Ghetto
- Bulletin of Oyneg Shabes containing information on the situation of Jews in various localities on the territory of the Polish Republic, in March 1942 [12.04.1942] (fragment)
- Descriptions of total or partial liquidation of Jewish population centers and other repressive actions against Jews in the following localities: Lublin (liquidation action in 03.1942), Hancewicze near Baranowicze, Kazimierz Dolny, Wąwolnica, and others.
- ***Description:*** original, handwritten manuscript (H*), pencil, Polish, 206×113 mm, very serious damage and losses of text, ss. 3, pp. 3.

  Index: Engineer Beker, Siegfried, Jew from Germany

  One of the copies of this bulletin survived in its entirety (original, handwritten, (H*), pencil, Polish, ss. 3, pp. 3) in AAN, no. 202/II-29, pp. 17–19 (collection of the Delegatura Rządu RP na Kraj).

## *STUDIES, SCHOLARLY WORKS, REPORTS*

### 39. RING. I/88. (Lb. 1574). Mf. ŻIH—776; USHMM—7

- Date unknown, Warsaw Ghetto
- NN., Article entitled "Vegn yidn un yidishkeyt. A vort tsu der diskusye" [About Jews and Judaism. A Word for the Discussion] (fragment)
- Decline among the Jewish people of the tradition of good works and compassion—indifference of the well-off to the need and hunger of the poor. The hallmark of Jewry should be beauty, good and spirituality, and now is the proper moment for demonstrating that the Mosaic commandments ought to be inscribed in the heart of each Jew.
- ***Description:*** transcript, typescript with additions, handwritten, ink, Yiddish, 208×295 mm, ss. 2, pp. 2.

  See Ring. I/86.

  Published: *Selected Documents*, 730–734.

---

He describes the lavish wedding of the only daughter of the Judenrat chairman, with much eating and drinking, in which the local Gestapo agents joined, too. "And they also received quite nice gifts from the local Neturei Karta [Aramaic: "Guardians of the City"]." The Ostrowiec ghetto is not sealed. The informant refers to the corrupt deals one of the local Gestapo officers makes with Jews. Two Gestapo men enjoy walking the ghetto streets with their big dog, Bruno, who likes to bite Jews. The liaison between the Judenrat and these two Gestapo men is a former Hasid named Funt, who is clean shaven and speaks only German. Reportedly, one of the German officers told Funt to provide him with a Jew to shoot. When he found he couldn't dissuade the German, Funt suggested he shoot one of the Jews locked up in the jail. Funt and the German went to the jail where the German shot down a Jewish prisoner and then cynically said about Funt, "This Jew is guilty in his death." Recent rumors of an approaching resettlement circulated. People were again being seized for forced labor.

**40. RING. I/507/5. Mf. ŻIH—789; USHMM—20**

- Date unknown, Warsaw Ghetto
- [Emanuel Ringelblum], Study on the fates of the Jewish people (fragment).
- ***Description:*** original, handwritten manuscript (ER*), ink, Yiddish, 142×177 mm, minor damage and losses of text, text is illegible in places, ss. 3, pp. 6.

**41. RING. I/457. Mf. ŻIH—786; USHMM—17**

- Date unknown, Warsaw Ghetto
- M. [Maurice] Landau, Study entitled "Demokratishe iluzies fun unzer tsayt. Mentshn un papirn" [Democratic Illusions of Our Time. People and Papers]
- Introduction to (or fragment of) a larger text on France's hospitality after World War I toward emigrants, including Jews, and the subsequent fate of foreigners in that country.
- ***Description:*** original[?], handwritten manuscript, ink, Yiddish, 110×355 mm, minor damage and losses of text, ss. 7, pp. 7.

  Attached note by H.W. in Polish, Yiddish: "Maurice Landau, Jew, Americ[an], journalist, died in the War[saw] ghetto of hunger. Article, fragment of a larger work."

**42. RING. I/336. Mf. ŻIH—781; USHMM—12**

- 1942, Warsaw Ghetto
- NN., Notes for a study about the fate of the Jews
- Past, present, and future of the Jews in Europe—postulate of building their own state.
- ***Description:*** original, handwritten manuscript, pencil, Yiddish, 187×292 mm, damage and losses of text, ss. 2, pp. 4.

  Published: *Selected Documents*, pp. 760–761.

**43. RING. I/166/2. Mf. ŻIH—779; USHMM—10**

- 17.06.1942, Warsaw Ghetto
- [Eliasz Gutkowski], Article entitled "Mikoyekh der poylisher zelbshtendikayt." [On Polish Independence] (17.06.1942)
- Analysis of the attitude of the USSR, of Polish society and government to the question of Poland's postwar borders. Author supports solution of the problem of the eastern borders of Poland according to ethnographic principles.
- ***Description:*** original, handwritten manuscript (LEG*), pencil, ink, Yiddish, 220×308, 195×85 mm, ss. 2, pp. 3.

**44. RING. I/1220/37. Mf. ŻIH—835; USHMM—47**

- Date unknown, Warsaw Ghetto
- NN., Note (letter, speech [?]) entitled "Etlekhe aktuele [. . .] tsum hayntikn khanike" [?], [Some Current [. . .] for Today's Hanukkah" [?]] (fragment)
- Reflections on the current situation of Jews during the occupation, references to religion.
- ***Description:*** transcript, handwritten manuscript (LEG*), pencil, Yiddish, 213×291, 211×156 mm, damage and losses of text, ss. 2, pp. 2.

**45. RING. I/144. (Lb. 257–258). Mf. ŻIH—778; USHMM—9**

- 06.1942, Warsaw Ghetto
- NN., Report entitled "Gehenna of Polish Jews under the Hitlerite Occupation"
- Course of the extermination of the Jewish population: forced resettlement and slave labor, pillage, ghettos; after June 1941 mass annihilation of Jews. Discussion of the liquidation actions in various parts of Polish territories. Attached tables: changes in the prices of foods, number of funerals and cases of typhus in the Warsaw Ghetto in 1941, list of liquidation actions of various Jewish population centers (approximate numerical data for particular localities) from July 1941 to June 1942.
- ***Description:*** transcript (2 copies), typescript, Polish, 210×290 mm, ss. 75, pp. 75.

  Missing p. 15 in the second copy.
  Inventory:[2] "Submitted [by] Jerzy Winkler."
  According to R.S., the text was compiled by the Oyneg Shabes group: E. Ringelblum, H. Wasser, and E. Gutkowski; see *Dwa etapy*, p. 140.
  See I/167 (condensed version of this report, contains table concerning liquidations actions as above).
  Published: *Dwa etapy*, pp. 140–160.
  See HWC, 2/1 (third copy, typescript, ss. 38). Fourth copy with corrections and additions by H.W.* is in AAN, catalog no. 202/II-30.

**46. RING. I/167. Mf. ŻIH—779; USHMM—10**

- 15.06.1942, Warsaw Ghetto
- [Eliasz Gutkowski], Study entitled "Dos oysrotn fun yidn" [The Extermination of Jews] (15.06.1942)
- Periodization of the Nazi extermination of Jews from September 1939 to June 1941: forced resettlement and forced labor, plunder, ghettos; after the start of the war with the USSR—mass extermination of Jewish population centers. Table: approximate numbers of Jewish population losses in particular localities in Polish territories.
- ***Description:*** original, handwritten manuscript (LEG*), pencil, Yiddish, 205×290 mm, ss. 5, pp. 5.

  Inventory: "Author is Eliahu Gutkowski."
  See Ring. I/144.
  Published: *Selected Documents*, pp. 687–690.

2. This refers to the original *inwentarz* (inventory or catalog) of the Ringelblum Archive. See the list of Abbreviations, p. 26.

**47. RING. I/448. (Lb. 1201). Mf. ŻIH—785; USHMM—16**

- After 10.1941, Warsaw Ghetto
- [M. Frenkel], Study of the fate of the Jews of Radomsko, Rawa Mazowiecka, Miechów, Pustków near Dębica (labor camp), Grodzisk, Szumowo near Zambrów, Zaręby Kościelne (1939–1941)
- Text based on the author's [?] own experiences and on statements of various persons. Incidents from September 1939, persecution of the Jewish population during the first years of the occupation (information about victims, ghettos, labor camps, deportatons, liquidation actions).
- ***Description:*** original or transcript, handwritten manuscript, notebooks, ink, Yiddish, 150×195, 155×200 mm, ss. 54, pp. 99.

  Attached note by H.W.: "Notes of the personal experiences of M. Frenkel, coworker of ŻTOS—Religious Leaders Section. Radomsko, Lubicz, Rawa Mazowiecka, Miechów, Pustków, Grodzisk, Szumowo, Zaręby Kościelne, 1939–1941."

  See Ring. I/400, I/669, I/901.

  Index: Kos from Radomsko, died during bombardment in 09.1939; Wolf Wajdenblat of Radomsko, died during bombardment on 10.09.1939; Mosze Bizajski of Radomsko, abused by Germans on "Black Tuesday" 12.09.1939; son-in-law of Fojgeltojb of Radomsko hanged himself after 12.09.1939; Ichiel Jakubowicz of Radomsko, abused; Szlomo Rabinowicz of Radomsko, abused; Abraham Goldberg of Radomsko, abused; Szlomo Najmark of Radomsko, abused; Awner Gurfinkiel of Radomsko, abused; Kwaśniewski, mayor of Radomsko, spoke out against the Jews; Roter, Gestapo agent in Radomsko; Engineer Zifter (Zifser [?]), supervised work on the highway to Przedbórz, exceptionally cruel; Mosze Wajnbaum of Rawa, died during bombardments 09.1939; Abraham Akiba Rapaport (age 25), son of the rabbi of Rawa, died during the bombardments 09.1939; Ichiel Blumberg with family from Rawa, died at the occupier's hand; Josel Szmidt of Rawy, died at the occupier's hand; Ichiel Berkowicz of Rawa, died at the occupier's hand; Jakub Aron Janowski of Rawa, died at the occupier's hand; Jakub Poznański of Rawa, died at the occupier's hand; Abram Lewkowicz of Rawa, died at the occupier's hand; Chenczyński of Rawa, died at the occupier's hand; Wolf Zylbering of Miechów, abused; Chaim, rabbi of Miechów, abused; Szachna Saliman of Miechów, abused; Lipa Rubinsztajn of Miechów, abused; Berl Akerman of Miechów, abused; Dawid Morgensztern (age 19), killed in a labor camp near Miechów; Pinchas Cukierman, died of hunger in the labor camp near Miechów; Jakub Grajcman, died of hunger in the labor camp near Miechów; Abraham Jakub Rozenbaum of Grodzisk, perished; Hanich Wajnguten of Grodzisk, perished; Mania Wajnguten of Grodzisk, perished; Icchak Goldberg of Grodzisk, perished; Icchak Ber Goldfarb of Grodzisk, perished; Abraham Hersz Rozenbaum of Grodzisk, perished; Meir Waserband of Grodzisk, perished

**48. RING. I/166/1. Mf. ŻIH—779; USHMM—10**

- 16.07.1942, Warsaw Ghetto
- [Eliasz Gutkowski], Article entitled "Der blutiker sakhakl" [The Bloody Balance] (16.06.1942)
- German extermination of Jews: extermination camp in Chełmno and liquidation of Jewish population centers in the Lublin region region and in former Galicia.
- ***Description:*** original, handwritten manuscript (LEG*), pencil, ink, Yiddish, 220×355 mm, ss. 4, pp. 4.

  Note by H.W. in Yiddish: "Eliahu [Eliasz] Gutkowski wrote this."

**49. RING. I/1220/40. Mf. ŻIH—835; USHMM—47**

- Date unknown, Warsaw Ghetto
- [Eliasz Gutkowski], Notes
- Notation on the situation of Jews in various localities on the territory of the Polish Republic, e.g., Warszaw, Marysin near Warsaw. Information on extermination of Jewish population centers, Gypsies.
- ***Description:*** original, handwritten manuscript (H*), pencil, Polish, 148×199 mm, text with portions barely legible, ss. 3, pp. 5.

  Doc. could have served for preparation of Oyneg Shabes bulletins [?]

**50. RING. I/318. Mf. ŻIH—781; USHMM—12**

- 06.1942, Warsaw Ghetto
- [Eliasz Gutkowski], Notes entitled "Fun der daytsher prese" [From the German Press], (3.06.1942)
- Information service intended for the underground press. Includes information, inter alia on honors for the winter campaign of 1941/42 in the East, on the German economic situation, on a conference of Jews in Moscow 25.05.1942, on the use of public parks for vegetable plots.
- ***Description:*** original or transcript, handwritten manuscript (LEG*), pencil, Yiddish, 207×295 mm, ss. 2, pp. 2.

  Attached note by H.W. in Yiddish: "Eliasz Gutkowski for the party press of Poalei Zion (ZS) [Zionists Socialists—Right]."

**51. RING. I/319. (Lb. 699). Mf. ŻIH—781; USHMM—12**

- 06–07.1941 [?], Warsaw Ghetto
- NN., Notes of radio communiqués on the situation at the fronts (fragments)

"Communiqués of the Soviet and English Headquarters," inter alia about battles on the eastern front, 06.07.1941.

- ***Description:*** original or transcript, handwritten manuscript (three handwritings: a) BB*, b) NN., c) NN.), pencil, Polish, 105×150, 143×220, 210×298 mm, minor damage and losses of text, (two ss.: significant damage and losses of text), ss. 16, pp. 17.

### 52. RING. I/1088 (1407). Mf. ŻIH–833; USHMM–45

- Date unknown, Warsaw Ghetto
- [Hersz Wasser], Notes (fragments)
- Notation about labor camp at Wilga,[3] sketch about the Order Service in the Warsaw Ghetto (profiles of functionaries).
- ***Description:*** original, handwritten manuscript, ink, Polish, Yiddish, 153×142 mm, serious damage and losses of text, ss. 6, pp. 9.

  Attached note by H.W. in Yiddish.

  Index: Aronson, Goldfeil, Ziegler, Paumeler, Kupczykier, Pagórek, Józef Szeryński, Stanisław Czapliński, Stefan Lubliner, Zundelewicz, councillor, Jakub Pinkiert, Henryk Nowogródzki, Maksymilian Lenbach, Marian Haendel, Erlich

### 53. RING. I/1175 (1494). (Lb. 1215). Mf. ŻIH–834; USHMM–46

- After 1940, Warsaw Ghetto
- [Hersz Wasser], Notes
- About kitchens and prices of meals, smuggled goods, about costs of services; fragments of an address by Chaim Rumkowski; information concerning deportations [?] of the Jewish population in the Warsaw vicinity (Warka, Lipno, Nasielsk, Karczew, Tarczyn, Żyrardów, Góra Kalwaria, Nowe Miasto).
- ***Description:*** original, handwritten manuscript (H.W.*), ink, Polish, Yiddish, 150×198 mm, ss. 2, pp. 4.

  Attached note by H.W. in Yiddish.

  Index: Mordcha Majzner, Salomon Siwek, Kaufman (ul. Pawia 20, apt. 3), Frajdenrajch, Rotenberg, Litenberg [?], Larpman [?]

### 54. RING. I/1089 (1408). (Lb. 1571). Mf. ŻIH–833; USHMM–45

- Date unknown, Warsaw Ghetto
- [Hersz Wasser], Notes concerning the situation of the Jewish population during the occupation in various localities
- Notation concerning Konin, Krośniewice, Żychlin (list of names of members of the Jewish Council in Konin). Description of the execution of Jews condemned for dealing in gold in the localities of NN. (Żychlin?) Fiszel Hirszberg age 44, Naftali Kon age 44, Eleazar Fażenczewski (Pażenczewski[?]) age 25, Chaim Lesman age 65, Moszkowicz age 55, and his son Jakub Moszkowicz age 28, Jakub [. . .] ger age 50, Kolski age 45, Jakub Wyszogrodzki age 46, Jakub Szpigel age 40.
- ***Description:*** original, handwritten manuscript, ink, Yiddish, 155×198 mm, ss. 2, pp. 3.

  Attached note by H.W. in Yiddish

  Index: Rozenberg, member of the Jewish Council in Konin; Józef Aberman age 28, member of the Jewish Council in Konin, chief of Order Service; Ajzyk Kelmer, member of the Jewish Council in Konin; Abraham Helman, member of the Jewish Council in Konin; Icchak Zajfer, member of the Jewish Council in Konin; Noach Helmer, member of the Jewish Council in Konin; Jecheskiel Zonder age 16 of Rypin; Mosze Gelbert age 12; Ruwen Gelbert; Grynbaum, of the Order Service in NN. (Żychlin?); Śliwkowicz, of Order Service in NN. (Żychlin?)

### 55. RING. I/113. Mf. ŻIH–777; USHMM–8

- After 03.1942, Warsaw Ghetto
- [Szymon Huberband], Study entitled "Tlies" [Gallows] on the basis of accounts about the collective executions of Jews in March 1942
- Description of the course of an execution (by hanging): in Zduńska Wola (10.03.1942)—10 persons (among others: Nachum Eliahu Zylberg, age 60, Nachum Jachimowicz, 60, Dr. Lemberg, chairman of the Jewish Council); in Łęczyca (17.03.1942)—10 persons (Moszkowicz, age 55, and his son Jakub Moszkowicz, age 28, Naftali Kon, age 44, Eliezer Fażenczewski, age 25, Fiszel Hirszenberg, age 44, Chaim Lutman, age 66, Szpringer, age 50, Kolski, age 45, Wyszogrodzki, age 46, Szpigel, age 40; in Poddębice (17.03.1942)—5 persons; in Bełchatów (17.03.1942)—10 persons; in Brzeziny (17.03.1942)—10 persons.
- ***Description:*** original, handwritten manuscript (HUB.*), notebook, ink, Yiddish, 152×195 mm, damage and losses of text, ss. 11, pp. 21.

  Inventory: "Szymon Huberband is the author of the text."

  Published: *Kiddush Hashem*, pp. 266–273.

### 56. RING. I/120. Mf. ŻIH–777; USHMM–8

- Date unknown, Warsaw Ghetto
- [Szymon Huberband], Study entitled "Kidesh-hashem" [Sanctification of God's Name = Martyrdom]
- About Jews who sacrificed their lives in defense of other Jews, saving synagogues, Torah scrolls, and

3. About 50 km from Warsaw.

sacred books: Awigdor Frydman (Warsaw—Praga 1939); Abram Wajshof, Tenenberg, Jakub Berliner, Wajngarten, Frajnd, Adler, Zojer and other activists of the Bund (Piotrków—1940); Rabbi Karnicer (Kornicer [?]), Rabbi Sz. Rapaport, Szapiro (Kraków—beginning of 1941); Szlajzinger with son and son-in-law (Będzin—September 1939); the chairman and deputy chairman of the Jewish Council (Wieluń—1942); Rabbi Ruskin, Rabbi Dawid Flek (Blek [?]) (Międzyrzec—18.04.1942); Rabbi Eliahu Laskowski and his son (near Łódź—first days of March [?] 1942); Motel Hochman (Aleksandrów—end of September 1939); Rabbi Abraham Mordechaj Maroko (Widawa—September 1939); Icchak Mordechaj Rabinowicz (Pławno—September 1939); Rabbi Lewi, Chairman of the Jewish Council Dr. Parnes (Lwów); Efraim Szechter (Bodzentyn); Rabbi Rapaport, Vice chairman of the Jewish Council (Rawa Mazowiecka); Mosze, Talmudic scholar (Sierpc—end of 09.1939); Icchak Meir Kominer (Kaminer [?]) (Radzymin—winter 1940).
- ***Description:*** original, handwritten manuscript (HUB.*), notebooks, ink, Yiddish, 160×195, 150×195 mm, minor damage and losses of text, ss. 21, pp. 42.

  Inventory: "Szymon Huberband is the author."

  See J. Leociak, *Tekst wobec Zagłady (O relacjach z getta warszawskiego)* [Text Regarding Extermination (About Accounts from the Warsaw Ghetto)], Wrocław 1997, pp. 286–302.

  Published: *Kiddush Hashem*, pp. 247–259.

## 57. RING. I/122. (Lb. 494). Mf. ŻIH—777; USHMM—8

- After 15.06.1942, Warsaw Ghetto
- [Szymon Huberband], Study concerning the fate of the Jewish population of Pilica, Pabianice, Słomniki and Otwock (1939–1942)
- Situation of the Jews in Pilica and events from the moment of the Germans' invasion (5.09.1939) until 15.06.1942. Division of the population of Pabianice into two groups: A) capable of work—deported to the Reich; and B) women and children up to age 10—18.05.1942 deported to an unknown destination [Chełmno] (many victims during liquidation of the ghetto). Residents of Słomniki were sent on 8.06.1942 to an unknown destination (attached copies of 2 letters from Słomniki to Warsaw: from Dawid, son of Lea and Efraim Fiszel, son of Małka, with requests for prayer). Searches (e.g., in the bakery of Mendel Leber—ul. Świderska), robberies (ul. Warszawska, ul. Cicha 2—where Henech Sieradzki, a prominent Hasid, was killed), roundups (e.g., 19.04.1942) and beating of the Jewish population in Otwock.
- ***Description:*** original, handwritten manuscript (HUB.*), notebook, ink, Yiddish, 150×195 mm, ss. 22, pp. 44.

  On p. 1. in Yiddish: "Pilica" and information by H.W. in Yiddish (ink): "June 1942. 23 ss."

  Index: Szternfeld—last rabbi of Pilica, [Szymon] Gurewicz, Chairman of the Jewish Council in Otwocku, Mordechaj Zeew Cigler—was killed by the Polish physician in Słomnik

## 58. RING. I/1220/3. Mf. ŻIH—835; USHMM—47

- Date unknown, Warsaw Ghetto
- [Szymon Huberband], Study concerning the fate of the Jewish population in various localities (fragments)
- Notation concerning localities of: Zduńska Wola, Lubień, Grodzisk, Sierpc, Skępe, Lipsko.
- ***Description:*** original, handwritten manuscript (HUB.*), ink, Yiddish, 30×50, 155×68, very serious damage and losses of text, damaged document, ss. 27, pp. 52.

  Index: Poznański, buried alive, Izrael Cukier

## 59. RING. I/452. (Lb. 1223). Mf. ŻIH—786; USHMM—17

- After 1939, Warsaw Ghetto
- [Szymon Huberband], Study entitled "Tsar ha-yokhed" [The Individual's Suffering]
- Fate of the Jewish population during the occupation (1939–early 1940) as exemplified by the experiences of individuals: Dr. Gonszer, vice prefect (starosta) of Kozienice, murdered because he did not confess to Jewish origin; martyr's death of Jezjasz Glikson; the suffering of a mother who lost a child.
- ***Description:*** original or transcript, handwritten manuscript (HUB.*?), notebook, ink, Yiddish, 145×200 mm, ss. 16, pp. 16.

  Attached note by H.W. in Polish, Yiddish: "Delivered by Szymon Huberband."

  See HWC, 61/1 (transcript in 2 copies, handwritten manuscript, pencil, ss. 7, pp. 7).

  Published: *Kiddush Hashem*, pp. 260–265.

  Index: Jezjasz Glikson's wife, daughter of the rabbi of Krasnosielec

## 60. RING. I/108. Mf. ŻIH—776; USHMM—7

- Date unknown, Warsaw Ghetto
- [Szymon Huberband], Study entitled "Der khurbn fun shiln, bote-midroshim, un beys-hakhaims" [The Destruction of Synagogues, Prayer and Study Halls, and Cemeteries]
- Concerning the localities: Otwock, Aleksandrów near Łódź, Serock, Piotrków, Sosnowiec, Będzin, Radomsk, Garwolin, Parysów near Garwolin, Pszonka near Parysów, Stoczek, Strzegowo, Sulejów, Przedborze, Brzeziny, Zgierz, Farniczów [?] near Zgierz, Wieluń, Gąbin, Warka, Dobrzyń-Golub, Pruszków, Mława, Praszka, Łódź, Rypin, Suwałki.
- ***Description:*** original, handwritten manuscript (HUB.*), notebooks, ink, Yiddish, 155×200 mm, damage and losses of text, ss. 67, pp. 119.

  Published: *Kiddush Hashem*, pp. 274–333.

## 61. RING. I/150. Mf. ŻIH—778; USHMM—9

- Date unknown, Warsaw Ghetto
- [Szymon Huberband], Study entitled "Dos religyeze lebn beys der milkhome" [Religious Life during the War], "Funem religyezn lebn beys der milkhome," Band IV ["Of Religious Life during War," vol. IV]
- Discussion of different areas of Jewish religious life (ritual slaughter, education, observances, rabbis, Sabbath, books, etc.). Letter from Rabbi Mosze Alter from 12.1940.
- ***Description:*** original, (handwritten manuscript—HUB.*, notebooks, ink, 164×200, 155×200 mm, significant damage and losses of text), transcript (2 copies in fragments, typescript, 150×270, 150×205 mm, significant damage and losses of text), Hebrew, Yiddish, ss. 120, pp. 170.

Study consists of four parts, the fourth part carries the somewhat altered title, "Funem religyezn lebn beys der milkhome" [Of Religious Life during the War] and the subtitle, "Yeshive un shtibl bokherim beys der milkhome" [Yeshiva and Shtibl Students during the War].

Published: *BFG*, vol. XXIX–XXX/1991–1992, pp. 193–207 (fragment); *Kiddush Hashem*, pp. 218–234 (notebook 1); pp. 188–198, 202–206 (notebook 2); pp. 207–217 (notebook 3), pp. 175–187 (vol. 4, notebooks 1–2)

## 62. RING. I/121. Mf. ŻIH—777; USHMM—8

- After 1940, Warsaw Ghetto
- [Szymon Huberband?], "Di poylishe rebeyim un 'gute yidn' beys der milkhome" [The Polish Rabbis and Hasidic Rebbes during the War]
- Fates of two renowned rabbis: Abraham Mordechaj Alter of Góra Kalwaria [Ger] and Icchak Menachem Danciger of Aleksandrów [Aleksander].
- ***Description:*** original or transcript, handwritten manuscript (HUB.*), notebook, ink, Yiddish, 152×195 mm, ss. 13, pp. 11.

On p. 1 notation by H.W. in Yiddish (ink): "June 1942. 4, 5 st[andard] pages"

Published: *Kiddush Hashem*, pp. 235–238.

## 63. RING. I/48. Mf. ŻIH—773; USHMM—4

- After 12.1941, Warsaw Ghetto
- [Szymon Huberband], Study concerning the situation of Jewish women during the war (fragment)
- Women's attitudes: relations with Germans, e.g., in the camp in Grodzisk, cooperation with the Gestapo, mixed marriages on the territory of the USSR, indifference towards destitution. Repressive actions directed at women: e.g., the snatching of girls from homes by the gendarmerie (Będzin, Sosnowiec, Dąbrowa, Zawiercie and other towns of Zagłębie—end of November 1941); order on the confiscation of fur coats (25.12.1941).
- ***Description:*** original, handwritten manuscript (HUB.*), notebook, ink, Yiddish, 152×205 mm, ss. 14, pp. 26.

Preserved fragment of a study contains part of notebook 2, entitled "Di moralishe laydn un moralishe yeride fun der yidisher froy beys der milkhome" [The Moral Suffering and Moral Decline of the Jewish Woman during the War] which consisted of 5 chapters, of which 3 (3–5) have been preserved: 1) "Di moralishe yeride fun der yidisher froy beys der milkhome" [The Moral Decline of the Jewish Woman during the War]; 2) "Hoysofes tsu kapitl alef" [Supplements to Chapter One]; 3) "Di troyrike faktn fun der futer gzeyre" [The Sad Facts of the Fur Decree]

Published: *Kiddush Hashem*, pp. 147–149, 239–243 (fragments).

Index: Guta Wajnberg (age 19), Chilewicz (age 18)

## 64. RING. I/146. Mf. ŻIH—778; USHMM—9

- 1940, Warsaw
- [Huberband Szymon], Memorandum on the Rescue of Relics of Jewish Culture
- Discussion of the wartime devastation to date of: synagogues in Pińczów, Przedborze, and Szydłów, synagogal items (among others, ark curtains, candlesticks, ritual goblets), historic tombstones, Jewish communal minute-books (pinkeysim); proposals: renewal of the activity of YIVO for the purpose of saving Jewish relics, to send delegates to Jewish population centers authorized to purchase historic objects, manuscripts, e.g., rabbinic responsa, and to conduct them to Warsaw; to make copies of old tombstones.
- ***Description:*** original, handwritten manuscript (HUB.*), ink, Yiddish, 205×218, 205×150 mm, minor damage and losses of text, ss. 4, pp. 4.

On p. 2 the abbreviation "YIVO" (aside from one instance) is crossed out with the [Yiddish] pronoun "men" (one).

Inventory: "Author of the text is Szymon Huberband, Rabbi."

Published: *BFG*, vol. I, no. 2/1948, pp. 105–110; *Kiddush Hashem*, pp. 454–459; *Selected Documents*, 437–441.

## 65. RING. I/34. Mf. ŻIH—772; USHMM—3

- After 04.1941, Warsaw Ghetto
- Jan Kapczan, Study entitled "Material vegn der finans-virtshaft fun di yid. kehiles in okupatsie-gebit beshas der milkhome" [Material about the Financial Management of the Jew[ish] Religious Communities in Occupation Territory during the War] (end of 04.1941)
- Abuses against the Jewish population by members of the Jewish communities in Łódź and in Warsaw.
- ***Description:*** transcript (2 copies), handwritten manuscript (MS*), pencil, Yiddish, 147×207 mm, ss. 12, pp. 12.

In the margin the Hebrew letter Ayin.
About Halber, see *Czerniaków*, p. 90.
Published: *Selected Documents*, pp. 294–297.
Index: Maurycy Halber, Pawecki

### 66. RING. I/147. Mf. ŻIH—778; USHMM—9

- After 11.1941, Warsaw Ghetto
- NN., Study entitled "A Note on Agriculture among Jews in 1941" about the activity of the Toporol society[4]
- Organization of seasonal work on farms for Jewish youth (information about estates to which youth were sent), attitude of the German authorities and of the Jewish Councils toward the activity of Toporol and the development of Jewish agriculture.
- ***Description:*** original or transcript (3 copies), handwritten manuscript (E*, ink, 150×195, 175×110 mm), transcript (2 copies., typescript, 205×295 mm), Polish, ss. 23, pp. 30.

  Typescript contains a somewhat shortened version of the text (several concluding sentences missing) in relation to the manuscript.

  On p. 1 (typescript, second copy) notation by H.W. in Yiddish: "No. 24. 109—1942/1 January."

### 67. RING. I/148. Mf. ŻIH—778; USHMM—9

- After 17.08.1941, Warsaw Ghetto
- NN., Information about the activity of Toporol (17.08.1941)
- Poor diet and difficult conditions of work on the land organized by Toporol for Jewish youth (enclosure: account about the situation at the Żerań estate in Łowicz district—from a letter by a sixteen-year-old boy, Zdzisław Gotlib, to his mother in Warsaw).
- ***Description:*** original [?,] (handwritten manuscript (E*), ink, 148×207, 148×103 mm, ss. 2, pp. 2); transcript (2 copies, handwritten manuscript—JG*, pencil, 148×207 mm, ss. 6, pp. 6), Polish, minor damage and losses of text, ss. 8, pp. 8.

  On p. 1 (transcript 1st copy) information from H.W.: "Kon. [Koniński], Contributions to the fate of Jewish youth through labor on the land."

  Date "17.VIII.1941" on p. 2 (original [?]) written in a different hand.

### 68. RING. I/173. Mf. ŻIH—779; USHMM—10

- Date unknown, Warsaw Ghetto
- NN., Study entitled "Dakh–pape oysarbetung" [Roofing Tarpaper Production]
- Significance of Jews in production of roofing tarpaper in Poland before the war and the changed situation during the occupation.
- ***Description:*** transcript (2 copies), handwritten manuscript (MS*), pencil, Yiddish, 145×208 mm, ss. 8, pp. 8.

  Attached note by H.W. in Yiddish: "Information delivered by Szyja Rabinowicz, member of the board of Oyneg Shabes."

### 69. RING. I/1220/56. Mf. ŻIH—835; USHMM—47

- Date unknown, place unknown
- NN., List of localities (labor camps [?])
- District of Opatów: Bogoria, Łagów, Iwanisko, Raków, Koprzywnica, Klimontów (50–60), Sandomierz (several do[zen]), Ożarów, Zawichost; county of Busko: Chmielnik, Pacanów, Stopnica, Nowy Korczyn; Zamość (100), Rejowiec, Ostrowiec (ca. 2 thousand), Wierzbnik.
- ***Description:*** original, handwritten manuscript, ink, German, Polish, 290×217 mm, ss. 1, pp. 1.

### 70. RING. I/194. Mf. ŻIH—779; USHMM—10

- Date unknown, place unknown
- Alphabetical list of selected localities in Poland under German occupation.
- ***Description:*** original, typescript (minor handwritten additions, ink), Polish, minor damage and losses of text, ss. 4, pp. 4.

## *GENERATED COLLECTIONS*

### "Kalisz" Letters

### 71. RING. I/542. (Lb. 1702). Mf. ŻIH—791; USHMM—22

- After 8.01.1942, Warsaw Ghetto
- "List of letters" submitted to the archive of Oyneg Shabes [?]
- Private and official letters from the years 1939–1941.
- ***Description:*** transcript (2 copies in fragments, together they include the entire text), handwritten manuscript (JG*), pencil, Polish, 205×293, 145×100 mm, damage and losses of text, ss. 7, pp. 7.

  Notation by H.W. in Yiddish (ink): "146 letters; January 1942. 110."

### 72. RING. I/599/43. Mf. ŻIH—812; USHMM—24

**Letter no. 4**

- After [27.01.1940], Warsaw Ghetto
- NN., Letter of [27.01.1940] to [M.K. T]ondawski (Jewish Hospital, Kalisz).
- ***Description:*** transcript, handwritten manuscript (JG*), ink, German, 83×100 mm, serious damage and losses of text, missing text of letter, ss. 1, pp. 1.

  Notation (pencil): "4."

### 73. RING. I/599/54. Mf. ŻIH—812; USHMM—24.

**Letter no. 5**

- After 27.12.1939, Warsaw Ghetto

4. Toporol was a society dedicated to the promotion and improvement of agriculture among Jews.

- [Mendel Eliasz (Stalag[5] XI[?] A), Letter of [27.12.1939] to [Hanna Eliasz] (Kalisz, [ul. POW 26]). Information concerning family.
- *Description:* transcript, handwritten manuscript (JG*), ink, German, 120×160 mm, serious damage and losses of text, ss. 1, pp. 2.
  Notation on p. 2 (ink): "[. . .] jasz, Kalisz, [. . .] 26" and (pencil): "5."

## 74. RING. I/599/48. Mf. ŻIH—812; USHMM—24

Letter no. 6

- After [24.10.1939], Warsaw Ghetto
- [M. Erlich (Kobierzyn near Kraków?)], Letter of [24.10.1939] to [Z. Erlich] (Kalisz, [R. D]ekerta 5).
- *Description:* transcript, handwritten manuscript (JG*), ink, Polish, 80×88 mm, serious damage and losses of text, missing text of letter, ss. 1, pp. 1.
  Notation (pencil): "6."

## 75. RING. I/599/5. Mf. ŻIH—812; USHMM—24

Letter no. 7

- Date unknown, Warsaw Ghetto
- [Dawid Sara[?] (Rzeszów)], Letter to [Jewish Council in Warsaw] (fragment)
  Notation concerning Birko [?] and Lejb Zajfe[l? . . .].
- *Description:* transcript, handwritten manuscript (JG*), ink, Polish, 88×85 mm, serious damage and losses of text, ss. 1, pp. 2.
  On p. 1 various notations (ink): "Community, Warsaw," some illegible; (pencil): "7."

## 76. RING. I/599/44. Mf. ŻIH—812; USHMM—24

Letter no. 9

- After [22.04.1940], Warsaw Ghetto
- [Majer Anszetewicz] (Stalag VI A [Hemer]), Letter of [22.04.1940] to Frani Szmidt (Kalisz, ul. R. Dekierta 3). Thanks for letters [?].
- *Description:* transcript, handwritten manuscript (JG*), ink, Polish, 85×73 mm, serious damage and losses of text, ss. 1, pp. 2.
  On p. 2 notation (ink): "Szmidt" and (pencil): "9."

## 77. RING. I/599/4. Mf. ŻIH—812; USHMM—24

Letter no. 10

- Date unknown, Warsaw Ghetto
- [B. Lemberger (Szpringer) (Włodawa)], Letter to the Committee for Refugees (Warsaw, ul. Tłomackie) (fragment)
- Request for help in finding son Icek Jakob. Information to be sent to the address: Szulim Kaufman (Warsaw, ul. Nowolipie 29).
- *Description:* transcript, handwritten manuscript (JG*), ink, German, Polish, 100×125 mm, serious damage and losses of text, ss. 1, pp. 2.
  On p. 1 notation (pencil): "10."

## 78. RING. I/599/40. Mf. ŻIH—812; USHMM—24

Letter no. 11

- After [. . . 12.1939], Warsaw Ghetto
- Abram [Gelbard] (Stalag II A [Neubrandenburg]), Letter of [. . . 12.1939] to [Eliasz] Frajnd (Kalisz, [ul. Babina[?] 17]). Question about mother.
- *Description:* transcript, handwritten manuscript (JG*), ink, German, serious damage and losses of text, 100×128 mm, ss. 1, pp. 2.
  On p. 2 notation (ink): "Herrn, Frajnd, Kalisz" and notation (pencil): "11."
  See Ring. I/599/39.

## 79. RING. I/599/47. Mf. ŻIH—812; USHMM—24.

Letter no. 12

- After [2.04.1940], Warsaw Ghetto.
- [Leizer Koft (Gąbin)], Letter of 2.04.1940 to the Jewish Community in Kalisz
- *Description:* transcript, handwritten manuscript (JG*), ink, Polish, 85×118 mm, serious damage and losses of text, missing text of letter, ss. 1, pp. 1.
  Notation (pencil): "12."

## 80. RING. I/599/46. Mf. ŻIH—812; USHMM—24

Letter no. 13

- After 15.04.1940, Warsaw Ghetto
- [Szmul Heida (Sieradz), Letter of 15.04.1940 to (J. Korzec [Kalisz, ul. Garbarska])].
- *Description:* transcript, handwritten manuscript (JG*), ink, German, 60×115 mm, serious damage and losses of text, missing text of letter, ss. 1, pp. 1.
  Notation (ink): "[. . .] strasse [. . .]" and (pencil): "13."

## 81. RING. I/599/39. Mf. ŻIH—812; USHMM—24

Letter no. 17

- After [21.01.1940], Warsaw Ghetto
- [Zenon Słomka] (no. 18876, Stalag II A [Neubrandenburg]), Letter of [21.01.1940] to Jadzia [Igielnik (Kalisz, [ul. POW 37])
- Questions about the health of family, whether brothers are at home.
- *Description:* transcript, handwritten manuscript (JG*), ink, Polish, 96×125 mm, extensive damage and losses of text, ss. 1, pp. 2.
  On p. 2 notation (ink): "Jadzia, Kalisz" and notation (pencil): "17."
  See Ring. I/599/40.

5. German abbreviation for Stammlager, main camp.

## 82. RING. I/599/45. Mf. ŻIH–812; USHMM–24

**Letter no. 18**

- After [17.06.1940], Warsaw Ghetto
- [Szmul Sznajnerman] (no. 9209A, Stalag VI F [Kreuzkrug]), Letter of [17.06.1940] to [P. Moszkowicz] (Kalisz, [ul. Ciasna 2]).
- ***Description:*** transcript, handwritten manuscript (JG*), ink, Polish, 90×115 mm, ss. 1, pp. 2.

  On p. 2 notation (ink): "[. . .] owicz, Kalisz" and (pencil): "18."

## 83. RING. I/599/41. Mf. ŻIH–812; USHMM–24

**Letter no. 22**

- After [1.01.1940], Warsaw Ghetto
- [Józef Djamend] (Stalag B78 [Moosburg]), Letter of [1.01.1940] to wife Ruchla Djamend (Kalisz, [ul. Harcerska 11]). Request for clothing.
- ***Description:*** transcript, handwritten manuscript (JG*), ink, Polish, 100×130 mm, serious damage and losses of text, ss. 1, pp. 2.

  On p. 2 notation (ink): "Ruchla Djamend, Kalisz" and information (pencil): "22."

## 84. RING. I/599/42. Mf. ŻIH–812; USHMM–24

**Letter no. 23**

- Date unknown, Warsaw Ghetto
- [Hemie Eich . . .] (Stalag and A [Stablack?]), Letter to Wolf [Pincze]wski, Kalisz, [ul. Browarna] 6). Request for a food parcel [?].
- ***Description:*** transcript, handwritten manuscript (JG*), ink, Polish, 93×124 mm, serious damage and losses of text, ss. 1, pp. 2.

  Notation (pencil): "23."

## 85. RING. I/599/57. Mf. ŻIH–812; USHMM–24

**Letter no. 24**

- After 21.[01.1941], Podedwórze near Wisznice
- [Nachum Segał] (Podedwórze near Wisznice), Letter of 21.[01.1941] to [Sz.] Groswirt (Warsaw, Lubeckiego 6, apt. 41). Information about stay in camp [?].
- ***Description:*** transcript, handwritten manuscript (JG*), Polish, 95×142 mm, serious damage and losses of text, ss. 1, pp. 2.

  On p. 2 notations (ink): "Herrn Groswirt, Warsaw, Lubeckiego 6/41" and (pencil): "24."

## 86. RING. I/599/66. Mf. ŻIH–812; USHMM–24

**Letter no. 26**

- [23.12.1941], [Łochów]
- [Goldsztejn (Łochów)], Letter of [23.12.1941] to [Laufer (Warsaw Ghetto)]. Request for medicine.
- ***Description:*** original, handwritten manuscript, ink, Polish, 85×205 mm, serious damage and losses of text, ss. 1, pp. 2.

  On p. 2 notation (pencil): "26."

## 87. RING. I/599/80. Mf. ŻIH–812; USHMM–24

**Letter no. 28**

- 7.01.1941, Parczew
- J. Zegał, Sz. Cukierkon, N.M. Segał, Jakub Sz. Herszberg, Isberscherg [?] (Mława Committee in Parczew), Letter of 7.01.1941 to the Joint [B. Horowic (Warsaw, ul. Zamenhofa 29, apt. 6)]. Request for aid.
- ***Description:*** original, handwritten manuscript, ink, Yiddish, 158×200 mm, serious damage and losses of text, ss. 2, pp. 3.

## 88. RING. I/599/101. Mf. ŻIH–812; USHMM–24

**Letter no. 29**

- After 12.1940, Mława
- [I. Zendel] (Mława), Letter to [F. Berman (Warsaw, ul. Lubeckiego 6, apt. 41)].
- ***Description:*** transcript, handwritten manuscript, pencil, Yiddish, 130×79 mm, minor damage and losses of text, ss. 1, pp. 1.

  Notation (pencil): "29" [?]

## 89. RING. I/599/11. Mf. ŻIH–812; USHMM–24

**Letter no. 30**

- 13.01.1941, Odrzywół
- Alter Weksler, Council of Elders of the Jewish Community in Odrzywól, Letter to Mława Hometown Association in the Warsaw Ghetto delivered to F. Berman (fragment). Request for aid.
- ***Description:*** original, handwritten manuscript, ink, stamp, Polish, 220×140, 225×75 mm, serious damage and losses of text, ss. 2, pp. 2.

## 90. RING. I/599/55. Mf. ŻIH–812; USHMM–24

**Letter no. 32**

- 31.01. [1941], Międzyrzec [Podlaski]
- [Doba Pasternak (Międzyrzec)], Letter of 31.01[1941] [postmark date] to M. Ch. Beker (Warsaw, ul. Zamenhofa 36 [apt. 27]).
- ***Description:*** original, handwritten manuscript on a postcard, ink, German and Yiddish in Roman transliteration, 108×140 mm, serious damage and losses of text, text is illegible in places, ss. 1, pp. 2.

## 91. RING. I/599/68. Mf. ŻIH–812; USHMM–24

**Letter no. 36 [?]**

- 18.[12?].1939, New York (USA)
- [S. Jakoby?] (1[0?]56 Kelly St., New York), Letter to [Traube ? (Kalisz)].
- ***Description:*** original, handwritten manuscript, ink, German, Yiddish in Roman transliteration, 128×164 mm, extensive damage and losses of text, ss. 1, pp. 1.

## 92. RING. I/599/35. Mf. ŻIH–812; USHMM–24

**Letter no. 38 [?]**

- 29.01.[1940], [Ja]dów

- Icek Izbicki [Symcha Perkal], Letter of 29.01.[1940], to Committee of Refugees from Kalisz (Warsaw)
- Concerning searches of the Jutkiewicz (Gołda) and Rozenfeld families from Kalisz.
- *Description:* original, handwritten manuscript, ink, German, 130×215 mm, serious damage and losses of text, ss. 1, pp. 2.

### 93. RING. I/599/49. Mf. ŻIH–812; USHMM–24

Letter no. 42 [?]

- Before 6.02.1940, place unknown., R[zeszów?]
- [Jewish Community in Rzeszów?], Letter of [29.01.1940?] [6.02.1940 postmark. Jewish Community in Warsaw?] to Jewish Community (Warsaw).
- Request for information about refugees from Kalisz: Alter Zyge and his wife, Jochewet, and Gucia Mintus.
- *Description:* original, typescript on a postcard, postmark and Jewish Community in Warsaw, handwritten manuscript, ink, pencil, German, 146×105 mm, serious damage and losses of text, ss. 1, pp. 2.

### 94. RING. I/599/82. Mf. ŻIH–812; USHMM–24

Letter no. 49

- 5.02.1940, Będzin
- [Hans Kielow] M. Rozenker (Będzin, ul. Kościuszki 66), Letter to [H] Frydman (Kalisz). Order for repayment of debt.
- *Description:* original, typescript, handwritten manuscript, pencil, Polish, German, 173×100 mm, significant damage and losses of text, ss. 1, pp. 1.

### 95. RING. I/599/103. Mf. ŻIH–812; USHMM–24

Letter no. 57

- Before 3[2?]1.01.1940, Brussels (Belgium)
- [Frohman] (Belgium), Letter to [H. Rauch (Kalisz, ul. Piłsudskiego 11)]
- Wedding invitation: [. . .]ady Cukier and [. . . .] Frohman, on 3[2?]1.01.1940 in Brussels (Belgium). Parents extending the invitation: Icchak and Hinda Cukier and Dawid and Jente Frohman. Address for correspondence: 91, Bd. M. Lemonnier, Bruxelles.
- *Description:* original, printed, French, Yiddish, 111×92 mm, serious damage and losses of text, ss. 2, pp. 2.

### 96. RING. I/599/1. Mf. ŻIH–812; USHMM–24

Letter no. 60

- 17.02.19[40], Łódź
- [Inf]ormationsabteilung des Roten Kreuzes Lodsch (Information Department of the Red Cross in Łódź) (Adolf Hitler Str. 2), Information on the people who were sought at the request of [Holc] (Kalisz, [ul. Harcer]ska 4).
- *Description:* original, hectographed[6] typescript, ink, German, 107×95 mm, serious damage and losses of text, ss. 1, pp. 2.

### 97. RING. I/599/23. Mf. ŻIH–812; USHMM–24

Letter no. 61 [?]

- [3.01.1940], [Baczki near Łochów]
- [M. Kowadło (Baczki, near Łochów)], Letter to Committee of Kalisz Exiles [Komitetu Kaliskich Wygnańców] (Warsaw, ul. Tłomackie 5)
- Request for information about: Wulew, Ziskin, Jakub [. . .].
- *Description:* original, handwritten manuscript on a postcard, ink, pencil, German, Polish, ink, 128×98 mm, serious damage and losses of text, ss. 1, pp. 2.

  On p. 1 notation: "Łochów."

  See I/599/21 and 24.

### 98. RING. I/599/31. Mf. ŻIH–812; USHMM–24

Letter no. 62

- Date unknown, Kirow [. . .]? (USSR)
- [H. Korzec], Letter to [D. Jud] [(Kalisz, ul. Ciasn]a 5).
- *Description:* original, handwritten manuscript on a postcard, postmark, ink, pencil, Russian, Yiddish, 110×100 mm, serious damage and losses of text, ss. 1, pp. 2.

### 99. RING. I/599/20A. Mf. ŻIH–812; USHMM–24

Letter no. 64 [?]

- [1.03.1940], [Włodawa]
- [Jewish Community in Włodawa], Letter to [Committee of Kalisz Refugees (Warsaw, ul. Tłomackie 12)] (fragment)
- Request for information about Szmul Jakub of Kalisz (former soldier of the 70th regiment of the Polish Army), wife Ruta and children in Włodawa.
- *Description:* original, handwritten manuscript, ink, Polish, 90×120 mm, serious damage and losses of text, ss. 1, pp. 1.

  Document glued from Ring. I/599/20.

  See Ring. I/599/24 and 25.

### 100. RING. I/599/20. Mf. ŻIH–812; USHMM–24

Letter no. 65

- [12.03.1940], Rz[eszów]
- [Jewish Community in Rzeszów], Letter to Committee of Kalisz Refugees (Warsaw, ul. Tłomackie 12) (fragment).
- *Description:* original, handwritten manuscript on a postcard, ink, Polish, 90×120 mm, serious damage and losses of text, ss. 1, pp. 1.

  Document glued from Ring. I/599/20a.

6. Hectography is duplication via methods such as mimeograph and spirit-masters.

### 101. RING. I/599/22. Mf. ŻIH—812; USHMM—24

Letter no. 66 [?]

- [22.03.1940], W[łodawa]
- [Jewish Community in Włodawia (R. Lias)], Letter to the Kalisz Association (Ziomkostwo Kaliskie) (Warsaw, ul. Tłomackie 12)
- Request for the address of Aron Rotstein and mother Taub[a?] [. . . ?] of Kalisz
- ***Description:*** original, handwritten manuscript on a postcard, ink, Polish, 100×100 mm, serious damage and losses of text, ss. 1, pp. 2.

    See Ring. I/599/21 and 25.

### 102. RING. I/599/38. Mf. ŻIH—812; USHMM—24

Letter no. 69

- 2[6].03.1940, Kalisz
- Nussen K[aufman] (Kalisz), Letter of 2[6].03.1940 to the Committee of Refugees from Kalisz (Warsaw)
- Request for information about author's daughter, Sura Zeifer[?] of 7 children (Kalisz, Pl. Kilińskiego[. . .]).
- ***Description:*** original, handwritten manuscript on a postcard, ink, postmark, German, 130×105 mm, serious damage and losses of text, ss. 1, pp. 2.

### 103. RING. I/599/21. Mf. ŻIH—812; USHMM—24

Letter no. 70 [?]

- [9.03.1940], [Rzeszów]
- [Jewish Community in Rzeszów], Letter to the Jewish Committee of Refugees from Kalisz (Warsaw, ul. Tłomackie 12)
- Request of H. Bajrach of Kalisz for information about those sought after NN. Attached address: ul. Sobieskiego.
- ***Description:*** original, typescript on a postcard, Polish, 100×100 mm, serious damage and losses of text, ss. 1, pp. 2.

### 104. RING. I/599/34. Mf. ŻIH—812; USHMM—24

Letter no. 82

- 2.01.1940, Wiernschau near Kępno
- [M. Bogań]ski ([W]iernschau, ul. Nowy Świat 4), Letter of 2.01.1940 to T. Moszkowicz (Kalisz, ul. 11 Listopada). Anxiety over the family's fate.
- ***Description:*** original, handwritten manuscript on a postcard, pencil, Polish, 140×103 mm, significant damage and losses of text, ss. 1, pp. 2.

    On p. 1 notations (pencil): "76" and "248" (crossed out) and "82."

### 105. RING. I/599/62. Mf. ŻIH—812; USHMM—24

Letter no. 83

- 2.01.1940, Ostrowo
- A. Szydłowski (Ostrowo, Ring [sic][7] 27), Letter of 2.01.1940 to Lapides (Kalisz, ul. POW 26).
- ***Description:*** original, handwritten manuscript on a postcard, postmark, ink, Polish, 145×100 mm, damage and losses of text, ss. 1, pp. 2.

    Notation on p. 1 (pencil): "83" (crossed out: "246").

### 106. RING. I/599/114. Mf. ŻIH—812; USHMM—24

Letter no. 84

- 4.01.1940, Bielitz [Bielsko]
- [German] commissioner of the firm Max Rappaport & Co., Two writings of 4.01.1940 to Fajwel Berger (Kalisz, [ul. Franciszkańska 4a]). Notices calling for payment of what is owed.
- ***Description:*** original, typescript, handwritten manuscript, ink, German, 215×168, 218×168 mm, significant damage and losses of text, ss. 2, pp. 2.

### 107. RING. I/599/71. Mf. ŻIH—812; USHMM—24

Letter no. 85

- 4.01.1940, Władysławów near Turek
- [W. Zbojnowski] (Władysławów near Turek), Letter of 4.01.1940 [postmark—Turek] to I. Z. Hendeles (Kalisz, ul. Szopena 16). Greetings.
- ***Description:*** original, handwritten manuscript on a postcard, postmark, ink, Yiddish in Roman transliteration, 100×130 mm, significant damage and losses of text, ss. 1, pp. 2.

    On p. 1 notation (pencil): "85" (crossed out: "241").

### 108. RING. I/599/104. Mf. ŻIH—812; USHMM—24. RING. I/595/3, I/595/5. Mf. ŻIH—792; USHMM—23

Letter no. 87

- 7.[10].1939, New York (USA)
- [Szalom Amsterdam] (New York), Letter of 7.[10].1939 to brother of [Icek] Szenk (Kalisz, ul. Piłsudskiego 1)]. Information on closest family (father, Ester).
- ***Description:*** original, handwritten manuscript, ink, Polish, 120×198 mm, significant damage and losses of text, ss. 1, pp. 2.

    Attached envelope (fragments) with addressee: Icek Szenk (Kalisz, Al. Aleksandry Piłsudskiej); and the sender: [Am]sterdam, New York (USA); with notation (pencil): "87" and German censorship band (original, handwritten manuscript, printed ink, postmark (23.01.1940, Geneva), English, German, Polish, 145×92 40×117 mm, serious damage and losses of text, ss. 2, pp. 2.

7. According to Epsztein's introductory essay, the Polish abbreviation [s] means [sic]. It might be that here the meaning is "street," as in Ringstrasse.

## 109. RING. I/599/107. Mf. ŻIH—812; USHMM—24

Letter no. 88

- 29[. . . .], Kiel [Kilonia]
- [Okonowski] (Kiel [Kilonia]-Elmschenhagen (Lager-Süd II [?]). Letter to Roman Warcka [Wartska ?] (Kalisz, ul. Piłsudskiego 3 or 5).
- Thanks for the cake and question whether the husband of the addressee is already home.
- ***Description:*** original, handwritten manuscript, ink, German, 150×180, 144×93 mm, serious damage and losses of text, ss. 2, pp. 3.
  Attached envelope, handwritten manuscript, ink, postmarks (Kiel), 150×95 mm, ss. 2, pp. 2. (On p. 1 notation (pencil): "88"; [. . .] in German: "return," "Jew"; on p. 2 notation (pencil): "[. . .] 3.02.1940."

## 110. RING. I/595/2. Mf. ŻIH—792; USHMM—23

Letter no. 90

- 21.08.1939, New York (USA)
- Szalom Szenk (114–120 E[. . . ?] 105th Street, New York), Letter of 21.08.1939 to son I. [Icek] Szenk (Kalisz, ul. Aleksandry Piłsudskiej 1). Information concerning family.
- ***Description:*** original, handwritten manuscript, ink, Yiddish, 213×277 mm, minor damage and losses of text, ss. 1, pp. 1. Attached envelope, postmark (21.08.1939), 165×95 mm, ss. 1.
  Letter on a printed letterhead: "Hebrew Home for the Aged of Harlem."

## 111. RING. I/595/4. Mf. ŻIH—792; USHMM—23

Letter no. 92

- 25.08.1939, New York
- [Szlama Amsterdam ?], Letter of 25.08.1939 to Dawid Szenk [I. Szenk] (Kalisz, ul. Aleksandry Piłsudskiej 1)
- Sister writes to brother in matter of a U.S. visa.
- ***Description:*** original, handwritten manuscript, ink, Yiddish, 123×198 mm, damage and losses of text, ss. 2, pp. 4. Attached envelope, postmark (25.08.1939, New York), address of the addressee and sender (damaged), information (pencil): "5.04. zurück," on the reverse of a censor's band with the date (pencil): "5.04.1940," "92" and crossed out: "40" (handwritten manuscript, ink, pencil, German, Polish, significant damage and losses of text, ss. 2, pp. 2).

## 112. RING. I/595/6. Mf. ŻIH—792; USHMM—23

Letter no. 93

- Date unknown [New York]
- [M. Ritz (New York, Brooklyn)], Letter to A. Sternberg (Kalisz, ul. Chodyń[skiego 5])
- Letter to sister and brother-in-law about dispatch of parcels [?].
- ***Description:*** original, handwritten manuscript, ink, Yiddish, 125×198 mm, damage and losses of text, ss. 1, pp. 2. Attached fragments of envelope with address with notation (pencil): "93" and crossed out: "39" and other illegible notations; fragment of the censorship band: "Oberkommando der Wermacht" (ink, pencil, 141×110, 135×80, 61×62 mm, significant damage and losses of text, ss. 3, pp. 3).

## 113. RING. I/599/53. Mf. ŻIH—812; USHMM—24

Letter no. 94

- [1940], Brody (USSR)
- Icek and Mendek [Ko]rsower) (Brody), Letter of [1940] to J. Szwarc (Kalisz, ul. Górnośląska 7/ Breslauer str. 7).
- ***Description:*** original, handwritten manuscript on a postcard, two handwritings, ink, Polish, ink, 145×98 mm, significant damage and losses of text, text illegible in places, ss. 1, pp. 2.
  On p. 1 notation (pencil): "94."

## 114. RING. I/599/97. Mf. ŻIH—812; USHMM—24

Letter no. 96

- 26.12.1940, Wola Uhruska
- Jewish Council in Wola Uhruska, Letter of 26.12.1940 to [F.] Berman (Warsaw, ul. Lubeckiego 6/41)
- There are no deportees from Kraków in Wola Uhruska; they should be sought in Świerż or in Sawin near Chełm.
- ***Description:*** original, handwritten manuscript on a postcard, postmark, ink, Polish, 144×105 mm, serious damage and losses of text, ss. 1, pp. 2.
  On p. 1 notation (pencil): "96."

## 115. RING. I/599/92. Mf. ŻIH—812; USHMM—24

Letter no. 97

- [18.[. . .].1940], Tomaszów Lubelski
- Władysława Hasiaków[na] (Tomaszów Lubelski, at Orlicz's [?]), Letter to (Izio)[I. Szwajcer, Kalisz, ul. POW 15).
- ***Description:*** original, handwritten manuscript, ink, Polish, 148×208 mm, serious damage and losses of text, ss. 1, pp. 1.

## 116. RING. I/599/98. Mf. ŻIH—812; USHMM—24

Letter no. 99

- 8.02.[40], Łódź
- Michał Rospscher (Łódź, [Se?]idstrasse 12), Letter of 8.02.[40] to Jewish Council [Jewish Hospital] (Kalisz)
- Notation concerning Berkowicz [?]; address in Kalisz [?] Oststrasse (ul. Piłsudskiego 37).
- ***Description:*** original, handwritten manuscript, ink, German, 108×134, 117×128 mm, serious damage and losses of text, ss. 4, pp. 4.
  On fragment of the envelope notation (pencil): "[. . .]9."

## 117. RING. I/599/63. Mf. ŻIH—812; USHMM—24

Nr. l. 100

- [13.11.]1939, USA

- [O. Busch (Chicago)], Letter to H. Hahn (Kalisz, ul. Widok [4]).
- ***Description:*** original, handwritten manuscript on a postcard, postmark, ink, pencil, German and Yiddish in Roman transliteration, 114×75 mm, serious damage and losses of text, text illegible in places, ss. 1, pp. 2.

  On p. 1 notation (pencil): "100," "13.02.40 W[. . . ?]."

  H. Hahn, chairman of the Jewish Council in Kalisz, see Ring. I/828.

### 118. RING. I/599/65. Mf. ŻIH–812; USHMM–24

**Letter no. 101**

- 28.02.1940, place unknown
- S. Horensztein, secretary of the Jewish Community in [?], letter of 28.02.1940 to the Jewish Community in Rzeszów
- Concerning missing persons including, among others, Reichman.
- ***Description:*** original, typescript on a postcard, Polish, 140×85 mm, serious damage and losses of text, ss. 1, pp. 2.

  On p. 1 notation (pencil): "101" (crossed out: "142").

### 119. RING. I/599/91. Mf. ŻIH–812; USHMM–24

**Letter no. 102**

- [15].04.1940, Łódź
- [Szlangier ?] (Łódź), Letter of [15].04.1940 to the Kalisz Committee (Warsaw, ul. Tłomackie 5).
- ***Description:*** original, handwritten manuscript on a postcard, postmark, ink, German and Yiddish in Roman transliteration, 100×145 mm, serious damage and losses of text, text illegible in places, ss. 1, pp. 2.

  On p. 1 signature (ink): "Honig [. . .]"[?] and information (pencil): "102."

### 120. RING. I/599/26. Mf. ŻIH–812; USHMM–24

**Letter no. 103**

- Date unknown, Woroszyłowgrad (Voroshilovgrad, USSR)
- NN. (Woroszyłowgrad [USSR], ul. Pocztowa 23), Letter to sister D. Pulwermacher ([Kalisz, ul. Pułaskiego 30])
- Author is living and working in Woroszyłowgrad.
- ***Description:*** original, handwritten manuscript on a postcard, ink, pencil, German, Russian, 140×103 mm, significant damage and losses of text, ss. 1, pp. 2.

  On p. 1 notation (pencil): "103."

### 121. RING. I/599/73. Mf. ŻIH–812; USHMM–24

**Letter no. 104**

- 30.01.1940, Poddębice
- [Sz. Adler], Letter to NN. (Jewish Hospital in Kalisz, Deutschestr [6]).
- ***Description:*** original, handwritten manuscript on a postcard, postmark, ink, Yiddish in Roman transliteration, 105×140 mm, serious damage and losses of text, ss. 1, pp. 2.

  On p. 1 notation (pencil): "104" (erased: "130").

### 122. RING. I/599/60. Mf. ŻIH–812; USHMM–24

**Letter no. 105**

- 15.02.1940, Poznań
- [E. Koschuk] (Poznań), Letter of 15.02.1940 to G. Hartmann (Kalisz, ul. Wodna 2/28)
- Notation on brother in Kalisz, lack of news from relative in Łódź. Greetings from Mr. Birkwahn.
- ***Description:*** original, handwritten manuscript on a postcard, postmark, ink, German, 148×100 mm, ss. 1, pp. 2.

  On p. 1 notation (pencil): "126" (crossed out), "105."

### 123. RING. I/599/72. Mf. ŻIH–812; USHMM–24

**Letter no. 106**

- 29.02.1940, Rzeszów
- [Ch. Kapłan] (Rzeszów, at W[. . .]er's), Letter of 29.02.1940 [date of postmark] to Cylka Kapłan (Jewish Hospital in Kalisz, Deutsche Strasse 6).
- ***Description:*** original, handwritten manuscript on a postcard, postmark, ink, German, 150×104 mm, serious damage and losses of text, ss. 1, pp. 2.

  On p. 1 notation (ink): "odp. 4.[. . .].40" and information (pencil): "106" (crossed out: "127").

### 124. RING. I/599/2. Mf. ŻIH–812; USHMM–24

**Letter no. 107**

- 30.01.1940, Kiejdany (Lithuania)
- [R.L. Glubowski] (Chaim Gryngras (Kiejdany), Letter of 30.01.1940 [postmark date Kiejdany] to [Ajzyk (?)] Kapłan (Kalisz, ul. Wodna 2). Information concerning exchange of correspondence.
- ***Description:*** original, handwritten manuscript on a postcard, ink, pencil, German, significant damage and losses of text, 135×175 mm, ss. 1, pp. 2.

  On p. 1 notation (pencil): "107," "Schulz," "6.02." and in German: "return."

  Index: Bluma Kapłan

### 125. RING. I/1220/7. Mf. ŻIH–835; USHMM–47

**Letter no. 108**

- 31.01.1940, Warsaw
- American Consulate General (Warsaw), letter of [31.01.1940] to Lajb Gelbchardt (Kalisz, ul. POW 28)
- Notation about the inclusion of the interested party's name on the registration list of persons seeking emigration visas, with the reservation that according to the consulate's calculations he would not be in possession of a number for a visa for several years and in the appropriate time will be notified about the required documents.
- ***Description:*** original, typescript on a postcard,

handwritten manuscript, pencil, German, Polish, 148×103 mm, damage and losses of text, ss. 1, pp. 2.
Notation on p. 1 (pencil): "108" and in German (pencil): "Return."

### 126. RING. I/557/2. Mf. ŻIH—791; USHMM—22

Letter no. 109 [?]

- [29.01.1940], Ozorków
- [Sz. F. (Frania?) Beatus] (Ozorków), Letter of [29.01.1940] to H. B[eatus] (Kalisz, Jewish Hospital).
- ***Description:*** original, handwritten manuscript on a postcard, ink, German, 135×100 mm, serious damage and losses of text, ss. 1, pp. 2.

### 127. RING. I/599/19. Mf. ŻIH—812; USHMM—24

Letter no. 110

- [31.01.1940], Warsaw
- American Consulate General (Warsaw), letter of [31.01.1940] to Ella Zalcberg (Kalisz, ul. Piłsudskiego 26, at Mr. B. Reichert's)
- Notation about placement of the interested party's name on the registration list of persons seeking emigration visas, with the reservation that according to the calculations of the consulate, she will not obtain a visa number for several years and in the appropriate time will be notified about the required documents.
- ***Description:*** original, typescript on a postcard, handwritten manuscript (two handwritings), pencil, German, Polish, 146×100 mm, significant damage and losses of text, ss. 1, pp. 2.
  Notation In German (pencil): "Breslauerstrasse 26," "Jew" and "Return."

### 128. RING. I/599/78. Mf. ŻIH—812; USHMM—24

Letter no. 112

- 22.02.1940, Karlsruhe
- The Physicians' Clearinghouse (Karlsruhe, Kriegsstrasse 47), letter of 22.02.1940 to Max Mühlstein, a tailor (Kalisz), concerning financial accounts.
- ***Description:*** original, typescript, German, 215×115 mm, serious damage and losses of text, ss. 1, pp. 1. Attached envelope (printed, typescript, 115×80, serious damage and losses of text, ss. 1, pp. 1.
  On the envelope information (pencil): "112."

### 129. RING. I/599/64. Mf. ŻIH—812; USHMM—24

Letter no. 115

- 3.03.1940, Rzeszów
- [L. Pulwermacher] (Rzeszów), Letter to father of A. Zalc (Jewish Hospital in Kalisz, Deutschestrasse [. . .])
- Author writes about mother and Mr. Jakub (Kalisz). Information about NN. District of Kostrzyń . . . , ul. Przechodnia . . . Jankiel.
- ***Description:*** original, handwritten manuscript., ink, German and Yiddish in Roman transliteration, 140×100 mm, ss. 1, pp. 2.
  On p. 1 notation (pencil): "115."

### 130. RING. I/599/110. Mf. ŻIH—812; USHMM—24

Letter no. 116

- 8.03.1940, Bielitz [Bielsko]
- Dr. Karl Schulz, attorney's chancellory (Bielitz), letter of 8.03.1940 to Helena Goldman (firm) [(Kalisz, ul. POW 14)]
- In the name of the Heinrich NN firm of Skawina near Kraków, seeks payment of amounts due.
- ***Description:*** original, typescript, German, 210×148 mm, serious damage and losses of text, ss. 2, pp. 2.

### 131. RING. I/1220/6. Mf. ŻIH—835; USHMM—47

Letter no. 119

- 18.04.1940, Berlin
- American Express Company New York (Berlin W8, Unter den Linden 73), Letter of 18.04.1940 to Zecharja Luser Leizerowicz (Kalisz)
- Notification of receipt of a money transfer at the order of Bernard Lazarus of New York.
- ***Description:*** original, printed, typescript, German, Polish, 159×42, 180×208 mm, serious damage and losses of text, ss. 6, pp. 8.

### 132. RING. I/599/36. Mf. ŻIH—812; USHMM—24

Letter no. 120

- 16.08.1939, Newberg (USA)
- Leib [Ralewicz], Letter of 16.08.1939 to daughter (Itta) and sister Łaja Markuszewicz (Kalisz, ul. POW 16).
- ***Description:*** original, handwritten manuscript, ink, Yiddish in Roman transliteration, 178×260 mm, ss. 1, pp. 2.
  Attached Envelope with address (ink, postmark), 156×90 mm, significant damage and losses of text, ss. 3, pp. 3; information in German (pencil): return.
  Remnant of the German censorship band.
  On the envelope notations (pencil): "53" (crossed out) and "120."

### 133. RING. I/599/27. Mf. ŻIH—812; USHMM—24

Letter no. 121

- [14.01.]194[0], Stoczek
- [M. Markowicz], Letter to (Minia) [Markowicz] ([Kalisz, ul. Targowa 1])
- Mother writes to daughter about arrival with the family in Stoczek. Greetings from Sala, Róza, Abramek, and Szmulek.
- ***Description:*** original, handwritten manuscript, ink, Polish, 125×197 mm, serious damage and losses of text, ss. 2, pp. 1.

### 134. RING. I/599/6. Mf. ŻIH—812; USHMM—24

**Letter no. 124, 125[?]**

- [28.08.1941, Ostrowiec] [?]
- [J. Halsztuk (Ostrowiec)], Letter[s?] of [28.08.1941] to [J. Szczeciński (Warsaw Ghetto)] (fragments)
- Inter alia, information concerning Rabbi Meier Stachelberg, Mojsze Witman, editor Hoher [?].
- ***Description:*** original, handwritten manuscript, ink, Yiddish, 200×103, 105×200, 205×230 mm, serious damage and losses of text, ss. 3, pp. 6.

    In the list in Ring. I/542 (see Ring I, entry 71) appear two letters (nos. 124 and 125) from J. Halsztuk to J. Szczeciński; the fragments preserved here could be remnants of both letters or of one of them.

### 135. RING. I/599/95. Mf. ŻIH—812; USHMM—24

**Letter no. 128**

- [20.12.1941], [Pacht] near Turek
- B. Gór[na] ([Pacht 11] near Turek, Judenkolonie),[8] Letter of [20.12.1941] to Maks Górny (Warsaw, ul. Miła 69, apt. 29).
- ***Description:*** original, handwritten manuscript on a postcard, postmark and [mark of] Jewish Council in Warsaw, ink, Polish, 105×148 mm, serious damage and losses of text, ss. 1, pp. 2.

    On p. 1 notation (pencil): "128."

    Other letters of Bronka Górny, see Ring. I/585, I/599/13–15.

### 136. RING. I/599/70. Mf. ŻIH—812; USHMM—24

**Letter no. 130**

- [22.12.]1939, Romania
- [K. Margules], Letter of [22.12.]1939 to Genia Tuszyńska (Kalisz, ul. Narutowicza 5).
- ***Description:*** original, handwritten manuscript on a postcard, postmark, ink, German, 144×105 mm, serious damage and losses of text, ss. 1, pp. 2.

    On p. 1 notation (pencil): "[1]30"

### 137. RING. I/599/51. Mf. ŻIH—812; USHMM—24

**Letter no. 131**

- [13.12.1939], [Rzeszów]
- [J. Gerst (Rzeszów)], Letter of [13.12.1939] to Ryfka Goldberg (Jewish Council, Kalisz, ul. POW/ Deutschestr.).
- ***Description:*** original, handwritten manuscript on a postcard, ink, Germany, 90×85 mm, serious damage and losses of text, ss. 1, pp. 2.

### 138. RING. I/599/32. Mf. ŻIH—812; USHMM—24

**Letter no. 134**

- Before 2.04.1940, [Łódź]
- [B. Grzmilas] ([Łódź]), Letter to Sz. Grzmilas (Jewish Hospital in Kalisz).

    Information on the family's situation.
- ***Description:*** original, handwritten manuscript on a postcard, postmark, ink, Polish, 110×95 mm, serious damage and losses of text, ss. 1, pp. 2.

### 139. RING. I/599/59. Mf. ŻIH—812; USHMM—24

**Letter no. 135**

- [18.02.]1940, Łódź
- [K. Lustig (Łódź], ul. Drewnowska [?] 9), Letter of [18.02.]1940 to Mendel Bloch (Jewish Hospital in Kalisz)
- Author (age 84) requests retrieval of his documents and prayer garb.
- ***Description:*** original, handwritten manuscript, ink, German, 150×108 mm, significant damage and losses of text, ss. 1, pp. 2.

    On p. 1 notations (pencil): "96" (crossed out) and "135."

### 140. RING. I/599/33. Mf. ŻIH—812; USHMM—24

**Letter no. 138**

- 2.04.1940, Brussels (Belgium)
- M. Makowski (Brussels, Ch.d. Haecht 584), Letter of 2.04.1940 to Natan Noskowicz [refugee] from Kalisz (Brody, USSR), ul. Szpitalna 12, at Jerma Arnowicz's [?])
- Lack of news about Natan's sister, promise to send a ticket [to the West] to the addressee.
- ***Description:*** original, handwritten manuscript on a postcard, postmarks, ink, Russian, Yiddish in Roman transliteration, 140×90 mm, damage and losses of text, text illegible in places, ss. 1, pp. 2.

    On p. 1 notation (pencil): "138."

### 141. RING. I/599/69. Mf. ŻIH—812; USHMM—24

**Letter no. 139**

- 28.11.1939, New York (USA)
- [P. Procel] (529 Bedford Ave., Brooklyn, New York), Letter to [E.] Pinczewska (Kalisz, ul. Harcerska 15).
- ***Description:*** original, handwritten manuscript on a postcard, postmark, ink, German and Yiddish in Roman transliteration, 85×138 mm, serious damage and losses of text, text legible in places, ss. 1, pp. 2.

    On p. 1 notation (pencil): "139"(crossed out: "84").

### 142. RING. I/599/25. Mf. ŻIH—812; USHMM—24

**Letter no. 141**

- 2.12.1939, Cincinnati (USA)
- [Stern] (Cincinnati [USA], Letter of 2.12.1939 to [A.L. Rozenst]raub ([Kalisz])

8. German for "Jewish colony," possibly referring to one of the handful of Jewish agricultural colonies that were for a time permitted by the Germans.

- Author of the letter recalls a visit in New York and his two brothers, Alfons and Leo.
- *Description:* original, typescript on a postcard, handwritten manuscript, ink, German, 120×80 mm, significant damage and losses of text, ss. 1, pp. 2.
  Index: Lev Gelbart

### 143. RING. I/599/24. Mf. ŻIH–812; USHMM–24

**Letter no. 142**

- 18.01.194[0], Włodawa
- [Sz. Jakubowicz (Włodawa), Letter of 18.01.4[0] to NN. [. . . J?]akubowicz (Kalisz Committee for Refugees, Warsaw, ul. Tłomackie 5)
- Request for information about Herman Et[?], Abram, Hanka E[t?], Icchak [?].
- *Description:* original, handwritten manuscript on a postcard, ink, pencil, Yiddish in Roman transliteration, 138×105 mm, significant damage and losses of text, ss. 1, pp. 2.

### 144. RING. I/599/37. Mf. ŻIH–812; USHMM–24

**Letter no. 143**

- [26.01.1940], [Meuheim?]
- [B. Działowski (Meuheim?)], Letter of [26.01.1940] to [R. Działowski (Kalisz, ul. Ciasna 6)].
- *Description:* original, handwritten manuscript on a postcard, ink, German, 130×105 mm, serious damage and losses of text, text illegible, ss. 1, pp. 2.
  On p. 1 notation in German, pencil): Gelbit[?] 8.02.4[. . .] and "143" and "88."

### 145. RING. I/599/30. Mf. ŻIH–812; USHMM–24

**Letter no. 144**

- 30.01.1940, Brussels (Belgium)
- M. Skiersabolski (Brussels, rue de Mirode 367), Letter of 30.01.1940 to sister Etka Bicz (Kalisz, ul. Piłsudskiego 16). Information on lack of response to several letters.
- *Description:* original, handwritten manuscript on a postcard, postmarks, ink, Polish, 203×130 mm, damage and losses of text, ss. 1, pp. 2.
  Notation in German (pencil): "return" and "144."

### 146. RING. I/599/58. Mf. ŻIH–812; USHMM–24

**Letter no. 145**

- [14.01.1940], [Brody] (USSR)
- [Sz. Kajler (Brody)], Letter of [14.01.1940] to [Sz. Sztarc (Kalisz, [ul. Piekarska 37])]. Letter of son to father [?].
- *Description:* original, handwritten manuscript on a postcard, postmark (26.02.1940, Berlin, Charlottenburg), pencil, French, German, Russian, significant damage and losses of text, text illegible in places, 140×100 mm, ss. 1, pp. 2.
  On p. 1 notation (pencil): "95" (crossed out) and "145."

### 147. RING. I/599/50. Mf. ŻIH–812; USHMM–24

**Letter no. 146**

- [7.12.1939], Bucharest
- Jeanette Niederhofer (Bucharest, Str. Matec Besarab 23/7), Letter of [7.12.1939] to M. Rosenblum (Kalisz, [Marian]ska 5)
- The author with brother Samuel requests contact with the Kapłan family ([Kalisz], ul. Parkowa 3).
- *Description:* original, handwritten manuscript on a postcard, postmarks, ink, pencil, German, 189×134 mm, significant damage and losses of text, ss. 1, pp. 2.
  Notation in German (pencil): "Return."

### 148. RING. I/595/4, I/595/7. Mf. ŻIH–792; USHMM–23

**a) Ring. I/595/4**

- Date unknown, USA
- NN., Letter to NN. (fragment)
- Author provides this address for correspondence [?]: "Hamil a[nd] Farnes [Farnus?] Inc., 6[?]10 Hamilton Ave, North Bergen."
- *Description:* original, handwritten manuscript, ink, Yiddish, serious damage and losses of text, ss. 1, pp. 1.
  Letter paper with the imprint "Diamond Crystal Salt Co. Inc., St. Clair, Michigan."

**b) Ring. I/595/7**

- Date unknown, place unknown
- Censorship band: "Oberkommando der Wehrmacht. Geöffnet." [German Army High Command. Opened] From letter NN. (fragment).
- *Description:* original, stamp, German, 141×29 mm, ss. 1, pp. 1.
  Doc. (a) and (b) are fragments of unknown letters from the "Kalisz" collection.

### 149. RING. I/1220/76. Mf. ŻIH–835; USHMM–47

- 11.08.1939, Washington (USA)
- Committee on Banking and Currency (Washington [USA], Robert F. Wagner, Letter of 11.08.1939 to Louis G. Holtzman (New York, 1452 Sterling Place, Brooklyn), concerning Frymeta Lipszyc of Poland.
- *Description:* original, typescript, English, 194×269 mm, ss. 1, pp. 1.
  Attached fragment of envelope (printed, handwritten manuscript, ink, postmark, English, 275×225 mm, ss. 1, pp. 1.

### 150. RING. I/1220/77. Mf. ŻIH–835; USHMM–47

- 19.08.1939, New York (USA)
- NN. (New York, 1709 Westchester Av., Brooklyn), Letter of 19.08.1939 to NN. (sister) (Poland).
- *Description:* original, handwritten manuscript, ink, Yiddish, 188×281 mm, text legible in places, ss. 1, pp. 1.

**151. RING. I/1220/78. Mf. ŻIH—835; USHMM—47**

- 24.12.1939, New York (USA)
- NN. (Dawid and Helena) (New York, 831 Hnuts Pt. [Hunts Point?] Ave., Brooklyn), Letter of 24.12.1939 to NN. (Izi and Regina) (Generalgouvernement.)
- Notation concerning family. Attached "postal censorship."
- ***Description:*** original, handwritten manuscript, ink, German, 199×262, 96×95 mm, ss. 2, pp. 3.

**152. RING. I/599/28. Mf. ŻIH—812; USHMM—24**

- 6[?].01.1940, place unknown
- NN., Letter to NN.
- ***Description:*** original, handwritten manuscript, ink, German, 120×83 mm, serious damage and losses of text, ss. 1, pp. 2.

**153. RING. I/599/61. Mf. ŻIH—812; USHMM—24**

- Date unknown, place unknown
- NN., Letter to NN. (Kalisz).
- ***Description:*** original, handwritten manuscript on a postcard, postmark, ink, Polish, 145×110 mm, serious damage and losses of text, text legible in places, ss. 1, pp. 2.

**154. RING. I/599/74. Mf. ŻIH—812; USHMM—24**

- Date unknown, place unknown
- NN. (Fela), Letter to NN.
- ***Description:*** original, handwritten manuscript, ink, Polish, 98×210 mm, serious damage and losses of text, ss. 1, pp. 2.

**155. RING. I/599/75. Mf. ŻIH—812; USHMM—24**

- Date unknown, place unknown
- NN., Letter to NN. concerning parcels.
- ***Description:*** original, handwritten manuscript, ink, German, 210×140 mm, significant damage and losses of text, ss. 1, pp. 2.

**156. RING. I/599/76. Mf. ŻIH—812; USHMM—24**

- Date unknown, place unknown
- NN, Letter to NN.
- ***Description:*** original, handwritten manuscript, ink, Yiddish, 100×175 mm, serious damage and losses of text, ss. 2, pp. 4.

**157. RING. I/599/81. Mf. ŻIH—812; USHMM—24**

- Date unknown, place unknown
- [Mława Committee?], Letter to Joint [Distribution Committee ?] (Warsaw Ghetto). Request for aid.
- ***Description:*** original, handwritten manuscript, ink, Yiddish, 110×115 mm, serious damage and losses of text, ss. 1, pp. 1.

**158. RING. I/599/96. Mf. ŻIH—812; USHMM—24**

- Date unknown, place unknown
- NN. [Millie], Letter to NN. (Zelda). Information about 10 dollars sent.
- ***Description:*** original, handwritten manuscript, ink, Yiddish, 152×230 mm, serious damage and losses of text, ss. 1, pp. 2.

**159. RING. I/599/100. Mf. ŻIH—812; USHMM—24**

- Date unknown, place unknown
- NN., Letter to NN.
- ***Description:*** original, handwritten manuscript, ink, Yiddish, 205×263 mm, serious damage and losses of text, ss. 1, pp. 1.

**160. RING. I/599/111. Mf. ŻIH—812; USHMM—24**

- Date unknown, place unknown
- NN., Letter to NN.
- ***Description:*** transcript, handwritten manuscript, pencil, Yiddish, 115×93 mm, serious damage and losses of text, ss. 2, pp. 1.

  Note: The document is integrated with other sheets from former catalog no. Ring. I/599, now found in no. 1067 (Ring. I/599/87).

**161. RING. I/599/117. Mf. ŻIH—812; USHMM—24**

- Date unknown, place unknown
- NN. [Zima?], Letter to NN.
- ***Description:*** original, handwritten manuscript, ink, Polish, 45×115 mm, ss. 1, pp. 2.

**162. RING. I/599/8. Mf. ŻIH—812; USHMM—24**

- Date unknown, Warsaw Ghetto
- NN., Notation: "Nowolipie 49a 17 [Miss?] Warcka."
- ***Description:*** original, handwritten manuscript, pencil, Polish, 190×24 mm, ss. 1, pp. 1.

**163. RING. I/599/10. Mf. ŻIH—812; USHMM—24**

- Date unknown, Mława
- NN., Letter to NN.
- ***Description:*** original, handwritten manuscript on letterhead of the limited liability company "[. . .] arka[. . .]" in Mława, ink Polish, Yiddish, 220×270 mm, significant damage and losses of text, ss. 1, pp. 2.

## "Płock" Letters

**164. RING. I/539. Mf. ŻIH—791; USHMM—22**

a)

- After 13.03.1941, Warsaw Ghetto
- Szlama Puterman (Białaczów), Letter of 13.03.1941 to NN. [Płockers' Association] (Warsaw Ghetto). Request for aid for Płockers in Białaczów (205 persons).
- ***Description:*** transcript (2 copies), handwritten manuscript (AA*), pencil, Polish, 148×208 mm, ss. 2, pp. 4.

  Index: Krawec [?]

b)

- After 15.04.1941, Warsaw Ghetto
- Szlama Puterman (Białaczów), Letter of 15.04.1941 to [Fiszel] Fliderblum and Eliasz Zylberberg [Płockers' Association] (Warsaw Ghetto)

- Thanks for news received about the money sent (100 zł).
- *Description:* transcript (3 copies), handwritten manuscript (AA*), pencil, Polish, 148×208 mm, ss. 3, pp. 6.

c)

- After 2.04.1941, Warsaw Ghetto
- Józef Zajde (Warsaw), Letter of 2.04.1941 to NN. (Warsaw Ghetto). Request for aid.
- *Description:* transcript (3 copies), handwritten manuscript (AA*), pencil, Polish, 148×208 mm, ss. 3, pp. 3.

d)

- After 1941, Warsaw Ghetto
- H. [Henoch Jakub] Zyman (Białaczów), Letter of 1941 to Fiszel Fliderbojm [Fliderblum, Płockers' Association] (Warsaw Ghetto). Request for aid.
- *Description:* transcript (4 copies), handwritten manuscript (TT*), pencil, Yiddish, 148×208 mm, damage and losses of text (only p. 3 in second and third copies.), ss. 16, pp. 16.

  In the margins (copies 1 and 4) a symbol (ink): "∇."

  Fragment of a larger set of copies (pp. 14–17); see Ring. I/541, I/537.

  Index: Puterman, Dawid Kryszek, Kilbert, Icek Rawicki, Zylberberg

## 165. RING. I/536. Mf. ŻIH—791; USHMM—22

a)

- After 14.03.1941, Warsaw Ghetto
- NN. (Beniamin) (Bodzentyn), Letter of 14.03.1941 to Eliasz [Zylberberg—Płockers' Association] (Warsaw Ghetto)
- Ca. 1,500 Płockers are staying in Bodzentyn—400 persons housed in the synagogue.
- *Description:* transcript (3 copies), handwritten manuscript (AA*), pencil, Polish, 148×210 mm, ss. 12, pp. 15.

  In the margins (copies 1–2) letter (ink): "M."

  Index: Szepski (gravedigger from Suchedniów), Żychlińska, Salek Żychliński, Grunwaldowa, Freidberg (Warsaw, ul. Franciszkańska 21, apt. 4), Fliderbaum

b)

- After 16.03.1941, Warsaw Ghetto
- Płockers Committee (Bodzentyn), Letter of 16.03.1941 to Płockers' Association (Warsaw Ghetto)
- Formation of the Płockers Committee on 16.03.1941: Dr. Jakub Bluman (chairman), Hersz Cytryn, Rabbi Jankiel Askanas, Engineer Izaak Rubin, Jojne Horowitz, Beniamin Lusiński, F.D. Elberg, J.A. Grojer, Hersz Strzyga, Jakub Eizyk (Ajzyk) (secretary), Amzel Kaliszer. Information on the situation of Płockers (ca. 1,500 persons) in Bodzentyn. 50 persons had died. Request for help.
- *Description:* transcript (2 copies), typescript, Polish, 210×293 mm, ss. 4, pp. 4.

c)

- After 17.03.1941, Warsaw Ghetto
- [Izaak] Rubin (Bodzentyn), Letter of 17.03.1941 to Eliasz [Zylberberg—Płockers' Association] (Warsaw Ghetto). Request for help for Chaim Flaks.
- *Description:* transcript (3 copies), handwritten manuscript (AA*), pencil, Polish, 148×208 mm, ss. 3, pp. 6.

  Index: Fiszel Fliderblum, Samuel Winter

d)

- After 5.04.1941, Warsaw Ghetto
- Chaim Flaks (Bodzentyn), Letter of 5.04.1941 to Eliasz [Zylberberg—Płockers' Association] (Warsaw Ghetto). Request for aid.
- *Description:* transcript (4 copies), handwritten manuscript (TT*), pencil, Yiddish, 148×208 mm, ss. 8, pp. 8.

  In the margins (copies 1 and 3) Hebrew letter (ink): "b" (beit).

  Fragment of a larger set of copies (pp. 41–42).

e)

- After 14.04.1941, Warsaw Ghetto
- Lejzor Granat (Bodzentyn), Letter of 14.04.1941 to Eliasz [Zylberberg—Płockers' Association] (Warsaw Ghetto)
- Situation of the deportees from Płock (ca. 1,300 persons) in Bodzentyn. Request for aid.
- *Description:* transcript (3 copies), handwritten manuscript (AA*), pencil, Polish, 148×208 mm, ss. 18, pp. 18.

  In the margins (copies 1, 3) letter (ink): "B."

  Index: Kubikowie, Ejzykowie, Szafran (Suchedniów), Ch. [Chaim] Flaks

f)

- After 1.05.1941, Warsaw Ghetto
- Chaim Flaks (Bodzentyn), Letter of 1.05.1941 to Eliasz [Zylberberg—Płockers' Association] (Warsaw Ghetto). Thanks for aid.
- *Description:* transcript (4 copies), handwritten manuscript (TT*), pencil, Yiddish, 148×208 mm, ss. 8, pp. 8.

  In the margins (copies 1 and 3) Hebrew letter (ink): "g" (giml).

  Fragment of a larger set of copies (*kopiariusz*) (pp. 43–44).

  Index: Tenenbaum (ul. Ostrowska 8, apt. 25)

g)

- After 13.05.1941, Warsaw Ghetto
- NN. (Roma) (Bodzentyn), Letter of 13.05.1941 to Teca [Zylberberg?] (Warsaw Ghetto). Thanks for aid.
- *Description:* transcript (3 copies), handwritten manuscript (AA*), pencil, Polish, 148×208 mm, ss. 6, pp. 6.

  In the margins (copies 1 and 3) symbol (ink): "∇"

  Index: J. Bursztyn

h)

- After 20.05.1941, Warsaw Ghetto
- Committee of the Płockers' Association (Bodzentyn), Letter of 20.05.1941 to Płockers' Association (Warsaw Ghetto)
- Difficult situation of the deportees from Płock (1,200 persons). Reckoning of the aid received and request for further assistance.
- ***Description:*** transcript (3 copies), handwritten manuscript (BTT*), pencil, Polish, 148×208, 115×195 mm, serious damage and losses of text (second copy), ss. 12, pp. 12.

  In the margins (1, 3 copies) symbol (ink): two "^" one above the other.

  Index: J. Rubin, Borenstejn of Joint

i)

- After 21.05.1941, Warsaw Ghetto
- Chaim Flaks (Council of Elders of the Jewish Community in Bodzentyn), Letter of 21.05.1941 to Eliasz [Zylberberg—Płockers' Association] (Warsaw Ghetto).
- Worsening of conditions in Bodzentyn, request for aid for himself and NN. (Michał).
- ***Description:*** transcript (4 copies), handwritten manuscript (TT*), pencil, Polish, Yiddish, 148×208 mm, ss. 12, pp. 12.

  In the margins (1, 3 copies) Hebrew letter (ink): "ts" (tsadi).

  Fragment of a larger set of copies (pp. 45–47).

j)

- After 25.06.1941, Warsaw Ghetto
- Committee of Płockers' Association (Bodzentyn), Letter of 25.06.1941 to Płockers' Association (Warsaw Ghetto)
- Request for further aid. Epidemic of typhus (200 persons sick), numerous deaths (among others, [Jankiel] Askenas, F.D. Elberg, Anszułowska, Luszyńska, Fuksowa), much aid from the Jewish Council in Bodzentyn; new makeup of the board of the Płock Committee: H. [Hersz] Cytryn, J.A. Grojer, Engineer I. [Izaak] Rubin, J. [Jakub] Eizyk, L. [Lejzor] Granat [. . . fragment damaged].
- ***Description:*** transcript (2 copies), handwritten manuscript (BTT*), pencil, Polish, 148×210 mm, numerous damaged areas and losses of text, ss. 16, pp. 16.

  Index: J. Elberg, Sztern, Ch.J. Kalman, H.L. Bzura, Flaksowie, G. Lichtensztajn, Grojer, M. Klopman, J. Rechtman, M. Horowic, Czarnołaski, Inowrocławski, Burdka, Borensztajn, Lewenberg, Belma [?], Markowicz

k)

- Date unknown, Warsaw Ghetto
- Committee of Płockers' Association (Bodzentyn), Letter [after 16.03.1941] to Płockers' Association [Fiszel] Fliderblum and E. [Eliasz] Zylberberg (Warsaw Ghetto). Request for aid.
- ***Description:*** transcript, handwritten manuscript (BTT*), pencil, Polish, 105×195 mm, damage and losses of text, ss. 1, pp. 1.

## 166. RING. I/531. Mf. ŻIH—790; USHMM—21

a)

- After 31.03.1941. Warsaw Ghetto
- NN. (Chmielnik near Busko), Letter of 31.03.1941 to [Eliasz Zylberberg—Płockers' Association]) (Warsaw Ghetto). Request for aid.
- ***Description:*** transcript (copies), handwritten manuscript (AA*), pencil, Polish, 150×208 mm, ss. 3, pp. 6.

  In the margins (in the third copy) three asterisks arranged in the form of a triangle ("∇") (ink).

  Index: Graubard, Szyfowa

b)

- After 29.05.1941, Warsaw Ghetto
- Płock Committee in Chmielnik near Busko, Letter of 29.05.1941 to Płockers' Association (Warsaw Ghetto)
- Composition of the Płock Committee chosen on 18.05.1941 in Chmielnik: Zelda Farbowa, Jakub Zeligman (chairman), Azriel Niedźwiedź (secretary), Nachman Tyk, Jechiel Fliderblum, Abram Cytrynblum, Izaak Kronenberg. Request for aid.
- ***Description:*** transcript (3 copies), handwritten manuscript (BTT*), pencil, Polish, 146×208, 120×140 mm, significant damage and losses of text (second copy), ss. 9, pp. 9.

  In the margins symbol (ink): "+" (underlined).

c)

- After 18.06.1941, Warsaw Ghetto
- Ch. M. (Chmielnik), Letter of 18.06.1941 to NN. [Płockers' Association?] (Warsaw Ghetto)
- Thanks for aid. Greetings to N.L. Zylberberg, Sz. Graubart, the Warszawskis, Guterman.
- ***Description:*** transcript, handwritten manuscript (AA*), pencil, Polish, 148×208 mm, ss. 3, pp. 6.

  Index: Sz. Wileński

## 167. RING. I/534. Mf. ŻIH—790; USHMM—21

- Date unknown, Warsaw Ghetto
- NN. (Abram) (Częstochowa), Letters (2) to Eliasz [Zylberberg] and Fiszel [Fliderblum (Płockers' Association) (Warsaw Ghetto)]
- Notation on the death of Sara, sister of Eliasz, about Jakub Józef Bursztyn.
- ***Description:*** transcript (4 copies, missing p. 7 in third copy), handwritten manuscript (TT*), pencil, Yiddish, 148×208 mm, significant damage and losses of text (only pp. 6 and 7 of the second and third copies), ss. 35, pp. 35.

  In the margins (1 and 4 copies) Hebrew–Yiddish letter [?] (ink): "v" [tsvey-vovn].

  Fragment of a larger set of copies [*kopiariusz*] (pp. 2–11).

  Index: Graubard

### 168. RING. I/540/2. Mf. ŻIH—791; USHMM—22

- After 18.06.1941, Warsaw Ghetto
- NN. (Daleszyce), Letter of 18.06.1941 to Płockers' Association ([Fiszel] Fliderblum and E[liasz] Zylberberg) (Warsaw Ghetto)
- Request for aid for the displaced persons from Płock (ca. 300 people), staying in Daleszyce since 3.03.1941.
- ***Description:*** transcript (2 copies), handwritten manuscript (BTT*), pencil, Polish, 148×208 mm, ss. 4, pp. 4.

  In the margins symbol (ink): "o."

### 169. RING. I/533. Mf. ŻIH—790; USHMM—21

a)

- 14.03.1941 and after 14.03.1941, Drzewica, Warsaw Ghetto
- NN. (Drzewica), Letter of 14.03.1941 to Fiszel [Fliderblum (Płockers' Association, Warsaw Ghetto)]. Description of his own experiences, request for aid.
- ***Description:*** original [?] (handwritten manuscript, ink, pencil, 220×350 mm, minor damage and losses of text), transcript (3 copies, handwritten manuscript—TT*, pencil, 148×206 mm, minor damage and losses of text), Yiddish, ss. 13, pp. 14.

  In the margins (original [?], transcript) Hebrew letter (ink): "t" (tof). On p. 1 (transcript, first copy) symbol (pencil): "+." On p. 4 (transcript) date: "2.08.1941."

b)

- After 7.06.1941, Warsaw Ghetto
- D.Z. (Drzewica), Letter of 7.06.1941 to Fiszel [Fliderblum (Płockers' Association, Warsaw Ghetto)]. Request for aid and news (letter).
- ***Description:*** transcript (4 copies), handwritten manuscript (TT*), pencil, Yiddish, 148×206 mm, ss. 36, pp. 36.

  In the margins symbol (ink): three dots (asterisks?) arranged in the form of a triangle ("∇").

  Fragment of larger set of copies (pp. 18–26).

c)

- After 25.07.1941, Warsaw Ghetto
- Jakow Josef [Bursztyn?] (Drzewica), Letters undated to Eliasz [Zylberberg] and Fiszel [Fliderblum (Płockers' Association, Warsaw Ghetto)]
- Attached letter from the author from 25.07.1941 to Szloma [Graubard [?] (Warsaw Ghetto)].

  Questions about acquaintances, request for facilitation of departure to Warsaw.
- ***Description:*** transcript (4 copies), handwritten manuscript (TT*), pencil, Polish, Yiddish, 148×206 mm, ss. 36, pp. 36.

  On p. 9 (35) postscript (handwritten manuscript—BW.*[?]) in Polish, of the wife of the author of the letter to Szloma [Graubard?].

  In the margins a letter (ink): "A."

  Fragment of a larger set of copies (pp. 27–35).

### 170. RING. I/540/1. Mf. ŻIH—791; USHMM—22. RING. I/1220/11. Mf. ŻIH—835; USHMM—47

- After 4.04.1941, Warsaw Ghetto
- Chana Borenstejn (Łączna near Suchedniów, at Herlinga 113), Letter of 1.04.1941 to Płockers' Association ([Fiszel] Fliderblum) (Warsaw Ghetto)
- Request for aid for mother. Attached supporting letter of Jewish Council of Suchedniów (4.04.1941).
- ***Description:*** transcript (3 copies), handwritten manuscript (BTT*), pencil, Polish, 148×208, 110×205, 106×163mm, damage and losses of text (three copies), ss. 6, pp. 6.

  In the margin symbol (ink): "- =."

  Third copy from Ring. I/1220/11.

  Attached note by H.W. in Polish and Yiddish

### 171. RING. I/532/1. Mf. ŻIH—790; USHMM—21

- After 9.04.1941, Warsaw Ghetto
- NN. [Ch. Szafran?] (Suchedniów), Letter of 9.04.1941 to [Eliasz] Zylberberg—[Płockers' Association] (Warsaw Ghetto)
- Request for remittance of money. Complaint about the behavior of the Jewish Community.
- ***Description:*** transcript (3 copies), handwritten manuscript (AA*), pencil, Polish, 148×205 mm, ss. 3, pp. 6.

  Index: Askanas, Morsztejnowie

### 172. RING. I/538/2. Mf. ŻIH—791; USHMM—22

- After 10.04.1941, Warsaw Ghetto
- Ch. Szafran [Suchedniów?], Letter of 10.04.1941 to [Eliasz] Zylberberg [Płockers' Association] (Warsaw Ghetto)
- Request for aid and intervention with Dir. Falk. Attitude of the Jewish Council in [. . .] toward deportees.
- ***Description:*** transcript (2 copies), handwritten manuscript (AA*), pencil, Polish, 148×208 mm, ss. 4, pp. 4.

  In the margins letter (ink): "P."

  Index: Szyja Askanas, Wajs, Kenig, Szawie, Morsztejn

### 173. RING. I/532/2. Mf. ŻIH—790; USHMM—21

- After 20.05.1941, Warsaw Ghetto
- Ch. Szafran (Suchedniów), Letter of 20.05.1941 to [Eliasz] Zylberberg [Płockers' Association] (Warsaw Ghetto)
- The Jewish Community does not agree to the appeal of the Płockers Committee, high cost of living, hunger in Suchedniów; request for aid.
- ***Description:*** transcript (3 copies), handwritten manuscript (AA*), pencil, Polish, 148×206 mm, ss. 9, pp. 9.

  In the margins letter (ink): "c."

  Index: Markowicz (Warsaw, ul. Krochmalna), Wiener, Szyja Askanas (Suchedniów, ul.

Handlowa, care of Jankel Borensztejn), Klara Żelaźniak, the Morsztejn family

### 174. RING. I/535. Mf. ŻIH—790; USHMM—21

a)

- After 14.03.1941, Warsaw Ghetto
- J. [Jakub] Lewin (Wierzbnik-Starachowice), Letter of 14.03.1941 to Eliasz [Zylberberg—Płockers' Association]) (Warsaw Ghetto)
- Information about 300 deportees from Płock in Wierzbnik and formation of the Committee of Płockers: 1) Jakub Lewin (Starachowice, ul. Dolna 54, care of Jabłoński); 2) Mordka (Motek) Głowiński (Wierzbnik-Starachowice, ul. Kolejowa 29); 3) Nusyn Wajnsztok (Starachowice, ul. Piłsudskiego 38b); Gerszon Bergson (Wierzbnik-Starachowice, ul. Iłżecka 18); Dawid Bok (Wierzbnik-Starachowice, Rynek 24). Request for aid.
- ***Description:*** transcript (3 copies), handwritten manuscript (AA*), pencil, Polish, 148×206 mm, extensive damage and losses of text (only in the second copy), ss. 6, pp. 6.

  In the margins letter (ink): "T"

  Index: Ewa Majzels (Warsaw, ul. Chłodna 34, apt. 28), Fliderblum, Winer

b)

- After 24.03.1941, Warsaw Ghetto
- J. [Jakub] Lewin, M. [Nusyn] Wajnsztok, M. [Mordka] Głowiński (Wierzbnik-Starachowice), Letter of 24.03.1941 to [Fiszel] Fliderblum and [Eliasz] Zylberberg [Płockers' Association] (Warsaw Ghetto)
- Request for aid; complaint about the behavior of the Jewish Council in Wierzbnik; increase of the Płockers group to ca. 400 persons with displaced persons from Bodzentyn.
- ***Description:*** transcript (3 copies), handwritten manuscript (AA*), Polish, 148×206 mm, minor damage and losses of text, ss. 12, pp. 12.

  In the margins (copies 1–2) letter, ink): "R."

### 175. RING. I/541. Mf. ŻIH—791; USHMM—22

a)

- After 2.03.1941, Warsaw Ghetto
- Icek Szpilman and his mother (Żarki), Letter of 2.03.1941 to NN. (Warsaw Ghetto)
- Deportees from Płock 20.02., were in a camp in Działdowo, from 28.02. in Żarki. Request for aid.
- ***Description:*** transcript (2 copies), handwritten manuscript (AA*), pencil, Polish, 147×208 mm, ss. 2, pp. 2.

b)

- After 1.05.1941, Warsaw Ghetto
- Copies of two letters
  1) NN. (Żarki), Letter of 3.03.1941 to Fiszel [Fliderblum] [Płockers' Association] (Warsaw Ghetto) (fragment). Deportee from Płock requests aid.
  2) NN., Letter from before 22.04.1941[?] to NN. [Mojsze].
- Deportation from Płock, stay in the camp in Działdowo, in Złoty Stok and Olsztyn.
- ***Description:*** transcript (2 copies), handwritten manuscript (BW*), pencil, Yiddish, 148×208 mm, minor damage and losses of text, ss. 10, pp. 10

  In the margins letter (ink): "E."

  On p. 2, date (22.04.1941) of forwarding of the letter (first or second [?]). On p. 5 date: "1.05.1941" of the making of the first copy [?]

c)

- After 14.03.1941, Warsaw Ghetto
- Jakub Strach (Żarki, ul. Piłsudskiego 11, u Ch. Fajnera), Letter of 14.03.1941 to NN. (Eliasz [Zylberberg] and Fiszel [Fliderblum]) (Warsaw Ghetto)
- Request for money for Z. Keselman (Żarki, ul. Kościelna 22, care of E. Kożuch).

  Question about brother: Abram Strach.
- ***Description:*** transcript (2 copies), handwritten manuscript (AA*), pencil, Polish, 148×208 mm, ss. 6, pp. 6.

  In the margins letter (ink): "S."

  Index: Mendel Grudland (Warsaw, ul. Bonifraterska 31), chairman of the Merchants Association, Zajderman, Froim Berland, Lajzer Brygard, Jakub Mańczyk Gąbiński, R. Peny [?]

d)

- After 14.03.1941, Warsaw Ghetto
- Jakub Strach, H. Sztern, and D. Rubinsztejn (Żarki), Letter of 14.03.1941 to NN. (Fiszel [Fliderblum]) (Warsaw Ghetto)
- Thanks for help and request for further aid. Information on the formation of the Committee of Płockers in Żarki (Jakub Strach, H. Sztern and D. Rubinsztejn).
- ***Description:*** transcript (2 copies), handwritten manuscript (AA*), pencil, Polish, 148×208 mm, ss. 4, pp. 4.

  In the margins Greek letter (ink): "α" [?]

  Index: Neustaber

e)

- After 15.04.1941, Warsaw Ghetto
- [Z. Keselman] (Żarki), Letter of 15.04.1941 to NN. (Warsaw Ghetto)
- Concerning amounts due from Zajderman.
- ***Description:*** transcript (2 copies), handwritten manuscript (AA*), pencil, Polish, 148×208 mm, ss. 2, pp. 4.

  See Ring. I/541/c.

  Index: Ruland (Berland [?])

f)

- Date unknown, Warsaw Ghetto
- Jewish Council in Żarki, [D.] Rubinsztejn, [H.] Sztern, [Z.] Keselman, Letter to NN. (Eliasz [Zylberberg] and Fiszel [Fliderblum]) (Warsaw Ghetto). Request for aid.

- *Description:* transcript (2 copies), handwritten manuscript (TT*), pencil, Polish, Yiddish, 148×208 mm, ss. 4, pp. 4.
  Fragment of a larger set of copies (pp. 12–13), see Ring. I/539, I/537.

g)

- After 25.04.1941, Warsaw Ghetto
- NN., (Żarki), Letter of 25.04.1941 to Zew N. Zylberberg
- Situation of Płock Jews in Żarki, request for a hernia belt.
- *Description:* transcript (4 copies, missing p. 1 in copies 2 and 3), handwritten manuscript (TT*), pencil, Yiddish, 1498×208 mm, ss. 6, pp. 6.
  On p. 1 in the margins a symbol (ink): two parallel lines crossed with a horizontal (letter: "H" [?]).
  Index: Fiszel [Fliderblum] and Graubart from Płock

### 176. RING. I/537. Mf. ŻIH—791; USHMM—22

a)

- After 7.04.1941, Warsaw Ghetto
- NN. (Felicja) (Żarnów), Letter of 7.04.1941 to Eliasz [Zylberberg—Płockers' Association]) (Warsaw Ghetto)
- Living conditions of displaced persons from Płock in Żarnów.
- *Description:* transcript (2 copies), handwritten manuscript (AA*), pencil, Polish, 148×208 mm, ss. 4, pp. 6.
  In the margins (copies 1, 2) letter (ink): "T."
  Index: Raciążerowa

b)

- After 18.06.1941, Warsaw Ghetto
- NN. (Żarnów), Letter of 18.06.1941 to Fliderbojm [Fiszel Fliderblum of the Płockers' Association] (Warsaw Ghetto)
- Ca. 250 deportees from Płock. Thanks for money (200 zł) and request for further aid. Jakub Aszkenazy died.
- *Description:* transcript (4 copies), handwritten manuscript (TT*), pencil, Yiddish, 148×208 mm, ss. 20, pp. 20.
  In the margins (copies 1 and 4) Hebrew letter (ink): "a" (alef).
  Fragment of a larger set of copies (pp. 36–40), see Ring. I/541, I/539.

### 177. RING. I/538/3. Mf. ŻIH—791; USHMM—22

- Date unknown, Warsaw Ghetto
- Jadzia Albert, Letter to Frydenblum [Fiszel Fliderblum—Płockers' Association] (Warsaw Ghetto). Request for coverage of leg treatment costs.
- *Description:* transcript (2 copies), handwritten manuscript (AA*), pencil, Polish, 148×208 mm, minor damage and losses of text, ss. 6, pp. 6.
  In the margins letter (ink): "m."

### 178. RING. I/538/1. Mf. ŻIH—791; USHMM—22

- After 14.03.1941, Warsaw Ghetto
- NN. (Abram from Płock), Letter of 14.03.1941 to NN. (Eliasz [Zylberberg—Płockers' Association]) (Warsaw Ghetto). Information concerning deportees from Płock.
- *Description:* transcript (2 copies), handwritten manuscript (AA*), pencil, Polish, 148×208 mm, ss. 2, pp. 2.
  See Ring. I/534.
  Index: Salomon Fiszel, Budnik Bruchman, Graubard

# III. Warsaw and the Warsaw Ghetto

## *DOCUMENTS OF GERMAN AUTHORITIES AND INSTITUTIONS*

### 179. RING. I/781/7. (1100). Mf. ŻIH—825; USHMM—37

- 02.1941, Warsaw
- Governor Dr. Fischer, District Chief in Warsaw, Proclamation of 27.02.1941
- Recruitment of guards for labor camps for Jews.
- *Description:* original, printed, German, Polish, 620×940 mm, ss. 1, pp. 1.
  Doc. was kept in a binder.

### 180. RING. I/308. (Lb. 1515). Mf. ŻIH—781; USHMM—12

- After 17.03.1941, Warsaw
- [Generalgouvernement. Office of the Chief of the Warsaw District. Resettlement Department.] Transferstelle [Transfer Station], Order of 17.03.1941 concerning forced labor for the Jewish population (fragment)
- Command for Jewish males born in the years 1881–1924 to report by the appointed times to ul. Prosta 12 for collection of labor cards.
- *Description:* transcript, typescript, German, Polish, 180×241 mm, serious damage and losses of text, ss. 1, pp. 1.

### 181. RING. I/211/3. (Lb. 881). Mf. ŻIH—779; USHMM—10

- After 28.05.1940, Warsaw
- Generalgouvernement. Office of the Chief of the Warsaw District, Letter of 28.05.1940 to AJDC (fragment)
- Reply to a letter from AJDC in the matter of display of 7 certificates for workers of the Joint [?] and

recovery of confiscated goods [?]. Signature [Karl] Massing.

- ***Description:*** transcript, typescript, German, 200×242 mm, serious damage and losses of text, ss. 1, pp. 1

**182. RING. I/208. (Lb. 1452). Mf. ŻIH—779; USHMM—10**

- O2.1942, Warsaw
- *Mitteilungsblatt für den jüdischen Wohnbezirk in Warschau* [News Gazette for the Jewish Residential District in Warsaw], no. 1, 1.02.1942
- Official bulletin of the Commissioner for the Jewish District in Warsaw. Contains the texts of orders of the German authorities (announced in the period: 2.10.1940–29.01.1942) concerning Jewish population and organizations as well as the functioning of the Warsaw Ghetto.
- ***Description:*** original, printed, German, 210×298 mm, ss. 4, pp. 8.

The newspaper was printed by the Monolit printshop in Warsaw.

Second copy: see Ring. II/323.

**183. RING. I/781/5. (1100). Mf. ŻIH—825; USHMM—37**

- 10.1941, Warsaw
- Heinz Auerswald, Commissioner for the Jewish Residential District in Warsaw, Announcement of 23.10.1941 on new boundaries of the ghetto.
- ***Description:*** original, printed, Polish, 607×370 mm, damage and losses of text, ss. 1, pp. 1.

Presumably missing upper part of the announcement in German

**184. RING. I/781/3. (1100). Mf. ŻIH—825; USHMM—37**

- 11.1941, Warsaw
- Heinz Auerswald, Commissioner for the Jewish Residential District in Warsaw, Announcement about the shooting of 8 Jews on 17.11.1941 for illegal departure from the ghetto, on the basis of the verdict of the Special Court of 12.11.1941.
- List of those shot: Rywka Kligerman, Sala Pasztejn, Josek Pajkus, Luba Gac, Motek Fiszbaum, Fajga Margules, Dwojra Rozenberg, Chana Zajdenwach.
- ***Description:*** original, printed, German, Polish, 350×298 mm, serious damage and losses of text (parts in German), ss. 1, pp. 1.

On the execution, see *Czerniaków*, p. 228.

Published: *Przewodnik*, pp. 206 (photocopy).

**185. RING. I/1220/85. Mf. ŻIH—835; USHMM—47**

- 12.1941, Warsaw Ghetto
- Heinz Auerswald, Commissioner for the Jewish Residential District in Warsaw, Order of 25.12.1941 on the command to turn in fur coats by 28.12.1941
- Notation on collection point for fur coats: ul. Grzybowska 26/28 and 27.
- ***Description:*** transcript, hectographed typescript, German, 203×158, serious damage and losses of text, ss. 1, pp. 1.

Attached note by H.W. in Yiddish.

**186. RING. I/781/4. (1100). Mf. ŻIH—825; USHMM—37**

- 01.1942, Warsaw
- Heinz Auerswald, Commissioner for the Jewish Residential District in Warsaw, Announcement of 8.01.1942 on the order to turn in skis and ski boots.
- ***Description:*** original, printed, German, Polish, 473×630 mm, ss. 1, pp. 2.

**187. RING. I/1220/64. Mf. ŻIH—835; USHMM—47**

- 9.07.1942, Warsaw Ghetto
- Office of Measures at the Commissioner for the Jewish District in Warsaw, Announcement of 9.07.1942:
- Concerning deadlines for mandatory registration of surveying tools in the Warsaw Ghetto (ul. Elektoralna 2).
- ***Description:*** original, printed, German, Polish, 468×618 mm, damage and losses of text, ss. 1, pp. 1.

Doc. printed in the Drukprasa Graphic Shop, ul. Nowy Świat 54.

**188. RING. I/273. (Lb. 542, 834). Mf. ŻIH—781; USHMM—12**

- 15.09.1941–11.06.1942, Warsaw
- The German Court in Warsaw, Letters of 15.09.1941 and 29.05.1942 to Eta Gulbas (Warsaw, ul. Muranowska 11/36 and Przebieg 1/29)
- The court's decision in the matter of not wearing an armband with the star of Zion. Summons to pay a fine in the amount of 250 zł and repeated summons to report to prison (ul. Daniłowiczowska 7) to serve 50 days for not paying the fine.
- ***Description:*** original, printed, typescript, German, 206×145, 170×124 mm, ss. 4, pp. 6.

Along with the letters, the original envelopes with postage stamps and with postmarks and seals of the Court and Jewish Council have been preserved. The latter indicate that the first letter was sent out only on 2.05.1942 and reached the ghetto 7.05.1942 [sic.], while the second arrived in the ghetto 11.06.1942. Address of Eta Gulbas (ul. Muranowska 11/36) on the envelope of 2.05.1942 was erased and a new one was written in pencil: "Przebieg 1/29"; on the second envelope was written only "Przebieg 1."

Attached H.W. notes in Polish and Yiddish: "H.W. delivered."

**189. RING. I/1087 (1406). (Lb. 760). Mf. ŻIH—833; USHMM—45**

- After 28.04.1942, Warsaw Ghetto
- Materials concerning Hinda (Chinda) Buki

1) Der Leiter der Anklagebehőrde beim Sondergericht—Warschau, Dr. Peter [Dr. Peter, Director of the Indictment Authority at the Special Court, Warsaw]. Bill of indictment of 28.04.1942 against Hinda Buki for leaving the Warsaw Ghetto without permission on 20.03.1942;
2) Chinda [Hinda] Buki (Warsaw Ghetto, jail at ul. Gęsiej 24, cell 24), Letter (smuggled note, after 28.04.1942) to Miss Sutkier (ul. Pawia 20 m.30) with a request for help.

- ***Description:*** original, printed, typescript, handwritten manuscript, pencil, Polish, Yiddish, 204×290 mm, ss. 1, pp. 2.
  Doc. 2 written on the back of doc. 1.
  Attached note by H.W. in Yiddish: "Delivered by Dir. Icchak Giterman."

**190. RING. I/1102 (1421). (Lb. 1263). Mf. ŻIH—833; USHMM—45**

- After 04.1942, Warsaw Ghetto
- Materials concerning Hirsz Rozenbaum (born 25.12.1925), son of Dawid and Sara
  1) Der Leiter der Anklagebehörde beim Sondergericht—Warschau, Baden [Director of the Indictment Authority at the Special Court—Warsaw, Baden], Bill of indictment of 2.12.1941 against Hirsz Rozenbaum (ul. Chłodna 35, apt. 26) for leaving the Warsaw Ghetto without permission on 18.11.1941;
  2) Jewish Council in Warsaw, Affadavit of 10.04.1942, on the release of Hirsz Rozenbaum from the Central Jail on 10.04.1942 "as a result of the governor's act of mercy of 9.01.1942."
- ***Description:*** transcript, handwritten manuscript, ink, German, Polish, 124×223, 223×354 mm, ss. 2, pp. 2
  Attached note by H.W. in Yiddish: "Delivered by Władysław Wajnblat of Łódź."

**191. RING. I/1220/81. Mf. ŻIH—835; USHMM—47**

- After 09.1939, place unknown
- [German authorities of the Generalgouvernement], List of documents needed to obtain a passport (fragment [?]).
- ***Description:*** original, hectographed typescript, German, 175×221 mm, serious damage and losses of text, ss. 1, pp. 1.

**192. RING. I/1103 (1422). (Lb. 1294). Mf. ŻIH—833; USHMM—45**

- After 13.10.1941, Warsaw Ghetto
- J. Lex GmbH Schuhleistenfabrik—Meschede/Westfalen [J. Lex, Ltd., Shoe lasts factory,—Meschede/Westphalia), Letter of 13.10.1941 to Transferstelle (Warsaw, ul. Królewska 23)
- Concerning possibility of using Jewish labor on the territory of the Generalgouvernement.
- ***Description:*** transcript, handwritten manuscript (H*), German, pencil, 208×296 mm, ss. 1, pp. 1.
  Attached note by H.W. in Yiddish: "Copy of letter from shoe last factory of Meschede in Westphalia was delivered to the ghetto archive by Jerzy [Icchak] Winkler, economist, employee of the statistical department of the Jewish Council."

**193. RING. I/278/1. (Lb. 766). Mf. ŻIH—781; USHMM—12**

- After 26.02.1942, Warsaw Ghetto
- Meuck, Krüger & Sohn Geflügelimport-Berlin (Warsaw branch), Letter of 26.02.1942 to Transferstelle (Warsaw, ul. Królewska 23)
- Request that a permit to leave the ghetto be issued to Maurycy Klar, an associate of the firm (specialist in liming of eggs [for preservation]).
- ***Description:*** transcript, handwritten manuscript (E*), ink, German, 220×350 mm, ss. 1, pp. 1.

## *DOCUMENTS OF OTHER INSTITUTIONS AND ORGANIZATIONS*

**194. RING. I/781/1. Mf. ŻIH—825; USHMM—37**

- 12.1939, Warsaw
- Capital Committee for Mutual Aid [Stołeczny Komitet Samopomocy Społecznej] in Warsaw, Announcement of 20.12.1939 about collection of underclothes for Polish prisoners in German camps.
- ***Description:*** original, printed, Polish, 207×293 mm, ss. 1, pp. 1.

**195. RING. I/1142 (1461). (Lb. 45). Mf. ŻIH—833; USHMM—45. RING. I/1199 (1518). ŻIH—835; USHMM—47**

- 1940–1941, Warsaw Ghetto
- Municipal Adminstration of the City of Warsaw. Directorate of Trolleys and Buses [Zarząd Miejski m. Warszawy. Dyrekcja Tramwajów i Autobusów], basic cards (monthly tickets for Jews).
- Tickets (5) entitling bearer to travel in cars designated for Jews for payment according to tariff A. Price 5 zł:
  1) no. 07638 for the month of Dec. 1940
  2) no. 22189
  3) no. 25101/1941
  4) no. 30081
  5) no. 32174.
- ***Description:*** original, printed, Polish, 93×52 mm, ss. 5, pp. 5.
  On documents 2–5 is the stamp: "9."
  Doc. 2—published in: *Przewodnik*, p. 119.

## *WORKSHOPS AND FACTORIES IN THE WARSAW GHETTO*

**196. RING. I/249. Mf. ŻIH—780; USHMM—11**

- After 24.12.1941, Warsaw Ghetto
- Organizing Committee for Self-Help of Workers of

the brushmakers' workshop, Letter of 24.12.1941 to Dir. Emil Weitz
- Difficult situation of workers: hunger, lack of clothing, they do not benefit from aid of welfare organizations, mistreatment of older workers; they propose creation of a relief fund, kitchen, cooperative store.
- ***Description:*** transcript (a) (handwritten manuscript—Ł*, ink, pencil, 225×355 mm), transcript (b) (3 copies, typescript, 210×295 mm), Yiddish, ss. 7, pp. 7.
  Date "24.12.1941" only on the handwritten manuscript.
  Attached note by H.W. in Yiddish: "Emil Weitz, 'king' of the brushmakers, handed large sums over to Dir. Guzik for social purposes, the document was delivered by Nechemia Tytelman."

### 197. RING. I/1112/3 (1431). (Lb. 1428). Mf. ŻIH—833; USHMM—45

- 03.[1942], Warsaw Ghetto
- Union of Brushmakers in the Jewish District [Zjednoczenie Szczotkarzy w Dzielnicy Żydowskiej], Invitation to an evening social gathering at the café "Na Pięterku" (ul. Nowolipki 29), on 25.03.[1942].
- ***Description:*** original, printed, Polish, 136×88 mm, ss. 1, pp. 2.
  On the back is handwritten in ink: "W.P. Blumsztejn [and illegible signature]"
  Published: *Przewodnik*, p. 565 (photocopy).

### 198. RING. I/1220/79. Mf. ŻIH—835; USHMM—47

- Date unknown, Warsaw Ghetto
- Ostdeutsche Bautischlerei Werkstätte [OBW: East German Construction Carpentry Workshops], Order concerning allocation of foods for workers employed in the workshop [?] (fragment).
- ***Description:*** original, typescript, stamp, German, Polish, 65×105 mm, serious damage and losses of text, ss. 1, pp. 1.

# *DOCUMENTS OF JEWISH AUTHORITIES, INSTITUTIONS, AND ORGANIZATIONS*

## Jewish Council

### 199. RING. I/276. (Lb. 172). RING. I/288. Mf. ŻIH—781; USHMM—12

- After 02.1941, Warsaw Ghetto
- [Office of the Chief of the Warsaw District.] Resettlement Department. Transfer Point [(Amt des Chefs des Distrikts Warschau) Abteilung Umsiedlung. Transferstelle], Two letters of 20.01.1941 to Jewish Council in Warsaw.
- Order for creation of 5–6 large tailor shops, 3 shoe factories, and a stocking and sock factory. Letters signed by Steyer [Steyert?].
- ***Description:*** Ring. I/276—transcript (2 copies), typescript, German, 202×295, 165×286 mm, damage and losses of text, ss. 2, pp. 2; Ring. I/288—transcript (2 copies); handwritten manuscript (MS*), pencil, German in Hebrew alphabet transliteration, 142×221 mm, ss. 2, pp. 2.
  Ring. I/288- In the margin Hebrew letter (in red pencil): "p." Doc. was kept in a binder.
  Ring. I/288—Attached note by H.W. in Yiddish: "For security Yiddish letters were used. Delivered by Mordechaj Szwarcbard."

### 200. RING. I/656/1. Mf. ŻIH—816; USHMM—28

- After 28.01.1941, Warsaw Ghetto
- Office of the Chief of the Warsaw District. Resettlement Department. Transfer Point [Amt des Chefs des Distrikts Warschau. Abteilung Umsiedlung. Transferstelle], Letter to [Jewish Council in Warsaw] (fragment)
- Concerning delivery of sewing machines. Doc. signed by [Aleksander] Palfinger.
- ***Description:*** transcript (2 copies), typescript, German, 148×175, 166×110, 138×120, 164×140 mm, serious damage and losses of text, ss. 4, pp. 4.

### 201. RING. I/656/2. Mf. ŻIH—816; USHMM—28

- After 16.02.1941, Warsaw Ghetto
- Office of the Chief of the Warsaw District. Resettlement Department. Transfer Point [Amt des Chefs des Distrikts Warschau. Abteilung Umsiedlung. Transferstelle], Letter to [Jewish Council in Warsaw] (fragment)
- Concerning creation of tailor workshops (shops) in the ghetto. Letter signed by [Aleksander] Palfinger.
- ***Description:*** transcript (2 copies), typescript, German, 162×222, 155×295 mm, serious damage and losses of text, ss. 2, pp. 2.

### 202. RING. I/274/1. Mf. ŻIH—781; USHMM—12

- After 28.02.1941, Warsaw Ghetto
- [Amt des Chefs des Distrikts Warschau. Abteilung Umsiedlung. Transferstelle], Letter from before 28.02.1941 to Jewish Council in Warsaw in the matter of supplying laborers for work
- Order for preparation by 28.02.1941 of 25,000 laborers for land improvement jobs, Jewish Council will secure work clothing. Letter signed by [Aleksander] Palfinger.
- ***Description:*** transcript, typescript, German, 177×200 mm, damage and losses of text, ss. 1, pp. 1.

### 203. RING. I/1105/3 (1424). Mf. ŻIH—833; USHMM—45

- After 03.1941, Warsaw Ghetto
- [Amt] des Chefs des Distrikts Warschau. Abteilung Umsiedlung. Transferstelle, Letter of 6.03.1941 to the Chairman of the Jewish Council in Warsaw.
- In connection with the typhus epidemic, labor battalions are banned from leaving the ghetto. Letter signed by Steyert.

- ***Description:*** transcript, typescript, German, 148×205 mm, minor damage and losses of text, ss. 1, pp. 1.

**204. RING. I/1105/4 (1424). Mf. ŻIH—833; USHMM—45**

- After 03.1941, Warsaw Ghetto
- Des Chefs des Distrikts Warschau. Abteilung Umsiedlung. Transferstelle, Letter of 6.[03.1941] to the Chairman of the Jewish Council in Warsaw
- Order to conduct delousing action (ul. Stawki 21 and Solna 4) beginning 7.03.1941 for persons applying for work outside the ghetto's boundaries. Letter signed by [Aleksander] Palfinger.
- ***Description:*** transcript, typescript, German, 148×205 mm, minor damage and losses of text, ss. 1, pp. 1.

**205. RING. I/656/3. Mf. ŻIH—816; USHMM—28**

- After 9.03.1941, Warsaw Ghetto
- Jewish Council in Warsaw, Letter of 9.03.1941 to Amt des Chefs des Distrikts Warschau. Abteilung Umsiedlung. Transferstelle (fragment)
- Notation on the number of skilled craftsmen within the ghetto. Letter signed by Adam Czerniaków.
- ***Description:*** transcript (2 copies), typescript, German, 154×252, 150×294 mm, serious damage and losses of text, ss. 2, pp. 2.

  Doc. was a reply to the letter in doc. Ring. I/656/2.

**206. RING. I/274/2. Mf. ŻIH—781; USHMM—12**

- After 24.04.1941, Warsaw Ghetto
- Amt des Chefs des Distrikts Warschau, Letter of 24.04.1941 to Jewish Council in Warsaw in the matter of labor duty
- 500 zł is to be charged for exemption from labor duty. A list of those exempted from work is to be delivered monthly. Letter signed by [Otto] Mohns.
- ***Description:*** transcript, typescript, German, 180×220 mm, damage and losses of text, ss. 1, pp. 1.

**207. RING. I/300. (Lb. 714). Mf. ŻIH—781; USHMM—12**

- After 23.07.1941, Warsaw Ghetto
- Amt des Chefs des Distrikts Warschau. Transferstelle, Letter of 23.07.1941 to Jewish Council in Warsaw
- Lack of consent to transfer a grand piano to Michał Michałowicz of Warsaw (refugees' house).
- ***Description:*** transcript, typescript, German, 208×292 mm, ss. 1, pp. 1.

  Inventory: "Delivered by archive coworker L. [Lipa] L. [Lejzer] Bloch."

  Attached note by H.W. in Yiddish.

**208. RING. I/656/4. Mf. ŻIH—816; USHMM—28**

- 1941, Warsaw Ghetto
- Amt des Chefs des Distrikts Warschau. Abteilung Umsiedlung. Transferstelle, Letter to [Jewish Council in Warsaw] (fragment)
- Concerning letter no. 1555.
- ***Description:*** transcript (2 copies), typescript, German, 130×154, 132×180 mm, serious damage and losses of text, ss. 2, pp. 2.

**209. RING. I/656/5. Mf. ŻIH—816; USHMM—28**

- 1941, Warsaw Ghetto
- Amt des Chefs des Distrikts Warschau. Abteilung Umsiedlung. Transferstelle, Letter to [Jewish Council in Warsaw] Letter signed by Aleksander Palfinger. (fragment)
- Concerning creation of carpenters' workshops in the ghetto.
- ***Description:*** transcript (2 copies), typescript, German, 153×169, 159×290, 125×150, 147×142 mm, serious damage and losses of text, ss. 4, pp. 4.

**210. RING. I/656/6. Mf. ŻIH—816; USHMM—28**

- Date unknown, Warsaw Ghetto
- Amt des Chefs des Distrikts Warschau. Abteilung Umsiedlung. Transferstelle, Letter to Jewish Council in Warsaw (fragment)
- Concerning the firm of Wiśniewski, Serejski.
- ***Description:*** transcript (2 copies), typescript, German, 135×190, 149×184 mm, serious damage and losses of text, ss. 2, pp. 2.

**211. RING. I/278/2. (Lb. 766). Mf. ŻIH—781; USHMM—12**

- Date unknown, Warsaw Ghetto
- Generalgouvernement der Distriktschef in Warschau. Abteilung Ernährung und Landwirtschaft [Generalgouvernement. The District Chief in Warsaw. Food and Agriculture Department], Letter to [Jewish Council in Warsaw] (fragment)
- Concerning allocation of eggs to the ZZRŻ [Provisioning Unit at the Jewish Council in Warsaw]. Letter signed: Meyer.
- ***Description:*** transcript (2 copies), typescript, German, 170×150 mm, serious damage and losses of text, ss. 2, pp. 2.

  Lack of encl.

**212. RING. I/1105/1 (1424). Mf. ŻIH—833; USHMM—45**

- After 02.1940, Warsaw Ghetto
- Präsident der Stadt Warschau [City President of Warsaw], Letter of 1.02.[1940] to [Zakład Oczyszczania Miasta (City Sanitation Department)] and Jewish Council in Warsaw
- In the matter of supplying 100 persons per day for city snow removal. The Jewish Council is to cover the costs. Letter signed by Suppinger.
- ***Description:*** transcript, typescript, German, 148×205 mm, minor damage and losses of text, ss. 1, pp. 1.

### 213. RING. I/310. Mf. ŻIH–781; USHMM–12

- After 26.09.1941, Warsaw Ghetto
- [Der Kommissar für den Jüdischen Wohnbezirk in Warschau (Commissioner for the Jewish Residential District)], Letter of 26.09.1941 to Jewish Council in Warsaw
- Order for the Jewish population to vacate by 5.10.1941 the buildings located on the south side of ul. Sienna and to the south of ul. Sienna from the streets: Twarda, Sosnowa, and Wielka. Letter signed by Heinz Auerswald.
- ***Description:*** transcript, typescript, Polish, 205×173 mm, minor damage and losses of text, ss. 1, pp. 1.

  On this letter, see *Czerniaków*, p. 218.

### 214. RING. I/299. (1099). (Lb. 597). Mf. ŻIH–781; USHMM–12. RING. I/778. Mf. ŻIH–825; USHMM–37

**a) Ring. I/778**

- After 21.10.1941, Warsaw Ghetto
- Der Kommissar für den Jüdischen Wohnbezirk in Warschau [Commissioner for the Jewish Residential District in Warsaw], Letter of 21.10.1941 to the Chairman of the Jewish Council in Warsaw
- Order for the Jewish population to vacate by 26.10.1941 the buildings excluded from the boundaries of the ghetto (attached list of streets).
- ***Description:*** transcript, typescript, German, 205×295 mm, minor damage and losses of text, ss. 1, pp. 1.

  On the planned displacement, see *Czerniaków*, p. 222.

**b) Ring. I/299. (Lb. 597)**

- 21.10.1941, Warsaw Ghetto
- Jewish Council in Warsaw, Circular of 21.10.1941 to apartment house administrators
- Order for all tenants to vacate the building by by 26.10.1941 on the basis of the German authorities' order of 21.10.1941. Apartments have to be cleaned and the keys delivered to the O[rder] S[ervice]. Letter signed by B. [Bolesław] Rozensztat [Rozenstadt].
- ***Description:*** original, typescript, Polish, 205×283 mm, minor damage and losses of text, ss. 1, pp. 1.

### 215. RING. I/656/7. Mf. ŻIH–816; USHMM–28

- After 8.01.1942, Warsaw Ghetto
- Der Kommissar für den jüdischen Wohnbezirk in Warschau [Commissioner for the Jewish Residential District in Warsaw], Letter of 30.12.1941 to Jewish Council in Warsaw
- Concerning supplying the Warsaw Ghetto with bread. Letter signed [Heinz] Auerswald.

  Transcript of 8.01.1942 for ZZ [Provisioning Unit at the Jewish Council in Warsaw] signed by Rodeck.
- ***Description:*** transcript, typescript, German, 185×294 mm, damage and losses of text, ss. 1, pp. 2.

  Attached note by H.W. in Yiddish

### 216. RING. I/575/3. Mf. ŻIH–792; USHMM–23

- After 26.02.1942, before 15.03.1942, Warsaw Ghetto
- Der Kommissar für den jüdischen Wohnbezirk in Warschau [Commissioner for the Jewish Residential District in Warsaw], Letter of 02/03.1942 to Chairman of the Jewish Council in Warsaw (fragment).
- ***Description:*** transcript, handwritten manuscript (WINK.*), ink, German, 140×160 mm, serious damage and losses of text, ss. 1, pp. 2.

  Doc. written on a Rusałka chocolate factory (Warsaw) label (Before 1915, printed, Polish, Russian).

### 217. RING. I/272. (Lb. 556). Mf. ŻIH–781; USHMM–12

- After 10.04.1942, Warsaw Ghetto
- Der Kommissar für den Jüdischen Wohnbezirk in Warschau [Commissioner for the Jewish Residential District in Warsaw], Letter of 8.04.1942 to Chairman of the Jewish Council in Warsaw
- Programs of all cultural performances in the ghetto must be presented to the German authorities for acceptance, ban on playing of musical works of non-Jewish composers (for breaking this ban, the symphony orchestra will be suspended for 2 months, starting from 15.04.1942), ban on selling or making accessible German and other foreign language books. Letter signed by Dr. [Franz] Grassler.
- ***Description:*** transcript (2 copies), handwritten manuscript (WINK.*, ink) and handwritten manuscript (H*, pencil), German, 206×293 mm, minor damage and losses of text, ss. 2, pp. 3.

  At the bottom of p. 1 information about the date of the letter's arrival at the Secretariat of the Jewish Council: "10.04.1942. Daily Registry No. 7810."

  About this document, see *Czerniaków*, p. 264.

### 218. RING. I/1220/66. Mf. ŻIH–835; USHMM–47

- 1942, Warsaw Ghetto
- Der Kommissar für den jüdischen Wohnbezirk in Warschau [Commissioner for the Jewish Residential District in Warsaw], Letter to Jewish Council in Warsaw (fragment)
- Concerning the registration obligation of Polish Army officers.
- ***Description:*** transcript, handwritten manuscript (WINK.*), ink, German, 191×147, 190×150, 65×70 mm, serious damage and losses of text, ss. 3, pp. 3.

### 219. RING. I/344. (Lb. 706). Mf. ŻIH–781; USHMM–12

- After 05.1942, Warsaw Ghetto
- NN., Study entitled "A Year under the Regime of the Commissioner for the Jewish District in Warsaw"

- Discussion of the ghetto's situation under the administration of Dr. Heinz Auerswald (15.05.1941–15.05.1942) based on a report from 18.05.1942 ("Die Verwaltung des Jüdischen Wohnbezirks in Warschau. Im Zeitraum von der Amtsübernahme des Herrn Kommissars (15 Mai 1941) bis zum 15 Mai 1942" [The Administration of the Jewish Residential District in Warsaw. During the period since the Commissioner took office (15 May 1941) until 15 May 1942]), produced at the request of Auerswald by a commission of the Jewish Council under the direction of Józef Jaszuński.
- ***Description:*** original, handwritten manuscript (WINK.*), ink, Polish, 200×277 mm, damage and losses of text, ss. 14, pp. 14.

  Manuscript written on the back of printed bills (filled out for the Adler firm in Warsaw, 11–12.1938) of the firm: "Przemysł Włókienniczy Ch.M.Pik. Łódź." [Ch. M. Pik Textile Industry of Łódź] (ink, stamp in India ink).

  Attached note by H.W. in Yiddish: "Delivered by Pinchas Wasserman."

### 220. RING. I/285. (Lb. 917). Mf. ŻIH—781; USHMM—12

- After 12.1940, place unknown
- Collection of documents (circulars) of the German occupation authorities of the Generalgouvernement concerning forced labor for the Jewish population (fragments)
- Order by [Hans] Frank of 26.10.1939 on introduction of forced labor for Jews in the Generalgouvernement; order of 12.12.1939 for a list of persons covered in the forced labor provision and other executive provisions for the order of 26.10.1939. Official letter to the Labor Offices of the Generalgouvernement and the Jewish Council in Warsaw concerning compulsory labor for Jews.
- ***Description:*** transcript, typescript, German, Polish, 198×255, 155×130 mm, serious damage and losses of text, ss. 14, pp. 14.

  Index: Krüger, Peemöller, Dr. Mueller

### 221. RING. I/275. (Lb. 993, 134). Mf. ŻIH—781; USHMM—12

- After 16.11.1940
- Labor Office in Warsaw, Letter of 16.11.1940 to Jewish Council in Warsaw in the matter of supplying laborers for work
- Order to provide 400 laborers for work in Puławy and 300 in Łęczna. Salary is according to the established tariff, but administration of both camps is in the hands of the Jewish Council. Letter signed by Dir. [Kurt] Hoffmann.
- ***Description:*** transcript (2 copies), typescript, German, 204×295 mm, minor damage and losses of text (second copy), ss. 2, pp. 2.

### 222. RING. I/1220/80. Mf. ŻIH—835; USHMM—47

- After 5.08.1940, Warsaw Ghetto
- [German authorities in the Generalgouvernement], Letter to the Jewish Council in Warsaw [?]
- Concerning work and payment of Jews. Letter signed by Dr. Frauendorfer.
- ***Description:*** transcript, typescript, German, 168×218 mm, extensive damage and losses of text, ss. 1, pp. 1.

### 223. RING. I/1105/2 (1424). Mf. ŻIH—833; USHMM—45

- After 06.1940, Warsaw Ghetto
- Firm of Wilh[elm] Kuhmichel, Engineer VDI (Saarbrücken 3, Am Homburg 35) in Warsaw, Letter of 6.06.1940 to Jewish Council in Warsaw
- Concerning provision of laborers (100) to the electricity plant at ul. Armatnia. Letter signed by Blum.
- ***Description:*** transcript, typescript, German, 148×205 mm, ss. 1, pp. 1.

  Attached note by H.W. in Yiddish.

### 224. RING. I/213. (Lb. 868, 869). Mf. ŻIH—780; USHMM—11

- After 8.10.1941, Warsaw
- [Jewish Council in Warsaw?], Note for the German authorities ("Notiz für Herrn Direktor Stark") concerning the fight against pediculosis. (8.10.1941)
- Proposal to fight pediculosis with the help of special health groups and disinfection bath facilities located in various parts of the city, instead of exclusively police methods (attached cost estimate for realizing the project).
- ***Description:*** transcript, typescript, German, 220×286 mm, minor damage and losses of text, ss. 2, pp. 2.

  See *Czerniaków*, pp. 176, 213.

### 225. RING. I/279. (Lb. 557). Mf. ŻIH—781; USHMM—12

- After 4.08.1941, Warsaw Ghetto
- Jewish Council in Warsaw, Correspondence concerning houses located near the Pawiak prison. (31.07–4.08.1941)
- 1) Letter of 31.07.1942 from the Gestapo to the Jewish Council ordering closure and sealing of the windows in houses facing the prison, forbidden to use balconies;

  2) Two letters (3.08 and 4.08.1941) from the Chairman of the Legal Department of the Jewish Council to the Technical Construction Desk of the Economic Department (Referatu Techniczno-Budowlanego Wydziału Gospodarczego) include: a list of houses covered by the aforementioned decree (ul. Dzielna 21, 23, 25, 27, 29; ul. Pawia 19, 26, 28, 30, 32, 34) and information about its enactment.

- *Description:* transcript, handwritten manuscript (WINK.*), ink, German, Polish, 210×290 mm, minor damage and losses of text, ss. 2, pp. 2.

### 226. RING. I/662, RING. I/664/1. Mf. ŻIH–816; USHMM–28

a) **Ring. I/662**

- After 03.1942, Warsaw Ghetto
- Jewish Council in Warsaw, Correspondence with the Financial Inspectorate of Warsaw City I and II (Inspektoratem Finansowym Warsaw-Miasto I i II). (with enclosures) (1941–1942)
- Concerning tax matters of the Jewish population in Warsaw (outstanding taxes due for the period 1939–1940).
- *Description:* transcript, typescript, handwritten manuscript (WINK.*), ink, German, Polish, 130×145, 195×290 mm, serious damage and losses of text, ss. 5, pp. 9.

  Attached note by H.W. in Polish.

b) **Ring. I/664/1**

- After 15.04.1942, Warsaw Ghetto
- Jewish Council in Warsaw, "Additional note in the mat[ter] of collection of sums due to the Revenue Offices [Urzędów Skarbowych] by the Jewish Council"
- Concerning collection of tax arrears in the period 5.02–7.04.1942.
- *Description:* transcript, handwritten manuscript (WINK.*), ink, Polish, ss. 1, pp. 1.

  Attached note by H.W.: "J. Winkler provided [this]."

### 227. RING. I/179. (Lb. 566). Mf. ŻIH–779; USHMM–10

- After 15.05.1942, Warsaw Ghetto
- Jewish Council in Warsaw, "Fifth and sixth report of the collection of tax sums due for the period of 14–30.04 and 1–15.05.1942"
- Balance sheet of the number of payers, settled cases, and amount of collected arrears.
- *Description:* transcript, handwritten manuscript (WINK.*), ink, Polish, 210×296 mm, minor damage and losses of text, ss. 2, pp. 2

  Handwritten on the back of a form of the Ministry of the Treasury: "Attachment to declaration of gross receipts" (Before 1939, printed, Polish).

  Attached note by H.W in Yiddish: "J. Winkler."

### 228. RING. I/295. (Lb. 563). Mf. ŻIH–781; USHMM–12

- After 03.1942, Warsaw Ghetto
- NN., "Note in the matter of the Social Insurance Administration (Ubezpieczalni Społecznej) in Warsaw"
- Financial account of the sums remitted by the ghetto's residents to the Social Insurance Administration. Number of those insured in the ghetto, proposal for creating a medical facility ("Pomoc Lekarska") for employees of the Jewish Council (copy of a fragment of a letter of 25.02.1942 from the Commissioner for the Jewish District to the Jewish Council in the above matter).
- *Description:* transcript, handwritten manuscript (WINK.*), ink, German, Polish, 202×295 mm, damage and losses of text, ss. 2, pp. 4.

### 229. RING. I/664/2. Mf. ŻIH–816; USHMM–28

- After 23.04.1942, Warsaw Ghetto
- Jewish Council in Warsaw, Correspondence
  1) Letter of [. . .] 1941. Chairman of the Jewish Council to the Social Insurance Administration, concerning insurance of employees of the Jewish Community in Warsaw;
  2) Letter of 23.03.1942. From the Legal Desk of the Jewish Council to the Personnel Department of the Jewish Council, concerning application of employees of the Jewish Council for social insurance (signed Z. Werner);
  3) Letter of 2.03.1942 from the Commissioner for the Jewish District in Warsaw to the Jewish Council containing a refusal to extend term for payment of a fine for smuggling for the following persons: Szmul Mincmacher (Krochmalna 7, apt. 13), Najman Brandler (Miła 56, apt. 5), Taube Hochberg (Ogrodowa 26a, apt. 86) and Norma Bursztyn (Ogrodowa 23, apt. 17) (signed Probst);
  4) See Ring. I/662 (Ring. I/664/1);
  5) See Ring. I/296 (Ring. I/664/3);
  6) See Ring. I/244 (Ring. I/664/4).
- *Description:* transcript, handwritten manuscript (WINK.*), ink, German, Polish, 144×205, 210×294 mm, damage and losses of texts, ss. 2, pp. 3.

  Attached Notes of H.W. to manuscripts 2), 3), 5), and 6): "J. Winkler wrote and delivered [this]."

### 230. RING. I/296. (Lb. 564). Mf. ŻIH–781; USHMM–12. RING. I/664/3. Mf. ŻIH–816; USHMM–28

a) **Ring. I/296**

- After 31.05.1942, Warsaw Ghetto
- NN., "Supplemental note in the matter of cleaning the streets in the Jewish District"
- Results of the decision (of 23.04.1942) by the German authorities on withdrawal from the ghetto of the ZOM [City Sanitation Dept.] from 1.06.1942. Course of discussions with ZOM, mutual settlement of accounts, selection of a new firm for keeping order (utrzymania porządku) in the Jewish District. Text produced, inter alia on the basis of correspondence and other official materials of the Jewish Council. Attached copies of 2 letters of 23.04.1942 from the Municipal Administration of Warsaw (Schulten) to ZOM (to Dir. [Kazimierz] Meyer) notifying of the discontinuation of service to the ghetto as of 1.06.1942.

- *Description:* original, transcript, handwritten manuscript (WINK.*), ink, German, Polish, 195×280, 205×295 mm, minor damage and losses of text, ss. 6, pp. 7.
  - Pp. 1–5 written on the back of printed bills (filled out for the Adler firm in Warsaw) from the firm Ch.M.Pik Textile Industry of Łódź (10.1938, ink, stamp in India ink, Polish).
  - Inventory: "Copied for O[yneg] Sh[abes], by J. [Jerzy] Winkler."
  - On decisions in the matter of cleaning the ghetto, see *Czerniaków*, p. 284.

b) **Ring. I/664/3**
- After 27.04.1942, Warsaw Ghetto
- Municipal Administration of the City of Warsaw. City Sanitation Department (ZOM) (ul. Ka[. . .]), Letter of 27.04.1942 to Jewish Council in Warsaw
- Notation on the termination of street cleaning on the terrain of the ghetto by ZOM as of 1.06.1942.
- *Description:* transcript, handwritten manuscript (WINK.*), ink, Polish, damage and losses of text, ss. 1, pp. 1.
  - Attached note by H.W.: "J. Winkler delivered."

### 231. RING. I/265. (Lb. 57). Mf. ŻIH—780; USHMM—11
- After 13.10.1940, Warsaw
- Jewish Council in Warsaw, "Communiqué 1 in the matter of a Jewish district in Warsaw" (13.10.1940)
- List of streets where the Jewish population may reside (attached list of numbers of houses on Żelazna, Krochmalna, Ogrodowa, Chłodna, Waliców, and Ciepła streets, that are excluded from the ghetto).
- *Description:* transcript, typescript (with handwritten additions in pencil), Polish, 220×340, 220×282 mm, minor damage and losses of text, ss. 3, pp. 3.
  - On p. 1 at the top is information: "Mr. [Sa]gan."

### 232. RING. I/778/1. (1099).Mf. ŻIH—825; USHMM—37
- After 10.10.[1941], Warsaw Ghetto
- [Jewish Council in Warsaw?], Announcement: "New boundaries of the Jewish District. Everyone from the newly annexed streets must leave their apartments by 10 October [1941]."
- Decree concerning the Polish population. Attached list of streets with addresses of buildings that were to be included in the ghetto.
- *Description:* transcript, typescript, Polish, 207×296 mm, minor damage and losses of text, ss. 1, pp. 1.
  - See *Przewodnik*, p. 96.

### 233. RING. I/778/2. (1099).Mf. ŻIH—825; USHMM—37
- [12.1941], Warsaw Ghetto
- [Jewish Council in Warsaw?], Announcement: "It is permissible to move into all of the remaining houses in the entire Jewish District with the exception of the following properties: . . ."
- Attached list of streets with addresses of buildings that were to be excluded from the ghetto [12.1941].
- *Description:* transcript, typescript, Polish, 206×296 mm, minor damage and losses of text, ss. 1, pp. 1.

### 234. RING. I/775 (1099). Mf. ŻIH—836; USHMM—67
- Date unknown, Warsaw Ghetto
- Jewish Council in Warsaw [?], Announcement concerning a public bathhouse
- Notation on closure of bathhouse.
- *Description:* original, handwritten manuscript, India ink, German, Polish, 530×370 mm, ss. 1, pp. 1.

### 235. RING. I/1082 (1401). (Lb. 601). Mf. ŻIH—833; USHMM—45
- 1942, Warsaw Ghetto
- [Jewish Council in Warsaw], Registration questionnaire for foreign nationals.
- *Description:* original, hectographed typescript, German, Polish, 202×295 mm, ss. 1, pp. 2.

### 236. RING. I/324. (Lb. 1632). Mf. ŻIH—781; USHMM—12
- After 4.01.1942, Warsaw Ghetto
- Adam Cz [Czerniaków], "Recollections about late Councilman Beniamin Zabłudowski." (4.01.1942)
- Oration at the funeral of a member of the Jewish Council in Warsaw (died 3.01.1942).
- *Description:* transcript, typescript, Polish, 210×294 mm, damage and losses of text, ss. 1, pp. 1
  - See Ring. II/147. (second copy)
  - The original of this document appeared in the form of a duplicated typescript; one copy is located in AAN 202/II-28, s. 18.

### 237. RING. I/1113 (1432). (Lb. 1673). Mf. ŻIH—833; USHMM—45
- [01.1942], Warsaw Ghetto
- Chairman of the Jewish Council in Warsaw, Adam Czerniaków, Notice of a memorial service in memory of deceased members of the Jewish Council
- Service in the communal synagogue of the Nożyk Foundation for the deceased: Herman Szwarc, Łazarz Łabędź, Henryk Grassberg, Meszulem Kaminer, Jakub Berman, and Beniamin Zabłudowski.
- *Description:* original, hectographed typescript, Polish, 206×292 mm, ss. 1, pp. 1.
  - On the service, see *Czerniaków*, p. 242.

### 238. RING. I/357. (Lb. 524). Mf. ŻIH—782; USHMM—13
- 28.06.1942 [?], Warsaw Ghetto
- Adam Czerniaków, "Oration on the occasion of Abraham Gepner's birthday" (Warsaw, 28.06.1942)

- Oration presented at the headquarters of the Jewish Council at the celebration of the 70th anniversary of Abraham Gepner's birth. Signed by Czerniaków.
- ***Description:*** original, hectographed typescript, Polish, 203×330 mm, ss. 1, pp. 1.
  Notation handwritten (hectographed): "3017."
  See *Czerniaków*, p. 293.

### 239. RING. I/224. Mf. ŻIH—780; USHMM—11

- After 15.12.1941, Warsaw Ghetto
- [Jewish Council in Warsaw. Central Jail?], Cards ("Personal details of the deceased") of 15 Jews shot on 15.12.1941 in the prison at ul Gęsia 24
- The cards concern persons sentenced to death for residing outside the ghetto:
  Majer Abramowicz
  Srul Lejb Drewnowicz
  Małka Elbaum
  Hela Kalksztajn
  Masza Kisielewicz
  Chana Kon
  Róża Mikanowska
  Mindla Prowizor
  Chaja Łaja Przychodzka
  Moszek Rotbard
  Ałta Rozenbaum
  Chaja Rubin
  Łaja Rywka Russ
  Hena Salwe
  Estera Śpiewak.
- ***Description:*** original (printed) and transcript [?] (handwritten), Polish, 108×140 mm, ss. 15, pp. 15.
  All the cards were filled out by one person on the basis of original [?] cards. On the back of Chaja Łaja Przychodzka's card in the same handwriting: "signature of physician, seal of Dr. Johan Frendler, physician, Warsaw, Elektoralna 14." Apparently the original cards were signed by the doctor [?].
  On this execution, see *Czerniaków*, p. 233. See also Ring. I/470.

### 240. RING. I/1201 (1520). Mf. ŻIH—835; USHMM—47

- 2.07.1942, Warsaw Ghetto
- Director of the C[entral] J[ail], Letter of 2.07.1942 to Public Kitchen (Kuchnia Ludowa) no. 43 (ul. Lubeckiego 5)
- Request for issuance of 110 fewer portions of soup on account of "reduction of the CJ's situation."
- ***Description:*** original, typescript, Polish, 167×133 mm, ss. 1, pp. 1.
  Doc. written on the back of a prewar matchbox label.
  On 2.07.1942, 110 persons were transported out of the jail on Gęsia Street sentenced to death; see *Czerniaków*, p. 295.

### 241. RING. I/28. Mf. ŻIH—772; USHMM—3

- 1941, Warsaw Ghetto
- [Jewish Council in Warsaw], "Labor Battalion general report for 1940"
- Reasons for formation of the Labor Battalion at the Jewish Council, organizational structure, number of workers, places of employment, labor camps, finances, supervisory authorities. List of enclosures: tables (I –XXIV) and printed models (1–41) (in attached tables I –V, inter alia the number of persons subject to compulsory labor in August 1940, list of Warsaw institutions and firms (addresses), where Jewish laborers were employed—middle of June 1940; "Memorandum of 28.04.1940 on the financing of the Labor Battalion at the Jewish Council").
- ***Description:*** transcript (3 copies, in fragments), handwritten manuscript (two handwritings, JG* and E*), German, Polish, damage and losses of text, ss. 166, pp. 166.
  In the margins notation by H.W.: "104–1[104/2]. Department of Labor/Materials."

### 242. RING. I/1123 (1442). Mf. ŻIH—833; USHMM—45. RING. I/97. Mf. ŻIH—776; USHMM—7. RING. I/1213. Mf. ŻIH—835; USHMM—47.

a) **Ring. I/1213**

- 12.03.1940, Warsaw
- Labor Battalion at the Jewish Council in Warsaw, Summons no. 14128A of 12.03.1940 for additional work days in March for Jakub Samson (ul. Nowolipie 12)
- Obligation to report on 15 and 17.03.1940 at 6 AM at ul. Twarda 6.
- ***Description:*** original, hectographed typescript, handwritten manuscript, ink, stamp, Polish, 208×168 mm, minor damage and losses of text, ss. 1, pp. 2.
  Stamp at the top: "The German Authorities have ordered the Labor Battalion itself to deliver lists of persons who are evading this obligation for the purpose of drawing them to compulsory labor and punishment."
  On the reverse, notation (pencil) and stamp: "16.03.[?] worked Ba . . . [. . .] group . . . [. . .][?]. [signature:] A. Kossower.
  See Ring. I/863.

b) **Ring. I/1123 (1442). (Lb. 2). Ring. I/97**

- 08.1940, after 08.1940, Warsaw, Warsaw Ghetto
- Labor Battalion, Circular of 1.08.1940 "To all Jews subject to compulsory labor"
- Regulations concerning compulsory labor for the Jewish population.
- ***Description:*** Ring. I/1123—original, hectographed typescript, Polish, 210×288 mm, ss. 1, pp. 1; Ring. I/97—transcript (2 copies), handwritten manuscript (MS*), pencil, Yiddish, 146×208 mm, minor damage and losses of text, ss. 2, pp. 2.

Ring. I/97—transcript of doc. translated into Yiddish or original printed in Yiddish
Docs. were kept in a binder.

c) **Ring. I/1123 (1442)**
- 1940, Warsaw
- Labor Battalion. Staff of Labor Camps, Form for a letter to the Accounting-Bursars Office (Referat Rachunkowo-Kasowy)
- Concerning relief grants for persons leaving for labor camps.
- ***Description:*** original (2 copies on one sheet), hectographed typescript, Polish, 210×288 mm, ss. 1, pp. 1.
  Doc. was kept in a binder.

**243. RING. I/1220/52. Mf. ŻIH—835; USHMM—47**
- Date unknown, place unknown
- Citizen's Committee at the Labor Battalion, Organizational chart
- Purpose of activity, organization, office work.
- ***Description:*** transcript, typescript, Polish, 172×243 mm, damage and losses of text, ss. 1, pp. 1.

**244. RING. I/778/3. (1099). Mf. ŻIH—825; USHMM—37**
- After 15.06.1942, Warsaw Ghetto
- Jewish Council in Warsaw. Housing Office, Letter of 15.06.1942 to residents of the apartment house at ul. Muranowska 2
- Notation about exclusion from the ghetto of buildings located on streets: Żoliborska, Pokorna, Bonifraterska, and Muranowska. Order to vacate this area. Letter signed by Ignacy Baumberg and St. Adler.
- ***Description:*** transcript, typescript, Polish, 218×283 mm, ss. 1, pp. 1.

**245. RING. I/19. (Lb. 164). Mf. ŻIH—771; USHMM—2**
- After 17.04.1941, Warsaw Ghetto
- Report of the Control Commission at the Jewish Community: "Report in the matter of allocation of administrator and superintendent positions in Jewish properties in the Jewish district"
- Discussion of abuses by the Building Administrators and Superintendents Desk (Committee) [Referat (Komitet) Administratorów i Rządców] in the registration of candidates for administrators of properties within the Warsaw Ghetto (attached list of names of several persons entered by the Desk on the list of administrators).
- ***Description:*** transcript, typescript, Polish, 210×295 mm, minor damage and losses of text, ss. 5, pp. 5.
  Index: Guta Gotlibowska, Łaja Palewska, Rafał Palewski, Maria Manela, J. Rozensztroch, Chaja Niemiec, Bronisława Chwat, Dawid Kronenberg, Joel Włodawer, Goldberg, Teszner, attorney

**246. RING. I/247. (Lb. 870, 220). Mf. ŻIH—780; USHMM—11**
- After 23.12.1940, Warsaw Ghetto
- Jewish Council, "Minutes of the session of the Labor Commission on 23.12.1940 at 5 PM in the Community's building"
- Seizure of the Opus firm, expansion of the Commission, supplies production, minutes of the carpentry subcommission of 20.12.1940, memorandum of the Artisans Association. Participated in the deliberations: Dr. M. Szpilfogel, Dr. S. Eiger, Director Braun, Mieczysław Orlean, Kazimierz Rechthand, and councilmen Józef Jaszuński, Rozental, and Leopold Kupczykier.
- ***Description:*** transcript, typescript, Polish, 205×295 mm, ss. 1, pp. 1.

**247. RING. I/1106/1 (1425). (Lb. 1716, 1717, 1718). Mf. ŻIH—833; USHMM—45**
- 13.01.1942, Warsaw Ghetto
- Jewish Council in Warsaw. Chairman of the Special Commission, A. [Abraham] Gepner, Invitation of 13.01.1942 for Josek Kukiełek (ul. Sienna 72) to a meeting on 14.01.1942 at the Community's building at ul. Grzybowska 26/28.
- ***Description:*** original, hectographed typescript, handwritten manuscript, pencil, Polish, 207×213 mm, ss. 1, pp. 1.

**248. RING. I/1084 (1403). (Lb. 592). Mf. ŻIH—833; USHMM—45**
- 22.04.1941, Warsaw Ghetto
- Commission for the Affairs of Displaced Persons at the Jewish Council in Warsaw, Warehouse, Rymarska 12, Announcement of 22.04.1941
- Summons to collect lost baggage by 1.05.1941, in connection with liquidation of the warehouse.
- ***Description:*** original, hectographed typescript, Polish, 208×290 mm, ss. 1, pp. 1
  Attached note by H.W. in Yiddish: "Submitted [by] H.W."

**249. RING. I/205. Mf. ŻIH—779; USHMM—10**
- After 31.08.1941, Warsaw Ghetto
- "Minutes of the Finance Commission at the Resettlement Commission at the Community," (31.08.1941)
- Taxation of affluent residents of the ghetto for the benefit of the starving. Present during the deliberations: Dir. Icchak Giterman, Lipe Eliezer Bloch, Emanuel Ringelblum, Daniel [Dawid] Chołodenko, Rabinowicz, Aleksander Landau, Menachem M. Kon.
- ***Description:*** transcript, typescript, Yiddish, 222×288 mm, minor damage and losses of text, ss. 1, pp. 1.
  Inventory: "Record submitted by Menachem M. Kon."

### 250. RING. I/103. Mf. ŻIH—776; USHMM—7

- After 1941, Warsaw Ghetto
- Economic Council of the Jewish District (Rada Gospodarcza Dzielnicy Żydowskiej) in Warsaw, Note concerning the flow of goods and funds between the ghetto and the "Aryan side"
- Difficulties in working out statistics of commercial exchange (attached balance sheet of the value of the ghetto's monthly "export" and "import" in 1941).
- *Description:* transcript, typescript, Polish, 210×293 mm, extensive damage and losses of text, ss. 2, pp. 3.
  See Ring. I/123, I/371.

### 251. RING. I/227. Mf. ŻIH—780; USHMM—11

- 1.06.1942, Warsaw Ghetto
- Official instruction for the Order Service[9] [Warsaw 1942]
- Official regulations of the Order Service, issued as an attached to pt. 1 of order no. 128 of 21.05.1942, includes particular ordinances regulating operation and tasks of the Order Service.
- *Description:* original (2 copies), printed, Polish, 125×174 mm, (k. 8, pp. 16) ss. 16, pp. 32.
  Printed by J. Rachman, ul. Chłodna 8, press-run 3,000 copies.
  Published: *Służba Porządkowa*, pp. 123–137.

### 252. RING. I/14. Mf. ŻIH—771; USHMM—2

- After 12.1940, Warsaw Ghetto
- [Jewish Council in Warsaw. Order Service], Orders of the day of Józef Szeryński [Szynkman], director of the Order Service (no. 8–11, 13–15, 17, 20–21, 38–53, 55, 57, 59–64; Nov. 1940–Jan. 1941)
- Organization of service, division into platoons and their number, allocation of guardposts (street names, apartment house numbers), personnel information (name lists of Order Service functionaries), instructions and orders.
- *Description:* original, typescript, and hectographed typescript with handwritten notations, Polish, 205×290 and 210×295 mm, minor damage and losses of text, ss. 46, pp. 70.

### 253. RING. I/206. (Lb. 523). Mf. ŻIH—779; USHMM—10

- After 14.01.1941, Warsaw Ghetto
- [Jewish Council in Warsaw. Order Service], Oskar Sekler, director of Region V of Order Service, Orders of the day (no. 3 and 4 of 12 and 14.01.1941)
- Personnel appointments, regulating ordinances, discharge, official duties, lists of functionaries of the Order Service (e.g., fight against usury and speculation).
- *Description:* transcript, typescript, Polish, 205×295 mm, ss. 2, pp. 3
  Attached Note by H.W. in Yiddish: "Submitted [by] Leon Wartski from Kalisz."
  Index: Rządziński Mojżesz, Najman Adam, Szpinger Herman, Rajmica Rudolf, Chaskielewicz Janusz, Abie Wajdenbaum, Jan Frenkel, Gustaw Kon, Mojżesz Bazyler

### 254. RING. I/229. Mf. ŻIH—780; USHMM—11

- After 29.01.1941, Warsaw Ghetto
- Adam Albek, Order Service group leader no. 1571, official report of 29.01.1941
- Reports on the conditions in the quarantine at ul. Leszno 109 and abuses tolerated by its director Halber.
- *Description:* transcript, typescript, Polish, 208×293 mm, minor damage and losses of text, ss. 1, pp. 1.
  Index: Korentajer, Order Service orderly (porządkowy) no. 1592, and underofficer (podobwodowy) Szper

### 255. RING. I/1143 (1462). Mf. ŻIH—833; USHMM—45

- 20.12.1941, Warsaw Ghetto
- Jewish Council in Warsaw. Order Service, Pass no. 4950 of 20.12.1941 authorizing removal on the basis of the quartering order
- Not filled in, with signature of J. [Jakub] Lejkin, Director of Department I of the Order Service.
- *Description:* original, printed, Polish, 148×105 mm, ss. 1, pp. 1.

### 256. RING. I/1135 (1454). (Lb. 171). Mf. ŻIH—833; USHMM—45

- 19.11.[. . . ?], Warsaw Ghetto
- Jewish Council in Warsaw. Inspectorate of the Order Service, Summons of candidate for Order Service NN. to report on 19.11.[. . . ?] before the medical commission at ul. Twarda 6.
- *Description:* original, hectographed typescript, handwritten manuscript, ink, Polish, 115×217 mm, ss. 1, pp. 1.
  Doc. was filled out, but the candidate's name and address, as well as the no. of the letter is smeared.
  Doc. was kept in a binder.

9. Order Service is the rendering of the German Ordnungsdienst, the Yiddish Ordnungsdinst, and the Polish Służba Porządkowa. All of the terms refer to the Jewish ghetto police. Use of the direct translation preserves an important element of the ambiguous use of language in the Nazi German-imposed circumstances.

### 257. RING. I/246. Mf. ŻIH—780; USHMM—11

- After 24.12.1940, Warsaw Ghetto
- Jewish Council in Warsaw, "Minutes of the session of the carpentry sub-commission of 24.12.1940, 5 PM in the Community's building"
- Production and employment possibilities in construction (reported by engineer Kuszner) and furniture-making (reported by engineer St. Margulis) (balance sheets). Also participated in the deliberations: Dr. M. Szpilfogel, Dr. S. Eiger, Herman Kalisz, Szwarc, Hałaj, engineer Hertz, and representatives of the Association of Craftsmen.
- ***Description:*** transcript, typescript, Polish, 206×290 mm, minor damage and losses of text, ss. 2, pp. 2.
  Attached note by H.W. in Yiddish: "Submitted [by] Dr. S. Eiger from Łódź."

### 258. RING. I/338/1. Mf. ŻIH—781; USHMM—12

- After 16.12.1941, Warsaw Ghetto
- Cemetery Department at the Jewish Council in Warsaw, Record in the matter of the massacred corpses found on 15.12.1941 at ul. Pańska 51 (16.12.1941, Warsaw)
- Noech Pinkiert, owner of the Ostatnia Posługa [Last Service] Funeral Establishment (ul. Grzybowska 21) announced the recovery of the massacred corpses. Post-mortem report signed: A.B. Ekerman, councilman and Adam Wiener, vice chairman of the Central Commission of Sponsors' Committees for Refugees.
- ***Description:*** transcript, typescript, Polish, 205×290 mm, ss. 1, pp. 1.

### 259. RING. I/777/4. (1099). Mf. ŻIH—825; USHMM—37

- 8.02.1942, Warsaw Ghetto
- Jewish Council in Warsaw. Department of Cemetery and Funeral Affairs, Certificate for Wolf Strzyg for entry to the cemetery (ul. Okopowa 49), in connection with a funeral on 9.02.1942.
- ***Description:*** original, printed, handwritten manuscript, ink, stamp, German, Polish, 165×117 mm, ss. 1, pp. 1.

### 260. RING. I/20. (Lb. 181). Mf. ŻIH—772; USHMM—3

- After 06.1940, Warsaw
- [Jewish Population Records Department (Wydział Ewidencji Ludności Żydowskiej) of the Jewish Council?], "List of baptized persons in the period 1.06–30.06.1940" and "Supplementary list for the m[onth] of May 1940"
- List includes 27 persons, residents of Warsaw, providing: name and surname, address, date of baptism, and religion.
- ***Description:*** original, hectographed typescript (with handwritten notation: "List no. 4"), Polish, 210×295 mm, pp. 1, ss. 1.
  Attached note by H.W. in Yiddish: "Submitted [by] Pinchas (Paweł) Wasserman, director of the Jewish Population Records Department at the Jewish Council."
  Index: Amsterdam Gennadij, merchant, ul. Hoża 39, apt. 16, Orth[odox]
  Apte Jan, advertising agent, ul. Kopernika 31, apt. 3, R.C. [Roman Catholic]
  Bregman Bronisława Regina, pl. Napoleona 1–5, apt. 8, R.C.
  Bregman Beata Halina, pl. Napoleona 1–5, apt. 8, R.C.
  Drucker Alicja Ewa, ul. Belwederwska 40, apt. 7, O.C. [Old Catholic]
  Drucker Gizela Anna, ul. Belwederska 40, apt. 7, O.C.
  Endelman Bogumił, ul. Poznańska 37, apt. 3, R.C.
  Endelman Ludwika, ul. Poznańska 37, apt. 3, R.C.
  Endelman Adolf Andrzej, ul. Poznańska 37, apt. 3, R.C.
  Fejgin Runa Irena, ul. Krasińskiego 29, apt. 6, R.C.
  Fejgin Piotr, ul. Krasińskiego 29, apt. 6, R.C.
  Fraenkel Gertruda, ul. Belwederska 40, apt. 7, O.C.
  Ginsberg Leja, pensioner, ul. Sienkiewicza 2, apt. 9, R.C.
  Olbert Szeme Szymon, office worker (urzędnik), ul. Wspólna 35, apt. 20, R.C.
  Olbert Paulina Antonina, Wspólna 35, apt. 20, R.C.
  Olbert Alma Irena Mieczysława, ul. Wspólna 35, apt. 20, R.C.
  Post Zofia, official (urzędniczka), ul. Boduena 5, apt. 5, R.C.
  Poznańska Tauba Teofila Maria, Al. Jerozolimskie 14 m.3, R.C.
  Safian Ludwik Jan, pensioner, ul. Wilcza 21, apt. 28, R.C.
  Totzek Ilsa Helena, schoolgirl, ul. Czerniakowska 205, apt. 20, R.C.
  Hermelin Halina Alicja, ul. Bagatela 14, apt. 10, R.C.
  Hopfenblum Salomea Zofia, ul. Moniuszki 3, apt. 4, R.C.
  Kanarek Paula Wacława, ul. Żurawia 23, apt. 9, R.C.
  Kanarek Tomasz Bogumił Stanisław, ul. Żurawia 23, apt. 9, R.C.
  Monis Klara Zofia, ul. Zgoda 4, apt. 18, O.C.
  Monis Elżbieta Jadwiga, ul. Zgoda 4, apt. 18, O.C.
  Silberstein Maryla Felicja, ul. Zgoda 4, apt. 13, R.C.

**261. RING. I/777/3. (1099). Mf. ŻIH—825; USHMM—37**

- 19.03.[. . .], Warsaw Ghetto
- Jewish Council. Jewish Population Records Department [Wydział Ewidencji Ludności Żydowskiej]. Address Division, Information cards
- 1) Luzer Rozental (born 1914), last address Karmelicka 27, place of residence Nowolipki 32/19, Information from 19.03.[. . .]; 2) Szlama Kornblit.
- ***Description:*** original, printed, handwritten manuscript, pencil, Polish, 103×158 mm, ss. 2, pp. 2.

**262. RING. I/257. (Lb. 522). Mf. ŻIH—780; USHMM—11**

a)

- 04.1942, Warsaw
- Jewish Council. Department of Real Estate and Facilities of Public Utility, Circular no. 82 of 20.04.1942
- Information pursuant to Circular no. 228 (of 10.04.1942) of the Commission Board for Insured Real Estate [Zarządu Komisarycznego Zabezpieczonych Nieruchomości] on eviction from apartments by administrative means of tenants who are "maliciously" refraining from payment of rent.
- ***Description:*** original, hectographed typescript, Polish, 140×200 mm, minor damage and losses of text, ss. 1, pp. 1.

  Document signed (stamp) by B. [Bolesław] Rozensztat, attorney, chairman of the Department of Real Estate and Facilities of Public Utility.

  See Ring. I/257b (originally attached to Ring. I/257a).

b)

- 02–04.1942, Warsaw
- Commission Board for Insured Real Estate [Komisaryczny Zarząd Zabezpieczonych Nieruchomości], Circulars no. 205 of 17.02.1942; 208 o 26.02.1942; 219 of 30.03.1942; 223 of 10.04.1942
- Ordinances concerning quartering services for the German Army, list of rental sums in arrears, amount of rent for Germans within Warsaw (attached list of streets), removal from apartments by administrative means of persons "maliciously" not paying rent.
- ***Description:*** original, hectographed typescript, German, Polish, 208×290 mm, minor damage and losses of text, ss. 8, pp. 16.

  Circulars signed by Gustaw Flemming.

  Inventory: "Submitted to the Archive [by] Dr. Berthold Dobrin."

**263. RING. I/230. (Lb. 219). Mf. ŻIH—780; USHMM—11**

- Date unknown, Warsaw Ghetto
- NN., Letter to Adam Czerniaków in the matter of the activity of the Department of Labor
- Author reproaches officials of the Department for breaking the law and exposing the people to repressive measures through various types of chicanery connected with labor cards and certificates of inability to work.
- ***Description:*** transcript, typescript, Polish, 206×295 mm, ss. 1, pp. 1.

**264. RING. I/244. (Lb. 204). Mf. ŻIH—780; USHMM—11. RING. I/664/4. Mf. ŻIH—816; USHMM—28**

a) **Ring. I/664/4**

- After 9.06.1942, Warsaw Ghetto
- Jewish Council in Warsaw, "Note in the matter of compulsory Sabbath rest"
- The Department of Religious Affairs of the Jewish Council sent on 4.06.1942 to the Legal Department for evaluation, "A Proposal for Organizing a Sabbath Watch (Mishmeret Ha-Shabat) and a Court for Sabbath Matters." By letter of 9.06.1942, the Legal Department replied that the proposal is not at all suitable for discussion and no changes in the matter of Sabbath rest are needed.
- ***Description:*** transcript, handwritten manuscript (WINK.*), ink, Polish, ss. 1, pp. 1.

  Attached note by H.W.: "Drawn up by J. Winkler."

  See Ring. I/244.

b) **Ring. I/244**

- Date unknown, Warsaw Ghetto
- NN., "Proposal for Organization of a Sabbath Watch (Mishmeret Ha-Shabat) and Court for Sabbath Affairs"
- Purposes, tasks, leadership, obligations and authority of the Watch and the Court, of organizations established by and functioning at the Jewish Council in Warsaw.
- ***Description:*** original or transcript, typescript, Polish, 195×288 mm, minor damage and losses of text, ss. 1, pp. 2.

  Attached note by H.W. in Yiddish: "Rabbi Huberband submitted this text."

  Notation about this document, see Ring. I/664/4.

**265. RING. I/333. Mf. ŻIH—781; USHMM—12**

- 30.04.1942 [?], Warsaw Ghetto
- Statistical Department of the Jewish Council in Warsaw, "Interim report on processing of results of the registr[ation] survey of the WELŻ [Jewish Population Records Department] [?] of 31.01.1942"
- Statistical analysis for the Jewish Council concerning the Jewish population in Warsaw divided by age and gender; number of persons subject to compulsory labor and possessing identification cards.
- ***Description:*** transcript, handwritten manuscript (WINK.*), ink, Polish, 205×258 mm, minor damage and losses of text, ss. 1, pp. 2.

**266. RING. I/1101 (1420). (Lb. 1536). Mf. ŻIH—833; USHMM—45**

- Before 03.1942, Warsaw Ghetto
- Jewish Council in Warsaw. School Department, Report Card
- Form of certificate of completion of the first half of the school year 1941/42 in elementary school (2.03.1942). Signature of school director B. [Bluma] Wasser.
- ***Description:*** original (2 copies), printed, handwritten manuscript, Hebrew, Polish, 208×300 mm, ss. 2, pp. 4.

  On both copies notations handwritten in Hebrew (ink): "Berek" [?] (certificate no. 30); "Jakub Fiszman" (certificate no. 5)

  Doc. printed by J. Rachman (ul. Chłodna 8).

  Attached note by H.W. in Yiddish: "From the school at Nowolipki 22 [Tarbut School; see *Przewodnik*, annex after p. 575], Submitted [by] Bluma Wasser."

  Published: *Dzieci*, pp. 260–262 (certificate no. 5).

**267. RING. I/7. Mf. (Lb. 73, 163). ŻIH—771; USHMM—2**

- 05.1941, Warsaw
- [Dr. Jakub Munwez], Memorandum addressed to the Chairman of the Administrative Commission of the Czyste Jewish Hospital at the Hospital Department of the Jewish Community in Warsaw in the matter of the Jewish Hospital's functioning
- Critical discussion of conditions reigning in the hospital: personnel matters, permanent residents (personnel with families), management of materials, X-ray equipment, the hospital's management and administrative records, and archive.
- ***Description:*** original (hectographed typescript with handwritten additions (ink); transcript (typescript and handwritten additions), Polish, 215×340 mm, minor damage and losses of text, ss. 30, pp. 30.

  On p. 16 (of the copy) signature checked off (zakreślony), signature beneath: "Dr. Munwez." On p. 14 (original) and 16 (copy): "Submitted, Warsaw, 11.05.1941; read out, 31.05.1941"

  See Ring. I/315.

**268. RING. I/350. (Lb. 296) Mf. ŻIH—782; USHMM—13**

- After 04.1941, Warsaw Ghetto
- Jewish Council in Warsaw Department of Production, Reports of activity for the period April–September 1941
- Information about meetings of the Board, lists of correspondence received from and sent to the Transferstelle, list of orders received and carried out for the Transferstelle, state of employment, financial reports. Doc. Signed by B. [Beniamin] Gliksman, director of the Department or Dr. S. Eiger, secretary of the Board. Attached cover letters [?].
- ***Description:*** original and transcript, typescript, Polish, 220×280 145×212 mm, damage and losses of text, ss. 17, pp. 21.

  Attached note by H.W. in Yiddish: "Submitted [by] Dr. S. Eiger."

  Reports were preserved for the period:

  a) 1–15.04.1941 (from 17.04.1941)
  b) 16–30.04.1941 (Date unknown)
  c) 1–15.05.1941 (Date unknown)
  d) 16–31.05.1941 (from 3.06.1941)
  e) 1–15.06.1941 (from 16.06.1941)
  f) 16–30.06.1941 (from 1.07.1941, attached cover letter of 5.07.1941 [original typescript] signed by Dr. S. Eiger)
  g) 1–15.07.1941 (of 15.07.1941)
  h) 16–31.07.1941 (of 1.08.1941)
  i) 1–15.08.1941 (of 16.08.1941)
  j) 16–31.08.1941 (Date unknown, fragment)
  k) 1–30.09.1941 (Date unknown).

  Docs. were kept in a binder.

**269. RING. I/163. (Lb. 514, 514A), I/164. Mf. ŻIH—779; USHMM—10**

- 8.12.1941, Warsaw Ghetto
- Jewish Council at the Jewish Community in Warsaw. Department of Production (ul. Prosta 14), Letter of 8.12.1941 from the director of the Department B. [Beniamin] Gliksman to the Statistical Department
- Report (to 30.11.1941) on the activity of workshops operated by the Department of Production and other firms on the territory of the ghetto (Jüdische Produktion G.m.b.H.—Warschau).
- ***Description:*** original, typescript, German, Polish, 208×229, 222×302 mm, minor damage and losses of text, ss. 2, pp. 2.

  Ring. I/163—Attached note by H.W.: "Document to the problem of work in Wars[aw] g[hetto]. B. Gliksman (former Łódź industrialist, social activist in a section of Jewish Mutual Aid, later assumed position of director of an autonomous department of the Jewish Council, the Department of Production). Document forwarded to archive [by] Dr. S. Eiger."

  Ring. I/164—Attached note by H.W.: "The firm Jüdische Produktion G.m.b.H. in Warschau was a sui generic clearinghouse for orders and deliveries for a segment of the Warsaw Ghetto."

**270. RING. I/191. Mf. ŻIH—779; USHMM—10**

- 01.1942, Warsaw Ghetto
- Jewish Council in Warsaw, Report on the activity of the Chemical-Bacteriological Institute at the Department of Health of the Jewish Council for the period from 7 July to 31 Dec. 1941 (fragments)
- History of the Institute (ul. Pańska 3), established in June 1941[?] at initiative of Dr. Sara Zofia Binsztejn-Syrkin, director of the Health Department; discussion of results of the research and analysis conducted

(chemical-bacteriological examination of food, medical analyses).
- *Description:* original, hectographed typescript, handwritten manuscript, Polish, l., 178×135 mm, serious damage and losses of text, ss. 9, pp. 9.
  On p. 1 dedication: "Tłomackie 5 (Ż.S.S.). To the Highly Esteemed Chairman Kirszenbaum with expressions of respect M. [Mieczysław] Centnerszwer."
  On p. 8 are illegible autographs (ink) of physicians, laboratory assistants [?] (inter alia Mieczysław Centnerszwer).

### 271. RING. I/260. (Lb. 1189). Mf. ŻIH—780; USHMM—11

- 03.1942, Warsaw Ghetto
- "Weekly Bulletin. Intended for all functionaries and employees of the Health Department," no. 1/8.03.1942
- Current information and orders (office hours, wages, personnel matters), reprint of a letter from the Secretariat of the Jewish Council in the matter of Regina Judt (ul. Leszno 42), recollection of Adam Czerniaków about the late Maksymilian Schoenbach, attorney, precinct officer (obwodowy) [?] of the Order Service. Document signed by Dr. Mieczysław Kon, director of the Health Department.
- *Description:* original, typescript, Polish, 208×295 mm, ss. 2, pp. 2.
  Attached note by H.W.: "Submitted to the archive by Dr. [Izrael] Milejkowski."
  About Maksymilian Schoenbach, see *Czerniaków*, p. 255.

### 272. RING. I/787/2. (1106). Mf. ŻIH—826; USHMM—38

- Date unknown, place unknown. (Warsaw Ghetto [?])
- [Jewish Council in Warsaw?], Instruction for district policemen in the area of health
- Collection of regulations concerning maintenance of order and cleanliness in the town.
- *Description:* original, hectographed typescript, Polish, 208×296 mm, ss. 1, pp. 1.
  Doc. was kept in a binder.

### 273. RING. I/180. (Lb. 1629). Mf. ŻIH—779; USHMM—10

- 23.10.1941, Warsaw Ghetto
- Jewish Council at the Jewish Community in Warsaw. Department of Hometown Associations,[10] Letter of 23.10.1941 of D. Ersler to the Section for Supervision over Refugees and Homeless Fire Victims
- Plan of activity of the Department of Hometown Associations: provisioning assistance, health-medical aid, emergency aid and constructive[11] aid.
- *Description:* original [?], typescript with handwritten additions, pencil, Polish, 202×285 mm, ss. 2, pp. 2
  Attached note by H.W. in Yiddish: "H. Wasser."

### 274. RING. I/364. (Lb. 1512). Mf. ŻIH—782; USHMM—13

- After 21.07.1941, Warsaw Ghetto
- [The Commissioner for the Jewish Residential District in Warsaw], "Statute of the Provisioning Unit for the Jewish Residential District in Warsaw" (Warsaw, 21.07.1941)
- Statute of the Provisioning Unit of the Jewish District confirmed by Commissioner Dr. Heinz Auerswald and Dr. Franz Grassler.
- *Description:* original, hectographed typescript (signatures of Auerswald and Grassler inscribed by hand (WINK.*), ink), German, 185×260 mm, damage and losses of text, ss. 2, pp. 2.
  On p. 1 glued-on fragments of handwritten manuscript (WINK.*).
  Attached note by H.W. in Polish and Yiddish: "Document forwarded by Szmul Winter."
  On the statute, see *Czerniaków*, p. 201.

### 275. RING. I/1080 (1399). (Lb. 818). Mf. ŻIH—832; USHMM—44

- 03–07.1941, Warsaw Ghetto
- ZZ [Provisioning Unit] at the Jewish Council in Warsaw, Circulars
- Concerning distribution of food articles and industrial items, directed to distribution points (shops, bakeries, apartment house committees). Most of the letters are signed by H.Grasberg, I. Drybiński, or J. Gomoliński.
  1) dated 4.03.1941, on allocation of sugar on February cards as well as its collection in the A. Zonszajn and Son storehouse at ul. Gęsia 13;
  2) dated 5.03.1941, on allocation of firewood on March cards;
  3) dated 14.03.1941, on change of the price of flour and bread in March;
  4) dated 14.03.1941, on prices of bread in March;
  5) dated 1941 (letter no. 1771/41), on allocation of salt and payment of sums due to the firm of Rafał Mławski, ul. Ciepła 28;
  6) dated 16.03.1941, on the possibility of acquiring salt at the firm of Rafał Mławski, ul. Ciepła 28;
  7) dated 16.03.1941, on allocation of salt to distribution points;
  8) dated 21.03.1941, on allocation of marmalade on March cards and its collection at the storehouse of A. Zonszajn at ul. Gęsia 13;
  9) dated 21.03.1941, on allocation of marmalade on March cards and its collection in the

10. Ziomkostwa = Landsmenshaftn or Hometown Associations.

11. "Constructive," as opposed to one-time emergency relief, is meant for longer term.

storehouse of Fliederbaum at ul. Rynkowa 1;10) dated 21.03.1941, on allocation of marmalade on March cards and its collection in the storehouse of Perle, Adler, and Joskowicz at ul. Nalewki 28;

11) dated 21.03.1941, reminder in the matter of advance payment for collection of potatoes, under threat of withdrawal of permit for operation of a [distribution] point;

12) dated 21.03.1941, on the ban on levying from consumers a fee for registration of potato cards and as advance payment for potatoes, under threat of withdrawal of permit;

13) dated 21.03.1941, on allocation of sugar as well as its collection in the storehouse of Front, Fiszerów and Szporn at ul. Grzybowska 30;

14) dated 21.03.1941, in the matter of allocation of sugar for March and its collection in the storehouse of A. Zonszajn at ul. Gęsia 13;

15) dated 21.03.1941, reminder in the matter of payment for salt to the Rafał Mławski firm, ul. Ciepła 28;

16) dated 30.03.1941, on allocation of soap and laundry powder on March cards, on the deadline for ordering goods at the firm of I. Chelemer and Z. Cederbaum at ul. Leszno 52;

17) dated 1.04.1941, on allocation of salt for March;

18) dated 1.04.1941, on allocation of salt for March and order for the commodity at Rafał Mławski's ul. Ciepła 28;

19) dated 3.04.1941, on allocation of marmalade for March and its collection in the storehouse of Fliederbaum at ul. Rynkowa 1;

19a) dated 3.04.1941, on allocation of marmalade for March and its collection in the storehouse of A. Zonszajn at ul. Gęsia 13;

19b) dated 3.04.1941, on allocation of marmalade for March and its collection in the storehouse of Perle, Adler and Joskowicz at ul. Nalewki 28;

20) dated 16.04.1941, on allocation of sugar for April and its collection in the storehouse of A. Zonszajn at ul. Gęsia 13;

21) dated 16.04.1941, on allocation of sugar for April and its collection in the storehouse of Front, Fiszerów and Szporn at ul. Grzybowska 30;

22) dated 16.04.1941, on invalidation of some of the May provisioning cards;

23) dated 26.04.1941, on allocation of salt on the April cards and its collection at the Rafał Mławski firm at ul. Ciepła 28;

24) dated 27.04.1941, on allocation of laundry powder on May cards and its collection at the firm of I. Chelemer and Z. Cederbaum at ul. Leszno 52;

25) dated 25.05.1941, on allocation of salt on June cards and its collection at the Rafał Mławski firm at ul. Ciepła 28.

26) dated 26.05.1941, on withdrawal of distribution authorizations of 8 shops with a reminder of the regulations governing distribution points;

27) dated 30.05.1941, on allocation of soap and laundry powder on June cards and their collection at the firm of I. Chelemer and Z. Cederbaum at ul. Leszno 52;

28) dated 30.05.1941, on allocation of pickled cabbage on May cards and its collection in the storehouse of Ch.Cymes, Ch. Tyk and L. Szpidbaum at ul. Nowolipie 30;

29) dated 30.05.1941, on allocation of sugar on June cards and its collection in the storehouse of Front, Fiszerów and Szporn at ul. Grzybowska 30 (on the letter is stamped: "deposit for a jute sack is zł 30");

30) dated 30.05.1941, on allocation of sugar on June cards and its collection in the storehouse of A. Zonszajn at ul. Gęsia 13;

31) dated 8.06.1941, warning about counterfeit June cards, methods of identifying them, list of numbers of stolen or lost cards;

32) dated 10.06.1941, on allocation of saccharine;

33) dated 13.06.1941, on allocation of matches on June cards, with collection in the storehouse of B. Halpern at ul. Leszno 24;

34) dated 17.06.1941, on allocation of 1 egg each and their collection in the firm of S. Segał and C. Sztybel at ul. Zimna 3;

35) dated 21.06.1941, on allocation of canned beets on June cards as well as the amount of deposit for barrels and cans;

36) dated 23.06.1941, on allocation of ersatz coffee (kawy zbożowej) on June cards;

37) dated 29.06.1941, list of numbers of stolen and lost food cards for July;

38) dated 17.07.1941, on allocation of rhubarb marmalade on July cards;

39) dated 17.07.1941, on the possibility of free sale of unrealized allotments of canned beets or return of unopened and not outdated barrels of beets;

40) Date unknown, "Instruction no. 2 for the distribution network of potatoes and vegetables."

- ***Description:*** original (no. 4, 16 in 2 copies), hectographed typescript, stamps, Polish, 150×204, 220×330 mm, minor damage and losses of text, ss. 43, pp. 43.

  Attached note by H.W. in Yiddish: "Submitted by Szmuel Winter from Włocławek, an Oyneg Shabes coworker."

  Doc. 33—Published: *Przewodnik*, p. 221 (photocopy).

276. **RING. I/775 (1099), I/776/1 (1099), I/777/5 (1099). Mf. ŻIH—825; USHMM—37. RING. I/775. Mf. ŻIH—836; USHMM—67. RING. I/1220/86. Mf. ŻIH—835; USHMM—47**

- 03.1941–03.1942, Warsaw Ghetto
- ZZ (Provisioning Unit) at the Jewish Council in Warsaw. Chairman of the Jewish Council in Warsaw, Announcements concerning allocation of foods and other products for the ghetto's residents

 Announcements: Ring. I/775
 1) dated 12.03.1941, provisioning cards for April 1941
 1a) dated 12.03.1941, allocation of marmalade
 2) dated 15.03.1941, price of bread on March cards
 3), 4), and 5) [respectively] dated 24.04 (no original), 26.04 (no original), and 28.04.1941, allocation of bread on May cards
 5a) dated 26.04.1941, allocation of salt
 5aa) dated 5.05.1941, allocation of bread and sugar for May
 6) and 7) dated 5.05. (no original) and 26.05.1941, allocation of salt on June cards
 7a) dated 1.06.1941, allocation of soap and laundry powder
 7aa) dated 5.06.1941, allocation of provisioning cards for July
 8) and 9) dated 5.06. (original missing) and 10.06.1941, allocation of saccharine on June cards
 10) dated 13.06.1941, allocation of matches on June cards
 11) dated 21.06.1941, allocation of saccharine on June cards
 12) dated 23.06.1941, allocation of bread on June cards ("additional for precincts with a predominantly poor population") as well as announcement of allocation of beets, grain coffee, sugar, and candies
 13) dated 24.06.1941, allocation of sugar on July cards
 14) dated 24.06.1941, allocation of candies on children's cards
 14a) dated 18.07.1941, allocation of provisioning cards for August
 14aa) dated 7.08.1941, allocation of provisioning cards for September
 15), 16), and 16a) dated 31.07. (no original), 7.08. (no original) and 11.08.1941, allocation of salt on August cards
 17) dated 15 08.1941, allocation of ersatz coffee on August cards
 18) dated 26.08.1941, allocation of soap on August cards
 19) dated 27.08.1941, allocation of candies on children's cards
 19a) dated 31.08.1941, surcharges on bread and sugar
 Ring. I/1220—19b) dated 20.12.1941, allocation of sugar on December cards, Ring. I/776/1—20) dated 15.01.1942, allocation of salt on January cards
 20a) dated 19.01.1942, allocation of cards for February
 20aa) dated 20.01.1942, allocation of bread and sugar
 21), 22), and 23) dated 19.01., 20.01. (original missing) and 23.01.1942, allocation of rutabaga on January cards
 24) dated 24.01.1942, allocation of sugar on January cards
 24a) dated 27.01.1942, allocation of soap and laundry powder
 24aa) dated 30.01.1942, allocation of free bread and sugar
 25) and 26) dated 30.01. (missing original), 13.02.1942, allocation of 2 eggs for children
 26a) dated 3.03.1942, allocation of soap and laundry powder
 26aa) dated 19.03.1942, allocation of bread and matzah (two variants of the same announcement)
 27) and 28) dated 3.03. (original missing) and dated 23.03.1942 (restamped 24.03.), allocation of sugar on March cards
 Ring. I/777/5—298) dated 11.1941, "Instructions" on procedure for frozen potatoes.

- ***Description:*** Ring. I/775—original (Announcement: 2), 9),12), 13), 14), 14aa), 16a), 17), 18), 19) in 2 copies; 10) in 3 copies), printed, German, Polish, Yiddish, 295×412, 470×632 mm, ss. 34, pp. 34; Ring. I/776/1—original (Announcement: 20), 23), 24), 24aa), 25), 26), 26a), 26aa), 27) in 2 copies; 20a), 21), 22), 24a) in 3 copies), printed, German, Polish, Yiddish, 313×424, 530×675 mm, ss. 23, pp. 23; Ring. I/777/5—original, printed, Polish, Yiddish, 204×148 mm, ss. 1, pp. 1; Ring. I/1220/86—original, printed, German, Polish,Yiddish, 275×340 mm, damage and losses of text, ss. 1, pp. 1.

 See HWC, 46/1–4 (4 copies of docs. dated 30.03.1941–21.06.1941); no information about which announcements are referred to).
 Docs. 26–28—Published: *Przewodnik*, pp. 409, 418, 422 (photocopy).

277. **RING. I/777/2. (1099). Mf. ŻIH—825; USHMM—37.**

- Date unknown, Warsaw
- [Provisioning Unit (ZZ) at the Jewish Council in Warsaw?] Leaflet: "Recipe for Preparation of Rutabaga"
- Recipes for: stewed rutabaga, baked rutabaga, and tsholnt stew (czulent).
- ***Description:*** original (2 copies), printed, Polish, Yiddish, 122×178 mm, ss. 1, pp. 2.

 Printed by A. Kejzman (ul. Leszno 24).
 Published: *Przewodnik*, p. 429 (photocopy).

## 278. RING. I/776/2. (1099). Mf. ŻIH–825; USHMM–37

a)

- 1941/1942, Warsaw Ghetto
- [Provisioning Unit (ZZ) at the Jewish Council in Warsaw], "Food Card no. 450000 for the month of January 1942."
- ***Description:*** original, printed, German, Polish, 209×194 mm, ss. 1, pp. 1.

  Sheet with overprint: "Hungry and cold. For the poor and homeless child. . ."

  In HWC, 46/5 are cards (2) no. 450000 for June and November 1941, as well as no. 187405 and 460000 dated 1941).

  Published: *Przewodnik*, after p. 372 (photocopy).

b)

- 1941/1942, Warsaw Ghetto
- Provisioning Unit (ZZ) at the Jewish Council in Warsaw, "Supplemental food card no. 003794 and 015000 for the month of January 1942."
- ***Description:*** original, printed, German, Polish, 162×193, 162×170 mm, minor damage and losses of text (no. 015000), ss. 2, pp. 2.

  Card no. 003794 drawn up for Hirsz Wasser, ul. Muranowska 6. Some of the coupons cut off. Registration no.: "586."

c)

- 01.1942, Warsaw Ghetto
- [Provisioning Unit (ZZ) at the Jewish Council in Warsaw], "Food Card no. 251183, 251184, 450000 for the month of February 1942."
- ***Description:*** original, printed, German, Polish, 210×192 mm, minor damage and losses of text (no. 450000), ss. 3, pp. 3.

  Cards no. 251183, 251184 drawn up for Hirsz and Bluma Wasser, ul. Muranowska 6. Some of the coupons cut off. Stamped on the reverse: "Sale of tea, cocoa . . ."

d)

- 01.1942, Warsaw Ghetto
- Provisioning Unit (ZZ) at the Jewish Council in Warsaw, "Supplemental Food Card no. 006375 and 022000 for month of February 1942."
- ***Description:*** original, printed, German, Polish, 160×173, 160×194 mm, ss. 2, pp. 2.

  Card no. 006375 drawn up for Hirsz Wasser, [ul. Muranowska 6]. Some of the coupons are cut off; stamped: "Mutual Aid Circle of Employees of the Jewish Social Welfare in Warsaw" (Koło Samopomocy Pracowników Żydowskiej Opieki Społecznej w Warszawie), stamped on the reverse: "Comradely Mutual Aid . . ." ("Samopomoc Koleżeńska . . .") and registration number "1761."

e)

- 02.1942, Warsaw Ghetto
- [Provisioning Unit (ZZ) at the Jewish Council in Warsaw], "Food Card no. 400000 for the month of March 1942."
- ***Description:*** original, printed, German, Polish, 208×194 mm, ss. 1, pp. 1.

  Card with the printed header: "Check the weight and quality of goods! Notify the Provisioning Unit about deficiencies."

f)

- 02.1942, Warsaw Ghetto
- Provisioning Unit (ZZ) at the Jewish Council in Warsaw, "Supplemental Food Card no. 016484 for the month of February 1942."
- ***Description:*** original, printed, German, Polish, 158×175 mm, ss. 1, pp. 1.

  Card drawn up for Hirsz Wasser, [ul. Muranowska 6]. On the reverse, an illegible stamp and registration number: "817."

g)

- Date unknown, Warsaw Ghetto
- Provisioning Unit (ZZ) at the Jewish Council in Warsaw, "Supplemental Card for Children no. 100000."
- ***Description:*** original, printed, German, Polish, 140×154 mm, ss. 1, pp. 1.

  Card with the header: "Remind Mama that each of us must help the poor child!"

  Published: *Przewodnik*, p. 410 (photocopy).

h)

- 09.1941–01.1942, Warsaw Ghetto
- Leaflet: Circular of the Humor Department of the Provisioning Unit of the Jewish District in Warsaw. (01.[1942])
- Information about allocation of humor on ration cards. [Invitation to the premiere of a skit entitled "Żarty na karty" (Jokes on Ration Card) on 17.01.[1942] at the office of the Provisioning Unit, ul. Leszno 12]
- ***Description:*** original, typescript, Polish, 211×297 mm, ss. 1, pp. 2.

  At the top, information by H.W. in Yiddish (ink): "108–1942/1 January."

  Doc. written on the reverse of Food Card no. 449777 drawn up for: "Rawicki F." This "Circular" was written before one of the control coupons of the card was cut off.

  Notation about the doc. on basis of the memoirs of A. Marianowicz, *Życie surowo wzbronione* [Life Is Strictly Prohibited], Warsaw 1995, pp. 73–78, illustration after p. 208.

  Pub. (photocopy): A. Marianowicz, op.cit.; *Przewodnik*, p. 572 (photocopy); *Dzieci*, pp. 288–289.

## 279. RING. I/82. Mf. ŻIH–776; USHMM–7

- 02.1942, Warsaw Ghetto
- Provisioning Unit (ZZ) of the Jewish District.

Statistical Desk, "Survey in the matter of consumption. Report. December 1941." (Feb. 1942)
- Purpose, method, and results of the survey conducted among various socio-occupational groups in the ghetto (attached 2 tables and questionnaire).
- ***Description:*** original and transcript [?], typescript and hectographed typescript (attached no. 1—"Survey"), Polish, 200×300 mm, 205×275 mm, 175×383 mm, 215×294 mm, damage and losses of text, ss. 33, pp. 39.

  Document was preserved in 4 copies (different) with uniform preserved content; attached in 2 or 4 copies.

  Published: *BFG*, vol. 2, no. 1–4 (1949), pp. 273–287.

**280. RING. I/1220/8. Mf. ŻIH—835; USHMM—47**

- 03.1941, Warsaw Ghetto
- Provisioning Unit (ZZ) at the Jewish Council in Warsaw. Desk for Bakeries and Distrib[ution] of Bread, Communiqué dated 31.03.1941, "To All Apartment house committees."
- Notation about issuance of bread on 2–4.04.1941 on cards dated Feb. 1941.
- ***Description:*** original, hectographed typescript, Polish, 218×168 mm, ss. 1, pp. 1.

**281. RING. I/1220/17. Mf. ŻIH—835; USHMM—47**

- After 09.1941, Warsaw Ghetto
- Administration of the Food Cooperative of Empl[oyees] of the Jewish Council in Warsaw, Note concerning activity of the Provisioning Unit (ZZ) (fragment)
- The Food Cooperative was established on 23.05.1940 [?].
- ***Description:*** original or transcript, typescript, Polish, 173×120, 208×160 mm, ss. 2, pp. 4.

**282. RING. I/575/1. Mf. ŻIH—792; USHMM—23**

- After 1941, Warsaw Ghetto
- Jewish Council in Warsaw, Correspondence concerning the Provisioning Unit (ZZ) (fragments)
- Concerning the legal charter of the Provisioning Unit (ZZ)
- ***Description:*** transcript, handwritten manuscript (WINK.*), ink, Polish, 210×270 mm, extensive damage and losses of text, ss. 3, pp. 5.

**283. RING. I/575/2. Mf. ŻIH—792; USHMM—23; RING. I/502/A. Mf. ŻIH—788; USHMM—19**

- 04.1942 [?], Warsaw Ghetto
- NN., "Note in the matter of the material situation of employees of the Jewish Council and the Provisioning Unit's (Zakł[adu] Zaopatr[ywania]) attitude toward them" (fragments)
- Differences in pay of employees of the Provisioning Unit (ZZ) and the Jewish Council.
- ***Description:*** Ring. I/572/2—original or transcript, handwritten manuscript (WINK.*), ink, Polish, 210×175, 170×130 mm, serious damage and losses of text, ss. 6, pp. 11; Ring. I/502/a—transcript (2 copies of the first page), typescript, Polish, 144×147, 145×128 mm, serious damage and losses of text, ss. 2, pp. 2.

  On the reverse of p. 5 [?] (handwritten) three original signatures (inter alia M. Zabłudowski [?])

  Attached note by H.W.: "J. Winkler." [note is in the manuscript Ring. I/663]

**284. RING. I/779/3. (1099). Mf. ŻIH—825; USHMM—37**

- 1942, Warsaw Ghetto
- Provisioning Unit (ZZ), Announcement about the *kashrut* ("kosherness") of candies distributed in bags with the inscription "Passover 1942."
- ***Description:*** original, printed, Yiddish, 280×210 mm, ss. 1, pp. 1.

**285. RING. I/1158/3 (1477). (Lb. 1592). Mf. ŻIH—833; USHMM—45**

- Date unknown, Warsaw Ghetto
- Provisioning Unit of the Jewish District [at the Jewish Council] in Warsaw, wrapper for ginger snaps (100 gr.).
- ***Description:*** original, printed, Polish, Yiddish, 138×150 mm, ss. 2, pp. 2.

  On p. 2 stamp: "Tea Biscuit Manufacturer Boruchowicz and [. . .] Warsaw."

  Published: *Przewodnik*, p. 416 (photocopy, p. 1); *Dzieci*, p. 290 (photocopy, p. 1).

**286. RING. I/1133 (1452). Mf. ŻIH—833; USHMM—45**

- Before 21.02. [. . . ?], Warsaw Ghetto
- [Provisioning Unit at the Jewish Council] Fuel Department (ul. Leszno 14), Invitation to an artistic evening on 21.02.[. . . ?] at ul. Leszno 14
- Income from the event is designated for the benefit of the "Broszków" shelter. Honorary Committee: Mr. and Mrs. Sztolcman, Mr. and Mrs. Marynower, Mr. and Mrs. Kramsztyk, Mr. and Mrs. Diamand, Mr. and Mrs. Czarnecki, Mr. and Mrs. Zabłudowski, Mr. and Mrs. Rozental.
- ***Description:*** original, printed, Polish, 160×98 mm, ss. 2, pp. 2.

  On p. 1 no. (printed): "12."

**287. RING. I/1126 (1445). (Lb. 24). Mf. ŻIH—833; USHMM—45**

- After 26.06.1940, Warsaw
- Jewish Council in Warsaw, Coupon no. 16001 entitling one to receive a food card without payment.
- ***Description:*** original, printed, stamp of the Jewish Council in Warsaw, Polish, 98×89 mm, ss. 1, pp. 1.

  See Ring. II/146.

## 288. RING. I/1092 (1411). (Lb. 576). Mf. ŻIH—833; USHMM—45

- 1942, Warsaw Ghetto
- [Jewish Council in Warsaw], "List of persons to whom were allotted fr[ee] provisioning coupons"
- Two lists (6 and 18 names) of persons entitled to pick up cards; they include address, number of family members, as well as the signature of the one picking up [the card].
- ***Description:*** original, printed, handwritten (several handwritings, inter alia H.W.*), ink, pencil, Polish, 208×290 mm, ss. 2, pp. 2.

  Attached note by H.W. in Yiddish: "By H.W."
  Index:
  Jakub Tytelman (ul. Muranowska 40)
  Perla Tytelman (ul. Gęsia 10)
  Hersz Klajman (Pl. Parysowski 15[?])
  Luba Majer [?] (ul. Nowolipki 19, apt. 7)
  Karmel [?] (ul. Leszno 15, apt. 27)
  Zysla Lebensold (ul. Nowolipie 36, apt. 6)
  Chaskiel Bratsztajn (ul. Nowolipie 14)
  Noel Zysman (ul. Nowolipie 57)
  Daniel Fligelman (ul. Śliska 24)
  Abram Blumsztajn (ul. Nowolipie 23)
  Szlama Gulbas (ul. Przebieg 1)
  Hersz Wasser (ul. Muranowska 6, apt. 15)
  Mosze Rajman (ul. Śliska 62)
  Hersz Rajman (ul. Śliska 62)
  Cyrla Rajman (ul. Śliska 62)
  Chaim Rajman (ul. Śliska 62)
  Rojza Rajman (ul. Śliska 62)
  Dwojra Sztatman (ul. Wołyńska 9)
  Izak Sztatman (ul. Miła 20)
  Frajda Wachenhauzer (ul. Nowolipki 60, apt. 8)
  Krauze Wolf

## 289. RING. I/1197 (1516). Mf. ŻIH—834; USHMM—46

- Date unknown, Warsaw Ghetto
- Sz. [Szmul Samuel] Winter, Letter "To the Chairman of the Jewish Council in Warsaw"
- Concerning the arrest by the Order Service of Salomon, chairman of an undetermined apartment house committee in the Warsaw Ghetto.
- ***Description:*** transcript, typescript, Polish, 185×235 mm, extensive damage and losses of text, ss. 1, pp. 1.

## 290. RING. I/1220/67. Mf. ŻIH—835; USHMM—47

- After 1.04.1942, Warsaw Ghetto
- Jewish Council in Siedlce, Letter to [Jewish Council in Warsaw] (fragment)

  Concerning Zylbersztejn and NN.
- ***Description:*** transcript, handwritten manuscript (WINK.*), ink, Polish, 160×145 mm, serious damage and losses of text, ss. 1, pp. 2.

## 291. RING. I/1220/69A. Mf. ŻIH—835; USHMM—47

- After 29.03.1942, Warsaw Ghetto
- Board of Mutual Aid (Samopomocy) [. . .], Letter of 29.03.1942 to Chairman of the Jewish Council in Warsaw (fragment)
- Concerning provision of food products in the Warsaw Ghetto.
- ***Description:*** transcript, typescript, Polish, 195×174, 200×156 mm, serious damage and losses of text, ss. 2, pp. 2.

  See Ring. I/776.

## 292. RING. I/215. Mf. ŻIH—780; USHMM—11. RING. I/322. Mf. ŻIH—781; USHMM—12

a) **Ring. I/215. (Lb. 867, 867a)**
- After 26.06.1941 [?], Warsaw Ghetto
- Letter [of 26.06.1941?] from workers of tailoring workshop no. 12 at ul. Prosta 14 (2nd floor)[12] to Adam Czerniaków
- Complaint against the difficult working conditions, without pay and suitable feeding, as well as against engineer Lipszyc, director of the workshop, who threatens repressive measures for lack of obedience. Letter was not delivered, since the workers feared that it would lead to worsening of their situation.
- ***Description:*** transcript (2 copies), typescript, Polish, minor damage and losses of text, ss. 4, pp. 4.

  On p. 1 notation of H.W. "By Mr. Ch." Attached note by H.W. in Yiddish: "Submitted by [Bencyjon] Chilinowicz, Jewish journalist."
  See HWC, 34/1 (different transcript with handwritten annotation, pp. 2).

b) **Ring. I/322**
- 6.07.1941 [?], Warsaw Ghetto
- Letter dated 6.07.1941 from workers of the tailors' workshop no. 12 at ul. Prosta 14 (2nd floor) to Adam Czerniakow
- Information about a workers' strike (1.07.1941) as a sign of protest against the mistreatment and bad food. Moldy bread was issued to workers who had to pay for it.
- ***Description:*** original or transcript, (handwritten manuscript, ink, 142×200 mm), transcript (handwritten manuscript—JG*, pencil, 142×200 mm), Polish, ss. 5, pp. 7.

  On p. 1 (transcript—JG*) information from H.W. (ink): "By [Bencyjon Chilinowicz?]"
  Part of the doc. was transferred from Ring. I/348.
  From this letter it appears that the first letter, despite the notation on it, was delivered to Czerniaków [?].

12. In American usage, this would be the third floor.

See HWC, 34/2 (two copies of the transcript, handwritten manuscript, pencil, ss. 3).

**293. RING. I/1125 (1444). (Lb. 23). Mf. ŻIH—833; USHMM—45**

- Before 25.11.1940, Warsaw
- Szmul Fersztenberg (ul. Mirowska 3, apt. 11), "Temporary Pass for Jews," no. 15953 issued by the Jewish Council in Warsaw, valid until 25.11.1940.
- ***Description:*** original, printed, manuscript, ink, stamp, German, 144×109 mm, ss. 1, pp. 1.
  Doc. was kept in a binder.

## *"THE THIRTEEN" ("TRZYNASTKA")*[13]

**294. RING. I/359. (Lb. 553). Mf. ŻIH—782; USHMM—13**

- After 25.01.1941, Warsaw Ghetto
- "Statut der Überwachungsstelle zur Bekämpfung des Schleichhandels und der Preiswucherei im jüdischen Wohnbezirk" (Statute of the Office to Combat Illicit Trade and Price Gouging in the Jewish Residential District) (fragment).
- ***Description:*** transcript, typescript, German, 207×290 mm, minor damage and losses of text, ss. 1, pp. 1.

**295. RING. I/1106/3 (1425). (Lb. 1716, 1717, 1718). Mf. ŻIH—833; USHMM—45**

- 6.03.1942, Warsaw Ghetto
- Kommissarische Verwaltung Sichergestelter Grunstücke in Warschau. Der Jüdische Sonderbeauftragte (Appointed Administration of Secured Real Estate in Warsaw. The Responsible Jewish Official), A. [Abraham] Gancwajch, Letter of 6.03.1942 to chairman of the apartment house committee at ul. Karmelicka 9 with invitation to a conference on 7.03.1942 at ul. Leszno 13.
- ***Description:*** original, typescript, stamp of "The Thirteen," Polish, 208×150 mm, ss. 1, pp. 1.
  Published: *Przewodnik*, pp. 221 (photocopy).

## *JEWISH SOCIAL SELF-HELP (ŻYDOWSKA SAMOPOMOC SPOŁECZNA)*

**296. RING. I/184. (Lb. 958, 52). Mf. ŻIH—779; USHMM—10.**

- After 09.1940, place unknown
- "Regulamin Żydowskiego Towarzystwa Opieki Społecznej" (Charter of the Jewish Social Welfare Association).
- ***Description:*** original or transcript, typescript, Polish, 205×285 mm, minor damage and losses of text, ss. 5, pp. 5

**297. RING. I/78. (Lb. 1443). Mf. ŻIH—775; USHMM—6**

- 15.12.1940, Warsaw Ghetto
- Bulletin "Statistik fun ISA" [Statistics of Jewish Social Self-Help], no. 8
- Report of activity for the period 09.1939–09.1940. Information concerning: number of persons aided by 30.06.1940; current registration and statistical records for the period 07–09.1940. Numerous tables and statistical analyses. Attached cover letter dated 15.12.1940 signed by Menachem Linder.
- ***Description:*** original, hectographed typescript, Polish, Yiddish, 205×294 mm, ss. 27, pp. 27.
  On reverse of p. 27 information in Yiddish (pencil): "Central Refugees Commission" [?]
  See Ring. I/79.

**298. RING. I/79. (Lb. 1057). Mf. ŻIH—775; USHMM—6**

- 15.02.1941, Warsaw Ghetto
- Bulletin "Statistik fun YISA" [Statistics of Jewish Social Self-Help], no. 9
- Statistical report of the activity for the period 11–12.1940 (number of persons benefitting from aid, participation in the aid campaign for people displaced into the ghetto, care of children). Tables and statistical analyses. Attached cover letter dated 15.02.1941 signed by Menachem Linder.
- ***Description:*** original, hectographed typescript, Yiddish, 208×295 mm, ss. 19, pp. 19.
  Attached note by H.W. in Yiddish: "Composed [by] M. Linder, MA, forwarded by H.W."
  About Menachem Linder, see *Kronika getta*, pp. 558–562.

**299. RING. I/80/1. Mf. ŻIH—775; USHMM—6**

- 19.12.1940, Warsaw Ghetto
- [Menachem Linder (Menakhem Linder)], "A yor YISA. Kitser fun a yor—barikht ofgegebn oyf farzamlungen fun YISA-askonim dem 3 tn, 11tn un 18tn XII 1940 durkh Menakhem Linder fun statistishn opteyl fun YISA" [A Year of Jewish Social Self-Help. Summary of an Annual Report Presented at Meetings of JSS Activists on the 3rd, 11th and 18th of Dec. 1940 by Menachem Linder of the Statistical Department of JSS]
- Report of JSS activity for the period 09.1939–09.1940. Lists, tables, diagram, discussion of the results of individual sections (collection of funds, levies, collection of clothing, consumers dept., training and supervision, youth desk, care of children, records).

13. "The Thirteen" (Trzynastka in Polish, Di draytsentl in Yiddish, after its address on Leszno Street) was a Jewish police "agency" affiliated with the Gestapo and headed by Abraham Gancwajch.

- *Description:* original, hectographed typescript, Yiddish, 205×295 mm, minor damage and losses of text, ss. 8, pp. 8.
  Published: *BFG*, vol. 1, no. 2 (1948), pp. 3–13.

### 300. RING. I/37/2. Mf. ŻIH—772; USHMM—3

- After 11.1940, Warsaw Ghetto
- [ŻSS (Jewish Social Self-Help)] NN., Article (report) on the activity of Jewish Social Self-Help (fragment)
- Polemical discussion of the activities of Jewish Social Self-Help: aid for the population, supplementary food, apartment house committees, etc. (attached list).
- *Description:* original, hectographed typescript with handwritten additions (pencil), Yiddish, text illegible in places, 217×338 mm, missing first page, ss. 4, pp. 4.
  Doc. was buried together with a doc. of Ring. I/76.

### 301. RING. I/37/1. Mf. ŻIH—772; USHMM—3

- 08.1941, Warsaw Ghetto
- [ŻSS (Jewish Social Self-Help)] Leaflet: "Yidishe gezelshaft far aleynhilf" [Jewish Society for Self-Help] (Warsaw, 08.1941)
- Appeal for contributions for social purposes.
- *Description:* original, hectographed typescript, Yiddish, 216×335 mm, ss. 1, pp. 1.

### 302. RING. I/210. (Lb. 884). Mf. ŻIH—779; USHMM—10

- After 15.01.1942, Warsaw Ghetto
- "Protokol fun der farzamlung vegn rateven di arestirte yidn far ibergeyn di grenitsn fun yidishn voyn-batsirk in Varshe, forgekumen in Varshe, dem 15 januar 1942, in lokal fun yidishn sotsyaln shuts (Tlomackie 5)" [Minutes of the Meeting about Rescuing the Jews Arrested for Crossing the Boundaries of the Jewish Residential District in Warsaw, Held in Warsaw on 15 January 1942, in the Offices of the Jewish Social Self-Help (Tłomackie 5)]
- Issue of buying the release of 300 Jews held in the prison at ul. Gęsiej, for 1500 sheepskin coats (kożuchów) worth 1.5 million zł.; organization of a collection for this purpose. Present: Emanuel Ringelblum, Icchak Giterman, Rabbi Rogoźnicki, Starobiński, Menachem M. Kon, A.Z. Frydman, Jewish Council member Rozen, Szymon Huberband, as well as representatives of the apartment house committees.
- *Description:* transcript, typescript, Yiddish, 205×290 mm, ss. 2, pp. 2.
  Attached note by H.W. in Yiddish: "Forwarded by Starobiński, director of the Finance Commission." In Inventory:[14] "F. Stabumiński [sic], director of the Finance Department in the ghetto."

### 303. RING. I/1220/44. Mf. ŻIH—835; USHMM—47

- 5.02.1942, Warsaw Ghetto
- I. [Izaak] Nisenbaum, Rabbi (Warsaw, ul. Ogrodowa 8a, apt. 21), Letter of 5.02.1942 to I. [Icchak] Giterman (ŻTOS, ul. Tłomackie 5)
- Proposal for acceptance into the ŻTOS (Jewish Society for Social Welfare) of the following persons: L. Szczarański (ul. Majzla [Mejzelsa] 4), Simcha Jubiler (ul. Dzielna 3), Jehuda Jafet (D. Szapiro) (ul. Nowolipie 55), Mosze Ginzburg (ul. Nalewki 38), Meir Merenwinder (ul. Twarda 27).
- *Description:* original, handwritten manuscript, ink, Yiddish, 224×290 mm, ss. 1, pp. 1.
  Published: *Selected Documents*, p. 354.

### 304. RING. I/1114 (1433). (Lb. 520). Mf. ŻIH—833; USHMM—45

- 3.05.1942, Warsaw Ghetto
- ŻSS-KOM [Jewish Social Self-Help—Municipal Guardian Committee]—Warsaw, engineer H. Kalnicki, Letter of 3.05.1942 to [Dawid] Chołodenko (ul. Żelazna 101)
- Invitation to the opening ceremony on 5.05.1942 of the preschool kindergarten of House of the Child (Dom Dziecka) at ul. Wolność 14.
- *Description:* original, typescript, Polish, 206×288 mm, k.1, pp. 1.
  On the reverse of the document calculations (pencil).
  Published: *Przewodnik*, p. 434 (photocopy); *Dzieci*, pp. 293–294.

### 305. RING. I/321. (Lb. 21). Mf. ŻIH—781; USHMM—12

- Date unknown, Warsaw Ghetto
- ŻSS [Jewish Social Self-Help], Letter to Amt des Distriktchefs Abteilung für Volksaufklärung und Propaganda in Warschau [Office of the District Governor Department for Public Enlightenment and Propaganda in Warsaw]
- Request for permission to open a lending library.
- *Description:* transcript, typescript, German, 214×274 mm, minor damage and losses of text, ss. 1, pp. 1.

### 306. RING. I/1220/68. Mf. ŻIH—835; USHMM—47

- After 04.1940, place unknown
- KK ŻSS [Coordinating Commission Jewish Social Self-Help]. Leaflet: *Nie jesteś sam! Nie żyjesz tylko dla siebie!* [You're not alone! You're not living only for yourself!] (fragment).

14. The abbreviation "inw." in the original refers to the first inventory or catalog of the Ringelblum Archive.

- ***Description:*** original, hectographed typescript, Polish 208×148 mm, ss. 1, pp. 1.
  On reverse, calculations and notations in Yiddish (pencil): names (Szlomo, Josef, Ruta, Mikel [?]).

## 307. RING. I/37/3. Mf. ŻIH—772; USHMM—3

- After 11.1941, Warsaw Ghetto
- Sign: *Jüdischer Wohlfahrtsverein in Warschau* [Jewish Welfare Association in Warsaw].
- ***Description:*** original, printed, German, Polish, 115×245 mm, signs of thumbtacks (2), ss. 1, pp. 1.
  At the top is a stamp (India ink): "Żydowska Opieka Społeczna Wydział Kuchen Ludowych w Warszawie" [Jewish Social Welfare Department of Public Kitchens in Warsaw].

## 308. RING. I/1220/9. Mf. ŻIH—835; USHMM—47

- 1941, Warsaw Ghetto
- ŻTOS (Jewish Society for Social Welfare), Form of a declaration filled out by persons seeking aid at ŻTOS.
- ***Description:*** original, hectographed typescript, Polish, 210×295 mm, ss. 1, pp. 1.

## 309. RING. I/1158/1 (1477). (Lb. 1592). Mf. ŻIH—833; USHMM—45

- Date unknown, Warsaw Ghetto
- ŻSS (Jewish Social Self-Help), Aid for war victims. Certificate acknowledging contribution of 20 groszy.
- ***Description:*** original, printed, Polish, Yiddish, 46×32 mm, ss. 1, pp. 1.

## 310. RING. I/197. Mf. ŻIH—779; USHMM—10

- After 9.07.1940, Warsaw
- "Memorandum from directors of boarding homes in the matter of the severe plight of Centos [Association of Societies for Care of Jewish Children and Orphans] orphanages at the present moment [addressed] to A.J.D.C. [American Joint Distribution Committee] and Ż.S.S." (9.07.1940)
- On 8.07.1940, at a gathering of directors of boarding homes supported by Centos, a list was prepared of the greatest shortages and needs of these institutions, connected with: expenditures for daily needs—institutional, pedagogical and didactical—as well as for employees' pay. The memorandum was signed by: A. [Aron] Koniński and Dr. [Rafał] Taubenszlag in the name of the directors of 12 orphanages (attached "List of boarding homes maintained and subsidized by Centos").
- ***Description:*** transcript, typescript, Polish, 224×288 mm, ss. 3, pp. 3.

## 311. RING. I/334. (Lb. 575). Mf. ŻIH—781; USHMM—12

- 1940, Warsaw Ghetto
- ŻSS [Jewish Social Self-Help]. Centos Society. Department of Social Work, "Instruction for Children's Guardians."
- At apartment house committees, children's guardians were hired to look after the children of the given building.
- ***Description:*** original, hectographed typescript, Polish, 210×285 mm, minor damage and losses of text, ss. 1, pp. 2.
  Doc. with notations and drawings (handwritten manuscript, ink) by Paulina Landau, MA.
  Published: *Dzieci*, pp. 173–175 (only p. 1).

## 312. RING. I/1121 (1440). (Lb. 1674). Mf. ŻIH—833; USHMM—45

- Before 15.11.[1941], Warsaw Ghetto
- Związek Towarzystw Opieki nad Dziećmi i Sierotami Żydowskimi "Centos" (Centos Association of Societies for Care for Jewish Children and Orphans) (ul. Leszno 2), Invitation to the opening of the central library for children on 15.11.1941 at the library (ul. Leszno 67, apt. 49)
- Program of the ceremony: Roza Symchowicz, Dir. L. [Lejb, Leon] Neustadt, and Dr. A. [Adolf] Berman; artistic portion: Chana Braz (recitation) and S. Gordon-Kamińska (song). Invitation signed by: A. [Adolf] Berman and I. Gitler.
- ***Description:*** original, hectographed typescript, stamp, Polish, Yiddish, 220×293 mm, ss. 1, pp. 1.
  Published: *Dzieci*, pp. 280–282.

## 313. RING. I/1220/10. Mf. ŻIH—835; USHMM—47

- Date unknown, Warsaw Ghetto
- [Centos?], Form: "Statement of Children's Attendance and Fees" for distribution points for supplementary food
- Printed form for preparation of financial reports.
- ***Description:*** original (2 copies on one sheet), hectographed typescript, Polish, 220×345 mm, ss. 1, pp. 1.

## 314. RING. I/657/3. Mf. ŻIH—816; USHMM—28

- 05.1942, Warsaw Ghetto
- [Centos"?], Invitation to "A Great Children's Presentation" on the occasion of "Holiday of the Child—5.05.1942," in the "Femina" hall (ul. Leszno 35) on 30.05.1942.
- ***Description:*** original, printed, Polish, Yiddish, 147×96 mm, ss. 2, pp. 4.
  On p. 4 information (printed): "33."
  Published: *Przewodnik*, p. 522 (photocopy); *Dzieci*, pp. 297–298.

## 315. RING. I/222. (Lb. 704). Mf. ŻIH—780; USHMM—11

- After 03.1941, Warsaw Ghetto
- "Report of the Activity of the Central Housing Commission [Centralna Komisja Lokalowa] for the month of March 1941"
- Description of several interventions by the Commission and lists of cases dealt with in particular districts (I–VI).

- *Description:* original, typescript, Polish, 220×280 mm, minor damage and losses of text, ss. 2, pp. 2
  On pp. 1 and 2 signature NN.and seal imprint: "Centralna Komisja Lokalowa."
  Attached note by H.W. in Yiddish: "Submitted by [Meir] Przedecz, coworker of ŻSS, killed in the camp at Poniatowa in Nov. 1943"

### 316. RING. I/201. (Lb. 515). Mf. ŻIH—779; USHMM—10. RING. I/298. Mf. ŻIH—781; USHMM—12

a) **Ring. I/201. (Lb. 515)**

- After 1.06.1942, Warsaw Ghetto
- Sponsors' committee [Patronat] of Kitchen no. 145 (ul. Nowolipki 68, 2nd floor), Letter of 1.06.1942 to Central Provisioning Commission at KOM [Komitet Opiekuńczy Miejski, Municipal Guardian Committee] in Warsaw
- Thanks for 75 kg of sugar and request for allocation of a further 75 kg of sugar for distribution among children.
- *Description:* transcript, typescript, Polish, 209×293 mm, ss. 1, pp. 1.

b) **Ring. I/298**

- After 4.06.1942, Warsaw Ghetto
- Sponsors' committee of the Kitchen (ul. Świętojerska 34), Letter of 4.06.1942 to Central Provisioning Commission at KOM in Warsaw
- Thanks for 75 kg of sugar and request for allocation of a further 75 kg.
- *Description:* transcript, typescript, Polish, 208×299 mm, ss. 1, pp. 1.

### 317. RING. I/219. (Lb. 260, 759). Mf. ŻIH—780; USHMM—11

- After 18.05.1941, Warsaw Ghetto
- [ŻTOS (Żydowskie Towarzystwo Opieki Społecznej; Jewish Society for Social Welfare)], "Proposed Regulations for the Departmental Collegium." (18.05.1941)
- The Departmental Collegium would consist of representatives of individual departments (Social Work Section, Refugees' Care Section, Clothing Department, and Public Kitchens) and serve as a coordinating organ for the departments.
- *Description:* original or transcript, typescript, Polish, 220×296, 220×198 mm minor damage and losses of text, ss. 2, pp. 2
  In the margin of p. 1, handwritten (pencil) entry: "Lamet, Ela"; on p. 2, office mark: "NA/ro 18.5.1941."
  See Ring. II/117.

### 318. RING. I/360/2. Mf. ŻIH—782; USHMM—13

- After 23.06.1941, Warsaw Ghetto
- Executive of the Circle of Honorary Employees of ŻTOS, Letter of 23.06.1941 to the Presidium of ŻTOS
- Demand for full equality of honorary employees of ŻTOS with regular employees (question of provisioning and participation in the Council of ŻTOS).
- *Description:* original, hectographed typescript, Polish, 210×290 mm, ss. 1, pp. 2.
  Attached note by H.W. in Yiddish: "Document forwarded by ŻSS member Naftali Hirszberg."

### 319. RING. I/1119 (1438). (Lb. 1538). Mf. ŻIH—833; USHMM—45

- 11.1941, Warsaw Ghetto
- ŻSS, Notice about a general meeting of workers of the self-help circles in the Warsaw Ghetto, on 29.11.1941 in the office at ul. Tłomackie 5
- Program of the meeting: situation in institution, rights and responsibilities of the employee, organization of the work of the self-help circle.
- *Description:* original, hectographed typescript, Yiddish, 147×210 mm, ss. 1, pp. 1.

### 320. RING. I/355. (Lb. 1714). Mf. ŻIH—782; USHMM—13

- 10.02.1942, Warsaw Ghetto
- ŻSS KOM in Warsaw. Employees' Self-Help Circle (ul. Tłomackie 5), Appeal in the matter of merging of the existing labor associations at the JHK (Jewish Relief Committee) (10.02.1942)
- Circle postulates maintenance in JHK of two autonomous workers' associations. The Board of the Section of Employees of JHK at ŻOS (Jewish Social Welfare) rejected this.
- *Description:* original, hectographed typescript, Polish, 207×251 mm, ss. 1, pp. 1.

### 321. RING. I/231. (Lb. 694). Mf. ŻIH—780; USHMM—11

- 07.1941, Warsaw Ghetto
- Commission for Deportees' Affairs (Komisja dla Spraw Przesiedleńców), *Bulletin*, no. 51/1.07.1941 (for the period from 1.06. to 1.07.1941)
- Report on the subject: number of deportees (12,371), housing matters (liquidation of the sites at: ul. Waliców 2/4, Niska 20—Stawki 21, Gęsia 24, Franciszkańska 11, Niska 59, Nowolipie 59, planned liquidation of the sites at: ul. Stawki 15, Dzika 9, Dzielna 7, site at ul. Smocza 47 was designated for repairs), supply, health conditions, child care (boarding homes: ul. Dzika 13 and 15, as well as the new site for Centos: Sienna 27). Doc. signed by: D. [Dawid] Chołodenko and G. Leszczyńska.
- *Description:* original, typescript, Polish, 205×280 mm, ss. 3, pp. 3.
  Office record number: "L.dz. 2895/41/G.L."
  Attached note by H.W. in Yiddish: "Submitted by Awigdor Epsztajn, died as director of the children's home (ul. Dzika 3), 18.01.1943 deported to Treblinka together with the children."

About Dawid Chołodenko, see *Archiwum Ringelbluma*, p. 176. On p. 1 notation, that the point for deportees (500 persons) at ul. Gęsia 24 was liquidated and the Central Jail was created there on 9.06.1941 (see *Ludzie*, p. 265; *Obozy*, p. 546; *Czerniaków*, pp. 190–191).

### 322. RING. I/200. Mf. ŻIH—779; USHMM—10

a)

- After 19.08.1940, Warsaw
- [ŻSS], "Minutes of session of Clothing Commission on 19.08.1940"
- List of those present: Sagan, Herman, Bloch, Cholewa, Braun, Sapir, Dr. Szwalbe, Bermanowa, Amster, Dobrzyński, Sz. Guzik, engineer Buchwitz. Reports of the Distribution, Emergency, Rules, Supply Subcommissions; motions and decisions; personnel matters.
- ***Description:*** original, typescript, Polish, 222×288 mm, ss. 3, pp. 3.

  On p. 1 notation handwritten: "Mr. Sz. [Szachno] Sagan"; on the reverse of p. 3 notation handwritten: "Hon. Mr. Sagan Żelazna 101/17" (single handwriting, ink). On p. 3 signature and note in red pencil (different handwriting).

  Index: Weinberg, Burakowska, Naparstek, Dr. Pfefferowa

b)

- After 10.02.1941, Warsaw Ghetto
- [ŻSS], "General report of the activity of the Clothing Warehouses and Workshops from 1 to 31 January 1941"
- Lists of clothing distributed (Warehouse of Old and New Clothing), activity of the sorting house and workshops.
- ***Description:*** original or transcript, typescript, Polish, 220×280 mm, ss. 3, pp. 3.

c)

- After 23.02.1940, Warsaw
- [ŻSS], "Minutes of the session of the Commission for Clothing Matters of 23 February [1940]"
- Discussion of report (attached lists of the Department of Clothing Collection); matter of the rules of the Clothing Distribution Commission. List of those attending the meeting.
- ***Description:*** original, typescript (handwritten addition—H.W.* and another hand, ink), Polish, Yiddish, 218×277 mm, minor damage and losses of text, text illegible in places, ss. 3, pp. 3.

  Index: Zylberberg, Sagan, Herman, Bloch, Sapir

d)

- After 23.07.1940, Warsaw
- [ŻSS], "Minutes of the conference concerning questions of clothing." (missing conclusion)
- List of those present: A.L. Bloch, Sz. Sagan, Dir. Faust, Dr. E. Ringelblum, engineer A. Sztolcman. Proposal for reorganization of the Clothing Commission.
- ***Description:*** original or transcript, typescript, Yiddish, 220×285, 218×72 mm, ss. 2, pp. 2.

  Attached note by H.W. in Polish, Yiddish

### 323. RING. I/13. (Lb. 101). Mf. ŻIH—771; USHMM—2

- After 09.1940, Warsaw
- ŻSS. Constructive Aid Commission, Documents concerning issuance of loans for needs of the population (July–September 1940)
  1) Study by Jerzy Winkler on the activity of the apartment house Funds [Kas Domowych] (8.07.1940);
  2) Letter from the ŻSS Constructive Aid Commission to the Social Work Section (E. Ringelblum) dated 9.07.1940 in the matter of cooperation in supervision of the issuance of loans (delegated to cooperate with the Section were: Nowogródzka, Gutgeld, J. Winkler, and Etkin), signed by Buchwitz (director of the Commission) and S. Nowogródzka (secretary);
  3) Reports by J. Winkler of 15.09.1940, "Results of inspection of workshops that received loans from the Constructive Aid Commission" (statistical information concerning the number of persons (craftsmen) who received loans with division into occupational groups) and of 20.09.1940, "Sections of Repayable Grants (Loan Funds)."
- ***Description:*** original (letter of 9.07.1940 office copy), transcript, typescript, Polish, l., 220×286 mm, slight damage and losses of text, ss. 15, pp. 15.

  Attached note by H.W.: "Submitted by Dr. E. Ringelblum."

  In typescript "Results of inspection. . . ." On all pages, at the top a symbol (ink): period with a circumflex over it.

### 324. RING. I/41. Mf. ŻIH—773; USHMM—4

- 1941, Warsaw Ghetto
- Annual Report for 1940 of the Department of Hometown Associations at the Section for Care for Refugees and Fire Victims. Jewish Society for Social Welfare. Department of Hometown Associations [Warsaw 1941]
- Descriptive and statistical report (tables) (movement of refugees and hometown associations, number of refugees registered in the Department, refugees' participation in the the social work of ŻTOS, grants and certificates, food matters, kitchens operated by hometown associations, clothing aid, medical treatment and health care, loans, employment of refugees).
- ***Description:*** original, hectographed typescript, Polish, 205×335 mm, ss. 18, pp. 18.

### 325. RING. I/356. (Lb. 1712). Mf. ŻIH—782; USHMM—13

- Date unknown, Warsaw Ghetto

- NN., "Proposal of CKU (Central Commission of Refugees) coordinated with the management of the Section for Care [of Refugees?]" (missing conclusion)
- CKU is subordinate to the Main Commission for Refugee Affairs [Głównej Komisji dla Spraw Uchodźców] of ŻTOS; comprised of representatives of hometown associations.
- ***Description:*** original or transcript, typescript (handwritten additions), Polish, 205×284mm, ss. 1, pp. 1.

  Attached note by H.W. in Yiddish: "Delivered by Eliezer Hirszberg, former deputy chairman of the Central Commission of Refugees."

### 326. RING. I/232. (Lb. 688). Mf. ŻIH—780; USHMM—11

- After 1940, Warsaw Ghetto
- NN., "Minutes of the joint meeting of the Presidium of the CKU and the Presidium of the Artisans' Commission at the CKU chaired by Dr. Dobryn [Bertold Dobrin] that took place on the 11th of last month on formation of sites of constructive labor"
- Adoption of the proposal and fixing of the costs for establishing a tailor-mending workshop [warsztatu łatutownictwa [sic] krawieckiego] (retouching and repairing clothing). Formation of a joint commission in the persons: Goldberg, Hofman, Dr. M. Reinhold, Frygland [Frydland?].
- ***Description:*** transcript, typescript (handwritten additions in ink), Polish, 215×280 mm, minor damage and losses of text, ss. 2, pp. 2.

  Attached note by H.W. in Yiddish: "Submitted by Eng[ineer] Reinberg, inspector of Joint."

  About Dr. Dobrin, see *Czerniaków*, p. 292.

### 327. RING. I/290. (Lb. 1065). Mf. ŻIH—781; USHMM—12

- After 11.12.1941, Warsaw Ghetto
- Koral, Report for the Section of Care for Refugees from an inspection on 10.12.1941 of the mortuary in the shelter at ul. Stawki 9. (11.12.1941)
- An inspection revealed disorder in documentation of the deceased, several persons are buried under others' names, bodies of several deceased lay in a state of decay. Attached list of several deceased.
- ***Description:*** transcript, typescript, Polish, 203×290 mm, ss. 1, pp. 1.

  Index:

  Abram Koper (died 28.11.1941)
  Perla Łokieć (died 27.11.1941)
  Gitla Meppen (died 24.11.1941)
  Gucia Troper (died 24.11.1941)
  Towia Lejb (died 14.11.1941)
  Gołda Lisner (died 19.11.1941)
  Moszek Berger (died 20.11.1941)
  Abram Zajdman (died 2.12.1941)
  Józef Bieliński (died 21.11.1941)
  Ruchla Popower (died 4.12.1941)
  Tema Koper (died 1.12.1941)
  Gołda Szlak (died 10.12.1941)
  Łaja Blutestein (died 10.12.1941)
  Icek Szmerlak (died 10.12.1941)
  Rajzla Plucer (died 10.12.1941)
  Estera Rajchgot (died 10.12.1941)
  Jankiel Grosfirt (died 10.12.1941)
  Mendel Salomon (died 10.12.1941)
  Dawid Goldberg (died 10.12.1941)

### 328. RING. I/182. Mf. ŻIH—779; USHMM—10

- After 05.1941, Warsaw Ghetto
- "Report of the activity of the Secretariat of the Artisans' Commission at the Central Commission for Refugees for month of May 1941"
- Contains, inter alia, a list of firms to which craftsmen were directed (professions, number of persons, amount of earnings), list of craftsmen by professions registered by 1.06.1941.
- ***Description:*** original, handwritten manuscript (two handwritings), ink, Polish, 222×350 mm, text is difficult to read in places, ss. 5, pp. 8.

  Attached note by H.W. in Yiddish with information : "Submitted by Friedland, coworker of the Artisans' Commission at the Central Commission for Refugees."

  Index:

  Epsztejn, engineer Schönfeld, engineer Cukier, Dr. Eiger, Braun (ul. Nowolipie 43/7a), Womberg & Lipman (ul. Nowolipie 43/7), engineer Feliks Strowajs (ul. Ogrodowa 5/1), Klingbeil (ul. Nalewki 40), Glezer (ul. Niska 65), Comter & Tepper (ul. Gęsia 6), engineer Michał Nirnberg (ul. Śliska 34/15), Dobroszklanka (ul. Nowolipie 65/17), Jakub Cacela, engineer Szerman (ul. Tłomackie 4), engineer Zajel, Mesyng, Herszenhorn (ul. Orla 10), Szwarce & Birman (ul. Krochmalna 52), Figower, engineer Bachrach, Wilner, Zylbersztajn (Łódź Hometown Association [Ziomkostwo Łódzkie]), Wilderbaum (ul. Elektoralna 20?), engineer Margulies (ul. Chłodna 33/9), Glatman

### 329. RING. I/923 (1242). Mf. ŻIH—829; USHMM—41

- 30.04.1941, Warsaw Ghetto
- J. Miedziński (Warsaw, ul. Nowolipki 43, apt. 32), Letter of 30.04.1941 to Central Commission for Refugees in Warsaw (for L. Hirszberg)
- Contains statistical data concerning the Jewish population in Łowicz (local population and refugees, report of activity of the Committee [of Refugees?]) in the years 1940–1941.
- ***Description:*** original, handwritten manuscript, ink, Polish, 222×350 mm, minor damage and losses of text, ss. 1, pp. 1.

At top is record number: "L.dz. [letter registry no.] 301/41."

### 330. RING. I/599/3. Mf. ŻIH—812; USHMM—24

- 19.11.1941, Warsaw Ghetto
- Provisioning Unit of the Jewish District [ZZ Dzielnicy Żydowskiej]. Department of Distribution, Letter of 19.11.1941 to Central Commission for Refugees at Jewish Society for Social Welfare [CKU ŻTOS] (ul. Tłomackie 5)
- Concerning allocation of marmalade [made from beets] and [artificial] honey.
- ***Description:*** original, printed, typescript, Polish, 220×100 mm, serious damage and losses of text, ss. 1, pp. 1.

### 331. RING. I/820 (1139). (Lb. 1506). Mf. ŻIH—826; USHMM—38

- 18.03.1942, Izbica Lubelska
- Jewish Council in Izbica, Szymon Szwartz, chairman, Letter of 18.03.1942 to Central Commission of Refugees (to Dr. B. Dobrin and [Hersz] Wasser, MA) (Warsaw, ul. Tłomackie 13)
- Notation about safeguarding Izrael Gross from Stawiszyn against deportation as well as a request for aid for Naftali Cząstkowski from Kłodawa.
- ***Description:*** original, handwritten manuscript, ink, stamp of the Jewish Council and Jewish Social Self-Help in Izbica, Polish, 206×297 mm, ss. 1, pp. 1.

### 332. RING. I/674/1. (Lb. 1688). Mf. ŻIH—816; USHMM—28

- 03.1942, Warsaw Ghetto
- Patronate for Sick Children of Refugees at the Central Commission for Refugees, Correspondence
- 1) Letter of 03.1942 to Provisioning Unit of the Jewish District in Warsaw (ul. Leszno 12) requesting free allocation of sweets for 800 children for the holiday of Passover; 2) Invitation dated 29.03.1942 to the seder celebration on 1.04.1942 at the Kitchen at ul. Leszno 14. Letters signed by H[ersz] Wasser and S. Mokrski.
- ***Description:*** transcript, handwritten manuscript (H.W.*), ink, Polish, 157×198 mm, minor damage and losses of text, ss. 1, pp. 2.

### 333. RING. I/360/1. Mf. ŻIH—782; USHMM—13

- After 13.05.1942, Warsaw Ghetto
- Central Commission of Refugees, Letter of 13.05.1942 to the Provisioning Unit of the Jewish District [ZZ Dzielnicy Żydowskiej] in Warsaw
- Request for a monthly allocation of 700 kg of honey, 700 kg of marmalade, and 140 kg of candies for quota prices [po cenach kontyngentowych]. Letter signed by: H. [Hersz] Wasser, MA, and L. Hirszberg.
- ***Description:*** transcript, typescript, Polish, 222×344 mm, ss. 1, pp. 1.

  Notation by H.W. (ink): "Frag." [Trag?]

  Letter written on the back of a form, "Declaration of the Circle of Honorary Employees of Ż.T.O.S." for members of that organization (1941, Warsaw, original, hectographed typescript, Polish). One of the questions on the form: "Are you a member of the Collegial Self-Help [Samopomocy Koleżeńskiej] (Leszno 14)?"

### 334. RING. I/577. Mf. ŻIH—792; USHMM—23

- Date unknown, Częstochowa
- NN. (Jutka, Jetka [Roter]), Letter to NN. [General Secretary of the Central Commission for Refugees—Bertold Dobryn]. (Warsaw Ghetto).
- Request for a letter from Central Commission of Refugees in Warsaw to the Jewish Social Self-Help in Częstochowa in the matter of arranging housing for the letter's author.
- ***Description:*** original, handwritten manuscript, ink, Polish, 115×198 mm, ss. 2, pp. 3.

  Index: Hendel, Przepiórka, Dr. [Bertold] Dobryn

### 335. RING. I/777/1. (1099). Mf. ŻIH—825; USHMM—37

- Date unknown, Warsaw Ghetto
- Jewish Social Self-Help. Central Commission of Refugees, Announcement about the availability of meals at the kosher kitchen at ul. Tłomackie 11.
- ***Description:*** original, printed, Hebrew, Yiddish, 227×246 mm, ss. 1, pp. 1.

### 336. RING. I/779/2 (1099). (Lb. 28). Mf. ŻIH—825; USHMM—37

- Date unknown, Warsaw Ghetto
- Central Commission of Refugees, Announcement about registration of cards for potatoes at the office of the Central Commission of Refugees (ul. Tłomackie 11).
- ***Description:*** original, printed, Polish, Yiddish, 470×310 mm, ss. 1, pp. 1.

### 337. RING. I/342. (Lb. 11). Mf. ŻIH—781; USHMM—12

- After 19.09.1940, Warsaw
- [Jewish Social Self-Help Social Work Section [ŻSS SPS]?], "Memorandum" on collection and distribution of clothing in Warsaw by the Jewish Social Self-Help. (Warsaw, 19.09.1940)
- Collection and distribution of clothing is divided among 3 sections: Social Work Section, Department of Provisioning and Department of Social Welfare—lack of coordination among them. Proposal for reorganization: Social Work Section [SPS] will undertake all of the tasks connected with the clothing action.
- ***Description:*** original or transcript, typescript, Polish, 223×288 mm, ss. 1, pp. 1

### 338. RING. I/343. (Lb. 15). Mf. ŻIH—781; USHMM—12

- 15.10.1940, Warsaw
- Jewish Social Self-Help. Department of Money Collection of the Social Work Section [Wydział Zbiórki Pieniężnej SPS], Circular letter dated 15.10.1940 notifying about a meeting on 16.10.1940 in the Department's office (ul. Tłomackie 5, II floor)
- In connection with preparation for displacements,[15] the Winter Aid Campaign was postponed; but a "Help the Homeless!" campaign was adopted. Letter signed by NN.
- ***Description:*** original, typescript, Polish, 222×143 mm, ss. 1, pp. 1.

### 339. RING. I/76. Mf. ŻIH—775; USHMM—6

- After 11.1940, Warsaw Ghetto
- [Jewish Society for Social Welfare, Social Work Section (ŻTOS SPS)], Draft of a lecture on the activity of the Jewish Society for Social Welfare [ŻTOS] in Warsaw from September 1939 to November 1940
- Paper for internal use of the Social Work Section of ŻTOS: statistics on the activity of ŻTOS, financial report for the period June–November 1940, information about various forms of aid for the population.
- ***Description:*** original, hectographed typescript, Polish, 220×335 mm, ss. 5, pp. 5.
  On p. 5 record number: "NE/nk/SPS."
  Doc. was buried together with doc. of Ring. I/37/2.

### 340. RING. I/80/2. Mf. ŻIH—775; USHMM—6

- After 02.1941, Warsaw Ghetto
- [Menachem Linder], "Report of the Activity of the Section for Social Work at the Jewish Society for Self-Help. For the month of February 1941"
- Information concerning the section, inter alia: collection of money and clothing, consumers, public kitchens, instruction and supervision, youth desk, women's desk, committee for entertainments, committee for aid to children.
- ***Description:*** original, hectographed typescript, Yiddish, 205×293 mm, ss. 9, pp. 9.
  On p. 1 handwritten notation: "CKU."

### 341. RING. I/307/1. (Lb. 1676, 1677). Mf. ŻIH—781; USHMM—12

- 08.1941, Warsaw Ghetto
- Jewish Social Self-Help, Social Work Section [ŻSS SPS]. Department of Money Collection, Circular letter dated 10.08.1941
- Call for a collection for the Fund for Emergency Grants for Intelligentsia.
- ***Description:*** original, hectographed typescript, Polish, 208×293 mm, ss. 1, pp. 1.

### 342. RING. I/307/2. (Lb. 1676, 1677). Mf. ŻIH—781; USHMM—12

- 12.1941, Warsaw Ghetto
- [(ŻSS SPS)] Winter Aid Campaign 1941–1942 (ul. Tłomackie 5, II floor), "Informational Circular," no. 1 of 12.1941
- Report of activity, inter alia information about: allocation of potatoes to individual districts, establishment of a kitchen for convalescents (ul. Leszno 40), coffee rooms (ul. Smocza 14, Pl. Grzybowski 10, ul. Gęsia 21, Dzika 9, Twarda 22), production of clothing and shoes, money collections, shows and donations (donation of Henryk Czerniawski, ul. Okopowa 46) for the benefit of the Campaign.
- ***Description:*** original, hectographed typescript, Polish, 208×293 mm, ss. 1, pp. 2.
  On p. handwritten notation (ink): "p.[16] Kon M."

### 343. RING. I/370. (Lb. 859). Mf. ŻIH—782; USHMM—13

- After 05.1941, Warsaw Ghetto
- "Jewish Social Self-Help. Municipal Guardians Committee Warsaw. Report of the Activity of 'Toporol' for the 1st Half-Year 1 Dec. 1940—31 May 1941" [Żydowska Samopomoc Społeczna. Komitet Opiekuńczy Miejski Warszawa. Sprawozdanie z działalności "Toporol-u" za I-wsze półrocze 1 XII 1940–31 V 1941]
- Financial matters (list of revenues and expenditures), agricultural training, dispatch of agricultural workers to landed estates, productivization of land within the ghetto (ul. Smocza 35, Zamenhofa 19, Gęsia 42, a garden farm at the Cemetery on ul. Okopowa and others), cooperation with the population.
- ***Description:*** original, hectographed typescript, Polish, 208×296 mm, minor damage and losses of text, ss. 11, pp. 11.
  Attached note by H.W. in Yiddish: "Document forwarded by engineer Kalnicki."
  Published: *Selected Documents*, 519–529.

### 344. RING. I/366. Mf. ŻIH—782; USHMM—13

- After 17.07.1940, Warsaw Ghetto
- ŻSS, Letter of 17.07.1940 to the Presidium ŻSS
- Concerning workshops designated for closure. Attached budget of workshops.
- ***Description:*** transcript, typescript, Yiddish, 210×286 mm, ss. 3, pp. 3.

15. May be an allusion to the displacement of Jews in conjunction with the impending creation of the Warsaw Ghetto.

16. The abbreviation "p." is Polish for Mr., Mrs., Miss, or Ms.

### 345. RING. I/780/3 (1099). Mf. ŻIH—825; USHMM—37

- Date unknown, Warsaw
- Advertising leaflets (2): "Handicraft Workshops of Ż.T.O.S." (ul. Leszno 29)
- Notation from the self-government of the Haluts[17] Point [Punktu Chalucowego] (ul. Nowolipki 7) about transfer of the handicraft workshops from ul. Długa 27 to ul. Leszno 29.
- ***Description:*** original (larger leaflet in 2 copies), printed Polish, 70×110, 153×228 mm, ss. 3, pp. 3.
  Docs. were kept in a binder.

### 346. RING. I/304. Mf. ŻIH—781; USHMM—12

- 26.02.1942, Warsaw Ghetto
- ŻOS. Personnel Department, Circular letter of 26.02.1942 (Warsaw) to departments of ŻOS
- Notification of extension to 10.11.1942 of identification cards for the month of March.
  Letter signed by M. [Michał] Brandstätter.
- ***Description:*** original, typescript, Polish, 208×132 mm, ss. 1, pp. 1.
  At top information (pencil): "CKU."
  Attached note by H.W.: "K.O.M (J.H.K) City Guardian Committee."
  About Brandstätter, see *Kronika getta*, p. 619.

### 347. RING. I/314. (Lb. 1669). Mf. ŻIH—781; USHMM—12

- After 12.1941, Warsaw Ghetto
- [ŻTOS], "Report of the activity of the Clothing Distribution Department for the year 1941"
- Increasing difficulties in obtaining clothing designated for distribution (balance sheet on distribution of clothing among the ghetto's population in the period January–December 1941).
- ***Description:*** original or transcript, typescript, Polish, 205×280, 205×198 mm, extensive damage and losses of text, ss. 6, pp. 6.

### 348. RING. I/32. (Lb. 1671). Mf. ŻIH—772; USHMM—3

- 11.1941, Warsaw Ghetto
- ŻSS. KOM in Warsaw. Statistical Department, "Internal Bulletin," no. 6, November 1941.
- Descriptive and statistical report (attached tables) of the activity of the Jewish social welfare sites: supplemental feeding campaign, allocation of clothing, money grants, care for children, residential care, medical and health care, activity of TOZ, Association for Aid to the Indigent Sick (Linas Cedek), mother and child care station, Zofiówka Hospital for the Mentally Ill in Otwock, ORT Society for the Spread of Professional and Agricultural Work among Jews, Toporol Association for Support of Agricultural and Handicraft Work among Jews.
- ***Description:*** original, hectographed typescript, Polish, 194×285 mm, ss. 12, pp. 24.
  On p. 1 handwritten notation: "WP Dir. Z [L?] Muszkat"

### 349. RING. I/170. Mf. ŻIH—779; USHMM—10

- After 12.1941, Warsaw Ghetto
- Sponsors' Committee for the Kitchen of the United Apartment House Committees of Ogrodowa and Biała Streets, Letter of 02.1942 [?] to KOM in Warsaw Statistical Department of ŻSS (fragment)
- Information about the genesis of the Union [Zjednoczenia] (Feb. 1941) and of the Sponsors' Committee (attached composition of the board of the Sponsors' Committee: St. Seydenbeutel—chairman, J. Perkal—vice chairman). Attached report of activity for period 1.06–31.12.1941 (fragments).
- ***Description:*** original, handwritten manuscript, typescript, Polish, 205×180 mm, serious damage and losses of text, ss. 4, pp. 5.
  Attached note by H.W. in Polish, Yiddish: "Submitted by Rita Krause, coworker of O[yneg]Sh[abes]."

## Jewish Institutions and Organizations Connected with ŻSS

### 350. RING. I/1096/2 (1415). (Lb. 654). Mf. ŻIH—833; USHMM—45

- 07.1942, Warsaw Ghetto
- Ch. [Chaim] N. [Nachman] Bialik Children's Home, Invitation for the opening of the home at Kitchen no. 135 (ul. Leszno 42, apt. 11), on 14.07.1942
- Attached program of the ceremony.
- ***Description:*** original, hectographed typescript, Hebrew, Yiddish, 206×290 mm, ss. 1, pp. 1.
  Published: *Dzieci*, pp. 299–300.

### 351. RING. I/306. (Lb. 573). Mf. ŻIH—781; USHMM—12

**a) 11.1940, Warsaw Ghetto**

- NN., Address to children on the opening of the new quarters of the Orphans' Home ("Communiqué of November 1940")
- Author, former ward of the Orphans' Home, tells about her memories connected with her stay in the home, mentions inter alia Dr. Janusz Korczak, Stefa [Wilczyńska], director, Hary [Hersz Kaliszer], Rózia [Lipiec-Jakubowska?] and [Róża] Sztokmanowa. Her son Oleś stayed in the orphanage in September 1939.
- ***Description:*** original, handwritten manuscript (with additions in another handwriting), ink, pencil, Polish,

17. Hebrew for "pioneer," term used for those preparing for agricultural pioneering in Palestine.

155×195 mm, minor damage and losses of text, ss. 2, pp. 4.

On p. 4 handwritten notation crossed out: ". . . 23 . . . 27/6 . . ."

According to R.S., the author of the text was Leonia Lengier-Aszowa; see *Dzieci*, p. 168.

Published: *Dzieci*, pp. 168–172.

b) **11.1940, Warsaw Ghetto**

- NN., Oration (handwritten card) entitled "We Welcome You, Doctor" in honor of Dr. Janusz Korczak
- The author, a child, a ward of the Orphans' Home, welcomes Korczak into the new quarters of the orphanage, after the sealing of the ghetto.
- ***Description:*** original, handwritten manuscript, ink, Polish, 210×293 mm, ss. 1, pp. 1.

  Published: *Dzieci*, pp. 61–62.

### 352. RING. I/178. Mf. ŻIH—779; USHMM—10

- 15.07.1942, Warsaw Ghetto
- Dom Sierot (Orphans' Home) (ul. Śliska 9), Janusz Goldszmit Korczak, director. Invitation to a presentation on 18.07.1942.
- ***Description:*** original, typescript, stamp, Polish, 208×128 mm, ss. 1, pp. 2.

  Stamps: "Żydowska Samopomoc Społeczna. Komitet Opiekuńczy Miejski [Jewish Social Self-Help City Guardians' Committee], Warsaw. Wydział Opieki nad Dzieckiem [Department of Child Care]"; "Dom Sierot. Krochmalna 92, obecnie Śliska 9 [Orphans' Home. Krochmalna 92, currently Śliska 9]"; "Goldszmit [?] Korczak."

  On the reverse a notation in handwriting of Stefania Wilczyńska (handwritten manuscript, ink, pencil): "Kitchen, ul. Dzielna 34, apt. 8, III fl. front, p. Cywia [Lubetkin], p. Ichak [Icchak Cukierman], p. [NN.], Timely." See also R. Sakowska's note in: *Dzieci*, p. 302.

  Published: *Selected Documents*, 484–485; *Przewodnik*, p. 521 (photocopy); *Dzieci*, pp. 301–303.

### 353. RING. I/303. Mf. ŻIH—781; USHMM—12

- 02.1941, Warsaw Ghetto
- [YIKOR (Yiddish Culture Organization)], Proclamation of the committee for celebrations in honor of Mendele Moykher Sforim inaugurated on 25.01.1941 in the 105th anniversary of the writer's birth
- Information on the central commemorative meeting at the office of the ŻSS (ul. Tłomackie 5) and district commemorative meetings; call for apartment house committees to organize evenings in honor of Mendele.
- ***Description:*** original (2 copies), hectographed typescript, Yiddish, 215×330 mm, minor damage and losses of text, ss. 2, pp. 2.

  First copy addressed for Izrael Lichtensztajn (Nowolipki 68); second copy for Hersz Wasser (ink)

  Attached note by H.W. in Yiddish: "Issued by Yikuf (Yiddish Culture Association), illegally; forwarded by H. Wasser." Error in H.W.'s note: the appeal was issued by YIKOR (Yidishe Kultur Organizatsye) the secret Yiddish Culture Organization.

### 354. RING. I/217. Mf. ŻIH—780; USHMM—11

- 15.12.1941, Warsaw Ghetto
- [YIKOR] Sponsors' Committee for Yiddish cultural activity. Yiddish School Committee, Appeal calling for support of schools with Yiddish as the language of instruction (15.12.1941)
- Appeal signed by: Sz. [Szyja] Braude, I. [Icchak] Giterman, B. [Beniamin] Wirowski, Sz. [Szachno] Sagan, M. [Menachem] Linder, M. [Mordechaj] Mazo, S. [Sonia] Nowogródzka, L. [Lejb (Leon)] Neustadt, and N. [Natan] Smolar. Encl. declaration form.
- ***Description:*** original, hectographed typescript, Yiddish, 205×300mm, minor damage and losses of text, ss. 1, pp. 1.

  Published: *Selected Documents*, pp. 463–464.

### 355. RING. I/1107 (1426). (Lb. 1463). Mf. ŻIH—833; USHMM—45

- 12.[1941], Warsaw Ghetto
- [YIKOR] Sponsors' Committee for Yiddish cultural activity, Letter to CKU (Central Commission of Refugees) in Warsaw with invitation to a commemorative meeting on 13.12.[1941] dedicated to Ber Borochow[18]
- On the program: I. [Icchak] Giterman, Dr. I. [Icchak] Schiper, and Menachem Linder as well as a musical quartet and recitations.
- ***Description:*** transcript, typescript, Yiddish, 200×291 mm, minor damage and losses of text, ss. 1, pp. 1.

### 356. RING. I/1110/2 (1429). (Lb. 1426). Mf. ŻIH—833; USHMM—45

- Before 4.01.1942, Warsaw Ghetto
- [YIKOR] Sponsors' Committee for Yiddish Cultural Activity in Warsaw. Yiddish School Committee, Invitation to a ceremony on 4.01.1942 to honor the memory of [Roza] Symchowicz at ul. Tłomackie 5, 30 days after her death.
- ***Description:*** original (4 copies), printed, Yiddish, 138×99 mm, ss. 4, pp. 4.

  Published: *Dzieci*, p. 239.

18. Borochow was the founder of the Poale Zion Labor Zionist movement and a proponent of Yiddish as a Jewish national language.

### 357. RING. I/1106/2 (1425). (Lb. 1716, 1717, 1718). Mf. ŻIH—833; USHMM—45

- 13.01.1942, Warsaw Ghetto
- [YIKOR] Sponsors' Committee for cultural activity, Invitation of 13.01.1942 to a gathering on 17.[01.1942] in the office at ul. Orla 6, apt. 42
- Program of the gathering signed by Icchak Giterman and Menachem Linder.
- ***Description:*** original, typescript, Yiddish, 205×154 mm, ss. 1, pp. 1.

### 358. RING. I/87. (Lb. 610). Mf. ŻIH—776; USHMM—7

- 03.1942, Warsaw Ghetto
- NN., "Protest Letter against the Behavior of the Artist Diana Blumenfeld"
- Protest against the departure by actors (Diana Blumenfeld, Miriam Orleska, and Jonasz Turkow) from the Yiddish language and stage.
- ***Description:*** transcript, typescript, Yiddish, 178×120 mm, ss. 1, pp. 1.

  Published: *Selected Documents*, p. 453.

### 359. RING. I/460. Mf. ŻIH—786; USHMM—17

- Date unknown, Warsaw Ghetto
- NN., Appeal entitled "To the Jewish Public"
- Call to society to rescue the elite of the Jewish people from death by starvation.
- ***Description:*** original or transcript, typescript, Yiddish, 208×275 mm, damage and losses of text, ss. 1, pp. 1.

  Published: *Selected Documents*, p. 353.

### 360. RING. I/89. (Lb. 1194). Mf. ŻIH—776; USHMM—7

- Date unknown, Warsaw Ghetto
- NN., Call for creation of an "Institute for Spiritual Provisioning" [Zakładu Zaopatrzenia Duchowego] of the Jewish population
- Significance of intellectual culture in the history of the Jewish people, need for organization of cultural life for the broad public in the ghetto: concerts, recital evenings, lectures, theater, etc.
- ***Description:*** original or transcript, typescript, Polish, 208×295 mm, ss. 2, pp. 2.

  Published: *Selected Documents*, pp. 456–457.

### 361. RING. I/1096/1 (1415). (Lb. 654). Mf. ŻIH—833; USHMM—45

- 01.[1941?], Warsaw Ghetto
- Pioneers' House [Dom chaluców][19] (ul. Nowolipki 7, workshops ul. Leszno 29), Invitation to the opening of a Hebrew club at ul. Leszno 29, on 26.01.[1941?].
- ***Description:*** original, hectographed typescript, Hebrew, 116×208 mm, ss. 1, pp. 1.

### 362. RING. I/1112/4 (1431). (Lb. 1429). Mf. ŻIH—833; USHMM—45

- 01.[1942], Warsaw Ghetto
- Pioneer Point [Punkt Chalucowy] (ul. Nowolipki 7), Invitation to the commemorative meeting on the occasion of the 40th year of existence of the Jewish National Fund (K.K.L.), 17.01.[1942] at the kitchen at ul. Leszno 14
- Program of the ceremony: I. [Icchak] Zaks Chorus, song performed by H. Silska.
- ***Description:*** original, printed, Polish, 148×98 mm, ss. 1, pp. 1.

### 363. RING. I/1187 (1506). (Lb. 669). Mf. ŻIH—834; USHMM—46

- 1941, Warsaw Ghetto
- Hebrew conversational circle (ul. Leszno 29), Membership declaration (1941).
- ***Description:*** original (2 copies), hectographed typescript, Hebrew, 145×210 mm, ss. 2, pp. 2.

  Docs. were kept in a binder.

### 364. RING. I/777/6. (1099). Mf. ŻIH—825; USHMM—37

- 05.1941, Warsaw Ghetto
- Apartment house committee (ul. Franciszkańska 30), Announcement: An Appeal to the Court[20] Tenants of ul. Franciszkańska 30
- Appeal for cooperation. Information about the composition of the committee: Mordechaj Szyfrys, chairman, Jehoszua Rozenfarb, secretary, B. Ber, B. Dorn, F. Szniur [Sznejer], M. Liburg, Sz. Lipniak, M. Wajsman, A. Handszua [Handszuh], Sz. Warum, M. Wolkin, I. Handkan, I. Jungerman, D. Tenenbaum.
- ***Description:*** original, printed, Yiddish, 166×245 mm, ss. 1, pp. 1.

  Printed by J. Wagerman (ul. Nowolipki 4).

### 365. RING. I/657/2. Mf. ŻIH—816; USHMM—28

- Before 3.04.1942, Warsaw Ghetto
- Kitchen (ul. Leszno 14), Invitation to the artistic evening of Chana Braz at the kitchen on 3.04.1942. Performers: H. Diksztajn (upright piano), A. Rajzer (dance), A. Osser (trio), H. Ostrowska (song), S. Fostel (humor), A. Kurc (recitations), M. Znicz (humor), Prof. Wolfson (grand piano).
- ***Description:*** original, printed, Polish, Yiddish, 122×69 mm, ss. 1, pp. 2.

### 366. RING. I/269. (Lb. 18, 19, 19A). Mf. ŻIH—780; USHMM—11

- 08.1941, Warsaw Ghetto
- Sponsors' Committee of Kitchen no. 145 (ul.

19. Center of He-Haluts, the Zionist Pioneer movement that prepared potential immigrants to Palestine.
20. Tenement houses were built around a central courtyard, with separate entrances to various stairwells of the building.

Nowolipki 68), Invitation to a dance in the garden of "Bagatela" (ul. Nowolipki 31)
- Program: dance for children under the direction of N. Tran-Herclich, singing, appearance of Adam Herszkowicz, orchestra under the direction of Bobby Fiedler.
- *Description:* Printed (2 copies), Polish, Yiddish, 80×92 mm, ss. 4, pp. 4.
  Published: *Dzieci*, pp. 272–273.

### 367. RING. I/777/7. (1099). Mf. ŻIH—825; USHMM—37

- Before 22.11.1941, Warsaw Ghetto
- Sponsors' Committee of the Kitchen-School for Children no. 145 (ul. Nowolipki 68), Invitation for tsholnt [czulent] on 22.11.1941.
- *Description:* original, printed, Yiddish, 87×140 mm, minor damage and losses of text, ss. 1, pp. 1.
  Published: *Dzieci*, p. 283.

### 368. RING. I/1205 (1524). Mf. ŻIH—835; USHMM—47

a)
- Before 10.12.1941, Warsaw Ghetto
- [Liza Nachtensztajn], Letter to NN
- Farewell letter with greetings for friends and coworkers.
- *Description:* original, handwritten manuscript, pencil, Yiddish, 120×205 mm and 145×203 mm, ss. 1, pp. 1.
  Index: [Natan] Smolar

b)
- Before 10.12.[1941], Warsaw Ghetto
- Kitchen-school (ul. Nowolipki 68), Invitation for a memorial meeting after the death of Liza Nachtensztajn, to be held on 10.12.[1941] at the children's kitchen at ul. Nowolipki 68
- Info. about the funeral of Liza Nachtensztajn, procession will set out from the home of the deceased at ul. Pawia 19.
- *Description:* original, typescript, Yiddish, ss. 1, pp. 1.
  Attached note by H.W. in Yiddish

### 369. RING. I/294. Mf. ŻIH—781; USHMM—12

- Date unknown, Warsaw Ghetto
- NN., Note of "Things taken to Kitchen no. 145 [ul. Nowolipki 68]"
- List includes several dozen items, mainly clothing designated for distribution [?].
- *Description:* original, handwritten manuscript, ink, Polish, 155×192 mm, ss. 2, pp. 3.

### 370. RING. I/594/2. Mf. ŻIH—792; USHMM—23

- 11.11.1941, Warsaw
- NN. (Warsaw), Letter to the Administration of the Kitchen for Children 145 (ul. Nowolipki 68)
- Author is a former official of LOPP [Liga Obrony Powietrznej i Przeciwgazowej (Air and Anti-Gas Defense League)]. Request for admission of children to the kitchen.
- *Description:* original, handwritten manuscript, ink, Yiddish, 125×198 mm, damage and losses of text, ss. 2, pp. 4.

### 371. RING. I/1098 (1417). (Lb. 655). RING. I/1111 (1430). Mf. ŻIH—833; USHMM—45

**a) Ring. I/1098 (1417)**
- After 02.1942, Warsaw Ghetto
- Sponsors' Committee of apartment house kitchen no. 22 (ul. Orla 13), Invitation to a commemorative meeting dedicated to Abraham Rajzen's (Raisin) fiftieth year as an author, on 22.02.1942 in the hall at ul. Tłomackie 5
- Attached program of the ceremony: Ester Goldenberg, Abraham Kurc, H. Silska, Z. Lewin, H. Kuczkowski, M. Bronsztajn [Bronsztejn ?] at the grand piano.
- *Description:* transcript, typescript, Yiddish, 192×285 mm, damage and losses of text, ss. 1, pp. 1.
  Published: *Selected Documents*, pp. 446–447.

**b) Ring. I/1111 (1430)**
- 13.02.1942, Warsaw Ghetto
- NN., Notification of 13.02.1942 about dispatch of 30 tickets for the evening dedicated to A. [Abraham] Rajzen, on 22.02.1942 in the hall at ul. Tłomackie 5
- Request for distribution of the tickets attached to the letter.
- *Description:* original, typescript, stamp, Yiddish, 150×207 mm, ss. 1, pp. 1.
  Postwar note by Laura Eichhornowa (pencil): "Not[ification] that 30 tickets were sent out for the evening dedicated to Rajzen."

### 372. RING. I/777/9. (1099). Mf. ŻIH—825; USHMM—37

- Date unknown, Warsaw Ghetto
- Sponsors' Committee of public kitchen no. 28 (ul. Orla 13), Invitation to tsholnt [czulent] on 14.[. . .]. [. . .] in the kitchen at ul. Orla 13
- Program: Sz. Rabinowicz, M. [Mordechaj] Mazo and I. Dąb signed the invitation.
- *Description:* original, typescript, Yiddish, 208×150 mm, ss. 1, pp. 1.
  Postwar notation by Laura Eichhornowa (pencil): "Invit[ation] to *czulent*."

### 373. RING. I/1220/25. Mf. ŻIH—835; USHMM—47

- 2.09.1940, Warsaw
- Sponsors' Committee of public kitchen no. 38 (Warsaw, ul. Świętojerska 11), Certificate of 2.09.1940 for Basia Getler (ul. Świętojerska 36) "with meal privileges on the basis of identification no. 12034/40."
- *Description:* original, handwritten manuscript, ink, stamp of the Kitchen and datemarkers (09–12.1940),

Polish, Yiddish, 175×110 mm, ss. 1, pp. 2.
Note at top (pencil): "7 leg."
Doc. was kept in a binder.

### 374. RING. I/1220/60. Mf. ŻIH—835; USHMM—47

- Date unknown, Warsaw Ghetto
- NN., "List of Consumers from Karczew"
- List of names of deportees from Karczew with privileges at a kitchen [?] in the Warsaw Ghetto.
- ***Description:*** original or transcript, handwritten manuscript (H.W.*), ink, Yiddish, 150×210 mm, ss. 1, pp. 2.
  Index: Aron Zilberberg of Karczew, Mosze Lazowert of Karczew, Icchak Melech of Karczew, Wolf Kirszenbaum of Karczew, Lejb Borowski of Karczew, Szymon Reinberg of Karczew, Mechl Goldfarb of Karczew, Sara Falk of Karczew, Lea Sommer of Karczew, Ita Przedecz of Karczew, Wolf Winkler of Karczew, Hersz Landau of Karczew, Icchak Felsztejn of Karczew, Aron Zelner of Karczew, Pesach Rabinowicz of Karczew, Blima Konińska of Karczew, Junger Lewin of Karczew, Josef Ber Natanblut of Karczew, Menachem Frajnd of Karczew

### 375. RING. I/1220/69B. Mf. ŻIH—835; USHMM—47

- Date unknown, Warsaw Ghetto
- Document (letter, appeal [?]) concerning the organization "Samopomoc" (fragment)
- Notation about establishment of the organization and its aims.
- ***Description:*** original or transcript (2 copies), typescript, Polish, 160×152, 185×150 mm, serious damage and losses of text, ss. 2, pp. 2.
  See Ring. I/1220/69a.

### 376. RING. I/329. Mf. ŻIH—781; USHMM—12

- After 02.1941, Warsaw Ghetto
- Sochaczew Aid Committee (Warsaw), Call for (Passover) holiday aid for poor refugees from Sochaczew
- Notation about the collection site—ul. Tłomackie 13 (room 13).
- ***Description:*** original, printed, Yiddish, 140×200 mm, ss. 1, pp. 1.
  Printed item sent out to the attention of (handwritten manuscript, ink): "Rabbi[?] Jantel."
  Attached note by H.W. in Yiddish: "Submitted by H.W."

### 377. RING. I/320. (Lb. 9). Mf. ŻIH—781; USHMM—12

- After 2.03.1941, Warsaw Ghetto
- Grodzisk and Area Hometown Association in Warsaw (ul. Żelazna 58), Appeal (Warsaw, 2.03.1941)
- The Grodzisk Hometown Association was called into being by the ŻSS in Warsaw 6.02.1941. Appeal for material aid for setting up of a kitchen for deportees from Grodzisk and environs. Document signed by Bernard Kampelmacher.
- ***Description:*** original or transcript, typescript, Polish, 208×293 mm, ss. 1, pp. 1.

### 378. RING. I/1128 (1447). (Lb. 5). Mf. ŻIH—833; USHMM—45

- Before 29.12.1940, Warsaw Ghetto
- Program of "Children's Show 29 December 1940"
- Chorus under Dir. Goldberg, Blitówna at the grand piano, Tran-Herclichówna leads dance.
- ***Description:*** original, hectographed typescript, Polish, Yiddish, 165×228 mm, ss. 2, pp. 4.
  Doc. was kept in a binder.
  Published: *Dzieci*, pp. 264–267.

### 379. RING. I/601. Mf. ŻIH—812; USHMM—24

- 8.02.1941, after 8.02.1941, Warsaw Ghetto
- Invitation for a concert entitled "Hour of Yiddish Writers and Artists." On 15.02.1941 in rooms of TOZ (ul. Gęsia 43)
- Program: Ewa Kozirόg—violin, Mina Maślanka—upright piano, Zula Kamińska—ballet, Herszele Sztern—song, Z. [Zygmunt] Szklar—recitations, Sz. [Szlomo] Gilbert, P. Wajland, Jechiel Lerer, I. [Icchak] Kacenelson—poetry, I. Smolarz, J. [Josef] Kirman, Z. [Zalman] Skałow, Jehuda Feld—short story, I. Sztern, I. Bernsztein, G. Szternberg, Rachel Auerbach—essays; Dr. I. Lajpuner—introductory word.
- ***Description:*** original (hectographed typescript, 210×220 mm), transcript (typescript, 148×210 mm), Yiddish, ss. 2, pp. 2.
  Transcript does not include the final fragment of original
  Docs. were kept in a binder.

### 380. RING. I/1097 (1416). (Lb. 655). Mf. ŻIH—833; USHMM—45

- Before 24.05.1941, Warsaw Ghetto
- Leaflet. Announcement about 14th [?] memorial meeting dedicated to Icchak Lejb Perec [Peretz], on 24.05.1941 at ul. Tłomackie 5.
- On the program: [Izrael] Lichtensztajn, M. [Mina] Abelman, Sz. Zagan, M. [Menachem] Linder, D. [Diana] Blumenfeld, A. [Ajzyk] Samberg, D. [Dawid] Szerman as well as a Yiddish children's chorus, dance.
- ***Description:*** original, hectographed typescript, Yiddish, 182×258 mm, ss. 1, pp. 1.
  Published: *Dzieci*, pp. 270–271.

### 381. RING. I/1110/1 (1429). (Lb. 1426). Mf. ŻIH—833; USHMM—45

- 02.1942, Warsaw Ghetto
- Invitation to an evening dedicated to the memory of

the poet Mieczysław Braun, on 8.02.1942 in the hall of the Judaic Library (ul. Tłomackie 5).[21]
- *Description:* original (2 copies), Printed Polish, 137×75 mm, ss. 2, pp. 2.

### 382. RING. I/1108/3 (1427). Mf. ŻIH—833; USHMM—45

- 02.1942, Warsaw Ghetto
- Committee of Friends and Colleagues of [J[akub?] Obarzanek?], Invitation to an evening of the work of J. Obarzanek (Ob-nek) entitled "Nadir un vayn nisht" [Here, Take It and Don't Cry] at Gospoda Artystów [Artists' Inn] (ul. Orla 6), on 8.02.1942
- Participants: Sz. J. Stopnicki, E. Cejtlin, editor H. Czerwiński, Zymra Zeligfeld, Chana Lerner, Symche Fostel, Jack Lewi, I.M. Moszkowicz, A. [Ajzyk] Samberg, Dawid Zajderman. First appearance of the community chorus under the direction of Prof. [Icchak] Zaks.
- *Description:* original, printed, Polish, Yiddish, 118×167 mm, ss. 1, pp. 1.

## Secret Jewish Organizations

### 383. RING. I/556. (Lb. 302). Mf. ŻIH—791; USHMM—22

- After 06.1940[?], Warsaw Ghetto [?]
- Correspondence of members of the Haszomer-Hacair [Ha-Shomer ha-Tsair][22] organization. (02–06.[1940?])
- Private matters, organizational matters, training (agriculture), emigration. Letters from members of the organization from different parts of Poland and abroad (e.g., Lithuania, Romania, Switzerland) addressed to NN. (inter alia Adam [Icek Randt], Józef [Kapłan], Józef [Diament], Tosia [Altman], Miriam [Hainsdorf], Janek, Mordechaj [Orensztajn], Szmuel [Bresław, Brasław], Zwi [Henszel Brandes], Chedwa [Russak], [Chaim Gelbard], Szaja [Wajner], Leibek [Leibowicz of Kraków]) in Warsaw.
- *Description:* copies, typescript, German, Polish, Yiddish, 204×290 mm, ss. 97, pp. 97.

  Inventory: "Letters of members of Ha-Shomer Ha-Tsair."

  Copies were backdated to 1930 for conspiratorial purposes. Information about several of the authors, addressees of the letters, and persons appearing in them in the 1946 list of documents.

### 384. RING. I/27. (Lb. 4). Mf. ŻIH—772; USHMM—3

a)

- After 04.1941, Warsaw Ghetto
- Appeal of 21.04.1941(Warsaw) "To all members of the nest"
- Call for boycott of the Jewish Council and Order Service, for going into hiding before the deportations to labor camps, announced by the Ha-Shomer Ha-Tsair organization.
- *Description:* transcript, typescript, Polish, 207×290 mm, ss. 1 pp. 1.

b)

- After 06.1941, Warsaw Ghetto
- Call of 22.06.1941 (Warsaw Ghetto) "To all guards [szomrów]"[23]
- Appeal for solidarity with the USSR after the attack by the Germans, announced by the Ha-Shomer Ha-Tsair organization.
- *Description:* transcript, typescript, Polish, 217×290 mm, ss. 1, pp. 1.

  Attached note by H.W.: "1940. Forwarded by Merenholc" (error in date; perhaps the note was made for a different document [?]).

### 385. RING. I/1207 (1526). Mf. ŻIH—835; USHMM—47

- [23.03. 1942?], Warsaw Ghetto
- [Eliasz Gutkowski], Minutes of the session of representatives of political parties in the Warsaw Ghetto. [23.03.1942?]
- Participating in the meeting at the kitchen at ul. Orla 2 were representatives of: the Bund ([Maurycy] Orzech, [Abrasza] Blum), Poale Syjon Lewica [Left Po'ale Tsiyon] (Melech Feinkind, [Hersz] Berliński), Poale Syjon Prawica [Right Po'ale Tsiyon] (L. [Lejzer] Lewin, [Stefan (Szalom) Grajek). The current situation in the Warsaw Ghetto and further prospects for cooperation were discussed (e.g., plan of armed action [?]).
- *Description:* original, handwritten manuscript (LEG*), ink,Yiddish, 90×94, 95×220 mm, damage and losses of text, ss. 2, pp. 2.

  Icchak Cukierman [Zuckerman] writes more extensively on this meeting; according to Cukierman, Gutkowski wrote the minutes on the basis of his account; see Cukierman, pp. 128–129.

  Attached lengthy postwar transcript by H.W. (ink, Yiddish).

### 386. RING. I/628. Mf. ŻIH—815; USHMM—27

- Date unknown, place unknown
- Instructions for drawing topographical maps (fragment)

21. Located adjacent to the Great Synagogue that was destroyed in May 1943, the Judaic Library building itself is now the renovated home of the Jewish Historical Institute (ŻIH) and the repository of the Ringelblum Archive.

22. Hebrew for "The Young Guard," a left-wing Zionist youth movement.

23. Combination of the Hebrew word *shomer* and the Polish suffix.

- Local field exercises for making measurements, sets of topographical symbols for drawing maps.
- *Description:* original (3 copies), hectographed typescript, Polish, 202×330 mm, ss. 12, pp. 21.

### 387. RING. I/1193 (1512). (Lb. 205). Mf. ŻIH–834; USHMM–46

- 11.03, 13.03, current year, Warsaw Ghetto
- Training instructions entitled "Mine Destruction"
- Methods of setting up explosive mine charges.
- *Description:* transcript (3 copies), typescript, drawings, pencil, Polish, 205×288 mm, minor damage and losses of text, ss. 6, pp. 6.

  On p. 1 (first copy) (pencil): "11/III"; on p. 1 (second copy): "13/III."

### 388. RING. I/1192 (1511). (Lb. 124). Mf. ŻIH–834; USHMM–46

- Date unknown, Warsaw Ghetto
- Training instructions entitled "Combat Gases" and "First Aid in Case of Emergencies"
- Info. concerning distribution, behavior, and effects of combat gases on humans. First aid for poisoning with gases and means of applying first aid in various cases.
- *Description:* transcript (3 copies), typescript, Polish, 215×288 mm, damage and losses of text, ss. 12, pp. 12.

## Other Jewish Institutions and Organizations

### 389. RING. I/780/1 (1099). Mf. ŻIH–825; USHMM–37

- 06.1941, Warsaw
- "Café-Chłodnia [Café Cooler] «Under the Seven »" (ul. Leszno 7), Advertising leaflet.
- *Description:* original, printed, Polish, 118×155 mm, ss. 1, pp. 1.

  At top notation by H.W. (ink): "June 1941."
  Printed at A. Kajzman (ul. Leszno 24).

### 390. RING. I/780/2 (1099). Mf. ŻIH–825; USHMM–37

- Date unknown, Warsaw
- Dining Spot [Jadłodajnia]. Dinners (ul. Leszno 48, apt. 1), Advertising leaflet.
- *Description:* original, printed, Polish, 110×164 mm, ss. 1, pp. 1.

### 391. RING. I/779/1. Mf. ŻIH–825; USHMM–37

- Before 22.[05.1942], Warsaw Ghetto
- Coffee Shop "Bagatela" (ul. Nowolipie 36), Advertising leaflet: *Blow on this leaflet!*
- Artistic program from 22.[05.1942]: Chana Lerner, Dawid Zajderman, Franciszka Mannówna, St. Stański, D. Birnbaum, and the orchestra of Bruno Heres and Bobby Fiedler.
- *Description:* original, printed, Polish, 120×154 mm, ss. 1, pp. 1.

  Printed at A. Kejzman (ul. Leszno 24).
  Published: *Przewodnik,* p. 566 (photocopy).

### 392. RING. I/1108/2 (1427). Mf. ŻIH–833; USHMM–45

- 02.1941, Warsaw Ghetto
- Coffee House—Restaurant "Nowoczesna" [Modern] (ul. Nowolipki 10), Invitation to: "Great Festival of Gypsy Romances," on 6.02.[1941], Thursday; "Great Children's Matinee," on 8.02.[1941], Saturday; "Great Matinee [Wielki Poranek] «In the Land of Tango», on 9.02.[1941], Sunday
- Participating: Artur Gold, Władysław Szpilman, Arkadi Flato, Halina Ajzenberżanka, Polcia Szwarcbard, Irka Rozenfried, Irenka Zylberberg, Lusia Cywiak, Michał Znicz, Salvatore Kuszes, Władysław Lin, Anna Fischerówna.
- *Description:* original, printed, Polish, 154×230 mm, ss. 1, pp. 1.

  Doc. was kept in a binder.
  Doc. printed at Melcer and Kotlar in Warsaw.

### 393. RING. I/1108/1 (1427). Mf. ŻIH–833; USHMM–45

- Date unknown, Warsaw Ghetto
- Eldorado Theater (ul. Dzielna 1), Program of L. Kobryn's play "Dorfs-Jung" [The Village Youth]
- Director M. Wiskind, musical illustrations Prof. I. [Icchak] Zaks, scenery A. Liberman, choreography Irena Prusicka. Performers: H. [Harry] Zajderman, E. Sztokfeder, J. Najwirt, I. Natan, D. Fakiel, A. Kurc, S. Rozen, M. Winder, D. Birnbaum, and M. Bryn.
- *Description:* original, printed, Polish 236×167 mm, ss. 2, pp. 3.

  Published: *Przewodnik,* p. 542 (photocopy).

### 394. RING. I/777/10. Mf. ŻIH–825; USHMM–37

- Date unknown, Warsaw Ghetto
- Jewish Symphony Orchestra, Poster of the II Symphonic Concert on Saturday, 2.08.[year ?] at "Melody Palace"[24] (ul. Rymarska 12) at 12:15 and in Great Hall (ul. Sienna 16) at 5 PM
- Participating: Marian Neuteich, Helena Ostrowska.
- *Description:* original, printed, Polish, 465×633 mm, minor damage and losses of text, ss. 1, pp. 1.

### 395. RING. I/1158/2 (1477). (Lb. 1592). Mf. ŻIH–833; USHMM–45

- Date unknown, Warsaw
- Wiktoria Sweets Factories. Paper candy wrapper.
- *Description:* original (3 copies), printed, Polish, Yiddish, 54×87 mm, ss. 3, pp. 3.

  Published: *Przewodnik,* p. 417 (photocopy); *Dzieci,* p. 290 (photocopy).

24. English theater name in original.

**396. RING. I/1158/4 (1477). (Lb. 1592). Mf. ŻIH—833; USHMM—45**

- Date unknown, Warsaw Ghetto
- Majestic Factory, Warsaw. Paper candy wrapper.
- ***Description:*** original, printed, Polish, Yiddish, 70×74 mm, ss. 1, pp. 1.

**397. RING. I/1158/5 (1477). (Lb. 1592). Mf. ŻIH—833; USHMM—45**

- Date unknown, Warsaw Ghetto
- Ormański Factory, Warsaw. Paper candy wrapper.
- ***Description:*** original, printed, Polish, Yiddish, 50×77 mm, ss. 1, pp. 1.

  Published: *Przewodnik*, p. 417 (photocopy).

**398. RING. I/1160 (1479). Mf. ŻIH—833; USHMM—45. RING. I/1199 (1518). Mf. ŻIH—834; USHMM—46**

- Date unknown, Warsaw Ghetto
- Omnibus Transportation Company in the Jewish District in Warsaw, Tickets
- 1) Regular ticket, no. 043847; 2) Subscription ticket (discount) no. 005232 valid for the B line.
- ***Description:*** Ring. I/1160—original, printed, Polish, 54×39 mm, ss. 1, pp. 1; Ring. I/1199—original, printed, Polish, 123×75mm, minor damage and losses of text, holes after cancellation by conductor, ss. 1, pp. 1.

  Doc. 2: Published: *Przewodnik*, p. 119.

**399. RING. I/1127 (1446). (Lb. 3). MISSING ORIGINAL**

- Date unknown, Warsaw Ghetto
- Jewish First-Aid Service, Invitation.
- ***Description:*** original, hectographed typescript, Polish, Yiddish, 240×170 mm, ss. 1, pp. 1.

  Missing before 1970

**400. RING. I/1220/59. Mf. ŻIH—835; USHMM—47**

- Date unknown, Warsaw Ghetto
- NN., Report [. . .]
- Notation on tailors' earnings. Apartment house addresses in the Warsaw Ghetto.
- ***Description:*** transcript, handwritten manuscript (Np.*), pencil, German, 145×155 mm, damage and losses of text, ss. 1, pp. 2.

  On p. 1 notation in Yiddish: "Report of member [. . .]"

**401. RING. I/1136 (1455). (Lb. 1535). Mf. ŻIH—833; USHMM—45**

- 1941–1942, Warsaw Ghetto
- Death Notices
  1) Beniamin Zabłudowski (died 3.01.1942), member of the Jewish Council;
  2) Hilary Fogel (died 1.10.[1941]), age 40, "delegate of the Łódź hometown association";
  3) Roza Symchowicz [died before 2.12.1941], educator and meritorious cultural activist;
  4) Liza Nachtensztejn [died before 10.12.1941], veteran teacher.
  5) Dr. Szymon Tenenbaum (died 28.11.1941), age 49, naturalist, member of the Warsaw Scientific Association [Towarzywstwa Naukowego Warszawskiego] and the Academy of Sciences in Kraków [Akademii Umiejętności], former director of the Laor secondary school.
- ***Description:*** original (doc. 1, 2, 4 [2 copies], 5, printed, transcript [?] [doc. 3, handwritten, ink], Polish, Yiddish, 470×332, 550×396, 542×392, 552×392 mm, extensive damage and losses of text (doc. 1), minor damage and losses of text (doc. 4), ss. 6, pp. 6.

  On doc. 3 notation at the bottom: "Sierakowska 6/6."

  Docs. 3 and 4—Published: *Dzieci*, pp. 180–182.

## *PERSONAL ACCOUNTS (DIARIES, CHRONICLES, REPORTS, MEMOIRS)*

**402. RING. I/25. (Lb. 8). Mf. ŻIH—772; USHMM—3**

- After 12.1941, Warsaw
- I.A., report entitled "Poles on Jews (From a conversation with Miss I.A., a Polish woman, an employee of the municipality in social welfare, a highly cultured and educated person, with political and democratic opinions, a believing Christian)"
- The author characterizes the attitudes and opinions of various Polish circles toward the Jewish population and German policy toward Jews.
- ***Description:*** original (o), handwritten manuscript (SB*), ink, Polish, 110×352 mm, ss. 4, pp. 7.

  Attached note by H.W. in Yiddish: "Samuel Bresław [Brasław] of Ha-Shomer Ha-Tsair conducted the interview."

  The author [Irena Adamowicz?] of the account had already heard about mass executions in Chełmno nad Nerem and Wilno.

**403. RING. I/1031 (1350). Mf. ŻIH—832; USHMM—44**

- 16.05 and 21.05.194[1 or 2 ?], Warsaw Ghetto
- NN. (Abraham), Report entitled "A bildl" [A little picture] about conflicts connected with quartering the homeless (refugees) in apartments in the Warsaw Ghetto (16.05 and 21.05.194[1 or 2?])
- The Goldwasser family (7 persons) and the author of the account moved into the 7-room apartment of the Fajermans (ul. Nalewki 38, apt. 2); 12 persons moved into the apartment of the Bramingers and Basióks (ul. Gęsia 49, apt. 49).
- ***Description:*** original or transcript, handwritten manuscript, pencil, Yiddish, 98×297, 117×297 mm, ss. 4, pp. 5.

  On the reverse of p. 3 notation by H.W. (ink): "bread—provisioning."

Published: *Selected Documents*, pp. 302–303 (fragment).

## 404. RING. I/1009 (1328). (Lb. 331). Mf. ŻIH—831; USHMM—43

- After 5.06.1941, Warsaw Ghetto
- NN. (Abraham), Report entitled "A bildl" [A little picture]
- Attitude of affluent residents of the Warsaw Ghetto (example of the Płatowski family, ul. Rynkowa 1, apt. 7) to poor deportees and refugees (inter alia the poet Szymański). Lack among the rich of understanding for and sensitivity to human misery and suffering.
- ***Description:*** transcript, handwritten manuscript (MS*), pencil, Yiddish, 148×209 mm, minor damage and losses of text, ss. 4, pp. 4.

  In the margins a symbol (ink): circle in a circle.

## 405. RING. I/641. Mf. ŻIH—815; USHMM—27. RING. I/654. (Lb. 640). Mf. ŻIH—816; USHMM—28

- 4.08.1941–26.07.1942, Warsaw Ghetto
- [Rachela Auerbach], Diary (4.08.1941–26.07.1942) (fragments, missing ending)
- Daily life in the Warsaw Ghetto: kitchen at Leszno 40, hunger, mass murders on the night of the 17th to the 18th of April 1942, German Jews (2,000 persons) at Tłomackie, "Frankenstein," German action against "13" (23/24.05.1942). Information about liquidation of the ghettos in Lublin, Tarnopol, Pabianice.
- ***Description:*** Ring. I/641—original, handwritten manuscript (RA*), ink, German, Polish, Yiddish, 216×340 mm, minor damage and losses of text, text illegible in places, ss. 31, pp. 61; Ring. I/654—original, handwritten manuscript (RA*), ink, Polish, Yiddish, and Yiddish in Roman transliteration, 122×190 mm, ss. 33, pp. 66.

  In Ring. I/654 on p. 66 list of valuables (jewelry, silver pieces, etc.) in two columns, below date and information (handwritten manuscript, different handwriting, pencil): "at Sam Landau's [?] 4.03./31.05.1924, at p. Friedt . . . [?]."

  Index: Braxmeier, Wajntraub, Roza Symchowicz; Nauman from ul. Pawia, dentist, shot in the ghetto (29/30.05.1942); Wilner, baker, shot in the ghetto (29/30.05.1942); [Mojżesz] Szklar, shot in the ghetto in 12.05.1942

## 406. RING. I/655. Mf. ŻIH—816; USHMM—28

- Date unknown, Warsaw Ghetto
- [Rachela Auerbach], Memoirs and Notes
- Experiences of war (September 1939) and occupation, daily life in the Warsaw Ghetto, author's work in the public kitchen [ul. Leszno 40]. Observations of behavior, reflections on hunger and human suffering. Sketches for a study on the public kitchen.
- ***Description:*** original, handwritten manuscript (RA*), notebook, ink, Yiddish, 155×193 mm, ss. 27, pp. 37.

  Index: Rajzeł [Rajzla] Żychlińska, poet, Bajla Sztumfeld, Braksmejer, Borensztejn, Pola Landau, Wajntraub, Berek Czebnicki, Izrael Sztern

## 407. RING. I/602. Mf. ŻIH—812; USHMM—24

- 16.12.1941–24.01.1942, Warsaw Ghetto
- [Icchak Cukierman?], "Notebook of the lessons conducted and exercises at the He-haluts (The Pioneer) seminar (III) end of 1941 and beginning of 1942—Warsaw"
- Notebook containing the daily schedule of classes (lists of lecture topics) at the secret seminar of the He-haluts youth organization from 16.12.1941 to 24.01.1942.
- ***Description:*** original, handwritten manuscript, ink, Hebrew, 100×156 mm, ss. 43, pp. 53.

  Description (title) doc. on p. 53 (handwritten manuscript—LEG*, ink, Yiddish).

  Published: BŻIH nr. 206/2003, pp. 209–226.

## 408. RING. I/1145 (1464) (Lb. 1115). Mf. ŻIH—833; USHMM—45

- After 12.1940, Warsaw Ghetto
- P. [Pesach] Cukierman, Note
- Notation on people who died in the last week from hunger and cold in the courtyard of the building at ul. Muranowska 13; among 7 dead were 5 children of Mrs. Cenesblat.
- ***Description:*** original, handwritten manuscript, ink, Yiddish, 112×180 mm, minor damage and losses of text, ss. 1, pp. 1.

  Written on a ŻTOS receipt form (7.12.1940) for contribution for war victims (printed, Polish, Yiddish). Postwar notations on reverse.

  Attached note by H.W. in Yiddish.

## 409. RING. I/177. Mf. ŻIH—836; USHMM—67

- After 07.[1941], Warsaw Ghetto
- NN. [Dora Sztatman], Account of the Warsaw Ghetto
- Author, a young woman, describes her meeting with two German soldiers on the grounds of the courts and a joint stroll along the Vistula.
- ***Description:*** transcript (2 copies), handwritten manuscript (JG*), pencil, Polish, 146×204, 146×90 mm, minor damage and losses of text, ss. 10, pp. 10.

  On p. 1 (first copy) on margin is notation by H.W. in Yiddish (ink): "Dora Sztatman" and letter (ink): "B."

  Attached note by H.W. in Yiddish: "Dora Sztatman."

## 410. RING. I/202. Mf. ŻIH—779; USHMM—10

- After 1941, Warsaw Ghetto
- [Jehuda Feld?], Report entitled "The Heating

Commission and the Transfer Station (Umschlagplatz)"
- The author, an employee of CKU, picked up transports of food for the ghetto's population in the warehouse at ul. Dzika 2 (smuggling, contacts with Poles, refugee housing points, trade in fuel at the ghetto Heating Commission at ul. Leszno 14, ul. Wołyńska 5).
- ***Description:*** transcript (2 copies), typescript (handwritten additions, handwritten manuscript, ink), Yiddish, 220×355 mm, ss. 42, pp. 42.
    On p. 1 (second copy) at top information in Yiddish: "Jehuda Feld."

**411. RING. I/263. (Lb. 186). Mf. ŻIH—780; USHMM—11**

- 05–06.1942, Warsaw Ghetto
- [Daniel Fligelman], Diary (28.05–22.06.1942) (fragment [?])
- Execution of smugglers (inter alia description of the death of Chaim Albert), activity of the navy blue police,[25] information about resettlement and liquidation actions (Włodawa, Hrubieszów).
- ***Description:*** original, handwritten manuscript (FLIG*), ink, Polish, 138×200 mm, minor damage and losses of text, text illegible in places, ss. 5, pp. 9.
    On pp. 1, 3, and 4 notation by H.W. in Yiddish (ink): "1942—1 standard page."
    Attached note by H.W. in Yiddish: "Daniel Fligelman, «Daily notes»."
    Inventory: "Author of the document is Daniel (Dawid) Fligelman (Fliegielman)."

**412. RING. I/464. Mf. ŻIH—786; USHMM—17**

- 3.04.1941 and after 3.04.1941, Warsaw Ghetto
- [Zygmunt (Zalmen) Frydrych], "Fun a tog-bukh" [From a diary].
- Conditions in the Provisioning Unit [ZZ], speculation and thefts intensifying before the holidays, prices of basic products in the Warsaw Ghetto.
- ***Description:*** original [?] (handwritten, ink, 22×288 mm, minor damage and losses of text), transcript (2 copies, handwritten manuscript—U*, pencil, 145×208 mm), Yiddish, ss. 3, pp. 3.
    In original [?] at top information handwritten—U* (pencil): "Frydrych." On p. 1 (transcript, first copy) notation by H.W. in Yiddish (ink): "Frydrych. 109–1942/1 January."
    Attached note by H.W.: "Warsaw 1941. Note of Zygmunt (Zalmen) Frydrych on cond[itions] in the Provisioning Unit for the Jewish District in Warsaw."
    Index: Gliszer, bakery (ul. Leszno 31)

**413. RING. I/435. Mf. ŻIH—785; USHMM—16**

- After 2.05.1942, Warsaw Ghetto
- [G.], Report entitled "News collected in conversation with a functionary of the Order Service." (2.05.1942)
- Text written on the basis of information of G., a former soldier of the Polish Army, from 11.1940 in the Order Service at the post at ul. Chłodna (corner of ul. Żelazna) (wages, sources of support in the Order Service, participation in smuggling, contacts with Germans, Erlich—Order Service liaison with Gestapo). Mentioned: Józef Szeryński, attorney Lederman, former law lecturer at the police school, Schönbach, major, Prusak, former sergeant of the Polish State Police.
- ***Description:*** original or transcript, handwritten manuscript (E*), notebook, ink, Polish, 150×195 mm, minor damage and losses of text, ss. 11, pp. 22.
    Published: *Selected Documents*, pp. 310–317.

**414. RING. I/29. (Lb. 119) Mf. ŻIH—772; USHMM—3. RING. I/96. Mf. ŻIH—776; USHMM—7. RING. I/264. Mf. ŻIH—780; USHMM—11. RING. I/895 (1215). Mf. ŻIH—828; USHMM—40. RING. I/1060 (1379). Mf. ŻIH—832; USHMM—44. RING. I/1220/87. Mf. ŻIH—835; USHMM—47**

- 04–07.1942, Warsaw Ghetto
- [Jechiel Górny], Daily notes (1942)
- Scenes of life of the Warsaw Ghetto, situation of the Jewish population in various localities on Polish lands (e.g., Sosnowiec, Rejowiec), part of the information on the basis of accounts of other people (NN.).
- ***Description:*** original, handwritten manuscript (U*), pencil, ink, Polish, Yiddish, 95×155–220×288 mm, minor damage and losses of text, ss. 49, pp. 72.
    Notes: 12.04.1942 (Ring. I/895); 22–25.05.1942 (Ring. I/264 and I/1060); 27–28.05.1942, 29–30.05.1942 (Ring. I/96), 1.06., 3–5.06., 5–7.06.1942 (Ring. I/96, I/1060, I/1220/87); 11–14.06.1942 (Ring. I/96); 11–27.06.1942 (notebook, Ring. I/29); 29.06–10.07.1942 (see below); 11–22.07.1942 (Ring. I/264).
    Ring. I/96 notation by H.W. (ink): "1 standard page"; at the end of the entry of 30.05.1942 H.W.'s note (pen): ". . . st[andard] page."
    Ring. I/1220; on p. 2 notation by H.W. (ink): "2 standard pages."
    Attached note by H.W. in Yiddish: "Daily notes of Jechiel Górny."
    In HWC 32.5 notebook including entries dated 29.06–10.07.1942 (handwritten by U*, Yiddish).
    Index: Elisabeth Kajzer (died 16.05.1942 in Warsaw Ghetto), Paul Harder (died 16.05.1942

25. The *policja granatowa* were the navy blue uniformed Polish collaborationist police force comprised of many ethnic Germans or Volksdeutsche, as well as ethnic Poles.

in Warsaw Ghetto), Walter Guttsman (died 17.05.1942 in Warsaw Ghetto), Windhajn (wife and son), Aleksander Borensztajn of *Gazeta Żydowska*

## 415. RING. I/432. (Lb. 1720). Mf. ŻIH—784; USHMM—15

- 20.07–3.08.1942, Warsaw Ghetto
- [Dawid Graber], Account entitled "A por ayndrukn un erinerungen" [A Few Impressions and Recollections]
- Author (born 22.05.1923) describes the situation in the Warsaw Ghetto, before the start of the liquidation action and during the action, his participation in collection and safeguarding of archival materials on the fate of the Jewish population during the occupation: persecutions and extermination; attached author's testament and biography written down while he and [Izrael] Lichtensztajn and [Nahum] Grzywacz were burying the Oyneg Shabes archive (3.08.1942).
- ***Description:*** original, handwritten manuscript, notebook, ink, Yiddish, 155×200 mm, ss. 19, pp. 32.

  At the end are traces left by photographs (preserved descriptions: 1) "At the daycamp of our kitchen. Year 1941. Summer. In the courtyard of the former barracks [ul.] Zamenhofa 19. Grzywacz and I are watering flowers"; 2) "Summer 1941. I with my friend on ul. Leszno. Graber Dawid, Zosia Dorn—refugee from Lipno").

  Inventory: "Author Dawid Graber."

  Published: *Selected Documents*, pp. 59–67 (fragment).

## 416. RING. I/1018 (1337). (Lb. 386). Mf. ŻIH—831; USHMM—43

- 07–08.1942, Warsaw Ghetto
- Nuchym [Nahum] Grzywacz (born 28.10.1924), Diary (20.07–3.08.1942), biography and testament
- Notes on events preceding the liquidation action of the Warsaw Ghetto and of the first days of the action (suicide of Adam Czerniaków, new authorities of the Jewish Council, active participation of the Order Service in the action), author's testament with biography. Information about how he, Izrael Lichtensztajn, and Dawid Graber (3.08.1942) buried the Oyneg Shabes materials.
- ***Description:*** original, handwritten manuscript, notebook, ink, Yiddish, 144×202 mm, ss. 17, pp. 32.

  Traces left by 2 photographs on pp. 24–25 (descriptions were preserved: 1) from the 1941 daycamp Grzywacz and Graber; 2) of the theatrical presentation entitled *Wszystkie okna ku słońcu* [All the windows facing the sun]).

  On the cover is the title written in the author's hand: "Zamlheft bashribn fun Nokhem Gzhivatsh" [Notebook Written by Nachum Grzywacz].

  Author assisted in concealing the ghetto archive; see *Kronika getta*, p. 18.

  Published: *BFG*, vol. II, no. 1–4 (1949), pp. 288–293.

  Index: Lichtensztajn, Graber, Bałaban, Czerniaków, Lichtenbaum, Sztolcman, Wielikowski, Szeryński [Józef], Lejkin

## 417. RING. I/218. Mf. ŻIH—780; USHMM—11

- After 09.1941, Warsaw Ghetto
- K. H. Band [Kalman Huberband], Report entitled "Der 'marsh' in mikve arayn, onhoyb yor tsh'a" [The "March" into the ritual bath, beginning of the year 5701 (Fall 1940)]
- Germans banned use of the ritual bath, despite which before Yom Kippur a rabbi recommended immersion in a mikve.
- ***Description:*** transcript (a) (1 copy, typescript, 220×175 mm, ss. 3, pp. 3), transcript (b) (2 copies, the second copy missing p. 4, typescript, 210×295 mm, ss. 7, pp. 7), Yiddish, minor damage and losses of text, ss. 10, pp. 10.

  On p. 1 (2nd and 3rd copies) information in Yiddish (ink): "Huberband."

  Attached note by H.W. in Yiddish: "Kalman Huberband [brother of Szymon] wrote, before the uprising he was a contact involved in purchase of weapons in the ghetto."

  See HWC, 40/1 (second copy of transcript (a), typescript, ss. 3 as well as one sheet (page 4) from transcript (b).

## 418. RING. I/347. Mf. ŻIH—782; USHMM—13

- After 06.1940, Warsaw Ghetto
- [Szymon Huberband?], Report entitled "Dinasn zumer 1940" [Dynasy[26] sport center, summer 1940]
- Author was seized with a colleague in the Praga district in June 1940 for compulsory labor (Schulz and Krieger beat them and treated them sadistically).
- ***Description:*** original, handwritten manuscript (HUB.*), ink, Yiddish, 210×292 mm, minor damage and losses of text, ss. 4, pp. 4.

  Published: *BFG*, vol. XXIX–XXX (1991–1992), pp. 208–213; *Kiddush Hashem*, pp. 66–70; *Selected Documents*, pp. 262–265.

## 419. RING. I/996 (1315). (Lb. 495). Mf. ŻIH—831; USHMM—43

- After 05.1942, Warsaw Ghetto
- [Szymon Huberband?], "Di khaperai fun yidn in

26. Dynasy, the name of which was derived from the palace of the Duke de Nassau that formerly stood there, was a small sport center in Warsaw, with a covered bicycle track, gymnastic facilities, and the like.

Varshe in mai 1942" [The Roundup of Jews in Warsaw in May 1942]

- Description of the action that commenced on 21.05.1942 with seizure of young males (1,330), who were sent out with a group of prisoners (160) from the jail (ul. Gęsia 24) to an unknown destination. On the terrain of the ghetto, only the Order Service took part in the action. Precise description of the Order Service post at ul. Zamenhofa 19, where those seized were gathered.
- ***Description:*** original or transcript, handwritten manuscript (HUB.*), notebook, ink, Yiddish, 150×194 mm, ss. 12, pp. 23.
  On p. 1 notation of H.W. in Yiddish (ink): "12 standard pages."
  Published: *Kiddush Hashem*, pp. 102–106 (fragment, to p. 12, to 8th line from the bottom).
  On the roundup in the ghetto, see *Czerniaków*, pp. 283–284.

### 420. RING. I/96. (Lb. 443). Mf. ŻIH—776; USHMM—7. RING. I/365. MF ŻIH—782; USHMM—13.

- 05.1942, Warsaw Ghetto
- [Szymon] Huberband, Diary (19–19.05.1942)
- Information about people killed on the streets of the ghetto, participation of Poles in persecution of Jews, about a Pole who aided the Jewish population. German film crew preparing a document[ary film] on the subjects: "Jewish demoralization," "Jewish cruelty," "Jewish debauchery," "Jewish funeral."
- ***Description:*** original, handwritten manuscript (HUB.*), ink, Yiddish, 160×200 mm, ss. 5, pp. 8.
  On p. 1, note by H.W. in Yiddish (ink): "5 st. pages."
  On p. 2 in another handwriting: "Huberband."
  This fragment of Huberband's diary was buried together (vivid traces survived of the second sheet were preserved on the back of the first sheet), but after the war the first sheet containing the entry of 9.05.1942 was separated from the rest and placed separately under the no. Ring. I/365.
  Index: Perkal, Rabbi who died winter 1942 in Warsaw; Dunenfeld, young man, son-in-law of Szlomo Grabski, murdered by the Germans in Warsaw 04/05.1942; Elimelech, butcher from Czerniaków, murdered by Germans in Warsaw 19.05. 1942

### 421. RING. I/446. Mf. ŻIH—785; USHMM—16

- 06.1942, Warsaw Ghetto
- [Szymon Huberband], Diary (21–27.06.1942)
- Notation on the situation and extermination of the Jewish population, e.g., in Olkusz, Chełm [Lubelski], Warsaw Ghetto (e.g., execution of a girl and her brother from ul. Nowolipki 51, fate of smugglers).
- ***Description:*** original, handwritten manuscript (HUB.*), ink, Yiddish, 155×195 mm, serious damage and losses of text, ss. 6, pp. 12.
  On p. 12 at the bottom is notation by H.W. in Yiddish (ink): "6.5 standard pages. June 1942"
  Attached note by H.W.: "Chronicle of Warsaw June 1942. Notes of R. Szymon Huberband."

### 422. RING. I/365. Mf. ŻIH—782; USHMM—13

NOTE: Document was shifted to no. 420.

### 423. RING. I/251. (Lb. 1290). Mf. ŻIH—836; USHMM—67

- After 6.01.1942, Warsaw Ghetto
- Icchak Kac, Rabbi, Report entitled "Vos ikh [hob] gevolt zogn . . . oyf der konferents fun JSS, vos iz forgekumen montog, dem 6 januar 1942, oyf velkher ikh bin geven a delegat" [What I wanted to say . . . at the conference of the JSS that took place on Monday, 6 January 1942, at which I was a delegate]
- Religious interpretation (based on the Talmud) of philanthropy for the benefit of the poor as a human obligation, accusation of a lack of charity on the part of Warsaw Jews, proposal for taxation of affluent residents of the ghetto for the needs of the starving.
- ***Description:*** original or transcript, typescript, Yiddish, 207×294 mm, ss. 2, pp. 2.
  Published: *Selected Documents*, pp. 355–357.

### 424. RING. I/235. Mf. ŻIH—780; USHMM—11

- After 20.08.1941, Warsaw Ghetto
- [Ojzer Koc], Report entitled "Epizodn fun 14 teg arbet in seym-gebayde" [Episodes from 14-days' labor in the building of the Sejm] (20.08.1941)
- Author, a teacher in clandestine study groups in Warsaw, seized at the start of December 1939 and forced to work on the grounds of the Sejm (mistreatment, beating of prisoners by guards) was witness to the execution of 8 Boy Scouts in the Sejm gardens and preparation for the next execution. Freed after 14 days.
- ***Description:*** transcript (2 copies), handwritten manuscript (BW*), pencil, Yiddish, 145×205 mm, ss. 20, pp. 20.
  Attached note by H.W.: "Personal statement of Ojzer Koc written down by Bluma Wasser."
  In the margins a letter (ink): "H."

### 425. RING. I/189. Mf. ŻIH—779; USHMM—10

- After 7.07.1941, Warsaw Ghetto
- [Menachem Mendel Kon], Report of: "Baratung fun 8 ratmener forgekumen dem 7 juli 1941 yor in kehile-binyen Gzhybovskie 26" [Conference of 8 councilmen held on 7 July 1941 in the Jewish Community building ul. Grzybowska 26]
- Compulsory taxation of affluent residents of the ghetto for the benefit of those who were starving; of the 8 present: 5 (e.g., Abraham Gepner, [Beniamin]

Zab[łudowski], the assimilator [Bolesław] Roz[enstadt], the corrupt [Leonard] Kupc[zykier], were opposed to taxation, while 3 (Git[erman], Dr. Wiel[ikowski], engineer [Stanisław] Szer[eszewski]) were for the introduction of compulsory taxation of the wealthy.

- ***Description:*** transcript (3 copies), typescript, Yiddish, 220x285 mm, minor damage and losses of text, ss. 9, pp. 9.
  Attached notes by H.W. in Polish and Yiddish: "Written [by] Menachem M. Kon, member of the board of Oyneg Shabes, member of the presidium."
  Published: *Selected Documents*, pp. 299–302.

### 426. RING. I/168. (Lb. 1292). Mf. ŻIH—779; USHMM—10

- After 5.09.1941, Warsaw Ghetto
- [Menachem Mendel Kon], Report entitled "A bliml fun der finants-komisye far individueler bashtajerung fun di milkhome-gvirim un stam raykhe yidn letoyves di pleytim un zeyere pleytim-heymen" [A flower from the Finance Commission for individual taxation of the war-rich and just rich Jews for the benefit of the refugees and their refugee homes]
- Description of a visit at the office of the Finance Commission (of M.M. Kon) by Order Service official [Marian] Haendel, Gestapo collaborator, who demanded exemption of Tabacznik from Łódź from the tax for the benefit of the starving. The Łódź hometown association taxed Tabacznik, and not the Commission.
- ***Description:*** transcript (3 copies), typescript, Yiddish, 208x295 mm, ss. 3, pp. 3.
  Attached note by H.W. in Yiddish: "Menachem Mendel Kon resided in the ghetto at ul. Przebieg 1, one of the most devoted coworkers of Oyneg Shabes."
  Published: *Selected Documents*, pp. 303–304.

### 427. RING. I/95. (Lb. 444). Mf. ŻIH—776; USHMM—7

- After 25.05.1942, Warsaw Ghetto
- [Menachem Mendel Kon?], Report entitled "Mayn bazukh in geto-tfise" [My visit in the ghetto prison]
- Author, at the invitation of the prisoner director [engineer Izaak] Rudniański, on 25.05.1942 visited the prison on ul. Gęsia (1,600 adults and 500 children, punished for leaving the ghetto, trade, lack of armband, and other minor offenses): overcrowded cells, poor sanitary conditions, persons sentenced to death.
- ***Description:*** original, handwritten manuscript (MK*), ink, Yiddish, minor damage and losses of text, ss. 7, pp. 14.
  On p. 1 notation by H.W. in Yiddish: "8 standard pages," "1942 June."
  Inventory: "Author is Menachem Mendel Kohn."

### 428. RING. I/221. Mf. ŻIH—780; USHMM—11

- 06.1942, Warsaw Ghetto
- [Natan Koniński?], Report entitled "First course for Jewish disinfection technicians (XI [19] 40)." (06. [19]42)
- Author in 28.10–9.11.1940 attended a course organized at the command of the German authorities by the State Department of Hygiene [Państwowy Zakład Higieny] (ul. Chocimska 24). Lectures were given and examinations conducted by the physicians: Marcin Kacprzak, Mirkowski, Zański, Stypułtowski, Radło. From the end of 1940 was employed in the Health Department in the mobile ambulance units.
- ***Description:*** original or transcript, handwritten manuscript (E*), ink, Polish, 180x214, 175x150 mm, minor damage and losses of text, ss. 5, pp. 5

### 429. RING. I/282. Mf. ŻIH—781; USHMM—12

- After 10.08.1941, Warsaw Ghetto
- [Natan Koniński?], Report about the funeral of a Catholic Jew in the Warsaw Ghetto (10.08.1941)
- Transcript of an obituary notice poster (klepsydra) and ceremony at the NMP church on ul. Leszno in connection with the funeral of Jerzy Blay on 9.08.1941 (died 6.08.1941), medical doctor, vice chairman of the Warsaw-Białystok Physicians' Chamber [Izba Lekarska Warszawsko-Białostocka].
- ***Description:*** transcript (3 copies), handwritten manuscript (BB*), pencil, Polish, 143x204 mm, damage and losses of text (1 and 3 copies), ss. 9, pp. 9.
  On p. 1 (second copy) information by H.W. (ink): "Kon."
  Inventory: "Author is N. Koniński."

### 430. RING. I/484. Mf. ŻIH—787; USHMM—18

- After 12.1941, Warsaw Ghetto
- [Natan Koniński], Report entitled "Hand over the fur coats"
- Reaction of the Warsaw Ghetto population to the order to give up fur coats (25.12.1941) (attached transcript of the above-mentioned order of Commissioner Auerswald).
- ***Description:*** original (handwritten manuscript -E*, pencil, 148x210 mm), transcript (handwritten manuscript—CA*, pencil, 148x210, minor damage and losses of text), German, Polish, ss. 15, pp. 15.
  Attached note by H.W.: "Written [by] N. Koniński."

### 431. RING. I/988 (1307). (Lb. 463). Mf. ŻIH—831; USHMM—43

- 05–06.1942, Warsaw Ghetto
- [Abraham Lewin], Diary (16.05–5.06.1942)
- Daily description of events of the Warsaw Ghetto, personal observations and overheard accounts, news concerning the Jewish population in other parts of Polish territory. Victims of Nazi violence: Winokur, worker killed 15.05.1942 at al. Szucha; Dziedzic, room

painter (ul. Dzielna 17); Lewiński (age 33), killed for smuggling 18.05.1942; Nadel from Łódź, killed in the Pawiak prison; Hurwic, peddler; Wilner with son and son-in-law Różycki (ul. Mylna 11) killed 30.05.1942; Erenberg family.

- ***Description:*** original, handwritten manuscript (Ś*), notebook, ink, Yiddish, 184×208 mm, minor damage and losses of text, ss. 36, pp. 71.

  On p. 1 notation by H.W. in Yiddish (ink): "27 standard pages"; on p. 50 (entry of 30.05.1942) information by H.W. in Yiddish (ink): "22 standard pages"; name and surname of the author written (Yiddish) in another handwriting.

  Other fragments of the diary of Abraham Lewin: see Ring. II/174, II/202.

  Published: *BFG*, vol. V (1952), no. 4, pp. 22–68; BŻIH, no. 19–20 (1956), pp. 175–206; A. Lewin, *A Cup of Tears. A Diary of the Warsaw Ghetto*, edited by Antony Polonsky, Oxford 1988, pp. 72–120 (also published in that text [pp. 120–144] is another fragment of the diary preserved in the HWC, 31/11 [8.04.1942, handwritten manuscript, ink, Yiddish, pp. 3] and HWC, 32/4 [6–12.06.1942, handwritten manuscript, ink, Yiddish, pp. 20]). Other parts of Abraham Lewin's diary are also in HWC: entries of 14–15.05.1942 (HWC 32.2, handwritten by S*, ink, Yiddish, pp. 5); entries of 13–15.06.1942 (HWC 32.7, handwritten by S*, ink, Yiddish, pp. 20); entries of 27.06–10.07.1942 (HWC 32.6, handwritten by S*, ink Yiddish, pp. 26).

  Index: Szymonowicz, Hurwicz, Mendel and Lewin, coworkers of the "13," killed 23.05.1942; [Abraham] Gancwajch, [Dawid] Szternfeld, Zachariasz brothers

## 432. RING. I/209. Mf. ŻIH—779; USHMM—10

- 1942, Warsaw Ghetto
- [Dr. Celina Lewin?], Memoirs titled "In besieged Warsaw. Tenants' Committee at ul. Nalewki 23"
- Activity of the Tenants' Committee in September 1939 in support of the OPL (anti-aircraft defense) post and its commander Jakub Kahan and coworkers: Szczerański, Elenberg, Mordko, Izydor and Mietek Haberman, Rozenberg, Skowronek, Frenklowa, Chil Moszkowicz and others (care for refugees, organization of a kitchen, provision of food, antifire defense). Attached supplement: "Issued to save the houses at Nalewki 23/25 [from fire]."
- ***Description:*** transcript, handwritten manuscript (D*), ink, Polish, 148×198 mm, extensive minor damage and losses of text, ss. 22, pp. 25.

  Probable fragment of the study from Ring. I/67. According to E.R., the author of the text was Dr. Celina Lewin; see *Kronika getta*, p. 489.

## 433. RING. I/1220/1. Mf. ŻIH—835; USHMM—47

- 1941, Warsaw Ghetto
- [Henryka Łazowert], Report entitled "Dziewi[ęć miesięcy na] Pawiaku" [Nine (months at) the Pawiak prison]
- The author describes conditions in the the prison, fellow prisoners, interrogations.
- ***Description:*** original or transcript, handwritten manuscript, ink, Polish, 198×160, 150×160 mm, extensive damage and losses of text, ss. 9, pp. 17.

  Attached note by H.W.: "1941. Nine months at Pawiak. Forwarded by Henryka Łazowert."

## 434. RING. I/234. (Lb. 350). Mf. ŻIH—780; USHMM—11

- After 08.1941, Warsaw Ghetto
- [Majlech Sztajnberg], Report entitled "Far vos yidn zitsn in Paviak" [Why Jews Are Being Held in Pawiak] (08.1941)
- Description of various cases (10), mainly minor offences (e.g., theft of a bottle of vodka, appearing without armband with star of David,[27] illegal trade, etc.), for which Jews ended up in prison.
- ***Description:*** transcript (2 copies), handwritten manuscript (two handwritings: a) H.W.*—ink; b) MS*—pencil), Yiddish, 147×208 mm, ss. 3, pp. 3.

  There are minor differences between the copies.

  Attached note by H.W. in Polish, Yiddish: "Report of Majlech [Sztajnberg], former prisoner of Pawiak."

  According to E.R., the account's author was Majlech Sztajnberg, a printer, activist of Poale Zion-Left; see *Kronika getta*, p. 485.

## 435. RING. I/100. Mf. ŻIH—776; USHMM—7

- After 04.1941, Warsaw Ghetto
- [Zygmunt Millet?], Recollection about work in the Order Service
- Author, an attorney, coworker of Leon Berenson, describes his efforts to be accepted into the Order Service and his work in it, describes the organization, staff (Józef Andrzej Szeryński, Nikodem Goldsztejn [Goldsztein], [Stanisław] Gąbiński [Gombiński], Szelbach, Marceli and Stanisław Czapliński, Lewin, [Albert] Szwalbe [Szeryński's brother-in-law], Kornblit, Stefan Lubliner, Lederman and others), conflicts around the activity of the Order Service and plan for its reorganization (memorandum of Mieczysław Goldsztejn, [Jerzy] Herc, Henryk Nowogródzki, Przeworski and others).

27. The original is "star of Zion."

- *Description:* transcript (2 copies), typescript, Polish, 208×290 mm, ss. 26, pp. 26.
  See Ring. I/233.

### 436. RING. I/480. Mf. ŻIH—787; USHMM—18

- After 11.1941, Warsaw Ghetto
- [Zygmunt Millet?], Report entitled "Courts"
- Author, an attorney, describes the building of the Courts (ul. Leszno), a place where the ghetto population and "the Aryan side" met, relations between the Polish and Jewish attorneys.
- *Description:* transcript (handwritten manuscript—E*, pencil, 146×210 mm), transcript (2 copies, handwritten manuscript—CA*, pencil, 150×210 mm), Polish, ss. 19, pp. 19.
  Inventory: "Author of the text is the attorney [Zygmunt] Milet [Millet]."
  Published: Palestra, XXXVI, no. 423–424, pp. 4–5 (fragment).

### 437. RING. I/52. Mf. ŻIH—774; USHMM—5

- After 10.1941, Warsaw Ghetto
- [Perec Opoczyński], Report entitled "Der shmugl in varshever geto. Dos Koze-gesl" [Smuggling in the Warsaw Ghetto: Kozia Street] (10.1941)
- Organization of smuggling, smugglers, demand for the work of smugglers, products brought into the ghetto.
- *Description:* original or transcript, handwritten manuscript (OP*), notebook, ink, Yiddish, 155×196 mm, minor damage and losses of text, with places difficult to read, ss. 25, pp. 45.
  Published: P. Opoczyński, *Reportazhn fun varshever geto*, ed. B. Mark, Warsaw 1954, pp. 62–74.

### 438. RING. I/207. ORIGINAL MISSING

- Date unknown, Warsaw Ghetto
- [Perec Opoczyński], Report entitled "Parówki" [Steambaths]
- Disinfection in the Warsaw Ghetto.
- *Description:* original or transcript, typescript, Yiddish, ss. 33, pp. 33.
  Doc. was mentioned (Perec [Opoczyński], "Paruvke," ss. 34) in the list made by H.W.: "Transport 108–1 January 1942"; see Ring. I/1176, p. 1.
  See HWC, 39/7 (another copy of transcript [?], typescript, ss. 34; author: Perec Opoczyński).
  Published: P. Opoczyński, *Reportazhn fun varshever geto*, ed. B. Mark, Warsaw 1954, pp. 25–48.

### 439. RING. I/242. ORIGINAL MISSING

- After 1946, Warsaw
- [Perec Opoczyński?], Report entitled "A Murder on Wolinska; Brother Kills His Little Sister Out of Need"
- On 7.12.1941 at ul. Wołyńska 21, Mosze Nadel (age 16) murdered his sick sister Perla Nadel (age 9) (orphans, parents died, second sister Estera Nadel [age 12]).
- *Description:* postwar transcript, typescript, Yiddish, ss. 4, pp. 4.
  Inventory: "Manuscript of Perec Opoczyński."
  Index: Awigdor Nadel [?] (ul. Wołyńska 2)

### 440. RING. I/981 (1300). (Lb. 492). ORIGINAL MISSING.

- 1948, Warsaw
- [Perec Opoczyński], "Warsaw Ghetto Chronicle: May 1942." (10–25.05.1942)
- Scenes of ghetto life, news from the front, arrests, information from Radom, Dęblin, Tomaszów Mazowiecki (pogrom; killed: Dr. [Efraim] Mortkowicz, Dir. of the Poznański Hospital in Łódź), Sosnowiec, Będzin, Zamość, obituary (Cwi Pryłucki, age 85, died 20.05.1942).
- *Description:* postwar transcript, typescript, Yiddish, 200×293 mm, ss. 14, pp. 14.
  Original perished, copy includes only part of the original's text (10–27.05., 9–18.07.1942)
  See Ring. II/289.
  Index: Siennicki (age 70) of Warsaw

### 441. RING. I/990/2 (1309). (Lb. 416). Mf. ŻIH—831; USHMM—43

- Date unknown, Warsaw Ghetto
- L.R., Report entitled "Kh'bet, helft mir!" [Please, help me!]
- Author (girl, age 16) from Germany, recounts search in Polish territory for her relatives—father and brothers arrested in 1938.
- *Description:* transcript, handwritten manuscript (MS*), pencil, Yiddish, 148×208 mm, minor damage and losses of text, ss. 1, pp. 2.
  In the margin Hebrew letter (ink): "b" (beit). (See Ring. I/990/a)
  Doc. was kept in a binder.

### 442. RING. I/674/3. (Lb. 1688). Mf. ŻIH—816; USHMM—28

- 15.11.1940, Warsaw Ghetto
- R., Report of a resident of the Warsaw Ghetto (ul. Gęsia). (15.11.1940)
- Author was abducted from ul. Leszno and deported from Warsaw, was beaten and tortured for 10 days.
- *Description:* original or transcript, handwritten manuscript, ink, Yiddish, 98×143 mm, ss. 1, pp. 2.

### 443. RING. I/1051 (1370). (Lb. 1476). Mf. ŻIH—832; USHMM—44

- Date unknown, Warsaw Ghetto
- Symche Rajchman (Rechtman?), called Blozer [Bluzer], Report of his stay at the Pawiak prison
- A porter from Warsaw's Praga neighborhood, a smuggler in the ghetto, describes his imprisonment at Pawiak, treatment of Jews by guards and fellow

prisoners (profile of Witold Pruszyński from Puławy, at whose hands many Jews suffered, as well as [Stanisław] Dubois, who defended Jews).

- *Description:* transcript, handwritten manuscript (Ł*), ink, Yiddish, 145×183 mm, minor damage and losses of text, ss. 3, pp. 5.

### 444. RING. I/368. Mf. ŻIH—782; USHMM—13

- After first half of 1940, Warsaw Ghetto
- [Szmuel Rejtowski], Report entitled "Di shkhite iber 53 yidn fun Nalevkes" [The Slaughter of 53 Jews of Nalewki]
- On 21.11.1939 Germans killed 53 men arrested in the apartment house at ul. Nalewki 9 (among others, the rabbi of Mińsk Mazowiecki) (description of arrest, execution at Żerań, the search for the missing by the families, exhumation and burial at Bródno).[28]
- *Description:* original, handwritten manuscript, pencil, Yiddish, 174×220, 150×198 mm, minor damage and losses of text, ss. 9, pp. 16.

  On p. 1 notation in Yiddish (ink): "Szmuel Rejtowski [?] age 29, Gęsia 17 [. . .]."

  Attached note by H.W. in Polish, Yiddish: "Execution Nalewki 9. Written down and delivered by Szmuel Rejtowski (Rajtowski)."

  Index: Kuba Zilberring (age 20), thief from ul. Nalewki 9

### 445. RING. I/503/1. (Lb. 459, 1501). Mf. ŻIH—788; USHMM—19

- 1942, Warsaw Ghetto
- [Emanuel Ringelblum], Notes (1942).
- *Description:* original, handwritten manuscript (ER*), ink, Yiddish, 100×125, 173×210, 150×222 mm, minor damage and losses of text, ss. 33, pp. 60.

  Published: BŻIH, no. 13–14/1955, pp. 211–267; *Kronika getta*, pp. 349–353 (8–26.01.1942, original, handwritten manuscript—ER*, ink, Yiddish, 221×149 mm, minor damage and losses of text, ss. 2, pp. 4); pp. 355–359 (01.1942, original, handwritten manuscript—ER*, ink, Yiddish, 172×210 mm, minor damage and losses of text, ss. 2, pp. 4; doc. was kept in a binder); pp. 359–360 (26.02.1942, original, handwritten manuscript—ER*, ink, Yiddish, 100×145 mm, minor damage and losses of text, ss. 1, pp. 2); pp. 360–361 (24.03.1942, original, handwritten manuscript—ER*, ink, Yiddish, 100×125 mm, ss. 1, pp. 1); pp. 361–362 and 383–384 (10, 12.04. and 05.1942, original, handwritten manuscript—ER*, ink, Yiddish, 150×195 mm, ss. 1, pp. 2); pp. (8–26.01.1942, original, handwritten manuscript—ER*, ink, Yiddish, 221×149 mm, minor damage and losses of text, ss. 2, pp. 4); pp. 362–364 (7.05.1942, original, handwritten manuscript—ER*, ink, Yiddish, 151×193 mm, ss. 2, pp. 3); pp. 364–369 (8.05.1942, original, handwritten manuscript—ER*, ink, Yiddish, 150×194 mm, minor damage and losses of text, ss. 3, pp. 6); pp. 370–374 (12.05.1942, original, handwritten manuscript—ER*, ink, Yiddish, 150×194 mm, minor damage and losses of text, ss. 2, pp. 4); pp. 374–376 ([18].05.1942, original, handwritten manuscript—ER*, ink, Yiddish, 150×194 mm, minor damage and losses of text, ss. 1, pp. 2 (fragment of manuscript omitted from the information repeated under the date 30.05.1942—about Judtowa); pp. 376–378 (19.05.1942, original, handwritten manuscript—ER*, ink, Yiddish, 158×194 mm, minor damage and losses of text, ss. 1, pp. 2); pp. 379–381 (22.05. and 05.1942, original, handwritten manuscript—ER*, ink, Yiddish, 150×194 mm, ss. 1, pp. 2); pp. 382–383 (25.05.1942, original, handwritten manuscript—ER*, ink, Yiddish, 149×194 mm, minor damage and losses of text, ss. 1, pp. 2); pp. 384–385 (26.05.1942, original, handwritten manuscript—ER*, ink, Yiddish, 144×180 mm, ss. 1, pp. 1); pp. 385–387 ([30].05.1942, original, handwritten manuscript—ER*, ink, Yiddish, 145×180 mm, minor damage and losses of text, ss. 2, pp. 3); pp. 387–388 (05.1942, original, handwritten manuscript—ER*, ink, Yiddish, 149×195 mm, ss. 1, pp. 2); pp. 388–391 (05.1942, original, handwritten manuscript—ER*, ink, Yiddish, 150×194 mm, ss. 1, pp. 2); pp. 391–395 (10.06.1942, original, handwritten manuscript—ER*, ink, Yiddish, 150×194 mm, minor damage and losses of text, ss. 3, pp. 6); pp. 395–397 (26.06.1942, original, handwritten manuscript—ER*, ink, Yiddish, 148×193 mm, minor damage and losses of text, ss. 1, pp. 2); pp. 397–399 (30.06.1942, original, handwritten manuscript—ER*, ink, Yiddish, 150×195 mm, minor damage and losses of text, ss. 2, pp. 4); pp. 399–401 (06.1942, original, handwritten manuscript—ER*, ink, Yiddish, 150×194 mm, ss. 2, pp. 4); pp. 401–402 (06.1942, original, handwritten manuscript—ER*, ink, Yiddish, 150×193 mm, ss. 1, pp. 2); pp. 402–403 (06.1942, original, handwritten manuscript—ER*, ink, Yiddish, 150×192 mm, minor damage and losses of text, ss. 1, pp. 2).

  Manuscript (Date unknown, original, handwritten manuscript—ER*, ink, Yiddish, 104×149 mm, ss. 1, pp. 2) undetermined whether it was published in print.

28. The site of the other Warsaw Jewish cemetery located in the Praga district, on the east bank of the Vistula River.

**446. RING. I/504. (Lb. 373). Mf. ŻIH–788; USHMM–19**

- 1941, Warsaw Ghetto
- [Emanuel Ringelblum], Notes (12.1940–06.1941).
- ***Description:*** transcript (2 copies), handwritten manuscript (MS*), pencil, Yiddish, 145×208, 150×210 mm, minor damage and losses of text, ss. 97, pp. 98.

Doc. was kept in a binder.

Published: BŻIH, no. 1(3)/1952, pp. 46–82 (Notes 02–04.1941); BŻIH no. 11–12/1954, pp. 122–166 (Notes 05–12.1941); *Kronika getta*, pp. 213–217 (12, 13, 14.12.1940, copy, handwritten manuscript—MS*, pencil, Yiddish, 148×208 mm, ss. 1, pp. 2; notation by H.W. in Yiddish (ink): "Little Flower" (Bliml); doc. was kept in a binder); pp. 278–279 (entry erroneously placed under the date 7.05.1942) (7.01.1941, transcript—2 copies, handwritten manuscript—MS*, pencil, Yiddish, 150×198 mm, minor damage and losses of text, ss. 2, pp. 2; at the top a symbol (ink): " ^^ "; notation in Yiddish: "current events"; doc. was kept in a binder); pp. 232–233 (19.02.1941, transcript—2 copies, handwritten manuscript—MS*, pencil, Yiddish, 147×208 mm, ss. 4, pp. 4; notation in Yiddish: "Little Flower"; in the margins a symbol (ink): "—="); pp. 239–243 (02.1941, transcript—2 copies, handwritten manuscript—MS*, pencil, Yiddish, 147×208 mm, ss. 6, pp. 6; notation in Yiddish: "Little Flower." In the margin a Hebrew letter [ink]: "b"; doc. was kept in a binder); pp. 245–250 (18.03.1941, transcript—2 copies, handwritten manuscript—MS*, pencil, Yiddish, 147×208 mm, ss. 8, pp. 8; notation in Yiddish: "Little Flower"; in the margins a symbol [ink]: "V" one above another, doc. was kept in a binder); pp. 257–260 (03.1941, transcript—2 copies, handwritten manuscript—MS*, pencil, Yiddish, 147×208 mm, ss. 4, pp. 4; notation in Yiddish: "Little Flower"; in the margins a symbol [ink]: " .-. "); pp. 260–263 (6.04.1941, transcript—2 copies, handwritten manuscript—MS*, pencil, Yiddish, 147×208 mm, ss. 6, pp. 6; notation in Yiddish: "Little Flower"; in the margins a symbol [ink]: "X" underlined top and bottom); pp. 263–266 ([10].04.1941, transcript—2 copies, handwritten manuscript—MS*, pencil, Yiddish, 148×208 mm, ss. 8, pp. 8; notation in Yiddish: "Little Flower"; in the margins Hebrew letter [ink]: "d"; doc. was kept in a binder); pp. 266–269 (17.04.1941, transcript—2 copies, handwritten manuscript—MS*, pencil, Yiddish, 150×208 mm, ss. 6, pp. 6; notation in Yiddish: "Little Flower"; in the margins a symbol [ink]: "circle with a dot in the middle"; pp. 269–277 (26.04.1941, transcript—2 copies, handwritten manuscript—MS*, pencil, Yiddish, 147×208 mm, minor damage and losses of text, ss. 18, pp. 18; notation in Yiddish: "Little Flower"; in the margins a letter [ink]: "R"); pp. 279–286 (11.05.1941, transcript—2 copies, handwritten manuscript—MS*, pencil, Yiddish, 147×206 mm, minor damage and losses of text, ss. 14, pp. 14; in the margins a letter [ink]: "T"); pp. 286–288 (18.05.1941, transcript—2 copies, handwritten manuscript—MS*, pencil, Yiddish, 147×208 mm, ss. 4, pp. 4; notation in Yiddish: "Little Flower"; in the margins a symbol [ink]: " ~ "); pp. 288–291 (20.05.1941, transcript—2 copies, handwritten manuscript—MS*, pencil, Yiddish, 145×206 mm, minor damage and losses of text, ss. 6, pp. 6; notation in Yiddish: "Little Flower"; in the margins a symbol [ink]: wavy vertical line); pp. 291–292 (Beginning 06.1941, transcript—2 copies, handwritten manuscript—MS*, pencil, Yiddish, 145×205 mm, ss. 2, pp. 2; notation in Yiddish: "Little Flower"; in the margins a symbol [ink]: " .-. "—vertically [pionowo]); pp. 292–294 ([Beginning 06.1941], transcript—2 copies, handwritten manuscript—MS*, pencil, Yiddish, 145×207 mm, ss. 4, pp. 4; notation in Yiddish: "Little Flower"; in the margins a symbol [ink]: dot in a semicircle—in a different composition than in the note of 10.06. [1941]); pp. 297–298 (10.06.[1941], transcript—2 copies, handwritten manuscript—MS*, pencil, Yiddish, 145×207 mm, ss. 4, pp. 4; notation in Yiddish: "Little Flower." In the margins a symbol [ink]: dot in a semicircle—in a different composition than in the note of [beginning 06.1941]).

**447. RING. I/505. (Lb. 1268). Mf. ŻIH–789; USHMM–20**

- After 1941, Warsaw Ghetto
- [Emanuel Ringelblum], Notes (1941).
- ***Description:*** transcript, typescript, Yiddish, 181×268, 207×294 mm, damage and losses of text, ss. 40, pp. 40.

Attached note by H.W. in Yiddish: "'Bliml' [Little Flower] [is the] cryptonym [of] Dr. E.R."

Published: BŻIH, no. 11–12/1954, pp. 122–166; *Kronika getta*, pp. 300–302 (08.1941, transcript—2 copies, typescript, Yiddish, 208×294 mm, minor damage and losses of text, ss. 8, pp. 8; on p. 1 (first copy) notation by H.W. in Yiddish (ink): "Little Flower"; pp. 309–311 (08.1941, transcript—2 copies, typescript, Yiddish, 208×293, 170×290 mm, minor damage and losses of text, ss. 6, pp. 6; on p. 1 (first copy) notation by H.W. in Yiddish (ink): "Bliml" (Little Flower); pp. 325–328

(10.1941, transcript—2 copies, typescript, Yiddish, 203×293, 170×290 mm, minor damage and losses of text, ss. 8, pp. 8; on p. 1 notation of H.W. in Yiddish [ink]: "Little Flower"; pp. 328–329 ([10.]1941, transcript (p. 1 in 2 copies), typescript, Yiddish, 165×290, 205×290 mm, damage and losses of text, ss. 3, pp. 3; on p. 1 notation of H.W. in Yiddish (ink): "Little Flower"; pp. 336–338 (22.11.1941, transcript—2 copies, typescript, Yiddish, 208×292 mm, minor damage and losses of text, ss. 6, pp. 6; on p. 1 notation of H.W. in Yiddish (ink): "Little Flower" and notation by H.W. in Yiddish [first copy]: "109–1942/1 January. no. 5") ; p. 347 (12.1941, transcript—3 copies, typescript, Yiddish, 170×275, 182×270 mm, serious damage and losses of text, ss. 3, pp. 3); ; p. 346 (12.1941, transcript—3 copies, Yiddish, 212×276 mm, significant damage and losses of text, ss. 3, pp. 3); pp. 346–347 (end of 1941, transcript—3 copies, typed, Yiddish, 205×280 mm, significant damage and losses of text, ss. 3, pp. 3; p. 347 (no date, transcript—3 copies, typed, Yiddish, 165×280, 187×268, 184×260 mm, significant damage and losses of text, ss. 3, pp. 3); two documents (12 1941, transcript—3 copies, typed, Yiddish, 190×277 mm, significant damage and losses of text, ss. 3, pp. 3)—not determined whether they were published in print.

See HWC, 31/6 (third copy of a fragment concerning 08.1941, typescript, ss. 4; on p. 1 notation in Yiddish [ink]: "Little Flower"; see *Kronika getta*, pp. 300–302); 31.7 (third copy of fragment, typed, ss. 3; on p. 1 a note by H.W. in Yiddish (ink): "Little Flower"; see *Kronika getta*, pp. 309–311); 31/9 (third copy concerning 10/1941, typescript, ss. 4, see *Kronika getta*, pp. 325–328).

### 448. RING. I/506. (Lb. 708). Mf. ŻIH—789; USHMM—20

- 1941, Warsaw Ghetto
- [Emanuel Ringelblum], Notes (1941).
- ***Description:*** original, handwritten manuscript (ER*), ink, Yiddish, 75×111, 142×205 mm, minor damage and losses of text, ss. 12, pp. 20.

Published: BŻIH, no. 3/1952, pp. 46–82 (Notes of 02–04.1941); no. 11–12/1954, pp. 122–166 (Notes of 05–12.1941); *Kronika getta*, pp. 235–239 ([27–28.02.1941], original, handwritten manuscript—ER*, ink, Yiddish, 150×198 mm, ss. 1, pp. 2); pp. 254–257 ([03.1941], original, handwritten manuscript—ER*, ink, Yiddish, 149×227 mm, ss. 1, pp. 1; enclosed H.W. note in ink: "March 1941"); pp. 299 ([08.1941], original, handwritten manuscript—ER*, ink, Yiddish, 145×212 mm, ss. 1, pp. 1); pp. 302–306 ([08.1941], original, handwritten manuscript—ER*, ink, Yiddish, 156×197 mm, ss. 2, pp. 4); pp. 312–313 ([31.08.1941], original, handwritten manuscript—ER*, ink, Yiddish, 140×205 mm, ss. 1, pp. 2); pp. 316–317 ([09.1941], original, handwritten manuscript—ER*, ink, Yiddish, 122×218 mm, ss. 1, pp. 2); pp. 317–319, 320–321 ([mid 09.1941], original, handwritten manuscript—ER*, ink, Yiddish, 144×109 mm, ss. 2, pp. 4).

Two manuscripts: a) ([Beginning 06.1941, original, handwritten manuscript—ER*, ink, Yiddish, 78×111 mm, ss. 1, pp. 2); b) (20, 26.09.1941, original, handwritten manuscript—ER*, ink, Yiddish, 75×111 mm, ss. 2, pp. 4)—not determined whether they were published in print.

### 449. RING. I/507/1, (Lb.. 708). RING. I/514. I/514. Mf. ŻIH—789; USHMM—20

**a) Ring. I/507/1**

- Warsaw Ghetto
- [Emanuel Ringelblum], Notes (1939–1941 [1942?])
- Chronicle of current events.
- ***Description:*** original, copy, handwritten manuscript (ER*), typescript, ink, Yiddish, 106×223, 117×336, 206×281 mm, k.121, pp. 177.

ER backdated some notes, e.g.: instead of 1939 he wrote "1937" or "1938."

Attached note by H.W. in Yiddish: "May 1941, notes ER."

Published: BŻIH, no. 2/1951, pp. 81–207 (Notes of 1940); no. 3/1952, pp. 46–82 (Notes of 02–04.1941); *Przewodnik*, before p. 609 (photocopy of a sheet with entry of 1–2.02.1942); *Kronika getta*, pp. 29–32 ([09.1939], original, handwritten manuscript—ER*, ink, Yiddish, 206×283 mm, ss. 1, pp. 2; doc. was kept in a binder) missing; pp. 32–33 ([09.1939], original, handwritten manuscript—ER*, ink, Yiddish, 94×155 mm, ss. 1, pp. 2; doc. was kept in a binder); pp. 33 ([09.1939], original, handwritten manuscript—ER*, ink, Yiddish, 93×155 mm, ss. 1, pp. 2; doc. was kept in a binder); pp. 35 ([1, 6, 7.12.1939], original, handwritten manuscript—ER*, ink, Yiddish, 95×109 mm, ss. 1, pp. 1; doc. was kept in a binder); pp. 34–35, 36–37, 37–39, 40 ([09.1939, 5–8.12., 6.12., 8.12.1939], original, handwritten manuscript—ER*, ink, Yiddish, 225×220 mm, ss. 2, pp. 3; doc. was kept in a binder); p. 41 ([10.12.1939], original, handwritten manuscript—ER*, ink, Yiddish, 93×153 mm, ss. 1, pp. 2; doc. was kept in a binder); pp. 42–43 (12.12.[1939], original, handwritten manuscript—ER*, ink, Yiddish, 205×281 mm, ss. 1, pp. 1; at the top a symbol (ink): "—"; doc. was kept in a binder); pp. 43–44 (13–14.12.[1939], original, handwritten manuscript—ER*, ink, Yiddish, 92×155 mm, ss. 1, pp. 1; doc. was kept in a binder); p. 44 (14.12.[1939], original, handwritten manuscript—ER*, ink, Yiddish, 206×143 mm, ss. 1, pp. 1; at the top a symbol (ink): "—"; doc. was kept in a binder); pp. 44–46 (15.12.[1939], original, handwritten manuscript—ER*, ink, Yiddish, 140×208 mm, ss. 1, pp. 2; at the top (p. 2) a symbol (ink): "—"; doc. was kept in a binder); pp. 47–48 (18.12.[1939], original, handwritten manuscript—ER*, ink, Yiddish, 157×150 mm, ss. 1, pp. 2; at the top a symbol (ink): "—"; doc. was kept in a binder); pp. 58–60 (after 18.12.[1939], original, handwritten manuscript—ER*, ink, Yiddish, 205×283 mm, text illegible in places, ss. 1, pp. 2; at the top a symbol (ink): "—"; doc. was kept in a binder); pp. 48–49 (18–19.12.[1939], original, handwritten manuscript—ER*, ink, Yiddish, 138×213 mm, text illegible in places, ss. 1, pp. 1; at the top a symbol (ink): "—"; doc. was kept in a binder); pp. 49–50 (19.12.[1939], original, handwritten manuscript—ER*, ink, Yiddish, 208×282 mm, text illegible in places, ss. 1, pp. 1; at the top a symbol (ink): "—"; doc. was kept in a binder); pp. 50–52 (21.12.[1939], original, handwritten manuscript—ER*, ink, Yiddish, 205×283 mm, text illegible in places, ss. 2, pp. 4; at the top a symbol (ink): "—"; doc. was kept in a binder); p. 60 (22.12.[1939], transcript—3 copies, typescript, Yiddish, 180×272, 205×280 mm, extensive damage and losses of text, ss. 3, pp. 3); pp. 54–56 (25.12.[1939], original, handwritten manuscript—ER*, ink, Yiddish, 205×283 mm, text illegible in places, ss. 1, pp. 2; at the top a letter (ink): "T"; doc. was kept in a binder); pp. 63–64 (28–31.12.[1939], original, handwritten manuscript—ER*, pencil, Yiddish, 206×153 mm, text illegible in places, ss. 1, pp. 2; at the top a symbol (ink): "—"; doc. was kept in a binder); pp. 61–63 (30.12.[1939], original, handwritten manuscript—ER*, pencil, Yiddish, 205×283 mm, text illegible in places, ss. 1, pp. 2; at the top a symbol (ink): "—"; doc. was kept in a binder); pp. 56–57 (12.[1939], original, handwritten manuscript—ER*, ink, pencil, Yiddish, 205×283 mm, text illegible in places, ss. 1, pp. 2; at the top a letter (ink): "T"; doc. was kept in a binder); pp. 61 (12.[1939], original, handwritten manuscript—ER*, ink, Yiddish, 93×155 mm, text illegible in places, ss. 1, pp. 2; at the top a symbol (ink): "—"; doc. was kept in a binder); pp. 65–67 ([Beginning 1940], original, handwritten manuscript—ER*, ink, Yiddish, 143×206 mm, text illegible in places, ss. 1, pp. 2; at the top a symbol (ink): "—"; doc. was kept in a binder); pp. 75–80 (7, 9.01.[1940], original, handwritten manuscript—ER*, ink, Yiddish, 110×176 mm, text illegible in places, ss. 2, pp. 4; doc. was kept in a binder); pp. 80–84 (17, 19, 20.01.[1940], original, handwritten manuscript—ER*, ink, Yiddish, 143×206 mm, text illegible in places, ss. 2, pp. 4; doc. was kept in a binder); pp. 84–86 (28, 30.01.[1940], original, handwritten manuscript—ER*, ink, Yiddish, 145×210 mm, ss. 1, pp. 2; doc. was kept in a binder); pp. 86–88 (1, 2.02.[1940], original, handwritten manuscript—ER*, ink, Yiddish, 154×185 mm, text illegible in places, ss. 1, pp. 2; doc. was kept in a binder); pp. 88–89 (7–8.02.[1940], original, handwritten manuscript—ER*, ink, Yiddish, 154×94 mm, text illegible in places, ss. 2, pp. 4; doc. was kept in a binder); pp. 90–92 (9, 12, 13, 14.02.[1940], original, handwritten manuscript—ER*, ink, Yiddish, 155×184 mm, text illegible in places, ss. 1, pp. 2; doc. was kept in a binder); pp. 92–94 (15, 18, 19.02.[1940], original, handwritten manuscript—ER*, ink, Yiddish, 155×184 mm, ss. 1, pp. 2; doc. was kept in a binder); pp. 95–98 (21, 22, 23.02.[1940], original, handwritten manuscript—ER*, ink, Yiddish, 155×190 mm, text illegible in places, ss. 1, pp. 2; doc. was kept in a binder); pp. 98–101 (6.03.[1940], original, handwritten manuscript—ER*, ink, Yiddish, 155×184 mm, text illegible in places, ss. 1, pp. 2; at the top a letter (ink): "T"; doc. was kept in a binder); pp. 101–105 (9, 12, 15, 16.03.[1940], original, handwritten manuscript—ER*, ink, Hebrew, Yiddish, 145×208 mm, text illegible in places, ss. 1, pp. 2; at the top a letter (ink): "T"; doc. was kept in a binder); pp. 109–113 (23, 28.03.[1940], original, handwritten manuscript—ER*, ink, Yiddish, 155×183 mm, ss. 1, pp. 2; at the top a letter (ink): "T"; doc. was kept in a binder); pp. 105–109 (27.03.[1940], original, handwritten manuscript—ER*, ink, Yiddish, 152×196 mm, ss. 1, pp. 2; at the top a letter (ink): "T"; doc. was kept in a binder); pp. 113–117 (29, 30.03.[1940], original, handwritten manuscript—ER*, ink, Hebrew, Yiddish, 155×184 mm, ss. 1, pp. 2; at the top a letter (ink): "T"; doc. was kept in a binder); pp. 117–118 (03.[1940], original, handwritten manuscript—ER*, ink, Yiddish, 146×197 mm, text illegible in places, ss. 1, pp. 2; at the top a letter (ink): "T"; doc. was kept in a binder); pp. 118–122 (end of 03.[1940], original, handwritten manuscript—ER*, ink, Yiddish, 143×199 mm, ss. 1, pp. 2; at the top a letter (ink): "T"; doc. was kept in a binder, handwritten manuscript published with omissions); pp. 122–125 (13.04.[1940], original, handwritten manuscript—ER*, pencil, Yiddish, 153×198 mm, ss. 2, pp. 4; doc. was kept in a binder); pp. 126–129 (26, 27.04.[1940], original, handwritten manuscript—ER*, ink, Yiddish, 145×200 mm, ss. 1, pp. 2; doc. was kept in a binder, manuscript published with omissions); pp. 134–135 (2, 4, 6, 7, 8.05.[1940], original, handwritten manuscript—ER*, ink, pencil, Yiddish, 99×159 mm, ss. 1, pp. 2; at the top a letter (ink): "T"; doc. was kept in a binder); pp. 135–138 (2–9.05.[1940], original, handwritten manuscript—ER*, ink, Yiddish, 120×336 mm, ss. 1, pp. 2; at the top a letter (ink): "T"; doc. was kept in a binder); pp. 138–142 (9, 13, 16, 21, 27, 28.05.[1940], original, handwritten manuscript—ER*, ink, Yiddish, 175×220 mm, text illegible in places, ss. 1, pp. 2; at the top a letter (ink): "T"; doc. was kept in a binder); pp. 142–144 (14, 16, 20, 22.08.[1940], original, handwritten manuscript—ER*, ink, Yiddish, 96×145 mm, ss. 1, pp. 2; at the top a letter (ink): "T"; doc. was kept in a binder, manuscript published with omission of closing fragments of text); pp. 144–145 (25, 28.08.[1940], original, handwritten manuscript—ER*, ink, Yiddish, 99×140 mm, minor damage and losses of text, ss. 1, pp. 2; at the top a letter (ink): "T"; doc. was kept in a binder); pp. 146–149 (6, 7, 8, 9.09.[1940], original, handwritten manuscript—ER*, ink, Yiddish, 97×135 mm, text illegible in places, ss. 2, pp. 4; at the top a letter (ink): "T"; doc. was kept in a binder);s. 149–151 (16.09.[1940], original, handwritten manuscript—ER*, ink, Yiddish, 96×135 mm, text illegible in places, ss. 1, pp. 2; at the top a letter (ink): "T"; doc. was kept in a binder); pp. 151–154 (17, 18, 19.09.[1940], original, handwritten manuscript—ER*, ink, Yiddish, 150×185 mm, minor damage and losses of text, ss. 1, pp. 2; at the top a letter (ink): "T"; doc. was kept in a binder); pp. 155–158 (24, 25, 29.09.[1940], original, handwritten manuscript—ER*, ink, Yiddish, 160×195 mm, ss. 1, pp. 2; at the top a letter (ink): "T"; doc. was kept in a binder); pp. 160–168 (2, 3, 4, 5.10.[1940], original, handwritten manuscript—ER*, ink, Yiddish, 216×276 mm, text illegible in places, ss. 1, pp. 2); pp. 170–174 (12–13.10.[1940], original, manuscript—ER*, ink, pencil, Yiddish, 207×230 mm, ss. 1, pp. 2; doc. was kept in a binder); pp. 174–177 (20.10.[1940], original, handwritten manuscript—ER*, ink, Yiddish, 100×137 mm, minor damage and losses of text, ss. 1, pp. 2; doc. was kept in a binder); pp. 177–180 (23–24.10.[1940], original, handwritten manuscript—ER*, ink, pencil, Yiddish, 98×150 mm, text illegible in places, ss. 2, pp. 4; doc. was kept in a binder; manuscript published with omissions); pp. 181–184 (25, 26, 27, 28, 29, 31.10.[1940], original, handwritten manuscript—ER*, ink, Yiddish, 150×197 mm, ss. 1, pp. 2; doc. was kept in a binder; on p. 1 notation (pencil): "INDOCHINY" [Indochina]); pp. 184–186 (1.11.[1940], original, handwritten manuscript—ER*, ink, pencil, Yiddish, 145×179 mm, ss. 1, pp. 2; doc. was kept in a binder); pp. 186–189 (2, 5, 6.11.[1940], original, handwritten manuscript—ER*, ink, Yiddish, 144×180 mm, ss. 1, pp. 2; doc. was kept in a binder); pp. 189–192 (8.11.[1940], original, handwritten manuscript—ER*, ink, Yiddish, 144×178 mm, ss. 1, pp. 2; doc. was kept in a binder); pp. 196–198 (15.11.[1940], original, handwritten manuscript—ER*, ink, Yiddish, 97×146 mm, ss. 1, pp. 2; at the top a letter (symbol) (ink): "X"; doc. was kept in a binder); pp. 198–201 (19, 20.11.[1940], original, handwritten manuscript—ER*, ink, Yiddish, 154×194 mm, ss. 1, pp. 2; on p. 1 at the bottom notation (pencil): "AMERYKA"; doc. was kept in a binder); pp. 201–204 (21, 23.11.[1940], original, handwritten manuscript—ER*, ink, Yiddish, 96×144 mm, ss. 1, pp. 2; at the top a letter (a symbol) (ink): "X"; doc. was kept in a binder; manuscript published with omission of the closing fragment); pp. 204–206 (26–27.11.[1940], original, handwritten manuscript—ER*, ink, Yiddish, 98×140 mm, minor damage and losses of text, text illegible in places, ss. 1, pp. 2; doc. was kept in a binder); pp. 206–210 (29.11–2.12.[1940], original, handwritten manuscript—ER*, ink, Yiddish, 155×195 mm, text illegible in places, ss. 1, pp. 2; on p. 2 at the bottom a letter (symbol) (ink): "X"; doc. was kept in a binder); pp. 217–221 (15, 17, 20.12.[1940], original, handwritten manuscript—ER*, ink, pencil, Yiddish, 150×177 mm, ss. 1, pp. 2); pp. 227–230 (31.12–5.01.[1941], original, handwritten manuscript—ER*, ink, Yiddish, 108×193 mm, minor damage and losses of text, ss. 1, pp. 2; doc. was kept in a binder); pp. 230–232 (15, 16.01.[1941], original, handwritten manuscript—ER*, ink, Yiddish, 105×167 mm, text illegible in places, ss. 2, pp. 4; doc. was kept in a binder; only a fragment of the manuscript was published [?]); pp. 306–307 (25.08.[1941], original, handwritten manuscript—ER*, ink, Yiddish, 144×213 mm, ss. 1, pp. 1); pp. 307–309 (26.08.[1941], original, handwritten manuscript—ER*, ink, Yiddish, 155×187 mm, ss. 1, pp. 2; manuscript published with omission of the closing fragment); pp. 314 (07–09.1941, copy, typescript, Yiddish, 205×292 mm, damage and losses of text, ss. 1, pp. 1; on p. 1 notation of H.W. in Yiddish (ink): "Little Flower"; pp. 314–315 ([09.1941], transcript—2 copies, typescript, Yiddish, 170×290, 208×292 mm, minor damage and losses of text, ss. 4, pp. 4; on p. 1 (second copy) notation by H.W. in Yiddish (ink): "Little Flower"); pp. 316–317 ([09.]1941, copy, typescript, Yiddish, 207×293 mm, ss. 1, pp. 1; in the margin notation by H.W. in Yiddish (ink): "Little Flower"); pp. 319–320 (poł. 09.[1941], original, handwritten manuscript—ER*, ink, Yiddish, 145×218 mm, ss. 1, pp. 2; only a fragment of the manuscript was published); pp. 318, 321–323, 323–325 (09.1941, 10.[1941], transcript—3 copies, typescript, Yiddish, 223×288 mm, damage and losses of text (second and third copies), ss. 12, pp. 12; on p. 1 notation of H.W. in Yiddish (ink): "109–1942/1 January. no. 8"; fragment concerning Morgensztern was published on p. 318); pp. 332–334 (10.11.1941, original, handwritten manuscript—ER*, ink, Yiddish, 140×204 mm, ss. 1, pp. 2); pp. 334–336 (14.11.1941, original, handwritten manuscript—ER*, ink, Yiddish, 142×203 mm, ss. 1, pp. 2); pp. 338–339 (23.11.[1941], original, handwritten manuscript—ER*, ink, Yiddish, 142×175 mm, minor damage and losses of text, ss. 1, pp. 2);s. 339–344 (24–25.12.1941, original, handwritten manuscript—ER*, ink, Yiddish, 140×204 mm, minor damage and losses of text, text illegible in places, ss. 1, pp. 2; on p. 2 notation (printed): "28"; doc. was kept in a binder); pp. 344–345 ([end of 1941], original, handwritten manuscript—ER*, ink, Yiddish, 105×158 mm, ss. 1, pp. 1); pp. 345–346 ([end of 1941], original, handwritten manuscript—ER*, ink, Yiddish, 148×192 mm, minor damage and losses of text, ss. 1, pp. 1).

Manuscripts for which it was not determined whether they were published in print: a) ([09.1939], original, handwritten manuscript—ER*, ink, Yiddish, 93×154 mm, ss. 1, pp. 2; on p. 1 symbol (ink): "- "; doc. was kept in a binder); b) ([09.1939 ?], original, handwritten manuscript—ER*, ink, Yiddish, 93×155 mm, ss. 1, pp. 1); c) ([1939?], original, handwritten manuscript—ER*, ink, Yiddish, 205×280 mm, text illegible in places, ss. 1, pp. 1; at the top a symbol (ink): "—"; doc. was kept in a binder); d) ([09.1939?], original, handwritten manuscript—ER*, ink, Yiddish, 98×142 mm, text illegible in places, ss. 1, pp. 1); e) ([1939?], original, handwritten manuscript—ER*, ink, Yiddish, 107×222 mm, text illegible in places, ss. 1, pp. 1; doc. was kept in a binder); f) [1939?], original, handwritten—ER*, ink, Yiddish, 188×158 mm, a torn sheet, ss. 1, pp. 2; symbol (ink): "-"; the document was stored in a binder; g) p. 395, no. 449; (after 30.09.[1940], original, handwritten manuscript—ER*, ink, Yiddish, 96×142 mm, text illegible in places, ss. 1, pp. 2; doc.); h) (02.1942 [?], original, handwritten manuscript—ER*, ink, Yiddish, 167×220 mm, serious damage and losses of text, ss. 1, pp. 1).

See HWC, 31/8 (Notes of 07–09.1941, typescript, ss. 4; on p. 3 notation in Yiddish: "Little Flower"; a text that touches on September 1941 and is published in *Kronika getta*, on pp. 315–316); 31/12 (Notes by ER, which are missing in the ŻIH collection of the ghetto archive; this part of the Wasser collection (catalog no. 31) includes other (e.g., 31/10) unidentified docs., which could belong to the literary estate of ER; see Prof. Epsztein's essay above).

b) Ring. I/514

- After 1940, Warsaw Ghetto
- [Emanuel Ringelblum], Notes [1940]
- Chronicle of current events (situation of the Jewish population in Romania, France, Belgium, Holland, the Czech lands, Slovakia).
- ***Description:*** transcript (2 copies), handwritten manuscript (MS*), pencil, Yiddish, ss. 1, pp. 2.

In the margins a Hebrew letter (ink): "g" (giml). On p. 1 on left at top notation in Yiddish: "Little Flower."

Text written in the form of a letter.

Doc. was kept in a binder.

Published: *Kronika getta*, pp. 224–226.

See Ring. I/511.

## 450. RING. I/510. Mf. ŻIH—789; USHMM—20

- After 11.1941, Warsaw Ghetto
- [Emanuel Ringelblum], Notes about Jews acting against the Jewish population and cooperating with the Germans
- Death of 30 Jews from Baranowicze (08.1941) as a result of denunciation by a member of the Jewish Council from Radom, swindle of money by NN., Order Service policeman in the tenement at ul. Dzielna 93; Jews cooperating with Germans: Anders (prewar boxer), Milek (ul. Pańska 52), Feferman (policeman of the II precinct: ul. Krochmalna 32), Fleischman from Galicia (chief of the II police precinct), Josełe Erlich (commandant of the Jewish prison at ul. Zamenhofa 19), NN. (director of the theater at ul. Nowolipki 52).
- ***Description:*** transcript, typescript, Yiddish, 102×146 mm, minor damage and losses of text, ss. 7, pp. 7.

Published: *Kronika getta*, pp. 330–332.

## 451. RING. I/511/1. Mf. ŻIH—789; USHMM—20

- After 09.1940, Warsaw Ghetto
- [Emanuel Ringelblum], Notes. (09.1940)

- Chronicle of current events.
- ***Description:*** transcript (2 copies), handwritten manuscript (MS*), pencil, Yiddish, 147×208 mm, ss. 4, pp. 4.
    In the margins Hebrew letter (ink): "a" (alef). On p. 1 notation in Yiddish (ink): "Little Flower."
    Text written in the form of a letter.
    Doc. was kept in a binder.
    Published: *Kronika getta*, pp. 158–160.
    Index: Dr. Berliński from Łódź; Koziołkiewicz, ONR activist; Dr. Rusic [Suryc]; Hilel Zajdman[29] of Gazeta Żydowska; Rozen F., journalist

### 452. RING. I/511/2. Mf. ŻIH—789; USHMM—20

- After 12.1940, Warsaw Ghetto
- [Emanuel Ringelblum], Notes. (7–10.12.1940)
- Chronicle of current events.
- ***Description:*** transcript, handwritten manuscript (MS*), pencil, Yiddish, 149×208 mm, minor damage and losses of text, ss. 1, pp. 2.
    On p. 1 on the left side a symbol (ink): "∴" and notation by H.W. in Yiddish (red pencil): "Bliml" [Little Flower].
    Text written in the form of a letter.
    Doc. was kept in a binder.
    Published: *Kronika getta*, pp. 210–213.
    Index: Baruch, [Josef?] Erlich

### 453. RING. I/511/3. Mf. ŻIH—789; USHMM—20

- After 1940, Warsaw Ghetto
- NN., [Emanuel Ringelblum?], Notes (23–24.12.1940)
- Description of Germans' brutalization of a group of Jews.
- ***Description:*** transcript, handwritten manuscript (MS*), pencil, Yiddish, damage and losses of text, 147×207 mm, ss. 2, pp. 3.
    In the margins Greek letter (ink): "β" and symbol: " I ." On p. 3 notation by H.W. in Yiddish (ink): "Current affairs."
    Doc. was kept in a binder.
    Published: *Kronika getta*, pp. 221–223.

### 454. RING. I/1039 (1358). Mf. ŻIH—832; USHMM—44

a)

- After 1939, Warsaw Ghetto
- [Emanuel Ringelblum], Notes. (5.11.1938 [sic])
- Economic matters, trade contacts with Łódź.
- ***Description:*** original (handwritten manuscript—ER*, ink, 206×280 mm, minor damage and losses of text, text illegible in places), transcript (3 copies, handwritten manuscript—MS*, pencil, 148×208 mm), Yiddish, ss. 5, pp. 10.
    Text written in the form of a letter. Transcript with minor changes (last three sentences are missing).

b)

- After 1939, Warsaw Ghetto
- [Emanuel Ringelblum], Notes : 1) from 2.01.1938[sic]; 2) from 19.04.1940; 3) from 1.01.1941; 4) Date unknown.
- ***Description:*** 1) original (handwritten manuscript—ER*, ink, 206×280 mm, text is difficult to read in places), transcript (3 copies), handwritten manuscript (MS*), pencil, Yiddish, 148×208 mm, ss. 4, pp. 8; 2) transcript, handwritten manuscript (MS*), pencil, Yiddish, 148×208 mm, ss. 1, pp. 1; 3) transcript (2 copies), handwritten manuscript (MS*), pencil, Yiddish, 148×208 mm, minor damage and losses of text, ss. 2, pp. 2; 4) transcript (2 copies), handwritten manuscript (MS*), pencil, Yiddish, 146×206 mm, extensive damage and losses of text, ss. 8, pp. 8.
    Texts written in the form of letters.
    Doc. (1) in original missing closing fragment.
    Doc. (2) was kept in a binder.
    On p. 1 (doc. 3), first copy) notation (ink): "11" (crossed out) and in Yiddish: "shaven."
    In *Kronika getta*, there is no data from these specific days.

### 455. RING. I/428. (Lb. 1468). Mf. ŻIH—784; USHMM—15

- 12.1941, Warsaw Ghetto
- Stanisław Różycki, Report entitled "To jest getto! (Reportaż z inferna XX wieku)." [This is the Ghetto! Reporting from the Inferno of the 20th Century] (7.12.1941)
- Daily life in the Warsaw Ghetto, the city's appearance, administrative offices, the Order Service, economics (smuggling—"everything's OK"), cultural and social life, interpersonal relations, family life (income and expenditures), future prospects.
- ***Description:*** original (handwritten manuscript—SR*, notebook, ink, 160×200 mm) and transcript (2 copies + 3 copies of a fragment of the chapter "Return to the Familial Nest," typescript, 223×290 mm), Polish, ss. 123, pp. 122.
    Text consists of the following chapters: 1) "First Impressions" ("Return to the Familial Nest,"

29. Possibly Hillel Seidman, who was the last student to submit a doctoral dissertation on a Jewish topic to Prof. Majer Bałaban at the University of Warsaw in August 1939. In the ghetto, Seidman was the director of the Judenrat Archives where he found employment for his teacher and other scholars, such as Yitshak Schipper. Seidman's doctoral dissertation on the history of the Warsaw Jewish Community was based on his access to the communal archives. The typescript, with Yitshak Schipper's notations made in the Warsaw Ghetto, survived and is in Seidman's family's possession.

"Walls, Walls, Walls . . . ," "Walled Up," "Inferno"); 2) "Jewish Administration" ("Dreams and Accomplishments," "The Community and Its Organs," "Police," "Economic Life: «'Everything's OK'»", "Everything's allowed! Nothing is prohibited!"); 3) "Social Life" ("Social Institutions," "Medical Treatment," "Cultural and Social Life," "Life of the Street and Home"); 4) "Right to Life" ("The Right of the More Powerful," "And the Rights of the Weaker . . . ," "Life of the Ghetto Man," "Perspectives"); 5) "The Middle Ages."

On p. 1 (transcript) of the chapter "Pierwsze wrażenia" (First impressions) is a postwar note by Laura Eichhornowa: "Stanisław Różycki Lb. 1468."

Pub. (fragments): *Eksterminacja Żydów*, pp. 134–137; BŻIH, no. 62/1967, pp. 113–123.

See Ring. I/427.

### 456. RING. I/429. (Lb. 266). Mf. ŻIH—784; USHMM—15

- 03.1942 [?], Warsaw Ghetto
- Stanisław Różycki, Collection of Reports entitled "Street Pictures of the Ghetto"
- Scenes from the life of the Warsaw Ghetto: Hesia and her family, Dawid Dobicki, manager of the cemetery on ul. Okopowa, funeral services for the ghetto, decline of manners and dishonesty, image of ul. Leszno, extortion by the the administration of the Community, story of Frania S. and Josek Kapusta.
- ***Description:*** original, handwritten manuscript (SR*), notebooks, ink, Polish, 150×197 mm, damage and losses of text, ss. 31, pp. 31.

On p. 1 notation of H.W. in Yiddish: "5 standard pages"; in another handwriting: "March 1942"; on p. 16 notation: "II–III/19[42?]."

Titles of individual reports: "Naked Corpse and Naked Facts," "Public Enemy no. 1," "Shamelessness," "About Substitutes, Forgeries and Incompetence," "Oriental Exoticism," "An Official Racket," "Mob Rule."

Index: Posner, Roland, Sztrauch, Szejnberg, Sztajner, Goldsztajn

### 457. RING. I/485. (Lb. 1591). Mf. ŻIH—787; USHMM—18

- After 02 1941, Warsaw Ghetto
- S. [Sommer], Report entitled "E pluribus una"
- Author, a group leader [grupowy] in the Skoda workshops in Warsaw describes the mistreatment of Jewish workers employed there (19.03.1940). Attached copies: medical certificate of 15.02.1941 and a work card of 11.09.1940 filled out for S. [Sommer].
- ***Description:*** original (o) (handwritten manuscript—FLIG*, ink, 210×295 mm), transcript (3 copies, handwritten manuscript -CC*, pencil, 148×207 mm), ss. 93, pp. 96.

Inventory: "Statement of Group Leader Sommer prepared by Daniel Fligelman."

### 458. RING. I/198. (Lb. 968). Mf. ŻIH—779; USHMM—10. RING. I/668. (Lb. 1158). Mf. ŻIH—816; USHMM—28. RING. I/1220/88. Mf. ŻIH—779; USHMM—47

- After 1.09.1941, Warsaw Ghetto
- [Michał Suryc], "Recollections from Pawiak, story of a Jew, citizen of the USSR."
- Author was arrested during the deportation of Jews from Żyrardów (27.02.1941), brought to Warsaw and imprisoned in Pawiak, where he was beaten and abused, then stayed in the prison on Daniłowiczowska and then the one on Rakowiecka, from which he was released 1.09.1941.
- ***Description:*** Ring. I/1220—transcript (a) (handwritten manuscript—FLIG*, ink, Polish, 220×350 mm, minor damage and losses of text, text illegible in places, ss. 3, pp. 6; Ring. I/198 and I/668—transcript (b) (Ring. I/198—2 copies, Ring. I/668—1 copy), handwritten manuscript (BTT*), pencil, Polish, 143×205 mm, damage and losses of text, ss. 60, pp. 60.

Ring. I/1220 On p. 1 In the margin is notation by H.W. (ink): "104/41—2."

Ring. I/198—Attached note by H.W.: "Recollections of the Pawiak, story of a USSR citizen of Jewish nationality. 2 copies, Cit[izen] B. Rotenberg of Żyrardów (Zionist activist) forwarded this statement of Cit[izen] Suryc. 1941."

On p. 1 (third copy Ring. I/668) notation by H.W. (ink): "By Kon." (note that H.W. in the postwar notation mentions nothing about notation written on the third copy of this document).

About Suryc [Michał], see *Kronika getta*, pp. 124, 145, 160, 371, 485, 627.

### 459. RING. I/1071 (1390, 1393). (Lb. 913, 1640). Mf. ŻIH—832; USHMM—44

- After 11.1940, Warsaw Ghetto
- H.S.L., Recollections of the Żoliborz district of Warsaw (1939–1940)
- The author, a female resident of the Warsaw Housing Cooperative [Warszawska Spółdzielnia Mieszkaniowa (WSM)] in Żoliborz, employee of the First Aid Desk at the Clothing Department of the Coordinating Commission (subsequently the ŻSS) [Referatu Pomocy Doraźnej przy Wydziale Odzieżowym Komisji Koordynacyjnej (późniejsza ŻSS)], describes the start of the war and the first year of occupation in Warsaw (care for fire victims, situation of the Jewish population in Żoliborz, preparations for transfer into the ghetto).
- ***Description:*** original (typescript with handwritten additions, pencil, ink, 100×210, 206×293 mm), transcript (2 copies, handwritten manuscript, pencil, 146×204 mm, extensive minor damage and losses of text), Polish, ss. 41, pp. 41.

On p. 1 (transcript, first copy) notation by H.W.: "Vel" [Alias]
Attached note by H.W.: "Recollections recorded by HSL, female resident of WSM (ask Mrs. Basia Berman)."
Index: Dr. Weichert

### 460. RING. I/176. (Lb. 854, 880). Mf. ŻIH—779; USHMM—10

- After 10.1940, Warsaw Ghetto
- H.S.L., Report about the treatment of Jews by the Polish population in Warsaw (September 1939–October 1940)
- Author describes several events exhibiting the negative stance of the Polish population toward Jews: public jeering, beating, theft of possessions, etc.
- ***Description:*** original or transcript (handwritten manuscript, pencil, 208×294 mm), transcript (2 copies; in the second copy p. 1 missing), handwritten manuscript, part 1 (09.1939): pp. 1–21—BB*, pp. 22–32—BTT*; part 2 (10.1940)—BTT*, pencil, 145×204 mm), German, Polish, damage and losses of text, ss. 59, pp. 59.

Manuscript (original and transcript) consists of two parts: part 1—"30 IX 1939"; part 2—"October 1940." In the copy, in part 1 at the top of the page is a symbol (ink): "—"; on p. 1 at the top is notation by H.W.: "Vel" [Alias]; in part 2 in the margins is a letter: "A" (ink), on p. 1 at the top is notation of H.W.: "Vel" [Alias].
See HWC, 31/1 (third copy of the transcript, handwritten, ss. 17, missing p. 2; on p. 1 notation: "Vel" [Alias]).

### 461. RING. I/984 (1303). (Lb. 1446). Mf. ŻIH—831; USHMM—43

- 04–07.1942, Warsaw Ghetto
- [Sz. Szejnkinder], "Fun mayn tog-bukh" [From My Diary]
- Author, a prewar journalist for Moment, comments upon current events, describes profiles of various people, e.g., journalists who died in the ghetto: Herman Czerwiński, Menachem Kipnis and Cwi Prylucki (died 21.05.1942), who perished at the hands of the Nazis (e.g., at ul. Leszno 41, apt. 21, Chaim [Heniek] Górka and his mother; ul. Nowolipki 54, Mojsze Szklar, typesetter, killed 12.05.1942; Abram Roman Fas from Galicia, military man, sport activist, street car operator, shot on 12.05.1942 in front of the building at ul. Zamenhofa 19). News about secret homicides: of Jan Kowalski, Kurzawa, Józef Lewiński-Lewensztajn; on 23.04.1942 two girls from Łódź were found killed: Rozen-Pomeranc and Wiślicka; on 24.04.1942 Rozin perished.
- ***Description:*** original, handwritten manuscript (Sz.*), ink, Yiddish, 150×165, 145×222 mm, minor damage and losses of text, ss. 15, pp. 15.

On the ss. beginning individual parts of the text, notation by H.W. in Yiddish (ink): p. 1—"4 standard [pages]"; p. 4—"1942. 5 standard pages"; p. 7—"1942. 3 standard pages"; p. 9—"11 standard pages"; p. 14—"[. . .] standard pages. June 1942."
Attached note by H.W.: "These notes for the period 21.04.–09.07.1942 are by the Jewish sport journalist Sz. Szajnkinder."
Published: *Selected Documents*, pp. 654–662 (fragment on Cwi Pryłucki).

### 462. RING. I/1040 (1359). (Lb. 490). Mf. ŻIH—832; USHMM—44

1) (a)

- After 27.12.1939, Warsaw Ghetto
- [Mordechaj Szwarcbard?], "Mey-inyoney-deyoyme" [On Current Events] (missing conclusion)
- Author seized for labor (27.12.1939) was employed in unloading trucks in Karolew near Łódź.
- ***Description:*** original or transcript, handwritten manuscript (MS*), pencil, Yiddish, 148×208 mm, ss. 1, pp. 1.

In the margin a letter (pencil [?]): "E"[?].
Title written out by H.W. (ink).
Doc. was kept in a binder.

2) (b)

- After 24.10.1940, Warsaw Ghetto
- [Mordechaj Szwarcbard?], "Mey-inyoney-deyoyme" (On Current Events)
- About the Łódź ghetto: system of tax collection, provisioning, activities of administration.
- ***Description:*** original or transcript, handwritten manuscript (MS*), pencil, Yiddish, 148×208 mm, ss. 1, pp. 1.

Notation by H.W. in Yiddish (ink), at top: "cleanshaven";[30] and on the bottom: "1, current events."
Doc. is written in the form of a letter for conspiratorial purposes.
Doc. was kept in a binder.

3) (c)

- After 26–30.12.1940, Warsaw Ghetto
- [Mordechaj Szwarcbard?], "Mey-inyoney-deyoyme" (On Current Events) (1) 26, 29, 30.12.1940
- Chronicle of the Warsaw Ghetto: registration books, daily life, news from abroad, filming of workers, robberies, smuggling.
- ***Description:*** original or transcript (of 26.12.1940 in 2 copies), handwritten manuscript (MS*), pencil, Yiddish, 148×208 mm, minor damage and losses of text, ss. 4, pp. 4.

30. The equivalent expression in Polish (*ogolony*) has the connotation of "cleaned out" as in "fleeced."

On the doc. (notation by H.W. [ink] or MS*), at top: "cleanshaven"; and on the bottom: "1, current events."
On doc. of 29.12.1940 notation (ink): "5"; on doc. of 30.12.1940 notation (ink): "6."
Docs. were kept in a binder.
Published: *BFG*, vol. VIII, nos. 3–4 (1955), pp. 106–145.

4) (cc)
- After 8.01.1941, Warsaw Ghetto
- [Mordechaj Szwarcbard?], "Mey-inyoney-deyoyme" [On Current Events]
- (8.01.1941)
- Chronicle of the Warsaw Ghetto: search at the Hering household at ul. Grzybowska 5; episode from ul. Karmelicka.
- ***Description:*** original or transcript (2 copies), handwritten manuscript (MS*), pencil, Yiddish, 147×207 mm, ss. 2, pp. 2.
  Doc. was kept in a binder.
  Published: *BFG*, vol. VIII, nos. 3–4 (1955), pp. 106–145.

5) (ccc)
- After 13.01.1941, Warsaw Ghetto
- [Mordechaj Szwarcbard?], "Mey-inyoney-deyoyme" [On Current Events] (13.01.1941)
- Scenes of street life of the Warsaw Ghetto.
- ***Description:*** original or transcript, handwritten manuscript (MS*), pencil, Yiddish, 147×208 mm, extensive damage and losses of text, ss. 1, pp. 1.
  Doc. was kept in a binder.
  Published: *BFG*, vol. VIII, nos. 3–4 (1955), pp. 106–145.

6) (ccca)
- After 5.02.1941, Warsaw Ghetto
- [Mordechaj Szwarcbard?], "Mey-inyoney-deyoyme" [On Current Events] (5.02.1941)
- On the influence of Hitler's speech on the situation of the Jews, Frank's visit to Warsaw and release of Jewish laborers from work ("at the outposts"). Smuggling in the Warsaw Ghetto.
- ***Description:*** original or transcript (2 copies), handwritten manuscript (MS*), pencil, Yiddish, 147×207 mm, ss. 2, pp. 2.
  In the margins a symbol (ink): "//" (underlined) or Hebrew letter: "v" (tsvey-vovn = V) and letter (pencil): "E" [?].
  Doc. was kept in a binder.
  Published: *BFG*, vol. VIII, nos. 3–4 (1955), pp. 106–145.

7) (cccb)
- After 15.03.1941, Warsaw Ghetto
- [Mordechaj Szwarcbard?], "Mey-inyoney-deyoyme" [On Current Events] (13.03., 14.03., 15.03.1941)
- Chronicle of the Warsaw Ghetto: search for Zofia Sidorow, about the "13," provisioning, high cost of living.
- ***Description:*** original or transcript (2 copies), handwritten manuscript (MS*), pencil, Yiddish, 147×207 mm, ss. 2, pp. 2.
  Doc. was kept in a binder.
  Published: *BFG*, vol. VIII, nos. 3–4 (1955), pp. 106–145.

8) (cccc)
- After 18.03.1941, Warsaw Ghetto
- [Mordechaj Szwarcbard?], "Mey-inyoney-deyoyme" [On Current Events] (18.03.1941)
- About the murder of residents (180 persons) at the home for the elderly from Kalisz. Flight of Jews from Głowno.
- ***Description:*** original or transcript (2 copies), handwritten manuscript (MS*), pencil, Yiddish, 147×207 mm, minor damage and losses of text, ss. 2, pp. 2.
  Doc. was kept in a binder.
  Published: *BFG*, vol. VIII, nos. 3–4 (1955), pp. 106–145.

9) (d)
- After 26.02.1941, Warsaw Ghetto
- [Mordechaj Szwarcbard?], "Mey-inyoney-deyoyme" [On Current Events] (26.02.1941)
- Chronicle of the Warsaw Ghetto: search connected with the robbery at ul. Nowolipki 23.
- ***Description:*** original or transcript (2 copies), handwritten manuscript (MS*), pencil, Yiddish, 147×207 mm, minor damage and losses of text, ss. 4, pp. 4.
  In the margins symbol (ink): ". . ."
  Doc. was kept in a binder.
  Published: *BFG*, vol. VIII, nos. 3–4 (1955), pp. 106–145.

10) (da)
- After 17.04.1941, Warsaw Ghetto
- [Mordechaj Szwarcbard?], "Mey-inyoney-deyoyme" [On Current Events] (17.04.1941)
- Report of a refugee from Kałuszyn about experiences of the Jewish population; beggars in the Warsaw Ghetto, smuggling.
- ***Description:*** original or transcript (2 copies), handwritten manuscript (MS*), pencil, Yiddish, 147×207 mm, minor damage and losses of text, ss. 4, pp. 4.
  In the margins a Greek letter (ink): "α."
  Doc. was kept in a binder.
  Published: *BFG*, vol. VIII, nos. 3–4 (1955), pp. 106–145.

11) (daa)
- After 5.05.1941, Warsaw Ghetto
- [Mordechaj Szwarcbard?], "Mey-inyoney-deyoyme" [On Current Events] (5.05.1941)
- Assault by German gendarmes on policemen of the Order Service in the Warsaw Ghetto; situation of the Jewish population in Germany, in Łódź and Wieluń; escapes from the Warsaw Ghetto.

- *Description:* original or transcript (2 copies), handwritten manuscript (MS*), pencil, Yiddish, 147×207 mm, minor damage and losses of text, ss. 8, pp. 8.

  In the margins a symbol (ink): "-."
  Published: *BFG*, vol. VIII, nos. 3–4 (1955), pp. 106–145.

12) (dd)
- After 13[14].05.1941, Warsaw Ghetto
- [Mordechaj Szwarcbard?], "Mey-inyoney-deyoyme." [On Current Events] (13[14].05.1941)
- Roundups in the Warsaw Ghetto, verification of young people's identity papers, forced labor, transport to a labor camp near Krosno; information from the camp of Wielki near Garwolin.
- *Description:* original or transcript (2 copies), handwritten manuscript (MS*), pencil, Yiddish, 147×207 mm, minor damage and losses of text, ss. 10, pp. 10.

  In the margins a symbol (ink): ". . ."
  Published: *BFG*, vol. VIII, nos. 3–4 (1955), pp. 106–145.

13) (dda)
- After 16.05.1941, Warsaw Ghetto
- [Mordechaj Szwarcbard?], "Mey-inyoney-deyoyme" [On Current Events] (16.05.1941)
- Numerous deaths on the streets and in points in the Warsaw Ghetto; prices; information from labor camps (list of persons murdered in camps: Meir Flint, Aron Josef Fajngeld, Alter Krawczyk, Izrael Gutweter, Maszek Nabożny, Abram Zuzholc, Lajzer Tisgarten, Szewes Dworecki, Pinkus Chanachowicz, Baruch Najhojz, Fajwel Tozleger, Bernard Bojmajl, Szlomo Cukierman, Gerszon Mordenfeld, Abram Artman, Waldberg, Chaim Pintowicz). Account of a meeting with Chaim Rumkowski (16.05.1941).
- *Description:* original or transcript, handwritten manuscript (MS*), pencil, Yiddish, 147×207 mm, minor damage and losses of text, ss. 7, pp. 7.

  In the margins a symbol (ink): "v." On p. 1 a symbol (red pencil): "+."
  Published: *BFG*, vol. VIII, nos. 3–4 (1955), pp. 106–145.
  See HWC, 31/5 (second and third copies, handwritten manuscript, ss. 14).

14) (ddb)
- After 20.05.1941, Warsaw Ghetto
- [Mordechaj Szwarcbard?], "Mey-inyoney-deyoyme" [On Current Events] (20.05.1941)
- Statistical chart concerning mortality in the Warsaw Ghetto; diseases; arrival of Chaim Rumkowski in Warsaw.
- *Description:* original or transcript (2 copies), handwritten manuscript (MS*), pencil, Yiddish, 148×208 mm, minor damage and losses of text, ss. 10, pp. 10.

  Published: *BFG*, vol. VIII, nos. 3–4 (1955), pp. 106–145.

15) (ddd)
- After 25.05.1941, Warsaw Ghetto
- [Mordechaj Szwarcbard?], "Mey-inyoney-deyoyme" [On Current Events] (25.05.1941)
- Hunger and high cost of living in the Warsaw Ghetto, provisioning, labor camps; assaults on Jews in the ghetto.
- *Description:* original or transcript (2 copies), handwritten manuscript (MS*), pencil, Yiddish, 147×207 mm, minor damage and losses of text, ss. 10, pp. 10.

  In the margins a Hebrew letter (ink): "s."
  Doc. was kept in a binder.
  Published: *BFG*, vol. VIII, nos. 3–4 (1955), pp. 106–145.

16) (ddda)
- After 4.06.[1941], Warsaw Ghetto
- [Mordechaj Szwarcbard?], "Mey-inyoney-deyoyme" [On Current Events] (4.06.[1941])
- About the funeral of the attorney [Józef] Wajcman from Łódź, about the "13"; smuggling in the Warsaw Ghetto, information from Zduńska Wola (destruction of holy books).
- *Description:* original or transcript (2 copies), handwritten manuscript (MS*), pencil, Yiddish, 148×208 mm, minor damage and losses of text, ss. 6, pp. 6.

  In the margins (first copy) a symbol (ink): "+."
  Published: *BFG*, vol. VIII, nos. 3–4 (1955), pp. 106–145.

17) (e)
- After 14.06.1941, Warsaw Ghetto
- [Mordechaj Szwarcbard?], "Mey-inyoney-deyoyme" [On Current Events] (14.06.1941)
- Hunger and destitution in the Warsaw Ghetto, escapes from the ghetto.
- *Description:* original or transcript (2 copies), handwritten manuscript (MS*), pencil, Yiddish, 147×207 mm, minor damage and losses of text, ss. 6, pp. 6.

  Published: *BFG*, vol. VIII, nos. 3–4 (1955), pp. 106–145.

18) (f)
- Date unknown, Warsaw Ghetto
- [Mordechaj Szwarcbard?], "Mey-inyoney-deyoyme" [On Current Events]
- Roundups for labor camps.
- *Description:* original or transcript (2 copies), handwritten manuscript (MS*), pencil, Yiddish, 147×207 mm, minor damage and losses of text, ss. 6, pp. 6.

  In the margins a symbol (ink): ". . ."

### 463. RING. I/248. (Lb. 995). Mf. ŻIH—780; USHMM—11

- 05.1941, Warsaw Ghetto
- [Nechemiasz (Nechemia) Tytelman], Diary (entries of 14 and 16.05.1941) (fragment [?])

- News from radio monitoring (e.g., flight of Hess to England, about Mussolini); about jokes in the Warsaw Ghetto, about the prison.
- ***Description:*** original, handwritten manuscript (Ł*), ink, Yiddish, 160×200 mm, ss. 5, pp. 10.

  Inventory: "Author of the text is Nechemiasz Tytelman."

  Attached note by H.W. in Yiddish: "Notes 14 and 16.05.1941 by Nechemia Tytelman coworker of Oyneg Shabes, actively took part in the distribution of information of the daily [bulletins] of the underground, already in 1941 he organized together with Natan Ostrowicz political groups that entered into the makeup of the combat units of the Anti-Fascist Bloc, [called] 'Fives.'"

  Published: *Selected Documents*, pp. 73–78.

### 464. RING. I/270. (Lb. 269). Mf. ŻIH—836; USHMM—67

- After 7.07.1942, Warsaw Ghetto
- [Dr. Akiba Uryson?], Report entitled "From a Physician's Stories" (7.07.1942)
- Methods of fighting typhus within the ghetto, graft among participants in the health campaign (ambulance company, physicians, Order Service).
- ***Description:*** transcript, handwritten manuscript (E*), ink, Polish, 215×256, 215×130 mm, minor damage and losses of text, ss. 4, pp. 7.

  Inventory: "Author of the account is Dr. [Akiba] Uryson from Łódź."

### 465. RING. I/195. (Lb. 66). Mf. ŻIH—779; USHMM—10

- 02.1941, Warsaw Ghetto
- [Regina Wajl], Recollections of the years 1939–1941 (27.02.1941)
- Author, a nurse from Łódź, her brother mobilized in 1939 perished in battle on the Bzura, displaced with mother in December of that year, settled in Warsaw, where she worked as a waitress in an eating house.
- ***Description:*** original, handwritten manuscript, ink, Polish, 160×200 mm, ss. 3, pp. 6

  See also Ring. I/196.

### 466. RING. I/196. (Lb. 54). Mf. ŻIH—779; USHMM—10

- Account of aid given to a certain child in the Warsaw Ghetto.
- ***Description:*** original, handwritten manuscript, ink, Polish, 148×210 mm, ss. 4, pp. 4.

  Attached note by H.W.: "History of a Certain Operation (picture). The matter occurs at Gęsia 65, 1941, is recounted [by] Regina Wajlówna—a refugee from Łódź, a certified nurse, employee of the Czyste Hospital."

  See also Ring. I/195.

### 467. RING. I/302. (Lb. 1202). Mf. ŻIH—781; USHMM—12. RING. I/490. (Lb. 620). Mf. ŻIH—788; USHMM—19. RING. I/853 (1172). Mf. ŻIH—827; USHMM—39. RING. I/1090 (1409). Mf. ŻIH—833; USHMM—45

- 1940–1942, Warsaw Ghetto
- [Hersz Wasser], Diary (1.12.1940–28.04.1941, 10.05., 26–30.05., 10.06.1942)
- Daily life in the Warsaw Ghetto and accounts concerning other ghettos on the basis of various sources (author gives the names of several informants)
- Parts I—IV: (account of the woman Gezerndheit [?] about the situation of the Jewish population in Łęczyca from 1939 to March 1942; account of Abraham Gips, representative of refugees from Gąbin, about exiles from the Reich; raids on smugglers in the Warsaw Ghetto; thoughts of "Jaga" [?] Czernowski; Itkin's account about the pogrom in Brzeżany 5.06.1941, ca. 500 Jews perished (among others, a Czech Jew, Skurecki); CKU (Central Commission of Refugees), public kitchens in the Warsaw Ghetto.
- ***Description:*** Ring. I/302—original, handwritten manuscript (H.W.*), notebook, ink, Yiddish, 155×200 mm, ss. 74, pp. 49; Ring. I/490—original, handwritten manuscript (H.W.*), ink, Yiddish, 150×198 mm, ss. 12, pp. 23; Ring. I/853—original, handwritten manuscript (H.W.*), ink, Yiddish, 150×198 mm, minor damage and losses, ss. 5, pp. 9; Ring. I/1090, original, ink, Yiddish, 150×198 mm, ss. 3, pp. 6.

  Ring. I/302 includes part I (1940–1941); Ring. I/1090, part II (10.05.1942), Ring. I/490, part III (26–30.05.1942); Ring. I/853, part IV (10.06.1942).

  In part II on p. 1, notation by H.W. (ink): "2.5 standard pages"; Part III was divided by the author into separate fragments concerning particular days and paginated. Fragment concerning 26.05. has notation by H.W. in Yiddish (ink): "4 standard pages"; fragments of 27, 29 and 30.05.: "2 standard pages." Part IV of 10.06.: "5 standard pages."

  Ring. I/1090: doc. was kept in a binder.

  Ring. I/490. Attached note by H.W. in Yiddish: "Diary H.W."

  See HWC, 32/1 (copy of Ring. I/302, postwar [?] typescript).

### 468. RING. I/491. Mf. ŻIH—788; USHMM—19

- After 01.1941, Warsaw Ghetto
- [Hersz Wasser?], Account entitled "Tsvey bilder fun geto-varshe" [Two Pictures of the Warsaw Ghetto]
- Scenes of life of the Warsaw Ghetto from 11.01. and 18.01.1941 (persecution of Jews by Germans, hunger).
- ***Description:*** original (2 copies), handwritten manuscript (H.W.*), pencil, Yiddish, 150×210 mm, ss. 2, pp. 2.

Attached note by H.W. in Polish, Yiddish: "Developed by H.W."
Doc. was kept in a binder.

### 469. RING. I/116. (Lb. 1187). Mf. ŻIH—777; USHMM—8

- 03.1941, Warsaw Ghetto
- [Mordechaj Wasser], Diary of a care-giver (opiekuna) in a shelter for refugees in the Warsaw Ghetto, 12–28.03.1941
- Organization of the shelter in a school building, 460 charges under care, refugees from the localities of Bolimów, Jeżów and Mogielnica, difficulties with feeding, hygiene and medical care, numerous deaths from hunger, situation of the elderly, handicapped, and mentally ill.
- ***Description:*** original, handwritten, ink, Polish, 158×199 mm; transcript (5 copies), handwritten manuscript (copies 1 and 2 JG*; copies 3–5 CA*), pencil, Polish, 146×210 and 150×210 mm, ss 53, pp. 58.

In the original, on p. 1, correction "biega" in a different handwriting in pencil, as well as on p. 3 (sheet 2) correction of the word "rządа" to "żąda". Both corrections were not taken into consideration by copyist JG*, but they were taken into account by copyist CA*, or both transcripts were produced on the basis of the original, the first by JG*, the second only after the correction of the original by CA*.

On p. 1, copy 1 (transcript—JG*), the year (1941) was added in the handwriting of H.W., as well as information in Yiddish: "109 1942/1 January," and the name of the author "Mordechai Wasser."

Attached note by H.W. with information about the author: "Luzer (Lutek) Rozental from Łódź"; that text is crossed out by the handwriting of H.W. and above is written: "Mordechaj Wasser."

### 470. RING. I/1099 (1418). (Lb. 730). Mf. ŻIH—833; USHMM—45

- 1941[?], Warsaw Ghetto
- [Dora Wajnerman], Account of a hospital in the Warsaw Ghetto
- Author, a female nurse, describes the process of gathering of more than 120 employees of the hospital (protest against irregular payment of wages and difficult situation of the employees—hunger); dramatic conditions in the children's hospital.
- ***Description:*** original or transcript, handwritten manuscript, ink, Yiddish, 177×205 mm, minor damage and losses of text, ss. 2, pp. 4.

Fragment of the account concerning the children's hospital bears the date: "20.05. [1941]."

Attached notations (2) of H.W. in Polish and Yiddish: "Written down by Dora Wajnerman, nurse—hospital employee, refugee from Łódź."

See Ring. I/989.

Published: (part 1) *BFG*, vol. XXXI (1993), pp. 75–76; *Dzieci*, pp. 134, 139.

On unrest among the hospital's employees in July 1941, see *Czerniaków*, p. 200.

### 471. RING. I/489. Mf. ŻIH—787; USHMM—18

- 8.01.1942 and after 8.01.1942, Warsaw Ghetto
- [Wojdysławski], Recollections, sketches, and reflections (8.01.1942)
- Scenes from the life of the Jewish population during the war and occupation (1939–1942); September 1939, ghetto; reflections on the tragic nature of human fate, on the attitude of the Germans.
- ***Description:*** original (handwritten manuscript, notebook, ink, 152×195 mm), transcript (2 copies, handwritten manuscript—CA*, pencil, 150×208 mm), Polish, ss. 90, pp. 89.

Attached note by H.W.: "Submitted by Dr. Em. [Emanuel] Ringelblum notes of Wojdysławski."

### 472. RING. I/1075 (1394). (Lb. 1412). Mf. ŻIH—832; USHMM—44

- Date unknown, Warsaw Ghetto
- J.Z., "Conversation with [F.W.] assessor of the Penal-Administrative Desk at the Dept. of the Fight against Usury. Leszno 13. Palace of Justice"
- Concerning the pseudo-judiciary at the "13" in the Warsaw Ghetto.
- ***Description:*** original, handwritten manuscript, ink, Polish, 137×110, 137×202, ss. 2, pp. 3.

On a postwar sheet was added: assessor—Feliks Wermus, labor camp inmate—Efroim Szkarłat

Index: Bramson, attorney, connected with the "13" in the Warsaw Ghetto

### 473. RING. I/466. (Lb. 1432). Mf. ŻIH—786; USHMM—17

a)

- After 14.01.1942, Warsaw Ghetto
- [Jakub Zylberberg (Zylberg?)], Account of collection of tax arrears by the Order Service in the Warsaw Ghetto
- Blockade of apartment houses at ul. Nowolipie 21 and 21a on 14.01.1942 by the Order Service.
- ***Description:*** original or transcript, handwritten manuscript (U* [?]), ink, Yiddish, 133×197 mm, ss. 1, pp. 1.

Attached note by H.W. in Yiddish: "Written [by] Jakub Zylberberg [sic]." See I/466/b.

b)

- 14.01.1942, Warsaw Ghetto
- Jewish Council in Warsaw. Order Service. Management of the III Region (ul. Leszno 10), Certificate issued for Jakub Zylberg.

- Ban on leaving the apartment house on 14.01.1942 at 1 PM in connection with completion of the formalities concerning back taxes on F.S.P. [Fundusz ? SP] [taxes for the Order Service].
- ***Description:*** original, typescript, pencil, stamp, Polish, 208×56 mm, ss. 1, pp. 1.
  Doc. was attached to the account (Ring. I/466/a).

**474. RING. I/185. Mf. ŻIH—779; USHMM—10**

- Date unknown, Warsaw Ghetto
- [Jakub Zylbersztajn], Account entitled "Prage" [Praga].
- The Jewish population in the Praga district (Warsaw) before the war (social and economic situation, religious life), in September 1939, and during the occupation (until resettlement into the ghetto).
- ***Description:*** original (o), handwritten manuscript (HUB.*), ink, Yiddish, 150×195 mm, minor damage and losses of text, ss. 14, pp. 23.
  Attached note by H.W. in Yiddish: "Sz. Huberband wrote, account of the rabbi of Praga Zylbersztajn."
  According to R. Sakowska, the account's author is Jakub Zylbersztajn, father-in-law of Szymon Huberband.
  Published: *BFG*, vol. XXXI (1993), pp. 11–22; *Kiddush Hashem*, pp. 443–453.

**475. RING. I/1011 (1330). (Lb. 314). Mf. ŻIH—831; USHMM—43**

- After 09.1939, Warsaw
- NN., "Fun a tog bukh" [From a Diary] (13.09.1939)
- Description of the events of one day—eve of the Jewish New Year (line for bread, bombardment of Warsaw).
- ***Description:*** transcript (2 copies), handwritten manuscript (MS*), pencil, Yiddish, 148×208 mm, ss. 2, pp. 2.
  Annotation by H.W. (ink): "1939."
  Published: *Selected Documents*, pp. 69–72.
  See Ring. I/1026.
  Doc. was kept in a binder.

**476. RING. I/467. (Lb. 1188). Mf. ŻIH—786; USHMM—17**

- After 09.1939, place unknown
- NN., Account entitled "Experiences during September 1939, of a member of the L.O.P [Liga Obrony Powietrznej (League for Anti-Aircraft Defense)] and of the Civil Guard [Straży Obywatelskiej]"
- Fulfilled duty in the apartment house at ul. Hoża 37. Description of the relations reigning among the residents (Jews and Poles) during the siege of Warsaw, various attitudes, behavior of the army.
- ***Description:*** transcript, typescript, Polish, 208×295 mm, ss. 1, pp. 1.
  Doc. written on the back of a questionnaire of the S[. . .] Commission (Komisji S[. . .]sowej) (hectographed typescript, Polish).
  Inventory: Attached note by H.W. in Yiddish: "Submitted to the archive by Abr. [Abraham] Lewin."

**477. RING. I/993 (1312). (Lb. 423). Mf. ŻIH—831; USHMM—43**

- After 10.1939, Warsaw Ghetto
- NN., Diary entitled "A bintl milkhome zikhroynes" [A Bundle of War Memories] (6.09–15.10.1939)
- Description of events from the first days of the war and occupation (construction of barricades, flight to the east, return to Warsaw, chaos, bombardments, capitulation, roundups on the streets, refugees' stories, observations of the behavior of the victorious Germans and defeated compatriots).
- ***Description:*** transcript (2 copies), handwritten manuscript (MS*), pencil, Yiddish, 148×210 mm, ss. 8, pp. 8.
  Title of the text by H.W.
  In the margins a Hebrew letter (ink): "g" (giml).
  Doc. was kept in a binder.

**478. RING. I/1019 (1338). (Lb. 383). Mf. ŻIH—831; USHMM—43**

- After 21.04.1941, Warsaw Ghetto
- NN., Account entitled "Di dermordung fun Lipe Kestin z"l" [The Murder of Lipe Kestin of blessed memory]
- Notation on the circumstances of the death (19.10.1939) of the Jewish journalist and poet.
- ***Description:*** transcript (2 copies), handwritten manuscript (BW*), pencil, Yiddish, 147×208 mm, ss. 2, pp. 2.
  Doc. was kept in a binder.

**479. RING. I/674/4. (Lb. 1688). Mf. ŻIH—816; USHMM—28**

- After 1940, Warsaw Ghetto
- NN., Account entitled "Nalewki"
- Picture of the street in Warsaw during the occupation (12.1939–02.1940).
- ***Description:*** original or transcript, handwritten manuscript (H.W.*), ink, Yiddish, 158×179 mm, ss. 1, pp. 1.

**480. RING. I/1007 (1326). (Lb. 334). Mf. ŻIH—831; USHMM—43**

- After 16.03.1940, Warsaw Ghetto
- NN., Account entitled "An epizod eyner far a sakh" [An Episode, One for Many]
- On the way (16.03.1940) to work, the author was seized by a gendarme and forced to clean the hall in the palace at Plac Krasińskich.
- ***Description:*** transcript, handwritten manuscript (MS*), pencil, Yiddish, 148×209 mm, ss. 2, pp. 2.
  At top of page is a symbol (ink): two dots in a circle.

Doc. was kept in a binder.
Published: *Selected Documents*, pp. 266–267.

**481. RING. I/1021 (1340). (Lb. 356). Mf. ŻIH—831; USHMM—43**

- After 06.1940, Warsaw Ghetto
- NN., Account entitled "A mayse fun Valove gas" [A Story of Wałowa Street]
- A German soldier did not allow ethnic Germans to rob Jewish merchants in Warsaw.
- ***Description:*** original or transcript (a) (handwritten manuscript—H.W.*, ink, 142×209 mm), original or transcript (b) (handwritten manuscript—MS*, pencil, 148×209 mm), Yiddish, ss. 2, pp. 2.

In both manuscripts, in the margins a letter (ink): "V."
Docs. were kept in a binder.

**482. RING. I/995 (1314). (Lb. 401). Mf. ŻIH—831; USHMM—43**

- After 15.06.[07?].1940, Warsaw Ghetto
- NN., Account of the memorial meeting in memory of Chaim Nachman Bialik and Theodor Herzl at the public kitchen at ul. Zamenhofa 13 (15.06.[07?].1940)
- About 200 people present, presidium: Dr. Nusblat, Mosze Limon, Dr. Bloch; addresses presented by: Menachem Kirszenbaum, Dr. Schiper, Dr. Nusblat.
- ***Description:*** transcript (2 copies), handwritten manuscript (BW*), pencil, Yiddish, 148×210 mm, ss. 18, pp. 18.

In the margins a Hebrew letter (ink): "t" (tof).
Doc. was kept in a binder.

**483. RING. I/1026 (1345). (Lb. 345). Mf. ŻIH—831; USHMM—43**

- After 12.1941, Warsaw Ghetto
- NN., Diary (19.10.1940–26.12.1940)
- Descriptions of daily roundups, beatings and persecution of Jews in Warsaw (e.g., events on Nowogródzka, Marszałkowska, Franciszkańska streets).
- ***Description:*** transcript (2 different transcripts in 2 copies each), handwritten manuscript (MS*), pencil, Yiddish, 148×209 mm, ss. 8, pp. 8.

First copy carries the title: "Fun a tog-bukh" [From a Diary]; in the margins is a Hebrew letter: "hey." Second copy carries the title: "A bintl iberlebungen in der milkhome tsayt" [A Bundle of Experiences in Wartime]; in the margins is a Hebrew letter: "v" [tsvey-vovn] as well as a symbol: triangle (∇) with a dot in the center.
The dating of parts of the entries is subject to doubt, for in both copies after 5 entries in chronological order from 19.10.1940 to 26.12.1940 there is an entry dated 1.01.1940 and subsequent dates, while the last is dated 3.11.1940. It is possible that the author of the diary erred, but the copyist did not correct the error and instead of 1.01.1940, it ought to be: 1.01.1941, while 3.11.1940 ought to be changed to 3.01.1941. However, it is not possible to exclude conscious choice and arrangement made by the copyist of only several of the entries from the original text of the diary. The author of both copies is the same person.
Doc. was kept in a binder.

**484. RING. I/1059 (1378). Mf. ŻIH—832; USHMM—44**

- Date unknown, Warsaw Ghetto
- NN., Account entitled "Anno 1940"
- A young boy describes a pogrom in Warsaw in spring 1940 and help that a passing Pole gave him.
- ***Description:*** original or transcript, handwritten manuscript (MM*[?]), ink, Polish, 152×201 mm, ss. 2, pp. 3.

**485. RING. I/361. Mf. ŻIH—782; USHMM—13**

- After 11.1940, Warsaw Ghetto
- NN., Account entitled "Closure of the Ghetto" (missing conclusion)
- Author (until 15.11.1940 resident of Pl. Żelazna Brama 8) describes the mood among the Jewish population before the closure of the ghetto and development of smuggling after closure of the Jewish district.
- ***Description:*** transcript (3 copies), handwritten manuscript (CA*), pencil, Polish, 150×210 mm, minor damage and losses of text, ss. 21, pp. 21.

Attached note by H.W. in Yiddish: "Submitted by Miriam Lewin from Łódź."
See HWC, 31/2 (original or another copy of this account, handwritten manuscript (E*), ink, ss. 5; on p. 1 notation by H.W. in ink: "Tilem" [Nechemia Tytelman?]).
Published: *Selected Documents*, pp. 143–145.

**486. RING. I/1012 (1331). (Lb. 380). Mf. ŻIH—831; USHMM—43**

- After 17.12.1940, Warsaw Ghetto
- NN., Account entitled "Di gasn-bavegung" [The Street Traffic]
- Female author describes the overcrowded streets of the Warsaw Ghetto on the way to the bathhouse, visit to the bathhouse and to a physician.
- ***Description:*** transcript (2 copies), handwritten manuscript (MS*), pencil, Yiddish, 147×208 mm, ss. 4, pp. 4.

In the margin a Hebrew letter (ink): "n" [nun].
Published: *Selected Documents*, pp. 154–155.

**487. RING. I/1025 (1344). (Lb. 346). Mf. ŻIH—831; USHMM—43**

- After 17.12.1940, Warsaw Ghetto
- NN., Account entitled "Arbet fun a sakh (farmitlung)" [Work of Many (Brokering)] (17.12.1940)

- After return from Russia to Warsaw, the author began to earn money as a matchmaker. Quotes a typical conversation with a client seeking a life's companion.
- ***Description:*** transcript (2 copies), handwritten manuscript (MS*), pencil, Yiddish, 147×206 mm, ss. 4, pp. 4.
  In the margins a symbol: "⧗" (hourglass).

488. **RING. I/22. Mf. ŻIH—772; USHMM—3**
- After 01.1941, Warsaw Ghetto
- NN., Account entitled "Stay in Quarantine (Leszno 109)"
- Resident of Jeziorna, near Warsaw, resettled with family to Warsaw, stayed for some dozens of hours together with a group of more than 600 deportees in the building at ul. Leszno 109; description of the housing conditions and treatment of the deportees by the quarantine manager (Helber).
- ***Description:*** transcript (2 copies), handwritten manuscript (JG*), pencil, Polish, 145×205 mm, minor damage and losses of text, ss. 14, pp. 14.,
  On p. 1 notation of H.W. illegible.
  Attached note by H.W. in Polish, Yiddish: "Helber, quarantine manager, Gestapo collaborator. Colleague Jechiel Górny recorded [this]."

489. **RING. I/1069 (1388). Mf. ŻIH—832; USHMM—44**
- After 02.1941, Warsaw Ghetto
- NN., Account of the work at quarantine for deportees into the Warsaw Ghetto (ul. Leszno 109) (fragments)
- Female author describes: conditions of work, difficult situation of the quarantine's residents, various categories of deportees, behavior of the Order Service, medical personnel.
- ***Description:*** transcript (2 copies), handwritten manuscript (CC*), pencil, Polish, 146×209 mm, serious damage and losses of text, ss. 32, pp. 32.

490. **RING. I/989 (1308). (Lb. 414). Mf. ŻIH—831; USHMM—43**
- After 28.03.1941, Warsaw Ghetto
- NN., Account entitled "Bilder fun a kinder-shpital" [Pictures from a Children's Hospital] (20 and 28.03.1941)
- Author describes her work in a hospital in the Warsaw Ghetto (difficult conditions, overcrowding, infectious diseases, starving children). Profiles of young patients (e.g., children from Kałuszyn, Abramek Cygler from Piaseczno).
- Description of transcript (part [b] in 2 copies), handwritten manuscript (BW*), Yiddish, pencil, 148×210 mm, ss. 12, pp. 12.
  Manuscript consists of 2 parts: a) and b). Part (a) is marked in the margins with a Hebrew letter (ink): "a" (alef); part (b) with Hebrew letters (ink): "k" (kof) and "t" (tes). In part (a) on p. 1 date of "20.03.[19]41" written by H.W.* Both parts have 4 pages each.
  Doc. (a) was kept in a binder.
  It is possible that the author of the account was Dora Wajnerman; see Ring. I/1099.
  Published: *BFG*, vol. XXXI (1993), pp. 68–74; *Selected Documents*, pp. 403–407; *Dzieci*, pp. 130–139.

491. **RING. I/1024 (1343). (Lb. 354). Mf. ŻIH—831; USHMM—43**
- After 11.04.1941, Warsaw Ghetto
- NN., Account entitled "Erev Peysekh in varshever geto, 2-ter yor fun milkhome 1941" [Eve of Passover in Warsaw Ghetto, 2nd Year of War 1941] (11.04.1941)
- Atmosphere on the streets of the Warsaw Ghetto on the eve of the holiday (11.04.1941) regarding the tragic provisioning situation, rising prices, and the daily struggle for survival.
- ***Description:*** transcript (2 copies), handwritten manuscript (BW*), pencil, Yiddish, 147×207 mm, ss. 10, pp. 10.
  In the margins a Hebrew letter: "l" [lamed].
  Doc. was kept in a binder.

492. **RING. I/1017 (1336). (Lb. 368). Mf. ŻIH—831; USHMM—43**
- After 20.04.1941, Warsaw Ghetto
- NN., Account entitled "Moment bildlekh fun varshever getto, 1941" [Snapshots of the Warsaw Ghetto, 1941]
- Tragic scenes from the ghetto's street life (hunger, beggars): ul. Karmelicka, Orla, Grzybowska. Announcement of 20.04.1941 by the Koło Młodych (Youth Circle) about a campaign against beggars (ul. Sienna 38).
- ***Description:*** original or transcript (2 copies), handwritten manuscript (MS*), pencil, Yiddish, 148×208 mm, ss. 2, pp. 2.
  In the margin a symbol (ink): "v," one above another.
  Published: *Selected Documents*, p. 78.

493. **RING. I/1020 (1339). (Lb. 365). Mf. ŻIH—831; USHMM—43**
- After 28.04.1941, Warsaw Ghetto
- NN., Account entitled "Milkh un kashe fun der vant" [Milk and Kashe from the Wall]
- About smugglers' inventiveness, description of various solutions for smuggling goods into the Warsaw Ghetto.
- ***Description:*** transcript (2 copies), handwritten manuscript (BW*), pencil, Yiddish, 148×208 mm, ss. 6, pp. 6.
  In the margins a letter (ink): "T."
  Doc. was kept in a binder.

**494. RING. I/1010 (1329). (Lb. 317). Mf. ŻIH—831; USHMM—43**

- After 30.07.1941, Warsaw Ghetto
- NN., Diary (1–8.05.1941). (29.07 and 30.07.1941)
- Author, an employee of the Joint, caring for refugees, describes daily life of the Warsaw Ghetto (hunger, high mortality, numerous human bodies waiting for burial, indifference of people toward death, corrupted Order Service).
- ***Description:*** transcript (2 copies), handwritten manuscript (BW*), pencil, Yiddish, 147×206 mm, minor damage and losses of text, ss. 22, pp. 22.
  Manuscript consists of two parts with separate pagination: 1) includes entries from 1, 2, and 8.05.1941 (at the end of the text is the date: 29.07.1941, in the margins letter in ink: "P"); 2) includes entry from 3.05.1941 (at the end dated: 30.07.1941, in the margins the letters: "PA").

**495. RING. I/1022 (1341). (Lb. 355). Mf. ŻIH—831; USHMM—43**

- After 3.05.1941, Warsaw Ghetto
- NN., Account entitled "A tsekholemoyd Peysekh . . ." [An Intermediate day Passover . . .] (3.05.1941)
- Roundup on the first intermediate day of Passover (15.04.1941) in the Warsaw Ghetto, description of the brutalization by Germans of 5 Jews caught in the roundup.
- ***Description:*** transcript (2 copies), handwritten manuscript (BW*), pencil, Yiddish, 148×208 mm, ss. 8, pp. 8.
  In the margins a Hebrew letter: "sh" (shin).

**496. RING. I/1015 (1334). (Lb. 369). Mf. ŻIH—831; USHMM—43**

- After 26.05.1941, Warsaw Ghetto
- NN., Account of life in the Warsaw Ghetto. (26.05.1941)
- Price increases, hunger among children, Order Service, trade in foreign currencies (scenes from Miła, Zamenhofa, Karmelicka, Wołyńska, Smocza streets).
- ***Description:*** transcript, handwritten manuscript (MS*), pencil,Yiddish, 146×208 mm, ss. 4, pp. 4.
  In the margin a Hebrew-Yiddish letter (ink): "v" [tsvey vovn] (or a symbol): " | | ."

**497. RING. I/1030 (1349). (Lb. 723). Mf. ŻIH—831; USHMM—43**

- 1–2.06.1941, Warsaw Ghetto
- NN., Account of the cemetery at ul. Gęsia (1–2.06.1941) (fragment of a diary [?])
- Funeral of Chmielnicki (died of hunger) and visit in the cemetery charnel house, in which are stored corpses brought from the ghetto to be buried in mass graves.
- ***Description:*** original or transcript, handwritten manuscript (Ł*), notebook, ink, Yiddish, 158×203 mm, ss. 8, pp. 16.

**498. RING. I/107. Mf. ŻIH—776; USHMM—7**

- After 2.06.1941, Warsaw Ghetto
- NN., Account entitled "Coronation of Young [Samuel] Gancwajch in an Eyewitness Account of the Festive Celebration Held in the Nowy Azazel Theater 2 VI 1941"
- Description of the festivities of the bar-mitzvah of the son of Abraham Gancwajch, founder and chief of the "13," an organization collaborating with the Germans, whose headquarters was at ul Leszno 13. In an ironic manner, the author describes the course of the gathering, names participants (inter alia Abram Gancwajch, Miriam Gancwajch, Białer, Czerwiński, Warszawiak, Kac), and summarizes their speeches.
- ***Description:*** original or transcript, typescript, Polish, 220×285 mm, slight mechanical damage and losses of text, ss. 5, pp. 5.
  See about "13": *Archiwum Ringelbluma*, p. 274; *Czerniaków*, pp. 169, 281, 341.

**499. RING. I/1005 (1324). (Lb. 338). Mf. ŻIH—831; USHMM—43**

- After 4.07.1941, Warsaw Ghetto
- NN., Account entitled "Varshe, an ekskursie tsu yidn velkhe dernern zikh mit hint, kets un shtshures . . . !!!" [Warsaw, an excursion to Jews who nourish themselves on dogs, cats, and rats . . . !!!] (4.07.1941)
- Description of the tragic living conditions of residents of apartment houses at ul. Wołyńska 7, 9, 25. During 3 months ca. 500 people died of hunger in 21 houses on Wołyńska Street.
- ***Description:*** transcript (2 copies), handwritten manuscript (BW*), pencil, Yiddish, 148×210 mm, ss. 6, pp. 6.
  In the margins a letter (ink): "N" [nun]
  On p. 1 a symbol (red pencil): "+."

**500. RING. I/362. Mf. ŻIH—782; USHMM—13**

- After 07.1941, Warsaw Ghetto
- NN., Account about Mrs. Bajnsztok of Warsaw (ul. Nowolipki 76). (07.1941)
- Mrs. Bajnsztok had four children, three died; remaining was Rachela [Rokhele] (age 14), sick, for whom she received bread from the baker Hilerowicz. After her death she continued to take bread and for two weeks did not admit that her daughter lay dead in the apartment.
- ***Description:*** transcript (2 copies), handwritten manuscript (TT*), pencil, Yiddish, 148×208 mm, ss. 4, pp. 4.
  On p. 1 (of the first copy) notation by H.W. in Yiddish (ink): "Weisberg" [Vaysberg]
  Attached note by H.W. in Yiddish: "Submitted by M. Weisberg, former librarian of the Judaic Library."

### 501. RING. I/326. Mf. ŻIH–781; USHMM–12

- After 09.1941, Warsaw Ghetto
- Record of a case before an honor court[31] between Natan [Tytelman] and Gerszon [Erdepl] on 6.09.1941
- Concerning distribution of the underground press.
- ***Description:*** original or transcript, handwritten manuscript, ink, Yiddish, damage and losses of text, ss. 1, pp. 1.

  Attached note by H.W. in Yiddish: "Honor Court between Natan Tytelman and Gerszon Erdepl concerning distribution of underground press communiqués. (6.09.1941)."

### 502. RING. I/93. Mf. ŻIH–776; USHMM–7. RING. I/291. (Lb. 1659). Mf. ŻIH–781; USHMM–12

- 03.1942, Warsaw Ghetto
- NN., Two accounts on the subject: "Health Action on Krochmalna Street" [in September 1941], dated 27.03 and 29.03.1942
- Description of the action with participation of ambulance units, Order Service, navy blue [Polish] police, and Germans. All residents were expelled from the apartment houses onto the street and kept there for many hours in the courtyard; there was compulsory bathing, disinfection of apartments and bedding.
- ***Description:*** Ring. I/93—original or transcript (handwritten manuscript (E*), ink, Polish, 198×160 mm, minor damage and losses of text, ss. 11, pp. 11); Ring. I/291—transcript (2 copies, typescript, Polish, 198×270, minor damage and losses of text (major in the second copy), ss. 6, pp. 6.

  Second account (dated 29.03.1942) recorded on the basis inter alia of the account of one of the participants in the action. According to information on the cover (Ring. I/291) the text's author is Schöntal.

  About the situation on ul. Krochmalna, see *Czerniaków*, pp. 202–203.

  Index: Dr. Syrkinowa, director of the Health Department, Dr. Hagen

### 503. RING. I/449. Mf. ŻIH–785; USHMM–16

- 7–15.10.1941, Warsaw Ghetto
- NN., Notes from life in the Warsaw Ghetto. (7–15.10.1941)
- Opening of the boarding and day school for children (7.10.1941 at ul. Nowolipki 25) with Czerniaków's wife, Wielikowski, Winter, Rozen, A. Gepner, Józef Szeryński present; effects of underfeeding of the Jewish population; attempts to construct a new wall at ul. Stawki; Adam Czerniaków and Józef Szeryński went to a boarding house (Otwock) but public kitchens in the ghetto close; racial restrictions and the situation of Jewish women.
- ***Description:*** original or transcript, handwritten manuscript, pencil, Polish, Yiddish, 105×160, 105×110 mm, ss. 5, pp. 5.

  Inventory: "Author is Ignacy Lipszyc, a functionary of the Order Service."

### 504. RING. I/212. (Lb. 876). RING. I/239. Mf. ŻIH–780; USHMM–11

- After 11.11.1941, Warsaw Ghetto
- NN., Account entitled "Reduction of the Warsaw Ghetto at the Beginning of October 1941" (11.11.1941)
- Course of eviction of the Jewish population 27.09–5.10.1941 from ul. Sienna (odd side) as well as from apartment houses on Wielka, Sosnowa, and Twarda streets crossed by ul. Sienna.
- ***Description:*** transcript (3 copies), typescript, Polish, 205×290 mm, minor damage and losses of text, ss. 9, pp. 9.

  On p. 1 (on the first copy) notation by H.W.: "Kon" as well as in the margins a symbol (letter): "X." Copies 1 and 2 were mixed before the symbol "X" was written on the first copy; p. 1 in the first copy originally belonged to the second copy, while p. 1 in the second belonged to the first copy.

  Attached notes by H.W. in Polish, Yiddish: a) (Ring. I/212) "Submitted by Aron Koniński"; b) (Ring. I/239) "Submitted by Szymon Wyszewiański (J.H.K)."

  See *Czerniaków*, p. 218; *Kronika getta*, pp. 617–618.

### 505. RING. I/240. Mf. ŻIH–780; USHMM–11

- After 10.1941 [?], Warsaw Ghetto
- NN., Account entitled "Dos aynmonen dire-gelt in geto" [Collection of Rent in the Ghetto]
- About methods of collection of rent arrears within the ghetto (ul. Krochmalna, Śliska).
- ***Description:*** transcript, handwritten manuscript (CHW*), notebook, pencil, Yiddish, 155×201 mm, ss. 8, pp. 16.

### 506. RING. I/158. (Lb. 971, 972). Mf. ŻIH–778; USHMM–9

- After 11.1941, Warsaw Ghetto
- Women's accounts of social work in September 1939 and during the occupation
- Profiles of 6 women social activists, written on the basis of their own recollections, inter alia about participation in rescue activity during the siege of Warsaw, situation of the Jewish population in Pabianice, work in welfare organizations in occupied

31. This refers to a clandestine underground court.

Warsaw (attached brief descriptions of these women written by NN.).
- *Description:* original, handwritten manuscript (different handwritings—4 [?]), ink, Polish, 210×295, 140×224 mm, minor damage and losses of text, ss. 12, pp. 14.
  The accounts were recorded by NN., assigned numbers from 1–6; numeration in texts 2–6 was made with a different handwriting than in the accounts. Text (no. 1) concerning Miss G. is written with a different handwriting than the rest. Added to texts no. 2–6 are brief characterizations of the women, produced by one person, but different from the one who recorded the accounts themselves.
  Part of the manuscript is written on the back of ŻTOS forms: certificates of employment at ŻTOS (Warsaw, 31.12.1940, typescript, German, Polish).

### 507. RING. I/1214. Mf. ŻIH—835; USHMM—47

- 12.1941, Warsaw Ghetto
- NN., Account entitled "Fragmentn fun 3 teg futer gzeyre" [Fragments from 3 days of Fur Edict] (26–28.12.1941)
- Mood in the Warsaw Ghetto during collection of fur coats for the Germans.
- *Description:* original or transcript, handwritten manuscript (Ł*), ink, Yiddish, 94×153, 150×190 mm, serious damage and losses of text, ss. 8, pp. 16.
  Author entered an erroneous date in the text: "26.12.1942" [sic]

### 508. RING. I/346. Mf. ŻIH—781; USHMM—12

- 1941, Warsaw Ghetto
- NN., Account entitled "Leyb Dembovski's avekgeyn" [Leyb Dembowski's Departure]
- Profile of a refugee and his family from the housing "point" for refugees in the Warsaw Ghetto (ul. Miła 2 [?] "M-2").
- *Description:* transcript, typescript, Yiddish, 220×287 mm, minor damage and losses of text, ss. 4, pp. 4.
  Doc. is part of a larger study, pages 7–10 preserved. On p. 9 is a mirror image, because the carbon paper was incorrectly inserted during preparation of the typescript.
  Attached note by H.W. in Yiddish: "Study by Izrael Winnik, coworker of O.Sh. (1941)."
  Published: *Tsvishn lebn un toyt*, ed. B. Mark, Warsaw 1955, pp. 20–23.

### 509. RING. I/86. Mf. ŻIH—776; USHMM—7

- Start of 1942 [?], Warsaw Ghetto
- Responses of Jewish intellectuals and scholars to a survey concerning appraisal of the situation of the Jewish population in the Warsaw Ghetto
- Attitudes to the conditions of life in the ghetto, problem of assimilation, role of the Jewish Council, demoralization, decline of religiosity, lack of social work among the lower social classes, trends in youth education, prospects for the Jewish people in Poland. Responses to the survey were provided by: Jehoszua (Szyja) Perle, Sz. [Szoel?] Stupnicki, Hilel Cajtlin [Hillel Zeitlin], A. [Aron] Einhorn, docent Dr. Edmund Sztejn, H. Rosen, Dr. [Izrael] Milejkowski. On one response the name is missing.
- *Description:* original, handwritten manuscript (three or four handwritings, e.g., pp. 39–54—LEG*—text of Dr. Milejkowski's questionnaire, additions in a different handwriting, ink), notebook, ink, pencil, Yiddish, 160×205 mm, 150×160 mm, damage and losses of text, ss. 71, pp. 74.
  Some of the names of those surveyed are entered in one handwriting (ink and pencil). Some of the document was written on printed order of payment forms of the Penny [grosz] Savings Bank ("Kasy Groszowej Oszczędności W.T.D.").
  Presumably, the article from Ring. I/88 is also a response to a similar survey.
  See HWC, 45/1 (transcript [?] of the survey of Dr. [Izrael] Milejkowski, typescript, ss. 7).
  Published: *BFG*, vol. I, no. 2 (1948), pp. 111–122 (questionnaires of: Hilel Cajtlin, Sz. Stupnicki, and A. Einhorn); *BFG*, vol. I, nos. 3–4 (1948), pp. 186–201 (surveys of: Dr. Izrael Milejkowski, H. Rosen, NN.); *Selected Documents*, pp. 734–737, 737–740, 741–746, 747–752, 753–754, 755–756, 757–760 (surveys of: Hilel Cajtlin, Sz. Stupnicki, Dr. Izrael Milejkowski, H. Rosen, NN., J. Perle, doc. Dr. E. Sztejn).

### 510. RING. I/253. Mf. ŻIH—780; USHMM—11

- After 01.1942, Warsaw Ghetto
- NN., Account summarizing news brought to the ghetto by a Polish underground activist [Irena Adamowicz ?] and her former pupil, a physician, an officer of the German Army. (01.1942) (fragment)
- Situation on the eastern front, moods in the German Army, training and armament of the Soviet armies; difficult living conditions in POW camp (near Warsaw) for Soviet soldiers, among the prisoners—including Poles incorporated into the Red Army after 1939; Poles better treated than Russians by the camp authorities.
- *Description:* transcript (2 copies), typescript, Yiddish, 207×295 mm, minor damage and losses of text, ss. 4, pp. 4.
  On p. 1 notation by H.W. in Yiddish (ink): "By Hober."
  Attached note by H.W. in Yiddish: "News comes from Shomer [Zionist pioneer] circles."
  Notation about Irena Adamowicz on the basis of R. Sakowska; see *Dwa etapy*, p. 106.
  Published: (Part in Polish translation) *Dwa etapy*, pp. 106–107.

### 511. RING. I/241. Mf. ŻIH—780; USHMM—11

a)

- After 19.02.1942, Warsaw Ghetto
- NN., Account entitled "Kanibalizm-fal oyf Krokhmalne 13" [Cannibalism Case at Krochmalna 13]
- Description of living conditions of the house's residents (hunger, diseases, demise of whole families, e.g., Kofmans, Rozenblums); in one of the apartments a boy died and his mother, dying from hunger, began to eat his body.
- ***Description:*** original or transcript, handwritten manuscript (CHW*), ink, Yiddish, 158×200 mm, ss. 3, pp. 5.

  On the back of p. 5 fragment of a copy of a document (a letter) from the start of XIX? (signed Müntzer) (handwritten manuscript, ink, Polish). Similar copies of documents, made in the same handwriting, are found in materials of Chaskiel Wilczyński in Ring. II.

  Attached note by H.W. in Yiddish: "Forwarded by Aleksander Landau?"

b)

- After 19.02.1942, Warsaw Ghetto
- Report by Group Leader D. Szwizgold (no. 1345) of the Order Service about confirmation of the instance of cannibalism at ul. Krochmalna 18, apt. 20. [19.02.1942]
- Rywka Urman admitted to consumption of the body of her son Berek, who died the previous day. She made the statement in the presence of: Jankiel Murawa, chairman, and Niuta Zajdman, secretary, of the apartment house committee, as well as M. Grosman, Order Service officer (no. 393).
- ***Description:*** transcript, typescript, Polish, 150×100 mm, ss. 1, pp. 1.

  Doc. (b) also cited by *Czerniaków* (p. 255).

### 512. RING. I/1052 (1371). Mf. ŻIH—832; USHMM—44

- After 26.03.1942, Warsaw Ghetto
- NN., Account entitled "In halbe sho" [In Half an Hour] (26.03.1942)
- Notes gathered on the streets of the Warsaw Ghetto from various persons about crimes committed against the Jewish population in Wąwolnica, Słonim, Nowogródek, Zduńska Wola, Łęczyca, Brzeziny, and Izbica Lubelska.
- ***Description:*** transcript (3 copies), handwritten manuscript (U*), pencil, Yiddish, 145×218 mm, ss. 9, pp. 9.

### 513. RING. I/203. (Lb. 922, 891). Mf. ŻIH—779; USHMM—10

- After 5.04.1942, Warsaw Ghetto
- NN., Account entitled "Apartment House Blockade (Nalewki)" (5.04.1942)
- Description of the disinfection campaign conducted in apartment houses within the ghetto by the Health Department with the aid of the Order Service and the related abuses. Description of one of the actions in an apartment house on ul. Nalewki (attempt at opposition to corruption in the Order Service by Hochman, chairman of the apartment house committee).
- ***Description:*** original or transcript (handwritten manuscript—E*, pencil, 145×208 mm), transcript (typescript—2 copies, 195×270 mm, damage and losses of text—second copy), Polish, ss. 13, pp. 13.

### 514. RING. I/470. Mf. ŻIH—786; USHMM—17

- After 10.04.1942, Warsaw Ghetto
- NN., Account about the fate of Bajla Keselberg [Kaselberg] alias Kociołek on the basis of her own recollections
- Protagonist of the account (born 8.02.1925), daughter of Lejzor and Glika, after formation of the Warsaw Ghetto supported her family by smuggling, was arrested 10.11.1941 on the "Aryan side" and imprisoned at Gęsia. She describes difficult prison conditions, executions, fellow prisoners (Salwerówna [Hena Salwe] and [Róża] Mikanowska—shot, Maniusia Frydman), prison personnel (e.g., Szwajcer, Szer, Flancer, Minc), released 10.04.1942. Attached copy of release from prison issued by the Jewish Council.
- ***Description:*** original or transcript, handwritten manuscript (I*), copy of the release in another handwriting (handwritten manuscript H*), notebook, ink, Polish, 150×195 mm, ss. 22, pp. 23.

  The account contains two chapters: "Before Imprisonment" and "In Prison."

  Attached note by H.W.: "Józef Honig prepared the text."

  Róża Mikanowska and Salwerówna were shot on 15.12.1941 together with a group of 15 prisoners. See Ring. I/224.

### 515. RING. I/243. (Lb. 207). Mf. ŻIH—780; USHMM—11

- After 15.04.1942, Warsaw Ghetto
- NN., Account entitled "Gravediggers"
- Author accompanies gravediggers in collection of human corpses, persons who died of hunger within the ghetto, inter alia at refugee centers at ul. Franciszkańska 21 and Gęsia 7 (15.04.1942).
- ***Description:*** transcript, typescript, Polish, 210×272 mm, ss. 1, pp. 1.

  Notation by H.W. in Yiddish (ink): "1 standard page"; and notation in another handwriting (ink): "Warsaw, 15.04.1942."

### 516. RING. I/434. (Lb. 208). Mf. ŻIH—785; USHMM—16

- After 04.1942, Warsaw Ghetto
- NN., Account entitled "Among Refugees from Germany" (04.1942)

- Arrival in the Warsaw Ghetto of a transport of Jews from the Reich (Berlin, Hanover, Braunschweig, Mannheim, inter alia Mündhausen, captain of the criminal police in Berlin until 1939, Protestant). Picture of the situation of Jews in the Reich, relations with Germans, conditions of deportation to the Generalgouvernement, life in quarantine (ul. Leszno 109), departures to labor camp (Treblinka) (Dr. Bloch, Gustaw Blumenbach, Dogobert Thal, Abraham Liess).
- ***Description:*** original or transcript, typescript with handwritten additions, ink, Polish, 215×272 mm, minor damage and losses of text, ss. 3, pp. 3.
  On p. 3 handwritten notation: "April 1942."

**517. RING. I/31. (Lb. 29). Mf. ŻIH—772; USHMM—3**

- 05.1942, Warsaw Ghetto
- NN. "Reflections of a Healthworker" (23–30.05.1942)
- Recollections of a participant in the units (columns) fighting epidemics in Warsaw, profiles of comrades, hunger.
- ***Description:*** original[?], handwritten manuscript, ink, Polish, 220×354 mm, ss. 2, pp. 4.

**518. RING. I/461. Mf. ŻIH—786; USHMM—17**

- 25.05.1942, Warsaw Ghetto
- NN., Account entitled "Ferofenbarte tsnies" [Defiled Modesty]
- 25.05.1942 at the corner of ul. Dzielna and Smocza a group of Germans snatched up elegantly dressed women, then took them to the mikve (ritual bath), where they were filmed during bathing.
- ***Description:*** original [?], handwritten manuscript, ink, Yiddish, damage and losses of text, ss. 1, pp. 2.
  Attached note by H.W. in Polish, Yiddish: "Note concerning filming of Jewish women driven to the rit[ual] bathing facility as well as a talk of a religious nature delivered by Menachem Kon."

**519. RING. I/1001 (1320). (Lb. 622). Mf. ŻIH—831; USHMM—43**

- 05.1942, Warsaw Ghetto
- NN., Notes concerning Warsaw Ghetto life. (05.1942)
- Descriptions of various events in the Warsaw Ghetto and the author's commentaries (demoralization among Jews, searches conducted by officials and the swindles under their cover, murders of several collaborators of the "13," information from letters arriving in the ghetto). Information about the Łódź ghetto.
- ***Description:*** original or transcript, handwritten manuscript (MS*), pencil, Yiddish, 155×196 mm, ss. 3, pp. 6.
  In the margins a symbol (pencil): "— = ."
  On p. 1 notation by H.W. in Yiddish (ink): "May 1942. 8 standard pages."
  Index: Gancwajch, Szternfeld, Lewin, Dr. Hurwicz, Mandel, Szymonowicz

**520. RING. I/289. (Lb. 1557, 561). Mf. ŻIH—781; USHMM—12**

- After 7.06.1942, Warsaw Ghetto
- NN., Sheets from a diary (7.06., 22.06., and 1.07.1942)
- Death of a Polish smuggler, shot at the ghetto's wall (ul. Przejazd 9), strike of manual laborers in TOZ, preparation of a grave at the Jewish cemetery in Warsaw for 200 people, profile of a gendarme nicknamed "Frankenstein," death of the superintendent of the apartment house at Dzielna 5, Eisen (and his wife) and the superintendent of the apartment house at Nowolipki 30, Mrs. Finkielsztajn (smugglers).
- ***Description:*** original or transcript, handwritten manuscript (E*), ink, pencil, Polish, 178×215, 152×198 mm, ss. 5, pp. 7.
  On p. 1 (7.06.1942) information by H.W. in Yiddish: "1 standard page."
  Attached note by H.W.
  About the grave, see *Czerniaków*, p. 294.

**521. RING. I/437. (Lb. 594). Mf. ŻIH—785; USHMM—16**

- 06.1942, Warsaw Ghetto
- NN., Diary (9–17.06.1942)
- Author, an official in the ghetto (worked with Bernstein); information about public executions, reduction of the Jewish district, Gypsies from Germany (ul. Pokorna 5), young smugglers.
- ***Description:*** original or transcript, handwritten manuscript (E*), pencil, Polish, 150×194 mm, minor damage and losses of text, ss. 4, pp. 7.

**522. RING. I/1036 (1355). Mf. ŻIH—832; USHMM—44**

- 13.06.1942, Warsaw Ghetto
- NN., Account of the moods in the Warsaw Ghetto. (13.06.1942)
- Troubles connected with the fight against smuggling, news about the fate of Jews in the provinces, fear of the future.
- ***Description:*** original or transcript, handwritten manuscript (MS*), pencil, Yiddish, 154×197 mm, ss. 1, pp. 2.

**523. RING. I/267. Mf. ŻIH—780; USHMM—11**

- 06.1942, Warsaw Ghetto
- NN., Daily notes (19.06–30.06.1942)
- Fates of the Jewish population in various localities on Polish territory, information concerning Warsaw, Janów [Lubelski?], Wieluń, Szawle, Miranów [?] (banishment of 24.06.1942), Mława, Wodzisław near Pińczów, about the rabbi of Radzymin (Radzyner [?]).
- ***Description:*** original or transcript, handwritten manuscript, notebook, ink, Yiddish, 150×194 mm, extensive damage and losses of text, ss. 15, pp. 24.
  On p. 1 (cover) notation by H.W. in Yiddish: "12 standard pages."

**524. RING. I/237. Mf. ŻIH—780; USHMM—11**

- After 26.06.1942, Warsaw Ghetto
- NN., Account entitled "Vos iz forgekumen baym mizrakh-vokzal" [What Happened at the Eastern Train Station]
- Group of Jewish laborers in response to provocations came to blows (26.06.1942) with Poles working at unloading wagons (one Pole perished and two Jews died in hospital as a result of wounds suffered—Tadeusz Robak, age 22, polytechnic student, ul. Pańska 35; and Grynberg, a butcher from Żyrardów; many Jews were wounded). The account was written on the basis of information provided by the leader of the Jewish group.
- ***Description:*** original or transcript, handwritten manuscript (Ł*), ink, Yiddish, 108×355 mm, ss. 1, pp. 2.

  Attached note by H.W. in Yiddish: "Nechemiasz Tytelman, a member Oyneg Shabes, recorded and edited the statement."

  About this incident, see *Czerniaków*, p. 292.

**525. RING. I/1032 (1351). (Lb. 728). Mf. ŻIH—832; USHMM—44**

- 07.1942, Warsaw Ghetto
- NN., Notes concerning life in the Warsaw Ghetto (1 and 17.07.1942)
- Threat to shoot 100 Jews and 10 members of the Order Service for opposition to German orders (posters); smuggling, corruption in the Order Service (Flajszman, Feferberg, Icze Buks [Anders]); information about the situation in the Łódź ghetto (provisioning) and in Lwów (letter of 28.06.1942 about prices of food products); fatalities in crossings to the "Aryan side"; death of the lawyer's wife Jaźwińska, maiden name Rywka Najman; corruption of the administration in the ghetto.
- ***Description:*** original or transcript, handwritten manuscript (MS*), pencil, Yiddish, 152×194 mm, minor damage and losses of text, ss. 4, pp. 7.

  On p. 5 notation by H.W. in Yiddish: "17.07.1942" and minor additions (ink).

  About the threat to shoot 100 Jews and 10 Order Service members, see *Czerniaków*, pp. 294–295.

  Index: Szmerling, Natan Ryba (age 29), section leader, shot by a German gendarme

**526. RING. I/768 (1093). Mf. ŻIH—825; USHMM—56; RING. I/1220/24. Mf. ŻIH—835; USHMM—47**

- After 15.07.1942, Warsaw Ghetto
- NN., Account entitled "History of a station [. . .] radio monitoring in the ghetto." (missing ending [?])
- Organization and functioning of a conspiratorial cell involved in radio monitoring, led by Szmuel Brasław and Mordechaj [Anielewicz ?] in the apartment of Mr. and Mrs. Gleser (ul. Leszno 6) (twice), finally at ul. Pawia 11.
- ***Description:*** original or transcript, handwritten manuscript (SB*), ink, Polish, 143×216 mm, a large part of the text is unreadable, damage and losses of text (one sheet from Ring. I/1220), ss. 9, pp. 17.

  Index: Towa Frenkiel

**527. RING. I/268. Mf. ŻIH—780; USHMM—11**

- 1942, Warsaw Ghetto
- NN., Recollections of a health unit employee
- Ineffectiveness of the unit's activity in preventing epidemics, lack of suitable means for disinfection, development of graft.
- ***Description:*** transcript (3 copies), handwritten manuscript (JG*), pencil, Polish, minor damage and losses of text, ss. 66, pp. 66.

  On p. 1 (first copy) H.W. in Yiddish (ink) : "Report of a disinfector."

  Author of the recollections could be the author of the text of Ring. I/221.

  Inventory: "Text transcribed by Jechiel Górny."

**528. RING. I/992 (1311). Mf. ŻIH—831; USHMM—43**

- Date unknown, Warsaw Ghetto
- NN., Account entitled "Khaye-oylem hot goyver geven . . ." [Eternal Life Triumphed . . .]
- Report of a meeting of a group of Zionist activists. Speakers attempt to raise the spirits of those gathered and not to enter into discussions of daily problems of the Warsaw Ghetto.
- ***Description:*** original or transcript, handwritten manuscript (MS*), pencil, Yiddish, 143×222 mm, ss. 2, pp. 3.

  At top of the page a letter (ink): "P."

**529. RING. I/442. Mf. ŻIH—785; USHMM—16**

- Date unknown, Warsaw Ghetto
- NN., Account entitled "A dinst, a shpion" [A Maid, a Spy]
- A maid in a Jewish family in Warsaw collaborated with the SS; after transfer of her employers into the ghetto, she remained in their apartment.
- ***Description:*** original or transcript, handwritten manuscript (CHW*), ink, Yiddish, 157×202 mm, ss. 3, pp. 5.

  Attached note by H.W. in Polish, Yiddish: "Jechaskiel Wilczyński edited."

  Index: Emilia Denkiewicz (born near Berlin)

**530. RING. I/439. (Lb. 1457). Mf. ŻIH—836; USHMM—67**

- Date unknown, Warsaw Ghetto
- NN., Account entitled "A Day in the Dayroom [świetlicy] or How to Escape from It" (fragment)
- Female author works in a dayroom for children in a refugees' point in the Warsaw Ghetto (hunger, poor sanitary conditions, diseases, numerous deaths of children). Named: Rywka Dura, Lichtensztajns, as

well as Hersz Lejb, Estera, Mojsie, Rajzla, Itka, Szejwa, Chaja, Hancia, Chaimek, Chemia, Dawid.
- ***Description:*** original or transcript, typescript, Polish, 182×265 mm, serious damage and losses of text, ss. 2, pp. 2.
    Published: *Dzieci*, pp. 235–238.

**531. RING. I/1220/27. Mf. ŻIH—835; USHMM—47**
- Date unknown, Warsaw Ghetto
- NN., Account about the Warsaw Ghetto
- Illegal trade and smuggling with participation of Germans.
- ***Description:*** original or transcript, handwritten manuscript, ink, Yiddish, 145×169 mm, 146×209 mm, minor damage and losses of text, ss. 2, pp. 2.
    In the margins a symbol (ink): a half-circle with a dot in the center.
    Doc. written in the form of a letter.
    Doc. was kept in a binder.
    Index: Fajgenbojm and Sznajderman, peddlers of the Warsaw Ghetto

**532. RING. I/1220/34. Mf. ŻIH—835; USHMM—47**
- Date unknown, Warsaw Ghetto
- NN., Note
- Author is an official (in the Jewish Council, a social activist [?]) in the Warsaw Ghetto; report of a conference (meeting).
- ***Description:*** original, or transcript, handwritten manuscript, ink, Yiddish, 100×146 mm, ss. 2, pp. 4.
    Doc. was kept in a binder.

**533. RING. I/426. (Lb. 1275). Mf. ŻIH—784; USHMM—15**
- Date unknown, Warsaw Ghetto
- NN., Accounts (2) entitled 1) "Fun plitim shtetl—Dzhike un Niske" [From the Refugees' Town—Dzika and Niska]; 2) "Froy Krashevitshes toyt" [The Death of Mrs. Kraszewicz]
- Situation of refugees in the Warsaw Ghetto (squalor, hunger, diseases), picture of the so-called refugee "points"[32] at ul. Stawki 9, 15 and Dzika 3 and 7/9 as well as Stawki 32 (place of Mrs. Kraszewicz's death).
- ***Description:*** original or transcript, typescript, Yiddish, 225×300 mm, ss. 6, pp. 6.
    According to B.M., author is presumably Józef Kirman; see *Tsvishn lebn un toyt*, ed. B. Mark, Warsaw 1955, pp. 39, 43.
    Published: *Tsvishn lebn un toyt*, ed. B. Mark, Warsaw 1955, pp. 39–45. *Ghetto: Berichte aus dem Warschauer Ghetto 1939–1945*, Berlin 1966, pp. 125–128 (doc. 2).

**534. RING. I/1220/73. Mf. ŻIH—835; USHMM—47**
- Date unknown, Warsaw Ghetto
- NN., Account of the Warsaw Ghetto (missing beginning)
- Displacement from ul. Żelazna.
- ***Description:*** transcript (2 copies), typescript, Yiddish, 195×130, 200×108 mm, page 2 preserved, ss. 2, pp. 2.

**535. RING. I/1220/74. Mf. ŻIH—835; USHMM—47**
- Date unknown, Warsaw Ghetto
- NN., Account [?] (conclusion).
- ***Description:*** original or transcript, typescript, Polish, 208×145, page 7 preserved, ss. 1, pp. 1.

**536. RING. I/674/2. (Lb. 1688). Mf. ŻIH—816; USHMM—28**
- Date unknown, Warsaw Ghetto
- NN., Account about confiscation of a Jewish shop by Germans
- Story of the shop owner.
- ***Description:*** original or transcript, handwritten manuscript (H.W.*), ink, Yiddish, 99×128 mm, ss. 3, pp. 5.

## Private Correspondence

**537. RING. I/1220/46. Mf. ŻIH—835; USHMM—47**
- After 4.12.1940, Warsaw Ghetto
- M. Askanaiser (Warsaw, ul. Nowolipie 27), Letter of 4.12.1940 to District Court in Chemnitz
- Concerning financial matters between the author of the letter and Häcker.
- ***Description:*** transcript, handwritten manuscript, ink, German, 210×296 mm, ss. 2, pp. 2.
    On the reverse of p. 1 is a fragment of a map of an unnamed city (pencil); on the reverse of p. 2 is text in Yiddish in Roman transliteration, in a different handwriting (pencil), entitled "Es werd werden Fug!"

**538. RING. I/517. Mf. ŻIH—789; USHMM—20**
- 22.03.1942, Warsaw Ghetto
- Hilel Cejtlin [Zeitlin] (Warsaw, ul. Śliska 60), Letter of 22.03.1942 to Pomerancblum. Request for financial aid.
- ***Description:*** original, handwritten manuscript, ink, Yiddish, 110×178 mm, ss. 2, pp. 4.
    Index: Zylbersztajn

**539. RING. I/598/1. Mf. ŻIH—792; USHMM—23**
- Date unknown, place unknown
- NN. (Heniek and [. . .]), Letter to NN. Greetings.
- ***Description:*** original, handwritten manuscript (two

32. The term *punkt* was used in Polish and Yiddish to refer to makeshift refugee shelters that came to house most of the more than 100,000 Jewish refugees from outside Warsaw who were in the ghetto. The term was also used in the Łódź ghetto to refer to shops where items were sold, distributed, or collected.

handwritings), ink, Polish, 89×132 mm, extensive damage and losses of text, ss. 1, pp. 1.

### 540. RING. I/589. (Lb. 26). Mf. ŻIH—792; USHMM—23

- Date unknown, Warsaw Ghetto
- Ela Janowska (Warsaw Ghetto), Letter to NN. (USSR). Troubles with support, lack of work.
- ***Description:*** transcript, typescript, Polish, 203×122 mm, ss. 1, pp. 1.
  Attached note by H.W. in Polish, Yiddish: "Submitted by H.W."

### 541. RING. I/543/3. Mf. ŻIH—791; USHMM—22

- After 24.02.1942, Warsaw Ghetto
- NN. (Jetka), Letter of 24.02.1942 to NN. (Dawid) (Warsaw Ghetto)
- Requests a meeting in Warsaw. Greetings for Frania Landau.
- ***Description:*** transcript, handwritten manuscript (H*), pencil, Polish, Yiddish, 118×135 mm, ss. 1, pp. 2.
  Notation in Yiddish over date "24.02.1942": "Warsaw Ghetto, postmark."

### 542. RING. I/1215. Mf. ŻIH—835; USHMM—47

- 1941, Warsaw Ghetto
- Alina Landau, Letter to [Eliezer Lipa] Bloch (Warsaw Ghetto)
- Request that he take an interest in Neufeld, locksmith. Information about Menche [?].
- ***Description:*** original, handwritten manuscript, two handwritings, pencil, Hebrew, Polish, 175×215 mm, ss. 1, pp. 1.
  On p. 1 notation in Hebrew: "author" and in Polish: "Paulina Landau . . . Alina Landau, a literary woman from Lwów was mentally ill. Died of typhus in the Warsaw Ghetto in fall 1941."

### 543. RING. I/1220/45. Mf. ŻIH—835; USHMM—47

- Date unknown, place unknown
- Dr. Jan Landau (Prison [?], cell 13), Letter (note [?]). List of dishes ordered for dinner.
- ***Description:*** original, handwritten manuscript, pencil, Polish, 91×209 mm, ss. 1, pp. 2.

### 544. RING. I/325. Mf. ŻIH—781; USHMM—12

- Before 21.12.1941, Warsaw Ghetto
- Maurice Landau, Letter to [I. Giterman] (Warsaw Ghetto). Request for aid.
- ***Description:*** original or transcript, handwritten manuscript, ink, Yiddish, 135×194 mm, minor damage and losses of text, ss. 9, pp. 9.
  Attached note by H.W. in Yiddish: "Maurice Landau to I. Giterman (1941)."

### 545. RING. I/507/6. Mf. ŻIH—789; USHMM—20

- After 19.11.1941, Warsaw Ghetto
- [Emanuel Ringelblum], Letter of 19.11.1941 to NN. concerning apartment house committees.
- ***Description:*** transcript, handwritten manuscript (ER*), ink, Yiddish, 150×115 mm, ss. 1, pp. 1.

### 546. RING. I/1100 (1419). (Lb. 727). Mf. ŻIH—833; USHMM—45

- Date unknown, Warsaw Ghetto
- Mendel Szmukler, rabbi from Grójec, letter to the firm Zelig Heller and Moryc Kohn (Warsaw Ghetto). Request for aid for the Passover holiday.
- ***Description:*** original, handwritten manuscript, ink, Yiddish, 90×156 mm, ss. 1, pp. 1.

### 547. RING. I/594/1. Mf. ŻIH—792; USHMM—23

- 21.11.1940, Warsaw Ghetto
- S. Wajnszbart [?], Letter of 21.11.1940 to [Mordechaj] Mazo [?]
- Notation about a loan (20 kg of wheat flour) figuring in the report of kitchen no. 27 (ul. Leszno 40), dated 18.11.1940.
- ***Description:*** original, handwritten manuscript, pencil, Polish, 218×165 mm, ss. 1, pp. 1.

### 548. RING. I/1210. Mf. ŻIH—835; USHMM—47

- 27.02.1942, Warsaw Ghetto
- P. Wejland (ul. Leszno 60, apt. 33), Letter of 27.02.1942 to [Dawid] Guzik
- Request for material aid.
- ***Description:*** original, handwritten manuscript, ink, Yiddish, 194×161 mm, ss. 1, pp. 2.

### 549. RING. I/598/8. Mf. ŻIH—792; USHMM—23

- 09.1940, Warsaw
- NN., Letter to Miss [Rachela?] Auerbach.
- ***Description:*** original, handwritten manuscript, ink, German, 142×200 mm, minor damage and losses of text, text illegible in places, ss. 1, pp. 1.
  In the margin notation (ink): "Volksküchen . . . onette, Warschau, im September 1940."
  On the top in another handwriting notation (ink): "Breszmerer"[?].

### 550. RING. I/586/3. Mf. ŻIH—792; USHMM—23

- After 15.12.1941, Warsaw Ghetto
- NN. (Warsaw Ghetto, prison at ul. Gęsia 24), Letter to NN. (Jakub and mother of the author) (Warsaw Ghetto) (missing conclusion)
- Female author witnessed the shooting of 15 persons on the grounds of the prison. Asks for food.
- ***Description:*** transcript, handwritten manuscript (H*), pencil, Polish, 100×155, 100×140 mm, extensive damage and losses of text, ss. 4, pp. 4.
  Execution, about which the author of the letter writes, took place 15.12.1941; see Ring. I/224.
  Index: Karliner

### 551. RING. I/316. Mf. ŻIH—781; USHMM—12

- After 03.1942, Warsaw Ghetto

- NN., Correspondence. (03.1942)
- Exchange of letters between long-time friends, a Pole and a Jew, the latter a resident of the Warsaw Ghetto. Picture of differences in daily life on both sides of the wall: "Aryan side" and the ghetto. Problem of Polish–Jewish relations.
- ***Description:*** transcript, handwritten manuscript (I*), notebook, ink, Polish, 155×198 mm, ss. 16, pp. 27.
  Inventory: "Written by Meir Czarny."
  Published: *Selected Documents*, pp. 635–644.

### 552. RING. I/1220/26. Mf. ŻIH—835; USHMM—47

- Date unknown, place unknown
- NN., Letter to NN.[?]
- Thanks for letter, information about prices of foodstuffs.
- ***Description:*** original, handwritten manuscript, ink, Polish, Yiddish, damage and losses of text, text legible in places, ss. 2, pp. 4.

### 553. RING. I/598/3. Mf. ŻIH—792; USHMM—23

- Date unknown, place unknown
- NN., Letter [?] to NN. (fragment).
- ***Description:*** original [?], handwritten manuscript, ink, Yiddish, 170×100, 80×65 mm, very serious damage and losses of text, ss. 5, pp. 10.

## *MONOGRAPHS (PLANS AND OUTLINES OF ESSAYS, SCIENTIFIC PAPERS, COMPILATIONS, TABLES, NOTES)*

### 554. RING.I/98. Mf. ŻIH—776; USHMM—7

- Date unknown, Warsaw Ghetto
- [Eliasz Gutkowski], List of subjects for a study of various areas of Warsaw Ghetto life.
- ***Description:*** original, handwritten manuscript (LEG*), ink, Yiddish, 220×350 mm, ss. 2, pp. 4
  On p. 4 notations in Polish and Yiddish (pencil, difficult to read, inter alia "Gutkowski . . .").

### 555. RING. I/130. (Lb. 112). Mf. ŻIH—777; USHMM—8

- Date unknown, Warsaw Ghetto
- NN., "Prison at Gęsia (theses)"
- Synopsis of a study on the operation of the prison (so-called Gęsiówka) at ul. Gęsia in Warsaw.
- ***Description:*** original or transcript, handwritten manuscript (H*), pencil, Polish, 220×350 mm, ss. 1, pp. 2.
  Published: *Selected Documents*, pp. 155–157.

### 556. RING. I/124. Mf. ŻIH—777; USHMM—8

- After 09.1941, Warsaw Ghetto
- NN., Summary of a study on libraries, bookstores, and reading among the Jewish population in Warsaw in the period from September 1939 to September 1941
- Attached draft questionnaire for owners of libraries and bookshops in the ghetto.
- ***Description:*** transcript (4 copies, part in fragments), handwritten manuscript (LEG*), pencil, Yiddish, 220×350, 220×155 mm, serious damage and losses of text, ss. 8, pp. 12.
  On p. 3 (second copy) (questionnaire) at the end of the text additions in a different handwriting (ink).
  Inventory: "Author is Barbara Berman."

### 557. RING. I/140. Mf. ŻIH—778; USHMM—9

- Date unknown, Warsaw Ghetto
- NN., "Housing Bureau (theses)"
- Summary of a study concerning housing affairs of the Warsaw Ghetto.
- ***Description:*** original or transcript (4 copies in fragments), handwritten manuscript (H*), pencil, Polish, 205×290, 205×160 mm, serious damage and losses of text (2–4 copies), ss. 4, pp. 8.

### 558. RING. I/125. Mf. ŻIH—777; USHMM—8

- Date unknown, Warsaw Ghetto
- NN., Summary of a study on "Street Children"
- Problems connected with the issue of "street children" (definition of the phenomenon, causes of its rise, children without families, "street children" who have a family, begging, vagrancy, and crime among "street children") and methods as well as prophylactic struggle with this phenomenon.
- ***Description:*** original [?] (handwritten manuscript—DD*, 202×135 mm, serious damage and losses of text), transcript (handwritten manuscript -H*, 218×350 mm, minor damage and losses of text), Polish, ss. 3, pp. 4.
  See Ring. I/47.
  Published: *Dzieci*, pp. 147–149.

### 559. RING. I/133. (Lb. 666). Mf. ŻIH—777; USHMM—8

- Date unknown, Warsaw Ghetto
- NN., "Yidisher handl in Varshe 1939–1942" [Jewish Commerce in Warsaw 1939–1942]
- Summary of a study on Jewish commerce in Warsaw: at the threshold of war (boycott), during the siege in 1939, in the occupied capital and in the ghetto.
- ***Description:*** original or transcript (2 copies), typescript, Yiddish, 205×287 mm, ss. 2, pp. 2.

### 560. RING. I/128. Mf. ŻIH—777; USHMM—8

- 1942, Warsaw Ghetto
- NN., "Di yidishe froy in geto varshe tsayt september 1939 biz ende 1941" [The Jewish Woman in Warsaw Ghetto in the period September 1939 until End of 1941]
- Summary and notes for a study on the situation during the war of Jewish women from various social and occupational environments (family, economic activity, social life).
- ***Description:*** original, handwritten manuscript (two handwritings: H* and NN.), ink, pencil (H*), Polish,

Yiddish, 205×295 mm, minor damage and losses of text, ss. 2, pp. 3.

According to Ringelblum, Cecylia Słapakowa was the author of the study "The Jewish Woman in the Second World War," but we do not know whether the author of *Kronika* had in mind the above notes or some other study unknown to us. See *Kronika getta,* p. 585; *Oneg Schabbat,* pp. 53–54.

**561. RING. I/138. (Lb. 540). Mf. ŻIH—778; USHMM—9**

- Start of 1942, Warsaw Ghetto
- NN., Synopsis of a study on the apartment house committees in the Warsaw Ghetto.
- ***Description:*** original or transcript, handwritten manuscript (ink, Polish) and handwritten manuscript (LEG*, pencil, Yiddish), 190×300, 195×295 mm, minor damage and losses of text (handwritten manuscript in Yiddish), ss. 2, pp. 4.

Text in two versions: Polish and Yiddish, with minor variations.

**562. RING. I/136. (Lb. 1087). Mf. ŻIH—777; USHMM—8**

- Start of 1942, Warsaw Ghetto
- NN., "Tezen tsu der teme: koruptsye—ganeives" [Theses on the Subject: Corruption—Theft]
- Synopsis of a study on corruption and theft in various bureaus, institutions, centers, and circles in the Warsaw Ghetto.
- ***Description:*** original or transcript (2 copies), typescript, Yiddish, 205×295, 145×292 mm, extensive damage and losses of text, ss. 6, pp. 6.

**563. RING. I/139. (Lb. 590). Mf. ŻIH—778; USHMM—9**

- Date unknown, Warsaw Ghetto
- NN., Summary of a study on the origins and operation of the public kitchens.
- ***Description:*** original or transcript (4 copies in fragments), typescript, Polish, 205×290, 203×100 mm, serious damage and losses of text, ss. 8, pp. 8.

**564. RING. I/137/1. Mf. ŻIH—777; USHMM—8**

- Date unknown, Warsaw Ghetto
- NN., "Order Service (theses)"
- Synopsis of a study on the Order Service in the ghetto.
- ***Description:*** original or transcript (2 copies), handwritten manuscript (H*), pencil, Polish, 220×350, 200×160 mm, extensive damage and losses of text (second copy), ss. 6, pp. 6.

On the back of the 3rd sheet (first copy) is a note (ink): "Goldbert Krakoska [sic] 9."

**565. RING. I/137/2. Mf. ŻIH—777; USHMM—8**

- Date unknown, Warsaw Ghetto
- NN., Synopsis of a study on the Order Service in the ghetto (fragment).
- ***Description:*** original or transcript, handwritten manuscript (H*), pencil, Polish, 205×295 mm, ss. 1, pp. 2.

**566. RING. I/129. Mf. ŻIH—777; USHMM—8**

- After 12.1941, Warsaw Ghetto
- NN., "Shops (thesis)"
- Synopsis of a study on the origin and operation of the factory workshops within the Warsaw Ghetto.
- ***Description:*** original or transcript (a) (handwritten manuscript—H*, pencil, 220×350 mm), transcript (b) (typescript, 200×295 mm, minor damage and losses of text), Polish, ss. 2. pp. 3.

Transcript (b) has a different title ("Thesis for a monograph on shops") and contains minor additions (in point 1) in relation to the original text (a).

**567. RING. I/135. Mf. ŻIH—777; USHMM—8**

- Start of 1942, Warsaw Ghetto
- NN., "Street"
- Synopsis of a study on the street in the ghetto, its appearance, life of residents, etc.
- ***Description:*** original or transcript (2 copies), handwritten manuscript (H*), pencil, Polish, 220×350 mm, ss. 2, pp. 4.

Published: *Selected Documents*, pp. 153–154.

**568. RING. I/1220/54. Mf. ŻIH—835; USHMM—47**

- After 1940, Warsaw Ghetto
- NN., Notes (Synopsis) for a study to concerning Warsaw (fragment)
- Notes about children, books, addresses, e.g., Leszno 67.
- ***Description:*** original or transcript, handwritten manuscript (LEG*), pencil, Yiddish, 223×173 mm, serious damage and losses of text, ss. 1, pp. 1.

**569. RING. I/674/13. (Lb. 1688). Mf. ŻIH—816; USHMM—28**

- Date unknown, Warsaw Ghetto
- [Hersz Wasser], Notes
- Notes of conversations conducted. Information about the Warsaw Ghetto; list of names.
- ***Description:*** original, handwritten manuscript (H.W.* and NN.), ink, pencil, Polish, Yiddish, 77×120, 155×185 mm, ss. 5, pp. 7.

Index: Sztajn, Horowicz, Rabinowicz, Staszewska, Moszek Weid (ul. Nowolipie 46), Izrael London (ul. Muranowska 47, apt. 23), Zalcfarb (ul. Karmelicka 15), Jerzy Kupfer (Warsaw), Gutkowski (ul. Nowolipie 50, apt. 23), Sadowska, Hinda and Mosze [?] Rozenwald (ul. Bonifraterska 25, apt. 6), Fryda Szwarc, Bor. (ul. Muranowska 44, apt. 22), Rozen, Rozenstatt, Lichtenbaum, Berman

**570. RING. I/1150 (1469) (Lb. 1466). Mf. ŻIH—833; USHMM—45**

- Date unknown, Warsaw Ghetto
- [Hersz Wasser], Notes
- Various data, inter alia about work in the CKU, notes of meetings, accounts, notes of radio monitoring [?].
- ***Description:*** original, handwritten manuscript (H.W.*), Polish, Yiddish, 155×185 mm, ss. 1, pp. 1.
  Attached note by H.W. in Polish, Yiddish
  Index: Gepner, Sztolcman, Szereszewski, Fisz, Dobrin, Wartski, Czerski, Frydmanówna, Rotenberg, Dr. Syrkin, Bursztyn, Wysomański [Wyszewiański ?]

**571. RING. I/674/15. (Lb. 1688). Mf. ŻIH—816; USHMM—28**

- Date unknown, Warsaw Ghetto
- [Hersz Wasser], Notes.
- ***Description:*** original, handwritten manuscript (H.W.*), ink, Yiddish, 206×293 mm, ss. 2, pp. 3.
  Second sheet is written on the back of a fragment (page no. 3) of a list of public kitchens in the Warsaw Ghetto (on ul. Miła and ul. Niska), gives date of creation of the kitchen, number of dinners issued, price of a dinner, etc. (original, typescript).

**572. RING. I/81. Mf. ŻIH—775; USHMM—6**

- After 09.1941, Warsaw Ghetto
- NN., Study concerning Jewish population statistics in Warsaw (1939–1941) (fragments)
- Quantity, social-occupational structure, mortality by age group, causes and places of death, physical development of children, food aid, wages, prices of food products, nutritional and caloric value of articles brought into the ghetto and issued on ration cards, budgets of the unemployed (tables with description).
- ***Description:*** transcript (2 copies), typescript, Polish, 210×295 mm (192×173 mm—damaged sheet), serious damage and losses of text, missing pages (second copy), ss. 64, pp. 64.
  Original pagination preserved in the first copy: pp. 1–31 (handwritten manuscript, ink)
  Part of the statistical material was collected on the basis of a survey conducted in 32 apartment houses in the ghetto, representing "centers of the greatest destitution, and of the average lower middle class" (see p. 20).

**573. RING. I/667. (Lb. 1456). Mf. ŻIH—816; USHMM—28**

- After 06.1941, Warsaw Ghetto
- Collection of various statistical tables and charts (fragments).
  Charts and tables concerning mortality in the Warsaw Ghetto produced on the basis of surveys; "Labor Camps. Chart of Camp Transports in the First Half of 1941" (list of labor camps and number of Jews sent out to them from January to April 1941); Occupational structure of those sent out to labor camps.
- ***Description:*** original, handwritten manuscript, several handwritings, ink, Polish, 152×147, 160×222, serious damage and losses of text, ss. 7, pp. 8.
  Attached note by H.W.: "1941. Tatters of survey tables and charts. J. Winkler edited the questionnaires."

**574. RING. I/1153 (1472). (Lb. 1228). Mf. ŻIH—833; USHMM—45**

- After 12.1941, Warsaw Ghetto
- [Hersz Wasser], Notes and charts concerning statistics of the Warsaw Ghetto for 1940–1941
- Statistics on population, forced labor (labor camps, Labor Battalion), funerals in 1941 (in particular months, including the number of suicides), activity of the outpatient clinic at ul. Twarda 6, Health Department, Labor Department, takeovers of firms, pauperization, ZZ [Provisioning Unit at the Jewish Council], vocational courses, Production Department [Wydział Wytwórczości], deportees.
- ***Description:*** original, handwritten manuscript, notebook, ink, Polish, 160×204 mm, ss. 10, pp. 13.
  Attached note by H.W.

**575. RING. I/1035 (1354). (Lb. 387). Mf. ŻIH—832; USHMM—44**

- After 1939, Warsaw Ghetto
- NN., Study entitled "May [19]39"
- Political and social life in Poland before the outbreak of war (e.g., Polish and Yiddish press, antisemitic propaganda, sports organizations).
- ***Description:*** transcript (2 copies), handwritten manuscript (MS*), pencil, Yiddish, 148×207 mm, minor damage and losses of text, ss. 8, pp. 8.
  In the margins letter (ink): "v."

**576. RING. I/175. Mf. ŻIH—779; USHMM—10**

- 07.1942, Warsaw Ghetto
- NN., Study entitled [?] (missing conclusion)
- Introduction to a longer text on the social life of the Jewish population in the Warsaw Ghetto, justification of commencement of work (notes about execution of 110 Jews in Babice 2.07.1942).
- ***Description:*** original or transcript, typescript, Yiddish, 195×284, 195×137 mm, minor damage and losses of text, ss. 2, pp. 2.

**577. RING. I/154. Mf. ŻIH—778; USHMM—9**

- 07.1942, Warsaw Ghetto
- [Stanisław Różycki?], Study entitled "Street," about the appearance and social life of the street in the Warsaw Ghetto (07.1942)
- Description of the pathology of social life in the ghetto, plagues: thefts, swindles, denunciation, spying, shakedowns, corruption, moral shamelessness,

mob rule, social egoism, caste system, begging, hooliganism, rowdyism, inconsiderateness, indifference toward other people, decline of religious life, etc. Street contrast: destitution and luxury.
- ***Description:*** original, handwritten manuscript (SR*), notebook, ink, Polish, 160×195 mm, minor damage and losses of text, text illegible in places, ss. 26, pp. 22.
  Text divided into two chapters: "Morality of the Street," "External Appearance." Preserved manuscript is presumably a fragment of a longer, unfinished study.

### 578. RING. I/512. (Lb. 1570). Mf. ŻIH—789; USHMM—20

- Date unknown, Warsaw Ghetto
- [Emanuel Ringelblum?], Notes entitled "Bikh[. . .]l" [Book(let ?)]; "Dos klasn-ponim fun der yidisher kehile" [The Class Face of the Jewish Community]
- The book in the Warsaw Ghetto (trade), social conflicts in the ghetto (attitudes of affluent Jews to the poorer social classes).
- ***Description:*** transcript (2 copies), typescript, Yiddish, 202×293 mm, minor damage and losses of text, ss. 6, pp. 6.
  On p. 1 (of the first copy) information by H.W. in Yiddish (ink): "Little Flower." 1942/[1] January. "[Nr?] 4"[?].
  See HWC, 37/1 (fragment, of third copy, typescript, ss. 1; concerning trade in books in the ghetto); 47/1 (fragment, of the third copy, typescript, ss. 2; concerning the social face of the Warsaw Ghetto).

### 579. RING. I/335. Mf. ŻIH—781; USHMM—12

- 1941–1942, Warsaw Ghetto
- A. M. Rogowy (ul. Nowolipie 58, apt. 8), Open letters dated 5.09., 16.09., 7.11., 7.12., 26.12.1941, 1.02., [. . .] 1942
- Statements on current problems of the Warsaw Ghetto (against the treatment to that point of human corpses, demand for creation of a Hevra Kadisha [Burial] Society, which would undertake supervision over the burial of the dead in accord with human and religious ethics; provisioning for Passover; proposal for uniform system of taxes; apartment house committees). Attached copies of Rogowy's articles from *Gazeta Żydowska* and letters to him (from engineer A. Sztolcman, Chaim Uszer Pużyc (ul. Zamenhofa 40 m 17), Dr. H. Glücksberg, councilman) touching on the same subjects.
- ***Description:*** original (letter dated 7.11.1941 in 2 copies), hectographed typescript, typescript (Yiddish), Polish, Yiddish, 218×345, 210×295, 217×120 mm, minor damage and losses of text, ss. 13, pp. 16.
  On p. 1, letter dated 7.12.1941, and on p. 3, letter of 26.12.1941, notation by H.W. in Yiddish: "108–1942/1 January." On p. 1 of letter of 7.12.1941 note: "Dr. Ringelblum ŻTOS."
  See Ring. II/114.
  Published: *Selected Documents*, pp. 317–323 (fragment).
  Index: Dr. Wielikowski

### 580. RING. I/990/1 (1309). (Lb. 416); RING. I/1002 (1321). Mf. ŻIH—831; USHMM—43

- 12.1940, after 12.1940, Warsaw Ghetto
- NN., Study entitled "Varshever-refleksn" [Warsaw Reflections] (12.1940)
- Material, physical, and spiritual devastation of the Jewish people by the German occupier.
- ***Description:*** Ring. I/1002—original [?], handwritten manuscript, ink, Yiddish, 219×353 mm, minor damage and losses of text, ss. 1, pp. 2; Ring. I/990/1—copy, handwritten manuscript (MS*), pencil, Yiddish, 152×211 mm, ss. 1, pp. 1.
  Copy contains minor differences in relation to the original [?]
  In the original [?] at the end is the date: "12.1940"; lack of title. In the copy (Ring. I/990) in the margin is a Hebrew letter (ink): "b" (beyt) and a Hebrew-Yiddish letter "v" (tsvey vovn) or Latin "v." Title "Varshever-refleksn" [Warsaw Reflections] written in by H.W.
  See Ring. I/966 (handwriting similar to Ring. I/1002).
  Doc. was kept in a binder.

### 581. RING. I/277. (Lb. 1151, 1152). Mf. ŻIH—836; USHMM—67

- 1941, Warsaw Ghetto
- [Rozenfeld], Sketches (5) presenting various places and scenes from ghetto life
- Attached to the sketches is a descriptive part: 1) "Staging Point"; 2) "Hospital on 'the Other Side'" 3) "A Carter's Funeral"; 4) "Chaimek Sztarkman [died 16.12.1941]"; 5) "Burial Fund."
- ***Description:*** original, sketches (quill—India ink, coal, pastel; 1)—200×158 mm; 2)—163×189 mm; 3)—178×255 mm; 4)—183×156 mm; 5)—178×209 mm, ss. 5, pp. 5), handwritten manuscript, ink, Polish, 210×297 mm, ss. 5, pp. 7.
  Attached note by H.W. in Yiddish: "Author is Rozenfeld."
  Doc. 5—Published: *Przewodnik*, p. 526 (photocopy).
  Docs. 1, 3, 4, and 5—Published: *Dzieci*, pp. 140–146.
  Index: Ber Ajzensztat, carter of the Warsaw Ghetto (ul. Muranowska)

### 582. RING. I/1220/83. Mf. ŻIH—835; USHMM—47

- After 10.1941, Warsaw Ghetto
- NN., Attached to a study [?] entitled "Displacement of the Jewish Population in October 1941" (fragment).
- ***Description:*** original, hectographed typescript, Polish, 195×97 mm, serious damage and losses of text, ss. 1, pp. 2.

## 583. RING. I/112. Mf. ŻIH—777; USHMM—8

- After 12.1941, Warsaw Ghetto
- [Szymon Huberband], Study entitled "Geto un ekzekutsies" [Ghetto and Executions]
- Description of several executions within the Warsaw Ghetto, chiefly of persons caught smuggling or illegally leaving the ghetto (e.g., 15.12.1941, preparations for and course of the execution, lists of those killed and biographical sketches of several of the victims).
- ***Description:*** original, handwritten manuscript (HUB.*), notebooks, ink, Yiddish, 153×191 mm, minor damage and losses of text, text legible [sic] in places, ss. 42, pp. 76.

  Index: Józef Fajkus; victims of the execution on 15.12.1941: Majer Abramowicz, Srul Lejb Drewnowicz, Małka Elbaum, Hela Kalksztajn, Masza Kisielewicz, Chana Kon, Róża Mikanowska, Mindla Prowizor, Chaja Łaja Przychodzka, Moszek Rotbard, Ałta Rozenbaum, Chaja Rubin, Łaja Rywka Russ, Hena Salwe, Estera Śpiewak.

  Published: *Kiddush Hashem*, pp. 150–174.

  See Ring. I/224.

## 584. RING. I/293. Mf. ŻIH—781; USHMM—12

- After 04.1942, Warsaw Ghetto
- NN., List of names of persons who were murdered on the night of 18/19.04.1942 within the Warsaw Ghetto
- Attached addresses and information about profession.
- ***Description:*** original, handwritten manuscript, ink, Yiddish, 150×187 mm, minor damage and losses of text, ss. 1, pp. 2.

## 585. RING. I/114. (Lb. 114). Mf. ŻIH—777; USHMM—8

- After 01.1942 [?], Warsaw Ghetto
- [Szymon Huberband], Study entitled "Gelt oyspresung bay yidn durkh yidn" [Extortion of Money from Jews by Jews]
- Denunciation and collaboration with the Germans or the navy blue police in the Warsaw Ghetto. Swindlers and thieves in the ghetto (collecting high sums from people for ostensible help).
- ***Description:*** original, handwritten manuscript (HUB.*), notebook, ink, Yiddish, 148×194 mm, minor damage and losses of text, ss. 14, pp. 28.

  Inventory: "Author of the text is Szymon Huberband."

  Published: *Kiddush Hashem*, pp. 136–146.

  Index: Kadisza (ul. Miła 5), the Judkowskis (ul. Gęsia 17), Abraham Ocap, Garniewicz, Abraham Piekarski, Rubinsztajn, Bartnbojm (ul. Miła 9), the Kanersztajns, Huberman, Rendlich, Roznbojm, Rozenfik, Pruwes, Liber, Ganc, Lichtenbojm, Urbach, Ganszer, Kamień, Bardt

## 586. RING. I/250. (Lb. 551). Mf. ŻIH—780; USHMM—11

a)

- After 07. 1941, Warsaw Ghetto
- [Szmul (Samuel) Bresław], Study entitled "Registrar (From the Series: Jewish Livelihoods)" (fragment)
- Abuses connected with distribution of food ration cards by registrars (for example the Naj family: Sanel, Różka, Symcha, ul. Nowolipki 51, apt. 20).
- ***Description:*** original or transcript, handwritten manuscript (SB*), ink, Polish, 174×218 mm, ss. 4, pp. 8.

b)

- After 07.1941, Warsaw Ghetto
- [Szmul (Samuel) Bresław], Study entitled "Disinfection Unit (From the Series: Jewish Livelihoods)"
- Principles of operation, recruitment of personnel, salary, collection of additional charges and extortion. Participation of Poles and Germans in the unit's work. Text produced on the basis of information from S. Rotszuld, unit section leader (ul. Nowolipki 34, apt. 24).
- ***Description:*** original, handwritten manuscript (SB*), ink, Polish, 178×219 mm, ss. 3, pp. 6. For information about the author, see HWC, 65/8.

  Inventory: "Statement written down by Samuel Breslauer [Bresław]."

  Index: Dr. Golde, Dr. Dyczkowski, Dr. Janicki, Dr. Fedorowski, Bursztyn

## 587. RING. I/292. (Lb. 562). Mf. ŻIH—781; USHMM—12

- After 05.1942, Warsaw Ghetto
- NN., "Note re[garding] escape of 2 prisoners from the Czyste Hospital at ul. Stawki"
- Polish police guarded the prisoners, but the blame was placed on the Order Service. The fugitives (Sz. and G. [Gomóliński]) were not caught.
- ***Description:*** original [?], handwritten manuscript (WINK.*), ink, Polish, 218×280 mm, minor damage and losses of text, ss. 2, pp. 2.

  Page 1 written on the back of a payroll sheet of an unknown firm in Poland during the period 09.1935–01.1936; names: Magda Scholz, Klara Kukowska, N. Lenczner, A. Awerbuch. Page 2 written on the back of a sheet from an account ledger of an unknown firm in Poland dated 21.04.1939.

  Inventory: "Author is Jerzy Winkler."

  According to the author, the escape took place in the middle of March 1942; *Czerniaków*, p. 261, recorded information about it under the date 22.03.1942

## 588. RING. I/143. Mf. ŻIH—836; USHMM—67

- After 09.1941, Warsaw Ghetto

- [Salomea Ostrowska?], Study entitled "Quarantine Leszno 109/III [?]"
- The author, an employee of the Quarantine Patronate [Patronatu Kwarantanny], describes its origin and activity (02–09.1941), number and categories of persons who underwent quarantine (deportees, hospital isolees, labor camp inmates), housing conditions, food, Patronate, benefactors of the quarantine. Tables concerning the traffic of labor camp inmates (dates, number, names of camps). Essay is based on reports and accounts (attached excerpts in the text) of the Quarantine Patronate [Patronatu Kwarantanny] Leszno 109 (established 11.02.1941).
- ***Description:*** original, handwritten manuscript (KK*), notebook, ink, Polish, 155×195 mm, minor damage and losses of text, ss. 58, pp. 113.

### 589. RING. I/309. Mf. ŻIH—781; USHMM—12

- After 12.1941, Warsaw Ghetto
- NN., Study entitled "Vi azoy 'lebn' di heymloze in di punktn?" [How Do the Homeless 'Live' in the Points?]
- Description of shelters for deportees sent into the Warsaw Ghetto (turn of the year 1941/42), e.g., ul. Pawia 51, Stawki 9 and 19; cold, filth, entire families perishing from hunger, population exiled from, inter alia, Płońsk, Żuromin, Nowy Dwór, Zgierz, Kalisz, Głowno, Łowicz, Żyrardów.
- ***Description:*** transcript, typescript, Yiddish, 218×268 mm, serious damage and losses of text, ss. 22, pp. 22.

  Inventory: "Author of the text J. [Jehuda] Feld"; according to R.S.: "Feldwurm."

### 590. RING. I/220. (Lb. 602). Mf. ŻIH—780; USHMM—11

- Date unknown, Warsaw Ghetto
- List of names of 242 refugees within the limits of the Warsaw Ghetto in the "point" at ul. Dzika 3
- Persons originating from Aleksandrów Kujawski, Będzin, Bielsko, Błaszki, Brześć Kujawski, Brzeziny, Chodecz, Chorzel, Chrzanów, Ciechocinek, Cieszyn, Częstochowa, Dąbrowa Górnicza, Dobrzyń, Dziedzice, Głowno, Izbica Kujawska, Jaworzno, Jędrzejów, Kalisz, Katowice, Kielce, Kleczewo, Koluszki, Koło, Konin, Koźminek, Kraków, Krośniewice, Kutno, Łask, Łęczyca, Łódź, Miechów, Mława, Modrzejów, Nasielsk, Olkusz, Ostrołęki, Oświęcim, Pabianice, Piotrków, Przedecz, Radomsko, Rypin, Serock, Sępolno, Sieradz, Słupiec, Sosnowiec, Tomaszów Mazowiecki, Trzebinia, Turek, Wadowice, Wieluń, Włocławek, Włodawa, Wolbrom, Zawiercie, Zduńska Wola, Zgierz, Żarki, Żywiec.
- ***Description:*** original [?], typescript, Polish, 206×295 mm, fascicule [poszyt], ss. 4, pp. 8.

  Attached note by H.W. in Yiddish: "List of residents in the refugees' 'place' at Dzika 3."

Index: Rozen Szymon, Łódź; Sakowski Szmul, Łódź; Wester Jakub, Łódź; Krowicki Abram, Łódź; Sendacz Josek, Łódź; Grodecki Izrael, Łódź; Zakheim Ichok, Łódź; Edelsztein, Łódź; Kamieniecki Izrael, Łódź; Zylberberg Henryk, Łódź; Kantor Dawid, Łódź; Milsztein Lajb, Łódź; Bornsztein Abram, Łódź; Liberman Tobiasz, Łódź; Nojman Saul, Łódź; Rotkopf Jacob, Łódź; Neuhaus Ichok, Łódź; Psiatowski Lajb, Łódź; Łupczyński Josek, Łódź; Sierakowiak Fiszel, Łódź; Weltman Jechiel, Łódź; Sztajnszneider Szulim, Łódź; Kamiński Jakow, Łódź; Zylbersztein Izrael, Łódź; Rozenberg Josek, Łódź; Minc, Łódź; Tyller, Łódź; Koperman Mordka, Łódź; Gdański, Łódź; Herszkorn Lajb, Łódź; Sznycer Szmul, Łódź; Ajzen Mordka, Łódź; Tugentrajch, Łódź; Krieger, Łódź; Włodawski Mojsze, Łódź; Tabak Szmul, Łódź; Gelbard Josef, Łódź; Milchman Ichok, Łódź; Kapelusz Moszek, Łódź; Kutner Jakow, Łódź; Szmul Nusen, Łódź; Gierman, Łódź; Duński Jechuda, Łódź; Kaufman Machel, Łódź; Poms Beniamin, Łódź; Goldfarb Lajb, Łódź; Ryszerfeld, Łódź; Kaczała Natan, Łódź; Aleksandrowicz Chaim-Zajwel, Łódź; Kuperman Mordcha, Łódź; Weiswohl Bernard, Łódź; Wolf Wiktor, Łódź; Ryczywół, Łódź; Wieruszewski, Łódź; Goldsztajn Hilel, Łódź; Targ, Łódź; Oliwensztajn Samuel, Włocławek; Izbicki Hanina, Włocławek; Cytryn Dawid, Włocławek; Gruza Szloma, Włocławek; Gontarz Izrael, Włocławek; Sztajer Michael, Słupiec; Lipka Aron, Dobrzyń nad Drwęcą; Olsztajn Josek, Dobrzyń nad Drwęcą; Pas, Dobrzyń nad Drwęcą; Blatt Fiszel, Koluszki; Walter, Kutno; Kruk, Kutno; Dancygier, Kutno; Kolski, Brześć; Kuj.[awski], Kaftański, Brześć; Kuj.[awski]; Szmulewicz, Brześć Kuj.[awski]; Wrzoński, Łódź; Szmidt, Tomaszów M.[azowiecki]; Szysler Lajbusz, Tomaszów M.[azowiecki]; Żółtowski Icek, Tomaszów M.[azowiecki]; Cukier Szlama, Piotrków; Lipszyc Mojsze, Kalisz; Jakubowicz Abram, Kalisz; Borensztajn, Kalisz; Śliwka, Kalisz; Faktor Michał, Będzin; Szlezyngier, Sosnowiec; Czapla Lajb, Będzin; Engler, Będzin; Rachelka, Rypin; Kozak, Rypin; Kłodowski, Przedecz; Kłodowski, Przedecz; Goldman, Przedecz; Tajchner Abram, Przedecz; Weisskohl Herman, Pabianice; Perelman Moszek, Pabianice; Nys Zelta, Pabianice; Szerman, Pabianice; Minc, Pabianice; Lewkowicz, Zgierz; Opatowski, Krośniewice; Markowicz Josef, Kielce; Gąsiorowski Icek, Włocławek; Szymański Wolf, Olkusz; Eljasz Szyja, Olkusz; Gross Szyja Eliezer, Chrzanów; Perelsztejn Moszek, Chrzanów; Chochbaum Johanan, Chrzanów; Wincelberg Pinkus,

Chrzanów; Apfelbaum Mojsze, Chrzanów; Klein Chaim, Chrzanów; Grubner Mordchaj, Chrzanów; Zimnowodzki Dawid, Chrzanów; Goldberg Michał, Jaworzno; Glicensztein, Kielce; Kune Berek, Brzeziny; Fortgang, Kraków; Berliński Abram, Kalisz; Braun Wigdor, Ciechocinek; Geisler, Włocławek, Mondziak; Mława, Fogiel, Koło; Rozentahl, Koło, Olsztajn; Koło; Lipka Izrael, Koło; Rotman, Koło; Bruchsztajn, Koło; Gelbard, Koło; Sierpc, Koło; Sedowski, Koło; Turek, Koło; Niewolski Josef, Kalisz; Michelsohn Wolf, Konin; Szumiraj, Głowno; Witelsohn Pinhas, Pabianice; Szwed Izrael, Błaszki; Kenigsberg Szulim, Chodecz; Tugentrajch Bajnysz, Łęczyca; Lisak Mojsze, Słupce; Śliwka Herman, Konin; Bocian Dawid, Łęczyca; Immergut Adolf, Cieszyn; Wajnsztok Szmul, Sieradz; Wilner, Zd. [Zduńska] Wola, Rotbart Josek, Zduńska Wola; Kamiński Szmul, Sosnowiec; Wolman Lajb, Sępolno; Bagno, Kleczew; Podolski Zyska, Wieluń; Wulkan Szloma, Oświęcim; Jasan, Oświęcim; Oksenhendler, Łódź; Berliński Nachman, Łódź; Adeltunger Herszel, Będzin; Rusinek Noech, Dąbrowa G. [Górnicza]; Groner Oziasz, Wadowice; Findberg Chaim, Chrzanów; Kurcfeld Moszek, Będzin; Lederman Mosza Josef, Sosnowiec; Ochband Johan, Sosnowiec; Zylberberg Maks, Trzebinia; Szychter Altar, Będzin; Książka Fiszel, Będzin; Kugelfrejer Mozes, Będzin; Frydman, Będzin; Goldfraund Oria, Miechów; Adlerfliegel Ichok, Będzin; Lokaj Abram, Będzin; Lewkowicz Mozes, Będzin; Śpiewak, Wolbrom; Szporn, Będzin; Markiewicz Pinkus, Włodawa; Perelberg, Nasielsk; Gelbhar Berek, Będzin; Kazimierski Jankiel, Dąbrowa G. [Górnicza]; Kazimierski Berek, Dąbrowa Górnicza; Czapa Abram, Sosnowiec; Ajzykowicz Beniek, Tomaszów M. [Mazowiecki]; Różański Szymsło, Tomaszów Mazowiecki; Herszkowicz, Jędrzejów, Jesion Jakow, Brześć Kuj.[awski]; Milsztajn Hersz, Tomaszów Maz. [Mazowiecki]; Chrzanowicz Boruch, Tomaszów Mazowiecki; Żychliński Motek, Brzeziny; Goldsztajn Chil Ber, Radomsko; Glicensztajn, Łódź; Markowski Rywen, Izbica; Kuj. [Kujawska], Markiewicz, Łódź; Berger Abram, Brzeziny; Dasau Abram, Łódź; Elembik, Tomaszów Maz. [Mazowiecki]; Pakin, Tomaszów Mazowiecki; Pinkus Fajwel, Częstochowa; Szechtman B., Sosnowiec; Blasberg, Bielsko; Siegel Szymon, Żywiec; Tymberg, Chrzanów; Nusbaum, Łódź; Szmul N., Łódź; Edelman Abram, Łódź; Horyniak Chemia, Łęczyca; Wasserzieher Chil, Łódź; Henrykowski Izaak, Łódź; Bajszwiger Natan, Chorzele; Kleiman Uszer, Serock; Lampart Abram, Łódź; Brom Hersz, Ostrołęka; Zylberman, Dziedzice; Ajzensztap J., Włocławek; Gostyński Josek, Włocławek; Krowicki Abram, Łódź; Berliński M., Koźminek; Goldzylber, Zawiercie; Weinberg Tanchem, Łask; Rawet, Łódź; Lewin Izrael, Dąbrowa G. [Górnicza]; Radzyński B., Dąbrowa Górnicza; Bergman Tobiasz, Dobrzyń nad Drwęcą; Grejcer, Katowice; Rubinsztajn Lajzer, Łódź; Kugelman, Będzin; Fränkel, Będzin; Zonenszajn Dawid, Zawiercie; Młynarski Hersz Ber, Dąbrowa G. [Górnicza]; Piekarski Izaak, Dąbrowa Górnicza; Stawski, Dąbrowa Górnicza; Tajchner Abram, Dąbrowa Górnicza; Pozmantir, Dąbrowa Górnicza; Gliksman, Łódź; Klausner Salo, Bielsko; Meisner Menachim, Żarki; Złocisty, Aleksandrów Kuj. [Kujawski]; Sendowski Abe, Turek; Szmul, Turek; Węgier Maks, Modrzejów; Brodkiewicz Mordka, Sosnowiec; Pluskwa Icek, Łódź; Grybnaum [Grynbaum ?], Łódź; Gioner, Wadowice; Goldhamer Fiszel, Będzin; Wajskopf, Będzin; Binder Mojżesz, Będzin; Cukierman, Będzin; Szulsinger, Będzin

### 591. RING. I/190. Mf. ŻIH—779; USHMM—10

- After 1941, Warsaw Ghetto
- NN., "Kosher-frage bay di pleytim in Varshe" [Kosher Question among the Refugees in Warsaw]
- Report of the rabbi of Skępe for the CKU on kosher food in the Warsaw Ghetto in 1941 (kosher kitchens in the Warsaw Ghetto: ul. Nalewki 37, Landenberg, director; ul Zamenhofa 11, Kobac, director; ul. Zamenhofa 22, Godszlak [? Goldszlak], director; ul. Zamenhofa 44, Kozłowski, director; ul. Ciepła 10, Feldmebel, director; ul. Nowolipki 15, Heber, director).
- ***Description:*** copy, typescript, Yiddish, 220×293 mm, ss. 1, pp. 1.

  Published: *Selected Documents*, 415–417.
  Index: Ersler, A.Z. Frydman

### 592. RING. I/358. (Lb. 516). Mf. ŻIH—782; USHMM—13

- Date unknown, Warsaw Ghetto
- NN., "Note. Financial liabilities of the population of the Jewish district"
- List of several dozen official and unofficial taxes, levies and other financial liabilities of Jews in the Warsaw Ghetto.
- ***Description:*** original or transcript, typescript, Polish, 207×293 mm, ss. 1, pp. 1.

### 593. RING. I/47. (Lb. 255, 255A, 265, 309). Mf. ŻIH—773; USHMM—4

- After 11.1941, Warsaw Ghetto
- Nusen Koniński, "The Face of the Jewish Child" (11.1941)

- Study on the situation of Jewish children during the occupation (private teaching, children of deportees, street children and their delinquency, child labor, fate of children from affluent homes, supervision of children by Centos, apartment house committees, and the Jewish Council.
- ***Description:*** original or transcript (a) (handwritten manuscript [E*], notebooks, ink, 156×193, ss. 38, pp. 73), transcript (b) (2 copies, typescript, 220×286 mm, ss. 32, pp. 32), Polish, minor damage and losses of text, ss. 70, pp. 105.

  On p. 9 handwritten manuscript (a) note (pencil, in another handwriting).

  On p. 1 (typescript 1st copy) notation by H.W., Yiddish: "20 standard pages."

  See Ring. I/125.

  Third copy of transcript (b) turned over to Yad Vashem.

  Published: *Selected Documents*, pp. 371–391; *Dzieci*, pp. 358–386.

## 594. RING. I/994 (1313). (Lb. 418). Mf. ŻIH—831; USHMM—43

- After 01.1941, Warsaw Ghetto
- NN., Study entitled "Di yesoymim heym, Milna 18" [The Orphanage, Mylna 18]
- Established in 10.1939 as a shelter for 80 children from destroyed apartment houses at Zamenhofa 5 and Pl. Grzybowski 7. Before the war, the building housed the Abraham Podliszewski Emigrants' Home. From 01.1941 the author organized a sponsors' committee (patronate) that engaged in provisioning the orphanage.
- ***Description:*** transcript (2 copies), handwritten manuscript (BW*), pencil, Yiddish, 148×210 mm, ss. 12, pp. 12.

  In the margins a Hebrew letter (ink): "t" (tes).

  For report of audit and activity of the institution, see Ring. II/95.

## 595. RING. I/149. MISSING ORIGINAL. Mf. ŻIH—778; USHMM—9

- After 1946, Warsaw
- NN., Study entitled "Youth in Vocational Courses"
- Biography of Bronek Segałowicz (born 1922), a young man, resident of the Warsaw Ghetto.
- ***Description:*** postwar transcript, typescript, Polish, 212×300 mm, ss. 4, pp. 4.

## 596. RING. I/46. Mf. ŻIH—773; USHMM—4

- Date unknown, Warsaw
- NN., Lecture on youth in the Warsaw Ghetto (fragment [?])
- Fates of Jewish youth during the war and occupation, internal divisions, attitudes to Germans and Nazism.
- ***Description:*** original or transcript, typescript, Polish, 217×279 mm, damage and losses of text, ss. 2, pp. 2,

  At top of page a Hebrew letter (ink): "p" (pei).

  On the back of p. 2 information in pencil: "2 [crossed out] 38/14."

  Published: *Selected Documents*, pp. 516–519.

## 597. RING. I/49. Mf. (Lb. 268, 279, 282). ŻIH—773; USHMM—4

- 1942, Warsaw Ghetto
- NN., Study "The Jewish Woman in Warsaw from September 1939 to the Present [1942]"
- Descriptions of various fates of, and attitudes among Jewish women through biographies of selected persons from the Warsaw Ghetto.
- ***Description:*** original or transcript, handwritten manuscript, notebooks, ink, Polish, 150×192 mm, extensive damage and losses of text, ss. 99, pp. 163.

## 598. RING. I/36. Mf. ŻIH—772; USHMM—3

- Date unknown, Warsaw
- NN. (Władko), Lecture entitled "[Assimila]tionists and Converts in the Era of War Actions and the Closed Jewish District"
- Attitudes of people of Jewish origin who converted to Christianity and assimilated into Christian society, before the war and during the occupation, situation of converts in the ghetto, plan for work among assimilationists and converts after the war.
- ***Description:*** original, typescript with handwritten additions, Polish, 220×355, minor damage and losses of text, ss. 11, pp. 11.

  According to J.K., the author of the text was Dr. Małowist; see *Selected Documents*, p. 634.

  Published: *Selected Documents*, pp. 620–634.

## 599. RING. I/91. (Lb. 357). Mf. ŻIH—776; USHMM—7

a)

- After 09.1939, Warsaw Ghetto
- NN., Study entitled "Di poylish–yidishe batsiungen (Beshas der balagerung fun Varshe)" [Polish–Jewish Relations (during the Siege of Warsaw)]
- Participation of Jews in the preparatory work for defense of the city in 1939 (digging of trenches, construction of fieldworks), care for refugees (including Poles, e.g., from Poznań and Bydgoszcz). Attitude of Poles to Jews and various attitudes among Jews.
- ***Description:*** transcript (2 copies), handwritten manuscript (MS*), pencil, Yiddish, 115×208 mm, ss. 12, pp. 12.

  In the margin Hebrew letter (ink): "ts" (tsadi).

b)

- After 09.1939, Warsaw Ghetto
- NN., Study entitled "Di poylish–yidishe betsiungen in okupirt Varshe" [Polish–Jewish Relations in Occupied Warsaw]
- Polish–Jewish relations in the period 10.1939–04.1940, report of conversations with representatives of various Polish political groups.

- *Description:* transcript (2 copies), handwritten manuscript (MS*), pencil, Yiddish, 115×208 mm, ss. 8, pp. 8.
  In the margins a Hebrew letter (ink): "z" (zayin)
  According to J.K., author of the doc. is E.R.; see *Selected Documents*, p. 611.
  Published: *Selected Documents*, pp. 611–614.

**600. RING. I/1091 (1410). (Lb. 199). Mf. ŻIH—833; USHMM—45**

- Date unknown, Warsaw Ghetto
- NN., Questionnaire entitled "General Directions for Home Visits"
- Set of questions for conducting an interview with pregnant women. On the back of the document is a poem entitled "Die Verscheuchte" [Scared Away].
- *Description:* original or transcript, handwritten manuscript, two handwritings (poem—H*), ink, pencil, German, Polish, 158×197 mm, ss. 1, pp. 2.

**601. RING. I/508. (Lb. 461) Mf. ŻIH—789; USHMM—20**

- Date unknown, Warsaw Ghetto
- [Emanuel Ringelblum], Study entitled "Di geshikhte fun sotsyaler hilf in Varshe beshas der milkhome" [History of Social Aid in Warsaw during the War]
- Organization of social welfare among the Jewish population from the outbreak of war.
- *Description:* original, handwritten manuscript (ER*), ink, Yiddish, 150×194, 176×77, 175×222 mm, ss. 10, pp. 17.
  Published: *Selected Documents*, pp. 338–344.

**602. RING. I/349. (Lb. 1451). Mf. ŻIH—782; USHMM—13**

- 12.1941, Warsaw Ghetto
- NN., Study entitled "Gutachten über Organisation und Taktig [Tätigkeit] der Fürsorge und Wohlfahrt im Jüdischen Wohnbezirk in Warschau (Warschau, Dezember 1941)." [Assessment of the Organization and Activity of Social Welfare Services in the Jewish Residential District in Warsaw (Warsaw, December 1941)]
- Number and structure of the Jewish population in Warsaw, food, changes and structure of prices, the ghetto's balance of payments, labor and employment, socioeconomic structure of the ghetto, food and clothing aid, care for children, for deportees, medical and health care, organization and forms of social aid. Numerous numerical balance sheets and tables attached.
- *Description:* original or transcript, handwritten manuscript (two handwritings: H* and NN.), ink, German, 210×280, 220×225 mm, serious damage and losses of text, ss. 29, pp. 56.

**603. RING. I/313. (Lb. 1661). Mf. ŻIH—781; USHMM—12**

- 28.06.1941 [?], Warsaw Ghetto
- Kazimierz Herszaft (ul. Chłodna 30), Memorandum: "In the matter of reorganization of social welfare" (Warsaw, 28.06.1941)
- Proposal to establish a new organization, the Jewish Social Welfare League (Żydowska Liga Opieki Społecznej), for the purpose of centralization of organization, locations, and tasks connected with social welfare. Attached charter of the proposed organization.
- *Description:* original or transcript, typescript, Polish, 225×285 mm, minor damage and losses of text, ss. 7, pp. 7.
  Attached note by H.W. in Yiddish: "Submitted by Meir Przedecz, former councilman of Warsaw."

**604. RING. I/1220/82. Mf. ŻIH—835; USHMM—47**

- After 1941, Warsaw Ghetto
- Fragment of a report concerning the situation in the Warsaw Ghetto
- Epidemics, number of cases of typhus, care for deportees.
- *Description:* original, hectographed typescript, Polish, 200×104 mm, serious damage and losses of text, ss. 1, pp. 1.

**605. RING. I/1211. Mf. ŻIH—835; USHMM—47**

- Date unknown, Warsaw Ghetto
- NN., Note entitled "Tsu erleydegn" [To Do]
- List of 12 different matters to be dealt with, connected inter alia with social welfare, fight against epidemic, winter aid.
- *Description:* original, handwritten manuscript, ink, pencil, Yiddish, 155×183 mm, ss. 1, pp. 1.
  Index: [Menachem] Kirszenbaum, [Szymon] Wyszewiański, [Gustaw] Wielikowski

**606. RING. I/204. Mf. ŻIH—779; USHMM—10**

- Date unknown, Warsaw Ghetto
- NN., "Plan fun der dertsierisher arbet in di bashpaizungs-punktn Karmelitske 29, Novolipki 68, Krokhmalne 36" [Plan of Educational Work in the Food Supply Points at ul. Karmelicka 29, Nowolipki 68, Krochmalna 36]
- Transformation of supplementary food supply points into centers of educational and welfare activity, care for the spiritual and social-ethical development of the child, list of readings, curriculum and methods of working with children.
- *Description:* transcript, typescript, Yiddish, 206×286 mm, minor damage and losses of text, ss. 2, pp. 2.
  Attached note by H.W. in Yiddish: "This plan forwarded by [Natan] Smolar, director of the school and kitchen at ul. Nowolipki 68."
  Published: *BFG*, vol. XXVIII (1990), pp. 15–17; *Selected Documents*, pp. 474–475; *Dzieci*, pp. 176–179.

## 607. RING. I/83. (Lb. 337). Mf. ŻIH—776; USHMM—7

- 1941, Warsaw Ghetto
- NN., Study entitled "Vegn gezunt-tsushtand fun der yid. bafelkerung in Varshe (sof 1939 un 1940)" [About the Health Condition of the Jewish Population in Warsaw (End of 1939 and 1940)]
- Reasons for the decline in resistance to disease among the Jewish population in the first weeks of the war; epidemics, increase in morbidity and mortality of Jews; medical care activity (hospitals: at Czyste, Bersohn, and Bauman).
- ***Description:*** transcript (2 copies), handwritten manuscript (MS*), pencil, Yiddish, 148×208 mm, ss. 8, pp. 8.

  In the margins Hebrew letter (ink): "p" (pei).
  Attached note by H.W.: "1941, Warsaw, J. Winkler."

## 608. RING. I/84. Mf. ŻIH—776; USHMM—7. RING. I/223. (Lb. 698). Mf. ŻIH—780; USHMM—11

a) **Ring. I/84**

- Date unknown, Warsaw Ghetto
- Eng. I. Einhorn, "Death Rate of Refugees in June of This Year in the Shelter at ul. Niska 20-Stawki 21"
- Monthly report of the shelter's director; number of refugees and of deaths by age group.
- ***Description:*** original or transcript, typescript, Polish, 217×278 mm, minor damage and losses of text, ss. 4, pp. 4,

  I. Einhorn is also the author of the text in Ring. I/70.

b) **Ring. I/84 and I/223**

- After 05.1941, Warsaw Ghetto
- NN., Fragment of a study concerning statistics of the Jewish population ("Supplements to Chapter III 'Deaths and Causes of Deaths' and to Chapter VIII 'The Jewish Child'")
- Changes in the number of deaths in May 1941; number of children in the year 1940–1941 in the Shelter for Children (ul. Dzielna 39).
- ***Description:*** transcript, typescript, Polish, 218×277 mm, minor damage and losses of text, ss. 2 (Ring. I/84), pp. 2 (Ring. I/84).

  Other copies of this text are in Ring. I/223 (copy, typescript, Polish, 190×280 mm, ss. 2, pp. 2.)

c) **Ring. I/223. (Lb. 698)**

- After 15.07.1941, Warsaw Ghetto
- NN., "Supplements to the Memorandum in the Matter of the Situation of the Jewish Population in Warsaw in June 1941" (supplements to Chapter III, "Deaths and Causes of Deaths"; IV, "Sanitary Conditions and State of Health"; VI, "Situation in the Jewish Hospital"; VII, "Situation in the Points"; VIII, "The Jewish Child")
- Changes in the number of deaths and their causes in the period May–mid-July 1941; statistics of the Czyste Hospital; number of children placed in June 1941 in the Shelter for Children (ul. Dzielna 39).
- ***Description:*** original or transcript, typescript, Polish, 215×280 mm, serious damage and losses of text (only p. 7), ss. 7, pp. 7.

  Attached note by H.W. in Yiddish: "Submitted by J. Winkler, coworker of Oyneg Shabes."

## 609. RING. I/85. Mf. ŻIH—776; USHMM—7

a)

- After 05.1940, Warsaw
- "Denkschrift über die Ursachen des Flecktyphus in Warschau und Vorschläge zu seiner Bekämpfung" [Memorandum on the causes of typhus in Warsaw and proposals for combating it] (15.05.1940, Warsaw)
- Typhus on Polish territories during the First World War and in the interwar period, causes of the increase of the threat of typhus among the Jewish population, and the program to combat it.
- ***Description:*** transcript, typescript, German, 210×295 mm, 210×150mm, minor damage and losses of text, ss. 6, pp. 6.

  Memorial from the Jewish Council to German authorities [?]

b)

- After 06.1941, Warsaw
- "Denkschrift über einige prophylaktische-soziale Massnahmen zur Bekämpfung des Fleckfiebers im Jüdischen Wohnbezirk in Warschau" [Memorandum on some prophylactic social measures to combat typhus in the Jewish residential district in Warsaw] (missing conclusion)
- Poor living conditions of the Jewish population cause an increase in cases of typhus; lacking suitable treatment means, the Jewish Community is unable to fight the epidemic effectively.
- ***Description:*** transcript, typescript, German, 210×295 mm, minor damage and losses of text, ss. 3, pp. 3,

  Memorandum from the Jewish Council to the German authorities [?]

c)

- Date unknown, Warsaw
- Studies (memoranda): "Denkschrift über die prophylaktische Massnahmen im Jüdischen Viertel" [Memorandum on prophylactic measures in the Jewish District] and "Denkschrift über die Epidemieverbreitung in Warschau" [Memorandum on spread of the epidemic in Warsaw]
- Impossibility of securing medical care for those in need and of assuring hygiene in the ghetto without introduction of the postulated treatment means. There is no basis for isolating the Jewish population, whose health condition is a result of external conditions and not racial ones.
- ***Description:*** transcript, typescript, German, 210×285 mm, damage and losses of text, ss. 4, pp. 4.

Studies by the Jewish Council for German authorities [?]

**610. RING. I/214. Mf. ŻIH—780; USHMM—11**

- After 28.06.1941, Warsaw Ghetto
- Memorandum of the Health Commission of the Ethnic Group of Jewish Physicians (Komisji Zdrowia Grupy Narodowościowej Lekarzy Żydowskich) in Warsaw in the matter of the epidemic threat in the Warsaw Ghetto (28.06.1941, Warsaw)
- Notes on the increase of morbidity and deaths due to typhoid fever, dysentery, tuberculosis. The number of hospital beds, medical personnel (training) must be increased, which raises the necessity of imposing a levy on the ghetto population for this purpose.
- ***Description:*** transcript, typescript, Polish, 208×294 mm, ss. 2, pp. 2.

**611. RING. I/363. Mf. ŻIH—782; USHMM—13**

- After 11.03.1942, Warsaw Ghetto
- NN., Study entitled "The Fight against Typhus" (11.03.1942)
- Methods of combatting typhus in the ghetto, their minimal effectiveness, corruption of the Polish and Jewish medical units, as well as physicians, preventive vaccinations, development of the epidemic (September–November 1941). Attached table: "Number of Cases of Typhus Reported to the Health Department," January 1941–February 1942.
- ***Description:*** transcript (3 copies), typescript, Polish, 210×300 mm, ss. 21, pp. 21.

  In HWC, 39/1-2 (handwritten—E*, ink, pencil, Polish, ss. 11+4) there is a manuscript of this document, containing an additional three charts.

**612. RING. I/102. (Lb. 1002). Mf. ŻIH—776; USHMM—7**

- Date unknown, Warsaw Ghetto
- Ch. Garbowicz [Garbawicz, Gorbowicz? Kh. Garbovitsh?] (ul. Nowolipie 23, apt. 30), Study entitled "Der kampf mit epidemies, vi azoy er iz un vi azoy er darf zayn" [The struggle with epidemics, how it is and how it should be]
- The struggle with epidemics conducted by the Jewish Council recalls the struggle with society. Lack of prophylactic activities; "steam baths" [parówki] and disinfection are a source of additional income for physicians and Order Servicemen. The inactivity of representatives of the Health Department (Dr. [Izrael] Milejkowski and Dr. Przeworski). Author's proposal for combatting the epidemics and means for its realization.
- ***Description:*** original, handwritten manuscript, notebook, ink, Yiddish, 155×194 mm, damage and losses of text, ss. 10, pp. 20.

**613. RING. I/64. (Lb. 347). Mf. ŻIH—836; USHMM—67**

- Date unknown, Warsaw Ghetto
- NN., Study entitled "Dos yidishe virtshaftlekhe lebn in Poyln in likht fun faktn in der tsayt fun milkhome un okupatsie" [Jewish economic life in Poland in light of facts in time of war and occupation]
- Participation of Jews in the Polish economy in the years 1933–1939, in the first days of the war, and during the occupation; destruction of the Jewish economy (industry, commerce and petty trade); situation of particular branches of commerce and handicrafts before and after closure of the Warsaw Ghetto, development of new economic branches.
- ***Description:*** transcript (2 copies), handwritten manuscript (MS*), pencil, Yiddish, 146×208 mm, ss. 26, pp. 26.

  On the right margin a symbol (ink): ">>."

**614. RING. I/503/2. (Lb. 460). Mf. ŻIH—789; USHMM—20**

- Date unknown, Warsaw Ghetto
- [Emanuel Ringelblum], Notes concerning economic affairs of the Warsaw Ghetto, calculations, tables.
- ***Description:*** original, handwritten manuscript (ER*), pencil, Polish, 88×156 mm, ss. 6, pp. 6.

**615. RING. I/53. Mf. ŻIH—774; USHMM—5**

- After 12.1941, Warsaw Ghetto
- [J.W.?], Note concerning the official census of useful animals in the Warsaw Ghetto (2–3.12.1941)
- Course of the census and its results (attached official census form).
- ***Description:*** original, handwritten manuscript (JW*), printed, ink, German, Polish, 205×295 mm, 417×293 mm, ss. 3, pp. 3.

  On p. 2 under the text, in a different handwriting (pencil): "J.W."

  Attached note by H.W.: "Recorded by J. Winkler."

**616. RING. I/99. Mf. ŻIH—776; USHMM—7**

- After 11.1940, Warsaw Ghetto
- NN., Study entitled "Dos virtshaftlekhe in der 'geto' mitn antshteyn fun der geto in november 1940" [Economics in the 'ghetto' with the establishment of the ghetto in November 1940]
- Jews' adaptation to the new situation. Production in the ghetto: internal (manual weaving, candy factories, confectionary shops [Wróblewski]; external [for German firms—workshops and homework]).[33] Illegal

33. American usage in regard to production in apartments is "homework," although the Polish term *chałupnictwo* alludes to cottage industry, i.e. work in a peasant's cottage.

economic activity of smugglers, Order Service, and provisioning institutions.
- ***Description:*** transcript (2 copies), handwritten manuscript (Z*), Yiddish, pencil, 148×208 mm, ss. 14, pp. 14.
  Published: *Selected Documents*, 535–537.

### 617. RING. I/1220/32. Mf. ŻIH—835; USHMM—47

- Date unknown, Warsaw Ghetto
- NN., Study entitled "Yidishe fakhn in der m[ilkhome . . .] un in geto" [Jewish trades in the w(ar) and in the ghetto]
- Jewish handicrafts in the Warsaw Ghetto, economic life.
- ***Description:*** original or transcript, handwritten manuscript (two handwritings: Ł* and NN.), ink, pencil, Yiddish, 128×186, 150×190 mm, serious damage and losses of text, ss. 7, pp. 13.

### 618. RING. I/65. Mf. ŻIH—836; USHMM—67

- Date unknown, Warsaw Ghetto
- NN., Study entitled "Boy branzhe" [Construction Branch]
- Situation of Jews in construction before the war and in the first weeks after the outbreak of war.
- ***Description:*** transcript (2 copies), handwritten manuscript (MS*), pencil, Yiddish, 145×207 mm, ss. 4, pp. 4.
  On the right margin three dots placed in the form of a triangle.

### 619. RING. I/216. Mf. ŻIH—780; USHMM—11

- 07.1941, after 07.1941, Warsaw Ghetto
- [Berliner Dawid], Study entitled "Naye fakhn in der milkhome tsayt" [New trades in wartime] (07.1941)
- Cause of the rise of new occupations in the Warsaw Ghetto (division into legal: brushmaking, production in workshops;[34] and illegal: production of soap, smuggling, vulcanization, tanneries, production of paper). Social situation of new occupational groups.
- ***Description:*** original [?] (handwritten manuscript—Ż*, ink, 223×288 mm), transcript (2 copies, typescript, 200×285 mm), Yiddish, minor damage and losses of text, ss. 21, pp. 21.
  On p. 1 (transcript, first copy) notation by H.W. in Yiddish (ink): "1942–109/1 January. no. 3. Berliner." On p. 1 (transcript, second copy) notation by H.W. in Yiddish (ink): "Berliner."
  Attached note by H.W. in Yiddish: "Written by Berliner, a former member of the board of the Warsaw Association of Small Shopkeepers."
  First name of Berliner determined on the basis of: *Selected Documents*, p. XX.
  Published: *Selected Documents*, pp. 538–542.
  In HWC, 33/4 (typescript, pp. 8) a third copy of the transcript.

### 620. RING. I/58. Mf. ŻIH—774; USHMM—5

- Date unknown, Warsaw Ghetto
- [Mojsze Zaks], Study entitled "Dos frizir fakh far un in der milkhome" [The barber profession before and during the war]
- Situation of Jewish barbers before and during the war (earnings, work conditions, degradation of the profession during the occupation, especially in the conditions of the ghetto, political awareness. and social circles).
- ***Description:*** transcript (2 copies), handwritten manuscript (Z*), pencil, Yiddish, pencil, 147×207 mm, ss. 38, pp. 38.
  Attached note by H.W. in Yiddish: "1941 Mojsze Zaks (ul. Nowolipki 3) is the author."

### 621. RING. I/59. (Lb. 894). Mf. ŻIH—774; USHMM—5

- After 06.1941, Warsaw Ghetto
- NN., Study "Processes of Wartime Adaptation of the Jewish Craftsman in Warsaw" (25–30.06.1941)
- Changes in production of various branches of handicrafts in connection with the evolution of the situation of the Jewish population in Warsaw (March 1940–June 1941).
- ***Description:*** transcript (2 copies in fragments: pp. 1–3), typescript, Polish, 206×295 mm, slight damage and losses of text, ss. 12, pp. 12.

### 622. RING. I/101. (Lb. 536). Mf. ŻIH—776; USHMM—7

- After 10.06. [1942?], Warsaw Ghetto
- NN., Study entitled "Barshtn-makher" [Brushmakers] (10.06.[1942?])
- A new Jewish "aristocracy," e.g., Krygier (ul. Dzielna) and Emil Wajc [Weitz] of the brushmaking branch. They obtained wealth and position thanks to contacts and connections among Germans and Jews.
- ***Description:*** original or transcript, typescript (title and corrections handwritten, ink), Yiddish, 225×288 mm, slight damage and losses of text, ss. 5, pp. 5.
  On p. 1 notation by H.W.: "6 standard pages."

### 623. RING. I/161. Mf. ŻIH—779; USHMM—10

- After 1940, Warsaw
- [Samuel Brasław ?], Biography of Henryk Gotland (born 1920)
- Henryk Gotland, former student at the University of

34. The Polish *szopy*, cognate with shop, is rendered as "workshops," and includes both mechanized and manual manufacturing. "Shop" has also been used in American industrial slang to refer to a factory or other workplace.

Warsaw, fled in September 1939 to the East; he lived in Białystok until March 1940, involved in trade, then made his way back into Warsaw, where he started with trade in gold and currencies. Profile of a person who was quite capable of adapting to the changing conditions.
- ***Description:*** original or transcript, handwritten manuscript (SB*), ink, Polish, 170×336 mm, minor damage and losses of text, text illegible in places, ss. 3, pp. 5.
  Attached note by H.W. in Yiddish: "Edited [by] Samuel Bresław [Brasław]."

## 624. RING. I/238. Mf. ŻIH—780; USHMM—11

- Date unknown, Warsaw Ghetto
- NN., "Relationship of Prices of Several Articles of Personal Use (Used, of Very Good Quality, with Little Damage) to Market Prices of Several Food Products." Daily fluctuations of prices of various articles of food (charts)
- Relation of the prices of a man's suit, shirt, sheet, and shoes to the prices of butter, salt bacon,[35] sugar, beef, horsemeat, milk, and bread. Daily fluctuations of the prices of rye and potatos, differences in prices of various food items (charts).
- ***Description:*** original, handwritten manuscript, ink, Polish, 215×353 mm, damage and losses of text, ss. 1, pp. 2.
  According to information from the inventory and attached note by H.W., the author of the charts is [Eliasz] Gutkowski; see also *Kronika getta*, p. 448.
  Attached note by H.W. in Yiddish.

## 625. RING. I/283. (Lb. 1157). Mf. ŻIH—781; USHMM—12

a)
- After 21.11.1941, Warsaw Ghetto
- NN., "Note in the matter of mass deliveries and export transactions in the carpentry and lathe industry in the Jewish District in Warsaw" (21.11.1941)
- Production of furniture in the Warsaw Ghetto for Germans' needs.
- ***Description:*** original or transcript, typescript, Polish, 210×264 mm, ss. 1, pp. 1.
  Inventory: "Jerzy Winkler author of the study."

b)
- After 23.11.1941, Warsaw Ghetto
- NN., "Note in the matter of export from the Jewish District with the omission of the Transferstelle." (23.11.1941)
- Handicraft production (tin, furs, brushes—250 workshops with 2,000 workers, carpentry, upholstery, locksmithing) for Germans and the Polish population.
- ***Description:*** original or transcript, typescript, Polish, 208×292 mm, ss. 2, pp. 2.
  Inventory: "Jerzy Winkler author of the study."

## 626. RING. I/371. (Lb. 867A). Mf. ŻIH—782; USHMM—13

- After 11.1941, Warsaw Ghetto
- NN., Notes concerning "export" production of the Warsaw Ghetto
- Development of production and semilegal export from the ghetto, timber industry, brushmaking. High prices of food and wages hamper further development. Resourcefulness of the ghetto's producers exemplified by the factory of Toba Zemsz (ul. Grzybowska 3).
- ***Description:*** transcript (3 copies), typescript, Polish, 207×293 mm, minor damage and losses of text, ss. 9, pp. 9.
  On p. 1, notation by H.W.: "Kler."
  See Ring. I/103, I/62.
  Published: *Selected Documents*, 546–548.

## 627. RING. I/123. (Lb. 951). Mf. ŻIH—777; USHMM—8

- 03.1942, Warsaw Ghetto
- [Rada Gospodarcza Dzielnicy Żydowskiej we Warszawie? (Economic Council of the Jewish District in Warsaw?)] NN., "Note on export production on the free market in the Jewish district"
- Influence of the general economic situation in the Generalgouvernement on development of production in the ghetto, adaptation of Jewish producers to the needs of the external market, scope of production for "export," cooperation with firms and "export" wholesalers.
- ***Description:*** transcript (a) (3 copies), typescript, Polish, 205×278, 205×70 mm, damage and losses of text, ss. 12, pp. 12; transcript (b) (typescript, Polish, 210×150, 210×110 mm, serious damage and losses of text, only fragments preserved, ss. 3, pp. 3.
  Copies a and b contain the same text.
  The themes of the study approximate the text in Ring. I/103; presumably one person created both "notes."
  See Ring. I/371.

## 628. RING. I/256. Mf. ŻIH—780; USHMM—11

- Date unknown, Warsaw Ghetto
- NN., Study entitled. "Dzhike–gas num. 4 (Transfershtele, Umshlagplats)" [Dzika Street no. 4 (Transferstelle, Umschlagplatz)]

35. Consumption of bacon by Jews in the ghetto reflected the sheer lack of options many Jews felt in the quest for bare endurance and survival during the years of occupation. This is related to the entire issue of *kashrut* in such a time of catastrophic oppression and deprivation.

- Transfer point for goods arriving into the ghetto (organization, work force—Jews, corruption and thefts, go-betweens).
- ***Description:*** transcript (a) (2 copies, handwritten manuscript—Z*, pencil, 147×208 mm), ss. 28, pp. 28; transcript (b) (typescript, 208×288 mm), Yiddish, ss. 8, pp. 8.

  On p. 1 (typescript) information by H.W. in Yiddish (ink): "Lew." nr [?] 26. 109—1942/1 January."

  Inventory: "M. Lew."

### 629. RING. I/62. Mf. ŻIH—774; USHMM—5. RING. I/284. Mf. ŻIH—781; USHMM—12

- After 11.1941, Warsaw Ghetto
- NN., Study: "The Ghetto Fights Economic Slavery"
- Development of the Warsaw Ghetto's economic relations with the "Aryan Side" and with the Germans; trade in recycled raw materials (surowcami wtórnymi), carpentry and brushmaking, smuggling.
- ***Description:*** Ring. I/284, I/62—original (handwritten manuscript (J.W.*), ink, Polish, 205×295 mm, damage and losses of text, some of the pages illegible, missing one sheet, ss. 44, pp. 44); Ring. I/62—transcript (2 copies, typescript with handwritten additions, ink and pencil, Polish, 210×297 mm, ss. 52, pp. 52).

  Because of damage, the original does not contain the entire text of the transcript.

  On p. 6 is described the history of the workshop of Toba Zemsz (ul. Grzybowska 3); a similar statement about this factory is in Ring. I/371, on p. 3.

  Ring. I/62—Attached note by H.W.: "J. Winkler is the author." According to information on the file jacket (Ring. I/284) the author of the text is J. Winkler.

  Published: *BFG*, vol. I, nos. 3–4 (1948), pp. 3–40; BŻIH, no. 35 (1960), pp. 55–86; *Selected Documents*, pp. 552–584.

### 630. RING. I/55. (Lb. 471). Mf. ŻIH—774; USHMM—5

- After 18.06.1942, Warsaw Ghetto
- [Sz. Szajnkinder], Study on the trade in old clothing and furniture in the Warsaw Ghetto (18.06.1942)
- Development and significance of the trade in used items (clothing, household items, etc.); sellers (Jews) and buyers (Poles); place of trade in the ghetto's street life.
- ***Description:*** transcript, typescript, Yiddish, 223×285 mm, slight damage and losses of text, ss. 5, pp. 5.

  On p. 1 notation by H.W. in Yiddish: "June 1942" and "5.5 standard pages."

  Attached note by H.W. in Yiddish: "Written by Sz. Szajnkinder."

  Published: *Selected Documents*, 548–552.

### 631. RING. I/56. Mf. ŻIH—774; USHMM—5

- Date unknown, Warsaw Ghetto
- NN., Study on trade in the Warsaw Ghetto
- Trade in used goods (rags, glass, scrap metal, waste paper) before the war and during the occupation and significance of Jews in its organization; rise of sorting firms. Development of "tram" smuggling and significance of the court house on ul. Leszno for the trade (smuggling headquarters).
- ***Description:*** transcript, handwritten manuscript (BW*), pencil, Yiddish, 150×207 mm, slight damage and losses of text, ss. 6, pp. 6.

  On p. 1 notation in Yiddish: "Forms of Jewish Trade XVIII–XXI"; in the margins a Hebrew letter "k" (kof).

### 632. RING. I/57. (Lb. 1552). Mf. ŻIH—774; USHMM—5. RING. I/104. (Lb. 1003, 1061). Mf. ŻIH—776; USHMM—7

- End of 1941, Warsaw Ghetto
- [T. Tykociński?], Study entitled "Altvarg—der eyntsiker handl bay di yidn in Varshe in der geto tsayt 1940 un 1941 yor" [Used goods—the sole business among the Jews in the Warsaw Ghetto during 1940 and 1941]
- Significance of the trade in used goods in the life of Warsaw Jews before the war; trade at "Wałówka" up to November 1940 and after formation of the ghetto, the new trading place "Gęsiówka" (corner of ul. Gęsia and Lubecki—from 09.1941), blossoming of trade at the beginning of winter 1941 (mass sale of goods by the ghetto's population). Association of Retail Traders (ul. Leszno 42), director Graf.
- ***Description:*** Ring. I/104—transcript (a) (2 copies), handwritten manuscript (NN*), pencil, Yiddish, 145×202 mm, extensive damage and losses of text, ss. 20, pp. 20; Ring. I/57—transcript (b) (2 copies), typescript, Yiddish, 207×295 mm, minor damage and losses of text, ss. 20, pp. 20.

  Ring. I/104 has a somewhat different title: "Valuvke. Der ayntsiker handl bay di yidn in Varshe in der geto-tsayt 1940 un 1941" [Wałówka. The only business among the Jews in Warsaw in the ghetto period 1940 and 1941]

  Ring. I/104—On p. 1 (in the second copy) at the top is information by H.W.: "Tykocinski."

  Ring. I/104—third copy transferred to Yad Vashem.

  Ring. I/57—On p. 1 (first copy) information by H.W. in Yiddish (ink): "109–1942/1 January. no. 25."

  Ring. I/57—See HWC, 33/3 (third copy, typescript, sheet 10; information about the author, "T. Tykociński").

  Published: *BFG*, vol. I, nos. 3–4 (1948), pp. 203–210.

### 633. RING. I/509. Mf. ŻIH—789; USHMM—20

- Date unknown, Warsaw Ghetto

- NN., Note concerning economic affairs of the Warsaw Ghetto (trade in lumber) (fragment).
- ***Description:*** transcript (2 copies), handwritten manuscript (MS*), pencil, Yiddish, 145×208 mm, minor damage and losses of text, missing pp. 1–2, ss. 2, pp. 2.
    In the margin a symbol (ink): three dots placed in the form of a triangle (∴).
    Inventory: "Dr. E. Ringelblum, Death Camp in Chełmno." [?]
    Index: Berl Glukson (ul. Sienna 64), lumber warehouse

### 634. RING. I/61. (Lb. 1224, 1439). Mf. ŻIH—774; USHMM—5

- After 12.1941, Warsaw Ghetto
- A. Ben-Jakub [Eliasz Gutkowski], Study entitled "Di shvartse birzhe" [The black market]
- Currency trade in the Warsaw Ghetto (1939–1941): organization, social composition, scope of activity of the "black market" (ul. Pawia near Pawiak)—currency headquarters for Warsaw and the Generalgouvernement; statement of fluctuation of the dollar's exchange rates (11.1940–12.1941) (table and chart).
- ***Description:*** original (handwritten manuscript LEG*, ink), transcript (2 copies) (handwritten manuscript—U*, pencil, notebook), Yiddish, various sizes: 144×187, 150×210 mm, 178×222, 236×640, very serious damage and losses of text (original), ss. 67, pp. 72.
    Chart drawn by Zelik. Transcript contains only part of the original (pp. 1–26) (missing the end, or pp. 27–31 and chart (p. 2).
    No. 1224—contains only a transcript (2 copies).
    Inventory: "Authors of the study: A. Ben-Jakow and E. Gutkowski." According to R.S., Eliasz Gutkowski used the pseudonym A. Ben-Jakub.
    See Ring. II/171.
    See HWC, 33/2 (third copy of the transcript, handwritten manuscript, ss. 16).

### 635. RING. I/51. (Lb. 446). Mf. ŻIH—774; USHMM—5

- 07.1942, Warsaw Ghetto
- NN., Study entitled "Shmugl" [Smuggling]
- History and organization of smuggling in the Warsaw Ghetto, activity of particular smuggling dens (points): ul. Biała (opposite no. 5), ul. Koźla, Pokorna 4, the wall at ul. Elektoralna from no. 14 to the corner of Orla, Sienna 22, Krochmalna; smugglers: Goldsztejn—"Jasz"; porters: Naftali—"Rabuś" ("the Robber"), Szlomo Bodnarz, Gedalja; participation of children in smuggling.
- ***Description:*** original or transcript, handwritten manuscript (TT* [?]), pencil, Yiddish, 110×170 mm, 150×195 mm and 170×207 mm, substantial damage and losses of text, ss. 36, pp. 36.
    Pages 6–11 are written on provisioning card forms: "Komisja Aprowizacyjna Akcji Przesiedleńczej. Tymczasowy bon" [Provisioning Committee of the Resettlement Action. Temporary Coupon] (hectographed typescript, 90×130 mm). Pages 25–29 are written on the back of filled-out (at the "Jewish Refugees Home, ul. Spokojna 13 [stamp, India ink]) application forms ("declarations") to the "Coordinating Commission of Social and Welfare Organizations TOZ, Centos and Others. Care for Refugees and Fire Victims in Warsaw" with a request for allocation of clothing, work, etc. for the following persons: Mojsze Płotniarz of Lubicz, Lipno district, tailor, age 18 (filled out on 18.05.1940); Mojsze Kowalski of Lipno, ul. Przekop, tailor, age 40, with wife Chana, age 37 (filled out on: 18.05.1940); Chawa Mądziak from Żuromin, age 17, with sisters Ruchla (age 13) and Idesa (age 10 [?]).

### 636. RING. I/226. (Lb. 976). Mf. ŻIH—780; USHMM—11

- Date unknown, Warsaw Ghetto
- [Berliner Dawid], Study entitled "Fun der serye yidishe parnoses in getto" [From the series Jewish Livelihoods in the Ghetto]
- Smuggling and trade with the "Aryan side" (organization, intermediaries, goods, earnings, tram smuggling).
- ***Description:*** original [?] (handwritten manuscript -Ż*, ink, 218×275 mm, ss. 2, pp. 4), transcript (2 copies, typescript, 203×294 mm, ss. 12, pp. 12), Yiddish, ss. 14, pp. 16.
    On p. 1 (copy) information by H.W. in Yiddish: "Berliner."
    Attached 2 notes by H.W. in Yiddish: "Berliner from Warsaw compiled, former member of the board of the Association of Retail Merchants, first half of 1941."
    Manuscript and analogous copies also in Ring. I/216.
    See HWC, 33/5 (third copy of transcript, typescript, ss. 6; on p. 1 notation [ink]: "Berliner").
    Berliner's first name was established on the basis of *Selected Documents*, p. XX.
    Published: *Selected Documents*, pp. 542–546.

### 637. RING. I/323. MISSING ORIGINAL

- After 1946, Warsaw
- [Perec Opoczyński], Study entitled "Goyim in geto" [Gentiles in the ghetto]
- Polish–Jewish trade relations before and after the war's outbreak, trade in used goods at the "Wołówka" marketplace (after formation of the ghetto at the intersection of Gęsia and Lubecki Streets), Poles buying in the ghetto; positive appraisal of smuggling in the ghetto, as one of the forms of cooperation between Poles and Jews.

- *Description:* postwar transcript, typescript, Yiddish, ss. 19, pp. 19.

## 638. RING. I/187. Mf. ŻIH—779; USHMM—10

- After 11.1941, Warsaw Ghetto
- NN., "Notitsn tsu der geshikhte fun aroysgeyn un araynkumen in varshever yidishn geto" [Notes on the history of leaving and entering the Warsaw Jewish ghetto]
- Imperfect isolation of the ghetto, petty smuggling by children and major smuggling with participation of the Order Service, Germans, officials, navy blue police, and the "Thirteen." From November 1941 sentences of death for leaving the ghetto without a pass.
- *Description:* transcript (2 copies), handwritten manuscript (U*), pencil, Yiddish, 145×204 mm, ss. 8, pp. 8.

  On p. 1 (on the first copy) information by H.W. in Yiddish: "Vink" [Winkler?].

  Inventory: "Author of text is Jechiel Górny."

## 639. RING. I/157. Mf. ŻIH—778; USHMM—9

- 13.07.1942, Warsaw Ghetto
- NN., Notes on smuggling in the Warsaw Ghetto
- Illegal trade with the "Aryan side," bribery of the navy blue police and gendarmes.
- *Description:* original or transcript, handwritten manuscript (MS*), pencil, ink, Yiddish, 175×320 mm, minor damage and losses of text, text illegible in places, ss. 4, pp. 4.

  On p. 4 information by H.W. in Yiddish: "2 standard pages."

  Manuscript written on the back of a "declaration," registration form of the Provisioning Department (Sekcji Aprowizacyjnej) (1940, printed, Polish, Yiddish). On p. 2 (on the back of the "declaration") information by H.W. in Yiddish: "June 1942. 6 standard pages."

## 640. RING. I/18. Mf. ŻIH—771; USHMM—2

- After 06.1941, Warsaw Ghetto
- Memorandum of representatives of Jewish society concerning the activity of the Commission at the Jewish Council in Warsaw (June 1941)
- Critique of the functioning of the Commission, which was to be an area of cooperation of representatives of Jewish society with the Jewish Council (personal conflicts, financial abuses).
- *Description:* transcript, typescript with handwritten additions (ink), Polish, 220×348 mm, minor damage and losses of text, ss. 9, pp. 9.

  On all the pages at the top two handwritten letters: "VV."

  Attached note by H.W. in Yiddish: "Submitted by colleague Szachno Sagan."

## 641. RING. I/54. Mf. ŻIH—774; USHMM—5

- Date unknown, Warsaw Ghetto
- NN., Study on the activity of the Department of Manufacturing (Wydziału Wytwórczości) (of Jewish Manufacturing [Wytwórczości Żydowskiej]) at the Jewish Council in Warsaw
- Start-up of the so-called "shops" (szopów), influence of the Transferstelle on the ghetto's economic life, the W.C. Toebbens firm.
- *Description:* transcript (2 copies), typescript with handwritten additions, ink, Polish, 215×285 mm, damages and minor losses of text, ss. 6, pp. 6,

  Attached note by H.W.: "Text was written down by J. Winkler."

  Index: Rotner, Głowiński, Bischoff, John of Żyrardów

## 642. RING. I/192. Mf. ŻIH—779; USHMM—10

- 07.1942, Warsaw Ghetto
- N.R. [Nechemiasz Tytelman], Study entitled "Arbets-amt, arbets-tsvang, koruptsye, shvindl, yidishe-unordenungs-dinst un andere mikol-haneorim gemeynheytn . . ." [Labor Office, forced labor, corruption, swindle, Jewish Disorder [sic] Service, and all sorts of other vulgarities]
- The Labor Office in the ghetto (behavior toward the population, forced labor, seizures, corruption, public opinion about the Office, the board: Councilman Rozen and Cygler).
- *Description:* original, handwritten manuscript (Ł*), ink, Yiddish, 108×352 mm, minor damage and losses of text, ss. 7, pp. 14.

  Attached note by H.W. in Polish, Yiddish: "Natan Tytelman, article in the form of an open letter to Councilman Rozen."

  Index: Silbermuenz, Ginsberg, Michał Tenenbaum

## 643. RING. I/315. (Lb. 687). Mf. ŻIH—781; USHMM—12

- After 07.1941, Warsaw Ghetto
- Memorandum from representatives of the Jewish public to Adam Czerniaków, chairman of the Jewish Council in the matter of the increase in mortality in the Warsaw Ghetto (missing conclusion)
- Statistics on deaths in the ghetto, hospital care, reference to the memorandum of Dr. Józef Stein dated 4.06.1941 on the tragic situation of the "Czyste" Hospital (attached extensive quotations from Stein's memorial), the Berson and Bauman Hospital, the need to intensify the fight against the epidemic, establishment of a new "public" hospital for adults and children.
- *Description:* transcript, typescript, Polish, 210×295, 210×150 mm, missing fragment of p. 7 with the conclusion, ss. 7, pp. 7.

  See Ring. I/7.

## 644. RING. I/507/2. Mf. ŻIH—789; USHMM—20

- After 12.1940, Warsaw Ghetto
- [Emanuel Ringelblum], Notes

- Charts concerning the activities of different departments of the Jewish Council in Warsaw in 1940.
- ***Description:*** original, handwritten manuscript (ER*), ink, Polish, 146×170 mm, ss. 1, pp. 1.

### 645. RING. I/233. Mf. ŻIH—780; USHMM—11

- After 10.1940, Warsaw Ghetto
- Memorandum in the matter of reform of the Order Service in the Warsaw Ghetto
- Necessity of introduction of changes into the Order Service: issuance of an instruction outlining its goals and tasks, convening a commission for evaluation of the current state of the Order Service, reduction and vetting of personnel, new rules of remuneration, encouragement of the population to cooperate with the Order Service, broadening the competence of the Disciplinary Department for real control over officers.
- ***Description:*** transcript (2 copies), handwritten manuscript (E*) and typescript, Polish, 150×220, 220×287 mm, ss. 4, pp. 4.

Attached note by H.W. in Polish, Yiddish: "Memorandum of opposition group within the Order Service in the matter of improving conditions in the police division. Forwarded by ghetto policeman attorney [Zygmunt] Milet [Millet], one of the close coworkers of the deceased attorney [Leon] Berenson."

A study located in Ring. I/115 refers to this memorial; perhaps it was originally attached to the above document.

See HWC, 42/2 (typescript, ss. 3).

### 646. RING. I/502. Mf. ŻIH—788; USHMM—19

a)

- After 04.1942, Warsaw Ghetto
- [T. Witelson], Study on the Order Service in the Warsaw Ghetto (fragments)
- Genesis of the Order Service, enlistment campaign, socio-occupational composition, profiles of several members of the Order Service (Józef Szeryński, Marian Wilhelm Händel [Hendel], Stanisław and Marian Czapliński, Bernard Szatensztajn, Jakub Lejkin, [Henryk] Nowogródzki, [Józef] Fels, Srul Borensztajn, Efraim Kalina, Albin Fleischman, Józef Erlich and others), charter, organizational chart, area of activity (theory and practice), participation in legal and illegal economic life, exploitation of authority, extortion, Order Service in satire, relations with the Germans. In the text are included transcripts of various documents concerning the Order Service (organizational chart, regulations, correspondence, account of group leader Mojżesz Passensztajn on a stay in the labor camp at Wilga—04.1942).
- ***Description:*** transcript (2 copies in fragments), typescript, Polish, 200×278, 175×135 mm, numerous severe damage and losses of text, ss. 148, pp. 148.

Attached note by H.W.: "Work of Witelson, prepared on the basis of archive's survey."

Published: *Służba Porządkowa*, pp. 108–109, 110 (fragments).

Index: Mieczysław Goldstein, Dr. Wihler, Trumper, attorney Solnik, S. Kroszczor, J. Hertz, A. Heiselman, N. Nadel, Brewda, K. Peczonik, Silberstein, Rode, L. Lindenfeld, Rose, attorney Schonbach, attorney Gombiński, Lubliner, J. Lejkin, Lederman

b)

- Date unknown, Warsaw Ghetto
- Jewish Council in Warsaw. Order Service, Pass for Aleksander Landau
- Authorization to enter the apartment at ul. Żelazna 99, apt. 28, on the basis of a housing order.
- ***Description:*** original, typescript, handwritten manuscript, ink, Polish, 60×206 mm, ss. 1, pp. 1.

c)

- 4.11.1941, Warsaw Ghetto
- Administration of the Medical Rescue Service (Kierownictwo Lekarskiej Służby Ratowniczej) at the Jewish Emergency Rescue Service in the Jewish District in Warsaw, acknowledgement of collection of four children from Order Service functionary no. 1067, dated 4.11.1941.
- ***Description:*** original, handwritten manuscript, pencil, stamp, Polish, 127×100 mm, ss. 1, pp. 1.

Index: Ber, Order Service member no. 1408

d)

- Date unknown, Warsaw Ghetto
- NN., Poem entitled "Rhyme of the Customer"
- Satire.
- ***Description:*** original or transcript, handwritten manuscript, ink, Polish, 128×98 mm, ss. 1, pp. 1.

On the document is the mirror image of a stamp from document (c), which indicates that both documents were buried together.

e)

- 4.03.1942, Kielce
- Medical document certifying that Samuel Józef Kapłan from Hrubieszów does not have lice and is not ill with infectious diseases.
- ***Description:*** original, typescript, handwritten manuscript, pencil, stamp, German, 140×206 mm, damages and minor losses of text, ss. 1, pp. 1.

### 647. RING. I/115. Mf. ŻIH—777; USHMM—8

- After 12.1941, Warsaw Ghetto
- NN., Fragment of a study on the Order Service in the Warsaw Ghetto
- Organization and activity of the Order Service—financial abuses and blackmail.
- ***Description:*** transcript (2 copies), handwritten manuscript (CA*), pencil, Polish, 150×210 mm, ss. 30, pp. 30.

See HWC, 42/1 (original or a different transcript of this document, handwritten—E*, ink, Polish, ss. 6.

Published: *Selected Documents*, pp. 304–309.

### 648. RING. I/181. Mf. ŻIH—779; USHMM—10

- After 5.08.1941, Warsaw Ghetto
- A[. . . ?], "Contemporary Tales of Hoffman. From a series of stories on the Bribe Service, or Order Service"
- Criticism of the activity of the Order Service in the Warsaw Ghetto (bribery, demoralization, abuse of authority).
- ***Description:*** transcript, typescript, Polish, 224×297 mm, ss. 6, pp. 6.

  Acc. to information on the file jacket, the author is "Amas Freund."

  Index: Józef Szeryński, Lederman (ul. Sienna 43), Solnik, Gancwajch, Lejkin

### 649. RING. I/174. Mf. ŻIH—779; USHMM—10

- After 10.1941, Warsaw Ghetto
- [Menachem Mendel Kon?], "Der tsveyter ofener briv tsu di askonim-'zitsers'" [The second open letter to the activist 'sitters']
- History of ŻTOS, accusations that the attitude of the Jewish Council and the Warsaw Committee of ŻSS toward the ghetto's poor is unjust, call to the activists of ŻTOS to shorten meetings and undertake work in the welfare institutions.
- ***Description:*** transcript, typescript, Yiddish, 205×290 mm, minor damage and losses of text, ss. 10, pp. 10.

  Inventory: "Author of the letter was Menachem Mendel Kon."

### 650. RING. I/1152/1 (1471). (Lb. 1228). Mf. ŻIH—833; USHMM—45

- Date unknown, Warsaw Ghetto
- NN., Outline of a plan for reorganization of the Department of Hometown Associations
- Establishment of a Committee for Refugee Affairs at the ŻOS, collaboration with the Social Welfare Section and CKU.
- ***Description:*** original, handwritten manuscript, ink, Polish, 145×192 mm, ss. 2, pp. 3.

  On the back of p. 3 a list of names (H.W.*, ink, Yiddish): "2nd list. Opoczyński Perec—Wolińska; Kirszenfeld Bluma; Zisman Wolf; Maks Zakrzewski—Żabia 15—Bureau of Mills initially with Szterner Kornkowski and then in Wagoniec near Nieszawa and then with him in the granary of Włocł[awek] until the war; Goldbas Szlomo; Rajnhold Mosze (Rejnhold); Szpiro Icchak; Zilberberg Jakow; Klajman (Klejman) Hersz—Now[olipie?] 44. Mil [?].; Brajtsztajn and Korn; Górny Jechiel; Iliard Hersz; Jungwic Pesach [first and surname crossed out]; Fiszman Guta; Bast [?] [crossed out]; Rapaport Genia—Grzybowska 48a."

  Doc. is on sheets torn from the notebook described in Ring. I/1151.

  Attached note by H.W.

### 651. RING. I/77. (Lb. 538). Mf. ŻIH—775; USHMM—6

- After 10.1940, place unknown
- [Bencjon Chilinowicz?], Report entitled "Di arbet fun der Dzhoynt centrale in Poyln, far di 13 milkhome khodoshim (september 1939—oktober 1940). Kurtser raport" [The Work of the Joint's Headquarters in Poland, during the 13 War Months (September 1939—October 1940). Short Report]
- Establishment, at the initiative of the Joint, of the Coordinating Committee (14.09.1939) for Jewish social and welfare organizations. Organization and assistance of miscellaneous aid for the Jewish population (feeding, public kitchens, Passover relief campaigns, aid for the homeless and displaced, clothing and financial aid, aid in establishing contacts with families, assistance of economic activity, courses, rescue of prisoners, apartment house committees, etc.).
- ***Description:*** transcript, typescript with handwritten manuscript additions, pencil, Yiddish, 215×282 mm, damage and losses of text, ss. 68, pp. 68.

  Attached note by H.W. in Yiddish: "Prepared [by] Bencjon Chilinowicz."

### 652. RING. I/66. Mf. ŻIH—774; USHMM—5

- Date unknown, Warsaw Ghetto
- NN., Study: "Internal Structure of the apartment house Committees"
- Origin of the apartment house committees, staffing, activity.
- ***Description:*** original or transcript, typescript, Polish, 210×294 mm, 210×148 mm, slight damage and losses of text, ss. 2, pp. 2.

  At the top of the page is a symbol (ink): a wavy line or the letter "w".

### 653. RING. I/297. (Lb. 569). Mf. ŻIH—781; USHMM—12

- 04.1942, Warsaw Ghetto
- [Stefa Szereszewska], Study on the activity of the apartment house committee at ul. Gęsia 19. (25.04.1942)
- Description of the building's residents, personal losses, kitchens, evolution of the material situation, deterioration of the committee's activity. The paper is based on the financial record book of the committee (for the period April–December 1941) and information from its chairman, Wajzer.
- ***Description:*** original, handwritten manuscript (D*), ink, Polish, 175×220, 147×195 mm, extensive damage and losses of text, ss. 14, pp. 15.

  On p. 1 later written (with pencil): "Prepared on the basis of the financial record book and conversations with the chair[man] of the apartment house Com[mittee]. The record book includes the period from April to December 41"; on p. 12 (pencil): "W[arsaw], 25 IV 42"

Attached note by H.W. in Polish, Yiddish: "Compiled [by] Stefa Szereszewska."
According to the Inventory, the text's author is Stefa Szereszewska.
Published: *Selected Documents*, pp. 148–152.

### 654. RING. I/68. (Lb. 285, 478, 478A). Mf. ŻIH—775; USHMM—6

- Date unknown, Warsaw
- Minutes of meetings of the apartment house committee at ul. Leszno 24 in Warsaw (fragment)
- Organizational, personnel and financial matters, aid for the needy, cooperation with other committees and institutions (attached lists of names of the committee's members) (July 1940–April 1942).
- ***Description:*** transcript, handwritten manuscript, notebooks, ink, Polish, 150×195 mm, damage and losses of text, text is illegible in places, ss. 57, pp. 105.

  On the title ss. (pp. 1 and 2): "Apartment House Committee of the Jewish Social Self-Help—apartment house at ul. Leszno no. 24. Minutes of meetings."

  On p. 2 (July 1940) list of the committee's members: Dawid Goldman, chairman; Izak Auster, vice chairman; Jakub Wasserkener, secretary; Moszek Nisenszal, financial department; Josek Pergament, clothing department; D. [. . .] Guman, sanitary department; Gerszon Atlas, Maksymilian Odesser, and Szyja Rapoport—audit commission; on pp. 13–14 list of committee's members after the election on 24.11.1940: Moszek Nisenszal, chairman; J. Lewkowicz, vice chairman; and representative of the refugees, Dawid Goldman; Jakub Wasserkener, secretary; M. Summer, sanitary department; Szyja Rapoport, clothing department; Josek Pergament, supplemental food department; Lipskier, Youth Circle department; Maksymilian Odesser, Izak Auster, Gerszon Atlas, D. [. . .] Guman, J. Szychman. On pp. 80 and 82 a list of the committee's members after the election on 8.11.1941: Apelblat J., chairman; Zadecki, treasurer; Landau, sanitary department; Moszek Nisenszal, Szyja Rapoport, provisioning department; J. Szychman, vice chairman and finance department; Sytner, vice chairman and cultural department; Audit Commission: Białer, Kociałkowski, and Zylberberg.

### 655. RING. I/106. MISSING ORIGINAL. Mf. ŻIH—776; USHMM—7

- After 1946, Warsaw
- [Perec Opoczyński], Study of the apartment house committee at ul. Muranowska 6
- History of the committee from the war's start in 1939 until March 1942 (organization, activity in different periods of the occupation).
- ***Description:*** postwar transcript, typescript, Hebrew, 214×278 mm, ss. 15, pp. 15.

  Published: *BFG*, vol. XIV/1961, pp. 171–179.

### 656. RING. I/67. (Lb. 278). Mf. ŻIH—774; USHMM—5

- After 04.1942, Warsaw Ghetto
- [Dr. Celina Lewin?], Study concerning the apartment house committee at ul. [Nalewki 23] in Warsaw (fragment). Minutes of meetings of the apartment house committee at ul. [Nalewki 23] in Warsaw (July 1939–April 1942) (fragments)
- Organizational, personnel and financial matters, aid for the needy, cooperation with other committees and institutions. Participants in the meetings, among others, were: Frenkiel, [Jakub] Kahan, Graf, M. [Mordka] Haberman, I. Haberman, Hamburger, Honigsfeld, Elenberg, Ihab, Białykamień, Szafir, Rozenberg, Skowronek, Szczarański (Szarański), Elbaum, Kotkowski, Kupersztein, Nauasbaum (Nanasbaum) [?], Committee treasurer, Zylbergleit. Numerous lists of names.
- ***Description:*** transcript, handwritten manuscript (two handwritings: D*), notebooks, ink, Polish, 150×195 mm, text illegible in places, ss. 285, pp. 536.

  Acc. to E.R., the paper's author was Dr. Celina Lewin; see *Kronika getta,* p. 489.

  See Ring. I/209.

### 657. RING. I/1220/63. Mf. ŻIH—835; USHMM—47

- Date unknown, Warsaw
- Table entitled "Record of inspections dated . . ."
- Concerning mutual food aid among residents of the apartment houses at ul. Nowolipki 60, 62, 64, 66, and 76.
- ***Description:*** original, handwritten manuscript, ink, Polish, 222×177 mm, ss. 1, pp. 1.

  On the back of a fragment of a study about the Jewish world Ba Omer[36] [??] (NN., handwritten manuscript, ink, German).

### 658. RING. I/40. (Lb. 923). Mf. ŻIH—773; USHMM—4

- Date unknown, Warsaw Ghetto
- NN., "Youth in the apartment house committees. Gurfinkiel Ewa, born 1921"
- Biographical sketch of an apartment house committee activist, family, education, intellectual

36. This may refer to a study of Jewish mourning customs that apply during the weeks between the holidays of Passover and Shavuot. Alternatively, this may be a corrupted reference to the minor holiday Lag ba-Omer, which occurs on the 33rd day of the period commencing from the second night of Passover.

interests, paid work (English lessons), social work, organization of the house library.
- *Description:* original or transcript, typescript, Polish, 210×295 mm (210×87 mm—pp. 3), ss. 3, pp. 3,

### 659. RING. I/92. Mf. ŻIH—776; USHMM—7

- After 11.1941, Warsaw Ghetto
- [Różycki Stanisław ?], Two studies: "Polish authors" and "Polish–Jewish Relations"
- Profiles of authors living in the ghetto (Janusz Korczak, Winawer, Fokszański, Jarecka, Sztajnberg [husband of Ćwiklińska], Włast, Szlengel, Frühling, Mark, Kraushar and others); various attitudes of Poles toward Jews: conflicts and cooperation.
- *Description:* original handwritten manuscript (SR*), notebook, ink, Polish, 155×195 mm, ss. 11, pp. 11

  Published: *Selected Documents*, pp. 615–620 ("Polish–Jewish Relations"), pp. 674–677 ("Polish Authors").

### 660. RING. I/1048 (1367). (Lb. 909). Mf. ŻIH—832; USHMM—44

- After 02.1942, Warsaw Ghetto
- NN., Study entitled "Khorn (dervaksene)" [Choirs (Adults)]
- Jewish choirs in Warsaw before the war and during the occupation (organization, personnel, program, public performances, supporters—attached list of names of people).
- *Description:* original or transcript, typescript (handwritten manuscript additions, pencil), Yiddish, 105×164, 172×271 mm, extensive damage and losses of text, ss. 4, pp. 4.

  Published: *Selected Documents*, 454–456.

### 661. RING. I/50. Mf. ŻIH—773; USHMM—4

a)

- Date unknown, Warsaw Ghetto
- [Stanisław Różycki], Study entitled "Theater in the Ghetto" (fragment)
- Circumstances of the formation of theaters, material situation, Polish and Yiddish theater, repertoire, actors, artistic level.
- *Description:* original, handwritten manuscript (SR*), notebook, ink, Polish, 155×200 mm (58×96 mm), serious damage and losses of text, missing page 53, ss. 55, pp. 55.

b)

- Date unknown, Warsaw Ghetto
- [Stanisław Różycki], Study entitled "Coffeehouses"
- Coffeehouses, restaurants, and hotels in the Warsaw Ghetto, description of individual establishments and their clientele.
- *Description:* original, handwritten manuscript (SR*), notebook, ink, Polish, 155×200 mm, minor damage and losses of text, ss. 27, pp. 27.

  Both texts (a and b) have common pagination inserted by the text's author.

### 662. RING. I/90. Mf. ŻIH—776; USHMM—7

- Date unknown, Warsaw Ghetto
- Jonasz Turkow, Study entitled "Varshe vaylt zikh . . ." [Warsaw Has a Good Time . . .]
- Description of Jewish cultural–entertainment life in Warsaw starting from mid-1940 and until after establishment of the ghetto (organization, survey of institutions, performers, activity of the Central Events Committee [Centralnego Komitetu Imprez; headed by Turkow], aid for the needy).
- *Description:* original or transcript, typescript (handwritten manuscript additions, ink, pencil), Yiddish, 208×295 mm, ss. 18, pp. 18.

  Index: Simcha Postel [?], Diana Blumenfeld, Michał Znicz, [Edmund] Minowicz, Grodzieńska, Wiera Gran, [Dawid] Zajderman, Ajzyk Pamberg [Bamberg?], Regina Cukier, Szlomo Kutner, Ester Goldberg [Goldenberg?], I. Zylberg, Maks Bryn [Brysz?], A[braham] Kurc, Żak Lewi, E. Sztokfeder, Sz. Kohn, Simcha Rozen, Dawid Birnbaum, I. Ajzensztat, Chaim Sandler, Dawid Hamburger, Jakow Wajnberg, Chana Lewin, Roza Gazel, Roza Sandler, Josef Gajwirt, Chana Lerner, Gladsztajn, J. Fajwisz [Fajwiszys?], [Marian] Neuteich, [Adam] Furmański

### 663. RING. I/186. Mf. ŻIH—779; USHMM—10

- After 07.1941, Warsaw Ghetto
- NN., Study entitled "Fotoplastikon in geto—fun der serie: farvaylungs-erter in geto" [Fotoplastikon[37] in the Ghetto—From the Series: Places of Entertainment in the Ghetto]. Ban on entry of Jews into cinemas, opening of a photo gallery (12.04.1941, ul. Leszno 27). Series of geographical presentations: Italy, Egypt, Japan, and others. Support of Janusz Korczak, excursions of youths from the secret school classes (kompletów), financial losses. and liquidation (10.07.1941). Proprietor was Icchak Grynwald from Łódź and his wife.
- *Description:* transcript [?], handwritten manuscript (LEG*), ink, Yiddish, 150×195 mm, minor damage and losses of text, ss. 7, pp. 7.

  On p. 1 notation by H.W. in Yiddish: "4 standard pages."

  Published: *Kiddush Hashem*, pp. 132–135.

37. This was apparently a commercial photo gallery where a series of exhibits on various themes were mounted from April 12 to July 10, 1941.

**664. RING. I/341. Mf. ŻIH–781; USHMM–12**

- Date unknown, Warsaw Ghetto
- NN., Study about artistic and cultural life in the Warsaw Ghetto
- Art schools (e.g., graphic schoool at ul. Sienna 34), material situation of artists (unemployment, hunger), vocational courses.
- ***Description:*** transcript (2 copies), handwritten manuscript (Z*), pencil, Yiddish, 150×206 mm, ss. 8, pp. 8.

  Published: *Selected Documents*, 515–516.

  See HWC, 35/1 (third copy, handwritten manuscript, ss. 4).

  Index: Regina Cukier, Artur Gold, Arkadi Flato, Prof. Hirszfeld, Cwajbaum

**665. RING. I/1220/75. Mf. ŻIH–835; USHMM–47**

- Date unknown, Warsaw Ghetto
- NN., Draft program of a celebration, an evening in the Warsaw Ghetto.
- ***Description:*** original, handwritten manuscript (LEG*), pencil, Hebrew, German, 150×106 mm, ss. 1, pp. 1.

  Document written on the back of a fragment of a (ŻSS "Centos" Society Department of Social Work) "Rulebook" [for a children's 'corner'?] in the Warsaw Ghetto (Date unknown, hectographed typescript, Polish).

## *EDUCATION IN THE WARSAW GHETTO*

**666. RING. I/345. Mf. ŻIH–781; USHMM–12**

- Date unknown, Warsaw Ghetto
- "Protokol fun der tsveyter plenarer farzamlung funem yidishn shulrat in Varshe" [Minutes of the Second Plenary Gathering of the Jewish School Council in Warsaw]
- Reports of the commissions (curricular, economic, personnel, etc.). Present: Sztajn, M. Klejman, I. Silberberg, M. Tauber, M. Brandszteter, Sz. Rozenblum and Mostkow, N. Frenkel, Szapiro, L. Kac, I. Sak, I. Morgensztern. Date of the next gathering: 15 and 19.[?].[?] ul. Nowolipki 35.
- ***Description:*** transcript, typescript, Yiddish, 210×294, 210×132 mm, ss. 3, pp. 3.

  Published: *Selected Documents*, 464–467.

**667. RING. I/70. Mf. ŻIH–775; USHMM–6**

- After 10.12.1940, Warsaw Ghetto
- Engineer I. Einhorn (Warsaw, ul. Nowolipki 44, apt. 5), Study "On Private, Supplementary, and Non-School Instruction in the Jewish Area in Warsaw" (10.12.1940)
- Need to develop private and supplementary instruction, to make up for the lack of school instruction, organization and program of supplementary courses for children and adults.
- ***Description:*** transcript, typescript, Polish, 218×318 mm, minor damage and losses of text, ss. 3, pp. 3.

**668. RING. I/71. (Lb. 896). Mf. ŻIH–775; USHMM–6**

- After 05.1941, Warsaw Ghetto
- Bernard Kampelmacher, Study entitled "Contribution to an Attempt to Solve the Question of Elementary Education in the Jewish District of the City of Warsaw" (05.1941)
- Plan for organizing schools in the ghetto on the basis of apartment house committees, appointment of the School Council, educational programs, funds.
- ***Description:*** transcript (2 copies), typescript, Polish, 185×280 mm, extensive damage and losses of text, ss. 8, pp. 8,

  On p. 1 note by H.W.: "Kampel—105/1"

**669. RING. I/74. Mf. ŻIH–775; USHMM–6**

- 05.1942, Warsaw Ghetto
- NN., Study entitled "Educational System"
- Situation of the Jewish educational system in Warsaw after 09.1939 (vocational courses [from spring 1941], elementary schools [from fall 1941], secret instruction on different levels; organization, programs, fees, instructors).
- ***Description:*** original or transcript, handwritten manuscript (SR*), notebook, ink, Polish, 150×195 mm, minor damage and losses of text, ss. 28, pp. 28.

  Attached note by H.W.: "Submitted by Jakub Zylberberg."

  Published: *Selected Documents*, 500–515 (fragments).

  Index: A. Wolfowicz, former Dir. of "Chinuch" Gimnazjum, Ornsztein, Dr. Tauter, former Dir. of the State Seminary for Teachers of the Mosaic Religion, Prof. Hirschfeld, Stein, Prof. Bałaban, Tauber, Dr. Cwajbaum, assistant professor of the University of Warsaw's Medical Department, Centnerszwer, assistant professor of the Jagiellonian University, Dr. Lachs, chemist

**670. RING. I/43. Mf. ŻIH–773; USHMM–4. RING. I/1220/89. Mf. ŻIH–835; USHMM–47**

a)

- Date unknown, Warsaw Ghetto
- NN., Study entitled "Di lerershaft un shul-yugnt fun efentlekhe folks-shuln far kinder (shabesuvkes) in Varshe beeys der milkhome" [The Faculty and student body of public elementary schools for children (shabasuvkes) in Warsaw during the war]
- Jewish schools before and during the war (teachers, management of schools, organization of schools, children).

- ***Description:*** original, handwritten manuscript, notebook, ink, Yiddish, 155×195 mm, ss. 67, pp. 120.
  Addendums (preserved), with the designation "aneks" (Yiddish) and numbering in the same handwriting, in the following sequence (no item 12):
  1) Table: Jewish schools before the war (date unknown, handwritten, Yiddish, ink, 155×194 mm, ss. 1, pp. 2);
  2) table of data for 1939/40. (Date unknown, Yiddish, ink, 355×440 mm, ss. 1, pp. 1);
  3) Appeal "To the Jewish Public, sent to the Directorate of the AJDC." (Date unknown, transcript, handwritten manuscript, Polish, ink, 210×295 mm, ss. 1, pp. 1);
  4) "Memorandum" in the matter of activation of care and educational centers for Jewish children in Warsaw. (Date unknown, transcript, handwritten manuscript, Polish, ink, 210×295 mm, ss. 4, pp. 4);
  5) "Memorandum to the Council of Elders of the Jews at the Jewish Community in Warsaw sent to Chairman engineer [Adam] Czerniaków." (Date unknown, transcript, handwritten manuscript, Polish, ink, 210×295 mm, ss. 3, pp. 3);
  6) Letter from a House Committee to the Jewish Council (date unknown, handwritten, ink, Polish, 49×155 mm, ss. 1, pp. 1);
  7) Secretariat of the Sponsors Committee of Former Public Elementary Schools for Jewish Children (Warsaw, ul. Fredry 10, offices of Centos), "Materiał in the Matter of Organization of Schools." (Contains a list of school premises withing the boundaries of the Warsaw Ghetto) (after 15.11.1940, original or transcript, typescript, Polish, 208×295 mm, ss. 4, pp. 4);
  8) two addendums: a) Minutes of the organizational meeting of the School Council for Jewish schools in Warsaw. (undated, but before 8.12.[. . .]), transcript, typescript, Yiddish, 208×297 mm, ss. 2, pp. 2.); b) "Plan of the School Council for Jewish schools in Warsaw." (Date unknown, original or transcript, typescript, Polish, 208×265 mm, ss. 1, pp. 1);
  9) "Memorandum to the Chairman of the Council of Elders at the Jewish Community in Warsaw." (missing ending?). (Date unknown, transcript, typescript, Polish, 210×294 mm, ss. 1, pp. 1);
  10) Memorandum in the matter of organization of care and vocational education for Jewish children and youth in Warsaw (attached "Proposal for care for children and Jew[ish] youth" in educational circles). (Original or transcript, handwritten manuscript, Polish, ink, 210×296 mm, ss. 2, pp. 2);
  11) Memorandum addressed "To the Chairman of the Jewish Council in Warsaw" in the matter of activation of schools. (transcript, handwritten manuscript, Polish, ink, 210×296 mm, ss. 2, pp. 2);
  13) Page from a study concerning schools (statistical data, tables). (Original, mimeographed typescript, Yiddish, 208×295 mm, ss. 1, pp. 1.);
  Attached without a number: Secretariat of the Council of Jewish Schools in Warsaw. Circular letter dated 19.12.1940 with information about the establishment of a School Council in Warsaw (attached list of organizations entering into the composition of the Council). (Transcript, typescript, Yiddish, 210×295 mm, ss. 1, pp. 1)
  Addenda no. 4, 5, 10, 11 are written in a single handwriting.
  Inventory: "Work of J. Silberberg."

b) **Ring. I/1220/2**
- Date unknown, Warsaw Ghetto
- "Memorandum in the matter of organization of Jewish schools in Warsaw for the school year 19[. . .]"
- Organization of schools, budget, list of school buildings with the number of rooms.
- ***Description:*** transcript, typescript, Polish, 222×284, 222× 256 mm, damage and losses of text, ss. 2, pp. 2.

## 671. RING. I/604. (Lb. 99). Mf. ŻIH—812; USHMM—24

- 1942, Warsaw Ghetto
- [Marian Małowist], Plan for a Study concerning the situation of Jewish secondary education during the war
- State of Jewish secondary education at the moment of the war's outbreak; the school issue in autumn 1939; beginnings of clandestine teaching; education in the Warsaw Ghetto: school year 1940/1941 and 1941/1942.
- ***Description:*** original, handwritten manuscript (MM*), ink, Polish, 160×195, 195×234 mm, ss. 2, pp. 4.
  Published: *Selected Documents*, 491–493.

## 672. RING. I/38. (Lb. 1562). Mf. ŻIH—773; USHMM—4. RING. I/69, I/72. Mf. ŻIH—775; USHMM—6

a) **Ring. I/38**
- Date unknown, Warsaw
- [Marian Małowist], Report about the Interests and Attitudes of Polish and Jewish Youth before the war and during the occupation
- Author was a history teacher in secondary schools in Warsaw. Profile of the attitudes of school youth: lack of broader interests, particularly humanistic, low intellectual level, strong influence of the current political situation (e.g., fascistic tendencies, rise of antisemitism), secondary school is a means for making a career and acquisition of a well-paid profession, interest in learning in school during the

occupation, situation of assimilated Jewish youth, general moral deterioration and depravity.

- ***Description:*** transcript (2 copies), handwritten manuscript (JG*), Polish, 115×207 mm, ss. 26, pp. 26.
  On p. 1 notation by H.W.: "[H? Małow?]ist."
  Attached note by R.S.: Prof. Marian Małowist confirmed authorship of this text, but was not certain who transcribed his text.
  Published: *Selected Documents*, 493–499 (fragment); *Polin*, vol. 13 (2000), pp. 147–162.

b) **Ring. I/69. (Lb. 691)**

- Date unknown, Warsaw Ghetto
- [Marian Małowist], Study about secret instruction of Jewish youth during the occupation (1939–1941)
- Jewish school system in autumn 1939, clandestine study groups, educational programs, changes in organization of instruction after sealing of the ghetto, material situation of the teachers.
- ***Description:*** transcript (2 copies), typescript, Polish, 210×295 mm, ss. 16, pp. 16,
  Published: *Polin*, vol. 13 (2000), pp. 153–158.

c) **Ring. I/72**

- 1941, Warsaw
- Marian Małowist, Fragment of a Study about the Jewish educational system in Warsaw before the war and during the occupation
- Problems of Jewish education before 1939, working conditions and material situation of teachers, educational system at the start of the occupation.
- ***Description:*** original, handwritten manuscript (MM*), pencil, Polish, 237×224, 220×345 mm, extensive damage and losses of text, ss. 6, pp. 10.
  It seems that the manuscript was a rough draft of a larger work, part II, entitled "Autumn 1939" in part similar to the text from Ring. I/69, but does not correspond with it; on p. 3 the author refers to a Study from Ring. I/38.
  Attached two notes: a) H.W.: "1941 Warsaw. Prepared by a coworker of the Archive, historian Dr. Małowist"; b) typescript: "Observations of H. Wasser, MA: Fragment of a work on Jewish education during the occupation in the ghetto. Forwarded by Jakub Zylberberg. 1940 Warsaw."
  Published: *Polin*, vol. 13 (2000), pp. 158–162.

## 673. RING. I/1064 (1383). Mf. ŻIH—832; USHMM—44

- 05.1941, Warsaw Ghetto
- Three compositions by children (Chaim Gluzsztejn [Glicsztejn, Gluzsztajn ?], Heniek Zygielman, and NN.) devoted to the celebration in honor of Icchak Lejb Perec (Isaac Leibush Peretz), which took place on 24.05.1941 in Warsaw (ul. Tłomackie 5). (28.05., 30.05.1941, date unknown)
- Speakers at the celebration: [Szachno] Zagan (Efroim Sagan), [Menachem] Linder, [Izrael] Lichtensztajn; there were performances by a choir, a dance group, and the singers [Sabina] Szyfman and Sorełe.
- ***Description:*** original, handwritten manuscript (three handwritings), ink, Yiddish, 210×230 mm, ss. 3, pp. 3.
  Published: *Dzieci*, pp. 83–87; *Selected Documents*, 445–446 (composition of Chaim Gluzsztejn [Gluzsztajn]).

## 674. RING. I/332. Mf. ŻIH—781; USHMM—12

- After 06.1941, Warsaw Ghetto
- Kitchen-school no. 145 (Warsaw, ul. Nowolipki 68), Reports of the children's council and pupils' compositions
- Organization and program of instruction, reports of various ceremonies, provision of food, teachers, reports of the committee of pupil self-government, school compositions. Authors of texts: E. Rozenblum, Charo, Sala Liliensztejn, Estera Honigsztok, Zelik Kryształ, Jankiel Frajnd, Cyrla Cymerman, Dora Błaszka, Złata Nadel, Estera Goldwaser, P. Jedwab, Frajda Sznajderman, Cymerman, Estera Frojnt, Motel Sznajderman, Rochenszwalb, Estera Nadel.
- ***Description:*** transcript, handwritten manuscript, notebook, ink, Polish, Yiddish, 155×190 mm, extensive damage and losses of text, ss. 26, pp. 25.
  Attached note by H.W. in Yiddish: "Forwarded by Izrael Lichtensztejn 1941."
  Published: *BFG*, vol. XXVIII (1990), pp. 18–27; *Dzieci*, pp. 88–107.

## 675. RING. I/1067 (1386). (Lb. 1117). Mf. ŻIH—832; USHMM—44

a)

- 07.1941, Warsaw Ghetto
- Heniek Zygielman, School compositions (2). (22.07., 30.07.1941)
- Concerning Germany's invasion of the USSR.
- ***Description:*** original, handwritten manuscript, ink, Yiddish, 135×155, 150×193 mm, minor damage and losses of text, ss. 2, pp. 3.
  Published: *Dzieci*, pp. 108–109, 110–111.

b)

- After 23.06.1941, Warsaw Ghetto
- Chaim Gluzsztejn [Glicsztejn ?], School composition about the German invasion of the USSR
- ***Description:*** original, handwritten manuscript, ink, Yiddish, 150×193 mm, minor damage and losses of text, ss. 1, pp. 1.
  Published: *Dzieci*, pp. 109 and 112.

c)

- After 23.06.1941, Warsaw Ghetto
- NN., School composition about the German invasion of the USSR
- ***Description:*** original, handwritten manuscript, ink, Yiddish, 251×200 mm, minor damage and losses of text, ss. 1, pp. 1.
  At the bottom is information (pencil) in Yiddish

in a different handwriting: "Tyzan Major [Meir?]"
Published: *Dzieci*, pp. 109 and 113.

### 676. RING. I/39. Mf. ŻIH—836; USHMM—67

- After 09.1941, Warsaw Ghetto.
- Responses to a questionnaire (entitled "What Changes Have Occurred among Us during the War?") by children of the boarding and day school (półinternat) in the Warsaw Ghetto at ul. Nowolipki 25. (09.1941)
- Recollections from the prewar period, of war and occupation, about their own experiences and those of their immediate family (children: H. Włodawer, M. Rubinsztein, Beniek Fryligsztejn, Jozue Gedalia Perlmutter, Cyrla Lajfer, Rozenblum Chana, Tadek Fruchtgarten, Fela Brzezińska, G. [Giela] Najman, Minia Mędra, Józef Kantorowicz, Pachucka, Beła Dymlecht, Fajga Blut, Cyla Rozenblum, B. Sztajman, Abram Brajtman, Estera Rudek, Z. Szejnberg, Chana Gluzman, Fajga Łazewnik, Chaja Perelman, Mania Salomończyk, Sz. J. Seluńczyk, L. Bakauer, Andzia Baranek, Aron Zajdner, Hela Gestel, Sonia Lerer, Szlama Zalewas, Hela Goldzand, Gitla Szulcman, Rywka Zelcer, Beniek Fredler).
- ***Description:*** transcript (3 copies), handwritten manuscript (JC*), Polish, pencil, 145×210 mm, missing pages 10–37 (three copies), ss. 83, pp. 83.

Except for the statements of Mania Salomończyk and Sz. J. Seluńczyk of 18.09. and Beniek Fredler of 19.09, all of the rest were written on 2.09.1941
Attached note by H.W.: "The children writing were probably instructed by Genia Sylkes"; and attached list of names of several children (as above) of the day school at ul. Nowolipki 25.
Published: *Dzieci*, pp. 3–45; (fragments) *Dwa etapy*, pp. 97–100.

### 677. RING. I/1065 (1384). Mf. ŻIH—832; USHMM—44

- [1941]-1942, Warsaw Ghetto
- Bergman, Kon and NN., Compositions entitled "Ma anakhnu roim ba-rehov?" [What Do We See in the Street?] (27.12.[1941], 1.06.1942)
- Image of the Warsaw Ghetto street with the eyes of children.
- ***Description:*** original, handwritten manuscript, three handwritings, ink, Hebrew, Polish, 140×85, 153×195 mm, damage and losses of text, ss. 3, pp. 3.

Doc. a) NN. dated 27.12.[1941], Polish; b) [Ja]fa Bergman (age 14) dated 1.06.1942, Hebrew; c) Kon (age 14) dated 1.06.1942, Hebrew. Children's age and dates (docs. b and c) and author's name (doc. c) written in a different handwriting (LEG*[?], pencil).
Published: *Dzieci*, pp. 119–122.

### 678. RING. I/44. Mf. ŻIH—773; USHMM—4

- After 04.1942, Warsaw Ghetto
- Collection of children's statements about occupation experiences
- Responses to a survey of children: Chil Brajtman, Zanwel Krigsman, Luba Glicensztejn, Bajla Grinberg, Izrael Lederman, Hejnoch Jarzębski, Sara Widawska, Sara Sborow [?].
- ***Description:*** transcript, handwritten manuscript, ink, Polish, 201×324, 206×323 mm, ss. 8, pp. 10.

Responses recorded by NN. Several sheets (1, 7, and 8) of the manuscript are written on the back of judicial forms ("Summons in the matter of a writ from a bill of exchange in the proceeding of art. 462 of the K.P.C." [Pozew w przedmiocie nakazu z weks. w trybie art. 462 K.P.C.] (before 1939, typescript, Polish).
Published: *Dzieci*, pp. 46–60; (fragments) *Dwa etapy*, pp. 137–139.

### 679. RING. I/1066 (1385). Mf. ŻIH—832; USHMM—44

- Date unknown, Warsaw Ghetto
- Abrasza, Composition entitled "My War Experiences"
- A boy's recollections of September 1939.
- ***Description:*** original, handwritten manuscript, ink, Polish, 112×245 mm, ss. 1, pp. 2.

On p. 1 notation : "Written by Abrasza" and lower (in a different handwriting, pencil): "He wrote at home, ended up in the orphanage."
Published: *Dzieci*, pp. 63–64.

### 680. RING. I/305. (Lb. 572, 582). Mf. ŻIH—781; USHMM—12

a)

- Date unknown, Warsaw Ghetto
- Hanka Zaksenhaus, School composition entitled "Our School."
- ***Description:*** original, handwritten manuscript, ink, Polish, 140×204 mm, ss. 2, pp. 2.

Published: *Dzieci*, pp. 114, 116.

b) (Lb. 572)

- After 06.1940, Warsaw Ghetto
- Estera Gluzman, School compositions entitled: "Already June" and "Recollection from the Period of the Last War"
- The bombardment of Warsaw 25.09.1939, expedition for bread.
- ***Description:*** original, handwritten manuscript, ink, Polish, 154×195 mm, ss. 2, pp. 3.

Published: *Dzieci*, pp. 115, 118.

c) (Lb. 582)

- Date unknown, Warsaw Ghetto
- Łaja Efrajmowicz, School composition entitled "How the Displacement Looked among Us"

• Fate of a Jewish community from an unknown locality in the vicinity of Warsaw.
• *Description:* original, handwritten manuscript, ink, Polish, 143×200 mm, minor damage and losses of text, ss. 1, pp. 1.
Inventory and attached note by H.W. in Polish, Yiddish: "Compositions of a girl pupil from the school-kitchen at ul. Nowolipki 68, forwarded by Izrael Lichtensztajn."
Published: *Selected Documents*, 485–487; *Dzieci*, pp. 114, 117.

### 681. RING. I/1068 (1387). Mf. ŻIH—832; USHMM—44

• Date unknown, Warsaw Ghetto
• NN., Class schedule (fragment)
• Schedule decorated with colorful illustrations.
• *Description:* original, handwritten manuscript, pencil, Hebrew, Yiddish, 353×218 mm, serious damage and losses of text, ss. 1, pp. 1.
Published: *Dzieci*, pp. 263.

### 682. RING. I/603. Mf. ŻIH—836; USHMM—67

• 1942, Warsaw Ghetto
• [Natan Smolar, Beniamin Wirowski], "Yidish-heft farn dritn lernyor" [Yiddish Workbook for the Third Grade], 1942
• Textbook, selections from world literature, poetry.
• *Description:* original, hectographed typescript, Yiddish, 210×290 mm, minor damage and losses of text, ss. 20, pp. 39
Published: *BFG*, vol. XXVIII/1990, pp. 28–59; *Dzieci*, pp. 304–357.

## *PHOTOGRAPHS FROM THE WARSAW GHETTO*

### 683. RING. I/1222. (Lb. 1297–1372).

• Date unknown, after 1946, Warsaw Ghetto, Warsaw
• Collection of photographs of the Warsaw Ghetto
The collection underwent dispersion after 1946 (see Prof. Epsztein's essay), but the original descriptions on the photographs were not preserved; therefore, the photographs were arranged and described on the basis of the 1946 list. Part of the photographs survived as original prints made in the Warsaw Ghetto, while others are exclusively in copies made after 1946, and some have been lost.
1) (Lb. 1297) "Construction of the wall at the tobacco shop on Dzielna."
• *Description:* original missing. The Photography Collections of ŻIH contain a copy from the collections of the Ghetto Fighters Kibbutz in Israel.
2) (Lb. 1298) "Street traffic in the ghetto before displacement."
• *Description:* original missing. ŻIH has a postwar copy. According to Jan Jagielski, the photograph shows a fragment of ul. Lubecki on the side of ul. Gęsia in the direction of ul. Pawia.
3) (Lb. 1299) "Chairman Czerniaków with the girl rescued from among eight Jews executed by firing squad, who had left the ghetto without permission (nearby, the mother of the rescued girl and a small group of people)."
• *Description:* original missing. There is a postwar copy at ŻIH. According to Jan Jagielski, the photograph dates to 11.03.1942 and shows Adam Czerniaków after freeing of 151 people from the prison at ul. Gęsia 24. (Third from left is Czerniaków, ninth is Winter.)
4) (Lb. 1300) "Allocation of bread."
• *Description:* original photograph, 125×178 mm, loose, ss. 1, pp. 1.
• The photograph is at ŻIH. According to Jan Jagielski, it dates to 11.03.1942 and shows a group of women released from the prison at ul. Gęsia 24 thanks to Adam Czerniaków's intervention (see photographs 3, 5 [Lb. 1299, 1301]).
5) (Lb. 1301) "A small group of women."
• *Description:* original, photograph, 118×179 mm, loose, ss. 1, pp. 1.
• The photograph is at ŻIH. According to Jan Jagielski, it dates to 11.03.1942 and shows a group of women released from the prison at ul. Gęsia 24 thanks to Adam Czerniaków's intervention (see photographs 3, 4 [Lb. 1299, 1300]).
6) (Lb. 1302) "A group on the street listens to radio (German propaganda loudspeaker)."
• *Description:* original, photograph, 123×178 mm, loose, ss. 1, pp. 1.
• The photograph is at ŻIH. According to Jan Jagielski, it dates to 11.03.1942 and shows a group of people waiting for the departure of 151 prisoners from the Central Prison at ul. Gęsia 24.
7) (Lb. 1303). "Order Service 'looks after' children."
• *Description:* missing original.
• ŻIH has a postwar print. According to Jan Jagielski, the photograph dates to 11.03.1942 and shows a group of people released from the Central Prison at ul. Gęsia 24. (See photograph 6 [Lb. 1302]).
8) (Lb. 1304) "Women standing in a line."
• *Description:* missing original.
9) (Lb. 1305) "People listen to radio communiqués (propaganda loudspeakers) on the street."
• *Description:* original, photograph, 120×175 mm, loose, ss. 1, pp. 1.
• The photograph is at ŻIH. According to Jan Jagielski, the photograph dates to 11.03.1942 and shows a group of people waiting for the departure of 151 prisoners from the Central Prison at ul. Gęsia 24. (See photograph 6 [Lb. 1302]).
10) (Lb. 1306) "Digging up potatoes."
• *Description:* original, photograph, 123×168 mm, loose, ss. 1, pp. 1.

- The photograph is at ŻIH. See Lb. 1328.

11) (Lb. 1307) "Smugglers toss sacks of flour over the wall."
- *Description:* missing original.
- ŻIH has a postwar print.

12) (Lb. 1308) "Jew[ish] order guard conducts a search of children 'smuggling' food into the ghetto."
- *Description:* original, photograph, 120×179 mm, loose, ss. 1, pp. 1.
- The photograph is at ŻIH. According to Jan Jagielski, the photograph shows the examination of little smugglers in front of the Central Prison at ul. Gęsia 24 in the presence of Adam Czerniaków.

13) (Lb. 1309) "A Jew working in a hothouse."
- *Description:* original, photograph, 122×165 mm, loose, ss. 1, pp. 1.
- The photograph is at ŻIH.

14) (Lb. 1310) "Women greedily eat 'issued' bread."
- *Description:* missing original.
- ŻIH has a postwar copy.

15) (Lb. 1311) "Tossing of smuggled flour over the wall."
- *Description:* missing original.
- ŻIH has a postwar copy.
- See Lb. 1307.

16) (Lb. 1312) "Ord[er] guard with Chairman Czerniaków and Polish police."
- *Description:* original, photograph, 121×175 mm, loose, ss. 1, pp. 1. In the lower left corner is a stamp impression: "foto/forber/Warszawa".
- The photograph is at ŻIH. According to Jan Jagielski, Adam Czerniaków and the leadership of the Order Service during an inspection conducted by the commandant of the navy blue police Col. Aleksander Reszczyński, who was later killed by the Gwardia Ludowa (People's Guard).
- See Lb. 1315, 1354.

17) (Lb. 1313) "Jewish children devastated by hunger in the ghetto."
- *Description:* missing original.
- ŻIH has a postwar copy.

18) (Lb. 1314) "Feeding poultry."
- *Description:* missing original.
- ŻIH has a copy from the collection of the Ghetto Fighters' Kibbutz in Israel.

19) (Lb. 1315) "Order guard with Chairman Czerniaków."
- *Description:* missing original.
- ŻIH has a postwar copy.
- See Lb. 1312, 1354.

20) (Lb. 1316) "Artificial incubator for poultry."
- *Description:* missing original.
- ŻIH has a postwar copy.

21) (Lb. 1317) "Obituaries."
- *Description:* original, photograph, 112×172 mm, loose, ss. 1, pp. 1.
- In ŻIH Photographic Archive.
- According to Jan Jagielski, the photograph was taken on ul. Karmelicka.

22) (Lb. 1318) "Order guard and Polish police."
- *Description:* missing original.

23) (Lb. 1319) "In the nursery."
- *Description:* missing original.
- ŻIH Photographic Archive has a postwar copy.

24) (Lb. 1320) "Ord[er] guard brings a crowd under control."
- *Description:* original, photograph, 123×179 mm, loose, ss. 1, pp. 1.
- Photograph is in the ŻIH Photographic Archive.
- According to Jan Jagielski the photograph was taken on the grounds of the Central Prison at ul. Gęsia 24.

25) (Lb. 1321) "Ord[er] guard unit."
- *Description:* original, photograph, 121×175 mm, loose, damages, ss. 1, pp. 1. In the lower right corner is the impression of a stamp: "foto/forber/Warszawa".
- Photograph is in the ŻIH Photographic Archive.
- See Lb. 1322, 1365, 1366, 1367, 1368.

26) (Lb. 1322) "Jewish policemen."
- *Description:* original, photograph, 84×146 mm, loose, ss. 1, pp. 2. On the back are traces of the stamp of the Foto Forbert photographic studio.
- Photograph is in the ŻIH Photographic Archive.
- According to Jan Jagielski, the photograph presents a unit of the Jewish Ambulance Service.

27) (Lb. 1323) "Wedding of Jew[ish] journalist Halina Zuckermann with a musician."
- *Description:* original, photograph, 116x164 mm, loose, ss. 1, pp. 1.
- Photograph is in the ŻIH Photographic Archive.

28) (Lb. 1324) "Ghetto wall at Elektoralna Street."
- *Description:* missing original.
- ŻIH has a postwar copy.

29) (Lb. 1325) "Obituaries."
- *Description:* original, photograph, 110×170 mm, loose, ss. 1, pp. 1.
- Photograph is in the ŻIH Photographic Archive.
- According to Jan Jagielski, the photograph was taken on ul. Karmelicka.
- See Lb. 1317.

30) (Lb. 1326) "Ruins on Twarda Street."
- *Description:* missing original.
- ŻIH has a postwar copy.
- See Lb. 1332.

31) (Lb. 1327) "Digging up potatoes."
- *Description:* original, photograph, 126×169 mm, loose, ss. 1, pp. 1.
- Photograph is in the ŻIH Photographic Archive.
- According to Jan Jagielski, the photograph was taken on the field near the cemetery on ul. Okopowa.

32) (Lb. 1328) "Collection of potatoes."
- *Description:* original, photograph, 122×164 mm, loose, ss. 1, pp. 1.
- Photograph is in the ŻIH Photographic Archive.

33) (Lb. 1329) "Jewish child at the ghetto's wall."

• *Description:* missing original.
• ŻIH has a postwar copy.

34) (Lb. 1330) "Bridge on Chłodna Street."
• *Description:* missing original.
• ŻIH has a postwar copy.

35) (Lb. 1331) "Gate to the cemetery."
• *Description:* original, photograph, 127×173 mm, loose, ss. 1, pp. 1.
• Photograph is in the ŻIH Photographic Archive.
• According to Jan Jagielski, it shows the cemetery gate on ul. Okopowa, looking from ul. Gęsia. Beyond the gate is visible the mortuary building that was destroyed in 1943 together with the Great Synagogue on Tłomackie Street.

36) (Lb. 1332) "Ruins at Twarda Street [5]."
• *Description:* original, photograph, 123×179 mm, loose, ss. 1, pp. 1.
• Photograph is in the ŻIH Photographic Archive.
• See Lb. 1326.

37) (Lb. 1333) "Gate at Plac Grzybowski."
• *Description:* original, photograph, 125×175 mm, loose, ss. 1, pp. 1.
• Photograph is in the ŻIH Photographic Archive.
• According to Jan Jagielski, shows the entrance to the ghetto at Pl. Grzybowski.

38) (Lb. 1334) "Wall on Przejazd."
• *Description:* missing original.
• ŻIH has a postwar copy.

39) (Lb. 1335) "Fence with barbed wire on Żelazna Street."
• *Description:* missing original.
• ŻIH has a postwar copy.

40) (Lb. 1336) "Mothers taking their children out 'for a stroll.'"
• *Description:* original, photograph, 107×174 mm, loose, ss. 1, pp. 1.
• Photograph is in the ŻIH Photographic Archive.

41) (Lb. 1337) "Distribution of soup."
• *Description:* missing original.
• ŻIH has a postwar copy.

42) (Lb. 1338) "Ruins on Pańska Street."
• *Description:* missing original.
• ŻIH has a postwar copy.

43) (Lb. 1339) "Ruins on Twarda Street."
• *Description:* missing original.

44) (Lb. 1340) "Trade on Miła Street."
• *Description:* original, photograph, 114×153 mm, loose, ss. 1, pp. 1.
• Photograph is in the ŻIH Photographic Archive.

45) (Lb. 1341) "Iron gate on Chłodna Street."
• *Description:* original, photograph, 127×173 mm, loose, ss. 1, pp. 1.
• Photograph is in the ŻIH Photographic Archive.
• According to Jan Jagielski, shows the passage along ul. Chłodna (corner ul. Żelazna) from the small to the large ghetto. In the building on the right side (that still exists) was a German police guardpost.

46) (Lb. 1342) "Ruins along Muranowska Street."
• *Description:* missing original.

47) (Lb. 1343) "Germans remove bricks from Nowolipki Street."
• *Description:* missing original.

48) (Lb. 1344) "Matsa for the holiday in the ghetto."
• *Description:* original, photograph, 121×168 mm, loose, ss. 1, pp. 1.
• Photograph is in the ŻIH Photographic Archive.

49) (Lb. 1345) "Courtyard in front of the K.S.P. [Order Service HQ, ul. Ogrodowa 17]"
• *Description:* original, photograph, 129×160 mm, loose, ss. 1, pp. 1.
• Photograph is in the ŻIH Photographic Archive.

50) (Lb. 1346) "Wall on Bonifraterska Street."
• *Description:* original, photograph, 123×172 mm, loose, ss. 1, pp. 1.
• Photograph is in the ŻIH Photographic Archive.

51) (Lb. 1347) "Line of vehicles (rickshaws) on Żelazna Street."
• *Description:* original, photograph, 121×154 mm, loose, ss. 1, pp. 1.
• Photograph is in the ŻIH Photographic Archive.
• According to Jan Jagielski, a line of rickshaws waiting before the entrance to the gate at the corner of ul. Żelazna and Chłodna.

52) (Lb. 1348) "Ban on walking on Bagno."
• *Description:* missing original.

53) (Lb. 1349) "Barbed wire on Waliców and Krochmalna."
• *Description:* original, photograph, 125×166 mm, loose, ss. 1, pp. 1.
• Photograph is in the ŻIH Photographic Archive.

54) (Lb. 1350) "Wire entanglements on ul. Wielka."
• *Description:* missing original.
• ŻIH has a copy from the collection of the Ghetto Fighters' Kibbutz in Israel.

55) (Lb. 1351) "Collection for winter aid."
• *Description:* missing original.
• ŻIH has a postwar copy.

56) (Lb. 1352) "Trade at 'Gęsiówka.'"
• *Description:* missing original.
• See 1355.

57) (Lb. 1353) "Karmelicka Street."
• *Description:* original, photograph, 113×166 mm, loose, ss. 1, pp. 1.
• Photograph is in the ŻIH Photographic Archive.

58) (Lb. 1354) "Chairman Czerniaków among Polish and Jewish policemen."
• *Description:* original, photograph, 120×174 mm, loose, ss. 1, pp. 1.
• Photograph is in the ŻIH Photographic Archive.
• According to Jan Jagielski, Adam Czerniaków is shown among members of the Order Service and the State Police on the courtyard of the Jewish Community building at ul. Grzybowska 26/28.

- See Lb. 1312, 1315.

59) (Lb. 1355) "Market at 'Gęsiówka.'"
- *Description:* original, photograph, 125×178 mm, loose, ss. 1, pp. 1.
- Photograph is in the ŻIH Photographic Archive.
- See 1352.

60) (Lb. 1356) "Demolition of walls on Ciepła."
- *Description:* missing original.
- ŻIH has a postwar copy.

61) (Lb. 1357) "Ban on walking on Sienna."
- *Description:* missing original.

62) (Lb. 1358) "Żelazna Brama and Grzybowska"
- *Description:* original, photograph, 116×179 mm, loose, ss. 1, pp. 1.
- Photograph is in the ŻIH Photographic Archive.
- According to Jan Jagielski, shows the gate to the ghetto at ul. Żelazna and Grzybowska.

63) (Lb. 1359) "Jew[ish] child begging near the wall."
- *Description:* missing original.
- ŻIH has a postwar copy.

64) (Lb. 1360) "Trade on Miła (fodder beets)."
- *Description:* missing original.
- ŻIH has a postwar copy.

65) (Lb. 1361) "Collection of cabbage."
- *Description:* original, photograph, 118×167 mm, loose, minor damage, ss. 1, pp. 1. In the lower right corner impression of a stamp: "foto/forber/warszawa."
- Photograph is in the ŻIH Photographic Archive.

66) (Lb. 1362) "Jewish store in the ghetto."
- *Description:* original, photograph, 113×156 mm, loose, ss. 1, pp. 1.
- Photograph is in the ŻIH Photographic Archive.

67) (Lb. 1363) "Jewish children in the ghetto."
- *Description:* missing original.
- ŻIH has a postwar copy.

68) (Lb. 1364) "Naked Jewish children ravaged by hunger in the Wars[aw] Ghetto."
- *Description:* missing original.
- ŻIH has a postwar copy.

69) (Lb. 1365) "Order Service in Wars[aw] ghetto, O.D. [Ordnungsdienst]"
- *Description:* original, photograph, 118×169 mm, loose, ss. 1, pp. 1.
- Photograph is in the ŻIH Photographic Archive.

70) (Lb. 1366) "Order Service in Wars[aw] gh[etto], O.D. [Ordnungsdienst]"
- *Description:* missing original.

71) (Lb. 1367) "Order Service O.D. [Ordnungs-dienst]"
- *Description:* missing original.

72) (Lb. 1368) "Order Service O.D. [Ordnungs-dienst]"
- *Description:* missing original.

73) (Lb. 1369) "Gathering potatoes."
- *Description:* original, photograph, 122×168 mm, loose, ss. 1, pp. 1.
- Photograph is in the ŻIH Photographic Archive.

74) (Lb. 1370) "A Jew[ish] woman worn out by hunger in the Wars[aw] Gh[etto]"
- *Description:* missing original.

75) (Lb. 1371) "Rivals [Zawodnicy] (prewar photogr[aph]) with later [member of] O.D. [Ordnungsdienst] Rotholz."
- *Description:* missing original, 80×130 mm (dimensions according to the 1946 list.

76) (Lb. 1372) "Hospital on Czyste."
- *Description:* original, photograph, 80×55 mm, loose, ss. 1, pp. 2. On the reverse a notation (handwritten—H.W.*, ink): "Typical picture of the hospital at 'Czyste'-Stawki, November 1941."
- Photograph is in the ŻIH Photographic Archive.

## IV. Materials on the History of Jewish Communities outside Warsaw

### 684. RING. I/789 (1108). Mf. ŻIH—826; USHMM—38

After the beginning of 1941, Warsaw Ghetto [Daniel Fligelman?], Account entitled "From Aleksandrów [Kujawski] to Warsaw (Aleksandrów-Łowicz)"

Author, resident of Aleksandrów, describes flight from the town (3.09.1939), massacre on Yom Kippur (23.09.) in Włocławek, plunder of Jewish property in Aleksandrów, [forced] contribution, destruction of the synagogue, escape in 11.1939 to Kutno, then to Łowicz, formation of the ghetto in Łowicz (05.1940), labor camp in Józefów and displacement from Łowicz in spring 1941.

- *Description:* original (handwritten manuscript—FLIG*, ink, 224×354 mm, damage and losses of text, text illegible in places), transcript (typescript, 208×296 mm, damage and losses of text), Polish, ss. 24, pp. 28.

On p. 1 notation by H.W. (ink): "Fligar."

Published: BŻIH, no. 137–138 (1986), pp. 174–181 (fragment).

See HWC, 2/7 (two copies of typed transcript, ss. 19).

Index: Jakubowski (Aleksandrów Kujawski, ul. Słowackiego), Izbicki (Aleksandrów Kujawski, ul. Słowackiego), Fligelman (Aleksandrów Kujawski, ul. Piłsudskiego 21), Szczeciński, (Aleksandrów Kujawski, ul. Piłsudskiego 23), Frydman and his wife from Aleksandrów Kujawski, perished during the bombardments in 09.1939, Sz. Wigder of Aleksandrów Kujawski, perished during the bombardments in 09.1939, M. Rozenfeld of Aleksandrów Kujawski, perished during the bombardments in 09.1939, Buchner of Jewish Council in Łowicz, Zylberman of Jewish Council in Łowicz, Atłas, Szapiro, chairman of the Jewish Council in Łowicz, D. Brand of Jewish Council in Łowicz, A. Urbach of Jewish Council in Łowicz, Miedziński, manager of the Committee for Aid to Refugees and the Poor in Łowicz, I. Natan, of the Order Service in Łowicz, Fefer of Łódź, Jakubowska, Schafrick, appointed mayor in Aleksandrów, Ritterski, mayor in Aleksandrów

**685. RING. I/566. (Lb. 945). Mf. ŻIH—792; USHMM—23; RING. I/599/94. Mf. ŻIH—812; USHMM—24**

- After 11.03.1942, Warsaw Ghetto
- NN. (Sala) (Aleksandrów Kujawski), Letter of 11.03.1942 to Luteczka [Luta?] (sister of the author of the letter) (Warsaw Ghetto)
- Husband and son of the author are in a labor camp; information about the approaching annihilation.
- ***Description:*** Ring. I/599/94—transcript (with clarifications by the copyist), handwritten manuscript (FLIG*), ink, Polish, 206×295 mm, serious damage and losses of text, text illegible in places, ss. 1, pp. 1; Ring. I/566—transcript (from Ring. I/599/94) (2 copies), typescript, Polish, 202×224 mm, damage and losses of text, ss. 2, pp. 2.

  At the top, information from the copyist: "Copy of the letter that arrived in the middle of March from Aleksandrów Kujawski. The sender writes to her sister." At the bottom a notation: "The parents of the sender, like her son Izuś, are long dead."

  Published: *Listy o Zagładzie*, pp. 71–73.

  Index: Landsman, Sied, Jakub Kac of Siedliszcze nad Wieprzem, Dudkiewicz

**686. RING. I/788 (1107). (Lb. 328). Mf. ŻIH—826; USHMM—38**

- After 25.04.1941, Warsaw Ghetto
- NN., Account entitled "Di gesheyenishn in Aleksander-Lodzher" [The events in Aleksandrów-Łódzki] (25.04.1941)
- Description of events preceding war's outbreak (arrests on 10.08.1939 of prominent Germans), September 1939, entry of the Germans (6.09.1939), start of the occupation, burning of the synagogue (8.09.1939), plundering and murder of Jews, [forced] contributions and requisitions, arrests among Jews and Poles, expulsion of the entire Jewish population (4,000) from the town to Głowno (27.12.1939).
- ***Description:*** transcript (2 copies), handwritten manuscript (BW*), pencil, Yiddish, 148×210 mm, ss. 10, pp. 10.

  In the margins a symbol (ink, green): "√."

  Document was kept in a binder.

**687. RING. I/436. Mf. ŻIH—785; USHMM—16**

- Date unknown, Warsaw Ghetto
- NN., Account entitled "Stu dziesięciu" [Hundred Tenth]
- Preparation for shootings and execution at the Women's Synagogue (pod Babicami) of 110 Jews (100 prisoners from the "Gęsiówka," among others Orlikówna and Komorowska, and 10 Order Service members).
- ***Description:*** original or transcript, typescript (handwritten additions, ink, pencil), Polish, 210×294 mm, extensive minor damage and losses of text, ss. 7, pp. 7.

  On p. 1 notation by H.W. in Yiddish (ink): "7 standard pages."

  Index: "Frankenstein," "schupowiec" [security policeman, Schupo], Dr. Adler, Ignacy Sterling, musician

**688. RING. I/258. (Lb. 1700). Mf. ŻIH—780; USHMM—11**

- After 9.08.1941, place unknown
- Srul Wajnberg, Letter of 9.08.1941 to Special Court in Warsaw (Brühl Palace)
- Appeal of verdict of 1.02.1941 in the matter of not wearing armband with star of Zion on the grounds of a factory in Baczki (community of Łochów).
- ***Description:*** transcript (2 copies), typescript, German, 205×285 mm, damage and losses of text (second copy), ss. 2, pp. 4.

  Attached note by H.W. in Yiddish.

  Inventory: "Submitted to the Archive by Sz. Laufer"

**689. RING. I/1016 (1335). (Lb. 367). Mf. ŻIH—831; USHMM—43**

- After 28.04.1941, Warsaw Ghetto
- NN., Account entitled "Zikhroynes fun yonkiper in yor 1939 in Belkhatov" [Memoirs of Yom Kippur in 1939 in Bełchatów] (28.04.1941)
- Order for the Jews to convey to the town headquarters all of their property; burning of a pile of Torah scrolls and religious books (they burned for 8 days).
- ***Description:*** transcript (2 copies), handwritten manuscript (BW*), pencil, Yiddish, 148×207 mm, ss. 6, pp. 6.

  In the margin a symbol (green ink): "+"

  Doc. was kept in a binder.

**690. RING. I/1083 (1402). (Lb. 591). Mf. ŻIH—833; USHMM—45**

- After 8.06.1942, Biała Podlaska
- Der Kreishauptman Kommunalaufsicht—Biała Podlaska, I.A. Lippkow, Circular letter dated 8.06.1942 to the commissioner in Wisznice [?] as well as to the mayors and village commune heads in the district of Biała Podlaska
- Ban on the sale of Jewish property.

- *Description:* transcript, typescript, German, 150×201mm, ss. 1, pp. 1.
  Attached note by H.W. in Yiddish: "Forwarded by Lejb Frydman, member of the Jewish Self-Help in Biała Podlaska."

### 691. RING. I/1000 (1319). Mf. ŻIH—831; USHMM—43

- After 12.1939, Warsaw Ghetto
- Cwi Klejnman, Account entitled "Zikhroynes fun a getribenem. Biale Podlask" [Memoirs of an Exile. Biała Podlaska]
- Author of the account, together with his wife and four children as well as a group of ca. 1,700 Jews, was exiled from Serock and via Nasielsk (6.12.1939) made his way by train to Biała Podlaska (7.12.1939). He describes living conditions of the Jewish population in Biała Podlaska.
- *Description:* original, handwritten manuscript (CK*), notebook, ink, Yiddish, 150×197 mm, minor damage and losses of text, ss. 22, pp. 40.
  On p. 1 on top is information in Yiddish (ink): "Klejnman Cwi. Mały [?] Serock."
  Index: Pinchas Mużyński of Łomazy, Menachem Kronenberg, former chairman of the Jewish Community in Serock
  See Ring. I/1169.

### 692. RING. I/1220/15. Mf. ŻIH—835; USHMM—47

- 22.09.19[41], Białystok
- [German army authorities], Pass dated 22.09.1941 for Nachman Zejtlin authorizing the transport of files for documents and 100 grams of tea.
- *Description:* original, typescript, stamp, German, 196×130 mm, damage and losses of text, ss. 1, pp. 1.

### 693. RING. I/1046 (1365). (Lb. 496). Mf. ŻIH—832; USHMM—44

- After 15.07.1941, Warsaw Ghetto
- NN., Account entitled "Iber a grenets. Epizod-Bialystok" [Across a Border. Białystok Episode] (15.07.1941)
- Author from Łódź, describes journey to the east (11.1939), manages to cross the German–Soviet border, situation of the Jewish refugees in Białystok (economic and cultural life).
- *Description:* transcript (2 copies), handwritten manuscript (BW*), pencil, Yiddish, 148×208 mm, minor damage and losses of text, ss. 70, pp. 70.
  In the margins a symbol (ink): "+."
  Attached note by H.W. in Polish and Yiddish: "Across a border. Białystok Episode. Copied 15.07.1941."
  Published: *Relacje z Kresów*, pp. 69–105.

### 694. RING. I/73. Mf. ŻIH—775; USHMM—6

- After 02.1940, Warsaw Ghetto
- NN., Account entitled "Jewish Education"
- Situation of Jewish education in Białystok region in the years 1939–1940 (organization, curriculum, problem of assimilation, schools in Kolno).
- *Description:* transcript (2 copies, page 4 in 3 copies), handwritten manuscript (BTT*), pencil, Polish, 145×208 mm, text barely legible in places (second copy), ss. 13, pp. 13.
  At top of page a letter (ink): "v."
  Published: *Relacje z Kresów*, pp. 106–110.

### 695. RING. I/488. Mf. ŻIH—787; USHMM—18

- After 11.1941, Warsaw Ghetto
- NN., Account of stay in Białystok (1939–1941)
- Author, a resident of Warsaw, describes flight with husband to Białystok (15.10.1939), ethnic relations, husband's illness, "passportization," deportation to the East, outbreak of the German–Soviet War, start of repressive actions against Jews, Jewish Council (Rozenberg, chairman), forced labor, deportation of Jews to Prużany (from 18.10.1941), journey to Warsaw (3.11.1941).
- *Description:* transcript (handwritten manuscript—KK*, notebook, ink, 150×198 mm), transcript (3 copies, handwritten manuscript—CA*, pencil, 150×210 mm), Polish, ss. 115, pp. 131.
  Attached note by H.W.: "Anonymous letter forwarded by Salomea Ostrowska, coworker of the archive. The author is the wife of a film director (from Warsaw), who on 22.05.1941 traveled from Białystok to Moscow, where on 30.05, he obtained a readership (docenturę) in the film academy and an assistantship with the director Eisenstein."
  Published: *Relacje z Kresów*, pp. 48–68.

### 696. RING. I/1070 (1389). (Lb. 1125). Mf. ŻIH—832; USHMM—44

- After 06.1941, Warsaw Ghetto
- NN., Account of the first days in Białystok after the German attack on the USSR (missing conclusion)
- Bombardments, lines in front of stores, evacuation of Soviet institutions, escape from Białystok.
- *Description:* original or transcript, handwritten manuscript, ink, Polish, 155×195 mm, damage and losses of text, ss. 2, pp. 4.
  Attached note by H.W.: "Forwarded by Abram Lewin."
  Published: *Relacje z Kresów*, pp. 142–146.

### 697. RING. I/791 (1110). (Lb. 1262). Mf. ŻIH—826; USHMM—38

- After 09.1941., Warsaw Ghetto
- NN., Account of the first months of the German occupation in Białystok
- Repressive actions against Jews after occupation of the city by the Germans (creation of the Jewish Council [Rabbi (J. Gedaliah) Rozenman, chairman, engineer (Efraim) Barasz, vice chairman, ul. Kupiecka]), formation of the ghetto (1.07.1941), arrests, forced labor, contribution, displacement to Prużany).

- *Description:* original or transcript, typescript, Polish, 210×298 mm, ss. 1, pp. 2.
  Published: *Relacje z Kresów*, pp. 111–115.
  Index: [Sebastian] Tilleman, attorney from Białystok (ul. Kilińskiego 16), Stein from Białystok, Gurewicz from Białystok

### 698. RING. I/792 (1111). (Lb. 440). Mf. ŻIH—826; USHMM—38

- 21.05.1942, Warsaw Ghetto
- NN., Account describing conditions of life in the Białystok ghetto (21.05.1942)
- Situation of the Jewish population, relations with Poles, activity of the Jewish Council (J. [Gedaliah] Rozenman, chairman, engineer [Efraim] Barasz, vice chairman, as well as Ajnsztajn and Pesach Kapłan of the Department of Culture), organization of educational system. Handwritten sketch of ghetto map.
- *Description:* transcript, handwritten manuscript (LEG*), ink, Polish, Yiddish, 150×195 mm, ss. 3, pp. 5.
  On the back of p. 5 information by H.W. in Yiddish (ink): "7.6. standard pages. June 1942."
  Published: *Relacje z Kresów*, pp. 308–314.

### 699. RING. I/795 (1114). (Lb. 342). Mf. ŻIH—826; USHMM—38

- After 22.04.1941, Warsaw Ghetto
- NN., Account entitled "Der intergang fun a kibuts in Brodnitse" [The End of a Community in Brodnica] (22.04.1941)
- History of the Jewish community in Brodnica before the war and information about the outbreak of war in 1939 (social composition, bombardments in September 1939, torching of the Jewish district after the Germans' entry [ul. Pocztowa], repressive actions, arrests and escape of Jews from the town).
- *Description:* transcript (2 copies), handwritten manuscript (BW*), pencil, Yiddish, 148×210 mm, ss. 6, pp. 6.
  In the margins a symbol (ink, green): "- =."
  Doc. was kept in a binder.

### 700. RING. I/972 (1291). (Lb. 344). Mf. ŻIH—831; USHMM—43

- After 20.07.1941, Warsaw Ghetto
- [Dr. Mojżesz Reinhold], Account about the situation of the Jewish population along the border with East Prussia (Brodnica, Lubawa, Nowe Miasto nad Drwęcą, Lidzbark, Działdowo, Iława) (20.07.1941)
- Information about cultural and social life, political involvement, about relations with Poles and Germans before 1939. Description of the author's escape with a group of 13 persons to Warsaw after the outbreak of war.
- *Description:* transcript, handwritten manuscript (BW*), pencil, Yiddish, 146×208 mm, minor damage and losses of text, ss. 14, pp. 14.
  In the margins a symbol (ink): "^" (underlined).
  Attached note by H.W. in Yiddish: "Mojżesz Reinhold is the author of the account, Bluma Wasser recorded it."

### 701. RING. I/888 (1208). (Lb. 999). Mf. ŻIH—828; USHMM—40

- Date unknown, place unknown
- NN., Account of stay in areas occupied by the USSR in 1939 (fragment)
- Situation of refugees, search for work (Brześć, Pińsk, Baranowicze), social relations, mood of the population.
- *Description:* transcript, handwritten manuscript, pencil, Yiddish, 210×297mm, minor damage and losses of text, missing pp. 1–21, ss. 24, pp. 24.

### 702. RING. I/1045 (1364). (Lb. 309). Mf. ŻIH—832; USHMM—44

- Date unknown, Warsaw Ghetto
- NN., Account entitled "Mayne iberlebenishn. Der loyfenish-psikhoz un di makhers" [My Experiences. The Flight Psychosis and the Bigshots]
- Author from Warsaw, departed on 20.11.1939, in order illegally to cross the border at the Bug (detailed description of the journey, stay in Brześć, plan to leave for Baranowicze).
- *Description:* transcript (2 copies), handwritten manuscript (MS*), pencil, Yiddish, 148×209 mm, ss. 42, pp. 42.
  In the margins a Hebrew letter (ink): "m" (mem).
  Doc. was kept in a binder.
  Published: *Relacje z Kresów*, pp. 225–248.

### 703. RING. I/1047 (1366). (Lb. 1474). Mf. ŻIH—832; USHMM—44

- After 03.1942, Warsaw Ghetto
- NN, Account entitled "Purim" (03.1942)
- Public mass executions of Jews in Brzeziny, Zduńska Wola, and Łęczyca during the holiday of Purim [3 or 4.03.]1942.
- *Description:* transcript (a) (handwritten manuscript—RR*, ink, 141×192 mm), transcript (b) (3 copies, handwritten manuscript—U*, pencil, 144×219 mm), Yiddish, ss. 11, pp. 13.
  Published: *Selected Documents*, pp. 686–687.

### 704. RING. I/382. (Lb. 1070). Mf. ŻIH—783; USHMM—14

a)

- After 25.03.1941, Warsaw Ghetto
- Letter dated 25.03.1941 (Bugaj) from the Jewish Colony (Bugitten and Neuhagen, Kreis Warthbrücken—Bugaj and Nowiny near Koło) to the ORT organization in Warsaw
- Information about the October 1940 deportation of 150 Jewish families from Koło and 50 Jewish families

from Babiak to the villages of Bugaj and Nowiny Brdowskie, where an agricultural colony (400 mórg)[38] was created for them; a request for expert assistance (agronomy instructor) for cultivation of the soil.
- ***Description:*** transcript, handwritten manuscript (E*, ink, 145×206 mm), typescript (2 copies, 210×298 mm), Polish, ss. 5, pp. 6.
  Notation by H.W. in Polish and Yiddish: "108–1942/1 January."
  Attached note by H.W.: "Letter received from engineer Sudowicz."

b)
- After 14.04.1941, Warsaw Ghetto
- Letter dated 14.04.1941 (Bugaj) from the Jewish Colony (Bugitten and Neuhagen, Kreis Warthbrück-en—Bugaj and Nowiny Brdowskie near Koło) to the Toporol organization in Warsaw
- Thanks for letter dated 7.04.1941 (no. 7308/41), information on soil conditions, stock and possibility for employment of 2 farming experts, without salary, for full maintenance.
- ***Description:*** transcript, handwritten manuscript (E*, ink, 145×206 mm), typescript (210×295 mm), Polish, ss. 3, pp. 4.
  See HWC, 48a/1 (second copy of transcript, typescript, ss. 2; with note by H.W. in Yiddish [ink]: "109–1942/1 January, nr 14").

### 705. RING. I/271. Mf. ŻIH—781; USHMM—12

- After 07.1941, place unknown
- Appointed village leader of Bychawa, letter of 27.07.1941 to the Jewish Council in Bychawa
- Order for delivery of all Talmuds to the front of the Village Office building by 5 PM.
- ***Description:*** transcript, handwritten manuscript, ink, Polish, 200×115 mm, ss. 1, pp. 1.
  Notation by H.W.in Yiddish (ink): "108—1942/1 January."
  Inventory: "Submitted to the archive by I. Falk."

### 706. RING. I/951 (1270). Mf. ŻIH—830; USHMM—42

- Date unknown, Warsaw Ghetto
- NN., Account entitled "Bychawa"
- About persecution of Jews by the mayor of Bychawa, August Świerkutt, an ethnic German.
- ***Description:*** original (o), handwritten manuscript (FLIG*), ink, Polish, 222×351 mm, minor damage and losses of text, text illegible in places, ss. 2, pp. 4
  Index: Grynsztajn, barber, member of the Jewish Council in Bychawa, Mojsze Suchota, German informer in Bychawa

### 707. RING. I/817 (1137). (Lb. 717). Mf. ŻIH—826; USHMM—38

- After 12.1940, place unknown
- Der Stadtkommissar der Stadt Chełm. Der Kreishauptman des Kreises Chełm, Correspondence with the Jewish Council in Chełm
  1) Letter of 31.10.1940 to [Marek] Frenkel (Fränkel), chairman of the Jewish Council in the matter of the boundaries of the ghetto in Chełm, attached list of streets that Jews must vacate by 10.11.1940;
  2) Letter of 7.11.1940 to Jewish Council in the matter of carrying out vaccinations, construction of barracks and sealing of the ghetto;
  3) Letter of 14.11.1940 to [Marek] Frenkel (Fränkel), chairman of the Jewish Council, with permission for his departure to Warsaw in order to purchase vaccine and reiteration of the order to vacate the enumerated streets located outside the ghetto by 10.12.1940;
  4) Letter of 27.11.1940 to the Jewish Council with an order for eviction of Jews from Lubelska Street;
  5) Jewish Council. Letter of 2.12.1940 to the Town Commissioner of Chełm with data about the number of those moved, cubic area of occupied and vacated residential units.
- ***Description:*** transcript, handwritten manuscript, ink, German, 208×295 mm, ss. 5, pp. 6.
  See Ring. I/818.

### 708. RING. I/818 (1136). (Lb. 1615). Mf. ŻIH—826; USHMM—38

- Date unknown, Warsaw Ghetto
- NN., Account entitled "Khelm far der tsayt fun 30.11.39 biz januar [1940]" [Chełm in the period from 30.11.39 until January (1940)]
- Jews' situation in the first months of the occupation (20,000 persons), Marek Frenkel, mill owner, chairman of the Jewish Council, absence of Order Service, forced labor (30.11.1939 dispatch of 900 men to work, ca. 500 have not returned), good relations with Poles.
- ***Description:*** transcript (2 copies), typescript, Yiddish, 208×296 mm, minor damage and losses of text, ss. 12, pp. 12.
  On p. 1 notation of H.W. in Yiddish (ink): "109—1942/1 January. no. 17."
  See Ring. I/817.
  See HWC, 14/1 (third copy, typescript, ss. 6).
  Index: Kirszenblat, glazier, member of the Jewish Council in Chełm; Szwarcblat, member of the Jewish Council in Chełm

38. A morga is a Polish land measure equal to 5,600 square meters.

**709. RING. I/1006 (1325). (Lb. 335). Mf. ŻIH—831; USHMM—43**

- After 21.04.1941, Warsaw Ghetto
- NN., Account entitled "Der pogrom in Khelm" [The Pogrom in Chełm] (21.04.1941)
- After Miller took over ca. 1,800 Jews were murdered in Chełm (2.11.1939).
- ***Description:*** transcript (2 copies), handwritten manuscript (BW*), pencil, Yiddish, 148×207 mm, ss. 6, pp. 6.
  In the margins a symbol (green ink): "-."
  Doc. was kept in a binder.

**710. RING. I/568/1. Mf. ŻIH—792; USHMM—23**

- After 13.04.1942, Warsaw Ghetto
- NN. (Chełm Lubelski), Letter of 10.04.1942 to NN. (Warsaw Ghetto)
- Information about the approaching extermination, request for aid.
- ***Description:*** transcript, handwritten manuscript (H*), ink, Hebrew, Yiddish in Roman transliteration, 96×125 mm, damage and losses of text, ss. 1, pp. 2.
  Published: *Listy o Zagładzie*, pp. 87–89.

**711. RING. I/870 (1189). (Lb. 451). Mf. ŻIH—828; USHMM—40**

- After 15.02.1941, Warsaw Ghetto
- NN., Account entitled "Khorzhele, pzhasnisher poviat (a mizrekh-praysishe grenets shtot)" [Chorzele, district of Przasnysz (an East Prussia border town)] (15.02.1941)
- Situation in the town before the war's outbreak (03–08.1939), September 1939 (flight of Jews from the town, fate of families who stayed); refugees from Chorzele in Maków and Warsaw.
- ***Description:*** transcript (2 copies), handwritten manuscript (MS*), pencil, Yiddish, 148×210 mm, ss. 8, pp. 8.
  In the margin a symbol (green ink): "o."
  Doc. was kept in a binder.

**712. RING. I/796 (1115). (Lb. 315). Mf. ŻIH—826; USHMM—38**

a)

- Date unknown, Warsaw Ghetto
- NN., Account entitled "Tsiekhotshinek" [Ciechocinek]
- About the German colony near Ciechocinek (relations between the settlers and Poles before the war), situation after the German invasion.
- ***Description:*** transcript (2 copies), handwritten manuscript (MS*), pencil, Yiddish, 148×210 mm, ss. 6, pp. 6.
  In the margins a symbol (ink): "o" [?]; on p. 1 a Hebrew letter: "f" (fey).
  Doc. was kept in a binder.

b)

- After 20.05.1941, Warsaw Ghetto
- NN., Account about the situation of Jews in Ciechocinek from 17.09.1939 until resettlement. (20.05.1941).
- ***Description:*** transcript, handwritten manuscript (BW*), pencil, Yiddish, 148×210 mm, ss. 7, pp. 7.
  In the margins a Hebrew letter (pencil): "e" (ayin).
  On p. 1 in the margin a symbol (red pencil): "+."
  Doc. a and b have common pagination.

**713. RING. I/592/8. Mf. ŻIH—792; USHMM—23**

- After 23.02.1942, Warsaw Ghetto
- NN., Fragment of a Study [?] (memoir [?])
- Attached letter from NN. from Cieszanów (ghetto [?]) to NN. (wife [?]) in the Warsaw Ghetto (compares his own situation and that of his companions [13] to refugees from the point at ul. Nowolipki 9).
- ***Description:*** transcript, typescript, Yiddish, 183×136 mm, serious damage and losses of text, ss. 1, pp. 1.

**714. RING. I/784 (1103). (Lb. 13). Mf. ŻIH—825; USHMM—37**

- 09.1941, Częstochowa
- Der Stadthauptmann [City Chief], Dr. Wendler, Announcement dated 30.09.1941
- Juda Smolarczyk (ul. Stary Rynek 30), Mendel Zaks (ul. Targowa 14), and Jakub Brat (ul. Nadrzeczna 36) are sentenced to 1 year of maximum security prison for evasion of compulsory labor.
- ***Description:*** original, printed, German, Polish, 675×480 mm, ss. 1, pp. 1.

**715. RING. I/183. Mf. ŻIH—779; USHMM—10. RING. I/245 (Lb. 594). Mf. ŻIH—781; USHMM—12. RING. I/1220/90. Mf. ŻIH—835; USHMM—47**

a) **Ring. I/183**

- After 12.1940, Warsaw Ghetto
- [Jewish Council in Częstochowa ?], Report of the Patent and Tax Office (Sprawozdanie Referatu Patentowego i Podatkowego) for the year 1940
- Analysis of the number of registration and industrial-tax cards purchased by branches of trades and commerce. Revenue of the Tax Office.
- ***Description:*** transcript (handwritten manuscript—F*, ink) and typescript (2 copies in fragments, typescript does not include the closing fragment of the manuscript from p. 3), Polish, 215×283 mm, damage and losses of text, ss. 6, pp. 8.
  In the manuscript on p. 4 is a copy of another text; see Ring. I/183b.
  On p. 1 (copy—typescript, second copy) notation by H.W. in Yiddish: "2[?] standard pages."
  Copy (typescript) does not include the closing fragment of the manuscript from p. 3.

b) **Ring. I/183, I/245 (Lb. 594), I/1220/90**
- After 12.1940, Warsaw Ghetto
- [Jewish Council in Częstochowa ?], Report of activity (fragment)
- Department of Forced Labor for the year 1940 (scope of activity, jobs carried out, local and out-of-town labor camps, organization of the the camp in Przyrów near Częstochowa, seasonal labor camp in the Lublin region), Social Welfare Department, statistics on the Jewish population in Częstochowa, tribute.
- ***Description:*** Ring. I/183—copy, handwritten manuscript (F*), ink, Polish, 205x285 mm, extensive minor damage and losses of text, ss. 1, pp. 1 (handwritten manuscript located on p. 4 of the manuscript Ring. I/183a); Ring. I/245—transcript, handwritten manuscript (F*), ink, Polish, 202x280 mm, minor damage and losses of text, ss. 1, pp. 1; Ring. I/1220—transcript, handwritten manuscript (two handwritings: F* and NN. [?]), ink, Polish, 146x214 mm, damage and losses of text, ss. 3, pp. 6.

  Page 1 from Ring. I/245, p. 2 from Ring. I/183.

  Ring. I/1220 on p. 1 notation H.W. (ink): "6 standard pages."

  Ring. I/245—Attached note by H.W. in Yiddish: "Submitted to archive by J. Winkler."

**716. RING. I/797 (1116). (Lb. 1218, 1627). Mf. ŻIH—826; USHMM—38**

- 12.1941, Warsaw Ghetto
- NN., Account entitled "Tshenstokhuv" [Częstochowa"] (12.1941)
- Situation of the Jewish population during the occupation (social divisions in the ghetto, Jewish Council's activity, forced labor, Order Service, corruption among Jewish officials, refugees from Płock, roundups and arrests).
- ***Description:*** transcript (a) (handwritten manuscript—RR*, ink, 143x185 mm), transcript (b) (2 copies, handwritten manuscript—Z*, pencil, 148x210 mm), Yiddish, ss. 27, pp. 27.

  On p. 1 (transcript—(b), first copy) notation by H.W. (ink): "Submitted by Dina Szaja, 109—1942/1 January, no. 15."

  Index: Kalenbrener, chief of the labor office in Częstochowa, Galster of the Order Service in Częstochowa, Kacinel of the Order Service in Częstochowa

**717. RING. I/867 (1186). Mf. ŻIH—828; USHMM—40**

- 04.1942, Warsaw Ghetto
- NN., Account entitled "Tshenstokhova. Yidishe moysrim, untervelt mentshn, untertroger, lobuzes, oysvorfn, zayn [sic] dinst bay di okupantn" [Częstochowa: Jewish informers, underworld figures, stool-pigeons, scoundrels, outcasts, (their) service for the occupiers]
- Situation of the Jewish and Polish population during the German occupation, ghetto, demoralization of the population, description of a group of the occupier's agents and collaborators.
- ***Description:*** transcript, handwritten manuscript (RR*), ink, Yiddish, 158x204 mm, ss. 5, pp. 9.

  On p. 1 under the heading Information, that the text is a continuation of another statement ("continuation").

  Index: Gecl Rozenberg, informer in Częstochowa; Herszl Jarząbek, tailor, informer in Częstochowa; Wolberg, informer in Częstochowa; Baruch Ginzburg, informer in Częstochowa; Kambrot, informer in Częstochowa; Samuel Wajnrib, dental technician, informer in Częstochowa; Samuel Wróblewski, informer in Częstochowa; Moniek F[P?]lawner, electrician, informer in Częstochowa; Beniek Kelenbrener [?], informer in Częstochowa, liaison between the Jewish Council and Germans; brothers Heniek and Maks Gnat, orderlies of high SS officer Delte [?]; Meir Sznikiewicz of Częstochowa, German collaborator; Epsztajn of Częstochowa, German collaborator

**718. RING. I/440. (Lb. 454, 454A, 455, 472). Mf. ŻIH—785; USHMM—16**

- After 2.07.1942, Warsaw Ghetto
- NN., Three personal statements (Studies [?]): 1) "Tshenstokhov" [Częstochowa] (2.07.1942); 2) "Ostroviets (keltser)" [Ostrowiec (kielecki)] (2.07.1942); 3) "Der arbetlager in Reyov (bay Skazhysko)" [The Labor Camp in Rejów (Near Skarzysko)]
- 1) Registration of Jews who have relatives in Palestine, situation in the ghetto, Polish–Jewish relations, persecution of the Polish population; 2) Situation of the Jewish population in Ostrowiec, relations with Germans; 3) Organization of camp (early in 1942), 1500 prisoners, living conditions, displacement of Jews from Kłobuck and Szczekocin.
- ***Description:*** original or transcript (handwritten manuscript—LEG*, notebook, ink, 150x195 mm, minor damage and losses of text, text illegible in places), transcript (2 copies, testimony "Labor camp in Rejów . . ." in 3 copies, typescript, 208x295 mm, extensive damage and losses of text), Polish, Yiddish, ss. 22, pp. 25.

  On the back of p. 3 (copy—typescript, first copy) notation by H.W. in Yiddish (ink): "June 1942. 8 standard pages."

  Part of the doc. was transferred from Ring. I/383. (Lb. 472). Ring. I/383—Inventory: "Submitted by Goldman."

  See HWC, 13/1 (fragment concerning Częstochowa, third copy [?], typescript, ss. 3).

**719. RING. I/497. Mf. ŻIH—788; USHMM—19**

- 24.04.1942, Częstochowa

- NN. (Częstochowa), Letter of 24.04.1942 to Alfreda Winnik (Warsaw, ul. Nowolipki 24, apt. 2[. . . ?])
- The author describes in detail her experiences, departure from Piotrków, arrest, the ghetto in Częstochowa [?].
- ***Description:*** original, handwritten manuscript, ink, Polish, 150×120, 140×203, 150×198 mm, text is difficult to read, ss. 6, pp. 12.

  Attached fragment of envelope: "Alfreda Winnik, Warsaw, ul. Nowolipki 24, apt. 2[. . . ?]" (handwritten manuscript, ink, stamp of the Jewish Council in Warsaw (4.05.1942), 149×119 mm, Polish, ss. 1, pp. 1.).

  Attached note by H.W.: "Anonymous."

**720. RING. I/799 (1118). (Lb. 1233). Mf. ŻIH—826; USHMM—38**

- After 26.02.1942, Warsaw Ghetto
- Wołkowicz, Account entitled "Dombye" [Dąbie] (26.02.1942)
- Author, a resident of Dąbie nad Nerem, describes the situation of the town's Jewish population from September 1939 until deportation to the death camp in Chełmno (12.1941). On 11.12.1941 he was sent by the Jewish Council to Koło to confirm the news about the deportation of the local Jews. He describes the deportation of the Jewish population in Koło (Brener and Engel, representatives of the Jewish Council in Koło, assisted the Germans) and passes on the information acquired about the death camp in Chełmno. On 14.12.1941 he fled from Dąbie to Grabowo, where he met 3 escapees from Chełmno ([Abram] Roj, Fajner [Szlamek (Shlomo) Wiener] of Izbica, and Michał (Mekhl) Podchlebnik of Bugaj). He then reached Warsaw via Łowicz on 21.02.1942. Attached list of names of members of the Jewish Council in Dąbie: Chairman Josef Diament; members Lejb Strykowski, Pinkas Elbojm, Mosze Gostyński, Gerszon Engel (sent out to labor in Poznań region), and Chaim Elie Lewin.
- ***Description:*** transcript (2 copies), handwritten manuscript (U*), pencil, Yiddish, 148×210 mm, ss. 12, pp. 12.

  See HWC, 15/1 (third copy, handwritten manuscript, ss. 6).

  Index: Błachowski, sequestrator; Nelter, mayor in Dąbie n. Nerem; Woltman, mayor in Dąbie n. Nerem

**721. RING. I/610. Mf. ŻIH—814; USHMM—26**

- After 02.1942, Warsaw Ghetto
- [Zygmunt Millet?], Account entitled "Vacation from the Ghetto" (02.1942)
- Author, a member of the Order Service who obtained from the German authorities a so-called rail pass and went (10.10.1941) to his hometown of Dębica for several days, compares the situation of the Jewish population in the Podkarpat (Sub-Carpathian) region (Dębica and Tarnów) and in the Warsaw Ghetto.
- ***Description:*** transcript (3 copies), handwritten manuscript (CA*), pencil, Polish, 150×210 mm, ss. 51, pp. 51.

  Attached note by H.W.: "Submitted by a Salomea Ostrowska, written by attorney [Zygmunt] Milet [Millet]."

**722. RING. I/1095 (1414). (Lb. 287). Mf. ŻIH—833; USHMM—45**

- 13.06.1940, Dobrzyń
- Edmund Milbradt Leather and Shoe Firm, Certificate dated 13.06.1940 of the employment of Szymon Wiewiórka during the period 15.09.1939–12.06.1940 and of dismissal on account of Jewish origin.
- ***Description:*** original, typescript, handwritten manuscript, ink, stamp, German, 188×145 mm, ss. 1, pp. 1.

  Attached note by H.W. in Yiddish.

**723. RING. I/802 (1121). (Lb. 1146). Mf. ŻIH—826; USHMM—38**

a)

- After 2.05.1941, Warsaw Ghetto
- NN., Account entitled "Dobrzin Drv[ents]—Golub Fam."[?] [Dobrzyń nad Drwęcą—Golub Fam."(?)] (2.05.1941)
- Repressive measures against the Jewish population in Dobrzyń and Golub nad Drwęcą in September and November 1939: ca. 230 men were transported from Dobrzyń to an unknown destination on Rosh Hashanah, confiscations of property, forced labor, abduction of pharmacist Adolf Riesenfeld (25.10.1939), transport of 35 of the wealthiest Jews to an unknown destination (8.11.1939), expulsion of the remaining Jewish population from both towns (9.11.1939) after exaction of a "contribution."
- ***Description:*** transcript (2 copies), handwritten manuscript (BW*), pencil, Yiddish, 148×210 mm, ss. 4, pp. 4.

  In the margins letter (ink, green): "G."

b)

- After 11.05.1941, Warsaw Ghetto
- NN., Account entitled "Dobrzin Drv[ents]—Golub Fam."[?] [Dobrzyń nad Drwęcą—Golub Fam."(?)] (2.05.1941)
- Repressive measures against the Jewish population in Dobrzyń nad Drwęcą and Golub nad Drwęcą in September and November 1939: transport of ca. 270 men to an unknown destination on Rosh Hashanah, searches, confiscations, forced labor, transport of 70 persons to an unknown destination (9.11.1939), expulsion of the remaining Jewish population (10.11.1939), after exaction of a "contribution," the majority (ca. 800) reached Warsaw. About 400 people perished.

- *Description:* transcript, handwritten manuscript (BW*), pencil, Yiddish, 148×210 mm, minor damage and losses of text, ss. 6, pp. 6.
  In the margins letter (ink): "A."

c)
- Date unknown, place unknown
- Lists of names of persons deported by the Germans from Dobrzyń and Golub in September and November 1939 (14.09. and 9.11.1939).
- *Description:* original, handwritten manuscript, ink, Polish, 225×310 mm, ss. 3, pp. 5.
  Attached note by H.W. in Yiddish: "List of Jewish residents of Dobrzyń-Golub killed by the Germans 9.11.1939."

**724. RING. I/674/5. (Lb. 1688). Mf. ŻIH—816; USHMM—28**

- After 1939, Warsaw Ghetto
- NN., Account from Dobrzyń and Górki near Gostynin
- Author left Grudziądz (2.09.1939), describes the situation of the Jewish population in Dobrzyń and his stay on the estate of Górki near Gostynin (until 19.09.1939).
- *Description:* original (o), handwritten manuscript (H.W.*), ink, Yiddish, 138×201 mm, ss. 2, pp. 2.
  On p. 4 various notes, calculations (handwritten manuscript, pencil, Polish).
  Index: Roterowa, Łaski, proprietor of the estate of Górki near Gostynin

**725. RING. I/801 (1120). (Lb. 363). Mf. ŻIH—826; USHMM—38**

- After 6.05.1941, Warsaw Ghetto
- NN., Account entitled "Protim vegn di iberlebungen fun di yidn in Drobien, zint der milkhome oysbrokh, biz zeyer teylvayzer oysvanderung fun shtetl" [Details of the experiences of the Jews in Drobin, from the war's outbreak until some of them left the town] (6.05.1941)
- Influx of refugees in September 1939 (ca. 100 families), repressive measures by the occupier, worsening Polish–Jewish relations; after 7.03.1941 half of the Jewish population was transferred to Działdowo (thence to the ghetto in Piotrków), while the remainder were driven into the ghetto on the town's periphery.
- *Description:* transcript (2 copies), handwritten manuscript (BW*), pencil, Yiddish, 148×210 mm, ss. 6, pp. 6.
  In the margins letter (ink, green): "B" (handwritten manuscript BB*).
  On p. 1 (first copy) a symbol (pencil, red): "+."

**726. RING. I/803 (1122). (Lb. 1477). Mf. ŻIH—826; USHMM—38**

- After 22.03.1942, Warsaw Ghetto
- NN., Account entitled "Dubienke" [Dubienka] (03.1942)
- Situation in the Dubienka ghetto after transfer to it of 800 women and children driven out of Mielec on 16.03.1942. Information from 22.03.1942.
- *Description:* transcript (handwritten manuscript -RR*, ink, 148×210 mm), transcript (3 copies) (handwritten manuscript—U*, pencil, 143×192 mm), Yiddish, ss. 7, pp. 8.

**727. RING. I/568/2. Mf. ŻIH—792; USHMM—23**

- 05–06.1942, Dubienka, Chełm, Warsaw Ghetto
- Luba Rozenberg (Dubienka), Letters dated 23.05., 1 and 4.06.1942 to Frania Zalcman (Warsaw, ul. Elektoralna 14, apt. 93)
- Annihilation of the Jews in Dubienka.
- *Description:* original, handwritten manuscript on postcards, postmarks and stamp of Jewish Council in Warsaw, ink, Polish, l., 146×104 mm, ss. 3, pp. 6.
  Attached copy of card dated 4.06., handwritten manuscript (H*), pencil, Polish, Yiddish, 206×147 mm, (insignificant changes of text in relation to the original), ss. 1, pp. 1.
  Published: *Listy o Zagładzie*, pp. 158–163.

**728. RING. I/581/1. Mf. ŻIH—792; USHMM—23**

- After 1.09.[. . .], Warsaw Ghetto[?]
- NN. (Dubienka), Letter of 1.09.[. . .] to NN.
- Request for delivery of parcels to Miss Lipszyc (ul. Tłomackie 2, apt. 16). Information about Moryc Garncarz.
- *Description:* original or transcript, handwritten manuscript, ink, Yiddish, 145×205 mm, ss. 1, pp. 2.

**729. RING. I/463. (Lb. 1486). Mf. ŻIH—786; USHMM—17**

- After 09.1939, Warsaw Ghetto
- NN., Account about Jews of Dynów
- Germans murdered several hundred Jews, and drove out of the town those who survived (09.1939).
- *Description:* original or transcript, handwritten manuscript, pencil, Yiddish, 148×208 mm, ss. 2, pp. 1.
  Attached note by H.W. in Yiddish: "Anonymous."
  Published: *Selected Documents*, p. 682.

**730. RING. I/1198 (1517). (Lb. 303). Mf. ŻIH—835; USHMM—47**

- 1.04.1942, Frankfurt (Oder)
- Materials concerning the confiscation of the property of Sara Färber (born 7.05.1924 in Hamburg) of Landwerk Neuendorf
  1) Der Regierungspräsident—Frankfurt (Oder). Order of 1.04.1942 about confiscation of the property of Sara Färber on the basis of the regulations concerning confiscation of the property of communists.
  2) Ober-Gerichtsvollzieher in Franfurt (Oder). Receipt dated 3.04.1942 about collection of the above-mentioned order by Sara Färber.
- *Description:* original, printed, typescript, handwritten manuscript, pencil, ink, stamp, German, 210×145, 205×295 mm, ss. 2, pp. 2

On the back of doc. 1 notation (ink): "Solna 17, apt. 37, groundfloor, Hanka?"

### 731. RING. I/986 (1305). (Lb. 1281, 1649). Mf. ŻIH—831; USHMM—43

- After 31.12.1941, Warsaw Ghetto
- NN., Account entitled "Grusn fun der provints" [Greetings from the Provinces] (31.12.1941)
- Female author describes the situation of the Jewish population in Garbatka near Radom from war's outbreak in 1939, relations with Poles (trade and work in the countryside, aid for refugees), typhus epidemic (summer 1941), formation of the ghetto (12.1941), change in Polish–Jewish relations in the second half of 1941, assaults on the Jewish population, antisemitic pronouncements (Skorupski, Krawczyk, Bolek Szczur, Gieniek, Rutka and Heniek Małolepszy).
- ***Description:*** original or transcript, (handwritten manuscript—Ś*, ink, 150×210 mm), transcript (3 copies, typescript, 210×297 mm, minor damage and losses of text), Yiddish, ss. 16, pp. 16.

On p. 1 (copy, typescript, first copy) notation by H.W. in Yiddish (ink): "Abraham Lewin."

Attached note by H.W. in Yiddish: "Prepared by Abraham Lewin."

In HWC (7/1) is a different [?] statement concerning Garbatka (handwritten manuscript, ink, Yiddish, ss. 2).

Index: Perelsztajn, chairman of the Jewish Council in Garbatka near Radom

### 732. RING. I/808 (1127). (Lb. 361). Mf. ŻIH—826; USHMM—38

a)

- After 1940, Warsaw Ghetto
- NN., Account entitled "Gombin" [Gąbin]
- Situation of the Jews from war's outbreak until March 1940 (numerous fatalities and material losses during the bombardments in 1939; more than 100 people, among others the Rotblid family, Szajna and Bluma Wolman), persecutions during the occupation, burning of the synagogue and adjacent Jewish homes (21.09.1939), arrests (of Poles, too)—11.11.1939 (among others, Abraham Zamość, a bank director and chairman of the Jewish Community, Icchak Benbaum [?], principal of an elementary school), rape and murder of Rajza Goldman (age 14) (31.12.1939), forced contribution (20,000 marks).
- ***Description:*** transcript, handwritten manuscript (MS*), pencil, Yiddish, 148×210 m, ss. 3, pp. 3.

In the margin a letter (ink): "K."

Doc. was kept in a binder.

b)

- After 1940, Warsaw Ghetto
- NN., Account entitled "Gombin" [Gąbin].
- ***Description:*** transcript (2 copies), handwritten manuscript (MS*), pencil, Yiddish, 148×210 m, ss. 8, pp. 8.

In the margins a letter (ink, green): "D."

See doc. a).

Doc. was kept in a binder.

Index: Mosze Ber (age 30), son of Mordechaj, shot by the Germans in Gąbin (21.09.1939)

c)

- After 1940, Warsaw Ghetto
- NN., Account entitled "Gombin" [Gąbin].
- ***Description:*** transcript (2 copies), handwritten manuscript (MS*), pencil, Yiddish, 148×210 m, ss. 6, pp. 6.

In the margins a letter (ink, green): "E."

See doc. a). Docs. a), b), and c) have very similar contents, including descriptions of similar events; a) is the most detailed. Statements b) and c) are almost identical.

### 733. RING. I/1220/4. Mf. ŻIH—835; USHMM—47

- 7.05.1942, Warsaw Ghetto
- NN., Account of escape from Łódź[?]
- A search conducted on the Gąbin-Łowicz road.
- ***Description:*** original or transcript, handwritten manuscript, Polish, 196×345 mm, serious damage and losses of text (fragments of these ss. are conserved separately), ss. 2, pp. 4.

### 734. RING. I/599/67. Mf. ŻIH—812; USHMM—24

- 21.01.1942, Gąbin
- NN., Letter of 21.01.1942 (postmarked Gąbin) to Tauba Różana (Warsaw, ul. Dzielna 1[. . . ?]). Request for remittance of money.
- ***Description:*** original, handwritten manuscript (NG*) on a postcard, postmark and stamp of Jewish Council in Warsaw (28.01.1942), pencil, ink, German, 95×100 mm, serious damage and losses of text, ss. 1, pp. 2.

### 735. RING. I/599/67A. Mf. ŻIH—812; USHMM—24

- 6.03.1942, Gąbin
- NN., Letter to Tauba Różana (Warsaw, ul. Dzielna [1 . . . ?]).
- ***Description:*** original, handwritten manuscript (NG*) on a postcard, postmark and stamp of Jewish Council in Warsaw, pencil, Yiddish in Roman transliteration, 113×105 mm, serious damage and losses of text, ss. 1, pp. 2.

### 736. RING. I/599/67B. Mf. ŻIH—812; USHMM—24

- Date unknown [Gąbin?]
- NN., Letter to Tauba Różana (Warsaw, ul. Dzielna [1 . . . ?]). Information about an illness.
- ***Description:*** original, handwritten manuscript (NG*) on a postcard, pencil, German and Yiddish in Roman transliteration, 108×100 mm, serious damage and losses of text, ss. 1, pp. 2.

### 737. RING. I/554. Mf. ŻIH—791; USHMM—22

- 28.02–3.03.1942, Gąbin

- Róża and Lusia [Gips] (Gąbin), Letters dated 28.02 and 3.03.1942 to A. [Abram] Gips (Warsaw, ul. Pawia 41, apt. 4)
- Living conditions in the ghetto in Gąbin and information about the approaching annihilation.
- *Description:* original, handwritten manuscript on postcards, postmarks and stamp of Jewish Council in Warsaw, ink, Polish, 148×104 mm, ss. 2, pp. 4.

**738. RING. I/1014 (1333). (Lb. 370, 370A). Mf. ŻIH—831; USHMM—43**

- After 1.05.1941, Warsaw Ghetto
- NN., Account entitled "Kurtser barikht iber gesheenishn fun di sinagogn-kehile in Dantsig fun 1.9.[19]39" [Short report about events of the synagogue community in Danzig from 1.9.(19)39]
- Notation concerning emigration of Jews from Danzig [Gdańsk] (since 1935) (inter alia about the Jewish fund that financed emigration).
- *Description:* transcript (2 copies), handwritten manuscript (MS*), pencil, Yiddish, 147×208 mm, ss. 4, pp. 4.

  In the margin a symbol (ink, green): " . " (square).

**739. RING. I/1023 (1342). (Lb. 353). Mf. ŻIH—831; USHMM—43**

- After 12.05.1941, Warsaw Ghetto
- NN., Account entitled "Rayze barikht. Dantsig–Varshe" [Travel report: Danzig–Warsaw]
- Course of deportation of Jews from Gdańsk [Danzig] (from 28.02.1941) and description of each stage of the journey via the transit camps in Tczew and Toruń to the Warsaw Ghetto.
- *Description:* transcript (2 copies), handwritten manuscript (BW*), pencil, Yiddish, 148×208 mm, ss. 6, pp. 6.

  In the margins a letter (green ink): "c."

  On p. 1 (first copy) a symbol in the margin (red pencil): "+."

**740. RING. I/16. (Lb. 31). Mf. ŻIH—771; USHMM—2**

- After 10.1939, Warsaw Ghetto
- [Ber Fisz], Account entitled "Gdynia"
- Author, a member of the Board of the Jewish Community in Gdynia, on the fate of the Jewish population in Gdynia in September and October 1939 (until the displacement on 17.10.1939).
- *Description:* original or transcript, typescript, Polish, l., 205×300 mm, ss. 2, pp. 2.

  Attached note by H.W. in Yiddish: "Written by the prominent activist from Gdynia Ber Fisz from Rzeszów, founder of the fishing kibbutz in Gdynia, in the ghetto was vice chairman of CKU, perished in Rzeszów, to which he had returned in 1941."

  Notation about the author on p. 1.

**741. RING. I/447. Mf. ŻIH—785; USHMM—16**

- 1939–1940, place unknown
- NN., "Tog bukh fun dem tog fun onfang krig tsvishn Poyln[. . . Doy]tshland 1939. den 31/8/" [Diary from the day of the start of the war between Poland (. . . Ger)many. 31/8/] (31.08.1939–27.03.1940)
- Author from Głowno, description of the September campaign, refugees from various nearby towns, entry of the Germans, religious life, forced labor, prices, daily life in the town during the occupation, registration of the Jewish population (4.03.1940).
- *Description:* original, handwritten manuscript, notebook, ink, pencil, Yiddish, 155×195 mm, minor damage and losses of text, ss. 38, pp. 73.

  Index: Hersz Piotrkowski, Samson Sochaczewski, Mosze Pomeranc, Landsberg

**742. RING. I/804 (1123). (Lb. 428). Mf. ŻIH—826; USHMM—38**

- After 04.1941, Warsaw Ghetto
- NN., Account entitled "Der glovner luekh" [The Głowno Calendar]
- Fate of the Jewish population from the entry of the Germans into the town (3.09.1939) until the deportation (5.04.1941) (displaced persons from Aleksandrów, Konstantynów, Zgierz, Stryków—ca. 8000 persons—Aid Committee, 12.1939, Jewish Council—02.1940, ghetto—05.1940, Order Service, sealing of the ghetto—09.1940, deportation—03/04.1941).
- *Description:* transcript (2 copies), handwritten manuscript (MS*), pencil, Yiddish, 148×210 mm, minor damage and losses of text, ss. 10, pp. 10.

  In the margins letter (ink): "M."

  Published: *Selected Documents*, pp. 120–123.

  Index: Ben Cijon Barszt of Głowno, killed in 09.1939; Icchak Rotenbach of Głowna, killed on 13.09.1939; Sochaczewski, father and son, of Głowno, killed 13.09.1939; Cwaj[g]enbaum, father and son, of Głowno, killed 15.09.1939; Abraham Cwek, community's clerk, Lejb Borensztajn, member of the Jewish Council in Głowno (05.1940)

**743. RING. I/438. Mf. ŻIH—785; USHMM—16**

- After 02.1941, Warsaw Ghetto
- NN., Recollections of a stay in Głowno (1940–1941) (fragments [?])
- The author and her family displaced from areas annexed to the Reich [?], describes stay from 10.02.1940 in Głowno, expulsion of 2,000 Jews (displaced persons) from the small town (20.04.1940), formation of ghetto, roundups for labor, fire in the town (27.09.1940), contacts with Poles, health campaigns, transportation to Warsaw (28.02.1941).
- *Description:* original handwritten manuscript, notebooks, ink, Polish, 150×192 mm, text illegible in places, ss. 48, pp. 90.

It appears from the surviving original (?) pagination of notebooks 1 and 2 that pp. 27–78 are missing; or there could be another two notebooks, which is indicated by the original (?) notebook numbering: on the first notebook "I," on the second notebook "IV," and on the third notebook "V."

In notebook 3, on p. 1, notation by H.W. in Yiddish (ink): "12 standard pages."

Index: Niewiadomski, Szwarc, Dr. Mierzejewski, Sztyller, Gruber, I. Flamcholc [?], B. Rozencwajg, Szumiraj, Rozenberg, Lenski, Lajzer Fas, Abram Szer, Ryt, Braun.

See Ring. I/447.

### 744. RING. I/952 (1271). Mf. ŻIH—830; USHMM—42

- After 04.1941, Warsaw Ghetto
- NN., Account entitled "Gostynin"
- Fate of the Jewish population from the entry of the Germans until formation of ghetto (requisitions, robberies, detention of hostages, torching of synagogue—11.1939, [forced] contribution, formation of ghetto—04.1941).
- ***Description:*** original (o), handwritten manuscript (FLIG*), ink, Polish, 196×351 mm, minor damage and losses of text, ss. 2, pp. 4.

Published: BŻIH, no. 137–138/1986, pp. 187–189.

Index: Moszek Szczygieł, killed in 09.1939 in Gostynin; Zając, arrested in 09.1939 in Gostynin, perished; Burak, arrested in 09.1939 in Gostynin, perished; Pinczewski, arrested in 09.1939 in Gostynin, perished; Dr. Merliński, arrested in 09.1939 in Gostynin, perished; Keller, arrested in 09.1939 in Gostynin, perished; Chil Majer, Tsadik of Gostynin; Bernsztajn, rabbi of Gostynin

### 745. RING. I/570. Mf. ŻIH—836; USHMM—67

- After 17.02.1942, Warsaw Ghetto
- M. Habergryc (Gostynin), Letter dated 17.02.1942 [postmark] to I. Kraut (Warsaw, Śliska 24, apt. 29)
- Letter addressed among others to Frania, about the annihilation of the Jewish population of surrounding towns and imposition of a head tax on the Jews in Gostynin.
- ***Description:*** transcript of a postcard (sketch of postmark: "Gasten" [Wartheland] 17.02.42), handwritten manuscript, ink, Polish, 152×107 mm, ss. 1, pp. 2.

Published: *Listy o Zagładzie*, pp. 25–27.

### 746. RING. I/809 (1128). (Lb. 1221). Mf. ŻIH—826; USHMM—38

- Date unknown, After 19.08.1941, Warsaw Ghetto
- NN., Account entitled "Gura Kalvarye (Ger)" [Góra Kalwaria (Ger)]
- Situation of the Jewish population before the war and during the war (1939) and occupation (formation of Jewish Council 15.01.1940, M. Skrzypek [?], chairman, development of illegal trade with Warsaw, 25–26.02.1941 deportation to the Warsaw Ghetto [2,700 people], hunger is cause of numerous deaths among displaced persons from Góra Kalwaria).
- ***Description:*** original or transcript (handwritten manuscript, ink, 220×355 mm), transcript (2 copies) (handwritten manuscript—BW*, pencil, 148×210 mm), Yiddish, ss. 29, pp. 35.

In the transcript are missing the concluding fragments of the original or transcript (from pp. 9–11). In the transcript on p. 12, at the bottom, is the date: "19.08.1941."

Published: *Selected Documents*, pp. 188–197.

See HWC, 9/1 (third copy of the transcript, handwritten manuscript, pencil, ss. 12; in the margin a symbol: "—").

Index: Dr. Szulman, Dir. of the Cooperative Bank (Banku Spółdzielczego) in Góra Kalwaria; Wajnsztok, proprietor of sawmill in Góra Kalwaria; Jechiel Czarnaczapka, chairman of the Jewish Community in Góra Kalwaria after 09.1939

### 747. RING. I/547. Mf. ŻIH—791; USHMM—22

a)

- 4.06.1942, Grabowiec; after 5.06.1942, Warsaw Ghetto
- NN. (Ita and [Icchak?]) (Grabowiec, staying with Chawa Szrojt [?]), Letter of 4.06.1942 [postmark] to I. [Icchak] Cukierman (Warsaw, ul. Dzielna 34, apt. 8)
- Information about the deportation from Werbkowice and request for aid.
- ***Description:*** original (handwritten manuscript on a postcard, postmark and stamp of Jewish Council in Warsaw, ink, Polish 148×104 mm), transcript (2 copies, handwritten manuscript—H*, pencil, Polish, Yiddish, 150×195 mm), ss. 3, pp. 4.

Published: *Listy o Zagładzie*, pp. 167–169.

b)

- After 5.06.1942, Warsaw Ghetto
- NN. (Icchak[?]) (Grabowiec), Letter of 5.06.1942[?] to NN. (Henoch) (Warsaw Ghetto).
- Information about the deportation from Werbkowice and the imminent danger. Request for aid.
- ***Description:*** original (handwritten manuscript, ink, 154×94 mm), transcript (includes only the beginning fragment of the original) (2 copies, handwritten manuscript—H*, pencil, 205×147 mm, minor damage and losses of text), Polish, ss. 3, pp. 4.

On p. 1 (original) in a different handwriting (H*): "2. 5.6.42—Grabowiec."

According to Ruta Sakowska the addressee of the letter was Henoch Gutman; see *Listy o Zagładzie*, p. 169.

Published: *Listy o Zagładzie*, pp. 169–170.

Index: Chaim Szydło, Klewak

### 748. RING. I/549. Mf. ŻIH—836; USHMM—67

a)

- 01.1942, Grabów near Łęczyca.
- A. Zontag (Grabów near Łęczyca), Letter of [2[. . .].01.1942] to M. Zontag (Warsaw, ul. Zamenhofa 10, apt. 74). Information about the approaching annihilation.
- ***Description:*** original (handwritten manuscript on a postcard, postmark and stamp of Jewish Council in Warsaw, Yiddish in Roman transliteration), transcript (3 copies, typescript, Polish, 213×115 mm), ss. 4, pp. 5.
  Transcript (typescript) has original pagination: "5"

b)

- 21.01.1942, Grabów near Łęczyca
- NN. (Grabów near Łęczyca), Letter from NN. (Warsaw Ghetto)
- Information about the annihilation at Chełmno nad Nerem of Jews from Koło, Dąbie, Kłodawa, Izbica Kujawska and other surrounding towns.
- ***Description:*** original (handwritten manuscript, ink, Yiddish, 144×210 mm, minor damage and losses of text), transcript (3 copies, typescript, Polish, 212×166 mm), ss. 4, pp. 5.
  According to Ruta Sakowska (*Listy o Zagładzie*, pp. 3), letter's author was Rabbi Jakub Szulman.
  Published: *Listy o Zagładzie*, pp. 3–7.
  Index: Milsztajn, Chanełe, Kenigsberg

c)

- 22.01.1942, Grabów near Łęczyca
- M [. . .] [A.? Mirł?] Jachimiak (Grabów near Łęczyca), Letter dated 22.01.1942 to A. Jachimiak (Warsaw, Dzika 19—point [for displaced persons]). Information about the approaching annihilation.
- ***Description:*** original (handwritten manuscript on a postcard, Yiddish and Yiddish in Roman transliteration, 148×104 mm), transcript (3 copies, typescript, Polish, 207×293 mm), ss. 4, pp. 5.
  On p. 1 (transcript, second copy) notation by H.W.: "Trans. from Yiddish."
  Published: *Listy o Zagładzie*, pp. 10–11.

d)

- Beginning of 1942, Grabów near Łęczyca
- NN. (Grabów near Łęczyca), Letter to Szymon Józef (Warsaw [?]). (missing conclusion). Information on the annihilation of Jews from Kłodawa.
- ***Description:*** original, handwritten manuscript, ink, German and Yiddish in Roman transliteration, 142×204 mm, damage and losses of text, ss. 1, pp. 2.
  On p. 1 notation (ink): "Grabów near Łęczyca."

### 749. RING. I/934 (1253). Mf. ŻIH—829; USHMM—41

- After 31.10.1941, Warsaw Ghetto
- NN., Account entitled "What a certain twenty-year-old Jewish woman newly arrived from Grodno tells about the life of Jews in Polish territories occupied by the Soviets." (31.10.1941)
- Author (age 20) describes Jewish society in Grodno and vicinity during the Soviet occupation (situation of the Jewish and Polish population) and after the entry of Germans (slaughter of several hundred Grodno Jews, forced labor, persecutions, liquidation of the Jewish communities in neighboring small towns).
- ***Description:*** transcript (3 copies), handwritten manuscript (JG*), pencil, Polish, 148×210 mm, minor damage and losses of text (second copy), ss. 24, pp. 24.
  In the margins (first and third copies) a symbol (ink): "+."
  Attached note by H.W.: "Grodno. Wilno. Białystok 1939–1941. Handful of news gathered by Chil Górny (anonymous female informant)."
  Published: *Relacje z Kresów*, pp. 147–158.

### 750. RING. I/805 (1124). (Lb. 1587). Mf. ŻIH—826; USHMM—38

- After 11.1941, Warsaw Ghetto
- NN., Account entitled "Grodno. War's Outbreak"
- Situation of the Jewish population in the first months of German occupation: bombardmant of the town and entry of Germans 23.06.1941, Polish population's attitude toward the Germans, arrest of 1,000 residents, terror, plunder, Spanish units in Grodno, formation (1.11.1941) of two ghettos: at Rybny Rynek (for artisans) and at Słobudka.
- ***Description:*** transcript (2 copies), handwritten manuscript (CC*), pencil, Polish, 148×210 mm, ss. 24, pp. 24.
  Published: *Relacje z Kresów*, pp. 159–168.

### 751. RING. I/327. Mf. ŻIH—781; USHMM—12

- After 14.01.1941, place unknown
- Kreishauptmann des Kreises Sochaczew-Błonie (I.V. Kramer), Letters (dated 16.12.1940 and 14.01.1941) to the Jewish School in Grodzisk
- Matter of courses for seamstresses will be regulated within the framework of the ghetto. In Jewish schools it is not permitted to teach or use German, Polish, or Ukrainian; only Yiddish and Hebrew (neo-Hebrew).
- ***Description:*** transcript (2 copies), typescript, German, 195×110, 180×128 mm, minor damage and losses of text, ss. 4, pp. 4.

### 752. RING. I/21/2. Mf. ŻIH—772; USHMM—3

- After 07.1941, Warsaw
- Council of Elders of the Jewish Community in Grodzisk Mazowiecki, copies of minutes of meetings (December 1939–March 1940)
- Three records (dated 31.12.1939, 27.01. and 9.03.1940) concerning: aid for those deported from Poznański and Konstantynów, financial matters, distribution of aid received from the Joint, activities of TOZ, register

of the Jewish population in the town, organizational and personnel matters, selection of new Council authorities (appended names of the participants in the meetings as well as of persons working in the Council's offices).

- ***Description:*** original, typescript, Polish, 202×296 mm, ss. 2, pp. 3.

  Index: F. Płachta, Michrowski; Benda, Zurych Rajnberg; Czerwonkówna, Perelmuttrowa [Perelmutter?]; A. Szulman; Moszek Goldfarb; Fiszel Mendel Goldfarb; Dr. S. Appel; Izak Appel; Applowa, doctor's wife; Najman; Krygsman; Abram Kalisiak; M. Ho[u]tt; Abram Zysman; Glicensztajn, [Lejb] Alefrant; Sierpski, Szulim Żurkowski; J. Flint; M. Gothard; E. Szwebelblit; Josek Libchaber; Jankiel Libchaber; F. Gancer; Abram Nyson Imber; Hopensztand; Zakon; Szmulewicz; Waserbart; Bąkówna; Najmanowa; Alefrantowa; Wajcerówna; Kac; Zacman; Gotard; Fobe, [Samuel] Lewkowicz; Moddel Hollender; L. Knopmacher

### 753. RING. I/21/3. Mf. ŻIH—772; USHMM—3

- 1940–1941, Grodzisk Mazowiecki
- Council of Elders of the Jewish Community in Grodzisk Mazowiecki, Correspondence (outgoing) with Jehuda Glicensztein (1940)
- Three letters (dated 6.07., 17.11.1940, and third date unknown) contain: two notices of selection as a member of the Council (one dated 17.11.1940, other Date unknown) and an invitation to a meeting of the Arbitration Court (ul. Wólczyńska 16) on 28.07.1940 (Sunday) in the matter of Wajnsztok and Walanowski (appended certificate of the Council dated 3.02.1941 for Jehuda Glicensztein and Leib Alefrant to travel on the EKD line to the Labor Office [Arbeitsamt] in Warsaw).
- ***Description:*** original Council's letterhead, handwritten manuscript, typescript, ink, German, Polish, 216×145 216×200, 215×145, 215×174 mm, ss. 4, pp. 4.

  Jehuda Glicensztein (Glicenszteјn) was a member of the Council by January 1940 (see Minutes of the meeting on 27.01.1940). (See Ring. I/8, I/9, I/10, I/15, texts from I/8, I/9, I/15, I/21 [aside from the Jehuda G. correspondence, see Ring. I/21/3] were prepared by one person [?] and were copied on one machine, with similar graphic image, style, etc.).

### 754. RING. I/1086 (1405). Mf. ŻIH—833; USHMM—45

- Date unknown, 11–12.[1940], Grodzisk Mazowiecki
- Jewish Council in Grodzisk Mazowiecki, Correspondence
- Copies of telegrams sent: 1) dated 27.11.[1940] to Rainsztajn and Glicensztajn [?] in Tomaszów Lubelski, with encrypted information;

  2) Date unknown, to Glicenstein regarding moneys dispatched (signed Feid[?]);

  3) dated 7.12.[1940] to Zelfrowicz in Hrubieszów (Rynek), with information concerning B[. . .] who is in the labor camp in Dołhobyczów.
- ***Description:*** original, handwritten manuscript on printed letterheads, 3 handwritings, pencil, Polish, 147×208 mm, ss. 3, pp. 3.

  Doc. were kept in a binder.

### 755. RING. I/1078 (1397). (Lb. 752). Mf. ŻIH—832; USHMM—44

- After 9.02.1941, Warsaw Ghetto
- Jewish Council [in Grodzisk Mazowiecki], Minutes no. 50 of the session of Jewish Council on 9.02.1941
- Concerning the closing of the office and convening of a transfer (deportation) commission. Appended lists of names of participants of meetings and members of the deportation commission.
- ***Description:*** transcript, typescript, Polish, 207×293 mm, minor damage and losses of text, ss. 1, pp. 1.

  Attached note by H.W. in Yiddish: "Submitted by (member of the Jewish Council in Grodzisk) Jehuda Glicensztein from Poznań."

  Index: M. Hutt, member of the Jewish Council in Grodzisk Mazowiecki; Zygmunt Lewkowicz, member deportation commission in Grodzisk Mazowiecki in 02.1941; Płachta, member of the Jewish Council in Grodzisk Mazowiecki; Michrowski, member of the Jewish Council in Grodzisk Mazowiecki; L. Alefrant, member of the Jewish Council in Grodzisk Mazowiecki; Lipszyc, member of the Jewish Council in Grodzisk Mazowiecki; Glicensztajn, member of the Jewish Council in Grodzisk Mazowiecki; Dytman, member of the Jewish Council in Grodzisk Mazowiecki; Libhaber, member of the Jewish Council in Grodzisk Mazowiecki; Appel Ajzyk, member deportation commission in Grodzisk Mazowiecki in 02.1941; Cymerman, member deportation commission in Grodzisk Mazowiecki in 02.1941

### 756. RING. I/806 (1125). (Lb. 351). Mf. ŻIH—826; USHMM—38

- After 3.05.1941, Warsaw Ghetto
- NN., Account about the deportation of Jews from Grodzisk Mazowiecki. (3.05.1941)
- Deportation (end of 01.1941) of ca. 1,200 Jews from Brwinów, Podkowa Leśna, Nadarzyn, Milanówek, and other localities to Grodzisk; the subsequent expulsion of the Jewish population from Grodzisk (ca. 5,400 people) to the Warsaw Ghetto. Behavior of the Grodzisk Jewish Council during the deportation.
- ***Description:*** transcript (2 copies), handwritten manuscript (BW*), pencil, Yiddish, 148×210 mm., ss. 8, pp. 8.

In the margins a letter (ink, green): "F." On p. 1 in the margin notation in Yiddish in another handwriting: "Grodzisk."

Index: Hering of Grodzisk, Rozencwajg of Grodzisk, Miler of Grodzisk, Hutt of the Jewish Council in Grodzisk, Lewkowicz of the Jewish Council in Grodzisk, Kaliszak of the Jewish Council in Grodzisk, Fejg of the Jewish Council in Grodzisk, Michrowski of the Jewish Council in Grodzisk, Jehuda Glicensztejn, chairman of the Jewish Council in Grodzisk, Szajndl Birnbojm of Grodzisk, Joanna Bendewa of Grodzisk, Appel of Grodzisk, Menasze Kirszenbaum of Grodzisk, Cadok Rumelsbojg of Grodzisk, Chumelsburg Joanna [?], Natan Zarodnik

757. **RING. I/8, I/9, I/15. (Lb. I/8–1633, 925; I/15—845, 925, 844B, 829, 596). Mf. ŻIH—771; USHMM—2**

a) **Ring. I/9**

- After 07.1941, Warsaw Ghetto
- [Bernard Kampelmacher], Study entitled "Grodzisk Mazowiecki"
- History of the Jews in Grodzisk Mazowiecki before the war and during the occupation.
- ***Description:*** original, typescript with handwritten manuscript additions, ink, Polish, 200×296 mm, ss. 4, pp. 4. Attached 2 notes by H.W. in Polish and Yiddish.

b) **Ring. I/8**

- After 07.1941, Warsaw Ghetto
- [Bernard Kampelmacher], Study entitled "Grodzisk Mazowiecki. Synagogue and Bet-Midrash"
- History of the construction of the synagogue and religious school in Grodzisk, destruction of the synagogue and the Talmud Torah building in 1939.
- ***Description:*** original, typescript with handwritten manuscript additions, ink, Polish, 202×295 mm, ss. 1, pp. 2.

Ring. I/8 notation by H.W. in Yiddish (ink): "no. 19. 109–1942/1 January."

Index: Lejwa Gutgield of Grodzisk, Lajb Mąka, tailor, donor of the funds for the building of the Talmudic school in Grodzisk, Dawid Frajerman of Grodzisk, Zylberberg, owner of the house at ul. Sienkiewicza 12 in Grodzisk, Hutt of Grodzisk, Lewkowicz of Grodzisk

c) **Ring. I/8**

- After 07.1941, Warsaw Ghetto
- [Bernard Kampelmacher], Study entitled "Grodzisk Mazowiecki. Public Bath—Mikva"
- History of the mikve (Jewish ritual bath) in Grodzisk.
- ***Description:*** original, typescript with handwritten manuscript additions, ink, Polish, 204×295 mm, ss. 1, pp. 2.

Ring. I/8 notation by H.W. in Yiddish (ink): "no. 21. 109–1942/1 January."

On the doc. is a copy of a drawing of a policeman of the Order Service with a truncheon (copy of a drawing from Ring. I/35—the drawing was probably copied [via bleeding of ink] while the documents were buried in the earth and were located next to each other).

Index: Strulak of Grodzisk, Lejwa Koper of Grodzisk

d) **Ring. I/8**

- After 07.1941, Warsaw Ghetto
- [Bernard Kampelmacher], Study entitled "Grodzisk Mazowiecki. Jewish Cemetery"
- History of the Jewish cemetery.
- ***Description:*** original, typescript with handwritten manuscript additions, ink, Polish, 203×297 mm, ss. 1, pp. 2.

Ring. I/8 notation by H.W. in Yiddish (ink): "no. 18. 109–1942/1 January."

Index: Majlech Szapiro, rabbi of Grodzisk: Wederman of Grodzisk; Izaak Bąk of Grodzisk, perished 09.1939: Rajnberg

e) **Ring. I/8**

- After 07.1941, Warsaw Ghetto
- [Bernard Kampelmacher], Study entitled "Grodzisk Mazowiecki. Hosiery and capmaking [bereciarski] industry"
- Handicrafts in Grodzisk before the war and during the occupation.
- ***Description:*** original, typescript with handwritten manuscript additions, ink, Polish, 203×295 mm, ss. 1, pp. 2.

Ring. I/8 notation by H.W. in Yiddish (ink): "no. 20. 109–1942/1 January."

f) **Ring. I/15**

- After 07.1941, Warsaw Ghetto
- [Bernard Kampelmacher], Study entitled "Grodzisk Mazowiecki. Labor Section of the Jewish Council"
- Organization of forced labor for the Jewish population (inter alia in the labor camp in the Lublin region). Appended "Extracts from the Minutes of Meetings of the Jewish Council in Grodzisk" concerning the Labor Section.
- ***Description:*** a) original, typescript with handwritten manuscript additions, ink, Polish, 203×297 mm, ss. 4, pp. 6; b) transcript (3 copies), handwritten manuscript (BB*), pencil, Polish, 150×208 mm, damage and losses of text, ss. 57, pp. 57.

In the copy the appended material is missing. Doc. b) in three parts, on p. 1 (second copy, of each part) notation by H.W. (ink): "Kampel."

Attached note by H.W. in Yiddish: "Submitted by Kampelmacher, who died of typhus in the ghetto in early 1942."

Index: Major Dolf

g) Ring. I/9
- After 07.1941, Warsaw Ghetto
- [Bernard Kampelmacher], Study entitled "Grodzisk Mazowiecki. Return of Jews to Grodzisk after the deportation"
- Deportation of the Jewish population of Grodzisk (20.02.1941) to Warsaw and return of several Jews to the town. Appended description of the letter from Grodzisk mayor E. Radgowski of 27.06.1941 to Bernard Kampelmacher of the Grodzisk Hometown Association (Warsaw) in the matter of the dispatch of a health commission to Grodzisk in connection with a typhus epidemic.
- ***Description:*** a) original, typescript with handwritten manuscript additions, ink, Polish, 201×295 mm, ss. 1, pp. 2; b) transcript (3 copies), handwritten manuscript (BB*), pencil, Polish, 146×205 mm, damage and losses of text, ss. 30, pp. 30; enclosure, copy, typescript, Polish, 203×148 mm, ss. 1, pp. 1.
  In transcript (b) missing copy of the attached. Document b) on p. 1 (second copy) has notation by H.W. (ink): "Kampel."
  Index: Hutt of Grodzisk, Lewkowicz of Grodzisk, Rajnberg of Grodzisk, Blajfeder of Grodzisk, building owner, Dr. Wodzyński, Dr. Klamczyński

### 758. RING. I/10. Mf. ŻIH—771; USHMM—2
- After 07.1941, Warsaw Ghetto
- [Bernard Kampelmacher], "Grodzisk Mazowiecki. Schooling for Jewish Youth"
- Study concerning the history of Jewish education in in Grodzisk before the war and during the occupation. (Attached extract from the Minutes of the Jewish Council meeting of 6.01.1940 concerning formation and activity of school, school's director Bernard Kampelmacher.)
- ***Description:*** original or transcript (2 copies), typescript, Polish, 190×275 mm, damage and losses of text, ss. 12, pp. 12.
  On p. 1 notation by H.W.: "Kampel." On p. 1 (attached) notation by H.W.: "Kampel. 105/1[. . . damaged]."
  See Ring. I/8, I/9, I/15, I/21.

### 759. RING. I/21/1. Mf. ŻIH—772; USHMM—3
- After 07.1941, Warsaw
- [Bernard Kampelmacher?], "Profile of Samuel Lewkowicz, vice chairman of the Jewish Council in Grodzisk"
- Author accuses Lewkowicz of collaboration with the Germans, exploitation of his position for private interests, ruthless treatment of his opponents, financial embezzlements.
- ***Description:*** original, typescript (handwritten manuscript additions), Polish, 202×296 mm, ss. 4, pp. 4,
  At the top of pages a symbol: "(-)."

### 760. RING. I/881 (1201). (Lb. 174). Mf. ŻIH—828; USHMM—40
- 21.01.1941, after 21.01.1941, Grójec, place unknown
- Order of 21.01.1941 concerning the transfer of Jews residing in rural communities in the district of Grójec
  Order to move to the nearest town (by 27.01.1941): Błędów, Tarczyn, Mogielnica, Góra Kalwaria, Warki, or Grójec. Document signed by Maurer.
- ***Description:*** original (typescript, stamp of Jewish Council in Grójec, 220×350 mm, evidence of thumbtacks), transcript (typescript, 203×293 mm), German, Polish, ss. 2, pp. 2.
  Doc. (copy) was kept in a binder.

### 761. RING. I/1054 (1373). Mf. ŻIH—832; USHMM—44
- Date unknown, Warsaw Ghetto
- NN., Account of events in the ghetto in Grójec
- Reduction of the ghetto's area, preparations for selection and transfer, good relations with Poles.
- ***Description:*** original or transcript, handwritten manuscript (Ł*), ink, Yiddish, 111×350 mm, damage and losses of text, ss. 1, pp. 2.
  Attached note by H.W. in Yiddish: "By Nechemiasz Tytelman."
  Index: Werber, killed in Grójec; A.N. Israel of Grójec, Mosze Goldsztajn of Grójec, Dawid Wajntraub of Grójec

### 762. RING. I/1173 (1492). Mf. ŻIH—834; USHMM—46
- Date unknown, Warsaw Ghetto
- NN., Account of the situation of Jews in Grudziądz in 1939
- There were about 550 Jews in the town, relations with Poles and Germans before the war. Flight from the town after war's outbreak.
- ***Description:*** original (o), handwritten manuscript (H.W.*), ink, Yiddish, 155×197 mm, ss. 1, pp. 2.
  Attached note by H.W. in Yiddish.

### 763. RING. I/807 (1126). (Lb. 352). Mf. ŻIH—826; USHMM—38
- After 12.05.1941, Warsaw Ghetto
- NN., Account entitled "Grudzhondz" [Grudziądz] (12.05.1941)
- After Germans entered the town and refugees had returned, the Germans killed a majority of the Jews (ca. 300 people).
- ***Description:*** transcript (2 copies), handwritten manuscript (BW*), pencil, Yiddish, 146×146 mm, ss. 2, pp. 2.
  In the margin (first copy) a symbol (red pencil): "+."

### 764. RING. I/816 (1135). (Lb. 955)
- After 03.1942, Warsaw Ghetto

- NN., Accounts of Jews from Hamburg, Hanover, and environs
- Information collected among German deportees (ul. Leszno 109) about the situation of Jews in Germany after 1939: housing conditions, working for Germans, food, persecutions, deportations, German–Jewish relations, mood reigning among the German civilian population, attitude to the army and Hitler, Gestapo terror, bombardments of German cities.
- ***Description:*** original or transcript, handwritten manuscript, ink, Yiddish, 110×218, 170×250 mm, ss. 19, pp. 24.

  Part of the account is written on the back of a ŻOS circular, "Help Your Brothers Survive Winter," addressed to apartment house committees (hectographed typescript, Polish, 214×335 mm).

### 765. RING. I/591. Mf. ŻIH—792; USHMM—23

- 5.02.1942, Höckendorf near Drezno [?]
- Adela Piętek (Höckendorf near Drezno [?]), Letter of 5.02.1942 to Marysia Landau (Warsaw Ghetto)
- Author, a Pole, (addressee's nanny [?]), deported to work in Germany.
- ***Description:*** original, handwritten manuscript, pencil, Polish, 150×208 mm, ss. 1, pp. 2.

### 766. RING. I/978 (1297). Mf. ŻIH—831; USHMM—43

- 1.01.1940, Hohenstein [Olsztynek]
- [Missing office name], Certificate of voluntary departure from the Third Reich for the purpose of reaching Soviet-occupied territory. Document signed by Mojżesz Szosna.
- ***Description:*** original, printed, handwritten manuscript, pencil, stamp, German, 198×147mm, ss. 1, pp. 1.

  Various additional notations on the doc. (pencil): "Sz[?]araki 38,[. . .] 15.5.18. Ostrołęka."

  Doc. was kept in a binder.

### 767. RING. I/1132 (1451). (Lb. 750). Mf. ŻIH—833; USHMM—45

- 23.10.1940, Hrubieszów
- Judenrat of the City of Hrubieszów, Pass no. 1662 of 23.10.1940 for Jehuda Glicensztejn of Grodzisk allowing freedom of movement on 23.10.1940 along the streets: Wehrmachtstrasse, Ostlandstrasse, Kasernenstrasse, Narutowiczastrasse, Górnastrasse, and Kilińskiegostrasse in Hrubieszów.
- ***Description:*** original, printed, handwritten manuscript, pencil, stamp of the Jewish Council in Hrubieszów, German, 153×113 mm, ss. 1, pp. 1.

  Doc. was kept in a binder.

### 768. RING. I/810 (1129). Mf. ŻIH—826; USHMM—38

- 10.07.1942, Warsaw Ghetto
- Dawid Mandelbaum, Account entitled "Hrubieshov" [Hrubieszów] (10.07.1942)
- Author, a resident of Warsaw (Praga district) in 1941 traveled from the Warsaw Ghetto to Hrubieszów; describes the situation of Jews in Hrubieszów (ca. 7,000 Jews, there was no hunger, good relations with Poles, after 01.1942 living conditions deteriorated, from 1.06.1942 the liquidation of the ghetto commenced: 500 persons were killed at the cemetery, 4,500 were shipped off to an unknown destination, and a [forced] contribution was exacted from those left. The author fled to Warsaw).
- ***Description:*** transcript, handwritten manuscript (Sz.*), ink, Yiddish, 140×223 mm, extensive minor damage and losses of text, ss. 6, pp. 6.

  Index: Bergman, brothers, killed on 27.04.1942 in Hrubieszów, Ben Cyjon, family, killed on 27.04.1942 in Hrubieszów

### 769. RING. I/811 (1130). (Lb. 486, 981). Mf. ŻIH—826; USHMM—38

- 06.1942, Warsaw Ghetto
- NN., Account entitled "Hrubieshov un di iberige shtetlekh beshas der 'aktsye'" [Hrubieszów and the other small towns during the 'action'] and an account of the ghetto in Częstochowa (15.06.1942)
- Report of journey to Werbkowice, also a description of the liquidation action in Hrubieszów—7.06.1942 (Sunday), Miączyn—8.06.1942 (Monday) (Germans gathered here ca. 5,000 persons from Grabowiec and surrounding localities, 700–800 healthy people were released to work, the rest were loaded onto wagons; attached sketch of the place where Jews were rounded up); Werbkowice, situation of the Jewish workers; Rejowiec, only 200 Jews remained here, the rest were deported at the end of May, there are also Czech Jews; Częstochowa, description of the local ghetto's life, positive activity of the Jewish Council (notation from early 05.1942).
- ***Description:*** transcript (a) (handwritten manuscript—LEG*, notebook, ink, 153×195 mm, minor damage and losses of text), transcript (3 copies, typescript, 203×138, 208×296 mm, damage and losses of text), Polish, Yiddish, ss. 31, pp. 40.

  On p. 1 (transcript—a) notation in Yiddish (ink): "Hrubieszów" and notation by H.W.: "16 standard pages. June 1942."

  Published: (reports on Hrubieszów and Werbkowice) *BFG*, vol. XXXI/1993, pp. 84–91; according to Ruta Sakowska, the author of the account of the journey to Werbkowice is Fruma Płotnicka, whom Chawa Folman accompanied (ibid.).

  Index: Lublink [?], chairman of the Jewish workers council in Częstochowa

### 770. RING. I/814 (1133). (Lb. 206, 231, 526). Mf. ŻIH—826; USHMM—38

- 30.06.1942, Warsaw Ghetto

- Dychterman, Account entitled "Hrubieszów—Poland's Granary" (30.06.1942)
- Author departed Warsaw 3.09.1941 with child and mother to join husband (F. Dychterman) in Hrubieszów. She describes living conditions of the Jewish population in Hrubieszów (trade, prices, Jewish Council—attached list of members, relations with Germans, forced labor, mortality), describes in detail the course of the deportation and liquidation actions in the vicinity of Hrubieszów and the liquidation action in the town itself (1 and 6.06.1942). Escape with her husband to Warsaw (11.06.1942).
- ***Description:*** transcript (3 copies), typescript (handwritten manuscript additions H.W.*, ink on the first copy), Polish, Yiddish in Roman transliteration, 207×292 mm, minor damage and losses of text, extensive damage and losses of text (first copy), ss. 21, pp. 21.

  On p. 1 (second copy) notation by H.W. (ink): "13 standard pages."

  Attached note by H.W.: "Forwarded by H.W."

  Index: Szmul Brand, chairman of the Jewish Council in Hrubieszów (Zionist); Joel Rabinowicz, secretary of the Jewish Council in Hrubieszów (Zionist); Fiszel Zylbersztajn, member of the Jewish Council in Hrubieszów (Zionist); Ajzyk Finger, member of the Jewish Council in Hrubieszów (Zionist); Szmul Zajd, member of the Jewish Council in Hrubieszów (Bund); Hersz Zylber, member of the Jewish Council in Hrubieszów (Aguda); Mojsze Sztecher, member of the Jewish Council in Hrubieszów; Jakub Perec, member of the Jewish Council in Hrubieszów; Mojsze Frymer, member of the Jewish Council in Hrubieszów (Bund); Srul Szpiler, member of the Jewish Council in Hrubieszów (Folkist); Ezryel Finkielsztajn, member of the Jewish Council in Hrubieszów (Aguda); Jukiel Brand, member of the Jewish Council in Hrubieszów; Akerman, director of the Arbeitsamt in Hrubieszów; Josel Feld, baker from Warsaw; Lejzor Mangel; Froim "Czuisz"-Feler; Szyfra Waldman; Berysz Dychterman, brother of the husband of the account's author; Matys Blas of Hrubieszów; Matys Kirszner; Szulim Kirszner (age 20); Basia Kirszner (age 21); Frajda Kirszner (age 16)

### 771. RING. I/550. Mf. ŻIH—791; USHMM—22

a)

- 2.05.[1942], [Hrubieszów?]
- Gutman [Hrubieszów?], Telegram dated 2.05.[1942] to NN. (Warsaw Ghetto). Request for aid.
- ***Description:*** original, printed, typescript, German, Polish, 210×145 mm, ss. 1, pp. 1.

  Attached note by H.W. in Yiddish: "Telegram sent 05.1942 during action."

  According to Ruta Sakowska, the telegram was sent from Hrubieszów by Henoch Gutman to the management of Hechaluc-Dror about the threat to the kibbutz at Werbkowice; see *Listy o Zagładzie*, pp. 80–81.

  Published: *Listy o Zagładzie*, pp. 80–81.

b)

- 1.06.1942, Warsaw Ghetto
- NN. (Brocha) (Hrubieszów), Letter of 1.06.1942 NN. (Warsaw Ghetto)
- Notation about the approaching annihilation of the ghetto in Hrubieszów and the kibbutz in Werbkowice.
- ***Description:*** original (handwritten manuscript, ink, 157×197 mm, minor damage and losses of text, text illegible in places), transcript (2 copies, handwritten manuscript—LEG*, pencil, 148×205 mm), Yiddish, ss. 3, pp. 4.

  Attached note by H.W. in Yiddish

  According to Ruta Sakowska, the letter was sent to the leadership of Hechaluc-Dror; see *Listy o Zagładzie*, p. 164.

  Published: *Listy o Zagładzie*, pp. 164–166.

  Index: Perec Piwnik, Chaim Sidło, Szoul [Dobuchno?]

### 772. RING. I/552/2. Mf. ŻIH—791; USHMM—22

- 21.03.1942, Hrubieszów
- Icek Pomaranc (Hrubieszów), Telegram to NN. (Warsaw Ghetto). Information about a past danger.
- ***Description:*** original, printed, typescript, German, Polish, 207×143 mm, ss. 1, pp. 1.

  Published: *Listy o Zagładzie*, pp. 81–82.

### 773. RING. I/812 (1131). Mf. ŻIH—826; USHMM—38. RING. I/998 (1317). Mf. ŻIH—831; USHMM—43

- After 26.06.1942, Warsaw Ghetto
- NN. (Hrubieszów), Letter of 26.06.1942 to NN. (Warsaw Ghetto [?])
- Account about preparations for and course of liquidation actions: Hrubieszów (31.05–9.06.1942), Bełz (3.06.1942), Dubienka (2.06.1942), Grabowiec (12.06.1942).
- ***Description:*** transcript (2 copies), handwritten manuscript (LEG*), pencil, Hebrew, 220×230, 215×350 mm, damage and losses of text, ss. 4, pp. 4.

  On p. 1 notation handwritten manuscript (LEG*): "A briv fun Hrubieshov vegn di aktsye-teg" [A Letter from Hrubieszów about the Action Days]

### 774. RING. I/815 (1134). (Lb. 143). Mf. ŻIH—826; USHMM—38

- 17.07.1942, Warsaw Ghetto
- NN., Account entitled "News about Events in Hrubieszów Area"
- Author (age 19) in May 1941 found his way from

Włocławek to work at the estate in Dłużniewo near Hrubieszów, describes the liquidation action during 1–10.06.1942 in the vicinity of Hrubieszów (of 10,000 Jews, 3,500 remained). Author procured a pass and left for Warsaw.
- ***Description:*** transcript, handwritten manuscript (E*), ink, Polish, 150×194 mm, ss. 2, pp. 4.

### 775. RING. I/954 (1273). (Lb. 996). Mf. ŻIH–830; USHMM–42

- Date unknown, Warsaw Ghetto
- NN., Account of repressive actions against the Jewish population of Iłowo near Płock.
- ***Description:*** original or transcript, handwritten manuscript, ink, Hebrew, 210×303 mm, minor damage and losses of text, ss. 3, pp. 5.

### 776. RING. I/819 (1138). (Lb. 382). Mf. ŻIH–826; USHMM–38

- After 3.07.1941, Warsaw Ghetto
- NN., Account entitled "Poyzn-Pomozhe. Inovrotslav" [Poznań–Pomorze, Inowrocław] (3.07.1941)
- History of the Jewish community in Inowrocław and its annihilation during the war (45 families). Annihilation of the Jewish population centers in the vicinity of Inowrocław.
- ***Description:*** transcript, handwritten manuscript (BW*), pencil, Yiddish, 148×210 mm, minor damage and losses of text, ss. 7, pp. 7.

  In the margins a letter (ink): "A."

  Index: Dr. [Leopold] Levi, chairman of the Jewish community in Inowrocław, perished in 09.1939; Dr. Warschauer of Inowrocław, Nachemstein of Inowrocław; Martin Grider, owner of a mill in Inowrocław; Artur Hirsch, owner of a mill in Inowrocław; Kirstein, merchant of Inowrocław; Rozenowicz, perished; Hirsch, brothers, perished; Przedborskis, perished

### 777. RING. I/949 (1268). Mf. ŻIH–830; USHMM–42

- After 04.1942, Warsaw Ghetto
- NN., Account entitled "Izbica Lub[elska]"
- In the town were ca. 5,000 Jews (inter alia deportees from Koło, Czech). Description of liquidation actions on 24.03. and 8.04.1942.
- ***Description:*** original or transcript, handwritten manuscript (GG *), ink, Polish, 100×149 mm, ss. 1, pp. 2.

### 778. RING. I/599/109. Mf. ŻIH–812; USHMM–24

- 04.1942, Izbica Lubelska [?]
- NN., Letter to [. . .]Konińska (Warsaw, ul. Ogrodowa 5, apt. 30)
- Inf.: 16 persons live in one room, typhus epidemic.
- ***Description:*** original, handwritten manuscript on a postcard, postmarks (inter alia Gorzków near Krasnystaw) and stamp of the Jewish Council in Warsaw, ink, Polish, 95×104 mm, serious damage and losses of text, ss. 1, pp. 2.

  On p. 1 in another handwriting (pencil): "from Izbica Lubelska."

  At ul. Ogrodowa 5 resided Natan Koniński, coworker of Oyneg Shabes; see Ring. I/1152/2.

### 779. RING. I/578. Mf. ŻIH–792; USHMM–23

- 06.1942, Janów Podlaski
- Jurberg [?], Letter of [11.06.1942] to Berek Lejb Jurberg (Warsaw, ul. Wołyńska 17, apt. 4 [?])
- Notation about the upcoming change of residence (concerning deportation [?]).
- ***Description:*** original, handwritten manuscript on a postcard, postmark (Janów Podlaski) and stamp of the Jewish Council in Warsaw, ink, Polish, 147×104 mm, extensive minor damage and losses of text, text illegible in places, ss. 1, pp. 2.

  On p. 1 notation: "Leszno 67/49" and in Yiddish: "Library 12–4."

  According to Ruta Sakowska, *Listy o Zagładzie*, p. 173, the letter was addressed to the name Hirberg.

  Published: *Listy o Zagładzie*, p. 173 (differences from the original text).

### 780. RING. I/821 (1140). (Lb. 1588). Mf. ŻIH–826; USHMM–38

- After 25.01.[1941], Warsaw Ghetto
- B. Janowski, Account entitled "Deportation from Jeziorna"
- Situation of the Jewish population in Jeziorna before deportation and the course of transfer to the ghetto in Warsaw (25.01.1941).
- ***Description:*** original (handwritten manuscript, ink, 200×260 mm), transcript (3 copies, handwritten manuscript-JG*, pencil, 146×207 mm, minor damage and losses of text), Polish, ss. 22, pp. 27.

  The third copy is missing the last page.

  See Ring. I/980.

### 781. RING. I/980 (1299). Mf. ŻIH–831; USHMM–43

- After 20.01.1941, Warsaw Ghetto
- NN., Account entitled "Tsvey faktn vegn vakhn. Yezhorne—januar 1941" [Two Facts about Keeping Watch. Jeziorna—January 1941] (missing conclusion)
- Occupation authorities' orders on sealing of the ghetto in Jeziorna.
- ***Description:*** transcript (2 copies), handwritten manuscript (H.W.*), pencil, Yiddish, 148×210 mm, ss. 2, pp. 2.

### 782. RING. I/564/2. Mf. ŻIH–791; USHMM–22

- 27.02.1942, Józefów near Zamość
- W. Wołkowicz (Józefów near Zamość), Letter of 27.02.1942 to NN. (Laiwe) (Warsaw, ul. Nowolipie 47, apt. 95, with Hinda Strykowska)

- Thanks for letter received. Information about past danger.
- ***Description:*** original, handwritten manuscript (two handwritings) on a postcard, postmark and stamp of Jewish Council in Warsaw, ink, Polish, 148×104 mm, ss. 1, pp. 2.

  Sender: "W. Wołkowicz," although the signature at the bottom of the letter is illegible. Added written greetings from: "Harry [?] G."

  See Ring. I/564/1.

**783. RING. I/826 (1145). (Lb. 842); I/825 (1144). (Lb. 842). Mf. ŻIH—826; USHMM—38. RING. I/476. Mf. ŻIH—786; USHMM—17. RING. I/830 (1149). (Lb. 866). Mf. ŻIH—827; USHMM—39. RING. I/1218. Mf. ŻIH—835; USHMM—47**

a) **Ring. I/826 (1145). (Lb. 842)**
- After 12.07.1941, Warsaw Ghetto
- [Natan Koniński?], Account by a Kalisz native from 1939, [part I], "Kalisz—August" (12.07.1941)
- Situation in the city before outbreak of war (moods of Jewish and Polish population, preparations for military operations, evacuation).
- ***Description:*** transcript (2 copies), handwritten manuscript (JG*), pencil, Polish, 147×201 mm, minor damage and losses of text, ss. 14, pp. 14.

b) **Ring. I/825 (1144). (Lb. 842)**
- After 2.08.1941, Warsaw Ghetto
- [Natan Koniński?], Account by a Kalisz native from 1939, part II, "September 1939. Koło" (19.07.1941); part III, "Jews in Kalisz from September to November 1939" (2.08.1941)
- Author fled (1.09.1939) from Kalisz to Koło, describes the first days of war, and the subsequent occupation in Koło (bombardments, taking of the city by Germans 16.09.1939, repressive measures against Jews, burning of the synagogue—19.09.), return to Kalisz. Situation of the Jewish population in Kalisz in the first months of the occupation (repressive measures, requisitions, forced labor, attitude of the Polish population to Jews, uprising (10.10.1939), and activities of the Jewish Council (ul. Kanonicka)—appended list of members, deportation of Jews from the city).
- ***Description:*** original or transcript, handwritten manuscript (E*), ink, Polish, 148×208 mm, ss. 71, pp. 82.

  Index:

  Dr. [Chil] Pfeffer, physician from Koło; Herszbajn, Bundist, member of the Civil Guard in Koło in 09.1939; Rozen, shot 19.09.1939 in Koło; Szlama Feldman (age 18) from Koło; Weingart, owner of an oil mill in Kalisz (ul. Górnośląska 28); Mendel Alter, rabbi of Kalisz; Heber of Kalisz; Rozenblum of Kalisz; Hahn, cantor, chairman of the Jewish Council in Kalisz; engineer Cukier, factory owner, member of the Jewish Council in Kalisz; Leon Rynek, factory owner, member of the Jewish Council in Kalisz; Zajdel, merchant, member of the Jewish Council in Kalisz; Lewkowicz, chairman of the Jewish bank and secondary school (gimnazjum), member of the Jewish Council in Kalisz; [Maurycy] Kacinel, attorney, member of the Jewish Council in Kalisz; [Tobiasz Józef] Perkal, attorney, chairman of ORT and TOZ, member of the Jewish Council in Kalisz; Dr. [Juda] Płocki, member of the Jewish Council in Kalisz; Mojżesz Szlumper, former city councilman, activist of Left Po'ale Tsiyon (Poale Syjon Lewicy), member of the Jewish Council in Kalisz; Michał Ajzenberg, former city councilman, Bundist, member of the Jewish Council in Kalisz; Dawid Herman, member of the Jewish Council in Kalisz; Luzer Mitz, Bundist, chairman of the Tailors' Association, member of the Jewish Council in Kalisz; Leon Siemiatycki, chairman of the Jewish bank, member of the Jewish Council in Kalisz; Rzepkowicz, member of the bank's board, member of the Jewish Council in Kalisz; Wiśniewski, factory owner, member of the Jewish Council in Kalisz; Samuel [Bengon] Arkusz, secretary of the Association of Jewish Artisans, member of the Jewish Council in Kalisz; Dr. [Rafał] Lubelski, member of the Jewish Council in Kalisz; Dr. [Dawid] Seid, member of the Jewish Council in Kalisz; Maks Górny of Kalisz; Bordowicz of Kalisz; Karo of Kalisz; Winter of Kalisz; Edelsztajn of Kalisz; Dr. Gross-Schinaglowa of Kalisz; Dr. [Edward] Beatus of Kalisz; Flinkier, co-owner of a mill, former editor of a Yiddish newspaper in Kalisz, killed by Germans in 1939

c) **Ring. I/830 (1149). (Lb. 866)**
- After 23.08.1941, Warsaw Ghetto
- [Natan Koniński?], Account of a Kalisz native from 1939, part IV, "From Kalisz to Warsaw" (23.08.1941)
- Author and his mother and younger brother flee from Kalisz to Warsaw (11.1939) (description of the journey with numerous changes of train, searches, and robberies carried out by German soldiers and railroad workers at the stations).
- ***Description:*** transcript (2 copies), typescript, Polish, 200×280 mm, minor damage and losses of text, ss. 12, pp. 12.

  On p. 1 notation by H.W. (ink): "Kon."

d) **Ring. I/476**
- After 31.08.1941, Warsaw Ghetto
- [Natan Koniński?], Account of a Kalisz native from 1939, [part] V, "Journey to Russia" (31.08.1941)
- Unsuccessful attempt to escape to territory occupied by the USSR at the end of November 1939.

- *Description:* original or transcript, handwritten manuscript (E*), ink, Polish, 148×208mm, ss. 6, pp. 12.
  - Attached note by H.W.: "1939—5th fragment. Manuscript 12 pages. Journey to Russia. Two unsuccessful attempts to cross the Bug River to the Soviet Union. Deposition of N. Koniński, coworker of the Archive."
  - Published: *Relacje z Kresów*, pp. 3–12.
  - Index: Judyta Horowicz of Kalisz, Głowiński of Kalisz, Wera Bakiel of Kalisz, Josef Weissberg of Kalisz

e) **Ring. I/825 (1144). (Lb. 842)**

- After 19.10.1941, Warsaw Ghetto
- [Tobiasz Józef] Perkal, Account on the situation of the Jewish population in Kalisz: "[. . .] from September to November 1939 [. . .] in conversation with att[orney] Perkal, former member of the Council of Elders in Kalisz" (19.10.1941)
- Flight of Jews from the city in the first months of occupation, formation and activity of the Jewish Council (appended list of members). Deportation of the Jewish population (11.1939).
- *Description:* transcript (a) (handwritten manuscript (E*), ink, 150×217 mm, minor damage and losses of text), transcript (b) (3 copies) handwritten manuscript—BTT*, pencil, 148×209 mm, damage and losses of text (first and third copies), Polish, ss. 63, pp. 66.
  - On pp. 1 and 5 of transcript a) is a symbol (in pencil): "V."
  - On p. 1 (transcript (b), second copy) notation by H.W. (ink): "Kon."
  - Index: Aleksander Poznański, member of the Jewish Council in Kalisz, Rotcejg, MA, member of the Jewish Council in Kalisz, Ulrych of Kalisza, Chmielnicki, industrialist of Kalisz

f) **Ring. I/1218**

- [1941], Warsaw Ghetto
- Sponsors' Committee of the Kalisz Hometown Association (Patronat Ziomkostwa Kaliskiego) in the Warsaw Ghetto, Circular with request for donations for the benefit of refugees from Kalisz
- Signed, inter alia, by the head of the Sponsors' Committee J. [Tobiasz Józef] Perkal and secretary Silberberg.
- *Description:* original, typescript, Polish, 205×228 mm, damage and losses of text, ss. 1, pp. 1.

### 784. RING. I/441. Mf. ŻIH—785; USHMM—16

- After 11.1939, Warsaw Ghetto
- Perla K., Account entitled "Di kalisher mark-hale als yidn-lager" [The Kalisz Market Hall as a Camp for Jews]
- Author and her family were evicted from apartment (11.1939) and settled in a camp in the former market hall, but subsequently escaped to Warsaw.
- *Description:* transcript, handwritten manuscript (CHW*), ink, Yiddish, 157×202 mm, ss. 3, pp. 6.
  - Attached note by H.W. in Yiddish: "Edited by Jechaskiel Wilczyński."

### 785. RING. I/827 (1146). (Lb. 1617). Mf. ŻIH—826; USHMM—38

- After 1.01.1941, Warsaw Ghetto
- NN., Account entitled "Milkhome notitsn vegn Kalish" [War Notes about Kalisz] (1.01.1941)
- Fate of the Jewish population in Kalisz from August until the deportation in November 1939. Entry of Germans into Brudzew. Activity of the Labor Battalion in Kalisz.
- *Description:* transcript (3 copies), handwritten manuscript (U*), pencil, Yiddish, 148×210 mm, ss. 15, pp. 15.
  - Index: Waksztan from Kalisz, Sodarkiewicz from Kalisz, Lewiński from Kalisz

### 786. RING. I/828 (1147). (Lb. 324). Mf. ŻIH—827; USHMM—39

- After 9.02.1940, Warsaw Ghetto
- NN., Account entitled "Kalish" [Kalisz] (9.02.1940)
- Situation of Jews in Kalisz from the entry of Germans (4.09.1939) until February 1940 (formation and activity of the Jewish Council—appended list of members, Labor Battalion, deportation in 11.1939, liquidation of the Jewish hospital in 02.1940).
- *Description:* transcript, handwritten manuscript (MS*), pencil, Yiddish, 148×210 mm, ss. 2, pp. 2.
  - In the margins a Hebrew letter (ink): "p" (pei) or "f" (fey) and a symbol, a dot beneath a horizontal line.
  - Doc. was kept in a binder.
  - Index: Wajngart from Kalisz (ul. Górnośląska 26); H. Hahn, chairman of the Jewish Council in Kalisz; engineer Cukier, member of the Jewish Council in Kalisz; M. Ajzenberg, member of the Jewish Council in Kalisz; attorney [Maurycy] Kacinel, member of the Jewish Council in Kalisz; Siemiatycki; attorney J. Perkal, member of the Jewish Council in Kalisz; D. Herman, member of the Jewish Council in Kalisz; M. Szlumper, member of the Jewish Council in Kalisz; Wiśniewski, member of the Jewish Council in Kalisz; B. Arkusz, member of the Jewish Council in Kalisz; Zajdel, member of the Jewish Council in Kalisz; Frenkel, member of the Jewish Council in Kalisz; K. Górny, member of the Jewish Council in Kalisz; B. Rzepkiewicz, member of the Jewish Council in Kalisz; Grinbojm, member of the Jewish Council in Kalisz; Dr. Zajd [Seid], member of the Jewish Council in Kalisz; Dr. [R.] Lubelski, member of the Jewish Council in Kalisz; Górny of the Labor Battalion in Kalisz; Bordowicz of the

Labor Battalion in Kalisz; Szenfeld of the Labor Battalion in Kalisz; Karo of the Labor Battalion in Kalisz; Winter of the Labor Battalion in Kalisz; Edelsztejn of the Labor Battalion in Kalisz; Kloc (Klotz) of the Labor Battalion in Kalisz

### 787. RING. I/829 (1148). Mf. ŻIH—827; USHMM—39

- Date unknown, Warsaw Ghetto
- NN., Account entitled "Kalish" [Kalisz]
- Author (age 40), horse dealer, resident of Kalisz, in first days of the war (1939) fled with family to Warsaw. On the way back they were seized by Germans near Rawa; they found their way to transit camp in Częstochowa.
- ***Description:*** transcript (2 copies), handwritten manuscript (MS*), pencil, Yiddish, 148×210 mm, ss. 16, pp. 16.

  In the margins a symbol (ink): circle in a circle.

### 788. RING. I/444. Mf. ŻIH—785; USHMM—16

- Date unknown, Warsaw Ghetto
- NN., Account entitled "Mayne nesies beys der milkhome–aktsies arum Kalish" [My Journeys during the Military Operations around Kalisz]
- Author from Kalisz, outbreak of war in 1939, evacuation from the city (Turek, Koło, Łęczyca) and return after conclusion of combat, first persecutions of the Jewish population, flight from Kalisz to Warsaw.
- ***Description:*** transcript, handwritten manuscript (CHW*), ink, Yiddish, 157×202 mm, ss. 4, pp. 8.

  Attached note by H.W. in Yiddish: "Edited by Jechaskiel Wilczyński."

### 789. RING. I/255. Mf. ŻIH—799; USHMN—30; RING. I/1219. Mf. ŻIH—835; USHMM—47

- After 1941, Warsaw Ghetto
- Manuscript contains transcripts of three accounts (fragments)

  1) NN., Account entitled "2.5 yor Varshe" [2.5 years Warsaw] (fragment)

  Deportation of Jewish population from Kalisz (16–17.11.1939), the road to Warsaw.

  2) NN., Account entitled "Kolo Bugay" [Bugaj Colony (?)].

  Formation in Bugaj of a "Jewish colony" of displaced persons from Koło and Babiak, Jewish Council (list of members), construction of housing, worsening relations in the Jewish Council.

  3) NN., Account from Lwów.

  Situation of the Jewish population on territories occupied by the USSR in 1939 (Lwów, Stanisławów, Tarnopol), refugees, formation of collective farms, beginning of war with the Germans (1941) (pogroms, mass executions, [forced] contributions, burning of synagogues, formation of ghetto).
- ***Description:*** transcript, handwritten manuscript (U*), notebook, pencil, Yiddish, 277×477, 242×343, 145×203 mm, substantial damage and losses of text, ss. 22, pp. 41.

  Part of the manuscript (sheet 5) is written on accounting forms ("Zestawienie kasowe") (Warsaw, 1941, printed, Polish); one sheet of an order form (date unknown, printed, Polish).

  Attached note by H.W. in Polish and Yiddish: "Jewish colony in Wartheland. Bugaj. On the back a fragment of a statement about Lwów."

  Index: Warnbrun, chairman of the Jewish Council in Bugaj; Nojman, secretary of the Jewish Council in Bugaj; Beatus, member of the Jewish Council in Bugaj (provisioning); Rzeszewski, member of the Jewish Council in Bugaj; Brawman, member of the Jewish Council in Bugaj; Babian [?], member of the Jewish Council in Bugaj; Krotowski, member of the Jewish Council in Bugaj; Frost, member of the Jewish Council in Bugaj; Laskowski, informer in Bugaj; Ladman [?], member of the Jewish Council in Bugaj; Kiwes, member of the Jewish Council in Bugaj; Przedecki, informer in Bugaj; Brawman, informer in Bugaj; Rozental, informer in Bugaj; Dr. Wachman; Halbersztam, Tsadik of Bobowa; Dr. I. Lewin; [Rabbi Aron] Lewin, former deputy to the Sejm of Poland; Henryk Heszeles, editor of [Warsaw's Yiddish daily] *Der Moment*

### 790. RING. I/557/1. Mf. ŻIH—791; USHMM—22

- 19.02.1942, Kalisz
- M. [Moniek] Gross (Kalisch [Kalisz], Wienerstrasse 13), Letter of 19.02.1942 to B. [Bronek] Lustig and Natan [Lustig?] (Warsaw, ul. Nowolipie 38, apt. 7)
- Information about loss of parents sent out together with a group of ca. 2,000 [sic] persons to death camp. In Kalisz 150 Jews remained.
- ***Description:*** original, handwritten manuscript on a postcard, postmark and stamp of the Jewish Council in Warsaw, ink, Polish, 147×105 mm, ss. 1, pp. 2.

  Published: *Listy o Zagładzie*, pp. 27–29.

### 791. RING. I/822 (1141). (Lb. 410). Mf. ŻIH—826; USHMM—38

- After 12.05.1941, Warsaw Ghetto
- NN., Account entitled "Kalishin" [Kałuszyn] (12.05.1941)
- Jewish population in Kałuszyn before the war (ca. 1,500 families), during war and occupation (significant destruction and numerous victims in 09.1939, at the end of 1940 ca. 4,000 Jews in the town, from 02.1941 intensified persecution).
- ***Description:*** transcript (2 copies), handwritten

manuscript (BW*), pencil, Yiddish, 148×210 mm, minor damage and losses of text, ss. 4, pp. 4.

In the margins letter (ink): "c"; on p. 1 (first copy) a symbol (red pencil): "+."

## 792. RING. I/823 (1142). (Lb. 434). Mf. ŻIH—826; USHMM—38

a)

- [Date unknown,] Warsaw Ghetto
- NN., Account entitled "Im lo yagid . . . (Kalushin)" [If he won't tell . . . (Kałuszyn)]
- Description of the first days of war (1–11.09.1939): panic, bombardments, numerous victims among the people (42 persons) and material losses.
- ***Description:*** transcript (2 copies), handwritten manuscript (MS*), pencil, Yiddish [but Hebrew title], 148×210 mm, ss. 8, pp. 8.

Text is divided into two parts with separate pagination.

In the margins a Hebrew letter (ink): "pey."

On p. 1 (second part) a symbol (red pencil): "+."

Doc. was kept in a binder.

Index: Judit Frucht (age 55) and daughter Rywka (age 25) and grandson (age 3) perished during bombardments in Kałuszyn (09.1939); Jona Telipc [Teplic?] (age 55) and daughters (age 16 and 22) and grandson (age 2) perished during bombardments in Kałuszyn (09.1939); Abrajnicki (?) (age 18), perished during bombardments in Kałuszyn (09.1939); Abrajnicka (?) (age 60), perished during bombardments in Kałuszyn (09.1939); Lajzer Gorzałka (age 48), perished during bombardments in Kałuszyn (09.1939); Gorzałka (age 45) and her daughter (age 24) and granddaughter (age 2) perished during bombardments in Kałuszyn (09.1939); Dawid Hersz, perished during bombardments in Kałuszyn (09.1939)

b)

- Date unknown, Warsaw Ghetto
- NN., Account about the fate of the Jewish population in Kałuszyn during the September Campaign and in the first days of the occupation (1939)
- Bombardment of 10.09.1939 (45 people died), battle for the town, occupation of Kałuszyn by Germans (11.09.1939) and start of the repressive measures against Jews (several hundred people perished).
- ***Description:*** transcript (2 copies), handwritten manuscript (BW*), pencil, Yiddish, 148×208 mm, ss. 12, pp. 12.

In the margins a symbol (ink): "| |." On p. 1 (first copy) notation by H.W. in Yiddish (ink): "Kałuszyn."

Index: Szymon Horończyk, coworker of [Warsaw Yiddish daily] *Der Moment*, committed suicide in Kałuszyn on 8.09.1939

## 793. RING. I/1220/12. Mf. ŻIH—835; USHMM—47

- Before 20.03.1942, Kielce
- [Al]testenrat der Juden. Abteilung Gesundheitswesen in Kielce [. . .] [Council of Elders of Jews, Health Department in Kielce] [, [Document?] no. 4728 for Szmul Kapłan (Radom, ul.[. . .]). Doc. valid until 20.03.1942.
- ***Description:*** original, printed, handwritten manuscript, ink, stamp, German, 130×137 mm, substantial damage and losses of text, ss. 1, pp. 1.

## 794. RING. I/211/4. (Lb. 881). Mf. ŻIH—779; USHMM—10

- After 19.06.1941, place unknown
- Record of inspection by the District Welf[are] Committee (KOP) in Kielce on 18 and 19 June 1941, by engineer A. Reinberg, delegate of the AJDC (fragments [?])
- Description of the activity of the KOP within the district (9 branches [delegatur]: Białogon, Bliżyn, Bodzentyn, Chęciny, Daleszyce, Łopuszno, Skarzysko, Słupia Nowa and Suchedniów); composition of board (Dr. E. Polak—chairman, Chaim Pachoł—vice chairman, Szymon Strawczyński, Wilhelm Gelbtuch, Jankiel Briks), public kitchens, outpatient clinic in Słupia Nowa, cooperation with the Jewish Councils. Proposal to appoint Józef Diament, chairman of the Supreme Council of Elders of the Jewish Population for the district of Radom, to be controller of the activity of KOP.
- ***Description:*** transcript, typescript (handwritten manuscript additions, pencil), Polish, 175×254 mm, damage and losses of text, ss. 3, pp. 3.

## 795. RING. I/1220/20. Mf. ŻIH—835; USHMM—47

- After 06.1941[?], Warsaw Ghetto
- [AJDC?], Memorandum concerning the situation of the Jewish population in the districts of Kielce and Radom. [?] (fragments)
- Sanitary conditions, diseases, nutrition, housing, social welfare.
- ***Description:*** transcript, typescript, Polish, 180×175, 200×270 mm, serious damage and losses of text, ss. 2, pp. 2.

Index: Diament, chairman of the Jewish Council in Kielce [?]

## 796. RING. I/1177 (1496). (Lb. 1215). Mf. ŻIH—834; USHMM—46

- 1941, Warsaw Ghetto
- NN., Account from Kielce
- Notation about a journey during 23.02–18.03.[1941] on the route Kielce–Opatów–Ostrowiec-Częstochowa–Radomsk–Piotrków–Lublin–Zamość–Hrubieszów–Łuków–Siedlce–Kraków–Nowy Sącz. Preserved text concerning only Kielce. Information about 1,200 Jews from Vienna in Kielce.

- *Description:* original (o), handwritten manuscript (H.W.*), ink, Yiddish, 155×198 mm, ss. 1, pp. 2.
  Attached note by H.W. in Yiddish: "Account of a Dror activist, recorded by H.W."

### 797. RING. I/560. Mf. ŻIH—791; USHMM—22

- 28.01.1942, Koluszki
- NN. (Leon) (Koluszki), Letter of 28.01.1942 to NN. (Warsaw Ghetto)
- Situation in the ghetto in Koluszki. Request for information about the Markowicz family, for financial aid and a railroad pass. About Icek [?] Honig [?].
- *Description:* original, handwritten manuscript, ink, Polish, 143×204 mm, minor damage and losses of text, ss. 2, pp. 3.
  On p. 3 notation in another handwriting (pencil): "Observations additional to these? Concerning 15 victims. Exit is currently impossible."

### 798. RING. I/843 (1162). (Lb. 362). Mf. ŻIH—827; USHMM—39

a)

- After 12.1940, Warsaw Ghetto
- NN., Account entitled "Koyl" [Koło] (12.1940)
- Author, a resident of Koło, describes experiences of the Jewish population from the entry of Germans into the town (09.1939) until 11.1939: forced labor, searches and robberies, arrests, closure of all Jews (2,000 people) into one barrack (11.1939). Author with wife and child fled the town.
- *Description:* transcript, handwritten manuscript (MS*), pencil, Yiddish, 148×210 mm, ss. 2, pp. 2.
  In the margins a symbol (ink): ":"; and on p. 1 a symbol (pencil, red): "+."
  Doc. was kept in a binder.

b)

- After 12.05.1941, Warsaw Ghetto
- NN., Account entitled "Koyl" [Koło]
- Experiences of the Jewish population in Koło from 09.1939 to 12.1939: searches, forced labor repairing the bridges on the Warta, burning of the synagogue (20.09.1939), ban on leaving the town, driving of all Jews into barracks (1.12.1939), and resettlement to Krasnystaw and Izbica Lubelska.
- *Description:* transcript (2 copies), handwritten manuscript (BW*), pencil, Yiddish, 148×210 mm, minor damage and losses of text, ss. 4, pp. 4.
  In the margins letter (ink): "F."
  Doc. was kept in a binder.

### 799. RING. I/844 (1163). (Lb. 860). Mf. ŻIH—827; USHMM—39

- After 12.1939, Warsaw Ghetto
- G.S., Account entitled "Bagatelles pour une massacre (Koło)"
- Experiences of the Jewish population from Germans' entry (12.09.1939) until the deportations in 12.1939 (forced labor, reconstruction of bridges, burning of synagogue—20.09., searches, transfer to Izbica Lubelska—4.12.1939). Information about mass shootings of Poles in Koło.
- *Description:* transcript (2 copies), typescript, Polish, 112×205, 190×290 mm, minor damage and losses of text, ss. 12, pp. 12.
  On p. 1 (first and second copies) notation by H.W. (ink): "Fligar."
  Published: BŻIH, no. 137–138/1986, pp. 183–187.
  Index: Bierzwiński, chairman of the Jewish Library, shot by the Germans in Koło (09.1939); Rozen (age 75), shot by Germans in Koło (09.1939); Sywosz, shot by Germans in Koło (09.1939); Koniński of Koło; Barab of Koło; Krośniewska of Koło, died on the road to Izbica (12.1939); Szubiewska of Koło, died on the road to Izbica (12.1939)

### 800. RING. I/845 (1164). (Lb. 1508). Mf. ŻIH—827; USHMM—39

- After 07.1941, Warsaw Ghetto
- NN., Account from Kołomyja
- Description of events of the first days of the German–Soviet War (abandonment of Kołomyja by the Soviet army, plundering of factories and warehouses by Ukrainians, and after entry of Hungarian troops a pogrom against the Jewish population).
- *Description:* original or transcript, handwritten manuscript, pencil, Yiddish, 155×195 mm, ss. 4, pp. 7.
  Published: *Relacje z Kresów*, pp. 906–911.

### 801. RING. I/841 (1160). (Lb. 848). Mf. ŻIH—827; USHMM—39

- After 07.1941, Warsaw Ghetto
- NN., Account entitled "Konin"
- Situation of the Jewish population in Konin after arrival of Germans (1939): arrests, Gestapo prison, forced labor, digging of graves for Poles shot in Konin, robberies, expulsion of Jews from Konin to Ostrowiec Kielecki, Grodźiec [?], Zagórów, Łódź, Izbica Lubelska (11.1939 and 07.1941).
- *Description:* original (o) (handwritten manuscript—FLIG*, ink, 220×354 mm, damage and losses of text, text illegible in places), transcript (3 copies, handwritten manuscript [MA*] pencil, 148×210 mm, extensive minor damage and losses of text), Polish, ss. 30, pp. 33.
  Published: BŻIH, no. 137–138/1986, pp. 189–193.
  Index: Słodki (age 70), merchant and house owner in Konin shot by the Germans, together with a Pole NN. at Pl. Wolności in September 1939; Kowalski of Konin, murdered in a labor camp near Gdańsk [Danzig]; Lewi of Konin; Mączki of Konin; Majer of Konin; Wienter [sic] of Konin; Gliksman of Konin; Lipszyc (age 72), rabbi of Konin; Aucer, perished in 07.1940 during the deportation of Jews from Konin; A. Lipszyc, perished in 07.1940 in Konin; Ajzen, perished in 07.1940 in Konin

**802. RING. I/842 (1161). Mf. ŻIH—827; USHMM—39**

- After 30.08.1941, Warsaw Ghetto
- NN., Paper on the annihilation of Jewish population centers in the Generalgouvernement (30.08.1941)
- Beginning of a longer study of the fate of the Jewish population of Konin from the occupation of the town by the Germans (09.1939) until the final deportations in June 1940 (robberies, burning of the synagogue, forced labor, beginning of resettlements—11.1939, expulsion of the Jews from the town—06.1940).
- *Description:* transcript (3 copies), handwritten manuscript (BW*), pencil, Yiddish, 148×210 mm, ss. 9, pp. 9.

  On p. 1 in the margins a symbol (pencil, red): "+."

**803. RING. I/674/14. (Lb. 1688). Mf. ŻIH—816; USHMM—28**

- Date unknown, Warsaw Ghetto
- NN., Notes
- Information about the Jewish population in Konin and Aleksandrów Kujawski.
- *Description:* original or transcript, handwritten manuscript (H.W.*), ink, Yiddish, 118×215 mm, ss. 1, pp. 2.

**804. RING. I/832 (1151). (Lb. 402). Mf. ŻIH—827; USHMM—39**

- After 2.05 1941, Warsaw Ghetto
- NN., Account entitled "Konstantinov" [Konstantynów] (2.05.1941)
- Fate of the Jewish population in Konstantynów from entry of the Germans until removal of ca. 1,000 persons to Głowno (22.12.1939).
- *Description:* transcript (2 copies), handwritten manuscript (BW*), pencil, Yiddish, 148×210 mm, ss. 6, pp. 6.

  In the margins a symbol (ink): two half-circles one over the other.

**805. RING. I/835 (1154). (Lb. 893). Mf. ŻIH—827; USHMM—39**

- After 12.07.1941, Warsaw Ghetto
- NN., Account entitled "Końskowola near Puławy" (12.07.1941)
- Author, policeman of the Order Service (from Warsaw), in labor camp in Końskowola, responds to survey questions about the situation of the Jewish population in the small town.
- *Description:* transcript (2 copies), handwritten manuscript (JG*), pencil, Polish, 148×210 mm, damage and losses of text, ss. 12, pp. 12.

  In the margins letter: "c."

  On p. 1 notation by H.W. in Yiddish (ink): "Lebensold."

**806. RING. I/500. Mf. ŻIH—788; USHMM—19**

- After 02.1940, Warsaw Ghetto
- Engineer Jan N., Account of the owner of the Kopojno farming estate (folwark) near Konin
- Author's intervention 3.09.1939 saved the lives of German colonists that a unit of the Polish Army wanted to shoot. After entry of the Germans, he was arrested by the SS at his estate 10.11.1939 and imprisoned in Konin (description of conditions under arrest and then in the prison in Konin), stayed in Warsaw from 02.1940.
- *Description:* original (o), handwritten manuscript (H.W.*), ink, Yiddish, 143×223 mm, ss. 2, pp. 3.

  In the margins a symbol (ink): "V" (with dot in the center).

  Doc. was kept in a binder.

  Attached note by H.W.: "Kopojno farming estate 21 km from Konin, owner Engineer Jan N. 1939–1940, testimony."

**807. RING. I/638. Mf. ŻIH—815; USHMM—27**

- 04.1942, Kosów [Lacki]
- Section for Feeding Children at the Social Welfare Department in Kosów, Leaflet from 04.1942 with appeal to the ghetto's residents for contributions for the benefit of children
- Information about the activity of the Section and report of work for the previous year.
- *Description:* original, handwritten manuscript hectographed, Polish, 225×373 mm., minor damage and losses of text, ss. 1, pp. 1

  Leaflet adorned with a drawing (two children's heads).

**808. RING. I/479. Mf. ŻIH—786; USHMM—17**

- 10.1941 and after 10.1941, Kosów Lacki [?], Warsaw Ghetto
- Hanna Lewkowicz, Account entitled "Notes on the life of deportees from Kalisz in Kosów Lacki 1939–1941" (10.1941)
- Arrival (13.12.1939) and stay of group of deportees (750 people), relations with the local population, housing conflicts, self-help organizations (Committee of Refugees, bread campaign, campaign for medical aid, health, fuel, and cooking campaigns, Department of Social Welfare and Health [Wydział Opieki Społecznej i Sanitarnej] of the Jewish Council led by Szyja Liberman), aid from Warsaw, transfer of some Kaliszans (150 persons) to Sterdynia (7.03.1940).
- *Description:* original (handwritten manuscript, several handwritings, main text: HL*, ink, Polish, 155×195 mm, text illegible in places), transcript (3 copies, typescript, 208×295 mm, minor damage and losses of text), ss. 47, pp. 58.

  Appended to the original are handwritten additions in a different handwriting. Within the text itself were written in the names of various prominent representatives of the Jewish population of Kosów and of deportees from Kalisz (J. Liberman, Perle, Engel, Kliniewski, Staszewski, Grüner, Rotenberg, physician). The author's surname and title were placed on p. 1 (handwritten manuscript E*) as well as signature with the name of the locality and date on p. 11—in a different handwriting than the rest of the text. In the transcript (typescript), additions were entered into the main text, but the name was omitted.

On p. 1 (transcript, second copy) notation by H.W. in Yiddish: "109—1942/1 January. no. 16."

Attached note by H.W.: "Recorded by Hanna Lewkowicz."

## 809. RING. I/997 (1316). Mf. ŻIH—831; USHMM—43

- 16.07.1942, Warsaw Ghetto
- NN., Account entitled "Kovel" [Kowel] (16.07.1942)
- Female author describes the fate of the Jews of Kowel (ghetto, mass executions, inter alia 8,000 persons shot in Bachowo in 06.1942, partisan activity).
- ***Description:*** transcript, handwritten manuscript (LEG*), pencil, Yiddish, 205×293 mm, ss. 4, pp. 4.

Published: *Relacje z Kresów*, pp. 916–923.

Index: Maurycy Mayzel, former chairman of the Jewish Religious Community in Warsaw (until 1939), murdered in Bachowo near Kowel at the beginning of 06.1942.

## 810. RING. I/846 (1165). (Lb. 1226). Mf. ŻIH—827; USHMM—39

- After 1940, Warsaw Ghetto
- NN., Account entitled "Kozenits" [Kozienice]
- The Jewish population before the war and during German occupation (relations with the German colonists, war's outbreak, bombardment of the town, flight of populace to surrounding forests, occupation of Kozienice by Germans, beginning of repressive measures, profile of Dr. Neuman,[39] a German physician, who aided Jews in Kozienice).
- ***Description:*** original (o) [?], handwritten manuscript (HUB.*), notebooks, ink, Yiddish, 155×195 mm, ss. 80, pp. 77.

Index: Rajzman of Kozienice; Józef Dembski of Wilno, Polish Army officer, committed suicide in Kozienice in 09.1939; Szmuel Mosze Korman, hanged by Germans in Kozienice (09.1939); Perłow, rabbi of Koziennice; Dr. [Aron] Abramowicz of Kozienice

## 811. RING. I/785/1. (1104). Mf. ŻIH—825; USHMM—37

- 09.1939–07.1940, Kraków
- Jewish Community (Provisional Board of the Religious Community) in Kraków, Announcements
- 1) Dated 17.09.1939, about formation of a board of the Provisional Board of the Religious Community in Kraków (list of members' names and addresses), call to assume a positive attitude toward the authorities' orders; 2) Date unknown, about compulsory appearance of the entire Jewish population of Kraków on 22.09.1939 for filling in anti-aircraft trenches; 3) Date unknown, about registration starting from 8.11.1939 of all Jews residing within the limits of the Community: Kraków, Skawina, Prokocim, Wola Duchacka, Bronowice Małe, Borek Fałęcki, Czernichów, Liszki, Mogiła, Piaski Wielkie, Prądnik Czerwony, Radziszów, Ruszcza, Świątniki Górne, Tyniec, Zabierzów, Zielonki, Ochojno, Rzeszotary, Jurczyce; 4) dated 25.07.1940 about compulsory displacement from Kraków on 15.06.1940 of part of the Jewish population.
- ***Description:*** original, printed, handwritten manuscript, German, Polish, 615×475, 625×470, 620×465, 235×314 mm, minor damage and losses of text (doc. 2), ss. 4, pp. 4.

Addresses of members of the Provisional Board of the [Jewish] Religious Community are written in next to their names on page 1 of document 1.

Index: Marek Bibersztein, chairman of the Provisional Board of the Religious Community in Kraków (Kraków, ul. Rejtana 10); Dr. Wilhelm Goldblatt, attorney (Kraków, ul. Grodzka 42); Teodor Dembitzer (Kraków, ul. Krowoderska 11); engineer Władysław Kleinberger (Kraków, ul. Starowiślna 8); Ferdynand Schenker (Kraków, ul. Bonifrater-ska 3); engineer Bernard Willer (Kraków, ul. Żuławskiego 1); Ascher Spira (Kraków, ul. Dietla 50); Schabse Rappaport, Rabbi (Kraków, ul. Dietla 63); Izydor Gottlieb (Kraków, ul. Dietla 3); Joachim Steinberg (Kraków, ul. Łokietka 11); Samuel Majer (Kraków, ul. Wrzesińska 7)

## 812. RING. I/785/2. (1104). Mf. ŻIH—825; USHMM—37

- Date unknown, Kraków
- Jewish Community in Kraków, Form for certification of compulsory registration of the Jewish population.
- ***Description:*** original, printed, German, Polish, 155×117 mm, ss. 1, pp. 1.

## 813. RING. I/785/3. (1104). Mf. ŻIH—825; USHMM—37

- After 09.1939, Kraków
- German occupation authorities, Announcement.

39. Spelling is Polish, not German, although the document is in Yiddish and the man is identified as a German, who would likely spell his name in German fashion, Neumann.

Collection of ordinances regulating behavior of Jews within Kraków.
- *Description:* original, printed, German, 425×500 mm, ss. 1, pp. 1.

### 814. RING. I/785/4. (1104). Mf. ŻIH—825; USHMM—37

- 01.1942, Kraków
- Polizeidirektion Krakau [Police Directorate, Kraków], Pass to leave the Kraków ghetto drawn up for Neustadt (5–10.01.1942).
- *Description:* original, printed, handwritten manuscript, ink, German, 106×75 mm, ss. 1, pp. 1.

### 815. RING. I/1220/13. Mf. ŻIH—835; USHMM—47

- 15.02.1941, Kraków
- Generalgouvernement. Aussiedlungsstelle II [Outsettlement Office II] (Kraków, ul. Lubicz 4), Notification dated 15.02.1941 for Riwka Wittenberg (Kraków, Kommandantur 5, apt. 14)
- Permission for continued stay in Kraków.
- *Description:* original, printed, typescript, stamp, German, Polish, 180×140 mm, damage and losses of text, ss. 1, pp. 2.

Stamp: "Aussiedlungsstelle II. Krakau, Lubicz 4."

### 816. RING. I/1220/14. Mf. ŻIH—835; USHMM—47

- 10.08.1940, Kraków
- NN., Notification for Zylkowicz [Żyłkowicz?] [. . .]cha (born 1912) (Kraków, [. . .]werstr. 19, apt. 4).
- *Description:* original, printed, typescript, stamps, German, 137×104 mm, major damage and losses of text, ss. 1, pp. 1.

### 817. RING. I/351. (Lb. 1144). Mf. ŻIH—782; USHMM—13

- Date unknown, Kraków
- Form for registration of the Jewish population in Kraków. Printed. Not filled in.
- *Description:* original, printed, German, Polish, 693×248 mm, ss. 1. pp. 1.

### 818. RING. I/1220/70. Mf. ŻIH—835; USHMM—47

- After 1940, place unknown
- [German Authorities of Generalgouvernement in Kraków?], Order concerning conduct of medical examinations among the Jewish population
- Examinations commence 15.11.1940. Appended medical questionnaire form.
- *Description:* transcript, typescript, German, 181×268, 207×244 mm, substantial damage and losses of text, ss. 2, pp. 2.

Attached note by H.W. in Yiddish

### 819. RING. I/286. (Lb. 918). Mf. ŻIH—781; USHMM—12

- After 05.1940, Warsaw
- ŻSS, Minutes of session of [. . .]05.1940 in Kraków
- Organization of social welfare, cooperation between Jewish communities, contacts with the RGO, Joint. Present at the meeting, inter alia: Dr. [Chaim] Hilfstein, Dir. Leinkram, engineer A. Reinberg, Dr. [Eliasz] Tisch, Dr. Michał Weichert, attorney Dr. Zimmermann.
- *Description:* transcript, typescript, Polish, 200×250 mm, serious damage and losses of text, ss. 2, pp. 2.

### 820. RING. I/211/1. (Lb. 881). Mf. ŻIH—779; USHMM—10

- After second half of 1940 [?], place unknown
- Agreement between the AJDC and the German authorities regulating the activity of the Joint in the Generalgouvernement (second half of 1940 [?]) (fragment)
- AJDC activity has to take place under the supervision of the Independent Welfare Desk of the Department for Internal Administration of Population Facilities and Relief (das Referat Freie Wohlfahrt der Abteilung Innere Verwaltung-Bevölkerungswesen und Fürsorge) of the Generalgouvernement. Announcement of the liquidation of the Joint's bureau in Warsaw by the end of 1940. Agreement signed on behalf of the AJDC by I. Bornstein and L. [Lejb (Leon)] Neustadt; on the German side by Heinrich.
- *Description:* transcript, typescript, German, 182×250 mm, serious damage and losses of text, ss. 1, pp. 1.

### 821. RING. I/287/1. (Lb. 919). Mf. ŻIH—781; USHMM—12

- After 13.09.1940, place unknown
- Minutes of meetings on [. . .] and 12.09.1941 of the AJDC representative I. Bornstein with German authorities at the Office of the General Governor in Kraków (13.09.1940)
- Discussions concerned, inter alia, transmission of funds and gifts from abroad for the benefit of Jewish social organizations, information bureau for separated families, interest-free loan funds, emigration, issuance of bonds among the Jewish population for social welfare purposes, matter of the Joint's employee, Benkel, rent for the premises (ul. Dietla 85), questionnaire for Jewish councils, budgets of social welfare institutions, recovery of annuities for Jews from the Reich. From the German side, Heinrich attended the meeting.
- *Description:* transcript, typescript, Polish, 190×273 mm, serious damage and losses of text, ss. 4, pp. 4.

### 822. RING. I/211/5. (Lb. 881). Mf. ŻIH—779; USHMM—10

- 09.1941, place unknown
- [AJDC?], Two documents concerning the demand

for materials for production and repair of shoes for the poor Jewish population (09.1941, Kraków)

1) Proposal to approach the German authorities for an allocation of 26,250 kg of rubber for repair of 75 thousand pieces of footware (16.09.1941);
2) Calculation of costs, quantity of materials (from quota and non-quota items) and volume of production of shoes with wooden soles ([. . . ?].09.1941).

- ***Description:*** transcript, typescript, Polish, 177×245 mm, minor damage and losses of text, ss. 2, pp. 2.

**823. RING. I/211/2. (Lb. 881). Mf. ŻIH—779; USHMM—10**

- After 16.10.1941, place unknown
- Minutes of three meetings of representatives of AJDC with German authorities at the Department for Internal Administration of Population Facilities and Relief (die Abteilung Innere Verwaltung-Bevölkerungswesen und Fürsorge) of the Generalgouvernement ([?] and October 1941, Kraków) (fragments)
- Conversations touched on, inter alia, a description of the AJDC's current activity, purchase of agricultural food items for social welfare institutions, establishment of farms on the terrain of the Generalgouvernement, aid for the Jewish population of Eastern Upper Silesia (Ost-Oberschlesien), Galicia [Eastern] and refugees from Vienna, allocation of coal, emigration, Jewish district in Piaski Lubelskie. Attending the conferences for the AJDC: I. Bornstein, L. [Lejb (Leon)] Neustadt, Dr. Rosenberg (only in discussions with Dr. Jehne); for the German side: Dr. Föhl and Heinrich (before 10.10.1941), Hexel (10.10.1941), and Dr. Jehne (before, or 16.10.1941).
- ***Description:*** transcript, typescript, Polish, 185×257 mm, serious damage and losses of text, ss. 16, pp. 16.

Minutes of the first conference were preserved in two versions differing in sequence of matters touched on and with minor changes and corrections of several words. Because of significant damage to the documents there were substantial difficulties in dating particular documents. We know the date of the second meeting only (10.10.1941) (Minutes of 12.10.1941); the first was earlier. Discussion with Dr. Jehne took place after 10.10., at the latest 16.10., since the minutes are from that date.

**824. RING. I/287/2. (Lb. 919). Mf. ŻIH—781; USHMM—12**

- After 1.08.1940, place unknown
- NN., Memorandum to AJDC and ŻSS in matter of taking over maintenance of property left behind by Jews who left Kraków in connection with the deportation action (fragment)
- Proposal for creation of a Jewish Social Trust Association (Żydowskiego Społecznego Towarzystwa Powierniczego), for the purpose of assumption of supervision of real estate, bank investments and deposits, moveable property, enterprises, etc. The AJDC and ŻSS would have control over the association.
- ***Description:*** transcript, typescript, Polish, 185×240 mm, serious damage and losses of text, ss. 2, pp. 2.

Text of the memorandum is a fragment of another document [?].

Attached note by H.W. in Yiddish.

**825. RING. I/674/11. (Lb. 1688). Mf. ŻIH—816; USHMM—28**

- Date unknown, Warsaw Ghetto
- NN., Account of September 1939
- Flight from Kraków [?] to the east (1–18.09.1939)—Wieliczka, Tarnobrzeg, Mielec, Lublin. Appended information (account [?]) concerning Warsaw.
- ***Description:*** original (o), handwritten manuscript (H.W.*), ink, Yiddish, 156×187 mm, ss. 1, pp. 2.

**826. RING. I/674/9. (Lb. 1688). Mf. ŻIH—816; USHMM—28**

- Date unknown, Warsaw Ghetto
- NN., Account entitled "Kroke" [Kraków]
- Situation of the Jewish population, labor camps (Pustków near Dębica, Lipie near Nowy Sącz).
- ***Description:*** original (o), handwritten manuscript (H.W.*), ink, pencil, Yiddish, 158×179 mm, ss. 1, pp. 1.

**827. RING. I/833 (1152). (Lb. 462). Mf. ŻIH—827; USHMM—39**

- 14.06.1942, Warsaw Ghetto
- NN., Account entitled "Di gesheenishn in Kroke 29.05–8.06.[1942]" [The Events in Kraków 29.05–8.06.(1942)"] (14.06.1942)
- Detailed description of the first liquidation action in the Kraków ghetto.
- ***Description:*** transcript, handwritten manuscript (LEG*), ink, Yiddish, 145×196 mm, minor damage and losses of text, ss. 3, pp. 5.

On p. 1 notation by H.W. in Yiddish (ink): "2 standard pages. June 1942."

**828. RING. I/573/1. Mf. ŻIH—792; USHMM—23. Mf. ŻIH—836; USHMM—67**

- 20.01.1942, after 20.01.1942, Krośniewice, Warsaw Ghetto
- Rózia [Kapłan] (Krośniewice), Letters dated 12.01., 20.01., 4.02., 9.02., 18.02., 20.02., 22.02.1942 to Dawid and Hela [Lewi] (Warsaw, ul. Leszno 60, apt. 25)
- Material aid, fate of closest relatives and friends, plan of escape to Warsaw, poll tax, information about the approaching annihilation.

- *Description:* original (Letter of 20.01.), handwritten manuscript on a postcard, postmark and stamp of the Jewish Council in Warsaw, German, Polish, 147×104 mm, ss. 1, pp. 2; copies (letters dated 12.01., 14.01., 4.02., 9.02., 8.02., 20.02., 22.02.1942, handwritten manuscript: letters dated 12.01(handwritten manuscript—H*, pencil, 118×180 mm, ss. 1, pp. 2), 4.02. (handwritten manuscript—H*, pencil, 170×120 mm, ss. 1, pp. 2), 9.02. (handwritten manuscript—H*, pencil, 190×115 mm, ss. 1, pp. 2), 18.02. (handwritten manuscript—H*, pencil, 130×116 mm, ss. 1, pp. 2), 20.02. (handwritten manuscript—H*, pencil, 140×98 mm, ss. 1, pp. 2), and 22.02. (handwritten manuscript—H*, pencil, 135×118 mm, ss. 1, pp. 2), handwritten manuscript (H*), Polish, information in Yiddish concerning postmarks in Krośniewice and stamps of the Jewish Council in Warsaw).

  Published: *Listy o Zagładzie*, pp. 31–34, 46–49, 53–54.

  Index: Rybicki, [Meir] Przedecz, Uszer Taube, [Balcia] Taube, Rybskis, Weksler, Tabaczyński, Trzaskowski, Dawid Taube, [Icchak] Borensztajn, Alek Szczeciński, Nasielskis, Korn, Sala Truman, Bronia Lajzer, Mela [Lewi?], Neuhaus, Birenbaumowa, M. Jachimowicz (Izbica Lubelska, at the home of Fingerhut), Gajzlers

## 829. RING. I/573/2. Mf. ŻIH—792; USHMM—23. Mf. ŻIH—836; USHMM—67

- 01.1942, After 01.1942, Krośniewice, Warsaw Ghetto
- Rózia [Kapłan] (Krośniewice), Letters dated 21.01., 22.01., 24.01., 27.01., 30.01. [postmark date], 20.02.1942 to Szmul [Kapłan] (Warsaw, ul. Nowolipie 28, apt. 18)
- Information about the annihilation of Jews of Turek, Koło, Dąbie, Łódź in Chełmno; request for intervention with [Adam] Czerniaków, Dr. [Izrael] Milejkowski and [Icchak] Borensztajn; escapees from Chełmno, special tax levied on the Jewish population.
- *Description:* original (letters dated 21.01., 22.01., 24.01., 27.01., 31.01. [postmark], 20.02., handwritten manuscript on postcards, postmarks and stamps of the Jewish Council in Warsaw, German, Polish, 147×104 mm), transcripts (2 copies) (letters dated 21.01., 22.01., 24.01., 27.01., 30.01. 1942), typescript (208×295 mm, ss. 4, pp. 4), Polish, ss. 10, pp. 16.

  Letters addressed to [Rywen] Gelbart (Warsaw, ul. Nowolipie 28, apt. 18); letters dated 21.01. and 20.02. missing sender, on the rest: "M. Święcicki, Krośniewice."

  Attached note by H.W. in Yiddish: "Letters from Róża Kapłan to Szmuel Kapłan, Bund activist from Kalisz, in Warsaw was esteemed activist of CKU, his wife traveled with three sons from Warsaw to Krośniewice for material reasons."

  The transcripts do not contain the full text of the originals. Transcripts of letters dated 21 and 22 January 1942 were preserved also in AAN, no. 202/II-29, ss. 8.

  Published: *Listy o Zagładzie*, pp. 35–46.

  Index: Parzęczewska, Aruś Kapłan, Chaimek Kapłan, Moniek Kapłan

## 830. RING. I/573/3. Mf. ŻIH—792; USHMM—23. Mf. ŻIH—836; USHMM—67

- 22.01.1942, After 22.01.1942, Krośniewice, Warsaw Ghetto
- Fela Mazierska (Krośniewice), Letters dated 22.01. and 23.01.1942 to Szymon Szymsio (Warsaw, ul. Miła 2, apt. 3)
- Information about the death of friends: Estera Kotowska, Hanka Ickowicz, Jakub Ickowicz, Rojewska (Ickowiczówna); plan of escape, request for help.
- *Description:* original (handwritten manuscript on postcards, postmarks and stamps of the Jewish Council in Warsaw, ink, Polish, 146×104 mm), transcript (2 copies, typescript, 212×280, 212×290 mm) Polish, ss. 4, pp. 6.

  Transcript includes letters dated 22.01. and 23.01., as well as Letter of 27.01. NN. (Fela). See Ring. I/573/4.

  Transcript (typescript) has old pagination: "4."

  Published: *Listy o Zagładzie*, pp. 11–15.

  Index: [Szmul] Winter from Włocławek, [Icchak] Borensztajn, Dzigański, Boruch Gerszt, Dawid Lewin (Warsaw, ul. Leszno 60, apt. 25).

## 831. RING. I/573/4. Mf. ŻIH—792; USHMM—23. Mf. ŻIH—836; USHMM—67

- After 27.01.1942, Warsaw Ghetto
- NN. (Fela) (Kutno), Letter of 27.01.1942 to NN. (Warsaw Ghetto)
- Information about the death camp at Chełmno (25,000 Jews perished there).
- *Description:* transcript, typescript, Polish. This letter is on the same sheet with the copies of the letters of Fela Mazierska; see Ring. I/573/3.

  Lack of information as to whether the author of the letter is Fela Mazierska [?]

  Published: *Listy o Zagładzie*, pp. 17–18.

## 832. RING. I/573/5. Mf. ŻIH—792; USHMM—23. Mf. ŻIH—836; USHMM—67

- 26.01.1942, Krośniewice
- Kopel Geisler (Krośniewice), Letter of 26.01.1942 to W. Dawid Lewi (Warsaw, ul. Leszno 60, apt. 25). Request for aid.
- *Description:* original, handwritten manuscript on a postcard, postmark and stamp of the Jewish Council in Warsaw, Polish, 147×104 mm, ss. 1, pp. 2.

  Published: *Listy o Zagładzie*, pp. 16–17.

## 833. RING. I/573/7. Mf. ŻIH—792; USHMM—23. Mf. ŻIH—836; USHMM—67

- After 02.1941, Warsaw Ghetto
- Copies of correspondence to the Warsaw Ghetto, inter alia from Krośniewice (fragment)

- Fragments of letters dated 1.12.1941 and 4.02.1942 (letter from Róza Kapłan to Dawid and Hela Lewi).
- ***Description:*** transcript, typescript, Yiddish, serious damage and losses of text, ss. 1, pp. 1.

**834. RING. I/836 (1155). (Lb. 312). Mf. ŻIH—827; USHMM—39**

- Date unknown, Warsaw Ghetto
- NN., Account entitled "Kutne" [Kutno]
- September 1939 and start of the occupation in Kutno. Situation of the Jewish population.
- ***Description:*** original (o), handwritten manuscript (H.W.*), ink, Yiddish, 148×210 mm, text is barely legible, ss. 2, pp. 3.

  In the margins a Hebrew letter (ink): "p" and a symbol (ink): "V" with a dot at the top. On p. 1 in the margin a symbol (pencil, red): "+."

**835. RING. I/837 (1156). (Lb. 311). Mf. ŻIH—827; USHMM—39**

- After 18.04.1941, Warsaw Ghetto
- NN., Account entitled "Kutne" [Kutno]
- Situation of the Jewish population in Kutno from 03.1940 to the beginning of 1941 (deportation to the camp on the terrain of the "Konstancja" sugar mill).
- ***Description:*** transcript (2 copies), handwritten manuscript (MS*), pencil, Yiddish, 148×210 mm, minor damage and losses of text, ss. 6, pp. 6.

  In the margins letter (ink): "E."

**836. RING. I/838 (1157). (Lb. 312, 735, 1208, 1672). Mf. ŻIH—827; USHMM—39**

- After 15.06.1940, Warsaw Ghetto
- Josef Piotrkowski Lubień, Account entitled "Geshikhte un milkhome iberlebenish fun Kutno" [History and War Experience of Kutno]
- History of the Jewish colonization in Kutno, September 1939, first months of German occupation, repression against the Jewish population and eviction of Jews to the camp on the grounds of the sugar mill in Konstancja (15.06.1940), living conditions in the camp (ghetto).
- ***Description:*** original (handwritten manuscript, notebook, ink, 140×200 mm), transcript (3 copies, handwritten manuscript—TT*, pencil, 148×210 mm), Yiddish, ss. 93, pp. 101.

  In the margins (copy, first and third copies) a Hebrew letter (ink): "hey."

  Transcript is a fragment of a larger copybook (pp. 48–74); see Ring. I/536/i.

  On the last page of the original a postscript by Aleksander Pakentreger, an employee of ŻIH (1993, ballpoint pen)

  Index: Lajzer Lewin of Kutno, Milke of Kutno

**837. RING. I/839 (1158). (Lb. 865). Mf. ŻIH—827; USHMM—39**

- After 06.1940, Warsaw Ghetto
- I. Ka., Account entitled "Kutno"
- Author, a resident of Kutno, describes September 1939, bombardments, start of the German occupation (from 16.09.1939), oppressive measures toward Jews, formation of the Jewish Council (appended list of members), chief of Gestapo, the sadist Geniek ("Nuchym"), care for deportees, removal of Jews to camp in the inactive sugar mill "Konstancja" (15.06.1940).
- ***Description:*** transcript, typescript, Polish, 193×290 mm, minor damage and losses of text, ss. 11, pp. 11.

  On p. 1 at the top is notation by H.W. (ink): "Fligar."

  See HWC, 27/1 (second copy, typescript, ss. 11; on p. 1 handwritten notation: "Fligar").

  Index: S. Falc, chairman of the Jewish Council in Kutno; M. Zandel; P[aweł] Goldszeider, attorney, member of the Jewish Council in Kutno; L. Praszkier, member of the Jewish Council in Kutno; I. Kubic, member of the Jewish Council in Kutno; Sz. Opoczyński, member of the Jewish Council in Kutno; Boas of Kutno; Przedborska of Kutno; Bagnówna, daughter of the chairman of the Jewish Council in Krośniewice; Blima Erdberg of Krośniewice; J. Borowski, secretary of the Jewish Council in Kutno; A. Ajke, bookkeeper of the Jewish Council in Kutno; L. Nejman of Kutno; Zelwerowiczowa (age 76) of Kutno; Kaila Krenig of Kutno; Gołda Krenig of Kutno (age 18); Igielski, a former sergeant from Kutno; Kwaśniewski of Kutno; L. Lewin, owner of a pharmacy in Kutno, taken away by Germans 15.02.1940, perished; Kilbert of Kutno; Rabe of Kutno; Kronzylber of Kutno; M. Korn, killed in Kutno in 1940

**838. RING. I/840 (1159). (Lb. 1138). Mf. ŻIH—827; USHMM—39. RING. I/599/16–17. Mf. ŻIH—812; USHMM—24**

- After 09.1940, Warsaw Ghetto
- NN., Account entitled "Kutne" [Kutno]
- Situation of the Jewish population in Kutno from September 1939 to September 1940 (oppressive measures after entry of Germans, arrival of ca. 3,000 Jews from the regions of Kłodawa, Koło, Włocławek, Aleksandrów, all Jews thrown into camp in inactive "Konstancja" sugar mill, description of living conditions in the camp).
- ***Description:*** transcript (2 incomplete copies), handwritten manuscript (Z*), pencil, Yiddish, 148×165 mm, serious damage and losses of text, ss. 25, pp. 25.

  On p. 1 (first copy) notation by H.W. in Yiddish: (ink): "Icchak Sz./typhus [?]"

  Two missing ss. included from Ring. I/599/16–17.

**839. RING. I/576. Mf. ŻIH—792; USHMM—23**

- 17.03.1940, Kutno

- NN. (Lilcia [?]) (Kutno), Letter to NN. (Mania) (Warsaw, ul. Śliska 35, apt. 6, with Wołkowicz[-owa?]). Information concerning family and friends.
- ***Description:*** original, handwritten manuscript (three handwritings) on a postcard, ink, Polish, 148×104 mm, ss. 1, pp. 2.

  Postscripted greetings from "Rachela" (child) and from "S. Menche" [?] ("Judis[z?]e Ol . . . Kutno, S. Kózka"[?])

  Index: Mendelson, Borkowska [?], Goldowa

### 840. RING. I/254. (Lb. 1563). Mf. ŻIH—780; USHMM—11

- Date unknown, Warsaw Ghetto
- [Bernard Kampelmacher], Study entitled "Requisition of furniture for the military" in Podkowa Leśna
- Profile and activity of Mieczysław Feldman, member of the Jewish Council [?] in Podkowa Leśna, later an employee of the housing bureau in the Warsaw Ghetto (ul. Krochmalna 22). Confiscations of furniture and other household effects from persons of Jewish origin (attorneys Landau and Ginsburg, dentist Wilner).
- ***Description:*** original[?] (typescript, 208×295 mm), transcript (2 copies, handwritten manuscript—CC*, pencil—147×208 mm), Polish, ss. 24, pp. 26.

  Attached note by H.W.: "Bernard Kampelmacher."

### 841. RING. I/854 (1173). (Lb. 931). Mf. ŻIH—827; USHMM—39

- After 16.12 1939, Warsaw Ghetto
- NN., Account about the Jewish community in Lipno
- Female author, a resident of Lipno, describes the situation of the Jewish population before the war and in the first months of occupation (ethnic relations, activity of social organizations [Jewish] in the town until 1939, September 1939, expulsion of Jews from Lipno—12.1939). Author traveled with husband to Warsaw 16.12.1939.
- ***Description:*** original (handwritten manuscript, notebook, ink, 145×207 mm, damage and losses of text), transcript (3 copies, handwritten manuscript—CC*, pencil, 148×210 mm, minor damage and losses of text), Polish, ss. 59, pp. 64.

  On p. 1 (transcript, second copy) notation by H.W. (ink): "Lipno" and "Zy[lber]."

  Author was chairwoman of the women's organization W.I.Z.O. in Lipno.

  Index: Klotzenberg, sculptor; Lewin Majeran, chairman of the Jewish community in Lipno (before 1939); Buchwaldowa; Mira Jakubowicz; Dir. Bloch; [Icchak] Borensztein of ŻTOS

### 842. RING. I/974 (1293). (Lb. 1586). Mf. ŻIH—831; USHMM—43

- After 1939, Warsaw Ghetto
- NN., Account about the fate of Jews in L[ipno]
- Author, an older woman from Lipno, describes the situation of the Jewish population in the first weeks of occupation in 1939 (roundups for forced labor, persecution of the rabbi, pastor's intervention in his defense, dragging of Jews at prayer from houses, plundering of Jewish houses and shops, requisitions, aid for the deportees from Lubicz and Dobrzyń nad Drwęcą).
- ***Description:*** transcript (3 copies), handwritten manuscript (JG*), pencil, Polish, 148×208 mm, ss. 36, pp. 36.

  Account was divided into three chapters: 1) "Yom Kippur in the town of L[ipno]"; 2) "10 X 1939 in the town of L[ipno]"; 3) "Fourteen (14) days later."

  Index: [Aron] Tr. [Trachtenberg], dentist from Lipno

### 843. RING. I/495. Mf. ŻIH—788; USHMM—19

- 1.01.1942, Warsaw Ghetto
- NN., Recollections of Lipno
- Female author, a resident of Lipno, describes the first months of occupation, destruction of the synagogue in mid-November 1939 (death of Elka Ickowicz, who ran out to save the burning synagogue), attempt to bribe Germans to extend stay in the town (collection of valuables for ransom), departure from Lipno (16.12.1939), journey to Warsaw, situation of refugees and Warsaw residents' attitude toward them.
- ***Description:*** original, handwritten manuscript, notebook, ink, Polish, 150×192 mm, sewn, ss. 16, pp. 28.

  On p. 29 notation (ink): "M.R."

  Recollections divided into chapters: "Demolition of the temple," "Collection of precious metals," "Road from L[ipno] to Warsaw," "Warsaw."

  Attached note by H.W.: "Submitted to archive by Dr. M. Reinhold."

### 844. RING. I/494. (Lb. 1634). Mf. ŻIH—788; USHMM—19

- After [09/10].1941, Warsaw Ghetto
- [Kac], Recollections of Lithuania from 1941
- Outbreak of the German–Soviet War, moods of the population, author's stay in labor camp in the peat bog of "Morg" (Jazowo near Kowalczuk) (companions from the camp: Kaufman from Wilno, engineer Rozental from Warsaw, Kinstler [?], Bułkin from Wilno, Boksza), extermination of Jews in Lithuania, attitude of Lithuanians and Poles toward Jews, escape from place of annihilation (Wieliczany near Nowa Wilejka).
- ***Description:*** transcript (3 copies), typescript, Polish, 208×295 mm, minor damage and losses of text, ss. 24, pp. 24.

  On p. 1 at top (first [?] copy) notation by H.W. in Polish, Yiddish: "Mr. Kac (Edelist) physician/

Łódź resident. 109–1942/1 January. no. 12." On p. 1 at top (third copy) notation by H.W. in Polish: "Mr. Kac (Edelist) physician/Łódź resident."

Inventory: "Statement of Kac, a medical student from Łódź, recorded by H.W."

Published: *Relacje z Kresów*, pp. 469–476.

**845. RING. I/487. Mf. ŻIH—787; USHMM—18**

- After 10.1941, Warsaw Ghetto
- [Arie (Jurek) Wilner?], Account entitled "Mon retour de l'URSS"
- Author, resident of Warsaw, member of Ha-Shomer Ha-Tsair, fled in fall 1939 with sister to USSR, and in November to Lithuania. He describes the attitudes reigning under Soviet occupation in Lithuania, Jews' living conditions, occupation of Lithuania by the USSR, war with Germans and start of the extermination of the Jewish population in Lithuania (ghetto in Wilno, executions in Ponary).
- ***Description:*** original (o) (handwritten manuscript—FLIG*, ink, 220×340 mm, minor damage and losses of text, text illegible in places), transcript (3 copies, handwritten manuscript—BTT*, pencil, 147×210 mm), Polish, ss. 157, pp. 164.

Title is found only on the transcript.

On p. 1 (handwritten manuscript—BTT*, first copy) notation by H.W. in Yiddish: "Wilno [member of Ha]-Shomer [Ha-Tsair]. 109–1942/1 January. no. 11." On p. 1 (handwritten manuscript—BTT*, second copy) notation by H.W. in Yiddish: "Wilno [member of Ha]-Shomer [Ha-Tsair]."

Inventory: "Text prepared by Daniel Fligelman."

Published: *Relacje z Kresów*, pp. 433–449.

**846. RING. I/864 (1183). (Lb. 847). Mf. ŻIH—828; USHMM—40**

- After 10.1939, Warsaw Ghetto
- NN., Account entitled "Lubicz [nad Drwęcą]"
- Oppressive measures against the Jewish population in the first weeks of the German occupation in Lubicz, until the deportation to Dobrzyń and Lipno (12.10.1939).
- ***Description:*** transcript (2 copies), handwritten manuscript (MA*), pencil, Polish, 147×210 mm, extensive minor damage and losses of text, ss. 18, pp. 18.

See HWC, 17A/1 (third copy, handwritten manuscript, ss. 9, on the sheets the letter "E"; on p. 1 notation "Fligar").

Index: Kernes, mill owner in Lubicz nad Drwęcą; Błotniarz, shot in Lubicz nad Drwęcą 12.10.1939; Bas from Lubicz nad Drwęcą, died during the deportation (10.1939); Klokmanówna from Lubicz nad Drwęcą; Szylszrajber of Lubicz nad Drwęcą, shot during the deportation (1939); Krajanek of Lubicz nad Drwęcą

**847. RING. I/852 (1171). (Lb. 427). Mf. ŻIH—827; USHMM—39**

- After 28.01.1941, Warsaw Ghetto
- NN., Account entitled "Lublin" (28.01.1941)
- Author reached Lublin 19.09.1939, describes the behavior of Germans toward Jews (e.g., action of 25.10.[1939?] on ul. Lipowa, where ca. 20,000 people were rounded up, of whom 8,000 were detained, interrogated, and persecuted).
- ***Description:*** transcript (2 copies), handwritten manuscript (MS*), pencil, Yiddish, 148×210 mm, minor damage and losses of text, ss. 4, pp. 4.

In the margins a Hebrew letter: "e" (ayin).

Doc. was kept in a binder.

**848. RING. I/855 (1174). (Lb. 1646). Mf. ŻIH—827; USHMM—39**

- After 7.01.1942, Warsaw Ghetto
- NN., Account entitled "Lublin" (01.1942)
- Situation of Lublin Jews from start of war until January 1942: increase in number of Jews to 90,000, [forced] contributions, smuggling, collaborators with the Germans (Grajer, brothers F[P?]inkier), forced labor, roundups, arrests (e.g., Szapiro, Nusbojm, Kunicki), march of war—prisoners from Lublin to Parczew, fate of 2,500 POWs from the east, deportation actions (March 1941), Jewish Council—24 persons (inter alia Dr. Elten [Alter?], engineer Beker, Kestenberg, attorney Szach, attorney Ergemajn), formation of ghetto (9.12.1941).
- ***Description:*** transcript (2 copies), handwritten manuscript (U*), pencil, Yiddish, 148×210 mm, ss. 22, pp. 22.

Index: Kestenberg, director of the labor department of the Jewish Council

**849. RING. I/948 (1267). Mf. ŻIH—830; USHMM—42**

- After 03.1942, Warsaw Ghetto
- NN., Account entitled "Lublin"
- Liquidation action in the Lublin ghetto in the second half of March 1942.
- ***Description:*** original or transcript, handwritten manuscript (GG *), ink, Polish, 100×149 mm, ss. 1, pp. 2.

**850. RING. I/1172 (1491). (Lb. 1215). Mf. ŻIH—834; USHMM—46**

- After 30.03.1942, Warsaw Ghetto
- NN., Account about the start of the liquidation action in the Lublin ghetto. (03.1942)
- Daily ca. 1,600 people were taken away, many were shot on the spot, inter alia ca. 150 children from the children's home, ca. 70 persons from the home for the elderly, hospital personnel 60 people, sick patients (600 people). Of 400 employees of the Jewish Council there remained 12 (taken away inter alia were the chairman of the Jewish Council, Beking,

Dr. Zygfryd. and Szlomo Roldersztat[?]). Kuperment[?] commanded the action, as well as [Harry] Sturm, Knitzki, [Herman] Worthoff.
- ***Description:*** original (o), handwritten manuscript (H.W.*), ink, Yiddish, 155×197 mm, ss. 1, pp. 2.
  Attached note by H.W. in Yiddish and Polish.

### 851. RING. I/1174 (1493). (Lb. 1215). Mf. ŻIH—834; USHMM—46

- After 03.1941, Warsaw Ghetto
- [Hersz Wasser], Notes
- 1) Mordechaj Auerbach, Account entitled "Nesiye Varshe–Lublin" [Journey Warsaw–Lublin]; report of a youth activist of a journey in March 1941 to a conference of the Zionist organization [Ha-Noar Ha-Tsiyoni] in Lublin (delegates from Zamość, Wąwolnica, Kraśnik, Chełm, Dęblin, Bodzentyn, Chmielnik, Staszów, Lipsko nad Wisłą, Sienna near Lipsko); 2) NN., Minutes dated 22.05.[1941?] of meeting of unspecified organization (presidium) [CKU?] in the Warsaw Ghetto; concerning organizational and personnel matters (refugees).
- ***Description:*** (1) original (o); and (2) original[?], handwritten manuscript (H.W.*), ink, Polish, Yiddish, 150×198 mm, ss. 1, pp. 2.
  Attached note by H.W. in Polish, Yiddish: "Report of journey of youth activist Mordechaj Auerbach to district conference in Lublin, recorded by H.W. 1941."

### 852. RING. I/1212. Mf. ŻIH—835; USHMM—47

- Date unknown, Warsaw Ghetto
- [Hersz Wasser], Notes.
- 1) NN., Account [Study?] entitled "Lublin" (Situation of the Jewish population in Lublin: persecutions, forced labor, forced contributions); 2) Report of meeting of CKU of 15.05.1942; 3) Roll of honoraria of Oyneg Shabes coworkers (Date unknown); 4) Accounts.
- ***Description:*** original or transcript, handwritten manuscript (H.W.*), ink, Yiddish, 145×200 mm, extensive damage and losses of text, ss. 2, pp. 4.
  Index: Dr. Alter, Beker, Kastenberg

### 853. RING. I/598/2. Mf. ŻIH—792; USHMM—23

- 10.06.1942[?]
- NN. [Lublin region?], Letter dated 10.06.1942 to NN. (fragment)
- ***Description:*** original, handwritten manuscript, ink, Polish, 160×149, 201×141, 94× 80 mm, extensive damage and losses of text, text illegible in places, ss. 3, pp. 6.

### 854. RING. I/599/85. Mf. ŻIH—812; USHMM—24

- After 24.03.1942, Warsaw Ghetto
- NN. (Lublin), Letter of 24.03.1942 to NN.
- ***Description:*** transcript, handwritten manuscript (LEG*), ink, Yiddish, 150×190 mm, serious damage and losses of text, text illegible in places, ss. 1, pp. 2.

### 855. RING. I/552/3. Mf. ŻIH—791; USHMM—22

- 27.03.1942, Lublin [Hrubieszów?]
- NN. (Lublin [?]), Telegram to NN. (Warsaw Ghetto). Request for money.
- ***Description:*** original, printed, typescript, German, Polish, 208×147 mm, ss. 1, pp. 1.

### 856. RING. I/552/4. (Lb. 1295). Mf. ŻIH—791; USHMM—22

- After 3.04.1942, Warsaw Ghetto
- NN. (Daniel) (Lublin), Letter of 29.03.1942 to sister (Warsaw Ghetto)
- Course of the liquidation action in Lublin ghetto.
- ***Description:*** transcript (from notation by copyist), typescript, Yiddish, 210×293 mm, ss. 1, pp. 1.
  Published: *Listy o Zagładzie*, pp. 83–86.

### 857. RING. I/552/5. Mf. ŻIH—791; USHMM—22

- 1942 [?], Lublin
- Dawid Lewkowicz (Lublin, ul. Szeroka 44), Letter to Krasnopolska of Kalisz (Warsaw, synagogue [?])
- Request to send news to Lublin. Letter sent to the address of the Jewish Council with a request to forward to the addressee.
- ***Description:*** original, handwritten manuscript on a postcard, postmark, German, Yiddish in Roman transliteration, 149×102 mm, major damage and losses of text, ss. 1, pp. 2.

### 858. RING. I/23. (Lb. 27). Mf. ŻIH—772; USHMM—3. RING. I/468. (Lb. 297). Mf. ŻIH—786; USHMM—17

- After 06.1941, Warsaw Ghetto
- NN., Recollections of stay in Lwów (1939–1941) (fragment [?])
- Author, resident of Warsaw, in 1939 fled with sister to Białystok, then they settled in Lwów. In February 1940 he commenced studies at the Pedagogical Institute. Social, political and economic situation in the regions occupied by the USSR in 1939, author's literary interests, academic life in Lwów, lecturers, youth, relations with Poles and Ukrainians, course of passportization, deportation of June 1940.
- ***Description:*** Ring. I/468—original or transcript, handwritten manuscript (I*), ink, Polish, 150×195 mm, text illegible in places, ss. 16, pp. 27; Ring. I/23—original or transcript, handwritten manuscript (I*), ink, Polish, 150×195 mm, text illegible in places, ss. 22, pp. 38.
  Manuscript was divided and preserved after excavation in 1946 under two file signatures: part 1 (fragment, perhaps missing the beginning [?]) (Ring. I/468); part 2, composed of two chapters: "Academic Life" and "Passportization" (Ring. I/23).

Ring. I/468: Inventory states that the author is Józef Honig, forwarded to the archive by A. [Abraham] Lewin.
Pub. (Ring. I/23): *Relacje z Kresów*, pp. 516–537.

### 859. RING. I/483. Mf. ŻIH—787; USHMM—18

- After 6.01.1942, Warsaw Ghetto
- Kr. [Krajn], Account entitled "What Mr. Kr. [Krajn] recounts after return from Lwów" (6.01.1942)
- Situation of Jews under Soviet occupation (deportation of the wealthy population, living conditions and work conditions, religious life, Jewish–Polish relations).
- ***Description:*** transcript, handwritten manuscript (E*), ink, Polish, 158×200 mm, k.2, pp. 4.
  Attached note by H.W.: "Krajn's statement, recorded by N. Koniński."
  Published: *Relacje z Kresów*, pp. 681–684.

### 860. RING. I/499. (Lb. 1583). Mf. ŻIH—788; USHMM—19. RING. I/955 (1274). (Lb. 1448). Mf. ŻIH—830; USHMM—42

- After 12.1941, Warsaw Ghetto
- [Ludwik Klaczko?], Account entitled "20 months in Red Lwów" (1939–1941)
- Author left Warsaw 6.09.1939. Describes entry into Poland of the Soviet military, stay in Lwów, population's living conditions, political, social, and economic relations, organization of labor, deportations, corruption, situation of the Jewish population, German occupation in Lwów, formation of ghetto and flight from Lwów (7.12.1941).
- ***Description:*** transcript (2 copies and third copy from Ring. I/955), handwritten manuscript (CA*), pencil, Polish, 148×208 mm, damage and losses of text, ss. 132, pp. 132.
  On p. 1 (first copy—Ring. I/499) notation by H.W.: "By Flig."
  Attached note by H.W.: "Ludwik Klaczko wrote."
  Published: *Relacje z Kresów*, pp. 685–720.

### 861. RING. I/1041 (1360). (Lb. 1278). Mf. ŻIH—832; USHMM—44

- After 11.1941, Warsaw Ghetto
- NN., Account entitled "Lemberg" [Lwów]
- Outbreak of German–Soviet War, social atmosphere, fate of the Jewish population, after entry of Germans, uprising of ghetto 15.11.1941 (Zamarstynów) and order to leave the city by 15.12.1941.
- ***Description:*** original or transcript, handwritten manuscript, notebook, ink, Yiddish, 173×222 mm, ss. 12, pp. 21.
  On p. 2 date (pencil).
  Published: *Selected Documents*, pp. 197–201; *Relacje z Kresów*, pp. 755–770.

### 862. RING. I/475. Mf. ŻIH—786; USHMM—17

- After 11.1941, Warsaw Ghetto
- NN., Account entitled "Migration to Lwów (1939) and back (1941): Impressions and Reflections"
- Female author, a resident of Łódź, flees with girlfriends to the east (24.10.1939), describes the journey, ethnic relations in the territories occupied by the USSR, outbreak of the German–Soviet War, beginning of repressive measures against Jews, escape to Warsaw (20.11.1941).
- ***Description:*** original (o) (handwritten manuscript—FLIG*, ink, 210×300 mm), transcript (2 copies, handwritten manuscript—CA*, pencil, 148×210 mm), Polish, ss. 55, pp. 55.
  Attached note by H.W.: "Prepared by Daniel Fligelman."
  See HWC, 19/1 (third copy of the transcript, handwritten manuscript, pencil, ss. 21).
  Published: *Relacje z Kresów*, pp. 667–680.

### 863. RING. I/1042 (1361). (Lb. 1257). Mf. ŻIH—832; USHMM—44

- 03.1942, Warsaw Ghetto
- NN., Account entitled "Lemberg" [Lwów] (Warsaw, 03.1942)
- Author left Warsaw 7.09.1939 for the east, from 17/18.09. was in Łuck, then reached Lwów (3.10.1939), describes the situation of refugees, conditions of life under Soviet occupation, German–Soviet War, repressive actions against the Jewish population, camp in Sokolniki, Lwów ghetto (15.11.1941, closure of ghetto postponed from 15.12.1941 to 28.02.1942), information about Stanisławów (Hungarian army) and persecution of the Jews there.
- ***Description:*** transcript (2 copies), handwritten manuscript (U*), pencil, Yiddish, 148×210 mm, ss. 50, pp. 50
  Published: *Relacje z Kresów*, pp. 771–787.

### 864. RING. I/420. (Lb. 930). Mf. ŻIH—783; USHMM—14

- After 10.1941, Warsaw Ghetto
- [Helena Kagan], Recollections of stay in Lwów (1939–1941)
- Author fled from Warsaw 12.11.1939 across the "green border" to Lwów, to husband. Difficulties crossing the border, situation in the territories occupied by the USSR, search for employment, exchange of money, courses for teachers, relations with Poles and Ukrainians, passportization and June 1940 deportations, German invasion, situation of Jews, departure to Warsaw (10.1941).
- ***Description:*** transcript (a) (handwritten manuscript—KK*, notebook, ink, 150×193 mm, damage and losses of text); transcript (b) (3 copies, typescript, 200×282, 163×80 mm, substantial damage and losses of text), Polish, ss. 35, pp. 45.
  Fragment of the testimony including the period from the Germans' entry into Lwów is on a separate sheet attached to the notebook (it was

preserved in a binder, with apparent traces on the last sheet of the notebook). The transcript does not include the text found on the aforementioned sheet.

Attached note by H.W.: "Statement of Helena Kagan, forwarded by Dr. Emanuel Ringelblum."

Published: *Relacje z Kresów*, pp. 590–613.

### 865. RING. I/481. Mf. ŻIH—787; USHMM—18

- After 18.12.1941, Warsaw Ghetto
- [Henryk Bursztyn], Account of escape from Lwów
- Author, a refugee in 1939, after occupation of Lwów by Germans left the city and fled to Warsaw (description of the journey Lwów–Przemyśl–Kraków–Warsaw—12.1941).
- ***Description:*** original or transcript (handwritten manuscript, ink, 215×236 mm), transcript (3 copies, typescript, 225×290 mm), Polish, ss. 21, pp. 21.

On the back of p. 9 (original) notation (ink): "H.B—n."

Attached note by H.W.: "Return from Lwów to Warsaw. Statement of Henryk Bursztyn—1941."

Published: *Relacje z Kresów*, pp. 745–754.

### 866. RING. I/450. Mf. ŻIH—785; USHMM—16

a)

- After 1941, Warsaw Ghetto
- St., Aau. [sic], Account entitled "Fun yener zayt [I]" [From the other side = the Soviet occupied zone (I)]
- Author (age 20) from Warsaw, [gymnasium] diploma in 1939; 6.09.1939 fled from Warsaw to the east; description of stay in the Polish regions occupied by USSR (Kowel, Lwów); in 1941 returned with wife to Warsaw.
- ***Description:*** original (o), handwritten manuscript (HUB.*), notebook, ink, Yiddish, 150×195 mm, ss. 18, pp. 32.

Published: *Kiddush Hashem*, pp. 383–399; *Relacje z Kresów*, pp. 886–905.

b)

- After 1941, Warsaw Ghetto
- Salomea L., Account entitled "Fun yener zayt II" [From the other side II]
- Author (about age 24), mathematics student at University of Warsaw; 25.10.1939 left Warsaw with family to the east; describes stay in Lwów; in 1941 returned to Warsaw.
- ***Description:*** original (o), handwritten manuscript (HUB.*), notebook, ink, Yiddish, 150×195 mm, ss. 22, pp. 40.

Attached note by H.W.: "Life of Jewish refugees in Western Belarus and Ukraine 1939–1941. 2 interviews conducted by Rabbi Szymon Huberband."

Published: *Kiddush Hashem*, pp. 399–420; *Relacje z Kresów*, pp. 116–141.

### 867. RING. I/1043 (1362). Mf. ŻIH—832; USHMM—44

- After 2.04.1942, Warsaw Ghetto
- Dr. [Mendel] Deliktish [Deliktysz (Deligtisch)], Account entitled "Lemberg" [Lwów] (Warsaw, 2.04.1942)
- Author, attorney from Pułtusk, describes his stay in Lwów during the Soviet occupation; he returned to Warsaw after outbreak of war.
- ***Description:*** transcript (3 copies), handwritten manuscript (U*), pencil, Yiddish, 148×210 mm, ss. 12, pp. 12.

Published: *Relacje z Kresów*, pp. 912–915.

Index: Ajzenberg, photographer from Pułtusk

### 868. RING. I/459. Mf. ŻIH—786; USHMM—17. RING. I/75. (Lb. 1054). Mf. ŻIH—775; USHMM—6

**a) Ring. I/459**

- After 06.1941, Warsaw Ghetto
- [Stanisław Różycki?], Account entitled "Lwów. Passportization and dispatch of refugees"
- Course of compulsory "passportization" on the territories occupied by the USSR in 1939, situation of refugees (Jews, Poles, and Ukrainians), German–Soviet repatriation commissions, deportations in June 1940, attitude of the population toward the refugees, attempts to endure in Lwów.
- ***Description:*** original, handwritten manuscript (OO*), notebooks, ink, Polish, 154×195, 145×200 mm, ss. 104, pp. 101.

Inventory: "Stanisław Różycki 'Genial bluff.'"

The document located in Ring. I/427 is probably a continuation of these memoirs.

Published: *Relacje z Kresów*, pp. 614–666.

**b) Ring. I/75**

- After 06.1941[?], Warsaw Ghetto
- [Stanisław Różycki ?], Account entitled "Lwów. Education 1939–41"
- Situation of educational system in Lwów after 09.1939 (changes in language of instruction, organization, teachers, political and social propaganda, textbooks, curricula, young people).
- ***Description:*** original, handwritten manuscript (OO*), notebooks, ink, Polish, 155×195 mm, ss. 123, pp. 119.

According to the list of 1946 (Lb. 1170) and inventory there was also a transcript of this doc. (3 copies, typescript, 3 x pp. 102).

The document located in Ring. I/427 is probably a continuation of these memoirs.

Published: *Relacje z Kresów*, pp. 792–885.

### 869. RING. I/427. Mf. ŻIH—784; USHMM—15

- After 09.1941, Warsaw Ghetto
- Stanisław Różycki, Account entitled "Part II. Ukraine 'liberated' again. Journal of a refugee in Lwów from 1.06–15[29].09.1941"

- Recollections recorded in the form of daily entries (June deportations, outbreak of the German–Soviet War, start of the German occupation, situation of the Jewish and Polish population, repressive measures against Jews, author's illness, flight from Lwów).
- ***Description:*** original (handwritten manuscript—SR*, notebook, ink, 155×195 mm, minor damage and losses of text), transcript (3 copies, typescript, 210×295 mm), Polish, ss. 116, pp. 113.

  On p. 1 (original) author's notation: "See part I. 'Genial bluff.' Experiences in 'liberated' Western Ukraine" (the author is probably writing about a text of which fragments or the entirety are now in Ring. I/459 and Ring. I/75). On p. 47 (46) author's notation: "See part 3. 'This is the ghetto' Report from the inferno of the XX century." On p. 2 (1) (original) title (subtitle [?]): "Lwów 1941"; on p. 42 (41) subtitle: "Departure from Lwów."

  See Ring. I/428, I/459.

  Published: *Relacje z Kresów*, pp. 538–589.

### 870. RING. I/431. Mf. ŻIH—784; USHMM—15

- After 12.1941, Warsaw Ghetto
- NN., Recollections from Lwów
- Beginning of the German occupation (30.06.1941), pogrom against the Jewish population, German repressive measures against Jews, labor camp in Sokolniki, conversations with German soldiers, formation of the ghetto, roundups and group executions, author's escape to Warsaw (8.12.1941).
- ***Description:*** original (handwritten manuscript, notebook, ink, 150×193 mm), transcript (2 copies, typescript, 218×284 mm, minor damage and losses of text), Polish, ss. 33, pp. 37.

  Published: *Relacje z Kresów*, pp. 721–744.

  Index: Weber, director of the Arbeitsamt in Lwów

### 871. RING. I/443. Mf. ŻIH—785; USHMM—16

- After 1941, Warsaw Ghetto
- NN., Account entitled "A mikhshl oyfn veg Lemberg–Varshe" [An Obstacle on the Lwów–Warsaw Route]
- Author, a refugee from Łódź, describes escape from Lwów to Warsaw, meeting with his brother in the Warsaw Ghetto.
- ***Description:*** transcript, handwritten manuscript (CHW*), ink, Yiddish, 157×202 mm, ss. 2, pp. 3.

  Attached note by H.W. in Yiddish: "Author anonymous, prepared [by] Jechaskiel Wilczyński."

  Published: *Relacje z Kresów*, pp. 788–791.

### 872. RING. I/851 (1170). (Lb. 424). Mf. ŻIH—827; USHMM—39

- After 25.12.1940, Warsaw Ghetto
- Sh. Yeshaya [Sz. Jeszaja], Account entitled "Laskazhev" [Łaskarzew] (25.12.1940)
- Picture of a small town after the entry of Germans on 17.09.1939 (ca. 400 Jewish families and 1,500 Polish families), torching of most of the houses, repressive actions against Jews and Poles, roundups, group executions (e.g., the shooting of 53 Jews and 70 Poles, later of 28 Jews, among others Eliezer Waldman with 3 sons perished). Author with his sons fled via Sobolewo to Warsaw. Appended list of victims [?].
- ***Description:*** transcript (a) (handwritten manuscript—H.W.*, ink, 145×210 mm, text illegible in places); transcript (b) (list of victims in 2 copies, handwritten manuscript—MS*, pencil, 145×210 mm, substantial damage and losses of text), Yiddish, ss. 11, pp. 14.

  In the margins of transcript (a) are letters (ink) "xx" and on p. 1 a symbol (red pencil): "+"; on transcript—b is a symbol (ink): "///."

  Doc. was kept in a binder.

  Index: Dr. Alter, Mordechaj Szalit (Szawit [?]), Stanisław Kełdziar [?], aided Jews

### 873. RING. I/973 (1292). (Lb. 722). Mf. ŻIH—831; USHMM—43

- 8.06.1942, Warsaw Ghetto
- NN., Account about the situation of the Jewish population in Łomazy and Biała Podlaska (8.06.1942)
- Authors, a woman and a man, after staying for 14 months in Łomazy returned to the Warsaw Ghetto. They describe the worsening living conditions in Łomazy and Biała Podlaska, the Nazis' bestiality, the psychological and physical terror imposed by the partisans from the nearby forests. Ca. 2,000–3,000 Jews were taken away from Biała Podlaska and their fate is unknown.
- ***Description:*** transcript, handwritten manuscript (Ł*), ink, Yiddish, 150×173 mm, damage and losses of text, ss. 6, pp. 6.

  Account was recorded by N.R. [Nechemiasz Tytelman] and in his handwriting is written the title: "Serie: Provints" [Series: Province].

  Attached note by H.W.: "Recorded [by] Natan Tytelman."

### 874. RING. I/847 (1166). (Lb. 360). Mf. ŻIH—827; USHMM—39

- After 12.02.1941, Warsaw Ghetto
- NN., Account entitled "Geyrush Lomianki bay Varshe" [Expulsion from Łomianki near Warsaw] (12.02.1941)
- Formation of the ghetto in Łomianki (15.09.1940); deportation of Jews from Łomianki to Legionowo and Warsaw (11.1940).
- ***Description:*** transcript (2 copies), handwritten manuscript (MS*), pencil, Yiddish, 148×210 mm, ss. 2, pp. 2.

  In the margin a symbol (ink): three dots arranged vertically and a symbol (letter [?]) (pencil, red): "+."

  Doc. was kept in a binder.

**875. RING. I/1149 (1468). (Lb. 1466). Mf. ŻIH—833; USHMM—45**

- Date unknown, Warsaw Ghetto
- [Czarnobroda], Account of the first days of the war in Łowicz
- Battle for the town, entry of German forces (17.09.1939), beginnings of the persecution of the Jewish population (roundups, forced labor).
- ***Description:*** original, handwritten manuscript (H.W.*), ink, Yiddish, 150×200 mm, ss. 1, pp. 2.
  Attached note by H.W. in Yiddish: "By a refugee from Łowicz, Czarnobroda."

**876. RING. I/848 (1167). (Lb. 379). Mf. ŻIH—827; USHMM—39**

- After 10.1939, Warsaw Ghetto
- NN., Account entitled "Loyvitsh" [Łowicz]
- About the treatment of Jewish laborers from Warsaw who were sent to work in Łowicz on 5.10.1939.
- ***Description:*** transcript, handwritten manuscript (MS*), pencil, Yiddish, 148×210 mm, minor damage and losses of text, ss. 1, pp. 1.
  On p. 1 notation by H.W. (ink): "10."
  Doc. was kept in a binder.

**877. RING. I/849 (1168). (Lb. 381). Mf. ŻIH—827; USHMM—39**

- After 11.05.1941, Warsaw Ghetto
- NN., Account about the persecution of displaced persons from Łowicz (11.05.1941)
- On 1.03.1941, near Sochaczew, I. A. Wołkowicz (age 52) was murdered, other persons were beaten. Children were also persecuted.
- ***Description:*** transcript (2 copies), handwritten manuscript (BW*), pencil, Yiddish, 97×148 mm, ss. 2, pp. 2.
  In the margin information in Yiddish: "Łowicz" and on p. 1 (copy 1) a symbol in red pencil: "+".

**878. RING. I/850 (1169). (Lb. 731, 958). Mf. ŻIH—827; USHMM—39**

- After 03.1941, Warsaw Ghetto
- NN., Account entitled "Loyvitsh" [Łowicz]
- Situation of the Jewish population from September 1939 until the deportation in March 1941: destruction and fatalities during the first days of the war, repressive actions against Jews after taking of Łowicz by the Germans, torching of the synagogue—11.11.1939, arrests, displaced persons from Łódź—20.12.1939; formation of the ghetto, relations with Poles, displacements in the vicinity of the town, and deportation of Jews from Łowicz to the Warsaw Ghetto (22.02–13.03.1941).
- ***Description:*** transcript (3 copies), handwritten manuscript (NN*), pencil, Yiddish, 148×210 mm, ss. 36, pp. 36.
  In the margins (first and third copies) a Hebrew letter (ink): "sh" (shin).
  Index: Gurt, perished in Łowicz in 09.1939; Bender, perished in Łowicz in 09.1939; Dr. [Icek] Jakubowski, former chairman of the Jewish Community in Łowicz, arrested 12.11.1939, perished; Abraham Grynberg and son, a merchant from Łowicz, arrested 12.11.1939, perished; Szreker, chairman of the "Makabi" organization of Łowicz, arrested 12.11.1939, perished; Wejnsztok, of the Order Service in Łowicz; Zilberg of Order Service in Łowicz; Munkel, vice mayor of Łowicz in 1941; Dr. Schwender

**879. RING. I/564/1. Mf. ŻIH—791; USHMM—22**

- 21.02.1942, Łowicz
- NN. (Laiwe) (Łowicz), Letter to Hinda Strykowska (Warsaw, ul. Nowolipie 47, apt. 95)
- Author was seized by the Germans and was to be shot (21.02.1942). Marek left him behind.
- ***Description:*** original, handwritten manuscript on a postcard, postmark and stamp of the Jewish Council in Warsaw, ink, Yiddish in Roman transliteration, 148×104 mm, ss. 1, pp. 2.
  About Marek, a guide, see *Listy o Zagładzie*, p. 59 and n.
  See Ring. I/564/2.

**880. RING. I/118. Mf. ŻIH—777; USHMM—8. RING. I/288/3. Mf. ŻIH—781; USHMM—12**

- 1940, Łódź [German authorities in Łódź], *Merkblatt für die Aussiedlung von Juden*
- Collection of regulations for Jews from Łódź resettled in the Generalgouvernement.
- ***Description:*** Ring. I/118—original, hectographed typescript, German, 207×294 mm, ss. 1, pp. 1; Ring. I/288—transcript, handwritten manuscript (MS*), pencil, German in Hebrew transliteration, 143×221 mm, minor damage and losses of text, ss. 1, pp. 1.
  Ring. I/288: on the margin a Hebrew letter in red pencil: "lamed" and a symbol (ink): "Δ."

**881. RING. I/331. Mf. ŻIH—781; USHMM—12**

- Date unknown, place unknown
- "Aufstellung sämtlischer Abteilungen des Arbeits-Ressorts und deren Erzeugnisse" [Statement of all the departments of factories and their products] in the Łódź ghetto (with addresses) (fragment)
- Notes about the nature of the production and services of individual departments (and factories).
- ***Description:*** original or transcript, typescript, German, 219×348 mm, ss. 2, pp. 2.

**882. RING. I/367. Mf. ŻIH—782; USHMM—13**

- Date unknown, Warsaw Ghetto.
- List of departments and establishments (with addresses) of the Jewish administration in the Łódź ghetto

- Appended list of names of members of the Central Committee of N.J.K. [N.I.K.?]: N. Szpet, chairman; members of the presidium: D. Fabrykant, H.B. Litwin, B. Strykowski; engineer M. Szyfer, secretary; Commission members: M. Perle, L. Rozenblatt, Dr. L. Szykier, J. Tenenbaum.
- ***Description:*** original or transcript, handwritten manuscript (Np*), pencil, Polish, 154×175, 154×196 mm, ss. 2, pp. 4.

### 883. RING. I/786 (1105). Mf. ŻIH–825; USHMM–37

a)

- 06.1940–02.1941, Łódź Ghetto
- Supreme Elder of the Jews in Litzmannstadt [Łódź], Chaim Rumkowski, Announcements.
  1) no. 60 of 12.06.1940, on the census of the population in the ghetto on 16.06.1940;
  2) no. 73 of 28.06.1940, on introduction in the ghetto of daycamps for children aged 4–7 and summer camps for children aged 7–15;
  3) no. 74 of 2.07.1940, on the ban on going outside after 6 pm on 3.07.1940;
  4) no. 104 of 12.08.1940, appeal to maintain calm in the ghetto;
  5) no. 107 of 13.08.1940, in the matter of submission of applications by the apartment house committees for permission to operate open-access kitchens;
  6) no. 123 of 20.09.1940, on the rules for granting of benefits in the budget of the Jewish Council;
  7) no. 133 of 4.10.1940, on introduction of curfew on 4.10.1940 at 9 pm;
  8) no. 134 of 11.10.1940, on the ban on doing business on Saturday;
  9) no. 136 of 11.10.1940, on illegal application for welfare benefits;
  10) no. 158 of 6.11.1940, on the creation of the Supreme Control Chamber (Najwyższej Izby Kontroli) for limiting offenses;
  11) no. 162 of 14.11.1940, on the allocation of food and fuel for winter (December 1940–February 1941);
  12) no. 166 of 19.11.1940, on the possibility of work for men (600 individuals) outside the ghetto, registration on 24.11.1940;
  13) no. 176 of 8.12.1940, on the ban on trade in articles of food acquired in the stores of Chaim Rumkowski;
  14) no. 177 of 10.12.1940, on the takeover of house kitchens from 12.12.1940;
  15) no. 178 of 12.12.1940, on the distribution of food ration cards on 15.12.1940;
  16) no. 182 of 20.12.1940, on payments for laborers working outside the ghetto;
  17) no. 185 of 24.12.1940, list of kitchens (addresses) in the Łódź ghetto taken over by Chaim Rumkowski;
  18) no. 186 of 27.12.1940, on introduction of food rationing in Rumkowski's shops;
  19) no. 187 of 28.12.1940, on a Hannuka gift for the poorest families in the ghetto;
  20) no. 195 of 16.01.1941, on an additional allocation of bread;
  21) no. 197 of 17.01.1941, on an increase of welfare grants for January 1941;
  22) no. 198 of 18.01.1941, on snow removal;
  23) no. 199 of 18.01.1941, appeal for lending tools for snow removal to the Department of Public Works;
  24) no. 200 of 21.01.1941, on allocation of bread;
  25) no. 206 of 1.02.1941, on formation of a committee for organizing the resettlement of the population in connection with the decision on reduction of the ghetto.
- ***Description:*** original (no. 123 in Yiddish in 2 different copies), printed, hectographed typescript, German, Polish, Yiddish, 206×290, 412×472 mm, ss. 48, pp. 48.

aa)[40]

- Date unknown, Warsaw Ghetto
- Supreme Elder of the Jews [Przełożony Starszeństwa Żydów] in Litzmannstadt [Łódź], Chaim Rumkowski. Announcement no. 123 of 20.09.1940
- Rules for awarding of welfare grants, budget of the Jewish Council.
- ***Description:*** transcript, handwritten manuscript (MS*), pencil, Yiddish, 144×222 mm, ss. 1, pp. 2.
  In the margin a Hebrew letter (pencil, red): "lamed."
  Doc. was kept in a binder.

b)

- 1941, date unknown, Łódź ghetto
- Supreme Elder of the Jews [Przełożony Starszeństwa Żydów] in Litzmannstadt [Łódź], Chaim Rumkowski, printed items
- 1) 12.1940, form (postcard) summoning [recipient] to labor outside the ghetto; 2) "Milk Card" for 03–05.1941 (handwritten pencil notation in German: "canceled"); 3) "Child's Food Card," 1941 (from a handwritten pencil notation in German: "canceled"); 4) Coupon for foodstuffs for the sick, 1941.
- ***Description:*** original (no. 1 in 5 copies, no. 4 in 2 copies), printed, handwritten manuscript, pencil, German, Polish, Yiddish, 143×86, 146×136 mm, ss. 9, pp. 17.

40. This (aa) reflects need to insert an additional item in the outline without having to change subsequent entries.

**884. RING. I/856 (1175). Mf. ŻIH—827; USHMM—39**

- After 15.05.1941, Warsaw Ghetto
- Chaim Mordechaj Rumkowski, "Lecture by the Chairman of the Council of Elders of the City of Łódź [. . .] presented on 15 May 1941 to representatives of the Łódź hometown association in Warsaw"
- Rumkowski's contributions to Jewish society in Łódź.
- ***Description:*** transcript, typescript, Polish, 117×205, 200×267 mm, damage and losses of text, ss. 2, pp. 2.
  Rumkowski's lecture in Yiddish: See Ring. I/193.
  Published: BŻIH, no. 54/1965, p. 23.

**885. RING. I/193. Mf. ŻIH—779; USHMM—10**

- After 15.05.1941, Warsaw Ghetto
- Chaim Rumkowski, "Barikht–referat funem eltestn funem yidishn rat in litsmanshtat–geto Kh. Rumkowski—gehaltn dem 15 maj 1941 far di forshteyer fun der lodzher landsmenshaft in Varshe" [Report Speech by the Chairman of the Jewish Council in Łódź Ch. Rumkowski presented 15 May 1941 before representatives of the Łódź hometown association in Warsaw]
- Rumkowski's contributions to the Łódź ghetto.
- ***Description:*** transcript (2 copies), handwritten manuscript (H.W.*), pencil, Yiddish, 147×208 mm, ss. 8, pp. 8.
  See Ring. I/856 (the identical document in Polish).
  Published: *Selected Documents*, pp. 297–299.
  See HWC, 17/5 (third copy, handwritten manuscript, ss. 4).

**886. RING. I/1144 (1144). Mf. ŻIH—833; USHMM—45**

- 15.05.1940, Łódź ghetto
- Paper money from the Łódź ghetto
- Banknotes ("Quittung") denominated: 1, 2, 5, 10, 50 marks and 50 pfenigs.
- ***Description:*** Printed, German, 85×56, 165×83 mm, extensive damage and losses of text, ss. 6, pp. 12.
  See HWC, 17/1 (banknote denominated 50 marks).

**887. RING. I/862 (1181). (Lb. 605). Mf. ŻIH—828; USHMM—40**

- 01–04.1942, Łódź Ghetto
- B. Cooperative (Litzmannstadt-Getto, Kirchgasse 4), bills dated 24.01., 14.03., 28.03., and 15.04.1942 filled out for B. Strykowski for various foodstuffs and industrial items included in the ration-card allocations in the Łódź ghetto.
- ***Description:*** original, printed, handwritten manuscript, pencil, German, 100×40, 122×248 mm, ss. 5, pp. 5.

**888. RING. I/857 (1176). (Lb. 326, 327). Mf. ŻIH—827; USHMM—39**

- After 09.1939, Warsaw Ghetto
- NN., Account entitled "Mayn aroysgeyn fun Lodzh" [My departure from Łódź]
- Author left Łódź before the Germans' entry, describes the route to Warsaw, via Stryków, Głowno, Łowicz (chaos, numerous refugees, air raids, bombardment of Łowicz).
- ***Description:*** transcript (2 copies), handwritten manuscript (MS*), pencil, Yiddish, 148×210 mm, minor damage and losses of text, ss. 6, pp. 6.
  In the margins a Hebrew letter (ink): "r" (reysh)
  Doc. was kept in a binder.
  Appended (Lb. 326) somewhat altered text of the same account (entitled "Dos antloyfn fun Lodzh" [Escape from Łódź]).
- ***Description:*** transcript, handwritten manuscript (MS*), pencil, Yiddish, 148×210 mm, minor damage and losses of text, ss. 3, pp. 3. In the margins a Hebrew letter (ink): "l" (lamed) underlined with symbol (ink): "- =." Doc. was kept in a binder.

**889. RING. I/858 (1177). (Lb. 404). Mf. ŻIH—827; USHMM—39**

- After 02.1940, Warsaw Ghetto
- C.T., Account entitled "Di organizatsie fun geto in Lodzh" [Organization of the ghetto in Łódź]
- Author, an official of the Łódź *gmina* (official Jewish communal organization, also known as *gmine* or *kehile* in Yiddish), describes events preceding the formation of the ghetto (from 02.1940), preparations for resettlements and displacements within the territory of the city, population's moods, corrupt practices, activity of the housing office at the gmina (ul. Południowa 14—gmina's seat, later at ul. Lutomirska 13), increasing housing problems of the Jewish population.
- ***Description:*** transcript (2 copies), handwritten manuscript (MS*), pencil, Yiddish, 148×210 mm, minor damage and losses of text, ss. 6, pp. 6.
  In the margins a Hebrew letter: "b" (beyt).

**890. RING. I/859 (1178). Mf. ŻIH—827; USHMM—39**

- After 10.1941, Warsaw Ghetto
- NN., Account entitled "My second flight from Łódź" (10.1941)
- Author, a journalist [?] from Łódź, describes the first months of occupation and his flight to Warsaw in December 1939.
- ***Description:*** transcript (3 copies), handwritten manuscript (CC*), pencil, Polish, 148×160, 148×210 mm, extensive damage and losses of text, missing page 9 (in second copy), ss. 26, pp. 26.
  Notation by H.W. [?]: "Submitted by Leon Morski."

**891. RING. I/991 (1310). (Lb. 307). Mf. ŻIH—831; USHMM—43**

- Date unknown, Warsaw Ghetto
- NN., Account entitled "Mayn antloyfn fun getto" [My escape from the ghetto]

- Description of a successful escape from the Łódź ghetto. Presents several examples of unsuccessful escapes, that generally ended tragically (e.g., Rozenzaft was shot). The men who were caught were tortured in the police precinct on ul. Brzezińska.
- ***Description:*** transcript (2 copies), handwritten manuscript (MS*), pencil, Yiddish, 148×208 mm, minor damage and losses of text, ss. 2, pp. 2.
  In the margin (first copy) a symbol (ink): "."(dot).
  Doc. was kept in a binder.

**892. RING. I/860 (1179). (Lb. 405). Mf. ŻIH—827; USHMM—39**

- After 12.1939, Warsaw Ghetto
- NN., Account entitled "Mayne lodzher iberlebungen (lager)" [My Łódź experiences (camp)]
- Notation about stay in a camp in Łódź [?] (12.1939[?]), persecution of prisoners (Poles and Jews), dispatch of many persons to an unknown destination. Information about persons: Rubin, attorney, Glater, attorney, Akawie, Gutman, Prof. Tomaszewski, Major Kowalczyk, Frankfurt, Ojerbach [Auerbach?], Gotlib.
- ***Description:*** transcript (2 copies), handwritten manuscript (MS*), pencil, Yiddish, 148×210 mm, ss. 6, pp. 6.
  Notation in Yiddish that the text is a continuation of another account.
  In the margins a Hebrew letter (ink): "a" (alef).

**893. RING. I/1013 (1332). (Lb. 371). Mf. ŻIH—831; USHMM—43**

- After 12.1940, Warsaw Ghetto
- NN., Account entitled "Zayer humor" [Their humor]
- German methods of humiliating and degrading Jews (Łódź December 1939, Warsaw 1940).
- ***Description:*** transcript (2 copies), handwritten manuscript (MS*), pencil, Yiddish, 148×210 mm, ss. 4, pp. 4.
  In the margins letter (ink): "J" or "I" [Yiddish yud]
  Doc. was kept in a binder.

**894. RING. I/30. Mf. ŻIH—772; USHMM—3**

- After 12.1939, Warsaw Ghetto
- NN., Recollections entitled "In occupied Łódź"
- Author, a resident of Łódź, worked for 20 years as a clerk in one of the Łódź firms. He describes the first months of the German occupation (September–18 December 1939): living conditions, relations with Germans, repressive actions against the Jewish population: requisitions, eviction from apartments, blackmailings, roundups for labor, introduction of yellow armbands and "stars," ban on walking along ul. Piotrkowska, restrictions for Jewish firms, mass departure of Jews from the city. After fleeing from Łódź, the author and his wife took up residence in Warsaw.
- ***Description:*** transcript (3 copies), handwritten manuscript, pencil, Polish, 150×205 mm, minor damage and losses of text, ss. 132, pp. 132.

**895. RING. I/957 (1276). Mf. ŻIH—830; USHMM—42**

- After 12.1939, Warsaw Ghetto
- [Eliasz (Eliahu) Gutkowski], Account entitled "Lodzh" [Łódź]
- First days of the war, mood of the population. Arrest of Jewish and Polish intelligentsia 12.12.1939 (also an account of the arrest of the author). Orders on introduction of "symbols of disgrace" for Jews. German–Soviet repatriation commission (ul. Zagajnikowa in Klejnman's factory). Eviction of Jews from ul. Zgierska. Mass flight of Jews from Łódź 12–17.12.1939.
- ***Description:*** original (handwritten manuscript—LEG*, ink, 104×295 mm, minor damage and losses of text), transcript (fragment) (handwritten manuscript—MS*, pencil, 148×210 mm), Yiddish, minor damage and losses of text, ss. 13, pp. 17.
  A copy of only part of the original preserved: pp. 1–4 and from the middle of page 8 to the end.
  In the original on p. 1 is notation by H.W. in Yiddish: "Łódź" and the Roman numeral: "I." In the transcript on pp. 1 and 2 is notation by H.W. in Yiddish: "Łódź" and Roman numeral: "II"; on p. 3, in the margin a Hebrew letter : "l" (lamed) and letter (or a symbol [?])":T" (for a similar marking, see e.g., Ring. I/964).
  The account is divided into two chapters: 1) "Fun onfang milkhome—1.IX.1939—biz 18-tn november" [From the war's start, 1 Sept. 1939 until 18 November]; 2) "Zikhrojnes fun noentn over" [Recollections from the recent past]
  Attached note by H.W. in Yiddish: "Eliahu Gutkowski, his own experiences."
  Doc. were preserved in binder.

**896. RING. I/958 (1277). (Lb. 430). Mf. ŻIH—830; USHMM—42**

- After 1939, Warsaw Ghetto
- NN., Account entitled "Di bank-hayzer in Lodzh" [The Banking Houses in Łódź]
- Rules of monetary exchange in the first months of the occupation of Łódź (restrictions for Jews, takeover of banks by Germans).
- ***Description:*** transcript, handwritten manuscript (MS*), pencil, Yiddish, 148×210 mm, minor damage and losses of text, ss. 1, pp. 2.
  In the margin a Hebrew letter (ink): "l."
  Doc. was kept in a binder.

**897. RING. I/959 (1278). (Lb. 433). Mf. ŻIH—830; USHMM—42**

- After 10.1939, Warsaw Ghetto
- NN., Account entitled "Fun der lodzer kehile lebn" [From the Łódź Jewish Community's life]

- Arrest of 50 Jewish prostitutes, plan for opening of a public house for Germans with Aryan prostitutes, Chaim Rumkowski's troubles (matter of the debt of NN. and Kenig [?], the Jewish Community's bookkeeper).
- ***Description:*** transcript, handwritten manuscript (MS*), pencil, Yiddish, 148×210 mm, minor damage and losses of text, ss. 2, pp. 2.
  In the margins a Hebrew letter (ink): "l" (lamed) and a symbol: "..."
  Doc. was kept in a binder.
  Attached note by H.W. in Yiddish.
  Index: Bunin, Nadel, Dr. Szloser

**898. RING. I/960 (1279). Mf. ŻIH—830; USHMM—42**

- After 09.1939, Warsaw Ghetto
- [Trajstman, Rabbi], Account entitled "Lodzh" [Łódź]
- Reorganization of the Łódź Jewish Community after outbreak of the war (09.1939), arrest of the author, Sochaczewer Rabbi Bornsztajn, and Natan Dawid Zelwer; account of the author's conversation of many hours with the Gestapo chief; experiences of Rabbis Segal and Mosze Dąb.
- ***Description:*** transcript (2 copies), handwritten manuscript (MS*), pencil, Yiddish, 148×209 mm, minor damage and losses of text, ss. 4, pp. 6.
  In the margins a Hebrew letter (ink): "l" (lamed) and a symbol: dot under a hyphen.
  Attached note by H.W. in Yiddish: "Via Mordechaj Szwarcbard, account of Łódź Rabbi Trajstman."
  Doc. was kept in a binder.
  Index: Pływacki, Światłowski, Sztol (Sztal?), Fajner, Dr. Szwalbe, Dr. Segal, attorney Rubin, Miss Lewitz, Chaim Rumkowski

**899. RING. I/961 (1280). Mf. ŻIH—830; USHMM—42**

- After 1939, Warsaw Ghetto
- NN., Account entitled "Lodzh" [Lódź]
- Description of the first days of the war in 1939, flight from Łódź, panic and chaos on the roads, battle near Brzeziny.
- ***Description:*** transcript, handwritten manuscript (MS*), pencil, Yiddish, 148×210 mm, minor damage and losses of text, ss. 1, pp. 2.
  In the margin of p. 1 a symbol (ink): "Δ" and a Hebrew letter (red pencil): "l" (lamed).
  Attached note by H.W. in Yiddish: "Mordechaj Szwarcbard."
  Doc. was kept in a binder.

**900. RING. I/962 (1281). Mf. ŻIH—830; USHMM—42**

- Date unknown, Warsaw Ghetto
- NN., Account entitled "Fun Lodzh" [From Łódź]
- Description of Germans' persecution of a group of 100 Łódź Jews at the SS headquarters (ul. Zgierska 116), subsequently 15 of them (among others, Mosze Szałdajewski) were shot in the forest near Ozorków [?].
- ***Description:*** original, handwritten manuscript, pencil, Yiddish, 148×210 mm, minor damage and losses of text, ss. 1, pp. 2.
  In the margin a Hebrew letter (red pencil): "l" (lamed).
  Doc. was kept in a binder.
  Attached note by H.W. in Yiddish: "November 1939 mass murder (Café Astoria), written down by Mordechaj Szwarcbard" (See Ring. I/970).
  Index: Chaim Rumkowski

**901. RING. I/963 (1282). Mf. ŻIH—830; USHMM—42**

- Date unknown, Warsaw Ghetto
- NN., Account entitled "Fun lodzher lebn" [From Łódź life]
- Łódź Jewish Community after outbreak of war (Chairman Lejb Mincberg left Łódź in September 1939), formation of the Jewish Council, operation of the financial commission and public assistance, delegation (Dr. [J.] Schlosser, Chaim Rumkowski, Dr. Szwalbe) that delivered to the authorities a memorandum against rounding people up for labor; composition of the Jewish Council: [Abraham Lejzer] Pływacki, first chairman of the Jewish Council, [Chaim] Rumkowski, second eldest of the Jews [drugi najstarszy Żydów], by order of the German authorities, [Samuel] Faust, director of social welfare, Dr. [D.] Helman, director of the financial department. Public kitchens: ul. Zachodnia, Smolna, Pomorska 18, Berka Joselewicza 16.
- ***Description:*** original or transcript, handwritten manuscript (MS*), pencil, Yiddish, 148×210 mm, minor damage and losses of text, ss. 1, pp. 1.
  In the margin a symbol (ink): "..."
  Doc. was kept in a binder.
  Attached note by H.W. in Yiddish: "By Mordechaj Szwarcbard."

**902. RING. I/964 (1283). (Lb. 425). Mf. ŻIH—830; USHMM—42**

- Date unknown, Warsaw Ghetto
- NN., Account entitled "Fun Lodzh" [From Łódź]
- Author, a social activist, imprisoned by the Germans; describes the beating of Jews and plundering of their houses by groups of young people and soldiers several days before the entry of Germans into the city; theft (for Hans Frank, governor) of the palace belonging to K., one of the wealthiest Jews in Łódź.
- ***Description:*** original or transcript, handwritten manuscript (MS*), pencil, Yiddish, 148×209 mm, minor damage and losses of text, ss. 2, pp. 3.
  In the margins a Hebrew letter (ink): "l" (lamed), under it a letter (or a symbol [?]): "T."
  Doc. was kept in a binder.

**903. RING. I/1008 (1327). (Lb. 332). Mf. ŻIH—831; USHMM—43**

- Date unknown, Warsaw Ghetto
- NN., Account entitled "Epizodn fun lodzher geto" [Episodes from the Łódź ghetto]
- Instances of policemen shooting at Jews who were approaching the boundaries of the ghetto (e.g., Lejbisz Blum was killed).
- *Description:* original or transcript (2 copies), handwritten manuscript (MS*), pencil, Yiddish, 148×209 mm, minor damage and losses of text, ss. 2, pp. 2.
  Doc. was kept in a binder.

**904. RING. I/1079 (1398). Mf. ŻIH—832; USHMM—44**

- [1941], Warsaw Ghetto
- NN., Account on the Łódź ghetto
- Arrests, Chaim Rumkowski, provisioning, food prices, education.
- *Description:* original or transcript, handwritten manuscript (MS*), pencil, Yiddish, 140×152 mm, damage and losses of text, ss. 2, pp. 3.
  Attached note by H.W. in Yiddish: "Łódź —1941—original, by Szwarcbard."
  Index: K[H]alska, teacher from Łódź; Ajzensztajnowa, teacher from Łódź; Jakubowiczowa, teacher from Łódź; Berliner, teacher from Łódź; Szmulewiczówna, teacher from Łódź; Kempflerówna, teacher from Łódź; Najfeld, teacher from Łódź; Wajsówna, teacher from Łódź

**905. RING. I/1029 (1348). (Lb. 397). Mf. ŻIH—831; USHMM—43**

- Date unknown, Warsaw Ghetto
- NN, Account entitled "Di martirologie fun a lodzher polit" [The martyrdom of a Łódź refugee] (missing conclusion)
- Author from Łódź (ul. Moniuszki 5), describes requisition of his apartment, search for a new place to live, decision to leave his hometown, and dramatic experiences on the road to Warsaw.
- *Description:* transcript, handwritten manuscript (MS*), pencil, Yiddish, 147×208 mm, minor damage and losses of text, ss. 12, s.12.
  In the margins letter (ink): "P" (pei)

**906. RING. I/1037 (1356). (Lb. 407). Mf. ŻIH—832; USHMM—44**

- After 20.12.1941[?], Warsaw Ghetto
- Mosze Szaja [?], Account of a boy from Łódź (20.12.[1941?])
- Author (age 15) caught and taken away from Łódź, finally finds his way to the Warsaw Ghetto.
- *Description:* transcript (2 copies), handwritten manuscript (MS*), pencil, Yiddish, 148×209 mm, minor damage and losses of text, ss. 2, pp. 2.
  In the margin a symbol (ink): circle made of dots.
  At top a title (H.W., red pencil): "Chronicle."
  Doc. was kept in a binder.

**907. RING. I/965 (1284). (Lb. 349, 415). Mf. ŻIH—830; USHMM—42**

- After 03.1940, Warsaw Ghetto
- L.G., Account about events in Łódź (December 1939–March 1940)
- Female author describes the situation of the Jewish population: displacements into the area of Bałuty and Stare Miasto on the night of 15/16.12.1939, preparations for formation of the Łódź ghetto, resettlement into the ghetto, roundup of 29.02.1940 and transport of those seized to the camp in Radogoszcz, Jewish Council and Chaim Rumkowski, numerous fatalities (ca. 100 people, e.g., the Joskowicz family, ul. Piotrkowska 9) during the displacement of residents from ul. Piotrkowska and al. Kościuszki (6–8.03.1940).
- *Description:* transcript, handwritten manuscript (MS*), pencil, Yiddish, 148×210 mm, minor damage and losses of text, ss. 12, pp. 12.
  Text of the account is divided into three chapters: 1) "December–January 1939–[19]40 in Łódź," ss. 3, pp. 3, in the margins a symbol: "·—·"; on p. 1 notation : "2"; 2) "Month of February 1940 in Łódź," ss. 3, pp. 3, in the margins a symbol: "..." (in slanting position); 3) "Month of March 1940 in Łódź," transcript (2 copies), ss. 6, pp. 6, in the margins a Hebrew letter (ink): final khaf.
  Notation by H.W. on the wrappers [na opaskach]: "Mordechaj Szwarcbard."

**908. RING. I/966 (1285). (Lb. 366, 997)**

- Date unknown, Warsaw Ghetto
- NN., Account from Łódź
- About the author's experiences in Łódź (in 3 months, he was seized 23 times for labor).
- *Description:* original or transcript (handwritten manuscript, ink, 220×354 mm, minor damage and losses of text), transcript (handwritten manuscript—MS*, pencil, 148×210 mm), Yiddish, ss. 5, pp. 7.
  Original or transcript; see Ring. I/1002 (similar handwriting).
  On p. 1 (original or transcript) title in Yiddish: "Łódź" (added after 1946 [?]); on p. 1 (transcript) title: "Impressions of Łódź."
  Attached note by H.W. in Yiddish: "Mordechaj Szwarcbard['s] own experiences" [?]
  Docs. were kept in a binder.

**909. RING. I/967 (1286). (Lb. 384). Mf. ŻIH—830; USHMM—42**

- After 09.1939, Warsaw Ghetto
- NN., Account entitled "Dos tsurikgeyn nokh Lodzh" [Return to Łódź]
- Three refugees from Łódź in September 1939

describe return to hometown from Warsaw via Pruszków, Skierniewice, Żyrardów, and Brzeziny.
- ***Description:*** transcript (2 copies), handwritten manuscript (MS*), pencil, Yiddish, 148×208 mm, minor damage and losses of text, ss. 6, pp. 6.
  In the margins a symbol (ink): "III"
  On the cover notation by H.W. in Yiddish: "Mordechaj Szwarcbard."
  Doc. was kept in a binder.

**910. RING. I/968 (1287). (Lb. 321, 413). Mf. ŻIH–830; USHMM–42**

- After 1939, Warsaw Ghetto
- NN., Account entitled "My experiences from my arrest on 8.11.[1939] to the camp in Radogoszcz"
- Author, former chairman of the association of factory owners, arrested 8.11.1939, describes stay in German prison together with a group of Jews and Poles, union activists, political and cultural activists, employees of economic institutions, scholars. Then he characterizes conditions reigning in the camp in Radogoszcz, to which he was brought with a group of fellow prisoners. People from the Łódź vicinity were there: from Ruda, Zgierz, Pabianice, Aleksandrów; e.g., attorney Rubin, attorney Glater, Auerbach, Rzepkowicz, Akawia, Jakow, Ajzner.
- ***Description:*** transcript, handwritten manuscript (MS*), pencil, ink, Yiddish, 148×210 mm, minor damage and losses of text, ss. 11, pp. 11.
  Manuscript consists of 2 parts: 1) includes ss. 3, pp. 3; in the margins a symbol ink): "÷" (slanted); on p. 1 at top a number (H.W.*, ink): "4." 2) contains (2 copies) ss. 8, pp. 8; in the margins a Hebrew letter (crossed out) (ink): "l" (lamed) twice underlined as well as a symbol, dot in a circle; on p. 1 at top notations in Yiddish: "continuation" (on the right side) and "Gimpy" [a pseudonym?] (on the left side).

**911. RING. I/969 (1288). (Lb. 388). Mf. ŻIH–830; USHMM–42**

- After 28.04.1941, Warsaw Ghetto
- NN., Account entitled "The tragedy of the Old Town Synagogue in Łódź" (28.04.1941)
- Significance of the Old Town Synagogue for Łódź Jews, course of the torching of the synagogue (10.11.1939); 90 Torah scrolls burned together with the synagogue.
- ***Description:*** transcript (2 copies), handwritten manuscript (BW*), pencil, Yiddish, 148×208 mm, ss. 8, pp. 8.
  In the margins a Hebrew letter (ink): "p" (pei).
  Attached note by H.W.: "Account of Abraham Blaszka, a Hasid from Łódź." See Ring. I/417; Ring. I/987.
  Doc. was kept in a binder.

**912. RING. I/970 (1289). Mf. ŻIH–831; USHMM–43**

- Date unknown, Warsaw Ghetto
- NN., Account entitled "Łódź"
- Creation of the ghetto in Łódź, displacement of the Jewish population into the ghetto (until 30.04.1940), living conditions in the closed district.
- ***Description:*** transcript (2 copies), handwritten manuscript (MS*), pencil, Yiddish, 148×208 mm, minor damage and losses of text, ss. 4, pp. 8.
  Transcript (first copy) has in the margins Hebrew letters (ink): "l" (lamed) and "sh" (shin); transcript (second copy) has in the margins a symbol (ink): "//" (or a Hebrew–Yiddish letter: "v" [tsvey-vovn]) . On p. 1 notation (first and second copies) in Yiddish (ink): "Astoria—create from [?] . . ." (See Ring. I/962)
  Doc. was kept in a binder.

**913. RING. I/482. Mf. ŻIH–787; USHMM–18**

- After 11.1939, place unknown
- Fela Wiernikówna, "Recollections and wartime experiences"
- The author, a resident of Łódź, a schoolteacher, describes the September Campaign and the first days of occupation, changed mood among the youth, repressive actions against the Jewish population.
- ***Description:*** original, handwritten manuscript, notebook, ink, Polish, 152×196 mm, ss. 16, pp. 29.
  Notebook signed by the author: "F. Wiernikówna."
  Attached note by H.W.: "Fela Wiernikówna of Łódź recorded these recollections."

**914. RING. I/971 (1290). Mf. ŻIH–831; USHMM–43**

- After 03.1941, Warsaw Ghetto
- NN., Account entitled "Refleksn fun Lodzh" [Łódź reflections] (03.1941)
- Germans' behavior toward Jews (roundups of people for labor, mistreatment, humiliation).
- ***Description:*** transcript (2 copies), handwritten manuscript (MS*), pencil, Yiddish, 148×206 mm, damage and losses of text, ss. 10, pp. 10.
  In the margins a Hebrew letter (ink): "t" (taf)

**915. RING. I/1004 (1323). (Lb. 366). Mf. ŻIH–831; USHMM–43**

- 1942, Warsaw Ghetto
- NN., Note on the role of Chaim Rumkowski in the Łódź ghetto
- Situation in the Łódź ghetto, Rumkowski's attitude and his role in the formation of the ghetto and in fulfillment of German demands.
- ***Description:*** original or transcript, handwritten manuscript (MS*), pencil, Yiddish, 155×197 mm, minor damage and losses of text, ss. 2, pp. 4.
  Attached note by H.W.: "By Mordechaj Szwarcbard."

**916. RING. I/999 (1318). Mf. ŻIH—831; USHMM—43**

- After 12.1941, Warsaw Ghetto
- NN., Recollections of Łódź and Warsaw (fragment)
- The female author, a resident of Łódź, describes the first months of the German occupation in Łódź, trips between Łódź and Warsaw, subsequent departure to Warsaw, and stay in the Warsaw Ghetto.
- ***Description:*** original or transcript, handwritten manuscript, notebook, ink, Polish, 153×193 mm, damage and losses of text, missing page, ss. 16, pp. 27.
  On p. 1 notation by H.W. in Yiddish (ink): "13 standard pages."

**917. RING. I/863 (1182). (Lb. 988). Mf. ŻIH—828; USHMM—40**

- After 03.1941, Warsaw Ghetto
- [Jakub Samson?], Account entitled "Iberlebenishn fun an arbeter-familie in Lodzh un Varshe, September 1939–merts 1941" [Experiences of a worker family in Łódź and Warsaw, September 1939–March 1941]
- The author, a married resident of Łódź (ul. Lipowa), describes his own experiences in Łódź after outbreak of the war in 1939 and his further fate after escape to Warsaw (from 4.12.1939), where he worked as an automotive mechanic at different sites. Description of the German employers. At the end is appended a copy of a certificate (favorable judgment) of the SS infantry regiment for the Jewish Council in Warsaw, about employment of the author in 1940.
- ***Description:*** transcript (3 copies), handwritten manuscript (TT* and BTT*), pencil, German (BTT*), Yiddish, 148×208 mm, damage and losses of text, ss. 39, pp. 39.
  In the margins a symbol (ink): three dots arranged in the form of a triangle—"∵"
  On p. 1 notation by H.W. in Yiddish (ink): "Samson."
  See Ring. I/1213.

**918. RING. I/674/10. (Lb. 1688). Mf. ŻIH—816; USHMM—28. RING. I/423. Mf. ŻIH—784; USHMM—15.**

**Ring. I/674/10.**

- Date unknown, Warsaw Ghetto
- NN., Account of various localities (fragment?)
- Łódź—confiscation of a Jewish shop on ul. Kilińskiego; Włocławek—situation in the town in August 1939, after outbreak of war and entry of Germans.
- ***Description:*** original (o), handwritten manuscript (H.W.*), ink, Yiddish, 158×179 mm, ss. 1, pp. 2.

**Ring. I/423.**

- Date unknown, place unknown
- NN., Fragment of a testimony.
- Refers to events in the vicinity of Łódź, 10–11 September 1939.
- ***Description:*** original, handwritten, ink, Yiddish, 155x88 mm, damage and losses of text, ss. 1, pp. 1.

**919. RING. I/544/1. Mf. ŻIH—791; USHMM—22**

- 5.01.1941, Łódź ghetto
- Ch. Częstochowski (Łódź, ul. Towiańskiego 8, apt. 1), Letter of 5.01.1941 to S. Schefner (Warsaw, ul. Leszno 64)
- Living conditions in the Łódź ghetto.
- ***Description:*** original, handwritten manuscript on a postcard, postmark, ink, German, 145×102 mm, minor damage and losses of text, ss. 1, pp. 2.

**920. RING. I/1220/47. Mf. ŻIH—835; USHMM—47**

- 29.12.1941, Łódź ghetto
- Maria Ulinower (Łódź ghetto, Rembrandtstr. 13), Letter of 29.12.1941 to Sara Brawelman (Częstochowa, ul. Katedralna 9, in care of I. M. Rotenberg)
- Information about family and friends, problems with correspondence.
- ***Description:*** original, handwritten manuscript on a postcard, ink, missing postmark, German, 148×105 mm, ss. 1, pp. 2.
  On p. 1 notation (printed): "99."
  Index: Hanka Rabinowicz

**921. RING. I/1208 (1527). Mf. ŻIH—835; USHMM—47**

- After 1939, Łódź ghetto
- Chaim Emanuel [Wołyński][?] (Łódź ghetto), Letter[s?] to Szachno [Sagan] (Warsaw) in Warsaw describing conditions reigning in Łódź
- Concerning situation in the Łódź ghetto (Chaim Rumkowski's activity) and financial aid (foreign) flowing in for the Jewish population; warning against transmission of funds into the hands of Chaim Rumkowski.
- ***Description:*** original, handwritten manuscript, ink, Yiddish, 212×304 mm, ss. 1 pp. 1.
  Index: Efraim Lezer, [Leon (Lejb)] Neustadt, [Icchak] Bernsztein, Trojstman [Trajstman?] of Łódź

**922. RING. I/63. Mf. ŻIH—836; USHMM—67**

- After 06.1940, Warsaw Ghetto
- Table entitled "Prayzn in Lodzh in yuni 1940" [Prices in Łódź in June 1940]
- Price differences for several food items between the ghetto and the "Aryan side" in Łódź.
- ***Description:*** transcript (2 copies), handwritten manuscript (MS*), pencil, Yiddish, 148×210 mm, ss. 2, pp. 2.

**923. RING. I/987 (1306). (Lb. 308). Mf. ŻIH—831; USHMM—43**

- After 5.05.1941, Warsaw Ghetto
- NN., Study on the Alte Shul in Łódź (5.05.1941)
- About the significance of the old Łódź synagogue for Jews, people fleeing antisemitism in the provinces

and settling en masse in Łódź in the final years before the war.

- ***Description:*** transcript (2 copies), handwritten manuscript (BW*), pencil, Yiddish, loose, 147×206 mm, minor damage and losses of text, ss. 10, pp. 10.
  In the margins a symbol (ink): "///" and on p. 1 (first copy) a symbol (red pencil): "+."
  See Ring. I/969.

**924. RING. I/60. (Lb. 947). Mf. ŻIH—774; USHMM—5**

- After 01.1941, place unknown
- NN., "Note on the economic situation of the Łódź ghetto at the end of January 1941" (30.01.1941) (fragment)
- Dictatorship of the Eldest (Rumkowski), provisioning, currency, education.
- ***Description:*** original or transcript, typescript, Polish, 223×287 mm, slight damage and losses of text, ss. 4, pp. 4.
  On p. 4, handwritten manuscript notation: "Mr. Winter, Councillor" [?] and typescript notation: "Dr/sb."

**925. RING. I/1034 (1353). (Lb. 1573). Mf. ŻIH—832; USHMM—44**

- After 06.1941, Warsaw Ghetto
- Cwi Klejnman, Account
- Fate of the Jewish population in northern Mazowsze, displacements, repressive actions (e.g., Ciechanów, Pułtusk); list of names of victims.
- ***Description:*** original, handwritten manuscript (CK*), notebook, ink, Yiddish, 144×209 mm, minor damage and losses of text, text illegible in places, ss. 7, pp. 10.
  Cover of the notebook was made out of a printed form: "Reports [of the activity of hometown associations] for the month of . . . 1941" (hectographed typescript); handwritten manuscript notation (ink): "VI."
  See Ring. I/1169.

**926. RING. I/558. Mf. ŻIH—791; USHMM—22**

- 5.05.1942, Międzyrzec Podlaski
- Masza Altman (Międzyrzec Podlaski, ul. Piłsudskiego 27), Letter of 5.05.1942 to NN. (Hela) (Warsaw, ul. Twarda 30, apt. 10)
- Information about mass executions (inter alia 18.04.1942) in Międzyrzec.
- ***Description:*** original, handwritten manuscript on a postcard, postmark and stamp of the Jewish Council in Warsaw, Hebrew, German, Polish, Yiddish, 147×105 mm, ss. 1, pp. 2.
  Letter's addressee: "J. Perkal, Warsaw, ul. Twarda 30, apt. 10"
  Published: *Listy o Zagładzie*, pp. 147–148.

**927. RING. I/866 (1185). (Lb. 200). Mf. ŻIH—828; USHMM—40**

- After 04.1942, Warsaw Ghetto
- NN., Account entitled "Mińsk" (04.1942)
- A young Jewish woman on Aryan papers travels in regions of the USSR occupied by the Germans. Describes stay in 02.1942 in Mińsk in Belarus, where there still resided ca. 900 Jews in the ghetto near the the rail station. 5 mass executions of Jews took place in the city.
- ***Description:*** transcript, handwritten manuscript (RR*), ink, Yiddish, 158×204 mm, ss. 2, pp. 4.
  Published: *BFG*, vol. XXXI/1993, pp. 82–83.
  According to Ruta Sakowska, the author of the account is Leja Koziebrodzka, ibid.

**928. RING. I/1220/30. Mf. ŻIH—835; USHMM—47**

- After 1941, Warsaw Ghetto
- NN., Account of a stay in the regions occupied by the USSR (fragment, missing conclusion)
- The author, a physician, refugee, stayed in Białystok, then worked in a hospital in Mir (situation of refugees on the territories of Poland occupied by the USSR, deportations, description of Mir, Jewish population, medical situation, aid for relatives in the Generalgouvernement [parcels], education, outbreak of the German–Soviet War in 1941).
- ***Description:*** transcript, handwritten manuscript (LEG*), pencil, Yiddish, 109×356, 109×301 mm, ss. 3, pp. 3.
  Sheets 1 and 2 were written on the back of a form: "Late payer certificate" (date unknown, printed, Polish); sheet 3 written on the back of a form (fragment): "[list of] late [pay]ers" (date unknown, printed, Polish).

**929. RING. I/865 (1184). (Lb. 390). Mf. ŻIH—828; USHMM—40**

- Date unknown, Warsaw Ghetto
- NN., Account entitled "Geyresh Mlave" [Mława Expulsion]
- Course of the expulsion of part of the Jewish population from Mława (5/6.12.1940) (despite payment of a "contribution" in the amount of 35 thousand marks, ca. 4,000 persons were removed to Działdowo, from where, after 8 days, they were distributed over the course of 3 days without food and drink to different localities of the Generalgouvernement).
- ***Description:*** original (o) (handwritten manuscript—H.W.*, ink, 148×210 mm, minor damage and losses of text), transcript (2 copies, handwritten manuscript—MS*, pencil, 148×210 mm, minor damage and losses of text), Yiddish, ss. 6, pp. 6.
  In the margins of both documents are a letter (ink) "F" (fei) and on p. 1 a symbol (red pencil): "+."
  Docs. were kept in a binder

Index: Perelmuter, chairman of the Jewish Council in Mława

**930. RING. I/580. Mf. ŻIH—792; USHMM—23**

- 06.1942, Mława
- Noach [Romaner] (Mielau [Mława]), Letter of 8.06.1942 to M. Romaner (Warsaw, ul. Gęsia 7, apt. 12)
- Information about the death (4.06.1942 in Mława) of the brother of the author and of the addressee: Mojsze and Lejb Romaner.
- ***Description:*** p. 1—original, handwritten manuscript on a postcard, postmark and stamp of the Jewish Council, p. 2—transcript (made in the Warsaw Ghetto and glued to the original postcard), ink, Yiddish, 144×103 mm, minor damage and losses of text, ss. 1, pp. 2.

Published: *Listy o Zagładzie*, pp. 171–173.

**931. RING. I/790 (1109). (Lb. 364). Mf. ŻIH—826; USHMM—38**

- After 2.05.1941, Warsaw Ghetto
- NN., Account entitled "Amshinov" [Mszczonów] (2.05.1941)
- Account in the form of a letter of son to father about the harassment of the Jewish population at the beginning of the German occupation: bombardment of the town (6.09.1939), persecution of the rabbi and more than 100 Jews on Yom Kippur, burning of 20 Jews in the house of Dawid Kojfman; Josef Nusbaum, Hersz Wejnrajch; the shooting of Josef Wejnrajch, forcing of the grandson of the miller Iczy Zasławski to set fire to the synagogue and beit midrash, where the following persons perished: a pregnant woman with three children (Gelbard), Zanwel [Gelbard?], Perkal, Szlomo Warszawski, Szaja Sztrejberg, and the shoemaker Meir Ber were shot. Also killed were 2 priests, the mayor, a physician, and other people.
- ***Description:*** transcript (2 copies), handwritten manuscript (BW*), pencil, Yiddish, 148×210 mm, ss. 4, pp. 4.

In the margins a Hebrew letter (ink): "b" (beit).

**932. RING. I/868 (1187). (Lb. 733). Mf. ŻIH—828; USHMM—40**

- After 1941, Warsaw Ghetto
- NN., Account entitled "Nadrazhin" [Nadarzyn]
- Situation of the Jews in Nadarzyn from the first bombardment (6.09.1939) until their expulsion to Grodzisk (winter 1941), and subsequently to Warsaw (those executed in 09.1939, composition of the Jewish Council).
- ***Description:*** transcript (3 copies), handwritten manuscript (NN*), pencil, Yiddish, 148×210 mm, ss. 15, pp. 15.

On p. 1 (second copy) at top is notation by H.W. in Yiddish (ink): "Hober."

In the margins (first and third copies) a Hebrew letter (ink): "t" (taf).

Index: Mosze Harman, killed in Nadarzyn in 1939; Ber (age 85), tailor, and son, killed in Nadarzyn in 1939; Abraham Górnik, Poles gave him away, killed in Nadarzyn in 1939; Jakub Mosze Goldsztajn, killed in Nadarzyn in 1939; Jechiel, rabbi, killed in Nadarzyn in 1939; Cymerman of Nadarzyn; Lejbisz Hamersztajn of Nadarzyn; Izrael Mosze Żychliński of Nadarzyn; Meir Hering, chairman of the Jewish Council in Nadarzyn; Feldman, member of the Jewish Council in Nadarzyn; Juda Mosze Feldman, member of the Jewish Council in Nadarzyn; Dawid Manhajt, member of the Jewish Council in Nadarzyn; Pinchas Dawid Zylberg, member of the Jewish Council in Nadarzyn

**933. RING. I/873 (1193). (Lb. 939). Mf. ŻIH—828; USHMM—40**

- Date unknown, Warsaw Ghetto
- NN., Account entitled "Nasielsk"
- Expulsion of Jews from Nasielsk (3.12.1939) and displacement to Międzyrzec [Podlaski].
- ***Description:*** original (o) (handwritten manuscript—DD*, ink, 202×273 mm), transcript (3 copies, handwritten manuscript JG*, pencil, 148×210 mm, minor damage and losses of text), Polish, ss. 13, pp. 14.

On p. 1 (transcript, first and second copies) notation by H.W. (ink): "Lebensold."

**934. RING. I/871 (1190). (Lb. 1063). Mf. ŻIH—828; USHMM—40**

- After 10.1939, Warsaw Ghetto
- NN., Account entitled "Nieszawa"
- Subjection of Jews to public whipping in Nieszawa: Graubart (father and 4 sons), Brańtuch, Gotlibowicz, Gross, Zakrzewski, and Jagoda.
- ***Description:*** original (o) [?], handwritten manuscript (FLIG*), ink, Polish, 203×296 mm, ss. 2, pp. 4.

Index: Jagoda, shot together with 2 Poles in Nieszawa (1939)

**935. RING. I/453. (Lb. 1229). Mf. ŻIH—786; USHMM—17**

- After 09.1939, Warsaw Ghetto
- NN., Account about the fate of Jews of Nowe Miasto on the Pilica in September 1939
- First days of the war, flight of the Jewish population from the town, plunder of property by Poles, Germans' repressive actions against Jews after their arrival in Nowe Miasto (8.09.1939) (numerous fatalities).
- ***Description:*** transcript (2 copies), handwritten manuscript (U*), pencil, Yiddish, 150×210 mm, ss. 10, pp. 10.

Index: Abraham Wolf Holcman, baker of Nowe Miasto, fatally beaten in 09.1939; Cwi Miler of Nowe Miasto, fatally beaten in 09.1939; Abraham Malewalczyk [?] of Nowe Miasto, severely wounded with a dagger; Alter Kahan (age 30) of Nowe Miasto, shot in 09.1939; Szlomo Józef Sztern (age 37) of Nowe Miasto, shot in 09.1939; Józef Majersdorf (age 27) of Nowe Miasto, shot in 09.1939; Gedali Lewin of Nowe Miasto, shot in 09.1939; Frenkel (age ca. 30) of Nowe Miasto, shot in 09.1939

### 936. RING. I/869 (1188). (Lb. 389, 389A). Mf. ŻIH—828; USHMM—40

a)

- After 22.03.1941, Warsaw Ghetto
- NN., Account entitled "Novi Dvor bay Varshe" [Nowy Dwór near Warsaw] (22.03.1941)
- ***Description:*** transcript (2 copies), handwritten manuscript (MS*), pencil, Yiddish, 148×208 mm, ss. 6, pp. 6.

  In the margins, letter (ink): "B." On p. 1 at top a date: "22.03.41" and a symbol (red pencil): "+."

b) (Lb. 389a)

- After 2.05.1941, Warsaw Ghetto
- NN., Account about experiences of the Jewish population in Nowy Dwór (Nowy Dwór, 2.05.1941)
- Chronology of events from 1.09.1939 to spring 1940.
- ***Description:*** transcript (2 copies), handwritten manuscript (BW*), pencil, Yiddish, 148×208 mm, ss. 4, pp. 4

  In the margins a Hebrew letter (ink): "g" (giml).

c) (Lb. 389)

- After 13.03.1941, Warsaw Ghetto
- NN., Account entitled "Mayn shtetl Novi Dvor un ir martyrologie" [My town Nowy Dwór and its martyrdom]
- History of the town (from the 14th century) and Jewish community, position of Jews during the interwar period, economic and cultural life, victims of persecutions during the war.
- ***Description:*** transcript (2 copies), handwritten manuscript (BW*), pencil, Yiddish, 148×210 mm, minor damage and losses of text, ss. 10, pp. 10.

  In the margins a Hebrew letter: "m" (mem).

  Doc. was kept in a binder.

  Index: Altsztajn, murdered when he refused to set fire to religious books; Beniamin Finker, Orthodox activist, died of terror of being arrested; Abratszych [?], tailor, fatally beaten in Legionowo

### 937. RING. I/872 (1191). (Lb. 1475). Mf. ŻIH—828; USHMM—40

- Date unknown, Warsaw Ghetto
- NN., Account concerning persons collaborating with the Germans
- Displaced persons from Nowy Dwór pass on information about Gestapo collaborators, informers, and blackmailers.
- ***Description:*** original or transcript, handwritten manuscript, ink, Yiddish, 145×184 mm, ss. 2, pp. 4.

  On p. 4 notation by H.W. in Yiddish (ink): "Groberg brothers (2), capmakers, trusted workers, former reds."

  Index: Melech Apelheim of Nowy Dwór; Moniek Diament, barber; Groberg (?) brothers

### 938. RING. I/501. (Lb. 1415). Mf. ŻIH—788; USHMM—19

a)

- After 1941, Warsaw Ghetto
- Berek Proza, Account about the expulsion of Jews from Okuniew
- Author, a merchant from Okuniew, describes the displacement to the Warsaw Ghetto (Thursday, date unknown), lists numerous fatalities.
- ***Description:*** transcript, handwritten manuscript, pencil, Polish, 214×300 mm, text is difficult to read in places, ss. 1, pp. 1.

  Doc. drawn up on the back of a registration card of a "point" (shelter) for displaced persons (date unknown, printed, Polish)

  Index: Srul Majer Naszewski, shot, Okuniew; Szlama Gurfinkiel, shot; Matys Powsinoga (age 18), shot; Szyja Zysman (age 20), Ryfka Zysman, shot; Dawid Stanisławski (age 17), Fajga Stanisławska [?] (age 14), Szlama Bursztyn, Łaja Rotsztajn, [. . . ?], (age 55), Dwojra Rubin, Jakub Rzetelny (age 70), shot near Rembertów

b)

- After 26.03.1942, Warsaw Ghetto
- Manes Puterman, Account about the expulsion of Jews from Wawer
- Author, age 41, a laborer from Wawer, describes the formation of a ghetto (10.11.1941) and displacement to the Warsaw Ghetto (Thursday, 23.03.1942).
- ***Description:*** transcript, handwritten manuscript, pencil, Polish, 205×293 mm, ss. 1, pp. 1.

  At top notation by H.W. (ink): "Wawer"; date "26.03.[1942?]" (ink) added later.

  Docs. a and b are written in the same handwriting.

  Index: Cybulski

c)

- After 27.03.1942, Warsaw Ghetto
- Maria Edelman, Account about the expulsion of Jews from Miłosna [?]
- Female author, age 25 from Miłosna, describes the expulsion of the Jewish population to the Warsaw Ghetto.
- ***Description:*** transcript, handwritten manuscript (KK*), ink, Polish, 154×200 mm, text is legible in places, ss. 1, pp. 2.

  Attached note by H.W.: "Okuniew and Wawer. Province and expulsion. Testimony of expellees: Berek Proza age 27—Okuniew, Manes Puterman age 40—Wawer, Maria Edelman, age 25—Miłosna."

**939. RING. I/875 (1195). (Lb. 1216). Mf. ŻIH—828; USHMM—40**

- 27.03.1942, Warsaw Ghetto
- Sara and Szymon Powsinoga, Mala Wisznia, Account about the displacement of Jews from Okuniew and Miłosna to the Warsaw Ghetto (27.03.1942)
- Situation of the Jewish population (84 families) in Okuniew during the occupation until expulsion (25.03.1942). Information about those killed during the displacement. Expulsion of Jews from Miłosna (26.03.1942).
- ***Description:*** transcript, handwritten manuscript (Ł*), ink, Yiddish, 162×180 mm, ss. 10, pp. 10.
  Index: Szyra and Rywka Zysman, killed during the expulsion from Okuniew (25.03.1942); Lea Rotsztajn, killed during the expulsion from Okuniew (25.03.1942); Jakub and Aszer Rzetelny, killed during the expulsion from Okuniew (25.03.1942); Izrael Mejer, butcher, killed during the expulsion from Okuniew (25.03.1942); Dawid Budny, killed during the expulsion from Okuniew (25.03.1942); Szlomo Bursztyn (age 15), killed during the expulsion from Okuniew (25.03.1942); Szlomo Gurfinkiel (age 42), gaiter maker from Rembertów, killed during the expulsion from Okuniew (25.03.1942); Rywka and Dawid Stanisławski (siblings, aged 17 and 18), killed during the expulsion from Okuniew (25.03.1942); Grifan [?], killed during the expulsion from Okuniew (25.03.1942); Nachman Szarsztajn, killed during the expulsion from Okuniew (25.03.1942); Rywka Sztern, killed during the expulsion from Okuniew (25.03.1942); Powsinoga, son of Sara and Szymon, killed during the expulsion from Okuniew (25.03.1942)

**940. RING. I/354. (Lb. 56). Mf. ŻIH—782; USHMM—13. RING. I/97. Mf. ŻIH—776; USHMM—7**

- After 2.12.1940, place unknown
- Der Kreishauptmann Warschau, Letter of 2.12.1940 to chairman of the Jewish Community in Młociny
- Order for the transfer of Jews from Młociny to Fort Solipse [?] near Warsaw[41] by 10.12.1940.
- ***Description:*** Ring. I/354—transcript, typescript, German, 207×293 mm, ss. 1, pp. 1; Ring. I/97—transcript, handwritten manuscript (MS*), pencil, German in Hebrew alphabet transliteration, 147×208 mm, ss. 1, pp. 1.
  Doc. (Ring. I/97) was kept in a binder. At top notation by H.W. (ink) in Yiddish: "Document."

**941. RING. I/199. Mf. ŻIH—779; USHMM—10**

- After 09.1941, Oleśnica near Busko
- A. [Anszel] Kurc (Oleśnica near Busko), Letter to the Central Refugees Commission (CKU) (Warsaw Ghetto)
- The author, a refugee from Łódź, was vice chairman of the Jewish Council in Oleśnica; information about troubles connected with a laundry sold in Warsaw.
- ***Description:*** original [?], handwritten manuscript, ink, Polish, 147×210 mm, ss. 2, pp. 4.
  Attached note by H.W. in Yiddish: "Anszel Kurc, a refugee from Łódź, a member of the Łódź sport group Gwiazda [Shtern, Star], wrote the letter."
  Index: Rywka Brylant (ul. Grzybowska 36, apt. 67), R. Kurc (ul. Nowolipie 21, apt. 25), Hinda and Izak Kac (ul. Leszno 47, apt. 9), Dr. Ludwik Podskocz, Grabowiecki (ul. Leszno 2, apt. 41), Bursztyn, Blumsztajn, Wasser, Vogel, Kapłan, Berliński, Dobrin, Bierzuński [Bieżuński ?]

**942. RING. I/567. Mf. ŻIH—792; USHMM—23**

- After 2.05.1942, Warsaw Ghetto
- NN. (Fela) (Opatów), Letter of 2.05.1942 to I. (Warsaw Ghetto)
- About an execution in Ostrowiec in April 1942.
- ***Description:*** transcript (2 copies), handwritten manuscript (H*), pencil, Polish, Yiddish, 205×158 mm, minor damage and losses of text, ss. 2, pp. 2.
  On p. 1 (first copy) note in Yiddish: "a copy."
  Published: *Listy o Zagładzie*, pp. 144–145.

**943. RING. I/587. Mf. ŻIH—792; USHMM—23**

a)

- 25.02.1941, Opole Lubelskie
- Samuel Stieber (Opole), Letter of 25.02.1941 to Józef Landau (Warsaw, ul. Śliska 59 [54?], apt. 26)
- About displaced persons from Vienna (1,000 persons).
- ***Description:*** original, handwritten manuscript on a postcard, ink, German, 144×102 mm, minor damage and losses of text, text illegible in places, ss. 1, pp. 2.
  The card was kept in a binder.

b)

- [29.03.]1942, Opole Lubelskie
- Mojsze Goldbaum (Opole Lubelskie), Letter to Josel (Josek) Goldbaum (Warsaw, ul. Zamenhofa 27)
- About displacements of Jews from Kazimierz Dolny, Puławy, Wąwolnice to Opole Lubelskie. About displaced persons from Vienna (2,500 persons). Request for aid.
- ***Description:*** original, handwritten manuscript, envelope (postmark and stamp of Jewish Council in

41. The original is "we Włochach." Włochy is a suburb of Warsaw.

Warsaw), pencil, ink, Polish, Yiddish, 110×176, 143×120 mm, ss. 4, pp. 6.

On the envelope the sender: "P. Goldbaum."

Published: *Listy o Zagładzie*, pp. 136–140.

Index: Joel [Goldbaum], Mojsze Welwel, Lejbel Markowicz

### 944. RING. I/1151 (1470). (Lb. 1228, 1466, 1537). Mf. ŻIH—833; USHMM—45

a)

- 1942, Warsaw Ghetto
- NN., Account entitled "Orsza"
- Author describes the first months of the Soviet-German war. Departure from Lwów (23.06.1941), journey to Kiev, service in the Red Army, participation in fighting near Orsza, German captivity (23.09.1941), POW camps in Khorol and Kremieńczuk (Kremenchug in Ukraine) (5.10.1941) (appended maps of the camps).

b)

- 1942, Warsaw Ghetto
- [Al. Graff], Account entitled "Mariupol"
- Situation of the Jewish population before outbreak of war in Ukraine (USSR), first months of the Soviet-German war, wandering on the coast of the Sea of Azov, Mariupol, Taganróg, Rostów, social relations, course of the German offensive, journey via Lwów to Warsaw.
- ***Description:*** original (o), handwritten manuscript (H.W.*), notebook (16 ss.), ink, Polish, 145×175, 156×187, 160×196 mm, ss. 29, pp. 39.

On sheet 6 (notebook) notation by H.W.: "3.03.1942"

Doc. a) includes ss. 1–8 (in the notebook numbered by H.W.) and sheet 9 (in the notebook); the rest of the ss. in the notebook not numbered.

Doc. b) includes pp. 1–10 (numbered by H.W.) and 2 loose ss. (conclusion).

Notebook also includes other materials (Notes) by H.W. in Polish and Yiddish: 1) Letter to ZZ [Zakład Zaopatrzenia, Supply Department] (Director Dybiński) concerning settlement (of a debt in the amount of 100 zł) of the vegetable-potato wholesaler Ryczke i Ska (ul. Smocza 19) with the distribution point of Fiszel Fliderblum (member of CKU) (Date unknown, transcript); 2) Roll of disbursements (relief grants, amounts due, fees [?]) of 9.01.1942 for the following persons: Weisberg, Tytelman, Winnik, Fligelman, Gutkowski, Wasser, Opoczyński, Huberband; 3) List of persons (with families) and addresses: "Breakfasts. 1) Gutkowski Eliahu, Gutkowska Luba, Gutkowski Gabriel, ul. Nowolipki 31/31; 2) Wilczyński Chaskiel, Wilczyńska Kalcia and Halina, ul. Ogrodowa 26/31; 3) Hornowicz Małka, ul. Ogrodowa 26/31; 4) Titelman Natan, ul. Muranow[ska] 31 [crossed out]; 5) Szrank Meir, Fajga, Małka, Rywka, Szejna, ul. Wołowa 2; 6) Opoczyński Perec, Mendel, Efraim-Dan, ul. Wołyńska 21; 7) Wasser Hersz, Blima, ul. Muran[owska] 6; 8) Zilberberg Jakow, Jochewed, Gotlib Rywka, ul. Nowolipie 21; 9) Tytelman Nechemja, ul. Muranow[ska] 31; 10) Tytelman Eliahu, Szymon, Abraham, ul. Pawia 5; 11) Fligelman Daniel, ul. Śliska 24."

Doc. b): Attached note by H.W.: "Experiences of Al. Graff [?] from the period of the liberation war of the Sov.Union, Mariupol-Rostów on Don-Warsaw," note by H.W., fragment.

E. Ringelblum writes about both accounts; see *Kronika getta*, pp. 478 and 483.

Index: Kazimierz Czerwiński from Lwów

### 945. RING. I/553. Mf. ŻIH—791; USHMM—22

- After 30.04.1942, Warsaw Ghetto
- NN. (Ostrowiec), Letter of 30.04.1942 to NN. (Warsaw Ghetto)
- About mass executions in Ostrowiec.
- ***Description:*** transcript (2 copies), handwritten manuscript (LEG*), pencil, Yiddish, 206×294 mm, minor damage and losses of text, ss. 2, pp. 2.

Published: *Listy o Zagładzie*, pp. 141–144.

Index: Szulc, Malkiel Lusternik

### 946. RING. I/782 (1101). Mf. ŻIH—825; USHMM—37

- 12.1939, Otwock
- Mayor of Otwock, Jan Gadomski, Announcement of 11.12.1939 about levy imposed by the German authorities on the Jewish population of Otwock
- Levy in the amount of 100,000 zł. to be paid by 20.12.1939. Appended list of names of the Special Committee created for collection of money.
- ***Description:*** original, printed, German, Polish, 470×402 mm, minor damage and losses of text, ss. 1, pp. 1.

Index: Ela Aroniak of Otwock, Chaim Bieloch of Otwock, Chonon Cetlin of Otwock, Rachmil Fleisyng of Otwock, Dawid Feldman of Otwock, Hersz From of Otwock, Jankiel Frydenzon of Otwock, Efroim Gójski of Otwock, Gustawa Kamińska of Otwock, Chaim Kenigsberg of Otwock, Izaak Lesman of Otwock, Mordka Landsberg of Otwock, Tobias Mokotowski of Otwock, Mordka Orliński of Otwock, Efroim Rikner of Otwock

### 947. RING. I/569. Mf. ŻIH—792; USHMM—23

- 03.1942, Ozorków ghetto
- Ita Aronowicz, Eda Kadysz and her mother (Ozorków, Feldstrasse 15), Letters of [13 and 20].03.1942 to M. Kadysz (Warsaw, ul. Szczęśliwa 15, apt. 20)

- Information about stay in the ghetto in Ozorków, about the situation of the closest relatives and friends (e.g., Aunt Tabaczyńska).
- ***Description:*** original, handwritten manuscript (three handwritings) on postcards, postmarks (Ozorków 13 and 20.03.42) and stamps of the Jewish Council in Warsaw, ink, German, Polish, 146×104 mm, text illegible in places, ss. 2, pp. 4.

  On letter of 20.03 Information about the address of the sender: Feldstrasse 15 "in care of Miss Landau."

  Published: *Listy o Zagładzie*, pp. 74–77.

### 948. RING. I/573/6. Mf. ŻIH—792; USHMM—23. Mf. ŻIH—836; USHMM—67

- 25.01.1942, Ozorków
- E. Prusinowska (Ozorków). Letter of 25.01.1942 to K. Poznański (Warsaw, ul. Dzielna 11, apt. 4).
- ***Description:*** original, handwritten manuscript on a postcard, pencil, ink, postmarks and stamp of Jewish Council in Warsaw, ink, Polish, 147×104 mm, text illegible in places, ss. 1, pp. 2.

  On p. 1 notation in Yiddish (pencil): "Lojzer [. . . ?]"

### 949. RING. I/585. Mf. ŻIH—792; USHMM—23

a)

- 10.1941–06.1942, Pacht near Turek
- Bronka Górna (Pacht 11 [?] near Turek), Letters dated 7.10.1941, 11.03. [postmark date], 9.04., 14.06.1942 to Maks Górny (Warsaw, ul. Miła 69, apt. 29)
- Author was transferred with family to a village ghetto [Judenkolonie-Heidemühle], where were collected the residents of Brudzewo, Turek, Władysławów, Tuliszków, Dobra, and Uniejów. Information on the approaching annihilation.
- ***Description:*** original, handwritten manuscript (BG*) on postcards, postmarks and stamps of Jewish Council in Warsaw, ink, Polish, 146×103 mm, damage and losses of text (letters of 11.03., 9.04.), text illegible in places (letter of 14.06.), ss. 4, pp. 8.

  Addressee of the letter dated 7.10.1941 was Maks Górny (Warsaw, ul. Miła 69, apt. 29), but from the contents of the correspondence it appears that he was at the time in a labor camp.

  Attached note by H.W. in Polish, Yiddish: "Period of murders in the region of Turek, 1942. Jechiel Górny's wife's final letter."

  Letter of 20.12.1941: See Ring. I/599/95.

  Published: *Listy o Zagładzie*, pp. 174–176, 178–179, 184.

  Index: Pola Sadorkiewicz, Herczyk, Ada Górna, Besser [?]

b)

- 04–06.1942, Pacht near Turek; after 8.06.1942, Warsaw Ghetto
- B.Najdat [and Bronka Górna] (Pacht 11 near Turek), Letters dated 28.04. [postmark] and 7.06.1942 to Jakub Langnas (Warsaw, ul. Zamenhofa 9, apt. 15)
- Information concerning living conditions, fate of immediate family, approaching annihilation.
- ***Description:*** original (Letter of 28.04. handwritten manuscript (BG*) on a postcard, postmark and stamp of Jewish Council in Warsaw, ink, 146×104 mm, minor damage and losses of text), transcript (Letter of 7.06.1942, handwritten manuscript -JG*, pencil, 146×208 mm), Polish, Yiddish, and Yiddish in Roman transliteration, ss. 2, pp. 4.

  On letter dated 7.06.1942 postscript of Hela [Waksztok].

  Published: *Listy o Zagładzie*, pp. 179–180, 183–184.

c)

- Before 15.05.1942, Pacht near Turek
- Hela Waksztok (Pacht near Turek), Letter dated 15.05.1942 [postmark date of Jewish Council in Warsaw] to Jakub Langnas (Warsaw, ul. Zamenhofa 9, apt. 15)
- Registration in ghetto, new ordinances in the matter of mailing parcels.
- ***Description:*** original, handwritten manuscript (BG*) on a postcard, postmark and stamp of Jewish Council in Warsaw, ink, Polish, 146×104 mm, minor damage and losses of text, ss. 1, pp. 2.

  Published: *Listy o Zagładzie*, pp. 180–181.

d)

- 7.04.1942, Pacht near Turek
- M. Sadorkiewicz (Pacht near Turek), Letter of 7.04.1942 to Abram Diament (Warsaw, Elektoralna 14, apt. 127)
- Information about mass annihilation of the Jewish population.
- ***Description:*** original, handwritten manuscript on a postcard, postmark, stamp of Jewish Council in Warsaw and stamp: "[Juden]kolo[nie] [Heide]mühle," ink, Yiddish in Roman transliteration, 146×104 mm, text illegible in places, ss. 1, pp. 2.

  Published: *Listy o Zagładzie*, pp. 177–178.

### 950. RING. I/599/13. Mf. ŻIH—812; USHMM—24

- 8.01.1942, Pacht near Turek
- B. [Bronka] Górna (Pacht 11, Fort Turek camp), Letter of 8.01.1942 to Maks Górny (Warsaw, Miła 69, apt. 29). Information about exchange of correspondence.
- ***Description:*** original, handwritten manuscript (BG*) on a postcard, postmarks and stamps of Jewish Council in Warsaw, ink, German, 146×103 mm, damage and losses of text, text illegible in places, ss. 1, pp. 2.

  Ada [Górna] added a postscript to the letter.

### 951. RING. I/599/14. Mf. ŻIH—812; USHMM—24

- 9.[?]02.1942, Pacht near Turek

- B. [Bronka] Górna (Pacht—camp), Letter of 9. [?]02.1942 to [Maks Górny (Warsaw, ul. Miła 69, apt. 29)][?].
- ***Description:*** original, handwritten manuscript (BG*) on a postcard, postmarks and stamps of Jewish Council in Warsaw, ink, pencil, Polish, 146×103 mm, substantial damage and losses of text, text illegible in places, ss. 1, pp. 2.

## 952. RING. I/599/15. Mf. ŻIH—812; USHMM—24

- 9.06.1942, Pacht near Turek
- B. [Bronka] Górna (Pacht—camp), Letter [postmarked 9.06.1942—Turek] to Maks Górny (Warsaw, ul. Miła 69, apt. 29).
- ***Description:*** original, handwritten manuscript (BG*) on a postcard, postmarks and stamps of Jewish Council in Warsaw, ink, Polish, 146×103 mm, minor damage and losses of text, text is illegible in places, ss. 1, pp. 2.

  Ada [Górna] wrote a postscript to the letter.

## 953. RING. I/763 (1087). Mf. ŻIH—823; USHMM—35

- 12.1939, Piotrków Trybunalski
- *Anordnungsblatt für Stadt und Landkreis Petrikau* [Regulation Gazette for the City and District of Piotrków], no. 7 of 1.12, no. 8 of 8.12.1939
- Bilingual weekly of the occupation authorities (Piotrków) containing official ordinances and announcements.
- ***Description:*** original, printed, German, Polish, 237×315 mm, ss. 10, pp. 20.

## 954. RING. I/659. Mf. ŻIH—816; USHMM—28

- After 6.12.1939, Piotrków [Trybunalski]
- Der Stadtkommissar Petrikau, [Hans] Drechsel, Letter of 6.12.1939 to the official Jewish Community in Piotrków
- Order to supply materials for construction of 2 barracks for refugees and expansion of the factory on ul. Garbarska, preparation of sleeping benches and adaptation of the interior of the synagogue on ul. Jerózolimska and the Jewish secondary school on ul. Pereca for refugees, construction of sheep-pens on ul. Curie-Skłodowska, construction of 2 barracks at the synagogue at ul. Piłsudskiego 25 and on the property at pl. Litewski. Jewish Community will bear full costs of these investments.
- ***Description:*** transcript, handwritten manuscript (MS*), pencil, German in Hebrew transliteration, Yiddish, 148×210 mm, minor damage and losses of text, ss. 1, pp. 1.

  Postwar note by Laura Eichhornowa in Polish (ink): "Piotrków."

  Attached note by H.W. in Yiddish

  Document was stored in a binder.

  See Ring. I/340.

## 955. RING. I/787/1. (1106). Mf. ŻIH—826; USHMM—38. RING. I/876 (1196), I/882 (1202). Mf. ŻIH—828; USHMM—40

**a) Ring. I/787/1, I/876, I/882**

- 11.1939–04.1940, Piotrków ghetto
- Jewish Community in Piotrków, announcements
- Announcements:
  1) dated 10.11.1939 on the Jewish population's obligation to register;
  1a) dated 11.1939, on prevention of spread of typhoid fever;
  2) dated 1.12.1939, summons to present 1,000 Jews daily for labor;
  3) after 1.12.1939, on the obligation of males from a given street to report for labor;
  4) dated 8.12.1939, on creation of the Emigration Committee;
  5) dated 14.12.1939, on registration for departure to the USSR;
  6) dated 19.12.1939, on the ban on taking in refugees;
  7) dated 26.12.1940, on registration of emigrants to the USSR and obligation of refugees passing through Piotrków to register at the Jewish Community;
  8) dated 27.12.1939, on the issuance of cards for bread for January 1940;
  9) dated 28.12.1939, on registration of merchants and artisans;
  10) dated 1940, on the requirement to submit to vaccination against typhoid fever;
  11) dated 4.01.1940, on sending letters through the bureau of the Jewish Community;
  12) dated 9.01.1940, summons for registration of all refugees by 12.01.1940;
  13) dated 9.01.1940, on the requirement to register economic activity by 16.01.1940;
  14) dated 12.01.1940, summons to immediate transfer into the ghetto for persons who previously obtained permission for an apartment or operation of a workshop outside the ghetto;
  15) dated 24.01.1940, on ban on the baking of white bread and confectionery products;
  16) dated 24.01.1940, on the requirement to wear an armband with a "Zionist star" (individuals over 10 years of age);
  17) dated 5.02.1940, on the issuance of new identification documents for those who have reached 15 years of age;
  18) dated 6.02.1940, on compulsory vaccinations;
  19) dated 22.02.1940, on prevention of epidemics;
  20) dated 28.02.1940, on the sale of bread rations (appended list of bakeries with the streets assigned to them);
  21) dated 29.02.1940, summons to males aged 16 to 60 to exchange their previous work identification cards for new ones;

22) before 1.03.1940, on the sale of bread rations;
22a) dated 9.03.1940, summons to register for forced labor;
23) dated 14.03.1940, summons for registration by 18.03.1940 of all residential rooms;
24) dated 18.03.1940, on the requirement to submit by 20.03.1940 all stores of seeds and fodder crops as well as on the ban on dealing in this commodity;
25) dated 21.03.1940, on the severe consequences of failing to report for forced labor;
25a) dated 13.04.1940, on the requirement to register for forced labor.

- ***Description:*** Ring. I/787/1—original (docs. 1, 6, 14, 15, 26, 28 in 2 copies; docs. 1a, 2, 4, 3 in 3 copies), transcript, printed, typescript, handwritten manuscript, German, Polish, Yiddish, 138×118, 335×490, 473×620 mm, ss. 46, pp. 46; Ring. I/876—transcript (doc. 5), handwritten manuscript (MS*), pencil, German in Hebrew transliteration, Yiddish, 210×287 mm, ss. 1, pp. 1;

Ring. I/882—transcript (doc. 20, without list of bakeries), typescript, Yiddish, 213×345 mm, ss. 1, pp. 1.

Doc. 1 has a stamp: "Print Shop of M. Rozensztajn, Piotrków Tryb[unalski], Rynek Trybunalski 4"; doc. no. 22a printed at Horowicz in Piotrków.

Doc. 3 printed on the back of ss. from an account ledger (after 1930, Piotrków, printed, Polish).

Ring. I/876: at top a Hebrew letter (red pencil): "p" (pei).

Some docs. were kept in a binder.

See HWC 22/1 for another copy of doc. 4, dated 8.12.1939.

b)

- 10–11.1939, Piotrków ghetto
- Jewish Community in Piotrków, Ration cards for bread for 11–12.1939.
- ***Description:*** original (cards dated 11.1939 in 2 copies), printed, stamp of the Jewish Community, German, Polish, 140×114, 137×107 mm, ss. 3, pp. 6.

c)

- Date unknown, Piotrków
- Police and Mayor of city of Piotrków, registration card form.
- ***Description:*** original (2 copies), printed, German, Polish, 174×245 mm, ss. 2, pp. 4.

d)

- After 09.1939, Piotrków
- Leaflet entitled *Żydzi są naszym nieszczęściem* (Jews are our misfortune)
- German propaganda publication.
- ***Description:*** original, printed, German, Polish, 157×276 mm, ss. 1, pp. 2.

**956. RING. I/877 (1197). (Lb. 400, 660, 1057). Mf. ŻIH—828; USHMM—40**

- 8.12.1939, Piotrków [Trybunalski]
- Jewish Community in Piotrków, Report of activity for the period 09–12.1939
- Information concerning operation of kitchens, children's home, housing commission, medical care, emigration, aid to refugees, budget, etc. Appended statistical breakdowns.
- ***Description:*** original (typescript, stamp of the Jewish Community in Piotrków, 205×290 mm, extensive minor damage and losses of text), transcript (handwritten manuscript—MS*, pencil, 143×222 mm, minor damage and losses of text), Yiddish, ss. 11, pp. 14.

On p. 1 (original) a Hebrew letter (red pencil): "p" (pei) and on p. 7 (original) illegible signature (handwritten manuscript).

In the margins (transcript) a symbol (ink): three dots arranged in the form of a triangle—"∴" and a Hebrew letter (red pencil): "p."

**957. RING. I/878 (1198). (Lb. 764). Mf. ŻIH—828; USHMM—40**

- 10.02.1940, Piotrków [Trybunalski]
- Jewish Council in Piotrków, Bill dated 10.02.1940 for Lieut. Sandner
- Balance due for materials (tailor's).
- ***Description:*** original, typescript, German, 135×208 mm, ss. 1, pp. 1.

At top notation: "codul" [?] and "103."

**958. RING. I/340. Mf. ŻIH—781; USHMM—12. RING. I/97. Mf. ŻIH—776; USHMM—7. RING. I/288. Mf. ŻIH—781; USHMM—12. RING. I/369. (Lb. 836). Mf. ŻIH—782; USHMM—13. RING. I/879 (1199). RING. I/880 (1200). (Lb. 593). Mf. ŻIH—828; USHMM—40**

a) **Ring. I/369. (Lb. 836) missing original Ring. I/97**

- After 23.11.1939
- Der Kommissar des Stadtkreises Petrikau, Letter of 23.11.1939 to Jewish Community in Piotrków
- Order for delivery by 11 AM of the sum of 350,000 zł. Document signed by Melles.
- ***Description:*** Ring. I/369—transcript, typescript, German, pp. 1; Ring. I/97—transcript, handwritten manuscript (MS*), pencil, German in Hebrew alphabet, 143×220 mm, ss. 1, pp. 1.

Doc. (Ring. I/97) was kept in a binder.

b) **Ring. I/340**

- After 28.10.1939, place unknown
- Board of the Jewish Religious Community in Piotrków, "Proclamation (Announcement) to the Jewish population of the city of Piotrków" (28.10.1939)
- Notification of the deadline (by 31.10.1939) for moving into the ghetto.

- ***Description:*** transcript, typescript with handwritten corrections, Polish, 218×328 mm, ss. 1, pp. 1.

c) **Ring. I/340**
- After 29.10.1939, place unknown
- Jewish Religious Community in Piotrków, "Announcement. To all Jewish producers and sellers of textile goods, hides, leather goods, shoes and so forth" (29.10.1939)
- Notification about the requirement to register a list of goods possessed.
- ***Description:*** transcript, typescript, Polish, 218×330 mm, ss. 1, pp. 1.

d) **Ring. I/340**
- After 26.11.1939, place unknown
- Announcement of the German authorities summoning to registration in the Jewish Community of children of poor families, for supplementary food (Piotrków, 26.11.1939).
- ***Description:*** transcript, typescript, German, Polish, 207×290 mm, ss. 1, pp. 1.

e) **Ring. I/340**
- After 27.11.1939, place unknown
- Jewish Community in Piotrków, Announcement "To the Jewish Population of the City of Piotrków" (27.11.1939)
- Summons to deliver designated furniture to apartments for Germans.
- ***Description:*** transcript, typescript, Polish, 205×148 mm, ss. 1, pp. 1.

  Date written in by hand.

f) **Ring. I/340**
- After 28.11.1939, place unknown
- Announcement: "Attention! Payday for substitutes (unemployed) every Thursday" (Piotrków, 28.11.1939)
- Those summoned to work are required to present themselves that very day, exemption only on the basis of a medical certificate.
- ***Description:*** transcript, typescript, German, Polish, 207×290 mm, ss. 1, pp. 1.

g) **Ring. I/879 (1199). (Lb. 284)**
- After 1.12.1939, place unknown
- Der Kommissar des Stadtkreises Petrikau, [Hans] Drechsel, Ordinance introducing various restrictions for the the Jewish population (Piotrków, 1.12.1939)
- Obligation of all residents of the ghetto to register by the evening of 2.12.1939; construction by the Community of a barrack for the homeless; submission on the preceding day of a list of 1,000 persons for labor on the next day; wearing armbands from 3.12.1939; ban on seeking compensation for losses sustained in result of the present orders.
- ***Description:*** transcript, typescript, German, 207×293 mm, ss. 1, pp. 1.

  Doc. was kept in a binder.

  Published: *Eksterminacja Żydów*, pp. 75–76.

gg) **Ring. I/880 (1200). (Lb. 593). Ring. I/97**
- After 4.12.1939, place unknown
- Der Kommissar des Stadtkreises Petrikau, [Hans] Drechsel, Correspondence with the Jewish Community in Piotrków
- 1) Letter of 4.12.1939 to Zelmen Tennenberg, chairman of the Jewish Community in matter of emigration of persons of Ukrainian descent; 2) document (order) dated 6.12.1939 in the matter of preparation of rooms and construction of barracks for refugees (Jews) at the expense of the Jewish Community.
- ***Description:*** Ring. I/880—transcript, typescript, German, Polish, 207×293 mm, ss. 2, pp. 2; Ring. I/97—transcript (doc. 1), handwritten manuscript (MS*), pencil, German in Hebrew alphabet, 143×220 mm, ss. 1, pp. 1.

  Ring. I/97—In the margin a Hebrew letter (red pencil): "p" (pei).

  Doc. (Ring. I/97) was kept in a binder.

ggg) **Ring. I/340**
- After 2.12.1939, place unknown
- Mayor of the city of Piotrków, Announcement of the order for wearing "star of Zion" (star of David) by Jews, baptized Jews, and individuals, one of whose parents is a Jew. (2.12.1939).
- ***Description:*** transcript, typescript, German, Polish, 207×293 mm, ss. 1, pp. 1.

  Doc. was kept in a binder.

h) **Ring. I/340**
- After 7.12.1939
- "Announcement regarding emigration of Jews from Piotrków" (7.12.1939)
- Notification about the formation at the the Jewish Community in Piotrków (ul. Piłsudskiego 27) of the Emigration Committee, which "established as its aim the task of organization and facilitation of emigration of Jews from Piotrków." The Committee serves from 8.12.1939.
- ***Description:*** transcript, typescript, German, Polish, Yiddish, 220×310 mm, ss. 1, pp. 1.

i) **Ring. I/340**
- After 20.12.1939
- Announcement of order for transfer of all Jews into the ghetto (20.12.1939).
- ***Description:*** transcript, typescript, German, Polish, Yiddish, 205×292 mm, ss. 1, pp. 1.

j) **Ring. I/288; Ring. I/880 (1200) (Lb. 593)**
- After 7.12.1939, place unknown
- National-Socialist Social Welfare. Special Delegate. Piotrków, Letter of 7.12.1939 to [Zelmen] Tennenberg, chairman of the Jewish Community in Piotrków
- Concerning takeover of control over Jewish social welfare organizations; volunteers for work (tailors).
- ***Description:*** Ring. I/880—transcript, typescript, German, Polish, 207×293 mm, ss. 1, pp. 1; Ring. I/288—transcript, handwritten manuscript (MS*),

pencil, German in Hebrew alphabet transliteration, 141×222 mm, ss. 1., pp. 1.

Ring. I/288 In the margin a Hebrew letter (red pencil): "p" (pei). Doc. was kept in a binder.

Ring. I/288—Attached note by H.W. in Yiddish: "For security Hebrew letters were used. Submitted by Mordechaj Szwarcbard."

### 959. RING. I/151. Mf. ŻIH—836; USHMM—67

- After 1940, Warsaw Ghetto
- [Szymon Huberband], Account entitled "Yontoyvim [Yomim-toyvim] beys der milkhome" [Holidays during the war]
- Author from Piotrków, describes the burning of Sulejów after the German bombardment in 1939 (1,700 perished), flight to Piotrków, Rosh Hashanah, and the ongoing roundups for forced labor and searches, persecution of the Jewish population, destruction of sacred books in the synagogue, Yom Kippur holiday, Sukkot, Hanukkah, arrival in Warsaw, holiday of Purim, trip to Piotrków for Passover and return to Warsaw, holiday of Lag ba-Omer, Shavuot; author also passes on information obtained from other persons about religious life during war and occupation (Warsaw, Łódź).
- ***Description:*** original, handwritten manuscript (HUB.*), notebooks, ink, Yiddish, 164×195, 155×198, 160×198 mm, minor damage and losses of text (z. 2), ss. 44, pp. 77.

Individual notebooks titled: 1) "Holidays of the year 1939/4"; 2) "High Holydays 1939/1940. Notebook II"; 3) "Holidays during the war 1939/1940."

Published: *BFG*, vol. XXIX–XXX/1991–1992, pp. 158–192; *Kiddush Hashem*, pp. 39–65. (without the initial fragment, notebook 1 to p. 5, 3 lines from the top).

Index: Miriam Rozenwald of Piotrków, Mosze Chaim Lau [, Rabbi] of Piotrków, Zalman Tenenberg, chairman of the Jewish Council in Piotrków, Mosze Chaim Zelmanowicz of Piotrków, killed on the way to Warsaw

### 960. RING. I/451. (Lb. 1222). Mf. ŻIH—786; USHMM—17

- After 1939, Warsaw Ghetto
- [Szymon Huberband], Account entitled "War Experiences of a Jewish Civilian"
- Author was a resident of Piotrków, member of the Jewish Council, married a rabbi's daughter. Situation in Piotrków before war's outbreak in September 1939, mood of the population, bombardments, author's flight with family to Sulejów (bombardment and fire in the shtetl, author's wife, son, and father-in-law perished, 4.09.1939), return to Piotrków, repressive actions against Jews (mass executions, thefts, beating), Jewish Council.
- ***Description:*** original, handwritten manuscript (HUB.*), notebook, ink, Yiddish, 155×200 mm, ss. 45, pp. 87.

Published: *Kiddush Hashem*, pp. 3–38 (without the concluding fragment of the manuscript: from p. 75, from line 8 from the top).

Index: [Zelmen] Tenenberg, chairman of the Jewish Council in Piotrków; Zigelman, member of the Jewish Council in Piotrków; Warszawski, member of the Jewish Council in Piotrków; [Stanisław] Silberstein, attorney, member of the Jewish Council in Piotrków; Icchak Aron Sochaczewski of Piotrków, imprisoned and transported 14.09.1939 to an unknown destination; Baruch Aszer Nodelman; Mosze Chaim Zelmanowicz of Piotrków, imprisoned and transported 14.09.1939 to an unknown destination; Perec Praszkier of Piotrków, imprisoned and transported 14.09.1939 to an unknown destination; Grosberg of Piotrków, owner of a shop; Synaj of Piotrków, owner of a shop; Ziskind of Piotrków; Frankel of Piotrków; Michelson of Piotrków; Zilberszac of Piotrków; Epsztajn of Piotrków, a painter, killed 6.09.1939; Lebl of Piotrków, died from injuries suffered; Jechiel Meir Promnicki, killed in Piotrków 5.09.1939; Lajzer Blumsztajn, killed in Piotrków 5.09.1939; Rajchman, killed in Piotrków 5.09.1939; Mosze Gomoliński of Piotrków; M.D. Rozenwald of Piotrków; D. Kamiński of Piotrków; Epsztajn, director of ORT in Piotrków, killed by a bomb 2.09.1939; Berliner, member of Jewish Community in Piotrków (before 09.1939); Pinkasiewicz, member Jewish Community in Piotrków (before 09.1939)

### 961. RING. I/1220/33. Mf. ŻIH—835; USHMM—47

- Date unknown, Warsaw Ghetto
- NN., Account about Płock
- About Polish–Jewish relations, about German colonists, Jews of service to the town (before 1939).
- ***Description:*** original or transcript, handwritten manuscript, Yiddish, ink, 55×67, 109×180 mm, serious damage and losses of text, ss. 5, pp. 8.

Index: Gustaw Szulc, chairman of the fire brigade, of the merchants association in Płock, Abraham Narwa of Płock, Izrael Asante[?] of Płock

### 962. RING. I/884 (1204). (Lb. 392). Mf. ŻIH—828; USHMM—40

- After 12.1940, Warsaw Ghetto
- NN., Account entitled "Plotsk" [Płock] (12.1940)
- Jewish community in Płock from the start of the occupation (9.09.1939) until formation of the ghetto (ul. Szeroka, ul. Złota). Appended list of persons responsible for collection of tribute payment.

- *Description:* transcript (2 copies), handwritten manuscript (MS*), pencil, Yiddish, 148×209 mm, minor damage and losses of text (first copy), ss. 4, pp. 6.
  In the margins a Hebrew letter (ink): "p" (pei) and a symbol beneath the letter (first copy): "=."
  Index: Alfred Blaj of Płock, Jakub Głowiński of Płock, Abraham Pantofel of Płock, Mosze Sochaczewer [?] of Płock, Henoch Szulim Graubard of Płock, Ajzyk Margules of Płock, Kiwa Benigsberg of Płock, Szmuel Kon of Płock, Lejb Kilbert of Płock, Szulit of Płock, Izaak Leon Klinkowstein, attorney from Płock

**963. RING. I/889 (1209). (Lb. 1625). Mf. ŻIH—828; USHMM—40**

- After 03.1941, Warsaw Ghetto
- NN., "Płock Expulsion 17–27 Febr. [19]41"
- Description of events preceding expulsion of Jews from Płock (removal of 42 elderly people—09.1940, assault on the residents of house at ul. Niecała 2—beginning of 02.1941, arrests—20.02.1941).
- *Description:* original (o) (2 copies), handwritten manuscript (H.W.*), pencil, Yiddish, 148×210 mm, ss. 12, pp. 12.
  See HWC, 24/1 (third copy, handwritten manuscript, pencil, ss. 6).

**964. RING. I/883 (1203). (Lb. 421). Mf. ŻIH—828; USHMM—40**

- After 6.04.1941, Warsaw Ghetto
- NN., Account entitled "Płock Expulsion 1941" (6.04.1941)
- Author (age 54), orderly of the Jewish hospital in Płock, describes the eviction on 21.02.1941 of the Jews (ca. 4,000 persons) from the town to the camp in Działdowo, subsequently via Jędrzejów to Chmielnik.
- *Description:* transcript (2 copies), handwritten manuscript (MS*), pencil, Yiddish, 148×210 mm, ss. 16, pp. 16.
  In the margins a Hebrew letter (ink): "d" (dalet).

**965. RING. I/886 (1206). (Lb. 1687). Mf. ŻIH—828; USHMM—40**

- Date unknown, Warsaw Ghetto
- NN., Account entitled "Pł—k" [Płock]
- Jews in Płock before the war as well as during the occupation (forced contribution on 15.10.1939 in the amount of 1 million złoty, Jewish Council, forced labor, social welfare, formation of the ghetto in 09.1940, Aid Committee, displacement from the city 22/23.02 and 1.03.1941 to Działdowo and further fate of Jews from Płock).
- *Description:* transcript (3 copies in fragments), handwritten manuscript (CA*), pencil, Polish, 148×210 mm, serious damage and losses of text (first and third copies), ss. 78, pp. 78.

**966. RING. I/674/8. (Lb. 1688). Mf. ŻIH—816; USHMM—28**

- After 02.1941, Warsaw Ghetto
- NN., Account of the expulsion of the Jewish population from the town of NN. [Płock?] to Działdowo (fragment)
- The expulsion (27.02.1941), stay in Działdowo, departure to Generalgouvernement (Kielce, Chmielnik, Żarki, Częstochowa).
- *Description:* original (o), handwritten manuscript (H.W.*), ink, Yiddish, 148×210 mm, missing page, ss. 2, pp. 1
  The second page was preserved.

**967. RING. I/885 (1205). (Lb. 682). Mf. ŻIH—828; USHMM—40**

- After 02.1941, Warsaw Ghetto
- NN., Study entitled "Płock"
- Situation of the Jewish population from the start of the war until displacement in February 1941 (living conditions, repressive actions, relations with Poles, formation of ghetto). Appended transcript of account (NN., of Płock), describing the displacement of Jews from the city to Działdowo.
- *Description:* original, handwritten manuscript (FLIG*), ink, Polish, 223×352 mm, text difficult to read in places, ss. 6, pp. 11.
  Index: Preszkiewicz, member City Council in Płock; Blaj of Płock, Graubart of Płock, Kilbert of Płock, Kaftan of Płock, Altman of Płock, Fryderson of Płock; Goldszyt of Płock, shot; Zawierucha of Płock

**968. RING. I/1050 (1369). Mf. ŻIH—832; USHMM—44. RING. I/454. Mf. ŻIH—786; USHMM—17**

- After 03.1940 and after 24.07.1941, Warsaw Ghetto
- P.B. [Paweł Bohm], Account entitled "The Outbreak of the [. . .]"
- Author from Poznań, description of return from vacation and departure with family to Łódź (30.08.1939), return to Poznań 20.10.1939, departure to Łódź after leaving prison, flight to Warsaw in March 1940.
- *Description:* Ring. I/1050—original or transcript, handwritten manuscript., ink (green), Yiddish, 222×351 mm, ss. 5, pp. 8; Ring. I/454—transcript (2 copies), handwritten manuscript—BW*, pencil, Yiddish, 150×210 mm, ss. 24, pp. 24.
  Ring. I/1050—on the back of p. 7 notes (calculations) in Yiddish (handwritten manuscript—BW*, pencil).
  Ring. I/454 contains text of Ring. I/1050 with minor changes; on p. 12 is the date 24.07.1941, which is missing in Ring. I/1050.
  Ring. I/454 -Attached note by H.W.: "1939–1940 Stages of wandering Poznań–Łódź, Poznań–Łodź – Łódź ghetto–Warsaw. [Paweł] Bohm, a former activist in the Zbąszyń effort, testifies."

**969. RING. I/1072 (1391). (Lb. 739, 913). Mf. ŻIH—832; USHMM—44**

- After unknown, Warsaw Ghetto
- NN., Account entitled "Displacement of Poznań Jews to the Sochaczew-Błonie district"
- Course of displacement of the Jewish and Polish population from Poznań region. Displacement to Buk from Nowy Tomyśl, Lwówek, Pniewy, Wronki, Szamotuły, Grodzisk Wielkopolski, Ryczywół, Kleck, Sieraków, Oborniki, Lubienie, and Kowal (ca. 1,300 Jews and ca. 3,000 Poles), camp Südhof, departure to Generalgouvernement, stay in Niepokalanów and aid of Franciscan fathers, and of the neighboring Jewish population.
- ***Description:*** transcript (2 copies), handwritten manuscript (BTT*), pencil, Polish, 145×204 mm, minor damage and losses of text, ss. 22, pp. 22.
  On p. 1 (first copy) notation by H.W. (ink): "Kampel."
  Index: Leopold Kohn of Zbąszyń, died in Südhof; Glicensztajn, member Jewish Community in Grodzisk Wielkopolski

**970. RING. I/892 (1212). (Lb. 452). Mf. ŻIH—828; USHMM—40**

- After 01.1941, Warsaw Ghetto
- NN., Account entitled "Expulsion from Pruszków"
- Situation of Jews in Pruszków during the occupation (ghetto, activity of the Jewish Council, forced labor, displacement to the Warsaw Ghetto—01.1941).
- ***Description:*** transcript, handwritten manuscript (BW*), pencil, Yiddish, 148×210 mm, ss. 9, pp. 9.
  On p. 1, in the margin notation by H.W. (ink): "19.03.41." and a symbol (red pencil): "+." In the margins a Hebrew letter (ink): "a" (alef).
  Doc. was kept in a binder.
  Index: Icchak Śliwkiewicz, director of the labor battalions in Pruszków

**971. RING. I/890 (1210). Mf. ŻIH—828; USHMM—40**

- After 12.1939, Warsaw Ghetto
- NN., Report on the Jewish community in Przasnysz
- Fate of Jews in Przasnysz from war's outbreak until displacement (until 09.1939 there were 500 Jewish families, destruction of Jews' property at the start of the war, displacement in 12.1939).
- ***Description:*** transcript (2 copies), handwritten manuscript (BW*), pencil, Yiddish, 148×210 mm, minor damage and losses of text, ss. 10, pp. 10.
  In the margins letter (ink): "c" [tsadi?]

**972. RING. I/891 (1211). Mf. ŻIH—828; USHMM—40**

- After 12.05.1941, Warsaw Ghetto
- NN., Account entitled "Pułtusk. Overview of the Fate of the Expelled Pułtusk Jews" (12.05.1941)
- Situation of the Jewish population after outbreak of war and resettlement on 22.09.1939 (886 persons from Pułtusk were registered in Warsaw in 1939).
- ***Description:*** transcript (2 copies), handwritten manuscript (BW*), pencil, Yiddish, 148×210 mm, minor damage and losses of text, ss. 4, pp. 4.
  In the margins letter (ink): "l" [lamed?].
  On p. 1 (copy 1) a symbol in red pencil: "+."

**973. RING. I/893 (1213). (Lb. 1539). Mf. ŻIH—828; USHMM—40**

- After 24.03.1942, Warsaw Ghetto
- NN., Account entitled "Expulsion 1942 (Pustelnik)"
- Fate of the Jewish population in Pustelnik (before 1939 ca. 200 families, ghetto—fall 1940, aid for Jews on the part of an ethnic German named Zientar, displacement—24.03.1942).
- ***Description:*** original or transcript, handwritten manuscript, notebook, ink, Yiddish, 153×170 mm, serious damage and losses of text, ss. 12, pp. 23.

**974. RING. I/898 (1218). (Lb. 1453). Mf. ŻIH—828; USHMM—40**

- After 1940, Warsaw Ghetto
- NN., Study on the history of the Jewish community in Raciąż
- Overview of the town's history from the times of the Swedish invasion until the interwar period.
- ***Description:*** original or transcript, handwritten manuscript, pencil, Yiddish, 214×298 mm, ss. 7, pp. 7.
  On pp. 1, 2 and 3 information in Polish (pencil): "Unit VII," "Unit V," "Unit IV."
  Doc. written on the back of official application forms for refugees (displaced persons) for allocation of coupons entitling receipt of free provisioning ration cards (Warsaw, 1940, hectographed typescript).

**975. RING. I/1157 (1476). (Lb. 81) Mf. ŻIH—833; USHMM—45**

- 12.1940–02.1941, Radom
- Main Council of the Elders of the Jewish Population of the Radom District, identity card of Samuel Bresław, issued 11.12.1940 in Radom
- ***Description:*** original, printed, handwritten manuscript, ink, stamp, German, Polish, 95×135 mm, ss. 2, pp. 3.
  Stamp of Dr. N. [Naum] Szenderowicz, physician of Radom, confirming that the holder of the identification card does not have pediculosis (from 1940 and 1941).

**976. RING. I/1220/19. Mf. ŻIH—835; USHMM—47**

- After 22.06.1941, Warsaw Ghetto
- Record of the inspection by the Municipal and District Welfare Committee [KOP] in Radom 15–22 June 1941, by [eng. A. Reinberg, delegate of AJDC?] (fragments, missing ending)

- Social activity within the district, composition of the projected board of KOP: Dr. Fastman, Hurwiczowa (Radom), Dr. Diament (Szydłowiec), Dr. Bułka (Białobrzegi), Halputer (Kozienice); information concerning placement of displaced persons from Płock (localities and number of persons).
- ***Description:*** transcript, typescript, Polish, 190×260 190×278 mm, serious damage and losses of text, ss. 3, pp. 3.
  Index: Wiener, MA

**977. RING. I/897 (1217). (Lb. 411). Mf. ŻIH—828; USHMM—40**

a)

- After 28.02.1941, Warsaw Ghetto
- NN., Account entitled "Radom" (28.02.1941)
- Situation of the Jewish population during the occupation (activity of Jewish Council). Comparison of the life of Radom and Warsaw Jews.
- ***Description:*** transcript (2 copies), handwritten manuscript (MS*), pencil, Yiddish, 148×210 mm, minor damage and losses of text, ss. 4, pp. 4.
  In the margins a Hebrew letter (ink): "h" (hei). On p. 1 a symbol (red pencil): "+."
  Doc. was kept in a binder.

b)

- After 12.1940, Warsaw Ghetto
- NN., Account entitled "Gzeyres Radom" [Persecutions in Radom]
- Displacement of Jews from Radom in 2–4.12.1940 (ca. 2,000) to Łagów, Ożarów near Opatów, Zawichost, Koprzywnica, Klimontów near Sandomierz, Połaniec, Chmielnik, Wiślica, Szydłów, Kurozwęki and Pacanów.
- ***Description:*** transcript (2 copies), handwritten manuscript (MS*), pencil, Yiddish, 148×210 mm, minor damage and losses of text, ss. 4, pp. 4.
  In the margins a Hebrew letter (ink): "h" (hei).
  Doc. was kept in a binder.
  Index: Dr. Szucer, member of the Jewish Council in Radom

**978. RING. I/236. Mf. ŻIH—780; USHMM—11**

- Date unknown, Warsaw Ghetto
- Jankiel Henig, Account entitled "Vos hert zikh" [What's going on] (missing conclusion)
- The author, a carpenter, describes the situation of the Jewish population in Radom (two ghettos, persecutions, murders, arrests, transports to Oświęcim).
- ***Description:*** transcript, handwritten manuscript (Ł*), ink, pencil, Yiddish, 108×355 mm, damage and losses of text, ss. 1, pp. 2.
  On p. 1 notation by H.W. in Yiddish: "4 standard pages" (ink).

**979. RING. I/900 (1220). (Lb. 1479, 1525). Mf. ŻIH—828; USHMM—40**

- After 04.1942, date unknown, Warsaw Ghetto
- NN., Account entitled "Radom" (04.1942)
- Situation of Jews in Radom during the occupation (refugees, two ghettos, Jewish Council, Order Service).
- ***Description:*** original or transcript (a) (handwritten manuscript—RR*, ink, 155×200 mm), transcript (b) (handwritten manuscript—U*, pencil, 145×218 mm), Yiddish, ss. 18, pp. 23.
  Index: [Józef] Diament, chairman of the Jewish Council in Radom; Abraham Salbe, attorney, member of the Jewish Council in Radom; Dr. [Naum] Szenderowicz, member of the Jewish Council in Radom; Gajger of the Order Service in Radom; Winer of the Order Service in Radom; Wajchindler of the Order Service in Radom

**980. RING. I/561. MISSING ORIGINAL**

- 1942 [?], Radom [?]
- NN. (Radom), Letter of 1942 to NN.
- ***Description:*** original or transcript, handwritten manuscript, pencil, Polish, ss. 2, pp. 4.

**981. RING. I/513. Mf. ŻIH—789; USHMM—20**

a)

- After 09.1939, Radomsko
- [Council of Elders of the Jewish Community in Radomsko], Official forms for obtaining discount when applying for an identity card
- ***Description:*** original (3 copies), typescript, German, 207×102 mm, ss. 3, pp. 3.
  Notation (pencil): "Certificate for discount on an identity card."

b)

- After 09.1939, Radomsko
- Form for listing residents: "Ausweis der Haushaltsangehörigen in Radomsko"
- ***Description:*** original (4 copies), printed, German, 180×145 mm, ss. 4, pp. 4.
  Notation (pencil): "Questionnaire in matter of bread ration cards"

c)

- After 09.1939, Radomsko
- Jewish Community in Radomsko, Form for registration of Jewish population
- ***Description:*** original (2 copies), printed, German, 270×207 mm, ss. 2, pp. 2.
  Inf. (pencil): "Questionnaire in matter of population census."

d)

- After 09.1939, Radomsko
- Council of Elders of the Jewish Community in Radomsko, Form of certificate for obtaining a pass

- ***Description:*** original (3 copies), typescript, German, 217×175 mm, ss. 3, pp. 3.
  Notation (pencil): "Pass."

e)

- After 09.1939, Radomsko
- Council of Elders of the Jewish Community in Radomsko, Form of certificate for members of the Jewish Council, exempting from forced labor
- ***Description:*** original (3 copies), typescript, German, 202×163 mm, ss. 3, pp. 3.
  Notation (pencil): "Certificate for members of the Council of Elders and Committees for the purpose of exemption from forced labor."

f)

- After 09.1939, Radomsko
- Council of Elders of the Jewish Community in Radomsko, Summons to pay dues for the Jewish Religious Community in Radomsko at the Community's cashier at ul. Mickiewicza 5
- ***Description:*** original (3 copies), printed, German, Polish, 227×245 mm, ss. 3, pp. 3.
  Notation (pencil): "Payment order for monthly dues."

g)

- After 09.1939, Radomsko
- Council of Elders of the Jewish Community in Radomsko, Summons to leave Radomsko and proceed to Piotrków. Passes must be purchased at the Community's cashier for 5 RM per person before departure.
- ***Description:*** original (3 copies), typescript, Polish, 200×160, 218×175 mm, ss. 3, pp. 3.
  Notation (pencil): "Summons to those who arrived after 1.09.1939 to leave the city."

h)

- After 09.1939, Radomsko
- Council of Elders of the Jewish Community in Radomsko, Summons for registration by persons moving permanently to Radomsko or who are departing permanently from the town
- ***Description:*** original (2 copies), typescript, Polish, 206×75 mm, ss. 2, pp. 2.
  Notation (pencil): "Registration."

i)

- 10.1939, Radomsko
- Council of Elders of the Jewish Community in Radomsko, bread ration cards for November 1939 (Bezugschein und Bestellschein, no. 1792, 1793, 1794)
- ***Description:*** original (3 copies), printed, German, 307×117 mm, ss. 3, pp. 3.
  Notation (pencil): "Bread ration card."
  Index: Moses Berger, chairman of the Jewish Council in Radomsko

j)

- After 09.1939, Radomsko
- Council of Elders of the Jewish Community in Radomsko, Summons to forced labor (during 3 days—Thursday, Friday, Saturday) (1939)
- ***Description:*** original (6 copies), printed, Polish, 120×157 mm, ss. 6, pp. 6.
  Doc. in two variants: a) with notation "1st round"; b) with notation "2nd round."
  Notation (pencil): "Summons to work."

k)

- After 09.1939, Radomsko
- Jewish Council in Radomsko, Summons to forced labor
- ***Description:*** original (3 copies), printed, Polish, 115×155 mm, ss. 3, pp. 3.
  Notation (pencil): "Summons to work during emergency increase in the number of those working."

l)

- After 09.1939, Radomsko
- Council of Elders of the Jewish Community in Radomsko, Summons to forced labor
- ***Description:*** original (3 copies), printed, Polish, 120×170 mm, ss. 3, pp. 3.
  Notation (pencil): "Summons to work during an increase in the number of workers."

ł)[42]

- After 09.1939, Radomsko.
- City council in Radomsko, Summons form to compulsory labor for women
- ***Description:*** original (3 copies), typed, city council stamp, German, Polish, 201×91, 201×101 mm, ss. 3, pp. 3.
  Notation (pencil): "Labor summons for women."

m)

- After 09.1939, Radomsko.
- City council in Radomsko, Summons form for admission of persons relocated from other towns
- ***Description:*** original, typed, city council stamp, German, Polish, 208×98 mm, ss. 1, pp. 1.
  Notation (pencil): "For 500 displaced persons expected to arrive from different towns."

### 982. RING. I/1206 (1525). Mf. ŻIH—835; USHMM—47

- Before 1.01.1940, Radomsko
- Jüdische Kultusgemeinde in Radomsko. Abteilung Verpflegung [Jewish Religious Community in Radomsko. Provisioning Department], Coupon Book no. 367 with 31 coupons for the kitchen of the Jewish Community for Jankiel Szlama Zelwer (Radomsko, ul. Reymonta), entitling him to receive 1 meal daily from 1.01.1940 to 31.01.1940.

42. In the Polish alphabet, the letter Ł or ł follows the letter L or l and precedes the letter M or m.

- *Description:* original, printed, handwritten manuscript, German, ink, 90×31, 97×68 mm, ss. 33, pp. 33.

983. **RING. I/901 (1221). (Lb. 1141). Mf. ŻIH—828; USHMM—40**

- After 12.1939, Warsaw Ghetto
- M. Frenkel, Account entitled "Radomsko 1.09.1939—15.12.1939"
- The author, a resident of Radomsko, describes situation of the Jewish population in the town from the beginning of the war until creation of the ghetto (September 1939, repressive actions, relations with Poles, forced labor, forced contribution, ghetto on ul. Limanowskiego).
- *Description:* transcript (2 copies), handwritten manuscript (U*), pencil, Yiddish, 148×210 mm, extensive minor damage and losses of text, ss. 76, pp. 76.

Index: Heszel Bass of Przedbórz, Mosze Bugajski of Radomsko, Minc brothers from Radomsko, Fojgeltojba from Radomsko, Libl Blas of Radomsko, Rapaport (age 15) of Radomsko, Rabinowicz of Radomsko, Jakubowicz of Radomsko, Abraham Goldberg of Radomsko, Awner Gurfinkel of Radomsko, Szlomo Nojmark of Radomsko

984. **RING. I/794 (1113). (Lb. 1445). Mf. ŻIH—826; USHMM—38**

- After 23.11.1941, Warsaw Ghetto
- U.[W?]B., Account entitled "The Situation of the Jewish population in the Radzyń region"
- Repressive actions in Radzyń and vicinity: arrest of the Jewish Council and transport on 15.07.1941 of 600 Jews to a labor camp near Łuków; shooting on 15.10.1941 of Chaim Haberman for giving food to a Soviet POW; and shooting of 11 Jews from Międzyrzec (1.11.1941); restriction of movement around the town; ban on buying from peasants (1.07.1941); death penalty for concealing Jews; death penalty on 25 peasants for failure to deliver quotas (23.11.1941); situation in Łuków.
- *Description:* original or transcript, handwritten manuscript, ink, Yiddish, 105×295 mm, ss. 5, pp. 5.

985. **RING. I/598/7. Mf. ŻIH—792; USHMM—23**

- After 04.1942, Warsaw Ghetto
- NN. (Dora [Bor?]ensztajn), Letter dated Wednesday [. . .] 04.1942 to husband NN. ("delegate from Rogów" [?] [Dawid Borensztajn (Bornsztein)?]) (Warsaw, ul. Gęsia 17, apt. 51)
- Mentions names of children [?]: Józio and Oleś. Information about Dawid [Borensztajn (Bornsztein) ?] (delegate) and Lusia [?]; Rejowiec, Krychów (post office at Hańsk).
- *Description:* transcript (from Information of the copyist), handwritten manuscript (JG*), pencil, Polish, 129×285 mm, ss. 1, pp. 2.

On p. 2 of text (handwritten manuscript—JG* and U*, pencil) in Polish, Yiddish: Information about a parcel dated 1.04.[. . .], about Rejowiec; fragment of a letter to Szmulek [. . . .] (Polish). Difficult to determine whether the doc. includes copies of several letters, or of one with different post scripts (by several persons).

See Ring. I/328/3–4.

986. **RING. I/328/3. Mf. ŻIH—781; USHMM—12**

- After 25.02.1941, Warsaw Ghetto
- Gendarmerieposten (German Police Post) at Rogów, Certificate dated 25.02.1941 for Dawid Bornstein, former chairman of the Jewish aid committee in Rogów
- Permission to transport money (8,200 zł) for Jews from Rogów who moved to Warsaw.
- ***Description:*** transcript (2 copies), handwritten manuscript (Np*), pencil, German, Yiddish, 148×160 mm, ss. 2, pp. 2.

In the margins a symbol (ink): "v."

See Ring. I/598/7.

987. **RING. I/328/4. Mf. ŻIH—781; USHMM—12**

- After 27.02.1941, Warsaw Ghetto
- Gendarmerieposten (German Police Post) at Rogów, Certificate dated 27.02.1941 for Dawid Bornstein about his work as chairman of the Jewish Council in Rogów
- ***Description:*** transcript (2 copies), handwritten manuscript (Np*), pencil, German, Yiddish, 148×160 mm, ss. 2, pp. 2.

In the margins a symbol (ink): "v."

See Ring. I/598/7.

988. **RING. I/559. Mf. ŻIH—791; USHMM—22**

a)

- 03.1942[?], place unknown
- NN., Letter to NN. (Mania)
- Description of mass execution of ca. 2,000 Jews with participation of SS and Ukrainians in Rohatyn [?].
- ***Description:*** original or transcript, handwritten manuscript, ink, Yiddish, 132×195, 147×118 mm, serious damage and losses of text, ss. 6 (two stuck together), pp. 11.

b)

- After 20.03.1942, Warsaw Ghetto
- NN. (Rohatyn), Letter of 20.03.1942 to NN. [Edward?] (Warsaw Ghetto)
- Notification about the death of immediate family during liquidation action (ca. 2,000 victims).
- ***Description:*** transcript (2 copies), typescript, Polish, 190×245 mm, minor damage and losses of text, ss. 2, pp. 2.

Published: *Listy o Zagładzie*, pp. 77–80.

989. **RING. I/899 (1219). (Lb. 1279). Mf. ŻIH—828; USHMM—40**

- After 09.1941, Warsaw Ghetto

- NN., Account entitled "Rutki"
- Jewish population in Rutki near Łomża before the war (40% of residents), during the Soviet and German occupations (slaughter of 450 Żydów from village in Gosie Małe near Rutki 6.09.941).
- ***Description:*** transcript (3 copies), typescript., Yiddish, 208×297 mm, minor damage and losses of text, ss. 15, pp. 15.
  On p. 1 (first copy) notation by H.W. in Yiddish (ink): "junior-Jasza" [?]
  Published: *Relacje z Kresów*, pp. 298–307.

**990. RING. I/896 (1216). (Lb. 732, 954). Mf. ŻIH—828; USHMM—40**

- Date unknown, Warsaw Ghetto
- NN., Account entitled "Rychwał (Konin̈ district)"
- Description of lynchings of Germans (Volksdeutschen) by Poles (09.1939) in Rychwał (30 people murdered), Germans' repressive actions against the Jewish population during the first months of the occupation (murder of Jakub Larech, age 23, and Jakub Obażanek, age 29; expulsion of Jews from the town in winter 1939). Jewish population of Rychwał in exile.
- ***Description:*** transcript (3 copies), handwritten manuscript (NN*), pencil, Yiddish, 148×210 mm, ss. 12, pp. 12.
  On p. 1 (second copy) notation in Yiddish H.W. (ink): "Hober."
  In the margins (first and third copies) a Hebrew letter (ink): "z" (zayin)
  Index: Krzeziński, mayor in Rychwał; Jecyński, director of elementary school in Rychwał

**991. RING. I/953 (1272). Mf. ŻIH—830; USHMM—42**

- Date unknown, Warsaw Ghetto
- NN., Account entitled "Rypin"
- Repressive actions against the Jewish population from Germans' invasion until displacement (14.11.1939) (forced labor, torching of synagogue, tribute payments, requisitions, Jewish Council, disappearance of 300 prisoners).
- ***Description:*** original (o), handwritten manuscript (FLIG*), ink, Polish, 194×350 mm, damage and losses of text, ss. 3, pp. 5.
  Published: BŻIH, no. 137–138/1986, pp. 181–183.
  Index: Binenfeld (elder and younger) of Rypin, perished in 1939; Smordin of Rypin, perished in 1939; Grynberg of Rypin, perished in 1939; Eliasz Szewczyn [?] of Rypin, perished in 1939; Bałaban of Rypin, perished in 1939; Szmelka Safersztajn and son, from Rypin, perished in 1939; Kon, member of the Jewish Council in Rypin, shot in 1939; Plucer, member of the Jewish Council in Rypin, shot in 1939; Gotlibowski, member of the Jewish Council in Rypin, shot in 1939; Cejtag, member of the Jewish Council in Rypin, shot in 1939; Luksemburg, member of the Jewish Council in Rypin, shot in 1939; Pukacz, member of the Jewish Council in Rypin, shot in 1939; Warszawiak [?] of Rypin, perished in 11.1939; Nadra [?] Hirszfeld of Rypin, perished in 11.1939; Izaak Buchman of Rypin, Biderman, died in Rypin fall 1939

**992. RING. I/1056 (1375). Mf. ŻIH—832; USHMM—44**

- After 1939, Warsaw Ghetto
- NN., Account about the fates of Jews in an unidentified district town [Rypin?] (fragment, missing beginning)
- Arrival of refugees from other towns in September 1939, German invasion and start of repression: beating of the chairman of the community in his apartment, daily punitive expeditions, expulsion of the Jewish population from the town to the accompaniment of a Polish orchestra (10.11.[1939]), march to Nowy Dwór, subsequently to Warsaw.
- ***Description:*** original or transcript, handwritten manuscript (TT*), pencil, ink,Yiddish, 210×298 mm, missing pages 1–7, ss. 2, pp. 4.
  Doc. has old pagination (pp. 8–10).
  Attached note by H.W.: "Account of Mojżesz Bursztyn from Rypin?"
  Index: Jankielewicz, Najfeld, Wadus, Józef Elefman, Motel Pechelmuter [?]

**993. RING. I/1104 (1423). (Lb. 1517). Mf. ŻIH—833; USHMM—45**

- 21.12.1941 and 23.01.1942, Rzeszów ghetto
- Jewish Community in Rzeszów. Department of Displaced Persons, L. Jakubowicz, Documents (2) dated 21.12.1941 and 23.01.1942 to CKU in Warsaw (in care of [Hersz] Wasser)
- Search for the family of family of Dr. Lipman Namiot, his wife and sister-in-law Aszkenazówna of Wilno (ul. Wiłkomirska 28, apt. 11).
- ***Description:*** original, typescript, handwritten manuscript, stamp, German, Polish, 224×250 mm, ss. 2, pp. 2.

**994. RING. I/905 (1224). (Lb. 394, 487). Mf. ŻIH—829; USHMM—41**

a)[43]

- After 12.1939, place unknown
- NN., Recollections of the first months of occupation
- The author, a resident of S. [Serock], describes the situation of Jews in his town after Germans' invasion in 1939 (repressive actions, expulsion from the town).

43. There is no b) in the Polish catalog text.

Author escapes and hides among peasants, returns to S. [Serock] and is again displaced to B. [Biała Podlaska?].

- ***Description:*** original or transcript (handwritten manuscript, notebook, ink, 125×198 mm, minor damage and losses of text), transcript (2 parts: I and II) (I is handwritten manuscript—MS*, pencil, 148×210 mm; II is in 2 copies, handwritten manuscript—MS*, pencil, 148×210 mm), Yiddish, ss. 50, pp. 91.

  Transcript (I): In the margins a symbol (ink): "^" and a Hebrew letter: "p" (pei).

  Transcript (II): In the margins a symbol (ink): "□" and notation by H.W. in Yiddish: "Of Serock's history."

**995. RING. I/907 (1226). (Lb. 313). Mf. ŻIH—829; USHMM—41**

- Date unknown, Warsaw Ghetto
- NN., Account entitled "Serock Expulsion"
- Displacement of the Jewish population from the town (5.12.1939) to Nasielsk, subsequently to Biała Podlaska.
- ***Description:*** transcript, handwritten manuscript (MS*), pencil, Yiddish, 148×210 mm, extensive minor damage and losses of text, ss. 6, pp. 6.

  In the margins letter (ink): "E" [ayin?]

  Notation on the postwar jacket: "Author of the account is Szpilka."

**996. RING. I/1168 (1487). (Lb. 1041, 1042). Mf. ŻIH—834; USHMM—46**

- Date unknown, Warsaw Ghetto
- Cwi Klejnman, Account of the events in Serock in September 1939
- Persecutions of the town's population, especially Jews (9–11.09.1939), commenced following the killing of a German soldier by a Pole (8.09.1939).
- ***Description:*** transcript (4 copies), typescript, Yiddish, 198×72, 205×297 mm, damage and losses of text, ss. 52, pp. 52.

  Text consists of two parts, the first without title, the second entitled "Misunderstandings and . . . forced labor."

  Attached note by H.W. in Yiddish: "By Hersz (Cwi) Klajnman (Klejnman) of Serock."

  See HWC, 26/1 (only the first part of the accont, typescript, ss. 6).

  Indeks: Abraham Bron [?] from Serock, Icchak Blachman (age 76) from Serock.

**997. RING. I/1169 (1488). (Lb. 1207). Mf. ŻIH—834; USHMM—46**

- Date unknown, Warsaw Ghetto
- Cwi Klejnman, Account entitled "Searches"
- Experiences of Jews displaced from Serock 6.12.1939, journey to Biała Podlaska (beatings, searches).
- ***Description:*** original, handwritten manuscript (CK*), notebook, ink, Yiddish, 158×200 mm, ss. 10, pp. 13.

  At the title of the account is a notation in Yiddish that this text is a continuation of another account.

  Attached note by H.W. in Yiddish: "Series of my wanderings. Fragment—journey Nasielsk–Wilenburg–Warsaw–Biała Podlaska, by Hersz Cwi Klajnman [Klejnman], refugee from Serock."

**998. RING. I/912 (1231). (Lb. 306). Mf. ŻIH—829; USHMM—41**

- After 22.04.1941, Warsaw Ghetto
- NN., Account about the displacement of Jews from Siennica (22.04.1941)
- Author, a delegate from Siennica, describes the events of 14.09.1939: arrest of all the residents (Poles and Jews), searches, shooting of 9 Jews, males sent out to Jackowo [?], displacement of the Jewish population from the village.
- ***Description:*** transcript (2 copies), handwritten manuscript (BW*), pencil, Yiddish, 110×148 mm, ss. 2, pp. 2.

  On p. 1 a symbol (red pencil): "+."

**999. RING. I/917 (1236). (Lb. 874). Mf. ŻIH—829; USHMM—41**

- After 1939, Warsaw Ghetto
- NN., Account entitled "Sierpc"
- Fate of the Jewish population in Sierpc from the German entry into the town (8.09.1939) until displacement (18.11.1939) (repressive actions, burning of the synagogue, forced contribution, successive stages of displacement [Pomiechówek, Nowy Dwór, Legionowo] to Warsaw).
- ***Description:*** transcript (3 copies), handwritten manuscript (MA*), pencil, Polish, 145×155, 145×206 mm, extensive damage and losses of text, ss. 45, pp. 45

  Index: Rzetelzer, died in 09.1939 in Sierpc; B. Poznański, mayor of Sierpc

**1000. RING. I/902 (1222). (Lb. 450). Mf. ŻIH—829; USHMM—41**

a)

- After 11.1939, Warsaw Ghetto
- NN., Account entitled "Sierpc"
- Persecution of Jews in Sierpc from the Germans' arrival until the displacement (11.1939).
- ***Description:*** transcript, handwritten manuscript (MS*), pencil, Yiddish, 148×208 mm, minor damage and losses of text, ss. 1, pp. 2.

  On p. 1 in the margin a Hebrew letter (underlined) (ink): "p" (pei) and a symbol (red pencil): "+."

  Doc. was kept in a binder.

b)

- After 13.05.1941, Warsaw Ghetto
- NN., Report entitled "Sierpc"
- Situation of the Jews in the town (ca. 4,000 people) from war's outbreak until the displacement in 11.1939 (to Pomiechówek, subsequently via Nowy Dwór to Jabłonna and Legionowo).
- ***Description:*** transcript (2 copies), handwritten manuscript (BW*), pencil, Yiddish, 148×210 mm, ss. 14, pp. 14.

  In the margins a symbol (ink): "√" and a symbol (red pencil): "+."

**1001. RING. I/1038 (1357). Mf. ŻIH—832; USHMM—44**

- After 11.1939, Warsaw Ghetto
- NN., Report from Sierpc
- Situation before and in the first days of the war, flight from the town, stay in Gostynin and return home. Sierpc after arrival of Germans: persecution of Jews. Flight via Płońsk to Warsaw (beginning of 11.1939 [?]).
- ***Description:*** transcript, handwritten manuscript (MS*), pencil, Yiddish, 148×210 mm, extensive damage and losses of text, ss. 2, pp. 2.

  In the margins a Hebrew letter (ink): "p" (pei) and a symbol consisting of three dots arranged in the form of a triangle ("∵").

  Doc. written in the form of a letter for clandestine purposes.

  Doc. was kept in a binder.

**1002. RING. I/903 (1223). Mf. ŻIH—829; USHMM—41**

- Date unknown, Warsaw Ghetto
- K., Account entitled "Brief outline of a study of the small town Sierpc according to the telling of one of its citizens, Mr. K.", Account entitled "Lubicz Settlement"
- History of the population of both villages before the war as well as the hell of displacement in the first period of the occupation: from Sierpc by freight wagons to Pomiechówek, from there by foot to Jabłonna and Warsaw, and from Lubicz by cart via Lipno to Dobrzyń, Płock and again to Dobrzyń.
- ***Description:*** transcript, handwritten manuscript, notebook, ink, Polish, 142×203 mm, minor damage and losses of text, ss. 13, pp. 20.

**1003. RING. I/1220/18. Mf. ŻIH—835; USHMM—47**

- 15.07.1942, Warsaw Ghetto
- NN., Account concerning the fate of the Jewish population in Skarżysko-Kamienna, Chmielnik Kielecki, and Janów Podlaski (15.07.1942)
- Descriptions of repressive actions, executions, situations in ghettos, relations with Poles, preparations for liquidation actions.
- ***Description:*** original or transcript, handwritten manuscript (SB*), ink, Polish, 197×215 mm, minor damage and losses of text, ss. 2, pp. 4.

  On p. 4 at bottom is notation (handwritten manuscript—H* [?], pencil): "W-wa, 15. VII.42."

  Doc. was used for preparation of the Bulletins of Oyneg Shabes; see Ring. I/472.

  Index: Andrzejczuk, "navy blue" policeman from Biała Podlaska

**1004. RING. I/906 (1225). (Lb. 497). Mf. ŻIH—829; USHMM—41**

- After 12.1939, Warsaw Ghetto
- NN., Account of the Jewish population in the town of Skępe
- August and September 1939, repressive actions, profile of Rabbi I. Gelernter (a speech by the rabbi attached), expulsion of Jews from the town (21.12.1939), homelessness of the population from Skępe.
- ***Description:*** transcript, handwritten manuscript (BW*), pencil, Yiddish, 148×210 mm, ss. 54, pp. 54.

  In the margins a Hebrew letter (ink): "p" (pei).

  See HWC, 2/3 (second copy, handwritten manuscript, pencil, ss. 54; information about the author [?]: "Kasel Enden?"; handwriting of Bluma Wasser?).

**1005. RING. I/908 (1227). (Lb. 435). Mf. ŻIH—829; USHMM—41**

- After 03.1941, Warsaw Ghetto
- NN., Account entitled "Skierniewice"
- Situation of the Jewish population from entry of the Germans (9.09.1939) until expulsion from the town (from 01.1941) (plundering, anti-Jewish orders, roundups for labor, labor camp—1.04.1940, ghetto—15.12.1940).
- ***Description:*** transcript (2 copies), handwritten manuscript (MS*), pencil, Yiddish, 148×210 mm, extensive minor damage and losses of text, ss. 14, pp. 14.

  In the margins letter (ink): "c" [tsadi ?]

  Index: Icchak Kałuszyn, rabbi of Skierniewice; Mosze Perkal, rabbi of Skierniewice; Menachem Binder, rabbi of Skierniewice (died in 1941); Franciszek Filipski, mayor of Skierniewice in 1940

**1006. RING. I/913 (1232). (Lb. 1238). Mf. ŻIH—829; USHMM—41**

- 01.1942, Warsaw Ghetto
- NN., Account entitled "Skryhiczyn" (01.1942)
- Fate of the Jewish population (farmers) in the village of Skryhiczyn during occupation (pogrom after entry of Germans in 1939—all the males in the Halpern family were shot; displacement 22.11.1941).
- ***Description:*** transcript, handwritten manuscript (RR*), ink, Yiddish, 150×194 mm, ss. 4, pp. 4.

  Published: *Selected Documents*, pp. 209–210.

**1007. RING. I/465. Mf. ŻIH–786; USHMM–17**

- After 10.1941, Warsaw Ghetto
- [Abram Gliklich], Account from Słonim
- Outbreak of the German–Soviet War, beginning of repressive measures against Jews, ghetto, annihilation of the residents of the town (15.10.1941).
- ***Description:*** original or transcript, handwritten manuscript, notebook, ink, Yiddish, 155×198 mm, text is difficult to read in places, ss. 32, pp. 31.

  Attached note by H.W. in Polish, Yiddish: "Abram Gliklich testified."

  Published: *Selected Documents*, pp. 172–181; *Relacje z Kresów*, pp. 202–224.

**1008. RING. I/938 (1257). Mf. ŻIH–830; USHMM–42**

- After 11.1941, Warsaw Ghetto
- NN., Account entitled "Słonim slaughter"
- Author, resident of Radom, describes flight to the east in September 1939, stay in Słonim, situation of the population in territories occupied by USSR (dispatches, mood of population, passportization), beginning of the German occupation in town, escalation of anti-Jewish decrees of Commandant Hick, Jewish Council, forced payment of tribute, formation of ghetto (09.1941), liquidation of Jewish population centers Żyrowice, Lachowicze, Mir, and Kosów, the liquidation action in Słonim 15.10.1941 (ca. 9,200 persons perished).
- ***Description:*** original (o) (handwritten manuscript FLIG*, ink, 220×287 mm, text illegible in places), transcript (3 copies, typescript, 218×290 mm, extensive minor damage and losses of text), Polish, ss. 35, pp. 40.

  Published: *Relacje z Kresów*, pp. 169–187.

**1009. RING. I/352. (Lb. 30). Mf. ŻIH–782; USHMM–13**

- After 31.01.1941, place unknown
- Der Kreishauptmann [District Governor of] Sochaczew-Blonie Reimann, Announcement: "Anordnung betreffend Freimachung des Kreises Sochaczew-Blonie von Juden" [Directive concerning making the Sochaczew-Blonie district free of Jews] (31.01.1941)
- Organization of displacement of Jews to the Warsaw Ghetto: from Żyrardów, Wiskitki, and Mszczonów 1–9.02.1941, from Grodzisk 10–14.02.1941, from Sochaczew 15–16.02.1941. and from Błonie 17–19.02.1941.
- ***Description:*** transcript, typescript, German, 210×295 mm, minor damage and losses of text, ss. 1, pp. 1.

**1010. RING. I/353. Mf. ŻIH–782; USHMM–13**

- 11.12.1940, Sochaczew
- Der Kreishauptmann [District Governor of] Sochaczew-Blonie, Reimann. Letter of 11.12.1940 to [Jakub] Baron, chairman of the Jewish Community in Żyrardów (appended "Anordnung über die Bildung eines jüdischen Wohnbezirk in der Stadt Żyrardów" [Directive on formation of a Jewish residential district in the town of Żyrardów]).
- Formation of a Jewish district in Żyrardów (appended description of boundaries) and order for the Jewish population to transfer to it by 15.12.1940; establishment of Order Service (50 individuals).
- ***Description:*** original ("Anordnung . . ." transcript), typescript, German, 208×296 mm, minor damage and losses of text, ss. 2, pp. 2.

  Document signed (handwritten manuscript, ink) by Reimann.

  Appended "Anordnung . . ." signed by Pott.

**1011. RING. I/1146 (1465). Mf. ŻIH–833; USHMM–45**

a)

- 1941, Warsaw Ghetto
- [Meir Medziński], Account of the fate of Jews of Sochaczew
- Author, a poet from Złoczów, describes the experiences of Jews displaced from Sochaczew in 1940.
- ***Description:*** transcript, handwritten manuscript, ink, Yiddish, 105×282 mm, extensive damage and losses of text, ss. 4, pp. 4.

  Account recorded by H. Grojł. Fragment of text of this account mixed into doc. b, pp. 1–2 of doc. a = pp. 25–26 of doc. b.

b)

- Date unknown, Warsaw Ghetto
- H. Grojł [Groyl], Account entitled "A shpatsir iber di punktn" [A stroll through the points]
- Situation of the displaced persons in shelters ("points") in the Warsaw Ghetto. Description of "points": ul. Ogrodowa (in the halls of a secondary school, displaced persons from Kalisz and Włocławek); ul. Dzika 3 (ca. 2,000 people); ul. Gęsia 24 (here lived the poet Meir Medziński from Złoczów and his wife); ul. Dzika 61 (former school, Margensztern [Morgensztern] of the Bund died here); ul. Stawki 9 (1,500 persons from Pomiechówek, Poznań, Płońsk); ul. Elektoralna 5 (former school); ul. Gęsia 11.
- ***Description:*** original or transcript, handwritten manuscript, ink, Yiddish, 110×355 mm, ss. 29, pp. 30.

  According to B.M., H. Grojł was the cryptonym of Zalman Skałow (Lejb Pluskałowski); see *Tsvishn lebn un toyt*, ed. B. Mark, Warsaw 1955, p. 73.

  Inventory: "[S. Gutgeld]."

  Published: *Tsvishn lebn un toyt, Między życiem a śmiercią*, ed. B. Mark, Warsaw 1955, pp. 73–96; *Ghetto. Berichte aus dem Warschauer Ghetto 1939–1945*, Berlin 1966, pp. 147–167.

Index: Abraham Kohn from Aleksandrów, a writer; Wengenborski from Łomianki, a Hebrew writer, died; Herszele (Danielewicz), folk writer, died in the point on ul. Pawia in 1941; Trzebucki—writer

**1012. RING. I/909 (1228). (Lb. 437). Mf. ŻIH—829; USHMM—41**

- Date unknown, Warsaw Ghetto.
- NN., Account entitled "A kleyn blimele fun der fareterisher tetikeyt fun sokhatshever yudenrat" [A small flower from the treacherous activity of the Sochaczew Judenrat]
- Personnel changes in Jewish Council in Sochaczew and activity of the new board of the Jewish Council (corruption).
- ***Description:*** transcript (2 copies), handwritten manuscript (MS*), pencil, Yiddish, 148×210 mm, damage and losses of text, ss. 6, pp. 6.

In the margins letter (ink): "D" [dalet]

Doc. was kept in a binder.

Index: Gelbsztejn, Sz. Libert

**1013. RING. I/915 (1234). (Lb. 1557, 1696). Mf. ŻIH—829; USHMM—41**

- [After 03.1941], Warsaw Ghetto
- NN., Collection of reports concerning expeditions from the Warsaw Ghetto to the provinces for food
- Experiences of children ("Zeldusia"—age 12) and young adults ("Pinio"—age 22; "Teacher" [Nauczycielka], Abramek—age 20), benefitting from aid from Poles and ethnic Germans (Volksdeutschów) (Kuschow [?], Perzyna from Kuklówka and others) in: Izdebna, Kozery, Skoliszew, Kuklówka, Podkowa Leśna, and other localities within the Sochaczew-Błonie district.
- ***Description:*** original, typescript (with annotations handwritten—E*, ink, 212×298 mm), transcript (3 copies, handwritten manuscript—CC*, pencil, 148×210 mm) Polish, ss. 51, pp. 54.

**1014. RING. I/914 (1233). (Lb. 1692). Mf. ŻIH—829; USHMM—41**

- Date unknown, Warsaw Ghetto
- [Bernard Kampelmacher], Study entitled "Sochaczew. Jewish cemetery"
- History of the Jewish cemetery in Sochaczew.
- ***Description:*** original, typescript (with handwritten manuscript additions, ink), transcript (3 copies, in the third copy pages 1 and 3 missing, typescript), Polish, 207×293 mm, ss. 11, pp. 12.

On p. 1 (transcript of the first copy) notation by H.W. in Polish and Yiddish (ink): "Kampel, 109.1942/1 January. no. 6."

Index: Praus, mayor of Sochaczew during the occupation; Balas, building contractor from Sochaczew; Marienfeld, murdered in Sochaczew by Germans; Szmelc, murdered in Sochaczew by Germans; Rozenpert family from Kampinos, murdered in Sochaczew at the Jewish cemetery by Germans; Biner from Kampinos, murdered in Sochaczew at the Jewish cemetery by Germans; Moszek Alter, rabbi, buried at the Jewish cemetery in Sochaczew; Abram Borensztajn, rabbi, buried in the Jewish cemetery in Sochaczew; Szmul Borensztajn, Rabbi, buried in the Jewish cemetery in Sochaczew; Luzer Kon, author and rabbi, buried in the Jewish cemetery in Sochaczew; Kampelmacher (age 13), son of Bernard, secondary school student in Sochaczew, buried at the Jewish cemetery in Sochaczew

**1015. RING. I/574. Mf. (Lb. 561). ŻIH—792; USHMM—23**

- 25.01.1942, Sosnowica near Parczew
- Hanka [Wermus] (Sosnowica near Parczew, care of T. Pogr[. . . ?]), Letter of 25.01. 1942 to NN. (Warsaw Ghetto)
- Author works on the farm of the village council chairman (description of the living conditions).
- ***Description:*** original, handwritten manuscript, pencil (improved with ink in archive [?]), 150×195 mm, Polish, Yiddish, damage and losses of text, ss. 4, pp. 8.

At the bottom of p. 8 a note in Yiddish: "There were no Jews in Sosnowica after the liquidation action."

Attached note by H.W. in Yiddish: "Letter from the village of Sosnowica near Parczew. Author Hanka Wermus, January 1942, forwarded by Abraham Lewin, coworker of Oyneg Shabes."

**1016. RING. I/5, I/11, I/12. Mf. ŻIH—771; USHMM—2**

**a) Ring. I/11, I/12**

- 09.1940, Sosnowiec
- *Bulletin*, no. 1 dated 15.09.1940, no. 2 dated 30.09.1940
- Official periodical of the Director of the Councils of Elders in Eastern Upper Silesia (Kierownik Rad Starszych GŻ w Ost-Oberschlesien). Statistical Department (Archival-Statistical), Sosnowiec. Prepared by, inter alia, Dr. I. Steinberg, director of the Statistical Department. Contents of no. 1: statistical data about the distribution of the Jewish population in Eastern Upper Silesia; no. 2: formation and organization of the Central Office of the Councils of Elders in Sosnowiec, report of activity, financial report (appended organizational chart of the Central Office).
- ***Description:*** original, duplicated typescript, German, 220×350 mm, ss. 9, pp. 9 (no. 1), ss. 5, pp. 5 (no. 2).

Ring. I/11 (*Bulletin*, no. 2) and Ring. I/12 (*Bulletin*, no. 1).

b) **Ring. I/5. (Lb. 12)**

- 10. 1940, Sosnowiec
- *Biuletyn Prawniczy* [Legal Bulletin], no. 1 dated 1.10.1940
- Official periodical of the Director of the Councils of Elders of the Jewish Communities in Eastern Upper Silesia. Central Legal Department, Sosnowiec. Prepared by Antoni Kon, Adolf Paradistal, and Eliasz Gertner. Contents: foreword, note on the bulletin's purposes, report of the Central Legal Department for August 1940, review of the decrees of the occupation authorities concerning property of Jews in the areas of Poland annexed to the Reich.
- ***Description:*** original, hectographed typescript, Polish, l., 210×335 mm, damage and loss of text, ss. 8., pp. 8.

Appended notation by H. W.: "Forwarded by H.W. Mehrin."

## 1017. RING. I/579. Mf. ŻIH—792; USHMM—23

- 05.1942, Sosnowiec
- Janina Szylska (Sosnowitz [Sosnowiec], Oderstrasse 11), Letter of 27.05.1942 to Ludwik Hirszberg (Warsaw, ul. Leśna 37 [?], Leszno 37, Ogrodowa 11/[?])
- Notation about the deportation of the Cukier couple to an unknown state and request for care for their child Atuś Cukier (signed the letter).
- ***Description:*** original, handwritten manuscript (two handwritings) on a postcard, postmark and stamp of the Jewish Council, ink, German, Polish, 148×104 mm, minor damage and losses of text, ss. 1, pp. 2.

On p. 1 in a different handwriting: "ul. Leśna 37[?]" crossed out and "Leszno 37" written in; also crossed out and written below "8 VI, Ogrodowa 11/[?]."

Published: *Listy o Zagładzie*, pp. 149–151.

## 1018. RING. I/1117 (1436). Mf. ŻIH—833; USHMM—45

- Date unknown, and 1942, Warsaw Ghetto
- Nickelberg, Account from Eastern Galicia
- Author, a dental student, son of a dentist from Warsaw, describes mass executions of the Stanisławów Jewish population (Żabie, Kosów, Stanisławów).
- ***Description:*** transcript (a) (handwritten manuscript, pencil, 208×292 mm, minor damage and losses of text), transcript (b) (2 copies, typescript, 208×292 mm), Polish, ss. 3, pp. 3.

In doc. (a) the surname: "Nickelberg" is crossed out. At the top (doc. (b), first copy) is notation by H.W. (ink): "108—1942/1 January."

Doc. (a) is written on the back of a printed sheet (fragment of the bulletin of ŻOS): *Winter Aid Campaign* (date unknown, hectographed typescript, Published: *Selected Documents*, pp. 358).

## 1019. RING. I/911 (1230). Mf. ŻIH—829; USHMM—41

- After 03.1941, Warsaw Ghetto.
- NN., Account entitled "Experiences of Stryków Jews until Arrival in Warsaw"
- Jews in Stryków before the war and during the occupation (Germans' entry, repressive actions and requisitions, displacement to Głowno—29.12.1939, bloody march to Stryków and back to Głowno, displacement from Głowno to Warsaw). Appended "Verse from the Life of Jews in the Neighborhood for Jews in Głowno, 'Little Statelet' [Małe państewko]," satire on the Jewish Council's corruption (09.1940).
- ***Description:*** original, handwritten manuscript, notebook, ink, Polish, 145×203 mm, ss. 8, pp. 8.

## 1020. RING. I/910 (1229). (Lb. 403). Mf. ŻIH—829; USHMM—41

- 6.01.1941, Warsaw Ghetto
- NN., Account entitled "Strzegowo" (6.01.1941)
- History of the Jewish community in Strzegowo and situation of the Jews in September 1939 in the first months of occupation.
- ***Description:*** transcript (2 copies), handwritten manuscript (MS*), pencil, Yiddish, 148×210 mm, minor damage and losses of text, ss. 8, pp. 8.

In the margins a symbol (ink): dot beneath horizontal line.

On p. 1 (in both parts) a symbol (red pencil): "+."

Account consists of two parts with the same title.

Doc. was kept in a binder.

## 1021. RING. I/918 (1237). (Lb. 1647). Mf. ŻIH—829; USHMM—41

- Date unknown, Warsaw Ghetto
- NN., Account of the expulsion of Jews from Suwałki
- Entry of Soviet troops into the town, then the Germans, and deportation of ca. 2,000 Jews to an unknown destination (1939).
- ***Description:*** original or transcript (handwritten manuscript, pencil, 210×296 mm), transcript (3 copies, handwritten manuscript—BW*, pencil, 148×208 mm, missing page 3 in the second copy), Yiddish, ss. 11, pp. 13.

On p. 3 (original) note by H.W. in Yiddish (ink): "4500–8000–3500 USSR (Lithuania)."

## 1022. RING. I/545. Mf. ŻIH—791; USHMM—22

a)

- 14.04.1942, after 19.04.1942, Szczebrzeszyn, Warsaw Ghetto.
- Fiszel Fryd (Szczebrzeszyn), Letter of 14.04.1942 to M. [Mojsze] Wulf (Warsaw, ul. Smocza 1, apt. 39a)
- Hunger in the Szczebrzeszyn ghetto; request for aid.
- ***Description:*** original (handwritten manuscript on a postcard, postmark and stamp of Jewish Council in

Warsaw, ink, Yiddish in Roman transliteration, 148×104 mm, damage and losses of text), transcript (2 copies, handwritten manuscript—LEG*, pencil, Yiddish, 150×190, 148×104 mm, extensive damage and losses of text), ss. 5, pp. 6.

Index: Lajbel Wajngarten, Sara Wulf, Joel Wulf

Published: *Listy o Zagładzie*, pp. 89–91.

b)

- 16.04.1942, after 20.04.1942, Szczebrzeszyn, Warsaw Ghetto
- S. [Sara] Wulf (Szczebrzeszyn), Letter of 16.04.1942 to Mojsze Wulf (Warsaw, ul. Smocza 1, apt. 39a)
- Lack of money and life full of fear.
- ***Description:*** original (handwritten manuscript—three handwritings—on a postcard, postmark and stamp of Jewish Council in Warsaw, ink, Yiddish in Roman transliteration, 148×104 mm, damage and losses of text), transcript (2 copies, handwritten manuscript -LEG*, pencil, Yiddish, 150×190, 150×140 mm, extensive damage and losses of text), ss. 5, pp. 6. Added greetings from Estera [Wulf] and Fiszel Fryd.

Published: *Listy o Zagładzie*, pp. 92–94.

c)

- 17.04.1942, after 20.04.1942, Szczebrzeszyn, Warsaw Ghetto
- Fiszel Fryd (Szczebrzeszyn), Letter of 17.04.1942 to Mojsze Wulf (Warsaw, ul. Smocza 1, apt. 39a)
- Attempt to rescue children. Request for further help.
- ***Description:*** original (handwritten manuscript on a postcard, postmark and stamp of Jewish Council in Warsaw, ink, Yiddish in Roman transliteration, 148×104 mm, damage and losses of text), transcript (2 copies, handwritten manuscript -LEG*, pencil, Yiddish, 150×190, 148×105 mm, significant damage and losses of text), ss. 5, pp. 6.

Published: *Listy o Zagładzie*, pp. 94–97.

**1023. RING. I/599/56. Mf. ŻIH—812; USHMM—24**

- 17.04.1942, Szczebrzeszyn
- NN., Letter to family. Request for information.
- ***Description:*** original, handwritten manuscript on a postcard, postmark, pencil, Polish, 126×100 mm, serious damage and losses of text, ss. 1, pp. 2.

Notation by H.W. in Yiddish (ink): "Distribution [?] . . ."

**1024. RING. I/920 (1239). (Lb. 724). Mf. ŻIH—829; USHMM—41**

- After 28.02.1941,Warsaw Ghetto
- NN., Account entitled "Tartshin" [Tarczyn]
- Experiences of the Jewish population in Tarczyn from Germans' entry until resettlement (temporary expulsion of male Poles and Jews from Tarczyn—09.1939, ghetto—01.1941, removal to Warsaw—28.02.1941).
- ***Description:*** transcript (2 copies), handwritten manuscript (NN*), pencil, Yiddish, 148×210 mm, ss. 34, pp. 34.

At the top a symbol (second copy) (ink): dot in a small circle. On p. 1 note by H.W. in Yiddish (ink): "Hober."

See HWC, 11/1 (third copy, handwritten manuscript, pencil, ss. 16, p. 1 missing).

Index: Chaim Wolfson (age 22), died during the resettlement from Tarczyn in 1939; Izrael Kaper (age 18), died during the resettlement from Tarczyn in 1939

**1025. RING. I/921 (1240). (Lb. 377). Mf. ŻIH—829; USHMM—41**

- After 28.02.1942, Warsaw Ghetto
- NN., Account entitled "Tartshin" [Tarczyn]
- Jews in Tarczyn before the war, in September 1939 (town fire), during the occupation (formation of the ghetto), until the expulsion [28.02.1942].[44]
- ***Description:*** transcript (2 copies), handwritten manuscript (BW*), pencil, Yiddish, 148×208 mm, ss. 10, pp. 10.

In the margins a symbol (ink): dot in a small circle and on p. 1 (first copy) a symbol (red pencil): "+".

**1026. RING. I/919 (1238). (Lb. 561) Mf. ŻIH—829; USHMM—41**

- 18.06.1942, Warsaw Ghetto
- NN., Account entitled "Tarnów" (18.06.1942)
- About the liquidation action in Tarnów—ca. 8,000 Jews murdered [11–13.06.1942].
- ***Description:*** transcript, handwritten manuscript (E*), pencil, Polish, 154×193 mm, ss. 1, pp. 2.

On p. 2 note by H.W. in Yiddish (ink): "1 standard page. 1942."

**1027. RING. I/922 (1241). (Lb. 489). Mf. ŻIH—829; USHMM—41**

- After 27.05.1942, Warsaw Ghetto
- NN., Account entitled "Tlushts" [Tłuszcz]
- Persecution of Jews in Tłuszcz (ca. 100 local families and 50 families of refugees) from the moment of the Germans' arrival in the small town until the expulsion of 27.05.1942. Victims, among others the first chairman of the Jewish Council, Popowski—died in Oświęcim; the second chairman, Meir Taub—shot

44. The Polish *wysiedlenie* is the equivalent of the German *Aussiedlung*, which has clear connotation of removal. The opposite would be *Einsiedlung*, resettlement or "in-settlement." The word had a distinctly negative connotation for Polish Jews, so it is being rendered as expulsion. In his 1962 Yiddish monograph on the Łódź ghetto, Isaiah Trunk employed the form "*oyszidlung*" in quotation marks to acknowledge his use of a form imitating the German usage.

during resettlement; the commander of the Jewish police,—Berl Gelbard; the rabbis: Jakub, Józef Brukman—tortured and killed in Jadów; Meir Radzimiński (died 26.05.1942).

- ***Description:*** original (o), handwritten manuscript (HUB.*), notebook, ink, Yiddish, 153×198 mm, minor damage and losses of text, missing pages [?], ss. 15, pp. 26.

  Published: *BFG*, vol. XXXI/1993, pp. 54–63; *Selected Documents*, pp. 201–209.

**1028. RING. I/925 (1244). (Lb. 1626). Mf. ŻIH—829; USHMM—41**

- Date unknown, Warsaw Ghetto
- [Monisz Szyk?], Account entitled "Tomashuv Maz[ovietski]" [Tomaszów Maz(owiecki)]
- Gradual removal of the Jewish population from the town (removal of Jews from the "small ghetto" on ul. Piłsudskiego to Opoczno and Rawa Mazowiecka, and from the "big ghetto"; numerous fatalities, escapes to the countryside).
- ***Description:*** original or transcript, handwritten manuscript, ink, Yiddish, 215×340 mm, ss. 1, pp. 2.

  Attached note by H.W.: "Written by Monisz Szyk."

  Title inserted in a different handwriting (pencil).

**1029. RING. I/1003 (1322). (Lb. 1414). Mf. ŻIH—831; USHMM—43**

- After 11.1939, Warsaw Ghetto
- NN., Report entitled "Toruń"
- Toruń Jews had to leave the city by 15.11.1939; most moved to Warsaw.
- ***Description:*** original or transcript, handwritten manuscript, ink, Polish, 152×200 mm, ss. 1, pp. 1.

**1030. RING. I/924 (1243). (Lb. 1269). Mf. ŻIH—829; USHMM—41**

- After 02.1942, Warsaw Ghetto
- NN., Account entitled "Turobin" (02.1942)
- Situation of the Jewish population during the occupation (influx of refugees from Łódź, Koło, Kleczew, Konin, Janów Lubelski—ca. 1,250–1,400 people, activities of the Jewish Council—Blajfeder and Jankiel Rozenfeld, [forced] contribution).
- ***Description:*** transcript (3 copies), typescript, Yiddish, 208×295 mm, minor damage and losses of text (first copy), ss. 6, pp. 6.

  On p. 1 (first copy) note by H.W. in Yiddish (ink): "Farb vintsik" [Little color ?]

**1031. RING. I/1061 (1380). (Lb. 663). Mf. ŻIH—832; USHMM—44**

- After 25.07.1942, Warsaw Ghetto
- [Rotring?], Account [entitled] "Tishevets" [Tyszowce] (fragment [?])
- Author from Warsaw, resided during the occupation with wife and children in the village of Podbór near Tyszowce. He describes the fate of the Jewish population from the war's outbreak until expulsion (fire in 09.1939, repressive actions, forced labor, Jewish Council, situation of Jews in the Tyszowce community, resettlement from Tyszowce on 25.07.1942 to neighboring localities).
- ***Description:*** transcript, handwritten manuscript (U*), pencil, Yiddish, 110×288 mm, minor damage and losses of text, ss. 1, pp. 2.

  Original pagination (2–3) indicates that the document could be a fragment of a larger whole.

  Index: Kleks, member of the Jewish Council in Tyszowce; Winter, member of the Jewish Council in Tyszowce; L. Elenbojm (Lilienbojm?), member of the Jewish Council in Tyszowce; Cukier, chairman of the Jewish Council in Tyszowce; Fiszleber, refugee from Germany, secretary of the Jewish Council in Tyszowce

**1032. RING. I/582. Mf. ŻIH—792; USHMM—23**

- 04.1942, Węgrów
- Idl Lajfer (Węgrów, Pl. Bóżniczy 8), Letter of 13.04.1942 to A. Blumsztajn (Warsaw, ul. Nowolipie 23, apt. 13)
- 500 persons transported from Węgrów to work in Mordy. Questions about acquaintances (relatives [?]): Wajnblat, Szwarcbard, Wasser, Zagan [Sagan?], and others. Greetings from Eli Szurek from Łódź.
- ***Description:*** original, handwritten manuscript on a postcard, postmark and stamp of Jewish Council, ink, Polish, 147×104 mm, ss. 1, pp. 2.

  On p. 1 in another handwriting a notation in Polish and Yiddish (pencil).

**1033. I/939 (1258) (Lb. 1142). Mf. ŻIH—830; USHMM—42**

- 04.1942, Warsaw Ghetto
- NN., Account entitled "Vyelun" [Wieluń] (04.1942)
- Murder of Abraham Kojten [?] by an ethnic German became the occasion for sentencing to death 10 Jews, hanged on the market square in Wieluń in 03.1941.
- ***Description:*** transcript, handwritten manuscript (RR*), ink, Yiddish, 163×208 mm, ss. 1, pp. 2.

**1034. RING. I/929 (1248). (Lb. 975). Mf. ŻIH—829; USHMM—41**

- After 1.03.1942, Warsaw Ghetto
- K.O., Account entitled "Jews in Wilno from 24 June to 4 November 1941" (1.03.1942)
- Author, a refugee from Łódź, worked at the Jewish Council in Wilno, describes the successive stages of liquidation of the Jewish population in Wilno (mass shootings at Ponary, formation of the ghetto, participation of Lithuanians in the murder of Jews, attitude of the Polish population). Author fled from the ghetto on 4.11.1941.
- ***Description:*** transcript (a) (handwritten manuscript—KK*, notebook, ink, 160×202 mm, text is only

partially legible); transcript (b) (3 copies, typescript, 200×280 mm, minor damage and losses of text, missing first page in third copy), Polish, ss. 25, pp. 34.
Attached note by H.W.: "Testimony recorded by Salomea Ostrowska."
Published: *Relacje z Kresów*, pp. 460–468.

**1035. RING. I/930 (1249). Mf. ŻIH—829; USHMM—41**

- After 12.10.1941, Warsaw Ghetto
- [Miriam Abramowska], Account entitled "Yedies vegn Vilne" [News about Wilno] (1941)
- Author (age 20) describes the situation of the Jewish population from Germans' arrival in Wilno until 12.10.1941 (formation of ghetto, executions at Ponary).
- ***Description:*** transcript, handwritten manuscript (TT*), pencil, Yiddish, 148×210 mm, ss. 4, pp. 4.
On p. 1 H.W note in Yiddish (ink): "A not very bright 20-year-old girl" [?].
Pages 1–2 and 4 of the first copy, p. 3 of the second copy.
Attached note by H.W.: "Testimony of Miriam Abramowska (age 20) from Wilno, written down by N. Tytelman."
See HWC, 10/2 (second copy, handwritten manuscript, pencil, ss. 4).
Published: *Relacje z Kresów*, pp. 456–459.

**1036. RING. I/931 (1250). Mf. ŻIH—829; USHMM—41**

- After 01.1942, Warsaw Ghetto
- NN., Account entitled "Wilno (general description until the ghetto)" (Warsaw, 01.1942)
- Persecution of the Jewish population in Wilno (occupation of the city by the Germans—24.06.1941, introduction of various restrictions for Jews, the Jewish Council, removal from apartments, robberies, forced labor, the first liquidation actions, removal to Ponary, removal of ca. 8,000 persons to an unknown destination on 26–28.08.1941).
- ***Description:*** transcript (3 copies), handwritten manuscript (JG*), pencil, Polish, 148×208 mm, ss. 18, pp. 18.
On p. 1 (first copy) note by H.W. in Yiddish (ink): "no. 7. 109—1942/1 January."
Published: *Relacje z Kresów*, pp. 450–455.
Index: Dr. [Jakub] Wygodzki, member of the Jewish Council in Wilno, died in August [?] 1941; Hinks [Hans Hingst], commissioner of Wilno in August 1941

**1037. RING. I/932 (1251). Mf. ŻIH—829; USHMM—41**

- 01.1942–2.03.1942, After 2.03.1942, Warsaw Ghetto
- NN., Account entitled "Jews in Wilno during German times" (01.1942–2.03.1942)
- Author (age 22), from the start of 1940 resided in the Betar dormitory in Wilno. He describes the situation of Jews in the USSR, relations with Lithuanians and Poles, entry of Germans into Wilno, and anti-Jewish repressive actions (arrests, decrees, robberies and murders, burning of the synagogue on Szkipiszki), formation of the Jewish Council with Dr. [Jakub] Wygodzki, liquidation action in the former Jewish District (2.09.1941 r), [forced] "contribution" (08.1941), formation of two ghettos with ca. 75,000 people, constant selections and slaughter of thousands of Jews at Ponary, composition of the second Jewish Council and Order Service, successive liquidation actions, hunger, selections until the start of 1942.
- ***Description:*** transcript (a) (handwritten manuscript—E*, notebooks, ink, 153×198 mm), transcript (b) (fragment, includes a handwritten copy of part 3) (3 incomplete copies, typescript, 195×275 mm, damage and losses of text), Polish, ss. 41, pp. 66.
Published: *Relacje z Kresów*, pp. 396–432.
Index: [Hans] Hingst, commissioner in Wilno

**1038. RING. I/979 (1298). (Lb. 498). Mf. ŻIH—831; USHMM—43**

- After 12.1941, Warsaw Ghetto
- NN., Account about the fate of Jews in Wilno during the German occupation
- Outbreak of the German–Soviet War, persecutions of the Jewish population, formation of the ghetto, mass executions at Ponary, situation in the ghetto at the end of 1941 (schools, library, orchestra, drama clubs). Appended sketches of the symbols that the Jews in Wilno had to wear.
- ***Description:*** transcript, handwritten manuscript (LEG*), pencil, Yiddish, 150×195 mm, ss. 7, pp. 6.
Attached note by H.W. in Yiddish: "By E. Gutkowski."
Published: *Relacje z Kresów*, pp. 490–499.
Index: Noach Pryłucki of Wilno; [Anatol] Fried, member of the Jewish Council in Wilno; Dr. [Jakub] Wygodzki, member of the Jewish Council in Wilno; [Szabtaj] Milkanowicki, member of the Jewish Council in Wilno; Rabbi Szub [?], member of the Jewish Council in Wilno; Werbliński, member of the Jewish Council in Wilno; Petuchewski, member of the Jewish Council in Wilno; Juszuński, member of the Jewish Council in Wilno; Gens from Lida, member Order Service in Wilno; Glazman, member Order Service in Wilno

**1039. RING. I/1209. Mf. ŻIH—835; USHMM—47**

- Middle of 02.1942, Warsaw Ghetto
- NN., Account entitled "Vilne" [Wilno] (middle of 02.1942)
- Author from Warsaw describes journey to the east (departure from Warsaw 13.11.1941, Siedlce—camp for Soviet POWs, Czyżew near Wysoki Mazowiecki, Białystok, relations with Germans, Sokółka,

information about the ghetto in Grodno, Wilno, about the participation of Lithuanians in persecutions of the Jewish population, hanging on Pl. Katedralny of Poles who aided Jews, return to Warsaw 8.02.1942).

- ***Description:*** transcript, handwritten manuscript (LEG*), pencil, Yiddish, 150×170 mm, serious damage and losses of text, ss. 5, pp. 10.

### 1040. RING. I/165. Mf. ŻIH—779; USHMM—10

- After 02.1942, Warsaw Ghetto
- NN., Account entitled "Anton Shmidt (fun serye 'Khsidei umes hooylem')" [Anton Szmidt (from the series: 'Righteous Among the Nations')][45]
- Profile of an Austrian from Vienna (age 38), a German Army sergeant, who helped and saved Wilno Jews and for this had to bear the death penalty [?] (prison in Łukiszki 02.1942).
- ***Description:*** transcript (2 copies), typescript, Yiddish, 208×293 mm, minor damage and losses of text, ss. 10, pp. 10.

  On p. 1 (first copy) a note by H.W. in Yiddish (ink): "14th page."

  Author of the account was probably Lonka Koziebrodzka; see *Relacje z Kresów*, pp. 477, 481.

  See HWC, 10/3 (third copy, typescript, ss. 5).

  Published: *Relacje z Kresów*, pp. 477–489.

### 1041. RING. I/433. (Lb. 1203). Mf. ŻIH—785; USHMM—16. RING. I/935 (1254). (Lb. 953). Mf. ŻIH—830; USHMM—42

**a) Ring. I/433, I/935**

- After 10.1941, Warsaw Ghetto
- NN., Account entitled "Der khurbn fun di kehiles oyf di farnumene shtokhim zumer 1941. Band I. Vilne un svive" [The destruction of the Jewish communities on the territories occupied in summer 1941. Volume I. Wilno and Vicinity]
- Author (age 22), fled from the Germans in September 1939 from Kraków to the east with a group of friends, journey through the Lublin region, entry of the Soviet military, departure to Lwów, then to Wilno (fall 1939), outbreak of the German–Soviet War, Wilno ghetto, escape to Warsaw (19.10.1941).
- ***Description:*** Ring. I/433—original (o), handwritten manuscript (HUB.*), notebooks, ink, Yiddish, 155×195 mm, ss. 42, pp. 75; Ring. I/935—transcript (2 copies), typescript, Yiddish, 210×297 mm, ss. 80, pp. 80.

  Ring. I/433—On p. 1 note by H.W. in Yiddish (ink): "108–1942/1 January."

  Ring. I/935—On p. 1 (transcript, first copy) note in Yiddish: "Sz. Huberband." On p. 1 (transcript, second copy) note by H.W. in Yiddish (ink): 108—1942/1 January."

  Ring. I/935—Attached note by H.W.: "Recorded and collected by Rabbi Szymon Huberband."

  According to Ruta Sakowska the account's author is Rachela Zylberberg.

  See HWC, 2/10 for third copy of the transcript (Ring. I/935), typescript, ss. 40.

  Published: *BFG*, vol. XXXI/1993, pp. 23–53; *Relacje z Kresów*, pp. 326–348, 363–381.

**b) Ring. I/433**

- After 09.1941, Warsaw Ghetto
- NN., Account entitled "Der khurbn fun di kehiles oyf di naye farnumene sovietishe gebitn. Band II. Bialestok un svive" [The destruction of the Jewish communities on the newly occupied Soviet regions. Volume II. Białystok and vicinity]
- On 13.09.1939, the author left Warsaw, fleeing to the east, arrested in Małkinia by the Germans, after release he escaped into regions taken by USSR (Zaręby Kościelne, Białystok; situation of refugees); departure to work in Brodnica near Pińsk, outbreak of the German–Soviet War, persecutions of the Jewish population (Jeziernica near Słonim, Słonim, Białystok ghetto), departure for Warsaw (09.1941).
- ***Description:*** original (o), handwritten manuscript (HUB.*), notebooks, ink, Yiddish, 152×192, ss. 36, pp. 59.

  Pub. (a and b): *Kiddush Hashem*, pp. 334–382; (a) *Relacje z Kresów*, pp. 348–362, 381–395.

### 1042. RING. I/1220/31. Mf. ŻIH—835; USHMM—47

- After 1939, Warsaw Ghetto
- NN., Account from: "Serye; Bialistok un andere [. . .], Sept-1939" [Series: Białystok and other [. . .], (September)-1939] (fragment?)
- Author (age 36), merchant, description of the situation on Polish lands occupied by the USSR in 09.1939 (Wilno).
- ***Description:*** original or transcript, handwritten manuscript (Ł*), ink, Yiddish, serious damage and losses of text, ss. 8, pp. 16.

  On the back of one of the ss. is a note in Yiddish: "From the cycle 2½ [years]."

### 1043. RING. I/1220/57. Mf. ŻIH—835; USHMM—47

- After 13.02.[1942], Warsaw Ghetto
- NN., Note concerning a journey [?] to Wilno and Białystok
- Inf. about Macerauer [?], the Adlers, a meeting in Białystok, ghetto in Wilno.
- ***Description:*** original or transcript (2 copies), handwritten manuscript (H*), pencil, Polish, 180×88 mm, ss. 2, pp. 2.

### 1044. RING. I/1220/58. Mf. ŻIH—835; USHMM—47

- Date unknown, Warsaw Ghetto

45. The Polish text renders this as "Friends of the Jews." The Yiddish-Hebrew original phrase is the one used by Yad Vashem to designate those non-Jews who saved Jews: Righteous among the Nations.

- NN., Note from an account (for editing [?]) about Wilno [?] (fragment)
- Inf.: Dr. Sołowiejczyk, Adler, Major Frucht, Rewel [?], Max Uppert of Bielsko.
- ***Description:*** original, handwritten manuscript (LEG*), pencil, Polish, 145×136 mm, damage and losses of text, ss. 1, pp. 2.

**1045. RING. I/551/2. Mf. ŻIH—791; USHMM—22**

- 8.05.1942, Wilno
- J. Dederko (Wilno, ul. Pohulanka 19, apt. 5), Letter of 8.05.1942 to G. Eisenberg (Warsaw, ul. Nowolipie 1, apt. 8)
- Attitudes in the Wilno ghetto.
- ***Description:*** original, handwritten manuscript (four handwritings) on a postcard, postmark and stamp of the Jewish Council in Warsaw, ink, pencil, German, Polish, 144×104 mm, damage and losses of text, ss. 1, pp. 2.

  Letter signed by 3 people: Parents of NN. [?] and their son Gabryś. On p. 1 is a handwritten note made in Warsaw and concerning the addressee: "according to K[. . . ?] and acc[ording to tenants of] apt. 8, Nowolipie 7, addressee does not fig[ure] and is unknown; [Nowolipie?] 24, apt. 5."[?]

**1046. RING. I/942 (1261). Mf. ŻIH—830; USHMM—42**

- After 11.1941, Warsaw Ghetto
- [Zimler (age 31)], Account entitled "Impressions from a stay in the environs of Wiskitki"
- Author, a barber, after resettlement to the Warsaw Ghetto, escaped three times with his wife (06.1941–17.11.1941) to go to his home region near Wiskitki, where he worked among peasants. List of Polish farmers who gave him work, fed them, and put them up for the night in villages: Oryszew (Znamirowski, head of the village council, Dokaszewski), Kolonia Oryszewska (Raczkowski), Drzewica (Jodłowski, Bodych, Paluch, Witkowski), Drybus (Krzyta), Kozłowice, Binderówka (Kiełbowicz), Buszyce (Sitarz), Wyczółki (Zieliński), and Janówka (Janicki, the Zawistowskis).
- ***Description:*** transcript (3 copies), handwritten manuscript (JG*), pencil, Polish, 148×206 mm, minor damage and losses of text, ss. 18, pp. 18.

  On p. 1 (first and second copies) a note by H.W. in Yiddish (ink): "Zimler, barber from Wiskitki, age 31, by [Jechiel] Górny. no. 10. 109—1942/1 January."

  Index: Barber Shop for Łódź Refugees (ul. Nowolipki 2) (Author worked here)

**1047. RING. I/941 (1260). (Lb. 883). Mf. ŻIH—830; USHMM—42**

- After 02.1941, Warsaw Ghetto
- [Bernard Kampelmacher], Study entitled "Wiskitki. Landkomisariat Żyrardów, Kreishauptman sochaczewski" [Sochaczew district governor]
- Description of Jewish society before the war, beginnings of the German occupation, [forced] contributions, roundups, Jewish Council, displaced persons, activity of the Social Aid Committee, resettlement on 3.02.1941 to Warsaw.
- ***Description:*** original (typescript, handwritten changes, ink, 206×295 mm, minor damage and losses of text), transcript (3 copies, typescript, 206×295 mm) Polish, minor damage and losses of text, ss. 22, pp. 25.

  On p. 1 (original) title: "Wiskitki, Sochaczew-Błonie District."

  Chapter titles: "Jewish Council," "Community Administration," "Aid Committee," and "Resettlement."

  On p. 1 (transcript, on all copies) a note by H.W. (ink): "Kampel."

  Index: Gelbsztajn, member of the Jewish Council in Sochaczew; Libert, member of the Jewish Council in Sochaczew; Sprangz, an ethnic German from Wiskitki

**1048. RING. I/456. (Lb. 1510). Mf. ŻIH—786; USHMM—17**

- 2[. . .].01.1941[?], Warsaw Ghetto
- NN., Account entitled "Fun Varshe kayn Vitebsk un tsurik. Mayn kurikulum vite" [From Warsaw to Vitebsk and back. My curriculum vitae] (2[. . .].01.1942)
- Author (born 21.11.1918 in Warsaw) of an artisan family, fled from Warsaw 7.09.1939 to the east, describes his stay in the USSR (Vitebsk); he returned to Warsaw in 1941.
- ***Description:*** transcript, handwritten manuscript (Ś*), ink, Yiddish, 145×220 mm, text illegible in places, ss. 42, pp. 42.

  Attached note by H.W.: "September 1939–January 1940. Warsaw–Vitebsk–Warsaw. Journeys in the 1st year of the war. Recorded by Abraham Lewin. A former youth activist and union activist (printers union) reports; I did not know his surname."

  Published: *Relacje z Kresów*, pp. 249–297.

**1049. RING. I/940 (1259). (Lb. 1449). Mf. ŻIH—830; USHMM—42**

- After 1939, Warsaw Ghetto
- NN., Account entitled "Włocławek"
- 1) First weeks of the German occupation of Włocławek (town taken 12.09.1939, action on Łęgska, torching of 2 synagogues, hunt for men, forced contributions, first resettlement of 11.1939); 2) Account of a resident (age 18) ul. 3 Maja 22, witness to the torching of a synagogue (ul. Żabia), description of a six-day stay in jail together with a group of Jews seized on 25.09.1939 as hostages.
- ***Description:*** original (o) (handwritten manuscript—

FLIG*, ink, 207×295, 223×350 mm, minor damage and losses of text, text illegible in places); transcript (3 copies, handwritten manuscript—JG*, pencil, 148×208 mm, damage and losses of text, missing pages (first and third copies), Polish, ss. 112, pp. 123.

On p. 1 (transcript, second copy) note by H.W. (ink): "Fligar."

Account in Ring. I/936 concerns these same events in Włocławek, but differs in details.

Index: Kanał, imprisoned in Włocławek in 09.1939; Eliasz Florman, imprisoned in Włocławek in 09.1939; Rathaus, imprisoned in Włocławek in 09.1939; Sztywelman, imprisoned in Włocławek in 09.1939; Maks Choroński, imprisoned in Włocławek in 09.1939; Zemelmans (father and son), imprisoned in Włocławek in 09.1939; Lichtensztajns (father and son), imprisoned in Włocławek in 09.1939; Pośladek, imprisoned in Włocławek in 09.1939; Żurawski, imprisoned in Włocławek in 09.1939; Lewczyński, imprisoned in Włocławek in 09.1939; J. Cygański, chairman of the Jewish Community in Włocławek; Pante, member of the Jewish Community in Włocławek; A. Czamański, member of the Jewish Community in Włocławek; Tenenbaum, member of the Jewish Community in Włocławek; Józef Rode, member of the Jewish Community in Włocławek (09.1939); Dębiński, killed in Włocławek (24.09.1939); [M.] Dyszel, killed in Włocławek (24.09.1939)

**1050. RING. I/936 (1255). (Lb. 1178). Mf. ŻIH—830; USHMM—42**

- Date unknown, Warsaw Ghetto
- [J. Bieżyńska ?], Account about the persecution of Jews in Włocławek in the second half of September 1939
- Author describes a public execution (ul. Łęgska), torching of synagogue, roundup of Jewish men. Appended copy of proclamation of 29.09.1939 of Commissioner of the City of Włocławek Cramer, regarding the Jewish population.
- ***Description:*** original (handwritten manuscript, notebook, ink, 153×198 mm), transcript (3 copies, typescript, 210×298 mm), Polish, ss. 25, pp. 29.

Information about the author, see HWC, 65/8.

Accounts in Ring. I/940 concern these same events in Włocławek, but vary in details from this account.

Index: M. Dyszel, shot in Włocławek (ul. Łęgska) 09.1939; [Wacław] Tomaszewski, editor of *A.B.C.*, and later the *Leslauer Bote* in Włocławek, shot by Germans 11.11.1939; [Stanisław] Dz. [Dziekanowski], pharmacist of Włocławek

**1051. RING. I/927 (1246). (Lb. 378). Mf. ŻIH—829; USHMM—41**

- After 1940, Warsaw Ghetto
- NN., Account entitled "Vlotslavek" [Włocławek]
- Before the war one of the wealthiest communities (18,000 Jews), after entry of Germans (14.09.1939) repressive actions and gradual resettlement of the Jewish population (3 forced contributions, forced labor).
- ***Description:*** transcript, handwritten manuscript (MS*), pencil, Yiddish, 148×120 mm, minor damage and losses of text, ss. 2, pp. 3.

On p. 1 in the margin a Hebrew letter (underlined) (pencil, red): "p" (pei). In the margins a symbol (ink): "//."

Doc. was kept in a binder.

**1052. RING. I/674/12. (Lb. 1688). Mf. ŻIH—816; USHMM—28**

- Date unknown, Warsaw Ghetto
- NN., Account entitled "Vlotslavek" [Włocławek]
- Author from Włocławek describes flight from the town and return after several days, the situation of the Jewish population after Germans' arrival until December 1939 (ban on gathering for prayer, burning of the old and new synagogues, [forced] contribution).
- ***Description:*** original (0), handwritten manuscript (H.W.*), ink, Polish, 156×188 mm, ss. 1, pp. 2. Title in Yiddish.

**1053. RING. I/565. Mf. ŻIH—792; USHMM—23**

- 03.1942, Włocławek
- Bronka Głowińska (Leslau [Włocławek]), Letter to husband [?] and Gołda Tabaczyńska (Warsaw, ul. Dzielna 18, apt. 5)
- Information about immediate family: father (father-in-law [?]) and daughter Celina.
- ***Description:*** original, handwritten manuscript (two handwritings) on a postcard, postmark (11.03.1942, Leslau) and stamp of the Jewish Council in Warsaw, German, Polish, 148×104 mm, text illegible in places, ss. 1, pp. 2.

On p. 2 postscript: "Feli." Letter addressed to: "E. Tabaczyńska (Warsaw, ul. Dzielna 18, apt. 5)"; see Ring. I/572.

**1054. RING. I/563. Mf. ŻIH—791; USHMM—22**

- After 1.06.1942, Warsaw Ghetto
- NN. (Włodawa), Letter to NN. (Warsaw Ghetto). Information about the approaching annihilation.
- ***Description:*** transcript (2 copies), handwritten manuscript (LEG*), pencil, Yiddish, 207×294 mm, ss. 2, pp. 2.

**1055. RING. I/926 (1245). (Lb. 1704). Mf. ŻIH—829; USHMM—41**

- 6.03.1941, Włoszczowa ghetto

- Jewish Council in Włoszczowa. Committee for Aid to Refugees and the Poor, Letter of 6.03.1941 to J. Falk (American Joint Distribution Committee, Kraków, ul. Dietla 85)
- Letter with appended report of activity in 1940 (Notation about refugees and displaced persons, e.g., from Włocławek, social welfare, aid received, formation of the ghetto—10.07.1940, photograph).
- ***Description:*** original, typescript, photograph, Polish, 112×170, 190×245 mm, serious damage and losses of text, ss. 18, pp. 18.

  Appended envelope.

  Attached note by H.W.: "Forwarded by D. Guzik."

  Index: Dr. Chaim Fargel, member of the Jewish Council in Włoszczowa; Josef Kochen, member of the Jewish Council in Włoszczowa

## 1056. RING. I/928 (1247). (Lb. 1556). Mf. ŻIH—829; USHMM—41

- Date unknown, Warsaw Ghetto
- [Chana Rajchman], Account entitled "Conversation with a 15-year-old young lady expelled from Wyszków"
- Relations with Poles, expulsion of Jews from Wyszków (Information about the author's relatives killed in 09.1939 by Germans: Mordka Rajchman [age 52], father; Icchak Rajchman [age 17], brother; Jankiel Majer Rajchman [age 49], father's brother; as well as the Holcman family, Hasidim—father, mother, and daughter).
- ***Description:*** transcript (3 copies), handwritten manuscript (CC*), pencil, Polish, 148×210 m, ss. 12, pp. 12.

  Attached note by H.W.: "Recorded by Chil Górny."

## 1057. RING. I/394. Mf. ŻIH—783; USHMM—14

- After 01.1942, Warsaw Ghetto
- [Tauba Omur?], Account concerning events in the Koło district 1941/1942
- Author from Kłodawa describes the liquidation of the community in Zagórów—09/10.1941 (information from Icchak Łaski, chairman of the Jewish Council in Zagórów), beginning of the selection of the population (11.1941), resettlement to an unknown destination (Izbica and Bugity [?]—12.01.1941), information about the death camp in Chełmno (Grabów, 18–19.01.1941) from refugees: [Szlamek Winer] Wiener, [Abram] Roj of Izbica, Mechl [Michał] Podchlebnik of Bugaj.
- ***Description:*** original or transcript (handwritten manuscript, notebook, ink, 142×200 mm), transcript (typescript, 208×295 mm, damage and losses of text), Yiddish, ss. 20, pp. 15.

  The notebook contains, apart from handwriting in Yiddish on ss. 12–14, notes (handwritten manuscript, Polish, pencil) of a child named Miriam Bretsztejn [?] from a Polish language lesson (5 and 12.01.19 . . . [?]).

  Attached note by H.W. in Yiddish: "Account of Tauba Omur [?] of Kłodawa, forwarded by H.W."

## 1058. RING. I/943 (1262). (Lb. 319). Mf. ŻIH—830; USHMM—42

- After 09.1939, Warsaw Ghetto
- NN, Account entitled "Zakrotshim" [Zakroczym]
- Situation of the Jewish population in Zakroczym several days before the outbreak and in the first days of the war until the moment of the Germans' arrival. First persecutions.
- ***Description:*** transcript (2 copies), handwritten manuscript (MS*), pencil, Yiddish, 148×210 mm, damage and losses of text (first copy), ss. 4, pp. 4.

  Two copies of this document preserved (without first [copy?]); pencil copies, variously marked, were preserved in different places, combined only after the war.

  In the margins (first copy) letter (ink): "E" [ayin?]. In the margins (second copy) a symbol (ink): "///."

  Doc. was kept in a binder.

## 1059. RING. I/946 (1265). (Lb. 719). Mf. ŻIH—830; USHMM—42

- After 6.06.1942, Warsaw Ghetto
- Fiszelson, Account entitled "Zamoshtsh" [Zamość]
- Author (age ca. 40), 5 children (ul. Nalewki 41 m 49), resided in Zamość from 06.1941 to 05.1942. He describes the situation of the Zamość Jews and three successive resettlement actions: 06.1941, 11.04. and 27.05.1942.
- ***Description:*** original (o), handwritten manuscript (H.W.*), notebook, ink, Yiddish, 153×197 mm, minor damage and losses of text, ss. 6, pp. 12.

  Doc. was kept in a binder.

  Index: Garfinkiel, chairman of the Jewish Council in Zamość

## 1060. RING. I/1220/5. Mf. ŻIH—835; USHMM—47

- After 06.1941, Warsaw Ghetto
- NN., Account entitled "[. . .]1940"
- Author, a Warsaw artisan, stayed from 28.09.1939 in Zaręby Kościelne (situation of the Jewish population in the small town after outbreak of war, relations with Poles, transfer point, outbreak of the German–Soviet War). Appended short description of the author written by the person who recorded the account.
- ***Description:*** original (o), handwritten manuscript (FLIG*), ink, Polish, 102×164, 210×299 mm, damage and losses of text, text is difficult to read in places, ss. 5, pp. 5.

**1061. RING. I/950 (1269). Mf. ŻIH—830; USHMM—42**

- 1941, Warsaw Ghetto
- Genia Landau, "Recollections and wartime experiences"
- Girl from Zduńska Wola describes her own and her family's experiences from 1.09.1939 to spring 1941 (beginning of war, first repressive actions, journeys to Łódź and Warsaw, settling in Warsaw).
- ***Description:*** original, handwritten manuscript, notebooks, ink, Polish, 153×194 mm, extensive minor damage and losses of text, ss. 24, pp. 48.

  Index: Głuchy, *melamed* (elementary Jewish religion teacher) from Zduńska Wola

**1062. RING. I/571. Mf. ŻIH—792; USHMM—23**

- 21.02.1942, Zduńska Wola
- I. Gutfreund (Zduńska Wola), Letter of 21.02.1942 to I. M. Heber (Warsaw, ul. Nowolipie 20, apt. 39)
- Appeal for rescue for the Jewish population threatened with annihilation.
- ***Description:*** original, handwritten manuscript on a postcard, postmark and stamp of Jewish Council in Warsaw, Yiddish in Roman transliteration, ss. 1, pp. 2.

  According to Ruta Sakowska (See *Listy o Zagładzie*, p. 32), the surname of the sender is fictive; in the place where the sender's name is inserted, the author wrote: "Se Psiru" (Hebrew code for "Secret Information" [?]); ibid., p. 31, note 1.

  Published: *Listy o Zagładzie*, pp. 29–32.

**1063. RING. I/478. Mf. ŻIH—786; USHMM—17**

- 10.1941 and after 10.1941, Kosów Lacki [?] and Warsaw Ghetto.
- [Hanna Lewkowicz], Account entitled "Journey to Russia" (Kosów Lacki in October 1941)
- Description of attempt to flee to the regions occupied by the USSR in September 1939.
- ***Description:*** original (handwritten manuscript—HL*, ink, 154×190 mm, extensive damage and losses of text), transcript (3 copies, typescript, 205×295 mm, minor damage and losses of text), Polish, ss. 27, pp. 33.

  On p. 1 (original) title at the top: "Journey to Russia" written in a different handwriting, as well as a subtitle: "Kosów Lacki in October 1941" in a different handwriting. On p. 1 (transcript, second copy) note by H.W. in Yiddish: "109–1942/1 January. no. 9."

  Attached note by H.W.: "Hanna Lewkowicz testifies, a young girl, a refugee from Kalisz."

  Published: *Relacje z Kresów*, pp. 13–22.

**1064. RING. I/474. Mf. ŻIH—786; USHMM—17**

- Date unknown, Warsaw Ghetto
- NN., Account entitled "Legal position of refugees"
- Situation of the population in regions of Poland occupied in 1939 by the USSR (matter of citizenship, situation of the intelligentsia, "passportization").
- ***Description:*** transcript (2 copies), handwritten manuscript (CC*), pencil, Polish, 147×208 mm, ss. 20, pp. 20.

  Attached note by H.W.: "Submitted to archive by Abram Lewin."

  Published: *Relacje z Kresów*, pp. 23–28.

**1065. RING. I/1220/29. Mf. ŻIH—835; USHMM—47**

- After 1941, Warsaw Ghetto
- NN., Account of a stay in the regions occupied by the USSR (fragment)
- Situation of the Jewish population.
- ***Description:*** transcript, handwritten manuscript (two handwritings: LEG* and [?]), pencil, Yiddish, 142×192 mm, serious damage and losses of text, ss. 9, pp. 18.

**1066. RING. I/1220/53. Mf. ŻIH—835; USHMM—47**

- 7.02.[194]2, Warsaw Ghetto
- NN., Account about an attempt to flee to the USSR (7.02.[194]2) (fragment, missing beginning)
- Author from Kalisz [?], description of stealing across the German–Soviet border.
- ***Description:*** original or transcript, handwritten manuscript (U*), ink, Yiddish, 111×205 mm, damage and losses of text, missing pages 1–13, ss. 1, pp. 2.

**1067. RING. I/599/87. Mf. ŻIH—812; USHMM—24**

- After 1939, Warsaw Ghetto
- NN., Account from 1939 (fragment)
- Escape from Warsaw, situation at the German–Soviet border, persecution of the Jewish population.
- ***Description:*** transcript, handwritten manuscript (LEG*), pencil, Yiddish, 115×190, 115×190, 107×190 mm, serious damage and losses of text, ss. 5, pp. 5.

**1068. RING. I/153. Mf. ŻIH—778; USHMM—9**

- After 06.1940, Warsaw Ghetto
- NN., Notes (account [?]) entitled "Jewish religion" on the attitude of the Soviet authorities to religion
- Legal situation of observant Jews (taxes on rabbis, compulsory work on Sabbath and holidays, antireligious education of youth, ritual slaughter impeded by lack of free trade).
- ***Description:*** original [?] (typescript with handwritten additions—ink, 220×300 mm), transcript (a) (2 copies, handwritten manuscript—(CC*), pencil, 150×208 mm); transcript (b) (3 copies, typescript, 208×293 mm), Polish, ss. 27, pp. 28.

  On p. 1 (transcript, typescript) a Hebrew letter (ink): "a" (alef).

  Copies a and b contain minor differences in text in relation to the original

  Published: *Relacje z Kresów*, pp. 29–32.

**1069. RING. I/944 (1263). (Lb. 323). Mf. ŻIH—830; USHMM—42**

- After 11.1939, Warsaw Ghetto
- NN., Account entitled "Zuromin" [Żuromin]
- Situation of Jews in Żuromin from war's outbreak (1.09.1939) until Germans' commencement of resettlement action (8.11.1939).
- *Description:* transcript (2 copies), handwritten manuscript (BW*), pencil, Yiddish, 148×210 mm, ss. 20, pp. 20.

  In the margins a symbol (ink): "Δ" and a symbol (red pencil): "t."

**1070. RING. I/945 (1264). (Lb. 441). Mf. ŻIH—830; USHMM—42**

- Date unknown, Warsaw Ghetto
- NN., Account entitled "Żuromin Expulsion"
- About the Jewish population expelled from Żuromin, beaten and abused in inhuman fashion, shipped out via Sierpc to Pomiechówek, then to Nowy Dwór.
- *Description:* transcript (2 copies), handwritten manuscript (MS*), pencil, Yiddish, 148×210 mm, minor damage and losses of text, ss. 6, pp. 6.

  In the margins letter (ink): "a" (alef) and a symbol (red pencil): "t."

  Doc. was kept in a binder.

**1071. RING. I/381. (Lb. 1280). Mf. ŻIH—783; USHMM—14**

- After 5.03.1942, Warsaw Ghetto
- NN., Account entitled "Vegn di eymefule teg in a.g. Varte-land" [About the fear-filled days in the so-called Wartheland]
- Author fled 16.02.1942 to Warsaw, describes the experiences of the Jews in Żychlin and neighboring localities (mass executions, inter alia committed by Modes, information about the annihilation of Jews in Kłodawa and Grabów). Information about engineer Borensztejn of Koło and Jakub Walrauch [?], chairman of the Jewish Council of Kłodawa.
- *Description:* transcript (3 copies), typescript, Yiddish, 208×295 mm, minor damage and losses of text, ss. 6, pp. 6.

  On p. 1 (first copy) note by H.W. in Yiddish (ink): "By Lewko."

  Attached note by H.W. in Yiddish: "Wartheland—Żychlinek, forwarded anonymously."

**1072. RING. I/572. Mf. ŻIH—792; USHMM—23**

a)

- 02.1942, Żychlin
- Lilka Opatowska (Żychlin), Letters (dated 22 [three letters] and 26.02.1942) to Gucia (Gołda) Tabaczyńska (Warsaw, ul. Dzielna 18, apt. 5)
- First days of the annihilation of the Jewish population in Żychlin.
- *Description:* original, handwritten manuscript on postcards (two handwritings), ink, German, Polish, 147×104 mm, ss. 4, pp. 8.

  Page 1 (letter of 22.02.) sent to L. Ejznerowicz (Warsaw, ul. Dzielna 20, apt. 25), sender: "W. Opatowski, Żychlin"; second letter dated 22.02. dispatched to E. Kadysz (Warsaw, ul. Dzielna 18, apt. 5), on it is a postscript in a different handwriting signed "Bulcio"; sender: "W. [crossed-out and written] "S. Opatowski"; third letter dated 22.02. sent to E. Tabaczyńska (Warsaw, ul. Dzielna 18, apt. 5), also with Bulcio's postscript, sender: "W. [crossed out and written] "S. Opatowski"; letter of 26.02. sent out to E. Kadysz (address as above), sender: "L. Opatowska, Żychlin." See Ring. I/565.

  Published: *Listy o Zagładzie*, pp. 57–65.

b)

- 24.02.1942, Żychlin
- NN. (Żychlin), Letter of 24.02.1942 to NN. (Warsaw Ghetto)
- Beginning of the liquidation of the ghetto in Żychlin, description of the death of the first victims (e.g., Józef Princ, shot 24.02.1942).
- *Description:* original [?], handwritten manuscript, ink, Yiddish, 144×195 mm, ss. 1, pp. 2.

  Published: *Listy o Zagładzie*, pp. 54–56.

**1073. RING. I/328/1. Mf. ŻIH—781; USHMM—12**

- After 20.01.1941, Warsaw Ghetto
- Der Kreishauptmann des Kreises Sochaczew-Blonie. Landkommissar Żyrardów [Sochaczew-Blonie district governor, Żyrardów regional commissioner], Letter (order) of 20.01.1941 to Jewish Council in Żyrardów
- The regulatory order concerning the apartments of the Jewish population transferred to Sochaczew.
- *Description:* transcript (2 copies), handwritten manuscript (Np*), pencil, German, Yiddish, 148×160 mm, ss. 2, pp. 2.

  In the margins a symbol (ink): "v."

**1074. RING. I/328/2. Mf. ŻIH—781; USHMM—12**

- After 3.02.1941, Warsaw Ghetto
- Arbeitsamt Sochaczew. Nebenstelle Żyrardów [Sochaczew Labor Office, Żyrardów Branch], Certificate dated 3.02.1941 for the Arbeitsamt employee Anders for taking washing machines from the Jewish district [?].
- *Description:* transcript (2 copies), handwritten manuscript (Np*), pencil, German, Yiddish, 148×160 mm, ss. 2, pp. 2.

  In the margins a symbol (ink): "v."

**1075. RING. I/947 (1266). (Lb. 943). Mf. ŻIH—830; USHMM—42**

- After 02.1941, Warsaw Ghetto
- NN., Account entitled "Zhirardov" [Żyrardów]
- Situation of the Jewish population in Żyrardów to 1939 (economic life, social and occupational

structure, relations with Poles, the Jewish community), as well as the most significant problems of Jews during the occupation until the moment of their expulsion from the town [February 1941].
- ***Description:*** transcript (2 copies), handwritten manuscript (U*), pencil, Yiddish, 146×204 mm, ss. 14, pp. 14.
  In the margins (first copy) a Hebrew letter (ink): "a" (alef).

1076. **RING. I/674/7. (Lb. 1688). Mf. ŻIH—816; USHMM—28**
- After 1939, Warsaw Ghetto
- NN., Account (accounts [?]) of the war of 1939
- Description of a journey along the route Żyrardów, Wiskitki, Łowicz, Zgierz, Stryków, Sochaczew (mood of the population, behavior of the Polish Army, Germans) (5–16.09.1939).
- ***Description:*** original or transcript, handwritten manuscript (H.W.*), ink, Yiddish, 150×185 mm, ss. 2, pp. 4.
  On p. 1 a date: "1940"[?].

1077. **RING. I/543/2. Mf. ŻIH—791; USHMM—22**
- 03/04.1942 [?], place unknown
- NN., Letter to NN. (Warsaw Ghetto) (fragment [?]). About the approaching annihilation.
- ***Description:*** original, handwritten manuscript on a postcard, Polish, 89×135 mm, damage and losses of text, ss. 1, pp. 1.

## V. Accounts of the September 1939 Campaign and of POW Camps

1078. **RING. I/983/1 (1302). (Lb. 763). Mf. ŻIH—831; USHMM—43**
- Date unknown, Warsaw Ghetto
- Dr. M.B., Account of the September 1939 campaign
- Author, physician (from Warsaw [?]), voluntarily reported to the Polish Army, as a private (szeregowy) in the 22nd regiment of light artillery; fought near Kamionka Strumiłowa, promoted to sergeant of artillery, in Pińczów he headed a hospital.
- ***Description:*** transcript, typescript, Polish, 220×350 mm, ss. 1, pp. 1.
  Published: BŻIH, no. 70/1969, pp. 110–111.

1079. **RING. I/983/2 (1302). (Lb. 763). Mf. ŻIH—831; USHMM—43**
- Date unknown, Warsaw Ghetto
- Dr. B., Account of the September 1939 campaign
- Author, physician, second lieutenant of the 2nd Sappers Battalion (2 baonu saperów kaniowskich) in Puławy, from 18.09.1939 in 26th regiment of light artillery, participant in the battle on the Bzura. After falling into captivity, he worked in a hospital for prisoners of war in Siedlce.
- ***Description:*** transcript, typescript, Polish, 210×295 mm, ss. 3, pp. 3.
  Published: BŻIH, no. 70/1969, pp. 108–110.

1080. **RING. I/145. (Lb. 1470). Mf. ŻIH—778; USHMM—9**
- 1.02.1942 and after 1.02.1942, Warsaw Ghetto
- Izrael Bursztyn, Account entitled "Di heldn fun der poylisher armey" [The heroes of the Polish army] (1.02.1942)
- Author (born 1908) before the war was a jeweler in Warsaw (ul. Mirowska 3), member of the sport club "Shtern" (Left Po'ale Tsiyon), took part in the September campaign (inter alia in the battle at the Bzura), as a private in the 65th regiment under the command of Lieutenant Wiśniewski. Bursztyn's address in the ghetto: ul. Ogrodowa 26.
- ***Description:*** transcript (a) (handwritten manuscript—Ł*, ink, 110×330–110×160 mm, damage and losses of text); transcript (b) (2 copies, handwritten manuscript—U*, pencil, 145×218 mm), Yiddish, ss. 29, pp. 34.
  Account written down by N.R. [Nechemiasz Tytelman].
  Index: Szymon Klejnic, husband of Bursztyn's sister; Major [Baruch] Steinberg and Rabbi Kestenberg, who administered the oath of allegiance of Jewish soldiers; soldier Elenberg, a locksmith from Radom—killed

1081. **RING. I/24. Mf. ŻIH—772; USHMM—3**
- After 09.1939, Warsaw
- M.D., Account entitled "Testimony of M.D. a [disa]bled corporal"
- Author, resident of Warsaw, was mobilized on 24.08.1939 as a reserve corporal into the 30th Regiment, took part in battles on the Warta; wounded 13.09 and was transported to Łódź. He describes stay in Łódź hospitals.
- ***Description:*** copies (2 copies), handwritten manuscript (JC*), Polish, pencil, 145×205 mm, minor damage and losses of text, ss. 10, pp. 10.
  Attached note by H.W. in Polish, Yiddish: "Account written down by Jechiel Górny, coworker of Oyneg Shabes, first and last names of informants in a majority of cases are not known out of conspiratorial considerations."

1082. **RING. I/983/3 (1302). (Lb. 763). Mf. ŻIH—831; USHMM—43**
- Date unknown, Warsaw Ghetto
- Dr. D., Account of the September 1939 campaign
- Author, physician, second lieutenant of the 31st regiment in Brześć; mood in the regiment after the outbreak of war, the journey from Brześć to Sochaczew.

• *Description:* transcript, typescript., Polish, 210×295 mm, ss. 1, pp. 1.
Notation by H.W.: "Submitted by Henryk Bieżuński."
Published: BŻIH, no. 70/1969, s.107–108.

**1083. RING. I/1027 (1346). (Lb. 343). Mf. ŻIH—831; USHMM—43**

• After 1940, Warsaw Ghetto
• F., Account entitled "Ekshumatsie fun a yidishn zelner" [Exhumation of a Jewish soldier]
• Author's brother, Eliezer F., a soldier in the Polish Army, died during combat in the region of Kampinos Forest of wounds sustained in the village K. and was buried together with other soldiers. Author, fulfilling the final wish of his dead brother, conducted an exhumation (spring 1940), in order to give him a Jewish burial. He describes the difficulties in preparing the exhumation. Appended copy of the journal (23.08–6.09.1939) of Eliezer F. found in the pocket of his uniform.
• *Description:* transcript (2 copies), handwritten manuscript (MS*), pencil, Yiddish, 148×208 mm, ss. 26, pp. 26.
In the margins letter (ink): "R" [reysh].
Published: *Selected Documents*, pp. 239–248.

**1084. RING. I/982 (1301). Mf. ŻIH—831; USHMM—43**

• After 06.1940, Warsaw Ghetto
• Two accounts by soldiers of the Polish Army about the September campaign in 1939 and stay in POW camps
1) J. Gr., sergeant of the 5th regiment of lancers in Ostrołęka, fought on the border of East Prussia, wounded near Kock (30.09.1939); later stayed in a hospital in Vienna and in POW camps: Kremnitz, Moosburg, and Ostrzeszów (from 4.05.1940); freed on 16.06.1940, returned to Warsaw;
2) L-in, private of the 115th regiment, fought in Podlasie, taken prisoner near Stoczek to Stalag Stablack in East Prussia; released on 13.05.1940 and sent to Warsaw.
• *Description:* transcript, typescript., Polish, 220×350 mm, ss. 2, pp. 2.
Attached note by H.W.: "Submitted by Henryk Bieżuński."

**1085. RING. I/462. (Lb. 1485). Mf. ŻIH—786; USHMM—17**

• After 1939, Warsaw Ghetto
• [M?]arek Kw-ny, Account entitled "Es volt mir liber geven a hiltserner krayts . . ." [I would have preferred a wooden cross . . .]
• Author, a soldier in the 8th Regiment in Płock, took part in the September campaign in defense of Modlin and spent four weeks in captivity in Stalag Soldau (Działdowo) and Iława (about the behavior of Polish soldiers and officers in relation to Jewish colleagues).
• *Description:* transcript, handwritten manuscript (Sz.*), ink, Yiddish, 160×195 mm, damage and losses of text, ss. 6, pp. 11.
Next to the account's title is a number (ink): "2."
Attached note by H.W.: "Sz. Szajnkinder recorded the testimony."

**1086. RING. I/1073 (1392). Mf. ŻIH—832; USHMM—44**

• After 02.1941, Warsaw Ghetto
• [Lewkowicz?], Account about Jewish prisoners from Stalag 21B
• Prisoners were transferred on 6.02.1941 from a camp [Thur (Tur)] to Częstochowa (6–10.02.1941), subsequently to Lublin (ul. Lipowa), whence they were marched to Biała Podlaska; author describes the several days of marching 14–16.02.1941.
• *Description:* original [?], handwritten manuscript, ink, Yiddish, 120×295 mm, minor damage and losses of text, ss. 4, pp. 4.
Attached note by H.W. in Yiddish: "By Lewkowicz, participant in the march."
Compare Ring. I/1154.

**1087. RING. I/422. (Lb. 1166). Mf. ŻIH—784; USHMM—15**

• 16.07.1941 and after 16.07.1941, Warsaw Ghetto
• [Marian Liberman], Recollections of a Polish Army soldier of stay in POW camp (09.1939–8.03.1940), (16.07.1941)
• Soldier of the 45th guard battalion in 1939, taken into German captivity near Ożarów. Stay in prison camps: in Częstochowa, Lamsdorf, Fallingbostel, and Alten Grabow-Stalag XIA, work in a sugar factory, relations with German workers and Polish colleagues.
• *Description:* original (handwritten manuscript, pencil, 220×355, 216×275 mm), transcript (2 copies, handwritten manuscript—JG*, pencil, 150×210 mm), Polish, ss. 29, pp. 32.
On p. 6 (original): "Marian Liberman wrote and dedicates to Mr.Wasser, a worthy friend and countryman."
On p. 1 (handwritten manuscript JG*) : "no. 4."
On p. 1 (original) information about articles on the author's inventions that ran in the *Głos Poranny* of 14 and 17.07.1939
Attached note by H.W.: "Jerzy Szaja (Łódź, Pabianice), recounts."[?]
Published: *Selected Documents*, pp. 215–221

**1088. RING. I/421. Mf. ŻIH—783; USHMM—14**

• 1942, Warsaw Ghetto
• Milo [?], account entitled "Fun gefangn-lager" [From the prison camp]
• Abuse of Jewish soldiers and residents of Wiskitki in 1939.
• *Description:* original or transcript, handwritten

manuscript, ink, Yiddish, 220×355 mm, minor damage and losses of text, ss. 1, pp. 2.

At the top of p. 1 a note by H.W. in Yiddish (ink): "3 standard pages" and [illegible].

Inventory: "Episodes of the [September] campaign of 1939 recorded by Hersz Weintraub."

**1089. RING. I/252. (Lb. 1526). Mf. ŻIH—780; USHMM—11. RING. I/496. (Lb. 473). Mf. ŻIH—788; USHMM—19**

- 06.1942, Warsaw Ghetto
- [Sz. Szajnkinder], Daily notes from the September campaign (18–21.09.1939) (fragment)
- Author, Polish Army sergeant, participant in the September campaign, service in the Warsaw area (Praga); assumption of company command, mood of the soldiers and civilian population, entry of Soviet Army into Poland, problems with food supply; stay in the quarters of Captain Ruczyński (Raczyński) in the region of ul. Kamionkowska and Terespolska in Praga.
- ***Description:*** Ring. I/252—original, typescript (handwritten manuscript—Sz.*, corrections and additions in ink), Yiddish, 202×187, 203×255 mm, damage and losses of text, ss. 5, pp. 5; Ring. I/496—original, typescript (handwritten manuscript—Sz.*, corrections and additions in ink), Yiddish, 205×295 mm, minor damage and losses of text, ss. 10, pp. 10.

Three chapters of the text survived: in Ring. I/496—chapter 24, entitled "Der nayer shef" [The New Chief]. Monday, 18.09.[1939]; chapter 25 entitled "Vos viln di Sovietn?" [What Do the Soviets Want?]. Tuesday and Wednesday, 19 and 20.09.[1939]; in Ring. I/252—chapter 26 entitled "Bay dem kapitan in der nayer kvartir" [With the captain in the new quarters]. Thursday, 21.09.1939.

Ring. I/252—On p. 1 note by H.W. in Yiddish: "5 standard pages."

Ring. I/252—Attached note by H.W. in Yiddish: "Szajnkinder, reporter, wrote personal recollections."

Ring. I/496—Attached note by H.W. in Yiddish: "Author Sz. Szajnkinder"; on p. 1 (chap. 24): handwritten note (See Ring. I/530) in Yiddish (ink): "Sz. Szajnkinder"; note by H.W. in Yiddish: "5 standard pages."; on p. 1 (chap. 25): note by H.W. in Yiddish: "6 standard pages" and "June 1942."

Inventory (Ring. I/252): "Text's author is Szymon Kincer." (According to Ruta Sakowska: "Szajnkinder ?".)

Inventory (Ring. I/496): "Text's author is Sz. Szajnkinder."

Index: Ołdak, Łukomski, Lieut. Domański, journalist and commander of the 1st platoon, Zapolski, Bugajski, Franke, Rogala, Corporal Zagórny

**1090. RING. I/458. (Lb. 1217). Mf. ŻIH—786; USHMM—17**

- After 03.1940, Warsaw Ghetto
- Samuel Zeldman, Account entitled "Oyf der defilade kayn Berlin" [On the march to Berlin]
- Author, soldier of the 14th regiment of the Polish Army (since 03.1938), fought in the September campaign, in German captivity (POW camps: Żyrardów, Ostrzeszów, Brandenburg, Frankfurt on the Oder, camp near Bydgoszcz), 11.03.1940 shipped out with 800 Jewish POWs to Biała Podlaska, then to Warsaw.
- ***Description:*** transcript, handwritten manuscript (Sz.*), ink, Yiddish, 145×224 mm, ss. 4, pp. 4.

Account written down by Sz. Szajnkinder (signature on p. 4).

Published: *Selected Documents*, pp. 227–231.

**1091. RING. I/498. (Lb. 1497). Mf. ŻIH—788; USHMM—19**

- After 09.1939, Warsaw Ghetto
- [Engineer Stefan Zuker?], Diary (August–September 1939) (fragment)
- Author, resident of Kalisz, owner or director of an industrial plant [?], preparation for war, protection of goods, escape to Warsaw, wartime destruction in the first days of September (Kalisz, Łódź, Łowicz).
- ***Description:*** transcript (2 copies), handwritten manuscript (CC*), pencil, Polish, 150×205 mm, serious damage and losses of text, ss. 48, pp. 48.

Attached note by H.W.: "Eng[ineer] Stefan Zucker of Kalisz."

Index: Lasman of Łowicz, Martinband [?], Stein of Kalisz, Lieut. Romski, Banasiak, Drejlich, locksmith from Kalisz, Corporal Norekowski [?], Wiktor Majorek, Landsberg, Ferenc, corporal of the 39th regiment of Lwów riflemen

**1092. RING. I/337. Mf. ŻIH—781; USHMM—12**

- After 27.09.1939, Warsaw Ghetto
- NN., Recollections of September 1939—siege of Warsaw (1–27.09.1939)
- Bombardment of the city, evacuation of the government, refugees, fate of the civilian population, destruction, capitulation.
- ***Description:*** transcript (2 copies), handwritten manuscript (CC*), pencil, Polish, 150×205 mm, minor damage and losses of text, ss. 26, pp. 26.

Published: BŻIH, no. 70/1969, pp. 101–105.

**1093. RING. I/159. Mf. ŻIH—778; USHMM—9**

- After 10.1939, place unknown
- NN., Recollections of the September campaign (27.08–15.10.1939)
- Author from Poznań region, mobilized at the rank of cadet (podchorążego) into the 68th regiment in September, participated in the battle on the Bzura, captured and held in Ostrów Wielkopolski, 15.10. was

released to go home. Describes the attitudes of Jewish soldiers and relations with Poles.
- ***Description:*** original, handwritten manuscript, notebook, ink, Polish, 157×198 mm, minor damage and losses of text, ss. 7, pp. 13.
  Published: *Selected Documents,* pp. 221–226 (fragment).

### 1094. RING. I/188. Mf. ŻIH—779; USHMM—10

- After 27.11.1941, Warsaw Ghetto
- NN., Account entitled "How anti-aircraft defense was organized during the siege of Warsaw in September 1939 in the Jewish building at ulica Franciszkańska 30" (27.11.1941)
- Discussion of the merit of Mr. K., the anti-aircraft defense commander of the apartment house at ul. Franciszkańska 30 in Warsaw (preparation of shelters, defense of the building against fire, protection of the belongings of residents of neighboring apartment houses, etc.).
- ***Description:*** transcript (2 copies), handwritten manuscript (JG*), pencil, Polish, 145×200 mm, minor damage and losses of text, ss. 10, pp. 10.
  In the margin of p. 1 a note by H.W.: "Kon."
  Inventory: "Prepared by A. [sic] Koniński." Presumably the data is based on lost postwar notes by H.W.

### 1095. RING. I/672. Mf. ŻIH—816; USHMM—28

- Date unknown, place unknown
- NN., Account of September 1939 (fragment)
- Description of a meeting with a group of soldiers (among others, with a sergeant, a Jew from Łódź, a teacher), bombardment of an unknown city.
- ***Description:*** original or transcript, handwritten manuscript, ink, Polish, 220×350 mm, damage and losses of text, text illegible in places, ss.1, pp. 2.
  On p. 1 a note (pencil): illegible.

### 1096. RING. I/985 (1304). Mf. ŻIH—831; USHMM—43

- After 1939, Warsaw Ghetto
- NN., Account entitled "Story of a Jewish private about experiences during the September campaign"
- Author, a rifleman with the 3rd machine gun platoon of the 3rd battalion of an unknown regiment, took part in battles near Ciechanów, later in the defense of Warsaw. He describes relations among soldiers, manifestations of antisemitism.
- ***Description:*** original (o), handwritten manuscript (FLIG*), ink, Polish, 220×353 mm, text difficult to read in places, ss. 6, pp. 12.
  Attached note by H.W.: "Recorded by Daniel Fligelman."
  Published: *Selected Documents,* pp. 231–239.

### 1097. RING. I/1028 (1347). (Lb. 398). Mf. ŻIH—831; USHMM—43

- After 4.07.1941, Warsaw Ghetto
- NN., "Derinerungen fun a yidishn dokter" [Recollections of a Jewish physician]
- Author, physician, soldier of the Polish Army, in 1939 worked in a field hospital near Lublin. He describes the evacuation to the east, situation of Jews in Łuck and Białystok after entry of Soviet forces, return to Warsaw.
- ***Description:*** transcript (2 copies), handwritten manuscript (BW*), pencil, Yiddish, 148×207 mm, minor damage and losses of text, ss. 12, pp. 12.
  In the margin a letter: "K"; on p. 1 (first copy) a symbol (red pencil): "+."

### 1098. RING. I/1076 (1395). (Lb. 1135). Mf. ŻIH—832; USHMM—44

- Date unknown, Warsaw Ghetto
- NN., Account about experiences from 7.09.1939 in Warsaw
- Author seeks mobilization point, journey under bombs to Saska Kępa and Grochów, return to the left bank of the Vistula. Description of chaos, panic, destruction.
- ***Description:*** original (handwritten manuscript, ink, 223×348 mm, minor damage and losses of text), transcript (3 copies, typescript, 217×277 mm, damage and losses of text), Polish, ss. 4, pp. 5.
  Attached note by H.W.: "Text forwarded by the Youth Department of ŻTOS."

### 1099. RING. I/445. Mf. ŻIH—785; USHMM—16

- After 1939, Warsaw Ghetto
- NN., Account of the September campaign 1939
- Author from Warsaw, mobilized on 1.09.1939 into the Polish Army (guard battalion, ul. Czerniakowska (fort [?]), was a clerk in the captain's office), Polish–Jewish relations in the military, participation in the defense of Warsaw.
- ***Description:*** original or transcript, handwritten manuscript, ink, Yiddish, 160×200 mm, ss. 6, pp. 12.
  Inventory: "Testimony of Zelman Kawa."

### 1100. RING. I/486. Mf. ŻIH—787; USHMM—18

- After 09.1939, place unknown
- NN., Student's Account of September 1939
- First day of war in a small town near Warsaw, description of German air raid, meeting with a longtime friend from school.
- ***Description:*** original [?] (handwritten manuscript, ink, 210×298 mm), transcripts (2 copies, handwritten manuscript—CA*, pencil, 145×210 mm), Polish, ss. 18, pp. 20.
  Inventory: "Forwarded by Salomea Ostrowska."

### 1101. RING. I/1220/50. Mf. ŻIH—835; USHMM—47

- After 09.1939, place unknown
- NN., Account of the September 1939 campaign (fragment)
- Author, resident of Warsaw, describes the city on 5/6.09.1939; instead of fleeing to the east, he reported to the army as a volunteer.

• *Description:* original, handwritten manuscript, ink, Polish, 209×296 mm, ss. 1, pp. 2.
 On p. 1 at top is a notation : "III" and title: "Warsaw at night. . . ."

**1102. RING. I/1220/51. Mf. ŻIH—835; USHMM—47**

• After 1939, place unknown
• NN., Account of stay in a POW camp (Germans)
• Living conditions, food, work.
• *Description:* original or transcript, handwritten manuscript, pencil, Polish, 208×108 mm, ss. 1, pp. 2.

**1103. RING. I/94. (Lb. 864). Mf. ŻIH—776; USHMM—7**

• After 03.1940, Warsaw Ghetto
• NN., Account entitled ". . . die waren in Deutschland gefangen" [. . . these were imprisoned in Germany]
• Author, Polish Army non-com, taken captive on 12.09.1939 in Siedlce, where he was initially imprisoned, then transferred to POW camp in Stablack (East Prussia). Description of relations among prisoners, treatment of Jewish soldiers by fellow prisoners and by Germans (separate quartering, slave labor and inadequate food). In November and December 1939 with a group of Jewish POWs, he was transported to the vicinity of Zatoka Kurońska to work on strengthening antiflood levees; returned to camp at the end of December and stayed there until 13.03.1940. After transfer to Warsaw he was released.
• *Description:* transcript (2 copies), typescript, Polish, 205×292 mm, minor damage and losses of text, ss. 34, pp. 34.
 On p. 1 (2 copies) handwritten note by H.W.: "Fligar."
 The account was recorded by Daniel Fligelman; see *Kronika getta*, p. 486.
 Index: Kazimierz Świtalski, Speaker of the Sejm of the Polish Republic, prisoner in Stablack

**1104. RING. I/377. (Lb. 1480). Mf. ŻIH—782; USHMM—13**

• 2.03.1942, after 2.03.1942, Warsaw Ghetto
• NN., "Vegn lager far idishe gefangene in Lublin" [On the camp for Jewish prisoners in Lublin] (2.03.1942)
• Text compiled from accounts of two former soldiers of the Polish Army taken into German captivity in 1939. Description of their stay in stalags (until the end of 1940) and in a camp outside Lublin (near Majdanek) 01.1941–17.02.1942 (murderous labor, collective punishment for escapes of prisoners, diseases, hunger, beating of prisoners, roundups in the Lublin ghetto; commandant of the camp was M.G. Dolf, who himself killed many Jews).
• *Description:* original or transcript (handwritten manuscript -Ś*, ink, 142×218, minor damage and losses of text, missing page 5), transcript (3 copies, handwritten manuscript -U*, pencil, 144×220 mm), Yiddish, ss. 49, pp. 49.
 Attached note by H.W. in Yiddish: "Prepared by Abram Lewin."
 Inventory: "Author of the text is Abraham Lewin."
 Index: Baran, Janusz Radziwiłł

## VI. Materials concerning Labor Camps, Transit Camps, and Annihilation Camps (Centers)

**1105. RING. I/671. Mf. ŻIH—816; USHMM—28**

a)

• After 05.1941, Warsaw Ghetto
• Order of German authorities concerning summoning to compulsory labor (labor camps) of Jews from the Warsaw Ghetto (fragment)
• Schedule of medical examinations for persons summoned to labor.
• *Description:* transcript, typescript, German, 175×250 mm, damage and losses of text, ss. 1, pp. 1.

b)

• After 31.12 1941, Warsaw Ghetto
• NN., Report (Memorial) concerning labor camps for Jews within the Generalgouvernement (fragment)
• Charts and tables: dates of transports, lists of camps as well as firms employing Jewish workers, occupation and number of those shipped out between January and December 1941.
• *Description:* transcript, typescript, German, Polish, 120×175, 175×250 mm, damage and losses of text, ss. 8, pp. 8.

**1106. RING. I/169. (Lb. 274, 275). Mf. ŻIH—779; USHMM—10**

• Date unknown, Warsaw Ghetto
• [Jewish Council in Warsaw], Registration form for persons returning from labor camps.
• *Description:* original, hectographed typescript, Polish, 208×285 mm, ss. 1, pp. 2
 Appended handwritten manuscript note by H.W.

**1107. RING. I/1220/41. Mf. ŻIH—835; USHMM—47**

• After 12.1941, Warsaw Ghetto
• NN., Study concerning labor camps (fragments)
• Tables: inter alia "Transports of workers to labor camps in 1941" (date of transport, camp, number of people, number of deaths in the camps).
• *Description:* original [?], handwritten manuscript, ink, Polish, 222×299 mm, damage and losses of text, ss. 2, pp. 2.
 Doc. written on the back of a record book [?] of persons with meal privileges in public kitchens in the Warsaw Ghetto (original, handwritten

manuscript, pencil, Polish). The preserved ss. (2) concern residents of ul. Pawia 12, 16, and 18, giving name and surname, apartment number, number of persons with paid and free dinner privileges, and the serial number of the kitchen.

**1108. RING. I/396. Mf. ŻIH—783; USHMM—14**

- Date unknown, Warsaw Ghetto
- [Goldman], Account entitled "Refleksn fun a rayze iber belzhetser lager-kompleks" [Reflections from a trip through the Bełżec camp complex]
- Situation in labor camps belonging to the Bełżec complex (10 camps, among others Bełżec, Płazów, Cieszanów, ca. 12,000–13,000 people, Commandant Dolf, housing, sanitation, medical and feeding conditions).
- ***Description:*** transcript, handwritten manuscript (MS*), pencil, Yiddish, 150×208 mm, extensive minor damage and losses of text, ss. 3, pp. 3.
  On p. 1 a note by H.W. in Yiddish: "Camp. . . [?]. In the margins a Hebrew letter: "mem."
  Attached note by H.W. in Yiddish: "Bełżec camp complex (1940). Account by Goldman, an inspector for the Joint, prepared by H.W."
  Index: Dr. Fajgeles of Lublin

**1109. RING. I/423. Mf. ŻIH—784; USHMM—15**

- 03.1942 and After 03.1942, Warsaw Ghetto
- [Perec Opoczyński], Study entitled "Belzhets. Tsvang arbet-lager unter Dolks [Dolfs] mamshole" [Bełżec. Forced Labor Camp under Dol[f]'s Reign] (03.1942)
- Improvement and fortification projects along the border, hunger, poor housing and sanitation conditions, beatings, shooting of prisoners. Prisoners from: Warsaw, Łowicz, Góra Kalwaria, Grójec, Biała Rawska, Skierniewice, Opatów, Kielce, Częstochowa, Radom, Lublin, Opole Lubelski, Chełm, Grabowiec, Izbica Lubelska, Lubartów, Piaski, and Gypsies from Hamburg. Text prepared on the basis of accounts of former camp inmates.
- ***Description:*** transcript, handwritten manuscript (RR*, ink, 155×200 mm, significant damage and losses of text), transcript (2 copies, handwritten manuscript—U*, pencil, 150×207 mm, significant damage and losses of text), Yiddish, ss. 35, pp. 44.
  Attached note by H.W.: "Prepared by Perec Opoczyński on the basis of testimonies."
  Index: Barteczko, boxer from Czech Lands; Dr. Fejgełes, physician; members of the aid commission of the Jewish Council in Lublin: Beker, engineer Hofnagel, Hersz Zylber, Szmul Wolman, Goldkrojt, Tenenbaum, Gradel, Zylbergelt, Panter, Goldberg (secretary); Beniamin Zabłudowski of the Jewish Council in Warsaw

**1110. RING. I/410. Mf. ŻIH—783; USHMM—14**

- After 12.1940, Warsaw Ghetto
- [Dr. Akiba Uryson], Account entitled "Di tsurikgekumene fun di arbet-lager" [Returnees from the labor camp]
- Serious condition of those returning from the labor camp in Bełżec (deadly labor, hunger, beating by the camp guards).
- ***Description:*** transcript (2 copies), handwritten manuscript (MS*), pencil, Yiddish, 145×208 mm, minor damage and losses of text (second copy), ss. 2, pp. 2.
  Attached note by H.W. in Yiddish: "Dr. Uryson's Account." For another text of Dr. Uryson's, see Ring. I/270.
  Index: Obernitz, camp manager

**1111. RING. I/599/113. Mf. ŻIH—812; USHMM—24**

- 29.10.1940, Bełżec
- NN. (Marysia) (Bełżec), Letter of 29.10.1940 to Jewish Community in Warsaw
- Information about extreme degradation, numerous victims, and extreme violence in the labor camp.
- ***Description:*** original, handwritten manuscript, ink, chancellory stamp ("Secretariat of the Labor Battalion" in Warsaw: 6.11.1940; stamp of the Jewish Council in Warsaw [?]: "2.11.1040"), Polish, 115×188 mm, minor damage and losses of text, text illegible in places, ss. 2, pp. 4.

**1112. RING. I/592/1. Mf. ŻIH—792; USHMM—23**

- After 30.10.1940, Warsaw Ghetto
- NN. (Biłgoraj), Letters of 28 and 30.10.1940 to NN. (Warsaw)
- Author released from labor camp on 23.10.1940 asks sister for aid.
- ***Description:*** transcript (2 copies), handwritten manuscript (MS*), pencil, Yiddish, 148×208 mm, minor damage and losses of text, ss. 2, pp. 2.
  Sheets have pagination (ink): "1" and "3" (missing p. 2 [?])
  Note by H.W. in Yiddish (ink): "Two letters for immediate aid from a returnee from camp."
  In the margin a Hebrew letter (ink): "t" (taf).
  Doc. was kept in a binder.
  Appended note by H.W.: "Warsaw residents in labor camps 1940, forwarded by H.W."

**1113. RING. I/592/9. Mf. ŻIH—792; USHMM—23**

- 30.04.1942, Britz near Eberswalde
- B. Taube (Waldlager Britz, Kreis Angermünde Wh. 15/3), Letter of 30.04.1942 to Uszer Taube (Warsaw, ul. Nowolipie 15, apt. 30)
- Living conditions in the camp, work in a factory, ethnic composition of prisoner population. Until 24.04.1942 he was in Pinnów [?] near Słubice.
- ***Description:*** original, handwritten manuscript on a postcard, postmark, stamp of Jewish Council in Warsaw, pencil, Yiddish in Roman transliteration, 145×104 mm, minor damage and losses of text, ss. 1, pp. 2.

Published: *Listy o Zagładzie*, pp. 232–234.
See Ring. I/592/10–11.
Index: Łajb Kleczewski

### 1114. RING. I/592/13. Mf. ŻIH—792; USHMM—23

- 7.06.1942, Broniewice near Mogilno
- Fela Rybska (Gemeinschaftslager Bronwitz [Broniewice] near Mogilno), Letter of 7.06.1942 to Uszer Taube (Warsaw, ul. Nowolipie 15 [m. 30])
- Notation about conditions in the labor camp.
- ***Description:*** original, handwritten manuscript on a postcard, postmark and stamp of Jewish Council in Warsaw, pencil, Polish, 146×103 mm, minor damage and losses of text, ss. 1, pp. 2.

Published: *Listy o Zagładzie*, pp. 234–235.
Index: Rózia Lewin

### 1115. RING. I/412. (Lb. 1000). Mf. ŻIH—836; USHMM—67

a)

- 1942, Warsaw Ghetto
- Jakow Grojnowski [Yankev Groynovski], Account entitled "Gvies-eydes funem tsvang-kabren . . ." [Testimony of the forced-labor gravedigger . . .]
- Author from Izbica Kujawska transported on 5.01.1942 to the death camp in Chełmno on the Ner. He worked at digging graves and unloading bodies from gas chamber trucks. He describes the organization of the mass destruction of Jews and Gypsies; he escaped from the camp on 19.01.1942.
- ***Description:*** transcript (3 copies), typescript, Yiddish, 207×142, 207×295 mm, minor damage and losses of text, (three copies: serious damage and losses of text), ss. 42, pp. 42.

Presumably, the authentic name of the author was Szlamek (Szlomo) Winer [Yiddish: Viner], which is affirmed by the testimony of Tauba Omur [?] (see Ring. I/394); and two postwar testimonies from 1945, by Michał Podchlebnik, also an escapee from Chełmno, and Bajla Altschuld [Altschul?] (Instytut Pamięci Narodowej, Warsaw, Record of the Judicial Investigation of Władysław Bednarz, catalog no. 271, vol. I, ss. 10–12; catalog no. 271, vol. IV, p. 314; Lucja Pawlicka-Nowak of the Museum in Konin provided copies of the aforementioned testimonies and further information about Szlamek Winer). In the testimony of Wolkowicz ("Dombie," Ring. I/799), Szlamek is called Fajner; Ruta Sakowska also accepts this spelling of his name (see *Dwa etapy*, p. 132; *Listy o Zagładzie*, p. 113). After escaping from Chełmno, Szlamek started to use the pseudonym Jakub Grojnowski. Hersz Wasser most likely did not know Szlamek's [real] name. Therefore, Wasser used Szlamek's pseudonym Jakub Grojnowski or his relatives' name Bajler when writing about him. See Ring. I/596 and the similar entry, Lb. 1000, in the 1946 "Katalog Archiwum dr Emanuela Ringelbluma," as well as in the Inw.: "Zeznanie o obozie śmierci Chełmno Abrahama Bajler (Grunowski) [sic] spisane przez Hersza Wassera" [Testimony about the Chełmno death camp by Abraham Bajler (Grunowski) [sic] recorded by Hersz Wasser].

Published: *Dwa etapy*, pp. 112–133; *Mówią świadkowie Chełmna*, Konin-Łódź 1996, pp. 17–34; Martin Gilbert, *The Holocaust*, New York 1985, pp. 252–279.
See HWC, 4/1 (fourth copy, typescript, ss. 14).

b)

- 5.02.1942, Piotrków
- Jewish Council in Piotrków, Certificate of 5.02.1942 of the registration of Jakub Grojnowski for a temporary stay (Piotrków, ul. Grodzka 3).
- ***Description:*** original, duplicated typescript, handwritten manuscript, ink, German, 210×103 mm, minor damage and losses of text, ss. 1, pp. 1.

Published: *Oneg Schabbat*, p. 37.

c)

- Before 18.03.1942, place unknown
- [Jakub Grojnowski] Szlamek [Winer?], Photograph.
- ***Description:*** original, photograph, 40×65 mm, ss. 1, pp. 2.

On p. 2 a note (handwritten manuscript, ink, Polish): "As a souvenir I offer my own likenesses [sic] to the Wassers, Szlamek. Warsaw, 18.03.1942."
Attached note by H.W. in Yiddish (fragment).
Published: *Oneg Schabbat*, pp. 36–37.

### 1116. RING. I/543/1. Mf. ŻIH—791; USHMM—22

- 01.1942, place unknown.
- Gelbart, Letter to Rywen [Gelbart] (Warsaw Ghetto)
- About mass murder of Jews in the death camp in Chełmno (inter alia, residents of Kłodawa).
- ***Description:*** original, handwritten manuscript, ink, Polish, 146×203 mm, ss. 1, pp. 2.

Published: *Listy o Zagładzie*, pp. 19–20.

### 1117. RING. I/413. Mf. ŻIH—783; USHMM—14

- After 01.1942, Warsaw Ghetto
- NN., Report entitled "Die Vorfälle in Kulmhof [Chełmno]" [The events in Chełmno]
- Organization of the death camp and process of mass executions of Jews (December 1941–January 1942).
- ***Description:*** (3 copies, p. 4 in 4 copies), typed, handwritten additions, ink (pp. 2 and 3 in the third copy), German, 210×x297 mm, damage and losses of text (third copy), ss. 16, pp. 16.

In individual copies, pages from different typed copies are mixed. Thus, pp. 3 and 5 of the first copy are in the third copy.
Text based inter alia on the account of Jakub Grojnowski from Ring. I/412; see also Ring. I/473, I/665, I/937.

**1118. RING. I/1055 (1374). Mf. ŻIH—832; USHMM—44**

- After 05.1941, Warsaw Ghetto
- Jakub Hoffnung (born 1895), Account of stay in the labor camp in Czyżew (missing conclusion)
- Author seized 8.05.1941[?] in the Warsaw Ghetto, was transported to labor camp in Czyżew (describes living conditions in the camp, food, mistreatment by Jewish guards).
- ***Description:*** original or transcript, handwritten manuscript (TT*), pencil, Yiddish, 150×222, 175×222 mm, ss. 3, pp. 6.
  Attached note by H.W.

**1119. RING. I/670. (Lb. 173). Mf. ŻIH—816; USHMM—28**

- After 28.10.1940, place unknown
- SS. Bauvorhaben Ostpolen. Der Baustab [SS. East Poland Construction Planning. Construction Headquarters] (Dębica), Circular letter of 28.10.1940 to subordinate firms
- Information about a ban on arbitrary beating and punishment of Jews working on the SS Bauvorhaben contract. Letter signed Heidelberg, chief of the Baustab.
- ***Description:*** transcript, typescript, German, 208×290 mm, ss. 1, pp. 1.

**1120. RING. I/1118 (1437). (Lb. 940). Mf. ŻIH—833; USHMM—45**

- After 7.11.1941, Warsaw Ghetto
- "Notice of departure from work" dated 4.11.1941 by the firm Continentale Wasserwerks-Gesellschaft, [Gmbh] Berlin Charlottenburg 2, Bau—Dębica, [regarding] the laborer Jeszai Syrkus (born 2.03.1924) of Warsaw (ul. Krochmalna 31, apt. 39) for the ZUS (Social Insurance Office)
- Information about the shooting of Jeszai Syrkus by an SS-man on 3.11.1941.
- ***Description:*** transcript (detailed copy of the filled-out ZUS form), handwritten manuscript, German, Polish, pencil, ink, 197×140 mm, ss. 1, pp. 1.
  Stamp (transcript): Continentale Wasserwerks-Gesellschaft, GmbH, Berlin Charlottenburg 2, Bau—Dębica.
  Notation by H.W. Yiddish (ink): "108–1942/1 January."

**1121. RING. I/592/6. Mf. ŻIH—792; USHMM—23**

- 8.08.1941, Jasło
- Fragment of a postal money order for the sum of 41 zł 78 gr sent out by Emil Ludwig Bauunternehmung [Construction Firm] in Jasło.
- ***Description:*** original, printed, handwritten manuscript, postmark, German, 40×102 mm, Polish, ss. 1, pp. 2.
  Letter carrier's stamp: "Paid."
  On the back is a note in German: "Employees of this camp were transferred to the labor camp in Dębica."

**1122. RING. I/592/5. Mf. ŻIH—792; USHMM—23**

- 20.06.1941, Dęblin—labor camp
- Salek Goldsobel (Dęblin, Air Field Labor Camp, in care of J. Grudka), Letter of 20.06.1941 to Ch. Goldsobel (Warsaw, ul. Nowolipie 31, apt. 10a)
- Poor housing conditions, efforts to obtain release from the camp.
- ***Description:*** original, handwritten manuscript on a postcard, postmark and stamp of the Jewish Council in Warsaw, pencil, Polish, 147×104 mm, minor damage and losses of text, ss. 1, pp. 2.

**1123. RING. I/1/2. (Lb. 678). Mf. ŻIH—770; USHMM—1**

- After 25.06.1940, Warsaw Ghetto
- [Olicki, Dr.], "Recollections of the labor camp in Drewnica" near Warsaw (April–June 1940)
- Account of the situation of Jewish prisoners and the kind of work carried out by them in the camp until 25.06.1940.
- ***Description:*** original or transcript, handwritten manuscript, notebook, ink, with pencil additions (different handwriting), Polish, 140×200 mm, ss. 10, pp. 8.
  Authorship determined on the basis of the list of 1946. The surname of Dr. Olicki also appears in the doc. on p. 7 (pencil).

**1124. RING. I/388. Mf. ŻIH—783; USHMM—14**

- Date unknown, Warsaw Ghetto
- NN., Account entitled "Varshe-Drevnitse. (Iberlebenishn, pasirungn, un epizodn inem tsvangs arbayts lager Drevnitse)" [Warsaw-Drewnica. (Experiences, events, and episodes in the Drewnica forced labor camp)]
- Hard conditions of labor, housing and food. Physician and manager of the camp were Jews.
- ***Description:*** original or transcript (handwritten manuscript—U* [?], ink, 110×350 mm, minor damage and losses of text, illegible in places), transcript (3 copies, handwritten manuscript- BW*, pencil, 147×205 mm), Yiddish, ss. 53, pp. 60.
  Page 15 (transcript, third copy) was found in Ring. I/1220; apparently, it was misplaced during the packing into the boxes, since there appear on it different traces of water stains, etc. In the margin it has a symbol (pencil): "x." In the transcripts (handwritten manuscript—BW*) in the margins is a symbol: "-"

**1125. RING. I/228. (Lb. 230). Mf. ŻIH—780; USHMM—11**

- After 20.05.1941, Warsaw Ghetto
- "Record of interview" of Zygmunt Dajtelbaum on 20.05.1941, regarding his stay in the labor camp in Drewnica

- Zygmunt Dajtelbaum, together with wife Berta, refugees from Kraków, were residents of the Shelter for Refugees at ul. Mławska 8; he reported voluntarily to the labor camp (Collection Point for Camp Laborers, ul. Leszno 84) and from 18.04. until the beginning of May 1941 stayed in the camp in Drewnica. He describes his wife's problems with sending parcels and money for him, describes attitudes reigning in the camp and personnel who tormented the camp inmates (camp physician NN., section head Messeing, former employee of the Order Service and another section head NN.).
- ***Description:*** original and transcript or transcript (2 copies), typescript, Polish, l., 210×293 mm, minor damage and losses of text, ss. 2, pp. 2

  In the lower left corner on first copy is an illegible signature.

### 1126. RING. I/397. (Lb. 964). Mf. ŻIH–783; USHMM–14

- After 06.1941, Warsaw Ghetto
- [Stefan Cukierman], Account entitled "Impressions of the labor camp" in Frysztak
- Author, a young man, an employee of "Toporol," seized on 14.05.1941 in the ghetto, sent to the camp; journey, work and housing in the camp; by accident released to go home.
- ***Description:*** original or transcript (handwritten manuscript, ink, 145×208 mm), transcript (3 copies, handwritten manuscript—JG*, pencil, 146×205 mm), Polish, ss. 12, pp. 14.

  On p. 1 (transcript, first and second copies) a note by H.W. (ink): "Frysztak"; on p. 1 (second copy) a note by H.W.: "Stefan Cukierman."

  Attached note by H.W.: "Testimony of Stefan Cukierman, student of Toporol, through the mediation of Chil Górny."

  Part of doc. was transferred from Ring. I/414. See also Ring. I/414 entry in Inventory: "Testimony of 'Toporol' student Izrael Bursztyn in camp."

  Published: *Selected Documents*, pp. 268–270.

### 1127. RING. I/607. Mf. ŻIH–814; USHMM–26

- After 05.1941, Warsaw Ghetto
- Records of accounts (interviews) concerning the situation in labor camps in Garwolin, Wilga, Narty, Łowicz, Dąbrowice near Skierniewice (30.04–8.05.1941)
- Authors of the accounts were chiefly camp inmates from Warsaw. Information about conditions of work, housing, feeding, treatment of prisoners, personnel matters. Appended records of testimonies of physicians treating former camp inmates.
- ***Description:*** transcript, typescript, German, 110×116, 200×255 mm, damage and losses of text, ss. 57, pp. 57.

  Attached note by H.W.

  Index: Matejac, camp commandant; Szyja Herbst (age 25), ul. Niska 71, apt. 2; Aron Bleifeder (age 24), ul. Prosta 19, apt. 27; Izrael Żelezny (age 25), ul. Dzielna 15; Aron Horenglas (age 28), ul. Prosta 19, apt. 31a; Icek Blutsztein, ul. Sapieżyńska 51; Aron Goldwasser, ul. Waliców 30; Matep[?] Aufgang (age 16), ul. Nowolipie 53; Mordcha Menachem Ocap (age 20), ul. Franciszkańska 5, apt. 12; Joel Feldman, ul. 22; Dawid Szpanin (age 35), ul. Parysowska 19; Abram Szczawiński (age 17), ul. Dzika 3, apt. 37; Abram Lubartowski (age 17), ul. Świętojerska 18, apt. 69; Jakub Fryd (age 18), ul. Pańska 59; Dawid Cwajgenhaft (age 36), ul. Nowolipki 32, apt. 48; Józef Tredler (age 23), ul. Nowolipie 30, apt. 69; Lejb Soliński (age 29), ul. Ostrowska 14, apt. 2; Szlama Szulc (age 17), ul. Krochmalna 54, apt. 22; Tojwja [. . .] zman (age 31), ul. Ogrodowa 34, apt. 22; Chil Guzik (age 27), ul. Nowolipie 23, apt. 55; Moszek Koper (age 19), ul. Śliska 16, apt. 3; Josek Durstmann (age 18), Wołyńska 11; Lejbuś Filcman (age 18), ul. Nowolipie 54, apt. 2; Jeremiasz Frenkiel (age 35), ul. Grzybowska 22; Jakub Szulim Bromberger (age 18), ul. Gęsia 24, apt. 39; Hersz Pasternak (age 38), ul. Gęsia 4; Szmul Pinkus (age 31), ul. Smocza 40, apt. 38; Boruch Icek Łodzeń (age 32), ul. Ogrodowa 46; Dr. Lipsztat; Daniel Letman (age 45), ul. Krochmalna 15, apt. 108; Natan Zylberman (age 18), ul. Miła 3, apt. 22; Abram Fetman (age 31), ul. Grzybowska 5; Mendel Cwajg (age 22), ul. Nowolipki 55; Chaim Kelter; Neuhaus; Chanachowski; Lejb Hersz, ul. Smocza 4; M. Rozenkranc; Sane Rozenfeld; Wolf Spektor; Idel Gros; Michael Kuper, ul. Śliska 62; Mordka Zylberberg; Josek Forman (age 22), tailor, ul. Grzybowska [. . .]; Józef Fiszer; Jankiel Lejderender (age 38), ul. Franciszkańska 11; Jankiel Grynberg (age 31), ul. Nalewki 30; Icek Szerar; Aron Hipsza; Moszek Lewkowicz, ul. Leszno; Gerszon Kornblum (age 33), ul. Dzielna 23; M. Grynberg, manager of the camp; Motek Rozenberg; Haskel Zalcman; Hersz Wasersztejn; Jankiel Borensztajn; Symcha Wajcel; Gejblum

### 1128. RING. I/385/7. Mf. ŻIH–783; USHMM–14

- Date unknown, Warsaw Ghetto
- NN., Note on beating of a boy in labor camp near Grójec [?] (fragment)
- Boy, after being beaten up by guards in camp, was released; on the way back to Warsaw, attacked and again beaten up by drunken Poles. He died in hospital.
- ***Description:*** transcript, typescript, Polish, 168×100 mm, extensive damage and losses of text, ss. 1, pp. 1.

  Document was probably a fragment of a larger text.

**1129. RING. I/404. (Lb. 1099). Mf. ŻIH—783; USHMM—14**

- Date unknown, Warsaw Ghetto
- NN., Account entitled "Hakhshore be-nusekh ashkenaz" [(Zionist) Pioneer Training in the German style]
- Author reported for work in a camp organized by Toporol (hard agricultural labor, unloading coal) near Skierniewice (Gzdów and vicinity).
- ***Description:*** transcript (3 copies), typescript, Yiddish, 208×292 mm, damage and losses of text, ss. 36, pp. 36.
  Attached note by H.W.: "Skierniewice. Agricultural work org[anized] by Toporol. Anonymous report, forwarded to the archive by Lajb Goldin."
  Index: Borowski, Kazimierz Blaucwirn[?] of Kalisz managed the work in Gzdów

**1130. RING. I/171. Mf. ŻIH—779; USHMM—10**

- After 8.08.1941, Warsaw Ghetto
- NN., Diary of stay in labor camp at the estate of Kamion near Skierniewice (4–8.08.1941)
- March through Warsaw to the station, attitude of Polish population to prisoners, conditions of housing, labor, and food in the camp, behavior of the administrators and group leaders.
- ***Description:*** original (handwritten manuscript, ink, 120×200 mm), transcript (2 copies, handwritten manuscript—JG*, pencil, 145×208 mm), Polish, minor damage and losses of text, ss. 24, pp. 32.
  Part of the doc. transferred from Ring. I/348. Ring. I/348—Inventory: "Written by an unknown camp inmate, a 17-year-old boy. Forwarded to the archive by engineer Kalnicki of 'Toporol.'"

**1131. RING. I/379. Mf. ŻIH—782; USHMM—13**

- After the first half of 1941, Warsaw Ghetto
- NN., Account entitled "Kampinos"
- Author from Warsaw, arrested during Passover 1941, shipped out with a group of ca. 200 persons to labor camp (Józefów near Kampinos) (description of camp, conditions of work in land improvement, housing, food, 53 fatalities, 6 weeks of work, information about a Catholic priest's call for aid for prisoners).
- ***Description:*** transcript (2 copies), typescript, 205×285 mm, minor damage and losses of text, ss. 68, pp. 68.
  On p. 1 (first copy) note in Yiddish (handwritten manuscript—LEC*, pencil): "Kampinos."
  Inventory: "Experiences of Rabbi Chitowski."
  Text written down by Szymon Huberband; see *Kronika getta*, pp. 473, 484.
  Published: *Kiddush Hashem*, pp. 71–101.

**1132. RING. I/425. (Lb. 920). Mf. ŻIH—784; USHMM—15**

- After 1940, Warsaw Ghetto
- [Engineer A. Reinberg], Memorandum entitled "Remarks [about] forced [labor camps?] in Lublin region and possibilities [of improving?] conditions in these camps"
- People who are unprepared or unable to perform hard labor (minors, elderly, sick) are often sent to camps; poor housing conditions, inadequate food, clothing and equipment for work, lack of medical and first-aid treatment; the requirements to correct this neglect, necessity of introducing decent wages similar to the earnings of Polish laborers; camps employ ca. 40,000 people.
- ***Description:*** transcript (2 copies), typescript, Polish, 185×280 mm, serious damage and losses of text, ss. 8, pp. 8.
  Attached note by H.W.: "Text's author is eng. Reinberg, 1940."

**1133. RING. I/390. Mf. ŻIH—783; USHMM—14**

- 15.08.1941 and after 15.08.1941, Warsaw Ghetto
- Lisser, Account entitled "In loyvitsher arbets-lager" [In the Łowicz labor camp] (15.08.1941)
- Author from Łódź, reported as a volunteer to the labor camp in Kapituła near Łowicz (work on regulation of the Bzura River, hunger, cruelty of Polish guards, and numerous escapes, inter alia the tailor Josef Raziński [age 28] was killed during an escape).
- ***Description:*** original, handwritten manuscript (ink, 222×354 mm), transcript (2 copies, handwritten manuscript—BW*, 150×210 mm), Yiddish, ss. 16, ss. 18.
  Attached note by H.W.: "Labor camp in Łowicz area 1941. Description of experiences written by his own hand by a refugee from Łódź cit[izen] Lisser."
  See HWC, 53/5 (third copy of transcript, typescript, ss. 7).
  Index: Aron Szemiantech [?], informer in camp in Kapituła near Łowicz; Dziubik, informer in camp in Kapituła near Łowicz; Henryk Akselfisz, engineer from Łódź, camp inmate in Kapituła near Łowicz; Kapłan (Motełe Kuk), cook in camp in Kapituła near Łowicz; Rozen from Wrocław, beat up prisoners in the camp in Kapituła near Łowicz; Lipszyc, physician, beat people up and informed in the camp in Kapituła near Łowicz

**1134. RING. I/6. Mf. ŻIH—771; USHMM—2**

- Beginning of 1941, Warsaw Ghetto
- "Winter camps." Memorandum [of the Jewish Council?] concerning camps in Końskowola and Milejów organized for the Jewish population November 1940–January 1941.
- Organization of camps, sanitary conditions, housing and work, diet, relations with authorities, aid from the Jewish Council (appended "Comparison of items

received by the camps in Końskowola and Milejów from the Jewish Council in Warsaw").

- *Description:* transcript, handwritten manuscript (JG*, 3 copies, pencil, 145×210 mm), typescript (2 copies, 210×300 mm), minor damage and losses of text, ss. 118, pp. 118.
  - On p. 1 handwritten manuscript note by H.W.: "104/41–2. Labor Department/Materials."
  - Attached note by H.W. in Yiddish: "Submitted by Order Serviceman [T.] Witelson, acquaintance of E.R., was on duty at ŻSS."
  - Original of the memorandum had attachments that were not preserved. Ring I/3 also contains data about "winter" camps in Końskowola and Milejów.

### 1135. RING. I/402. Mf. ŻIH—783; USHMM—14

- After 12.1940, Warsaw Ghetto
- NN., Account entitled "Der konskovoler lager" [The Końskowola camp]
- Description of stay (from 16.11.1940): camp under escort of the Order Service from Warsaw, work for the benefit of German firms, construction of the Końskowola-Puławy highway, poor sanitary conditions, wage—3.20 zł per day.
- *Description:* transcript, handwritten manuscript (MS*), pencil, Yiddish, 147×208 mm, ss. 2, pp. 2.
  - In the margin a Hebrew letter (ink): "z."
  - Inventory: "Author of the text is Mordechaj Szwarcbard."

### 1136. RING. I/783 (1102). Mf. ŻIH—825; USHMM—37

- Before 11.10.1941, Kutno
- Estera Kopel (Kutno, Judenlager Konstancja), Letter to Ch.[?] Gałecka (Warsaw, ul. Nowolipie 53, apt. 6[?])
- Greetings sent from camp on the grounds of the former "Konstancja" sugar mill, on a prepared form, "Herzliche Glückwunsch zum Neuen Jahr 5702" [Happy New Year wish for 5702].
- *Description:* original, printed, handwritten manuscript on a postcard, postmark, stamps of police in Kutno (11.10.1941) and of the Jewish Council in Warsaw (15.10.1941), German, 135×83 mm, ss. 1, pp. 2.
  - On p. 1 a printed notation: "Verlag: Vereinigte Hilfskomitet in Konstancja" [United Aid Committee in Konstancja].

### 1137. RING. I/592/7. (Lb. 1489). Mf. ŻIH—792; USHMM—23

- 13.02.1942, Steineck [Krzyżowniki] near Poznań
- O. Łenczycki (Arbeitslager 12, Steineck [Krzyżowniki] near Poznań, Post Office 15, for no. 1580), Letter of 13.02.1942 to M. Gelernter (Warsaw, ul. Dzika 10, apt. 24)
- Notation about stay of 5 months in the labor camp with son Luzer Manes; request to sister and brother-in-law for help.
- *Description:* original, handwritten manuscript on a postcard, postmark, stamps of camp and of the Jewish Council in Warsaw, pencil, Yiddish in Roman transliteration, 146×104 mm, ss.1, pp. 2.
  - In the address, beneath the street name "Dzika," author wrote in: "Zamenhofa 10, apt. 24," the prewar name of the street.
  - Attached note by H.W.: "Lb. 1489. Letter from labor camp in Poznań. February 1942."
  - Published: *Listy o Zagładzie*, pp. 21–24.
  - Index: Dancygier

### 1138. RING. I/392. (Lb. 1047). Mf. ŻIH—783; USHMM—14

- After 04.1941, Warsaw Ghetto
- A. Kelcer, Account entitled "Obóz Ksanyi" [Camp Ksany] (1941)
- Author seized in 04.1941 in Kielce ended up in the labor camp in Ksany near Opatów (preparations for being sent to the camp, journey, housing at the "castle," first days of stay). Information about camp manager Jan Kowalski.
- *Description:* transcript (3 copies), typescript, Yiddish, 215×285 mm, minor damage and losses of text (damage and losses of text—second copy), ss. 25, pp. 25.
  - On p. 1 (second and third copies) a note by H.W. in Yiddish: "24 standard pages" and [. . . ?]."
  - Inventory: "Account of Jehuda Szełman of Kielce."

### 1139. RING. I/592/10. Mf. ŻIH—792; USHMM—23

- 1.06.1942, Camp Lautawerk Süd (Lauta near Cottbus)
- Szymon Józef [Taube] (Camp Lautawerk Süd [Lauta near Cottbus]), Letter of 1.06.1942 to U. [Uszer] Taube (Warsaw, ul. Nowolipie 15, apt. 30)
- Request for aid, information about family and acquaintances.
- *Description:* original, handwritten manuscript on a postcard, postmark and stamp of Jewish Council in Warsaw, ink, Yiddish in Roman transliteration, 146×104 mm, minor damage and losses in text, text illegible in places, ss. 1, pp. 2.
  - See Ring. I/592/9 and I/592/11.
  - Index: W.D. Lewin, Wierzbicki,[Ruwen?] Wiśniewski, Mojsze Lejb[. . .], Fela Rybska

### 1140. RING. I/592/11. Mf. ŻIH—792; USHMM—23

- 14.06.[1942], Camp Lautawerk Süd (Lauta near Cottbus)
- [Szymon Józef Taube] (Lautawerk Süd—labor camp [Lauta near Cottbus]), Letter of 14.06.[1942] to [Uszer Taube] (Warsaw Ghetto)
- Information about death of author's parents, about work in the camp in Liebenau [Lubrza] and Lauta.

Appended letter of M. Targacz of Grabów to author in matter of the death camp in Chełmno (missing enclosure).[46]

- ***Description:*** original, handwritten manuscript, ink, German, Hebrew and Yiddish in Roman transliteration, 140×200 mm, extensive minor damage and losses in text, ss. 1, pp. 2.

See Ring. I/592/10 and I/592/9.
Published: *Listy o Zagładzie,* pp. 235–243.
Index: Mojsze Mendel Kibel of Szydłowiec, Wolner, Ruwen Wiśniewski, Binem Taube

### 1141. RING. I/598/5. Mf. ŻIH—792; USHMM—23

- Date unknown, place unknown
- [Szymon Józef Taube], Letter to NN. (fragment)
- Information regarding: M. [Moniek] Mazur, L. [Libcia] Pińczewska.
- ***Description:*** original, handwritten manuscript (two handwritings), ink, German, Hebrew in Roman transliteration, 139×77 mm, extensive damage and losses of text, ss. 1, pp. 2.

Letter in Hebrew (fragment) on the back (or glued) with letter of Szymon Józef Taube (Concerning saving the life of . . . ?)

### 1142. RING. I/384. Mf. ŻIH—783; USHMM—14

- After 1940, Warsaw Ghetto
- [Eng. A. Reinberg], Account entitled "The labor camp in Lipe (Nowy Sącz)"
- Camp numbered 650 persons, difficult hygienic conditions, lack of suitable care for the sick, insufficient diet.
- ***Description:*** transcript (2 copies), handwritten manuscript (MS*), pencil, Yiddish, 148×208 mm, minor damage and losses of text, ss. 2, pp. 2.

Attached note by H.W.: "Labor camp in Lipe (Nowy Sącz). Note of engineer A. Reinberg insp. of Joint, prepared by M. Szwarcbard. 1940"
Index: Dr. Finder

### 1143. RING. I/387. (Lb. 920). Mf. ŻIH—783; USHMM—14

- After 16.09.1940
- NN., Report of inspection of the labor camp in Lipe in 10–16.09.1940 (Kraków, 16.09.1940)
- Ca. 200 Jewish laborers, wage of 40 gr/h, less than for Poles (50 gr/h), difficult housing conditions, insufficient food, inspector's efforts to improve pay and conditions in the camp.
- ***Description:*** transcript, typescript, Polish, 205×265 mm, serious damage and losses of text, ss. 3, pp. 3.

Appended note by H.W.: "Report of Joint's inspector engineer A. Reinberg."
See Ring. I/384.

### 1144. RING. I/3. Mf. ŻIH—770; USHMM—1. RING. I/4. Mf. ŻIH—771; USHMM—2. RING. I/416. Mf. ŻIH—783; USHMM—14

a) **Ring. I/3**

- Beginning of 1941, Warsaw
- Memorandum [of the Jewish Council] concerning labor camps organized in the Lublin region for Jewish population, autumn 1940
- Organization of camps, location, number of workers, conditions of work and housing, attached statistical data, instructions ("Pointers [for] delegates of the Jewish Council in Labor Camps" [fragment]), reports of inspection of particular camps, copies of letters of laborers and other documents.
- ***Description:*** transcript, handwritten manuscript (2 copies, different handwritings, inter alia JG*, E*, FLIG*, pencil, 145×200 mm) and typescript (205×295 mm), German, Polish, slight damage and losses of text (handwritten manuscript, typescript), ss. 502, pp. 502.

On p. 1 (handwritten manuscript—JG*, first copy) note by H.W.: "[. . .] Department [. . .]"
In the document, there is also information about the labor camp in Falente [?] near Warsaw (p. 12). In the attachments to the memorandum (attachments no. 1–36 and a–h) are reports and accounts about camps in: Józefów on the Wieprz, Bełżec, Cieszanów, Płazów, Dzików Stary, Lipsko Narolu [?], Zamość, Białobrzegi (near Zamość), Tyszowce, Witków, Wereszyn, Dołhobyczów-Oszczów, Sawin, Luta (near Włodawa), Ossów, Ruda Opalin near Chełm, Dorohusk, Siedliszcze nad Wieprzem, Biała Podlaska, Ortel Książęcy, Terespol, Końskowola, Milejów, Chełm, Włodawa.
Published: *BFG,* vol. II, no. 1–4/1949, pp. 242–272 (fragments).

b) **Ring. I/416**

- After 06.1940, Warsaw Ghetto
- NN., Memorandum (report) regarding labor camps within the Lublin district (06.1940) (missing beginning [?])
- Camps for Jews of the Generalgouvernement, land improvement projects, control of rivers, work on the land, employing ca. 30,000 people, work conditions (beating and intimidation of workers, poor housing conditions, inadequate food, bad sanitary condition of the camps, lack of medical care, lack of pay),

46. According to Ruta Sakowska, the text of the letter from M. Targacz of Grabowo is one of those in Ring. I, no. 549, for which no author is identified. See *Listy o Zagładzie,* p. 241, where the letter is published in Polish translation.

requirements for improvement of the existing conditions. Convening in the camp in Bełżec (for camps: Bełżec, Lipsko, Płazów and Cieszanów) of a Camp Council (records of those working, organization of feeding, etc.).

- ***Description:*** transcript, handwritten manuscript (3 copies, JG*, pencil, 145×206 mm, minor damage and losses of text) and typescript (190×290 mm, damage and losses of text), German, Polish, ss. 26, pp. 26.

  Pages 11–17 of the handwritten document survived; transcript (typescript) contains the text with handwritten manuscript (pp. 11–17).

  It cannot be excluded that the remaining fragments of the handwritten manuscript contained text concerning other matters (camps), etc. See Ring. I/3

**1145. RING. I/1154 (1473). (Lb. 1228). Mf. ŻIH—833; USHMM—45**

- After 02.1941, Warsaw Ghetto
- [Lejb Frydman(?)], Account about Jews, prisoners of war moved from Lublin to Biała Podlaska
- A total of 700 prisoners left Lublin, 275 reached Biała (some escaped, the rest died) and were placed in the camp. Information about Langer (camp commandant [?]) and Szwarc, a German official in Biała.
- ***Description:*** original (o), handwritten manuscript (H.W.*), ink, Yiddish, 143×175 mm, ss. 1, pp. 1.

  Attached note by H.W. in Polish, Yiddish: "Death march of Jewish war prisoners from Lublin to Biała Podlaska, data gathered from Lejb Frydman (?), a member of the Jewish aid committee in Biała Podlaska."

**1146. RING. I/376. Mf. ŻIH—782; USHMM—13**

- After 01.1942, Warsaw Ghetto
- NN., Account from: "Serye: arbets-lagern. Band III. Der froyen arbets-lager in Lublin" [Series: Labor Camps. Volume III. The Women's Labor Camp in Lublin]
- Author from Warsaw describes the camp's organization (01.1942), the rounding up of women for the camp by the Jewish Council in the Lublin ghetto, living conditions, work, food, departure to Warsaw on a pass.
- ***Description:*** original (o), handwritten manuscript (HUB.*), notebooks, ink, Yiddish, 145×205, 150×208, 157×197 mm, ss. 45, pp. 77.

  Attached note by H.W. in Yiddish: "Collected by Szymon Huberband."

  Published: *Kiddush Hashem*, pp. 421–442.

**1147. RING. I/411. (Lb. 1102). Mf. ŻIH—783; USHMM—14**

- Date unknown, Warsaw Ghetto
- NN., Account entitled "Notes of a camper from 1941 (Łęki near Siedlce)"
- Author seized in a roundup in Warsaw, held in "Collegium." She describes the camp, work conditions, personnel (Gomel, commandant, personally killed one of the camp laborers), numerous deaths of prisoners, attitudes of local Polish population, attempts to obtain release, after 3 weeks released to go home.
- ***Description:*** original (o) (handwritten manuscript—FLIG*, ink, 218×286 mm, minor damage and losses of text, text illegible in places), description (3 copies, typescript, 220×288 mm, extensive damage and losses of text), Polish, ss. 33, pp. 37.

  Inventory: "Account written down by Daniel Fligelman."

  Index: Szabikiewicz, Bekerman, fellow-prisoners

**1148. RING. I/666. (Lb. 1124). Mf. ŻIH—816; USHMM—28**

- 1941[?], Warsaw Ghetto
- NN., Account of stay in labor camp in [Łęki near Siedlce]
- Conditions of work, feeding, camp commandant Gomel. Information about Arbeitsamt inspections.
- ***Description:*** original or transcript (handwritten manuscript, ink, 145×222 mm, minor damage and losses of text), transcript (3 copies) (typescript, 178×70, 192×280 mm, extensive damage and losses of text), Polish, ss. 9, pp. 9.

**1149. RING. I/372. (Lb. 886). Mf. ŻIH—782; USHMM—13**

- After 06.1941, Warsaw Ghetto
- [Bronisław Braff], Report entitled "Łowicz labor camp (seen in June 1941)"
- Organization and living conditions in "Arbeitshaus" (Labor Center) in Łowicz. Labor camps in Kapituła and Małszyce (15.04–19.06.1941). Food supply activity of Gurt and Szapiro, former members of the Jewish Council of Łowicz; death of Abram Rozensztajn (born 1915); camp managers: Tenenbaum and Rozenkranc as well the physicians Liwszyc and Halperin. Attempts to improve sanitary conditions; financial settlements with the Meermann firm.
- ***Description:*** transcript (3 copies, third copy in fragments, abreviated), typescript, Polish, 210×295, 163×140 mm, minor damage and losses of text (third copy: extensive damage and losses of text), ss. 24, pp. 24.

  On p. 1 (first copy) note by H.W. in Polish and Yiddish: "108–1942/1 January" and "Department."

  Attached note by H.W. with data: "Report prepared by Bronisław Braff, delegate of the Arbeitsamt."

**1150. RING. I/419. Mf. ŻIH—783; USHMM—14**

- Date unknown, Warsaw Ghetto
- J.[?]Z., Account entitled "Łowicz labor camp"
- Text prepared on the basis of recollections of one of

the camp laborers. Camp authorities: management designated by the Jewish Council, guards (Lagerschutz), team leaders named from among the camp laborers. Management and team leaders contributed to abuse of prisoners. Killing of two of the workers released to go home.

- ***Description:*** original, handwritten manuscript, ink, Polish, 214×135 mm, ss. 1, pp. 2.

  Attached note by H.W.: "Anonymous notes, forwarded by E. Gutkowski."

### 1151. RING. I/398. Mf. ŻIH—783; USHMM—14. RING. I/1220/91. Mf. ŻIH—835; USHMM—47

- After 23.08.[. . . ?], Warsaw Ghetto
- NN., Account of stay in the labor camp in Małoszewice near Terespol and Ortel Książęcy near Biała Podlaska
- Author, resident of Warsaw, was qualified by the commission at ul. Kawęczyńska for labor camp (23.08. [. . . ?]). Description of journey and conditions in the camp, abuse of prisoners (220 men, including 50 from Warsaw).
- ***Description:*** Ring. I/398—original [?], handwritten manuscript, ink, Yiddish, 156×197 mm, ss. 2, pp. 4; Ring. I/1220—transcript, handwritten manuscript (MS*), pencil, Yiddish, 149×209 mm, minor damage and losses of text, ss. 1, pp. 2.

  Ring. I/398 and I/1220—On p. 1 a Hebrew letter (ink): "d" (dalet) (or "ts" [tsadi ?]). In Ring. I/1220 in the margin a note in Yiddish (ink): "Camp."

  Ring. I/398—Attached note by H.W. in Polish, Yiddish: "Anonymous, forwarded by Izrael Lichtensztajn."

  Documents were kept in a binder.

### 1152. RING. I/592/14. Mf. ŻIH—792; USHMM—23

- 06.1942, Mogilno
- Jakub Topolski of Osięciny and Rafał Olewski (labor camp in Mogilno—monastery), Letter of 16.06.1942[?] to Icchak Borensztajn (Warsaw Ghetto)
- Lack of news about families in Osięciny and Piotrków Kujawski. Request for aid.
- ***Description:*** original, handwritten manuscript (two handwritings), ink, German, Yiddish, 145×208 mm, ss. 2, pp. 2.

  On p. 1 in a different handwriting is written: "Mogilno, 16.06.42."

### 1153. RING. I/389. Mf. ŻIH—783; USHMM—14. RING. I/375. (Lb. 1079). Mf. ŻIH—782; USHMM—13

- After 04.1941, Warsaw Ghetto
- [Abram Erlich?], Account entitled "Labor camp in Mordy—1941"
- Author (age 24), before the war a warehouseman, reported as a volunteer for camp, describes the journey to the camp, the camp (appended map of the camp and barrack), work conditions, feeding, treatment by personnel, pay, daily schedule and the worsening situation in the camp after the passage of several weeks.
- ***Description:*** Ring. I/375—original (o) (handwritten manuscript—FLIG*, ink, pencil, 204×319, 80×100 mm, minor damage and losses of text, text difficult to read in places, extensive damage and losses of text, ss. 4, pp. 6); Ring. I/389—transcript (3 copies, typescript, pencil, 197×280, 197×197 mm, ss. 15, pp. 15), Polish, ss. 19, pp. 21.

  On p. 5 a note: "Camp laborer did not show up to continue the account."

  Ring. I/375—Attached note by H.W.: "Labor camp in Marki [sic] near Warsaw. Testimony prepared by Daniel Fligelman." Ring. I/389—Attached note by H.W.: "Labor camp in Mordy near Siedlce 1941 (Judenlager Mordy). Fragment of the testimony presented by Erlich Abram, prepared by H. Wasser."

### 1154. RING. I/562. Mf. ŻIH—791; USHMM—22. RING. I/663. Mf. ŻIH—816; USHMM—28

- 18.10.1941, after 18.10.1941, Nowa Słupia, Warsaw Ghetto
- NN. (Dawid) (Nowa Słupia—camp [?]), Letter of 18.10.1941 to mother. Request for aid.
- ***Description:*** Ring. I/562—original [?] (handwritten manuscript, ink, Yiddish, 148×208 mm, minor damage and losses of text), ss. 2, pp. 4; Ring. I/663—transcript (2 copies) (handwritten manuscript—U*, pencil, Yiddish, 167×218, 145×208 mm, damage and losses of text), ss. 6, pp. 6.

  On p. 1 at top (original [?]) note in Polish: "Nowa Słupia 18.10.41."

  On p. 1 at top (transcript, first copy) note by H.W. in Yiddish (ink): "Letter." In the margin: "104/41." and in another handwriting a note in Polish (pencil): "Nowa Słupia 18.10.41."

  Index: Winter

### 1155. RING. I/555. Mf. ŻIH—791; USHMM—22

- 03.1942, Obernick [Oborniki near Poznań]
- Female prisoners of the labor camp in Oborniki, Letter of 7.03.1942 [postmark date] to NN. (Warsaw Ghetto)
- Request for help and information on people deported from Izbica Kujawska, Koło, and other localities.
- ***Description:*** original, handwritten manuscript on a postcard, postmark (Obernick 07.03.42) and stamp of Jewish Council in Warsaw, ink, Polish, 147×103 mm, text is barely legible and in places is illegible, ss. 1, pp. 2.

### 1156. RING. I/385/2. Mf. ŻIH—783; USHMM—14

- After 8.09.1941, Warsaw Ghetto
- NN., Two declarations (of 7 and 8.09.1941)

concerning an execution in camp in Ossów [Osowa ?] near Włodawa
- Information about the shooting (30.08.1941) of 51 laborers and 2 managers (Moszkowicz and Libert); survived: Akawie Gelbsz, Dr. Lipszyc, medic Rotleder, cooks Ciechanowiecki and Zylbernerg [?], medic Hirszbein, and 8 orderlies.
- ***Description:*** transcript, typescript (handwritten additions, ink), Polish, 160×226 mm, serious damage and losses of text, ss. 1, pp. 1.

## 1157. RING. I/385/3. Mf. ŻIH—783; USHMM—14

- After 21.09.1941, place unknown
- NN., Account concerning an execution in the camp in Ossów [Osowa] near Włodawa (21.09.1941) (fragment)
- Preparations for execution and execution of prisoners (30.08.1941). Among the victims: Libert, Moszkowicz, and Żelazny.
- ***Description:*** transcript, typescript, German, Polish, 190×268, 165×140 mm, serious damage and losses of text, ss. 4, pp. 4

Index: Rojter, chairman of Jewish Council in Sawin, Dr. Chomyn, Dr. Rot

## 1158. RING. I/424. (Lb. 1050). Mf. ŻIH—784; USHMM—15

- After 19.10.1941, Warsaw Ghetto
- Fayvl Koyfman [Fajwel Kaufman], Account entitled "Der arbet-lager in oshedle Osuv (Osove)" [The labor camp in the area Ossów (Osowa)] (19.10.1941)
- Author (age 25), bachelor (ul. Franciszkańska 9), before 1939 clerk in the firm "Wasser and Feldman" (Warsaw, ul. Gęsia 3), father a rabbi in Łódź; at start of 06.1941 he left Warsaw in search of food and work. Arrested near Warsaw, he ended up in labor camp, description of conditions in the camps in Osowa and Krychów near Włodawa, beating, behavior of the camp doctor; as a result of the treatment in camp he partially lost speech. After return to home he was in hospital for 8 weeks. At the end, a copy of record from 20.08.1941 regarding events in the camp in Osowa (shooting of 52 young people, prisoners of the camp).
- ***Description:*** transcript (3 copies), handwritten manuscript (TT*), pencil, Yiddish, 148×208, 148×140 mm, damage and losses of text (second copy), significant damage and losses of text (first and third copies), ss. 57, pp. 57.

On p. 1 (second copy) a note by H.W. in Yiddish (ink): "Guter."

Attached note by H.W. "Ossowa-Krychów (Lublin area) concentration (labor) camp 1941. Testimony of Fajwel Kaufman, prepared by E. Gutkowski."

See HWC, 53/1 (transcript, handwritten manuscript—LEG*, ink, Yiddish, ss. 4; date: Warsaw, 20.10.1941).

## 1159. RING. I/401. Mf. ŻIH—783; USHMM—14

- After 12.1940, Warsaw Ghetto
- NN., Account entitled "Der arbetslager in Oshtshuv. Der marsh in lager" [The labor camp in Oszczów. The march to the camp]
- Journey from Warsaw (5 people died), stay in camp (from 12.09.1940), work conditions (road building), housing (hunger, diseases), and poor treatment of prisoners (the Ukrainian camp manager Choroszko and jailer Brodowski). Help from Jewish Council of Hrubieszów and local peasants.
- ***Description:*** transcript, handwritten manuscript (MS*), pencil, Yiddish, 154×210 mm, minor damage and losses of text, ss. 3, pp. 3.

In the margin a Hebrew letter (ink): "hey"

Inventory: "Text's author is Mordechaj Szwarcbard."

Index: Komendacki [?], Jur, Makiewicz [?] (Poles-technicians, favorable reference)

## 1160. RING. I/1085 (1404). (Lb. 768). Mf. ŻIH—833; USHMM—45

- After 6.11.1940, Auschwitz (camp)
- Der Leiter der Verwaltung des KL Auschwitz [Director of the Administration of KL Auschwitz], Letter of 6.11.1940 to Leja Nejman (Warsaw, ul. Targowa 64, apt. 9)
- Concerning Chil Nejman (born 5.04.1894), who died in camp.
- ***Description:*** transcript (a) (handwritten manuscript—WINK.*, ink, German, 157×133 mm, minor damage and losses of text), transcript (b) (handwritten manuscript—MS*, pencil, Yiddish, 147×209 mm), ss. 2, pp. 3.

Doc. was kept in a binder.

Attached note by H.W. in Polish and Yiddish: "Forwarded by Gutkowski."

## 1161. RING. I/395. Mf. ŻIH—783; USHMM—14

- After 20.08.1941, Warsaw Ghetto
- NN., Account entitled "Mayn iberlebung fun obuz pratsy in Plazov" [My experiences in the labor camp in Płazów] (20.08.1941)
- Author (age 16), volunteer from Warsaw, describes trip to camp and work and living conditions in the camp (1940).
- ***Description:*** transcript (2 copies), handwritten manuscript (BW*), pencil, Yiddish, 147×204 mm, ss. 6, pp. 6.

In the margins a symbol (red pencil): "+".

## 1162. RING. I/658. (Lb. 1137). Mf. ŻIH—816; USHMM—28

- Date unknown, Warsaw Ghetto
- NN., Account, "My experiences in the forced labor camp for Jews in Płazów near Bełżec" (fragment)
- Author, an apprentice tailor, a prewar political prisoner for leftist activity. He describes the journey from Grodzisk Mazowiecki with a group of 63

persons to Lublin, then a stay in the labor camp in Płazów (sadism of guards, epidemic of dysentery, difficult work conditions).

- ***Description:*** transcript (2 copies), handwritten manuscript (CC*), pencil, Polish, 145×155 mm, serious damage and losses of text, ss. 18, pp. 18.
  On p. 1 at top a note by H.W. (ink): "Kampel" [Bernard Kampelmacher]. "105/1"
  Index: Tudo [?] Wajberg, Zajdner

### 1163. RING. I/374. (Lb. 928). Mf. ŻIH—782; USHMM—13

- After 16.08.1941, Warsaw Ghetto
- [Salomea Ostrowska], Study entitled "Death camp—Pomiechówek"
- Course of transfer of Jews from Nowy Dwór and Płońsk to camp in Pomiechówek (fort). Living conditions in camp, abuse of prisoners, numerous fatalities, help from outside, infectious disease, camp commandant Zydler, behavior of Majloch Hoppenblum, commander of the Order Service, transfer to the Generalgouvernement (Warsaw) (ca. 700 people, 16.08.1941), torching of wagons with prisoners on the road to Jabłonna. Text created on the basis of reports by, among others, Abram Błaszki [Blaszki?] from Nowy Dwór, Szyja Sokół from Płońsk, Pola Szpilman from Żuromin, Sala Gabler from Nowy Dwór, Fiszel Lipsztejn, Rojza Końskowolska, Rafał (Icek) Herckowicz from Płońsk, Chaskiel Rejbak from Płońsk, Pejsach Surgał from Nowy Dwór, Chaim Srogal from Sierpc, Szajndel Gutkowicz from Nowy Dwór, Chana Michałowicz from Płońsk, Małka Czarnoczapka from Raciąż, Hersz Blumert, Josek Kapłan from Nowy Dwór, Szajna Frydlender. Names of several persons tortured in camp were also submitted.
- ***Description:*** original (handwritten manuscript—KK*, notebook, ink, 140×140, 140×200 mm, serious damage and losses of text), transcript (2 copies, typescript, 207×290 mm), Polish, ss. 64, pp. 85.
  Attached note by H.W.: "Report on the basis of testimonies of camp inmates, prepared by Salomea Ostrowska, coworker of Dr. Ringelblum's archive."
  See Ring. I/415, I/417 and I/956.

### 1164. RING. I/301. (LB 1261). Mf. ŻIH—781; USHMM—12. RING. I/956 (1275). (Lb. 921). Mf. ŻIH—830; USHMM—42

- 08.1941, Warsaw Ghetto
- Records (9) of conversations with former prisoners of the camp in Pomiechówek
- Accounts of stay in camp in the period 07–08.1941 (Paweł Robota, Szmul Krzak from Nowy Dwór, Majer Magid from Nowy Dwór, Zelig Top from Nowy Dwór, Azryel Górecki of Nowy Dwór, Mordka Całka of Nowy Dwór, Natan Ruda, Lejzor Ajzenberg, rabbi from Zakliczyn, Róża Kapłan). Descriptions of experiences, of treatment by guards (beating, executions, coerced sexual relations, burial of living people). Appended lists of names of victims and torturers of Pomiechówek (missing conclusion).
- ***Description:*** original, handwritten manuscript (three handwritings: a) H.W.*, b) POM*, c) NN.), ink, pencil, Polish, 210×295, 210×255 mm, ss. 7, pp. 9.
  Pages 7–10 were found in Ring. I/956. On p. 6. is a note: "N.pk 27/13."
  Attached note by H.W. in Yiddish: "Recorded by H.W. in quarantine at ul. Leszno 109."
  Accounts ("Records" 1–6) as well as the list of names on pp. 4–5, written down in the handwriting of H.W.*
  Missing account no. 7.
  Index: Paweł Robota; Szmul Krzak from Nowy Dwór; Majer Magid from Nowy Dwór; Zelig Top from Nowy Dwór; Azryel Górecki from Nowy Dwór; Mordka Całka from Nowy Dwór; Natan Ruda; Lejzor Ajzenberg, rabbi of Zakliczyn; Róża Kap łan; Tuchendler; Motyl [?]; Natan Ruda; Krzak; Kręć; Lajbuś Sosiń; Szyja Aksamit; Mosze Dobrowicz; Chaskiel Flajszhakiel; Hersz Perelmutter; Majlech Perelmutter; Iser Elbaum; Szmul Łokieć; Eliasz Rzeszotka; Szulin [Szulim?] Rzetelny; Pejsach Surgal; Mordka Michałowicz; Boruch Frydman; Josek Furman; Chaskiel Karmel; Wolf Młynarski; Moszek Korensztajn; Szeps Top (died 7.08.1941); Lejb Towia [?]; Gołda Wagman; Hersz Całka (died 10.08.1941 r.); Jankiel Ewenberg [?], rabbi; *Guards:* Schultz; Fitzner (father and son); Holtz, settler from Wólka Górska; Netzel from Nowy Dwór, blacksmith; Paweł, coal dealer; Auch [?]; Repsch; Fredek Kelm [?]; Edek Wendt, carpenter from Nowy Dwór; Majloch Hopentreger [Hopenblum?] of the Order Service; Hersz Tarngojł of the Order Service; Icek Moszkowicz of the Order Service.

### 1165. RING. I/956 (1275). Mf. ŻIH—830; USHMM—42. RING. I/374

**a) Ring. I/374, Ring. I/956**

- 09.1941, after 09.1941, Warsaw Ghetto
- Collection of accounts of former prisoners of camp in Pomiechówek
- Accounts of persons resettled from various towns to the camp in Pomiechówek, then to the Generalgouvernement: inter alia Szyja Sokół (age 33) of Płońsk, Pola Szpilman (age 20) of Płońsk, Chana Michałowicz (age 16) of Płońsk, Małka Czarnoczapka (age 60) of Raciąż, Rafał Herckowicz (age 52) of Płońsk, Pejsach Surgał (age 18) of Płońsk, Rojza Końskowolska (age 30) of Żuromin (8.09.1941), Szajndel Gutkowicz (age 25) of Nowy Dwór, Irka Grzebieniakówna (age 21) of Bieżuń, Sala Gabler (age 19) of Nowy Dwór, Szajna Frydlender, and

Chaskiel Rejbak (age 28) of Płońsk. Information about other prisoners and victims of the camp.
- *Description:* Ring. I/374—original (handwritten manuscript—KK* and original signatures of the authors of the account, ink, damaged document, small fragments of pieces of paper survived: ss. 14, pp. 28), Ring. I/956—transcript (3 incomplete copies, typescript, 83×154, 195×285 mm, serious damage and losses of text), Polish, ss. 21, pp. 21.

These accounts were used in preparation of the report on the camp in Pomiechówek; see Ring. I/374.

Appended notes (2) by H.W. in Yiddish: "Materials collected in the quarantine at ul. Leszno 109; fragments about Pomiechówek, camp prisoners' testimonies, written down by Salomea Ostrowska."

b) **Ring. I/956**
- After 09.1941, Warsaw Ghetto
- NN. ("Refugee"), Account of stay in camp in Pomiechówek
- Interview conducted in the quarantine at ul. Leszno 109.
- *Description:* transcript (3 copies), typescript, Polish, 195×232 mm, serious damage and losses of text, ss. 6, pp. 6.

### 1166. RING. I/415. (Lb. 1098). Mf. ŻIH—783; USHMM—14

a)
- After 08.1941, Warsaw Ghetto
- NN., Account of stay in camp in Pomiechówek
- Author, a resident of Zakroczym, at the end of June and early July 1941 was resettled together with a group of local Jews to a camp in Pomiechówek (fort), stayed there until 14.08.1941, when they were tossed out and into the Generalgouvernement (Warsaw). Living conditions in the camp, abuse of prisoners, activity of the chief of Order Service Majloch [Hoppenblum], torching of wagons with prisoners on the way to Jabłonna.
- *Description:* original or transcript, handwritten manuscript, ink, Polish, 157×196 mm, serious damage and losses of text, ss. 4, pp. 7.

Inventory: "Author NN., text forwarded by Salomea Ostrowska."

See Ring. I/374.

b)
- Date unknown, place unknown
- NN., Account (fragment)
- Fragment of description of stay in camp [?].
- *Description:* original or transcript, handwritten manuscript, ink, Polish, 100×169 mm, very serious damage and losses of text, ss. 1, pp. 2.

### 1167. RING. I/887 (1207). (Lb. 1001). Mf. ŻIH—828; USHMM—40. RING. I/1057 (1376). Mf. ŻIH—832; USHMM—44

- Date unknown, Warsaw Ghetto
- NN., Account entitled "Płońsk"
- Fate of Jews deported from Płońsk (13.07.1941) to camp in Pomiechówek (expulsion from Płońsk, stay in Pomiechówek, numerous fatalities, removal of survivors into the Generalgouvernement).
- *Description:* Ring. I/1057—original or transcript, handwritten manuscript, pencil, Yiddish, 190×276 mm, ss. 3, pp. 5; Ring. I/887—transcript (2 copies), handwritten manuscript (TT*), pencil, Yiddish, 145×185 mm, serious damage and losses of text, ss. 22, pp. 22.

Ring. I/1057—doc. written on ss. from an account ledger [?] (Printed, Polish).

See HWC, 23/1 (third copy of transcript, handwritten manuscript, ss. 11).

Attached note by H.W.: "Collected by H. Wasser."

Index: Jenta Prost, killed in Pomiechowek; Dwojra Baliban, killed in Pomiechówek; Miriam Tans, killed in Pomiechówek; Rachela Heler, killed in Pomiechówek; Cytrynowski (age 17), killed in Pomiechówek; Hagelewicz was in Pomiechówek; Etka Iliart, raped in Pomiechówek; Icze Dancygier from Nowy Dwór, with daughter, shot in Pomiechówek; Gutsztat from Drobin, shot in Pomiechówek; Jare Top, shot in Pomiechówek; Lejb Top, shot in Pomiechówek; Hene Wróbel from Nowy Dwór, shot in Pomiechówek; Borensztajn from Nowy Dwór, shot in Pomiechówek; Szaszyński brothers from Nowy Dwór, shot in Pomiechówek; Karaś, tortured and killed in Pomiechówek; Szlomo Fuks, imported parcels of food from Płońsk to Pomiechówek; Markiewicz from Warsaw, killed near Legionów; Mosze Krzyński killed near Legionów; Szmuel Krzyński killed near Legionów; Mendel Szwajger from Nowy Dwór, killed near Legionów

### 1168. RING. I/417. (Lb. 928). Mf. ŻIH—783; USHMM—14

- After 08. 1941, Warsaw Ghetto
- Adam Blaszka, Account entitled "Impressions from a stay in the concentration camp in Pomiechówek"
- Author (ul. Stawki 9), a teacher of Jewish studies from Nowy Dwór, sent with family to the camp on 7.07.1941. Description of the camp's personnel (Zydler, Szulc, Netzel—"Chawer[47] Nisn"), hunger, abuse of prisoners, barter, aid from Jews of Nowy Dwór and Płońsk, activity of Order Service (Majloch

47. Yiddish-Hebrew for "friend" or "comrade."

Hoppenblum, commandant, Hersz Tarnegol [Tarngojł], Icchak Sowiński, Abram Braun, Abram Goldbroch, Szmul Dobski, Abe Jarząbek, Abram Lejzerowicz, Icek Moszkowicz, Moszek Fejer), execution by shooting of sick and elderly (ca. 800 people), childbirth in the camp (Brandstein, Berta Rozensztajn, midwife). Released after 6 weeks and deported into Generalgouvernement. Appended autobiography of the author.
- ***Description:*** original or transcript (handwritten manuscript, pencil, 220×295 mm, serious damage and losses of text), transcript (3 copies, typescript, 208×296, 100×240 mm, much and significant damage and losses of text in the third copy), Polish, ss. 45, pp. 53.

    Attached note by H.W.: "Abram Błaszka's testimony of stay in concentration ca[mp] in Pomiechówek, Salomea Ostrowska conducted the int[erview]."

### 1169. RING. I/418. (Lb. 928). Mf. ŻIH—783; USHMM—14

- After 08.1941, Warsaw Ghetto
- NN., Account entitled "Pomiekhuvek" [Pomiechówek]
- Author from Sierpc, stayed in Płońsk, whence he was resettled to Pomiechówek (together with ca. 1,200), describes stay in camp, executions (600 people). After release he stayed in a shelter for refugees in the Warsaw Ghetto.
- ***Description:*** original or transcript, handwritten manuscript, ink, Yiddish, 156×220 mm, ss. 6, pp. 6.

    On the back of ss. a series of numbers: 13926–13928, 13931–13933.

### 1170. RING. I/1155 (1474). (Lb. 1228). Mf. ŻIH—833; USHMM—45

- After 14.08.1941, Warsaw Ghetto
- Miriam Fasa, Account of expulsion from Płońsk (6.07.1941) and stay in camp in Pomiechówek
- Displacement of 1,200 Jews from Płońsk. Description of conditions reigning in the camp in Pomiechówek (ca. 200 people died, numerous fatalities as a result of beating, Frydlander shot, ca. 100 persons escaped). Survivors were transported on 14.08. into the Generalgouvernement. Appended list of fatalities of the camp in Pomiechówek.
- ***Description:*** original (o), handwritten manuscript (H.W.* and POM*), notebook, ink, pencil, Yiddish, 156×200 mm, ss. 8, pp. 8.

    On p. 1 (cover), stamp: "Central Commission of Refugees, Warsaw, Tłomackie 13, II fl. room 8," notation (pencil): "Educational System"; on p. 2 a note by H.W. (ink): "Koplowicz—Sierpc"; on p. 3 heading (pencil): "Professional Education System. Delegates and their families." On p. 4 two names were inscribed in pencil (handwritten manuscript).

    In Polish compare Ring. I/1216.

    Appended note by H.W. in Yiddish: "Account of Miriam Fasa from Sierpc; incomplete list of those killed and those who died in the camp in Pomiechówek, compiled by H.W. at the quarantine (ul. Leszno 109)."

    Index: Bursztyn from Nasielsk, Majloch [Hoppenblum]

### 1171. RING. I/1216. Mf. ŻIH—835; USHMM—47

a)

- After 09.1941, Warsaw Ghetto
- NN. and [Hersz Wasser], List of names of Jews murdered in the camp in Pomiechówek
- ***Description:*** original, handwritten manuscript, three handwritings (H.W.* and NN.), Polish, 95×151 mm and 117×198 mm, ss. 1, pp. 2.

    Compare Ring.I/1155.

    Index: Sura Asz (born 1877), murdered in Pomiechówek; Mojżesz Herdlisz (born 1891), died in Pomiechówek; Wolf Grapa (born 1912), died in Pomiechówek; Josek Rubin (born 1914), died in Pomiechówek; Dawid Tuchendler (born 1901), murdered in Pomiechówek; Łemeł Rzeszotka (born 1900), murdered in Pomiechówek; Poze Kletczewski (born 1880), murdered in Pomiechówek; Ester Ruda (born 1890), murdered in Pomiechówek; Hena Ostaszewer (born 1890), murdered in Pomiechówek; Chaja Motyl (born 1894[?]), murdered in Pomiechówek; Sura Tuchendler (born 1900), murdered in Pomiechówek; Tauba Rzetelna (born 1895), murdered in Pomiechówek; Frajdes Lesman (born 1896), murdered in Pomiechówek; Rywka Blum (born 1914), was in Pomiechówek, missing; Hersz Lesman (born 1891), was in Pomiechówek, went missing; Icek Dancygier (age 54) from Drobin, murdered in Pomiechówek for possession of gold; Ita Dancygier (age 28) from Drobin, murdered in Pomiechówek for possession of gold; Mojsze Kohn (age 39) from Drobin, murdered in Pomiechówek; Ruchla Borenschaft-Altman [?] (age 36) from Drobin, murdered in Pomiechówek; Gutsztat [?] Josel Icek (age 43) from Drobin, murdered in Pomiechówek

b)

- After 09.1941, Warsaw Ghetto
- NN., "List of those from Kikół [?] killed in Ponichówki [sic]"
- List of names of people originating from the village of Kikół killed or who died in the camp in Pomiechówek.
- ***Description:*** original, handwritten manuscript (minor supplements by H.W.*, ink), pencil, Polish, 97×152 mm, ss. 1, pp. 1.

    Index: Szyja Złotak (age 68) from Kikół, died in Pomiechówek; Dan Złotak (age 31) from

Kikołów [sic], died in Pomiechówek; Aron Dawid Złotak (age 35) from Kikołów, died in Pomiechówek; Mordcha Chomont (age 42) from Kikołów, died in Pomiechówek; Ester Złotak (age 58) from Kikołów, died in Pomiechówek; Mojsze Goldrejch (age 42) from Kikołów, died in Pomiechówek; Mania Goldrejch (age 41) from Kikołów, died in Pomiechówek; Sura Lipiec (age 32) from Kikołów, died in Pomiechówek; Wolf Grofia [Grapa?] from Kikołów, died in Pomiechówek

**1172. RING. I/400. Mf. ŻIH—783; USHMM—14**

- After 1.10.1940, Warsaw Ghetto
- [Eng. A. Reinberg], Account entitled "Arbets lager in Pustkuv" [Labor camp in Pustków]
- Report of an inspection of the camp by a representative of the Joint on 1.10.[1940] (1,200 workers, housing conditions, sanitary conditions, food, work conditions).
- ***Description:*** transcript (2 copies), handwritten manuscript (MS*), pencil, Yiddish, 148×208 mm, minor damage and losses of text, ss. 2, pp. 2.

  See Ring. I/448, I/669.

  Attached note by H.W.: "Labor camp in Pustków (Dębica). Notes prepared by M. Szwarcbard on the basis of information from engineer A. Reinberg, 1940"

**1173. RING. I/669. Mf. ŻIH—816; USHMM—28**

- Date unknown, Warsaw Ghetto
- NN., Report of visit in labor camp in Pustków (near Dębica) (fragments)
- Organization of camp authorities (Scharf, commandant; Jewish Council in camp: Immerglik from Dębica, Bitkower from Tarnów and Weksberg; physicians: Dr. Thau and Dr. Saksowa, Schuhmacher); housing conditions, food, work, pay, medical care, social composition of the camp inmates, Order Service.
- ***Description:*** transcript, typescript, Polish, 180×225 mm, damage and losses of text, ss. 5, pp. 5.

  See Ring. I/400, I/448.

  See HWC, 53/7 (a fuller version of this document: "Report of the labor camp [in] Pustków near Dębica," typed, Polish, ss. 4).

**1174. RING. I/894 (1214). (Lb. 393). Mf. ŻIH—828; USHMM—40**

- After 16.12.1939, Warsaw Ghetto
- NN., Account entitled "Ruda Pabianitska bay Lodzh" [Ruda Pabianicka near Łódź]
- Author, resident of Łódź, on 16.12.1939 was arrested and sent to the labor camp in Ruda Pabianicka (description of treatment of prisoners).
- ***Description:*** transcript, handwritten manuscript (MS*), pencil, Yiddish, 148×210 mm, minor damage and losses of text, ss. 1, pp. 2.

  On p. 1 the title in Yiddish is written by H.W. (ink) and a notation: "9" (See "10").

**1175. RING. I/393. Mf. ŻIH—783; USHMM—14**

- After 01.1942, Warsaw Ghetto
- NN., Account entitled "Rudniki, yidn oyf tsvang arbet in der fabrik 'Wapnorud'" [Rudniki, Jews at forced labor in the 'Wapnorud' factory] (01.1942)
- Author, a member of the Jewish Council of Radomsko, describes the conditions in the camp at the factory in Rudniki near Częstochowa (he brought a shipment of food for prisoners—01.1942).
- ***Description:*** transcript (3 copies), typescript, Yiddish, 210×296 mm, minor damage and losses of text, ss. 6, pp. 6.

  On p. 1 (first copy) a note by H.W. (ink): "Kapłan Wincyk [?]."

  Appended notation by H.W. in Yiddish: "Submitted by Kapłan, the Hebrew writer (01.1942)."

**1176. RING. I/916 (1235). (Lb. 1641). Mf. ŻIH—829; USHMM—41**

- After 13.08.1941, Warsaw Ghetto
- NN., Account entitled "Saytshitse—pov. khelmski," [Sajczyce—Chełm dist(rict)]
- Author voluntarily reported for trip to labor camp in Sajczyce (9.05.1941). He describes conditions in camps (escapes, food, housing, and labor). Released from the camp with sick inmates on 13.08.1941, he returned to Warsaw. Appended map of the camp.
- ***Description:*** original (o), handwritten manuscript (H.W.*), ink, Polish, Yiddish, 154×198 mm, minor damage and losses of text, ss. 2, pp. 4.

**1177. RING. I/385/4. Mf. ŻIH—783; USHMM—14**

- Date unknown, Warsaw Ghetto [?]
- Edward P[. . .]ry, manager of camp in Sajczyce, Letter to Jewish Council in Warsaw[?]
- Information about the shooting of two prisoners from Warsaw for attempted escape from the camp: Chaim Michlewicz (born 1901, ul. Ogrodowa 7) and Szaja Finkielsztein (born 1907, ul. Dzielna 57).
- ***Description:*** transcript, typescript, Polish, 170×190 mm, damage and losses of text, ss. 1, pp. 1.

**1178. RING. I/385/5–6. Mf. ŻIH—783; USHMM—14**

- Date unknown, Warsaw Ghetto [?]
- a) NN., Extract from "Report of inspection trip [. . .]" through labor camps Sawin, Krychów, Sajczyce, and Ossów [Osowa] near Włodawa (July 1941) (fragment)
- Escape of 2 prisoners from Sawin; in Krychów (commandant Napieralla) ca. 400 Jews and 280 Poles; behavior of the Order Service (trade, bribery, and receipt of stolen goods); Sajczyce, commandant Roliksmann.
- b) NN., "Report of second trip [through] Chełm

[area camps]. Departure [. . .] return 28.08[?].1941" (Sawin, Sajczyce, Krychów)
- Changes in the management of camps (Sawin, the Pole Korol; in Sajczyce, Augustyniak); in Sawin grave of those shot (7 people) for attempted escape and 16 graves of deceased from diseases and emaciation, release of Izrael Rechtdiner.
- ***Description:*** transcript, typescript, Polish, 175×270, 145×95 mm, serious damage and losses of text, ss. 13, pp. 13.

Attached note by H.W.

Index: Beike, commandant of the camp in Osowa; Oberkoch, Schrumpf, commandant in Krychów

### 1179. RING. I/619. (Lb. 408). Mf. ŻIH—814; USHMM—26

- After 7.12.1940, Warsaw Ghetto
- NN., Account entitled "Der lager in Shedlishtshe" [The camp in Siedliszcze]
- Author (age 17) from Warsaw, reported for labor camp (24.08.1940, point at ul. Kawęczyńska), sent together with a group of 2,300 persons to Chełm, then to Siedliszcze (only 150 people). Description of trip, living and work conditions in camp. Released 7.12.1940.
- ***Description:*** transcript, handwritten manuscript (MS*), pencil, Yiddish, 148×210 mm, minor damage and losses of text, ss. 2, pp. 2

In the margins a Hebrew letter (ink): "t" (tet). Doc. was kept in a binder.

### 1180. RING. I/409. (Lb. 396). Mf. ŻIH—783; USHMM—14

- After 5.05.1941, Warsaw Ghetto
- Mosze Herdyk (ul. Nalewki 9, apt. 2), Account entitled "A barikht fun a lager in Sobin" [A report about a camp in Sobienie] (5.05.1941)
- Information about labor camp in Wilga obtained by author in the Jewish Council in Sobienie-Jeziory near Garwolin.
- ***Description:*** transcript (2 copies), handwritten manuscript (BW*), pencil, Polish, Yiddish, 145×208 mm, extensive minor damage and losses of text, ss. 2, pp. 2.

Beneath the text of the account is a notation in Polish: "The Wilga camp, near S[obienie]-Jeziory, Garwolin district, 12 km. of road [?] to Minów [?]. Herdyk Moszek, Nalewki 9/2. 5.05.1941."

Attached note by H.W. in Polish, Yiddish: "Account of Mojsze Herdyk, recorded by Bluma Wasser."

In the margins a symbol (red pencil): "+".

### 1181. RING. I/546, I/548. Mf. ŻIH—791; USHMM—22

**a) Ring. I/548**
- 20.02.1942, Sobienie-Jeziory
- I. Rajczet [?] (Sobienie-Jeziory, ul. Garwolińska 7), Letter of 22.02.1942 to Rotblit (Warsaw, ul. Miła 7, apt. 35, in care of Szlama Sztern)
- Request for money for travel to Warsaw.
- ***Description:*** original, handwritten manuscript on a postcard, postmark and stamp of Jewish Council in Warsaw, ink, Polish, 148×104 mm, ss. 1, pp. 2.

**b) Ring. I/546**
- 20.02.1942[?], Sobienie-Jeziory
- NN. (Sobienie-Jeziory), Letter of 20.02.1942[?] to NN. (Warsaw Ghetto)
- Request for aid in leaving camp and travel to Warsaw.
- ***Description:*** original, handwritten manuscript, ink, Yiddish, 148×206 mm, ss. 1, pp. 2.

The same person probably wrote both letters.

### 1182. RING. I/408. Mf. ŻIH—783; USHMM—14

- After 07.1941, Warsaw Ghetto
- NN., Account of stay in labor camp in Sochaczew and Tarczyn
- Author (born 10.06.1899) from Warsaw (ul. Miła 67), seized on ul. Zamenhofa, was sent to camp in Sochaczew, then to Tarczyn (Unger firm). Description of living and work conditions in camps. As a result of injuries suffered in the camp he was released and transferred to hospital in Warsaw.
- ***Description:*** original or transcript, handwritten manuscript (Ś*), ink, Yiddish, 143×220 mm, minor damage and losses of text, ss. 3, pp. 3.

### 1183. RING. I/1/1. (Lb. 53, 102, 103, 221, 222, 229, 274, 275, 292, 293) Mf. ŻIH—770; USHMM—1

- After 03.1940, Warsaw Ghetto
- [Pola Mordkowicz (Mordkiewicz)], Journal (03.1940–02.1941)
- Author, after resettlement from Łódź to Limanowa, stayed there in the labor camp in Sowliny. Via Nowy Sącz and Kraków, from June 1940 she found herself in Sochaczew until February 1941; i.e., until the resettlement of Sochaczew Jews to the ghetto in Warsaw. She describes in detail the circumstances of her wandering: resettlement from Łódź, daily life in the camp in Sowliny, living conditions in Kraków and Sochaczew, the deportations of Jews in Żyrardów and Sochaczew as well as first impressions of stay in Warsaw Ghetto.
- ***Description:*** original or transcript, handwritten manuscript, ink, pencil, Polish, 140×200 mm, minor damage and losses of text, ss. 174, pp. 319.

Authorship established by H.W. in 1946. Text written in 11 school notebooks, with one handwriting. Individual notebooks written in the same handwriting: 1. "On the path of exile, Łódź –Limanowa 10 III—16 III 1940"; 2. "On the path of exile, Sowliny–Limanowa, March–April 1940"; 3. "Sowliny–Limanowa"; 4. "Sowliny–Limanowa–Nowy Sącz"; 5. "Nowy Sącz, April–May 1940"; 6. "Kraków 1940"; 7. "Kraków, May–June 1940"; 9. "Sochaczew"; 10.

"Soch[aczew]"; 11. "Soch[aczew], January–February 1941"; 12. "S[ochaczew], February 1941"

On the cover of notebook 10 is a notation (ink): "M[ordkowicz?]."

Notebooks 1–4 were preserved in binders.

Notebook 8 is missing. It could contain texts of poems (see Ring. I/2).

Other texts of Pola Mordkowicz, see Ring. I/2.

**1184. RING. I/2. Mf. ŻIH—770; USHMM—1**

- After 06.1940, place unknown.
- [Pola Mordkowicz], "Pokłosie obozowe—Sowliny pod Limanową-Nowy Sącz-Bochnia-Kraków—15 III Rok 1940 10 VI" [Camp gleanings—Sowliny near Limanowa-Nowy Sącz-Bochnia-Kraków—15 March to 10 June 1940]
- Songs and satirical poems ("Here we have a camp . . . ," "Long live the camp . . . ," "On Lustig. To the chairman of the community of the Piedmont townlet Limanowa . . . ," "Cheers to you, Marin. To the vice chairman of the Jewish Community of Nowy Sącz," "Most meritorious of the personnel in the orphanage's kitchen . . . ," "Farewell to Marin!," "Departure from Nowy Sącz," "The Pass," "To Fus the janitor in the Department for Resettlement Affairs at the J[ewish] Community in Kraków," "Synagogue," "Application") concern the author's experiences in camp in Sowliny and stay in Nowy Sącz, Bochnia, and Kraków in the period 03.–06.1940.
- ***Description:*** original or transcript, handwritten manuscript, ink, Polish, 160×220 mm, damage and losses of text, ss. 14, pp. 26.

On the title sheet are the dates 15.03.–10.06.1940. Manuscript inscribed by the same handwriting as the manuscript Ring I/1.

**1185. RING. I/592/12. (Lb. 583). Mf. ŻIH—792; USHMM—23**

- After 7.06.1942, Warsaw Ghetto
- Ajzenberg Fiszek (Schwanningen [Swarzędz], Gemeinschaftslager a. D.A.F 24, Zimmer 87, [prisoner's no.?]—668), Letter of 1.06.1942 to NN. (Warsaw Ghetto)
- Notation about death of author's father (19.04.1942) and deportation of closest relatives (Uncle Izak Lejb with family). Request for bread.
- ***Description:*** transcript (2 copies), handwritten manuscript (H*), pencil, German, Yiddish, 150×196 mm, ss. 2, pp. 4.

On p. 1 a note in Yiddish: "Copy of postcard sent by a young Łódźer from a labor camp near Poznań."

Published: *Listy o Zagładzie*, pp. 155–157.

**1186. RING. I/386. Mf. ŻIH—783; USHMM—14**

- After 11.11.1941, place unknown
- German authorities in Generalgouvernement, Letters (dated 4.12.1940, 3.05., 11.07., 11.11.1941 and Date unknown) to Dr. Mieczysław Finder (Swoszowice), chairman of Jewish Council (fragments)
- Concerning administration of peat yard (torfowni) (and camp [?]) in Swoszowice (inter alia congratulations for increasing production of peat) and other official matters. Letters signed by Dr. Fr. Schmidt (commissioner of Nowy Sącz) or Frenzel (commissioner of Wieliczka).
- ***Description:*** transcript, typescript, German, 208×260, 130×240, serious damage and losses of text, ss. 4, pp. 4.

Index: Chemala, Nelly Finder, Fanny Heistlinger, Stefanie Askenase

**1187. RING. I/592/3. Mf. ŻIH—792; USHMM—23**

- Date unknown, Szymanów near Sochaczew
- NN. (Szymanów near Sochaczew, labor camp), Letter to NN. (Warsaw Ghetto)
- Author, volunteer in labor camp, employed in the region of Puszcza Kampinowska. Colleagues: Gedali Rozenberg, Zelig Wolfowicz, Mojsie Kepojer[48] (from Łódź).
- ***Description:*** original, handwritten manuscript, pencil, Polish, 148×92 mm, minor damage and losses of text, ss. 1, pp. 2.

Index: Pinkiert, Dora Kaufman (Warsaw, ul. Sienna 46, apt. 34)

**1188. RING. I/406. Mf. ŻIH—783; USHMM—14**

- After 06.1941, place unknown
- NN., Notes regarding the camp in Trawniki
- Organization after 22.06.1941 of a camp for Soviet prisoners in Trawniki, and later of a death camp for Jews (gas chamber and crematorium), where ca. 1,500 people are killed daily, mainly Jews from the Czech lands and Slovakia [sic].
- ***Description:*** original (handwritten manuscript) and transcript (typescript), Polish, 195×150, 136×100 mm, ss. 2, pp. 3.

In the transcript is the sentence: "On the Lublin–Chełm rail track is the small station Trawniki and a settlement of the same name," that is not in the original, while in the original there is the notation "Trawniki near Chełm."

**1189. RING. I/373. Mf. ŻIH—836; USHMM—67**

- After 12.1941, Warsaw Ghetto
- NN., Account entitled "Labor camp in Tyszowce in 1940"

48. "Mojsie Kepojer" is a comic nickname in Yiddish (Moyshe-kepoyer). It may originate from a pseudo-Hebrew phrase meaning "Moses like a peasant," that a Jew did something quite foolishly. Moyshe-kepoyer is more commonly used to imply that something has been done entirely backwards or upside-down.

- Author, from Warsaw, was taken to labor camp in August 1940. After a short stay in camp in Lublin he was sent to Tyszowce, where he stayed until 10.12.1940, working on regulation of the Huczwa River. Work conditions, food, watchtowers, relations with local Jewish and Polish population.
- ***Description:*** original (o) (handwritten manuscript—FLIG*, ink, 220×288, 160×204 mm), transcript (typescript, 210×298 mm), Polish, ss. 23, pp. 33.
  Attached note by H.W.: "Daniel Fligelman from Aleksandrów Kujawski."
  See HWC, 53/4 (second copy of transcript, ss. 11).

**1190. RING. I/26. Mf. ŻIH—772; USHMM—3**

- 1941, Warsaw Ghetto
- Collection of accounts and documents concerning labor camps near Warsaw (1941)
- Accounts of workers, copies of extracts from forensic medical examinations, physicians' reports, telephone messages, camp records concerning treatment of camp inmates (frequent beatings and deaths), conditions of work and lodging in the camps in: Stok Ruski, Narty, Piekło (Kampinos), Garwolin, Łęki, Sobienie-Jeziory, Kałuszyn, Roztoki near Błonie, Łowicz.
- ***Description:*** transcript, typescript, Polish, 205×293 mm, minor damage and losses of text, ss. 14, pp. 14.
  Copies made from documents obtained by the Jewish Council in Warsaw [?]. Among others, accounts of: Majer Lejb Fiszbin, Dr. Lipsztadt, Dr. Hirsch, Dr. J. Kahan (Warsaw, Nalewki), H. Żuchowski.
  On p. 1 note by H.W.: "108 -1942/1 January. Department."

**1191. RING. I/391. (Lb. 949). Mf. ŻIH—783; USHMM—14**

- Date unknown, Warsaw Ghetto
- A. L. [Limonad (?)], Account entitled "How was I captured for labor camp and saved ? Not[es?] by a certain professor of music A.L."
- Author seized in a roundup at ul. Leszno, held in "Collegium" [ul. Żelazna 84], evaded transfer to labor camp, released to go home the same day. During escape one of those seized was shot.
- ***Description:*** transcript (3 copies), typescript, Polish, 200×277, 190×54 mm, extensive damage and losses of text, ss. 6, pp. 6.
  Attached note by H.W.: "Statement of prof. of music A. Limonad (?) submitted by I. Giterman."

**1192. RING. I/405. (Lb. 322). Mf. ŻIH—783; USHMM—14**

- After 2.05.1941, Warsaw Ghetto
- [M. Landau], Account entitled "Der etapn-punkt fun di lageristn" [The staging point for camp inmates] (2.05.1941)
- Conditions reigning in the "Collegium" building (ul. Leszno 84) and quarantine at ul. Leszno 109, where people summoned (volunteers and those seized in the ghetto) for labor camps were assembled.
- ***Description:*** transcript (2 copies), handwritten manuscript (MS*), pencil, Yiddish, 147×205 mm, minor damage and losses of text, ss. 10, pp. 10.
  In the margin a Hebrew letter (ink): "g" (giml).
  Attached note by H.W. in Yiddish: "Recorded by Mordechaj Szwarcbard on the basis of the account of Arbeitsamt coworker M. Landau."

**1193. RING. I/407. (Lb. 305). Mf. ŻIH—783; USHMM—14**

- After 11.05.1941, Warsaw Ghetto
- Judel Moszman (ul. Nalewki 32, apt. 2), Account concerning labor camp in Wilga near Garwolin (11.05.1941)
- Stay in camp in 04/05.1941; labor in land improvement; hunger and mistreatment by Ukrainian warders, nighttime roll calls.
- ***Description:*** transcript (2 copies), handwritten manuscript (BW*), Polish,Yiddish, 147×207 mm, minor damage and losses of text, ss. 2, pp. 2.
  Over the text of the account is a note in Polish: "Camp of Wilga near Garwolin. 0,330 [sic]. Moszman Judel, Nalewki 32/2."

**1194. RING. I/592/4. Mf. ŻIH—792; USHMM—23**

- After 05.1941, Warsaw Ghetto
- NN. (Wilga), Letter from early 05.1941 to NN. (Warsaw)
- Letter from a prisoner after 8-day stay in labor camp with request to parents to obtain his immediate release from the camp.
- ***Description:*** transcript (2 copies), handwritten manuscript (MS*), pencil, Yiddish, 148×208 mm, ss. 2, pp. 2.
  Attached note by H.W. in Yiddish: "Copied from original and submitted to Oyneg Shabes by Eliasz Gutkowski."

**1195. RING. I/661. Mf. ŻIH—816; USHMM—28**

- After 25.04.1941, Warsaw Ghetto
- Mojżesz Passenstajn, Order Service group leader, record no. 535, Letter to the Chairman of the Jewish Council in Warsaw [A. Czerniaków]
- Complaint about abduction on 25.04.1941 from the Warsaw Ghetto of 3 officers of the Order Service (the letter's author and 2 orderlies: Rotsztein and Wizenfeld) by Lagerschutz to the labor camp Wilga-Casino. Description of living conditions in camp.
- ***Description:*** transcript (2 copies), typescript, Polish, 115×166, 188×248 mm, damage and losses of text, missing ending (first copy), ss. 5, pp. 5.
  Index: Hirszkowicz, Order Service group leader

**1196. RING. I/592/15. Mf. ŻIH—792; USHMM—23**

- After 28.06.[1942], Warsaw Ghetto
- NN. (Mojsze, Mundek) (labor camp Bautruppe "Nord"—Wilkowiecko near Opatów), Letters dated 21 and 28[?].06.[1942] to NN. (Warsaw Ghetto)
- Information about author's and addressee's father (works in camp in Kamyk).
- ***Description:*** transcript, handwritten manuscript (H*[?]), Yiddish and Yiddish in Roman transliteration, pencil, ink, 148×193 mm, minor damage and losses of text, ss. 1, pp. 1.

**1197. RING. I/385/1. Mf. ŻIH—783; USHMM—14**

- After 05.1941, Warsaw Ghetto
- NN., Account concerning stay in Wojaszówka labor camp near Krosno (05.1941) (fragment)
- Author, a journalist, sent to the labor camp, where he spent 10 days (from 16.05.1941). Behavior of the Jewish managers of the camp, Order Service (commandant Krawczyk), the medic (Sztajnfeld) (sending of the sick to work, lack of medical care, beating of prisoners, trade, profiteering, and bribery).
- ***Description:*** transcript, typescript, Polish, 180×260, 180×110 mm, serious damage and losses of text, ss. 4, pp. 4.

  On p. 4 a note (ink): "Rawicz."

  Index: Dr. Neuman, Pantela, camp's manager, Mendel Sonabend, fellow prisoner

**1198. RING. I/592/16. Mf. ŻIH—792; USHMM—23**

- After 5.06.1942, Warsaw Ghetto
- L. Schnurbach (Września, Ohlendorff Lager, Am Bahnhoff), Letter of 27[?].05.1942 to S. Włocławska (Warsaw, ul. Świętojerska 43, apt. 36, with Świder)
- Author deported from Włocławek, stays in camp and works in rail line construction.
- ***Description:*** transcript (from copyist's note), handwritten manuscript (FLIG*), ink, Polish, 138×203 mm, text is difficult to read in places, ss. 1, pp. 2.

  On p. 1 copyist's note: "Copy of a letter sent from one of the men displaced in April 1942 from Włocławek, the sheet is addressed to a wife's friend."

**1199. RING. I/378. Mf. ŻIH—782; USHMM—13**

- After 7.12.1940, Warsaw Ghetto
- NN., Account entitled "About the labor camp in Zamość in 1940"
- Author seized 3.09.1940 by Camp Commission (Warsaw, ul. Kawęczyńska) and sent to the labor camp in Zamość. He worked on drainage of swamplands, and for a certain time constructed an airfield in the vicinity of the village Mokre (near Zamość). He obtained release and 7.12.1940 returned to Warsaw. He also describes: arrival of the delegation of the Jewish Council from Warsaw in Zamość 1.11.1940 (Dr. Lewin, Braff, and Norski Nożyca); and on the basis of accounts of friends the camp in Białobrzegi (near Zamość), inter alia commandant Sobota, one of Schultz's "blacks" [?], Jewish commandant Ryniek Handelsman.
- ***Description:*** transcript (3 copies), handwritten manuscript (CA*), pencil, Polish, 150×210 mm, minor damage and losses of text, ss. 138, pp. 138.

  Attached note by H.W.: "Author NN, text submitted to the archive by Salomea Ostrowska."

**1200. RING. I/380. (Lb. 1149). Mf. ŻIH—783; USHMM—14**

- After 28.10.1940, Warsaw Ghetto
- NN., Letter from the labor camp in Zamość to NN. in Warsaw ("Verbatim copy of excerpt from camp inmate's letter to an acquaintance in Warsaw, 28.10.1940")
- Description of the housing (barracks in Zamość), march out to construct airfield near Mokre (near Zamość), dinner in a small village store, return to barracks, common meal, food supply help from outside, position in camp of the Jewish commandant "Negus."
- ***Description:*** transcript (a) (handwritten manuscript, several handwritings: FLIG*, ink, 210×300, 160×202 mm); transcript (b) (2 copies, typescript, 210×295 mm), Polish, ss. 34, pp. 40.

  See HWC, 53/9 (third copy of copy (b), typescript, ss. 11).

**1201. RING. I/403. (Lb. 325). Mf. ŻIH—836; USHMM—67**

- After 29.01.1941, Warsaw Ghetto
- [Józef Fersztenberg], Account entitled "Zamoshtsh–Bialobzhegi" [Zamość–Białobrzegi] (29.01.1941)
- Author (age 19) from Warsaw, describes stay in labor camps (from 9.09.1940) in Zamość and Białobrzegi; land improvement jobs, without pay; mistreatment of prisoners and sanitary conditions (diseases); assistance from peasants. Attempt to escape to USSR.
- ***Description:*** original (o) (2 copies), handwritten manuscript (H.W.*), pencil, Yiddish, 150×210 mm, ss. 8, pp. 8.

  In the margin of p. 1 a note in Yiddish: "camps"; in the margins a Hebrew letter (ink): "yud."

  On p. 4 near the date is a note : "told" (or a note about the date of writing down of the account).

  Attached note by H.W.: "Testimony of Josef Fersztenberg, recorded by H.Wasser."

**1202. RING. I/280. Mf. ŻIH—781; USHMM—12**

a)

- Date unknown, Warsaw Ghetto
- NN., Account entitled "Di doktoyrim komisies fun

tsvangs-lagern" [The doctors committees for forced (labor) camps]
- Author, physician, describes the activity of the committee at ul. Kawęczyńska in Warsaw.
- *Description:* transcript (2 copies), handwritten manuscript (MS*), pencil, Yiddish, 148×210 mm, minor damage and losses of text, ss. 2, pp. 2.

b)
- Date unknown, Warsaw Ghetto
- NN., Account entitled "Di praktik fun di doktoyrim-kom. fun di arb. lagern" [The practice of the physicians com(mittee) for lab(or) camps]
- Activity of the committee in one of the points in Warsaw (bribed officials—a Volksdeutsch [ethnic German] and a Pole, they issue false documents, permitting evasion of labor camp).
- *Description:* transcript (2 copies), handwritten manuscript (MS*), pencil, Yiddish, 148×210 mm, minor damage and losses of text, ss. 4, pp. 4.

  In the margins pp. 3–6 a symbol: "/.," or a Hebrew letter (ink): "u" [vov]

**1203. RING. I/399. Mf. ŻIH—783; USHMM—14**

- 12.06.1941, Warsaw Ghetto
- NN., Account entitled "Zeks vokhn tsvangs-arbets-lager" [Six weeks of forced labor camp] (12.06.1941)
- Author from Warsaw, about the Order Service in Warsaw Ghetto, trip to camp [?], description of camp, housing, hunger, work conditions, return home after six weeks.
- *Description:* original or transcript, handwritten manuscript, notebook, ink, Yiddish, 150×200 mm, text illegible in places, ss. 16, pp. 19.

  Published: *Selected Documents*, pp. 270–276.

**1204. RING. I/493. (Lb. 1052). Mf. ŻIH—788; USHMM—19**

- Date unknown, Warsaw Ghetto
- [Marian Liberman], Account of forced labor in a sugar mill
- Influence of war on the sugar mill's work.
- *Description:* transcript (2 copies), handwritten manuscript (JG*), pencil, Polish, damage and losses of text, ss. 6, pp. 6.

  On p. 1 letter "D" and a note by H.W. in Yiddish: "Liberman."

  Attached note by H.W.: "Author Liberman Marian—from Łódź."

**1205. RING. I/592/2. Mf. ŻIH—792; USHMM—23**

- After 17.12.1940
- NN. (Saul), Letter of 17.12.1940 NN. (Warsaw Ghetto)
- Author finding himself in labor camp asks parents for help in getting out of it.
- *Description:* transcript, typescript, Polish, 216×139 mm, ss. 1, pp. 1.

**1206. RING. I/622. (Lb. 715). Mf. ŻIH—814; USHMM—26**

- Date unknown, Warsaw Ghetto
- NN., Account entitled "Our day in camp"
- Unnamed labor camp (field work, drainage of marshlands, and clearing of forests). Appended sketch: jobs in clearing forest under supervision of SS men.
- *Description:* original, handwritten manuscript, ink, pencil, Polish, 200×295 mm., ss. 2, pp. 2.

  Manuscript on the back of: "Questionnaire C" of the Jewish Council in Warsaw, a record form for institutions in the Warsaw Ghetto (after 1.04.1941, printed, German, Polish)

  Attached note by H.W.: "Delivered by E. Gutkowski."

  Published: *Selected Documents*, pp. 267–268.

**1207. RING. I/1171 (1490). Mf. ŻIH—834; USHMM—46**

- Date unknown, Warsaw Ghetto
- NN., Satirical songs sung in labor camps

  1) "Marshall Śmigły Rydz gave us nothing . . ."—a song that Jews had to sing in labor camp in Józefów in 1941;

  2) "Oh, how pleasant to stand in line for bread . . ."—a song sung in Łódź and Zgierz in 1940.
- *Description:* transcript, printed, handwritten manuscript, ink, Polish, 102×180, 180×206 mm, ss. 2, pp. 2.

  Doc. written on the back of a distribution list of food products for community center (świetlicy) no. 24 at ul. Twarda 22 in the Warsaw Ghetto, dated 9.10.[. . .] as well as the community center at ul. Stawka 9, dated 8[9].10.[. . .] (Printed, handwritten manuscript, ink).

  Attached note by H.W.

**1208. RING. I/1156 (1475). Mf. ŻIH—833; USHMM—45**

- Date unknown, Warsaw Ghetto
- Aron Gips, Collection of songs entitled "From the Bzura (a bundle of camp songs)"
- Songs: 1) "We arrived here from around Warsaw . . ."; 2) "Bzura, our Bzura . . ."; 3) "Our red barrack stands on the river . . ."; 4) "Reveille to get up . . ."; 5) (6) "We have with us wheelbarrows, spades, spades . . ."; 6) (7) "Lorry, our lorry . . ."; 7) "We have to mow the slope . . ."; 8) "Hey dredge, dredge . . ."; 9) "Because behind the wire stands the Lagerschutz . . ."[49]

49. The Polish original does not provide transliteration of the Yiddish titles, but only Polish translation.

- *Description:* original, handwritten manuscript, ink, Yiddish, pencil, 150×199 mm, minor damage and losses of text, text difficult to read in places, ss. 2, pp. 4.

  Annotation (pencil): "Sienna 24/4—Rysiek."

  Error in numbering of the songs, missing no. 5, while no. 7 appears twice.

  Attached note by H.W. in Yiddish: "Author Aron Gips from Gąbin, wrote down songs that were sung in camp near Łowicz."

## VII. Literary Texts

### 1209. RING. I/1137 (1456). Mf. ŻIH—833; USHMM—45

- After 1941, Warsaw Ghetto
- [Icchak Berensztein?], Essays (4) entitled "Oyf khurves" [On ruins]
- Reflections on the current situation, about human indifference, about hunger, coexistence with death, about the Warsaw Ghetto's "philosopher" Rubinsztajn, about the war that no one can evade, about Mendele Moykher Sforim.
- *Description:* original or transcript, typescript, Yiddish, 210×297 mm, extensive damage and losses of text, ss. 34, pp. 32.

  Titles of individual essays: 1) "Hunger—1941"; "2) "On ruins"; 3) "Dialogues about literature in difficult times."

  Doc. was sewn and bound in cardboard covers.

  Inventory: "Author is I. [Icchak] Berensztejn."

### 1210. RING. I/600. (Lb. 585). Mf. ŻIH—812; USHMM—24

- Date unknown, Warsaw Ghetto
- [Icchak Berenstein], Essays entitled: 1) "Hunger—1941"; 2) "Dialogues about literature in difficult times"
- Reflections on the situation of Jews in the face of the tragedy of war and occupation; sketches from the history of Jewish literature.
- *Description:* transcript, typescript, Yiddish, 100×176, 204×292 mm, extensive damage and losses of text, missing one sheet, ss. 31, pp. 31.

  On p. 1 a postwar note in Yiddish (ink): "Icchak Bernstein."

  Published: doc. 1) *Tsvishn lebn un toyt* [Between life and death], ed. B. Mark, Warsaw 1955, pp. 66–69; *Ghetto. Berichte aus dem Warschauer Ghetto* 1939–1945, Berlin 1966, pp. 121–125.

### 1211. RING. I/1138 (1457). (Lb. 1596). Mf. ŻIH—833; USHMM—45

- Date unknown, Warsaw Ghetto
- [Icchak Berensztein], Prose poems (6) entitled 1) "Warsaw, 5701 [1941/42]"; 2) "The Walls"; 3) "Yom Kippur."; 4) "Kiddush Ha-Shem" [Martyrdom]; 5) "Head and Heart"]; 6) "The Kelmer[50] Preacher"
- Martyrdom of the Jewish population during occupation.
- *Description:* transcript, typescript, Yiddish, 210×294 mm, ss. 15, pp. 13.

  Poem "Warsaw 5701": pp. 2 and 3 in 2 copies.

  On p. 1 of the poem "The Kelmer Preacher" is a note by H.W. (ink): "109–1942/1 January, no. 23."

  On p. 1 at top (in docs. 2, 4, 5) a note by H.W. (red pencil): "I. Ber."

  Inventory: "Author I. [Icchak] Berensztejn."

  See HWC, 61/13 (second copy [?] of doc. 3, typescript, ss. 1).

### 1212. RING. I/522. (Lb. 531). Mf. ŻIH—790; USHMM—21

- Date unknown, place unknown
- I.D. Berkowicz, Program of a theatrical play entitled *Amkho*[51] [Your people] based on Sholem Aleichem's drama, "Dos groyse gevins" [The big win][52]
- Directors: C. Frydland and B. Czemeryński; assistant director: I. Rubinsztajn; set design: M. Szmid; music: A.W. Szterenberg; scenery: D. Sznajder; crew: B. Czemeryński, T. Robens, Ch. Hendler, Klaczkin, A. Meskin, Sz. Bruk, Sz. Finkel, M. Batami, M. Bnimini, A. Barac, T. Judelewicz, Ch. Amti, M. Gnesin, G. Szajn. Synopsis in Yiddish and text of the play in Hebrew.
- *Description:* transcript, typescript, Hebrew, Yiddish, 208×290 mm, ss. 51, pp. 51.

### 1213. RING. I/1164 (1483). (Lb. 589). Mf. ŻIH—833; USHMM—45

- Date unknown, Warsaw Ghetto

50. Presumably the preacher originated in the Lithuanian Jewish community of Kelem, not to be confused with Chełm (Khelm or Khelem in Yiddish), the community near Lublin.

51. Hebrew–Yiddish expression that literally means "Your people," but is used figuratively in Yiddish for "common folk" or for "Jews" as opposed to Gentiles.

52. The Sholem Aleichem story and play is also known as "200,000."

- Pedro Calderón de la Barca, Drama entitled "Keter David" [Crown of David]
- About intrigues at the court of King David and the struggle for the throne after the ruler's death. Appended program of the play with synopsis.
- ***Description:*** transcript, typescript, Hebrew, Yiddish, 210×295 mm, ss. 80, pp. 80.
  Doc. was kept in a binder and bound in a paper cover (similar in Ring. I/1163).

**1214. RING. I/527. (Lb. 1569, 1569A, 1569B). Mf. ŻIH—790; USHMM—21**

- After 05.1941, Warsaw Ghetto
- Jehuda Feld [Feldwurm], Collection of stories entitled "In di tsaytn fun Homen dem tsveytn" [In the time of Haman the Second]
- Expulsion of Jews from Płock, tragic fate of the population of the Warsaw Ghetto, hunger as a social problem, story of a 10-year-old boy, an orphan from an orphanage.
- ***Description:*** original or transcript, typescript (handwritten additions, ink), Yiddish, 220×345 mm, minor damage and losses of text, ss. 69, pp. 69.
  Titles of individual texts: 1) "Expulsion from P—k [Plock?]" (11.05.1941), pp. 22; 2) missing title (no page) (21.05.1941), pp. 7 (missing p. 1); 3) "Hunger," pp. 5; 4) "Homeless" (2.05.1941), pp. 9; 5) "Fifteen Minutes after Five" (date unknown), pp. 8; 6) "A Mother's Dream"; 7) "Sorele Grober." On p. 1 (second copy [?]) ("Fifteen Minutes after Five") a note in Yiddish (one handwriting with addition in the text, ink): "for revision."

**1215. RING. I/528. (Lb. 1568). Mf. ŻIH—790; USHMM—21**

- Date unknown, Warsaw Ghetto
- Jehuda Feld [Feldwurm], Stories entitled "Khaykl, Paykl un Baykl (klal-tuer fun a hoyz- komitet)" [Khaykl, Paykl, and Baykl (officials of an apartment house committee)]
- Satirical story about officials of an apartment house committee (chairman, secretary, and treasurer).
- ***Description:*** original or transcript, typescript (handwritten additions, ink), Yiddish, 220×350 mm, minor damage and losses of text, ss. 8, pp. 8.
  On p. 1 a note in Yiddish (same handwriting as additions in text, ink): "Document finished" [?].

**1216. RING. I/521. Mf. ŻIH—789; USHMM—20**

- Date unknown, Warsaw Ghetto
- [Bruno Frank], Drama
- Period of the American War of Independence; an English envoy arrives at the court of a German prince in order to hire 12,000 soldiers.
- ***Description:*** transcript, typescript, Yiddish, 210×275 mm, extensive minor damage and losses of text, ss. 77, pp. 77.
  Inventory: "Bruno Frank, Ten Thousand."

**1217. RING. I/1162 (1481). (Lb. 508). Mf. ŻIH—833; USHMM—45**

- Date unknown, Warsaw Ghetto
- [Szymon] Dżigan, Monologue entitled "A klog tsum gelekhter" [Damn the joking]
- About adversity, unemployment, assimilation—in reference to the current situation in Europe (before 1939).
- ***Description:*** transcript, typescript, Yiddish, 210×294 mm, minor damage and losses of text, ss. 3, pp. 3.

**1218. RING. I/1166 (1485). (Lb. 963). Mf. ŻIH—834; USHMM—46**

- 1941, Warsaw Ghetto
- Glater, Story entitled "Bay komunikat" [In announcement]
- Story of Warsaw Ghetto life.
- ***Description:*** transcript (2 copies), handwritten manuscript (MA*), pencil, Yiddish, 147×207 mm, ss. 30, pp. 30.
  On p. 1 a note by H.W. in Yiddish (ink): "Glater."
  Attached note by H.W. in Yiddish: "Scene based on authentic events, N. Tytelman's handwriting."

**1219. RING. I/1167 (1486). (Lb. 1594). Mf. ŻIH—834; USHMM—46**

- After 08.1941, Warsaw Ghetto
- [Lejb Goldin], Story entitled "Kronik fun [mes-les]" [Chronicle of (24 Hours)] (08.1941)
- Meditations of a hungry person, waiting for the longed-for soup in a public kitchen. Description of life in the Warsaw Ghetto.
- ***Description:*** transcript, typescript, Yiddish, 208×293 mm, damage and losses of text, ss. 8, pp. 8.
  Attached note by H.W. in Yiddish: "Lejb Goldin."
  Published: *Tsvishn lebn un toyt* [Between life and death], ed. B. Mark, Warsaw 1955, pp. 49–65; *Dwa etapy*, pp. 84–96. *Ghetto. Berichte aus dem Warschauer Ghetto 1939–1945*, Berlin 1966, pp. 132–147 [also: Leyb Goldin, "Chronicle of a Single Day," in *The Literature of Destruction*, ed. David G. Roskies (Philadelphia, 1988), pp. 424–434].

**1220. RING. I/631. (Lb. 1734). Mf. ŻIH—815; USHMM—27**

- Before 1939, place unknown
- Ber Horowitz, Poem entitled "Legende fun dorf" [Legend of the village]
- Scenes of village life.
- ***Description:*** original, printed (clippings from a newspaper), Yiddish, 130×185 mm, ss. 1, pp. 1.
  At top a note: "Poem dedicated to Masza and Lejb Roskes."

**1221. RING. I/519. Mf. ŻIH—789; USHMM—20**

- Date unknown, Warsaw Ghetto
- Jurandot, Drama entitled "Love Seeks a Home. Comedy in 3 Acts with Music of Iwo Wesby"
- ***Description:*** original or transcript, handwritten manuscript, ink, Polish, Yiddish (in Roman transliteration), 210×300 mm, ss. 86, pp. 86.
  Attached note by H.W.: "Play performed in 'Femina' [theater] in 1941."
  Published: *Przewodnik*, pp. 549–550 (fragment and photocopy of one page).

**1222. RING. I/630. (Lb. 1735). Mf. ŻIH—815; USHMM—27**

- Date unknown, place unknown
- Rachela H. Korn, Poem entitled "A Song of Night"
- About ill-fated love for a missing lover.
- ***Description:*** transcript, typescript, Yiddish, 156×232 mm, minor damage and losses of text, ss. 1, pp. 1.

**1223. RING. I/618. Mf. ŻIH—814; USHMM—26**

- Date unknown, Warsaw Ghetto
- Kalman Lis, Poems (3): "Berg-motiv" [Mountain motif]; "A briv mit a entfer (folkstimlekher motivn)" [A letter with a response (folk motifs)]; "Vos shvaygstu velt . . ." [Why are you silent, world . . .]
- Poetry of morals; the world and the annihilation of the Jews.
- ***Description:*** transcript, handwritten manuscript (TW*), ink, Yiddish, 153×195 mm, ss. 11, pp. 11.
  Manuscripts of the first two poems were kept in a binder.
  Published: Poem "Why are you silent, world . . ." in: *Yidishe Shriftn* (1948); *Antologia*, pp. 327–329.

**1224. RING. I/1139 (1458). (Lb. 634). Mf. ŻIH—833; USHMM—45**

- Date unknown, Warsaw Ghetto
- [Kalman Lis?], Poems (3): 1) "Ikh zing dos lid fun rozn gloybn" [I sing the song of rosy faith]; 2) "Reb Khaim Kuzmirer"; 3) "Ver zogt az alts fargeyt" [Who says that everything passes].
- ***Description:*** transcript, typescript (handwritten additions, ink, postwar), Yiddish, 162×295 mm, damage and losses of text, ss. 7, pp. 7.
  Published: Poem "Ikh zing dos lid fun rozn gloybn" appeared in *Naye Folks-tsaytung*, no. 123, 29.04.1938.

**1225. RING. I/520. Mf. ŻIH—789; USHMM—20; RING. I/621. Mf. ŻIH—814; USHMM—26**

- Date unknown, place unknown
- L. Maloch, Drama entitled "In shtub—in klub" [At home—in the club]
- On the occasion of Mothers' Day, the children of a poor cobbler prepare a surprise for their mother.
- ***Description:*** transcript (2 copies, second copy from Ring. I/621), typescript, Yiddish, 205×294 mm, minor damage and losses of text, ss. 18, pp. 18.

**1226. RING. I/515. Mf. ŻIH—789; USHMM—20**

- Date unknown, Warsaw Ghetto
- Kadie Mołodowska [Kadya Molodowska], Poems (3): 1) "A mayse mit a balie" [A story with a washtub]; 2) "Di oremheyt" [Poverty]; 3) "A mayse mit a mantl" [A story with a coat]
- Dramatic stories: about a washtub that haunts an apartment where there was linen to wash and washed it itself; about the dreams of poor girls; about the children of a tailor who one after the other wear the same coat.
- ***Description:*** transcript, typescript, Yiddish, 177×220, 220×347 mm, ss. 3, pp. 5.

**1227. RING. I/1044 (1363). MISSING ORIGINAL**

- After 1955, Warsaw
- Perec Chasyd [Perec Opoczyński], Story entitled "Din Toyre" [Torah Court]
- Story about a poor Jew who cannot marry off his daughter due to the high marriage tax. Story dedicated to Menachem Kohn (05. or 06.1942).
- ***Description:*** postwar transcript, typescript, Hebrew, 215×280 mm, ss. 6, pp. 6.

**1228. RING. I/1140 (1459). MISSING ORIGINAL**

- Date unknown, place unknown
- [Perec Opoczyński?], Story entitled "Dom no. 21" [House no. 21]
- ***Description:*** original or transcript, typescript, Yiddish, ss. 11, pp. 11.
  Missing before 1970.
  Published: P. Opoczyński, *Reportazhn fun varshever geto* [Reports from the Warsaw Ghetto], ed. B. Mark, Warsaw 1954, pp. 9–24 [; David Roskies, ed., *The Literature of Destruction* (Philadelphia, 1988), pp. 408–423].

**1229. RING. I/33. MISSING ORIGINAL Mf. ŻIH—772; USHMM—3**

- After 1946, Warsaw
- [Perec Opoczyński], Narrative entitled "Di geshikhte fun a hoyz-komitet, a hoyz komitet oyf Volinska" [The History of an apartment house committee, An apartment house committee on Wołyńska]
- Creation, activity, and gradual degradation of an apartment house committee in the Warsaw Ghetto (ul. Wołyńska 21). Overview of human attitudes, unsatisfied ambition, dishonesty (1939–winter 1941).
- ***Description:*** postwar transcript, typescript, Yiddish, ss. 22, pp. 22.

**1230. RING. I/455. MISSING ORIGINAL**

- After 1946, Warsaw
- [Perec Opoczyński?], Essay entitled "Der yidisher brivn-treger" [The Jewish Letter Carrier]
- Work and problems of a letter carrier in the Warsaw Ghetto.

• *Description:* postwar transcript, typescript, Yiddish, 215×279 mm, ss. 24, pp. 24.
Published: P. Opoczyński, *Reportazhn fun varshever geto*, ed. B. Mark, Warsaw 1954, pp. 75–93.

**1231. RING. I/430. MISSING ORIGINAL**

• After 1946, Warsaw
• [Perec Opoczyński], Essay entitled “Kinder oyfn bruk” [Children on the Pavement]
• *Description:* postwar transcript, typescript, Yiddish, 214×278 mm, ss. 16, pp. 16.
Inventory “Author is Perec Opoczyński.”
Published: P. Opoczyński, *Reportazhn fun varshever geto*, ed. B. Mark, Warsaw 1954, pp. 49–60.

**1232. RING. I/162. Mf. ŻIH—779; USHMM—10**

• After 1940, Warsaw Ghetto
• Anatol Pomeranc, Poems entitled “Komitet Domowy” [Apartment House Committee], “Ż.T.O.S.,” and “Dzielnica Żydowska w Warszawie” [The Jewish District in Warsaw]
• Author (age 13), satirical works.
• *Description:* transcript (2 copies), handwritten manuscript (BTT*), pencil, Polish, 146×205 mm, ss. 14, pp. 14.
In the margins of the manuscript of the poem “Komitet Domowy,” there is the letter: “v.” On the manuscript of the poem “Ż.T.O.S.” is a symbol in the margin: “^” (or Hebrew letter “t” (taf).
Attached note by H.W. in Yiddish (missing).

**1233. RING. I/605. Mf. ŻIH—813; USHMM—25**

• After 06.1941, Warsaw Ghetto
• Lejb [Zelman] Skalow [Pluskałowski], Novel in two parts: 1) “Di hak un kroyts” [The Swastyka]; 2) “Kvo vadis?” [Quo vadis?]
• Fates of the residents of a tenement on ul. Graniczna in Warsaw in the years 1939–1941 (war in 1939, labor camps, ghetto, steam-disinfection baths [parówki], hunger, diseases).
• *Description:*
doc. 1) in two versions a (larger) and b:
(a) original (2 copies) (typescript with handwritten manuscript corrections, ink, 206×290 mm; in the second copy pp. 35 and 36 are missing, text starts from p. 2);
(b) transcript (4 copies, typescript, 206×293 mm, minor damage and losses of text. (copies 1–3), copy 1 (missing pp. 37, 43–47), copy 3 (fragments), copy 4 (serious damage and losses of text), Yiddish, ss. 297, pp. 297;
doc. 2)—original or transcript (2 copies), typescript, Yiddish, 208×293 mm, minor damage and losses of text, ss. 208, pp. 208.
Published: *Di hak un kroyts, Swastyka*, ed. B. Mark, Warsaw 1954; *Ghetto. Berichte aus dem Warschauer Ghetto 1939–1945*, Berlin 1966, pp. 17–116 (“Swastyka”).

**1234. RING. I/653. (Lb. 1656). Mf. ŻIH—816; USHMM—28**

• Date unknown, Warsaw Ghetto
• Sul [?], Poems (4): 1) “Slupkes” [Posts]; 2) “Nekht” [Nights]; 3) “Es brent” [It's Burning]; 4) “Goyrl” [Fate].
• *Description:* original or transcript, handwritten manuscript, ink, Yiddish, 224×356 mm, ss. 2, pp. 2.

**1235. RING. I/639. Mf. ŻIH—815; USHMM—27**

• Date unknown, place unknown
• Sh. Shayev [Simcha Bunim Szajewicz], Poems: 1) “S'lid fun der mamen vos hot farloyrn ir kind in der milkhome” [Song of the mother who lost her child in the war]; 2) “Mayn veg” [My way]; 3) “S'kind in harbst” [The Child in Autumn]; 4) “Balade fun der vayser nakht” [Ballad of the white night]
• *Description:* original, handwritten manuscript (Szaj.*), ink, Yiddish, 157×472 mm, ss. 7, pp. 9
Poem 1) in 2 copies.

**1236. RING. I/652. Mf. ŻIH—816; USHMM—28**

• Date unknown, Warsaw Ghetto
• [Simcha Bunim Szajewicz], Poems (4): 1) “Minkhe” [Afternoon prayer]; 2) “Oktober” [October]; 3) “Bay nakht” [At night]; 4) “Harbst lid” [Autumn song]
• *Description:* original or transcript, handwritten manuscript (Szaj.*), ink, Yiddish, 148×210 mm, ss. 4, pp. 7.
Inventory: “Author—[Simcha Bunim] Szajewicz.”

**1237. RING. I/530. Mf. ŻIH—790; USHMM—21**

• After 2.06.1942, Warsaw Ghetto
• [Sz. Szajnkinder], Story entitled “4 meydlekh” [Four Girls]
• Story about the happy childhood and dramatic life in the ghetto of Ala, Bela, Guta, and Zula, girls from one Warsaw tenement.
• *Description:* original, typescript (handwritten additions—Sz.*, ink), Yiddish, 220×288 mm, minor damage and losses of text, ss. 6, pp. 6.
On p. 1 note by H.W. in Yiddish (ink): “July 1942. 6 st. pages.” and in a different handwriting (as in Ring. I/496) (ink): “Sz. Szajnkinder.”

**1238. RING. I/1170 (1489). (Lb. 1010). Mf. ŻIH—834; USHMM—46**

• 1941, Warsaw Ghetto
• [Sz. Szajnkinder], Poem entitled “R' Abe der prezes” [Reb Abba the Chairman]
• Satirical work about attitudes in the Warsaw Ghetto.
• *Description:* original, typescript, handwritten manuscript (Sz.*), ink, Yiddish, 220×185 mm, extensive damage and losses of text, ss. 1, pp. 1.
Attached note by H.W. in Yiddish: “Sz. Szajnkinder, 1941.”

**1239. RING. I/525. (Lb. 1711). Mf. ŻIH—790; USHMM—21**

- Start of 1942, Warsaw Ghetto
- [Władysław Szlengel?], Poem "Raz kupiłem sobie sak . . ." [Once I bought myself a sack . . .]
- Satire on requisition of fur coats in the Warsaw Ghetto.
- ***Description:*** transcript, typescript, Polish, 203×285 mm, minor damage and losses of text, ss. 1, pp. 1.

Attached note by H.W.: "Beginning of 1942, author is presumably W. [Władysław] Szlengel."

**1240. RING. I/526. Mf. ŻIH—790; USHMM—21**

- After 09.1941, Warsaw Ghetto
- [Władysław Szlengel?], Collection of satiric compositions: "Opaski" [Armbands], "Kiedy . . ." [When], "Chleb" [Bread], "Matura" [Diploma], "Ryksza" [Ricksha], "Ogródek" [A Little Garden], "Komitet Domowy przy ul. Świętojerskiej 16—szopka" [Apartment house committee at ul. Świętojerska 16—The outhouse], "Szukam mieszkania" [I'm Looking for an Apartment]
- Daily life in the Warsaw Ghetto in satire.
- ***Description:*** transcript (2 copies), typescript, Polish, 165×290, 172×140, 187×90 mm, serious damage and losses of text, ss. 34, pp. 34.

Inventory: "Author is [Władysław] Szlengel."

**1241. RING. I/111. (Lb. 466). Mf. ŻIH—777; USHMM—8**

- 06.1942, Warsaw Ghetto
- N.R. [Nechemiasz Tytelman], "Aktuele geshprekhn (vitsn un humor)" [Topical Conversations (Jokes and Humor)]
- Jokes and songs recorded during a courtyard concert performed by the Berkowicz family from Głowaczów near Warka (mother Sara—age 36, Srulek—age 13, Fajga—age 9, and Abramełe—less than a year old); data on the fate of the family.
- ***Description:*** original, handwritten manuscript (Ł*), ink, Yiddish, 175×220 mm, ss. 3, pp. 5.

Texts signed with the initials N.R. [Nechemiasz Racheles] pseudonym of Nechemiasz Tytelman.

Inventory and list of 1946: "Author is Tytelman."

**1242. RING. I/172. Mf. ŻIH—779; USHMM—10**

a)

- 06.1942, Warsaw Ghetto
- N. Rocheles [Nechemiasz Tytelman], Study entitled "Fun der serye 'Hoyf-zinger, betler-kinder, zayere milkhome-lider'" [From the Series: 'Yard Singers, Child Beggars, Their Wartime Songs'] (06.1942)
- Street song composers of the Warsaw Ghetto (appended texts of songs).
- ***Description:*** original, handwritten manuscript (Ł*), ink, Polish, Yiddish, 130×195 mm, damage and losses of text, ss. 4, pp. 7.

See Ring. I/1053.

Published: *Dzieci*, pp. 152–163.

Index: Jakub Lejb Solnicki (age 16) (ul. Lubeckiego 11), Abraham Solnicki (ul. Lubeckiego 11), Chaja Landau (ul. Lubeckiego 11), Herszman, tailor (ul. Gęsia 45)

b)

- 15.06.1942, Warsaw Ghetto
- N.R. [Nechemiasz Tytelman, ed.], Study entitled "Fun der milkhome vitsn-serye" [From the Wartime Joke Series]
- Sketches and jokes about the situation of the Jewish population and concerning different areas of life (e.g., Lwów under Soviet occupation, identity cards, German policies toward Jews).
- ***Description:*** original, handwritten manuscript (Ł*), ink, Polish, Yiddish, 130×195 mm, damage and losses of text, ss. 4, pp. 7.

c)

- Date unknown, Warsaw Ghetto
- [Nechemiasz Tytelman, ed.], Songs (2): 1) "Humen" [Haman]; 2) "Mendele"
- ***Description:*** original or transcript, handwritten manuscript (Ł*), ink, Yiddish, 218×355 mm, ss. 1, pp. 2.

**1243. RING. I/1053 (1372). Mf. ŻIH—832; USHMM—44**

- 1942, Warsaw Ghetto
- [Nechemiasz Tytelman], "[Se]rie hoyf-zinger un zayre lider" [Series: Courtyard Singers and Their Songs]
- Profiles of courtyard singers of the Warsaw Ghetto and lyrics of their songs. NN., age 12, ul. Szczęśliwa 3, Szlomo Wadowski (age 10) and his sister Chana Wadowska (age 13). Songs: 1) "Obuz lid" [Camp Song]; 2) "On mues geyt nit" [Can't Get By Without Money].
- ***Description:*** original or transcript, handwritten manuscript (Ł*), ink, Yiddish, 111×350 mm, significant damage and losses of text, ss. 2, pp. 4.

Attached note by H.W. in Yiddish: "By Nechemiasz Tytelman. 1942."

Compare from Ring. I/172.

Published: *Dzieci*, pp. 156–159, 164–167.

Index: Rywkełe Wadowska (age 6), Ides Wadowska (age 5), Małka Wadowska, Josł Drimlewicz, Żebrocki

**1244. RING. I/627. Mf. ŻIH—815; USHMM—27**

- After 1939, Warsaw Ghetto [?]
- Kubi Wahl, Poem entitled "Horia" (1935)
- Composition dedicated to [Nikolae] Horia, leader of the revolt of the Romanian highlanders against the

Hungarian nobility in Transylvania in 1784. Horia died 28.02.1785 by public execution (quartered).
- *Description:* transcript, handwritten manuscript (TT*[?]), ink, Yiddish, 206×337 mm, ss. 1, pp. 1.
  On p. 2 a note in Polish (ink): list of clothing and bedclothes.

### 1245. RING. I/612. Mf. ŻIH—814; USHMM—26

- Date unknown, Warsaw Ghetto
- Berysz Wajnsztejn, Poem entitled "A neger" [A Black Person] from the collection "Fun yener zayt yam" [From the Other Side of the Sea]
- About the murder of a black person by a white person.
- *Description:* transcript, handwritten manuscript (TW*), ink, Yiddish, 143×220, 198×300 mm, minor damage and losses of text, ss. 2, pp. 2.
  Manuscript was written on letterhead paper of "Centos" (printed, Yiddish).

### 1246. RING. I/611. Mf. ŻIH—814; USHMM—26

- Before 1939, date unknown, place unknown
- Icchak Winer, Poems (5) entitled "Mayn kindhayt" [My Childhood]; "Zol zayn ruik in mayn tsimer" [Be Quiet in My Room]; "Gut iz hobn oygn cwey . . ." [It's Good to Have Two Eyes . . .]; "Dos lidl fun meydl—a milkh hendlerin" [The Song of a Girl, a Milk Peddler]; "Tsvey lider (kontrastn)" [Two Songs (Contrasts)]
- *Description:* Printed handwritten manuscript, ink, Yiddish, 118×142, 120×243 mm, ss. 4, pp. 6.
  On back of p. 2 is a note (pencil): illegible address (street) and surname.
  Published: Compositions: "The Song of a Girl . . ." and "Two Songs . . ." were published in the prewar Yiddish press (their clippings were preserved).

### 1247. RING. I/523. Mf. ŻIH—790; USHMM—21

- Date unknown, place unknown
- Miniature Theater "Bałaganajdn"[53] (artistic director M. Broderson)[54] [Łódź]. Program entitled "Eyns in der velt" [One in the World]
- Selection of different texts, compositions, and satiric dialogues. Cast (authors of the texts [?]): M. Broderson, Lejzer Wolf, Perec Mirański, S. Juszkiewicz.
- *Description:* transcript (2 copies of p. 40), typescript (On p. 1 handwritten manuscript—ink, translation of Yiddish headline, and list of scenes in Roman transliteration), Polish, Yiddish, 207×295 mm, ss. 45, pp. 45.

### 1248. RING. I/651. (Lb. 448). Mf. ŻIH—816; USHMM—28

- Date unknown, Warsaw Ghetto
- Poetry
- 1) Josef Rubinstein, "Friling in shtot" [Spring in the City] from the book *Modeln* [Models];
- 2) Rajzla Żychlińska, "Regn" [Rain] from the book *Der regn zingt* [The rain sings] and "Der zumer iz groy gevorn . . ." [Summer turned gray . . .];
- 3) Chaim Grade, "Dos bin ikh . . ." [It's Me] from the book *Musernikes* [English edition: *The Yeshiva*];
- 4) Mojsze [Mojżesz] Broderson, "Ikh bin shuldik" [I Am Guilty] from the book *Yo* [Yes];
- 5) F. Wejland, "Wayser shwan" [White swan] from the book *Shiksal un shpil—sonatn und shtrofn* [Fate and play—sonatas and penalties].
- *Description:* transcript, handwritten manuscript (TW*), ink, pencil, Yiddish, 155×198 mm, ss. 6, pp. 6.

### 1249. RING. I/1165 (1484). (Lb. 532). Mf. ŻIH—833; USHMM—45

a)
- Date unknown, Warsaw Ghetto
- Kalman Lis, Poem entitled "Tsu gast in der heym" [Visiting at home]
- *Description:* transcript (3 copies), typescript, Yiddish, 208×294 mm, missing page 7 (second and third copies), ss. 19, pp. 19.

b)
- Date unknown, Warsaw Ghetto
- Efroim Kaganowski, Short stories (4)
- 1) "Bletelekh fun umet" [Leaves of Sadness]; 2) "Simkhele treger" [Simkhe the Porter]; 3) "Altkeyt" [Old Age]; 4) "Tsvey alte khaveyrim" [Two Old Friends].
- *Description:* transcript, typescript, Yiddish, 210×293 mm, damage and losses of text, ss. 17, pp. 17.

c) [Efroim Kaganowski], Short stories (2)
- 1) "Kleyne meydelekh" [Little Girls]; 2) "Manspar-shoyn" [A Male].
- *Description:* transcript, typescript, Yiddish, 210×293 mm, damage and losses of text, ss. 6, pp. 6.

d)
- Date unknown, Warsaw Ghetto
- I. Rapaport, Article entitled "Farlorene glaykhge-vikht" [Lost Balance]
- Response to Yankev Glatszteyn's "Yidishe barikadn" [Jewish Barricades] that appeared in the periodical *In zikh*, no. 48 (1939) (situation of Jews in the Nazi era).
- *Description:* transcript, typescript, Yiddish, 210×293 mm, damage and losses of text, ss. 6, pp. 6.

53. The name is a play on the Slavic–Yiddish *bałagan* (mess, disorder) and the biblical Hebrew *gan-eden*, Garden of Eden, Paradise.

54. Moshe Broderson fled the German occupation and survived the war in the Soviet Union, returning to Poland in 1955 after release from Gulag imprisonment as a Yiddish-language author.

**1250. RING. I/650. (Lb. 503). Mf. ŻIH—816; USHMM—28**

- Date unknown, Warsaw Ghetto
- Synopsis and adaptations of short scenic compositions
  1) Synopsis of the play "Kajdany" [Shackles], original or transcript (handwritten manuscript, ink), transcript (3 copies, typescript), Polish, Yiddish;
  2) Chaim N. Bialik's "Kur[tser fray]to[g]" [Short Friday], dir. B. Czemeryński;
  3) Dawid Piński, "Der yid [eybiker] vanderer" [The Jew (Eternal) Wanderer], ed. W. Meczedinow;
  4) [Szymon Dżigan and Izrael Szumacher], "A klog tsum gelekhter" [Damn the Laughter] (2 copies);
  5) I. Sz. Goldstein and M. Nodlman, Sketch entitled "M [. . .] bekers," [(. . .) bakers].
- ***Description:*** transcript, typescript, handwritten manuscript, ink, Polish, Yiddish, 210×295 mm, damage and losses of text, ss. 30, pp. 30.

**1251. RING. I/606. Mf. ŻIH—814; USHMM—26**

- Date unknown, place unknown
- Poems and articles
- Eliezer Grinberg, Poem entitled "Zumer frimorgns bam yam (fun der poeme "Fishn-dorf"[?]) [Summer Mornings at the Sea (from the poem "Fishn-dorf"[?])]; I. Segalovitsh [Segałowicz], Poems (3) from the collection *Fun shures akht* [From Eight Lines]: "Vi a nes" [Like a Miracle]; "Do kumt nisht a yeder" [Not Everybody Comes Here]; "Dos lid" [The Song]. Appended articles: "'Shures akht' fun I. Segalovitsh" ["Eight Lines" by I. Segalovitsh]; "Fun poetishn varshtat" [From the Poetry Workshop]; "Tsu lange shaferishe yor" [To Many Creative Years] (about the poet [H. Leivick]).
- ***Description:*** original or transcript, handwritten manuscript (two handwritings: TW*), ink, pencil, Yiddish, 110×213, 200×280 mm, damage and losses of text, ss. 7, pp. 7.

  Manuscript written on forms of "Centos" (printed, Yiddish).

  Index: Dawid Kenigsberg, translator of [Mickiewicz's] *Pan Tadeusz*, Mosze Szymel, [Abraham] Sutzkewer

**1252. RING. I/676. Mf. ŻIH—816; USHMM—28**

- Date unknown, Warsaw Ghetto
- Collection of poems
- Yehoash [Szlomo Blumgarten], "Folks motiv" [Folk motif]; Icyk Manger, 1) "Di balade fun dem podolier rov" [The ballad of the Podolian rabbi]; 2) "Tfile" [Prayer]; 3) "Di muter Sore zingt Yitskhokln a shloflid" [Mother Sarah sings little Isaac a lullaby]; Nokhem Bomze, "Oyf der gildener brik" [On the golden bridge]; Abraham Wajneman, "Klog-lid" [A dirge]; Z. Szneur[?], "Ameratsim" [Ignorant people]; NN., "Der khalef un der zeg" [The knife and the saw]. Appended copy of a letter from the Mendele Committee dated 02.1941 to an unnamed apartment house committee NN. in the matter of organization of an evening devoted to Mendele Moykher-Sforim [Shalom Yaakov Abramowicz].
- ***Description:*** transcript, typescript, handwritten manuscript, pencil, Polish, Yiddish, 110×172, 220×288 mm, ss. 10, pp. 14.

  Published: Poem by Yehoash [Szlomo Blumgarten], "Folks motiv" [Folk motif] in Polish translation in: *Antologia*, p. 61.

**1253. RING. I/17. (Lb. 127). Mf. ŻIH—771; USHMM—2**

- Date unknown, Warsaw Ghetto
- Poems (4): 1) Jan Witlin, "Matka żegna jedynaka" [A Mother Says Goodbye to Her Only Child], 2) "Hymn o łyżce ciepłej zupy" [Hymn to a Spoonful of Warm Soup]; 3) Ludwik Akierman, "Wojna" [War]; 4) Antoni Słonimski, "Nalot" [Air raid]
- Compositions illustrating experiences of people affected by the misfortune of war.
- ***Description:*** copies, handwritten manuscript, Polish, pencil, loose, 207×295 mm, ss. 3, pp. 5.

**1254. RING. I/648. Mf. ŻIH—816; USHMM—28**

a)

- Date unknown, Warsaw Ghetto
- [Sz. Berliński?], Story entitled "Tekhter" [Daughters] (fragment)
- About 6 daughters of a poultry dealer, who move from the provinces to Warsaw in search of work.
- ***Description:*** transcript, typescript, Yiddish, damage and losses of text, missing pages, 210×280 mm., ss. 19, pp. 19.

  Appended text of a continuation of the story or of another [story] (concerning the daughters' meeting with family members at the bed of their dying mother) (transcript, typescript, Yiddish, 183×77, 208×270 mm, damage and losses of text, missing beginning, ss. 6, pp. 6.

  Inventory: "Author, Sz. Berliński, 'Daughters'"

b)

- Date unknown, Warsaw Ghetto
- NN., Story about a young married couple (fragment)
- Housing problems.
- ***Description:*** transcript, typescript, Yiddish, 201×106, 204×282 mm, damage and losses of text, ss. 4, pp. 4.

c)

- Date unknown, Warsaw Ghetto
- NN., Story about a butcher's family (fragment)
- About poverty and hunger.
- ***Description:*** transcript, typescript, Yiddish, 208×270 mm, 208×285 mm, damage and losses of text, ss. 6, pp. 6.

d)

- Date unknown, Warsaw Ghetto
- NN., Story about love during the occupation
- Protagonist, a young man, meets a girl.

- *Description:* transcript, typescript, Yiddish, 207×120, 208×282 mm, damage and losses of text, missing pages, ss. 6, pp. 6.

e)

- Date unknown, Warsaw Ghetto
- NN., Various texts. 1) Story about Estusia (fragment); 2) Story about a shelter for refugees in the Warsaw Ghetto (about a young boy, Yankl).
- *Description:* transcript, typescript, Yiddish, 203×140, 201×290 mm, serious damage and losses of text, missing pages, ss. 4, pp. 4.

### 1255. RING. I/629. Mf. ŻIH—815; USHMM—27

- Date unknown, place unknown
- NN., Poems (6): "Himn tsu der aynzamkeyt" [Hymn to Loneliness]; "Zilber–necht" [Silver nights]; "Vi a stade oksn . . ." [Like a herd of oxen . . .]; "Bin ikh antlofn fun ayere hayzer . . . ," [So I fled from your houses . . .]; "Vi voyl iz mir . . ." [How happy I am . . .]; "Ahasver" [Ahasuerus = Akhashveyres].
- *Description:* original or transcript, handwritten manuscript, ink, Yiddish, 110×175 mm, ss. 5, pp. 5.

### 1256. RING. I/524. Mf. ŻIH—790; USHMM—21

a)

- 01.1942, Warsaw Ghetto
- Collection of poems: "Father of the Jew-stricken,"[55] "Bells Are Ringing," "With the New Marks . . ."
- Satire of the Jewish administration (inter alia Chaim Rumkowski) and attitudes reigning in the Łódź ghetto. Appended information about the genesis of the creation of the aforementioned compositions.
- *Description:* transcript, handwritten manuscript (H* and LEG*), notebook, ink, Polish, Yiddish, 150×190 mm, ss. 12 pp. 10.

b)

- Date unknown, place unknown
- Collection of poems: "Biją dzwony" [They're Ringing Bells], "Lokomotywa" [Locomotive], "Oda do getta" [Ode to the Ghetto], "Oda do młodości" [Ode to Youth], "Kuplety gettowe" [Ghetto Couplets]
- Satire of the Jewish administration and attitudes reigning in the Łódź ghetto.
- *Description:* transcript, handwritten manuscript, ink, Polish, 173×323, 88×110 mm, damage and losses of text, text illegible in places, ss. 3, pp. 3.

  Compositions written on the back of a form, Provisioning Department registration cards (1940, printed, Polish, Yiddish).

### 1257. RING. I/109. (Lb. 457, 992). Mf. ŻIH—777; USHMM—8

a)

- Date unknown, Warsaw Ghetto
- Collection of various compositions entitled "Milkhome folklor" [War Folklore]
- Jokes, sayings, catch phrases, predictions, legends, stories concerning the situation of the Jews during the German occupation (inter alia the image of Jewish-Polish relations).
- *Description:* original (o), handwritten manuscript (HUB.*), notebook, ink, Yiddish, 155×195 mm, minor damage and losses of text, ss. 36, pp. 56.

  On the title sheet of the notebook is a note in Yiddish (ink): "Huberband."

  Collection consists of several parts:
  1) "Vitsn und vort-shpil" [Jokes and Wordplay];
  2) "Remozim fun geula" [Hints of Redemption]
  3) "Legendes" [Legends]. In the list of contents are also mentioned still other chapter titles, which are missing in the doc.:
  4) "Lider" [Songs];
  5) "Rednsartn un naye werter" [Figures of Speech and New Words];
  6) "Kloles" [Curses];
  7) "Politishe remozim" [Political Allusions];
  8) "Plotkes" [Rumors].

  Published: *Kiddush Hashem*, pp. 113–129.

b)

- Date unknown, Warsaw Ghetto
- Collection of different compositions entitled "Folklor, band II" [Folklore, Volume II]
- Jokes, sayings, curses, songs, new words, legends, stories concerning the situation of Jews during the German occupation. Several texts of Rubinsztajn from the Warsaw Ghetto.
- *Description:* transcript, handwritten manuscript (Z*), pencil, Yiddish, 112×119 mm, minor damage and losses of text, missing pages, ss. 9, pp. 9.

  Doc. (b) is presumably a copy of additions to doc. (a).

  Doc. (b) includes the following chapters:
  1) "Hoysofe tsu remozim fun geula" [Supplement to Hints of Redemption];
  2) "Rubinshtayn zogt" [Rubinsztajn says];
  3) "Kloles" [Curses];
  4) "Brukhes" [Blessings];
  5) "Geto–reklame" [Ghetto-advertisement];
  6) "Hoysofe tsu di vitsn" [Supplement to the Jokes];
  7) "Naye verter" [New Words];
  8) "Hoysofe tsu legendes" [Supplement to Legends].

  About Rubinsztajn, see *Przewodnik*, pp. 573–575.

  See HWC, 38/1 (second copy, handwritten manuscript, ss. 9).

  Index: Kominer [? Kaminer], informer in Warsaw Ghetto

55. Play on the words "Ojciec zadżumionych" (father of the plague-stricken) by Słowacki.

**1258. RING. I/1163 (1482). (Lb. 584). Mf. ŻIH—833; USHMM—45**

- Date unknown, Warsaw Ghetto
- Copy entitled "M'lakht fun der velt" [People Laugh at the World], comedic compositions, songs, sketches, etc. performed before 1939 on the stage of the Ararat Theater in Warsaw (artistic director Mojżesz Broderson)
- Compositions:
  1) "Dos yingl" [The boy];
  2) "Monolog" [Monologue];
  3) "Mekhl";
  4) "Tango";
  5) "Duet";
  6) "Khuhele";
  7) "Gripe" [Flu];
  8) "Andulatsye" [Undulation?];
  9) "Zay gezunt mayn libster" [Be well my dearest];
  10) "Tsvey toybe" [Two deaf people];
  11) "Der freylekher kabtsn" [The merry pauper];
  12) "Fir bonim" [Four sons];
  13) "Madagaskar";
  14) "Valts" [Waltz];
  15) "Revelersn" [Barbershop quartet ?];
  16) "Fayvl un Getsl" [Fayvl and Getsl];
  17) "An eytse" [A solution];
  18) "Der merder" [The murderer];
  19) "Deklamatsye" [Declamation];
  20) "Ikh oder der zlote" [Me or the złoty].
- ***Description:*** transcript, typescript, Yiddish, 210×293 mm, minor damage and losses of text, ss. 49, pp. 47.

  Doc. was kept in a binder and bound in a paper cover.

**1259. RING. I/119. (Lb. 1693). Mf. ŻIH—777; USHMM—8**

- Date unknown, Warsaw Ghetto
- NN., Story entitled "A shpogl-naye krenk bay di 'shpitsn'" [A Brand New Disease among the "Higher Ups"]
- Satire of the extended conferences and meetings of the administration of the ŻSS.
- ***Description:*** original or transcript, typescript, Yiddish, 205×290, 205×157 mm, ss. 2, pp. 2.

  Inventory: "Author is Menachem M. Kohn."

**1260. RING. I/516. Mf. ŻIH—789; USHMM—20**

- Date unknown, Warsaw Ghetto
- NN., Poems: "Gmina Żydowska" [Jewish Community] and "Gmina i Rodzina" [Community and Family]
- Satire of the officials of the Jewish Community in Warsaw, mentioning their surnames.
- ***Description:*** original or transcript, handwritten manuscript, pencil, typescript, Polish, 220×305, 209×295 mm, ss. 2, pp. 3.

  On p. 1 ("Gmina Żydowska") is a note at the top, "Szafa gra" [Everything's all right].

**1261. RING. I/609. Mf. ŻIH—814; USHMM—26**

- 07.1942, Warsaw Ghetto
- NN., Poem entitled "In the Margins of a Certain Nativity Scene in the Year of Our Lord 1942 at ul. Chłodna 22"
- About the approaching destruction of the ghetto.
- ***Description:*** original or transcript, handwritten manuscript, pencil, Polish, 210×290 mm, extensive minor damage and losses of text, ss. 1, pp. 1.

**1262. RING. I/617. Mf. ŻIH—814; USHMM—26**

- After 2.06.1942, Warsaw Ghetto
- NN., Poem entitled "Ale vaybelakh . . ." [All the Young Married Women . . .] (2.06.1942)
- Song sung at ul. Smocza 42 by the streetsinger Szloma Elbaum (age 13).
- ***Description:*** transcript from copyist's note, handwritten manuscript (LEG*), ink, Yiddish, 150×195 mm, ss. 1, pp. 2.

  Published: *Dzieci*, pp. 150–151.

**1263. RING. I/635. Mf. ŻIH—815; USHMM—27**

- After 1930, place unknown
- NN., Poems (2): 1) "Du" [You]; 2) "Tsu der mamen fun unzer dor" [To the Mother of Our Generation].
- ***Description:*** original or transcript, handwritten manuscript., ink, Yiddish, 150×226 mm, minor damage and losses of text, ss. 1, pp. 2.

  Handwritten on letterhead of Mrs. Eug. Jaszuńska-Zeligmanowa's Private Girls' Secondary School in Łódź (ul. Południowa 18) (after 1930, printed, Polish).

**1264. RING. I/643. (Lb. 534). Mf. ŻIH—815; USHMM—27**

- Date unknown, place unknown
- NN., Study entitled "Di formulirung fun der problem" [The Formulation of the Problem]
- Philosophy of poetry, attitude of the creator to the work, role of the reader, poetic material, a word's function, artistic idea, subject, timbre, form, and contents of the piece. Reflections on kitsch, style of the epoch, and its influence on the poet's creativity.
- ***Description:*** original or transcript, typescript, Yiddish, 210×290 mm, minor damage and losses of text, ss. 62, pp. 62.

**1265. RING. I/644. Mf. ŻIH—815; USHMM—27**

- Date unknown, place unknown
- NN., Play entitled: "Der payats" [The Clown]
- Purim burlesque on the canvas of the biblical story of Joseph and his brothers.
- ***Description:*** original or transcript, handwritten manuscript, ink, Yiddish, 160×205 mm, damage and losses of text, ss. 15, pp. 29.

1266. **RING. I/646. (Lb. 467). Mf. ŻIH–816; USHMM–28**

- After 1941, Warsaw Ghetto
- NN., Poem entitled "Dos varshever geto" [The Warsaw Ghetto] (Warsaw, 1941)
- Hunger, public kitchens, smuggling, fate of the intelligentsia, the youth in labor camps, suffering and death.
- ***Description:*** transcript, handwritten manuscript (U*), ink, Yiddish, 204×283 mm, text difficult to read in places, ss. 1, pp. 2.

  Attached note by H.W. in Yiddish: "Poem was copied by Jechiel Górny."

1267. **RING. I/649. (Lb. 504). Mf. ŻIH–816; USHMM–28**

- Date unknown, place unknown
- NN., Play entitled "Akhdes" [Unity]
- Comedic scene (one more guest moves into the already occupied single room in a hotel).
- ***Description:*** transcript, typescript, Yiddish, 211×280 mm, damage and losses of text, ss. 11, pp. 11.

  Inventory: "From the prewar repertoire of the actors [Szymon] Dżigan and [Izrael] Szumacher."

1268. **RING. I/1093 (1412). (Lb. 1533). Mf. ŻIH–833; USHMM–45**

- Date unknown, Warsaw Ghetto
- "Circular no. 1 for All Delegates [of apartment house committees] and Users of the Kitchens"
- Contains "Procedure for Assignment to Kitchens"—method of obtaining privileges at [house] kitchens—satire of the bureaucracy of an institution in the Warsaw Ghetto.
- ***Description:*** original or transcript, typescript, Polish, 220×226 mm, ss. 1, pp. 1.

1269. **RING. I/1131 (1450). (Lb. 269, 575). Mf. ŻIH–833; USHMM–45**

- Date unknown, Warsaw Ghetto
- NN., Poem: "The Jewish Community Stands at Grzybowska [Street] . . ."
- Satire on the Jewish Council in Warsaw (mentions members of the Jewish Council).
- ***Description:*** original or transcript, handwritten manuscript, green ink, Polish, 208×270 mm, minor damage and losses of text, k.1, pp. 2.

  Doc. was kept in a binder.

  According to H.W., this is "Gmina Żydowska. Szafa gra" [Jewish Community. Everything's All Right], satire by an anonymous author written in the style of Julian Tuwim's "Lokomotywa" [Locomotive].

1270. **RING. I/1220/22. Mf. ŻIH–835; USHMM–47**

- Date unknown, Warsaw Ghetto
- NN., Notes: "The calm of those people was a result not of readiness for death, but of a stubborn, tenacious will to live."
- ***Description:*** original,or transcript, handwritten manuscript (H*), ink, 158×93 mm, Polish, ss. 1, pp. 1.

1271. **RING. I/1220/71. Mf. ŻIH–835; USHMM–47**

- Date unknown, place unknown
- NN., Poem (fragment)
- ***Description:*** transcript, typescript, Yiddish, 176×122 mm, serious damage and losses of text, ss. 1, pp. 1.

1271a. **RING. I/616. Mf. ŻIH–814; USHMM–45.**

- 04, 1941, Warsaw Ghetto.
- NN., Poem entitled "In a roytn tsigl-hoyz . . ." [In a red brick house]
- Satire of TOŻ [?].
- ***Description:*** original or transcript, handwritten, pencil, Yiddish, 220×340 mm, minor damage and losses of text, ss. 2, pp. 3.
- At the end of the poem is a note in different handwriting: "Warsaw, April 1941, teachers' banquet in the TOŻ hall [?]."

  In the margins a symbol (ink): "∇".

# VIII. Periodicals and Other Printed Matter

## *JEWISH PRESS FROM THE PERIOD OF THE SEPTEMBER CAMPAIGN OF 1939*

1272. **RING. I/679 (1003). Mf. ŻIH–816; USHMM–28**

- 09.1939, Warsaw
- *Folkstsaytung* [People's Newspaper], no. 270, dated 19.09.1939
- Daily, press organ of the Bund.
- ***Description:*** original, printed, Yiddish, 357×497 mm, extensive minor damage and losses of text, ss. 1, pp. 2.

  See Ring. II/326.

## *NEWSPAPERS AND OFFICIAL PERIODICALS ISSUED IN GERMANY AND OCCUPIED TERRITORIES*

1273. **RING. I/734 (1058). Mf. ŻIH–822; USHMM–34**

- 09–11.1939, Włocławek
- *ABC dla Włocławka i Kujaw*, dated 29.09.1939
- *Leslauer Bote. ABC dla Włocławka i Kujaw*, no. 46, dated 25.11.1939
- Newspaper issued by the occupation authorities in bilingual version.
- ***Description:*** original, printed, German, Polish, 285×403, 345×500mm, ss. 3, pp. 6.

**1274. RING. I/1182 (1501). Mf. ŻIH–834; USHMM–46**

- 24.07.1941, Berlin
- *Berliner Ilustrierte Zeitung*, no. 30, dated 24.07.1941
- Contains inter alia extensive photo essay on the Warsaw Ghetto.
- ***Description:*** original, printed, German, 270×370 mm, ss. 11, pp. 22.

**1275. RING. I/1180 (1499). Mf. ŻIH–834; USHMM–46**

- 12.1941, Brussels
- *Brüsseler Zeitung*, no. 336, dated 4.12.1941
- German daily published in Brussels.
- ***Description:*** original, printed, German, 428×615 mm, ss. 5, pp. 10.

**1276. RING. I/759 (1083). (Lb. 1293). Mf. ŻIH–824; USHMM–36**

- 04–10.1941, Kraków
- *Die Burg*, no. 2 (04.1941), no. 3 (07.1941), and no. 4 (10.1941)
- Quarterly published by the Institut für Deutsche Ostarbeit [Institute for German Eastern Work] in Kraków.
- ***Description:*** original, printed, German, 208×295 mm, damage and losses of text, ss. 199, pp. 382.

**1277. RING. I/755 (1079). (Lb. 1543). Mf. ŻIH–823; USHMM–35**

a)

- 07.1941, Kraków
- *Krakauer Zeitung*, no. 155, 5.07.1941
- German daily.
- ***Description:*** original, printed, German, 320×467 mm, missing pp. 5–6, ss. 4, pp. 8.

b)

- 1941–1942, date unknown, Kraków, place unknown
- Clippings from the *Krakauer Zeitung*, e.g., from 09.1940, no. 50 dated 4.03., no. 92 dated 23.04., no. 157 dated 8.07., no. 158 dated 9.07., no. 159 dated 10.07., no. 160 dated 11.07., no. 169 dated 22.07., no. 170 dated 23.07.1941, no. 128 dated 2.06.1942
- Articles and press information concerning Jews.
- ***Description:*** original, printed, German, Polish, 65×70, 320×470 mm, ss. 23, pp. 31.

**1278. RING. I/766 (1090). Mf. ŻIH–823; USHMM–35**

- 03.1940, Łódź
- *Lodscher Zeitung*, no. 77 dated 17.03.1940
- German daily published in Łódź.
- ***Description:*** original, printed, German, 315×468 mm, ss. 2, pp. 4.

**1279. RING. I/1181 (1500). Mf. ŻIH–834; USHMM–46**

- 24.07.1941, Munich
- *Münchner Ilustrierte Presse*, no. 30 dated 24.07.1941 (fragment [?])
- ***Description:*** original, printed, German, 275×365 mm, ss. 12, pp. 24.

**1280. RING. I/757 (1081). (Lb. 753). Mf. ŻIH–823; USHMM–35**

a)

- 06.1942, Berlin
- *Novoe Slovo*, no. 44 (426) dated 3.06.1942
- German newspaper published in Russian.
- ***Description:*** original, printed, Russian, 302×462 mm, ss. 4, pp. 8.

  See Ring. II/325.

b)

- 06–07.1942, Berlin, Warsaw Ghetto
- Collection of clippings from the newspaper *Novoe Slovo*
- Articles and information concerning Jews.
- ***Description:*** original, printed, handwritten manuscript (H*, LEG*), notebooks, ink, Polish, signed, Yiddish, 95×172, 155×195, 280×400 mm, ss. 51, pp. 51.

  Most of the clippings were arranged according to the numerical sequence of the newspapers (from no. 45 dated 7.06.1942 to no. 57 dated 19.07.1942), glued into 2 notebooks and described in a single handwriting (H* and LEG*).

**1281. RING. I/765 (1089). (Lb. 1707). Mf. ŻIH–823; USHMM–35**

- 02–12.1941, Warsaw
- *Nowy Kurier Warszawski*, no. 47 dated 25.02., no. 266 dated 10.11., and no. 294 dated 12.12.1941
- German daily published in Polish in Warsaw.
- ***Description:*** original, printed, Polish, 365×545 mm. ss. 3, pp. 6.

  See HWC, 58/1–6 (no. 299 from 1940; no. 16, 44, 95, 110, 229 from 1941).

**1282. RING. I/785/5. (1104). Mf. ŻIH–825; USHMM–37**

- 02–03.1941, Kraków, Warsaw Ghetto
- Collection of press clippings (*Nowy Kurier Warszawski*, dated 27.02., 2.03.1941; *Krakauer Zeitung*, dated 28.02. and 2.03.1941)
- Articles and information concerning Jews.
- ***Description:*** original, printed, German, 70×298, 86×70, 132×138, 170×205 mm, ss. 7, pp. 7.

  Clippings described by H.W.* (handwritten manuscript, ink).

**1283. RING. I/266. Mf. ŻIH–780; USHMM–11**

- 10.1940, Warsaw

- "Wykaz ulic na których Żydzi nie powinni zajmować mieszkań i z których muszą się przeprowadzić do strefy przewidzianej dla przesiedlenia, Wykaz ulic do których Żydzi mogą się wprowadzić i Plan dzielnicy żydowskiej." [List of Streets on Which Jews Are Not Allowed to Occupy Apartments and from Which They Must Move to the Area Foreseen for Resettlement, List of Streets to Which Jews May Move, and Map of the Jewish District.]
- Documents published in *Nowy Kurier Warszawski* dated 15.10.1940.
- ***Description:*** original, printed, Polish, 235×314 mm, minor damage and losses of text, ss. 2, pp. 3.
  Document was kept in a binder.

1284. **RING. I/1134 (1453). Mf. ŻIH—833; USHMM—45**
- After 06.1940, Warsaw
- Clippings from the *Nowy Kurier Warszawski* with reports: "Jewish Speculators on Corsica"
- Notation about emigration of 3,000 French Jews to Corsica, where they organized a "black market."
- ***Description:*** original, printed, Polish, 75×25 mm, ss. 1, pp. 1.
  After excavation glued onto a sheet.

1285. **RING. I/1178 (1497). Mf. ŻIH—834; USHMM—46**
- 1941–1942, Berlin
- *Das Reich*, no. 10 dated 9.03., no. 12 dated 23.03., no. 14 dated 6.04., no. 15 dated 13.04., no. 16 dated 20.04., no. 17 dated 27.04., no. 26 dated 29.06., no. 46 dated 16.11., no. 48 dated 30.11.1941, 22.03.1942 and 29.03.1942 (fragments)
- Weekly. no. 10 dated 9.03.1941 contains two photographs from the Warsaw Ghetto.
- ***Description:*** original, printed, German, 130×265, 370×525 mm, damage and losses of text, missing several columns, ss. 77, pp. 152.

## *OTHER GERMAN PRINTED MATERIALS*

1286. **RING. I/738 (1062). (Lb. 1460). Mf. ŻIH—822; USHMM—34**
- After 1.10.1941, place unknown
- Leaflet: *Kontyngenty* [Quotas]
- German propaganda publication to Polish peasants concerning levies of agricultural products.
- ***Description:*** original, printed, Polish, 210×295 mm, ss. 1, pp. 2.

1287. **RING. I/746 (1070). (Lb. 129). Mf. ŻIH—823; USHMM—35**
- 07.1941, place unknown
- Proclamation: *Offiziere, Soldaten des russischen Heeres, Genossen!*
- German leaflet addressed to soldiers of the Red Army calling for them to surrender.
- ***Description:*** original, printed, German, Russian, 268×373 mm, ss. 1, pp. 2.

1288. **RING. I/747 (1071). (Lb. 110). Mf. ŻIH—823; USHMM—35**
- Date unknown, place unknown
- Leaflet entitled *O Rosji Sowieckiej. Pytania i odpowiedzi* [About Soviet Russia: questions and answers].
- Anti-Soviet propaganda publication.
- ***Description:*** original, printed, Polish, 125×174 mm, ss. 2, pp. 4.

1289. **RING. I/1033 (1368). (Lb. 761). Mf. ŻIH—832; USHMM—44**
- After 19.07.1942, Warsaw Ghetto
- NN., Excerpts of propaganda texts from the German press and publications
  a) "Dr. Ley un di frantsoyzishe arbeter" [Dr. Ley and French Workers]. Speech by Dr. Ley, leader of the Deutsche Arbeitsfront, to French workers about the common enemy, Bolshevism (excerpt from newspaper [damaged fragment] of 12.07.1942);
  b) "Fun vanen nemt zikh tsu zey aza akshones" [Where Do They Get Such Stubborness From]. Fragment of an article from *Nowe Słowo*, no. 57/19.07.1942 (reprint from the SS press organ) about the peril of Bolshevism;
  c) "Briv tsu di front-kameradn! fun raykhsminister Dr. Gebels" [Letter to Frontline Comrades! From Reichsminister Dr. Goebbels]. Request to soldiers to write from the front full of humor and hope, because the Fatherland and their relatives need only such letters (excerpt from NSDAP publication in Munich).
- ***Description:*** original, handwritten manuscript (LEG*), pencil, Yiddish, 205×293, 219×353 mm, minor damage and losses of text, ss. 6, pp. 6.
  On the jacket a note by H.W. in Yiddish: "Eliahu Gutkowski."

1290. **RING. I/1202 (1521). Mf. ŻIH—835; USHMM—47**
- Date unknown, place unknown
- Der Chef der Oberkommandos der Wehrmacht. Kriegsgefangenen-Lagergeld, Gutschein über 10 Reichspfennig
- Scrip used as money in a German POW camp.
- ***Description:*** original, printed, German, 83×42 mm, ss. 1, pp. 1.

## *JEWISH NEWSPAPERS AND OFFICIAL PUBLICATIONS WITHIN THE AREA OF GERMAN OCCUPATION*

1291. **RING. I/861 (1180). (Lb. 1656). Mf. ŻIH—828; USHMM—40**
- 1941, Łódź Ghetto
- Der Aelteste der Juden in Litzmannstadt. *Kalender*

*für das Jahr* 1942 [The Eldest of the Jews in Litzmannstadt. Calendar for year 1942]
- Wall calendar containing information about dates concerning the history of the ghetto as well as numerous quotations from speeches of Chaim Rumkowski; also notes his private "anniversaries," inter alia the dates of his birth and the death of his wife Ita.
- ***Description:*** original, printed, German, Yiddish, 98×185, 148×222 mm, ss. 60, pp. 60.

### 1292. RING. I/702 (1026). Mf. ŻIH—820; USHMM—32

- 01.1942, Kraków
- *Gazeta Żydowska*, no. 2 dated 4.01.1942
- Daily, the official organ of the Jewish Communities in the Generalgouvernement.
- ***Description:*** original, printed, Polish, 290×427 mm, ss. 2, pp. 4.

See Ring. II/318.
See HWC, 58/7–8 (no. 84 from 1941 and no. 4 from 1942).

### 1293. RING. I/678 (1002). Mf. ŻIH—816; USHMM—28

- 03–05.1941, Łódź Ghetto
- *Geto-tsaytung* [Ghetto Newspaper], no. 1 dated 7.03.1941, no. 2 dated 14.03.1941, no. 3 dated 21.03.1941, no. 4 dated 28.03.1941, no. 5 dated 4.04.1941, no. 6 dated 11.04.1941, no. 7 dated 17.04.1941, no. 8 dated 25.04.1941, no. 9 dated 2.05.1941, and no. 10 dated 11.05.1941
- Weekly of the "Eldest of the Jews" Chaim Mordechai Rumkowski. Editorial office: Łódź, ul. Dworska 1.
- ***Description:*** original (no. 3 in 2 copies, second copy incomplete), printed, Yiddish, 245×350 mm, minor damage and losses of text (no. 7), damage and losses of text (no. 3, second copy), ss. 24, pp. 48.

## *JEWISH PRESS PUBLISHED IN THE USSR*

### 1294. RING. I/688 (1012). (Lb. 1090). Mf. ŻIH—817; USHMM—48

- 06.1941, Kiev
- *Der shtern* [The Star], dated 22.06.1941 (fragment)
- Daily of the Communist Party of Ukraine.
- ***Description:*** original, printed, Yiddish, 70×150, 140×295 mm, serious damage and losses of text, ss. 4, pp. 7.

## *UNDERGROUND PRESS OF THE WARSAW GHETTO*

### 1295. RING. I/741 (1065). Mf. ŻIH—823; USHMM—35

- Date unknown, Warsaw Ghetto
- *A koyl in der midbar* [A Voice in the Wilderness], date unknown [1940?], not numbered (two issues)
- Periodical of the Agudat Israel organization.
- ***Description:*** original (one issue in 2 copies), hectographed typescript, Yiddish, 215×306 mm, minor damage and losses of text, ss. 13, pp. 13.

See *Żydzi Warszawy*, p. 230.

### 1296. RING. I/686 (1010). Mf. ŻIH—817; USHMM—29

- 02–06.1942, Warsaw Ghetto
- *Avangard* [Vanguard], no. 1 dated 02.1942 and no. 2 dated 06.1942
- Underground publication of Left Po'ale Tsiyon.
- ***Description:*** original, typescript, hectographed typescript, Yiddish, 30×42, 208×295 mm, damage and losses of text, ss. 16, pp. 16.

See *Centralny katalog*, p. 30.
See HWC, 60/5 (no. 3 of 1942).

### 1297. RING. I/697 (1021). Mf. ŻIH—818; USHMM—30

- 08–12.1941, Warsaw Ghetto
- *Awangarda Młodzieży. Pismo Żydowskiej Młodzieży Marksistowskiej* [Vanguard of Youth. Publication of the Jewish Marxist Youth], no. 2 (5) dated 30.08, no. 6–7 (9–10) dated 4.10, no. 11 dated 7.11, and no. 12 dated 1.12.1941
- Underground monthly of the Left Po'ale Tsiyon organization.
- ***Description:*** original, typescript, hectographed typescript [?], Polish, 225×287mm, damage and losses of text (no. 2 and 11), ss. 55, pp. 55.

See *Centralny katalog*, p. 30.
Published: *The Jewish Underground Press*, vol. 3, pp. 171–180, 429–453 (nos. 2 [5], 6–7 [9–10]).

### 1298. RING. I/695 (1019). (Lb. 1503). Mf. ŻIH—818; USHMM—30

- [12].1940, Warsaw Ghetto
- *Bafrayung* [Liberation], no. 1 of [12].1940
- Underground publication of the Right Po'ale Tsiyon organization.
- ***Description:*** original, hectographed typescript, Yiddish, 206×295 mm, ss. 30, pp. 30.

According to H.W., the author of the article on the Jewish ghetto (pp. 20–24) is Eliasz Gutkowski; see Ring. I/1058.
See *Żydzi Warszawy*, p. 230.
Published: *The Jewish Underground Press*, vol. 1, pp. 178–207.
Doc. was kept in a binder.

### 1299. RING. I/1058 (1377). (Lb. 1130). Mf. ŻIH—832; USHMM—44

- [12].1940, Warsaw Ghetto
- Spektator, "Dos yidishe geto—a historishe iberzikht" [The Jewish Ghetto—a Historical Overview]
- Short historical sketch of Jewish ghettos in Europe from the Middle Ages until modern times. Article from *Bafrayung*, no. 1 of 1940, pp. 20–24.

- *Description:* original, hectographed typescript, Yiddish, 206×294 mm, ss. 5, pp. 5.
  Attached note by H.W.: "Article by E. Gutkowski, MA, from Yedies[56] no. 31."
  Doc. was buried together with no. 1 of the publication *Bafrayung;* see Ring. I/695.
  Doc. was kept in a binder.

**1300. RING. I/682 (1006). Mf. ŻIH—817; USHMM—29**

- 04–12.1941, Warsaw Ghetto
- *Biuletin* [Bulletin], no. 4 (14) of 04.1941, no. 6 (16) of 05.1941, no. 9 (19) of 10.08.1941, no. 10 (20) of 31.08.1941, no. 11 (21) of 10.09.1941, and no. 14 (24) of 20.12.1941
- Underground periodical of the Bund.
- *Description:* original, hectographed typescript, Yiddish, 110×140, 216×350 mm, serious damage and losses of text (nr. 14 (24)), ss. 74, pp. 74.
  Appended collection of loose fragments of different pages from no. 14 (24) or from other issues [?]—ss. 23, pp. 23.
  See *Centralny katalog,* p. 33.
  See HWC, 60/1–2 (no. 1 (11) and 4 (14) of 1941).
  Published: *The Jewish Underground Press,* vol. 2, pp. 191–207, 252–267 (no. 4 [14], 6 [16]); vol. 3, pp. 131–170, 265–291 (no. 9 [19], 10 [20], 11 [21]).

**1301. RING. I/680 (1004). (Lb. 1284). Mf. ŻIH—816; USHMM—28**

- 11–12.1941, Warsaw Ghetto
- *Tsayt-fragn* [Contemporary Issues], no. 2 of 11.1941 and no. 3 of 12.1941
- Underground monthly of the Bund.
- *Description:* original, hectographed typescript, Yiddish, 142×218 mm, serious damage and losses of text (no. 3, no. 2 is miising only p. 21), ss. 60, pp. 60.
  See *Centralny katalog,* p. 49.
  Published: *Przewodnik,* p. 651 (photocopy of the title page of no. 3).
  Index: Nojach, posthumous memoir; Włodzimierz Kosowski, activist of the Jewish labor movement, notification about death; Sigmund Freud; Rabindranath Tagore; Kazimierz Czapiński; Norbert Barlicki; Herman Liberman

**1302. RING. I/716 (1040). Mf. ŻIH—821; USHMM—33**

- 12.1940–07.1941, Warsaw Ghetto
- *Czerwony Sztandar* [Red Banner], no. 2 of 12.1940, no. 3 of 02.1941, no. 4 of 03.1941, no. 5 of 06.1941, and no. 6 of 07.1941
- Underground monthly of the Trotskyites.
- *Description:* original, hectographed typescript, Polish, 210×325, 230×305, 222×350 mm, ss. 46, pp. 51.
  Nos.2, 3 were kept in a binder.
  See *Centralny katalog,* p. 53.
  Published: *The Jewish Underground Press,* vol. 3, pp. 45–64 (no. 6/1941).

**1303. RING. I/705 (1029). (Lb. 679). Mf. ŻIH—820; USHMM—32**

- 07.1940–05/06.1941, Warsaw Ghetto
- *Dror* [Freedom], no. 3 of 07.1940, no. 4 of 10.1940, 5 (9) of 01–02.1941, 6 (10) of 1.05.1941; and 7–8 (13) of 05–06.1941
- Underground social-political-cultural publication of the youth movement He-haluts Dror of the Right Po'ale Tsiyon.
- *Description:* original (no. 4 in 2 incomplete copies), hectographed typescript, Yiddish, 132×180, 208×287, 208×294 mm, damage and losses of text (no. 4 of 1940), missing pages (no. 4 and 5 [9]), ss. 66, pp. 117.
  No. 3 was kept in a binder.
  See *Centralny katalog,* p. 60.
  Published: *The Jewish Underground Press,* vol. 1, pp. 30–43, 99–115, 350–379; vol. 2, pp. 268–275, 380–441 (nos. 3, 4, 5 [9], 6 [10], 7–8 [13]).
  See Ring. I/706.
  Index: Bialik, A.L. Sztater, and A. Domski, I.E. Fis, Dowa Hoz, Kurt Tucholski, Ch. Goldberg, Berl Sztajnman, A. Frajnd

**1304. RING. I/706 (1030). Mf. ŻIH—820; USHMM—32**

- 05.1941, Warsaw Ghetto
- *Dror-Wolność* [Freedom], no. of 05.1941
- Underground periodical issued by the He-haluts Dror organization in Polish; no. 5 of May 1941 is the equivalent of no. 7–8 (13) dated 1.05.1941 of the publication *Dror* in Yiddish (See Ring. I/705).
- *Description:* original, hectographed typescript, Polish, 210×322 mm, ss. 11, pp. 19.
  See *Centralny katalog,* p. 60.
  Published: *The Jewish Underground Press,* vol. 2, pp. 304–321.

**1305. RING. I/701 (1025). Mf. ŻIH—836; USHMM—67**

- 04.1941–01.1942, Warsaw Ghetto
- *El-Al* [Ascending], no. 1 of 04.1941, no. 2 of [06].1941, no. 3 (8) of 08.1941, no. 4 (9) of 11.1941, and no. 5 of 01.1942
- Underground biweekly of the Ha-Shomer Ha-Tsair organization.
- *Description:* original, hectographed typescript, Hebrew, Polish, 25×40, 205×283 mm, damage and losses of text, ss. 47, pp. 90.
  See *Centralny katalog,* p. 70.

56. Probably refers to the underground bulletin published by the Oyneg Shabes group.

Published: *The Jewish Underground Press*, vol. 2, pp. 226–251, 459–481 (nos. 1, 2); vol. 3, pp. 181–200 (no. 3 [8]).

**1306. RING. I/737 (1061). Mf. ŻIH—822; USHMM—34**

- After 14.08.1940, Warsaw
- *Ha-medinah* [The State], date unknown
- One-time publication of the Betar youth organization dedicated to Zeew [Włodzimierz] Żabotyński [Vladimir Zeev Jabotinsky] in connection with his death on 14.08.1940.
- ***Description:*** original (2 copies), printed, Hebrew, Yiddish, 150×220 mm, ss. 20, pp. 36.

See *Żydzi Warszawy*, p. 230; *Kronika getta*, p. 258.
Published: *The Jewish Underground Press*, vol. 1, pp. 63–74.
In the text, the date of Jabotinsky's death is 3.08.1940

**1307. RING. I/740 (1064). Mf. ŻIH—822; USHMM—34**

- 11.1941- 05.1942, Warsaw Ghetto
- *Iton ha-Tnua* [Newspaper of the Movement], nos. dated 12.1940/01.1941 and 03./04.1942
- Underground publication of Ha-Shomer Ha-Tsair.
- ***Description:*** original, printed, hectographed typescript, Hebrew, Polish, Yiddish, 155×212 mm, minor damage and losses of text, ss. 143, pp. 280.

Appended jacket: *Przegląd Rolniczy* [Agricultural Review], Warsaw-Poznań 1932.
Publisher of the newspaper: Samuel Bresław.
See *Żydzi Warszawy*, p. 230.
See HWC, 61/5 (second copy of issue dated 04.1942, pp. 165).
Published: *The Jewish Underground Press*, vol. 1, 260–349 (no. dated 12.1940/01.1941).

**1308. RING. I/690 (1014). Mf. ŻIH—817; USHMM—29. RING. I/975 (1293). Mf. ŻIH—831; USHMM—43**

- 03–07.1942, Warsaw Ghetto
- *Yedies* [News], no. from 1941 [?], no. 1 dated 26.03.1942, unnumbered issue [?], no. 4 dated 25.05.1942, no. 5 dated [2.06.]1942, no. 6 dated 9.06.1942, no. 7 dated 13.06.1942, no. 8 dated 20.06.1942, no. 9 dated 27.06.1942, and no. 10 dated [11.]07.1942
- Underground weekly of the He-haluts-Dror organization.
- ***Description:*** Ring. I/690—original (no. 4, 5, 8 in 2 incomplete copies, no. 7 in 2 copies), hectographed typescript, typescript, Yiddish, 192×228, 200×297 mm, damage and losses of text, serious damage and losses of text, missing pages (no. 1, unnumbered issue [?]), ss. 97, pp. 97; Ring. I/975—(no. from 1941 [?], no. 6 from 1942) original, hectographed typescript, typescript, Yiddish, damage and losses of text, missing pages [?], 192×282, 205×298 mm, ss. 13, pp. 13.

See *Centralny katalog*, p. 95.
See HWC, 60/8 (second copy of no. 4 dated 25.05.1942).

**1309. RING. I/684 (1008). Mf. ŻIH—817; USHMM—29**

- 01.1941–04.1942, Warsaw Ghetto
- *Yugnt-Ruf* [Call to Youth], (a) no. 1 dated 01.1941, (b) no. 2 dated 10.1941, no. 4 dated 01–02.1942, no. 5 dated 03.1942, and no. 6 dated 04.1942
- Underground monthly of Poalei Zion Left.
- ***Description:*** original, (a) (typescript, 208×294 mm), (b) (in no. 6, pp. 19–20 in 2 copies, hectographed typescript, 220×295, 214×345 mm, damage and losses of text—nos. 2, 4), Yiddish, ss. 71, pp. 78.

Doc. (a) was kept in a binder.
See *Centralny katalog*, p. 96.
Published: *The Jewish Underground Press*, vol. 1, pp. 395–405 (no. 1); vol. 3, pp. 475–494 (no. 2).

**1310. RING. I/685 (1009). (Lb. 1012, 1078). Mf. ŻIH—817; USHMM—29**

- 10.1940–01.1942, Warsaw Ghetto
- *Yugnt Shtime* [Voice of the Youth], no. 2 from 10.1940, no. 3 from 12.1940, no. 1–2 (4–5) from 01–02.1941, no. 5 (8) from 05.1941, no. 10 (13) from 11.1941, and no. 1 (14) from 01.1942, no. 2–3 (15–16 from 02–03.1942.
- Underground monthly of the Bund. Title pages adorned with drawings (e.g., fighting youth and a fist crushing snakes entangled in a swastika).
- ***Description:*** original, hectographed typescript, Yiddish, 148×213, 205×298 mm, damage and losses of text, missing pages, title page in no. 3, three pages of undetermined provenance (pp. 2, 7 [?], and 14 from a no. from 1941), ss. 91, pp. 91.

Several issues were kept in a binder.
The following issues appear in Lb. 1012: no. 2 of 10.1940, no. 1–2 of 01.02.1941, no. 5 (8) of 05.1941, no. 10 (13) of 11.1941, and no. 2–3 (15–16) of 02-03.1942. The latter issue was discovered in 2007 in Varia [Miscellany], catalog no. 230, j. 84, and included into the Ringelblum Archive.
See *Centralny katalog*, p. 96.
See HWC, 60/3 (second copy of no. 10 [13] from 11.1941).
Published: *The Jewish Underground Press*, vol. 1, pp. 148–166, 217–229, 425–444; vol. 2, pp. 276–289 (no. 2, 3, 1–2 [4–5], 5 [8]).

**1311. RING. I/687 (1011). Mf. ŻIH—817; USHMM—29**

- 07.1941, Warsaw Ghetto
- *Yunge Gvardie* [Young Guard], no. 1 from 07.1941
- Underground periodical of the Bund.
- ***Description:*** original, hectographed typescript, Yiddish, 182×240 mm, ss. 18, pp. 18.

See *Centralny katalog*, p. 96.
Published: *The Jewish Underground Press*, vol. 3, pp. 1–18.

**1312. RING. I/731 (1055). (NO. 944). Mf. ŻIH–822; USHMM–34**

- 02–04.1942, Warsaw Ghetto
- *Jutrznia* [Before Dawn], no. 1 dated 14.02., no. 2 dated 21.02., no. 3 dated 1.03., no. 4 dated 8.03., no. 5 dated 14.03., no. 6 dated 21.03., no. 7 dated 28.03., no. 8 dated 4.04., no. 9 dated 11.04., and no. 10 dated 18.04.1942
- Underground periodical of Ha-Shomer Ha-Tsair. In no. 4 a table of mortality in the Warsaw Ghetto in particular months of 1941; in no. 6 a table depicting the fluctuation of prices of staple foods during 1941.
- ***Description:*** original (nos. 1, 5, 6, 7, 8, 9 in 2 copies, no. 2 in 3 incomplete copies), hectographed typescript, Polish, 203×93, 210×296 mm, substantial damage and losses of text (no. 1 [first copy], no. 2 [second and third copies], 4, 5, 7, 8, 9,10), missing pages (no. 5 [second copy], 7 and 10), extensive minor damage and losses of text (nos. 3, 8), ss. 147, pp. 147.

  Attached note by H.W.

  See *Centralny katalog*, p. 98.

**1313. RING. I/769/1. (1093). Mf. ŻIH–825; USHMM–37**

- 01.1941, Warsaw Ghetto [?]
- [missing title] Bulletin with announcements from radio monitoring, no. dated 13.01.1941.
- ***Description:*** original, hectographed typescript, Polish, 208×300 mm, minor damage and losses of text, ss. 1, pp. 1.

  Doc. was kept in a binder.

**1314. RING. I/769/2. (1093). Mf. ŻIH–825; USHMM–37**

- 01–02.1941, Warsaw Ghetto
- Announcements from radio monitoring, dated 9.01., 10.01., 02.1941.
- ***Description:*** original, handwritten manuscript, pencil, Polish, 110×290 mm, ss. 10, pp. 16.

  Doc. was kept in a binder.

**1315. RING. I/769/3. (1093). Mf. ŻIH–825; USHMM–37**

- 06–08.1941, Warsaw Ghetto [?]
- Announcements from radio monitoring dated 23.06., 24.06., 25.06., 26.06., 27–28.06., 29.06., 30.06., 1.07., 28.08.1941.
- ***Description:*** original (no. dated 25.06. in 2 copies), typescript, Polish, 217×140, 216×343, mm, ss. 13, pp. 13.

**1316. RING. I/744 (1068). Mf. ŻIH–823; USHMM–35**

- Date unknown, Warsaw Ghetto
- *Magen Dawid* [Star of David], date unknown, no number
- Publication of Zionist-Revisionists.
- ***Description:*** original, hectographed typescript, Hebrew, Polish, Yiddish, 203×298, 210×320 mm, ss. 17, pp. 34.

  According to Gutman a publication of the Betar organization from 1942; see *Żydzi Warszawy*, p. 230.

  Index: Uri Cwi Grynberg, Ben-Zeew, Zeew Żabotyński [Uri Zvi Greenberg, Ben-Zeev, Vladimir Zeev Jabotinsky]

**1317. RING. I/692 (1016). (Lb. 1036). Mf. ŻIH–818; USHMM–30**

- 03–11.1941, Warsaw Ghetto
- *Morgen fray* [Tomorrow Free], no. 2 dated 20.03.1941, no. 4 dated 1.05.1941, no. 6 dated 15.06.1941, no. 15 dated 8.11.1941, and no. 18 dated 8.12.1941
- Underground monthly, subsequently a biweekly, of the organization Sierp i Młot [Hammer and Sickle] and Robotniczo-Chłopska Organizacja Bojowa [Worker–Peasant Combat Organization]. Continuation of the newspaper was *Morgen frayhayt* [Tomorrow Freedom] (See Ring.I/691).
- ***Description:*** original, hectographed typescript, typescript, Yiddish, 210×294, 212×335 mm, minor damage and losses of text, ss. 5, pp. 7 .

  See *Centralny katalog*, p. 122.

  Published: *The Jewish Underground Press*, vol. 2, pp. 117–119, 300–303, 454–458 (no. 2, no. 4, no. 6).

  No. 2 and 4 were kept in a binder.

**1318. RING. I/691 (1015). (Lb. 1036, 1084). Mf. ŻIH–817; USHMM–29. RING. I/933 (1252). Mf. ŻIH–829; USHMM–41**

- 11.1941–03.1942, Warsaw Ghetto
- *Morgen frayhayt* [Tomorrow Freedom], no. dated 3.11., 2 (two different numbers), 5, 6, 9, 10, 13, 18, 22, 23, 24, 28, 29.12.1941; 2, 4, 6, 7, 8, 9, 10, 11, 12, 13, 14.01.1942; no. 151 dated 15.01., no. 152 dated 16.01., no. 153 dated 17.01., no. 155 dated 19.01., no. 156 dated 20.01., no. 157 dated 21.01., no. 158 dated 22.01., no. 159 dated 23.01., 26.01., 27.01., 28.01., no. 164 dated 29.01., no. 166 dated 30.01., no. 167 dated 31.01., no. 168 dated 1.02., no. 169 dated 2.02., no. 170 dated 3.02., no. 172 dated 4.02., no. 173 dated 6.02., no. 174 dated 7.02., no. 175 dated 8.02., no. 176 dated 9.02., no. 177 dated 10.02., no. 178 dated 11.02., no. 179 dated 12.02., no. 179 [sic] dated 13.02., no. 182 dated 15.02., no. 184 dated 17.02., no. 185 dated 18.02., no. 186 dated 19.02., no. 187 dated 20.02., no. 188 dated 21.02., no. 189 dated 22.02., no. 190 dated 23.02., 25.02., no. 197 dated 27.02., no.[198] dated 28.02., no. 199 dated 1.03., no. 200/201 dated 2/3.03., no. 202 dated 4.03., no. 203/204 dated 6.03., no. 205 dated 7.03., no. 206 dated 8.03., no. 207/208 dated 10.03.1942
- Underground newspaper of the Robotniczo-Chłopska Organizacja Bojowa [Worker–Peasant Combat Organization], subsequently the Polska Partia Robotnicza (Polish Workers' Party), continuation of the newspaper *Morgen fray* [Tomorrow Free]. (See Ring.I/692).

- ***Description:*** original (no. dated 5.12.1941, no. 188, no. [198] dated 28.02. in 2 copies), hectographed typescript, typescript, Yiddish, 222×288, 214×352 mm, damage and losses of text, ss. 79, pp. 138.
  Ring. I/933 (1252)—nos. dated 5 and 9.12.1941 and three issues (without number) erroneously described as the title: *Fraye Prese* [Free Press], nos. dated 5 and 22.12.1941; see *Centralny katalog*, p. 71.
  See *Centralny katalog*, pp. 122–123.
  See HWC, 60/4 (no. dated 27.12.1941).

### 1319. RING. I/699 (1023). Mf. ŻIH—819; USHMM—31

- 01–08.1941, Warsaw Ghetto
- *Nasze Hasła* [Our Mottos], no. dated 01.1941 and no. 3 dated 08.1941
- Underground newspaper of Poalei Zion Left.
- ***Description:*** original (no. dated 01.1941 in 2 incomplete copies), typescript, Polish, 208×295 mm, illegible text, missing pages (second copy of no.dated 01.1941), ss. 25, pp. 25.
  See *Centralny katalog*, p. 134.
  Published: *The Jewish Underground Press*, vol. 1, pp. 417–424 (no. dated 01.1941); vol. 3, pp. 201–213 (no. 3).

### 1320. RING. I/698 (1022). Mf. ŻIH—819; USHMM—31

- 1941–1942, Warsaw Ghetto
- *Neged Hazerem* [Against the Current], no. 2 (13) from 02/03.1941, no. 3 (14) from 04.1941, 4 (15) of 05.1941, 5 (16), 6 (17) of 05/06.1941, 7–8 (18–19) of 09/10.1941, 20 of 03.1942 and 21 of 05.1942
- Underground monthly of the Ha-Shomer Ha-Tsair organization.
- ***Description:*** original (no. 6 [17], no. 21 in 2 copies), hectographed typescript, Hebrew, Polish, Yiddish, 220×295 mm, substantial damage and losses of text (no. 20), missing pages (no. 21, second copy), ss. 153, pp. 280.
  See *Centralny katalog*, p. 135.
  Published: *The Jewish Underground Press*, vol. 2, pp. 26–88, 163–190, 322–362 (no. 2 [13], 3 [14], 4 [15]); vol. 3, pp. 33–44, 95–130, 364–408 (no. 5 [16], 6 [17], 7–8 [18–19]); *Przewodnik*, p. 653 (photocopy of the title page of no. 2 [13]).

### 1321. RING. I/477. (Lb. 518). Mf. ŻIH—786; USHMM—17

- 05.1941, Warsaw Ghetto
- *Neged Hazerem* [Against the Current], no. 4 (15) of 05.1941 (fragment, pp. [19–23])
- Includes: "Thesis for a programmatic lecture: The Ideological and Political Path of the Movement in the Age of the Second Imperialistic War and of the Ghetto." "Thesis for a lecture: Path of Shomer Education in Time of War."
- ***Description:*** original, reproduced typescript, Polish, 205×288 mm, ss. 3, pp. 5.
  Published: *The Jewish Underground Press*, vol. 2, pp. 322–362.
  See Ring. I/698.

### 1322. RING. I/704 (1028). (Lb. 546). Mf. ŻIH—820; USHMM—32

- 03.1942 [?], Warsaw Ghetto
- *Nowe Tory* [New Tracks], no. of 03.[?] 1942
- Underground magazine of Hechaluc (He-Haluts).
- ***Description:*** original, hectographed typescript, Polish, 215×315 mm, minor damage and losses of text, missing title page, ss. 11, pp. 11.
  See *Centralny katalog*, p. 139.
  According to Gutman (*Żydzi Warszawy*, p. 230) organ of the Poalei Zion Right.

### 1323. RING. I/689 (1013). Mf. ŻIH—817; USHMM—29

- 06.1942, Warsaw Ghetto
- *Der oyfbroyz* [The Upheaval], no. 1 (16) dated 7.06.1942, no. 2 (17) dated 14.06.1942, and no. 4 (19) dated 29.06.1942
- Underground weekly of the Ha-Shomer Ha-Tsair organization.
- ***Description:*** original (no. 4 [19] in 2 copies), hectographed typescript, Yiddish, 220×345 mm, minor damage and losses of text, ss. 32, pp. 32.
  See *Centralny katalog*, p. 145.
  See HWC, 60/10–11 (second copy of no. 1 [16] dated 7.06.1942 and no. 3 [18] dated 22.06.1942).

### 1324. RING. I/754 (1078). Mf. ŻIH—823; USHMM—35

- 08.1941, Warsaw Ghetto
- *Oysdoyer* [Endurance], no. 4 dated 25.08.1941
- Underground periodical of Gordonia.
- ***Description:*** original (2 copies), hectographed typescript, Yiddish, 214×336 mm, ss. 2, pp. 4.
  See *Centralny katalog*, p. 145; *Żydzi Warszawy*, p. 230.

### 1325. RING. I/751 (1075). (Lb. 1655). Mf. ŻIH—823; USHMM—35

- 1940, Warsaw
- *Payn un gvure* [Suffering and Heroism], no. of 07–08.1940
- Underground publication of He-Haluts Dror.
- ***Description:*** original, hectographed typescript, Yiddish, 20×30, 156×200 mm, damage and losses of text, ss. 98, pp. 98.
  See *Żydzi Warszawy*, p. 230.
  Published: *The Jewish Underground Press*, vol. 1, pp. 44–52 (Pub. of fragments).

**1326. RING. I/707 (1031). Mf. ŻIH—820; USHMM—32**

- 09–10.1940, Warsaw
- *Płomienie* [Flame], no. dated 1.09.1940 and no. dated 10.10.1940
- Underground newspaper of Left Po'ale Tsiyon (Ha-Shomer Ha-Tsair).
- ***Description:*** original, hectographed typescript, Polish, 200×280 mm, damage and losses of text, missing pages, ss. 13, pp. 25.

See *Centralny katalog*, p. 154.

Published: *The Jewish Underground Press*, vol. 1, pp. 87–98, 131–147.

**1327. RING. I/733 (1057). Mf. ŻIH—822; USHMM—34**

- 10.1941–02.1942, Warsaw Ghetto
- *Podziemne Getto* [Underground Ghetto], no. 1 dated 14.10.1941
- *Getto Podziemne* [Ghetto Underground], no. 2 dated 3.02.1942
- Underground monthly of the Polish Socialists.
- ***Description:*** original, hectographed typescript, Polish, 210×294, 215×330 mm, ss. 4, pp. 8.

See *Centralny katalog*, p. 73.

Published: *The Jewish Underground Press*, vol. 3, pp. 500–505 (no. 1).

**1328. RING. I/694 (1018). Mf. ŻIH—818; USHMM—30**

- 03.1941–02.1942, Warsaw Ghetto
- *Proletarisher gedank* [Proletarian Thought], no. of 03./04.1941, no. 3 of 07.1941, no. 4 of 09.1941, and no. 5 of 02.1942
- Underground newspaper of Left Po'ale Tsiyon.
- ***Description:*** original (no. 3 and no. 4 in 2 copies; one copy of no. 3 is missing a page), hectographed typescript, Yiddish, 185×195, 208×295 mm, damage and losses of text (nos. 4, 5), ss. 86, pp. 86.

See *Centralny katalog*, p. 175.

Published: *The Jewish Underground Press*, vol. 2, pp. 143–162 (no. of 03/04.1941); vol. 3, pp. 19–32, 311–327 (nos. 3, 4).

**1329. RING. I/742 (1095, 1066). (Lb. 587, 1006). Mf. ŻIH—823; USHMM—35**

a)

- After 02.1942, Warsaw Ghetto
- Appeal entitled "Yidishe arbeter un folksmasn!" [Jewish Workers and Masses of the People!]
- Call for a boycott of the German orders concerning collection of winter clothing. Reprint from Proletarisher gedank no. 5 of 02.1942.
- ***Description:*** original, hectographed typescript, Yiddish, 210×295 mm, serious damage and losses of text, ss. 1, pp. 1.

b) **Ring. I/742 (1095) (Lb. 587)**

- After 22.06.1942, Warsaw Ghetto
- Appeal entitled "Tsu der yidisher arbetndiker folks-mase!" [To the Jewish Working Masses!]
- Issued on the first anniversary of the German attack on the USSR. Summons to demonstration of solidarity with the Red Army in the ghettos. Reprint from *Proletarisher gedank*, no. 3 dated 22.06.1942.
- ***Description:*** original, hectographed typescript, Yiddish, 217×315 mm, ss. 2, pp. 2.

**1330. RING. I/703 (1027). (Lb. 225, 226, 227, 228, 547). Mf. ŻIH—820; USHMM—32**

- 05.1942, Warsaw Ghetto
- *Przedwiośnie* [Early Spring], no. 11 dated 2.05.1942, no. 13 dated 17.05.1942, no. 14 dated 24.05.1942, and no. 15 dated 31.05.1942
- Underground weekly of the Ha-Shomer Ha-Tsair organization.
- ***Description:*** original, hectographed typescript, Polish, 221×295, 222×302 mm, ss. 25, pp. 25.

See *Centralny katalog*, p. 177.

Published: *Przewodnik*, p. 655 (photocopy of the title page of no. 11).

**1331. RING. I/720 (1044). Mf. ŻIH—821; USHMM—33**

- 02–08.1941, Warsaw Ghetto
- *Przegląd Marksistowski* [Marxist Review], no. 6 of 02/03., no. [7] of 04/05., and no. 8 of 08.1941
- Underground periodical of the Trotskyites.
- ***Description:*** original, hectographed typescript, Polish, 150×98, 208×320, 220×345 mm, substantial damage and losses of text (no. [7] and 8), ss. 67, pp. 75.

On no. [7] on p. 3 is a note (pencil) "Trotskyite 'Red Banner.'"

No. 8 dedicated to Trotsky.

See *Centralny katalog*, p. 178.

Published: *The Jewish Underground Press*, vol. 3, pp. 214–243 (no. 8).

**1332. RING. I/677 (1001). Mf. ŻIH—836; USHMM—67**

- 15.05.1942, Warsaw Ghetto
- *Der ruf* [The Call], no. 1 dated 15.05.1942
- Underground newspaper issued by the Blok Antyfaszystowski [Anti-fascist Bloc].
- ***Description:*** original, hectographed typescript, Yiddish, 210×293 mm, ss. 12, pp. 12.

See *Centralny katalog*, p. 197.

Published: *BFG*, vol. IV, issue 1/1951, pp. 64–80 (fragments); BŻIH, no. 1(5)/1953, pp. 4–8 (fragments).

**1333. RING. I/696 (1020). (Lb. 269, 685). Mf. ŻIH—818; USHMM—30**

- 07.1941–03.1942, Warsaw Ghetto

- *Słowo Młodych. Pismo Młodzieży Gordonistycznej* [Word of the Young. Newspaper of Gordonist Youth], no. 5 (19) of 07.1941, no. 6–7 (20–21), no. 8 (22) of 11/12.1941, and 9–10 (23–24) of 02./03.1942.
- Underground monthly of a Zionist youth organization.
- ***Description:*** original, hectographed typescript, Polish, Yiddish, 208×270 mm, damage and losses of text, ss. 73, pp. 139.

  From information in the 1946 "Katalog Archiwum dr Emanuela Ringelbluma" (Lb. 269), it appears that the newspaper was issued by Eleazer (Eliezer) Geller (pseudonym Eugeniusz Kowalski), a ŻOB courier and a participant in the Warsaw Ghetto uprising.

  See *Centralny katalog*, p. 206.

  Published: *The Jewish Underground Press*, vol. 3, pp. 65–94, 328–363 (no. 5 [19], 6–7 [20–21]); *Przewodnik*, p. 652 (photocopy of the title page of no. 5 [19]).

### 1334. RING. I/752 (1076). (Lb. 933). Mf. ŻIH—823; USHMM—35

- [1940–1941], Warsaw Ghetto
- *Shviv* [Spark], no. [12.1940], no. 5 of [06–07.1941]
- Underground periodical of the youth organization of the General Zionists.
- ***Description:*** original, printed, hectographed typescript, Hebrew, 204×280 mm, ss. 55, pp. 75.

  No. (without cover, date unknown, no issue no.) was kept in a binder.

  See *Żydzi Warszawy*, p. 231.

  Published: *The Jewish Underground Press*, vol. 1, pp. 230–259, vol. 2, pp. 482–517.

  See HWC, 61/4 (no. 6).

### 1335. RING. I/724 (1048). Mf. ŻIH—821; USHMM—33

- After 03.1941, Warsaw Ghetto
- *Trybuna Młodych* [Tribune of the Young], date unknown, and without number (fragment)
- Underground newspaper of the Bund.
- ***Description:*** original, hectographed typescript, Polish, 214×340 mm, only pp. 1 and 11–12,14 survived, ss. 4, pp. 4.

  See *Centralny katalog*, pp. 198–199.

### 1336. RING. I/693 (1017). (Lb. 1113). Mf. ŻIH—818; USHMM—30

- 03–04.1942, Warsaw Ghetto
- *Unzer hofnung* [Our Hope], no. 1 dated 1.03.1942, no. 2 dated 1.04.1942, and no. [?]
- Underground periodical of the General Zionists organization.
- ***Description:*** original (no. 2 in 2 incomplete copies, no. dated [?] in 3 copies), hectographed typescript, typescript., Yiddish, 15×65, 208×292mm, damage and losses of text, missing pages, ss. 56, pp. 95.

  See *Centralny katalog*, p. 227.

### 1337. RING. I/683 (1007). Mf. ŻIH—817; USHMM—29

- 12.1941–05.1942, Warsaw Ghetto
- *Unzer veg* [Our Path], no. (a) of 12.1941 and no. (b) of 1.05.1942
- Underground periodical of the He-Haluts-Dror organization.
- ***Description:*** original, (a) (pp. 22–23 in 2 copies, hectographed typescript, 214×320 mm, damage and losses of text); (b) (typescript, 210×290 mm, major damage and losses of text), Yiddish, ss.18, pp. 30.

  See *Centralny katalog*, p. 227.

### 1338. RING. I/681 (1005). Mf. ŻIH—817; USHMM—29

- 01–04.1942, Warsaw Ghetto
- *Der veker.* Informatsie biuletin [The Alarm. Information Bulletin], no. 1 (25) dated 18.01.1942, no. 2 (26) dated 25.01.1942, no. 3 (27) dated 1.02.1942, no. 4 (28) dated 8.02.1942, no. 5 (29) dated 15.02.1942, no. 6 (30) dated 23.02.1942, no. 7 (31) dated 1.03.1942, no. 8 (32) dated 8.03.1942, no. 11 (35) dated 6.04.1942, and no. 12 (36) dated 12.04.1942
- Underground weekly of the Bund.
- ***Description:*** original (no. 1 [25] in 2 incomplete copies), hectographed typescript, Yiddish, 188×220, 220×346 mm, damage and losses of text, missing pages [?], ss. 47, pp. 47.

  See *Centralny katalog*, p. 237.

  See HWC, 60/6 (no. 9 [33] dated 15.03.1942).

### 1339. RING. I/768 (1092). (Lb. 604). RING. I/769. Mf. ŻIH—825; USHMM—37

a)

- 11.1941–07.1942, Warsaw Ghetto
- *Wiadomości i Komunikaty* [News and Announcements], no. of 22.11., 24.11., 25.11., 27.11., 28.11., 30.11., 2.12., 3.12., 5.12., 7.12., 8.12., 9.12., 10.12., 13.12., 14.12., 16.12., 17.12., 21.12., 24.12., 25.12., 27.12., 29.12. (fragment), 31.12.1941; 1.01., 2.01., 3.01., 4.01., 5.01., 6.01., 7.01., 8.01. (two different numbers), 9.01., 10.01., 11.01., 12.01., 13.01., 14.01., 15.01., 16.01., 17.01., 23.01. (fragment), 31.01.,12.02., 17.02., 19.02., 27.02., 28.02., 28.02. (without title), 2.03., 3.03., 10.03. (without title), 14.03. (two different numbers), 17.03., 26.03., 1.04., 2.04., 3.04. (two different numbers), 4.04., 5.04., 6.04., 8.04., 9.04., 10.04., 11.04., 12.04., 13.04., 14.04., 15.04., 16.04., 17.04.,18.04., 22.04., 23.04., 26.04., 28.04., 29.04., 30.04., 2.05., 3.05., 5.05., 6.05., 8.05. (two different numbers), 9.05., 10.05., 11.05.[?], 12.05., 13.05., 14.05, 16.05., 18.05., 19.05., 23.05., 27.05., 28.05. (two different numbers [?]), 30.05., 31.05., 1.06., 2.06., 3.06, 4.06., 5.06., 6.06., 7.06., 8.06., 11.06., 12.06., 13.06., 15.06., 16.06.[?], 19.06., 22.06., 26.06. (missing title), 11.07., 12.07., and 16.07.1942.
- Daily with announcements from monitoring of London radio. [Prepared and issued by Oyneg Shabes?].

- ***Description:*** original (no. dated 21.12.1941, 14.01., 17.02., 2.03., 3.04., 8.04., 18.04., 11.07.1942 in 2 copies, and 28.02.1942 in 3 incomplete), typescript, handwritten manuscript (SB*), pencil, Polish, 85×90, 210×347 mm, damage and losses of text, numerous loose pages (date unknown, and without number), ss. 235, pp. 237.

  On the back of the issue dated 1.06.1942 is a note by H.W.* in Yiddish: "21 daily announcements, June 1942, 8."

  See Ring. II/317.

  See *Centralny katalog*, p. 240.

  See HWC, 59/3 (no. of 12, 20 and 26.12.1941).

b)

- 02–04.11942, Warsaw Ghetto
- [missing title, *Wiadomości i Komunikaty* (News and Announcements) ?] Announcements from radio monitoring, no. dated 27.01., 27.02.[?], 28.02., 10.03. and 30.04.1942.
- ***Description:*** original, handwritten manuscript (various handwritings), pencil, Polish, 146×103, 203×296 mm, damage and losses of text (no.z 30.04.1942), ss. 12, pp. 12.

### 1340. RING. I/700 (1024). (Lb. 1, 14). Mf. ŻIH—819; USHMM—31

- 03.1941–01/02.1942, Warsaw Ghetto
- *Za Naszą i Waszą Wolność* [For Our and Your Freedom], no. 2 of 03.1941, no. 3 05.1941, no. 7 of 08.1941, no. 8 [?] of 10.1941 [erroneously labeled no. 7], no. ca. 12.1941, and no. of 01/02.1942
- Underground newspaper of the Bund.
- ***Description:*** original, hectographed typescript, Polish, 200×295, 215×350 mm, damage and losses of text (no. of 01/02.1942), missing title page (no. 2 from ca. 03.1941 and no. from ca. 12.1941), ss. 78, pp. 78.

  See *Centralny katalog*, p. 260.

  Published: *The Jewish Underground Press*, vol. 2, pp. 120–142, 363–379 (no. 2, 3); vol. 3, pp. 244–264, 506–527 (no. 7, no. [8] 7).

### 1341. RING. I/714 (1038). (Lb. 217). Mf. ŻIH—820; USHMM—32

- 07.1942, Warsaw Ghetto
- *Zarzewie* [Embers], no. 1 (20) dated 15.07.1942
- Underground weekly of the Ha-Shomer Ha-Tsair organization.
- ***Description:*** original, hectographed typescript, Polish, 198×288 mm, damage and losses of text, missing last page, ss. 8, pp. 8.

  See *Centralny katalog*, p. 262.

### 1342. RING. I/730 (1054). Mf. ŻIH—822; USHMM—34

- 02–05.1942, Warsaw Ghetto
- *Żagiew* [Torch], no. 1 of 02.1942, no. 3, 03.1942, and no. 5 of 05.1942
- Underground monthly of Jewish army veterans.
- ***Description:*** original, hectographed typescript, Polish, 208×322, 205×308 mm, substantial damage and losses of text (no. 5), damage and losses of text (no. 1 and 3), ss. 16, pp. 27.

  See *Centralny katalog*, p. 268. According to Gutman, a newspaper of assimilated Jews; see *Żydzi Warszawy*, p. 231.

  See Ring. II/316/1.

### 1343. RING. I/1220/35. Mf. ŻIH—835; USHMM—47

- Date unknown, Warsaw Ghetto
- Fragment of a periodical [?]
- Story signed by Rosa.
- ***Description:*** transcript, hectographed typescript [?], Yiddish, 135×171, 171×223 mm, substantial damage and losses of text, missing pages, ss. 4, pp. 4.

### 1344. RING. I/1220/36. Mf. ŻIH—835; USHMM—47

- After 1941 [?], Warsaw Ghetto
- Fragment of a periodical.
- ***Description:*** original, hectographed typescript, Yiddish, 176×116, 202×262 mm, serious damage and losses of text, missing pages, ss. 5, pp. 10.

### 1345. RING. I/1220/72. Mf. ŻIH—835; USHMM—47

- Date unknown, Warsaw Ghetto
- Fragment of a periodical.
- ***Description:*** original, hectographed typescript, Yiddish, 208×332 mm, only page 4 survived, ss. 1, pp. 1.

  Doc. was kept in a binder.

### 1346. RING. I/599/105. Mf. ŻIH—812; USHMM—24

- Date unknown, place unknown
- Fragments of a periodical [?].
- ***Description:*** original, copied typescript, Yiddish, 85×43 mm, serious damage and losses of text, ss. 2, pp. 2.

### 1347. RING. I/1220/42. Mf. ŻIH—835; USHMM—47

- Date unknown, Warsaw Ghetto
- Fragment of a periodical or bulletin [?]
- Statistical data about education, postal service in the Warsaw Ghetto.
- ***Description:*** original, hectographed typescript, Polish, 160×113 mm, serious damage and losses of text, ss. 1, pp. 1.

## *OTHER UNDERGROUND PUBLICATIONS OF THE WARSAW GHETTO*

### 1348. RING. I/160. Mf. ŻIH—778; USHMM—9

- After 12.1941, Warsaw Ghetto
- [Lea Rotkop], *Roze Symkhovitsh* [Roza Symchowicz] (1887–1941), Warsaw 1942
- Underground pamphlet with the biography of a teacher (born 1887), an educational activist, author of works in the field of pedagogy, died before 2.12.1941 in the Warsaw Ghetto.

- ***Description:*** original (2 copies in fragments, only one cover jacket), hectographed typescript, Yiddish, 215×304 mm, damage and losses of text, (ss. 6, pp. 11), ss. 10, pp. 19.
  On p. 2 (cover jacket) in Yiddish: "Ji.Sz.K. [Yi. Sh.K. ?], Warsaw 1942."
  Inventory: Pamphlet's author is Lea Rotkop.
  About Roza Symchowicz and the pamphlet, see *Kronika getta*, pp. 607–610.
  Published: *Dzieci*, pp. 240–251.

**1349. RING. I/35. Mf. ŻIH—772; USHMM—3**

- 08.1941, Warsaw Ghetto
- *Sylwetki znakomitych mężów Służby Porządkowej* [Profiles of Famous Figures of the Order Service]. Warsaw, August 1941
- Collection of satirical rhymes dedicated to selected members and coworkers of the Order Service in the Warsaw Ghetto.
- ***Description:*** original, duplicated typescript with handwritten manuscript notations (ink, pencil), on the cover is a sketch (caricature) of an Order Service policeman, 203×295 mm, ss. 7, pp. 12.
  On p. 1 the number: "42" (printed).
  Attached note by H.W. in Polish and Yiddish: "Forwarded to the archive by attorney [Gerszon Juda?] Wichler."
  Published: *Służba Porządkowa*, pp. 111–122.
  Index: Szeryński, Czapliński (Moniak, Dymiński, Major Przymusiński), Berek Rabinowicz, Handel, Firstenberg, Mieczysław Lichtenbaum, Fels, Schonbach, Stefan Lubliner, Nikodem Goldsztein, Albert Szwalbe, Lederman, Leikin, Lindelfeld, Blaupaper, Dr. Fajncyn, Peczenik, Hertz, Capt. Fleischman, Landau, Trumper, Brewda, Nadel, Kroszczor, Adler, Tondowski, Dir. Szatensztajn, Talmus, Dr. Gombiński, Wichler, Szmerling, Rode, Gutgold, Wajsblat, Seweryn Spotkowski, Kerner, Melania Wasserman, Kornbergowa, Koplówna, Kacowa

**1350. RING. I/739 (1063). Mf. ŻIH—822; USHMM—34. RING. I/1220/92. Mf. ŻIH—835; USHMM—47**

- 1942, Warsaw Ghetto
- *Z problematyki ruchu w chwili obecnej* [Of the Movement's Issues at the Present Moment], [Warsaw, 1942]
- Pamphlet issued by the chief headquarters of the Gordonia movement, includes movement's political program and educational tasks, inter alia, "On the Trail of Bankrupt Phraseology," "Scouting Education in the Present Day."
- ***Description:*** original (2 incomplete copies), printed hectographed typescript, Polish, 160×237 mm, damage and losses of text, very serious damage and losses of text (second copy—Ring. I/1220), ss. 46, pp. 88.
  Third copy, see Ring. II/343.
  See *Bibliografia druków*, p. 262.
  "Na tropach zbankrutowanej frazeologii" [On the Trail of Bankrupt Phraseology]—comprehensive article placed in no. 8 (22) of 11.1941 and 9–10 (23–24) of 02–03.1942 of *Słowo Młodych* containing polemic with the position of Ha-Shomer Ha-Tsair.

**1351. RING. I/743 (1067). (Lb. 911). Mf. ŻIH—823; USHMM—35**

- 1.05.1941, Warsaw Ghetto
- Proclamation: *Do Ludu Pracującego Polski!* [To the Working People of Poland!]
- Pub. of the Bund for 1st of May.
- ***Description:*** original, printed, Polish, Yiddish, 164×260 mm, ss. 1, pp. 2.
  Leaflet was kept in a binder.

**1352. RING. I/1077 (1396). (Lb. 1266). Mf. ŻIH—832; USHMM—44.**

- [After 06.1941], Warsaw Ghetto
- Leaflet entitled *Kol-korei* [Proclamation] (missing conclusion)
- Concerning the problem of funerals in the Warsaw Ghetto.
- ***Description:*** original or transcript, typescript, Hebrew, 220×288 mm, ss. 1, pp. 1.
  On p. 1 a note by H.W. in Yiddish (ink): "108–1942/1 January."
  Compare Ring. I/767.
  Attached note by H.W. in Yiddish: "Delivered by Rabbi Józef Gelernter of Saska Kępa." [A list of rabbis includes Josef Gelertner (?) of Skierniewice. Compare Ring. II/210].

## *POLISH UNDERGROUND PRESS*

**1353. RING. I/769/5 (1093). (Lb. 25). Mf. ŻIH—825; USHMM—37**

- 07.1941–07.1942, Warsaw
- *Agencja Radiowa* [Radio Agency], no. 577 dated 30.07., 31.07., no. 594 dated 16.08., no. 603 dated 25.08., 17.08., no. 612 dated 3.09., 4.09., no. 615 dated 6.09., no. 616 dated 7.09.1941, no. 816 dated 26.03., and no. 914 dated 2.07.1942
- Announcements from radio monitoring (Delegatura Rządu [Government Delegacy, head of the underground state in occupied Poland]).
- ***Description:*** original, hectographed typescript, Polish, 220×305, 220×345 mm, minor damage and losses of text, ss. 13, pp. 21.
  See Ring. II/315.
  See *Centralny katalog*, pp. 24–26.

**1354. RING. I/712 (1036). (Lb. 10). Mf. ŻIH—820; USHMM—32**

- 12.1940–04.1942, Warsaw

- *Barykada Wolności* [Barricade of Freedom], no. 27 of 29.12.1940; no. 56 of 20.07., no. 57 of 27.07, no. 58 of 3.08., no. 59 of 11.08., no. 60 of 17.08., no. 62 of 31.08., no. 63 of 7.09., no. 67 of 5.10., no. 68 of 12.10., no. 70 of 26.10., no. 71 of 2.11., no. 74 of 23.11., no. 75 of 30.11., no. 77 of 14.12., no. 78 of 21.12. and no. 79 of 28.12.1941; no. 79 [error in numbering] of 4.01., no. 80 of 18.01., no. 82 of 15.02., no. 84 of 15.03., and no. 86 of 15.04.1942
- Underground weekly, then biweekly of the group Barykada Wolności, later of the Polish Socialists.
- ***Description:*** original (no. 75, pp. 3 and 4 in 2 copies; no. 77 pp. 5 and 6 in 2 copies; no. 79 of 28.12.1941—1 sheet, no. 79 of 4.01.1942, 80, 84 in 2 copies), printed hectographed typescript, Polish, 120×175, 220×320 mm, minor damage and losses of text (no. 27, 74, 78, 82), damage and losses of text (no. 77, 79, 84—second copy), ss. 87, pp. 174.

No. 27 was kept in a binder.

See *Centralny katalog*, p. 31.

See HWC, 59/4 (no. 81 of 31.01.1942).

**1355. RING. I/719 (1042, 1043). (Lb. 22). Mf. ŻIH—821; USHMM—33**

- 04.1941–07.1942, Warsaw
- *Biuletyn Informacyjny* [Information Bulletin], no. of 3.04., 14.08. and 30.10.1941, no. 6 (110) of 12.02., no. 7 (111) of 19.02., no. 10 (114) of 12.03., no. 11 (115) of 19.03., no. 12 (116) of 26.03., no. 13 (117) of 2.04., no. 14 (118) of 9.04., no. 16 (120) of 23.04., no. 19 (123) of 14.05., no. 20 (124) of 21.05., no. 21 (125) of 28.05., no. 22 (126) of 3.06., no. 23 (127) of 11.06., no. 24 (128) of 18.06., no. 26 (130) of 2.07., no. 27 (131) of 9.07.1942; and no.[?]
- Weekly of the ZWZ-AK [Association for Armed Combat—Home Army].
- ***Description:*** original (no. 12 [116], 13 [117] and 22 [126] in 2 copies), printed Polish, 115×175, 145×221 mm, minor damage and losses of text, missing pages (no. 12 [116] in the second copy, no.[?]), ss. 101, pp. 200.

See Ring. II/314.

See *Centralny katalog*, pp. 35–38.

**1356. RING. I/769/4. (1093). Mf. ŻIH—825; USHMM—37**

- 08.1941, Warsaw
- *Biuletyn Radiowy* [Radio Bulletin], no. 17 of 19.08.1941
- Announcements from radio monitoring of the Związek Walki Wyzwoleńczej [Union of the Liberation Struggle].
- ***Description:*** original, hectographed typescript, Polish, 205×295 mm, ss. 3, pp. 6.

See *Centralny katalog*, p. 43.

**1357. RING. I/769/7. (1093). Mf. ŻIH—825; USHMM—37**

- 02.1942, Warsaw
- *Biuletyn Radiowy* [Radio Bulletin], no. 7 of 16.02.1942, no. 8 of 19.02.1942
- Announcements from radio monitoring (Publication of the Warsaw Committee of the Polish Workers Party [Polska Partia Robotnicza]).
- ***Description:*** original, hectographed typescript, Polish, 218×340, 218×332 mm, minor damage and losses of text (no. 8), ss. 2, pp. 4.

See *Centralny katalog*, p. 43.

**1358. RING. I/727 (1051). (Lb. 1602, 1602A). Mf. ŻIH—821; USHMM—33**

- 01.1942, Warsaw
- *Do Broni!* [To Arms!], no. 2 of 20.01.1942
- Underground biweekly of the Konfederacja Narodu [Confederation of the Nation].
- ***Description:*** original, printed, Polish, 155×234 mm, ss. 4, pp. 8.

See *Centralny katalog*, pp. 56–57.

**1359. RING. I/717 (1041). (Lb. 193). Mf. ŻIH—821; USHMM—33**

- 07–08.1941, date unknown, Warsaw
- *Do Zwycięstwa* [To Victory], no. 1 of 14.08. and no. 2 of 20.08.1941
- Underground weekly of the Association of Friends of the USSR
- Appended fragment of a leaflet of this group of 27.07.1941, a leaflet of August 1941, and an unsigned proclamation "Workers! Peasants! Intelligentsia!"
- ***Description:*** original (no. 1 and leaflet of 08.1941 in 2 copies), hectographed typescript, Polish, 131×206, 206×285 mm, minor damage and losses of text, ss. 12, pp. 19.

See *Centralny katalog*, p. 58.

**1360. RING. I/710 (1034). Mf. ŻIH—820; USHMM—32**

- 08.1941–01.1942, Warsaw
- *Gwardia* [Guard], no. 15 of 08.1941, no. 17 of 10.1941, no. 20 of 01.1942, and no. 22 of 03.1942
- Underground monthly of the Polish Socialists.
- ***Description:*** original (appended to no. 22 in 2 copies), printed, Polish, 135×177 mm, damage and losses of text (no. 17), ss. 28, pp. 56.

See *Centralny katalog*, p. 83.

**1361. RING. I/711 (1035). Mf. ŻIH—820; USHMM—32**

- 06.1942, Warsaw
- *Gwardia Ludowa* [People's Guard], no. 4 (7) of 06.1942
- Underground monthly of the Polska Partiai Socjalistyczna (Wolność Równość Niepodległość) [Polish Socialist Party (Freedom Equality Independence)].
- ***Description:*** original, printed, Polish, 120×155 mm, ss. 4, pp. 8.

See *Centralny katalog*, p. 84.

**1362. RING. I/709 (1033). Mf. ŻIH–820; USHMM–32**

- 06.1942, Warsaw
- *Gwardzista* [Guardsman], no. 2 of 10.06.1942
- Underground biweekly of the Gwardia Ludowa.
- ***Description:*** original (1 copy printed and 3 copies hectographed typescript in an abbreviated version, 2 copies of a fragment of text: "Gwardzista i broń" [Guardsman and Arms], printed, duplicated typescript, Polish, 105×150, 208×290 mm, minor damage and losses of text (hectographed typescript), ss. 32, pp. 38.

In Ring. II/320 is a duplicated version (hectographed typescript) of this no.

See *Centralny katalog*, p. 85.

**1363. RING. I/760 (1084). (Lb. 182). Mf. ŻIH–823; USHMM–35**

- 07–10.1941, Warsaw
- *Der Hammer* [The Hammer], no. 13 of 25.07. and no. 18 of 14.10.1941
- Underground magazine of ZWZ-AK [Association for Armed Combat—Home Army] issued in the framework of "akcja N" [?].
- ***Description:*** original, printed, German, 153×215 mm, ss. 4, pp. 8.

See *Centralny katalog*, p. 85.

**1364. RING. I/773 (1097). Mf. ŻIH–825; USHMM–37**

- 05.1941, Warsaw
- *Jedna Karta* [One Sheet], no. 139 of 10.05.1941
- Newspaper of a group of students of the prewar School of Political Science.
- ***Description:*** original, hectographed typescript, Polish, 210×330 mm, ss. 1, pp. 2.

See *Centralny katalog*, p. 95.

**1365. RING. I/761 (1085). (Lb. 104). Mf. ŻIH–823; USHMM–35**

- 08.1941, Warsaw
- *Jutro PN* [Tomorrow Independent Poland], no. 109 of 15.08.1941
- Underground weekly of the organization Polska Niepodległa [Independent Poland].
- ***Description:*** original, printed, Polish, 150×207 mm, ss. 3, pp. 6.

See Ring. II/322.

See *Centralny katalog*, pp. 96–97.

**1366. RING. I/769/6. (1093). Mf. ŻIH–825; USHMM–37**

- 05.1941, Warsaw
- *K.O.* [?], no. of 7.05. and 9.05.1941
- Announcements from radio monitoring.
- ***Description:*** original, hectographed typescript, Polish, 205×290 mm, ss. 2, pp. 4.

See *Centralny katalog*, p. 98.

**1367. RING. I/726 (1050). (Lb. 250, 251). Mf. ŻIH–821; USHMM–33**

- 03–05.1942, Warsaw
- *Miecz i Pług* [Sword and Plow], no. 9 of 23.03., no. 10 of 5.04., no. 15 of 31.05.1942
- Underground weekly of the organization Miecz and Pług [Sword and Plow].
- ***Description:*** original, printed, Polish, 110×155 mm, ss. 12, pp. 24.

No. 15 has title: *Ruch Miecz i Pług* [Sword and Plow Movement].

See *Centralny katalog*, p. 118.

**1368. RING. I/721 (1045). (Lb. 247, 248). Mf. ŻIH–821; USHMM–33**

- 05–06.1942, Warsaw
- *Myśl Państwowa* [State Thought], no. 17 of 12.05., no. 18 of 19.05., and no. 19 of 2.06.1942
- Underground biweekly of the Konwent Organizacji Niepodległościowych [Convention of Organizations for Independence].
- ***Description:*** original, printed, Polish, 138×181 mm, damage and losses of text (no. 19), ss. 14, pp. 28.

See *Centralny katalog*, p. 125.

**1369. RING. I/728 (1052). (Lb. 950). Mf. ŻIH–821; USHMM–33**

- 12.[1941]-02.1942, Warsaw
- *Nowa Polska* [New Poland], no. 15 of 22.12 [1941], no. 2 (18) of 20.01., and no. 3 (19) of 4.02.1942
- Underground biweekly of the Konfederacja Narodu [Confederation of the Nation].
- ***Description:*** original, printed, Polish, 156×228 mm, extensive minor damage and losses of text (no. 15, no. 3 [19]), ss. 12, pp. 24.

See *Centralny katalog*, p. 137.

**1370. RING. I/735 (1059). Mf. ŻIH–822; USHMM–34**

- 05.1941, Warsaw
- *Polsce Służ. Nasz Biuletyn. Agencja Prasowa* [Serve Poland. Our Bulletin. Press Agency], no. 44 of 20.05.1941
- Underground newspaper of ZWZ-AK [Association for Armed Combat—Home Army].
- ***Description:*** original, printed, Polish, 230×312 mm, ss. 1, pp. 2.

See *Centralny katalog*, p. 159.

**1371. RING. I/718 (1042). (Lb. 1373). Mf. ŻIH–821; USHMM–33.**

- 12.1941, Warsaw
- *PONS. Biuletyn Informacyjny* [PONS. Information Bulletin], no. 29 of 12.1941 and no. 30 of 23.12.1941
- Underground newspaper of the Polska Organizacja Narodowo-Syndykalistyczna [Polish National-Syndicalist Organization].
- ***Description:*** original, hectographed typescript,

Polish, 208×275, 208×292 mm, damage and losses of text, missing pages and erroneously linked fragments of surviving ss. (no. 29), ss. 10, pp. 20.

See *Centralny katalog*, p. 150.

**1372. RING. I/976 (1295). Mf. ŻIH—831; USHMM—43**

- 12.05.1942, Warsaw
- *Robotnik* [Worker], no. 88 of 12.05.1942 (fragment)
- Underground biweekly of the Polish Socialists.
- ***Description:*** original, printed, Polish, 147×205 mm, minor damage and losses of text, missing end, ss. 1, pp. 2.

See *Centralny katalog*, p. 194.

**1373. RING. I/723 (1047). (Lb. 1377). Mf. ŻIH—821; USHMM—33**

- 04.1941–05.1942, Warsaw
- *Rzeczpospolita Polska* [Polish Republic], no. 3 of 25.04., no. 19/20 of 11.12.1941, no. 4 (24) of 10.03., and no. 9 (29) of 23.05.1942
- Underground biweekly of the Delegatura Rządu na Kraj [Government Delegacy in the Homeland].
- ***Description:*** original (No. 19/20 in 2 copies), printed, Polish, 150×210, 171×244 mm, damage and losses of text (no. 19/20), ss. 40, pp. 80.

See *Centralny katalog*, pp. 198–199.

**1374. RING. I/762 (1086). (Lb. 107). Mf. ŻIH—823; USHMM—35**

- 08.1941, Warsaw
- *Sprawa* [The Cause], no. 17 (55) of 15.08.1941
- Underground weekly of the Związek Syndykalistów Polskich [Union of Polish Syndicalists].
- ***Description:*** original, printed, Polish, 117×173 mm, ss. 8, pp. 16.

See *Centralny katalog*, p. 208.

**1375. RING. I/736 (1060). Mf. ŻIH—822; USHMM—34**

- 10.1941, Warsaw
- *Uwagi Polityczne* [Political Observations], no. 20 of 3.10.1941
- Underground biweekly of the Polish Socialists.
- ***Description:*** original, hectographed typescript, Polish, 205×288 mm, ss. 1, pp. 2.

See *Centralny katalog*, p. 228.

**1376. RING. I/725 (1049). (Lb. 253, 254). Mf. ŻIH—821; USHMM—33**

- 05.1942, Warsaw
- *Wiadomości Codzienne Organizacji Miecza i Pługa* [Daily News of the Sword and Plow Organization], no. 116 of 23.05. and no. 119 of 28.05.1942
- Underground newspaper of the organization Miecz i Pług [Sword and Plow].
- ***Description:*** original, printed, Polish, 160×217 mm, minor damage and losses of text, ss. 2, pp. 4.

See Ring. II/336.

See *Centralny katalog*, pp. 239–240.

**1377. RING. I/715 (1039). Mf. ŻIH—821; USHMM—33**

- 02–06.1942, Warsaw
- *Wiadomości Polskie* [Polish News], no. 4 (61) of 12.02., [no. 5 (62)] of 1.04., and no. 10–11 (67–68) of 10.06.1942
- Underground biweekly of ZWZ-AK [Association for Armed Combat—Home Army].
- ***Description:*** original, printed, Polish, 160×240 mm, substantial damage and losses of text (no. of 1.04.1942), ss. 16, pp. 32.

See Ring. II/339.

See *Centralny katalog*, pp. 241–242.

**1378. RING. I/732 (1056). (Lb. 192). Mf. ŻIH—822; USHMM—34**

- 02.1940–08.1941, Warsaw
- *Wieści ze Świata* [News of the World], no. 28 of 1.02., no. 43 of 15.05.1940, no. 46 of 12.06., no. 49 of 4.06., and no. 55 of 9.08.1941
- Underground weekly of the Association of Friends of the USSR.
- ***Description:*** original (no. 28, 55 in 2 copies), hectographed typescript, Polish, 206×294 mm, minor damage and losses of text (no. 55, second copy), ss. 7, pp. 14.

See *Centralny katalog*, p. 250.

**1379. RING. I/708 (1032). Mf. ŻIH—820; USHMM—32**

- 02–06.1941, Warsaw
- *Wolność* [Freedom], no. 1 of 1.02., no. 2 of 10.02., no. 3 of 20.02., no. 4 of 1.03., no. 5 of 10.03., no. 6 of 20.03., no. 7 of 1.04., no. 8 of 10.04., no. 9–10 of 20.04., no. 11 of 15.05., and no. 12 of 5.06.1941
- Underground newspaper of the Polska Partia Socjalistyczna (Wolność Równość Niepodległość) [Polish Socialist Party (Freedom Equality Independence)].
- ***Description:*** original, printed, Polish, 135×176 mm, ss. 46, pp. 92.

Publications were kept in a binder.

See Ring. II/337.

See *Centralny katalog*, pp. 255–256.

**1380. RING. I/722 (1046). (Lb. 7, 1376). Mf. ŻIH—821; USHMM—33**

- 09.1940, 06.1942, Warsaw
- *WRN*, of 11–19.09.1940, no. 5 (87), of 9–23.03.1942, no. 6 (88) of 24.03–11.04., no. 8 (90) of 11.05., no. 9 (91) of 22.05.. and no. 10 (92) of 8.06.1942
- Underground biweekly of the Polska Partia Socjalistyczna (Wolność Równość Niepodległość) [Polish Socialist Party (Freedom Equality Independence)].

- *Description:* original, printed, Polish, 120×154, 125×176 mm, extensive minor damage and losses of text (no. 9), ss. 25, pp. 50.
  No. of 11–19.09.1940 was kept in a binder.
  See *Centralny katalog*, pp. 228–230.

**1381. RING. I/729 (1053). (Lb. 96). Mf. ŻIH—821; USHMM—33**

- 11/12.1940, Warsaw
- *Zagadnienia* [Issues], nos. 3–4 of 11–12.1940
- Underground publication of the Polish Socialists.
- *Description:* original, hectographed typescript, Polish, 210×294 mm, ss. 10, pp. 20.
  Appended blank sheet (from another doc.) with torn [odbitą] first page of the periodical *Zagadnienia*.
  Publication was kept in a binder.
  See *Centralny katalog*, p. 261.

**1382. RING. I/713 (1037). Mf. ŻIH—820; USHMM—32**

- 01.1942, Warsaw
- *Zwyciężymy* [We Shall Prevail], no. 8 of 15.01.1942
- Underground biweekly of the Związek Walki Wyzwoleńczej "Za Naszą i Waszą Wolność" [Union of the Struggle for Liberation "For Our and Your Freedom"].
- *Description:* original, hectographed typescript, Polish, 223×350 mm, minor damage and losses of text, text illegible in places, ss. 3, pp. 6.
  See *Centralny katalog*, p. 268.

**1383. RING. I/769/8. (1093). Mf. ŻIH—825; USHMM—37**

- 05.1941, place unknown
- [missing title] no. 288 of 18 [?] 05.1941
- Announcements from radio monitoring.
- *Description:* original, hectographed typescript, Polish, 215×343 mm, minor damage and losses of text, missing p. 1, ss. 1, pp. 2.

## *OTHER UNDERGROUND PUBLICATIONS OF THE WARSAW GHETTO*

**1384. RING. I/772 (1096). (Lb. 567). Mf. ŻIH—825; USHMM—37**

a) (1096). (No. 567)
- 05.[1942], Warsaw
- Proclamation: *Do Oddziałów Gwardii Ludowej wyruszających w pole. Rozkaz z dnia 15 maja [1942]* [To Units of the People's Guard Moving into the Field. Order of 15 May (1942)].
- Order of the "High Command of the People's Guard" in connection with movement into the field of the partisan unit [of Franciszek Zubrzycki].
- *Description:* original, hectographed typescript, Polish, 201×283 mm, ss. 1, pp. 1.

b)
- Date unknown, place unknown
- Leaflet entitled *Rozważania na temat partyzantki w Polsce* [Reflections on Partisan Warfare in Poland]
- On the necessity of conducting partisan activities.
- *Description:* original (2 copies), hectographed typescript, Polish, 201×283 mm, ss. 2, pp. 4.

**1385. RING. I/338/2. Mf. ŻIH—781; USHMM—12**

- Date unknown, place unknown
- Leaflet (poster [?]): *Deutschland [verfallen an] allen Fronten / Niemcy gin[ą na wsz]ystkich frontach* [Germans Are Los[ing on a]ll Fronts]
- Underground publication.
- *Description:* original, printed, German, Polish, 188×49 mm, torn and missing the middle fragment, losses of text, ss. 1, pp. 1.
  On the left side a letter: "V" of the height of two lines.

**1386. RING. I/977 (1296). Mf. ŻIH—831; USHMM—43**

- 1940, Warsaw
- [Leon Marszałek] Andrzej Brzoza, *O powołaniu naszego pokolenia* [On the Calling of Our Generation], Warsaw 1930 [1940]
- Underground pamphlet, issued by the Headquarters of the Gray Ranks [Scouts] (Kwatera Główna Szarych Szeregów). On the causes of Poland's downfall, economic and foreign policies, on the national character of the Poles.
- *Description:* original, printed, Polish, 120×160 mm, ss. 16, pp. 29.
  See *Bibliografia druków*, p. 134.

**1387. RING. I/748 (1072). (Lb. 1705). Mf. ŻIH—823; USHMM—35**

- After 01.1942, Warsaw
- Leaflet entitled: *Do robotników, chłopów i inteligencji, do wszystkich patriotów polskich* [To Workers, Peasants and Intelligentsia, to All Polish Patriots]
- Programmatic proclamation of the Polska Partia Robotnicza [Polish Workers Party].
- *Description:* original, hectographed typescript, Polish, 215×316 mm, ss. 1, pp. 2.
  See Ring. II/332.

**1388. RING. I/774 (1098). Mf. ŻIH—825; USHMM—37**

- Before 1.05.1942, [Warsaw]
- Leaflet entitled *1 Maja 1942* [1 May 1942]
- May Day proclamation of the group of Trotskyites.
- *Description:* original, hectographed typescript, Polish, 211×335 mm, damage and losses of text, ss. 1, pp. 2.

## PREWAR JEWISH PRESS, PERIODICALS, AND PUBLICATIONS

**1389. RING. I/749 (1073). (Lb. 1572). Mf. ŻIH—823; USHMM—35**

- 1921, place unknown
- *Di frayhayts shtime* [The Voice of Freedom], no. 1 of [1921]
- Anarchist publication devoted, inter alia, to the memory of Piotr Kropotkin, (died 8.02.1921), the conference of anarchists in Moscow (15.05.1921); the tragic death of Jasza Ali (Jakow Suchowolski), Josef Gutman, and A. Safianow.
- ***Description:*** original, printed, Yiddish, 227×298 mm, damage and losses of text, missing pages 3–4, 13–14, ss. 6, pp. 12.

**1390. RING. I/767 (1091). (Lb. 1610). Mf. ŻIH—823; USHMM—35**

- Before 1939 [?], place unknown
- *Kol korei* [Proclamation]
- One-time publication of the religious association of Orthodox Jews Szomrej Sta"m [Shomrei Sta"m].[57]
- ***Description:*** original, printed, Hebrew, 527×710 mm, ss. 1, pp. 1.

**1391. RING. I/750 (1074). (Lb. 1577). Mf. ŻIH—823; USHMM—35**

- 1930–1931, Radom
- *Literarishe grupe* [Literary Group], no. 2 of 09.1930 and no. 4 of 03.1931
- Literary monthly.
- ***Description:*** original, printed, Yiddish, 150×225 mm, ss. 16, pp. 32.

**1392. RING. I/753 (1077). (Lb. 1578). Mf. ŻIH—823; USHMM—35**

- 09.1928, Radom
- *Dos literarishe Radom. Oysgabe far literatur un teatr* [Literary Radom. Publication for Literature and Theater]
- Special publication. Editor and publisher: B. Sztrajman (Radom, ul. Lubelska 85).
- ***Description:*** original, printed, Yiddish, 265×380 mm, minor damage and losses of text, ss. 4, pp. 8.

**1393. RING. I/756 (1080). (Lb. 1509). Mf. ŻIH—823; USHMM—35**

- 05.1933, Warsaw
- *Nasz Przegląd Ilustrowany* [Our Review Illustrated], no. 19
- Illustrated supplement to *Nasz Przegląd*, no. 127 of 7.05.1933.
- ***Description:*** original, printed, Polish, 255×348 mm, ss. 4, pp. 8.

**1394. RING. I/764 (1088). (Lb. 1719). Mf. ŻIH—823; USHMM—35**

- 12.1935, place unknown
- *Sifriyat ha-menahel* [The Director's Library], no. 15 of 12.1935
- Weekly of the Zionist-Socialist youth organization.
- ***Description:*** original, printed, Hebrew, 120×120, 120×160 mm, damage and losses of text, ss. 24, pp. 48.

**1395. RING. I/1220/43. Mf. ŻIH—835; USHMM—47**

- Before 1914, place unknown [Germany?]
- Periodical (newspaper), missing title, missing no. (fragment)
- Jewish periodical in German.
- ***Description:*** original, printed, German, 199×244 mm, damage and losses of text, preserved are pages 1825–1828, ss. 2, pp. 4.

**1396. RING. I/777/14. (1099). Mf. ŻIH—825; USHMM—37**

- 1937, Warsaw
- *Gościnne występy teatru palestyńskiego "Habima" w Polsce. I. "Krótki Piątek." II."Żyd Wieczny Tułacz." Sezon* 1937/1938 [Guest Appearances of the "Habima" Palestinian Theater in Poland. I. "Short Friday." II. "The Eternally Wandering Jew." 1937/1938 Season] [Warsaw 1937]
- Theater program.
- ***Description:*** original, printed, Polish, Yiddish, 153×207 mm, ss. 6, pp. 12.

**1397. RING. I/777/15. (1099). Mf. ŻIH—825; USHMM—37**

- Before 1939, Tel Aviv
- "Habima" Theater. Program of a play in three acts entitled *Amkha* [Your People], by Sholem Aleichem, adapted by I.D. Berkowicz
- Directed by C. Fridland and B. Czemeryński.
- ***Description:*** original, printed, Hebrew, 173×244 mm, ss. 2, pp. 4.

  On p. 2 a note, handwritten (pencil).

**1398. RING. I/777/16. (1099). Mf. ŻIH—825; USHMM—37**

- Before 1939, Tel Aviv
- "Habima" Theater. Program of a play in three acts entitled *Kavalim* [Chains], by H. Leivik
- Directed by B. Czemeryński.
- ***Description:*** original, printed, Hebrew, 176×250 mm, ss. 2, pp. 4.

57. Shomrei Sta"m refers to an organization committed to proper observance of the religious rules regarding the writing of sacred texts for Torahs, Tefillin (phylacteries), and Mezuzot.

# IX. Bequests

## *DOCUMENTS OF RACHEL AUERBACH (PAPERS OF ICYK [ITZIK] MANGER)*

### 1399. RING. I/608. (Lb. 1723). Mf. ŻIH–814; USHMM–26

- Before 1939, Bucharest
- Icyk [Itzik] Manger, *Megile lider* [Megilla Poems]
- Collection of poems illustrated with drawings.
- ***Description:*** Printed, Yiddish, 55× 65, 135×195mm, serious damage and losses of text, ss. 38, pp. 64.

### 1400. RING. I/613. Mf. ŻIH–814; USHMM–26

- Date unknown, Warsaw Ghetto
- Abraham Goldfaden, Drama entitled *Di kishef-makherin* [The Witch]
- Play in 3 acts, adapted by Itzik Manger.
- ***Description:*** transcript, typescript, Yiddish, 205×295, 220×295 mm, damage and losses of text, missing pages, ss. 67, pp. 67.

  Published: in 1902 [?]; see Ring. II/456.

### 1401. RING. I/614. Mf. ŻIH–814; USHMM–26

- Before 1939, place unknown
- Icyk [Itzik] Manger, Poems
  1) "Kinder yorn" [Childhood years] (published in the magazine *Lid* [Song]);
  2) "Na peronie w Kołomyi" [On the platform in Kołomyja]. Polish translation from Yiddish by Henryk Luft;
  3) "[Vol]kns" [Clouds];
  4) "Der ovnt tunklt" [Night falls];
  5) "Khinezishe folks-lider" [Chinese folk songs];
  6) "Der orimer gvir" [The impoverished tycoon];
  7) "Ikh bet dir Tshang Tsoy" [I ask you, Tshang Tsoy];
  8) "Der vayser general kholemt in Pariz" [The white general dreams in Paris];
  9) "Lid" [Song];
  10) "Itzik Manger-a foygl" [Itzik Manger-a bird];
  11) "Idilye" [Idyll];
  12) "Di balade fun Itzik Manger dem shnayder-jung un der sheyner grafine fun Duptse" [The ballad of Itzik Manger the tailor-boy and the beautiful countess of Dupce];
  13) "Dwie siostry" [Two sisters] (translation from the Yiddish by Horacy Safrin);
  14) "In bordel" [In the bordello];
  15) "Khad-gadye";
  16) "Idele" [Little Jew];
  17) "Viglid" [Lullaby];
  18) "Lid" [Song] (poem dedicated to Rachel);
  19) "Di balade fun Petlura" [The ballad of Petlura]. Attached fragments of literary criticism.
- ***Description:*** original, transcript, printed, typescript, Polish, Yiddish, 58×238, 220×342, damage and losses of text, ss. 29, pp. 30.

  Published: in the prewar press in Polish and Yiddish (e.g., in the periodical entitled *Lid* [Song])

### 1402. RING. I/615. Mf. ŻIH–814; USHMM–26

- 1925–1935 and Date unknown, place unknown
- [Itzik Manger], Poems and other works
  1) "Mir hobn zikh bagegnt . . ." [We met . . .];
  2) ". . .Un oyb men hot dos lid dergraykht . . ." [. . . And if the song was achieved . . .];
  3) "Bagegnt zi a shvartse" [She encounters a black];
  4) "A idilye" [An idyll];
  5) "Amerike, Amerike di goldene medine" [America, America, the golden land];
  6) ". . . Hotsmakh iz geven der melekh fun altn yidishn teater" [Hotsmakh was the king of the old Yiddish theater] (fragment of a poem);
  7) "A khopte shnayders. In shenk . . ." [A bunch of tailors. In a saloon . . .];
  8) "Katulus. [?] [Katon?]. Nyanye oyfn toyt fun a shperling" [Catullus. A nanny at the death of a young sparrow];
  9) "Lomir zikh lib hobn" [Let's fall in love];
  10) "Katsyzne un Morevski" [Kacyzna and Morewski] (a scene);
  11) "Der tsug loyft. Felder, statsyes, felder . . ." [The train speeds. Fields, stations, fields . . .];
  12) "Stsene tsvishn Aron Tsaytlin un Noyekh Prilutski" [A scene between Aron Zeitlin and Noah Prylucki];
  13) "Mit neplke hor, sandaln oyf di fis . . ." [With misty hair, sandals on the feet . . .];
  14) "Lid" [Song];
  15) "Brutus kum, ikh gey mit . . ." [Come, Brutus, I'm going along . . .];
  16) "Dos lid hobn dorfs layt gezungen . . ." [Village folk sang this song . . .];
  17) "Tsvey lobuzlekh" [Two little urchins] (two versions of the same poem);
  18) "Di blonde froy zitst un vart . . ." [The blond woman sits and waits . . .];
  19) "Banal lid" [A banal song];
  20) "A layt iz frum vi a galekh . . ." [A respectable fellow is pious as a priest . . .];
  21) "Fun bukh Harbstige oygn" [From the book Autumnal eyes]. (The book was supposed to appear in the publishing house Kultura in Czerniowce [Czernowitz] in 1925);
  22) "Vanderlid" [Vagabond's song];
  23) "Mayn tate der shnayder Hilel Manger . . ." [My father, the tailor Hillel Manger . . .];
  24) "Un khotsh s'klapt der regn . . ." [And even though the rain's pounding . . .];

25) "Alte frantsoyzishe folkslider" [Old French folksongs];
26) "Brutus kum ikh . . ." [Brutus come I . . .];
27) "Di broder zinger" [The Brody Singers]. Appended poem titled
28) "Ciobă naşul" (1920).
Attached fragments of different works.

- ***Description:*** original, printed, handwritten manuscript (two handwritings: IM* and another), ink, Polish, Romanian, Yiddish, Yiddish in Roman transliteration, 44×120, 220×350 mm, damage and losses of texts, ss. 51, pp. 60.

  Works no. 5–6 and 8–9 are on a single sheet. On the back of work no. 25 is a list of poetry. Two handwritten manuscripts on the back of a proclamation of the Central Committee for Celebrations of the 100th anniversary of the birth of Mendele Moykher Sforim (Sholem Yankev Abramovitsh), Warsaw, December 1935, ul. Tłomackie 13, apt. 24 (printed, Yiddish). One work is on a form of the Bank dla Handlu i Przemysłu (Bank for Business and Industry) in Warsaw, ul. Traugutta 6/8 (printed, Polish).

  Index: Prof. O. Densusianu

**1403. RING. I/637. Mf. ŻIH–815; USHMM–27**

- 1938, date unknown, Warsaw, place unknown
- Icyk [Itzik] Manger, Various works of poetry, fragments of plays
- Works: 1) "Toyt tsetlekh" [Death certificates] (fragment); 2) "Ikh vil onshraybn a lid . . ." [I want to compose a poem . . .]; 3) "Bay nakht in der teyve" [At night in (Noah's) ark], fragments of a play in different versions; 4) Fragment of a play about Esther; Poem about Naomi (two versions).
- ***Description:*** original, printed (clippings from an unidentified newspaper, Warsaw, 18.02.1938), handwritten manuscript (IM*), ink, Polish, Yiddish, 48×44, 145×209, 190×230, 105×238 mm, ss. 16, pp. 20.

  Three ss. of manuscript written on the back of: "Dyplom Komitetu Obywatelskiego Pożyczki Narodowej" [Certificate of the Civil Committee for the National Loan] (Warsaw, 1933) (Printed, Polish). One sheet of manuscript written on the back of a circular letter (12.1933, Warsaw, hectographed typescript) from the leadership of the colony (at the Kultur-Lige Society) inviting support of the Bronisław Grosser Library of the Kultur-Liga Society. Clipping from an unknown newspaper (Warsaw), no. 4 (6), dated 18.02.1938, with a fragment of the play, *Bay nakht in der teyve* [At night in (Noah's) ark].

**1404. RING. I/626. Mf. ŻIH–815; USHMM–27**

- 1935, Stary Warchałów near Głowno
- Miriam Ulinower, Poems (4):
  "Meydl on kam" [Girl without comb];
  "Meydl on zeyf" [Girl without soap];
  "Meydl mit beygel" [Girl with bagel];
  "Meydl—eyne aleyn" [Girl—all alone]
- Works on traditional subject matter. Appended. Letter of 28.06.1935 to [Itzik] Manger with a request to forward the poems to the editors of *Haynt* (Warsaw).
- ***Description:*** original, handwritten manuscript, ink, Yiddish, 95×152, 152×190 mm, ss. 5, pp. 7.

**1405. RING. I/632. (Lb. 1736). Mf. ŻIH–815; USHMM–27**

- Date unknown, place unknown
- [Itzik Manger], Poems (4):
  "Nakht protsesye" [Nocturnal procession];
  "Fiber balade" [Fever ballad];
  "Kin" [Kindling?];[58]
  "Un dershis dem vint mit dayn payn in oygn . . ." [And shoot down the wind with the pain in your eyes . . .]
- Lyrical poetry. Attached list of various poems.
- ***Description:*** original [?], handwritten manuscript, notebooks, ink, pencil, Yiddish, minor damage and losses of text, 162×202 mm, ss. 27, pp. 18.

  Notebooks (Printed, Romanian)

  On the title page of notebook 1 is a note (ink): "Balade de I. Manger."

**1406. RING. I/633. (Lb. 1721). Mf. ŻIH–815; USHMM–27**

- Date unknown, place unknown
- Itzik Manger, Drama entitled Ahasver [Ahasuerus][59] (fragment, missing ending)
- Draft of the first act of a burlesque about a cruel and foolish king.
- ***Description:*** original, handwritten manuscript (IM*), ink, Yiddish, 220×360 mm, minor damage and losses of text, ss. 11, pp. 8.

**1407. RING. I/636. Mf. ŻIH–815; USHMM–27**

- 1932–1938, date unknown, Warsaw, place unknown
- [Itzik Manger], Manuscripts and various documents
- Literary works, poems (e.g., "Shtern in fenster . . ." [Stars in the window . . .]; "Fun mayn notitsbukh" [From my notebook]; "Tsu a meydl" [To a girl]; "Entfer" [Answer]; "Barekhtikung" [Justification]), reviews, excerpts, notes, correspondence (letter from writer's father Hilel Manger dated 7.11.1934; letter to Jakub Glatszteyn [Jacob Glatstein] dated 30.03.1938). Poem entitled: "Mayn ershte bagegenish mit mayn

58. The Yiddish word kin can mean either kindling or chin.

59. The Persian monarch in the biblical Book of Esther.

unshterblikhen gayst" [My first encounter with my immortal spirit] (11.04.1932).
- ***Description:*** original, handwritten manuscript (two handwritings): IM* and NN.—Author or copyist of the poem: "Moje pierwsze spotkanie . . ." [My first encounter . . .], printed, ink, pencil, Polish, Yiddish, 113×175, 215×343 mm, damage and losses of text, ss. 22, pp. 30.

  Part of the manuscript is written on the back of different printed forms, e.g., on the letterhead of "El-Hahar Corporation," address in Warsaw: M. Kirszenbaum, ul. Leszno 54, apt. 33 (after 1930); circular letter (12.1933, Warsaw, hectographed typescript) from the leadership of the colony (summercamp?) (at the Kultur-Liga Society [?]) inviting support for the Bronisław Grosser Library at the Kultur-Lige Society.

  Index: Rawicz

### 1408. RING. I/623. Mf. ŻIH—815; USHMM—27

- Date unknown, place unknown
- Collection of poems and songs
- Anthology of poetry of various nations and authors.
- ***Description:*** transcript, handwritten manuscript (IM*), ink, Yiddish, 95×155, 158×195 mm, ss. 207, pp. 235.

### 1409. RING. I/624. Mf. ŻIH—815; USHMM—27

- 21.11.1932–19.05.1938, New York, Bucharest, Warsaw
- Itzik Manger, Private Documents
  1) *Jewish Daily Forward* (New York). Certification dated 21.03.1938 for Izydor [Itzik] Manger (Warsaw, ul. Tłomackie 13, apt. 24) of his accreditation in Poland (original, typescript, English, ss. 1, pp. 1);
  1a) *Jewish Daily Forward* (B. Charney Vladeck, New York), Letters dated 28.02. and 21.03.1938 to Izydor [Icyk] Manger (Warsaw, ul. Tłomackie 13, apt. 24) (original, typescript, English, Yiddish, ss. 2, pp. 2);
  2) *Lumea* (Iaşi). Identification no. 206 of the correspondent I. Manger in Warsaw (5.10.1935) (original, printed, handwritten manuscript, ink, Romanian, missing photograph, ss. 2, pp. 3);
  3) *Lumea* (Iaşi). Certification dated 4.03.1937 of the correspondent Izydor Helfer or Manger (born 30.05.1901 in Cernauti) in Warsaw (since 1934) (original, typescript, stamp, French, ss. 1, pp. 1);
  4) *Reporter* (Bucharest). Certificate dated 4.03.1939 of correspondent Izydor Helfer alias Manger (born 30.05.1901 in Cernauti) in Warsaw (since 1934) (original, typescript, French, Romanian, photograph damaged, ss. 2, pp. 2);
  5) Agreements of Izydor Manger with Kurt Kacz, actor, dated 25.03.1936 and 27.12.1936 (Warsaw) on translation of books and staging as well as performance of theatrical plays (original, typescript, handwritten manuscript, ink, Yiddish, ss. 2, pp. 2. On the back are notes, inter alia, names: Dr. Herman Halpern, Prof. Ernst Arndt);
  5a) Agreement of Izydor Manger with Zygmunt Turkow, dated 5.08.1937 (Warsaw) on preparation of plays of Goldfaden (original, typescript, Yiddish, ss. 1, pp. 1);
  6) Agreements of Izydor Manger with the publishing house Ch. Brzoza in Warsaw (ul. Chłodna 16, apt. 4), undated, (2), 11.04. and 19.05.1938 (addendum dated 22.11.[1938?]) (original, handwritten manuscript, ink, Polish, Yiddish, ss. 4, pp. 5);
  7) *Der Moment* (Warsaw, ul. Nalewki 38). Certification dated 10.06.1937 for I. Manger for payment of an honorarium for the year 1935 (50 zł)(original, typescript, stamped "Nasza Prasa" [Our Press], Polish, ss. 1, pp. 1);
  8) Transcript of the birth certificate of: Izydor Helfer [Manger], born 30.05.1901 in Cernauti, son of Hilel and Haia (née Wolliner) (original, printed, typescript, Romanian, ss. 1, pp. 1);
  9) *Völkermagazin* [Magazine of Peoples], no.[?], pp. 49–50. (inter alia, a collection of poems by Romanian poets in German translation) (original, printed, German, ss. 1, pp. 2).
- ***Description:*** original, printed, typescript, handwritten manuscript (different handwritings: IM* and others), ink, English, Polish, Romanian, Yiddish, 66×90, 240×345 mm, minor damage and losses of text, ss. 18, pp. 20.

### 1410. RING. I/518. (Lb. 1729). Mf. ŻIH—789; USHMM—20

- 03.1937, Warsaw
- *Kinder-Fraynd* [Children's Friend], no. 11–12 (20.03.1937)
- Biweekly for children. Articles on topics of geography, natural sciences, technology, literary texts, poems (e.g., by Icyk [Itzik] Manger), puzzles.
- ***Description:*** original, printed, Yiddish, 173×250 mm, ss. 12, pp. 24.

## *DOCUMENTS OF MOJŻESZ KAUFMAN (MOJSZE MEZRYCZER, MOYSHE MEZRITSHER)*

### 1411. RING. I/1183 (1502). (Lb. 1581, 1581A, 1581B, 1581C). Mf. ŻIH—834; USHMM—46

- Date unknown, place unknown
- Mojżesz Kaufman (Mojsze Mezryczer, Moyshe Mezritsher) (Falenica, ul. Cicha 10), Notes for preparation of a history of the labor movement in Polish lands
- Author, member of the Jewish organization at the PPS (Polish Socialist Party). Information about the PPS's Jewish Organization in Warsaw.

- *Description:* transcript, handwritten manuscript, several handwritings, ink, Polish, Yiddish, 55×127, 127×365 mm, minor damage and losses of text, ss. 131, pp. 133.
  Individual fragments of the study entitled: "Pierwsze żydowskie socjalistyczne kółko w Warszawie" [The First Jewish Socialist Circle in Warsaw]; "Udział żydowskich pepesowców w rewolucyjnych występach stycznia 1905" [Participation of Jewish PPS members in Revolutionary Demonstrations of January 1905]; "Walka żydowskiego robotnika z wyrzutkami społeczeństwa" [Struggle of the Jewish Worker with Outcasts of Society]; "Pierwszy napad złodziejów na politycznych w ratuszu" [The First Robbery of Politicians by Thieves at the City Hall]; "Rola żydowskich robotników PPS" [Role of Jewish Workers of the PPS]; "Reorganizacja w pracy żydowskiej" [Reorganization in Jewish Work].
  Compare Ring. I/1185.

### 1412. RING. I/1184 (1503). (Lb. 1652). Mf. ŻIH—834; USHMM—46

- [Before 1936], place unknown
- Mojżesz Kaufman (Mojsze Mezryczer, Moyshe Mezritsher) (Falenica, ul. Cicha 10), Notes for a history of the labor movement in Polish lands
- Jews in the labor movement, organizations (Proletariat, PPS, Bund), ideological and ethnic divisions, activity, Revolution of 1905.
- *Description:* original, handwritten manuscript, notebook, ink, pencil, Polish, Yiddish, 134×180, 118×313 mm, damage and losses of text, ss. 31, pp. 26.
  In the notebook are exercises in Polish orthography in a childish handwriting.

### 1413. RING. I/1185 (1504). Mf. ŻIH—834; USHMM—46

- [Before 1936], place unknown
- Mojżesz Kaufman (Mojsze Mezryczer, Moyshe Mezritsher) (Falenica, ul. Cicha 10), Recollections, notes, documents, and correspondence
- Origin of the PPS, activity, ideological and ethnic character of the organization "Robotnik," beginnings of the Jewish socialist movement in Warsaw, profiles of worker activists, copies of proclamations. Appended foreign texts concerning the labor movement [?]. Attached letter to the author dated 16.09.1933 from Białystok in the matter of an article about the PPS in Grodno.
- *Description:* original, handwritten manuscript, three handwritings, ink, Yiddish, 40×130, 130×450 mm, damage and losses of text, ss. 147, pp. 164.

### 1414. RING. I/1186 (1505). Mf. ŻIH—834; USHMM—46

- [Before 1936], place unknown
- Mojżesz Kaufman (Mojsze Mezryczer, Moyshe Mezritsher), Collection of poems
  1) "Dos iz geshen in yenem moment ven di zun [. . .] unter a shvartsn volkn . . ." [It happened when the sun [. . .] behind a black cloud . . .];
  2) ". . . zi hot dokh dem gresten ferbrekh bagangen gegen mir . . ." [. . . she committed the biggest crime against me . . .];
  3) ". . . di gantse velt iz shtil gevorn, der vint dem otem hot ayngehaltn . . ." [. . . the whole world grew still, the wind held its breath . . .];
  4) ". . . bin ikh zikh avek ahin vu dos harts vert geglivert un di oygen farloshen . . ." [. . . I went away to where the heart becomes hard and the eyes extinguished . . .];
  5) "Mit tsvey shvartse melankholishe oygen blikt zi tif arayn . . ." [With two black, melancholic eyes, she gazes in deeply . . .];
  6) "[. . .] loyft oyf di Vaysl brik a bahn . . ." [. . . a train runs on the Vistula bridge . . .];
  7) "Giftige gazn" [Poison gases];
  8) "Di blumen getn!" [The flowers are divorcing!];
  9) "Libes gebeyt" [Love's prayer];
  10) "Visn iz makht" [Knowledge is power];
  11) "Gezikhn un nit gefinen!" [Search and not find!].
- *Description:* original, handwritten manuscript (one handwriting [?]), ink, pencil, Yiddish, 104×168, 110×345 mm, damage and losses of text, ss. 12, pp. 17.
  On the back of pp. 8–9 is a certificate and stamp of a midwife: "Akuszerka Ostrogórska-Kaufman. Falenica." [Midwife Ostrogórska-Kaufman. Falenica.]

### 1415. RING. I/634. (Lb. 1219). Mf. ŻIH—815; USHMM—27

- After 1931[?], place unknown.
- [Mojżesz Kaufman ?], Poems (35):
  1) "Host fargesn!" [You forgot!], (30.09.1922)
  2) "Mayn lebn" [My life]
  3) "Ikh muz shwaygn!" [I must keep silent!], (2.11.1922)
  4) "Far mayn shifl. Fir mir shifl . . ." [For my boat. Carry me, boat . . .], (31.10.1922)
  5) "Ikh zing nisht mer . . ." [I don't sing anymore . . .], (18.01.1924)
  6) "Vos zikh ikh do" [What I am looking for here], (23.06.1923)
  7) "Ikh rayt tsu der zun" [I ride to the sun], (1.05.1931)
  8) "Tsu di yunge blumen" [To the young flowers], (21.06.1921)
  9–10) "Nisht geklibn" [Not chosen] [poem in two versions], (23.07.1921)
  11) "Beynkshaft" [Longing], (4.01.1924)
  12) "Oygn tsvey" [Two eyes], (25.12.1928)

13) "Bayde begegenen mir" [Both meet me], (15.11.1928)
14) "Dos frimer ketsl" [The pious kitten], (30.12.1928)
15) "Gekumen iz der friling" [Spring has arrived], (27.10.1928)
16) "Biter iz der vayn" [Bitter is the wine], (8.11.1923)
17) "On verter" [Without words], (10.07.1921)
18) "Der dikhter" [The poet]
19) "Gekumen un avek" [Came and went], (17.08.1922)
20) "Far di zun vel ikh zingen" [I'll sing for the sun], (17.08.1922)
21) "Zol di erd tsufaln" [Let the earth fall apart], (15.09.1922)
22) "Mayne begleter" [My caressers?]
23) "Ikh kum dir nisht beshuldigen" [I don't come to blame you], (20.06.1921)
24) "Visn iz makht" [Knowledge is power]
25) "Mayn letster ferlang" [My last wish]
26) "Farnakht" [Dusk], (17.01.1922)
27) "Mayn letst vort" [My final word], (10.01.1922)
28) "Kum mit mir" [Come with me], (18.01.1922)
29) "A haylige shvester in shvartsn geklayd" [A holy sister in black dress]
30) "Zol shoyn kumen" [Let (it/him) come soon]
31) "Biter lebn" [Bitter life]
32) [corrected version of poem no. 30]
33) "Shtimung" [Mood]
34) "Tsu der zun" [To the sun]
35) "Soydesful" [Full of secrets].

- ***Description:*** original or transcript, handwritten manuscript, ink, pencil, Yiddish, 158×194 mm, ss. 20, pp. 39.

On p. 9 (poem: "I ride to the sun") is a note (pencil): "sent to Gishir" [?].

For poems of this author, see Ring. I/642, I/645, and I/647.

### 1416. RING. I/642. (Lb. 1651). Mf. ŻIH—815; USHMM—27

- After 1923, Falenica, place unknown
- [Mojżesz Kaufman?], Various documents
  a) Łazarz Geller, Letters dated 8. and 18.05.1923 to the Appellate Court in Warsaw. Request for commutation of a sentence for espionage activity for Soviet Russia;
  b) NN., Article entitled "Der kosmopolitizm un zayn bankrot" [Cosmopolitanism and its bankruptcy];
  c) [Mojżesz Kaufman?], Poems:
    1) "Vi yene fun mir shoyn lang dervartete nakht . . ." [Like the night I have long awaited . . .], (Falenica, 1.01.1929);
    2) "Geyt oyf a zin, shaynt a zin . . ." [A sun rises, a sun shines . . .], (Falenica, 6.08.1929);
    3) "Gekumen iz der friling" [Spring has arrived], (27.10.1928);
    4) "Oygn tsvey" [Two eyes], (25.12.1928);
    5) "Ikh rayt tsu der zun!" [I ride to the sun!], (1.02.1931).
  d) Letter from Zofia and Gabriel Plewicki to the Zarząd Kasy Chorych m. Warszawy [Board of the Health Care Fund of the City of Warsaw] in connection with the costs of childbirth as well as certification of collection of payment by the midwife.
- ***Description:*** original or (i) transcript, handwritten manuscript (different handwritings), notebook, ink, Polish, Yiddish, 113×158, 158×205 mm, ss. 12, pp. 21.

### 1417. RING. I/645. Mf. ŻIH—816; USHMM—28

a)

- After 1931, place unknown
- [Mojżesz Kaufman ?], Collection of poems, inter alia:
  1) "Dos letste vort" [The last word], (10.01.1922)
  2) "Farnakht" [Dusk], (17.01.1922)
  3) "Du bist mayn troym!" [You are my dream!]
  4) "Ikh rayt tsu der zun" [I ride to the sun], (1.02.1931)

b)

- Date unknown, place unknown
- M. [Mojżesz] Kaufman, Poem entitled "Ostatnie me pragnienie" [My last desire]. Translation from Yiddish by Z. Przygodzki.
- ***Description:*** a) original or transcript, handwritten manuscript (two handwritings [?]), ink, pencil, Yiddish, damage and losses of text, text illegible in places; b) original or transcript, handwritten manuscript, ink, Polish, 117×206 mm, ss. 16, pp. 30.

On many pages are written (in a child's hand [?]) numbers (pencil): "5," "4+," etc.

Poems (a): 1), 2) and 4) appear in Ring. I/634 (poems: 7), 26–27). With the poem "I ride to the sun" in Ring. I/634 is a different date: "1.05.1931." Poem 1) in Ring. I/634 has a different version of the title.

Manuscript (a and b) in one notebook; attached sheet with the letterhead of the laboratory of the Warsaw Veterinary Institute (before 1915) (printed, Russian). Old pagination survived (pencil). On sheet 14 is a note in Polish (ink): "In the notebook are fourteen pages (14). On 3.09.[19]23 Inspector [. . . surname illegible]."

### 1418. RING. I/647. Mf. ŻIH—816; USHMM—28

- 1921–1922, place unknown
- [Mojżesz Kaufman?], Poems:
  1) "Nisht geklibn" [Not chosen], (23.07.1921)
  2) "Kum mit mir" [Come with me], (18.01.1922)
  3) "Visn iz makht" [Knowledge is power]
  4) "Ikh kum dir nisht bashuldign" [I don't come to blame you] and others.
- ***Description:*** original [?], handwritten manuscript, pencil, Yiddish, 117×206 mm, damage and losses of text, ss. 24, pp. 16.

Manuscript in a notebook imprinted with the letterhead of the laboratory of the Warsaw Veterinary Institute (before 1915) (printed, Russian). On one sheet is a stamp: "Akuszerka /Ostrogorska-Kaufm[ann]/Falenica" [Midwife/ Ostrógorska-Kaufm(ann)/Falenica]. On sheet 10 is a note in Polish (different handwritings, pencil): "M. Kaufman, Hela Kaufman, Cesia Kaufman, Sabina Kaufman."

For Kaufman's poems, see also: Ring. I/634, I/642, I/645.

**1419. RING. I/1109 (1428). (Lb. 1500). Mf. ŻIH—833; USHMM—45**

- 12.1934–07.1935, Paris
- Institut Scientifique Juif [YIVO Institute for Jewish Research], Section Historique, E. Tsherikover, Cherikover], Letters (4) dated 21.12.1934, 1.02.1935, 11.06.1935, and 26.07.1935 to Mojżesz Kaufman of Falenica.
- In the matter of an article sent by Kaufman to a collective publication on the history of the Jewish labor movement, prepared by the Historical Section of the Jewish Research Institute (YIVO).
- ***Description:*** original, typescript, handwritten manuscript, ink, French, Hebrew, Yiddish, 210×265 mm, ss. 4, pp. 4.

## *DOCUMENTS OF MENACHEM MENDEL KON (KOHN)*

**1420. RING. I/1124 (1443). (Lb. 17). Mf. ŻIH—833; USHMM—45**

- 24.11.1938, Warsaw
- Menachem Mendel Kon (born 9.12.1881 in Ostrów), Identity card, Ser. E. No 3754[. . . ?]5, issued in Warsaw on 24.11.1938 by the municipality in Warsaw.
- ***Description:*** original, printed, handwritten manuscript, ink, Polish, 81×120 mm, minor damage and losses of text, lacking photograph, ss. 2, pp. 4.

**1421. RING. I/1189 (1508). Mf. ŻIH—834; USHMM—46**

- Before 5.05.[1942], Warsaw Ghetto
- School Department of the Jewish Council, Invitation to a "School Matinée" on 5.05.[1942] at the "Femina" [theater] (ul. Leszno 35), for [Menachem Mendel] Kohn (ul. Przebieg 2)
- Program of the celebration: participation of children from the schools at: Nowolipki 22 and 68, Kurza 10, Gęsia 9, Prosta 8, Świętojerska 34, and Karmelicka 29. Invitation signed by the chairman of the Department, A. [Abram] Wolfowicz and director S. [Samuel] Horensztejn.
- ***Description:*** original, hectographed typescript, handwritten manuscript, ink, Polish, 145×210 mm, ss. 1, pp. 1.

Published: *Dzieci*, pp. 295–296.

**1422. RING. I/281. Mf. ŻIH—781; USHMM—12**

- 1942, date unknown, Jadów [?], Warsaw Ghetto
- Menachem Mendel Kohn (Kon), Correspondence (1942)
  1) NN. (Warsaw, ul. Pawia [?] 88, apt. 6), Letter of 1942 with greetings
  2) Eliezer (Iława), Letter of 1.04.1942 with holiday wishes and on the occasion of return to health after illness
  3) Teachers and employees of the kitchen and school at ul. Nowolipki 68 (signatures: Natan Smolar and Fejga Herclich—directors, Izrael Lichtensztajn, Gela Seksztajn, Ł. Fajnsztajn, D. Perelman, NN.), Letter of 3.04.1942 with wishes for a speedy return to health
  4) Mostowicz (Jadów [?]), Letter of thanks for help and with request for further aid.
- ***Description:*** original, handwritten manuscript, ink, pencil, Hebrew, Yiddish, 185×210, 215×170, 200×130, 140×220, damage and losses of text, ss. 4, pp. 4.

**1423. RING. I/660. Mf. ŻIH—816; USHMM—28**

- 26.03.1942, place unknown
- Eliezer of Iława, rabbi, Letter of 26.03.1942 to Menachem Kohn (Kon) (Warsaw Ghetto)
- Request for aid via [Szymon] Huberband.
- ***Description:*** original, handwritten manuscript, ink, Yiddish, 222×350 mm, substantial damage and losses of text, ss. 1, pp. 1.

Attached note by H.W. in Yiddish

**1424. RING. I/593. (Lb. 659). Mf. ŻIH—792; USHMM—23**

a)

- 05. or 06.1942, Warsaw Ghetto
- Perec Chasyd [Perec Opoczyński, Perets Opotshinski], Letter of 05. or 06.1942 to Menachem Mendel Kohn (Kon) (Warsaw Ghetto)
- Concerning stories that the author sent to the addressee.
- ***Description:*** original, handwritten manuscript (OP*), ink, Hebrew, 84×105, ss. 1, pp. 2.

See Ring. I/1044.

b)

- Date unknown, place unknown
- [Kalonimus Kalmisz] Szapiro, Rabbi, Letter to Menachem Mendel Kohn (Kon) (Warsaw Ghetto)
- Author awaits the addressee's visit.
- ***Description:*** original, handwritten manuscript, ink, stamp (Kalonimus [Szapiro] Rabbi, in Piaseczno), Hebrew, 110×154 mm, minor damage and losses of text, ss. 1, pp. 1.

c)

- 05.1942, Warsaw Ghetto
- NN. (Eliezer of Iława, a rabbi), Letter to Menachem Mendel Kohn (Kon) (Warsaw Ghetto)
- Shavuot holiday greetings.

- *Description:* original, handwritten manuscript, ink, Yiddish, 219×245 mm, ss. 1, pp. 1.
  Attached note by H.W. in Yiddish.
  See Ring. I/660.

d)

- 1.04.1942 [?], place unknown
- NN., Letter (note) (1.04.1942).
- *Description:* original, handwritten manuscript, ink, Hebrew, 216×68 mm, minor damage and losses of text, ss. 1, pp. 2.

## *MATERIALS OF IZRAEL LICHTENSZTAJN AND GELA SEKSZTAJN (ISRAEL LIKHTNSHTAYN AND GELA SEKSHTAYN)*[60]

### 1425. RING. I/156. Mf. ŻIH—778; USHMM—9

- After 1938, place unknown
- "Kolonie-rat fun der Borokhov shul, Kuzmir 1938" [Camp council of the Borochow School, Kazimierz 1938]. Minutes of the meetings of the children's camp government during 7–22 July 1938 in Kazimierz Dolny.
- Editorial staff of the camp newspaper; nature, sport and library commissions; list of names of children and teachers (Izrael Lichtensztajn and Rotenberg).
- *Description:* transcript, handwritten manuscript, notebook, ink, Yiddish, 140×204 mm, ss. 10, pp. 9.
  Notation by H.W.: "Submitted by Izrael Lichtensztajn."
  Index: Wajsblat, Hochman, Elbojm, Jedwach, Elencwajg, Hurwicz, Zajcman, Lerman, Kelman, Knopmacher, Lewczyn, Augen, Szlapak, Tarnegoj, Szwarc, Graber, Sznajer, Halinka Szlengel, Cederbojm, Blitental, Bigelman, Aubfal

### 1426. RING. I/597/2. (Lb. 1116). Mf. ŻIH—792; USHMM—23

- 1927, Wilno
- Medem Library in Wilno, Admission Card no. 1882 for Izrael Lichtensztajn, seminar participant (1927).
- *Description:* original, printed, handwritten manuscript, ink, Yiddish, 77×123 mm, ss. 1, pp. 1.

### 1427. RING. I/597/3. (Lb. 1116). Mf. ŻIH—792; USHMM—23

- 01.1929, place unknown
- Editorial board of *Mezritsher tribune* [Międzyrzec Tribune], Invitation for Izrael Lichtensztajn to a press evening on 19.01.1929.
- *Description:* original, printed, handwritten manuscript, ink, Yiddish, 139×90 mm, ss. 2, pp. 2.

### 1428. RING. I/597/4. (Lb. 1116). Mf. ŻIH—792; USHMM—23

- 10.10.1929, Wilno
- Union of Jewish Writers and Journalists in Wilno (ul. Bendyktyńska 4, apt. 2), Authorization dated 10.10.1929 for Izrael Lichtensztajn to collect contributions from members of the union
- *Description:* original, printed, handwritten manuscript, ink, stamp, Polish, Yiddish, 121×137 mm, ss. 1, pp. 1.

### 1429. RING. I/597/12. (Lb. 1116). Mf. ŻIH—792; USHMM—23

- 20.01.1931, Wilno
- [YIVO.] Żydowski Instytut Naukowy [Jewish Scientific Institute]. Central Board (Wilno, ul. Pohulanka 18), Invitation to a gathering of the philological section on 24.01.1931 for Izrael Lichtensztajn
- On the program was a lecture by N. Sztyft [Shtif ?], with participation of M. Weinreich, Zelig Kalmanowicz [Kalmanovitsh], and Załmen Rajzen [Reisin].
- *Description:* original, printed, duplicated typescript, handwritten manuscript, ink, Yiddish, 208×288 mm, ss. 1, pp. 1.

### 1430. RING. I/597/6. (Lb. 1116). Mf. ŻIH—792; USHMM—23

- 03.1931, Białystok
- Invitation to the opening of an exhibition of paintings by Michał Duńc in Białystok (ul. Sienkiewicza 5) on 24.03.1931
- *Description:* original, printed, Yiddish, 137×88 mm, minor damage and losses of text, ss. 1, pp. 2.
  On the back is a note in Yiddish (pencil): "Izrael" [Lichtensztajn].

### 1431. RING. I/597/7. (Lb. 1116). Mf. ŻIH—792; USHMM—23

- 23.12.1931, Wilno
- Society of the Gimnazjum Realne [nonclassical secondary school] in Wilno (ul. Rudnicka 6), Invitation for Izrael Lichtensztajn to the inaugurational meeting on 26.12.1931
- *Description:* original, printed, handwritten manuscript, ink, Yiddish, 127×197 mm, ss. 1, pp. 1.

60. The names might also be rendered Israel Lichtenstein and Gela Sekstein, but the Polish spellings are used in the English-language catalog, *Scream the Truth at the World: Emanuel Ringelblum and the Hidden Archive of the Warsaw Ghetto,* ed. Louis Levine (New York and Warsaw: Museum of Jewish Heritage and Żydowski Instytut Historyczny, 2001), no pagination; see photographs and texts beneath documents no. 31 and no. 39, as well as docs. nos. 32–34.

**1432. RING. I/597/5. (Lb. 1116). Mf. ŻIH—792; USHMM—23**

- 03.1933, Warsaw
- Parents Committee of the Elementary School [Szkoła Powszechna] at Muranów 16 (ul. Muranowska [?]), Invitation to an evening of entertainment on 11.03.1933
- *Description:* original, printed, Yiddish, 107×76 mm, ss. 1, pp. 1.

  On the back an illegible stamp.

**1433. RING. I/1220/48. Mf. ŻIH—835; USHMM—47**

- 1935, Warsaw
- Society of Friends of Working Palestine [Towarzystwo Przyjaciół Pracującej Palestyny], Membership card no. 182 issued on 4.04.1935 for Izrael Lichtensztajn (born 1906) (Warsaw, ul. Miła 41, apt. 50)
- *Description:* original, printed, handwritten manuscript, ink, Polish, Yiddish, 70×105 mm, missing photograph, ss. 8, pp. 8.

**1434. RING. I/597/10. (Lb. 1116). Mf. ŻIH—792; USHMM—23**

- Before 1.09.1939, Wilno
- First Pro-Palestinian Labor Congress [I Kongres Robotniczy Propalestyński] in Wilno, Electoral card no. 8307 for Izrael Lichtensztajn
- *Description:* original, printed, handwritten manuscript, ink, Yiddish, 62×88 mm, ss. 1, pp. 2.

  On p. 2 a note in Polish: "Izrael Lichtensztajn, Radzyń Podlaski, Ostrowiecka 17."

**1435. RING. I/1220/49. Mf. ŻIH—835; USHMM—47**

- Before 1939, Wilno
- Załmen Rejzen [Reisen] (Wilno, ul. Wielka Pohulanka 11, apt. 10, editor of Vilner tog [Wilno Day]), Calling card with letter to NN.
- Request to give [Izrael] Lichtensztajn of the Pen Club a ticket to Grosbart's presentation.
- *Description:* original, printed, handwritten manuscript, ink, Yiddish, 91×40 mm, ss. 1, pp. 2.

**1436. RING. I/597/8. (Lb. 1116). Mf. ŻIH—792; USHMM—23**

- Before 1.09.1939, Wilno [?]
- Teachers Seminary in Wilno [?] (ul. Końska 1), Invitation to a Purim performance
- *Description:* original, printed, Yiddish, 104×77 mm, ss. 1, pp. 1.

**1437. RING. I/597/9. (Lb. 1116). Mf. ŻIH—792; USHMM—23**

- Before 1.09.1939, Wilno
- Society of Friends of the [YIVO] Jewish Scientific Institute (Wilno, ul. Pohulanka 18), Notice of receipt of a shipment for Izrael Lichtensztajn
- *Description:* original, handwritten manuscript, printed, ink, Yiddish, 137×87 mm, ss. 1, pp. 2.

**1438. RING. I/551/1. Mf. ŻIH—791; USHMM—22**

- Before 1.09.1939, Wilno
- M. Szatan (Szutan [?]) (Wilno, Int. Clinic USB [?] at Antokol, room III), Letter of 3.01.193 . . . [postmark date] to I. Lichtensztajn, editor Literarishe bleter [Literary Pages], Warsaw, ul. Grzybowska 24) (fragment, missing p. 2 [?])
- Concerning subscription [?] to the publication *Literarishe bleter.*
- *Description:* original, handwritten manuscript on a postcard, ink, Polish, Yiddish, 142×100 mm, damage and losses of text, ss. 1, pp. 1.

**1439. RING. I/597/1. (Lb. 1116). Mf. ŻIH—792; USHMM—23**

- 01.1931, place unknown
- NN., Letter of 01.1931 to Izrael Lichtensztajn
- Thanks for aid.
- *Description:* original, handwritten manuscript, ink, Yiddish, 143×100 mm, damage and losses of text, ss. 1, pp. 1.

**1440. RING. I/225. Mf. ŻIH—780; USHMM—11**

- 1939–1941, Lublin, Warsaw
- Papers of Izrael Lichtensztajn
  - a) Certificate dated 13.09.1939 authorizing journey by slow train from Lublin to Warsaw (original, printed, handwritten manuscript, Polish, ink, 128×186 mm, ss. 1, pp. 1);
  - b) Jewish Community in Warsaw, Verification dated 12.02.1940 for Izrael Lichtensztajn about registration for forced labor (original, printed, handwritten manuscript, German, Polish, pencil, 155×81 mm, ss. 1, pp. 1);
  - c) Dr. P. [Paulina (Perla)] Edelsburg-Feimanowa (TOZ, ul. Gęsia 43), Certificate for Izrael Lichtensztajn about vaccinations against typhoid fever administered on 2.01.1940 and 12.01.1940 (original, hectographed typescript, handwritten manuscript, Polish, ink, 218×104 mm, ss. 1, pp. 1);
  - d) Labor Battalion at the Jewish Council in Warsaw, Certificate dated 28.10.1940 for Izrael Lichtensztajn about work order, obligation to report at Plac Muranowski (enclosures 1–6 control stubs) (original, printed, handwritten manuscript, pencil, German, Polish, pencil, 88×167, 70×84 mm, ss. 7, pp. 7);
  - e) Invitation for a school celebration on 21.12.1941 in the "Femina" hall (ul. Leszno 35) (original, printed, handwritten manuscript, ink, Hebrew, Polish, Yiddish, 102×144 mm, ss. 3, pp. 4);
  - f) Izrael Lichtensztajn, Letter of 17.12.1940 to D. [Dawid] Guzik (transcript, typescript, Yiddish, 203×288 mm, ss. 1, pp. 1);
  - g) Izrael Lichtensztajn, Letter of 17.12.1940 to G. [Gustaw] Wielikowski (ŻSS) (transcript, typescript, Yiddish, 193×287 mm, ss. 1, pp. 1);

h) Izrael Lichtensztajn, Letter of 17.12.1940 to Falek (ŻSS) (transcript, typescript, Yiddish, 220×287 mm, ss. 1, pp. 1).

- ***Description:*** original, printed, typescript, handwritten manuscript, pencil, ink, German, Polish, Yiddish, 80×155, 220×286 mm, ss. 16, pp. 17.

Correspondence (docs.: f, g, h) regarding purchase of coal by Izrael Lichtensztajn.

All the documents are made out in the name of Izrael (Peltę) Lichtensztajn (addresses: b) and c) ul. Okopowa 29, apt. 29, in e) ul. Pawia 81.

Doc. h) was kept in a binder.

Attached note by H.W. in Yiddish: "Delivered by Izrael Lichtensztajn, coworker of 'Oyneg Shabes.'"

Doc. e)—Published: *Dzieci*, pp. 284–287.

Index: Adam Czerniaków, Dir. [Izrael] Fajwiszys, A. Wolfowicz, chairman of the School Department of the Jewish Council, Dr. Felicja Czerniaków, Chana Bras, Marysia Ajzensztadt, Wajman, Klin, Wileński

### 1441. RING. I/1081/1 (1400). RING. I/1115 (1434). Mf. ŻIH—833; USHMM—45

- 01–04.1940, Warsaw
- TOZ, Certificates (3) dated 29.01., 25.[02?], and 4.04.1940 for Izrael Lichtensztajn regarding employment at TOZ, in children's kitchen no. 145 (ul. Nowolipki 68). Doc. signed by Dr. J. [Jakub] Rozenblum, Secretary General of TOZ
- In the certificate dated 29.01.1940 is a note about Lichtensztajn's employment in the position of warehouseman.
- ***Description:*** Ring. I/1081—original, typescript, German, Polish, stamp of TOZ, 208×287 mm, minor damage and losses of text, ss. 2, pp. 2; Ring. I/1115 (certificate dated 29.01.1940)—original, typescript, German, Polish, stamp of TOZ, 208×287 mm, minor damage and losses of text, ss. 1, pp. 1.

### 1442. RING. I/1220/21. Mf. ŻIH—835; USHMM—47

- 21.05.1940, Warsaw
- Jewish Council in Warsaw. Tax Department [. . .], Order of payment dated 21.05.1940 for Izrael Lichtensztajn (ul. Okopowa 29 m.[. . .]
- ***Description:*** original, printed, handwritten manuscript, pencil, 150×190 mm, substantial damage and losses of text, ss. 1, pp. 1.

### 1443. RING. I/1220/61. Mf. ŻIH—835; USHMM—47

a)

- 06.1940, Warsaw
- Labor Battalion at the Jewish Council in Warsaw, Certificate no. 3531 dated 20.06.1940 for Izrael Lichtensztejn [Lichtensztajn] (ul. Okopowa 29) about fulfillment of forced labor in June 1940
- ***Description:*** original, printed, stamp, German, Polish, 95×139 mm, ss. 2, pp. 2.

No. punched: "20*6*ROFO."

b)

- 07.1940, Warsaw
- Labor Battalion at the Jewish Council in Warsaw, "Call-up notice for the month of August [1940]" to forced labor for Izrael Lichtensztajn (ul. Okopowa 29, apt. 23) dated 27.07[?].1940
- Attached control stubs.
- ***Description:*** original, printed, handwritten manuscript, pencil, ink, German, Polish, 80×92, 157×92 mm, ss. 11, pp. 12.

c)

- 07.1940, Warsaw
- Labor Battalion at the Jewish Council in Warsaw, "Call-up notice for month of July [1940]" to forced labor for Berek Lichtensztajn (ul. Okopowa 29, apt. 23) dated [?].07.1940
- Attached control stubs.
- ***Description:*** original, printed, handwritten manuscript, pencil, ink, German, Polish, 80×92, 157×92 mm, ss. 11, pp. 12.

d)

- 07.1940, Warsaw
- Labor Battalion at the Jewish Council in Warsaw, "Call-up notice for the month of August [1940]" to forced labor for Berek Lichtensztajn (ul. Okopowa 29, apt. 23) dated 31.07.1940
- Appended control stubs.
- ***Description:*** original, printed, handwritten manuscript, pencil, ink, German, Polish, 80×92, 157×92 mm, ss. 11, pp. 12.

### 1444. RING. I/1200 (1519). Mf. ŻIH—835; USHMM—47

a)

- 29.[?][. . .].1940, Warsaw
- [ŻSS] Coordinating Commission of Communal and Welfare Organizations TOZ, Centos and others. (Warsaw, ul. Leszno 13), Receipt dated 29[?][. . .]. 1940 of payment in the amount of 20 zł "for the benefit of kitchens as well as for refugees and fire victims" made by [Izrael] Lichtensztajn (ul. Okopowa 29, apt. 23)
- ***Description:*** original, printed, handwritten manuscript, pencil, stamps, Polish, 119×92 mm, damage and losses of text, ss. 1, pp. 1.

Stamp: "Pomoc świąteczna" [Holiday Aid].

b)

- 7.10.1940, Warsaw
- ŻSS Coordinating Commission (Warsaw, ul. Leszno 13), Receipt dated 7.10.1940 of payment in the amount of 4 zł "for the benefit of kitchens as well as for refugees and fire victims" made by [Izrael] Lichtensztajn (ul. Okopowa 29, apt. 23)
- ***Description:*** original, printed, handwritten manuscript, pencil, Polish, 119×92 mm, damage and losses of text, ss. 1, pp. 1.

Printed inscription.: "Let's save the hungry!"

**1445. RING. I/1204 (1523). Mf. ŻIH—835; USHMM—47**

- 1940, Warsaw
- Municipal Government of the City of Warsaw, Heating Fuel Card 1940/1941
- Ration cards for coal for Izrael Lichtensztajn (ul. Okopowa 29, apt. 23).
- ***Description:*** original, printed, handwritten manuscript, ink, German, Polish, 98×86 mm, ss. 1, pp. 1.

**1446. RING. I/1220/62. Mf. ŻIH—835; USHMM—47**

- Before 10.02.1941, Warsaw
- City Government in Warsaw. Finance Department, Form for payment of levy by residents filled out for Berek Lichtensztejn (ul. Okopowa 29, apt. 23)
- ***Description:*** original, printed, handwritten manuscript, pencil, German, Polish, 103×160 mm, ss. 3, pp. 6.

**1447. RING. I/1081/2 (1400). Mf. ŻIH—833; USHMM—45**

- 10.05.1941, Warsaw Ghetto
- Dr. P. [Paulina (Perla)] Edelsburg-Feiman, Certificate dated 10.05.1941 about administration of vaccinations against typhus for Izrael Lichtensztajn (ul. Pawia 81)
- ***Description:*** original, printed, handwritten manuscript, ink, physician's stamp (stars of David on each side, in ink), German, Polish, 108×148 mm, ss. 1, pp. 2.

  Attached note by H.W. in Yiddish: "Submitted by Izrael Lichtensztajn, coworker of "Oyneg Shabes."

**1448. RING. I/1094 (1413). (Lb. 16, 16a). Mf. ŻIH—833; USHMM—45**

- 05–06.1941, Warsaw Ghetto
- Centos Association of Societies for Supervision over Children and Orphans (Warsaw, ul. Leszno 2), Certificates (2) dated 22.05.1941 and 21.06.1941, about employment, filled out for Izrael Lichtensztajn (born 1904) (ul. Pawia 81) (no. work card 1708/04)
- Doc. signed by Seweryn Majzner.
- ***Description:*** original, hectographed typescript, handwritten manuscript, ink, stamp of Centos, Polish, 165×218 mm, ss. 2, pp. 2.

  Attached note by H.W. in Yiddish: "By H.W."

**1449. RING. I/597/11. Mf. ŻIH—792; USHMM—23**

- 11.1941, Warsaw Ghetto
- Sponsors board (Patronat) of school (kitchen) for children no. 145 (ul. Nowolipki 68), Invitation for meal of tsholnt (czulent) on 22.11.1941 on the occasion of the first anniversary of the formation of the patrons board
- ***Description:*** original, printed, Yiddish, 140×87 mm, ss. 1, pp. 1.

**1450. RING. I/1190 (1509). (Lb. 670). Mf. ŻIH—834; USHMM—46**

- 1942, Warsaw Ghetto
- Izrael Lichtensztajn, Account of the liquidation action in the Warsaw Ghetto in the 2nd half of July 1942
- Orders for displacement, roundups, arrests, accusations regarding the attitude of Jewish activists, the Jewish Council and the Order Service, trade in "life cards" [lebn-shaynen].[61] Appended testament of Author dated 31.07.1942, with request to remember him, his wife, and daughter Margelit (20 months).
- ***Description:*** original,handwritten manuscript (IL*), notebook, ink, Yiddish, 142×200 mm, minor damage and losses of text, ss. 12, pp. 15.

  Text is divided into several parts:
  1) "Un es iż geshen . . ." [And it happened . . .]
  2) "Tsen teg 'iberzidlungs-aktsie' funem varshever yidntum ongehoybn erev tisha be-av 1942" [Ten days of "resettlement action" of Warsaw Jewry commenced on the eve of Tisha be-Av 1942]
  3) "Mayn tsavoe" [My will].

  Four photos were enclosed with the doc.: 1) Izrael Lichtensztajn; 2) Gela Seksztajn (date unknown, original, photograph, 85×135 mm; handwriting on the back by IL*, pencil, Yiddish, as well as postwar notations in Polish); 3) Margelit, daughter of Izrael and Gela; 4) Margelit with Gela Seksztajn (date unknown, original, photograph, 84×60 mm; handwriting on the back by IL*, pencil, Yiddish, as well as postwar notations and stamp in Polish). The remaining photographs 2 and 4 are now in the ŻIH Photograph Collection. Publication of the enclosures: photo. 2 in *Oneg Schabbat*, p. 64, and in *Scream the Truth at the World*, p. 60; photo. 4 in *Ocalone z warszawskiego getta*, p. 17.

  In HWC (31/16, 31/18) are also copies (typescript) of Izrael Lichtensztajn's texts, regarding the liquidation action in the Warsaw Ghetto in 1942, but the lack of precise descriptions in the available catalog (see essay by Epsztein) prevented comparison of them with the doc. in Ring. I/1190.

  In HWC (61/6) is the doc. "Mayn tsavoe" [My will] dated 31.07.1942, typescript, ss. 2 (postwar transcript of fragment of doc. Ring. I/1190 [?]).

  Published: *BFG*, vol. II, no. 1–4/1949, pp. 3–8; *Selected Documents*, pp. 29–31 (fragment of will); 696–700 (fragment of chapter 2).

61. Slang term for the employment ID cards that might protect one from forced resettlement to an unknown destination.

Index: Emanuel Ringelblum, Lejb Sznajderman, Szachno Sagan, Mini Ruchajson [?], teacher, [Bencjon] Chilinowicz, journalist, Dr. Frenkel, Cukierman, Grynkraut, Wajnsztajn, Auerbach, Lichtenbaum of the Jewish Council in Warsaw, Sztolcman, [Gustaw] Wielikowski, [Józef] Szeryński, [Jakub] Lejkin, Józef Erlich ("Josełe Kapota"), a German agent

**1451. RING. I/552/1. Mf. ŻIH—791; USHMM—22**

- 9.02.1942, Lublin
- F. [Fiszel?] Finkielsztejn (Lublin, ul. Lubartowska 31, apt. 14), Letter of 9.02.1942 to Izrael Lichtensztejn (Warsaw, ul. Pawia 81, apt. 38)
- Inquiry about the possibility of moving to Warsaw.
- ***Description:*** original, handwritten manuscript on a postcard, postmark and stamp of Jewish Council in Warsaw, ink, German, Polish, 146×104 mm, minor damage and losses of text, ss. 1, pp. 2

**1452. RING. I/1195 (1514). (Lb. 674). Mf. ŻIH—834; USHMM—46**

- 9.11.1931–13.03.1939, Warsaw
- Gela Seksztajn, Collection of press clippings regarding prewar exhibitions of the paintings of Jewish artists
- Press clippings, inter alia, from the *Nasz Przegląd Ilustrowany* and *Nowy Głos* (reviews and photographs of works of Gela Seksztajn, photographs of the Jewish art galleries at ul. Leszno 13, Leszno 10 and Granicznej 10). Attached catalog of an unidentified exhibition of paintings and sculptures.
- ***Description:*** original, printed, handwritten manuscript, ink, pencil, Polish, Yiddish, 122×177, 150×204 mm, ss. 24, pp. 40.

  Attached note by H.W.

  Doc. was kept in a binder.

**1453. RING. I/777/12. (Lb. 673). Mf. ŻIH—825; USHMM—37**

- 1932–1938, Warsaw.
- Żydowskie Towarzystwo Krzewienia Sztuk Pięknych [Jewish Society for the Propagation of Fine Arts] (Warsaw). Exhibition catalogs:
  1) *Salon Zimowy LXIX, grudzień 1932–styczeń 1933* [Winter Salon LXIX, December 1932–January 1933] [Warsaw 1932]
  2) *Wystawa Zbiorowa LXXX, styczeń 1935* [Collective Exhibition LXXX, January 1935] [Warsaw 1935]
  3) *Salon Doroczny LXXXVII, styczeń–luty 1938* [Annual Salon LXXXVII, January–February 1938] [Warsaw 1938].
- ***Description:*** original, printed, Polish, 114×150, 120×177 mm, ss. 12, pp. 24.

  From the estate of Gela Seksztajn.

  Docs. were kept in a binder.

**1454. RING. I/777/13. (Lb. 673). Mf. ŻIH—825; USHMM—37**

- 1939, Warsaw
- Stowarzyszenia Żydowskich Artystów Plastyków w Polsce [Association of Jewish Artists in Poland] (Warsaw, ul Długa 26). Exhibition catalog.
- *V Salon Jubileuszowy luty–marzec 1939. Malarstwo, rzeź ba, metaloplastyka, grafika* [V Jubilee Salon February–March 1939. Painting, Sculpture, Metalwork, Graphics] [Warsaw 1939].
- ***Description:*** original, printed, Polish, 120×167 mm, ss. 8, pp. 13.

  From the estate of Gela Seksztajn.

  Docs. were kept in a binder.

**1455. RING. I/1203 (1523). Mf. ŻIH—835; USHMM—47**

- Date unknown [Warsaw]
- Shekel (Zionist), Contributions paid for the benefit of the World Zionist Organization by Gela Seksztajn and [her husband] Izrael Lichtensztajn
- ***Description:*** Printed, handwritten manuscript, ink, English, Hebrew, Yiddish, minor damage and losses of text, 98×110 mm, ss. 4, pp. 8.

**1456. RING. I/1196 (1515). (Lb. 672). Mf. ŻIH—834; USHMM—46**

- Beginning of 08.1942, Warsaw Ghetto
- Gela Sekshtayn [Seksztajn], "Mayn tsavoe" [My will] and "A por datn fun mayn lebn" [A few dates from my life]
- Autobiographical information, requests: to transfer her works to a Jewish museum in Poland; to convey information about her to relatives and friends.
- ***Description:*** transcript, handwritten manuscript (IL*), notebook, ink, Yiddish, 140×200 mm, ss. 14, pp. 7.

  On p. 1 (cover) subtitle "'Iberzidlungs-aktsye' fun varshever yidntum. Oysrotung" ["Resettlement action" of Warsaw Jewry. Extermination]

  Section titles: "Vos ken ikh in itstikn moment zogn un farlangen" [What can I say and ask for in the present moment]

  Index: Margelit and Izrael Lichtensztajn, Yentka and Abraham Lichtensztajn of Buenos Aires, Szloma Lichtensztajn and his wife Noemi Fridman in Tel Aviv, B.C. Hariton in New York, I.J. Singer, author.

  Published: *Selected Documents*, pp. 672–674.

**1457. RING. I/1221 (Lb. 675, 676).**

Gela Seksztajn, Watercolors, drawings, sketches.

Watercolors, pencil and pastel sketches, some signed by the artist, others described by Izrael Lichtensztajn in the Warsaw Ghetto shortly before the concealment of the entire collection together with the Ringelblum Archive. After 1947, Gela Seksztajn's works were included into the Jewish Historical Institute's museum collections, where they still remain. In the present inventory, they are listed according to their museum catalog numbers.

A-26

- Date unknown [1932–39], place unknown
- Gela Seksztajn, Portrait of a man with a book.
- ***Description:*** original, watercolor, paper, 725×550 mm, ss. 1, pp. 1.

A-28

- Date unknown [1932–1939], place unknown
- Gela Seksztajn, Portrait of a girl.
- ***Description:*** original, watercolor, paper, 780×450 mm, ss. 1, pp. 1.
  Signed at the bottom left with a copy pencil: "G. Seksztajn."

A-29

- Date unknown [1932–1939], place unknown
- Gela Seksztajn, Portrait of the writer Baruch Gelman.
- ***Description:*** original, water color, card-board, 680×425 mm, ss. 1, pp. 1.
  Signed at the bottom left with pencil: "G. Seksztajn."

A-30

- Date unknown [1932–1939], place unknown
- Gela Seksztajn, Portrait of a boy with a bowl of apples.
- ***Description:*** original, watercolor, paper, 817×474 mm, ss. 1, pp. 1.
- Signed at the bottom left with pencil: "G. Seksztejn."

A-31

- Date unknown [1932–1939], place unknown
- Gela Seksztajn, Portrait of a girl begging.
- ***Description:*** original, watercolor, paper, 715×440 mm, ss. 1, pp. 1.
  Signed at the bottom left with pencil: "G. Seksztejn."

A-32

- Date unknown [1932–1939], place unknown
- Gela Seksztajn, Portrait of a girl with a basket of apples.
- ***Description:*** original, watercolor, paper, 740×465 mm, ss. 1, pp. 1.
  Signed at the bottom left with blue copy pencil: "G. Seksztejn."

A-33

- Date unknown [1932–1939], place unknown
- Gela Seksztajn, Portrait of a girl with a thrown-on shawl.
- ***Description:*** original, watercolor, paper, 783×465 mm, ss. 1, pp. 1.
  Signed at the bottom left with pencil: "G. Seksztejn."

A-34

- Date unknown [1932–1939], place unknown
- Gela Seksztajn, Portrait of a girl with braids.
- ***Description:*** original, watercolor, paper, 710×460 mm, ss. 1, pp. 1.
  Signed on the bottom left with blue ink: "G. Seksztejn."

A-35

- Date unknown [1932–1939], place unknown
- Gela Seksztajn, Portrait of a girl with a bucket.
- ***Description:*** original, watercolor, paper, 760×455 mm, ss. 1, pp. 1.
  Signed at the bottom right with pencil: "G. Seksztejn."

A-193

- Date unknown [1932–1939], place unknown
- Gela Seksztajn, Portrait of a girl with a doll.
- ***Description:*** original, watercolor, paper, 600×442 mm, ss. 1, pp. 1.
  Signed at the bottom left with blue pencil: "G. Seksztejn."
  On the back a postwar number in pencil: "44."

A-328

- Date unknown [1932–1939], place unknown
- Gela Seksztajn, Portrait of the writer Szymon Horończyk.
- ***Description:*** original, watercolor, paper, 525×417 mm, ss. 1, pp. 1.
  Signed at the bottom left with pencil: "G. Seksztejn."
  On the back inscribed in pencil in Yiddish: "Szymon Horończyk/G. Seksztejn."

A-329

- 1938, place unknown
- Gela Seksztajn, Portrait of a girl with a doll.
- ***Description:*** original, watercolor, paper, 556×428 mm, ss. 1, pp. 2.
  At bottom left of page signed in ink: "G. Seksztejn 1938."
  On the back is a postwar number in pencil: "6."

A-537

- Date unknown [1932–1939], place unknown
- Gela Seksztajn, Portrait of a smiling boy.
- ***Description:*** original, charcoal sketch [rys. węglem], paper, 326×242 mm, ss. 1, pp. 2.
  On the back are two numbers in pencil: "114" and "9."

A-538

- Date unknown [1932–1939], place unknown
- Gela Seksztajn, Portrait of a girl.

- *Description:* original, charcoal sketch [rys. węglem], paper, 371×286 mm, ss. 1, pp. 2.
  On the bottom left side written in blue crayon [kredka] in Yiddish [IL*]: "G. Seksztajn"; in the upper right corner is visible a fragment of a water-mark: "Canson and M. . .".
  On the back are two numbers in pencil: "10" and "136."

### A-539

- Date unknown [1932–1939], place unknown
- Gela Seksztajn, Portrait of a boy with a bandaged eye.
- *Description:* original, charcoal sketch [rys. węglem], paper, 380×318 mm, ss. 1, pp. 2.
  On the lower left side is an inscription in blue crayon [kredka] in Yiddish [IL*]: "G. Seksztajn"; on the left part of the upper edge is a partial water-mark: ". . . ONTGOLFIER France".
  On the back are two numbers in pencil: "135" and "12".

### A-540

- Date unknown [1932–1939], place unknown
- Gela Seksztajn, Portrait of a boy.
- *Description:* original, charcoal sketch [rys. węglem], paper, 325x242 mm, ss. 1, pp. 2.
  On the back is a postwar number in pencil: "121."

### A-541

- Date unknown [1932–1939], place unknown
- Gela Seksztajn, Portrait of a girl.
- *Description:* original, charcoal sketch [rys. węglem], 364× 244 mm, ss. 1, pp. 2.
  On the back is a postwar number in pencil: "123."

### A-542

- Date unknown [1932–1939], place unknown
- Gela Seksztajn, Portrait of a girl.
- *Description:* original, charcoal sketch [rys. węglem], paper, 326× 243 mm, ss. 1, pp. 2.
  On the bottom left side is an inscription in blue crayon [kredka] in Yiddish [IL*]: "G. Seksztajn."
  On the back are two numbers in pencil: "86" and "7."

### A-891

- Date unknown [1932–1939], place unknown
- Gela Seksztajn, Self-portrait.
- *Description:* original, charcoal sketch [rys. węglem], paper, 228x170 mm, ss. 2, pp. 2.
  On the lower left side of the paper, to which the sketch is glued, is an inscription in blue crayon [kredka] in Yiddish [IL*]: "G. Seksztajn—self-portrait."

### A-892

- 1938, place unknown
- Gela Seksztajn, Portrait of a seated girl.
- *Description:* original, watercolor, cardboard, visible pencil sketch, 565× 427 mm, ss. 1, pp. 1.
  On the upper left side signed in ink: "G. Seksztejn 1938."[62]

### A-893

- Date unknown [1932–1939], place unknown
- Gela Seksztajn, Portrait of a girl sleeping at a table.
- *Description:* original, watercolor, cardboard, 706× 465 mm, ss. 1, pp. 1.
  On the lower left side signed in pencil: "G. Seksztejn."

### A-894

- 1938, place unknown
- Gela Seksztajn, Portrait of a girl.
- *Description:* original, watercolor, paper, 561× 427 mm, ss. 1, pp. 2.
  On lower left side signature in ink: "G. Seksztejn 1938."

### A-895

- Date unknown [1932–1939], place unknown
- Gela Seksztajn, Portrait of a girl with a basket.
- *Description:* original, watercolor, paper, 556× 428 mm, ss. 1, pp. 1.
  On lower left side signature in pencil: "G. Seksztejn."

### A-896

- Date unknown [1932–1939], place unknown
- Gela Seksztajn, Portrait of a man.
- *Description:* original, watercolor, paper, 495× 429 mm, ss. 1, pp. 1.

### A-897

- 1938, place unknown
- Gela Seksztajn, Portrait of a girl.
- *Description:* original, watercolor, paper, 550×410 mm, ss. 1, pp. 2.
  On the lower right side signed in ink: "G. Seksztejn 1938."
  On the back a [postwar] number in pencil: "43."

### A-898

- Date unknown [1932–1939], place unknown

62. Trans. note: The artist's name is rendered variously as Seksztajn and Seksztejn in the catalog, reflecting Polish spelling and transcription of Yiddish. Seksztajn's name in YIVO standard transcription is Sekshteyn, although it was likely pronounced Sekshtayn.

- Gela Seksztajn, Portrait of a girl.
- ***Description:*** original, watercolor, paper, 370×315 mm, ss. 1, pp. 1.

### A-899

- Date unknown [1932–1939], place unknown
- Gela Seksztajn, Portrait of a seated little boy.
- ***Description:*** original, watercolor, paper, 553×440 mm, ss. 1, pp. 2.
  On the lower left side signed with blue crayon: "G. Seksztejn."
  On the back with blue copy pencil is inscribed: "G. Seksztejn—G. Seksztejn."

### A-900

- 1938, place unknown
- Gela Seksztajn, Portrait of a girl with braids.
- ***Description:*** original, watercolor, cardboard, 532×420 mm, ss. 1, pp. 2.
  Signed at the bottom in black ink: "G. Seksztejn 1938."
  On the back inscribed in pencil: "Może to RS" [?].

### A-901

- Date unknown [1932–1939], place unknown
- Gela Seksztajn, Portrait of a girl with a ball.
- ***Description:*** watercolor, paper, 764×482 mm, ss. 1, pp. 2.
  Signed on the lower left side in blue crayon: "G. Seksztejn."
  On the back a [postwar] number in pencil: "10."

### A-902

- Date unknown [1932–1939], place unknown
- Gela Seksztajn, Portrait of a girl with flowers.
- ***Description:*** original, watercolor, paper, 658×432 mm, ss. 1, pp. 2.
  Signed in blue crayon on the lower right side: "G. Seksztejn."
  On the back a [postwar] number in pencil: "39."

### A-903

- Date unknown [1932–1939], place unknown
- Gela Seksztajn, Portrait of a seated boy.
- ***Description:*** original, watercolor, paper, 612×478 mm, ss. 1, pp. 2.
  Signed with blue crayon on the lower left side: "G. Seksztejn."
  On the back a [postwar] number in pencil: "17."

### A-904

- Date unknown [1932–1939], place unknown
- Gela Seksztajn, Portrait of a girl.
- ***Description:*** original, watercolor, paper, 580×445 mm, ss. 1, pp. 2.
  Signed on the lower right side: "G. Seksztejn."
  On the back is a [postwar] number in pencil: "30."

### A-905

- Date unknown [1932–1939], place unknown
- Gela Seksztajn, Still life. Flowers in a vase.
- ***Description:*** original, watercolor, paper, 582×446 mm, ss. 1, pp. 2.
  Signed with blue crayon on the lower right side: "G. Seksztejn."
  On the back a [postwar] number in pencil: "45."

### A-906

- Date unknown [1932–1939], place unknown
- Gela Seksztajn, Still life. Flowers in a vase and fruit.
- ***Description:*** original, watercolor, paper, 500×440 mm, ss. 1, pp. 1.
  Signed with blue copy pencil at the bottom: "G. Seksztejn"

### A-907

- Date unknown [1932–1939], place unknown
- Gela Seksztajn, Portrait of a man.
- ***Description:*** original, watercolor, paper, 578×443 mm, ss. 1, pp. 2.
  On the back is a crossed-out [postwar] number in pencil: "60."

### A-908

- 1938, place unknown
- Gela Seksztajn, Woman sewing.
- ***Description:*** original, watercolor, paper, 444×583 mm, ss. 1, pp. 2.
  Signed in ink on the lower left side: "G. Seksztejn 1938."
  On the back a crossed-out [postwar] number in pencil: "13."

### A-909

- Date unknown [1932–1939], place unknown
- Gela Seksztajn, Portrait of a girl.
- ***Description:*** original, watercolor, paper, 553×403 mm, ss. 1, pp. 2.
  Signed in ink at the bottom: "G. Seksztejn."
  On the back is a postwar number in red crayon: "ŻIH inw. 1304."

### A-910

- 1938, place unknown
- Gela Seksztajn, Portrait of a boy.
- ***Description:*** original, watercolor, paper, 463×364 mm, ss. 1, pp. 1.
  Signed in ink on the lower right side: "G. Seksztejn 1938."

### A-911

- Date unknown [1932–1939], place unknown
- Gela Seksztajn, Still life. Flowers in a vase.
- ***Description:*** original, watercolor, paper, 579×446 mm, ss. 1, pp. 2.

Signed in ink on the lower left side: "G. Seksztejn."
On the back is a crossed-out [postwar] number in pencil: "15"; as well as an inscription in red crayon: "ŻIH inw. 1304."

### A-912

- Date unknown [1932–1939], place unknown
- Gela Seksztajn, Portrait of a boy.
- ***Description:*** original, watercolor, paper, 545×376 mm, ss. 1, pp. 2.

Signed in ink on the lower right side: "G. Seksztejn."
On the back is a crossed-out [postwar] number in pencil: "18."

### A-913

- Date unknown [1932–1939], place unknown
- Gela Seksztajn, Still life. Vegetables.
- ***Description:*** original, watercolor, paper, 444×573 mm, ss. 1, pp. 2.

Signed in ink on the lower right side: "G. Seksztejn."
On the back is a crossed-out [postwar] number in pencil: "20."

### A-914

- Date unknown [1932–1939], place unknown
- Gela Seksztajn, Still life. Flowers and fruit.
- ***Description:*** original, watercolor, paper, 444×581 mm, ss. 1, pp. 2.

Signed in ink on the lower left side: "G. Seksztejn."
On the back is a crossed-out [postwar] number in pencil: "24."

### A-915

- Date unknown [1932–1939], place unknown
- Gela Seksztajn, Portrait of a man in a hat.
- ***Description:*** original, watercolor, paper, 442×370 mm, ss. 1, pp. 2.

Signed with watercolor on the lower left side: "G. Seksztajn."
On the back is a crossed-out [postwar] number in pencil: "26"; as well as an inscription in red crayon: "ŻIH inw. 1304."

### A-916

- Date unknown [1932–1939], place unknown
- Gela Seksztajn, Riverside landscape.
- ***Description:*** original, watercolor, paper, 404×580 mm, ss. 1, pp. 2.

Signed in ink on the lower right side: "G. Seksztejn 1938."
On the back is a crossed-out [postwar] number in pencil: "28"; and an inscription in red crayon: "ŻIH inw. 1304. G. Seksztajn."

### A-917

- Date unknown [1932–1939], place unknown
- Gela Seksztajn, Portrait of a woman.
- ***Description:*** original, watercolor, paper, 413×305 mm, ss. 1, pp. 2.

On the back is a crossed-out [postwar] number in pencil: "29"; and an inscription in red crayon: "ŻIH inw. 1304. G. Seksztajn."

### A-918

- Date unknown [1932–1939], place unknown
- Gela Seksztajn, Portrait of a man.
- ***Description:*** original, watercolor, paper, 459×373 mm, ss. 1, pp. 2.

On the back is a [postwar] number in pencil: "33."

### A-919

- Date unknown [1932–1939], place unknown
- Gela Seksztajn, Portrait of a woman.
- ***Description:*** original, watercolor, paper, 296×269 mm, ss. 1, pp. 2.

On the back is a crossed-out [postwar] number in pencil: "34."

### A-920

- Date unknown [1932–1939], place unknown
- Gela Seksztajn, Landscape. View of a bridge
- ***Description:*** original, watercolor, paper, 194×280 mm, ss. 1, pp. 2.

On the back is a crossed-out [postwar] number in pencil: "35"; and an inscription in red crayon: "ŻIH inw. 1304. G. Seksztajn."

### A-921

- Date unknown [1932–1939], place unknown
- Gela Seksztajn, Landscape with a lake.
- ***Description:*** original, watercolor, paper, 195×292 mm, ss. 1, pp. 2.

On the back a [postwar] number in pencil: "36"; and an inscription in red crayon: "ŻIH inw. 1304. G. Seksztajn."

### A-922

- Date unknown [1932–1939], place unknown
- Gela Seksztajn, Landscape. A solitary tree.
- ***Description:*** original, watercolor, paper, 351×233 mm, ss. 1, pp. 2.

On the back is a crossed-out [postwar] number in pencil: "37."

### A-923

- 1933 [?], place unknown
- Gela Seksztajn, Portrait of a boy in a cap.
- ***Description:*** original, watercolor, paper, 440×344 mm, ss. 1, pp. 2.

Signed with watercolor on the lower left side: "Seksztajn"; and in pencil: "33".

On the back is a crossed-out [postwar] number in pencil: "38."

### A-924

- Date unknown [1932–1939], place unknown
- Gela Seksztajn, Portrait of a woman.
- ***Description:*** original, watercolor, paper, 484×400 mm, ss. 1, pp. 2.
  On the back is a crossed-out [postwar] number in pencil: "40."

### A-925

- Date unknown [1932–1939], place unknown
- Gela Seksztajn, Still life. Flowers in a vase.
- ***Description:*** original, watercolor, paper, 582×445 mm, ss. 1, pp. 2.
  Signed with blue crayon on the lower left side: "G. Seksztejn."
  On the back is a [postwar] number in pencil: "46"; and the same number crossed out: "46."

### A-926

- Date unknown [1932–1939], place unknown
- Gela Seksztajn, Portrait of a boy.
- ***Description:*** original, watercolor, paper, 381×305 mm, ss. 1, pp. 2.
  Signed in ink on the lower left side: "G. Seksztejn."
  On the back is a crossed-out [postwar] number in pencil: "49."

### A-927

- Date unknown [1932–1939], place unknown
- Gela Seksztajn, Portrait of a boy in eyeglasses.
- ***Description:*** original, watercolor, paper, 700×482 mm, ss. 1, pp. 2.
  Signed in pencil on the lower right side: "G. Seksztejn."
  On the back is a crossed-out [postwar] number in pencil: "50."

### A-928

- Date unknown [1932–1939], place unknown
- Gela Seksztajn, Still life. Jug, bottle, and apple.
- ***Description:*** original, watercolor, paper, 421×360 mm, ss. 1, pp. 2.
  Signed in watercolor on the lower right side: "G. Seksz."
  On the back is a crossed-out [postwar] number in pencil: "51"; and an inscription in red crayon: "ŻIH inw. 1304."

### A-929

- Date unknown [1932–1939], place unknown
- Gela Seksztajn, Portrait of a girl with a doll.
- ***Description:*** original, watercolor, paper, 360×290 mm, ss. 1, pp. 2.
  On the back is a crossed-out [postwar] number in pencil: "54."

### A-930

- Date unknown [1932–1939], place unknown
- Gela Seksztajn, Still life with a flower pot.
- ***Description:*** original, watercolor, paper, 350×277 mm, ss. 1, pp. 2.
  Signed with black crayon on the back: "G. Seksztejn"; and a crossed-out [postwar] number in pencil: "55."

### A-931

- Date unknown [1932–1939], place unknown
- Gela Seksztajn, Portrait of a woman.
- ***Description:*** original, watercolor, paper, 350×270 mm, ss. 1, pp. 2.
  On the back a crossed-out [postwar] number in pencil: "56."

### A-932

- Date unknown [1932–1939], place unknown
- Gela Seksztajn, Still life: bread and vegetables.
- ***Description:*** original, watercolor, paper, 397×390 mm, ss. 1, pp. 2.
  On the reverse a crossed-out [postwar] number in pencil: "57."

### A-933

- Date unknown [1932–1939], place unknown
- Gela Seksztajn, Still life.
- ***Description:*** original, watercolor, paper, 353×444 mm, ss. 1, pp. 2.
  On the reverse a crossed-out [postwar] number in pencil: "58."

### A-934

- Date unknown [1932–1939], place unknown
- Gela Seksztajn, Flowers in a vase.
- ***Description:*** original, watercolor, paper, 542×428 mm, ss. 1, pp. 2.
  At the bottom of the left side signed in ink: "G. Seksztajn"; on the reverse crossed-out [postwar] number in pencil: "61."

### A-935

- Date unknown [1932–1939], place unknown
- Gela Seksztajn, Portrait of a woman.
- ***Description:*** original, watercolor, paper, 364×295 mm, ss. 1, pp. 2.
  On the reverse two crossed-out numbers in pencil: "37/29" and "62."

### A-936

- Date unknown [1932–1939], place unknown
- Gela Seksztajn, Portrait of a man.
- ***Description:*** original, charcoal drawing, paper, 416×315 mm, ss. 1, pp. 2.
  At the bottom left side signature in blue indelible pencil in Yiddish (handwriting IL*): "G. Seksztajn"; on the reverse crossed-out [postwar] number in pencil: "63."

A-937

- Date unknown [1932–1939], place unknown
- Gela Seksztajn, Portrait of a man.
- ***Description:*** original, charcoal drawing, paper, 370×288 mm, ss. 1, pp. 2.
  At the bottom of the left side signature in blue indelible pencil in Yiddish (handwriting IL*): "G. Seksztajn," in the upper left corner visible decorative detail of a watermark; on the reverse a crossed-out [postwar] number in pencil: "64."

A-938

- Date unknown [1932–1939], place unknown
- Gela Seksztajn, Portrait of a woman.
- ***Description:*** original, charcoal and colored crayon drawing, paper, 388×318 mm, ss. 1, pp. 2.
  At the bottom of the right side signed in crayon: "G. Seksztajn," at the top of the left side visible inscription of a watermark: "Canson i Mo[. . .]"; on the reverse crossed-out [postwar] number in pencil: "66."

A-939

- Date unknown [1932–1939], place unknown
- Gela Seksztajn, Portrait of a man.
- ***Description:*** original, charcoal drawing, paper, 361×318 mm, ss. 1, pp. 2.
  At the bottom right side signed in pencil: "G. Seksztajn"; and on the left signature in blue indelible pencil in Yiddish (handwriting IL*): "G. Seksztajn"; on the reverse a crossed-out [postwar] number in pencil: "67."

A-940

- Date unknown [1932–1939], place unknown
- Gela Seksztajn, Portrait of a boy.
- ***Description:*** original, charcoal drawing, paper, 484×310 mm, ss. 1, pp. 2.
  In the upper right corner visible watermark with inscription: "JCA France," and on the left: "[. . .] RES"; on the reverse crossed-out [postwar] number in pencil: "68."

A-941

- Date unknown [1932–1939], place unknown
- Gela Seksztajn, Portrait of a boy.
- ***Description:*** original, charcoal drawing, paper, 484×310 mm, ss. 1, pp. 2.
  At bottom right side signed in pencil: "G. Seksztajn," in the upper right corner visible watermark: "ING[RES]," and on the left: "JCA France"; on the reverse crossed-out [postwar] number in pencil: "69."

A-942

- Date unknown [1932–1939], place unknown
- Gela Seksztajn, Interior of a room.
- ***Description:*** original, charcoal drawing, paper, 510×398 mm, ss. 1, pp. 2.
  At the bottom left signature in blue indelible pencil in Yiddish (handwriting IL*): "G. Seksztajn," visible watermark with inscription: "INGRES JCA France"; on the reverse crossed-out [postwar] number in pencil: "70."

A-943

- Date unknown [1932–1939], place unknown
- Gela Seksztajn, Portrait of a man.
- ***Description:*** original, charcoal drawing, paper, 405×318 mm, ss. 1, pp. 2.
  At the bottom of the left side signature in blue indelible pencil in Yiddish (handwriting IL*): "71."

A-944

- Date unknown [1932–1939], place unknown
- Gela Seksztajn, Still life on a table.
- ***Description:*** original, charcoal drawing, paper, 480×316 mm, ss. 1, pp. 2.
  At the bottom right side signed in pencil: "G. Seksztajn," alongside visible watermark with inscription: "J.A.V. écoles"; on the reverse crossed-out [postwar] number in pencil: "72."

A-945

- Date unknown [1932–1939], place unknown
- Gela Seksztajn, Portrait of a man.
- ***Description:*** original, charcoal drawing, paper, 382×313 mm, ss. 1, pp. 2.
  At the bottom of the left side signature in blue indelible pencil in Yiddish (handwriting IL*): "G. Seksztajn," in upper left corner fragment of inscription of watermark: "[. . .]ES[. . .]"; on the reverse signature in blue indelible pencil in Yiddish (handwriting IL*): "L. Seksztajn—AL Toff" [?] as well as crossed-out [postwar] number in pencil: "138."

A-946

- Date unknown [1932–1939], place unknown
- Gela Seksztajn, Portrait of a little girl.
- ***Description:*** original, charcoal drawing, paper, 579×446 mm, ss. 1, pp. 2.
  On the reverse crossed-out [postwar] number in pencil: "73" and marked inscription in red crayon: "ŻIH. Inw. 1304 G. Seksztajn."

A-947/1

- Date unknown [1932–1939], place unknown
- Gela Seksztajn, Female nude.
- ***Description:*** original, colored crayon drawing, paper, 324×241 mm, ss. 1, pp. 1.

A-947/2

- Date unknown [1932–1939], place unknown
- Gela Seksztajn, Portrait of a woman seated on a stool.
- In the upper part of the drawing is an outline sketch of a face

- ***Description:*** original, crayon drawing, paper, 326×240 mm, ss. 1, pp. 2.

### A-947/3

- Date unknown [1932–1939], place unknown
- Gela Seksztajn, Portrait of a woman seated on a stool.
- ***Description:*** original, crayon drawing, paper, 325×240 mm, ss. 1, pp. 2.

### A-947/4

- Date unknown [1932–1939], place unknown
- Gela Seksztajn, Portrait of a recumbent woman.
- ***Description:*** original, crayon drawing, paper, 325×240 mm, ss. 1, pp. 2.
  On the back a postwar number in pencil: "77."

### A-947/5

- Date unknown [1932–1939], place unknown
- Gela Seksztajn, Face of a girl.
- ***Description:*** original, crayon drawing, paper, 325×240 mm, ss. 1, pp. 2.
  On the back a postwar number in pencil "78" and "ŻIH inw. 1304."

### A-947/6

- Date unknown [1932–1939], place unknown
- Gela Seksztajn, Portrait of a man.
- ***Description:*** original, crayon drawing, paper, 326×240 mm, ss. 1, pp. 2.
  On the back a postwar number in pencil "79."

### A-947/7 A, B

- Date unknown [1932–1939], place unknown
- Gela Seksztajn, A seated man.
- ***Description:*** original, crayon drawing, paper, 206×338 mm, ss. 1, pp. 2.
  On the back an unfinished sketch of the same seated man as well as the inscribed postwar number in pencil: "80."

### A-947/8

- Date unknown [1932–1939], place unknown
- Gela Seksztajn, Portrait of a sleeping child.
- ***Description:*** original, crayon drawing, paper, 325×240 mm, ss. 1, pp. 2.
  Signature in Yiddish (handwriting of IL*) with blue indelible pencil on the lower left side: "G. Seksztajn."

### A-947/9

- Date unknown [1932–1939], place unknown
- Gela Seksztajn, Portrait of a girl with a kerchief on her head.
- ***Description:*** original, charcoal drawing, paper, 325×240 mm, ss. 1, pp. 2.
  Signature in blue indelible pencil in Yiddish (handwriting IL*) on the lower left side: "G. Seksztajn."

### A-947/10

- Date unknown [1932–1939], place unknown
- Gela Seksztajn, Portrait of a child.
- ***Description:*** original, crayon drawing, paper, 325×240 mm, ss. 1, pp. 2.
  Signature in blue indelible pencil in Yiddish (handwriting IL*) in the lower left corner: "G. Seksztajn"; on the back a postwar number in pencil: "85"; as well as an inscription in red crayon: "ŻIH inw. 1304."

### A-947/11

- Date unknown [1932–1939], place unknown
- Gela Seksztajn, Portrait of a sleeping child.
- ***Description:*** original, crayon drawing, paper, 325×241 mm, ss. 1, pp. 2.
  Signature in Yiddish (handwriting IL*) with blue indelible pencil in the lower left corner: "G. Seksztajn"; on the back a postwar number: "87."

### A-947/12

- Date unknown [1932–1939], place unknown
- Gela Seksztajn, Portrait of a girl with a bow.
- ***Description:*** original, crayon drawing, paper, 325×240 mm, ss. 1, pp. 2.
  Signature in Yiddish (handwriting IL*) with blue indelible pencil in the lower left corner: "G. Seksztajn"; on the back a postwar number: "88."

### A-947/13

- Date unknown [1932–1939], place unknown
- Gela Seksztajn, Portrait of a girl with braids.
- ***Description:*** original, charcoal drawing, paper, 325×241 mm, ss. 1, pp. 2.
  Signature in Yiddish (handwriting IL*) with blue indelible pencil in the lower right corner: "G. Seksztajn."

### A-947/14

- Date unknown [1932–1939], place unknown
- Gela Seksztajn, Portrait of a man.
- ***Description:*** original, charcoal drawing, paper, 325×241 mm, ss. 1, pp. 2.
  On the back an inscription in blue indelible pencil in Yiddish (handwriting IL*): "Czubik" [Tshubik]; and a signature: "G. Seksztajn"; on the back is a postwar number in pencil: "91."

### A-947/15

- Date unknown [1932–1939], place unknown
- Gela Seksztajn, Portrait of a child.
- ***Description:*** original, crayon drawing, paper, 324×240 mm, ss. 1, pp. 2.
  On the back is a postwar number in pencil: "92"; and an inscription in red crayon: "G. Seksztajn ŻIH inw. 1304."

### A-947/16

- Date unknown [1932–1939], place unknown
- Gela Seksztajn, Portrait of a woman.
- ***Description:*** original, crayon drawing, paper, 325×240 mm, ss. 1, pp. 1.

### A-947/17

- Date unknown [1932–1939], place unknown
- Gela Seksztajn, Portrait of a small boy
- ***Description:*** original, charcoal drawing, paper, 325×240 mm, ss. 1, pp. 1.

### A-947/18

- Date unknown [1932–1939], place unknown
- Gela Seksztajn, Portrait of a woman from the back.
- ***Description:*** original, crayon drawing, paper, 330×244 mm, ss. 1, pp. 1.

### A-947/19

- Date unknown [1932–1939], place unknown
- Gela Seksztajn, Portrait of a young girl.
- ***Description:*** original, pencil drawing, paper, 326×242 mm, ss. 1, pp. 2.

  On the back is a postwar number in pencil: "97."

### A-947/20

- Date unknown [1932–1939], place unknown
- Gela Seksztajn, A sleeping child.
- ***Description:*** original, crayon drawing, paper, 324×241 mm, ss. 1, pp. 2.

  Signature in Yiddish (handwriting IL*) with blue indelible pencil on the lower left side: "G. Seksztajn"; on the back is a postwar number in pencil: "98"; and an inscription with red crayon: "ŻIH inw. 1304."

### A-947/21

- Date unknown [1932–1939], place unknown
- Gela Seksztajn, A seated little boy.
- ***Description:*** original, pencil drawing, tissue paper, 332×216 mm, ss. 1, pp. 2.

  On the back is a postwar number in pencil: "99."

### A-947/22

- Date unknown [1932–1939], place unknown
- Gela Seksztajn, A little boy with a blindfold on his eye.
- ***Description:*** original, crayon drawing, paper, 296×238 mm, ss. 1, pp. 2.

  On the back is a postwar number in pencil: "100."

### A-947/23

- Date unknown [1932–1939], place unknown
- Gela Seksztajn, Portrait of a sleepy adolescent boy.
- ***Description:*** original, charcoal drawing, paper, 330×244 mm, ss. 1, pp. 2.

  On the back is an inscription in Yiddish (handwriting IL*) in blue indelible pencil: "M. Knapais" and "G. Seksztajn."

### A-947/24

- Date unknown [1932–1939], place unknown
- Gela Seksztajn, A sleeping woman.
- ***Description:*** original, crayon drawing, paper, 326×240 mm, ss. 1, pp. 2.

  On the back is a postwar number in pencil: "103."

### A-947/25

- Date unknown [1932–1939], place unknown
- Gela Seksztajn, Head of a sleeping child.
- ***Description:*** original, crayon drawing, paper, 325×240 mm, ss. 1, pp. 2.

  In the lower left corner is a signature with blue indelible pencil in Yiddish (handwriting IL*): "G. Seksztajn"; on the back is a postwar number in pencil: "104".

### A-947/26

- Date unknown [1932–1939], place unknown
- Gela Seksztajn, A boy sitting by a stove.
- ***Description:*** original, charcoal drawing, paper, 325×241, ss. 1, pp. 2.

  On the back is a postwar number in pencil: "105."

### A-947/27

- Date unknown [1932–1939], place unknown
- Gela Seksztajn, Portrait of a little boy.
- ***Description:*** original, crayon drawing, paper, 325×240 mm, ss. 1, pp. 2.

  On the back is a postwar number in pencil: "106" and an inscription in red crayon: "G. Seksztajn ŻIH inw. 1304."

### A-947/28

- Date unknown [1932–1939], place unknown
- Gela Seksztajn, A boy and a girl.
- ***Description:*** original, charcoal drawing, paper, 233×325 mm, ss. 1, pp. 2.

  On the back is a postwar number in pencil: "107."

### A-947/29

- Date unknown [1932–1939], place unknown
- Gela Seksztajn, Image of a seated woman.
- ***Description:*** original, crayon drawing, paper, 326×242 mm, ss. 1, pp. 2.

  On the back is a postwar inscription in pencil: "108."

### A-947/30

- Date unknown [1932–1939], place unknown
- Gela Seksztajn, A seated man.
- ***Description:*** original, crayon drawing, paper, 332×242 mm, ss. 1, pp. 2.

  Signed in ink on the lower right side: "G.

Seksztejn"; on the back is a postwar number in pencil: "109."

### A-947/31

- Date unknown [1932–1939], place unknown
- Gela Seksztajn, Portrait of a child.
- ***Description:*** original, crayon drawing, paper, 325×240 mm, ss. 1, pp. 2.
  On the back is a postwar number in pencil: "110" and an inscription in red crayon: "G. Seksztajn ŻIH inw. 1304."

### A-947/32

- Date unknown [1932–1939], place unknown
- Gela Seksztajn, Female nude.
- ***Description:*** original, crayon drawing, paper, 325×241 mm, ss. 1, pp. 2.
  On the back is a crossed-out number in ink: "75" and inscribed postwar number in pencil: "111."

### A-947/33

- Date unknown [1932–1939], place unknown
- Gela Seksztajn, Study of a hand.
- ***Description:*** original, charcoal drawing, paper, 330×244 mm, ss. 1, pp. 2.
  On the back is a postwar number in pencil: "112" and twice inscribed in red crayon: "G. Seksztajn."

### A-947/34

- Date unknown [1932–1939], place unknown
- Gela Seksztajn, Portrait of a boy.
- ***Description:*** original, crayon drawing, paper, 325×241 mm, ss. 1, pp. 2.
  Signature in blue indelible pencil in Yiddish (handwriting IL*) on the lower left side: "G. Seksztajn"; on the back is a postwar number in pencil: "113" and inscribed in red crayon: "ŻIH inw. 1304."

### A-947/35

- Date unknown [1932–1939], place unknown
- Gela Seksztajn, Portrait of a young girl.
- ***Description:*** original, charcoal drawing, paper, 326×242 mm, ss. 1, pp. 2.
  Signed in ink on the lower left side: "G. Seksztejn"; on the back a postwar number in pencil: "115."

### A-947/36

- Date unknown [1932–1939], place unknown
- Gela Seksztajn, Portrait of a crying girl.
- ***Description:*** original, crayon drawing, paper, 330×244 mm, ss. 1, pp. 2.
  On the back a postwar number in pencil: "116."

### A-947/37

- Date unknown [1932–1939], place unknown
- Gela Seksztajn, Portrait of a man.
- ***Description:*** original, charcoal drawing, paper, 325×241 mm, ss. 1, pp. 2.
  On the back is a postwar number in pencil: "117."

### A-947/38

- Date unknown [1932–1939], place unknown
- Gela Seksztajn, Portrait of a boy.
- ***Description:*** original, charcoal drawing, paper, 326×240 mm, ss. 1, pp. 2.
  On the back is a postwar number in pencil: "118."

### A-947/39

- Date unknown [1932–1939], place unknown
- Gela Seksztajn, Portrait of a seated woman.
- ***Description:*** original, charcoal drawing, paper, 330×244 mm, ss. 1, pp. 2.
  On the back is a postwar number in pencil: "119."

### A-947/40

- Date unknown [1932–1939], place unknown
- Gela Seksztajn, Portrait of a boy.
- ***Description:*** original, charcoal drawing, paper, 325×241 mm, ss. 1, pp. 1.

### A-947/41

- Date unknown [1932–1939], place unknown
- Gela Seksztajn, Study of a face.
- ***Description:*** original, charcoal drawing, paper, 326×242 mm, ss. 1, pp. 2.
  Signed in ink on the lower right side: "G. Seksztajn"; on the back is a postwar number in pencil: "122" and mirror-image of an inscription in Yiddish (handwriting IL*): "G. Seksztejn."

### A-947/42

- Date unknown [1932–1939], place unknown
- Gela Seksztajn, Portrait of a boy carrying a box.
- ***Description:*** original, crayon drawing, paper, 326×242 mm, ss. 1, pp. 2.
  On the back is a postwar number in pencil: "124."

### A-947/43

- Date unknown [1932–1939], place unknown
- Gela Seksztajn, Head of a little boy in a cap.
- ***Description:*** original, charcoal drawing, paper, 326×242 mm, ss. 1, pp. 2.
  Signed in ink at the lower middle: "G. Seksztejn"; on the back is a postwar number in pencil: "125."

### A-947/44

- Date unknown [1932–1939], place unknown
- Gela Seksztajn, Portrait of an old woman.
- ***Description:*** original, charcoal drawing, paper, 265×184 mm, ss. 1, pp. 2.
  On the back is a postwar number in pencil: "126."

A-947/45

- Date unknown [1932–1939], place unknown
- Gela Seksztajn, Portrait of a child.
- ***Description:*** original, charcoal drawing, paper, 324×241 mm, ss. 1, pp. 2.
  On the back is a postwar number in pencil: "127."

A-947/46

- Date unknown [1932–1939], place unknown
- Gela Seksztajn, Head of a child in profile.
- ***Description:*** original, crayon drawing, paper, 325×241 mm, ss. 1, pp. 2.
  Signature in Yiddish (handwriting IL*) in blue indelible pencil on the lower left side: "G. Seksztajn"; on the back is a postwar number in pencil: "128."

A-947/47

- Date unknown [1932–1939], place unknown
- Gela Seksztajn, Portrait of a boy.
- ***Description:*** original, crayon drawing, paper, 325×242 mm, ss. 1, pp. 2.
  Signature in Yiddish (handwriting IL*) with blue indelible pencil on the lower left side: "G. Seksztajn"; on the back is a postwar number in pencil: "129."

A-948/48

- Date unknown [1932–1939], place unknown
- Gela Seksztajn, Portrait of a boy.
- ***Description:*** original, crayon drawing, paper, 325×240 mm, ss. 1, pp. 2.
  On the back is a postwar number in pencil: "130" and an inscription in red crayon: "G. Seksztajn ŻIH inw. 1304."

A-947/49

- Date unknown [1932–1939], place unknown
- Gela Seksztajn, Portrait of a little boy.
- ***Description:*** original, crayon drawing, paper, 325×241 mm, ss. 1, pp. 2.
  Inscription in Yiddish (handwriting IL*) with blue indelible pencil on the lower left side: "G. Seksztajn"; on the back is a postwar number in pencil: "131."

A-947/50

- Date unknown [1932–1939], place unknown
- Gela Seksztajn, Portrait of a man.
- ***Description:*** original, charcoal drawing, paper, 356×256 mm, ss. 1, pp. 2.
  Inscription in Yiddish (handwriting IL*) with blue indelible pencil on the lower left side: "G. Seksztajn"; on the back is an inscription in blue indelible pencil in Yiddish: "Sz. Berliński" and "G. Seksztajn," besides a postwar number in pencil: "134."

A-947/51

- Date unknown [1932–1939], place unknown
- Gela Seksztajn, Portrait of a boy.
- ***Description:*** original, mixed media drawing with crayon and charcoal, paper, 240×207 mm, ss. 1, pp. 2.
  On the back is a postwar number in pencil: "133."

A-947/52

- Date unknown [1932–1939], place unknown
- Gela Seksztajn, Sketch of a girl's head in profile.
- ***Description:*** original, crayon drawing, paper, 324×240 mm, ss. 1, pp. 2.
  On the back is a postwar number in pencil: "81"; and an inscription in red crayon: "G. Seksztajn ŻIH inw. 1304."

A-948

- 1938, place unknown
- Gela Seksztajn, Portrait of a man.
- ***Description:*** original, charcoal drawing, paper, 463×311 mm, ss. 1, pp. 2.
  At bottom of right side signature: "G. Seksztajn 1938." On the reverse of the drawing inscription in Yiddish made twice: in blue indelible pencil and pencil: "Toff—Tof" [?].

A-949

- 1934 [?], place unknown
- Gela Seksztajn, Portrait of a man.
- ***Description:*** original, charcoal drawing, paper, 424×310 mm, ss. 1, pp. 2.
  At bottom of right side signature: "G. Seksztajn 34." On the reverse of the drawing inscription in blue indelible pencil in Yiddish: "Pomerants Hebrew author. G. Seksztajn."

A-950

- Date unknown [1932–1939], place unknown
- Gela Seksztajn, Portrait of a man.
- ***Description:*** original, charcoal drawing, paper, 326×243 mm, ss. 1, pp. 2.
  On the reverse signature in blue indelible pencil in Yiddish (handwriting IL*): "G. Seksztajn—N. Szternberg."

A-951

- Date unknown [1932–1939], place unknown
- Gela Seksztajn, Portrait of a man.
- ***Description:*** original, colored crayon drawing, paper, 326×243 mm, ss. 1, pp. 2.
  On the reverse signature in blue indelible pencil in Yiddish (handwriting IL*): "G. Seksztajn—M. Szulsztajn."

A-952

- 1938, place unknown
- Gela Seksztajn, Portrait of a man.
- ***Description:*** original, colored crayon drawing, paper, 327×243 mm, ss. 1, pp. 2.

On the reverse signature in blue indelible pencil in Yiddish (handwriting IL*): "G. Seksztajn—'Herszele'" as well as date in pencil: "1938."

**A-985/1**

- Date unknown [1932–1939], place unknown
- Gela Seksztajn, Young girl with bow.
- ***Description:*** original, pencil drawing, paper, 202×159 mm, sheet 1, pp. 2.
  On the back [a postwar] number in pencil: "139."

**A-985/2**

- Date unknown [1932–1939], place unknown
- Gela Seksztajn, Portrait of a young woman.
- ***Description:*** original, pencil drawing, Oxford paper [bibułka], 188×143 mm, sheet 1, pp. 2.
  On the back [a postwar] number in pencil: "140."

**A-985/3**

- Date unknown [1932–1939], place unknown
- Gela Seksztajn, Portrait of a man.
- ***Description:*** original, pencil drawing, tissue paper [bibułka], 190×140 mm, sheet 1, pp. 2.
  On the back written with a blue indelible pencil an inscription in Yiddish (handwriting IL*): "Goruelov" [?]] and signature: "G. Seksztajn"; also on the back is [a postwar] number in pencil: "141."

**A-985/4**

- Date unknown [1932–1939], place unknown
- Gela Seksztajn, Portrait of a man en face.
- ***Description:*** original, colored crayon drawing, Oxford paper [bibułka], 198×140 mm, sheet 1, pp. 2.
  On the back [a postwar] number in pencil: "142."

**A-985/5**

- Date unknown [1932–1939], place unknown
- Gela Seksztajn, Man in eyeglasses
- ***Description:*** original, colored crayon drawing, paper, 198×175 mm, sheet 1, pp. 2.
  Signed at the bottom of the left side in pencil: "Seksztajn"; on the back [a postwar] number in pencil: "143."

**A-985/6**

- Date unknown [1932–1939], place unknown
- Gela Seksztajn, Male portrait.
- ***Description:*** original, pencil drawing, paper, 189×145 mm, sheet 1, pp. 2.
  Signed at the bottom of the left side in pencil: "Seksztajn"; on the back [a postwar] number in pencil: "144."

**A-985/7**

- Date unknown [1932–1939], place unknown
- Gela Seksztajn, Horse in harness.
- ***Description:*** original, pencil drawing, paper, 198×161 mm, sheet 1, pp. 2.
  On the back [a postwar] number in pencil: "145."

**A-985/8**

- Date unknown [1932–1939], place unknown
- Gela Seksztajn, Female nude.
- ***Description:*** original, pencil drawing, paper, 190×138 mm, sheet 1, pp. 2.
  On the back [a postwar] number in pencil: "146."

**A-985/9**

- Date unknown [1932–1939], place unknown
- Gela Seksztajn, Little boy.
- ***Description:*** original, pencil drawing, paper, 180×133 mm, sheet 1, pp. 2.
  On the back [a postwar] number in pencil: "147."

**A-985/10**

- Date unknown [1932–1939], place unknown
- Gela Seksztajn, Girl with braids.
- ***Description:*** original, pencil drawing, paper, 179×149 mm, sheet 1, pp. 2.
  On the back [a postwar] number in pencil: "148."

**A-985/11**

- Date unknown [1932–1939], place unknown
- Gela Seksztajn, Portrait of a little girl.
- ***Description:*** original, colored crayon drawing, paper, 205×162 mm, sheet 1, pp. 2.
  On the back [a postwar] number in pencil: "149."

**A-985/12**

- Date unknown [1932–1939], place unknown
- Gela Seksztajn, Portrait of a young man.
- ***Description:*** original, pencil drawing, paper, 194×158 mm, sheet 1, pp. 2.
  On the back [a postwar] number in pencil: "150."

**A-985/13**

- Date unknown [1932–1939], place unknown
- Gela Seksztajn, Portrait of a young man.
- ***Description:*** original, pencil drawing, paper, 193×160 mm, sheet 1, pp. 2.
  On the back [a postwar] number in pencil: "151."

**A-985/14**

- Date unknown [1932–1939], place unknown
- Gela Seksztajn, Male portrait.
- ***Description:*** original, pencil drawing, paper, 194×145 mm, sheet 1, pp. 2.
  On the back two numbers in pencil: "20/16" and "152."

**A-985/15**

- Date unknown [1932–1939], place unknown
- Gela Seksztajn, Portrait of a man.
- ***Description:*** original, pencil drawing, paper, 195×162 mm, sheet 1, pp. 2.
  On the back in blue indelible pencil is an inscription in Yiddish: "Kelner fun literarishe ferayn 'Leon'" [Waiter at the Literary Society,

Leon] as well as the signature: "G. Seksztajn" [both inscriptions are in the handwriting of Izrael Lichtensztajn]; in addition, [a postwar] number in pencil: "153."

### A-985/16

- Date unknown [1932–1939], place unknown
- Gela Seksztajn, Portrait of a boy.
- ***Description:*** original, pencil drawing, paper, 183×149 mm, sheet 1, pp. 2.

On the back [a postwar] number in pencil: "154."

### A-985/17

- Date unknown [1932–1939], place unknown
- Gela Seksztajn, Portrait of a young woman.
- ***Description:*** original, pencil drawing, paper, 195×159 mm, sheet 1, pp. 2.

On the back [a postwar] number in pencil: "155."

### A-985/18

- Date unknown [1932–1939], place unknown
- Gela Seksztajn, Girl with braids.
- ***Description:*** original, pencil drawing, paper, 200×175 mm, sheet 1, pp. 2.

Signed at the bottom of the left side in pencil: "Seksztajn"; on the back [a postwar] number in pencil: "156."

### A-985/19

- Date unknown [1932–1939], place unknown
- Gela Seksztajn, Seated man.
- ***Description:*** original, pencil drawing, paper, 210×162 mm, sheet 1, pp. 2.

On the back [a postwar] number in pencil: "157."

### A-985/20

- Date unknown [1932–1939], place unknown
- Gela Seksztajn, Male nude.
- ***Description:*** original, pencil drawing, paper, 202×159 mm, sheet 1, pp. 2.

On the back [a postwar] number in pencil: "158."

### A-985/21

- Date unknown [1932–1939], place unknown
- Gela Seksztajn, Portrait of a man.
- ***Description:*** original, pencil drawing, paper, 200×162 mm, sheet 1, pp. 2.

Signed at the bottom of the left side in pencil: "Seksztajn"; on the back [a postwar] number in pencil: "159."

### A-985/22

- Date unknown [1932–1939], place unknown
- Gela Seksztajn, Man seated on a stool.
- ***Description:*** original, pencil drawing, paper, 201×154 mm, sheet 1, pp. 2.

On the back [a postwar] number in pencil: "160."

### A-985/23

- Date unknown [1932–1939], place unknown
- Gela Seksztajn, Male nude.
- ***Description:*** original, pencil drawing, paper, 208×160 mm, sheet 1, pp. 2.

On the back [a postwar] number in pencil: "161."

### A-985/24

- Date unknown [1932–1939], place unknown
- Gela Seksztajn, Portrait of a man.
- ***Description:*** original, colored crayon drawing, Oxford paper [bibułka], 192×145 mm, ss. 1, pp. 2.

On the back in blue indelible pencil is an inscription in Yiddish (handwriting IL*): "N. [Y]ankele Dantsigen" as well as the signature: "G. Seksztajn"; in addition, [a postwar] number in pencil: "162."

### A-985/25

- 1934, place unknown
- Gela Seksztajn, Portrait of a man.
- ***Description:*** original, colored crayon drawing, Oxford paper [bibułka], 190×145 mm, ss. 1, pp. 2.

At the bottom on the right side is the date, "1934"; on the back in blue indelible pencil is an inscription in Yiddish (handwriting IL*): "Michal Natish" as well as the signature: "G. Seksztajn"; on the back [a postwar] number in pencil: "163."

### A-985/26

- Date unknown [1932–1939], place unknown
- Gela Seksztajn, Portrait of a man in eyeglasses.
- ***Description:*** original, pencil drawing, paper, 197×171 mm, sheet 1, pp. 2.

At the bottom in the left corner signed in pencil: "Sekszt[ajn]"; on the back in blue indelible pencil an inscription in Yiddish (handwriting IL*): "Borukh Tshebutshini" [?] and signature: "G. Seksztajn"; moreover, also on the back, [a postwar] number in pencil: "164."

### A-985/27

- Date unknown [1932–1939], place unknown
- Gela Seksztajn, Portrait of a man in a hat.
- ***Description:*** original, pencil drawing, paper, 200×157 mm, ss. 1, pp. 2.

On the back in blue indelible pencil in Yiddish (handwriting IL*): "W. Godin" and signature "Seksztajn"; moreover, [a postwar] number in pencil: "165."

### A-985/28

- Date unknown [1932–1939], place unknown
- Gela Seksztajn, Head of a man.
- ***Description:*** original, pencil drawing, 140×101 mm, sheet 1, pp. 2.

On the reverse [a postwar] number in pencil: "166."

### A-985/29

- Date unknown [1932–1939], place unknown
- Gela Seksztajn, Portrait of a boy.
- ***Description:*** original, pencil drawing, paper, 140×101 mm, ss. 1, pp. 2.

  On the reverse [a postwar] number in pencil: "167."

### A-985/30

- Date unknown [1932–1939], place unknown
- Gela Seksztajn, Nude of an old man.
- ***Description:*** original, pencil drawing, paper, 190×145 mm, ss. 1, pp. 2.

  On the reverse [a postwar] number in pencil: "168."

### A-985/31

- Date unknown [1932–1939], place unknown
- Gela Seksztajn, Male nude.
- ***Description:*** original, pencil drawing, paper, 197×145 mm, ss. 1, pp. 2.

  On the reverse [a postwar] number in pencil: "169."

### A-985/32

- Date unknown [1932–1939], place unknown
- Gela Seksztajn, Male nude.
- ***Description:*** original, pencil drawing, paper, 194×140 mm, ss. 1, pp. 2.

  On the reverse [a postwar] number in pencil: "170."

### A-985/33

- Date unknown [1932–1939], place unknown
- Gela Seksztajn, Portrait of a woman.
- ***Description:*** original, pencil drawing, paper, 198×148 mm, ss. 1, pp. 2.

  On the reverse [a postwar] number in pencil: "171."

### A-985/34

- Date unknown [1932–1939], place unknown
- Gela Seksztajn, Man seated on a barrel.
- ***Description:*** original, pencil drawing, paper, 194×148 mm, ss. 1, pp. 2.

  On the reverse [a postwar] number in pencil: "172."

### A-985/35

- Date unknown [1932–1939], place unknown
- Gela Seksztajn, Female nude.
- ***Description:*** original, pencil drawing, paper, 211×162 mm, ss. 1, pp. 2.

  On the reverse [a postwar] number in pencil: "173."

### A-985/36

- Date unknown [1932–1939], place unknown
- Gela Seksztajn, Male nude.
- ***Description:*** original, pencil drawing, paper, 193×143 mm, ss. 1, pp. 2.

  On the reverse [a postwar] number in pencil: "174."

### A-985/37

- Date unknown [1932–1939], place unknown
- Gela Seksztajn, Female nude.
- ***Description:*** original, pencil drawing, paper, 192×146 mm, ss. 1, pp. 2

  On the reverse [a postwar] number in pencil: "175."

### A-985/38

- Date unknown [1932–1939], place unknown
- Gela Seksztajn, Seated figure.
- ***Description:*** original, pencil drawing, paper, 198×149 mm, ss. 1, pp. 2.

  On the reverse [a postwar] number in pencil: "176."

### A-985/39

- Date unknown [1932–1939], place unknown
- Gela Seksztajn, Female nude.
- ***Description:*** original, pencil drawing, paper, 197×140 mm, ss. 1, pp. 2.

  On the back [a postwar] number in pencil: "177."

### A-985/40

- Date unknown [1932–1939], place unknown
- Gela Seksztajn, Female nude.
- ***Description:*** original, pencil drawing, paper, 194×148 mm, ss. 1, pp. 2.

  On the reverse [a postwar] number in pencil: "178."

### A-985/41

- Date unknown [1932–1939], place unknown
- Gela Seksztajn, Male nude.
- ***Description:*** original, pencil drawing, paper, 212×166 mm, ss. 1, pp. 2.

  On the reverse [a postwar] number in pencil: "179."

### A-985/42

- Date unknown [1932–1939], place unknown
- Gela Seksztajn, Female nude.
- ***Description:*** original, pencil drawing, paper, 197×147, ss. 1, pp. 2.

  On the reverse [a postwar] number in pencil: "180."

### A-985/43

- Date unknown [1932–1939], place unknown
- Gela Seksztajn, Female nude.
- ***Description:*** original, pencil drawing, paper, 185×148 mm, ss. 1, pp. 2.

  On the reverse [a postwar] number in pencil: "181."

A-985/44

- Date unknown [1932–1939], place unknown
- Gela Seksztajn, Female nude.
- ***Description:*** original, pencil drawing, paper, 197×146 mm, ss. 1, pp. 2.
  On the reverse [a postwar] number in pencil: "182."

A-985/45

- Date unknown [1932–1939], place unknown
- Gela Seksztajn, Female nude.
- ***Description:*** original, pencil drawing, paper, 197×146 mm, ss. 1, pp. 2.
  On the reverse [a postwar] number in pencil: "183."

A-985/46

- Date unknown [1932–1939], place unknown
- Gela Seksztajn, Female nude.
- ***Description:*** original, pencil drawing, paper, 191×144 mm, ss. 1, pp. 2.
  On the reverse [a postwar] number in pencil: "184."

A-985/47

- Date unknown [1932–1939], place unknown
- Gela Seksztajn, Children.
- ***Description:*** original, pencil drawing, paper, 201×155 mm, ss. 1, pp. 2.
  On the reverse [a postwar] number in pencil: "185."

A-985/48

- Date unknown [1932–1939], place unknown
- Gela Seksztajn, Male nude.
- ***Description:*** original, pencil drawing, paper, 197×144 mm, ss. 1, pp. 2.
  On the reverse [a postwar] number in pencil: "186."

A-985/49

- Date unknown [1932–1939], place unknown
- Gela Seksztajn, Male nude.
- ***Description:*** original, pencil drawing, paper, 197×145 mm, ss. 1, pp. 2.
  On the reverse [a postwar] number in pencil: "187."

A-985/50

- Date unknown [1932–1939], place unknown
- Gela Seksztajn, Female nude.
- ***Description:*** original, pencil drawing, paper, 192×145 mm, ss. 1, pp. 2.
  On the reverse [a postwar] number in pencil: "188."

A-985/51

- Date unknown [1932–1939], place unknown
- Gela Seksztajn, Female nude.
- ***Description:*** original, pencil drawing, paper, 197×147 mm, ss. 1, pp. 2.
  On the reverse [a postwar] number in pencil: "189."

A-985/52A

- Date unknown [1932–1939], place unknown
- Gela Seksztajn, Female nude.
- ***Description:*** original, pencil drawing, paper, 188×144 mm, ss. 1, pp. 2.
  On the reverse [a postwar] number in pencil: "190."

A-985/52B

- Date unknown [1932–1939], place unknown
- Gela Seksztajn, Walking.
- ***Description:*** original, pencil drawing, paper, 153×142 mm, ss. 1, pp. 2.
  On the reverse is a fragment of an anonymous text in pencil: "Dear Sir, At the recommendation of Mr. Bielski [?], I turn to you with a request to kindly make available to me information in the matter of joining the group of artists organized by you, which I would like [. . .] to join"; also on the reverse of the sketch, [a postwar] number in pencil: "191."

A-985/53

- Date unknown [1932–1939], place unknown
- Gela Seksztajn, Dogs.
- ***Description:*** original, pencil drawing, paper, 149×160 mm, ss. 1, pp. 2.
  On the reverse [a postwar] number in pencil: "192."

A-985/54

- Date unknown [1932–1939], place unknown
- Gela Seksztajn, Female nude.
- ***Description:*** original, pencil drawing, paper, 180×146 mm, ss. 1, pp. 2.
  On the reverse [a postwar] number in pencil: "193."

A-985/55

- Date unknown [1932–1939], place unknown
- Gela Seksztajn, Man dressing.
- ***Description:*** original, pencil drawing, paper, 190×140 mm, ss. 1, pp. 2.
  On the reverse [a postwar] number in pencil: "194."

A-985/56

- Date unknown [1932–1939], place unknown
- Gela Seksztajn, Man standing with raised arms.
- ***Description:*** original, pencil drawing, paper, 192×138 mm, ss. 1, pp. 2.
  On the reverse [a postwar] number in pencil: "195."

### A-985/57

- Date unknown [1932–1939], place unknown
- Gela Seksztajn, Two standing women.
- ***Description:*** original, pencil drawing, paper, 188×147 mm, ss. 1, pp. 2.
  On the reverse [a postwar] number in pencil: "196."

### A-985/58

- Date unknown [1932–1939], place unknown
- Gela Seksztajn, Man with arm held up.
- ***Description:*** original, pencil drawing, paper, 190×144 mm, ss. 1, pp. 2.
  On the reverse [a postwar] number in pencil: "197"; the latter crosses out a previous number: "210."

### A-985/59

- Date unknown [1932–1939], place unknown
- Gela Seksztajn, Man leaning on a stick.
- ***Description:*** original, pencil drawing, paper, 190×145 mm, ss. 1, pp. 2.
  On the reverse [a postwar] number in pencil: "198."

### A-985/60

- Date unknown [1932–1939], place unknown
- Gela Seksztajn, Female nude.
- ***Description:*** original, quill pen drawing, India ink, paper, 180×148 mm, ss. 1, pp. 2.
  On the reverse [a postwar] number in pencil: "199."

### A-985/61

- Date unknown [1932–1939], place unknown
- Gela Seksztajn, Female nude.
- ***Description:*** original, pencil drawing, paper, 177×144 mm, ss. 1, pp. 2.
  On the reverse [a postwar] number in pencil: "200."

### A-985/62

- Date unknown [1932–1939], place unknown.
- Gela Seksztajn, Female nude.
- ***Description:*** original, quill pen drawing, paper, 180×146 mm, ss. 1, pp. 2.
  On the reverse [a postwar] number in pencil: "201."

### A-985/63

- Date unknown [1932–1939], place unknown
- Gela Seksztajn, Female nude.
- ***Description:*** original, pencil drawing, paper, 145×183 mm, ss. 1, pp. 2.
  On the reverse twice [a postwar] number in pencil: "203."[63]

### A-985/64

- Date unknown [1932–1939], place unknown
- Gela Seksztajn, Seated female nude.
- ***Description:*** original, pencil drawing, paper, 182×143 mm, ss. 1, pp. 2.
  On the reverse [a postwar] number in pencil: "204."

### A-985/65

- Date unknown [1932–1939], place unknown
- Gela Seksztajn, Female nude.
- ***Description:*** original, pencil drawing, paper, 144×175 mm, ss. 1, pp. 2.
  On the reverse [a postwar] number in pencil: "205."

### A-985/66

- Date unknown [1932–1939], place unknown
- Gela Seksztajn, Female nude.
- ***Description:*** original, quill pen drawing, paper, 180×143 mm, ss. 1, pp. 2.
  On the reverse [a postwar] number in pencil: "206."

### A-985/67

- Date unknown [1932–1939], place unknown
- Gela Seksztajn, Female nude.
- ***Description:*** original, pencil drawing, paper, 149×183 mm, ss. 1, pp. 2.
  On the reverse twice [a postwar] number in pencil: "207."

### A-985/68

- Date unknown [1932–1939], place unknown
- Gela Seksztajn, Portrait of a young girl.
- ***Description:*** original, colored crayon drawing, paper, 141×100 mm, ss. 1, pp. 2.
  On the reverse [a postwar] number in pencil: "208."

### A-985/69

- Date unknown [1932–1939], place unknown
- Gela Seksztajn, Portrait of a young man.
- ***Description:*** original, colored crayon drawing, paper, 141×100 mm, ss. 1, pp. 2.
  On the reverse [a postwar] number in pencil: "209."

### A-985/70

- Date unknown [1932–1939], place unknown
- Gela Seksztajn, Male portrait.

63. There is no item numbered "202."

- *Description:* original, colored crayon drawing, Oxford paper [bibułka], 128×102 mm, ss. 1, pp. 2.
  On the back in blue indelible pencil in Yiddish (handwriting IL*): "umr gener" [?] as well as signature: "G. Seksztajn"; also on the reverse, [a postwar] number in pencil: "210."

**A-985/71**

- Date unknown [1932–1939], place unknown
- Gela Seksztajn, Portrait of a boy.
- *Description:* original, colored crayon drawing, paper, 138×100 mm, ss. 1, pp. 2
  On the reverse [a postwar] number in pencil: "211."

**A-985/72**

- Date unknown [1932–1939], place unknown
- Gela Seksztajn, Portrait of a girl.
- *Description:* original, colored crayon drawing, paper, 141×100 mm, ss. 1, pp. 2.
  On the reverse [a postwar] number in pencil: "212."

**A-985/73**

- Date unknown [1932–1939], place unknown
- Gela Seksztajn, Portrait of a young girl.
- *Description:* original, colored crayon drawing, paper, 139×100 mm, ss. 1, pp. 2.
  On the reverse [a postwar] number in pencil: "213."

**A-985/74**

- Date unknown [1932–1936], place unknown
- Gela Seksztajn, Portrait of a young woman.
- *Description:* original, colored crayon drawing, paper, 139×100 mm, ss. 1, pp. 2.
  On the reverse [a postwar] number in pencil: "214."

**A-985/75**

- Date unknown [1932–1939], place unknown
- Gela Seksztajn, Male portrait.
- *Description:* original, colored crayon drawing, paper, 153×121 mm, ss. 1, pp. 2.
  On the reverse [a postwar] number in pencil: "215."

**A-985/76**

- Date unknown [1932–1939], place unknown
- Gela Seksztajn, Portrait.
- *Description:* original, pencil drawing, paper, 233×141 mm, ss. 1, pp. 2.
  On the reverse [a postwar] number in pencil: "216."

**A-985/77**

- Date unknown [1932–1939], place unknown
- Gela Seksztajn, Standing man.
- *Description:* original, pencil drawing, paper, 197×148 mm, ss. 1, pp. 2.
  On the reverse [a postwar] number in pencil: "217."

**A-985/78**

- Date unknown [1932–1939], place unknown
- Gela Seksztajn, Female nude.
- *Description:* original, pencil drawing, paper, 204×144 mm, ss. 1, pp. 2
  On the reverse [a postwar] number in pencil: "218."

**A-985/79**

- Date unknown [1932–1939], place unknown
- Gela Seksztajn, Female nude.
- *Description:* original, pencil drawing, paper, 152×204 mm, ss. 1, pp. 2.
  On the reverse [a postwar] number in pencil: "219."

**A-985/80**

- Date unknown [1932–1939], place unknown
- Gela Seksztajn, Man seated on a bench.
- *Description:* original, pencil drawing, paper, 196×150 mm, ss. 1, pp. 2.
  On the reverse [a postwar] number in pencil: "220."

**A-985/81**

- Date unknown [1932–1939], place unknown
- Gela Seksztajn, Seated women.
- *Description:* original, pencil drawing, paper, 197×152 mm, ss. 1, pp. 2.
  On the reverse [a postwar] number in pencil: "221."

**A-985/82**

- Date unknown [1932–1939], place unknown
- Gela Seksztajn, Female nude.
- *Description:* original, pencil drawing, paper, 188×142 mm, ss. 1, pp. 2.
  On the reverse [a postwar] number in pencil: "222."

**A-985/83**

- Date unknown [1932–1939], place unknown
- Gela Seksztajn, Female nude.
- *Description:* original, pencil drawing, paper, 195×144 mm, ss. 1, pp. 2.
  On the reverse [a postwar] number in pencil: "223."

**A-985/84**

- Date unknown [1932–1939], place unknown
- Gela Seksztajn, Female nude.
- *Description:* original, pencil drawing, paper, 194×144 mm, ss. 1, pp. 2.
  On the reverse [a postwar] number in pencil: "224."

### A-985/85

- Date unknown [1932–1939], place unknown
- Gela Seksztajn, Female nude.
- ***Description:*** original, pencil drawing, paper, 185×135 mm, ss. 1, pp. 2.
  On the reverse [a postwar] number in pencil: "225."

### A-985/86

- Date unknown [1932–1939], place unknown
- Gela Seksztajn, Two dogs.
- ***Description:*** original, pencil drawing, paper, 140×190 mm, ss. 1, pp. 2.
  On the reverse [a postwar] number in pencil: "226."

### A-985/87

- Date unknown [1932–1939], place unknown
- Gela Seksztajn, Portrait of a woman.
- ***Description:*** original, pencil drawing, paper, 174×144 mm, ss. 1, pp. 2.
  On the reverse [a postwar] number in pencil: "227."

### A-985/88

- Date unknown [1932–1939], place unknown
- Gela Seksztajn, Dogs.
- ***Description:*** original, colored crayon drawing, paper, 148×185 mm, ss. 1, pp. 2.
  On the reverse [a postwar] number in pencil: "228."

### A-985/89

- Date unknown [1932–1939], place unknown
- Gela Seksztajn, Man dressing.
- ***Description:*** original, colored crayon drawing, paper, 197×144 mm, ss. 1, pp. 2.
  On the reverse [a postwar] number in pencil: "229."

### A-985/90

- Date unknown [1932–1939], place unknown
- Gela Seksztajn, Man putting on an overcoat.
- ***Description:*** original, pencil drawing, paper, 197×150 mm, ss. 1, pp. 2.
  On the reverse [a postwar] number in pencil: "230."

### A-985/91

- Date unknown [1932–1939], place unknown
- Gela Seksztajn, Male nude.
- ***Description:*** original, pencil drawing, paper, 161×203 mm, ss. 1, pp. 2.
  On the reverse [a postwar] number in pencil: "231."

### A-985/92

- Date unknown [1932–1939], place unknown
- Gela Seksztajn, A dog.
- ***Description:*** original, pencil drawing, paper, 155×196 mm, ss. 1, pp. 2.
  On the reverse [a postwar] number in pencil: "232."

### A-985/93

- Date unknown [1932–1939], place unknown
- Gela Seksztajn, In the park on a bench.
- ***Description:*** original, pencil drawing, paper, 204×156 mm, ss. 1, pp. 2.
  On the reverse [a postwar] number in pencil: "233."

### A-985/94

- Date unknown [1932–1939], place unknown
- Gela Seksztajn, A dog.
- ***Description:*** original, pencil drawing, paper, 150×196 mm, ss. 1, pp. 2.
  On the reverse [a postwar] number in pencil: "234."

### A-985/95

- Date unknown [1932–1939], place unknown
- Gela Seksztajn, Portrait of a boy.
- ***Description:*** original, pencil drawing, paper, 183×153 mm, ss. 1, pp. 2.
  On the reverse [a postwar] number in pencil: "236 a."

### A-985/96

- Date unknown [1932–1939], place unknown
- Gela Seksztajn, Female nude.
- ***Description:*** original, quill pen drawing, paper, 180×153 mm, ss. 1, pp. 2.
  On the reverse [a postwar] number in pencil: "236."

### A-985/97

- Date unknown [1932–1939], place unknown
- Gela Seksztajn, Portrait of an old man.
- ***Description:*** original, colored crayon drawing, paper, 208×155 mm, ss. 1, pp. 2.
  On the reverse [a postwar] number in pencil: "237."

### A-985/98

- Date unknown [1932–1939], place unknown
- Gela Seksztajn, Seated female nude.
- ***Description:*** original, pencil drawing, paper, 196×150 mm, ss. 1, pp. 2.
  On the reverse [a postwar] number in pencil: "238."

### A-985/99

- Date unknown [1932–1939], place unknown
- Gela Seksztajn, Male nude.
- ***Description:*** original, pencil drawing, paper, 210×149 mm, ss. 1, pp. 2.
  On the reverse [a postwar] number in pencil: "239."

### A-985/100

- Date unknown [1932–1939], place unknown
- Gela Seksztajn, Male nude.
- ***Description:*** original, pencil drawing, paper, 204×155 mm, ss. 1, pp. 2.
  On the reverse [a postwar] number in pencil: "240."

### A-985/101

- Date unknown [1932–1939], place unknown
- Gela Seksztajn, Male nude.
- ***Description:*** original, pencil drawing, paper, 196×147 mm, ss. 1, pp. 2.
  On the reverse [a postwar] number in pencil: "241."

### A-985/102

- Date unknown [1932–1939], place unknown
- Gela Seksztajn, Male nude.
- ***Description:*** original, pencil drawing, paper, 208×153 mm, ss. 1, pp. 2.
  On the reverse [a postwar] number in pencil: "242."

### A-985/103

- Date unknown [1932–1939], place unknown
- Gela Seksztajn, Nude old man.
- ***Description:*** original, colored crayon drawing, paper, 208×153 mm, ss. 1, pp. 2.
  On the reverse [a postwar] number in pencil: "243."

### A-985/104

- Date unknown [1932–1939], place unknown
- Gela Seksztajn, Nude old man.
- ***Description:*** original, colored crayon drawing, paper, 209×157 mm, ss. 1, pp. 2.
  On the reverse [a postwar] number in pencil: "244."

### A-985/105

- Date unknown [1932–1939], place unknown
- Gela Seksztajn, Male nude.
- ***Description:*** original, colored crayon drawing, paper, 207×156 mm, ss. 1, pp. 2.
  On the reverse [a postwar] number in pencil: "245."

### A-985/106

- Date unknown [1932–1939], place unknown
- Gela Seksztajn, Portrait of a woman.
- ***Description:*** original, pencil drawing, paper, 204×159 mm, ss. 1, pp. 2.
  On the reverse [a postwar] number in pencil: "246."

### A-985/107

- Date unknown [1932–1939], place unknown
- Gela Seksztajn, Female portrait.
- ***Description:*** original pencil drawing, paper, 197×150 mm, ss. 1, pp. 2.
  On the reverse [a postwar] number in pencil: "247."

### A-985/108

- Date unknown [1932–1939], place unknown
- Gela Seksztajn, A hen.
- ***Description:*** original, pencil drawing, paper, 197×146 mm, ss. 1, pp. 2.
  On the reverse [a postwar] number in pencil: "248."

### A-985/109

- Date unknown [1932–1939], place unknown
- Gela Seksztajn, Male portrait.
- ***Description:*** original, pencil drawing, paper, 196×147 mm, ss. 1, pp. 2.
  On the reverse [a postwar] number in pencil: "249."

### A-985/110

- Date unknown [1932–1939], place unknown
- Gela Seksztajn, Woman in a hat.
- ***Description:*** original, pencil drawing, paper, 196×149 mm, ss. 1, pp. 2.
  On the reverse [a postwar] number in pencil: "250."

### A-985/111

- Date unknown [1932–1939], place unknown
- Gela Seksztajn, Portrait of a child.
- ***Description:*** original, pencil drawing, paper, 195×153 mm, ss. 1, pp. 2.
  On the reverse [a postwar] number in pencil: "251."

### A-985/112

- Date unknown [1932–1939], place unknown
- Gela Seksztajn, Man seated on a bench.
- ***Description:*** original, pencil drawing, paper, 196×150 mm, ss. 1, pp. 2.
  On the reverse [a postwar] number in pencil: "252."

### A-985/113

- Date unknown [1932–1939], place unknown
- Gela Seksztajn, Portrait of a woman in a hat.
- ***Description:*** original, pencil drawing, paper, 198×142 mm, ss. 1, pp. 2.
  On the reverse [a postwar] number in pencil: "253."

### A-985/114

- Date unknown [1932–1939], place unknown
- Gela Seksztajn, Portrait of a man in profile.
- ***Description:*** original, pencil drawing, paper, 197×143 mm, ss. 1, pp. 2.

On the reverse [a postwar] number in pencil: "254."

A-985/115

- Date unknown [1932–1939], place unknown
- Gela Seksztajn, Rooster.
- ***Description:*** original, pencil drawing, paper, 197×147 mm, ss. 1, pp. 2.
  On the reverse [a postwar] number in pencil: "255."

A-985/116

- Date unknown [1932–1939], place unknown
- Gela Seksztajn, Female nude.
- ***Description:*** original, pencil drawing, paper, 207×160 mm, ss. 1, pp. 2.
  On the reverse crossed out [postwar] number in pencil: "207," and number inserted in pencil: "256."

A-985/117

- Date unknown [1932–1939], place unknown
- Gela Seksztajn, Female nude with jug.
- ***Description:*** original, pencil drawing, paper, 196×148 mm, ss. 1, pp. 2.
  On the reverse [a postwar] number in pencil: "257."

A-985/118

- Date unknown [1932–1939], place unknown
- Gela Seksztajn, Study of a lying figure.
- ***Description:*** original, pencil drawing, paper, 159×209 mm, ss. 1, pp. 2.
  On the reverse [a postwar] number in pencil: "258."

A-985/119

- Date unknown [1932–1939], place unknown
- Gela Seksztajn, Portrait of a little girl.
- ***Description:*** original, pencil drawing, paper, 196×156 mm, ss. 1, pp. 2.
  On the reverse [a postwar] number in pencil: "259."

A-985/120

- Date unknown [1932–1939], place unknown
- Gela Seksztajn, Portrait of a boy.
- ***Description:*** original, pencil drawing, paper, 195×155 mm, ss. 1, pp. 2.
  On the reverse [a postwar] number in pencil: "260."

A-985/121

- Date unknown [1932–1939], place unknown
- Gela Seksztajn, Female nude.
- ***Description:*** original, pencil drawing, paper, 145×160 mm, ss. 1, pp. 2.
  On the reverse [a postwar] number in pencil: "261."

A-985/122

- Date unknown [1932–1939], place unknown
- Gela Seksztajn, Man in hat seated on a bench.
- ***Description:*** original, pencil drawing, paper, 195×149 mm, ss. 1, pp. 2.
  On the reverse [a postwar] number in pencil: "262."

A-985/123

- Date unknown [1932–1939], place unknown
- Gela Seksztajn, Portrait of a young girl.
- ***Description:*** original, pencil drawing, paper, 195×154 mm, ss. 1, pp. 2.
  On the reverse [a postwar] number in pencil: "263."

A-985/124

- Date unknown [1932–1939], place unknown
- Gela Seksztajn, Portrait of a woman.
- ***Description:*** original, pencil drawing, paper, 194×152 mm, ss. 1, pp. 2.
  On the reverse [a postwar] number in pencil: "264."

A-985/125

- Date unknown [1932–1939], place unknown
- Gela Seksztajn, Male portrait in profile.
- ***Description:*** original, pencil drawing, paper, 195×156 mm, ss. 1, pp. 2.
  On the reverse [a postwar] number in pencil: "265."

A-985/126

- Date unknown [1932–1939], place unknown
- Gela Seksztajn, Study of a female head and seated man.
- ***Description:*** original, pencil drawing, gray wrapping paper, 220×158 mm, ss. 1, pp. 2.
  On the reverse [a postwar] number in pencil: "266."

A-985/127

- Date unknown [1932–1939], place unknown
- Gela Seksztajn, Woman in kerchief with bundle.
- ***Description:*** original, pencil drawing, gray wrapping paper, 192×143 mm, ss. 1, pp. 2.
  At the bottom on the left side signature [of the author] in ink: "Seksztajn"; on the reverse [a postwar] number in pencil: "267."

A-985/128

- Date unknown [1932–1939], place unknown
- Gela Seksztajn, Portrait of a woman in a beret.
- ***Description:*** original, pencil drawing, paper, 195×157 mm, ss. 1, pp. 2.
  On the reverse [a postwar] number in pencil: "268."

**A-985/129**

- Date unknown [1932–1939], place unknown
- Gela Seksztajn, Portrait of a child.
- ***Description:*** original, pencil drawing, paper, 195×156 mm, ss. 1, pp. 2.
  On the reverse [a postwar] number in pencil: "269."

**A-985/130**

- Date unknown [1932–1939], place unknown
- Gela Seksztajn, At the market.
- ***Description:*** original, pencil drawing, paper, 171×152 mm, ss. 1, pp. 2.
  In the upper right corner signed in pencil: "Sekszt[ajn]"; on the reverse [a postwar] number in pencil: "270."

**A-985/131**

- Date unknown [1932–1939], place unknown
- Gela Seksztajn, Two males sitting on a bench.
- ***Description:*** original, pencil drawing, paper, 159×185 mm, ss. 1, pp. 2.
  On the reverse [a postwar] number in pencil: "271."

**A-985/132**

- Date unknown [1932–1939], place unknown.
- Gela Seksztajn, Portrait of a girl with a bow.
- ***Description:*** original, charcoal drawing, gray wrapping paper, 204×158 mm, ss. 1, pp. 2.
  On the reverse [a postwar] number in pencil: "272."

**A-985/133**

- Date unknown [1932–1939], place unknown
- Gela Seksztajn, A sleeper.
- ***Description:*** original, pencil drawing, paper, 199×164 mm, ss. 1, pp. 2.
  On the reverse [a postwar] number in pencil: "273."

**A-985/134**

- Date unknown [1932–1939], place unknown.
- Gela Seksztajn, At a market stall.
- ***Description:*** original, pencil drawing, gray wrapping paper, 225×168 mm, ss. 1, pp. 2.
  At the bottom left side signed in ink: "G. Seksztajn"; on the reverse [a postwar] number in pencil: "274."

**A-985/135**

- Date unknown [1932–1939], place unknown
- Gela Seksztajn, At the market.
- ***Description:*** original, pencil drawing, paper, 166×153 mm, ss. 1, pp. 2.
  On the reverse [a postwar] number in pencil: "275."

**A-985/136**

- Date unknown [1932–1939], place unknown
- Gela Seksztajn, Portrait of a little girl.
- ***Description:*** original, charcoal drawing, paper, 207×159 mm, ss. 1, pp. 2.
  On the reverse [a postwar] number in pencil: "276."

**A-985/137**

- Date unknown [1932–1939], place unknown
- Gela Seksztajn, Portrait of a man.
- ***Description:*** original, colored crayon drawing, Oxford paper [bibułka], 200×145 mm, ss. 1, pp. 2.
  On the reverse [a postwar] number in pencil: "277."

**A-985/138**

- Date unknown [1932–1939], place unknown
- Gela Seksztajn, Male portrait en face.
- ***Description:*** original, colored crayon drawing, Oxford paper [bibułka], 191×155 mm, ss. 1, pp. 2.
  On the reverse twice [a postwar] number in pencil: "278."

**A-985/139**

- Date unknown [1932–1939], place unknown
- Gela Seksztajn, Portrait of a man.
- ***Description:*** original, colored crayon drawing, paper, 195×156 mm, ss. 1, pp. 2.
  On the reverse [a postwar] number in pencil: "279."

**A-985/140**

- Date unknown [1932–1939], place unknown
- Gela Seksztajn, Portrait of a young woman.
- ***Description:*** original, colored crayon drawing, paper, 327×243 mm, ss. 1, pp. 2.
  On the reverse [a postwar] number in pencil: "280."

**A-985/141**

- Date unknown [1932–1939], place unknown
- Gela Seksztajn, Portrait of a man.
- ***Description:*** original, pencil drawing, Oxford paper [bibułka], 199×149 mm, ss. 1, pp. 2.
  On the back in blue indelible pencil in Yiddish (handwriting IL*): "Pomerants" and "G. Seksztajn" as well as [a postwar] number in pencil: "281."

**A-985/142**

- Date unknown [1932–1939], place unknown
- Gela Seksztajn, Portrait of a man with a short mustache.
- ***Description:*** original, pencil drawing, paper, 162×132 mm, ss. 1, pp. 2.

On the back of the drawing, in blue indelible pencil, an inscription in Yiddish (handwriting IL*): "Shneur"; and signature: "G. Seksztajn" as well as [a postwar] number in pencil: "282."

### A-985/143

- Date unknown [1932–1939], place unknown
- Gela Seksztajn, Female portrait.
- ***Description:*** original, watercolor, paper, 195×154 mm, ss. 1, pp. 2.

On the back in blue indelible pencil in Yiddish (handwriting IL*): "first watercolor" and: "G. Seksztajn"; on the reverse [a postwar] number in pencil: "283."

### A-985/144

- Date unknown [1932–1939], place unknown
- Gela Seksztajn, Portrait of a man.
- ***Description:*** original, charcoal drawing, paper, 201×166 mm, ss. 1, pp. 2.

On the back in blue indelible pencil in Yiddish (handwriting IL*): "Efroim Kaganowski" and "G. Seksztajn" as well as [a postwar] number in pencil: "284."

### A-985/145

- Date unknown [1932–1939], place unknown
- Gela Seksztajn, At the easels.
- ***Description:*** original, pencil drawing, paper, 225×164 mm, ss. 1, pp. 2.

At the bottom of the left side signed in pencil: "Seksztajn"; on the reverse [a postwar] number in pencil: "285."

### A-985/146

- Date unknown [1932–1939], place unknown
- Gela Seksztajn, Portrait of a little girl.
- ***Description:*** original, pencil drawing, 199×167 mm, ss. 1, pp. 2.

At the bottom of the left side signed in ink: "Seksztajn"; on the reverse [a postwar] number in pencil: "286."

### A-985/147

- Date unknown [1932–1939], place unknown
- Gela Seksztajn, Woman working in a field.
- ***Description:*** original, pencil drawing, paper, 224×162 mm, ss. 1, pp. 2.

In the lower-left corner signed in ink: "G. Seksztajn"; on the reverse [a postwar] number in pencil: "287."

### A-985/148

- Date unknown [1932–1939], place unknown
- Gela Seksztajn, Portrait of a young woman.
- ***Description:*** original, pencil drawing, paper, 195×157 mm, ss. 1, pp. 2.

On the reverse [a postwar] number in pencil: "288."

### A-985/149

- Date unknown [1932–1939], place unknown
- Gela Seksztajn, Friends.
- ***Description:*** original, charcoal drawing, paper, 164×220 mm, ss. 1, pp. 2.

On the reverse [a postwar] number in pencil: "289."

### A-985/150

- Date unknown [1932–1939], place unknown
- Gela Seksztajn, Nude with a chair.
- ***Description:*** original, colored crayon drawing, paper, 196×147 mm, ss. 1, pp. 2.

On the reverse [a postwar] number in pencil: "290."

### A-985/151

- Date unknown [1932–1939], place unknown
- Gela Seksztajn, Old man.
- ***Description:*** original, colored crayon drawing, gray paper, 226×167 mm, ss. 1, pp. 2.

On the reverse [a postwar] number in pencil: "291."

### A-985/152

- Date unknown [1932–1939], place unknown
- Gela Seksztajn, Male portrait in profile.
- ***Description:*** original, colored crayon drawing, paper, 199×172 mm, ss. 1, pp. 2.

On the reverse [a postwar] number in pencil: "292."

### A-985/153

- Date unknown [1932–1939], place unknown
- Gela Seksztajn, Girls sitting on a bench—study.
- ***Description:*** original, pencil drawing, paper, 204×162 mm, ss. 1, pp. 2.

On the reverse [a postwar] number in pencil: "293."

### A-985/154

- Date unknown [1932–1939], place unknown
- Gela Seksztajn, Child lying in a baby carriage.
- ***Description:*** original, colored crayon drawing, paper, 158×199 mm, ss. 1, pp. 2.

On the reverse [a postwar] number in pencil: "294."

### A-985/155

- Date unknown [1932–1939], place unknown
- Gela Seksztajn, Standing nude.
- ***Description:*** original, pencil drawing, paper, 196×151 mm, ss. 1, pp. 2.

On the reverse [a postwar] number in pencil: "295."

### A-985/156

- Date unknown [1932–1939], place unknown

- Gela Seksztajn, Female nude.
- ***Description:*** original, pencil drawing, paper, 196×149 mm, ss. 1, pp. 2.
  On the reverse [a postwar] number in pencil: "296."

### A-985/157

- Date unknown [1932–1939], place unknown
- Gela Seksztajn, Portrait of a man in a hat.
- ***Description:*** original, pencil drawing, paper, 200×174 mm, ss. 1, pp. 2.
  On the reverse [a postwar] number in pencil: "297."

### A-985/158

- Date unknown [1932–1939], place unknown
- Gela Seksztajn, Study of the palm of a hand.
- ***Description:*** original, pencil drawing, paper, 145×195 mm, ss. 1, pp. 2.
  On the reverse [a postwar] number in pencil: "298."

### A-985/159

- Date unknown [1932–1939], place unknown
- Gela Seksztajn, Portrait of a man en face.
- ***Description:*** original, colored crayon drawing, paper, 199×174 mm, ss. 1, pp. 2.
  On the reverse [a postwar] number in pencil: "299."

### A-985/160

- Date unknown [1932–1939], place unknown
- Gela Seksztajn, Male nude.
- ***Description:*** original, pencil drawing, paper, 214×165 mm, ss. 1, pp. 2.
  On the reverse number crossed out with pencil: "21/18" and inscribed: "300."

### A-985/161

- Date unknown [1932–1939], place unknown
- Gela Seksztajn, Portrait of a man.
- ***Description:*** original, pencil drawing, paper, 195×154 mm, ss. 1, pp. 2.
  On the reverse [a postwar] number in pencil: "301."

### A-985/162

- Date unknown [1932–1939], place unknown
- Gela Seksztajn, Male nude
- ***Description:*** original, pencil drawing, paper, 196×128 mm, ss. 1, pp. 2.
  On the reverse [a postwar] number in pencil: "302."

### A-985/163

- Date unknown [1932–1939], place unknown
- Gela Seksztajn, Portrait of a young girl.
- ***Description:*** original, colored crayon drawing, paper, 195×150 mm, ss. 1, pp. 2.
  On the reverse [a postwar] number in pencil: "303."

### A-985/164

- Date unknown [1932–1939], place unknown
- Gela Seksztajn, Child.
- ***Description:*** original, colored crayon drawing, Oxford paper [bibułka], 196×143 mm, ss. 1, pp. 2.
  On the reverse [a postwar] number in pencil: "304."

### A-985/165

- Date unknown [1932–1939], place unknown
- Gela Seksztajn, Rumors—a study.
- ***Description:*** original, pencil drawing, paper, 203×160 mm, ss. 1, pp. 2.
  On the reverse [a postwar] number in pencil: "305."

### A-985/166

- 1934, place unknown
- Gela Seksztajn, Portrait of a man with a short mustache.
- ***Description:*** original, colored crayon drawing, paper, 202×161 mm, ss. 1, pp. 2.
  At the bottom of the drawing on the right side a number in pencil: "34" [signed by the artist]; on the reverse [a postwar] number in pencil: "306."

### A-985/167

- Date unknown [1932–1939], place unknown
- Gela Seksztajn, Male nude.
- ***Description:*** original, pencil drawing, paper, 216×169 mm, ss. 1, pp. 2.
  On the reverse [a postwar] number in pencil: "307."

### A-985/168

- Date unknown [1932–1939], place unknown
- Gela Seksztajn, Portrait of a man in eyeglasses.
- ***Description:*** original, colored crayon drawing, paper, 199×172 mm, ss. 1, pp. 2.
  On the reverse [a postwar] number in pencil: "308."

### A-985/169

- Date unknown [1932–1939], place unknown
- Gela Seksztajn, Portrait of a child.
- ***Description:*** original, colored crayon drawing, paper, 200×171 mm, ss. 1, pp. 2.
  On the reverse [a postwar] number in pencil: "309."

### A-985/170

- Date unknown [1932–1939], place unknown
- Gela Seksztajn, Portrait of a man en face.
- ***Description:*** original, pencil drawing, paper, 195×158 mm, ss. 1, pp. 2.

On the reverse [a postwar] number in pencil: "310."

A-985/171

- Date unknown [1932–1939], place unknown
- Gela Seksztajn, Man sitting on a bench—a study.
- ***Description:*** original, pencil drawing, paper, 151×190 mm, ss. 1, pp. 2.
  On the reverse a crossed-out [postwar] number in pencil: "209" and entered in ink: "311."

A-985/172

- Date unknown [1932–1939], place unknown
- Gela Seksztajn, Portrait of a young boy.
- ***Description:*** original, colored crayon drawing, paper, 195×143 mm, ss. 1, pp. 2.
  On the reverse [a postwar] number in pencil: "312."

A-985/173

- Date unknown [1932–1939], place unknown
- Gela Seksztajn, Male nude.
- ***Description:*** original, pencil drawing, paper, 206×166 mm, ss. 1, pp. 2.
  On the reverse [a postwar] number in pencil: "313."

A-985/174

- Date unknown [1932–1939], place unknown
- Gela Seksztajn, Female nude.
- ***Description:*** original, colored crayon drawing, paper, 197×149 mm, ss. 1, pp. 2.
  On the reverse [a postwar] number in pencil: "314."

A-985/175

- Date unknown [1932–1939], place unknown
- Gela Seksztajn, Portrait of a girl in a beret.
- ***Description:*** original, colored crayon drawing, paper, 200×170 mm, ss. 1, pp. 2.
  On the reverse [a postwar] number in pencil: "315."

A-985/176

- Date unknown [1932–1939], place unknown
- Gela Seksztajn, Portrait of a man en face.
- ***Description:*** original, colored crayon drawing, paper, 200×170 mm, ss. 1, pp. 1.

A-985/177

- Date unknown [1932–1939], place unknown
- Gela Seksztajn, Portrait of a girl.
- ***Description:*** original, pencil drawing, paper, 195×153 mm, ss. 1, pp. 2.
  On the reverse a number in pencil: "20/16."

A-1391 A, B

- Date unknown [1932–1939], place unknown
- Gela Seksztajn, Flowers in a vase.
- ***Description:*** original, watercolor, karton, 730×510 mm, ss. 1, pp. 2.
  On the reverse an unfinished watercolor (date unknown, place unknown): Gela Seksztajn, Akt kobiecy tyłem [Female nude from the back].

## *MATERIALS OF EMANUEL RINGELBLUM*

1458. RING. I/777/8. (1099). Mf. ŻIH—825; USHMM—37

- 01.1942, Warsaw Ghetto
- Kibuc Szomrowy [Ha-Shomer Kibbutz] (ul. Nowolipki 23), Invitation for Dr. E. Ringelblum for meal of tsholnt on 17.01.1942
- ***Description:*** original, printed, handwritten manuscript, ink, Hebrew, Yiddish, 106×84 mm, ss. 2, pp. 2.
  Originally printed date 10.01.1942, manually corrected to 17.01.1942.

1459. RING. I/657/1. Mf. ŻIH—816; USHMM—28

- Before 1.04.1942, Warsaw Ghetto
- Orphans Home (ul. Śliska 9, formerly at Krochmalna 92). Janusz Korczak, director, Invitation for Emanuel Ringelblum (ul. Leszno 18) to the [Passover] seder celebration on 1.04.[1942]
- ***Description:*** original, printed, typescript, Polish, 145×99 mm, ss. 1, pp. 2.
  Signature (ink) of Janusz Korczak; invitation addressed to: "Dir. Ringienblum [sic] and Wife, Leszno 18."
  Published: *Dzieci*, pp. 291–292.

1460. RING. I/673. Mf. ŻIH—816; USHMM—28

- 8.06.1941, Warsaw Ghetto
- Frieda Katz (Warsaw Ghetto), Letter of 8.06.1941 to NN. [Judyta Ringelblum?]
- Thanks for help and request for further assistance.
- ***Description:*** original, perforated document, Polish, 224×175 mm, ss. 3, pp. 3.
  Inventory: "Letter to [Judyta] Ringelblum, wife of E.R."

## *MATERIALS OF HERSZ WASSER*

1461. RING. I/1220/84. Mf. ŻIH—835; USHMM—47

- 23.10.1939, Łódź
- Feldkommandantur 530, Fragment of document filled out for NN. [Hersz Wasser?]
- ***Description:*** original, handwritten manuscript, stamps, German, 116×163 mm, ss. 1, pp. 1.
  Doc. was kept in a binder.

**1462. RING. I/1161 (1480). Mf. ŻIH—833; USHMM—45. RING. I/288. Mf. ŻIH—781; USHMM—12**

- Before 13.11.1939, Łódź
- Vorstand der Isr[aelitische] Kultusgemeinde [Board of the Jewish Religious Community] in Lodz, Arbeitszuteilungsschein [Labor summons] no. 22148 for Hirsz Herman Wasser (Łódź, ul. Żeromskiego 9)
- Summons for 13.11.1939 to ul. Lipowa 31.
- ***Description:*** Ring. I/1161—original, printed, handwritten manuscript, ink, stamps, German, Polish, 110×140 mm, ss. 1, pp. 1; Ring. I/288—transcript, handwritten manuscript (MS*), pencil, German in Hebrew alphabet transliteration, 143×220 mm, ss. 1, pp. 1.

    Ring. I/288 in the margin a Hebrew letter (pencil, red): "lamed" and a symbol (ink): "Δ."

    Ring. I/288—Attached note by H.W. in Yiddish: "For security, Jewish letters were used. Delivered by Mordechaj Szwarcbard."

    Doc. was kept in a binder.

    This manuscript (Ring. I/288) also contains a copy of a doc. from Ring. I/1188.

    Stamps: "Stawiennictwo osobiste obowiązkowe" [Personal appearance obligatory]; "Die Arbeit wurde geleistet. Der Aufseher der isr. Kultusgemeinde, Lodz" [The work will be performed. The inspector of the Jewish Religious Community, Łódź].

**1463. RING. I/1188 (1507). (Lb. 608). Mf. ŻIH—834; USHMM—46. RING. I/288. Mf. ŻIH—781; USHMM—12**

- 13.11.1939, Łódź
- Feldkommandantur [Field Command] [5] 30, Lange, Certificate made out for H. [Hersz] Wasser authorizing him to walk along Piotrkowska Street in Łódź
- ***Description:*** Ring. I/1188- original, hectographed typescript, handwritten manuscript, pencil, stamps, German, 155×214 mm, minor damage and losses of text, ss. 1, pp. 1; Ring. I/288—transcript, handwritten manuscript (MS*), German in Hebrew alphabet transliteration, 143×220 mm, ss. 1, pp. 1.

    Ring. I/288 In the margin a Hebrew letter (red pencil): "lamed" and a symbol "Δ." This manuscript (Ring. I/288) also contains a transcript of a doc. from Ring. I/1161.

    Ring. I/288—Attached note by H.W. in Yiddish: "For security, Jewish letters were used. Delivered by Mordechaj Szwarcbard."

    Docs. were kept in a binder.

**1464. RING. I/1129 (1448). (Lb. 1002). Mf. ŻIH—833; USHMM—45. RING. I/288. Mf. ŻIH—781; USHMM—12**

a) **Ring. I/1129. (1448). (Lb. 6)**

- 15.11.1939, Łódź
- Polizeipräsident Lodsch [Police-President of Łódź], Pass dated 15.11.1939 for Hirsz Herman [Hersz] Wasser (born 13.06.1912 in Suwałki) for trip to Białystok
- ***Description:*** original, handwritten manuscript, ink, stamp, German, 208×100 mm, ss. 1, pp. 1.

    Doc. was kept in a binder.

b)

- 23.11.1939, Łódź, after 1939, Warsaw Ghetto
- Polizeipräsident Lodsch [Police-President of Łódź], Permit dated 23.11.1939 for Hersz Wasser to move about the streets of Łódź until 17.00 [5 PM], valid until 23.12.1939
- ***Description:*** Ring. I/1129—original, printed, handwritten manuscript, ink, stamp, German, 210×148 mm, ss. 1, pp. 1; Ring. I/288—transcript, handwritten manuscript (MS*), pencil, German in Hebrew alphabet transliteration, 142×186 mm, ss. 1, pp. 1.

    Ring. I/288 in the margin a Hebrew letter (red pencil): "lamed" and a symbol (ink): "Δ."

    Ring. I/288—Attached note by H.W. in Yiddish: "For security, Jewish letters were used. Delivered by Mordechaj Szwarcbard."

    Docs. were preserved in binders.

**1465. RING. I/834 (1153). (Lb. 673). Mf. ŻIH—827; USHMM—39**

- 10–11.1941, Warsaw Ghetto, Kraków
- Devisenstelle Krakau. Genehmigungsabteilung (Foreign Currency Office in Kraków, Department of Permits), Permits (2) dated 6.11.1941 for dispatch of things for Leib Wasser and Szmul Elbirt (Litzmannstadt [Łódź]—Ghetto, Steinmetzstr. 12/101)
- Docs. filled out for Hirsch Wasser and Bluma Kirszenfeld [Wasser] (Warsaw, ul. Muranowska 6, apt. 15). Appended list of things (linens, clothing, footwear) for Leib Wasser (19.10.1941).
- ***Description:*** original, typescript, German, stamp, 147×210, 220×300 mm, ss. 3, pp. 3.

    Attached note by H.W.

**1466. RING. I/1148 (1467). (Lb. 1466). Mf. ŻIH—833; USHMM—45**

- After 1.09.1939, Łódź
- Firma I. Kolner, Łódź, ul. Sienkiewicza 6, Certificate of employment of Herman Wasser (Łódź, ul. Żeromskiego 9) as a bookkeeper
- ***Description:*** original, typescript, stamp, German, Polish, 114×163 mm, ss. 1, pp. 1.

    Doc. was kept in a binder.

    Attached note by H.W.: "Submitted by H.W. certificate of labor intended to protect from constant roundups."

**1467. RING. I/1112/2 (1431). (Lb. 1427). Mf. ŻIH—833; USHMM—45**

- 01.1941, Warsaw Ghetto

- ŻTOS, Invitation to inaugural celebration of the "Winter Relief" campaign on 9.01.1941 in the offices of ŻTOS, ul. Tłomackie 5, for Hirsz [sic] Wasser (ul. Muranowska 6)
- Program of the ceremony.
- *Description:* original, printed, handwritten manuscript, ink, 140×100 mm, ss. 1, pp. 2.

1468. **RING. I/1130 (1449). (Lb. 20). Mf. ŻIH—833; USHMM—45**
- 20.03.1941, Warsaw Ghetto
- Apartment house committee at ul. [Muranowska 6?], Notification dated 20.03.1941 about taxation of [Hersz] Wasser in the sum of 10 zł for the benefit of the poor and refugees on the occasion of the Passover holiday
- *Description:* original, typescript, Polish, 220×78 mm, ss. 1, pp. 1.

1469. **RING. I/1122 (1441). (Lb. 1494). Mf. ŻIH—833; USHMM—45**
- 05 [?].1941, Warsaw Ghetto
- Invitation to the Haszomer Hacair [Ha-Shomer Ha-Tsair]seminar for activists and alumni
- Program: "Ideological and political position of Ha-Shomer Ha-Tsair in the time of the second imperialist war and the ghetto"; "Ha-Shomer Ha-Tsair's public educational posture at the present time."
- *Description:* original, typescript, Hebrew, 190×150 mm, minor damage and losses of text, ss. 1, pp. 1.

  Surname of the invitation's addressee crossed out (ink): H. [Hersz] [?] [Wasser][?].

1470. **RING. I/1120 (1439). (Lb. 1675). Mf. ŻIH—833; USHMM—45**
- 3.12.1941, Warsaw Ghetto
- Invitation dated 3.12.1941 to the Ha-Shomer Ha-Tsair conference for H. [Hersz] Wasser
- Program: the Jewish population's economics and demography, history of the Hebrew labor movement in the Diaspora, history of Palestine and of the new settlement in Palestine, Ha-Shomer Ha-Tsair's pedagogy and education.
- *Description:* original, typescript., ink, Hebrew, Yiddish, 205×148 mm, ss. 1, pp. 1.

  Notation by H.W. in Yiddish (ink): "108—1942/1 January."

1471. **RING. I/1112/1 (1431). Mf. ŻIH—833; USHMM—45**
- 12.1941, Warsaw Ghetto
- Jewish Council in Warsaw. School Department, Invitation dated 16.12.1941 for H. [Hersz] Wasser "in connection with the establishment of elementary schools for Jewish children" at a school celebration on 21.12.1941 in the "Femina" hall (ul. Leszno 35)
- In the program speeches and appearances by A[dam] Czerniaków, chairman of the School Department A. Wolfowicz, and Dr. F[elicja] Czerniaków; children's choir of [Izrael] Fajwiszys, M[aria] Ajzensztadt, Ch. Bras [Chana Braz].
- *Description:* original, printed, Hebrew, Polish, Yiddish, 100×153 mm, ss. 3, pp. 4.

1472. **RING. I/1116 (1435). (Lb. 1495). Mf. ŻIH—833; USHMM—45**
- 01.1942, Warsaw Ghetto
- [He-Haluts Dror], Invitation for [Hersz] Wasser to celebration of the end of the II national seminar of Dror, on 31.01.1942 in the Dror kibbutz at ul. Dzielna 34, apt. 8
- *Description:* original, printed, handwritten manuscript, Hebrew, Polish, Yiddish, 101×148 mm, ss. 2, pp. 1.

  Postwar notation by Laura Eichhornowa, at the bottom handwritten (pencil): "to the Dror banquet."

1473. **RING. I/594/3. Mf. ŻIH—792; USHMM—23**
- 31.03.1942, Warsaw Ghetto
- NN., Receipt dated 31.03.1942 for 50 zł received, filled out for [Hersz] Wasser
- *Description:* original, handwritten manuscript, pencil, Polish, 143×94 mm, ss. 1, pp. 1.

1474. **RING. I/529. Mf. ŻIH—790; USHMM—21**

a)
- 12.1939–1941[42?], Warsaw
- [Hersz Wasser], Financial records ledger
- List of daily expenditures from 19.12.1939 to 30.05.1941. Various notes.
- *Description:* original, handwritten manuscript (H.W.* and another handwriting: BW*), notebook, ink, pencil, French, Polish, 95×155 mm, ss. 80, pp. 154.

  Attached note by H.W.: "1939–1942, W[arsaw], original, financial records ledger of the H.W. family in W[arsaw]."

b)
- Date unknown, Warsaw.
- [Bluma Wasser], Receipts for household purchases [?]
- List of products with prices.
- *Description:* original, handwritten manuscript (BW*), pencil, Yiddish, 145×210 mm, ss. 2, pp. 2.

1475. **RING. I/598/6. Mf. ŻIH—792; USHMM—23**
- Date unknown, place unknown
- NN. (Josef), Letter to NN. (Hersz Wasser [?]) (fragment)
- Request for news about Pinkas, Icchak, Jakub, Tobcia. Thanks for Wasser for the postscript.
- *Description:* original, handwritten manuscript, ink, Yiddish, 124×205 mm, damage and losses of text, (sheet preserved with no. "4"), ss. 1, pp. 2.

**1476. RING. I/588. Mf. ŻIH—792; USHMM—23**

- 18.04.1940, after 18.04.1940, Małkinia, Warsaw Ghetto
- [Kirszenfeld (Małkinia)], Letter of 18.04.1940 to Hersz Wasser (Warsaw)
- Request for aid in moving to Warsaw.
- ***Description:*** original (handwritten manuscript, pencil, 120×203 mm), transcript (handwritten manuscript—MS*, pencil, 148×208 mm), Yiddish, ss. 4, pp. 8.
  On p. 1 (original) note in Polish: "S.O.S."
  Transcript does not contain the concluding fragment of the original ("P.S." from p. 5 [6]). On p. 1 (transcript) note in Yiddish by H.W. (ink) and in the margin a Hebrew letter (ink): "ts" (tsadi).
  Original and transcript were kept in a binder.

**1477. RING. I/584. Mf. ŻIH—792; USHMM—23**

- 06.1941–07.1942, Biłgoraj
- Josif [Józef] Kirszenfeld with wife (Biłgoraj), Letters dated 27.06.1941, 15.02., 15.03., 17.06., 19.06.1942 to Hersz and Bluma Wasser (Warsaw, ul. Muranowska 6, apt. 15)
- Requests for aid. Thanks for money received. Information about the difficult situation in Biłgoraj: hunger. Prices of foodstuffs.
- ***Description:*** original, handwritten on postcards, postmarks and stamp of the Jewish Council in Warsaw, ink, pencil, Polish, 146×104 mm, minor damage and losses of text, ss. 5, pp. 10.
  On card dated 27.06.1941 the sender's address: Biłgoraj, ul. 3 Maja 3 [35?]; on the cards dated 15.02. and 15.03.1942: Biłgoraj, ul. Kościelna 35 (3 Maja = Kościelna [?]); on the cards dated 17.06. and 19.06.1942: Biłgoraj, ul. Nadstawna 42.
  Index: Brafmans, Kasners

**1478. RING. I/599/102. Mf. ŻIH—812; USHMM—24**

- After 02.1941, Biłgoraj
- Josif Kirszen[feld (Biłgoraj)], Letter to NN. [(Warsaw Ghetto)?]
- Request for aid and rescue as well as forwarding of the contents of the letter to brother- and sister-in-law Szaja and Bluma.
- ***Description:*** original, handwritten manuscript on a postcard, pencil, Polish, 103×69 mm, serious damage and losses of text, ss. 1, pp. 2.

**1479. RING. I/544/3. Mf. ŻIH—791; USHMM—22**

- 25.03.1942, Łódź Ghetto
- Chaim Rumkowski (Łódź Ghetto.), Letters (2) dated 25.03.1942 to H. [Hersz] Wasser (Warsaw, ul. Muranowska 6, apt. 15)
- Official notifications that Dora and Sulamita Elbirt as well as Lejb and Estera Wasser are healthy and residing in the Łódź Ghetto at ul. Hohensteiner 43/45, apt. 101.
- ***Description:*** original, printed, handwritten manuscript, German, ink, 146×102 mm, ss. 2, pp. 4.
  See Ring. II/393.
  Published: *Listy o Zagładzie*, pp. 201–205.

**1480. RING. I/581/2. Mf. ŻIH—792; USHMM—23**

- 10.1941, Dubienka
- Genia Segal (Dubienka), Letter of [14.10.1941 postmark date] to Bluma and Heńiek [Hersz] Wasser (Warsaw, ul. Muranowska 6, apt. 15). Request for information
- ***Description:*** original, handwritten manuscript on a postcard, postmark and stamp of Jewish Council, ink, Polish, 147×104 mm, ss. 1, pp. 2.

**1481. RING. I/596. Mf. ŻIH—792; USHMM—23**

- Correspondence concerning Szlamek (Szłojme) [Winer] [pseudonym Jakub Grojnowski]

a)

- 02–03.1942, Zamość
- [Fela] Bajler (Zamość), Letters (2) dated 11.02. and 18.03.1942 to NN. (Szlamek [Winer]) (Warsaw, ul. Muranowska 6, apt. 15, in care of H. [Hersz and Bluma] Wasser)
- Matter of departure of Szlamek to Zamość. Information concerning family and friends.
- ***Description:*** original, handwritten manuscript (Letter of 11.02., handwritten manuscript, ink, 115×194 mm) (Letter of 18.03.1942, handwritten manuscript on a postcard, postmark, stamps of Jewish Councils in Zamość and Warsaw, ink, 148×106 mm), Polish, ss. 3, pp. 6.
  On letter dated 18.03.1942 sender's address: "Zamość, ul. Św. Piątka 21."
  Published: *Listy o Zagładzie*, pp. 112–113, 124–125.
  Index: Reichenbachowa, Ule Bore (ul. Nowolipki 7, apt. 9), Radzymińscy (ul. Pawia 41, apt. 28, at Puttermilch), [Rafał?] Grabiński, Majer

b)

- 17.02.1942, Koluszki
- Izrael Szlamowicz (Koluszki, ul. 11 November 60), Letter of 17.02.1942 to NN. (Szlamek [Winer]) (Warsaw, ul. Wołyńska 9, apt. 1, in care of Dwojra Sztatman)
- Notation from Szlamek's sister-in-law [Fela Bajler of Zamość] and about a friend who departed for Wierzbnik.
- ***Description:*** original, handwritten manuscript on a postcard, postmark and stamp of Jewish Council in Warsaw, ink, Polish, 148×105 mm, ss. 1, pp. 2.
  In the address author's correction: ul. "Wołyńska" written beneath crossed-out ul. "Nowolipki"; added below: "for Szlamek."
  According to Ruta Sakowska, the friend of Szlamek mentioned in the letter was named Abram Roj, who on 18.01.1942 escaped from Chełmno (a day before Szlamek); see *Listy o*

*Zagładzie*, pp. 116 and 118; see also Ring. I/394 and I/799.
Published: *Listy o Zagładzie*, pp. 116–117.

c)

- 20.02.1942, Wierzbnik
- NN. (Abram [Roj?]) (Wierzbnik, ul. Kolejowa 71, at H. [Helena] Auerbach), Letter of 20.02.1942 to NN. (Szlamek [Winer]) (Warsaw, ul. Wołyńska 9, apt. 1, at Dewojra [Dwojry?] Sztatman)
- Difficult situation in Wierzbnik.
- ***Description:*** original, handwritten manuscript (two handwritings) on a postcard, postmark and stamp of Jewish Council in Warsaw, ink, Polish, 148×104 mm, ss. 1, pp. 2.

Postscript with greetings from Helena [Auerbach], who figures as the sender of the letter.
According to Ruta Sakowska, the letter's author is Abram Roj, one of the escapees from the extermination camp in Chełmno; see *Listy o Zagładzie*, pp. 118; Ring. I/394.
Published: *Listy o Zagładzie*, pp. 118–119
Index: Herber

d)

- 02.1942, Radziejów
- NN. (Hinda) (Radziejów), Letter of 20.02.1942 [postmark] to NN. (Szlamek [Winer]) (Warsaw, ul. Wołyńska 9, apt. 1, at Dwojra Sztatman)
- Information about the search for Szlamek by German police (inter alia, in Osięciny), about the deaths of closest members of family.
- ***Description:*** original, handwritten manuscript on a postcard, postmark and stamp of Jewish Council in Warsaw, ink, Polish, 146×104 mm, ss. 1, pp. 2.

The letter's sender was: "Juda Radziejewski (Radziejów)."
Published: *Listy o Zagładzie*, pp. 120–122.
Index: Ch. Lewi (Warsaw, ul. Nalewki 18, apt. 18 or Nowolipki 18, apt. 18)

e)

- 7.03.1942, Przygłów
- M. Rokman (Przygłów), Letter of 7.03.1942 to Grojnowski [Szlamek Winer] (Warsaw, ul. Muranowska 6, apt. 15, in care of Heńiek [Hersz] Wasser)
- Information about the rescue of the author's brother (Sz. J.).
- ***Description:*** original, handwritten manuscript on a postcard, postmark and stamp of Jewish Council in Warsaw, ink, Polish, 148×104 mm, ss. 1, pp. 2.

Published: *Listy o Zagładzie*, pp. 122–123.
Index: Bibrowskie, Izbicki, Majer Łaski of Zelów

f)

- 03–04.1942, Zamość
- NN. (Szlamek [Winer]) (Zamość, ul. Św. Piątka 21), Letters (3) dated 21.03., 5.04., after 5.04.1942 to Heńiek [Hersz] Wasser (Warsaw, ul. Muranowska 6, apt. 15)
- Information regarding living conditions in the Zamość ghetto, material aid, fate of closest relatives, extermination camp in Bełżec.
- ***Description:*** original, handwritten manuscript (letters dated 21.03. and 5.04.1942 on postcards, postmarks and stamps of the Jewish Council in Zamość and Warsaw), Polish, Yiddish in Roman transliteration, 145×105 mm, ss. 4, pp. 8.

On letters dated 21.03. and 5.04.1942, the sender was: "Fela Bajler, Zamość, Św. Piątka 21." Letter of 5.04.1942, Szlamek signed with the surname "Grojnowski" (Szlamek's pseudonym; see *Listy o Zagładzie*, p. 113), another fragment with the surname: "Praszkier" (Gerszon Praszkier from Izbica Kujawska was together with Szlamek in the camp in Chełmno, where he died; see *Listy o Zagładzie*, p. 130).
Published: *Listy o Zagładzie*, pp. 126–134.
Attached note by H.W.: "Grojnowski—Bajler."
Index: Kohn, Zysman, Rubinsztein, Groj[nowski?], Knopmacher, Chaim Rywen Izbicki

g)

- 24.04.1942, Zamość
- Abram Bajler (Zamość, ul. Św. Piątka 21), Letter to H. [Hersz] Wasser (Warsaw, ul. Muranowska 6, apt. 15)
- Information about loss of entire family (also including Szlamek's uncle) in liquidation action in Zamość.
- ***Description:*** original, handwritten manuscript on a postcard, postmark and stamp of Jewish Council in Warsaw, minor damage and losses of text, Polish, ss. 1, pp. 2.

Address erroneously written: "ul. Muranowska 16 apt.[?]," alongside handwritten note [by a postal official?]: "Mur. 6, apt. 15."
Published: *Listy o Zagładzie*, pp. 134–135; *Przewodnik*, p. 647 (photocopy of fragment).

## 1482. RING. I/583. Mf. ŻIH—792; USHMM—23

- 05—06.1942, Otwock
- Władysław Wajnblat (Otwock, "Brius" [Hebrew for "Health"] Sanatorium), Letters (2) dated 31.05.1942 and 29.06.194[2?] to H. [Hersz, Henryk] Wasser (Warsaw, ul. Muranowska 6, apt. 15)
- Information about stay for treatment in Otwock.
- ***Description:*** original, handwritten manuscript (Letter of 31.05.1942 on a postcard, postmark and stamp of the Jewish Council in Warsaw, ink, 144×102 mm, damage and losses of text), (Letter of 29.06.1942, pencil, 123×201 mm), Polish, ss. 2, pp. 4.

## 1483. RING. I/586/2. Mf. ŻIH—792; USHMM—23

- 12.11.1941, Warsaw Ghetto
- Hersz and Bluma Wasser (Warsaw, Muranowska 6, apt. 15.), Letter of 12.11.1941 to I.M. Kirszenfeld (Dubno, ul. Kantorska 15, at J. Sekier). Request for a letter
- ***Description:*** original, handwritten manuscript on a

postcard, postmark, ink, Polish, 147×104 mm, ss. 1, pp. 2.

Letter returned to sender ("Unzulaessig" [Inadmissible]).

**1484. RING. I/586/1. Mf. ŻIH—792; USHMM—23**

- 18.07.1940, Warsaw
- Hersz and Bluma Wasser (Warsaw, ul. Bielańska 15/17, apt. 26), Letter of 18.07.1940 to L. [Lejb and Estera] Wasser (Łódź, ul. Ceglana 7 m 3)
- Information regarding cost of living in Warsaw.
- ***Description:*** original, handwritten manuscript on a postcard, postmark, ink, Polish, 144×102 mm, ss. 1, pp. 2.

Card was kept in a binder.

Letter returned to Warsaw, was not delivered to the addressee.

**1485. RING. I/544/2. Mf. ŻIH—791; USHMM—22**

- 07–12.1941, Łódź Ghetto
- L. [Lejb] and Estera Wasser (Łódź, Steinmetzgasse [Ceglana] 12, apt. 101), Letters (4) dated 3.07., 4.09., 6.09., 12.12.1941 to H. [Hersz] Wasser (Warsaw, ul. Muranowska 6, apt. 15)
- Information regarding family and friends; material aid.
- ***Description:*** original, handwritten manuscript (several handwritings), letters dated 4.09., 6.09., 12.12.1941 on postcards, postmarks and stamps of the Jewish Council in Warsaw, German, (letter of 3.07.: ink, 165×200, ss. 1, pp. 2), postcards: 147×104 mm, minor damage and losses of text (Letters of 3.07., 4.09.), ss. 4, pp. 8.

On letters dated 4.09., 6.09., 12.12.1941 postscripts by Dora [Elbirt].

On letters dated 4.09. and 6.09.1941 to the address of H. [Hersz] Wasser is added: "bei Herrn Dunkielang" [at Mr. Dunkielang].

Index: Rubin, Samuel Faust, Chaim M. Rumkowski, Szalamcia [Sulamita] Elbirt, Szmul Elbirt, Józef Podlaski, Hilary Wodnicki

**1486. RING. I/594/4. Mf. ŻIH—792; USHMM—23**

- 1.04.1942, Warsaw Ghetto
- NN. (Warsaw Ghetto), Letter of 1.04.1942 to [Hersz] Wasser (Warsaw Ghetto)
- Matter of dinners for sister of the letter's author (Kapłańska).
- ***Description:*** original, handwritten manuscript, ink, Polish, 148×181 mm, minor damage and losses of text, ss. 1, pp. 1.

**1487. RING. I/598/4. Mf. ŻIH—792; USHMM—23**

- 1.06.1942, place unknown
- NN., Letter of 1.06.1942 to Hersz [Wasser?] (missing conclusion)
- Thanks for money sent.
- ***Description:*** original [?], handwritten manuscript, ink, Yiddish, 145×207 mm, extensive minor damage and losses of text, ss. 1, pp. 2.

**1488. RING. I/586/4. Mf. ŻIH—792; USHMM—23**

- 27.07.1942, Warsaw Ghetto
- NN. (Warsaw Ghetto), Letter of 27.07.1942 to [Hersz] Wasser (Warsaw Ghetto, Nowolipki 29, apt. 16)
- Request for a document exempting from deportation.
- ***Description:*** original, handwritten manuscript, ink, Yiddish, 190×127 mm, minor damage and losses of text, ss. 1, pp. 2.

Address in Polish: "Waser, Nowolipki 29, apt. 16."

Date: "27.7.1942" written in by H.W.

**1489. RING. I/544/4. Mf. ŻIH—791; USHMM—22**

- Date unknown, Łódź
- NN., Telegram to [Hersz Wasser?] (Warsaw, ul. Muranowska 6 [m. 15])
- Concern over the lack of news.
- ***Description:*** original, printed, German, 205×99 mm, damage and losses of text, ss. 1, pp. 1.

## X. Miscellaneous

**1490. RING. I/1141 (1460). Mf. ŻIH—833; USHMM—45**

- 1916, Warsaw
- Z.S. M. W. [Zarząd Stołeczny miasta Warszawy (Municipal Government of the Capital City of Warsaw)]. Commission for Distribution of Flour and Bread, Form with ration cards for bread, flour and sugar (valid from 26.06. to 9.07.1916)
- ***Description:*** original, printed, German, Polish, 52×93 mm, ss. 1, pp. 2.

Inscription on the cards: "Karta szpitalna" [Hospital card].

On the reverse stamp (Polish, Yiddish): "[H]ouse dinners, ul. Nalewki 17 in the courtyard, [. . . ?]."

**1491. RING. I/595/1. Mf. ŻIH—792; USHMM—23**

- Before 11.03.192[4?]
- NN. (Hela, Cesia and others), Letter to NN.
- Letter from children to father being held in prison (camp [?]).
- ***Description:*** original, handwritten manuscript (several handwritings), ink, Polish, 120×200 mm, text legible in places, ss. 2, pp. 4.

Letter imprinted three times by the censor's seal with the date (11.03.192[4?]) written in and inspector's signature (India ink, pencil).

**1492. RING. I/1220/28. Mf. ŻIH—835; USHMM—47**

- 1[. . .].04.1924, place unknown
- NN., Note (letter [?]) (1[. . .].04.1924)
- Information regarding publication matters [?].
- *Description:* original, or transcript, handwritten manuscript, Yiddish, damage and losses of text, text difficult to read, ss. 1, pp. 2.

**1493. RING. I/1220/16. Mf. ŻIH—835; USHMM—47**

- 1929, Warsaw
- Zarząd Stowarzyszenia Głuchoniemych Żydów "Spójnia" [Board of the Association of Deaf-mute Jews] (Secretariat: Warsaw, ul. Miła 38, apt. 7), Member share [consists] of a one-time contribution to the center
- *Description:* original, printed, Yiddish, 120×90 mm, ss. 1, pp. 2.

On reverse a note (ink) in Hebrew.

**1494. RING. I/770 (1094). (Lb. 261). Mf. ŻIH—825; USHMM—37**

- After 19.11.1930, Warsaw
- Investigative Bureau of the Capital City of Warsaw, Information from informants (I Brigade) from 22.10.1930–19.11.1930
- Information and materials concerning the activity of leftist organizations in Warsaw (inter alia, Polish Socialist Party—Left, Communist Party of Poland). Appended lists of names of activists, texts of documents.
- *Description:* original, typescript, handwritten manuscript, pencil, seal of the Investigative Bureau (Urząd Śledczy), Polish, 209×295 mm, minor damage and losses of text, ss. 17, pp. 17.

Document was kept in a binder.

**1495. RING. I/110. Mf. ŻIH—777; USHMM—8**

- 5.09.1932, place unknown
- NN., Study concerning presence of Jews in various fields throughout the world
- Culture and civilization (philosophy, music, sculpture, engineering, etc.).
- *Description:* original, handwritten manuscript (several handwritings), ink, Yiddish, 166×255, 195×290 mm, damage and losses of text, text is difficult to read in places, ss. 43, pp. 86.

Document was kept in a binder.

**1496. RING. I/824 (1143). (Lb. 500). Mf. ŻIH—826; USHMM—38**

- 08.1938, place unknown
- NN., Study entitled "Kazimir, 1938"
- Notes for a study on the history and monuments of Kazimierz on the Vistula.
- *Description:* original, handwritten manuscript, notebook, ink, Polish, Yiddish, 147×198 mm, ss. 13, pp. 19.

**1497. RING. I/592/17. Mf. ŻIH—792; USHMM—23**

- 1938, Paris [?]
- NN. (Paris [?]), Letter of 1938 to NN.
- Concerning subsequently undetermined party matters.
- *Description:* original, handwritten manuscript, ink, Yiddish, 205×270 mm, serious damage and losses of text, ss. 1, pp. 1.

Doc. written on the letterhead of the firm: "Fabrique de [. . .] Nade[. . .], Paris, 25 bis rue de la For[. . .] 1938."

**1498. RING. I/1220/23. Mf. ŻIH—835; USHMM—47**

- After 1940, Warsaw Ghetto
- NN., Account (or Study [?]) on unknown subject matter
- *Description:* original or transcript, handwritten manuscript, notebook, ink, Polish, 144×205 mm, illegible text, ss. 16, pp. 29.

On p. 1 (cover) note by H.W. in Yiddish (ink): "7 st. pages."

**1499. RING. I/1220/65. Mf. ŻIH—835; USHMM—47**

- 26.06.1941, place unknown
- Band for wrapping banknotes (26.06.1941).
- *Description:* original, handwritten manuscript, stamp, pencil, German, 175×40 mm, ss. 1, pp. 1.

Stamp: "Geprüft" [Verified]. Note (pencil): "100 RR" and illegible.

**1500. RING. I/599/86. Mf. ŻIH—812; USHMM—24**

- 1941, without place
- Note of a religious nature regarding a fast [?].
- *Description:* original or transcript, handwritten manuscript, pencil, Hebrew, 190×100 mm, damage and losses of text, ss. 1, pp. 1

**1501. RING. I/590. Mf. ŻIH—792; USHMM—23**

- 6.01.1942, Floss[?]
- NN. (Floss [?]), Letter of 6.01.1942 to NN. (Fritz)
- Letter from a German soldier to a friend.
- *Description:* original, handwritten manuscript, pencil, German, 205×288 mm, minor damage and losses of text, ss. 1, pp. 2.

Doc. presumably found within the Warsaw Ghetto, e.g., in a military overcoat sent to be repaired [?]

**1502. RING. I/620. (Lb. 718). Mf. ŻIH—814; USHMM—26**

- Date unknown, place unknown
- NN., Study about Jewnie (Junie) Azefie [Yevnye (Yunye) Azefye] (1869–1918) (fragment)
- Reflections on the conduct of a provocateur and agent of the tsarist police within the revolutionary movement.

- *Description:* original, handwritten manuscript, ink, Yiddish, 35×75, 110×270 mm, damage and losses of text, ss. 41, pp. 41.

**1503. RING. I/781/6. Mf. ŻIH—825; USHMM—37**

- Date unknown, place unknown
- Form for certificate of award of wartime Cross of Merit (with swords) (Germany).
- *Description:* original (12 copies, 3 sets of 4 certificates each), printed, German, 335×496 mm, ss. 3, pp. 3.

**1504. RING. I/1159 (1478). (Lb. 86). Mf. ŻIH—833; USHMM—45**

- Date unknown, place unknown
- Keren Kayemet (Jewish National Fund), Certificate of contribution for the planting of trees in Palestine on the occasion of the holiday of Tu be-Shvat [New Year of Trees]
- *Description:* original, printed, Hebrew, 95×107 mm, ss. 1, p. 2.

  Document was was kept in a binder.

**1505. RING. I/599/116. Mf. ŻIH—812; USHMM—24**

- Date unknown, place unknown
- Miscellany. Various fragments (8) conserved on 1 sheet, among others a fragment of a municipal transit ticket.
- *Description:* original, printed, handwritten manuscript, ink, German, Polish, 20×10–60×65 mm, serious damage and losses of text, ss. 8, pp. 13.

**Unless otherwise noted, all photos are courtesy of the Żydowski Instytut Historyczny imienia Emanuela Ringelbluma (Emanuel Ringelblum Jewish Historical Institute), Warsaw.**

Figure 1. The first examination of the Ring. II documents discovered in December 1950 in two sealed milk canisters.
USHMM, courtesy of Yad Vashem Photo Archives, Jerusalem.

Figure 2. Three of the ten metal boxes in which the first cache of Oyneg Shabes documents was buried in August 1942. The boxes were recovered in September 1946.

Figure 3. One of the two large milk canisters in which the second cache of Oyneg Shabes documents was buried in February 1943. The canisters were recovered in December 1950.

4

5

6

7

8

9

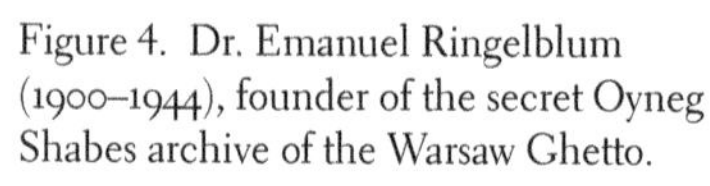

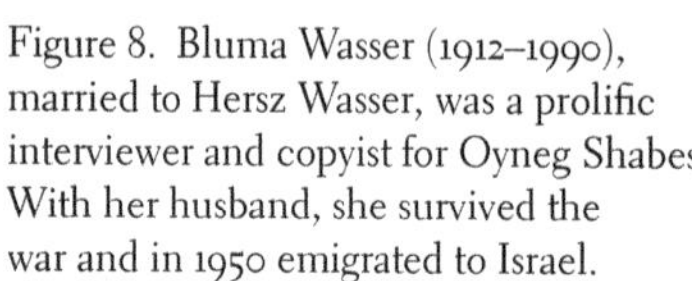

Figure 4. Dr. Emanuel Ringelblum (1900–1944), founder of the secret Oyneg Shabes archive of the Warsaw Ghetto.

Figure 5. Ringelblum posing with son Uri in 1938.
USHMM, courtesy of YIVO Institute, New York.

Figure 6. Eliasz (Eliyahu) Gutkowski (1900–1943) was a teacher active in the socialist Zionist movement Poalei Tsion. As one of the group's two secretaries, he was a key figure in Oyneg Shabes.

Figure 7. Hersz Wasser (1912–1980) was a trained economist and Left Poalei Tsion activist. As one of the group's two secretaries, he was a key figure in Oyneg Shabes. In September 1946, he guided searchers to the first cache of Oyneg Shabes documents.

Figure 8. Bluma Wasser (1912–1990), married to Hersz Wasser, was a prolific interviewer and copyist for Oyneg Shabes. With her husband, she survived the war and in 1950 emigrated to Israel.

Figure 9. Icchak (Yitshak) Giterman (1889–1943) headed the Polish section of the American Jewish Joint Distribution Committee and created the Jewish Self-Help organization that employed Emanuel Ringelblum and other Oyneg Shabes members.

Figure 10. Izrael Lichtensztajn (Israel Lichtenstein, 1904–1943) was a teacher of Yiddish and an editor active in the Left Poalei Tsion. In the Warsaw Ghetto, he worked in orphan care and was guardian of the Oyneg Shabes archive. He oversaw the burial of three caches of documents.

10

11

12

13

14

15

16

17

Figure 11. Rachel Auerbach (Oyerbakh, 1903–1976), a writer and essayist in Polish and Yiddish, managed a soup kitchen in the Warsaw Ghetto and collected testimonies for the secret ghetto archive. In March 1943 she escaped from the ghetto and was one of only three Oyneg Shabes members to survive the war.

Figure 12. Jehoszua Perle (1888–1943) was a prominent Yiddish-language author who worked in the Warsaw Ghetto's supply department designing posters. He contributed to Oyneg Shabes his accounts of experiences in occupied Lwów and of the annihilation of Warsaw's Jews.

Figure 13. Jonas Turkow (1898–1988), a prominent actor and director in Yiddish theater, was active in cultural projects in the Warsaw Ghetto. He contributed essays on ghetto theater to Oyneg Shabes. With his wife and daughter, he escaped from the ghetto and survived the war.

Figure 14. Eliezer (Aleksander) Lipe Bloch (1889–1944), a leader of the Jewish Self-Help in the Warsaw Ghetto, was active in underground Jewish cultural life.

Figure 15. Fruma Plotnicka (1914–1943) served as a courier for the Dror Zionist youth movement and provided Oyneg Shabes with information concerning provincial communities and the Sobibór death camp.

Figure 16. Icchak ("Antek") Cukierman (Zuckerman, 1914–1981) was a leader of the Dror Zionist youth movement and a founder of the Jewish Fighting Organization (Żydowska Organizacja Bojowa, ŻOB), who cooperated with Oyneg Shabes.

Figure 17. Icchak Kacenelson (Yitshak Katzenelson, 1886–1944) was a prominent poet, author, and teacher of Yiddish whose works were preserved by Oyneg Shabes.

18

19

20a

Figure 18. Dawid Nowodworski (1916–1944) was a leader of the Jewish resistance in the Warsaw Ghetto who escaped from Treblinka in 1942 and reported to Oyneg Shabes about the death camp.

Figure 19. Rabbi Szymon Huberband (1909–1942) was a Talmud scholar and historian who directed the Religious Affairs Department of the Jewish Self-Help and wrote on a variety of themes for Oyneg Shabes.

Figure 20a. Szlamek Winer (also known as Szlamek Bajler or Fajner) escaped from the Chełmno death camp and reached the Warsaw Ghetto in early 1942. Under the pseudonym Jakub Grojnowski, he provided Oyneg Shabes with detailed testimony about Chełmno and later sent word to Hersz Wasser about the Bełżec death camp. Winer was killed in Bełżec no later than April 1942. Ring. I/1115

Figure 20b. First page of the eyewitness testimony in Yiddish of "Jakub Grojnowski" (Szlamek Bajler/Szlamek Winer) describing the organization of the mass destruction of Jews and Gypsies at the Chełmno death camp in January 1942. Ring. I/1115

20b

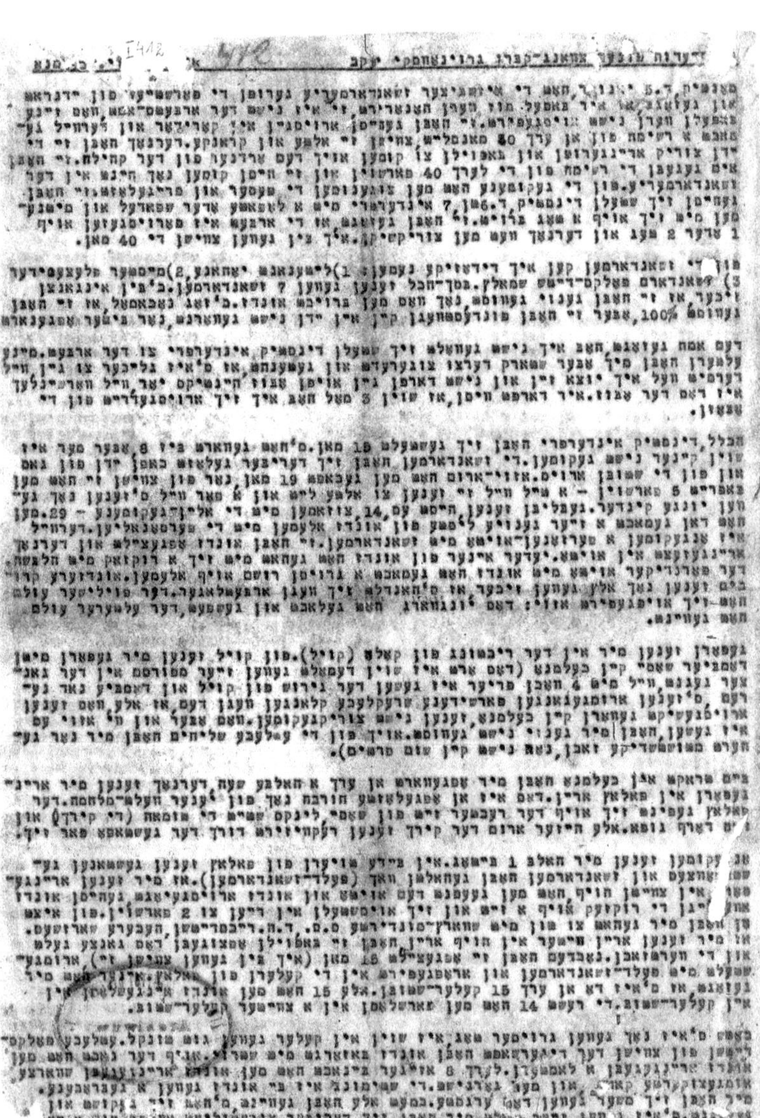

21 

22 

23 

24 

25 

26 

27 

Figure 21. Chawa Folman (b. 1924) was a courier for the Jewish resistance. She provided Oyneg Shabes with confirmation about the Sobibór death camp.

Figure 22. Jakub Abram Krzepicki (ca. 1917–1943) escaped from Treblinka death camp in September 1942, returned to the Warsaw Ghetto, and gave detailed testimony to Oyneg Shabes.

Figure 23. Shmuel Brąsław (Breslav, 1920–1942) was a leader of the Ha-Shomer Ha-Tsair youth movement who joined the Oyneg Shabes executive committee. Brasław was a talented writer and journalist who contributed to the underground press and Oyneg Shabes.

Figure 24. Josef Kaplan (1913–1942), a leading member of Ha-Shomer Ha-Tsair, was active in the underground press and Jewish Self-Help. He was a founder of the Jewish Fighting Organization and was named to the Oyneg Shabes executive committee.

Figure 25. Shmuel Winter (1891–1943) was a successful importer-exporter, arts patron, and collector of Jewish folklore, as well as a supporter of the Bund, Yiddish culture, and YIVO. Active in the ghetto's provisioning department, he was a key supporter of Oyneg Shabes.

Figure 26. Władysław Szlengel (1919–1943), whom Ringelblum called "the poet of the ghetto," wrote exuberant satire, lyrics, and poetry in Polish.

Figure 27. Janusz Korczak (Dr. Henryk Goldszmit, 1878–1942) was a renowned author, teacher, physician, radio personality, and child advocate who managed an orphanage in the Warsaw Ghetto. On August 6, 1942, he chose to accompany his orphans on the journey that ended at Treblinka.

28

29

30

31

32

33

Figure 28. Rabbi Kalman Kalonimus Szapiro (1889–1944), the Piaseczner Rebbe and founder of a yeshiva, was a prominent preacher and author of works on religion and education. Texts of his sermons in the ghetto were preserved by Oyneg Shabes.

Figure 29. Lea Koziebrodzka (1917–1943) was a university student active in the Dror youth movement. She served Oyneg Shabes as an intercity courier.

Figure 30. Menachem Mendel Linder (1911–1942), an attorney, was active in YIVO's economics section. In the ghetto, he headed the statistics department of the Jewish Self-Help and worked closely with Oyneg Shabes.

Figure 31. Mordechai Szwarcbard (1896–1942), a Łódź native active in the Left Poalei Tsion, worked at a soup kitchen for refugees from Łódź in the Warsaw Ghetto. Active in Oyneg Shabes, he contributed a diary, materials about Łódź, and copies of Ringelblum's writings.

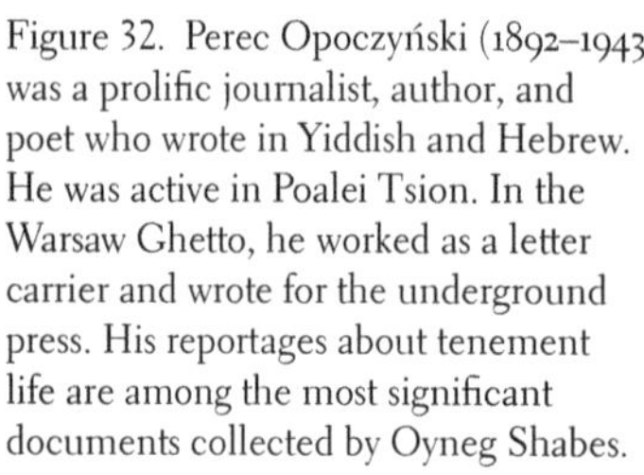
Figure 32. Perec Opoczyński (1892–1943) was a prolific journalist, author, and poet who wrote in Yiddish and Hebrew. He was active in Poalei Tsion. In the Warsaw Ghetto, he worked as a letter carrier and wrote for the underground press. His reportages about tenement life are among the most significant documents collected by Oyneg Shabes.

Figure 33. Abraham Lewin (1893–1943), a high school teacher, historian, and a member of the General Zionists, headed the youth division of the Jewish Self-Help in the ghetto and was one of the most important members of the Oyneg Shabes archive. His ghetto diary was preserved in the Oyneg Shabes collection.

Figure 34a. Gela Seksztajn (1907–1943) was a painter, educator, and the wife of Izrael Lichtensztajn. Many of her paintings and sketches were included in the Oyneg Shabes archive. Ring. I/1450

34a

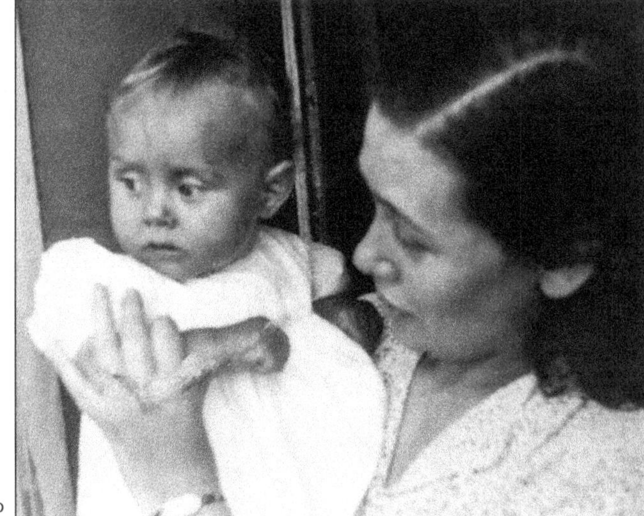
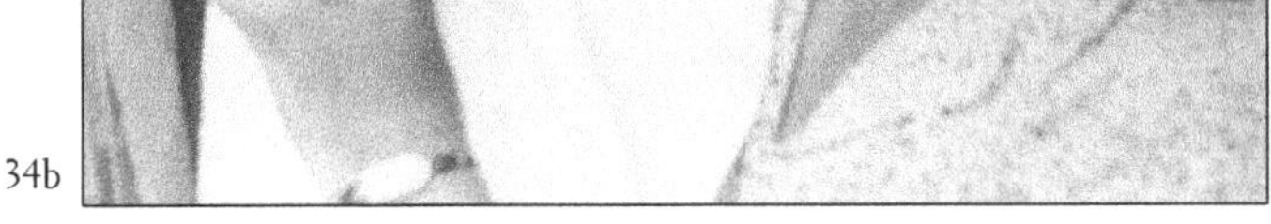

34b

35

36

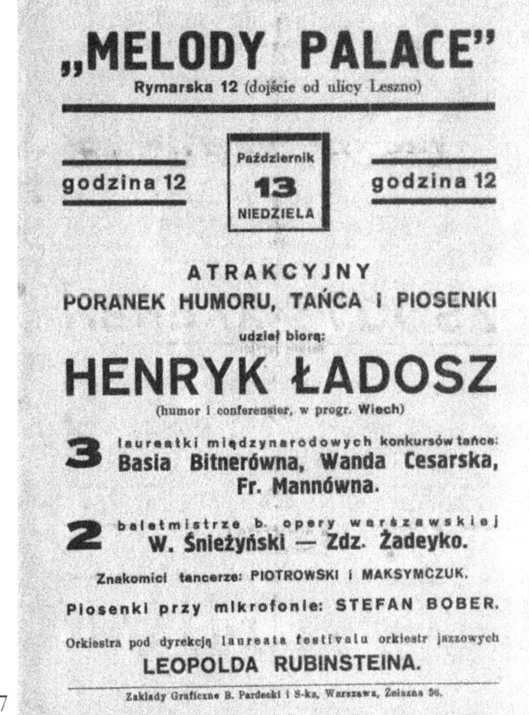

„MELODY PALACE"
Rymarska 12 (dojście od ulicy Leszno)

godzina 12 | Październik 13 NIEDZIELA | godzina 12

ATRAKCYJNY
PORANEK HUMORU, TAŃCA I PIOSENKI
udział biorą:
HENRYK ŁADOSZ
(humor i conferensier, w progr. Wiech)
3 laureatki międzynarodowych konkursów tańca: Basia Bitnerówna, Wanda Cesarska, Fr. Mannówna.
2 baletmistrze b. opery warszawskiej W. Śnieżyński — Zdz. Żadeyko.
Znakomici tancerze: PIOTROWSKI i MAKSYMCZUK.
Piosenki przy mikrofonie: STEFAN BOBER.
Orkiestra pod dyrekcją laureata festiwalu orkiestr jazzowych
LEOPOLDA RUBINSTEINA.
Zakłady Graficzne B. Pardecki i S-ka, Warszawa, Żelazna 36.

37

Figure 34b. Gela Seksztajn with her daughter Margalit. Ring. I/1450

Figure 35. Portrait of a young woman, by Gela Seksztajn. Ring. I/1457

Figure 36. Portrait of a girl begging, by Gela Seksztajn. Ring. I/1457

Figure 37. "Melody Palace" flyer announcing "a matinee of humor, dance, and song" on 13 October [1940]. Ring. II/240

Raz kupiłem sobie sak,
A to było wtedy tak:
Na wieszaku, tuż u ściany
Wisiał piękny płaszcz futrzany.
Przyszedł gość, a był grandziarzem,
Moje futro zabrał razem.
Taki chłop to był wesoły,
Więc zostałem całkiem goły......

Będąc jednak przy gotówce,
Sak nabyłem na Wałówce.
Co za sak!! Och, o mój Boże!!
Gorszy w świecie być nie może.
Kusy, brudny, wąski, stary,
W łokciach dziury, jak talary.
To nie sak, ale saczyna!!
Tak wyzywa mnie rodzina.

Rumieniłem się ze złości
I wstydziłem chodzić w gości.
W takiej szmacie nie wypada,
Lecz cóż robić, trudna [illegible].
Straszne rzeczy! Czy wiesz [illegible]?
Przeklinałem własne życie.
Ci złodzieje, co za dranie!!
Hania grozi mi zerwaniem!

Serce jedna wielka rana,
Gdy tu nagle wielka zmiana:
Zarządzenie, że od jutra
Trzeba oddać wszystkie futra.
Los odmienił mi się w mig,
Co za radość! Co za krzyk!
Wszyscy dają, a ja nic!
Ze szczęścia skakać mi się chce!

Aby uczcić to zdarzenie,
Do cukierni poszłem z Heniem.
Lecz nie miła tam zabawa:
Czarny nastrój, czarna kaw[illegible]
Sala pełna i napchana,
Cała giełda tam futrzana.
Te spojrzenia wszystkich gości
Były pełne strasznej złości.

Zazdrość im wierciła duszę,
Że ja saka dać nie muszę!
Powiesiłem sak na ścianie
I poszedłem zjeść śniadanie.
Gdy usiadłem przy stoliku,
Zamówiłem ćwierć befsztyku,
A że radość była wielka,
Poszła na stół też "kropelka".

I przed samym więc jedzeniem
Trąciłem się mocno z Heniem.
Jedno było niezbyt miłe,
Że do saka siadłem tyłem.
A gdy wstałem - co za draka!
Nie ma, nie ma mego saka!!
Boże! Cóż ja zrobię jutr[illegible]
Zamienili sak - na [illegible]

Figure 38. Poem in Polish by Władysław Szlengel: "Once I bought myself a net bag." Ring. I/1239

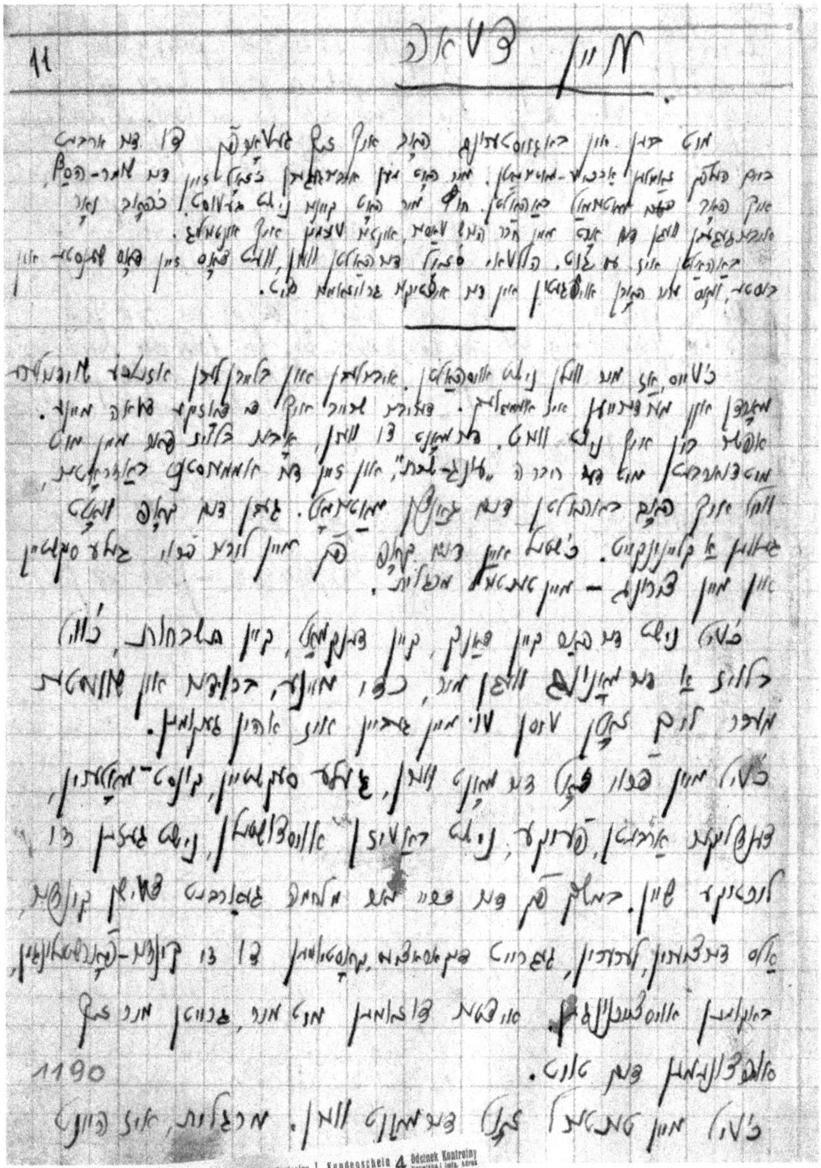

Figure 39. (ABOVE) Izrael Lichtensztajn's will, August 1942: "I want my little daughter to be remembered. Margalit is today 20 months old." Ring. I/1450

Figure 40. (LEFT) Food ration card for January 1942 overprinted with the red slogan, "THE POOR, HOMELESS CHILD IS HUNGRY AND COLD." Ring. I/278

Figure 41. (RIGHT) A candy wrapper imprinted in Polish and Yiddish: "FOR EVERYBODY." Ring. I/395

Figure 42. (BELOW) Warsaw Ghetto bus ticket. Ring. I/398

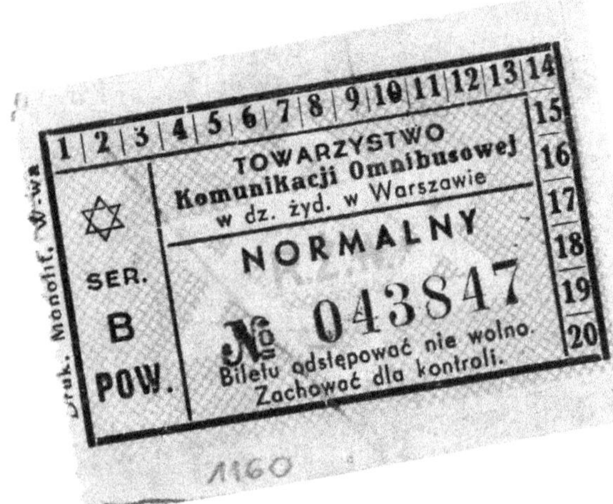

Figure 43. Paper money from the Łódź Ghetto. Ring. I/886

קײן באראנאװיטש זענען ד[illegible]יטשן ארײן
אויפן 5טן טאג מלחמה, ד.ה. ד.[illegible] יוני. 941
קײן קאמפן צוליב דער שטאט ז[illegible] נישט פאר
געקומען. די ערשטע עטלעכע טע[illegible] ס'איז
נאך געװען די בלויזע מיליטער[illegible] פארװאל-
טונג, איז נאך געװען פארהעלטע[illegible]עסיק צו
דערטראגן. אבער שוין אין די ערשטע טעג יול
איז די לאגע געװארן זײער שװער - װי אומע-
טום.

אנה"ב אויגוסט האט זיך דער מיליטע-
רישער װעטערינאר-דאקטאר געװאנדן (צו דער
קהילה, מסתמא) װעגן צושטעלן אים 32 ײדן
אויף צו קאנװאירן פערד קײן ראדעם - װײזט
אוים, אז דארט איז א [illegible] פערד-לאזא-
רעט. ס'האט די 32 ײדן צעטײלט צװישן א גע-
װיסער צאל פערד, פארלאדן אין בהמות-װאגא-
נען און אריבערגעפירט קײן ראדעם. אויפן פּפּ
װעג האט מען זײ, ד.ה. די ײדן, געגעבן פארהעל-
טענישמעסיק נישט שלעכט צו עסן און קײן
ספעציעלע נגישות נישט אנגעטון.
אנגעקומען קײן ראדעם האבן זײ די פערד
צוגעשטעלט אין ארדענונג, װאס דער מיטפארנ-
דיקער לײטענאנט-װעטערינאר האט בפירוש אונ-
טערגעשטראכן. ער איז מיט די 32 מאן אװעק
אין דער ײדישער גמינע אין ראדעם און, אלס
אנערקענונג פאר זײער גוטער ארבעט, געהײסן
אויסשטעלן פאר יעדן שאפירשײנען, װוהין יע-
דער װיל.
פאר אויסשטעלן א פאסירשײן נעמט די
ראדעמער קהילה בדרך-כלל צו [illegible] זלאטעם.
דא איז קײן געלט, פארשטײט ז[illegible]שט געװען.
די 32 האבן אבער פארלאנג[illegible]כוים, מען
זאל האנארירן דעם אפיצירס [illegible] ס'איז.
./.

Figure 44. Typed notes in Yiddish, dated November 1941, about the arrival of German troops in Baranowicze and the mass killing of 30 Jews in June 1941. (front) Ring. I/450

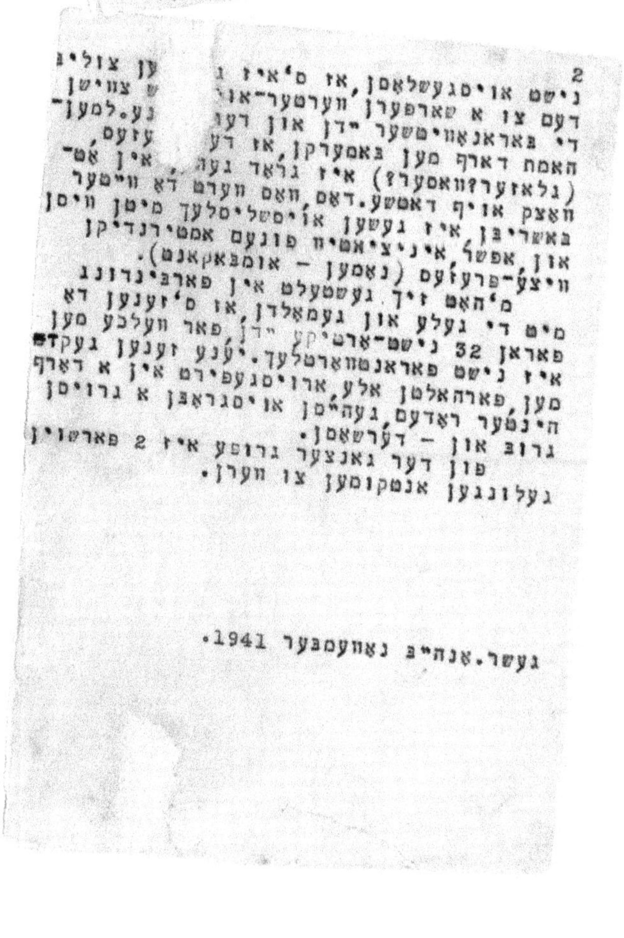

2
נישט אויסגעשלאסן, אז ס'איז ג[illegible]ען צוליב
דעם צו א שארפערן װערטער-או[illegible]ש צװישן
די באראנאװיטשער ײדן און דער[illegible]נע. למען-
האמת דארף מען באמערקן, אז דע[illegible]עזעם,
(גלאזערזװאסער?) איז גראד געװ[illegible] אין אט-
װאצק אויף דאטשע. דאס, װאס װערט דא װײטער
באשריבן, איז געשען אויסשליסלעך מיטן װיסן
און אפשר, איניציאטיװ פונעם אמטירנדיקן
װיצע-פרעזעס (נאמען - אומבאקאנט).
מ'האט זיך געשטעלט אין פארבינדונג
מיט די געלע און געמאלדן, אז ס'זענען דא
פאראן 32 נישט-ארטיקע ײדן, פאר װעלכע מען
איז נישט פאראנטװארטלעך. ס'זענען געקו
מען, פארהאלטן אלע, ארויסגעפירט אין א דארף
הינטער ראדעם, געהײסן אויסגראבן א גרויסן
גרוב און - דערשאסן.
פון דער גאנצער גרופע איז 2 פארשוין
געלונגען אנטקומען צו װערן.

געשר. אנה"ב נאװעמבער 1941.

Figure 45. Typed notes in Yiddish, dated November 1941, about the arrival of German troops in Baranowicze and the mass killing of 30 Jews in June 1941. (back) Ring. I/450

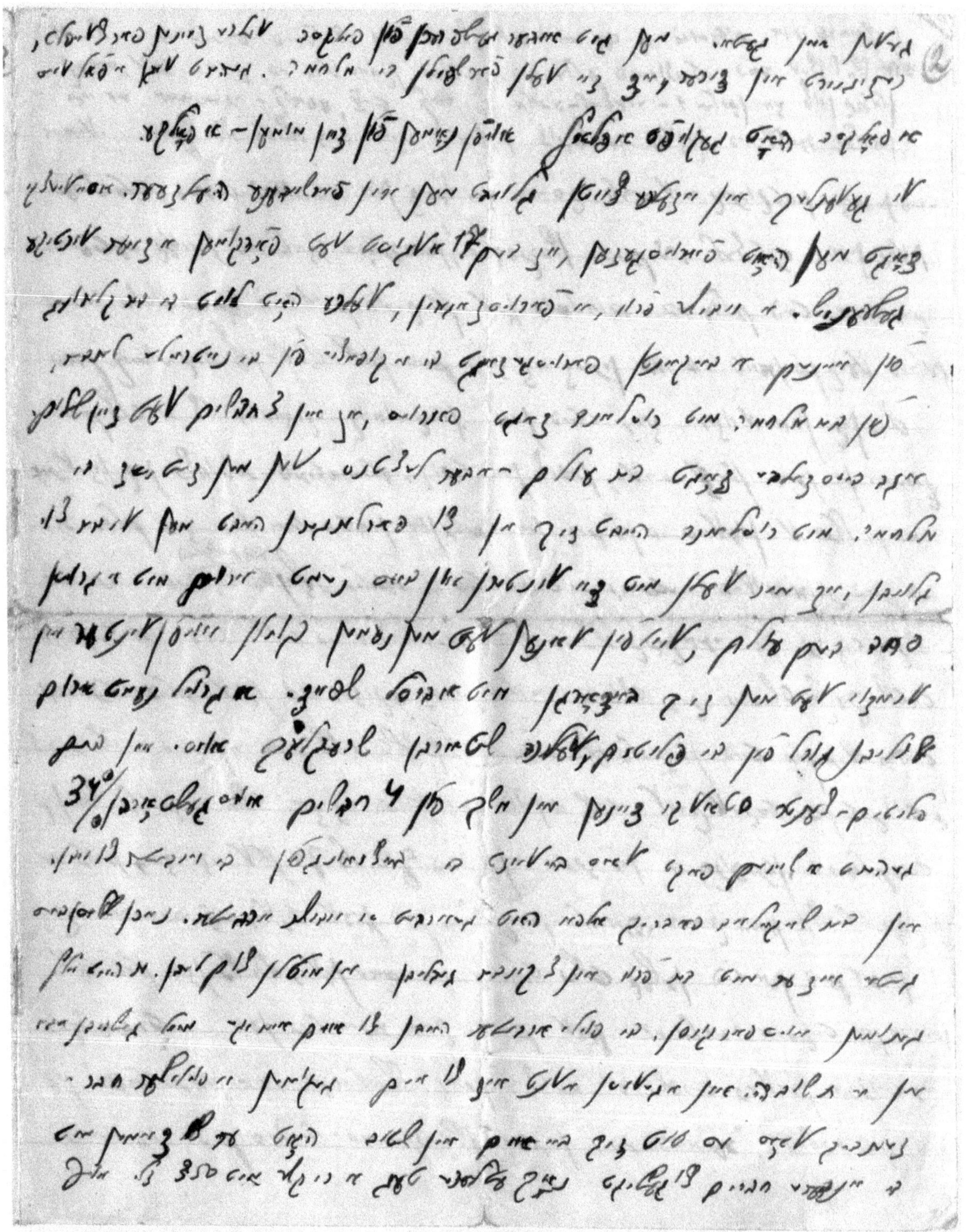

Figure 46. Diary notes by Emanuel Ringelblum, 1941. Ring. I/448

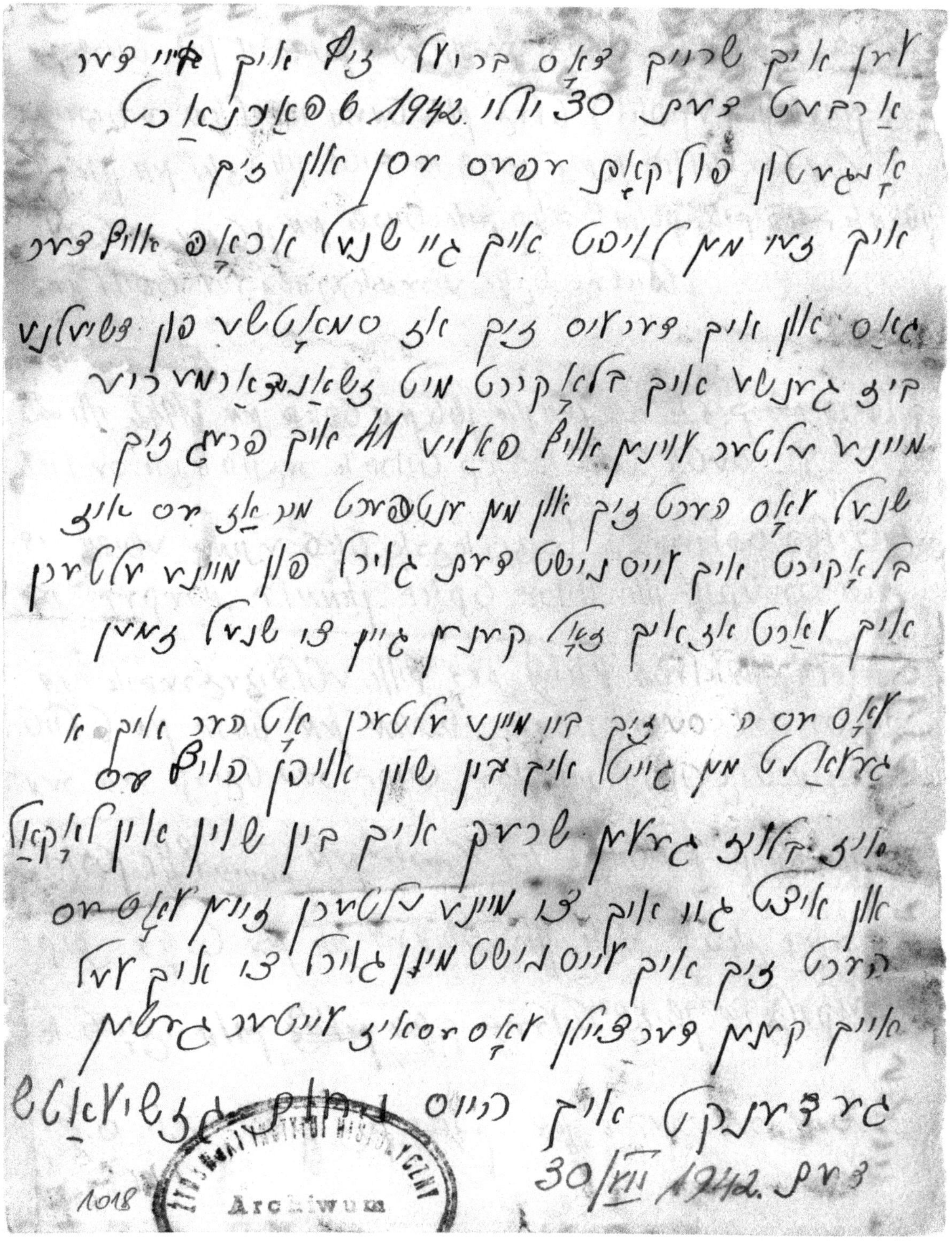

ווען איך שרייב דאָס בריוול זיצ איך [illegible]

אַרבעט דינסטיק 30 יולי 1942 6 אַזייגער נאַכט

[illegible]

[illegible]

[illegible]

[illegible]

[illegible]

[illegible]

[illegible]

[illegible]

[illegible]

[illegible]

[illegible]

[illegible]

[illegible]

[illegible]

געדענקט איך הייס נחום גשיוואַטש

30/יולי 1942. [illegible]



Figure 47. ". . . I don't know what's going to happen to me. *Remember, my name is Nachum Grzywacz.*" The last-minute testament of teenager Nachum Grzywacz, who assisted in the concealment of the first cache of the Oyneg Shabes archive. Ring. I/416

Nr. 9 (22) WARSZAWA LISTOPAD 1942 R.

Śmierć żołnierza na wojnie jest rzeczą zwykłą. Jest również cząstką ceny, którą okupujemy utraconą wolność. I każda śmierć żołnierska zbliża nas do tej wolności.

**DEPRAWACJA WOJENNA ŻOŁNIERZA I OBYWATELA**

Niszcząca siła wojny godzi najboleśniej w charakter człowieka. Nie miasta zburzone, nie plony zniszczone, lecz ofiary burzy szalejącej w duszach i umysłach ludzi — to ciosy wojny, od których rany najtrudniej zagoić.

W czasie pokoju na postępo anie jednostek wpływają władze, ustalone prawa i obyczaje. Wojna obezwładnia wiele z tych środków oddziaływania, przerywa kontakty utarte i pewne, wysuwa na pierwszy plan wolę i instynkt człowieka.

Zwłaszcza pobyt na froncie jest egzaminem charakteru. Wymaga woli dla pokonania zwierzęcego strachu, szlachetnego serca dla ukochania idei, rozumu dla uświadomienia sobie potrzeby znoszonych trudów. Brak tych elementów skieruje żołnierza poprzez strach i słabość ku zdradzie obowiązku. A jak każde zwycięstwo nad sobą nosi w sobie zaród przyszłej wielkości charakteru — tak przeżyta hańba zapowiada jego deprawację.

Żołnierz-okupant deprawuje się bardzo łatwo. Sytuacja zachęca go do wykorzystania swojej przewagi fizycznej, daje możność upojenia się władzą i brutalizowania bezbronnego otoczenia. Widzi dokoła siebie nadużycia i okrucieństwa nieukarane. Takie przeżycia zawsze zostawiają osad w duszy.

Ludność cywilną staje w okresie wojennym przed szerokimi możliwościami wyboru. Od donosicielstwa, paskarstwa, wykorzystywania swojej kaniunkturalnie korzystnej sytuacji, przez uczciwe wypełnianie obowiązków aż do służby i ofiarności społecznej. I tu wojna jest próbą wartości jednostki.



Figure 48. An underground Polish periodical, *Żołnierz Polski* (Polish Soldier), November 1942. Ring. II/449

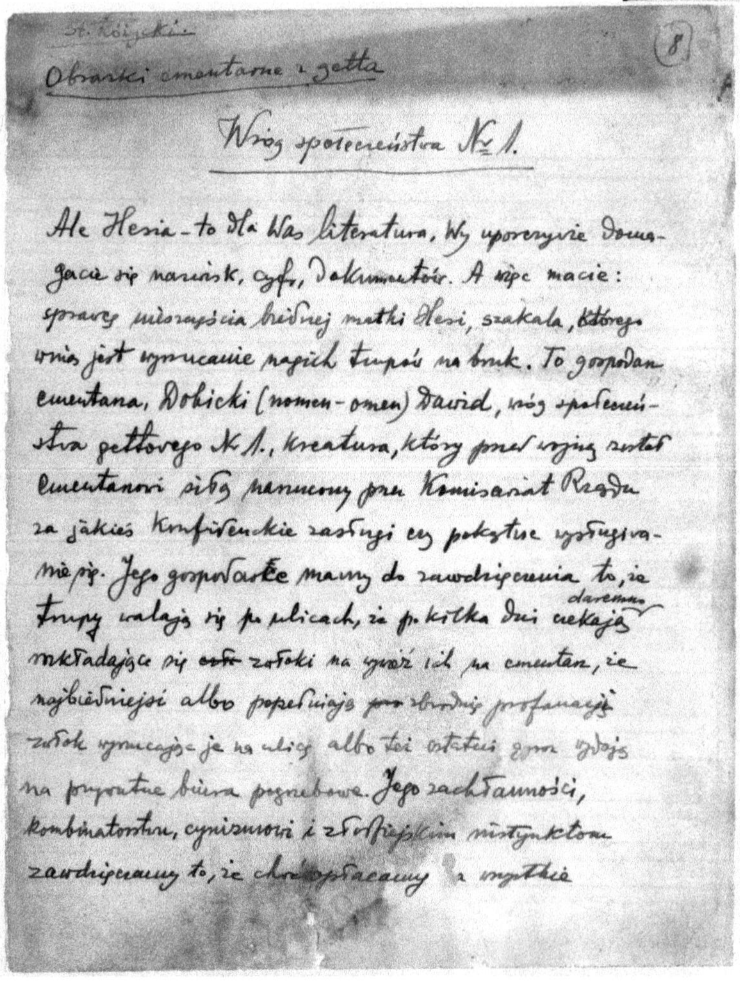

St. Różycki

8

Obrazki cmentarne z getta

Wróg społeczeństwa Nr 1.

Ale Hesia – to dla Was literatura. Wy uporczywie domagacie się nazwisk, cyfr, dokumentów. A więc macie: sprawcę nieszczęścia biednej matki Hesi, szakala, którego [illegible] jest wyrzucanie nagich trupów na bruk. To gospodarz cmentarza, Dobicki (nomen-omen) Dawid, wróg społeczeństwa gettowego Nr 1., kreatura, który przed wojną został cmentarzowi siłą narzucony przez Komisariat Rządu za jakieś konfidenckie zasługi czy pokątne wysługiwanie się. Jego gospodarce mamy do zawdzięczenia to, że trupy walają się po ulicach, że po kilka dni daremnie czekają rozkładające się zwłoki na wywóz ich na cmentarz, że najbiedniejsi albo popełniają zbrodnię profanacji zwłok wyrzucając je na ulicę albo też ostatni grosz wydają na prywatne biura pogrzebowe. Jego zachłanności, kombinatorstwu, cynizmowi i złodziejskim instynktom zawdzięczamy to, że [illegible] wszystkie

Figure 49. From a series of sketches, “Street Cartoons of the Ghetto,” by Stanisław Różycki: “Public Enemy no. 1.” Ring. I/456

Absender: DER AELTESTE DER JUDEN
in LITZMANNSTADT
Wohnort, auch Zustell- oder Leitpostamt
Straße, Hausnummer, Gebäudeteil, Stockwerk oder Postschließfachnummer

Postkarte
Litzmannstadt
DRUCKSACHE
Textil-Industrie
im Osten

An
Hirsz Wasser
Warschau
Muranowska 6/15
Straße, Hausnummer, Gebäudeteil, Stockwerk oder Postschließfachnummer

Δ C154 Din A 6

Figure 50. A printed postcard from the Łódź Ghetto administration to Hirsz (Hersz) Wasser in the Warsaw Ghetto. (front) Ring. II/529

Litzmannstadt-Getto, den .................... 1942.

An Hirsch Wasser
in Warschau
Strasse Muranowska Nr. 6/15

Familie Estera Lejb Wasser, wohnhaft hier,
Strasse Hohensteinstr. 43-45/101, befindet sich gesund.

(—) CH. RUMKOWSKI
Der Aelteste der Juden in Litzmannstadt

Figure 51. A printed postcard dated 1942 from Chaim Rumkowski of the Łódź Ghetto administration to Hersz Wasser. It affirms the address and good health of Estera and Lejb Wasser, Hersz's parents. Ring. II/529

Abschrift.

Der Leiter der Anklagebehörde
beim Sondergericht
Akt. Z.: 6 Js 1024/42

Warschau, den 28. April 1942.

An
das Sondergericht
in
Warschau.

HAFT!

**Anklage.**

B u k i Hinda, Juedin,

geb. am 22.2.1919, Buerstenmacherin, ledig,
wohnh. in Warschau, Krochmalnastr. 17 .171
z.Zt. im Gefgs. Gaensestrasse 24

klage ich wegen unbefugten Verlassens des jüdischen Wohnbezirkes an.

~~Er~~ /Sie hat als ~~Jude~~/ Jüdin am 20. Maerz 1942 in Warschau den den Juden zugewiesenen Wohnbezirk unbefugt verlassen.

Verbrechen nach § 4 b der Verordnung über die Aufenthaltsbeschränkungen im Generalgouvernement vom 13.9.40 /15.10.41/ V. Bl. GG 1941 Seite 595

**Beweismittel:**

Einlassung der Beschuldigten.

**Ermittlungsergebnis:**

~~Der~~ /Die Beschuldigte ist ~~Jude~~/ Jüdin. ~~Er~~ /Sie hat, wie ~~er~~/ sie selbst einräumt, am 20. Maerz 1942 in Warschau den jüdischen Wohnbezirk ohne Erlaubnis verlassen, um zu betteln.

**Antrag:**

Ich beantrage: 1) Hauptverhandlung vor dem Sondergericht Warschau (Kammer) anzuberaumen,
2) Haftfortdauer gegen ~~den Beschuldigten~~/ die Beschuldigte wegen Fluchtverdachts zu beschliessen.

J.A. Dr. Peter.
I. Staatsanwalt.

Figure 52. German indictment dated 28 April 1942 against Hinda Buki for the crime of leaving the Warsaw Ghetto without permission on 20 March 1942. Ring. I/189

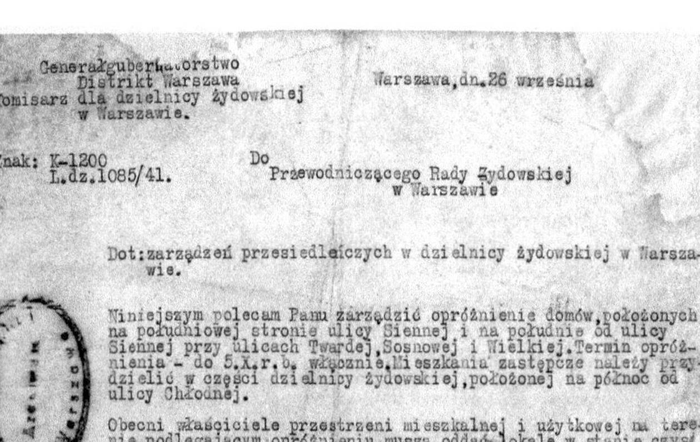

Generalgubernatorstwo
Distrikt Warszawa
Komisarz dla dzielnicy żydowskiej
w Warszawie.

Warszawa, dn. 26 września

Znak: K-1200
L.dz.1085/41.

Do
Przewodniczącego Rady Żydowskiej
w Warszawie

Dot: zarządzeń przesiedleńczych w dzielnicy żydowskiej w Warszawie.

Niniejszym polecam Panu zarządzić opróżnienie domów, położonych na południowej stronie ulicy Siennej i na południe od ulicy Siennej przy ulicach Twardej, Sosnowej i Wielkiej. Termin opróżnienia – do 5.X.r.b. włącznie. Mieszkania zastępcze należy przydzielić w części dzielnicy żydowskiej, położonej na północ od ulicy Chłodnej.

Obecni właściciele przestrzeni mieszkalnej i użytkowej na terenie, podlegającym opróżnieniu, muszą oddać lokale w stanie czystym zamiecionym. Oddać należy administratorowi domu, któremu należy również wręczyć klucze od mieszkania. Administrator domu ma [illegible]cze swego domu dostarczyć zebrane właściwemu Rejonowi Żydow[illegible] Służby Porządkowej.

Żydowska Służba Porządkowa ma w okresie opróżnienia urządzić wzmocnioną służbę nadzorującą, aby zapewnić prawidłowość przesiedlenia, w szczególności, aby zapobiec uszkodzeniu lokali, podlegających opróżnieniu, przez zabranie części budowlanych lub w inny sposób. Gdyby się mimo to zdarzyły uszkodzenia, wówczas na wypadek niewykrycia sprawcy lub niemożności osiągnięcia od niego odszkodowania, uczyniłbym za nie odpowiedzialnym Pana.

/-/ Auerswald

Figure 53. Transcript in Polish of a letter dated 26 September [1941] from German official Heinz Auerswald notifying the Warsaw Jewish Council that Jews must vacate all buildings along designated streets by 5 October 1941, with the Jewish Council and Jewish police responsible for arranging the evictions.

W-wa dn. 2. lipca 1942
Nr Dz. Int/319

Do
Kuchni Ludowej Nr 43
Lubeckiego 5

Ze względu na zmniejszenie się stanu A.C. o 110 osób, proszę o zmniejszenie ilości zup o 110 porcji z racji popołudniowej.

Kierownik A.C.

z/r ..............

Figure 54. Letter from the director of the ghetto's central jail dated 2 July 1942 to Public Kitchen no. 43 noting that, due to the reduction in its population, the jail will require 110 fewer portions of soup. (Jewish Council Chairman Adam Czerniaków's diary refers to the transporting of 110 prisoners sentenced to death.) Ring. I/240

DER JUDENRAT
in Warschau

Warschau, den 12. März 1941

# BEKANNTMACHUNG

**Gemäss Anordnung des Beauftragten des Distriktschefs für die Stadt Warschau gelangen in der Zeit vom 20. bis 25. März 1941 Lebensmittelkarten für den Monat April 1941 zur Ausgabe.**

1. Die Meldeführer haben in der Zeit vom 20. bis 25. März 1941 in dem zuständigen Bezirksbüro für Verteilung vom Lebensmittelkarten die ausgefüllten Bedarfsscheine auf Lebensmittelkarten für die Hausbewohner samt quittiertem Verzeichnis der verteilten Lebensmittelkarten der vorhergehenden Serie vorzulegen.
2. Die ausgefüllten Vordrucke sind zusammen mit den Meldebüchern in dem Bezirksbüro für Verteilung von Lebensmittelkarten vorzulegen, wo die Uebereinstimmung der Bedarfsscheine mit dem in den Meldebüchern aufgewiesenen Stande nachgeprüft wird.
3. **Die Vordruke sind laut dem Einwohnerstand am 19. März 1941 auszufüllen.**
4. Bis zum 19. März 1941 sind den Meldeführern 10 Groschen für jede Lebensmittelkarte einzuzahlen. Ausserdem ist jeder Hausbewohner verpflichtet, zu Gunsten des Judenrates zl. 1.— für jede Lebensmittelkarte zu entrichten. Diese Beträge sind bei Abgabe der Bedarfsscheine einzuzahlen.
   Für Lebensmittelkarten, die nicht im obigen Termin abgeholt werden, erhebt der Judenrat einen Zuschlag von 50 Groschen für jede Karte.
5. Die Meldeführer sind verantwortlich für die eingereichten Bedarfsscheine, die Abnahme der Karten und deren Verteilung unter die Hausbewohner in den festgesetzten Fristen.
6. Die Meldeführer haben sich in den nachstehenden Bezirksbüros für Verteilung von Lebensmittelkarten zu melden:

| | | | | |
|---|---|---|---|---|
| Bezirk | I. des Ordnungsdienstes | — | Bezirksbüro | Walicòw 10 |
| „ | II. „ | „ | — „ | Ogrodowa 39 |
| „ | III. „ | „ | — „ | Ogrodowa 39 |
| „ | IV. „ | „ | — „ | Gęsia 6 |
| „ | V. „ | „ | — „ | Gęsia 6 |
| „ | VI. „ | „ | — „ | Lubeckiego 4 |

## TERMINE

17–19.III.1941 — Die Meldeführer übernehmen in den Bezirksbüros für Verteilung von Lebensmittelkarten die Verzeichnisvordrucke (zu 5 Groschen das Stück)

20–25.III.1941 — Die Meldeführer legen in den Bezirksbüro für Verteilung von Lebensmittelkarten die Bedarfsscheine vor und erhalten dortselbst die Lebensmittelkarten.

26–28.III.1941 — Die Kunden melden den Abschnitt I der Lebensmittelkarten in den Verteilungsstellen von Lebensmitteln an und den Abschnitt II—in den Verteilungsstellen für Seifenartikel.
Die Anmeldefrist anderer Abschnitte wird besonders bekanntgegeben werden.

29–31.III.1941 — Die Verteilungsstellen legen die Kundenlisten samt Kundenscheinen und Meldungen in den Bezirksbüro für Verteilung von Lebensmittelkarten vor.

**Der Obmann des Judenrates in Warschau**
**( ) Dipl. Ing. Adam Czerniaków**

---

RADA ŻYDOWSKA
W WARSZAWIE.

Warszawa, dnia 12 marca 1941 r.

# Obwieszczenie

Zgodnie z zarządzeniem Pełnomocnika Szefa Dystryktu dla m. Warszawy wydawane będą w marcu 1941 r. karty aprowizacyjne na miesiąc kwiecień 1941 r.

1. Prowadzący meldunki obowiązani są w czasie od dnia 20 do 25 marca 1941 r. złożyć we właściwym Okręgowym Biurze Rozdziału Kart Aprowizacyjnych wypełnione zapotrzebowanie kart aprowizacyjnych dla mieszkańców domu, wraz z wykazami pokwitowań rozdanych kart aprowizacyjnych poprzedniej serii.
2. Wypełnione blankiety wraz z księgami meldunkowymi winny być przedstawione w Okręgowym Biurze Rozdziału Kart Aprowizacyjnych, które sprawdzi zgodność zapotrzebowania ze stanem wykazanym w księgach meldunkowych.
3. **Blankiety należy wypełnić zgodnie ze stanem zamieszkania w dniu 19 marca 1941 r.**
4. Prowadzącym meldunki należy do dnia 19 marca 1941 r. wpłacić po 10 groszy na każdą kartę żywnościową. Prócz tego każdy mieszkaniec wpłaca na rzecz Rady Żydowskiej zł 1.—od każdej karty żywnościowej. Sumy te winny być wnoszone równocześnie ze zgłoszeniem zapotrzebowania.
   Za karty aprowizacyjne, nie wykupione w powyższym terminie, Rada Żydowska pobiera dodatkową opłatę w wysokości 50 groszy od każdej karty.
5. Prowadzący meldunki są prawnie odpowiedzialni za dokonane zgłoszenia, odbiór kart i ich rozdział mieszkańcom w wyznaczonych terminach.
6. Prowadzący meldunki zgłaszają się do następujących Okręgowych Biur Rozdziału Kart Aprowizacyjnych:

| | | | | | | | | |
|---|---|---|---|---|---|---|---|---|
| Rejon | I | Służby | Porządkowej | — | O. B. R. K. A. | przy | ulicy | Walicòw 10 |
| „ | II | „ | „ | — | „ | „ | „ | Ogrodowej 39 |
| „ | III | „ | „ | — | „ | „ | „ | Ogrodowej 39 |
| „ | IV | „ | „ | — | „ | „ | „ | Gęsiej 6 |
| „ | V | „ | „ | — | „ | „ | „ | Gęsiej 6 |
| „ | VI | „ | „ | — | „ | „ | „ | Lubeckiego 4 |

## KALENDARZ CZYNNOSCI

17. — 19.III.1941 — Prowadzący meldunki odbierają w Okręgowych Biurach Rozdziału Kart Aprowizacyjnych formularze wykazów (po 5 groszy za sztukę).

20. — 25.III.1941 — Prowadzący meldunki składają zapotrzebowania i odbierają karty aprowizacyjnej w Okręgowych Biurach Rozdziału Kart Aprowizacyjnych.

26. —28. III.1941 — Konsumenci rejestrują odcinek I kart aprowizacyjnych w punktach rozdzielczych artykułów spożywczych, zaś odcinek II — w punktach rozdzielczych artykułów mydlarskich.

29 — 31. III.1941 — Punkty Rozdzielcze przedstawiają listy konsumentów wraz z odcinkami kontrolnymi i meldunkiem w Okręgowych Biurach Rozdziału Kart Aprowizacyjnych.

**Przewodniczący Rady Żydowskiej w Warszawie**
**(—) Inż. Adam Czerniaków**

Druk. A. Kejzmana, Warszawa, Leszno 34 w podwórzu

---

יידישער ראַט
אין ווארשע

ווארשע, 12 מערץ 1941

# מודעה

אין הסכם מיט דער פאראָרדענונג פון באפולמעכטיקטן פון דיסטריקט-שעף פאר דער שטאט ווארשע, וועלן אין חודש מערץ 1941 ארויסגעגעבן ווערן אפּראָוויזאציע-קארטעס אויפן חודש אפּריל 1941.

1. די פּערזאָנען, וואָס פירן די מעלדונגס-ביכער, זיינען מחויב אין טערמין פון 20-טן ביז דעם 25-טן מערץ 1941 צו באליפערן אין די געהעריקע קרייז-ביוראָען פארן פארטייל פון אפּראָוויזאציע-קארטעס אויסגעפילטע באדארף-רשימות פאר אפּראָוויזאציע-קארטעס פאר די הויז-איינוווינער, צוגלייך מיט די קבלות פון די פונאנדערגעטיילטע אפּראָוויזאציע-קארטעס פון דער פריערדיקער סעריע.
2. די אויסגעפילטע בלאנקעטן דארפן צוזאמען מיט די מעלדונגס-ביכער פארגעלייגט ווערן אין קרייז-ביוראָ פארן פארטייל פון אפּראָוויזאציע-קארטעס, ווו עס וועט קאָנטראָלירט ווערן צי דער באדארף שטימט מיטן פאקטישן צושטאנד לויט די מעלדונגס-ביכער.
3. די בלאנקעטן דארף מען אויספילן לויטן וווינונג-צושטאנד פון 19 מערץ 1941.
4. פאר יעדער אפּראָוויזאציע-קארטע דארף מען ביזן 19-טן מערץ 1941 באצאָלן דער פּערזאָן, וואָס פירט די מעלדונגס-ביכער צו 10 גר. חוץ דעם באצאָלט יעדער איינוווינער צו —.1 זל. פון אן אפּראָוויזאציע-קארטע פאר דער יידישער קהילה. דאָס געלט דארף איינגעצאָלט ווערן איינצייטיק מיטן איבערגעבן די באדארף-רשימות.
   פאר אן אפּראָוויזאציע-קארטע, וועלכע ווערט אויסגעקויפט נאכן טערמין, האט דער יידישער ראט באשטימט א צוגאב-אָפּצאָל אין דער הויך פון 50 גראָשן.
5. די פּערזאָנען, וואָס פירן די מעלדונגס-ביכער, זיינען רעכטלעך פאראַנטוואָרטלעך פארן איבערגעבן דעם באדארף, פארן אָפּנעמען די קארטעס און פארן פארטיילן זיי צווישן די איינוווינער אין די באשטימטע טערמינען.
6. די פּערזאָנען, וואָס פירן די מעלדונג-ביכער, מעלדן זיך צו די ווייטערדיקע קרייז-ביוראָען פארן פארטייל פון אפּראָוויזאציע-קארטעס:

1-ער ראַיאָן פון אָרדענונג דינסט — קרייז ביורא פארן פארטייל פון אפּר.-קארטעס וואליצוו 10
2-ער „ „ „ „ „ „ „ — „ „ „ „ אגראדאווע 39
3-ער „ „ „ „ „ „ „ — „ „ „ „ אגראדאווע 39
4-ער „ „ „ „ „ „ „ — „ „ „ „ גענשע 6
5-ער „ „ „ „ „ „ „ — „ „ „ „ גענשע 6
6-ער „ „ „ „ „ „ „ — „ „ „ „ לובעצקי-גאס 4

## אַרבעט-לוח

17 — 19 מערץ 1941: די פּערזאָנען, וואָס פירן די מעלדונג-ביכער, נעמען אָפּ אין די קרייז-ביוראָען פארן פארטייל פון אפּראָוויזאציע-קארטעס די פאָרמולארן פון די רשימות (5 גר א שטיק).

20 — 25 מערץ 1941: די פּערזאָנען, וואָס פירן די מעלדונג-ביכער באלייגן דעם באדארף און נעמען אָפּ די אפּראָוויזאציע-קארטעס אין די קרייז-ביוראָען פארן פארטייל פון די אפּראָוויזאציע-קארטעס.

26 — 28 מערץ 1941: די קאָנסומענטן רעגיסטרירן דעם אָפּשניט I. פון די אפּראָוויזאציע-קארטעס אין די פארטייל-פונקטן פאר שפייז-ארטיקלען און דעם אָפּשניט II.—אין די פארטייל-פונקטן פון זייף-ארטיקלען.

29 — 31 מערץ 1941: די פארטייל-פונקטן לייגן פאר די קאָנסומענטן-רשימות מיט די קאָנטראָל-אָפּשניטן און מיט א דין-וחשבון אין די קרייז-ביוראָען פארן פארטייל פון אפּראָוויזאציע-קארטעס.

דער פארזיצער פון יידישן ראט אין ווארשע
(—) אינזש' א. טשערניאַקאָוו

Figure 55. Poster in German, Polish, and Yiddish, dated 12 March 1941 and signed by Jewish Council Chairman Adam Czerniaków, announcing rations fixed for food and other items for ghetto residents. Ring. I/276

Figure 56. (TOP) Warsaw Ghetto air raid warden's armband imprinted in German and Polish. Ring. II/69

Figure 57. (BOTTOM) Paper band printed in German indicating that a letter had been opened by German military censors. Ring. I/148

Figure 58. (ABOVE) Ruins on Twarda Street. Ring. I/683 photo 30

Figure 59. (RIGHT) Ruins on Twarda Street. Ring. I/683 photo 36

Figure 60. (BELOW) Ghetto wall at Elektoralna Street (with overhead sign announcing in German and Polish, "Typhus Quarantine Zone"). Ring. I/683 photo 28

Figure 61. (above) Iron gate on Chłodna Street. Ring. I/683 photo 45

Figure 62. (left) Wooden gate at Plac Grzybowski. Ring. I/683 photo 37

Figure 63. (below) Ghetto wall on Przejazd Street. Ring. I/683 photo 38

Figure 64. Pedestrian traffic on a ghetto street before the deportation. Ring. I/683 photo 2

Figure 65. Pedestrian bridge over Chłodna Street. Ring. I/683 photo 34

Figure 66. Men of the Warsaw Ghetto's Order Service (Jewish police). Ring. I/683 photo 69

Figure 67. Jewish policemen (with white armbands on right arms) with Council Chairman Adam Czerniaków (wearing civilian garments, bowler hat, Jewish star armband) and Polish policemen (in uniforms without Jewish armbands). Ring. I/683 photo 16

Figure 68. Adam Czerniaków (left of center), Szmul Winter (on extreme right), and others with a girl rescued from the fate of eight Jews executed by firing squad for leaving the ghetto without permission. (Unknown if the rescued girl is standing at the center or second from left). Ring. I/683 photo 3

Figure 69. Jewish police, Adam Czerniaków (at right in fedora), and ghetto children. Ring. I/683 photo 7

Figure 70. Jewish police with Jewish Council Chairman Adam Czerniaków (right of center, bald man holding fedora), apparently speaking with uniformed Polish police. Ring. I/683 photo 19

Figure 71. Women with their bread rations. Ring. I/683 photo 14

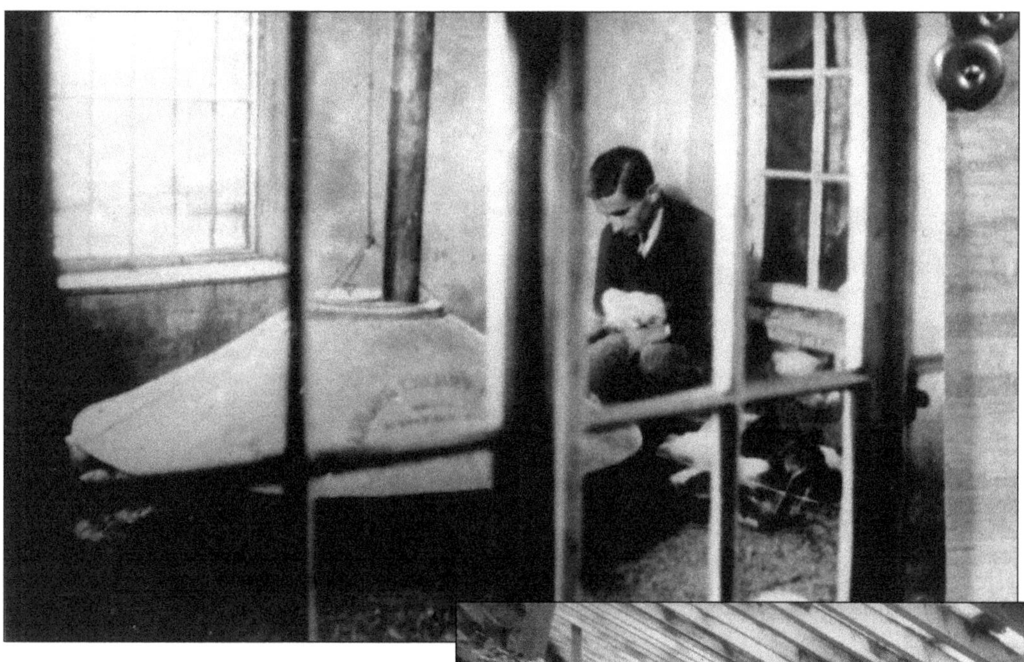

Figure 72. (ABOVE) A poultry incubator in the Warsaw Ghetto. Ring. I/683 photo 20

Figure 73. (RIGHT) A Jew working in a ghetto hothouse. Ring. I/683 photo 13

Figure 74. (BELOW) Mothers with their children in the Warsaw Ghetto. Ring. I/683 photo 40

Figure 75. Journalist Halina Zuckermann's wedding to a musician. Ring. I/683 photo 27

Figure 76. Children and teachers in the ghetto. Ring. I/683 photo 23

Figure 77. Trade on Miła Street. Ring. I/683 photo 44

Figure 78. Fodder beets for sale on Miła Street. Ring. I/683 photo 64

Figure 79. (ABOVE) Harvesting potatoes in the Warsaw Ghetto. Ring. I/683 photo 10

Figure 80. (LEFT) Harvesting cabbages in the Warsaw Ghetto. Ring. I/683 photo 65

Figure 81. (BELOW) Café selling matzah: “Large selection of matzah at factory prices” (Polish); “Sale of kosher matzahs, square and round, under the supervision of the Warsaw Rabbinate” (Yiddish). Ring. I/683 photo 48

Figure 82. (above) Line of rickshaws on Żelazna Street in the ghetto. Ring. I/683 photo 51

Figure 83. (right) Smuggling flour over the ghetto wall. Ring. I/683 photo 11

Figure 84. (below) Market on "Gęsiówka" in the ghetto. Ring. I/683 photo 59

Figure 85. (ABOVE) Jewish police searching children caught smuggling food into the ghetto. Ring. I/683 photo 12

Figure 86. (RIGHT) Jewish children in the Warsaw Ghetto. Ring. I/683 photo 67

Figure 87. Posted death notices. Ring. I/683 photo 21

Figure 88. (BELOW) Two patients sharing a bed in the Czyste Hospital in the Warsaw Ghetto. Ring. I/683 photo 76

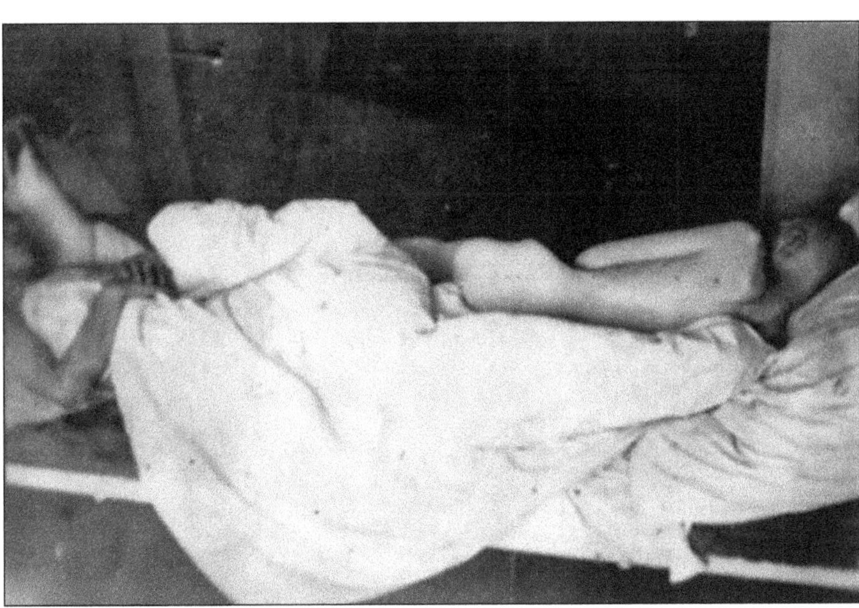

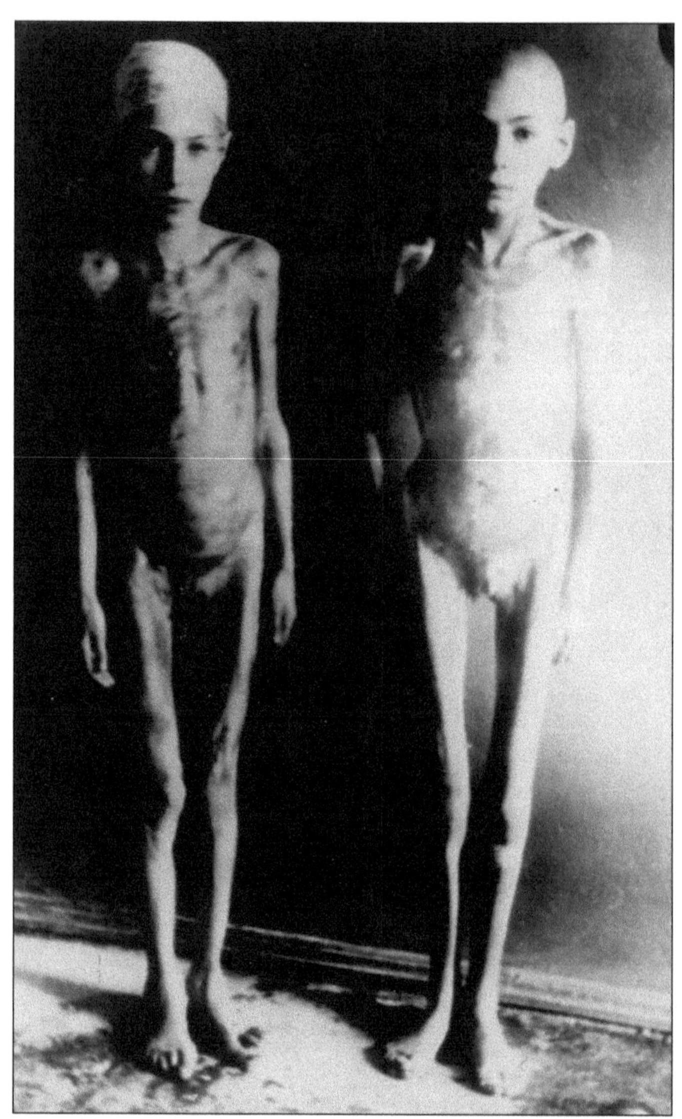

Figures 89 and 90. Emaciated Jewish children in the ghetto. Ring. I/683 photos 17 and 68

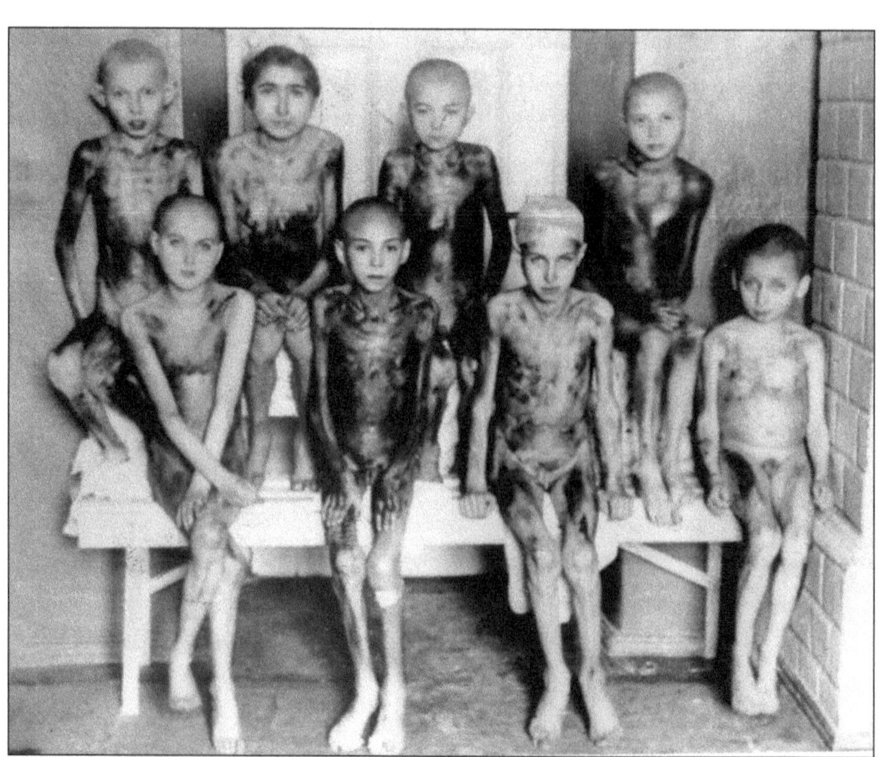

# Catalog of Ringelblum II

## I. Oyneg Shabes Records: Ring. II

1. RING. II/212. Mf. ŻIH—798; USHMM—53.
   - 11.1940–08.1942, Warsaw Ghetto
   - [Menachem Mendel Kohn], Cash ledger of the Oyneg Shabes group (9.11.1940–7.08.1942)
   - Lists of revenues and expenditures, salaries (lists of persons), addresses, notes, notation about the founding meeting of Oyneg Shabes on 5.10.1940.
   - ***Description:*** original, handwritten manuscript (MK*, H.W.*), notebook, ink, Yiddish, 143×158, 137×202, 167×213 mm, ss. 37, pp. 71.
     Index: [Szymon] Huberband, Dr. [Emanuel] Ringelblum, [Nechemiasz] Tytelman, [Salomea] Ostrowska, [Perec] Opoczyński, [Daniel] Fligelman, [Mordechaj] Szwarcbard, Goldsztajn, Grojnowski, [Eliasz] Gutkowski, [Jechiel] Górny, [Hersz] Wasser, Menachem Kohn, [Abraham] Lewin, Szajnkinder, [Lejb] Goldin, [Rita?] Krauze, [Natan] Smolar, Herclich, [Izrael] Winnik, [Izrael] Lichtensztajn

2. RING. II/236/2. Mf. ŻIH—798; USHMM—53.
   - Date unknown, Warsaw Ghetto
   - NN., Notes
   - Surnames, addresses (inter alia, coworkers of Oyneg Shabes)
   - ***Description:*** original, handwritten manuscript (LEG*i H*), pencil, Polish, Yiddish, 150×195 mm, ss. 1, pp. 2.

## II. General Monographs on the Situation of the Jewish Population during the War

3. RING. II/126. Mf. ŻIH—794; USHMM—49.
   - After 01.1940, place unknown.
   - NN., Memorandum entitled, "Die Zerstörung der jüdischen wirtschaftlichen Positionen in Polen" [The destruction of Jewish economic positions in Poland]
   - Social and economic situation of the Jewish population in Poland before the war and in the first months of occupation (losses during the war, anti-Jewish legislation and economic policies of the German occupier, displacements).
   - ***Description:*** transcript, typescript, German, 216×281 mm, ss. 9, pp. 9.
     On p. 1 at top a note (ink): "VII–VIII 1940"

4. RING. II/125. Mf. ŻIH—794; USHMM—49.
   - Date unknown, place unknown
   - NN., Memorandum entitled, "Uwagi o produktywizacji ludności Żydowskiej w Guberni Generalnej" [Observations on the productivization of the Jewish population in the Generalgouvernement]
   - Role and significance of the Jewish population in the economic life of the Polish lands before the war and in the Generalgouvernement. Demands to lift legal restrictions on the Jewish population and reconstruct the economic system.
   - ***Description:*** transcript, typescript, Polish, 219×282 mm, ss. 9, pp. 9.

5. RING. II/168. Mf. ŻIH—795; USHMM—50.
   - Date unknown, place unknown
   - [Friedrich] Gollert, *Zwei Jahre Aufbauarbeit im Distrikt Warschau* [Two years of constructive work in the Warsaw District], Warschau 1941 (fragment)
   - Fragments of a book concerning German policy toward the Jewish population.
   - ***Description:*** transcript, typescript, German, 208×298 mm, minor damages and losses of text, ss. 4, pp. 4.

6. RING. II/290. Mf. ŻIH—800; USHMM—55.
   - After 28.10.1942, Warsaw Ghetto
   - Max Gröters, Article entitled "Ein Fetzen Papier? Genfer Konvention und 'Soldaten Christi'" [A shred of paper? The Geneva Convention and "Soldiers of Christ"], (*Warschauer Zeitung*, no. 255, dated 28 [6?].10.1942) (fragment)
   - Concerning obedience by Germans to the Geneva Convention on protection of the civilian population during war.
   - ***Description:*** transcript (in German and in Polish translation), handwritten manuscript (H*), ink, German, Polish, 160×223 mm, ss. 2, pp. 2.
     A copy of this doc. was inserted in the report

entitled "Likwidacja Żydowskiej Warszawy" [Liquidation of Jewish Warsaw]; see Ring. II/192 (pub.: *Archiwum Ringelbluma*, p. 311).

7. **RING. II/292. Mf. ŻIH—800; USHMM—55.**
   - After 19.12.1942, Warsaw Ghetto
   - Note entitled "Official German Note on the Jewish Problem. Berlin, 19 December 1942"
   - Transcript of article from *Corriere della Sera* (no date and no issue no.).
   - ***Description:*** transcript (2 copies), typescript, Polish, 210×295, 205×295 mm, ss. 2, pp. 2.

8. **RING. II/429. Mf. ŻIH—806; USHMM—61.**
   - Beginning of 1942, Warsaw Ghetto
   - Rabbi Shimon Huberband, Study entitled "Mekoyrim tsu der yidisher geshikhte in di slavishe lender, bifrat in Poyln, Rusland un Lite" [Sources for Jewish history in the Slavic lands, particularly in Poland, Russia, and Lithuania] (Warsaw, winter 1942)
   - Review of sources for history of Jews in Slavic lands from the Middle Ages to the 16th century. Work dedicated to Director [Daniel] Guzik.
   - ***Description:*** original or transcript, typescript, Yiddish, 215×306 mm, ss. 44, pp. 43.

     On p. 1 (cover) note in Yiddish (pencil): "M. Kohn"

     Published: BFG, vol. IV, no. 4/1951, pp. 93–130; BŻIH, no. 2/1951, pp. 16–46.

9. **RING. II/430. Mf. ŻIH—806; USHMM—61.**
   - Date unknown, place unknown
   - A. Bluman, "Yidishe geoynim[1] vos hobn geshmakhtet in tfises bay di araber" [Jewish leaders who languished in prison among the Arabs]
   - Concerning Jews living within the territory of Iraq in the 5th to 11th centuries.
   - ***Description:*** transcript (pp. 5 in 2 copies), typescript, Yiddish, 221×285 mm, ss. 6, pp. 6.

10. **RING. II/184. Mf. ŻIH—797; USHMM—52.**
    - Date unknown, Warsaw Ghetto
    - NN., Notes concerning the situation of the Jewish people
    - Effects of emancipation, problem of place for settlement, financial situation.
    - ***Description:*** original, handwritten manuscript, pencil, Yiddish, 158×200 mm, ss. 2, pp. 3.

      On p. 3 calculations (ink).

11. **RING. II/433. Mf. ŻIH—807; USHMM—62.**
    - Date unknown, place unknown
    - NN., Fragment of a study concerning the economic situation of the Jewish population
    - Issue of productivization of Jews in the 20th century.
    - ***Description:*** original, handwritten manuscript, ink, Yiddish, 212×264 mm, minor damages and losses of text, ss. 2, pp. 3.

12. **RING. II/239/1. Mf. ŻIH—799; USHMM—54.**
    - 1942, Warsaw Ghetto
    - [Hersz Wasser], Notes (lack of beginning)
    - Information concerning the situation of the Jewish population in various localities (Baranowicze, Koło); food prices.
    - ***Description:*** original, handwritten manuscript (H.W.*), ink, Yiddish, 151×200 mm, missing pp. 1–2, ss. 2, pp. 3.

      Doc. was kept in a binder.

      Index: Dr. Hochman, Lippkow

13. **RING. II/304. Mf. ŻIH—801; USHMM—56.**
    - After 1.01.1943, Warsaw Ghetto
    - U. Zilb., Study entitled "Gezamlte faktn fun geyrushim un redifes" [Collected facts about expulsions and persecutions]
    - Collection of accounts about: Łosice (beginning of the liquidation action 15.12.1942), Lublin and Izbica (about the Bornhard [Bernhard ?] family of Lublin); about the blockade of apartment blocks in the Warsaw Ghetto at ul. Miła 38–46, belonging to "Ursus," transfer of men to the branch factory in Czechowice.
    - ***Description:*** original, handwritten manuscript, notebook, ink, Yiddish, 144×205 mm, ss. 16, pp. 27.

      On p. 1 (cover) stamp: content illegible.

      Index: Lipszyc, physician

14. **RING. II/431. Mf. ŻIH—806; USHMM—61.**
    - Date unknown, place unknown
    - Kalonimus Szapiro, rabbi of Piaseczno, Study entitled "Tsav ve-zariz" [Command and the conscientious person]
    - Philosophical discussion of relation to God and fellow men.
    - ***Description:*** original, typescript (handwritten additions, ink), Hebrew, 210×297, 210×146 mm, ss. 20, pp. 20.

      Appended note (handwritten manuscript, ink, Hebrew, 83×53 mm, ss. 1, pp. 1).

15. **RING. II/370. Mf. ŻIH—803; USHMM—58.**
    - 1939–1942, Warsaw
    - [Kalonimus Kalmisz] Szapiro, rabbi of Piaseczno, Sabbath sermons
    - Enclosures 1) a note with request for conveyance of the manuscript to the address: "Rabbi I. Szapiro, Tel Aviv, Palestine"; 2) letter to rabbis: I. Szapiro,

1. The Hebrew–Yiddish word refers to the heads of the great Talmudic schools of Babylonia (Iraq). The word *gaon* originally meant "excellence" and came to be used in Yiddish and Hebrew to characterize a "brilliant genius."

Blumental, Elimelekh,[2] with request for publication of the transmitted text.
- *Description:* original, handwritten manuscript, ink, Hebrew, Yiddish, 208×297, 222×357 mm, ss. 52, pp. 100.

  See J. Leociak, *Tekst wobec Zagłady. (O relacjach z getta warszawskiego)* [Text regarding the Holocaust: On personal accounts from the Warsaw Ghetto], Wrocław 1997, pp. 303–313.

  Published: Kalonimus Kalmish [Shapiro], *Sefer Esh Kodesh*, Jerusalem 1959–1960; fragments published in English translation: N. Polen, *The Holy Fire: The Teachings of Rabbi Kolonymus Kalman Shapira, the Rebbe of Warsaw Ghetto*, Northvale, New Jersey 1994.

16. RING. II/432. Mf. ŻIH—806; USHMM—61.
- Date unknown, 10.08.1942, place unknown, Warsaw Ghetto
- Kalonimus Szapiro, rabbi of Piaseczno, "Hakhsharat ha-avrekhim" [Preparation of young scholars]
- Recommendations for educating the young. Attached notes and corrections.
- *Description:* original, handwritten manuscript (several handwritings), ink, Hebrew, 104×148, 210×297, 223×166, 223×355 mm, ss. 74, pp. 144.

  Index: Rabbi Abraham Moses Grinsztajn of Łódź.

17. RING. II/434. Mf. ŻIH—807; USHMM—62.
- Date unknown, place unknown
- NN., "Tsi hot der Bund egzistents barekhtikung" [Does the Bund have a justification for its existence]
- Significance of the Bund in the history of the Jewish labor movement.
- *Description:* original or transcript, handwritten manuscript, pencil, Yiddish, 157×195 mm, ss. 8, pp. 15.

18. RING. II/482. Mf. ŻIH—809; USHMM—64.
- Date unknown, Warsaw Ghetto
- NN., Notes for a lecture on 28th anniversary of the creation of the first kibbutz[3] in Palestine
- *Description:* original, handwritten manuscript, pencil, Polish, 155×110, 155×196 mm, ss. 7, pp. 13.

19. RING. II/478. Mf. ŻIH—809; USHMM—64.
- After 11.1938, place unknown
- List of books and periodicals from an unidentified collection.
- *Description:* original or transcript, typescript, Yiddish, 205×292 mm, ss. 4, pp. 4.

# III. Warsaw and the Warsaw Ghetto

## *DOCUMENTS OF GERMAN AUTHORITIES AND INSTITUTIONS*

20. RING. II/399. Mf. ŻIH—804; USHMM—59.
- After 6.07.1942, Warsaw
- Der Kommandant Sicherheitspolizei und des SD für den Distrikt Warschau [Commander Security Police and SD for the Warsaw District], Proclamation about offering of a reward for assistance in apprehension of the perpetrators of the holdup murder of Paulina Krüger (née Rüger), committed on 6.07.1942 at ul. Moniuszki 9 in Warsaw
- *Description:* original, printed, German, Polish, 590×464 mm, ss. 1, pp. 1.

  Doc. printed at the business of J. Dreszcz (ul. Teatralna 5, apt. 7).

21. RING. II/397. Mf. ŻIH—804; USHMM—59.
- 30.04.1942, Warsaw
- City Governor in Warsaw. Director of Police Dr. [Otto] Bethke, Proclamation dated 30.04.1942 on the requirement to obey the street traffic regulations
- *Description:* original, printed, German, Polish, 592×411 mm, minor damages and losses of text, ss. 1, pp. 1.

22. RING. II/323. Mf. ŻIH—801; USHMM—56.
- 02.1942, Warsaw
- *Mitteilungsblatt für den jüdischen Wohnbezirk in Warschau*, no. 1 dated 1.02.1942
- Official bulletin of the Commissioner for the Jewish District in Warsaw. Includes texts of German authorities' decrees (published in the period:

2. The Polish catalog text erroneously transliterates the name as Alimelech, which reflects a misreading of the Hebrew name, Elimelekh. Spelling of names, especially surnames, of Polish Jews is a complex issue, aggravated by different systems of transliteration. To minimize confusion between the English edition of the present catalog of the Ringelblum Archive and the Polish edition, spelling generally follows the Polish pattern, unless there is an alternative spelling known to have been used by the person named. Researchers dealing with Polish Jews will have to be aware of the possibility of spelling, e.g., Shapiro as Szapiro or as Shapira or as Szapira or as Szpira or as Schapira or as Schapiro, all of which are extent spellings for the Hebrew surname spelled shin-pei-yud-reish-alef (sh-p-i-r-a). An attempt to impose consistency could create more problems.

3. The first agrarian kibbutz (*kevutsa*) was Deganya established in 1909. En Harod, founded in 1921, was the first larger collective village, combining agriculture with industry, to be designated a kibbutz.

2.10.1940–29.01.1942) regarding the Jewish population and organization and functioning of the Warsaw Ghetto.
- *Description:* original, printed, German, 208×298 mm, ss. 4, pp. 8.
  Newspaper was printed at the Monolit printworks in Warsaw.
  Second copy, see Ring. I/208.

### 23. RING. II/143. Mf. ŻIH—795; USHMM—50.

- 17.11.1941, Warsaw Ghetto
- Der Kommissar für den jüdischen Wohnbezirk in Warschau [Commissioner for the Jewish Residential District in Warsaw], Proclamation dated 17.11.1941 on execution of the sentence of death on 8 Jews for crossing the boundaries of the ghetto
- Names of those murdered: Rywka Kligermann, Sala Pasztejn, Josek Pajkus, Luba Gac, Motek Fiszbaum, Fajga Margules, Dwojra Rozenberg, Chana Zajdenwach.
- *Description:* original, printed, German, Polish, 340×497 mm, ss. 1, pp. 1.
  Printed by Monolit (ul. Elektoralna 3).

### 24. RING. II/144. Mf. ŻIH—795; USHMM—50.

- 25.12.1941, Warsaw Ghetto
- Der Kommissar für den jüdischen Wohnbezirk in Warschau [Commissioner for the Jewish Residential District in Warsaw], Order dated 25.12.1941 obligating Jews to turn in all furs and fur clothing under threat of death by firing squad
- *Description:* original (2 copies in a different format), printed, German, Polish, 468×625, 450×596 mm, minor damages and losses of text (first copy), damages and losses of text (second copy), ss. 2, pp. 2.

### 25. RING. II/190. Mf. ŻIH—797; USHMM—52.

- After 22.07.1942, Warsaw Ghetto
- [Das Beauftragten für die Umsiedlung, Hermann Höffle] [Plenipotentiary for Resettlement Matters, Herman Höffle], "Eröffnung und Auflagen für den Judenrat" (22.07.1942)
- Guidelines transmitted orally at meeting of the Jewish Council on 22.07.1942 at the community's seat at ul. Grzybowska 26 by the plenipotentiary for resettlement matters, Hermann Höffle, on the subject of organization of the "movement to the East" of Jews of Warsaw.
- *Description:* transcript, typescript, German, 224×287 mm, minor damages and losses of text, ss. 3, pp. 3.
  Inf. on "guidelines," see Ring. II/191.
  Published: *Archiwum Ringelbluma*, pp. 33–35.

### 26. RING. II/294. Mf. ŻIH—800; USHMM—55.

- 1941, Warsaw
- Generalgouvernement (Warsaw), Official Form of "Identification Card 'J'" for Jews
- Printed item intended for the Warsaw Ghetto.
- *Description:* original, printed, German, Polish, 97×142 mm, ss. 3, pp. 6.
  Published: BŻIH, no. 71–72/1969, pp. 138–139.

### 27. RING. II/265. Mf. ŻIH—799; USHMM—54.

- Date unknown, Warsaw Ghetto
- NN., "Internal Regulations for Employees of the Labor Office"
- Collection of regulations.
- *Description:* original or transcript, typescript, Polish, 220×354 mm, ss. 1, pp. 2.
  Doc. was kept in a binder.
  According to Ruta Sakowska, the Labor Office [Urząd Pracy] in the Warsaw Ghetto was a unit of the Arbeitsamt.
  Published: *Archiwum Ringelbluma*, pp. 65–66.

## *DOCUMENTS OF OTHER AUTHORITIES AND INSTITUTIONS*

### 28. RING. II/383/2. Mf. ŻIH—803; USHMM—58.

- 1940, Warsaw
- Municipal Administration in Warsaw [Zarząd Miejski w Warszawie], "Fuel Card for 1940/1941."
- *Description:* original, printed, German, Polish, 99×88 mm, part of the coupons cut out, ss. 1, pp. 1.
  On the reverse stamp: "Skład węgla F. Osiński, ul. Ogrodowa 67" [F. Osiński Coal Yard, ul. Ogrodowa 67].

### 28a. RING. II/13. Mf. ŻIH—803; USHMM—58.

a)

- Date unknown, place unknown
- "Charter of the Polish Main Welfare Council" [Statut Polskiej Rady Głównej Opiekuńczej]
- *Description:* transcript, typescript, Polish, 225×289 mm, ss. 5, pp. 5.

b)

- Date unknown, place unknown
- "Rules of the Main Welfare Council" [Regulamin Rady Głównej Opiekuńczej]
- *Description:* transcript, typescript, Polish, 225×288 mm, ss. 7, pp. 7.

## *WORKSHOPS [SZOPY] IN THE WARSAW GHETTO*

### 29. RING. II/240. Mf. ŻIH—799; USHMM—54.

- Before 12.1942, Warsaw Ghetto
- [Emanuel Ringelblum?], "Regulations of the Central Commission for Support of Labor in Workshops at the Department of Providing Aid [Jewish Council in Warsaw] (CKPP)" [Regulamin Centralnej Komisji Popierania Pracy w Szopach przy Wydziale Niesienia Pomocy [RŻ w Warszawie] (CKPP)]
- Goals and tasks, organization, personnel, finances.
- *Description:* original, typescript, Polish, 208×294 mm, ss. 3, pp. 3.

On p. 1 a note (ER*, ink): "Ringelbl[um], Hallma[nn's workshop]."
Author determined on basis of *Kronika getta*, p. 519.
Published: *Archiwum Ringelbluma*, pp. 329–331.

## 30. RING. II/247. Mf. ŻIH—799; USHMM—54.

- 09–10.1942, Warsaw
- Firm of Bernhard Hallmann & Co KG, Announcements
  1) dated 10.09.1942, on ban on unregistered persons staying in houses belonging to the workshop;
  2) dated 13.10.1942, about hours of distribution of food cards and of the sale of rationed products on cards.
- ***Description:*** original, typescript, stamp, German, 208×147, 207×294 mm, ss. 2, pp. 2.
  In doc. 1 at the bottom is an illegible signature (pencil); in corners damage from thumbtacks.
  See *Archiwum Ringelbluma*, pp. 60, 63 (summary).

## 31. RING. II/253. Mf. ŻIH—799; USHMM—54.

a)

- 10.09.1942, Warsaw Ghetto
- OBW [Eastern Construction Carpentry Workshops] (ul. Gęsia 30), Letter dated 10.09.1942 to the firm Bernhard Hallmann & Co. (ul. Nowolipki 66)
- OBW's request that former employees of OBW (Hirszel Berliński, Pola Elster, Hirsz and Blima Wasser, Pinia Rzomska, Jechiel Górny, Lewek Rubinstein, Helena Szyf-Lifszyc) be allowed to return to their firm.
- ***Description:*** original, typescript, stamp, German, 208×148 mm, ss. 1, pp. 1.
  At bottom is an illegible signature (ink).
  See *Archiwum Ringelbluma*, p. 60 (summary).
  Published: BŻIH, no. 71/72/1969, pp. 160–161.

b)

- After 24.10.1942, Warsaw Ghetto
- [ZZ]. Distribution point no. 18 (ul. Nowolipki 68), Order of 24.10.1942
- Regarding performance of the order contained in the attached letter. Attached: ZZ, Letter dated 21.10.1942 to the firm Bernhard Hallmann & Co. (ul. Nowolipki 66) (order for collection of food issued on ration cards of 09.1942 with the printed inscription 08.1942 to 27.10.1942).
- ***Description:*** transcript, typescript, German, 218×175 mm, ss. 1, pp. 1.
  See *Archiwum Ringelbluma*, pp. 64 (summary).
  Published: BŻIH, no. 71/72/1969, pp. 168–169.

c)

- After 30.10.1942, Warsaw Ghetto
- Bernhard Hallmann & Co, Letter dated 30.10.1942 to managers of Workshops I and II, the Housing Office, Construction Bureau, Order Service and Werkschutz [Factory Guard], Kitchens
- Regarding security matters, maintenance of discipline. Letter signed B. Hallmann.
- ***Description:*** transcript, typescript, Polish, 218×153 mm, ss. 1, pp. 2.
  On p. 1 at the top is a note (pencil): "to inform the workers of the II floor 2.11.[1942] [illegible signature]"; on p. 2 at the bottom a note (pencil): "employees of the kitchen read over and took note."
  See *Archiwum Ringelbluma*, pp. 65 (summary).
  Published: BŻIH, no. 71/72/1969, pp. 163, 165.

## 32. RING. II/254. Mf. ŻIH—799; USHMM—54.

a)

- 08–09.1942, Warsaw Ghetto
- Bernhard Hallman & Co. K.G. Werkschutz [Factory Guard]. Dawid Szafran, "Dienstnotizbuch" [Service Notebook]
- Course of service during 19.08–22.09.1942.
- ***Description:*** original, handwritten manuscript (various handwritings), ink, pencil, German, Polish, 96×156 mm, sewn, ss. 16, pp. 6.
  See *Archiwum Ringelbluma*, p. 45 (summary).

b)

- 08–09.1942, Warsaw Ghetto
- Bernhard Hallman & Co. K.G. Werkschutz [Factory Guard]. Hersz Klepfisz (registration card 27056, work card 622), "Dienstbuch für Werkschutzmann" [Service book of factory guard]
- Course of duty during 31.08–22.09.1942.
- ***Description:*** original, handwritten manuscript (various scripts), ink, pencil, German, Polish, 96×156 mm, sewn, ss. 20, pp. 9.
  Stamp on the cover: "Bernhard Hallmann & Co. K.G. Holzverarbeitung, Warschau C 1, Künstlerstr. 10, Fernruf 65820"; on the cover (sheet 20) a note (ink): "628 Kurewa."
  See *Archiwum Ringelbluma*, p. 45 (summary).

c)

- 08–10.1942, Warsaw Ghetto
- Bernhard Hallman & Co. K.G. Werkschutz. Wolf Graubart (registration card no. 79305, work card 152), "Dienstbuch für Werkschutzmann" [Service book of factory guard]
- Record of duty during 31.08–1.10.1942.
- ***Description:*** original, handwritten manuscript (various scripts), ink, pencil, German, Polish, 96×156 mm, sewn, ss. 10, pp. 9.
  On the cover stamp: "Bernhard Hallmann & Co. K.G. Holzverarbeitung, Warschau C 1, Künstlerstr. 10, Fernruf 65820."
  See *Archiwum Ringelbluma*, p. 45 (description, photocopy—fragment—pp. 1–2).

d)

- 09.1942, Warsaw Ghetto
- Bernhard Hallman & Co. K.G. Werkschutz. Josef Winogron (registration card no. 57766, work card

399), "Dienstbuch für Werkschutzmann" [Service book of factory guard]
- Record of duty during 3–30.09.1942.
- ***Description:*** original, handwritten manuscript (various handwritings), ink, pencil, German, Polish, 96×156 mm, sewn, ss. 34, pp. 11.
  On the cover stamp: "Bernhard Hallmann & Co. K.G. Holzverarbeitung, Warschau C 1, Künstlerstr. 10, Fernruf 65820."
  See *Archiwum Ringelbluma*, p. 45 (summary).

## 33. RING. II/235. Mf. ŻIH—798; USHMM—53.

- 11.1942–01.1943, Warsaw Ghetto
- [Self-help Committee at Hallmann's workshop (ul. Nowolipki 59), CKPP ?]. Relief Commission, Minutes of sessions of 2.12., [6].12., 9.12., 14.12., 18.12., 28.12.1942–5.[?]01., 10.01., 27.01.1943
- Decisions on allocation of food, monetary and medical aid. Attached minutes of the session of 9.12. [1942] of the Aid Commission, opinions, medical certificates, vouchers for distribution of aid, lists of names of the needy, notes; Jozowa, letter [before 4.01.1943?] to [Emanuel] Ringelblum and [Lipe Lejzer] Bloch (request for food aid).
- ***Description:*** original, typescript, handwritten manuscript (several handwritings: ER* et al.), ink, pencil, Polish, Yiddish, 128×70, 102×64, 155×196 mm, ss. 31, pp. 41.
  About the self-help committee at Hallmann's workshop, see *Kronika getta*, p. 519.
  Regulations of CKPP, see Ring. II/240.

## 34. RING. II/255. Mf. ŻIH—799; USHMM—54.

- 26.12.1942, Warsaw Ghetto
- H.S.V. [Heeresstandortverwaltung (Army Site Administration)—brushmakers' workshop, ul. Świętojerska 34]. Management of the Sentry Unit (of the Werkschutz), Announcement of 26.12.1942
- Order for persons not employed in the workshop to leave the residential block, under threat of death penalty.
- ***Description:*** original, typescript, German, Polish, 215×175 mm, ss. 1, pp. 1.
  See *Archiwum Ringelbluma*, p. 89 (summary).
  Published: BŻIH, no. 71/72/1969, pp. 167–168.
  Index: Brenner

## 35. RING. II/293/5.

- 1942, Warsaw Ghetto
- H.S.V. [Heeresstandortverwaltung (Army Site Administration)—brushmakers' workshop, ul. Świętojerska 34], Emblem from the cap of an employee of the factory guard [Werkschutz], no. 13.
- ***Description:*** original, cloth with an embroidered number "13" and the letters "HSV," 32×50 mm.
  Published: BŻIH, no. 71/72/1969, p. 168 (photo.).

## 36. RING. II/216. Mf. ŻIH—798; USHMM—53.

- 07.1942, Warsaw Ghetto
- [Workshop] Holzverarbeitungsunternehmen Ing.T. Tepicyn und M. von Szaniawski [Carpentry firm] (ul. Gęsia 69), Pass no. 389 dated 23.07.1942 for Szymon Heller (ul. Nalewki 23)
- Attached: Der SS und Polizeiführer Brest Kommandeur der Ordnungspolizei—Wirtschaftsdienstelle [SS and Police Leader Brest Commander of the Order Police—Economic Bureau], Certificate dated 3.06.1942, that the firm Holzverarbeitungsunternehmen Ing.T. Tepicyn und M. von Szaniawski is their supplier of wooden goods.
- ***Description:*** original, printed, photocopy (attached), typescript, German, 99×138, 147×88 mm, missing photograph, ss. 3, pp. 4.
  Published: *Archiwum Ringelbluma*, pp. 246–248 (photocopy without attachment; ibid., p. 249, reproduction of photograph of Szymon Heller from 1938).

## 37. RING. II/248. Mf. ŻIH—799; USHMM—54.

- 28.10.1942, Warsaw Ghetto
- Werkschutz [Factory Guard] of the OBW workshop, Order no. 1/42 of 28.10.1942
- Order to turn in all electric heaters from the OBW block on ul. Miła.
- ***Description:*** original, typescript, Polish, 204×136 mm, ss. 1, pp. 1.
  At bottom signature of the manager of the OBW Werkschutz (pencil): "Kurtsch [?]"
  See *Archiwum Ringelbluma*, p. 64 (summary).
  Published: BŻIH, no. 71/72/1969, p. 162.

## 38. RING. II/249. Mf. ŻIH—799; USHMM—54.

a)

- [23.09.1942], [After 23.09.1942], Warsaw Ghetto
- OBW (Warsaw Ghetto), Announcement
- Order to carry out the instructions of the workshop's management and return to work within 36 hours.
- ***Description:*** a) original, handwritten manuscript, ink, German, Polish, 512×610 mm, minor damages and losses of text, ss. 1, pp. 1; b) transcript, handwritten manuscript (H.W.*), ink, Yiddish, 209×142 mm, ss. 1, pp. 1.
  Date: "23.09.1942" from doc. b).
  At top in doc. b) a note (H.W.*, pencil, Polish): "translation of the German original [in addition to] transcript."
  Doc. a): beneath the text in German, illegible signature of the factory's manager (ink).
  Doc. b), see *Archiwum Ringelbluma*, p. 61 (summary).
  Published: BŻIH, no. 71/72/1969, pp. 161–162.

b)

- 29.10.1942, Warsaw Ghetto
- OBW, "Factory Regulations" (29.10.1942)
- Regulations for workers of the workshop.
- ***Description:*** original, typescript, stamp, German, Polish, 208×543 mm, ss. 1, pp. 2.

At bottom (beneath text in German and beneath translation into Polish) stamp of OBW and under the text in German an illegible signature (ink); under the text in Polish signature (ink): "Landau."
See *Archiwum Ringelbluma*, p. 64 (summary).
Published: BŻIH, no. 71/72/1969, pp. 162–164.

### 39. RING. II/250. Mf. ŻIH—799; USHMM—54.

a)

- 3.12.1942, Warsaw Ghetto
- Carpenters Commission of the OBW workshop, Letter dated 3.12.1942 [?] to Józef Landau, director (Warsaw Ghetto, OBW)
- Regarding organization of labor in the workshop.
- ***Description:*** transcript, handwritten manuscript (LEG*), pencil, Yiddish, 218×288 mm, ss. 2, pp. 2.
  Date: "3.12.42" (H*, ink).
  Published: *Archiwum Ringelbluma*, p. 323.

b)

- 2.12.1942, Warsaw Ghetto
- NN., Letter of 2.12.1942 to Józef Landau
- Request for a meeting.
- ***Description:*** original, handwritten manuscript, pencil, Yiddish, 143×200 mm, ss. 1, pp. 2.
  See *Archiwum Ringelbluma*, p. 198 (summary).

### 40. RING. II/256. Mf. ŻIH—799; USHMM—54.

- After 10.12.1942, Warsaw Ghetto
- Firm of [Fritz] Schultz[, ul.Nowolipie 44/46], Announcement dated 10.12.1942
- About introduction of a new system of inspection of workers from 14.12.1942
  Doc. signed by: F. Schultz, R. Neumann, F. Scherf.
- ***Description:*** original or transcript, typescript, German, 208×295 mm, ss. 1., pp. 1.
  See *Archiwum Ringelbluma*, p. 84 (summary).
  Published: BŻIH, no. 71–72/1969, pp. 165–167.

### 41. RING. II/260. Mf. ŻIH—799; USHMM—54.

- Date unknown, Warsaw Ghetto
- Program of an artistic event in an unspecified workshop of the Warsaw Ghetto
- Participants: Samberg, Fostel, M. Miodowski, R. Gurfinkiel, Hadasa Wein (age 10), M. Bogaty, Sz. Inwentarz [sic], Endewelt.
- ***Description:*** original, typescript, Polish, 117×156, 218×280 mm, ss. 3, pp. 2.
  See *Archiwum Ringelbluma*, p. 155 (summary).

## *DOCUMENTS OF JEWISH AUTHORITIES, INSTITUTIONS, AND ORGANIZATIONS*

## Jewish Council

### 42. RING. II/134. Mf. ŻIH—795; USHMM—50.

- After 19.02.1941, Warsaw
- Generalgouvernement. Amt des Chefs des Distrikts Warschau. Abteilung Umsiedlung [Office of the Chief of the Warsaw District. Resettlement Department]. Transferstelle [Transfer Station], Letter dated 19.02.1941 to Chairman of the Jewish Council in Warsaw
- Permit for employees of the Jewish post office to wear special armbands. Letter signed J. [Josef] A. Steyert.
- ***Description:*** transcript, stamp, German, 84×120 mm, ss. 1, pp. 1.

### 43. RING. II/139. Mf. ŻIH—795; USHMM—50.

- 09–12.1941, Warsaw Ghetto
- Jewish Council in Warsaw, Correspondence with the Commissioner for the Jewish District in Warsaw (Der Kommissar für den jüdischen Wohnbezirk in Warschau).
  1) Der Distriktchef in Warschau. Abteilung Innere Verwaltung. Unterabteilung Gesundheitswesen [The District Chief in Warsaw. Department of Internal Administration. Health Facilities Subdepartment], Letter of 28.08.1941 (refusal to open a central distribution warehouse for medications, signed Dr. W. Sydow);
  2) Jewish Council in Warsaw, Letter [after 12.11.1941] (concerning Litauer, an attorney—who does not appear in the Jewish Council's registration card index);
  2a) Der Kommissar . . . , Letter dated 13.10.1941 (cover letter with the attached letter dated 13.10.1941 to Litauer, an attorney, in the matter of documents of the Radziwiłł brothers from Ołyka, letter and attachment signed [Hermann] Probst);
  3) Jewish Council in Warsaw, Letter [after 16.10.1941] (cover letter to the encl. letter of Józef Jerzy Hertz [Order Service] and record of the testimony of Moszek Lipa, janitor [ul. Pańska 51, apt. 18] concerning theft in the house at ul. Sienna 33; testimony of Moszek Lipa was recorded by Mieczysław Hufnagel, of the Order Service no. 797);
  4) Jewish Council in Warsaw, Letter dated 21.10.1941 to the Bureau of Banking Clearance (Biura Rozrachunku Bankowego) (ul. Nowolipki 10) (regarding transfer of 100.000 zł. to the account of the firm Schmidt and Münstermann);
  5) Jewish Council in Warsaw, Letter dated 22.10.1941 (regarding printing of a newspaper by the Monolit firm within the ghetto) (2 copies);
  6) Jewish Council in Warsaw, Letter dated 28.10.1941 (Sura Wajsberg of ul. Walicόw 22, apt. 6, does not appear in the Jewish Council's registration card index);
  7) Jewish Council in Warsaw, Letter dated 28.10.1941 (Chamel Lilienblum of ul. Zimna 5,

apt. 3, 26.10.1941 apparently had to leave for Łowicz);
8) Jewish Council in Warsaw, Letter dated 28.10.1941 (regarding electricity supply to the "Czyste" hospital);
9) Jewish Council in Warsaw, Letter dated 29.10.1941 (regarding archival materials connected with combating epidemics in the Warsaw Ghetto);
10) Jewish Council in Warsaw, Letter dated 29.10.1941 (regarding the announcement about compulsory vaccination against dysentery);
11) Jewish Council in Warsaw, Letter dated 31.10.1941 (regarding formation of schools in closed social welfare institutions and with request for agreement to open a school in the orphanage at ul. Dzielna 39);
12) Der Kommissar . . . , Letter dated 12.11.1941 (regarding documents of the Radziwiłłs of Ołyka, signed [Hermann] Probst);
13) Der Kommissar . . . , Letter dated 16.11.1941 (regarding restriction of issuance of permits for travel of Jews, signed Dr. [Franz] Grassler);
14) Jewish Council in Warsaw, Letter dated 17.11.1941 (regarding rules for posting of announcements in the Jewish district);
15) Jewish Council in Warsaw, Letter dated 19.11.1941 (regarding courses for auxiliary pharmaceutical personnel);
16) Jewish Council in Warsaw, Letter dated 19.11.1941 (Lejzor Szlama Kamień of ul. Lubeckiego 17, apt. 2, was on 24.11.1940 reported to have moved to Otwock);
17) Der Kommissar . . . , Letter dated 19.11.1941 (regarding place of residence of Jenny Daehling, widow of a postal superintendent, signed [Heinz] Auerswald);
18) Der Kommissar . . . , Letter dated 21.11.1941 (regarding death certificate of Jankiel Kossower [died 12.05.1941], ul. Grzybowska 20, apt. 45);
19) Der Kommissar . . . , Letter dated 21.11.1941 (regarding ascertainment of the address of J.W. Gantz of ul. Zielna 29 as well as of the owner of the firm Landau and Sliozberk);
20) Der Kommissar . . . , Letter dated 21.11.1941 (regarding request of Wiktor Nuss of ul. Grzybowska 36);
21) Der Kommissar . . . , Letter dated 22.11.1941 (regarding timetable of the lines of horse-drawn buses in the ghetto);
22) Jewish Council in Warsaw, Letter dated 25.11.1941 (regarding Litauer, attorney, who does not appear on the roll of residents of the ghetto);
23) Der Kommissar . . . , Letter dated 25.11.1941 (regarding synagogues in the ghetto, signed [Heinz] Auerswald);
24) Jewish Council in Warsaw, Letter dated 26.11.1941 (regarding payment of fines);
25) Jewish Council in Warsaw, Letter dated 26.11.1941 (Sucher Zawadzki does not appear in the Jewish Council's registration card index);
26) Jewish Council in Warsaw, Letter dated 28.11.1941 (request for extension of permission not to wear armband for these persons: Altberg Lucjan [ul. Ogrodowa 26], Jerzy Graff [ul. Grzybowska 9], Kazimierz Rechthand [ul. Elektoralna 11], Chiel Rozen [ul. Sądowa 13], Józef Andrzej Szeryński [ul. Dzika 25]);
27) Jewish Council in Warsaw, Letter dated 3.12.1941 (regarding confiscation of furniture);
28) Der Kommissar . . . , Letter dated 5.12.1941 (regarding heirs of Wolf Binem Gefilhaus of ul. Mariańska 6, apt. 7, who died 15.06.1941);
29) Der Kommissar . . . , Letter dated 5.12.1941 (refusal of permission for Chana Różycka of ul. Nowolipki 25, apt. 8, to travel to Klimontów, signed [Franz] Grassler);
30) Jewish Council in Warsaw, Letter dated 8.12.1941 (regarding horse transport in the ghetto).

- ***Description:*** transcript, typescript (handwritten additions, ink, pencil), German, 204×148, 210×297 mm, ss. 36, pp. 36.

  Docs. 1–30 are office file copies of the Jewish Council in Warsaw. Incoming correspondence was marked with register numbers, dates of arrival, and other office markings, as well as handwritten notes. Attachments to correspondence were not preserved.

  Some of the docs. were kept in a binder.

## 44. RING. II/140. Mf. ŻIH—795; USHMM—50.

- 09.1941–03.1942, Warsaw Ghetto
- Jewish Council in Warsaw, Correspondence with the Commissioner for the Jewish District in Warsaw (Der Kommissar für den jüdischen Wohnbezirk in Warschau)

  1) Der Kommissar . . . , Letter dated 26.09.1941 (concerning change of the ghetto's boundaries, order to vacate houses by 5.10.1941, all houses on the southern side of ul. Sienna as well as on Sosnowa, Wielka, and Twarda);
  2) Der Kommissar . . . , Letter dated 21.10.1941 (concerning change of the ghetto's boundaries, order to vacate houses by 26.10.1941—attached list of streets);
  3) Der Kommissar . . . , Letter dated 25.12.1941 (concerns compulsory collection of fur garments);
  4) Der Kommissar . . . , Letter dated 9.02.1942 (receipt for collection of 1,500 sheepskin coats, delivered by the Jewish Council to the Transferstelle at ul. Stawki);
  5) Der Kommissar . . . , Letter dated 12.02.1942 (concerning requirement to register all persons held in the jail at ul. Gęsia);

6) Der Kommissar . . . , Letter dated 2.03.1942 (order for Władysława Radzka [Rudzka?] [ul. Mariańska 11, at Jankiel Ajzenberg] to leave the ghetto by 12.03.1942);
7) Der Kommissar . . . , Letter dated 10.03.1942 (concerns 151 prisoners held in the jail [at ul Gęsia], who are to leave the jail as a result of the amnesty of 9.01.1942).

- ***Description:*** transcript, typescript, German, 208×147, 208×288 mm, ss. 7, pp. 7.
  Docs. 1–5 and 7 were signed by Heinz Auerswald.
  Docs. 1–7 are office file copies of the Jewish Council in Warsaw. On several of the copies were recorded register numbers, dates of arrival and other office markings, as well as handwritten notes (docs. 3 and 7) (ink): "copy for the Chairman."

## 45. RING. II/138. Mf. ŻIH—795; USHMM—50.

- 08–11.1941, Warsaw Ghetto
- Jewish Council in Warsaw, Correspondence with Transferstelle [Transfer Station]

1) Transferstelle, Letter dated 25.08.1941 (permission for K. Rechthand and R. Wundheiler to move about Warsaw by carriage and rickshaw with ban on using streetcar and bus, signed [Max] Bischof);
2) Jewish Council in Warsaw, Letter dated 14.09.1941 to Transferstelle (concerns printing equipment for the Monolit printworks as well as passes for Jono[?] Rachman [ul. Leszno 56] and Józef Hirszowicz [ul. Waliców 17/19]);
3) Transferstelle, Letter dated 16.09.1941 (concerns transport and distribution of cabbage for the Jewish district);
4) Transferstelle, Letter dated 24.09.1941 (concerns Industrie und Handelsgesellschaft "Prohan," signed [Max] Bischof);
5) Jewish Council in Warsaw, Letter dated 6.10.1941 (concerns the illegal bakery at Gerichtsstr. 65 of Josek Groswurcel [ul. Krochmalna 5, apt. 54] and Jankiel Goldsztejn [ul. Pawia 50, apt. 15]);
6) Transferstelle, Letter dated 6.10.1941 (about confiscation and ban on distribution of Dr. Simon Nichtberger's publication, *Produktionsmöglichkeiten und Voraussetzungen des jüdischen Gewerbes* [Production possibilities and postulates of Jewish business], as well as the order to send to that office copies of the book *Aufstellung der Betriebe nach Branchen* [Establishment of workshops by branches] immediately after its appearance, signed [Max] Bischof);
7) Transferstelle, Letter dated 7.10.1941 to the Jewish Production Company (Żydowska Spółka Produkcyjna) (ul. Prosta 12/14) (concerns production of denim clothing, signed Küchenhoff);
8) Transfelstelle, Letter dated 8.10.1941 (in the matter of payments for postal shipments to labor camps, signed Dr. Rathje);
9) Transferstelle, Letter dated 8.10.1941 (concerns cooperation with the firm Schenker & Co., signed Dr. Rathje);
10) Jewish Council in Warsaw, Letter dated 9.10.1941 to Transferstelle (concerns confiscated parcels, signed B. [Beniamin] Zabłudowski);
11) Transferstelle, Letter dated 9.10.1941 (concerns lack of permission to dispatch books and articles of religious worship);
12) Transferstelle, Letter dated 10.10.1941 (concerns refund of the relief grant allotted to Irena Głogowska and Irena Landau [ul. Ogrodowa 27, apt. 23], signed Berrens);
13) and 14) Transferstelle, Letters (2) dated 16.10.1941 (letters principally concern social security [benefits], signed [Max] Bischof);
15) Transferstelle (Social Security Bureau [Ubezpieczalnia Społeczna] in Warsaw), Letter dated 14.10.1941 (concerns reporting of cases of sickness and death);
16) Transferstelle, Letter dated 16.10.1941 (concerns transport into the ghetto of products for which there is no permission for sale);
17) Transferstelle, Letter dated 16.10.1941 (concerns application of Nuchim Prezmann for permission to import into the ghetto parcels received from Paris);
18) Transferstelle, Letter dated 16.10.1941 (concerns confiscation of merchandise from Elkan Milchior [ul. Świętojerska 34], A. Tarnower [ul. Sienna 32], Gdali Szyff [ul. Nalewki 32] and Samuel Wachtel [ul. Sienna 24], signed [Max] Bischof);
19) Jewish Council in Warsaw, Letter dated 20.10.1941 to Transferstelle (concerns issuance of a pass to Leopold Lindenfeld, director of the jail in the Warsaw Ghetto);
20) Tranferstelle, Letter dated 21.10.1941 (concerns refund of money in connection with the complaint of Robert Nosek [?] [ul. Hopfenstr. 25] for the 4,000 zł owed him from Abraham Koral [ul. Nowolipie 20, apt. 17], signed Berrens);
21) Transferstelle, Letter dated 23.10.1941 (concerns payment of fines, signed Berrens);
22) Transferstelle, Letter dated 23.10.1941 (concerns paying out of pension of 169 zł monthly to Stefan Skubiszewski [ul. Cząstkowska 6, apt. 1], signed Berrens);
23) Nursing school, Letter dated 27.10.1941 (concerns deposit of 3,450 zł for meals [za posiłki] for 58 trainees working in Jewish hospitals);
24) Jewish Council in Warsaw, Letter dated

28.10.1941 to Transferstelle (concerns permit to deposit 100,000 zł to the account of the firm Schmidt u. Münstermann for construction work at the wall of the Warsaw Ghetto);
25) Jewish Council in Warsaw, Letter dated 28.10.1941 to Transferstelle (Icek Herschberg of Rawa Mazowiecka is absent from the directory of those registered in the ghetto);
26) Jewish Council in Warsaw, Letter dated 29.10.1941 (concerns payment of 3,450 zł for the benefit of the nursing school [ul. Pańska 34] for feeding trainees working in hospital);
27) Transferstelle, Letter dated 14.11.1941 (concerns foundation of the firm J. Margoses & Co. [ul. Nowolipie 17], signed [Max] Bischof);
28) Der Stadthauptmann für die Stadt Warschau, Letter dated 19.11.1941 with attached certification that Elisabeth Wilhelmine Dreimann née Werner (born 1.01.1890 in Wiesbaden), residing in Warsaw at ul. Górnośląska 7a, apt. 26, since 19.11.1941, is not of the Mosaic faith, signed Becher;
29) Transferstelle, Letter dated 24.11.1941 (cover letter to doc. 28 [?], signed Dr. Rahtje).

- ***Description:*** transcript, typescript (handwritten notations, ink, pencil), German, 210×150, 210×297 mm, ss. 29, pp. 29.

  Docs. 1–29 are office copies of the Jewish Council in Warsaw. On incoming correspondence are written register numbers, dates of arrival, and other office markings, also handwritten notes. Attachments to the correspondence were not preserved.

  Index: Marceli Seydengart

  Docs. were kept in a binder.

### 46. RING. II/127. Mf. ŻIH—794; USHMM—49.

- After 26.03.1940, Warsaw
- Chairman of the Jewish Council in Warsaw A[dam] Czerniaków, Memorandum entitled "Die neuen Aufgaben der Jüdischen Gemeinde in Warschau und die Lage der jüdischen Bevölkerung" [The new tasks of the Jewish Community in Warsaw and the situation of the Jewish population] (26.03.1940)
- Organizational and financial situation of the Jewish Council in the period of the occupation. Changes in the economic and legal position of the Jewish population in Warsaw, security, nourishment, and state of health. Proposal to remove restrictions for Jews.
- ***Description:*** transcript, typescript, German, 220×349 mm, ss. 8, pp. 8.

  Doc. was kept in a binder.

  See *Czerniaków*, pp. 97–98.

### 47. RING. II/29. Mf. ŻIH—793; USHMM—48.

- 15.01.1941, Warsaw Ghetto
- Jewish Council, Circular letter of 1940 to house committees in the matter of coupons exempting from the obligation to pay for food cards (15.01.1941).
- ***Description:*** original, printed, Polish, 207×293 mm, ss. 1, pp. 1.

  Date entered in ink.

  Published: *Przewodnik*, p. 404 (photocopy).

### 48. RING. II/135. Mf. ŻIH—795; USHMM—50.

- 15.04.1941, Warsaw Ghetto
- Jewish Council in Warsaw, Order dated 15.04.1941 on introduction of compulsory Saturday rest for residents of the Jewish quarter (in place of heretofore compulsory Sunday rest)
- From Friday sunset and during the whole of Saturday, only enterprises of public utility may operate.
- ***Description:*** original, printed, German, Polish, Yiddish, 580×837 mm, minor damages and losses of text, ss. 1, pp. 1.

### 49. RING. II/136. Mf. ŻIH—795; USHMM—50.

- 7.05.1941, Warsaw Ghetto
- Jewish Council in Warsaw, Announcement dated 7.05.1941 about preparations for anti-aircraft defense
- Obligation to designate an anti-aircraft defense post in each house, as well as to complete specified projects by 15.05.1941.
- ***Description:*** original, printed, German, Polish, Yiddish, 412×587 mm, ss. 1, pp. 2.

### 50. RING. II/152. Mf. ŻIH—795; USHMM—50.

- Before 5.06.1941, Warsaw Ghetto
- [Jewish Council in Warsaw?], Notification about deadline for registration of businesses, institutions, and employees (fragment)
- Leaflet addressed to the residents of the house at ul. Ogrodowa 43.
- ***Description:*** original, printed, Polish, 209×297 mm, missing second part of the item printed in German [?], ss. 1, pp. 1.

  Address and deadline for registration (5.06.1941) inscribed with ink.

### 51. RING. II/141. Mf. ŻIH—795; USHMM—50.

a)

- 21.10.1941, Warsaw Ghetto
- Jewish Council in Warsaw, Circular letter dated 21.10.1941 to the administration of houses and to house committees
- Announcement concerning changes in the ghetto's borders with an order for vacating houses (attached list of streets with house numbers) by 26.10.1941. Letter signed by Adam Czerniaków.
- ***Description:*** original, duplicated typescript, typescript, Polish, 220×340 mm, minor damages and losses of text, ss. 1, pp. 1.

b)

- After 21.10.1941, Warsaw Ghetto
- "List of houses excluded on 21 October 1941"
- List of streets and house numbers.
- ***Description:*** original or transcript, typescript, Polish, 208×295 mm, ss. 1, pp. 1.

### 52. RING. II/186. Mf. ŻIH—797; USHMM—52.

- 07–09.1942, Warsaw Ghetto
- Jewish Council in Warsaw, Announcements
  1) dated 22.07.1942, on "resettlement to the East" of Warsaw's Jews, with a list of groups excluded from "resettlement";
  2) dated 22.07.1942, informing that those employed in German enterprises cannot interrupt work during the "resettlement" action (fragment);
  3) dated 15.08.1942, about vacating residences in the apartment blocks listed on 16 streets of the northern ghetto;
  4) dated 16.08.1942, only those employed in enterprises located in the southern part can stay there; order that all unemployed should report to the Umschlagplatz ("trans-shipping site");
  5) dated 24.08.1942 about leaving vacated rooms and streets clean;
  6) dated 25.08.1942 about ban on spending the night on the streets;
  7) dated 5.09.1942 about the reporting of all residents of the ghetto on 6.09. within the limits of the streets Smocza—Gęsia—Zamenhofa—Szczęśliwa—pl. Parysowski "for the purpose of registration."
- ***Description:*** original (doc. 3 in 3 incomplete copies, doc. 4 in 2 copies), printed, German, Polish, 300×452, 307×464, 307×470, 292×460, 470×684, 338×487, 310×263, 314×472 mm, minor damages and losses of text (docs. 1, 4), damages and losses of text (docs. 3, 4, 6, 7), severe damages and losses of text (docs. 2, 3—third copy), ss. 10, pp. 10.

  Doc. 1 printed at J. Rachman (ul. Chłodna 8), kept in a binder; docs. 3, 4, 5, 6 and 7 printed at Leszno 24.

  Docs. 2, 3, 4, 5, 6)—Published: *Archiwum Ringelbluma*, pp. 37–38, 48, 49–52, 55–56 (photocopy). Doc. 1 published: *Kronika getta*, p. 668 (photocopy).

### 53. RING. II/189. Mf. ŻIH—797; USHMM—52.

a)

- 25.08.1942, Warsaw Ghetto
- Jewish Council in Warsaw, Announcement dated 25.08.1942 about the order of 24.08.1942 by the Labor Bureau in Warsaw
- Ban on changing place of work without permission of the Labor Bureau. Order signed by [Friedrich] Ziegler.
- ***Description:*** original, printed, German, Polish, 347×479 mm, minor damages and losses of text, ss. 1, pp. 1.

  Published: *Archiwum Ringelbluma*, pp. 53–54 (photocopy).

b) **See Ring. II/191.**

### 54. RING. II/187. Mf. ŻIH—797; USHMM—52.

- After 09.1942, Warsaw Ghetto
- Jewish Council in Warsaw, Announcements
  1) dated 24.07.1942, about "voluntary resettlement of the nonproductive population to eastern territories";
  2) dated 5.09.1942, about the obligation of all residents of the large ghetto residing within the limits of the streets Smocza-Gęsia-Zamenhofa-Szczęśliwa-pl. Parysowski to report on 6.09.1942 for the purpose of registration;
  3) dated 28.09.1942, about restrictions on moving about in the Jewish district.
- ***Description:*** transcript, typescript, handwritten manuscript (H*, ink—doc. 2), German, Polish, 205×296, 350×222 mm, ss. 4, pp. 4.

  Docs. 1, 2, and 3 published: *Archiwum Ringelbluma*, pp. 38–39, 57–59, 62.

### 55. RING. II/266. Mf. ŻIH—799; USHMM—54.

- 4.10.1942, Warsaw Ghetto
- Chairman of the Jewish Council in Warsaw, Circular letter dated 4.10.1942 to employees of the Jewish Council in Warsaw
- About combating harmful activity and sluggishness in work.
- ***Description:*** original, duplicated typescript, Polish, 203×164 mm, ss. 1, pp. 1.

  Published: *Archiwum Ringelbluma*, pp. 62–63.

### 56. RING. II/262. Mf. ŻIH—799; USHMM—54.

- 12.1942–01.1943, Warsaw Ghetto
- Jewish Council in Warsaw, Announcements
  1) dated 23.12.1942, about the directive for "Cleanliness Week" from 3–9.01.1943, Commissioner of the campaign—superintendent of the Order Service;
  2) dated 30.12.1942, about restoration of the general registration obligation within the area of the Jewish district and of the workshop blocks lying outside the ghetto;
  3) dated 3.01.1943, about precise observance of the instructions connected with "Cleanliness Week";
  4) dated 5.01.1943, leaving and entering the Jewish district is possible only with a pass from the Sonderkommando of the Sicherheitspolizei.
- ***Description:*** original (docs. 3 and 4 in 2 copies), printed, German, Polish, Yiddish, 345×485, 138×180, 153×210, 159×209, 300×427 mm, ss. 6, pp. 10.

On doc. 4) (first copy) at the top a note (handwritten manuscript—H*, pencil): "Posted on 7 I 43 (Monday)."
Doc. 4) printed on the reverse of a fragment of a PKO form: "blocked account."
Docs. 1–2, 4 printed in the Printworks of the Jewish Council in Warsaw (ul. Muranowska 40).
Doc. 1—Published: *Archiwum Ringelbluma*, pp. 84–86 (photocopy).
Doc. 2—Published: *Archiwum Ringelbluma*, pp. 90–91 (photocopy).
Doc. 3—See *Archiwum Ringelbluma*, p. 93 (summary); *Kronika getta*, p. 176 (photocopy).
Doc. 4—Published: *Archiwum Ringelbluma*, pp. 94–95; *Kronika getta*, p. 112 (photocopy).

### 57. RING. II/263. Mf. ŻIH—799; USHMM—54.

- 29.12.1942, Warsaw Ghetto
- Jewish Council in Warsaw, Commissioner of the Cleanliness Week, "Rules of 29.12.1942 for 'Cleanliness Week' in the Jewish district in Warsaw"
- Instruction about the security campaign in the ghetto during 3–9.01.1943. Announcement signed by J. [Józef] Szeryński.
- ***Description:*** original, printed, German, Polish, 474×630 mm, ss. 1, pp. 1.

See *Archiwum Ringelbluma*, p. 89 (summary).

### 58. RING. II/191, II/189. Mf. ŻIH—797; USHMM—52.

- After 30.09.1942, Warsaw Ghetto
- [Jewish Council in Warsaw], "Report for the period 22 July–30 September 1942" (fragments)
- The "resettlement" in the Warsaw Ghetto (encl. copies of documents, announcements, orders, etc.). Organizational and personnel changes in the Jewish Council. Enclosed "Organizational diagram of the Jewish Council adopted at the session of the Jewish Council's Presidium on 15 August 1942" (Notes concerning personnel appointments, new addresses of Jewish Council agents). "Addendum" with a copy of the Jewish Council's announcements dated 8, 9, 25.08.1942.
- ***Description:*** original or transcript, typescript, Polish, 208×296 mm, missing pages 1–5 and 14, ss. 13, pp. 13.

"Addendum" was preserved in Ring. II/189.
Published: *Archiwum Ringelbluma*, pp. 67–79; "Addendum": pp. 44–45 (fragment).
Index: Eng. Marek Lichtenbaum, Chairman of the Jewish Council in Warsaw; Bernard Zundelewicz, member of the Jewish Council in Warsaw, chairman of the Department of the Order Service, manager of the Bureau of Control and Complaints; Natan Grodziński, member of the Jewish Council in Warsaw, chairman of the Department of the Post Office, manager of the Personnel Department; Bolesław Rozensztat, member of the Jewish Council in Warsaw and chairman of the Administrative Department and of the Department of Real Estate, manager of the Legal Department; Józef Jaszuński, chairman of the General Department of the Jewish Council in Warsaw; Stanisław Szereszewski, chairman of the Finance-Budget Department of the Jewish Council in Warsaw; Dr. Izrael Milejkowski, member of the Jewish Council in Warsaw, chairman of the Department of Public Health; Dr. Henryk Glücksberg, member of the Jewish Council in Warsaw, manager of the Department of Pharmacies and of the Social Security Office; Dr. Gustaw Wielikowski, member of the Jewish Council in Warsaw, chairman of the Department of Services and Social Welfare; Leopold Kupczykier, member of the Jewish Council in Warsaw; Boruch Wolf Rozenthal, member of the Jewish Council in Warsaw; Hirsz Rottenberg, manager of the Department of Nourishment of the Population (Referatu Wyżywienia Ludności) of the Jewish Council in Warsaw; Eng. Alfred Sztolcman, chairman of the Economic Department of the Jewish Council in Warsaw; Abram Wolfowicz, member of the Jewish Council in Warsaw, chairman of the Department of Craftsmen Services; Hiel Rozen, member of the Jewish Council in Warsaw, chairman of the Department of Labor; Abraham Gepner, member of the Jewish Council in Warsaw, chairman of the Department of Supply; Zygmunt Hurwicz, member of the Jewish Council in Warsaw, chairman of the Cemetery Department; Ajzyk Ber Ekerman, member of the Jewish Council in Warsaw; Jakub Kobryner of the Cemetery Department of the Jewish Council in Warsaw; [Dawid] Spiro [member of the Jewish Council in Warsaw], manager of the Department of Registration Matters (Referatu Spraw Metrykalnych); Simon Stokhamer, member of the Jewish Council in Warsaw

### 59. RING. II/124. Mf. ŻIH—794; USHMM—49.

- After 01.1940, Warsaw
- [Jewish Council in Warsaw?], "List of those arrested 18–25 January 1940 registered in the Community" and "List of those arrested 18–25 January 1940 registered in the Community, who have since died"
- List of names of persons arrested by the Germans in connection with the escape from custody of Kazimierz Andrzej Kott of the group Polish People's Action for Independence (Polska Ludowa Akcja Niepodległościowa).
- ***Description:*** original, typescript (handwritten additions), ink, pencil, Polish, 209×294, 224×287 mm, ss. 10, pp. 10.

About those arrested in January 1940, see *Czerniaków*, pp. 78–79; *Kronika getta*, pp. 83–84, 613, 626, 628.
Published: BŻIH, no. 62/1967, pp. 68–75.

### 60. RING. II/147. Mf. ŻIH–795; USHMM–50.

- After 4.01.1942, Warsaw Ghetto
- A. [Adam] Czerniaków, "Reminiscences about the late Councilman Beniamin Zabłudowski" (4.01.1942)
- Speech at the funeral of a member of the Jewish Council.
- ***Description:*** original, duplicated typescript, Polish, 219×338 mm, ss. 1, pp. 1.

See Ring. I/324 (second copy).

### 61. RING. II/148. Mf. ŻIH–795; USHMM–50.

- 12.1941, Warsaw Ghetto
- Prisoners of the Central Jewish Jail, Application to Superintendent Rose for consent to prepare an artistic-literary evening on 24.12.[1941]
- Program and list of performers: Feilorn, Chaba, Lerner, Helena Apelbaum, Henia Czerska, Genia Ejgenberg, Anita Kalinowska, Basia Lajfer, Irena Hertz, Zuzanna Kornberger, Ruta Finkielstern, Landau, [Leon] Ryszfeld, Grünstein, Rubinstein, Klemański, Kobryń. Application signed Leon Ryszfeld.
- ***Description:*** original, handwritten manuscript, ink, Polish, 200×264 mm, ss. 1, pp. 2.

### 62. RING. II/151. Mf. ŻIH–795; USHMM–50.

- 11.03.1942, Warsaw Ghetto
- Headquarters of the Central Jail Guard. J. Rudniański, subcommander, Telefonogram dated 11.03.1942 to the Chairman of the Jewish Council in Warsaw

Concerns 151 prisoners released on 11.03.1942. Doc. signed J. Rudniański, subcommander.

- ***Description:*** original or transcript, typescript (additions and underlinings, pencil), Polish, 208×147 mm, ss. 1, pp. 1.

Index: Lustberg, superintendent of the jail; Lewiński, subcommander of the Order Service; Boraks, group leader of the Order Service

### 63. RING. II/150. Mf. ŻIH–795; USHMM–50.

- After 25.03.1942, Warsaw Ghetto
- Central Jail of the Jewish District in Warsaw. NN., Notes concerning the transfer of 16 prisoners to the Germans on 25.03.1942
- Course of visit in the jail by noncommissioned officers of the Sonderdienst and of policemen of the Schutzpolizei.
- ***Description:*** original typescript, Polish, 210×300 mm, ss. 1, pp. 1.

At bottom of the Doc. an illegible signature (ink). Czerniaków writes about this event under the date 27.03.1942, that these prisoners "were reportedly sent at 10 AM to Treblinka from the Eastern Station"; see *Czerniaków*, p. 262.
Index: [J.] Rudniański, sub-commander of the Order Service

### 64. RING. II/382. Mf. ŻIH–803; USHMM–58.

- 24–25.03.1941, Warsaw Ghetto
- Jewish Council in Warsaw, Housing Bureau (ul. Elektoralna 5), Letter dated 24.03.1941 to Josef Nusyn Herman (ul. Nowolipki 31, apt. 6)
- Inf. about occupation by the Bureau of 1 room in an apartment at ul. Nowolipki 31, apt. 6. Letter delivered 25.03.1941. Attached receipt dated 28.03.1941 for Josef Nusyn Herman for a sum (5 zł) paid to the Housing Bureau's cash office.
- ***Description:*** original, printed, handwritten manuscript, pencil, stamp, Polish, 171×54, 187×202 mm, ss. 2, pp. 2.

### 65. RING. II/264. Mf. ŻIH–799; USHMM–54.

- 12.1942, Warsaw Ghetto
- Jewish Council in Warsaw, Administrative Department IV. Census Bureau (Biuro Ewidencji Ludności) (ul. Kurza 9), Circular letters
  1) dated 24.12.1942, about restoration of the general registration obligation in the Jewish district from 1.01.1943 (letter signed by B. [Bolesław] Rozensztat, chairman of the Administrative Department, P. [Paweł] Wasserman, manager of the Census Bureau);
  2) dated 24.12.1942, about restoration of the general registration obligation in the Jewish district from 1.01.1943, letter directed to those keeping registration books (letter signed by B. [Bolesław] Rozensztat, chairman of the Administrative Department, P. [Paweł] Wasserman, manager of the Census Bureau [Biura Ewidencji]). Attached: "Notification of Place of Residence" (printed, Polish).
- ***Description:*** original (Docs. 1 and 2 in 3 copies, attachment in 2 copies), duplicated typescript, printed matter (attachment), Polish, 208×294, 198×279, 105×190 mm, ss. 8, pp. 10.

Attachment: See *Archiwum Ringelbluma*, p. 93 (summary).
Published: *Archiwum Ringelbluma*, pp. 86–89 (without attachment).

### 66. RING. II/153. Mf. ŻIH–795; USHMM–50.

- After 22.07.1942, Warsaw Ghetto
- B.E.L.Ż [Biuro Ewidencji Ludności Żydowskiej w Warszawie (Bureau of Jewish Census Records in Warsaw)], Record card
- Personal data, address before 22.07.1942 and current.
- ***Description:*** original, printed matter, Polish, 122×144 mm, ss. 1, pp. 1.

See *Archiwum Ringelbluma*, p. 92 (description and photocopy).

### 67. RING. II/116. Mf. ŻIH—794; USHMM—49.

- [After 15.11.1941], Warsaw Ghetto
- NN., "Draft of official record in the matter of care for refugees"
- Decision of representatives of the Social Welfare Department of the Jewish Council, Commission for Matters of Displaced Persons and the ŻSS-KOM about formation of a Commission for Care of Refugees at the Jewish Council [15.11.1941].
- ***Description:*** original or transcript, typescript, Polish, 207×292 mm, ss. 1, pp. 1.

### 68. RING. II/188. Mf. ŻIH—797; USHMM—52.

- 07.1942, Warsaw Ghetto
- Order Service in Warsaw, Announcements
  1) dated 26.07.1942, summons for residents of the house at ul. Miła 56 subject to "resettlement" (wysiedlenie) to report the following day at ul. Stawki;
  2) dated 29.07.1942, summons for voluntary reporting to Stawki [Street] at the corner of Dzika [Umschlagplatz]; everyone who does so on 29, 30, and 31 July receives 3 kg of bread and 1 kg of jam.
- ***Description:*** original (doc. 2 in 2 copies), printed matter, German, Polish, 443×576 mm, 445×577, 460×443 mm, minor damages and losses of text (Docs. 1 and 2 first copy), serious damages and losses of text (doc. 2, second copy), ss. 3, pp. 3.

  Doc. 1—address and date entered in red pencil; printed at J. Rachman (ul. Chłodna 8). Doc. 2 first copy was kept in a binder.

  Docs. 1, 2)—Published: *Archiwum Ringelbluma*, pp. 40–43 (photocopy).

  Doc. 2—Published: *Kronika getta*, p. 674 (photocopy).

### 69. RING. II/293/3. Mf. ŻIH—800; USHMM—55.

- Date unknown, Warsaw Ghetto
- Jewish Council in Warsaw, Order Service, Anti-Aircraft Defense Department, Employee armband.
- ***Description:*** original, printed matter (pasted with binding cloth, strings for binding armband on the arm), stamps, German, Polish, 245×65 mm, ss. 1, pp. 1.

  On sheet 1 (printed matter): "Hausluftschutz O.P.L.W" [House Anti-Aircraft Defense Warsaw] and stamp: "R.Ż.W. Kierownictwo Służby Porządkowej. Referat Obrony Przeciwlotniczej" [Jewish Council of Warsaw, Management of the Order Service, Anti-Aircraft Defense Department]

  Published: *Kronika getta*, p. 198.

### 70. RING. II/36. Mf. ŻIH—793; USHMM—48.

- 1941/1942, Warsaw Ghetto
- Jewish Council, Social Welfare Department, Draft budgets of the campaign for "Winter Relief 1941/1942"
- Separate breakdowns for: ŻOS, "Centos," and TOZ.
- ***Description:*** transcript, typescript, Polish, 214×290, 290×313 mm, ss. 7, pp. 7.

### 71. RING. II/396. Mf. ŻIH—803; USHMM—58.

- 15.09.1941, Warsaw Ghetto
- Jewish Council in Warsaw, Department of Payments for Hospitals and Health Service. Social Work Section (ul. Ceglana 7), Letter dated 15.09.1941 to Icek Mordka Łabędź (ul. Ogrodowa 43, apt. 8)
- Request to come in for the purpose of submitting personal data. Letter signed Hilary Ekerman, Department manager.
- ***Description:*** original, duplicated typescript, handwritten manuscript, ink, stamp, Polish, 219×133 mm, ss. 1, pp. 1.

### 72. RING. II/220. Mf. ŻIH—798; USHMM—53.

- 17.09.1942, Warsaw Ghetto
- Jewish Council in Warsaw, Department [of Labor], Norbert Goldfeil, manager, Letter dated 17.09.1942 to the Chairman of the Jewish Council in Warsaw
- Concerns settlement of sums transmitted by the Jewish Council to the following persons: Norbert Goldfeil, Witalis Aronzon, Eug[eniusz] Merenholc, M. Wajcentregier, Zuzanna Lanes, Zofia Rozen.
- ***Description:*** original, typescript, Polish, 210×297 mm, ss. 1, pp. 1.

### 73. RING. II/261. Mf. ŻIH—799; USHMM—54.

- 11.1942, Warsaw Ghetto
- Jewish Council in Warsaw, Announcements of the Department of Labor and the Labor Commission
  1) dated 4.11.1942, call for 700 people to report for work at the Werterfassung [Property Collection Agency] (ul. Niska 20);
  2) dated 16.11.1942, about acceptance of applications for work from men and women aged 16–50 years;
  3) dated 20.11.1942, call for registration of all unemployed at the Labor Department of the Jewish Council (ul. Zamenhofa 19) for work in the Werterfassung.
- ***Description:*** original, printed matter, German, Polish, 420×575, 300×456, 328×480 mm, minor damages and losses of text (doc. 2), ss. 3, pp. 3.

  Doc. printed in the printing shop of the Jewish Council (ul. Muranowska 40).

  Doc. 1—Published: *Archiwum Ringelbluma*, pp. 79–80 (photocopy).

  Doc. 3—Published: *Archiwum Ringelbluma*, pp. 81–82 (photocopy).

### 74. RING. II/142. Mf. ŻIH—795; USHMM—50.

- 09–10.1941, Warsaw Ghetto
- Jewish Council, Registry Department (Wydział Spraw Metrykalnych), Letter dated 29.10.1941 to the chairman of the Jewish Council

- Concerns the custom of arranging weddings of poor couples at cemeteries for alleviating plague. Attached letter to M. Kaminer, chairman of the Department of Religious Affairs, with resolution of the Assembly of Rabbis (signed: [N. (Noach) Rogoźnicki, J. (Jankiel) A. Zamczyk, J.A. Biderman, E. (Efraim) Majmin, I.M. Kanał, Sz. (Szlama) Merkier, M. (Menachem) Ziemba, A. (Aron) N. (Naftali) Zawłodawer (Zabludower?), D. (Dawid) Kahane-Szpiro), dated 28.09.1941 with proposal for a wedding at the cemetery in Warsaw in order to stop the epidemic in the Warsaw Ghetto.
- ***Description:*** original, typescript, handwritten manuscript, ink, Hebrew, Polish, 205×298, 208×295 mm, ss. 2, pp. 2.

  Letter dated 29.10.1941 signed by (ink): "Dr. M. [Majer] Bałaban."

**75. RING. II/133. Mf. ŻIH—795; USHMM—50.**

- 3.05.1940–4.09.1940, Warsaw
- [Jewish Council in Warsaw,] Statistical Department, Internal Bulletin, no. 1 of 3.05., no. 2 of 17.05., no. 3 of 2.06., no. 4 of 17.06., and no. 8 of 4.09.1940
- Statistics on the Jewish population in Warsaw (location, age, occupational structure, illnesses, deaths, etc.); reports of the Jewish Council's activities. Bulletins signed by J. [Józef] Jaszuński, chairman of the Statistical Department, and M. [Michał] Alpern, manager of the Department. In no. 8 a list of the contents of no. 1–8.
- ***Description:*** original, duplicated typescript, Polish, 207×294, 213×332 mm, ss. 90, pp. 86.

  On the first pages (cardboard covers) no. of the issues (stamp).

  Published: BŻIH, no. 73/1970, pp. 101–132.

**76. RING. II/28. Mf. ŻIH—793; USHMM—48.**

- Date unknown, Warsaw
- [Jewish Council?] Department for Fighting Epidemics. Coupons entitling to discount for laundering of linens at the TOZ Cleaning Facility.
- ***Description:*** original (6 copies on one sheet), duplicated typescript, Polish, 208×280 mm, ss. 1, pp. 1.

**77. RING. II/137. Mf. ŻIH—795; USHMM—50.**

- After 26.09.1941, Warsaw Ghetto
- Jewish Council, Department of Production (ul. Grzybowska 26–28/ul. Prosta 14), Letter dated 26.09.1941 to the Labor Department at the Social Welfare Section
- Bill for 6 purchased sewing machines. Letter signed Dr. S. [Salomon] Eiger.
- ***Description:*** transcript, typescript, Polish, 230×150 mm, ss. 1, pp. 1.

**78. RING. II/146. Mf. ŻIH—795; USHMM—50.**

a)

- After 26.06.1940, Warsaw Ghetto
- Jewish Council in Warsaw, Coupon no. 98624 entitling holder to receive a food card without charge in July of the current year.
- ***Description:*** original, printed matter, Polish, 98×80 mm, ss. 1, pp. 1.

  On p. 1 stamp: "Chairman of the Jewish Council in Warsaw. Administration of the Jewish Quarter in Warsaw."

b)

- 06.1942, Warsaw Ghetto
- Jewish Council in Warsaw, Coupon no. 18936 entitling holder to receive a food card without charge in July 1942.
- ***Description:*** original, printed matter, Polish, 93×84 mm, ss. 1, pp. 2.

  On p. 1 stamp: "Chairman of the Jewish Council in Warsaw. Administration of the Jewish Quarter in Warsaw."; on the reverse, stamp: "Issued for property . . . [missing inf.]" and stamp: ŻSS-KOM, SPS with illegible signature (pencil).

  See Ring. I/1126.

**79. RING. II/383/4. Mf. ŻIH—803; USHMM—58.**

- 1940/41, Warsaw Ghetto
- ZZ, "Potato Card for 1941 no. 342087" filled out for Fajga Krauze (ul. Pawia 1, apt. 3).
- ***Description:*** original, printed matter, handwritten manuscript, ink, German, Polish, 143×88 mm, ss. 1, pp. 2.

  On reverse a stamp: "Distribution Point for Potatoes and Vegetables F. [Fiszel?] Fliderblum [?] Pawia 60."

**80. RING. II/383/8. Mf. ŻIH—803; USHMM—58.**

- Before 10.1942, Warsaw Ghetto
- [ZZ], "Food Card" no. 003465, 003466, 003467 for 10.1942.
- ***Description:*** original, printed matter, German, Polish, 207×196 mm, some of the coupons torn off, ss. 3, pp. 3.

**81. RING. II/383/6. Mf. ŻIH—803; USHMM—58.**

- Date unknown, Warsaw Ghetto
- ZZ, "Supplemental Card for children of preschool age no. 014183" filled out for Erika Grasberg (ul. Nowolipki 29, apt. 16).
- ***Description:*** original, printed matter, handwritten manuscript, ink, German, Polish, 141×153 mm, some of the coupons torn off, ss. 1, pp. 2.

  Card has inscription: "Remind Mommy that each of us must help a poor child!"

  On the reverse a stamp: "Groceries Distribution Shop G. Warg Warsaw, ul. Smocza 16."

  Erika (Rika) Grasberg, daughter of Anna Grasberg-Górna, See Ring. II/209.

**82. RING. II/154. Mf. ŻIH—795; USHMM—50.**

- Date unknown, Warsaw Ghetto
- ZZ., Sign of a Groceries Distribution Point.

- *Description:* original, printed matter, German, Polish, Yiddish, 570×200 mm, ss. 1, pp. 1.

### 83. RING. II/130. Mf. ŻIH—795; USHMM—50.

- 31.10.1940, Warsaw
- [Jewish Council]. Dr. I. [Izrael] Milejkowski, Letter dated 31.10.1940 to Dr. Paulina Folmanowa Edelsburg (ul. Gęsia 49, apt. 16)
- Cover letter with attachment: Distriktsgesundheitskammer Warschau. Aerztekammer [District Health Chamber, Warsaw. Physicians Chamber] (ul. Koszykowa 37), Letter dated 26.10.1940 to Dr. I. [Izrael] Milejkowski, chairman of the Association of Jewish Physicians, in the matter of ban on confiscation of equipment and apartments of Jewish physicians. Letter (attached) signed by Dr. Alkiewicz and Dr. Lambrecht.
- *Description:* original, photocopy (attachment), typescript, German, Polish, 214×139 mm i 238×299 mm, ss. 2, pp. 2

  On the letter and attachment is stamped: "422."

### 84. RING. II/272/2. Mf. ŻIH—799; USHMM—54.

- 10.10.1942, Lwów
- Ewa Bornstein (Lwów, ul. Warszawska 3), Letter dated 10.10.1942 to Jewish Council in Warsaw
- Request for information about: Dr. Roman, Gertruda and Rozalia Bornstein (ul. Chłodna 24, apt. 14), Dr. Mikołaj Bornstein (ul. Leszno 8, apt. 12), Zygmunt and Irena Jakubowicz (ul. Śliska 18, apt. 8). Attached postcard with return address.
- *Description:* original, typescript, German, 208×148, 147×105 mm, ss. 2, pp. 2.

  Attached envelope (typescript, postmark and stamp of the Jewish Council in Warsaw, German, 158×114 mm, ss. 1, pp. 2).

  See *Archiwum Ringelbluma*, p. 181 (summary).

  Published: *Listy o Zagładzie*, pp. 229–231.

### 85. RING. II/271/2. Mf. ŻIH—799; USHMM—54.

- 14.10.1942, Berlin
- Heinrich Israel Cohn (Berlin N. 113, Wicherstr. 48a), Letter dated 14.10.1942 to Jewish Council in Warsaw
- Request for information about Bertha Sara Jacobsohn née Blumenfarb of Popowo near Toruń, later resided in Berlin (Spichernstr. 5), lately in Warsaw (ul. Ogrodowa 27, room 5), lack of news since 10.09.1942. Attached postcard with return address.
- *Description:* original, typescript on postcard, postmark and stamp of the Jewish Council in Warsaw, ink, German, 148×103 mm, ss. 2, pp. 4.

  On p. 1 notation (ink, pencil): "Ewidencja wg. właściwości, 20.10.42, Kwaterunek, Kurza 9" [Records according to validity, 20.10.42, Housing Office, Kurza 9].

  See *Archiwum Ringelbluma*, p. 181 (summary).

  Published: *Listy o Zagładzie*, pp. 258–260.

### 86. RING. II/270/7. Mf. ŻIH—799; USHMM—54.

- 25.12.1942, Rembertów
- Franka Cybulska (Rembertów, Judenlager, ul. Kościuszki 6), Letter of 25.12.1942 to Jewish Council in Warsaw
- Request for information about Stella Berland (ul. Pańska 59, apt. 24).
- *Description:* original, handwritten manuscript on a postcard, postmark and stamp of Jewish Council in Warsaw, pencil, Polish, 147×105 mm ss. 1, pp. 2.

  On p. 1 stamp: "Mun. Lager Rembertów Distrikt Warschau" [Rembertów Camp in Warsaw District ?] and note (ink): "Zensiert, Bauer, 30.12.42 (belanglos)" [Censored, Bauer, 30.12.42 (unimportant)].

  See *Archiwum Ringelbluma*, p. 200 (summary).

  Published: *Listy o Zagładzie*, pp. 333–335.

### 87. RING. II/269/2. Mf. ŻIH—799; USHMM—54.

- [30.11.1942], Kraków
- Alfred Dafner (Kraków 14, Julag I [Płaszów camp]), Letter of [30.11.1942 postmark] to Jewish Council in Warsaw
- Request for information about Hela Weinsberg (ul. Nowolipie 23, apt. 2).
- *Description:* original, handwritten manuscript on a postcard, postmark and stamp of the Jewish Council in Warsaw, ink, German, 147×107 mm ss. 1, pp. 2.

  On p. 1 information (pencil): "Kurza 9."

  Published: *Listy o Zagładzie*, pp. 302–304.

### 88. RING. II/275/4. Mf. ŻIH—799; USHMM—54.

- 3.10.1942, Kraków
- Ginzigs (E. Ginzig) (Heitler, tricot factory, Kraków, ul. Długosza 8), Letter of 3.10.1942 to [Jewish Council in Warsaw?]
- Request for information about Balbina Cajtagowa, teacher, and son Janek (ul. Szpitalna 33, lately in care of Mr. and Mrs. Duński, ul. Solna 17, apt. 25a).
- *Description:* original, typescript, Polish, 208×135 mm, ss. 1, pp. 1.

  See *Archiwum Ringelbluma*, p. 179 (summary).

  Published: *Listy o Zagładzie*, pp. 224–225.

### 89. RING. II/272/1. Mf. ŻIH—799; USHMM—54.

- 30.09.1942, Lwów
- Mania Goldberg (Lwów, ul. Wybranowskiego 11, apt. 3), Letter of 30.09.1942 to Jewish Council in Warsaw
- Request for information about: Beniamin, Sara, and Lunia Grines (ul. Leszno 65, apt. 11).
- *Description:* original, handwritten manuscript on a postcard, postmark and stamp of the Jewish Council in Warsaw, ink, Polish, 148×105 mm, ss. 1, pp. 2.

  See *Archiwum Ringelbluma*, p. 178 (summary).

  Published: *Listy o Zagładzie*, pp. 218–220.

### 90. RING. II/163. Mf. ŻIH—795; USHMM—50.

- 9.02.1942, Warsaw Ghetto

- Henryk Goldszmit (Janusz Korczak) (ul. Sienna 16—Śliska 9), Letter dated 9.02.1942 to Personnel Bureau of Jewish Council in Warsaw
- Autobiography with application to be hired for work at the boarding school for orphans at ul. Dzielna 39.
- ***Description:*** original, typescript (crossing-outs, ink), Polish, 222×355 mm, ss. 2, pp. 4.

  Published: *Selected Documents*, 488–491; *Dzieci*, pp. 252–259.

### 91. RING. II/268/4, II/268/5. Mf. ŻIH—799; USHMM—54.

a)

- 29.10.1942, Staszów near Opatów
- K. Hajman [Hajlman?] (Staszów, ul. Długa 7, at M. Rosz), Letter of 29.10.1942 to Jewish Council in Warsaw
- Request for information about husband Berek Hajlmann [Hajman] (ul. Nalewki 43, apt. 86). Encl. card for reply with return address.
- ***Description:*** original, handwritten manuscript on a postcard, postmark and stamp of the Jewish Council in Warsaw, ink, Polish, 147×105 mm, ss. 2, pp. 3.

  On p. 1 notation (pencil): "Kurza 9" and stamp: "B."

  See *Archiwum Ringelbluma*, p. 185 (summary).

  Published: *Listy o Zagładzie*, pp. 275–277.

b)

- 5.01.1943, Warsaw Ghetto
- Jewish Council in Warsaw, Department of Census of Jewish Population, Address Department, "Information Card" of Berek (Henryk) Hajlman. (5.01.1943)
- Addresses in the Warsaw Ghetto: ul. Nalewki 43, then Nowolipie 67 and lastly ul. Leszno 76.
- ***Description:*** original, printed matter, handwritten manuscript, ink, Polish, 103×155 mm, ss. 1, pp. 2.

  See *Archiwum Ringelbluma*, p. 93 (summary).

### 92. RING. II/269/1. Mf. ŻIH—799; USHMM—54.

- 8.11.1942, Augsburg
- Felicja Hammer (Firm of Ch. Drierig, Augsburg, Fichtelbacherstr. 1), Letter of 8.11.1942 to Jewish Council in Warsaw
- Request for information about: Sz. Hammer (ul. Muranowska 13, apt. 6), J. Katz (ul. Majzelsa 4, apt. 16).
- ***Description:*** original, handwritten manuscript on a postcard, postmark and stamp of the Jewish Council in Warsaw, ink, Polish, 147×104 mm, ss. 1, pp. 2.

  See *Archiwum Ringelbluma*, p. 187 (summary).

  Published: *Listy o Zagładzie*, pp. 281–282.

### 93. RING. II/271/3. Mf. ŻIH—799; USHMM—54.

- 25.11.1942, Ferramonti di Tarsia (Italy)
- Feibus Holzman (Ferramonti di Tarsia [Italy], [camp]), Letter of 25.11.1942 to Jewish Council in Warsaw
- Request for information about brother Lejzor Jakub Holzman (ul. Nowolipki 46, apt. 64, at Glatt), lack of news for year and a half.
- ***Description:*** original, typescript on a postcard, postmark, stamps of camp and of Jewish Council in Warsaw, ink, German, 146×103 mm, ss. 1, pp. 2.

  See *Archiwum Ringelbluma*, p. 188 (summary).

  Published: *Listy o Zagładzie*, pp. 295–297.

### 94. RING. II/268/1. Mf. ŻIH—799; USHMM—54.

- 10.10.1942, Piotrków
- Szlomo Kac (Piotrków, ul. Litewska 6, at Miedziński), Letter of 10.10.1942 to Jewish Council in Warsaw
- Request for new address of Jakub Blender (ul. Majzelsa 4, apt. 4), employed in one of the workshops in the Warsaw Ghetto.
- ***Description:*** original, handwritten manuscript on a postcard, postmark and stamp of the Jewish Council in Warsaw, ink, Polish, 147×105 mm, ss. 1, pp. 2.

  See *Archiwum Ringelbluma*, p. 180 (summary).

  Published: *Listy o Zagładzie*, pp. 227–228; *Kronika getta*, p. 709 (photocopy of fragment).

### 95. RING. II/271/1. Mf. ŻIH—799; USHMM—54.

- 24.09.1942, Genf [Geneva]
- Komitee zur Hilfeleistung für die kriegsbetroffene jüdische Bevölkerung, Genf [Committee to provide aid for the war-impacted Jewish population, Geneva], 52, rue des Pâquis (no. 247), Letter dated 24.09.1942 to Jewish Council in Warsaw
- Request for information about: Hanna Altman (ul. Śliska 31, apt. 24) and Łaia Kac (ul. Pawia 41, apt. 26).
- ***Description:*** original, typescript on a postcard, postmark, stamps of German military censorship and of Jewish Council in Warsaw, German, 149×104 mm, ss. 1, pp. 2.

  On p. 1 note (pencil): "Majzelsa 9"; on pp. 1 and 2 stamp: "Komitee zur Hilfeleistung . . ."

  See *Archiwum Ringelbluma*, p. 177 (summary).

  Published: *Listy o Zagładzie*, pp. 215–218.

  Index: Arnold A. Cohn of Copenhagen

### 96. RING. II/270/5. Mf. ŻIH—799; USHMM—54.

- 12.11.1942, Rembertów
- M. Korentajer (Rembertów-Judenlager, ul. Kościuszki 6), Letter of 12.11.1942 to Jewish Council in Warsaw
- Request for information about fate of mother Małka Korentajer (age ca. 60), who before 5.11.1942 was at the Umschlagplatz. Attached postcard with return address.
- ***Description:*** original, handwritten manuscript on a postcard, postmark and stamp of the Jewish Council in Warsaw and of the Secretariat General of the Jewish Council (21.11.1942, no. 20542), pencil, Polish, 147×105 mm, ss. 2, pp. 3.

  On p. 1 beneath the stamp of the Secretariat a note (pencil): "B. Ewidencji."

  Published: *Archiwum Ringelbluma*, p. 188; *Listy o Zagładzie*, pp. 291–293.

**97. RING. II/268/2. Mf. ŻIH—799; USHMM—54.**

- 24.10.1942, Oleśnica near Busko Zdrój
- Henryk Kurc (Oleśnica near Busko Zdrój), Letter of 24.10.1942 to A. [Anszel] Kujawski (Gęsia 13, apt. 2) or to the Jewish Council in Warsaw (ul. Kurza 9)
- Request for information about Chemja Dawidowicz (ul. Smocza 2, apt. 8), Anszel Domb (ul. Smocza 7, apt. 34), Izrael Lejb Wejntraub (ul. Nowolipie 21, apt. 25), Abram Lejb Domb (ul. Zamenhofa 24, apt. 41), Anszel Kujawski (ul. Gęsia 13, apt. 2), Abram Naparstek, Roza and Chana Kurc (ul. Nowolipie 21, apt. 25), Symcha Grabowiecki (ul. Leszno 2, apt. 41), H. [Hersz] Wasser, MA (ul. Muranowska 6, apt. 15).
- ***Description:*** original, handwritten manuscript on a postcard, postmark and stamp of the Jewish Council in Warsaw, ink, Polish, 147×105 mm ss. 1, pp. 2.
  Published: *Archiwum Ringelbluma*, pp. 182–183 (photocopy, fragment); *Listy o Zagładzie*, pp. 264–266

**98. RING. II/223/5. Mf. ŻIH—798; USHMM—53.**

- 18.12.1942, Hohensalza [Inowrocław]
- Icek Leszczyński (Hohensalza [Inowrocław]-labor camp), Letter of 18.12.1942 to Jewish Council in Warsaw
- Request for information about Isaak Glitzenstein, rabbi of Toruń, and J. Rochow (Warsaw, pl. Krasińskich).
- ***Description:*** original, handwritten manuscript on a postcard, postmark and stamp of the Jewish Council in Warsaw, pencil, Polish, 148×104 mm, ss. 1, pp. 2.
  See *Archiwum Ringelbluma*, p. 198 (summary).
  Published: *Listy o Zagładzie*, pp. 331–333.

**99. RING. II/272/5. Mf. ŻIH—799; USHMM—54.**

- 26.12.1942, Lwów
- J. Litwakowa (Lwów-Kleparów, ul. Dzielna 10), Letter of 26.12.1942 to Jewish Council in Warsaw
- Request for information about Ewa Buk (ul. Puławska), in 1941 was manager in hospital kitchen in the Warsaw Ghetto. Attached postcard with return address.
- ***Description:*** original, handwritten manuscript on a postcard, postmark and stamp of the Jewish Council in Warsaw, ink, German, 148×105 mm, ss. 2, pp. 3.
  See *Archiwum Ringelbluma*, p. 189 (summary).
  Published: *Listy o Zagładzie*, pp. 335–337.

**100. RING. II/272/3. Mf. ŻIH—799; USHMM—54.**

- 28.11.1942, Lwów
- Emil Mangel (Lwów, ul. Zamarstynowska 23, apt. 22), Letter of 28.11.1942 to Jewish Council in Warsaw
- Request for information about: Izaak Mangel, dentist (ul. Śliska 47, apt. 5), H. Steinerowic, dentist (ul. Nowolipki 44, apt. 22), Erna Mangel-Herlingowa (ul. Zamenhofa 36, apt. 3), Helena Mangel, seamstress (ul. Dzielna 25, apt. 136). Attached postcard.
- ***Description:*** original, handwritten manuscript on a postcard, postmark and stamp of the Jewish Council in Warsaw, ink, Polish, 148×105 mm, ss. 2, pp. 3.
  On p. 1 notation (pencil): "Kurza 9."
  See *Archiwum Ringelbluma*, p. 190 (summary).
  Published: *Listy o Zagładzie*, pp. 300–302.

**101. RING. II/270/4. Mf. ŻIH—799; USHMM—54.**

- 5.11.1942, Rembertów
- Josef Müller (Rembertów-Judenlager [ul. Kościuszki 6]), Letter of 5.11.1942 to Jewish Council in Warsaw
- Request for the new address of Józef Kiselsztejn (ul. Solna 16) and for forwarding of letter (attached to the same card).
- ***Description:*** original, handwritten manuscript on a postcard, postmark and stamp of the Jewish Council in Warsaw, ink, Polish, 147×105 mm, ss. 1, pp. 2.
  See *Archiwum Ringelbluma*, p. 186 (summary).
  Published: *Listy o Zagładzie*, pp. 277–279.

**102. RING. II/270/3. Mf. ŻIH—799; USHMM—54.**

- [12.11.1942], Lublin
- B. [Bolesław] Norski-Nożyca (Lublin, Camp of SS—DAW [Deutsche Ausrüstungswerke (German Armament Works)], ul. Lipowa 7), Letter of [12.11.1942 postmark] to [Paweł] Wasserman, manager [of the Department of Census of Jewish Population (Wydziału Ewidencji Ludności Żydowskiej)] of the Jewish Council in Warsaw (ul. Zamenhofa 19) (fragment—envelope survived).
- ***Description:*** original, handwritten manuscript, postmark, stamps of camp censor and of the Jewish Council in Warsaw, ink, Polish, 154×125 mm, ss. 1, pp. 2.
  See *Archiwum Ringelbluma*, p. 189 (summary).
  Published: *Listy o Zagładzie*, pp. 293–294.

**103. RING. II/269/4. Mf. ŻIH—799; USHMM—54.**

- 13.12.1942, Lublin
- B. [Bolesław] Norski-Nożyca (Lublin, Camp of SS, ul. Lipowa 7), Letter of 13.12.1942 to [Paweł] Wasserman, manager of the Department of Census of the Jewish Population (Wydziału Ewidencji Ludności Żydowskiej) of the Jewish Council in Warsaw (ul. Franciszkańska 30)
- Request for promised money and for forwarding of letter (attached to the same card) from Abuś Nisenbaum (Lublin, SS Camp, ul. Lipowa 7) to Szmul Ejlman (ul. Majzelsa 10).
- ***Description:*** original, handwritten manuscript, typescript on a postcard, postmark and stamp of the Jewish Council in Warsaw, ink, Polish, 147×105 mm, ss. 1, pp. 2.
  See *Archiwum Ringelbluma*, p. 192 (summary).
  Published: *Listy o Zagładzie*, pp. 312–314.

**104. RING. II/269/3. Mf. ŻIH—799; USHMM—54.**

- 13.12.1942, Pinne [Pniewy]
- M. Nüssenbaum (Schloss Pinne [Pniewy—chateau,

labor camp ?]), Letter of 13.12.1942 to Jewish Council in Warsaw
- Request for information about medical Dr. S. [Stanisław] Bzura (ul. Muranowska 44, apt. 84); lack of information since 21.07.1942.
- ***Description:*** original, handwritten manuscript on a postcard, postmark and stamp of the Jewish Council in Warsaw, pencil, German, ss. 1, pp. 2.
  See *Archiwum Ringelbluma*, p. 192 (summary).
  Published: *Listy o Zagładzie*, pp. 310–312.

### 105. RING. II/268/6. Mf. ŻIH—799; USHMM—54.

- 6.11.1942, Reichshof [Rzeszów]
- Jewish Council in Rzeszów, Letter of 6.11.1942 to Jewish Council in Warsaw
- Request for information about: Moniek and Stella Herschenfuss (ul. Muranowska 7, apt. 9, in care of the Dębstocks).
- ***Description:*** original, typescript on a postcard, postmark and stamp of the Jewish Council in Warsaw, Polish, 147×105 mm, ss. 1, pp. 2.
  On p. 1 notation (pencil): "Kurza 9."
  See *Archiwum Ringelbluma*, p. 186 (summary).
  Published: *Listy o Zagładzie*, pp. 279–280.

### 106. RING. II/271/4. Mf. ŻIH—799; USHMM—54.

- [28.11.1942], Prague [Praha, Czechoslovakia]
- Marta Reich-Vidor (Prag II, Krakauergasse 7), Letter of [28.11.1942 postmark] to Jewish Council in Warsaw
- Request for information about Ludwik and Emilia Vidor, transported from Prague on 20.06.1942.
- ***Description:*** original, handwritten manuscript, ink, German, 159×208 mm, ss. 2, pp. 1.
  Encl. envelope (original, handwritten manuscript, postmark and stamp of the Jewish Council in Warsaw, ink, German, 170×110 mm, ss. 1, pp. 2.). On p. 1 (envelope) note (pencil, Polish): "Soc. Welfare." Paper and envelope with imprint: "R.L."
  See *Archiwum Ringelbluma*, p. 190 (summary).
  Published: *Listy o Zagładzie*, pp. 297–300 (here according to Ruta Sakowska, the name of the letter's author is Vider, although it appears that the correct reading is Vidor).

### 107. RING. II/268/3. Mf. ŻIH—799; USHMM—54.

- 25.10.1942, Rawa Ruska
- Roman Segal (Rawa Ruska), Letter of 25.10.1942 to Jewish Council in Warsaw
- Request for information about: Maria Lemberger (ul. Leszno 49); Genia Fromberg (ul. Nowolipie 46); M. Buchwald (bakery, ul. Parysowska 4)
- ***Description:*** original, handwritten manuscript on a postcard, postmark and stamp of the Jewish Council in Warsaw, ink, 147×105 mm, ss. 1, pp. 2.
  See *Archiwum Ringelbluma*, p. 184 (summary).
  Published: *Listy o Zagładzie*, pp. 271–273.

### 108. RING. II/268/7. Mf. ŻIH—799; USHMM—54.

- 3.12.1942, Sambor
- Arje Szrajbman (Sambor, ul. Wałowa 6, at P. Twurski), Letter of 3.12.1942 to Jewish Council in Warsaw
- Request for information about M.C. and M. Alter.
- ***Description:*** original, handwritten manuscript on a postcard, postmark and stamp of the Jewish Council in Warsaw, ink, Yiddish in Roman transcription, ss. 1, pp. 2.
  See *Archiwum Ringelbluma*, p. 191 (summary).
  Published: *Listy o Zagładzie*, pp. 304–306.

### 109. RING. II/162. Mf. ŻIH—795; USHMM—50.

- 10.12.1940, Warsaw Ghetto
- Mina Tyńska (ul. Miła 23, apt. 42), Letter dated 10.12.1940 to Jewish Council in Warsaw
- Author (age 22), former student of UW (Romance philology and English studies) at the French Institute. Request to be hired for work at the post office.
- ***Description:*** original, handwritten manuscript, ink, Polish, 210×298 mm, ss. 2, pp. 1.

### 110. RING. II/268/8. Mf. ŻIH—799; USHMM—54.

- 12.12.1942, Bendsburg [Będzin]
- Dawid Izrael Unger (Bendsburg [Będzin], ul. Markstr. 57), Letter of 12.12.1942 to Jewish Council in Warsaw
- Request for information about Moritz Unger (ul. Zamenhofa 17, apt. 21).
- ***Description:*** original, handwritten manuscript on a postcard, postmark and stamp of the Jewish Council in Warsaw, ink, German, 147×105 mm, ss. 1, pp. 2.
  See *Archiwum Ringelbluma*, p. 202 (summary).
  Published: *Listy o Zagładzie*, pp. 308–309.

### 111. RING. II/270/6. Mf. ŻIH—799; USHMM—54.

- 14.12.1942, Kawęczyn near Warsaw
- J. Wajnberg (Kawęczyn near Warsaw, Labor Camp [Schmidt und Junk]), Letter of 14.12.1942 to Jewish Council in Warsaw
- Request for information about brother Abram Wajnberg (ul. Twarda). Attached postcard with return address.
- ***Description:*** original, handwritten manuscript on a postcard, postmark and stamp of the Jewish Council in Warsaw, ink, Polish, 147×105 mm ss. 2, pp. 3.
  See *Archiwum Ringelbluma*, p. 194 (summary).
  Published: *Listy o Zagładzie*, pp. 314–316.

### 112. RING. II/166. MF ŻIH—795; USHMM—50.

- 21.04.1942, Warsaw Ghetto
- Michał Weichert [?], Letter of 21.04.1942 to [Adam Czerniaków]
- Thanks for help extended during illness.
- ***Description:*** original, typescript, Polish, 212×297 mm, minor damages and losses of text, ss. 1, pp. 1.

### 113. RING. II/267. Mf. ŻIH—799; USHMM—54.

- 10.1942, Warsaw
- Dr. [Eduard Wilhelm] von Wendorff (Warsaw, Siegestrasse [Zwycięzców] 41), Letters of 7, 23 and 30.10.1942 to Jewish Council in Warsaw (ul. Ceglana 7)
- Concerns determination of new addresses of the following persons:
  1) Moszek Perlmutter (ul. Nowolipki 42); 2) Gerszon Sapir (ul. Pawia 4, apt. 37); 3) Maurycy Gutgisser (ul. Sienna 45, apt. 61).
- ***Description:*** original, typescript on postcards, postmark and stamp of the Jewish Council in Warsaw, German, 147×105 mm, ss. 3, pp. 6.
  On p. 1 notation (pencil): "Kurza 9."
  See *Archiwum Ringelbluma*, pp. 180, 182, 185 (descriptions).

### 114. RING. II/272/4. Mf. ŻIH—799; USHMM—54.

- 8.12.1942, Lwów
- J. Zandel (Lwów ghetto, Jewish Council), Letter of 8.12.1942 to Jewish Council in Warsaw
- Request for information about: H. Zandel (ul. Pańska 10, apt. 12), H. Zandel (ul. Komitetowa 1), Adam Szenberg, Order Service constable.
- ***Description:*** original, handwritten manuscript on a postcard, postmark and stamp of the Jewish Council in Warsaw, ink, Polish, 147×105 mm, ss. 1, pp. 2.
  See *Archiwum Ringelbluma*, p. 191 (summary).
  Published: *Listy o Zagładzie*, pp. 306–307.

### 115. RING. II/268/9. Mf. ŻIH—799; USHMM—54.

- 10–11.1942, place unknown, Czech Lands [Czechy]
- NN., Letters (2) of [21.10. and 25.11.1942 postmark] to Jewish Council in Warsaw [Records Department, ul. Kurza 9]. (fragments—only the envelopes preserved).
- ***Description:*** original, handwritten manuscript, postmark and stamp of the Jewish Council in Warsaw, ink, pencil, German, 175×126, 162×113 mm, ss. 2, pp. 3.

### 116. RING. II/293/2. Mf. ŻIH—800; USHMM—55.

- 1942, Warsaw Ghetto
- Jewish Council in Warsaw, Armband of employee no. 436 (Rozengarten).
- ***Description:*** original, printed on cloth ("Judenrat in Warschau. Umsiedlugsaktion" [Jewish Council in Warsaw. Resettlement Action]), stamps, German, 373×103 mm, ss. 1, pp. 2.
  On the reverse a note (pencil): "Rozengarten."
  On p. 1 a stamp: "436" and circular seal of the Jewish Council in Warsaw.
  Published: *Kronika getta*, p. 664 (photocopy).

## Jewish Social Self-Help (Żydowska Samopomoc Społeczna)[4]

### 117. RING. II/1. Mf. ŻIH—793; USHMM—48.

1)

- After 9.01.1940, Warsaw
- SKSS [Capital Committee for Social Self-Help]. Executive Department, Supply Section (Warsaw, ul. Warecka 11), Letter dated 9.01.1940 to Coordinating Committee of Social and Welfare Organizations (KKOSiO) (Warsaw, ul. Leszno 13)
- Summons to a meeting with Dir. Grebsch (ul. Warecka 11, apt. 2) on 10.01.1940.
- ***Description:*** transcript, typescript, Polish, 213×278 mm, ss. 1, pp. 1.
  Doc. was kept in a binder.

2)

- After 10.01.1940, Warsaw
- [Coordinating Committee] MW [Michał Weichert], "Report I of the conference with Mr. Blumenthal and Mr. Grebsch, on 10 January 1940"
- Jewish population cannot count on help from the SKSS, which will only care for the Aryan population.
- ***Description:*** transcript, typescript, Polish, 208×294 mm, ss. 1, pp. 1.
  Doc. was kept in a binder.

3)

- After 10.01.1940, Warsaw
- Hilfsaktion für notleidende Juden in Polen [Aid campaign for needy Jews in Poland] (Zürich, Badenerstrasse 18/Zetthaus), Letter dated 10.01.1940 to Jewish Council in Warsaw
- Concerns shipments of clothing and medications for the Jewish population in Warsaw.
- ***Description:*** transcript, typescript, German, 225×288 mm, ss. 1, pp. 1.
  Doc. was kept in a binder.

4)

- After 12.01.1940, Warsaw
- [Coordinating Committee] MW. [Michał Weichert], "Bericht ueber die Fuersorge fuer die juedische Bevoelkerung" [Report on care for the Jewish population] (12.01.1940)
- Report of the activity of the Coordinating Committee for German authorities.
- ***Description:*** transcript, typescript, German, 208×292 mm, ss. 3, pp. 3.
  Doc. was kept in a binder.

5)

- After 13.01.1940, Warsaw
- [Coordinating Committee] [Michał Weichert], "Report II of the conference with Mr. Graebsch on 13 January 1940"

4. The term *samopomoc* literally means "self-help" but it also has the connotation of mutual aid within the community. *Społeczna* literally means "social" but it also has the connotation of privately organized, nongovernmental, and nonprofit.

- Concerns aid for the poor Jewish population.
- ***Description:*** original or transcript, typescript (handwritten additions, ink), Polish, 208×297 mm, ss. 2, pp. 2.

  Doc. was kept in a binder.

6)

- After 15.01.1940, Warsaw
- [Coordinating Committee] MW. [Michał Weichert], "Report of the conference with Mr. Olesiński, inspector of kitchens of SKSS on 15 January 1940"
- Concerns activity of SKSS kitchens in Warsaw.
- ***Description:*** transcript, typescript, Polish, 223×289 mm, ss. 1, pp. 1.

  Doc. was kept in a binder.

7)

- After 15.01.1940, Warsaw
- Der Chef des Distrikts Warschau. Abteilung Volkswohlfahrt [Chief of the Warsaw District, Public Welfare Department] (Warsaw, ul. Warecka 11), Letter dated 15.01.1940 to [Coordinating Committee]
- Concerns report of 12.01.1940 and ban on extension of care by the Coordinating Committee to the "Aryan" population.
- ***Description:*** transcript, typescript, German, 213×280 mm, ss. 1, pp. 1.

  Doc. was kept in a binder.

8)

- After 16.01.1940, Warsaw
- Jewish Council in Warsaw, Engineer Adam Czerniaków, Letter dated 16.01.1940 to Das Amt für Volkswohlfahrt [Office for Public Welfare] (Warsaw, ul. Warecka 11)
- Concerns permission for a collection for the needs of 2 new hospitals (quarantine) for the Jewish population.
- ***Description:*** transcript, typescript, German, 223×287 mm, ss. 1, pp. 1.

  Doc. was kept in a binder.

9–10)

- After 18.01.1940, Warsaw
- [Coordinating Committee] MW. [Michał Weichert], "Report III of conference with Mr. Graebsch on 18 January 1940"
- Concerns activity of the Coordinating Committee; matter of Ms. Szedliskier of Düsseldorf. Enclosed: Szedliskier, wife of Jakub (Düsseldorf, Mintrogstr. 1, bei Wallach), Letter of 10.12.1939 to the local group of the NSV [National Socialist People's Welfare] (Warsaw) (request about bringing her children from Warsaw: Leo Szedliskier, age 13, and Fanny Szedliskier, age 11).
- ***Description:*** transcript, typescript, Polish, 209×297 mm, ss. 3, pp. 3.

  Doc. was kept in a binder.

11)

- After 18.01.1940, Warsaw
- [Coordinating Committee] MW. [Michał Weichert], Letter dated 18.01.1940 to Der Chef des Distrikts Warschau. Abteilung Volkswohlfahrt [Chief of Warsaw District, Public Welfare Department] (Warsaw, ul. Warecka 11)
- Concerns clothing aid for the needy organized by Lejzor Lipa Bloch (ul. Leszno 19, apt. 20).
- ***Description:*** transcript, typescript, German, 208×297 mm, ss. 1, pp. 1.

  Doc. was kept in a binder.

12)

- After 19.01.1940, Warsaw
- Jewish Council in Warsaw, engineer Adam Czerniaków, Letter dated 19.01.1940 to Das Amt für Volkswohlfahrt [Office for Public Welfare] (Warsaw, ul. Warecka 11)
- Cover letter with notation about the attached copy of a letter from the Hilfsaktion für notleidende Juden in Polen [Aid Campaign for Needy Jews in Poland] (Zürich).
- ***Description:*** transcript, typescript, German, 225×288 mm, ss. 1, pp. 1.

  See Ring. II/1/4.

  Doc. was kept in a binder.

13)

- After 20.01.1940, Warsaw
- [Coordinating Committee] [Michał Weichert], "Report IV of conference with Mr. Graebsch of the Depart[ment of] Soc[ial] Wel[fare] on 20 January 1940"
- Concerns withdrawal of 100 and 500 zł banknotes in the Generalgouvernement and exchange of money in the possession of the Coordinating Committee.
- ***Description:*** original or transcript, typescript (handwritten additions, ink), Polish, 208×297 mm, ss. 1, pp. 1.

  On the bottom signature of Michał Weichert (ink).

  Doc. was kept in a binder.

14)

- After 20.01.1940, Warsaw
- Der Chef des Distrikts Warschau. Abteilung Volkswohlfahrt [Chief of Warsaw District, Public Welfare Department] (Warsaw, ul. Warecka 11), Letter dated 20.01.1940 to Jewish Council in Warsaw
- Concerns a shipment of clothing and medications from Switzerland. Letter signed Blumenthal.
- ***Description:*** transcript, typescript, German, 226×289 mm, ss. 1, pp. 1.

  Doc. was kept in a binder.

15)

- After 24.01.1940, Warsaw
- [Coordinating Committee] [Michał Weichert], "Report V of conference with Mr. Graebsch of the Depart[ment of] Soc[ial] Wel[fare] on 24 January 1940"
- Concerns exchange of money.
- ***Description:*** original or transcript, typescript

(handwritten additions, ink), Polish, 209×297 mm, ss. 1, pp. 1.
At bottom signature of Michał Weichert (ink).
Doc. was kept in a binder.

16)
- After 24.01.1940, Warsaw
- Jewish Council in Warsaw, engineer Adam Czerniaków, Letter dated 24.01.1940 to Das Amt für Volkswohlfahrt [Office for Public Welfare] (Warsaw, ul. Warecka 11)
- Concerns transport of clothing and medications from Switzerland.
- ***Description:*** transcript, typescript, German, 226×288 mm, ss. 1, pp. 1.
Doc. was kept in a binder.

17)
- After 26.01.1940, Warsaw
- [Coordinating Committee] [Michał Weichert], "Report VI of conversation with Mr. Blumenthal of the Depart[ment of] Soc[ial] Wel[fare] on 26 January 1940"
- Concerns exchange of money.
- ***Description:*** original or transcript, typescript (handwritten additions, ink), Polish, 209×297 mm, ss. 1, pp. 1.
Signature of Michał Weichert at bottom (ink).
Doc. was kept in a binder.

18)
- After 27.01.1940, Warsaw
- [Coordinating Committee] [Michał Weichert], "Report VII of conversation with Mr. Graebsch of the Depart[ment of] Soc[ial] Wel[fare] on 27 January 1940"
- Concerns exchange of money.
- ***Description:*** original or transcript, typescript, Polish, 209×296 mm, ss. 1, pp. 1.
At bottom signature of Michał Weichert (ink).
Doc. was kept in a binder.

19)
- After 27.01.1940, Warsaw
- [Coordinating Committee] MW. [Michał Weichert], Letter dated 27.01.1940 to Der Chef des Distrikts Warschau. Abteilung Volkswohlfahrt [Chief of Warsaw District, Public Welfare Department] (Warsaw, ul. Warecka 11)
- Concerns exchange of money.
- ***Description:*** transcript, typescript, German, 222×285 mm, ss. 1, pp. 1.
Doc. was kept in a binder.

20)
- After 27.01.1940, Warsaw
- [Coordinating Committee] [Michał Weichert], "Report VIII of conversation with Mr. Graebsch on 29 January 1940"
- Concerns exchange of money.
- ***Description:*** original or transcript, typescript, Polish, 209×296 mm, ss. 1, pp. 1.
At bottom signature of Michał Weichert (ink).
Doc. was kept in a binder.

21)
- After 30.01.1940, Warsaw
- [Coordinating Committee] MW. [Michał Weichert], Letter dated 30.01.1940 to Der Chef des Distrikts Warschau. Abteilung Volkswohlfahrt [Chief of Warsaw District, Public Welfare Department] (Warsaw, ul. Warecka 11)
- Concerns care for the "Aryan" population by Jewish organizations.
- ***Description:*** transcript, typescript, German, 226×289 mm, ss. 1, pp. 1.
Doc. was kept in a binder.

22)
- After 3.02.1940, Warsaw
- [Coordinating Committee] [Michał Weichert], "Report of conversation with Mr. Blumenthal and Mr. Graebsch on 3 February 1940"
- Concerns farewell with Blumenthal and Graebsch in connection with transfer of the Coordinating Committee to the authority of a different department of the municipal government.
- ***Description:*** transcript, typescript, Polish, 224×289 mm, ss. 1, pp. 1.
Doc. was kept in a binder.

23)
- After 10.02.1940, Warsaw
- [Coordinating Committee] [Michał Weichert], "Information ueber die Taetigkeit der Koordinierungs-Kommission der juedischen Wohlfahrts und Fuersorge Organisationen zu Warschau, [ul.] Leszno 13." [Information about the activity of the Coordinating Committee of Jewish Welfare and Social Service Organizations in Warsaw, Leszno 13] (12.02.1940)
- Concerns report of activity for the period 12.1939–01.1940.
- ***Description:*** transcript, typescript, German, 209×296 mm, ss. 1, pp. 1.
Doc. was kept in a binder.

24)
- After 12.02.1940, Warsaw
- [Coordinating Committee] MW. [Michał Weichert], "Report of the conference with Doctor [Alfons] Ilg on 12 February 1940"
- Concerns current activity of the Coordinating Committee.
- ***Description:*** transcript, typescript, Polish, 209×296 mm, ss. 2, pp. 2.
Doc. was kept in a binder.

25)
- After 16.02.1940, Warsaw
- [Coordinating Committee] MW. [Michał Weichert], "Report of conference with Dr. [Alfons] Ilg on 16 February 1940"

• Concerns purchases of products, permits for travel into the provinces, roundups for work, aid from Zürich, transformation of the Coordinating Committee into the JSS.
• ***Description:*** transcript, typescript, Polish, 209×296 mm, ss. 2, pp. 2.
Doc. was kept in a binder.

26)
• After 23.02.1940, Warsaw
• [Coordinating Committee] [Michał Weichert], "Report of conference between Dr. Arldt, superintendent of Social Welfare in the Generalgouvernement, Colonel Wiecki, department head [Karl] Massing (Department of Social Welfare of the Chief of the Warsaw District), as well as I. Bornstein, P. Czerski (AJDC), Dr. M. Weichert (Coordinating Committee of Social and Welfare Organizations) at the premises of AJDC on 23 February 1940"
• Concerns organization of social welfare for the Jewish population in the Generalgouvernement.
• ***Description:*** transcript, typescript, Polish, 223×287 mm, ss. 3, pp. 3.
Doc. was kept in a binder.

27)
• After 26.02.1940, Warsaw
• [Coordinating Committee] [Michał Weichert], "Report of conference with Dr. [Alfons] Ilg on 26 February 1940"
• Concerns allocations of products, matter of the organization of the ŻSS (JSS), supervisory authorities, immunities, identification and insurance for employees, exchange of banknotes, contributions for communal purposes.
• ***Description:*** transcript, typescript, Polish, 216×279 mm, ss. 3, pp. 3.
Doc. was kept in a binder.

28–29)
• After 29.02.1940, Warsaw
• [Coordinating Committee] [Michał Weichert], "Report of conference in the Generalgouvernement in Kraków on 29 February 1940"
• Concerns the material situation of the Jewish Community in Kraków, organization of public assistance. List of participants of the conference: Dr. [Fritz] Arlt, Heinrich, I. [Izaak] Borenstein, M. [Marek] Bieberstein, chairman of the Jewish Community in Kraków, Dr. M. Weichert.
• ***Description:*** transcript (2 copies), typescript, Polish, 218×286, 222×284 mm, ss. 8, pp. 8.
Doc. was kept in a binder.

30)
• After 2.03.1940, Warsaw
• [Coordinating Committee] [Michał Weichert], "Report of conference in the Generalgouvernement in Kraków on 2 March 1940"
• Plan of new reorganization of Jewish social welfare; delivery of a memorandum concerning the activity of the AJDC and Coordinating Committee. List of participants of the conference: Dr. [Fritz] Arlt, Serafin, Heinrich, I. [Izaak] Borenstein, Dr. M. Weichert. Encl. memoranda (2): "Bemerkungen über die Aufgaben der jüdischen Wohlfahrtspflege" [Remarks about the tasks of Jewish welfare work] (Kraków, 2.03.1940) and "Notiz über die Tätigkeit der American Joint Distribution Committee" [Note on the activity of the AJDC] (Kraków, 2.03.1940).
• ***Description:*** transcript (2 copies, encl. in 1 copy), typescript, Polish, 224×289, 224×283, 219×345 mm, ss. 17, pp. 17.
Doc. was kept in a binder.

31)
• After 2.03.1940, Warsaw
• [Coordinating Committee] [Michał Weichert], "Note of the conference at the Kraków Jewish Community on 2 III 1940"
• Concerns RGO, contacts with German authorities, district bureaus of AJDC, social welfare in Kraków. List of participants of the conference: M. [Marek] Bieberstein, attorney [Wilhelm] Goldblatt, Engineer Willer, S. Majer, member of the Council of Elders of the Jewish Community in Kraków, [Leon] Salpeter, MA, member of the Council of Elders of the Jewish Community in Kraków, Uszer [Aszer] Szpira, member of the Council of Elders of the Jewish Community in Kraków, I. [Izaak] Borenstein, Dr. M. Weichert.
• ***Description:*** transcript, typescript, Polish, 225×287, 210×251 mm, ss. 2, pp. 2.
Doc. was kept in a binder.

32)
• After 11.03.1940, Warsaw
• AJDC (Warsaw), Letter dated 11.03.1940 to Der Chef des Distrikts Warschau. Abteilung Volkswohlfahrt [Chief of Warsaw District, Public Welfare Department] [Warsaw, ul. Warecka 11]
• Concerns holiday food aid for the Jewish population in the Generalgouvernement from AJDC.
• ***Description:*** transcript, typescript, German, 228×288 mm, ss. 1, pp. 1.
Doc. was kept in a binder.

33)
• After 13.03.1940, Warsaw
• [Coordinating Committee] [Michał Weichert], "Report of conference with Dr. [Fritz] Arlt, manager of the Unterabteilung Bevölkerungswesen und Fürsorge [Sub-department for population and welfare] and Mr. Heinrich, department head of Freie Wohlfahrt [Public Welfare] held on 13 March 1940 in Kraków in the building of the Generalgouvernement in the Mining Academy"
• Delegation of the American Red Cross, issue of the Karaites, contacts with German authorities, permits for import of food products from abroad, suspension of insurance payments for Jews, allocation of rationed

products, subsidies for social welfare institutions, purchase and import of products and materials, matter of the name for the new social welfare organization, displaced persons, issue of ghettos, transfer of money to the regions incorporated into the Reich.
- ***Description:*** transcript, typescript (additions, handwritten, ink), Polish, 208×290 mm, ss. 6, pp. 6.
  Doc. was kept in a binder.

34)
- After 14.03.1940, Warsaw
- [Coordinating Committee] [Michał Weichert], "Report of conference with Dr. [Fritz] Arlt, manager of the Unterabteilung Bevölkerungswesen und Fürsorge [Subdepartment for population and welfare] and Mr. Heinrich, department head of Freie Wohlfahrt [Public Welfare], held on 14 March 1940 in Kraków in the Building of the Generalgouvernement in the Mining Academy"
- Reorganization of social welfare (final confirmation of the name for the new organization: ŻSS [JSS], travel by train, passes, identification cards and armbands for employees of Jewish social welfare, protection of warehouses and residences of employees, aid for war prisoners and displaced persons, forced labor, development of social welfare in Warsaw).
- ***Description:*** transcript, typescript (additions, handwritten, ink), Polish, 208×291, 215×276 mm, ss. 5, pp. 5.
  Doc. was kept in a binder.

35)
- After 27.03.1940, Warsaw
- [Coordinating Committee] [Michał Weichert], "Note on conversation held [in Kraków] on 27.3.40"
- Description of the situation of the Jewish population in Warsaw. List of those present: Dr. [Fritz] Arlt, Dr. Gordon and Heinrich as well as engineer [Adam] Czerniaków, Dr. Weichert, Milejkowski, Jaszuński and Sztolcman.
- ***Description:*** transcript, typescript, Polish, 224×288 mm, ss. 5, pp. 5.
  Doc. was kept in a binder.

36)
- After 28.03.1940, Warsaw
- Amt des Generalgouverneurs für die besetzen polnischen Gebiete. Innere Verwaltung-Bevölkerungswesen und Fürsorge [Office of the Generalgovernor for the occupied Polish territories. Internal administration—Population and welfare] (Kraków), Letter dated 28.03.1940 to Dr. [Michał] Weichert (Warsaw), chairman of JSS
- Concerns response to the proposals of the ŻSS. Letter signed Heinrich.
- ***Description:*** transcript, typescript, German, 215×276 mm, ss. 1, pp. 1.
  Doc. was kept in a binder.

37)
- After 2.04.1940, Warsaw
- Amt des Generalgouverneurs für die besetzen polnischen Gebiete. Innere Verwaltung-Bevölkerungswesen und Fürsorge [Office of the Generalgovernor for the occupied Polish territories. Internal administration-Population and welfare] (Kraków), Letter dated 2.04.1940 to [Dr. Michał Weichert (Warsaw)]
- Concerns [social ?] insurance of the Jewish population. Letter signed Heinrich.
- ***Description:*** transcript, typescript, German, 216×278 mm, ss. 1, pp. 1.
  Doc. was kept in a binder.

## 118. RING. II/2. Mf. ŻIH—793; USHMM—48.

1)
- After 2.04.1940, Warsaw
- [Coordinating Committee] [Michał Weichert], "Note on conference with Mr. [Karl] Massing, director of the Department of Welfare of the Chief of the Warsaw District on 2 April 1940"
- Concerns current matters connected with activity of the Coordinating Committee.
- ***Description:*** transcript, typescript, Polish, 211×274 mm, ss. 1, pp. 1.
  Doc. was kept in a binder.

2)
- After 4.04.1940, Warsaw
- [Coordinating Committee] MW. [Michał Weichert], "Note on conversation with Mr. [Karl] Massing, director of the Department of Welfare in the Management of the District on 4 April 1940"
- Delivery of Jaszuński's memoranda, "Remarks about Forced Labor" and "Memorandum about emigration."
- ***Description:*** transcript, typescript, Polish, 215×277 mm, ss. 1, pp. 1.
  Doc. was kept in a binder.

3)
- After 4.04.1940, Warsaw
- [Coordinating Committee] MW. [Michał Weichert], "Note on conversation with the att[orney] Hertzog in the Office of the Chief of the District on 4 April 1940"
- Concerns forced labor and Karaites.
- ***Description:*** transcript, typescript, Polish, 215×277 mm, ss. 2, pp. 2.
  Doc. was kept in a binder.

4)
- 11.04.1940, Warsaw
- [Coordinating Committee] MW. [Michał Weichert], "Note on conference with the Central Guardian Council [Rada Główna Opiekuńcza] on 9 April 1940" (11.04.1940)
- Concerns allocation of grant for social welfare for the Polish and Jewish population. List of those present: [Andrzej] Jałowiecki, [Henryk] Kułakowski, Dir.

[Stefan] Łopato [Łoppato], [Izaak] Borenstein, Dr. [Michał] Weichert, Heinrich.
- *Description:* transcript, typescript, Polish, 220×284 mm, ss. 2, pp. 2.
 Doc. was kept in a binder.

5)
- After 9.04.1940, Warsaw
- Amt des Generalgouverneurs für die besetzen polnischen Gebiete. Innere Verwaltung-Bevölkerungswesen und Fürsorge [Office of the Generalgovernor for the occupied Polish territories. Internal administration-Population and welfare] (Kraków), Letter dated 9.04.1940 to Dr. Michał Weichert (Warszawa, ul. Długa 8a)
- Concerns financial matters. Letter signed Heinrich.
- *Description:* transcript, typescript, German, 217×281 mm, ss. 1, pp. 1.
 Doc. was kept in a binder.

6)
- 10.04.1940, Warsaw
- [Coordinating Committee] MW. [Michał Weichert], "Note. Report about the conference with Mr. Heinrich, department head of Public Welfare in the Department of Population and Welfare in the Generalgouvernement in Kraków on 8 and 9 April 1940" (10.04.1940)
- New charter of the RGO for confirmation in 05.1940 (Jewish sector in RGO is to bear the name "Jüdische Soziale Selbsthilfe" [Jewish Social Self-Help[5]]), budget, rations, Jewish hackney drivers, packages from abroad, etc. List of those present: Heinrich, Borenstein, Dr. M. Weichert.
- *Description:* original or transcript, typescript (handwritten additions, ink), Polish, 222×283 mm, ss. 4, pp. 4.
 Doc. was kept in a binder.

7)
- After 10.04.1940, Warsaw
- MW. [Michał Weichert], Letter dated 10.04.1940 to Presidium of the Coordinating Committee (Warsaw)
- Concerns allocation of coal for the Coordinating Committee.
- *Description:* typescript, Polish, 220×287 mm, ss. 1, pp. 1.
 Doc. was kept in a binder.

8)
- 11.04.1940, Warsaw
- [Coordinating Committee] MW. [Michał Weichert], "Note on conference with Mr. Artur Śliwiński, Chairman of the Capital Committee for Mutual Aid [Stołeczny Komitet Samopomocy Społecznej] on 11 April 1940" (11.04.1940)
- Concerns anti-Jewish incidents in Warsaw, financial matters.
- *Description:* transcript, typescript, Polish, 221×287 mm, ss. 2, pp. 2.
 Doc. was kept in a binder.

9)
- 11.04.1940, Warsaw
- [Coordinating Committee] MW. [Michał Weichert], "Note on conference with Mr. [Karl] Massing, director of the Department of Welfare in the Office of the Chief of the District on 11 April 1940" (11.04.1940)
- Concerns financial matters
- *Description:* transcript, typescript, Polish, 220×285 mm, ss. 2, pp. 2.
 Doc. was kept in a binder.

10)
- 14.04.1940, Warsaw
- [Coordinating Committee] MW. [Michał Weichert], "Note on conference with Mr. Wenderoth, Head of the Department of Agriculture and Food of the Chief of the Warsaw District on 12 April 1940" (14.04.1940)
- Concerns allocation of wheat flour for baking of [Passover] matzo.
- *Description:* transcript, typescript, Polish, 220×286 mm, ss. 3, pp. 3.
 Doc. was kept in a binder.

11)
- 14.04.1940, Warsaw
- [Coordinating Committee] MW. [Michał Weichert], "Note on conference with Mr. [Karl] Massing, Head of the Department of Welfare of the Chief of the Warsaw District on 13 April 1940" (14.04.1940)
- Concerns financial matters.
- *Description:* transcript, typescript, Polish, 220×287 mm, ss. 3, pp. 3.
 Doc. was kept in a binder.

12)
- 15.04.1940, Warsaw
- [Coordinating Committee] MW. [Michał Weichert], "Note of conference with Mr. Min[ister] [Janusz] Machnicki, Chairman of the Provisioning Section of the Capital Committee for Mutual Aid [Prezes Sekcji Zaopatrywania Stołecznego Komitetu Samopomocy Społecznej] on 14 April 1940" (15.04.1940)
- Concerns cooperation of Coordinating Committee with the SKSS.
- *Description:* transcript, typescript, Polish, 223×288 mm, ss. 3, pp. 3.
 On p. 3 at bottom an initial (pencil).
 Doc. was kept in a binder.

13)
- After 15.04.1940, Warsaw
- [Coordinating Committee] MW. [Michał Weichert], "Note on visit at the Mayor's Department of Provisioning on 15 April 1940"

5. The German *Selbst-Hilfe*, like the Polish *samopomoc*, might also be rendered "mutual aid" or "cooperative aid."

- Meeting with Dr. Bauer, Spindler, Dir. Marian Drozdowski, Chlebiński regarding provision of food.
- ***Description:*** transcript, typescript, Polish, 219×288 mm, ss. 1, pp. 1.
  Doc. was kept in a binder.

14)
- After 15.04.1940, Warsaw
- [Coordinating Committee] MW. [Michał Weichert], "Note of conference with Mr. Szarwenke at the Economic Association [Związek Gospodarczy] on 15 April 1940"
- Regarding provision of food.
- ***Description:*** transcript, typescript, Polish, 219×287 mm, ss. 1, pp. 1.
  At bottom initials (pencil).
  Doc. was kept in a binder.

15)
- After 15.04.1940, Warsaw
- [Coordinating Committee] MW. [Michał Weichert], "Note on conference with Mr. Min[ister] [Janusz] Machnicki, Chairman of the Provisioning Section of SKSS on 15 April 1940"
- Concerns purchase of potatoes.
- ***Description:*** transcript, typescript, Polish, 221×287 mm, ss. 1, pp. 1.
  At bottom initials (pencil).
  Doc. was kept in a binder.

16)
- After 16.04.1940, Warsaw
- [Coordinating Committee] MW. [Michał Weichert], "Note on conference with Mr. Artur Śliwiński, Chairman of SKSS on 16 April 1940"
- Concerns financial matters.
- ***Description:*** transcript, typescript, Polish, 219×284 mm, ss. 2, pp. 2.
  Doc. was kept in a binder.

17)
- After 16.04.1940, Warsaw
- [Coordinating Committee] MW. [Michał Weichert], "Note on conference with Mr. [Karl] Massing, Manager of the Department of Social Welfare of the Chief of the District on 16 April 1940"
- Concerns confiscation of flour from Terespolski, baker in Henryków.
- ***Description:*** transcript, typescript, Polish, 220×287 mm, ss. 1, pp. 1.
  Doc. was kept in a binder.

18)
- After 16.04.1940, Warsaw
- [Coordinating Committee] MW. [Michał Weichert], "Note on conference with Mr. Bohlenbach, Manager of the Mayor's Department of Social Welfare on 16 April 1940"
- Concerns relations of Coordinating Committee with German authorities.
- ***Description:*** transcript, typescript, Polish, 219×282 mm, ss. 3, pp. 3.
  Doc. was kept in a binder.

19)
- After 17.04.1940, Warsaw
- [Coordinating Committee] MW. [Michał Weichert], "Note on conference with Chairman Strzelecki [of SKSS], on 17 April 1940"
- Concerns purchase of foodstuffs for the Coordinating Committee.
- ***Description:*** transcript, typescript, Polish, 220×284 mm, ss. 2, pp. 2.
  Doc. was kept in a binder.

20)
- After 17.04.1940, Warsaw
- [Coordinating Committee] MW. [Michał Weichert], "Note of conference with Mr. Minister [Janusz] Machnicki, on 17 April 1940"
- Concerns purchase of foodstuffs for the Coordinating Committee.
- ***Description:*** transcript, typescript, Polish, 221×285 mm, ss. 2, pp. 2.
  Doc. was kept in a binder.

21)
- After 18.04.1940, Warsaw
- [Coordinating Committee] MW. [Michał Weichert], "Note on conference with Dr. Zahn of the Sub-prefecture of Warsaw District [ze Starostwa Powiatu Warszawskiego] on 18 April 1940"
- Concerns confiscation of flour in Henryków.
- ***Description:*** transcript, typescript, Polish, 219×284 mm, ss. 2, pp. 2.
  Doc. was kept in a binder.

22)
- After 19.04.1940, Warsaw
- [Coordinating Committee] MW. [Michał Weichert], "Note of conference with Mr. Captain Rochling of the Order Police [Policja Porządkowa] [Al. Szucha 23] on 19 April 1940"
- Concerns wearing of armbands by Jews, confiscation of furniture in the Precinct Committee [Komitecie Dzielnicowym] (ul. Leszno 52).
- ***Description:*** transcript, typescript, Polish, 222×282 mm, ss. 1, pp. 1.
  At bottom initials (pencil).
  Doc. was kept in a binder.

23)
- After 19.04.1940, Warsaw
- [Coordinating Committee] MW. [Michał Weichert], "Note on conversation with Dr. Bauer, Manager of the Mayor's Food Bureau on 19 April 1940"
- Concerns confiscation of flour in Henryków.
- ***Description:*** transcript, typescript, Polish, 222×285 mm, ss. 1, pp. 1.
  At bottom initials (pencil).
  Doc. was kept in a binder.

24)
- After 19.04.1940, Warsaw
- [Coordinating Committee] MW. [Michał Weichert], "Report of conference at the Capital Committee of Mutual Aid [SKSS] on 19 April 1940"

- Concerns relations between SKSS and KK, provision of food products to the KK. List of those present: Jan Strzelecki, vice chairman of SKSS, Prof. Staniszkis, vice chairman of SKSS, Min[ister] [Janusz] Machnicki, chairman of the Provisioning Section of SKSS, Engineer Piechocki, vice chairman of the Provisioning Section of SKSS, Engineer Andrzej [Artur] Śliwiński, manager of the Department of Purchases of the Provisioning Section of SKSS [kierownik Wydziału Zakupów Sekcji Zaopatrywania SKSS], Dr. M. Weichert (KK), Engineer A. Sztolcman (KK), Prof. Sz. Braude (KK).
- ***Description:*** original or transcript, typescript (handwritten additions, ink), Polish, 220×285 mm, ss. 5, pp. 5.

  At bottom an initial (pencil).

  Doc. was kept in a binder.

25)

- After 20.04.1940, Warsaw
- [Coordinating Committee] [Michał Weichert], "Ueberblick über die Tätigkeit des Koordinierungs-Ausschusses der Jüdischen Sozialen Selbsthilfe Warschau" [Overview of activity of the Coordinating Committee of the Warsaw Jewish Self-Help] (20.04.1940)
- Concerns activity of KK in period 1939–1940.
- ***Description:*** transcript, typescript, German, 214×276 mm, ss. 4, pp. 4.

  Doc. was kept in a binder.

26)

- After 29.04.1940, Warsaw
- [Coordinating Committee] MW. [Michał Weichert], "Note on conference with Mr. [Heinrich] Bollenbach, Director of the Mayor's Department of Social Welfare on 29 April 1940"
- Concerns home for refugees (ul. Leszno 14), issue of identification, armbands, and certificates for employees of ŻSS [KK].
- ***Description:*** transcript, typescript, Polish, 222×288 mm, ss. 2, pp. 2.

  Doc. was kept in a binder.

27)

- After 6.05.1940, Warsaw
- [Coordinating Committee] MW. [Michał Weichert], "Note on conference with Mr. Min[ister] [Janusz] Machnicki, Chairman of the Provisioning Section of SKSS on 6 May 1940"
- Concerns financial matters, relations between SKSS and KK.
- ***Description:*** transcript, typescript, Polish, 222×284 mm, ss. 2, pp. 2.

  Doc. was kept in a binder.

28)

- After 7.05.1940, Warsaw
- [Coordinating Committee] [Michał Weichert], "Report of conference with Mr. H. Heinrich, Director of the Department of Public Welfare of the Generalgouvernement in Kraków on 7.5.1940"
- Concerns new charter of RGO for confirmation (also concerns creation of ŻSS within the framework of RGO), sources of revenue and food products for ŻSS in Warsaw.
- ***Description:*** transcript, typescript, Polish, 206×288, 208×295 mm, ss. 5, pp. 5.

  Doc. was kept in a binder.

29)

- After 8.05.1940, Warsaw
- [Coordinating Committee ŻSS] [Michał Weichert], "Report about conference with Mr. Heinrich, Director of the Department of Public Welfare in the Generalgouvernement on 8.5.1940"
- Concerns emergency aid, allocation of food and other products, allowances for closed medical facilities.
- ***Description:*** transcript, typescript, Polish, 205×290 mm, ss. 2, pp. 2.

  Doc. was kept in a binder.

30)

- After 8.05.1940, Warsaw
- [Coordinating Committee ŻSS] [Michał Weichert], "Report of conference with Dr. [Fritz] Arlt and Mr. Heinrich, in the presence of Chairman Bieberstein on 8 May 1940 in Kraków"
- Concerns organization of ŻSS in Kraków at the RGO, sources of revenue of KK ŻSS in Warsaw, emergency aid, allocations of food products.
- ***Description:*** transcript, typescript, Polish, 208×291 mm, ss. 2, pp. 2.

  Doc. was kept in a binder.

31)

- After 8.05.1940, Warsaw
- [Coordinating Committee ŻSS] MW. [Michał Weichert], "Note on conversation with Chairman Bieberstein in Kraków on 8 May 1940"
- Concerns personnel of the Board of ŻSS in Generalgouvernement.
- ***Description:*** transcript, typescript, Polish, 219×283 mm, ss. 1, pp. 1.

  Doc. was kept in a binder.

32)

- After 9.05.1940, Warsaw
- [Coordinating Committee ŻSS] [Michał Weichert], "Report of conference with Mr. Heinrich, Director of the Department of Public Welfare on 9 May 1940"
- Concerns the new charter of RGO, emergency aid for KK ŻSS in Warsaw.
- ***Description:*** transcript, typescript, Polish, 205×290 mm, ss. 2, pp. 2.

  Doc. was kept in a binder.

33)

- After 9.05.1940, Warsaw
- [Coordinating Committee ŻSS] MW. [Michał Weichert], "Report of conference with Mr. Heinrich, Director of the Department of Public Welfare in the Generalgouvernement in Kraków on 9 May 1940 (Afternoon)"

- Concerns sources of revenue for ŻSS, new charter of RGO.
- ***Description:*** transcript, typescript, Polish, 220×285 mm, ss. 3, pp. 3.
  Doc. was kept in a binder.

34)
- After 11.05.1940, Warsaw
- [Coordinating Committee ŻSS] Wt. [Michał Weichert], "Note on conference at the Provisioning Section of the SKSS on 11 May 1940"
- Concerns allotment of food products, charter of RGO, information about plan to reduce the allocation of food rations for the Jewish population by 50 percent. List of those present: Janusz Machnicki, Jarkowski, Dr. M. Weichert, Engineer A. Sztolcman.
- ***Description:*** transcript, typescript, Polish, 222×285 mm, ss. 2, pp. 2.
  Doc. was kept in a binder.

35)
- After 11.05.1940, Warsaw
- [Coordinating Committee ŻSS] Wt. [Michał Weichert], "Note on conference at the SKSS on 11 May 1940 in the matter of abuses committed during disinfection of apartments"
- Concerns abuses in the northern district in Warsaw. List of those present: Chairman Artur Śliwiński, Inspector Dr. Łącki, Dr. Kaczyński, Dr. M. Weichert, Engineer A. Sztolcman.
- ***Description:*** transcript, typescript, Polish, 222×283 mm, ss. 2, pp. 2.
  Doc. was kept in a binder.

36)
- After 14.05.1940, Warsaw
- [Coordinating Committee ŻSS] Wt. [Michał Weichert], "Report of conference at the home of Prince Janusz Radziwiłł on 14 May 1940"
- Concerns financial aid for ŻSS, distribution of foreign gifts. List of those present: Prince Janusz Radziwiłł, Count Adam Ronikier, Chairman A. Gepner, Dir. I. Borenstein, Dr. M. Weichert.
- ***Description:*** transcript, typescript, Polish, 223×286 mm, ss. 4, pp. 4.
  Doc. was kept in a binder.
  For information concerning this meeting, see A. Ronikier, *Pamiętniki*, Kraków 2001, p. 52.

37)
- After 14.05.1940, Warsaw
- [Coordinating Committee ŻSS] Wt. [Michał Weichert], "Report of conference with Mayor [Julian] Kulski on 14 May 1940"
- Concerns distribution of food products for KK ŻSS. List of those present: Mayor Julian Kulski, Chairman Strzelecki, Minister [Janusz]Machnicki, Engineer A. Sztolcman, Dr. Reicherowa, M. Weichert.
- ***Description:*** transcript, typescript, Polish, 220×287 mm, ss. 2, pp. 2.
  Doc. was kept in a binder.

38)
- After 14.05.1940, Warsaw
- [Coordinating Committee ŻSS] [Michał Weichert], "Report of conference with Mr. [Karl] Massing, Director of the Department of Social Welfare of the Chief of the Warsaw District on 14 May 1940"
- Refugee shelter at ul. Leszno 14, allocation of rationed articles, identification papers and certificates for employees of ŻSS, housing tax, repatriants from the USSR.
- ***Description:*** transcript, typescript (handwritten additions, ink), Polish, 214×272 mm, ss. 3, pp. 3.
  Doc. was kept in a binder.

39)
- After 04.1940, Warsaw
- [Coordinating Committee ŻSS] [Michał Weichert], "Die jüdische Fürsorge in Stadt und Distrikt Warschau" [Jewish welfare in the city and district of Warsaw] (ending missing)
- Report of activity of KK in Warsaw and in the Warsaw district (04.1940).
- ***Description:*** transcript, typescript, German, 223×289 mm, ss. 1, pp. 1.
  Doc. was kept in a binder.

40)
- After 15.05.1940, Warsaw
- [Coordinating Committee ŻSS] [Michał Weichert], "Note about the conference with Director of the Bank of Issue Mr. F. [Feliks] Młynarski, on 14 May 1940"
- Concerns credit for KK ŻSS. List of those present: F. Młynarski, A. Gepner, Dr. M. Weichert.
- ***Description:*** original or transcript, typescript, Polish, 208×273 mm, ss. 2, pp. 2.
  Doc. signed by Michał Weichert (ink).
  Doc. was kept in a binder.

41)
- 17.05.1940, Warsaw
- [Coordinating Committee ŻSS] [Michał Weichert], Letter dated 17.05.1940 to SKSS in Warsaw
- Concerns allocation of rationed products for KK. Encl. (3): 1) [KK ŻSS] Department of the Fight against Epidemics [Wydział Walki z Epidemiami] (ul. Tłomackie 11, apt. 14), Letter dated 8.05.1940 to Presidium of KK ŻSS; 2) "Order for food products for Coordinating Committee"; 3) KK ŻSS, Presidium, "Informational Note for Mayor [Julian] Kulski" (17.05.1940).
- ***Description:*** transcript, typescript, Polish, 222×283 mm, ss. 7, pp. 7.
  Encl. in transcripts, missing encl. 2.
  Doc. was kept in a binder.

42)
- After 18.05.1940, Warsaw
- [Coordinating Committee ŻSS] [Michał Weichert], "Report about the conference with Mr. [Karl] Massing, Manager of the Department of Social Welfare of the Chief of District on 18 May 1940"

- Safe-conduct passes [Glejty] for KK's warehouses and offices, identification cards for office workers, contributions, charter of RGO, distribution of American gifts.
- ***Description:*** transcript, typescript, Polish, 211×273 mm, ss. 2, pp. 2.
  Doc. was kept in a binder.

43)
- After 18.05.1940, Warsaw
- [Coordinating Committee ŻSS] [Michał Weichert], "Note on conference with Min[ister] [Janusz] Machnicki, Chairman of the Provisioning Section of the SKSS on 18 May 1940"
- Concerns charter of RGO, allocation of products on loan account of KK.
- ***Description:*** transcript, typescript, Polish, 211×272 mm, ss. 1, pp. 1.
  Doc. was kept in a binder.

44)
- After 19.05.1940, Warsaw
- [Coordinating Committee ŻSS] [Michał Weichert], "Note of conference with Dr. Syrkin-Binsteinowa of the Commission of the Struggle against Epidemics on 19 May 1940"
- Concerns activity of the Commission.
- ***Description:*** transcript, typescript, Polish, 220×287 mm, ss. 1, pp. 1.
  Doc. was kept in a binder.

45)
- After 21.05.1940, Warsaw
- [Coordinating Committee ŻSS] Wt. [Michał Weichert], "Report of conference with Mr. Heinrich, Manager of the Department of Voluntary Social Welfare in the Department of Soc[ial] Welfare of the Generalgouvernement on 21 May 1940 in Warsaw"
- Concerns identification cards and certificates for KK, facilities of KK in the program of the delegation of the American Red Cross, home for displaced persons (ul. Leszno 14), housing tax, charter of RGO.
- ***Description:*** transcript, typescript, Polish, 223×290 mm, ss. 3, pp. 3.
  Doc. was kept in a binder.

46)
- 24.05.1940, Warsaw
- [Coordinating Committee ŻSS] Wt. [Michał Weichert], "Note on conversation with Mr. Artur Śliwiński, Chairman of the SKSS" (24.05.1940)
- Concerns delegation of the American Red Cross.
- ***Description:*** transcript, typescript, Polish, 222×140 mm, ss. 1, pp. 1.
  Doc. was kept in a binder.

47)
- 25.05.1940, Warsaw
- [Coordinating Committee ŻSS] [Michał Weichert], Note regarding activity of KK ŻSS (25.05.1940)
- Concerns description of particular departments of KK ŻSS.
- ***Description:*** original or transcript, typescript, German, 222×287 mm, ss. 2, pp. 2.
  Doc. was kept in a binder.

48)
- 28.05.1940, Warsaw
- [Coordinating Committee ŻSS] Wt. [Michał Weichert], "Note about visit of Delegation of American Red Cross on 24 and 25 May 1940" (28.05.1940)
- Inf. about social welfare institutions in Warsaw visited by the delegation. List of those present: American Red Cross—House and Shephardt; RGO—Dir. Iłowiecki, Count Plater; PCK—Skrzyński; SKSS—Śliwiński, Dir. H. Drozdowski; AJDC—Dir. I. Borenstein; KK ŻSS—Dr. M. Weichert. Appended "Program of visits of the Delegation of the American Red Cross, communicated telephonically by Dir. H. Drozdowski."
- ***Description:*** original or transcript, typescript, Polish, 218×286 mm, ss. 3, pp. 3.
  Doc. was kept in a binder.

49)
- 28.05.1940, Warsaw
- [Coordinating Committee ŻSS] Wt. [Michał Weichert], "Report about conference at [office of] Mayor [Julian] Kulski on 28 May 1940" (28.05.1940)
- Concerns financial matters.
- ***Description:*** transcript, typescript, Polish, 211×273 mm, ss. 4, pp. 4.
  Doc. was kept in a binder.

50)
- 28.05.1940, Warsaw
- [Coordinating Committee ŻSS] Wt. [Michał Weichert], "Note on conversation with Chairman [Adam] Czerniaków on 28 May 1940" (28.05.1940)
- Concerns conversation at office of Julian Kulski.
- ***Description:*** transcript, typescript, German, 210×269 mm, ss. 1, pp. 1.
  Doc. was kept in a binder.

51)
- 29.05.1940, Warsaw
- [Coordinating Committee ŻSS] Wt. [Michał Weichert], "Report about conference with Mr. [Heinrich] Bollenbach, Manager of the Mayor's Department of Social Welfare on 29 May 1940" (29.05.1940)
- Concerns eviction of a home for refugees (ul. Leszno 14), contributions for ŻSS, identification cards and certificates for employees of ŻSS, housing tax.
- ***Description:*** transcript, typescript, Polish, 214×276 mm, ss. 2, pp. 2.
  Doc. was kept in a binder.

52)
- 31.05.1940, Warsaw
- [Coordinating Committee ŻSS] Wt. [Michał Weichert], "Note about on-site inspection at the

Shelter at [ul.] Leszno 14 on 30 May 1940" (31.05.1940)
- Concerns eviction of shelter for refugees.
- ***Description:*** transcript, typescript, Polish, 219×284 mm, ss. 1, pp. 1.
  Doc. was kept in a binder.

53)
- 31.05.1940, Warsaw
- [Coordinating Committee ŻSS] Wt. [Michał Weichert], "Report of conference at the Presidium of SKSS on 30 May 1940" (31.05.1940)
- Concerns financial matters, aid for KK. List of those present: Chairman Artur Śliwiński, Treasurer Fabierkiewicz, Chairman A. Gepner, Dr. Weichert, engineer A.Sztolcman.
- ***Description:*** original or transcript, typescript (handwritten additions, pencil), Polish, 210×272 mm, ss. 3, pp. 3.
  Doc. was kept in a binder.

54)
- 31.05.1940, Warsaw
- [Coordinating Committee ŻSS] Wt. [Michał Weichert], "Report about conference with Mr. [Heinrich] Bollenbach, Manager of the Mayor's Department of Social Welfare on 30 May 1940" (31.05.1940)
- Concerns eviction of a home for refugees (ul. Leszno 14), identification cards and certificates for employees of ŻSS.
- ***Description:*** original or transcript, typescript, Polish, 220×283 mm, ss. 1, pp. 1.
  Doc. was kept in a binder.

55)
- After 31.05.1940, Warsaw
- [Coordinating Committee ŻSS] Wt. [Michał Weichert], "Report about conference with Mr. [Heinrich] Bollenbach, Manager of the Mayor's Department of Social Welfare on 31 May 1940"
- Concerns eviction of a home for refugees (ul. Leszno 14), identification cards and certificates for employees, membership contributions [cegiełki] for ŻSS.
- ***Description:*** original or transcript, typescript (handwritten additions, ink), Polish, 213×272 mm, ss. 2, pp. 2.
  Doc. was kept in a binder.

## 119. RING. II/3. Mf. ŻIH—793; USHMM—48.

1)
- 2.06.1940, Warsaw
- [Coordinating Committee ŻSS] Wt. [Michał Weichert], "Report of conference with Mr. [Heinrich] Bollenbach, Manager of the Mayor's Department of Social Welfare on 1 June 1940" (2.06.1940)
- Printing of certificates of contribution, eviction of the [refugees'] shelter at ul. Leszno 14, allotment of products, budget of KK.
- ***Description:*** original or transcript, typescript, Polish, 224×290 mm, ss. 1, pp. 2.
  Doc. was kept in a binder.

2)
- 4.06.1940, Warsaw
- [Coordinating Committee ŻSS] Wt. [Michał Weichert], "Report of conference at [office of] Mr. Artur Śliwiński, chairman of the SKSS on 3 June 1940" (4.06.1940)
- Matter of distribution of American aid for the population of the Generalgouvernement. List of those present at the conference: [Artur] Śliwiński, [Janusz] Machnicki, Minister; Dir. [Henryk] Drozdowski, Dr. Brzeziński (SKSS), Dir. [Mieczysław] Jastrzębowski (RGO), Countess [Maria] Tarnowska (PCK), Count [Jan] Zamoyski (PCK), Dir. [Izaak] Bornstein (AJDC), Dr.Weichert (KK ŻSS).
- ***Description:*** original or transcript, typescript, Polish, 224×290 mm, ss. 1, pp. 2.
  Doc. was kept in a binder.

3)
- After 3.06.1940, Warsaw
- [Coordinating Committee ŻSS] Wt. [Michał Weichert], "Report of conference at the Chamber of Industry and Commerce on 3 June 1940"
- Concerns American aid for the population of the Generalgouvernement. List of those present at the conference: John Hartigan (Hoover Commission—Commission for Polish Relief, New York), Dr. Sanne, general (manager of the German Red Cross), Handtke (German Red Cross), Dr. J.G. Lohmann (Ministry of Foreign Affairs in Berlin), H. Heinrich (director of the Department of Social Welfare of Generalgouvernement in Kraków), C. [Karl] Massing (manager of the Department of Social Welfare of the Chief of the District), Dir. Makowski (bureau manager of Municipal Adminstration), Countess [Maria] Tarnowska (PCK), Count [Jan] Zamoyski (PCK), Dir. Gorczycki (PCK), Dir. Brzezińska (German Red Cross), Artur Śliwiński (chairman of SKSS), Janusz Machnicki (chairman of Provisioning Section of SKSS), Piotr Drzewiecki (chairman of the Auditing Commission of SKSS), Henryk Drozdowski (secretary general of SKSS), Dir. [Mieczysław] Jastrzębowski (RGO), Dr. Brzeziński (chief of the Presidial Bureau of SKSS), Izaak Bornstein (AJDC), Dr. M. [Michał] Weichert (ŻSS), Dr. J. Rozenblum (TOZ). Encl. TOZ (Dr. J. Rozenblum) (Warsaw), Letter dated 3.06.1940 to ŻSS (M. Weichert) notifying about meeting with representatives of the American Mission of the Red Cross at the office of SKSS at ul. Wiejska 10, on 3.06.1940 (transcript).
- ***Description:*** original or transcript, typescript, Polish, 224×290 mm, missing encl. 2–6, ss. 3, pp. 3.
  Doc. was kept in a binder.

4)
- After 3.06.1940, Warsaw
- [Coordinating Committee ŻSS] Wt. [Michał

Weichert], "Note on conversation with Mr. Heinrich on 3 June 1940"
- Concerns aid from AJDC for ŻSS.
- ***Description:*** original or transcript, typescript, Polish, 224×290 mm, ss. 1, pp. 1.
  At top a note: "Private."
  Doc. was kept in a binder.

5)
- After 21.06.1940, Warsaw
- [Coordinating Committee ŻSS] [Michał Weichert], "Report of conference at the Population and Social Welfare Department of the Generalgouvernement on 21 June 1940"
- "Haupthilfsausschuss" [Central Relief Committee], Jewish Councils and ŻSS, subventions for ŻSS, displacement of Jews from Kraków. List of those present at the conference: Dr. [Fritz] Arlt, Heinrich, Col. Wieck, M. Bieberstein, Dir. J. Jaszuński, Dr. M. Weichert.
- ***Description:*** original or transcript, typescript, Polish, 224×290 mm, ss. 5, pp. 5.
  Doc. was kept in a binder.

6)
- After 11.07.1940, Warsaw
- [Coordinating Committee ŻSS] [Michał Weichert], "Report of conference with Mr. Heinrich, manager of the Department of Freie Wohlfahrt of the Gen[eral] Gov[ernment] in the presence of secretary and chairman [Marek] Bieberstein on 11 July 1940"
- Economic and financial matters, management of Jewish property, theft of American gifts, ghetto in Mińsk Mazowiecki, dismissal of Jewish employees, unblocking of bank accounts belonging to Jews, displacement of Jews from Krynica and Kraków, gifts from AJDC, matter of bowing to Germans, nonacceptance of foreign letters from Jews.
- ***Description:*** original or transcript, typescript, Polish, 210×278 mm, minor damages and losses of text, ss. 4, pp. 4.
  Doc. was kept in a binder.

7)
- After 12.07.1940, Warsaw
- [Coordinating Committee ŻSS] [Michał Weichert], "Note of conference with Minister [Janusz] Machnicki on 12.07.1940"
- Concerns participation of KK ŻSS in finances of SKSS.
- ***Description:*** original or transcript, typescript, Polish, 210×278 mm, ss. 1, pp. 1.
  Doc. was kept in a binder.

8)
- After 15.07.1940, Warsaw
- [Coordinating Committee ŻSS] [Michał Weichert], "Report of conference at the Mayor's Department of Social Welfare on 15 July 1940, in the presence of Chairman B. Zabłudowski"
- Financial matters.
- ***Description:*** original or transcript, typescript, Polish, 224×285 mm, ss. 4, pp. 4.
  Doc. was kept in a binder.

9)
- After 16.07.1940, Warsaw
- [Coordinating Committee ŻSS] [Michał Weichert], "Note about telephone conversation with Mr. Heinrich, Director of the Department of Public Welfare of the Generalgouvernement on 16 July 1940 at 9:30 AM"
- Financial matters, Orphanage at ul. Leszno 127.
- ***Description:*** original or transcript, typescript, Polish, 220×285 mm, ss. 1, pp. 1.
  Doc. was kept in a binder.

10)
- After 17.07.1940, Warsaw
- [Coordinating Committee ŻSS] [Michał Weichert], "Note about telephone conversations with Mr. [Karl] Massing on 17 July 1940"
- Financial matters (participation of ŻSS in streetcar tax).
- ***Description:*** original or transcript, typescript, Polish, 225×290 mm, ss. 1, pp. 1.
  Doc. was kept in a binder.

11)
- After 17.07.1940, Warsaw
- [Coordinating Committee ŻSS] [Michał Weichert], "Report of meeting at Warsaw bureau of the RGO on 17 July 1940"
- Division of gifts. List of those present: Dir. [Mieczysław] Jastrzębowski of RGO, Dr. Gorczycki, [Jan] Zamoyski (PCK), Chairman Piechocki (SKSS), Dr. Weichert, A. Perlmutter.
- ***Description:*** original or transcript, typescript, Polish, 222×285 mm, ss. 2, pp. 2.
  Doc. was kept in a binder.

12)
- After 18.07.1940, Warsaw
- [Coordinating Committee ŻSS] [Michał Weichert], "Report of conference with Mr. [Heinrich] Bollenbach at the Mayor's Department of Social Welfare in Warsaw, on 18 July 1940"
- Aid for boarding schools [internatów], eviction of a shelter for refugees (ul. Leszno 52), requisition of the Home for the Elderly (ul. Górczewska 9).
- ***Description:*** original or transcript, typescript (handwritten additions, ink), Polish, 222×280 mm, ss. 2, pp. 2.
  Doc. was kept in a binder.

13)
- After 19.07.1940, Warsaw
- [Coordinating Committee ŻSS] [Michał Weichert], "Note about the conversation with Minister [Janusz] Machnicki at RGO in Kraków on 19 July 1940"
- Share of the Warsaw district in distribution of American gifts, RGO, lottery, aid from the Hoover Committee.

- ***Description:*** original or transcript, typescript, Polish, 222×280 mm, ss. 1, pp. 1.
  Doc. was kept in a binder.

14)
- After 19.07.1940, Warsaw
- [Coordinating Committee ŻSS] [Michał Weichert], "Note about a telephone conversation with Mr. Heinrich on 19.07.1940 at 12 o'clock"
- Financial matters (share of ŻSS in the streetcar tax).
- ***Description:*** original or transcript, typescript, Polish, 222×280 mm, ss. 1, pp. 1.
  Doc. was kept in a binder.

15)
- After 23.07.1940, Warsaw
- [Coordinating Committee ŻSS] [Michał Weichert], "Report of conference with Heinrich, Director of the Department of Public Welfare in the Generalgouvernement with the participation of Major Raga, in presence of Dr. Wielikowski and Mr. Zabłudowski on 23 July 1940"
- Activity of ŻSS, ghetto in Mińsk Mazowiecki, removal of Jewish employees, displacement of Jews from Kraków, streetcar tax.
- ***Description:*** original or transcript, typescript, Polish, 222×285 mm, ss. 3, pp. 3.
  Doc. was kept in a binder.

16)
- After 25.07.1940, Warsaw
- [Coordinating Committee ŻSS] [Michał Weichert], "Report of conference with Mr. [Heinrich] Bollenbach in the Mayor's Department of Social Welfare on 25 July 1940" and "Note about visit of Mr. [Heinrich] Bollenbach at the Home for the Elderly at ul. Górczewska 9 on 25 July 1940"
- Entertainment tax for the benefit of ŻSS, agricultural ranch at Grochów, permission to settle 100 families in Otwock.
- ***Description:*** original or transcript, typescript, Polish, 219×287 mm, ss. 2, pp. 2.
  Doc. was kept in a binder.

17)
- After 26.07.1940, Warsaw
- [Coordinating Committee ŻSS] [Michał Weichert], "Report of conference with Mr. [Heinrich] Bollenbach and Mr. [Karl] Massing on 26 July 1940"
- Home for the Elderly (ul. Górczewska 9), allocations of food, permission to settle 100 families in Otwock, streetcar tax, children's sanatorium in Długosiodło.
- ***Description:*** original or transcript, typescript, Polish, 218×284 mm, ss. 2, pp. 2.
  Doc. was kept in a binder.

18)
- After 29.07.1940, Warsaw
- [Coordinating Committee ŻSS] [Michał Weichert], "Note on conversation with Dr. [Fritz] Arlt, Director of the Department of Population Services and Welfare [Bevölkerungswesen und Fürsorge] in the Generalgouvernement in Kraków on 29 July 1940"
- Displacement of Jews from Kraków, financial situation of the Coordinating Committee ŻSS.
- ***Description:*** original or transcript, typescript, Polish, 218×275 mm, ss. 2, pp. 2.
  Doc. was kept in a binder.

19)
- After 30.07.1940, Warsaw
- [Coordinating Committee ŻSS] [Michał Weichert], "Note on conferences with the Chairman of the Central Guardianship Council [Naczelnej Rady Opiekuńczej] Count Adam Ronikier in Kraków on 29 and 30 July 1940. in presence of Chairman Bieberstein and Dr. Wielikowski"
- Displacement of Jews from Kraków, streetcar tax, distribution of American gifts.
- ***Description:*** original or transcript, typescript, Polish, 208×278 mm, ss. 2, pp. 2.

20)
- After 30.07.1940, Warsaw
- [Coordinating Committee ŻSS] [Michał Weichert], "Note on conference with Dr. Colonel Wick, manager of the Department of Displacement of the Department of Population Services and Welfare [Bevölkerungswesen und Fürsorge] of the Generalgouvernement in Kraków on 30 July 1940 with participation of Chairman [Marek] Bieberstein and Chairman [Wilhelm] Goldblatt"
- Displacement of Jews from Kraków.
- ***Description:*** original or transcript, typescript, Polish, 220×288 mm, minor damages and losses of text, ss. 2, pp. 2.

21)
- After 2.08.1940, Warsaw
- [Coordinating Committee ŻSS] [Michał Weichert], "Note on conversations with Mr. [Heinrich] Bollenbach and [Karl] Massing in the Mayor's Department of Social Welfare on 2 August 1940"
- Streetcar tax, food supply issues.
- ***Description:*** original or transcript, typescript, Polish, 224×285 mm, ss. 5, pp. 5.

22)
- After 3.08.1940, Warsaw
- [Coordinating Committee ŻSS] [Michał Weichert], "Note about the inspection conducted by Mr. [Heinrich] Bollenbach on 2 August 1940"
- Public kitchens, shelters, orphanages, agricultural ranch in Grochów. Encl. report of the inspection in German and list of public kitchens with addresses.
- ***Description:*** original or transcript, typescript, German, Polish, 208×276, 225×288 mm, ss. 6, pp. 6.
  Report in German is more extensive than the text in Polish.

### 120. RING. II/16. Mf. ŻIH—793; USHMM—48.

- 11.01.1940, Warsaw

- Coordinating Committee of the Social and Welfare Organizations TOZ, Centos and Others. At the SKSS in Warsaw (ul. Leszno 13), Circular letter of 11.01.1940 with request for aid.
- ***Description:*** original (2 copies), duplicated typescript, Polish, 220×295 mm, ss. 2, pp. 2.
  At bottom stamp of the Coordinating Committee and signature (ink): "S. Starobiński." At bottom notation (printed): "S. XII.39. 5000."

121. **RING. II/7. Mf. ŻIH—793; USHMM—48.**

- After 4.04.1940, Warsaw
- [ŻSS?], "Protokol fun der tsveyter zitsung fun der reorganizir-komisye dem 4-tn april 1940, 8 a zeyger fri" [Minutes of the second session of the reorganization commission on 4 April 1940, 8 AM]
- Concerns house committees, public kitchens, need for collection of money and raw materials (of textiles, leather, accessories). List of participants at the session: I. [Icchak] Giterman (chairman), [Abraham] Sztolcman, M. [Michał] Weichert, M. [Menachem] Linder (secretary), Hip[olit] Czerski and E. [Emanuel] Ringelblum.
- ***Description:*** transcript, typescript, Yiddish, 210×295 mm, ss. 4, pp. 4.
  On p. 1 note in Yiddish (ink): "E. Ringelblum."

122. **RING. II/14. Mf. ŻIH—793; USHMM—48.**

- 05.1940, Warsaw
- ŻSS. Coordinating Committee, Warsaw. Circular no. 1 of 30.05.1940
- Report of ŻSS from 09.1939 to 03.1940 and report of activity of specific departments of ŻSS in 04.1940 (care for refugees and fire victims, activity of office for care of returning captives, Department of Individual Aid, constructive aid, public kitchens, etc.).
- ***Description:*** original, duplicated typescript, Polish, Yiddish, 220×340 mm, ss. 23, pp. 23.

123. **RING. II/8. Mf. ŻIH—793; USHMM—48.**

- 05.1940, Kraków
- [ŻSS?], Memorandum entitled "Observations in the matter of division of American gifts for the Jewish population" directed to RGO in Kraków. (Kraków, 05.1940)
- Data concerning the Jewish population centers in the Generalgouvernement, percentage share of the Jewish population in specific districts and towns, number of refugees registered in Jewish social welfare institutions on the territory of Generalgouvernement on 1.02.1940, situation of the Jewish population, list of public kitchens and kitchens for children together with the number of dinners issued from 30.09.1939 to 29.02.1940. Encl. tables (2).
- ***Description:*** original, duplicated typescript, Polish, 220×340 mm, ss. 7, pp. 7

124. **RING. II/10. Mf. ŻIH—793; USHMM—48.**

- After 12.06.1940, Warsaw
- [ŻSS]. J. [Józef] Jaszuński, "Report of the Commission for Affairs of Headquarters of ŻSS" (12.06.1940)
- Discussion of resolutions of the sessions of the Commission for Affairs of the Headquarters of ŻSS on 8 and 10.06.1940 concerning the charter of ŻSS. List of members of the Commission: I. Berenstein, I. Giterman, J. Jaszuński, B. Rozensztat, Engineer A. Sztolcman, Dr. M. Weichert.
- ***Description:*** transcript, typescript, Polish, 225×286 mm, ss. 2, pp. 2.

125. **RING. II/17. Mf. ŻIH—793; USHMM—48.**

- After 07.[1940], Warsaw
- [ŻSS. Coordinating Committee], Report of activity during the period 04–07.[1940] (fragment)
- Inf. concerning food supply, care for fire victims and refugees, home for refugees in Warsaw (ul. Długa 27), sanitary-medical campaign (TOZ) and care for the child ("Centos").
- ***Description:*** original, duplicated typescript, Polish, 220×340 mm, missing pages, preserved pages: 7–9, 11–13 and 15, ss. 7, pp. 7.

126. **RING. II/22. Mf. ŻIH—793; USHMM—48.**

- 4.09.1940, Warsaw
- ŻSS. Coordinating Committee. "Report of the Finance Department of District VI for the month of August 1940"
- Inf. about the "Month of the Child" campaign, emergency campaigns, general financial results, instructors of the Department (Lichtenstein, Torner, Zylberberg, Łaznowski, Kirszbraun, Bajer, Lewin, Rozenbaum, Dr. Lew; dismissed [odwołani] in August 1940: Chmielnicki, Goldman and, Lotte).
- ***Description:*** original, typescript (crossing-outs, ink), Polish 224×285 mm, ss. 2, pp. 2.
  On p. 1 office stamps, "Reporting department" and the date "15.09.1940," and a note (red pencil): illegible signature and no. "3625." On p. 2 at bottom the date 4.09.1940 and two illegible signatures and other notations (ink).

127. **RING. II/20. Mf. ŻIH—793; USHMM—48.**

- 8.09.1940, Warsaw
- [ŻSS. Coordinating Committee], Department of Women's Social Work. R. Gamarnikowa, Report of activity during the month of August 1940 (8.09.1940)
- Cooperation with the Finance Department, Department of Child Care, Clothing Department (opening of sewing rooms: ul. Nalewki 35, apt. 47—Mrs. Lewowa; ul. Nalewki 27, apt. 7—Dr. Goldbard, ul. Rymarska 16, apt. 4; ul. Twarda 18—Feferbergowa; ul. Alberta 3—Mrs. Heymanowa; ul. Żurawia 23, apt. 3—Kohenówna, Rajfeldowa; opening of workshops for slippers and gloves: ul. Nalewki 27—Miss Moczydlińska; ul. Senatorska 32—Binkwasser and Szwalbe; ul. Żurawia 23—Miss Milsteinówna);

formation of ladies' circles connected to apartment house committees, monetary collections, etc.

- ***Description:*** original, typescript (handwritten additions, ink), stamp, Polish, 225×290 mm, ss. 3, pp. 3.

  On p. 1 office stamps: "Reporting department" and the date: "15.09.1940," as well as notations (red pencil): illegible signature and no. "3645"; on p. 3 signature (ink): "R. Gamarnikowa."

### 128. RING. II/23. Mf. ŻIH—793; USHMM—48.

- 10.09.1940, Warsaw
- ŻSS. Coordinating Committee. B. [Barbara] Bermanowa, "Report for the month of August [19]40. Department for Children's Issues at the W.Z.O. [Wydziale Zbiórki Odzieży? (Department of Clothing Collection?)]"
- Statement of the collected clothing and its distribution in particular districts in various social welfare institutions, boarding schools of Centos and others (the point for refugees at ul Spokojna 13 received the most).
- ***Description:*** original, typescript, stamps, Polish, 217×296 mm, ss. 1, pp. 1.

  On p. 1 office stamps: "Reporting department" and the date "15.09.1940" and illegible signature (red pencil). Signature of B. [Barbara] Bermanowa, clerk.

### 129. RING. II/21. Mf. ŻIH—793; USHMM—48.

- 11.09.1940, Warsaw
- ŻSS. Coordinating Committee. Department of Monetary Collections, "Report of the Dep[artment] of Monetary Collections for the first 10 days of the month of September 1940" (11.09.1940)
- Statement of receipts in particular districts in recognition of various monetary collections.
- ***Description:*** original, typescript, stamps, Polish, 222×288 mm, ss. 1, pp. 1.

  On p. 1 office stamps: "Reporting department" and the date: "15.09.1940" and illegible signature (red pencil). Illegible signature of the Department's manager and bookkeeper.

### 130. RING. II/25. Mf. ŻIH—793; USHMM—48.

- 12.09.1940, Warsaw
- [ŻSS] "Report of the Department of Foreign Letters on work in the first 10 days of September [1940]"
- Inf. about correspondence arriving from America, about searches for relatives. Encl. "Ten-day compilation of news from America according to senders" and "Ten-day compilation of news from the USA as well as countries of Central and South America according to contents" (10.09.1940).
- ***Description:*** original, typescript, duplicated typescript, stamps, Polish, 225×287, 210×294 mm, ss. 2, pp. 2.

  On p. 1 office stamps: "Reporting department" and date: "15.09.1940" and illegible signature (red pencil). On encl. date stamp: "15.09.1940"

### 131. RING. II/18. Mf. ŻIH—793; USHMM—48.

- Before 15.09.1940, Warsaw
- [ŻSS. Coordinating Committee], M. [Meir] Przedecz, "Monthly report of the Department of Training and Control [Wydziału Instrukcji i Kontroli] for the month of August 1940"
- Inf. regarding arbitration activity, inspection of apartment house committees (activity, number). Appended table with results of inspection of house committees.
- ***Description:*** original, typescript (handwritten additions, ink), stamps, Polish, 218×347 mm, ss. 12, pp. 12.

  On p. 1 office stamps: SPS receipt stamp of 15.09. [1940], date stamp: "15.09.1940"; stamp: "Reporting department" and illegible signature (red pencil); on p. 11 signature (ink): "M[Meir] Przedecz."

### 132. RING. II/19. Mf. ŻIH—793; USHMM—48.

- Before 15.09.1940, Warsaw
- [ŻSS. Coordinating Committee], Department of Women's Social Work, Districts IV and V. E. Secemska, Report of activity for the month of August 1940. ([. . .].09.1940)
- Inf. regarding the establishment of the circle of supporters [patronat] of the Orphans' Home (ul. Leszno 127), formation of workshops for girls: seamstress workshop at ul. Twarda 18 (manager: Feferbergowa) and a slipper- and capmaking workshop at Senatorska 32 (Linwasser and Szwalbe); circle of supporters of a kitchen (ul. Zielna 15) (Rozenblumowa); "cleanliness week," "Ladies' Circles."
- ***Description:*** original, typescript, stamps, Polish, 225×288 mm, ss. 1, pp. 1.

  At top office stamps: "Reporting department" and date stamp: "15.09.1940" and illegible signature (red pencil); signature (ink): "E. Secemska."
  
  Index: Dr. Oderfeld of ŻSS

### 133. RING. II/24. Mf. ŻIH—793; USHMM—48.

- Before 15.09.1940, Warsaw
- [ŻSS] Provisioning Section, "Report of the food warehouse for the month of August 1940." List of products issued from the food warehouse to individual institutions in August 1940
- Financial report with list of food items in the Section's warehouse. Encl. tables (4): "List of products issued from the food warehouse in the month of August 1940 to the institutions specified below" (lists of products and institutions).
- ***Description:*** original, typescript, stamps, Polish, 220×346, 225×440 mm, ss. 5, pp. 5.

  On p. 1 office stamps: "Reporting department"; date-stamp "15.09.1940"; and illegible signature (red pencil).

**134. RING. II/26. Mf. ŻIH–793; USHMM–48.**

- Before 15.09.1940, Warsaw
- ŻSS. Coordinating Committee, "Report no. 5 of meeting of the Clothing Commission of 9 September 1940"
- Report of the Distributing Subcommission and of the Emergency Distribution Subcommission. List of meeting's participants: Sagan, Braun, Gliksman, Cholewa, Pfeferowa, [Barbara] Bermanowa, Szwalbe, Dobrzyński, Herman, Engineer Buchweitz.
- ***Description:*** original, typescript, stamps, Polish, 224×287 mm, ss. 2, pp. 2.

  On p. 1 office stamps: "Reporting department," date-stamp "15.09.1940," and illegible signature (red pencil). On p. 2 illegible signature of the secretary of the Welfare Section.

**135. RING. II/122. Mf. ŻIH–794; USHMM–49.**

- Before 29.12.1940, Warsaw Ghetto
- ŻTOS, Invitation to the VI symphonic concert on 29.12.1940
- Program and performers (director Adam Furmański, grand piano Tadeusz Pasternak).
- ***Description:*** original, duplicated typescript, Polish, 163×230 mm, ss. 2, pp. 3.

**136. RING. II/15. Mf. ŻIH–793; USHMM–48.**

- 1940, place unknown
- [ŻSS Coordinating Committee?], Memorandum entitled "Bemerkungen ueber die Wohnverhältnisse der Juden im Generalgouvernement am Rande der angeordneten Judenaussiedlung aus Krakau" (Observations on the housing conditions of Jews in the Generalgouvernement on the verge of the directed displacement of Jews out of Kraków)
- Concerns harmful effects of the planned displacement of the Jewish population from Kraków.
- ***Description:*** original or transcript, typescript, German, 218×280 mm, ss. 3, pp. 3.

**137. RING. II/31. Mf. ŻIH–793; USHMM–48.**

- 9.05.1941, Warsaw Ghetto
- ŻTOS, Department of Monetary Collection SPS, "Monthly Levy." (9.05.1941)

  Cashier's report of receipts from 28.01.1941 to 8.05.1941. Doc. signed by: Mr. Starobiński, manager, and by p. Z. Ringartowa, cashier.
- ***Description:*** original, typescript, Polish, 224×145 mm, ss. 1, pp. 1.

  At top notation (ink): "Hon[orable] Dir. [Icchak] Giterman."

**138. RING. II/117. Mf. ŻIH–794; USHMM–49.**

- After 18.05.1941, Warsaw Ghetto
- [ŻTOS], "Draft regulations of the 'Departmental Administrative Board' ['Kolegium Wydziałowego']"
- Departmental Administrative Board was to assemble representatives of individual departments (Social Work Section, Refugee Care Section, Clothing and Public Kitchens Department) and serve as a negotiating organ for them.
- ***Description:*** original or transcript, typescript, Polish, 205×165, 225×298 mm, ss. 2, pp. 2.

  See Ring. I/219.

**139. RING. II/32. Mf. ŻIH–793; USHMM–48.**

- After 20.07.1941, Warsaw Ghetto
- [ŻTOS], Executive Commission, "List of services on 20.07.1941"
- Statement regarding social activity in specific districts (dinners, monetary collection, foods).
- ***Description:*** original or transcript, typescript, Polish, 304×214 mm, ss. 1, pp. 2.

  On the reverse illegible signatures (ink): I. [Icchak] Giterman [?] and calculations.

**140. RING. II/35. Mf. ŻIH–793; USHMM–48.**

- After 08.1941, Warsaw Ghetto
- [ŻTOS], Draft budget and execution of the provisioning budget for the month of August 1941
- Statement with list of organizational units of social welfare institutions.
- ***Description:*** original or transcript, typescript, Polish, 445×580 mm, ss. 1, pp. 1.

**141. RING. II/34/2. Mf. ŻIH–793; USHMM–48.**

- Before 14.09.1941, Warsaw Ghetto
- ŻTOS. Section for Care of Refugees and Fire Victims (ul. Tłomackie 11), "Report for the month of August 1941"
- Inf. regarding the Commission for Refugee Affairs, so-called "points" for refugees, provision of food and clothing, medical care, housing issues, organizational matters, circles of supporters.
- ***Description:*** original, typescript, stamps, Polish, 225×288 mm, ss. 4, pp. 4.

  On p. 1 stamp "Reporting department"; and illegible signature (ink) "Rot . . . [?]"; on p. 4 stamps and signatures (ink): "Section of Care for Refugees and Fire Victims," "M. Chmielewski, secretary."

**142. RING. II/33. Mf. ŻIH–793; USHMM–48.**

- After 14.09.1941, Warsaw Ghetto
- [ŻTOS], "Minutes of meeting of the Commission for Refugee Affairs held on 10.09. and 14.09.1941"
- Budget of CKP, matter of the boarding facility at ul. Stawki 9, Inspectorate of the Points (Inspektorat Kontroli Punktów), CKU and Department of Hometown Associations (Wydział Ziomkostw), circle of supporters for the points on ul. Dzika and ul. Stawka. List of those present: [Icchak] Giterman, Ginsberg, [Dawid] Chołodenko, [Aleksander] Landau, [Józef] Sak; from CKP: Wiener, Rozenfarb, Kahane, Wajsberg; from CKU: Ersler and Dr. Dobryń.

- *Description:* original, typescript (handwritten additions, green ink), stamp, Polish, 208×295 mm, ss. 3, pp. 3.
  On p. 3 stamp and signature (green ink): "M. Chmielewski, secretary."

### 143. RING. II/34/1. Mf. ŻIH—793; USHMM—48.

- 17.09.1941, Warsaw Ghetto
- ŻTOS, Main Secretariat. N. Asz, Letter dated 17.09.1941. to I. [Icchak] Giterman
- Cover letter with attachment "Concise numerical report of the activity of the Jewish Social Welfare Society (ŻTOS) in the month of August 1941" (15.09.1941).
- *Description:* original, transcript (encl.), typescript, stamp, Polish, 224×150, 225×288 mm, ss. 3, pp. 3.
  On p. 2 (encl.) stamp "Reporting department" and illegible signature (ink).

### 144. RING. II/90. Mf. ŻIH—794; USHMM—49.

a)

- 18–26.09.1941, Warsaw Ghetto
- ŻSS-KOM, Inspection Section (Sekcja Kontroli) (ul. Tłomackie 11), Letter dated 26.09.1941 to Dir. I. [Icchak] Giterman
- Cover letter with attachment: "Report of the inspection conducted at the Department of Public Kitchens of the Jew[ish] Social Welfare Soc[iety] in Warsaw" (inspection carried out by M. Goldfarb and D. Towbin in July and August 1941) (18.09.1941).
- *Description:* original, typescript, Polish, 205×111, 209×297 mm, minor damages and losses of text, ss. 24, pp. 24.
  On p. 1 (letter) signatures (ink, pencil): D. [Dawid] Chołodenko and G. Leszczyńska; on p. 23 (encl.) signatures (ink): M. Goldfarb and D. Towbin.

b)

- After 13.08.1941, Warsaw Ghetto
- [ŻSS-KOM], "Detailed list of the cash balances of the Department of Public Kitchens on 12.08.1941 in the sum of zł. 61.015.50" (13.08.1941)
  Balance of expenditures. Doc. signed by A. Kaszuka [?].
- *Description:* original or transcript, typescript, Polish, 209×297 mm, ss. 1, pp. 1.
  Index: Engineer Cyge, Szklar, Asz, Etkin, Larner

### 145. RING. II/30. Mf. ŻIH—793; USHMM—48.

a)

- After 10.1940, Warsaw Ghetto
- ŻTOS, "Report of district guardian"
- Form to be filled out during inspection of house committees.
- *Description:* original, duplicated typescript, Polish, 208×140 mm, ss. 1, pp. 1.
  Inf. (ink): "Ogrodowa 53."

b)

- 1941, Warsaw Ghetto
- ŻTOS, Receipt for collection of questionnaire "Annual report of the [House Committee]."
- *Description:* original (4 copies—2 copies per sheet), duplicated typescript, Polish, 210×150 mm, ss. 2, pp. 2.

### 146. RING. II/99. Mf. ŻIH—794; USHMM—49.

- 11.1941–05.1942, Warsaw Ghetto
- ŻSS-KOM, Provisioning Department, Correspondence with Dir. I. [Icchak] Giterman
- Cover letters dated 9.11.1941, 12.02.1942, and 17.05.1942 with lists of the forwarded encl. (various monthly reports). Letters signed by K. Bresler, director of the Department. Attachment missing.
- *Description:* original, typescript, Polish, 218×295 mm, ss. 3, pp. 3.

### 147. RING. II/37. Mf. ŻIH—793; USHMM—48.

- After 22.11.1941, Warsaw Ghetto
- [ŻOS], "Protokol fun der zitsung fun revir-rat in ershtn revir, den 22-tn november 1941 yor" [Minutes of the session of the district council in the First District, on 22 November 1941]
- Concerns activity of the house committees in the Warsaw Ghetto. List of those present: Winnykamień, Sztajngerner, Liberman, Ajzenberg, Wreglum, Hobberg, Kronenberg, Przepiórko, Rozen, Lipszyc, Wisengrot, Marmursztejn, Szlamberg, attorney Berkman, Rajndorf, Goldblat, Kadisz, Otman, Grinberg (ul. Miła 13), Grinberg (ul Miła 44), Szmerański, and [Dawid] Raduński (district manager).
- *Description:* transcript, typescript, Yiddish, 208×295 mm, ss. 2, pp. 2.

### 148. RING. II/91. Mf. ŻIH—794; USHMM—49.

- 30.12.1941, Warsaw Ghetto
- ŻSS-KOM, Inspection Section, "Report of the inspection of Provisioning Department of the Municipal Welfare Committee (Wydziału Zaopatrywania Komitetu Opiekuńczego Miejskiego)" (30.12.1941)
- Inspection conducted by M. Goldfarb and I. Wajnman on 10 and 11.1941. Information furnished by: H. [Hirsz] Rotenberg, K. Bresler, Domb, Frydman, Szlamowicz, Czerski (history of the Department, tasks and goals, organization, activity, distribution of products, warehouses, personnel matters, list of employees).
- *Description:* original, typescript (handwritten additions, ink, pencil), Polish, 208×148, 445×288, 208×290 mm, minor damages and losses of text, ss. 30, pp. 30.
  On p. 30 signature (ink): M. Goldfarb, inspector.

### 149. RING. II/84. Mf. ŻIH—794; USHMM—49.

- After 05.1942, Warsaw Ghetto

- [ŻSS-KOM], Care for Refugees Section. M. Chmielewski, secretary, Correspondence with Dir. I. [Icchak] Giterman
- Cover letters with encl.:
  1) Health Center IV, Warsaw, Letter dated 10.01.1942 to the Sanitary Department (Referatu Sanitarnego) of the Jewish Council's Department of Health in the matter of the point for refugees at ul. Stawki 9;
  2) Dr. Einhorn, physician of the point at Stawki 9, Letter dated 15.01.1942 to the Sanitary Department (Wydziału Sanitarnego) of "TOZ," including report about the catastrophic situation in the facility entrusted to him;
  3) Jewish Council, Department of Health, Sanitary Department (Referat Sanitarny), Dr. J. Landau, inspector, Letter dated 11.05.1942 to the Care for Refugees Section (ul. Tłomackie 11) with encl. report of Dr. Wajshof, chief physician, dated 5.05.1942 about inspection of the point for refugees at ul. Dzika 3;
  4) S. Ginsbarg, Note dated 11.05.1942, regarding lack of fuel for the Shelter (Dom Etapowy) at ul. Leszno 9; 5) Center for Orphans (ul. Nowolipki 76). J. Zylberstein, manager, Letter of 23.05.1942. to the Care for Refugees Section in the matter of the spoiled food received from "Centos."
- ***Description:*** original, typescript, Polish, 210×294, 228×335 mm, ss. 5, pp. 5.
  Cover letters with signatures (pencil) of M. Chmielewski, written directly on the encl., not dated, except for the letter (of 11.05.1942) in encl. 4. Encl. 4 is original, the rest are transcripts. On encl. 4 an illegible signature (ink).
  Docs. 1 and 2 written on the reverse of inventory ss. (fragments) for so-called "points" for refugees (printed matter, Polish); Doc. 2 sheet from point no. 2 (ul. Nalewki 23).
  Index: Dr. Fajgenblat, physician in the Warsaw Ghetto

## 150. RING. II/38. Mf. ŻIH—793; USHMM—48.

- 01.1942, Warsaw Ghetto
- "Winter Relief Campaign 1941–1942, Informational Circular," no. 2 of 01.1942
- Informational letter from ŻOS meant for the house committees.
- ***Description:*** original, duplicated typescript, Polish, 208×295 mm, ss. 1, pp. 2.
  On p. 1 at top notation (ink): "Dir. [Icchak] Giterman."

## 151. RING. II/39. Mf. ŻIH—793; USHMM—48.

- After 01.1942, Warsaw Ghetto
- [ŻOS], "Finances of the House Committees in the month of January [19]42"
- Inf. about activity of the house committees on the basis of the survey conducted. Appended tables concern the financial situation of the committees.
- ***Description:*** transcript, typescript, Polish, 226×290 mm, ss. 5, pp. 5.

## 152. RING. II/40. Mf. ŻIH—793; USHMM—48.

- After 01.1942, Warsaw Ghetto
- [ŻOS], Department of Individual Assistance, "Report of the Department of Individual Assistance for the month of January 1942"
- General and financial report.
- ***Description:*** original, typescript (additions, ink), stamps, Polish, 218×285 mm, ss. 2, pp. 2.
  On p. 1 stamps: "Department of Individual Assistance"; "Reporting department," date-stamp "9.02.1942" and illegible signature (pencil). On p. 2 illegible signature (pencil), on reverse notation (red pencil): "[Icchak] Giterman, Kirszenbaum, Sagan."

## 153. RING. II/41. Mf. ŻIH—793; USHMM—48.

- 02.1942, Warsaw Ghetto
- [ŻOS?], Memorandum entitled "Memorandum for the delegation of Jewish Social Welfare" (10.02.1942)
- About the overburdening of house committees by orders of the Jewish Council and its agenda in the Warsaw Ghetto.
- ***Description:*** original or transcript, typescript, Polish, 210×295 mm, ss. 3, pp. 3.

## 154. RING. II/98. Mf. ŻIH—794; USHMM—49.

- 11.02.1942, Warsaw Ghetto
- ŻSS-KOM, Central Social Services Registry, Declaration of 11.02.1942 [of] Miriam Rogozik (born 1920) (ul. Leszno 54, apt. 36)
- Request for right to use the public kitchen (ul. Leszno 14) for herself and for mother, Luba Rogozik (born 1892).
- ***Description:*** original, printed matter, handwritten manuscript, ink, Polish, Yiddish, 156×233 mm, ss. 1, pp. 2.

## 155. RING. II/66. Mf. ŻIH—793; USHMM—48.

- 17.02.1942, Warsaw Ghetto
- KOM. Commission for the Improvement of the Work of the Kitchens. Letter dated 17.02.1942 to Dir. [Icchak] Giterman
- Cover letter with encl.: M. Wajsberg, "Minutes of session of the Commission for Improvement of the Work of the Kitchens of 9 February 1942" (report of activity, personnel and organizational matters, activity of committees of supporters [patronatów], List of those present: Dir. H. [Hirsz] Rottenberg, M. Sukiennik, Dir. H. Spindler, Dr. [Emanuel] Ringelblum, Dr. [Adolf] Berman, H. Rabinowicz, Kalksztajn, Chonowski instead of Dr. [Szya] Braude, L. Nowik, L. Barenbaum, Gutgold, M. Wajsberg).

- *Description:* original, typescript, Polish, 210×141, 210×295 mm, ss. 7, pp. 7.
  On p. 1 (letter) and on p. 6 (encl.) signature (ink): "M. Wajsberg."
  Index: Dir. Gitler, Sarna-Płucer, Ch. Szpringer

### 156. RING. II/58. Mf. ŻIH—793; USHMM—48.

- After 23.02.1942, Warsaw Ghetto
- I. [Icchak] Giterman (Warsaw Ghetto), Letter of 23.02.1942 to Dr. Michał Weichert (Warsaw Ghetto)
- Regarding reorganization of KOM.
- *Description:* transcript (3 copies), typescript, Polish, 210×295 mm, ss. 3, pp. 3.

### 157. RING. II/42. Mf. ŻIH—793; USHMM—48.

- 23–24.02.1942, Warsaw Ghetto
- [ŻOS], Population statistics for several apartment buildings of the Warsaw Ghetto (23–24.02.1942)
- Compilation regarding individual districts (I, IV, V, and VI), number of residents, of the dead (from 1.09.1939), of orphans, and cases of typhus. Addresses of investigated buildings are provided.
- *Description:* original or transcript, typescript, Polish, 208×295 mm, ss. 8, pp. 8.

### 158. RING. II/43. Mf. ŻIH—793; USHMM—48.

- After 25.02.1942, Warsaw Ghetto
- [ŻOS], "Protokol fun der baratung vegn 'khoydesh fun gezunt' forgekumen dem 25-tn februar 1942 yor" [Minutes of the consultation of 25th of February 1942 about "Health Month"]
- Fight against infectious diseases (inoculations, collection of funds for purchase of medicines, sanitary-hygienic campaign). List of those present: Dr. [Emanuel] Ringelblum, Dr. Bajn, Dr. Szwalbe, M. [Menachem Mendel] Kirszenbaum, Dr. [Eliezer Lipa (Lipe)] Bloch, Dr. [Zofia] Rozenblum.
- *Description:* transcript, typescript, Yiddish, 208×293 mm, ss. 1., pp. 1.
  At top notation in Yiddish (ink): "for I. Giterman."

### 159. RING. II/44. Mf. ŻIH—793; USHMM—48.

- 25.02.1942, Warsaw Ghetto
- W. Braun (Warsaw), Letter dated 25.02.1942 to administration of SPS
- Concerning increase of the number of free provisioning coupons.
- *Description:* original, typescript, Polish, 208×290 mm, ss. 1, pp. 1.
  At top notation (ink): "Hon. Dir. Giterman."

### 160. RING. II/59. Mf. ŻIH—793; USHMM—48.

a)

- 1.03.1942, Warsaw Ghetto
- [ŻOS]., "Minutes of the meeting of the Dep[artment] of Women's Social Work of 24 February 1942" (1.03.1942)
- Report of activity, Winter Relief Campaign, personnel matters (inter alia, selection of a new board: Zofia Poznańska of ul. Ogrodowa 26a, chairwoman, Mrs. Grützsändlerowa and Mrs. Kasmanowa, vice chairwomen, Miss Gulmanówna, secretary). List of those present.
- *Description:* original, typescript, stamps, Polish, 210×295 mm, ss. 2, pp. 2.
  On p. 1 stamp and note of the office of SPS: "came in on 9.03.[1942] no. 397"; on the margin an illegible note (ink); on p. 2 stamp: "Manager District IV" and two signatures (ink): "Z. Poznańska" and NN.
  Index: Secemska, Wekslerowa (ul. Chłodna 22), Mokrska, Sztückgoldowa (ul. Grzybowska 16), Sztückgoldowa, Dobrecka, R. Dancygier, Krymkierowa [Krymkiewiczowa?] (ul. Ceglana 21), Najmanowa, Majerczykowa, attorney Haltrechtowa (ul. Grzybowska 23), Jubiler, Mendelsburgowa, Sznapmanowa (ul. Grzybowska 16), Faustówna, Rubinlicht, Gitlerowa, Eksztajnowa, Hurwiczówna,

b)

- After 5.03.1942, Warsaw Ghetto
- ŻOS, District V (ul. Twarda 11), Department of Women's Social Work. E. Secemska, "Emergency Guardian Service for Street Children. Report for month of February 1942"
- Inf. about opening of the Emergency service at ul. Śliska 40 (4.02.1942); description of the facility's activity.
- *Description:* transcript, typescript, Polish, 224×288 mm, ss. 1, pp. 1.

### 161. RING. II/105. Mf. ŻIH—794; USHMM—49.

- 10.04.1942, Warsaw Ghetto
- Józef Rosenblatt (born 1878) (ul. Nowolipie 38, apt. 27), Letter dated 10.04.1942 to Council of Social Welfare [ŻSS?] in Warsaw
- Request for a loan.
- *Description:* original, handwritten manuscript, ink, Polish, 220×278 mm, ss. 2, pp. 1.
  Beneath a postscript dated 10.04.1942 in a different handwriting (ink, illegible signature, dr[. . .]): "in support of Józef Rosenblatt, founder of the literary-musical society 'Ha-zomir' in Łódź." At the Jewish Musical-Literary Society in Łódź there was a choir, "Ha-Zomir," led by Icchak Zaks.

### 162. RING. II/45. Mf. ŻIH—793; USHMM—48.

- 12.06.1941–2.03.1942, Warsaw Ghetto
- ŻOS, Manager of District V, Letter dated 2.03.1942 to SPS
- Regarding aid for 2 families: of Josef Wyszegrodzki (Wyszogrodzki) (Pl. Grzybowski 10, apt. 14, at Mr. Weinberg), refugees from Łomża, 6 children; Blumenkranc, 2 children (ul. Pańska 5, caretaker's

apartment), fire victims. Encl. copy of report dated 1.03.1942 by the district guardian Ch. Bender. Encl. 2 reports by district guardian of District V R. [Roza] Simchowicz of 12.06.1941 in support of the proposal for aid for the above-mentioned families.

- ***Description:*** original, typescript, handwritten manuscript, stamps, ink, Polish, Yiddish, 213×148, 157×178 mm, ss. 3, pp. 3.
  Office stamps of SPS: arrived and date 6.03[1942] and stamp: "Manager District V" and illegible signature (ink)
  Index: Dr. Lipowski

### 163. RING. II/60. Mf. ŻIH—793; USHMM—48.

- After 10.03.1942, Warsaw Ghetto
- [ŻSS-KOM], "Minutes of meeting of KOM on 10 March 1942"
- Inf. about induction into KOM of social welfare institutions; organizational chart and principles of operation of KOM after reorganization; personnel matters
- List of those present: St. [Stanisław] Szereszewski, I. [Icchak] Giterman, H. [Hirsz] Rotenberg, Sz. [Szymon] Wyszewiański.
- ***Description:*** transcript, typescript, Polish, 210×297 mm, ss. 2, pp. 2.

### 164. RING. II/46. Mf. ŻIH—793; USHMM—48.

- 11.03.1942, Warsaw Ghetto
- ŻOS. SPS, Letter dated 11.03.1942 to Board of ŻOS
- Cover letter with attached memorandum of 8.03.1942 prepared by M. [Meir] Przedecz and directed to the Department of Health of the Jewish Council (concerns reduction of the burdens of house committees from the excessive obligations of an administrative nature piled on by the Health Department of the Jewish Council, demand for reduction of the amount of various fees).
- ***Description:*** original, typescript, stamp, Polish, Yiddish, 217×134, 210×295 mm, ss. 5, pp. 5.
  On p. 1 stamp (Yiddish) "Section SPS" and illegible signature; at top a note (pencil): "Board"; on p. 1 (attachment) note (ink): "To the Board of ŻOS."

### 165. RING. II/61. Mf. ŻIH—793; USHMM—48.

- 11.03.1942, Warsaw Ghetto
- ŻSS-KOM in Warsaw, Letter dated 11.03.1942 to Dir. I. [Icchak] Giterman
- Cover letter with encl.: Main Board of the Society for the Propagation of Vocational and Agricultural Labor among Jews (Zarząd Główny Towarzystwa Szerzenia Pracy Zawodowej i Rolnej wśród Żydów), formerly "ORT" in liquidation. J. [Józef] Jaszuński, Letter dated 9.03.1942 to ŻSS-KOM, Concerns opposition to the name of the organization directed by him: Vocational Training Section (Sekcją Kształcenia Zawodowego).
- ***Description:*** original, transcript (encl.), typescript (handwritten additions, ink), Polish, 219×145, 205×295 mm, ss. 2, pp. 2.
  At bottom (letter dated 11.03.1942) illegible signature (ink).

### 166. RING. II/92. Mf. ŻIH—794; USHMM—49.

- 11.03.1942, Warsaw Ghetto
- ŻSS-KOM, Control Section. M. Goldfarb, inspector, "Report of inspection at the TOZ Society for Protection of Health in Warsaw at ul. Gęsia 43" (11.03.1942)
- Inspection conducted in the presence of I. Wajnman on 25.11.1941–30.01.1942. Information furnished by: Dr. J. Rozenblum; Dr. M. Szwalbe; Dr. J. Chain; Dr. M. Thursz; Dr. Ch. Zajdengart; N. Finkielsztejn; Sz. Kaliska; R. Wachmanóna; J. Rabinowicz. (History of TOZ, board from 13.11.1940: Dr. M. Kenigstein, chairman; Dr. Mesz, vice chairman; N. Finkielsztejn, treasurer; Dr. J. Rosenblum, secretary; Dr. Sz. Wyszewiański; J. Rudnicki; L. Neustadt; Dr. Wohl; Dr. Mitz; Dr. Braude-Hellerowa; Dr. J. Chain; P. Czerski; Dr. M. Szwalbe; activity of particular units of TOZ, financial and personnel matters, statistical charts and tables).
- ***Description:*** original, typescript, Polish, 445×290, 208×290 mm, ss. 49, pp. 49.
  On p. 49 signature (ink): M. Goldfarb.

### 167. RING. II/47. Mf. ŻIH—793; USHMM—48.

a)

- 12.03.1942, Warsaw Ghetto
- [ŻOS] SPS. CKP, M. Wajsberg, Letter dated 12.03.1942 to Dir. [Icchak] Giterman. With the attached 4 reports of activity in January and February 1942
  Cover letter with attachments (3): 1) CKP, "Report for the Month of February 1942" (financial matters, encl. "Cumulative results of collection of [contributions of] plates of soup and bread from CKP of Districts and individual Sponsors' Committees [Patronatów] on 1.03.[19]42." Doc. signed by M. Wajsberg); 2) "Sponsors' Committee of the 'Dzika-Stawki' Shelters. Report for the period January–February 1942" (inf. regarding "points" at ul. Dzika 3, 9, 19 as well as Stawki 9, personnel matters, composition of the Sponsors' Committee: [Eliahu] Kahan, Blimbaum, Nadel, Sznejer, Gercwolf, Lipskier [Lipskierowa], Praszkier, Jagodziński, Majnemer, Dr. Trachtenhorc [Trachtenherc], Rabbi Majzels, [Abraham] Hendel, Bagno, Dr. Landau, Grajpner, Dr. Rywoszowa, Löscher, Pomper, Segał, Rozencwajg, Dębiński, Kirszencwajg, Kon, Cybula; doc. signed by Chairman [Eliahu] Kahan and secretary M. Wajsberg); 3) "Minutes of the meeting of the Sponsors'

Committee for the 'Dzika-Stawki' shelters of 24.02.1942" (financial matters, provision of extra food, Sponsors' Committee for the kitchen, clothes collection; List of those present: E. Kahan, Dr. Trachtenherc, Dr. Majnemer, Praszkier, Debiński, Nadel, Pomper, Löscher, Rywoszowa, Segał, Wajsberg).
- ***Description:*** original, transcript (attached), typescript, stamp, Polish, 210×145, 225×290 mm, ss. 8, pp. 8.
  On the letter a stamp: SPS.CKP and signature (ink): M. Wajsberg.

b)
- 02.1942, Warsaw Ghetto
- ŻTOS. Sponsors' Committee over Refugees, "Yanuar barikht funem 'pleytim-shtetl' Dzike-Stavki" [January report from the "refugees-shtetl" Dzika-Stawki] (02.1942)
- Information on the number of refugees and their origin, mortality, housing, hygienic state of the points, etc. (concerns "points" at ul. Dzika 3, 9, 19 and ul. Stawki 9).
- ***Description:*** transcript, typescript, Yiddish, 220×290 mm, ss. 6, pp. 6.
  See HWC, 48/2 (another transcript [?], typescript, ss. 4 [two copies]).
  Published: *Selected Documents*, pp. 326–331.

## 168. RING. II/67. Mf. ŻIH—793; USHMM—48.

- 12.03.1942, Warsaw Ghetto
- KOM, Commission for Improvement of the Work of Kitchens, Letter dated 12.03.1942 to Dir. [Icchak] Giterman
- Cover letter with attachment: "Report for the month of February 1942" (results of inspection of Sponsors' Committees, discussion of Sponsors' Committees' reports, list of selected kitchens under the care of the Sponsors' Committees).
- ***Description:*** original, typescript, Polish, 227×160, 227×290 mm, ss. 3, pp. 3.
  On p. 1 (letter) and on p. 2 (attachment) signature (ink): "M. Sukiennik."

## 169. RING. II/48. Mf. ŻIH—793; USHMM—48.

- After 15.03.1942, Warsaw Ghetto
- [ŻOS] CKP, "Minutes of the meeting of the Presidium of CKP that occurred on 15.03.[1942]"
- Plan for work, fundraising, recruiting volunteers, purchase of products, holiday campaign. List of those present: [Eliahu] Kahan, Mokrska, Wiener, Weinstein, Weishof, [Stanisław] Szereszewski, Pomper, [M.] Wajsberg. Minutes signed by Chairman of CKP E. Kahan, and secretary M. Wajsberg.
- ***Description:*** transcript, typescript, Polish, 208×292 mm, ss. 1, pp. 1.
  At top notation (ink): "Hon. Dir. Giterman."

## 170. RING. II/74. Mf. ŻIH—794; USHMM—49.

- 20.03.1942, Warsaw Ghetto
- [ŻSS-KOM], Section for Vocational Restructuring and Training (Sekcja Zawodowego Przewarstwowienia i Kształcenia), Letter dated 20.03.1942 to Financial-Budgeting Department
- Regarding the proposed budget for 04.1942. Letter signed by J. [Józef] Jaszuński, manager of the section.
- ***Description:*** original, typescript, Polish, 208×150 mm, ss. 1, pp. 1.
  Letter written on the reverse of letterhead of the Main Board of the Society for Propagation of Vocational and Agricultural Work among Jews, formerly ORT (ul. Żabia 9) (printed, Polish, Yiddish.).

## 171. RING. II/93. Mf. ŻIH—794; USHMM—49.

- 23.03.1942, Warsaw Ghetto
- ŻSS-KOM, Inspection Section. Dr. J. Szalman, inspector, "Report of the inspection at the boarding school of 'Centos' at Dzielna 67 on 15.03.1942" (23.03.1942.)
- Description of the rooms of the boarding school, children, meals, conducted classes, personnel (Ablówna, director of the boarding school, Szenberg, educators).
- ***Description:*** original, typescript, Polish, 209×297 mm, ss. 7, pp. 7.
  On p. 7 signature (ink): J. Szalman.

## 172. RING. II/94. Mf. ŻIH—794; USHMM—49.

- 22.03.1942, Warsaw Ghetto
- ŻSS-KOM, Control Section. M. Goldfarb and D. Towbin, "Report of inspection at the Jewish Society for Assistance to Indigent Mothers in Warsaw, at ul. Ceglana 17 (Waliców 8)" (22.03.1942)
- Inspection conducted on 23.02.1942–5.03.1942; information furnished by: Dr. B. Muszkatblatt, administrative director and F. Kornblumówna, bookkeeper (history of the society, personnel matters with lists of names of personnel, residence and its cost of upkeep, inventory, illnesses, financial report, attached "List of the inventory of the Gynecological-Obstetrical Facility of the Jewish Society for Assistance to Indigent Mothers in Warsaw, at ul. Ceglana 17 on 1 March 1942," missing ending).
- ***Description:*** original, typescript (handwritten additions, ink), Polish, 210×295 mm, ss. 15, pp. 15.
  On p. 1 notation (ink): "encl. aa"; on p. 13 signatures: M. Goldfarb and D. Towbin.

## 173. RING. II/95. Mf. ŻIH—794; USHMM—49.

- 24.03.1942, Warsaw Ghetto
- ŻSS-KOM, Inspection Section, Dr. J. Szalman, inspector, "Report of the inspection at the boarding school of 'Centos'—Mylna 18 in Warsaw on 16 March 1942" (24.03.1942)
- Premises of the boarding school, number of children,

wages of personnel, meals, state of the warehouse, fuel, laundry, activity of the Sponsors' Committee, financial report. Director of the boarding school [Aron] Koniński.

- *Description:* original, typescript, Polish, 209×295 mm, ss. 7, pp. 7.
  On p. 7 signature (ink): J. Szalman.
  On the boarding school and its director, see *Kronika getta*, pp. 617–618.
  Index: Zylberberg, honorary employee of the boarding school of "Centos" (ul. Mylna 18), Reichman, member of the Sponsors' Committee of the boarding school of "Centos" (ul. Mylna 18), R. [Roman] Lichtenbaum, attorney, member of the Sponsors' Committee of the boarding school of "Centos" (ul. Mylna 18), Dr. Szeinkalk, member of the Sponsors' Committee of the boarding school of "Centos" (ul. Mylna 18)

### 174. RING. II/63. Mf. ŻIH—793; USHMM—48.

- After 03.1942, Warsaw Ghetto
- [ŻSS-KOM], "Execution of the provisioning budget for the month of March 1942"
- Inf. regarding costs of distribution of food for different institutions in the Warsaw Ghetto (addresses).
- *Description:* original or transcript, typescript, Polish, 226×288 mm, ss. 1, pp. 1.

### 175. RING. II/56. Mf. ŻIH—793; USHMM—48.

- [03.1942], Warsaw Ghetto
- [ŻSS-KOM], "Reshime fun di loynen fun di mitarbeter in gezelshaftlekhn sektor" [List of the wages of the coworkers in the public sector].
- *Description:* original or transcript, typescript (handwritten additions, ink), Yiddish, 207×237, 210×295 mm, ss. 5, pp. 5.

### 176. RING. II/96. Mf. ŻIH—794; USHMM—49.

- 18.04.1942, Warsaw Ghetto
- ŻSS-KOM, Inspection Section, Dr. J. Szalman, "Report of the inspection in the boarding school named 'Dobra Wola' [Goodwill] (Warsaw, Dzielna 61) conducted on 17 April 1942" (18.04.1942)
- Organization, Sponsors' Committee—list of names, premises, number of children, meals, education and study, health of the wards, personnel, financial report).
- *Description:* original, typescript, Polish, 224×288 mm, ss. 7, pp. 7.
  On p. 7 signature (ink): J. Szalman.
  Index: A. [Abraham] Gepner, member of the Sponsors' Committee of the boarding school "Dobra Wola" (ul. Dzielna 61), engineer S. [Stanisław] Szereszewski, member of the Sponsors' Committee of the boarding school "Dobra Wola" (ul. Dzielna 61), Engineer Z. Cederbaum, secretary of the Sponsors' Committee of the boarding school "Dobra Wola" (ul. Dzielna 61), E. [Edward] Kobryner, member of the Sponsors' Committee of the boarding school "Dobra Wola" (ul. Dzielna 61), D. Mauer, chairman of the board of the Sponsors' Committee of the boarding school "Dobra Wola" (ul. Dzielna 61), K. Wajsberżanka, treasurer of the Sponsors' Committee of the boarding school "Dobra Wola" (ul. Dzielna 61), M. [Maria] Pinkertowa, member of the Sponsors' Committee of the boarding school "Dobra Wola" (ul. Dzielna 61), N. Rothnerowa, member of the Sponsors' Committee of the boarding school "Dobra Wola" (ul. Dzielna 61), T. Rotsztejnowa, member of the Sponsors' Committee of the boarding school "Dobra Wola" (ul. Dzielna 61)

### 177. RING. II/62. Mf. ŻIH—793; USHMM—48.

- 30.04.1942, Warsaw Ghetto
- [ŻSS-KOM], Social Work Section. Department of Training and Control (ul. Nowolipki 25), Letter dated 30.04.1942 to Dir. I. [Icchak] Giterman
- Cover letter with encl. (2): 1) "Regulations of Apartment House Committees prepared by the Legal Department of the Jewish Council"; 2) "Remarks about the draft charter concerning the rights and obligations of Apartment House Com[mittees] submitted by attorney B. [Bolesław] Rozensztadt."
- *Description:* original, transcript (attached), typescript (handwritten additions duplicating contents of typescript), Polish, 206×145, 207×295 mm, minor damages and losses of text, ss. 5, pp. 5.

### 178. RING. II/75. Mf. ŻIH—794; USHMM—49.

- 05–06.1942, Warsaw Ghetto
- ŻSS-KOM, Department of Labor Aid and Economic Aid [Wydział Pomocy Pracy i Pomocy Gospodarczej], A. [Abram] Prowalski, Reports and studies concerning activity of ŻSS
  1) "Note in the matter of the brushmaking workshop at ul. Leszno 29" (proposal for monetary aid for development of the workshop) (11.05.1942);
  2) "Note in the matter of establishing a carpentry workshop for the internal needs of ŻSS and possibly the Jewish Council" (proposal) (11.05.1942);
  3) "Note in the matter of establishment of a vocational card index" (proposal of a register of those employed in the Warsaw Ghetto) (12.05.1942);
  4) "Note in the matter of the so-called Haluts [Zionist pioneer] workshops" (aid for the existing Haluts workshops: ul. Leszno 29, Dzielna 34 and 95, Nalewki 10 and 23) (12.05.1942.);

4)[6] "Note in the matter of establishing a 'Brigade of domestic helpers' [Brygady pomocnic domowych] at the Department of Labor Aid and Economic Aid of ŻSS" (13.05.1942);
5) "Note in the matter of the Economic Bureau at KOM" (7.06.1942).

- ***Description:*** original, typescript, handwritten manuscript (AP*), ink, Polish, 147×205, 220×285 210×295 mm, ss. 8, pp. 12.

## 179. RING. II/64. Mf. ŻIH—793; USHMM—48.

- [After 11.05.1942], Warsaw Ghetto
- ŻSS-KOM in Warsaw, Provisioning Department, Chart of distribution of food for welfare institutions in the Warsaw Ghetto in the first 10 days of May 1942
- Tables (4): 1) "List of products issued to various institutions of the distribution campaign"; 2) "List of products issued to various institutions of the supplemental food campaign"; 3) "List of the movement of products in the warehouse of the distribution campaign"; 4) "List of the movement of products in the warehouse of the supplemental food campaign."
- ***Description:*** original, typescript, stamps, Polish, 448×289, 448×310 mm, ss. 4, pp. 4.

At the bottom stamps of ŻSS-KOM and illegible signatures (ink).

On reverse of table 1 note (handwritten manuscript, ink): "His Honor Mr. Dir. I. [Icchak] Giterman w/m [?]."

## 180. RING. II/71. Mf. ŻIH—793; USHMM—48.

- 28.05.1942, Warsaw Ghetto
- ŻSS-KOM, SPS.WZO, Letter dated 28.05.1942 to Dir. [Icchak] Giterman
- Cover letter with encl.: compilation regarding clothing collected and handed out from 01.1941 to 04.1942.
- ***Description:*** original, transcript [?] (encl.) typescript, stamp, Polish, 212×148, 212×294 mm, ss. 5, pp. 5.

At bottom (letter) stamp: "Wydział Zbiórki Odzieżowej" [Department of Clothing Collection] and two illegible signatures (R. Zylberberg . . .[?]).

## 181. RING. II/65. Mf. ŻIH—793; USHMM—48.

- After 05.1942, Warsaw Ghetto
- [ŻSS-KOM], "Cumulative results of collection of bowls of soup and bread by districts and individual Sponsors' Committees for the month of May 1942"[7]
- Table includes data for six districts.
- ***Description:*** original or transcript, handwritten manuscript, pencil, Polish, 210×249 mm, ss. 1, pp. 1.

## 182. RING. II/82. Mf. ŻIH—794; USHMM—49.

- After 30.05.1942, Warsaw Ghetto
- [ŻSS-KOM, Interest-free Loans Section], Report
- Balance sheet of loans granted during the period 1.04.1941–31.05.1942. Occupational structure of borrowers.
- ***Description:*** transcript, typescript, Polish, 208×294 mm, ss. 3, pp. 3.

## 183. RING. II/97. Mf. ŻIH—794; USHMM—49.

- After 30.05.1942, Warsaw Ghetto
- [ŻSS-KOM, Inspection Section], Report of inspection of Department of Provisioning of KOM of activity during the period 01–05.1942 (fragment)
- Organization of labor, food allocations for the Department, Supplemental Feeding Campaign, Distribution Campaign (Akcja Rozdawnictwa), provisioning of public kitchens, allocations for the Committee of Care for Refugees.
- ***Description:*** original, typescript, Polish, 224×288 mm, missing pages (pp. 1–9, 20 and n.?), ss. 10, pp. 10.

## 184. RING. II/108. Mf. ŻIH—794; USHMM—49.

- After 05.1942, Warsaw Ghetto
- [ŻSS-KOM], Report about the Provisioning Commission
- Call for changes in operation of the Commission, which is not fulfilling its statutory tasks. Encl. fragment (transcript) of report of Commission's activity dated 30.12.1941.
- ***Description:*** original or transcript (2 copies, typescript with supplements, handwritten manuscript, ink, 218×298 mm, missing pp. 1 and 6–7 [in second copy]); transcript (3 copies, typescript, 213×295, 208×295 mm, Yiddish, ss. 38, pp. 38).

## 185. RING. II/50. Mf. ŻIH—793; USHMM—48.

- 1.06.1942, Warsaw Ghetto
- [ŻOS. CKP], "Minutes of the meeting of the Presidium of the 'Dzika-Stawki' Sponsors' Committee together with the Health Commission of 30 May 1942" (1.06.1942)
- Organizational matters, duty-hours of members of the Sponsors' Committee, closure of the Convalescent Home, organization of the Commission of First-aid Stations (Komisji Sanitarnych). List of those present: Wiener, Sznajer, Rozencwajg, chairman of the Economic Commission, Löscher, Pomper, Dr. Trachtenherc, Dr. Szachnerowicz, Dr. Majnemer, Wajsber [Wajsberg?].
- ***Description:*** original, typescript, Polish, 210×295 mm, ss. 1, pp. 1.

At top notation (ink): "Dir. Giterman"; at bottom illegible signature (red pencil).

6. Sic.

7. Tenants were asked to donate a spoonful or more of soup or a piece of bread for those who were in even greater need.

Index: Weisshoff, member of the "Dzika-Stawki" Sponsors' Committee, Dębiński, member of the "Dzika-Stawki" Sponsors' Committee, Jagodziński, member of the "Dzika-Stawki" Sponsors' Committee, Ajzenberg, member of the "Dzika-Stawki" Sponsors' Committee, Grajpner, member of the "Dzika-Stawki" Sponsors' Committee, Segał, member of the "Dzika-Stawki" Sponsors' Committee

### 186. RING. II/88. Mf. ŻIH—794; USHMM—49.

a)

- 2.06.1942, Warsaw Ghetto
- [ŻSS-KOM], "Statement of expenditures and disbursements of Money Collection, of global (ryczałtowych) receipts, the Emergency Grants Campaign and various remittances for the month of May 1942" (2.06.1942)
- Financial reports.
- ***Description:*** original or transcript, typescript, Polish, 202×296, 224×285 mm, ss. 2, pp. 2.

b)

- 1.07.1942, Warsaw Ghetto
- [ŻSS-KOM], "Cashier's report of receipts of the Money Collection in the month of June 1942" (1.07.1942)
- Receipts by Districts I–VI.
- ***Description:*** original, typescript, Polish, 210×296 mm, ss. 1, pp. 1.

    At bottom illegible signature (ink) of the bookkeeper.

c)

- 1.07.1942, Warsaw Ghetto
- [ŻSS-KOM], "Statement of expenditures and disbursements of the Money Collection, of global receipts, of the Emergency Grants Campaign and various payments in the month of June 1942" (1.07.1942)
- Financial reports.
- ***Description:*** original, typescript, Polish, 210×278, 210×296 mm, ss. 2, pp. 2.

    On p. 1 top notation (ink): "Dir. I. Giterman," on p. 2, at bottom illegible signature (ink) of the bookkeeper.

d)

- 5.07.1942, Warsaw Ghetto
- [ŻSS-KOM], "Statement of receipts of the Aid for Displaced Persons Campaign (Akcji Pomocy Przesiedlonym) for the period 9–30.06.1942." (5.07.1942)
- Payments by Districts I–VI.
- ***Description:*** original, typescript, Polish, 204×345 mm, ss. 1, pp. 1.

    At bottom illegible signature (ink) of the bookkeeper.

### 187. RING. II/49. Mf. ŻIH—793; USHMM—48.

- 3.06.1942, Warsaw Ghetto
- [ŻOS]. CKP, "Report for the month of May 1942" (3.06.1942)
- Financial reports, expenditures of individual Sponsors' Committees in the Warsaw Ghetto (attached addresses of Sponsors' Committees).
- ***Description:*** original or transcript, typescript, j. Polish, 210×295 mm, ss. 1, pp. 1.

    At top notation (ink): "Dir. Giterman."

### 188. RING. II/77. Mf. ŻIH—794; USHMM—49.

- 9.06.1942, Warsaw Ghetto
- Handicrafts Committee (Komisja Rzemieślnicza) at CKU (ul. Leszno 6, apt. 31), "Proposal" of 9.06.1942 for granting of loans for establishment of workshops, directed to Dir. [Icchak] Giterman (Department of Labor Aid and Economic Aid of [ŻSS] KOM in Warsaw)
- Funds needed for start up of 3 workshops for refugees: tailoring, shoemaking, and hosiery (cost estimates).
- ***Description:*** original, typescript, stamp, Polish, 228×300, 205×335 mm, ss. 2, pp. 2.

    On p. 2 at bottom stamp: "ŻSS-KOM in Warsaw. CKU" and two signatures (ink): H.W. and NN.; date written in by hand of H.W.*

    Published: *Selected Documents*, 363–365.

### 189. RING. II/69. Mf. ŻIH—793; USHMM—48.

- 10.06.1942, Warsaw Ghetto
- [ŻSS], SPS, Letter dated 10.06.1942 to Dir. Icchak Giterman.
- Cover letter with attachment: "Excerpt from minutes of the meeting of the Governing Council (Kolegium Działaczy) at District VI of 16 May 1942" (concerns activity of Sponsors' Committees at kitchens. Minutes signed by: chairman M. Mazor and secretary Z. Dywan).
- ***Description:*** original, transcript (encl.), typescript, stamp, Polish, Yiddish, 208×148, 208×290 mm, ss. 2, pp. 2.

    At bottom (letter) stamp: "Section of SPS" and illegible signature.

    Index: [A]. Freund, director of District VI, Pelc

### 190. RING. II/70. Mf. ŻIH—793; USHMM—48.

- 16.06.1942, Warsaw Ghetto
- [ŻSS], SPS, Letter dated 16.06.1942 to Dir. Icchak Giterman.
- Cover letter with encl.: ŻSS-KOM, SPS—District VI (ul. Nowolipki 29). A. Freund, director of District VI, Letter dated 12.06.1942 to SPS with encl. "Demand for individual, discount and collective (free) dinners" (List of apartment houses with addresses). Letter with attachment signed by A. Freund.
- ***Description:*** original, transcript (attachment), typescript, Polish, Yiddish, 214×152, 214×305 mm, ss. 6, pp. 6.

### 191. RING. II/68. Mf. ŻIH—793; USHMM—48.

- 24.06.1942, Warsaw Ghetto
- [ŻSS-KOM], M. Wajsberg, "Minutes of meeting of the Commission for Improvement of the Work of Kitchens of 22 June 1942" (24.06.1942)
- Report of current activity, relation of the Department of Public Kitchens to Sponsors' Committees, control of the work of Sponsors' Committees. List of those present: Dir. H. [Hirsz] Rotenberg, H. Spindler, M. Sukiennik, Sz. [Szyja—Jehoszua] Rabinowicz, T. [Tadeusz] Płucer-Sarna, Kalksztein, G. Mirabel, Szpryngier, Rudomin, [L.] Nowik, M. Wajsberg.
- ***Description:*** original, typescript (handwritten additions, ink), Polish, 209×297 mm, ss. 3, pp. 3.

  On p. 3 signature (ink): M. Wajsberg. On p. 1 at top notation (pencil): "Dir. Giterman."

### 192. RING. II/85. Mf. ŻIH—794; USHMM—49.

- After 24.06.1942, Warsaw Ghetto
- [ŻSS-KOM], Letter for Dir. I. [Icchak] Giterman
- Cover letter with encl.: [Jewish Council], Committee of Care for Refugees, Letter dated 24.06.1942 to ŻSS-KOM (concerns employment of displaced persons).
- ***Description:*** original, transcript (encl.), typescript, Polish, 208×294 mm, ss. 1, pp. 1.

  Published: *Selected Documents*, 361–362.

### 193. RING. II/87. Mf. ŻIH—794; USHMM—49.

a)

- After 06.1942, Warsaw Ghetto
- [ŻSS-KOM], "8 Report of the Section of Care for Refugees. June 1942" (06.1942)
- Financial, administrative, housing matters (list of shelters with addresses), provisioning, fuel, health care, mortality, child care, sponsors' committees.
- ***Description:*** original or transcript, typescript, Polish, 232×310, 220×295 mm, ss. 16, ss. 15.

  Doc. in cardboard cover, on which a note at bottom: "His honor Dir. I. Giterman mentioned above."

b)

- After 9.07.1942, Warsaw Ghetto
- [ŻSS-KOM], Section of Care for Refugees, "Report of the displacement action of the newly arrived to the district from Biała Rawska and Nowe Miasto on 9 July 1942" (9.07.1942)
- Organization of aid for the displaced persons (760 people from Mszczonów, Grójec, Grodzisk, Żyrardów, Skierniewice, Biała Rawska, Nowe Miasto) newly arrived into the Warsaw Ghetto 8.07.1942.
- ***Description:*** original or transcript, typescript, Polish, 220×295 mm, ss. 2, ss. 2.

  On reverse of p. 2 notation in Yiddish (pencil).

  Compare *Czerniaków*, p. 298.

  Index: Prof. Ginzbarg, director of the Section of Care for Refugees, Mieczysław Rozenberg (ul. Ceglana 7), H. Ekerman, director of the Hospital Department, Prof. Ch. Kahane, Folman (ul. Ceglana 5)

### 194. RING. II/185. Mf. ŻIH—797; USHMM—52.

- 1.07.1942[?], Warsaw Ghetto
- ŻSS-KOM, Employee's identification no. 1541 dated 1.07.1942 [?] of Hinda Weltman (ul. Nalewki 35)

  Doc. signed by B. [Bolesław] Rozenstadt.
- ***Description:*** original, printed matter, handwritten manuscript, ink, stamps, German, Polish, 86×140 mm, photograph, ss. 2, pp. 4.

  According to Ruta Sakowska, the identification card was issued after 22.07.1942 and deliberately backdated; see *Archiwum Ringelbluma*, pp. 250–251 (photocopy and summary).

### 195. RING. II/79. Mf. ŻIH—794; USHMM—49.

- 2.07.1942, Warsaw Ghetto
- ŻSS-KOM, Department of Labor Aid and Economic Aid. Agricultural Labor Section, Engineer H. Kalnicki, Letter dated 2.07.1942 to delegate of KOM in the Department of Labor Aid and Economic Aid
- Cover letter with attachment "Agricultural report for the month of June 1942" (concerns gardening jobs, cultivation of vegetables, on the terrain of the Warsaw Ghetto, agricultural courses, employment in agriculture outside the ghetto).
- ***Description:*** original, transcript (attachment), typescript, stamp, Polish, 222×144, 210×298 mm, ss. 4, pp. 4.

  At the bottom (letter) stamp "ŻSS-KOM, Of the Department of Labor Aid and Economic Aid. Of the Agricultural Work Section" and signature of H. Kalnicki (ink).

  Published: *Selected Documents*, pp. 529–532.

### 196. RING. II/78. Mf. ŻIH—794; USHMM—49.

a)

- 07.1942, Warsaw Ghetto
- ŻSS-KOM, "Cashier's report of the Occupational Restructuring and Training Section at KOM in Warsaw for the month of June 1942"

  Doc. directed to the Department of Labor Aid and Economic Aid at KOM (2.07.1942).
- ***Description:*** original, typescript, stamps, Polish, 204×290 mm, ss. 1, pp. 1.

  Stamps: "ŻSS-KOM, Occupational Restructuring and Training Section," at bottom an illegible signature (ink).

b)

- 07.1942, Warsaw Ghetto
- ŻSS-KOM, Occupational Restructuring and Training Section, "Report of activity in June 1942"
- Inf. about the Department of Professional Training, courses and seminaries.
- ***Description:*** original, typescript, stamp, Polish, 202×295 mm, ss. 2, pp. 2.

c)

- 07.1942, Warsaw Ghetto
- ŻSS-KOM, Occupational Restructuring and Training Section, Department of Professional Training in institutions for children and teenagers (ul. Leszno 2), "Report for June 1942"
  Inf. about establishment of groups of tailors, locksmiths and carpenters and of the toymaking workshop. Doc. signed by F. Kiełbikowa.
- ***Description:*** original, typescript (additions, handwritten manuscript, ink), stamp, Polish, 208×295 mm, ss. 2, pp. 2.

197. RING. II/72. Mf. ŻIH—793; USHMM—48.

- 3.07.1942, Warsaw Ghetto
- ŻSS-KOM, Department of Provisioning. Clothing Section (ul. Ogrodowa 27). L. Michelson, director, Letter dated 3.07.1942 to Dir. [Icchak] Giterman
- Cover letter with attachment: "Report of the activity of clothing stores and workshops for the month of June 1942" (inf. about procured, produced, repaired, distributed, and sold clothing and shoes).
- ***Description:*** original, typescript, stamps, Polish, 210×152, 210×298 mm, ss. 2, pp. 2.
  At top and at bottom (letter) stamps "ŻSS-KOM," at bottom (letter and encl.) signature (ink): "L. Michelson."

198. RING. II/89. Mf. ŻIH—794; USHMM—49.

- 6.07.1942, Warsaw Ghetto
- [ŻSS-KOM], Temporary Commission for affairs of the Communal Sector [Tymczasowa Komisja dla spraw Sektora Społecznego], Letter dated 6.07.1942 to the Presidium of the Commission for General and Budget-Financial Affairs [Prezydium Komisji dla spraw Ogólnych i Budżetowo-Finansowych] [ŻSS] KOM (missing ending)
- Concerns reorganization of KOM.
- ***Description:*** original or transcript, typescript (handwritten additions, ink), Polish, 205×330 mm, ss. 1, pp. 1.
  Index: [Menachem] Kirszenbaum, [Michał] Mazor, [Emanuel] Ringelblum, [Adolf] Berman, [Lejb] Neustadt

199. RING. II/86. Mf. ŻIH—794; USHMM—49.

- 7.07.1942, Warsaw Ghetto
- [ŻSS-KOM], "Report of insp[ection by] J. Cwajgel of activity of Dist[ricts] I, II, VI of ŻS of the Campaign for Aid for Displaced [Persons] for the period until 30 June 1942" (7.07.1942)
- Personnel matters (lists of members of the Campaign for Aid to Displaced Persons [Akcja Pomocy Przesiedleńcom = APP] committees), financial matters, organizational matters.
- ***Description:*** original, typescript, Polish, 206×340 mm, ss. 5, pp. 5.
  Index: B. Kaduszyn, member of APP in District I; Gliner, member of APP in District I; Praszkier, member of APP in District I; Frydman, member of APP in District I; I. Szojchet, member of APP in District I; Towbinowa, member of APP in District I; Krukówna, member of APP in District I; Rubinsztajnówna, member of APP in District I; Jagodzińska, member of APP in District I; Wajsbardówna, member of APP in District I; Tytelmanówna, member of APP in District I; Rudnicki, member of APP in District I; Rapke, member of APP in District II; Goldraj, member of APP in District II; Górka, member of APP in District II; Turkienicz, member of APP in District II; Gąsiorowa, member of APP in District II; Kacowa, member of APP in District II; Gerlitz, member of APP in District II; Segał, member of APP in District II; Blajwajs, member of APP in District II; Wiślicki, member of APP in District II; Gelerówna, member of APP in District II; Frydmanówna, member of APP in District II; engineer Műhlstein, member of APP in District VI; Pelc, member of APP in District VI; Wajnsztejn, member of APP in District VI; Waksberg, member of APP in District VI; Machonbaumówna, member of APP in District VI; Rozenowicz, member of APP in District VI; Kwekzylber, member of APP in District VI.

200. RING. II/73. Mf. ŻIH—794; USHMM—49.

- 15.07.1942, Warsaw Ghetto
- ŻSS-KOM Warsaw. SPS. Collection and Distribution of Clothing [Zbiórka i Rozdawnictwo Odzieży], "Memorandum" dated 15.07.1942 concerning the material situation of employees of Collection and Distribution of Clothing of SPS, directed to the address of Dir. I. [Icchak] Giterman
  Report of previous activity 1940–1942, personnel difficulties, proposal for regular payment of wages. Encl. "Minutes of inspection of the sorting shop of the Department of Clothing Collection of 17 May 1942 by Sapir, Glazer, and Rudniański" (Doc. signed by Rudniański and G. Sapir).
- ***Description:*** original, typescript, Polish, 208×293 mm, ss. 4, pp. 4.
  On p. 3 ("Memorandum") and on p. 1 (attachment) stamp: "ŻSS-KOM Warsaw. SPS Collection and Distribution of Clothing" and illegible signature (ink): "R. Zylberberg . . .[?]."

201. RING. II/55. Mf. ŻIH—793; USHMM—48.

- Date unknown, Warsaw Ghetto
- [ŻSS], "Forshlogn vegn tsuzamenshtel fun di opteyl–komisyes" [Proposals concerning composition of the departmental commissions]

- List of names of people and list of organizations entering into the composition of various commissions.
- *Description:* original or transcript, typescript, Yiddish, 210×295 mm, ss. 1, pp. 1.
  Index: Muszkat, Rogosz, Brojn, Rudnejski, Gewirc, Szapiro, Etkin, Chołodenko, Sz. Mazur, W. Brojn, Kirszenbaum, Mazur, Landau, Trokenhajm, Sak, Mermelsztajn [?], [Szachno] Sagan, Rabinowicz, Frydman, Guzik, Sukiennik, L. Klajn, Nowogródzka, Dr. Wdowiński

### 202. RING. II/76. Mf. ŻIH—794; USHMM—49.

- Date unknown, Warsaw Ghetto
- [ŻSS-KOM], Department of Labor Aid and Economic Aid. [Abram Prowalski?], "Budget of the General Bureau of the Department of L[abor] A[id] and Econ[omic] A[id of ŻSS-KOM]"
- Plan
- *Description:* original, handwritten manuscript (AP*), ink, Polish, 143×180 mm, ss. 1, pp. 1.

### 203. RING. II/112. Mf. ŻIH—794; USHMM—49.

- Date unknown, place unknown
- "Di foderungen fun der IGA[8] laytung be-negeye der aprovizatsye" [Demands of the Jewish Social Self-Help (ŻTS ?)[9] concerning provisioning]
- Concerning activity of public kitchens.
- *Description:* original, typescript, Yiddish, 205×295 mm, ss. 1, pp. 1.

### 204. RING. II/123. Mf. ŻIH—794; USHMM—49.

- 5.03.[year unknown], Warsaw Ghetto
- ŻTOS, Central Entertainment Committee, Invitation to a show on 5.03.[year unknown] organized in the premises of the public kitchen at ul. Leszno 29.
- *Description:* original (2 copies), printed matter, stamps, handwritten manuscript, ink, Polish, 104×62 mm, ss. 2, pp. 2
  Stamps: "For the benefit of the Jew[ish] Social Self-Help Soc[iety] 10 gr"; "Department of Individual Assistance." On the reverse stamps: "88."

### 205. RING. II/160. Mf. ŻIH—795; USHMM—50.

- Date unknown, Warsaw Ghetto
- Khalutsim (Zionist Pioneers) Point [Dror] (ul. Dzielna 34), Letter to [Henryk] Rotenberg [ŻKOM?]
- Request for consent to start a laundry at ul. Dzielna 34. Encl. list of needed equipment.
- *Description:* original, typescript, Yiddish, 210×144, 210×295 mm, ss. 2, pp. 2.
  At bottom notation (pencil): "Health Services Department Dr. [Szymon] Wyszewiański, I v[ery much] request granting of allowance for establishment of a laundry, R. . . [initial of Rotenberg?]."

### 206. RING. II/217. Mf. ŻIH—798; USHMM—53.

a)

- Before 27.07.1942, Warsaw Ghetto
- ŻSS-KOM, Notification about obligation to report for work on 27.07.[1942].
- *Description:* original, typescript, stamp, Polish, 218×77 mm, ss. 1, pp. 1.

b)

- 3.08.1942, Warsaw Ghetto
- [ŻSS-KOM], Receipt dated 3.08.1942 for collection of 30 kg of bread.
- *Description:* original, handwritten manuscript, pencil, Polish, 72×106 mm, ss. 1, pp. 1.

c)

- 4.08.[1942], Warsaw Ghetto
- [ŻSS-KOM], Note dated 4.08.[1942] concerning allocation of bread [?] for Bartman and Fiszman.
- *Description:* original, handwritten manuscript, pencil, Polish, 115×80 mm, ss. 1, pp. 1.
  Name "Fiszman" crossed out.
  Doc. written on the reverse of a fragment of printed material (article): "Dawid Loyd George, Prawda o traktacie wersalskim" [David Lloyd George, The Truth about the Versailles Treaty].

d)

- 3.08.1942, Warsaw Ghetto
- ŻSS-KOM, Warehouse receipt dated 3.08.1942, no. 3360, for 50 kg of bread
- *Description:* original, printed matter, handwritten manuscript, pencil, Polish, 129×182 mm, ss. 1, pp. 1.
  On the reverse order of 4.08.[1942] for disbursement of 20 zł to Zalcsztajn and Zielony for delivery of bread (handwritten manuscript, pencil).

e)

- 08.1942, Warsaw Ghetto
- [ŻSS-KOM], Lists of names of white-collar workers and manual laborers dated 3.08., 4.08. and 5.08.1942.
- *Description:* original (list of 4.08. in 2 copies, of 5.08. in 3 copies), typescript (numerous handwritten additions, pencil), Polish, 210×223, 212×294 mm, damages and losses of text, ss. 6, pp. 6 .
  Docs. written on the reverse of certificates of service provided by ŻTOS (1941, duplicated typescript).

8. IGA = Idishe gezelshaftlekhe aleynhilf, Jewish Social Self-Help in Yiddish.

9. Unclear if the reference is to ŻSS or ŻTOS, as date is unknown. Name of the organization was changed in October 1940.

Published: *Archiwum Ringelbluma*, pp. 251–254 (photocopy, fragment, summary).

207. RING. II/218. Mf. ŻIH—798; USHMM—53.

- 07–08.1942, Warsaw Ghetto
- [ŻSS-KOM?], "Special provision[ing] campaign" (25.07–7.08.1942)
- Book of income and expenditure of money and food articles during the liquidation action in the Warsaw Ghetto.
- ***Description:*** original, handwritten manuscript, notebook, pencil, Polish, 150×202 mm, ss. 12, pp. 11.
  On p. 2 notation (pencil): "Ada N.—28.07.—25 (Sala z d. Kandel)" [Sala née Kandel?]
  According to Ruta Sakowska, the doc. collects notations of the aid campaign conducted at the Umschlagplatz; see *Archiwum Ringelbluma*, p. 255 (summary).

## Correspondence of Icchak Giterman

208. RING. II/251. Mf. ŻIH—799; USHMM—54.

- Date unknown, Warsaw Ghetto
- [Dawid] Chołodenko (brushmakers workshop), Letter to I. [Icchak] Giterman
- Request for food aid.
- ***Description:*** original, handwritten manuscript, ink, Yiddish, 145×175 mm, ss. 1, pp. 2.
  See *Archiwum Ringelbluma*, p. 176 (summary).
  Published: *Selected Documents*, pp. 287–288.

209. RING. II/165. Mf. ŻIH—795; USHMM—50.

- 02–04.1942, Wilno ghetto.
- [Zelig Hersz Kalmanowicz], Letters (4) of 16.02., 19.02., 23.03., and 21.04.1942 to [Icchak] Giterman (Warsaw Ghetto)
- Living conditions in the Wilno ghetto. Tidying up of Jewish collections at Germans' order (manuscripts, printed matter and other collections brought to the YIVO building).
- ***Description:*** original, handwritten manuscript, Yiddish, ink, 122×170, 144×223 mm, ss. 5, pp. 7.
  On p. 2 (letter of 16.02.1942) notation in Polish (pencil): "Dr. Dzont Gutermanowski [Icchak Giterman], W[arsa]w, unpaid."
  On p. 2 (letter of 23.03.[1942] notation in Polish (pencil): "Giterman [. . .]." [further text illegible]
  Published: *Listy o Zagładzie*, pp. 97–111; *Goldene Keyt* (Tel-Aviv), no. 110–111/1983.

210. RING. II/106. Mf. ŻIH—794; USHMM—49.

- 25.06.1941, Warsaw Ghetto
- Jakub Karo (ul. Żelazna 89, apt. 76), Letter of 25.06.1941 to Dir. Izaak [Icchak] Giterman
- Thanks for allocation of food parcel, request for another parcel and for privileges for his 5-member family benefit at the public kitchen at ul. Leszno 14.
- ***Description:*** original, handwritten manuscript, ink, Polish, 223×295 mm, ss. 2, pp. 1.

211. RING. II/181/7. Mf. ŻIH—797; USHMM—52.

- Date unknown, Lublin.
- Josef Kenigsberg (Lublin), Letter to [Dir. Icchak Giterman] (Warsaw Ghetto)
- Request for aid.
- ***Description:*** original, handwritten manuscript, ink, Yiddish, 144×166 mm, text legible in places, ss. 1, pp. 2.
  Published: *Selected Documents*, pp. 368–369.
  Index: Blok

212. RING. II/219/1. Mf. ŻIH—798; USHMM—53.

- [1942], Warsaw Ghetto
- Josef Kirman (Umschlagplatz), Letter to I. [Icchak] Giterman (ul. Lubeckiego 6, apt. 15)
- Request for aid.
- ***Description:*** original, handwritten manuscript, pencil, Yiddish, 125×88 mm, ss. 1, pp. 1.
  Published: *Archiwum Ringelbluma*, p. 161 (photocopy).

213. RING. II/103. Mf. ŻIH—794; USHMM—49.

- 16.08.1941—10.01.1942, Warsaw Ghetto
- Moris (Maurice) Landau (ul. Waliców 22), Letters of 16, 18, 19.08.1941 and 10.01.1942 to Icchak Giterman
- Living conditions in the Warsaw Ghetto, requests for help (inter alia, concerning opportunity to teach an English-language class).
- ***Description:*** original, handwritten manuscript, ink, English, Yiddish, 160×178, 145×210, 135×195 mm, ss. 10, pp. 16.
  On sheet 10 notation: "Maurice Landau, [Warsaw Ghetto, ul.] Waliców 22."

214. RING. II/181/6. Mf. ŻIH—797; USHMM—52.

- Date unknown, place unknown
- Milsztejn, Letter to Dir. Icchak Giterman (Warsaw Ghetto)
- Request for money.
- ***Description:*** original, handwritten manuscript, ink, Yiddish, 116×199 mm, ss. 1, pp. 2.

215. RING. II/181/8. Mf. ŻIH—797; USHMM—52.

- 14.01.1942, Warsaw Ghetto
- NN. (Rabbi Moshe), Letter of 14.01.1942 to [Dir. Icchak] Giterman (Warsaw Ghetto)
- Request for shipment of matzo.
- ***Description:*** original, handwritten manuscript, ink, Hebrew, 158×213 mm, ss. 1, pp. 1.

216. RING. II/104. Mf. ŻIH—794; USHMM—49.

- 5.02.1942, Warsaw Ghetto
- Sponsors' Committee for Students of Torah (Sponsors' Committee for Orthodox Youth) (ul. Gęsia 21, apt. 7), Letter dated 5.02.1942 to Dir. I. [Icchak] Giterman

- Request for material aid. Letter signed by: Mordechai Alter, A. [T.?] Kaczyński, I. Ch. Grabski.
- *Description:* original, typescript, stamp, Yiddish, 213×294 mm, ss. 1, pp. 1.
  Stamp (Polish): "Patronat Młodzieży Ortodoksyjnej [Sponsors' Committee for Orthodox Youth], Warsaw, Gęsia 21/7."
  Published: *Selected Documents*, pp. 417–418.

**217. RING. II/119. Mf. ŻIH—794; USHMM—49.**

- 03–04.1942, Warsaw Ghetto
- Sponsors' Committee for Care for the Remains of Poor Jews "Halwajat Hamet" [Hebrew: Accompanying the Dead] (ul. Gęsia 17), Letter dated 20.04.1942 to Dir. I. [Icchak] Giterman
- Cover letter with encl.: "Memorandum" of 31.03.1942 from a group of Orthodox communal activists of Warsaw directed to the chairman of the Jewish Council (proposal for creating at the Cemetery Department of the Jewish Council a Sponsors' Committee for Care for the Remains of Poor Jews "Halwajat Hamet," a list of names of members of the Sponsors' Committee, attached "Regulations" of the Sponsors' Committee). Memorandum signed by: Rabbi Dawid Borensztajn, the Tsadik of Sochaczew, Rabbi Jakub Icek Landau, Rabbi Izrael Szapiro, the Tsadik of Grodzisk [Mazowiecki], Rabbi Icchak Mendel Dancygier, the Tsadik of Aleksandrów, Zysia Fraydman [Friedman ?] and Dir. Dawid Guzik, Meszulam Kaminer.
- *Description:* original, typescript, stamps, Polish, Yiddish, 205×148, 210×295 mm, ss. 5, pp. 5.
  Stamps on the documents "Memoranda" and "Regulations": "'Hałwajat Hamet' Care for Remains of the Poor in Warsaw" and signatures: Rabbi I. [Icchak Hirsz] Adalberg.
  Published: *Selected Documents*, pp. 418–421.
  Index: Rabbi Jakub Icchak Landau, member of the Sponsors' Committee for Care for the Remains of Poor Jews "Halwajat Hamet" in Warsaw, Tsadik of Stryków (ul. Nowolipki 23, apt. 7); Rabbi I. Adelberg of Maków (ul. Gęsia 15), member of the Sponsors' Committee for Care for the Remains of Poor Jews "Halwajat Hamet" in Warsaw; Majer Zylberberg of Warsaw (ul. Nowolipki 16), member of the Sponsors' Committee for Care for the Remains of Poor Jews "Halwajat Hamet" in Warsaw; Noe Zonszajn of Warsaw (ul. Gęsia 13), member of the Sponsors' Committee for Care for the Remains of Poor Jews "Halwajat Hamet" in Warsaw; Dr. Gadt of Kalisz (ul. Świętojerska 32), member of the Sponsors' Committee for Care for the Remains of Poor Jews "Halwajat Hamet" in Warsaw; Salom Litwak of Warsaw (ul. Świętojerska 34), member of the Sponsors' Committee for Care for the Remains of Poor Jews "Halwajat Hamet" in Warsaw; Joel Syrkus of Warsaw (ul. Miła 42), member of the Sponsors' Committee for Care for the Remains of Poor Jews "Halwajat Hamet" in Warsaw; Izaak Nadel of Łódź (ul. Zamenhofa 16), member of the Sponsors' Committee for Care for the Remains of Poor Jews "Halwajat Hamet" in Warsaw; Chananel Rozenblum from Kalisz (ul. Muranowska 18), former Dir. KKO, member of the Sponsors' Committee for Care for the Remains of Poor Jews "Halwajat Hamet" in Warsaw

**218. RING. II/181/4. Mf. ŻIH—797; USHMM—52.**

- Date unknown, place unknown
- NN. (G. Rap . . . [?], Grap . . . . [?]), Letter to Dir. Icchak Giterman (Warsaw Ghetto)
- Request for a meeting.
- *Description:* original, handwritten manuscript, pencil, Yiddish, 103×76 mm, ss. 1, pp. 2.

**219. RING. II/181/3. Mf. ŻIH—797; USHMM—52.**

- 7.06.1942, Warsaw Ghetto
- Engineer A. Russak (Warsaw), Collection of Monetary Levy [Pobór Daniny Pieniężnej], Letter of 7.06.1942 to Dir. Icchak Giterman (Warsaw Ghetto)
- Request for meeting.
- *Description:* original, handwritten manuscript, ink, Polish, 143×143 mm, ss. 1, pp. 1.

**220. RING. II/181/1. Mf. ŻIH—797; USHMM—52.**

- 12.11.1941, Warsaw Ghetto
- L. Tenenbaum, Letter of 12.11.1941 to Dir. [Icchak Giterman] (Warsaw Ghetto)
- Concerning meeting with Adam Czerniaków.
- *Description:* original, handwritten manuscript, ink, Polish, 180×102 mm, ss. 1, pp. 2.

**221. RING. II/181/2. Mf. ŻIH—797; USHMM—52.**

- Before 2.10.1941, Königsberg (Królewiec)
- NN. Königsberg (Królewiec) . . . 12, Letter predates 2.10.1941 to Dir. Icchak Giterman (Warsaw Ghetto, ul. Thomackie [Tłomackie] 5)
- Envelope of a letter.
- *Description:* original, typescript, handwritten manuscript, ink, postmark and stamp of the Jewish Council in Warsaw (2.10.1941), German, 153×109 mm, ss. 2, pp. 2.
  On the reverse surname and address of the sender (ink): different to read.

**222. RING. II/181/5. Mf. ŻIH—797; USHMM—52.**

- Date unknown, place unknown
- NN., Letter to Dir. I.G. [Icchak Giterman] (Warsaw Ghetto).
- *Description:* original, handwritten manuscript, ink, Yiddish, 143×109 mm, ss. 1, pp. 1.

## 223. RING. II/101. Mf. ŻIH—794; USHMM—49.

- 18.11.1941–9.04.1942, Warsaw Ghetto
- Icchak Giterman, Incoming Correspondence
  1) Association of Jewish Artisans in Warsaw (ul. Elektoralna 6). Bakers' Section (ul. Leszno 12), Letter dated 18.11.1941, concerns financial matters;
  2) Jewish Production Cooperative L.L.C. Organization and support of production in the Jewish District in Warsaw (ul. Chłodna 4), Letter dated 23.01.1942, notation about a meeting, to take place on 25.01.1942 in the apartment of [Józef] Jaszuński (ul. Żelazna 78);
  3) P. Kamień, I. Wajnberg and J. [Johanan] Morgensztern, Letter dated 10.02.1942, concerning foreign food aid arriving for private persons;
  4) A. [Abraham] Gepner, Letter dated 3.03.1942, concerning unpaid March installment for dinners;
  5) B. Goldsztadt (ul. Chłodna 6, apt. 6), Letter dated 9.04.1942, Request for a meeting;
  6) ŻSS-KOM, SPS, Letter dated 28.06.1942, concerning postponement of date of meeting from 28.06. to 30.06.1942.
- ***Description:*** original, typescript, handwritten manuscript, Polish, Yiddish, 223×146, 206×298, 220×353 mm, ss. 7, pp. 8.

  On the reverse of doc. 2 notation in Yiddish (ink): [?]; on doc. 5 at top notation (pencil): "14.04., 9:30"; on doc. 2 Giterman's address: "Żelazna 101"; on doc. 4: "Leszno 2," on doc. 6: "Żelazna 101[3]."

  Index: Jakub Neuman, attorney

## 224. RING. II/100. Mf. ŻIH—794; USHMM—49.

- 11.1941–06.1942, Warsaw Ghetto
- ŻSS-KOM, Correspondence with Dir. I. [Icchak] Giterman
  1) Letter dated 30.11.1941 with notation about efforts to obtain a subsidy for the IFO [Yidishe Froyen-Organizatsye; Jewish Women's Organization], missing attachment;
  2) [Gustaw] Wielikowski, Letter dated 18.03.1942 in matter of foreign aid;
  3) Letter dated 12.05.1942 concerns exemption of chaluc (Haluts, Zionist Pioneer) workshops from rent payment (opłaty komornego);
  4) [Gustaw] Wielikowski, Letter dated 16.06.1942 concerning clothing collection.
- ***Description:*** original, typescript, German, Polish, 218×145, 207×290 mm, ss. 4, pp. 4.

  On doc. 3 at bottom notation (ink): "transcript to Mr. Prowalski [?]."

  Index: Paul Israel Meyerheim of the Reichsvereinigung der Juden in Deutschland [Reich Association of Jews in Germany] (Berlin, Charlottenburg 2, Kantstr. 158)

## 225. RING. II/102. Mf. ŻIH—794; USHMM—49.

- 31.01.1942, 7.07.1942, Date unknown, Lwów ghetto, Rejowiec ghetto, place unknown
- Icchak Giterman, Incoming correspondence
  1) [ŻSS] JSS. Jüd. Hilfskomitee Lemberg-Stadt [Lwów City Jewish Aid Committee]. Dr. Schaff, chairman, Dr. Sucher, secretary, Letter dated 31.01.1942, regarding employment of Krischer;
  2) [ŻSS] JSS. Delegatur in Rejowiec, Letter dated 7.07.1942, concerns a travel permit for p. S[. . .];
  3) [ŻSS] JSS in [Lwów?]. Landau, Letter to engineer J. [Józef] Jaszuński (ul. Żelazna 78, apt. 5), Request for transmission to Icchak Giterman of information about Abraham Seinfeld, who is in Jezierna near Tarnopol.
- ***Description:*** original, typescript, handwritten manuscript on a postcard (doc. 2), ink, stamps, Polish, 205×145, 205×290, 148×105 mm, ss. 3, pp. 4.

  On doc. 1 notation (ink): "Warm regards and I shake Landau's hand"; on Docs. 1–3 stamps of JSS.; on doc. 2 postmark and stamp of the Jewish Council in Warsaw.

# Jewish Institutions and Organizations Connected with ŻSS

## 226. RING. II/121. Mf. ŻIH—794; USHMM—49.

- Date unknown and 10.1941, Warsaw Ghetto
- "Centos," Invitations and tickets to cultural performances organized in the Warsaw Ghetto
  1) Concert of oratorio music at the Great Synagogue on ul. Tłomackie on 19.10.1941 organized by "Centos" on the occasion of Children's Month (09–10.1941). Performers: Choir of the Great Synagogue—Dir. D. [Dawid] Ajzensztadt, the Jewish Symphonic Orchestra—Dir. M. [Marian] Neuteich, soloists: M. [Marysia] Ajzensztadtówna (singing), H. [Henryk] Reinberg (violin), I. [Izrael] Fajwiszys (organ) (2 copies, printed matter, Polish, Yiddish, 139×98 mm, ss. 4, pp. 8);
  2) Sponsors' Committee and Ladies' Kitchen and Hearth Circle of "point" no. 118 of the "Centos" Society, Invitation to 2 vocal-musical teas in the garden of the "point" at ul. Nowolipki 35, no date (printed matter, stamp: "Sponsors' Committee of the Communal Kitchen for Children no. 118," ul. Nowolipki 35, Polish, 144×102 mm, ss. 1, pp. 1.);
  3) "Centos—Children's Month." Ticket of admission to the tournament of children's choirs in the "Femina" hall (ul. Leszno 35), on 13.[10].[1941]. Taking part are children's choirs of the "Centos" institutions under the direction of I. [Izrael] Fajwiszys, I. [Izrael] Gladsztein, L.

Goldberg, p. Kamińska-Gurdusowa, Mr. Z. [Zygmunt] Szklar. Jury: Dir. D. Ajzensztadt, Dir. Dawidowicz, Prof. J. [Józef] Fiszhaut, Editor [Menachem] Kipnis, Dir. M. [Marian] Neuteich, Dir. Sz. [Szymon] Pullman, T. [Tadeusz] Płucer-Sarna, Prof. Z. [Zygmunt] Wolfson (printed matter, Polish, Yiddish, 137×98 mm, ss. 1, pp. 2).

- *Description:* original (doc. 1 in 2 copies), printed matter, Polish, Yiddish, 139×98, 144×102, 137×98 mm, ss. 6, pp. 11.

  Doc. 1, 3—Published: *Kronika getta*, pp. 277–279, 274–275.

## 227. RING. II/159. Mf. ŻIH—795; USHMM—50.

- 1941–1942, Warsaw Ghetto
- [Centos], H. Peker and J. Zylberberg, common room supervisors, Notebook of entries regarding supplemental feeding of children in the "points" at ul. Franciszkańska (07.1941–04.1942)
- Daily numeration of food products, lists of names of children, calculations.
- *Description:* original, handwritten manuscript (several handwritings), notebook, ink, pencil, Polish, 80×104, 155×196 mm, ss. 16, pp. 25.

  Index: Żychlińska

## 228. RING. II/110. Mf. ŻIH—794; USHMM—49.

- 12.1941, Warsaw Ghetto
- [Centos] Collection of reports of common room supervisors about work with children from the shelters for refugees
  1) T. Bokse[nbaum–] Nigelszporn, "Report from the common room at ul. Dzika 3" (16.12.1941);
  2) G. Konowa and S. [Sima] Rydygerowa, "Report of the activity of the common room at ul. Stawka 9" (16.12.1941);
  3) Stefania Halberstat, "Report of the common room at the point at Nowolipki 25" (17.12.1941);
  4) A. Motrolowa, "Report of the common room at ul. Nowolipki 76" (12.1941);
  5) Br. Żychlińska, "Report of the work in the area of the common room at ul. Żelazna 58a" (12.1941);
  6) Cajtagowa, "Report of the work in the common room at ul. Ogrodowa 27" (no date);
  7) B. Frenzel, "Report" concerning the common room at ul. Twarda 18 (no date);
  8) Rega Czarka, "Report—common room Nalewki 31" (17.12.1941);
  9) H. Brams, "Report of the work in common room no. 10 at ul. Grzybowska 48" (17.12.1941);
  10) Bronisława Dostal, "Report. Point at ul. Dzika 19" (18.12.1941);
  11) N. [Noemi] Danielowa, "Report of the common room at ul. Miła 2" (no date);
  12) S. Przedborska, "Report. Common Room—Bagno 3/5" (12.1941);
  13) Estera Karasiówna, "Common Room at ul. Śliska 28. Report" (17.12.[1941]);
  14) J. Zylberberg, "Draft in the matter of the educational state, care, and supplemental feeding in the common room in the p[oint] for children of refugees at ul. Franciszkańska [21]" (no date);
  15) C. Marzyńska, "Report of the condition of points under the supervision of a mobile common room supervisor" (17.12.1941);
  16) J. Alfabetówna, "Report of common room supervisor J. Alfabetówna of her activity from April to December 1941" (concerns the common room at ul. Nowolipa 30) (12.1941);
  17) Cecylia Apel, "Report of my work as a mobile guardian (lotnej opiekunki)" (12.1941);
  18) E. Justmanówna, "Report of the work in the common room [ul. Bagno 1]" (12.1941);
  19) R. Nutkiewicz, "Report of the work in point no. 31 [ul. Twarda 22]" (17.12.1941);
  20) W. Hantowerówna, Report of work of the mobile guardian in points for refugees at ul. Zimnej 3 and 4, Zamenhofa 2, 6, 8, 9, and 16, Pawia 12 and 18, Nowolipki 5, and Lubecki 12 (1.12.1941).
- *Description:* transcript, typescript (handwritten additions, ink), Polish, 208×295 mm, minor damages and losses of text, ss. 34, pp. 34.

  Docs. 9, 13, 18: Published: *Selected Documents*, pp. 483–484, 479–483, 476–478.
  Published: *Kronika getta*, pp. 183–234
  Index: [Erna] Peker, common room supervisor, Moszek Bok, orphan, died in the Warsaw Ghetto in a point for refugees (ul. Lubecki 12)

## 229. RING. II/111. Mf. ŻIH—794; USHMM—49.

- After 01.1942, Warsaw Ghetto
- [Centos] W. Braun, Reports of inspection of points for refugees, boarding schools for children
  1) "Note of Mr. W. Braun about inspection of the point for refugees [ul. Stawki 9]" (inspection conducted on 24.01.1942 together with Icchak Kacnelson);
  2) "Note of II inspection of the boarding school at Dzika 9—2 February 1942";
  3) "Note of visit at the boarding school at ul. Dzika 9 on 14 February 1942";
  4) "Note of the inspection of the Boarding school for Children at ul. Ogrodowa 29 on 28.02.1942";
  5) "Note of the inspection [on 1.03.1942] of the Boarding school Nests (Gniazda) for Orphans at ul. Śliska 28";
  6) "Note of inspection [on 1.03.1942] of the Nest for children at ul. Nowolipki 76";
  7) Fragment [?] of a memorandum on the subject of the situation of orphans left by refugees and displaced persons;

8) "Plan for placing orphans left by refugees and displaced persons at points" (plan for organization of care for orphans with the support of more prosperous apartment houses in the Warsaw Ghetto).

- *Description:* original, transcript (doc. 1 in 2 copies), typescript, Polish, 188×252, 223×298 mm, ss. 8, pp. 8.

  Doc. 7 and 8 signed (ink) by W. Braun.

  On the reverse of doc. 2. drawings and notes. (pencil).

### 230. RING. II/51. Mf. ŻIH—793; USHMM—48.

- 9.02.1942, Warsaw Ghetto
- [Centos], "Information about child care and about the major works of 'Centos' during January 1942"
- Care for street children, establishment of the boarding school "Dobra Wola" ("Good Will") (ul. Dzielna 61), orphanage for children of refugees (ul. Ogrodowa 29), Lodging House (Domu Noclegowego) (ul. Nowolipie 1), organization of the Children's Home (Domu Dziecka) and the Emergency Protective Service for Homeless and Abandoned Children (Pogotowia Opiekuńczego dla Dzieci Bezdomnych i Opuszczonych) (ul. Zegarmistrzowska 14), inspections of half-boarding[10] schools, new facilities for children, organizational matters.
- *Description:* original or transcript, typescript, Polish, 210×295 mm, ss. 2, pp. 2.

  Index: Prof. Dr. Hirszfeld, Dr. Milejkowski

  Published: *Selected Documents*, pp. 366–368.

### 231. RING. II/54. Mf. ŻIH—793; USHMM—48.

- 16.02.1942, Warsaw Ghetto
- Centos, Presidium, Letter dated 16.02.1942 to Dir. I. [Icchak] Giterman
- Inf. about the resolution of "Centos" of 15.02.1942 questioning the proposals for reorganization of KOM.
- *Description:* original, typescript, Polish, 223×294 mm, ss. 1, pp. 1.

  At bottom four illegible signatures (ink).

### 232. RING. II/52. Mf. ŻIH—793; USHMM—48.

- After 20.02.1942, Warsaw Ghetto
- "Centos," Soc[ial]-Propag[anda] Department. Welfare Bureau (Referat Opiekuńczy), Circular letter of 20.02.1942 directed to house committees
- Concerns possibility of feeding children in children's kitchens (noted fall in attendance of children in kitchens). Letter signed by: A. Szmidt and H. [Helena] Merenholc.
- *Description:* transcript, typescript, Polish, 210×294 mm, minor damages and losses of text, ss. 1., pp. 1.

### 233. RING. II/53. Mf. ŻIH—793; USHMM—48.

- 6.03.1942, Warsaw Ghetto
- "Centos," Secretary, Letter dated 6.03.1942 to Dir. I. [Icchak] Giterman
- Cover letter with attachment: "Data about the principal works of 'Centos' during February 1942" (6.03.1942) (establishment of the Children's Home at ul. Zegarmistrzowska 14, the children's kitchen at ul. Świętojerska 34, supplemental feeding of children, formation of new committees of social welfare for children, questionnaire for gifted children).
- *Description:* original, transcript (encl.), typescript, stamps, Polish, 225×144, 227×285 mm, ss. 2, pp. 2.

  On p. 1 (letter) stamp: "Jewish Social Self-Help. City Welfare Committee. Care for Children and Orphans 'Centos', Warsaw, Leszno no. 2."; "Secretary" and illegible signature (ink).

### 234. RING. II/109. Mf. ŻIH—794; USHMM—49.

- Date unknown, Warsaw Ghetto
- ["Centos"?], List of names of displaced children from [Germany?] located in an undetermined shelter for displaced persons in the Warsaw Ghetto.
- *Description:* original, handwritten manuscript, pencil, German, 220×340, 220×348, 112×350 mm, ss. 6, pp. 9.

  List preserved in three versions: 1) Initial list with numerous additions and cross-outs (ink, pencil); 2) Second list (in 2 copies) (pencil); 3) Transcript of list 2.

  List 2) prepared on the reverse of two personnel questionnaires: a) Of Jankiel Zylberberg (age 35) (ul. Nowolipie 21, apt. 5), MA in pedagogy, teacher (Elementary School no. 138); b) NN. [name and surname smeared] (age 34) (ul. Nowolipie, MA in pedagogy, teacher (Elementary School no. 81), manager of kitchen no. 25 from 11.12.1939 (original, typescript, handwritten manuscript, ink, pencil, Polish, docs. were preserved in binder).

  First page of list 3) prepared on a fragment of an application for work to NN.: Of Luba Włodawer (ul. Złota 71, apt. 2). (After 1939, original, typescript, Polish).

  Index: Hoch Karl (age 7), Hoch Fritz (age 12), Katz Brunhilde (age 9), Meier Gusti (age 13), Gottschalk Güntler (age 14), Boroschek Inge (age 10), Zander Helma (age 11), Zander Ruth (age 7), Korona Alfred (age 13), Kahn Norbert (age 6), Domke Erwin (age 12), Domke Ruth (age 4), Lipholz Heinz (age 10), Lipholz Margot (age 13), Frank Wiliam (age 4), Lichtblum Dawid (age 2 and 9 months), Lichtblum Bernhard (age 4), Kupowsky Wiera

10. "Half-boarding" homes provided meals but not necessarily a place to sleep. Perhaps they could be equated with daycare facilities.

(age 12), Kupowsky Sonia (age 14), Will Arnold (age 13), Heilbrunn Usla (age 14), Heilbrunn Gerd (age 12), Gelbart Ruth (age 12), Gelbart Margot (age 15), Kirsch Helga (age 12), Kirsch Gisla (age 9), Kamp Ursla (age 13), Josel Horst (age 10), Falk Bella (age 12), Samt Elwira (age 8), Friedmann Deni (14 miesięcy), Friedmann Ilse (age 9), Friedmann Sonia (age 11), Lopian Wolfgang (7 weeks), Winkelfeld Berta (age 13), Winkelfeld Norberth (age 6), Löwy Lutz (age 13), Schwarz Wolfgang (age 10), Fried Eva (age 12), Hirsch Rachel (age 3), Stein Hans (age 8), Stein Irich (age 7), Wapnitzky Jakob (age 5), Wapnitzky Elie (age 8), Wapnitzky Scharlotte (age 12), Rosenthal Gerda (age 13), Rosenthal Inge (age 11), Rosenthal Gitel (age 1 and 6 months), Rosenthal Gehard (age 14), Tworoger Ruth (age 1), Tworoger Manfred (age 4), Lehmann Helga (age 11), Lehmann Renate (age 9), Steinhand Margot (age 5), Hähnlein Rosa (age 10), Hähnlein Heinrich (age 13), Putziger Chana (age 9), Hahn Ruth (age 10), Hahn Günther (age 13), Freundlich Eva (age 11), Juker Harald (age 9), Gerson Wolfgang (age 10), Friedmann Lea (age 11), Sondheim Helmut (age 9), Denemark Wolfgang (age 9), Wirth Dawid (age 12), Schul Edite (age 13), Schul Hilde (age 14), Kowalsky Regina (age 14), Tenenbaum Hermann (age 2 and 6 months), Bick Regina (age 8), Edelmand Ida (age 14), Matias Horst (age 4), Matias Gehard (age 12), Menschenfreund Dagobert (age 11 or 13), Menschenfreund Leon (age 14), Freiberg Gitel (age 2 and 9 months), Freiberg Deni 6 weeks), Cohn Rudolf (age 11 or 12), Gruno Ruth (age 12), Neumann Ruth (age 6), Neumann Miriam (age 11), Neumann James (age 13), Neumann Hans (age 15), Neumann Marianne (age 15), Sinasohn Gerda (age 14), Sinasohn Rita (age 12), Siburth (Abraham) Irene (age 6), Schuster Inge (age 14), Liebermann Inge (age 13), Heide Wolfgang (age 12), Posner Heinz (age 6), Baruch Gerda (age 10), Baruch Paul (age 12), Baruch Berndt (age 14), Baruch Hilde (age 15), Aron Hari (age 14), Steinbock Lote (age 15), Becker Marian (age 15), Mannes Lilo (age 15), Sänger Manfred (age 15), Abrahamsohn Alfred (age 15), Milewsky Rose (age 14), Gans Margitt (age 15 or 14), Laufer Betty (age 15), Lesser Hermine (age 15), Adler Lili (age 4), Aron Manfred Wolfberg Friede (age 26), Jura Markus Spiro Lesser Lundner Miriam (age 4), Lundner Babette (age 5), Lundner Rachel (age 7), Lundner Eli (age 9), Lundner Sula (age 13), Schönskols (?) Regina (age 7 and 6 months), Berensohn Bernhard (age 4), Wangenheim Edith (age 5), Wangenheim Bernhard (age 4), Bierwald Hainz (age 8), Bierwald Ilse (age 5), Zelhide (?) Dolfi (age 15), Jokutowski Klaus Gerwanish Berlinger Wolfberg Friede Litzmersky Kurt (age 12)

## 235. RING. II/367. Mf. ŻIH—803; USHMM—58.

- 02.1941, Warsaw Ghetto
- *Głos Domu Chłopców* (Voice of the Boys' Home), no. 1, 10.02.1941
- Newsletter of children of the boarding school at ul. Gęsia 6/8. Authors of texts: M. Lipman, S. Hajtler, J. Denda, Sz. Gogol, Josef Fibich (age 10), Jankiel Hanower (age 11), Jakub Lerych (age 12), I. Rutowicz, M. Bafilis, J. Cwikiel.
- ***Description:*** original, typescript, Polish, 178×222, 185×222 mm, ss. 15, pp. 15.

  Published: BŻIH, no. 97/1976, pp. 79–87; *Kronika getta*, pp. 65–82; *Kronika getta*, pp. 318 (photocopy of title page).

  Index: Mojsze Hanower of the boarding school at ul. Gęsia 6/8, Fliderbaum of the boarding school at ul. Gęsia 6/8, Lewiner of the boarding school at ul. Gęsia 6/8, Borensztajn of the boarding school at ul. Gęsia 6/8, Redlich of the boarding school at ul. Gęsia 6/8, Klapp of the boarding school at ul. Gęsia 6/8, Dr. Taubenszlak

## 236. RING. II/177. Mf. ŻIH—797; USHMM—52.

- Before 19.04.1941, Warsaw Ghetto
- Dom Dziecka (Children's Home) (ul. Krochmalna 36), Invitation to children's performance on 19.04.1941.
- ***Description:*** original, printed matter, handwritten manuscript, ink, Yiddish, 120×85 mm, ss. 1, pp. 2.

  On reverse a stamp: "Supplemental feeding kitchen for children no. 143 at ul. Krochmalna 36."

  Published: *Kronika getta*, pp. 268–269.

## 237. RING. II/27. Mf. ŻIH—793; USHMM—48.

- Date unknown, Warsaw
- House Committee. Public appeal for a money collection for hungry and sick residents of the house.
- ***Description:*** original or transcript, typescript, Polish, 210×295 mm, ss. 1, pp. 1.

## 238. RING. II/293/1. Mf. ŻIH—800; USHMM—55.

- Before 9.09.1942, Warsaw Ghetto
- "Czyste" Infectious Diseases Hospital, Armband for employee (no. 636).
- ***Description:*** original, printed matter, stamps, German, 251×97 mm, ss. 1, pp. 2.

  On p. 1 stamps of hospital "Czyste" and "636."

  On reverse notation (pencil): "9.9.42 6.00 o'clock—wife, sister, 10.09.1942—parents (no. 636)."

See *Archiwum Ringelbluma*, p. 120 (summary); *Kronika getta*, p. 260 (photocopy).
Published: BŻIH, no. 71–72/1969, p. 147 (photograph).

### 239. RING. II/179. Mf. ŻIH—797; USHMM—52.

a)

- 08.1941, Warsaw Ghetto
- Invitation to special evening of folklore devoted to the 40th birthday of Szmuel Leman at ul. Tłomackie 5 on 3.08.1941.
- ***Description:*** original, printed matter, Yiddish, 135×89 mm, damages and losses of text, ss. 1, pp. 1.

b)

- 03.[1942], Warsaw Ghetto
- Artists' Inn [Gospoda Artystów] (ul. Orla 6), Invitation to special literary-artistic evening of Jakub Rajzenfeder in 7.03.[1942]
- Appearing: Sz. Stupnicki, J. [Jehoszua] Perle, Al. Cajtlin, I. Bernsztajn, J. [Jacek] Lewi, Z. Zeligfeld, Ester Goldinberg, I. Zaks' folk choir, Diana Blumenfeld, Dawid Zajderman, Abraham Kurc, H. Diksztajn.
- ***Description:*** original, printed matter, Yiddish, 96×138 mm, ss. 1, pp. 1.

## Other Jewish Institutions and Organizations

### 240. RING. II/178. Mf. ŻIH—797; USHMM—52.

a)

- Before 13.10.1940, Warsaw
- "Melody Palace" (Rymarska 12), Invitation to "Matinée of humor, dance and song" on 13.10.[1940] with participation of: Henryk Ładosz, Basia Bitner, Wanda Cesarska, Fr. Mann, W. Śnieżyński, Zdz. Żadeyko, Leopold Rubinstein, Stefan Bober, Piotrowski, and Maksymczuk.
- ***Description:*** original printed matter, Polish, loose, 157×212 mm, ss. 1, pp. 1.

Invitation printed at the B. Pardecki and Co. Graphics, Warsaw, ul. Żelazna 56.

b)

- Date unknown, Warsaw Ghetto
- "Na Pięterku" Kawiarnia [On the Mezzanine Coffeehouse] (Nowolipki 29), Invitation to program entitled "Znicz [Torch] on the Mezzanine" with participation of: Michał Znicz, Irena Prusicka, Maria Dwoińska, Józef Kinelski, Maria Hinterhoff, Irena Drybińska, Zygmunt Szklar and Izrael Weisfeld.
- ***Description:*** original, printed matter, Polish, 113×155 mm, ss. 1, pp. 1.

Invitation printed at A. Kejzman (ul. Leszno 24)
Doc. presumably from Ring. I [?]

### 241. RING. II/279. Mf. ŻIH—800; USHMM—55.

- 7.01.1943 [?], Warsaw Ghetto
- Announcement: "We serve dinners, breakfasts, and suppers, Nalewki 33, apt. 89, gate 2, II floor [2 brama II piętro]."
- ***Description:*** original, handwritten manuscript, ink, Polish, 138×125 mm, ss. 1, pp. 1.

At bottom notation (handwritten manuscript—LEG*, ink) in Yiddish: "on 7 January 1943."
See *Archiwum Ringelbluma*, p. 156 (summary).

## *ACCOUNTS (DIARIES, CHRONICLES, MEMOIRS) ABOUT THE WARSAW GHETTO*

### 242. RING. II/170. Mf. ŻIH—795; USHMM—50.

- After 07.1942, Warsaw Ghetto
- Dawid Bryner, Account entitled "Shabrovnikes" [Looters]
- Author (age 18), son of a Warsaw carpenter (ul. Skaryszewska 11), after loss of entire family during action in 1942, took up looting, together with his friend Malina Kaufman.
- ***Description:*** transcript, handwritten manuscript, ink, Yiddish, 223×355 mm, ss. 2, pp. 3.

Index: Perla Bryner, sister of Dawid
Printed material (photocopy in Polish translation): *Archiwum Ringelbluma*, pp. 153–154, 344–346.

### 243. RING. II/494.

- 6.01.1943, Warsaw Ghetto
- B.G., Account entitled "Dullness of the moment" (6.01.1943)
- Reflections on the situation of Jews in the vestigial ghetto in Warsaw.
- ***Description:*** original, handwritten manuscript, ink, Polish, 210×298 mm, ss. 1, pp. 1.

Text dedicated by the authoress [?] NN. ("To the Doctor" [Emanuel Ringelblum?]).
Document was not entered into the old inventory and was found among the materials of the group of loose fragments (rozsypu) of Ring. I (see T. Epsztein's essay).

### 244. RING. II/205. Mf. ŻIH—797; USHMM—52. RING. II/207. Mf. ŻIH—798; USHMM—53.

- 28.08–2.09.1942, Warsaw Ghetto
- [Lejzor Czarnobroda?], Account of the liquidation action of the Warsaw Ghetto and diary (22.07–2.09.1942)
- Author, employee of a workshop [OBW (Ostbau-werke?), residential buildings inter alia at ul. Miła 58]; events preceding and the first days of the action; mood reigning among the people rescued from selection, work in the workshops, blockades; bombardment of the ghetto by Soviet air force.
- ***Description:*** Ring. II/205—original, handwritten manuscript, notebook, pencil, Polish, 145×205 mm, sewn, ss. 16, pp. 18; Ring. II/207—original, handwritten manuscript, pencil, Polish, 145×205 mm, ss. 14, pp. 24.

Ring. II/205 includes description regarding the days: 22.07–28.07.1942; Ring. II/207: 1–2.09.1942.

On the cover of Ring. II/207 notation (in a different handwriting, pencil): "Mr. Czarnobroda."

Index: Prof. [Franciszek] Raszeja, physician from Poznań, on 21.07.1942 was shot in the Warsaw Ghetto during a medical consultation in the apartment [of the antiquarian Abe Gutnajer] (ul. Chłodna [6]), see PSB, vol. 30, p. 605], Wacławski, manager in a workshop.

Published: *Archiwum Ringelbluma*, pp. 111–120 (Ring. II/205: 22.07–28.08.1942); BŻIH, no. 62/1967, pp. 143–148 (Ring. II/207: 1–2.09.1942).

## 245. RING. II/209. Mf. ŻIH—798; USHMM—53.

- 08–09.1942, Warsaw Ghetto
- Anna [Grasberg-Górna] (born 8.08.1906), Diary (25.08–4.09.1942) and correspondence (08–09.1942)
- Author, employee of the workshop of OBW, describes work within the ghetto and outside the ghetto (cemetery) (trade with Poles). Encl. two letters of 30.08. and 6.09.1942 to NN. (Maria) (so-called Aryan side), with whom the author's daughter, Rika, stayed (request for care for the child and for aid for the authoress and her mother in getting out of the ghetto).
- ***Description:*** original (letters: transcript), handwritten manuscript, ink, Polish, part of diary in stenographic notation, 159×198 mm, ss. 8, pp. 13.

According to Ruta Sakowska, Anna Grasberg-Górna; see *Archiwum Ringelbluma*, p. 120 (summary).

Published: BŻIH, no. 71–72/1969, pp. 140–144 (fragment); Diary: *Archiwum Ringelbluma*, pp. 107–110 (entries of 27–28.08.1942); Correspondence: *Archiwum Ringelbluma*, pp. 168–169, 171–173.

Index: Miller, Dals, Wentla, Fröhlich, team leader of Order Service, Siennickis, Hulanickis, Kintoffówna

## 246. RING. II/237. Mf. ŻIH—799; USHMM—54. RING. II/287. Mf. ŻIH—800; USHMM—55.

- 11–12.1942, Warsaw Ghetto
- [Jechiel Górny], Diary (4.11.–21.12.1942)
- Current events in the Warsaw Ghetto (inter alia behavior of the Order Service); information received from fugitives from other ghettos (e.g., from Kraków and Sandomierz); detailed description of events, selections, street executions, excerpts from newspapers, workshops, rumors.
- ***Description***: Ring. II/237—original, handwritten manuscript (JG*i U*), notebook, ink, Polish, Yiddish, 160×198 mm, sewn, ss. 12, pp. 17; Ring. II/287—original, handwritten manuscript (U*), ink, Yiddish, 143×204 mm, sewn, ss. 15, pp. 27.

Ring. II/237: on p. 1 (cover) notation in Yiddish (handwritten manuscript—LEG* [?], pencil): "1. Górny."

Ring. II/287: on p. 1 (cover) notation w Yiddish (handwritten manuscript—LEG*[?], pencil): "2. Górny" and "Bibersztajn, Kacyzne."

Ring. II/237 contains entries from the period: 4–10.11.1942; Ring. II/287: 10.11–21.12.1942.

Ring. II/237, see *Archiwum Ringelbluma*, p. 157 (summary).

Ring. II/237: Published in BFG, vol. IV, nr. 1/1951(fragments); *Selected Documents*, pp. 94–101.

Ring. II/287: Published: *Selected Documents*, pp. 86–94.

Index: Offerman; Hochman, carpenter of OBW; Sztiler, official of OBW; Rozenberg, factory guardsman; Dr. Jabłoński of OBW; Grinberg of OBW; Kirszenbaum, employee of OBW, killed in the house at ul. Miła 52; Herszkowicz of OBW; Gilde of OBW; three Suchecki brothers were killed for smuggling meat at ul. Franciszkańska 22 (26.11.1942), [Izrael] First (age 36) (ul. Muranowska 40), employee of Jewish Council, shot on 29.11.1942 by an unknown perpetrator [see *Czerniaków*, p. 72]; F. Salbe of OBW

## 247. RING. II/288. Mf. ŻIH—800; USHMM—55.

- 28.01.1943, Warsaw Ghetto
- [Jechiel Górny], Account entitled "Aktsye no. 2" [Action nr. 2] (28.01.1943)
- Description of the January action to liquidate the Warsaw Ghetto during 18–28.01.1943 (author lived at ul. Gęsia 30, worked at the site on ul. Leszno, information about the attitude of the young people).
- ***Description:*** original, handwritten manuscript (U*), pencil, Yiddish, 151×196 mm, sewn, ss. 8, pp. 8.

Published: BFG, vol. IV, no. 1/1951, pp. 88–91; *Selected Documents*, pp. 591–594.

Index: Józef Landau, extracted from Umschlagplatz (01.1943); Aleksander Landau, escaped on the way to Umschlagplatz (01.1943); Chaim Srebrnik, escaped from transport to Treblinka; Emilka Landau, daughter of Aleksander, killed during the resistance of the Haluts and Ha-Shomer young people (01.1943); Liberman, perished (01.1943); I. [Icchak] Giterman, killed 18.01.1943 at ul. Miła 69; Fogel, took money from Jews in hiding (ul. Miła 64)

## 248. RING. II/183. Mf. ŻIH—797; USHMM—52.

- 24.04.1941, Warsaw Ghetto
- Kik. [?], Accounts about the lawlessness of the Lagerschutz (camp guards) in the Warsaw Ghetto (24.04.1941)
- Theft and swindling of goods.
- ***Description:*** original, handwritten manuscript,

pencil, Polish, Yiddish, 220×204, 207×124 mm, ss. 3, pp. 5.
Index: S[econd-]lieut[enant] D. Reichman of "13"

## 249. RING. II/208. Mf. ŻIH—798; USHMM—53.

- 08–10.1942, Warsaw Ghetto
- [Menachem Mendel Kohn], "Togbukh" [Diary]
- Author, employee of a workshop, description of events in the Warsaw Ghetto (6.08–1.10.1942), Information about transport of Rabbi [Szymon] Huberband and his wife to Treblinka (18.08.1942).
- ***Description:*** original, handwritten manuscript (MK*), ink, Yiddish, 97×324, 146×185, 145×203, 103×270 mm, ss. 18, pp. 19.
  See *Archiwum Ringelbluma*, p. 121 (summary).
  Published: *Selected Documents*, pp. 80–86.
  Index: Dir. Bloch, Dr. Ringelblum, Cukierman

## 250. RING. II/282. Mf. ŻIH—800; USHMM—55.

- 5.11.1942, Warsaw Ghetto
- [Menachem Mendel Kohn], "Lezikorn unzer gelibtn fraynd, Oyneg-Shabes khaver, horav Shimen Huberband" [In memory of our beloved friend, member of Oyneg Shabes, Rabbi Shimon Huberband]
- Inf. about the works of Huberband in the Oyneg Shabes group; on 18.08.1942 he was transported together with his wife and workers (1,670 people) from the brushmakers workshop to Treblinka.
- ***Description:*** original, handwritten manuscript (MK*), ink, Yiddish, 165×252 mm, ss. 4, pp. 4.
  See *Archiwum Ringelbluma*, p. 130 (summary).
  Published: *Selected Documents*, pp. 54–57; *Kiddush Hashem*, pp. 107–109.

## 251. RING. II/174. Mf. ŻIH—795; USHMM—50.

a)

- 26.03.1942, Warsaw Ghetto
- [Abraham Lewin?], Diary (Entry entitled "In eyn halbe sho . . ." [In a half-hour . . .] (26.03.1942)
- Miscellaneous data (accounts) concerning: Wąwolnice (22.03.1942 slaughter of ca. 90 Jews), Słonim (liquidation action), Zduńska Wola (hanging of 10 Jews), Łęczyca, Bieżuń, Izbica Lubelska.
- ***Description:*** original, handwritten manuscript (Ś*), ink, Yiddish, 141×222 mm, ss. 2, pp. 2.
  Published: BŻIH no. 3–4/1956, pp. 169–170; A. Lewin, *A Cup of Tears. A Diary of the Warsaw Ghetto*, edited by Antony Polonsky, Oxford 1988, pp. 61–62.

b)

- 05.1942, Warsaw Ghetto
- [Abraham Lewin?], Diary (Entries entitled "Gehert-gezen" [Heard-seen]) 9.05–13.05.1942.
- Miscellaneous data (accounts), concerning: Ostrowiec (several hundred fatal victims), Hanka Tauber, daughter of Dr. Meir Tauber, freed from prison after 7 months; plan to displace beggars and street children from the Warsaw Ghetto; jobs for women in the Warsaw Ghetto; roundup on the "Aryan" side in Warsaw at Karcelak (12.05.1942); scenes from the life of the Warsaw Ghetto.
- ***Description:*** original, handwritten manuscript (Ś*), ink, Yiddish, 155×196, minor damages and losses of text, ss. 4, pp. 8.
  Index: Dr. [Zofia Sara] Syrkin-Binsztejnowa
  Published: BFG, vol. V, no. 4/1952, pp. 22–68; BŻIH, no. 3–4/1956, pp. 170–175; A. Lewin, *A Cup of Tears. A Diary of the Warsaw Ghetto*, edited by Antony Polonsky, Oxford 1988, pp. 65–72.
  HWC contains other fragments of the diary of Abraham Lewin [?]; see Ring. I/988.

c)

- 1942, Warsaw Ghetto
- [Abraham Lewin], Diary (fragment)
- Analysis of the Jewish people's self-evaluation [autooceny].
- ***Description:*** original, handwritten manuscript (Ś*), ink, Yiddish, 150×198 mm, ss. 1, pp. 2.
  Sheet has author's pagination: pp. 28–29. Possible that the sheet is the final fragment of doc. from HWC 32/6 (handwritten manuscript, ink, Yiddish, ss. 26, pages numbered 3–27, missing pp. 1–2 and ending).
  Index: Śliwiński

## 252. RING. II/202. Mf. ŻIH—797; USHMM—52.

- 08.1942–16.01.1943, Warsaw Ghetto
- [Abraham Lewin], Diary 11.08.1942–16.01.1943 (missing beginning)
- First liquidation action in the Warsaw Ghetto.
- ***Description:*** original, handwritten manuscript (Ś*), ink, pencil, Hebrew, 95×155, 150×195, 104×254, 105×302 mm, missing pages (pp. 1–12), ss. 53, pp. 106.
  Pp. 35–38 written on paper with the inscription: "Kalisz, dnia. . . . 193. . . . ul. K. Pułaskiego 11."
  Pp. 1–12, including description of events from 22.07.1942 to 10.08.1942 disappeared after 1955.
  Published: BFG, vol. VII, no. 1/1954, pp. 42–99; no. 2–3/1954, pp. 210–240; BŻIH, no. 21/1957, pp. 136–137; no. 22/1957, pp. 85–114; no. 23/1957, pp. 71–79; no. 24/1957, pp. 42–55; no. 25/1958, pp. 119–130; A. Lewin, *A Cup of Tears. A Diary of the Warsaw Ghetto*, edited by Antony Polonsky, Oxford 1988, pp. 152–242.

## 253. RING. II/173. Mf. ŻIH—795; USHMM—50.

- 02–05.1942, Warsaw Ghetto
- NN. (Margalit [Emilia (?)]), Diary and notes. (14/15.02–9.05.1942)
- Author (age 17), from a well-to-do family, describes personal feelings and meditations. Encl. note entitled "Working youth" with thesis for discussion or analysis concerning the fates of young people in the Warsaw

Ghetto; names mentioned: Sarna, Ludwik, Jonatan, Oliwa, Irka, Izrael.
- *Description:* original, handwritten manuscript, ink, pencil, Polish, 221×354 mm, ss. 2, pp. 3.
  Author of the doc. could be Margalit (Margolit) Landau (born 1925), daughter of the director of the workshop of OBW in the ghetto, Aleksander Lejb Landau. Margalit Landau was an active member of Ha-Shomer Ha-Tsair and ŻOB; see *Archiwum Ringelbluma*, p. 36

## 254. RING. II/245. Mf. ŻIH—799; USHMM—54.

- After 10.1942, Warsaw Ghetto
- [Jehoszua Perle], Account "4580"
- Reflections of a workshop employee, who has a "certificate of life" [lebns-shayn] in the Warsaw Ghetto.
- *Description:* original, handwritten manuscript (JP*), ink, Yiddish, 120×193 mm, ss. 19, pp. 19.
  Published: BFG, vol. V, no. 3/1952, pp. 53–62; *Tsvishn lebn un toyt* [Between Life and Death], ed. B. Mark, Warsaw 1955, pp. 142–149; *Ghetto. Berichte aus dem Warschauer Ghetto 1939–1945*, Berlin 1966, pp. 179–187; *Archiwum Ringelbluma*, pp. 223–228; *Selected Documents*, pp. 662–668; David Roskies, ed., *The Literature of Destruction* (Philadelphia, 1988), pp. 450–454.

## 255. RING. II/201. Mf. ŻIH—797; USHMM—52.

- Before 10.12.1942, Warsaw Ghetto
- NN. (Noske) [Natan Smolar?], Recollections (1941–1942)
- Author from Zambrow, fates of immediate family (mother, sisters: Etla, Estera, Chana, brother Herszel), stay in Białystok, departure to Warsaw, liquidation action in the Warsaw Ghetto, loss of wife and daughter (Estera and Nikełe—age 3) (7.08.1942), selection on 6.09.1942. Recollections addressed to sister: Polin (Pesza) Dajczman, 1468 Leyland Avenue, Bronx, New York.
- *Description:* original, handwritten manuscript, pencil, Yiddish, 157×200 mm, ss. 12, pp. 11.
  On the reverse of p. 1 notation in Yiddish (LEG*, pencil): "10.12.1942."
  Published: *Archiwum Ringelbluma*, pp. 134–139.
  Index: Felka and Rutka Fajnlicht, Dr. R. [Emanuel Ringelblum ?]

## 256. RING. II/289. Mf. ŻIH—800; USHMM—55.

- 09-1942–01.1943, Warsaw Ghetto
- [Perets Opoczyński (Opotshinski)], "Varshever geto-khronik" [Warsaw Ghetto chronicle]
- Description of current events in the period 1[3].09.1942 to 5.01.1943 (first liquidation action, selections in the workshops, blockades, news of other ghettos, daily life, dance for children 28.12.1942 at ul. Miła 13, robbery and murder at ul. Miła 46).
- *Description:* original, handwritten manuscript (OP*), notebooks (6), ink, Yiddish, 152×196, 147×209, 144×204, 146×203, 187×145, 210×146 mm, sewn, ss. 87, pp. 163.
  On p. 1 (notebook 5, cover) notation in Yiddish (pencil): "Opoczyński" [Opotshinski].
  See *Archiwum Ringelbluma*, p. 155 (summary).
  Published: *Selected Documents*, pp. 101–111 (fragment concerns 09.1942).
  Index: Brekman [?], attorney, shot on the "Aryan" side; Samuel Fiber of Ha-Shomer, shot in 09.1942; Kefman, Kopel Kinigsberg of Lublin, prisoner of Pawiak; Ali [Eli, Eliasz] Gutkowski, historian, taken during blockade of the carpenters workshop on ul. Gęsia, managed to free himself; Mosze Świec, carpenter, and his wife and children on 13.09.1942 were sent to Treblinka; Blumenfeld, rabbi, killed during blockade (09.1942); Hensel of OBW; Kasparek of OBW; Gajze of *Haynt*, journalist, committed suicide (09.1942); Wajn, poison dealer; [Jakub] Lejkin, chief of Order Service, shot on the street 29.10.1942; Czaplicki of Order Service, wounded 29.10.1942; Dr. Jabłoński; the Suchecki brothers killed at Franciszkańska 22; [Izrael] First of the Jewish Council (ul. Muranowska 24), killed probably by Jews [see *Czerniaków*, p. 72]; Szepsl[?], master carpenter; Walter, killed 23.12.1942; Bibersztejn, shot 25.12.1942 by sentry Brener; Kadiszewicz, shot 25.12.1942 by sentry Brener; Klotzermeyer, German, murderer

## 257. RING. II/227. Mf. ŻIH—798; USHMM—53.

- 10–12.1942, Warsaw Ghetto
- [Emanuel Ringelblum], Notes (10–12.1942)
- Inf. regarding the first liquidation action in the Warsaw Ghetto. Lists of names.
- *Description:* original, handwritten manuscript (ER*), notebook, ink, pencil, Yiddish, 150×192 mm, ss. 41, pp. 57.
  See *Archiwum Ringelbluma*, p. 241 (summary).
  Published: BFG, vol. V, no. 3/1952, pp. 32–52 (fragments); *Kronika getta*, pp. 404–428 (with the exception of loose notes and notes on covers).

## 258. RING. II/228. Mf. ŻIH—798; USHMM—53.

- 5.12.1942, Warsaw Ghetto
- [Emanuel Ringelblum], Note entitled "Di sine tsu der politsey" [Hatred toward the police] (5.12.1942)
- Role of the Order Service during the first liquidation action in the Warsaw Ghetto.
- *Description:* original, handwritten manuscript (ER*), ink, Yiddish, 157×198 mm, ss. 3, pp. 6.
  Manuscript written on ss. of a record book (of vaccinations) from a medical clinic [?], before 1939. (See Ring. II/230, II/231, II/232, II/234.)

See *Archiwum Ringelbluma*, p. 241 (summary).
Published: BFG, vol. IV, no. 1/1951, pp. 85–87; *Kronika getta*, pp. 428–431.
Index: [Jakub] Lejkin, Kalman Zylberberg

## 259. RING. II/229. Mf. ŻIH—798; USHMM—53.

- 24.12.1942, Warsaw Ghetto
- [Emanuel Ringelblum], "Baheltenishn" [Hideouts] (24.12.1942)
- About hideouts, shelters, and bunkers in the Warsaw Ghetto (after 07.1942).
- ***Description:*** original, handwritten manuscript (ER*), notebook, ink, pencil, Yiddish, 145×200 mm, ss. 14, pp. 17.

See *Archiwum Ringelbluma*, p. 242 (summary).
Published: *Kronika getta*, pp. 436–441.

## 260. RING. II/230. Mf. ŻIH—798; USHMM—53.

- 14–15.12.1942, Warsaw Ghetto
- Emanuel Ringelblum, Notes. (14–15.12.1942)
- Titles of sketches: "Mir veln blaybn oder nisht?" [Will we remain or not?] (14.12.1942); "Galokhim viln rateven yidishe kinder" [Priests want to save Jewish children] (14.12.1942); "Aseres ha-shvotim" [The Ten Tribes] (15.12.1942); "Shtivl, shtivl" [Boots, boots]; "Zayer perfidye" [Their perfidy].
- ***Description:*** original, handwritten manuscript (ER*), ink, Yiddish, 155×198 mm, ss. 20, pp. 39.

See *Archiwum Ringelbluma*, p. 242 (summary).
Published: BFG, vol. V, no. 3/1952, pp. 32–52 (fragments: "Boots, boots," "Their perfidy"); *Kronika getta*, pp. 431–436, 441–447.
Manuscript written in a record book (of vaccinations) from a medical clinic [?], before 1939 [?] with lists of patients' names (children). (See Ring. II/228, II/231, II/232, 234.)

## 261. RING. II/231. Mf. ŻIH—798; USHMM—53.

- After 07.1942, Warsaw Ghetto
- [Emanuel Ringelblum], Notes containing lists of names of Jewish authors, scholars, journalists, attorneys, painters, rabbis, public activists, and others murdered during the first liquidation action of the Warsaw Ghetto.
- ***Description:*** original, handwritten manuscript (ER*) (additions in another handwriting: LEG* and NN.), ink, pencil, Polish, Yiddish, 126×139, 103×157, 247×303 mm, ss. 14, pp. 24.

Notes written on pieces of paper of various origins, e.g., label of fruit wine: "Santos" of the "Oryginał" Wines and Mead Producer of Warsaw (printed matter, Polish); bill of the Wholesale Store of Fashionable and Lace Merchandise "Freidkin and Lewit" [Hurtowego Składu Towarów Modnych i Koronkowych "Freidkin i Lewit"] in Warsaw (ul. Długa 50) (before 1915, printed matter, Polish, Russian); advertisement sheet from a notebook (before 1939, printed matter, Polish); sheet from an accounting ledger: Accounting "Hero" [Księgowość «Hero»] (before 1939, printed matter, Polish); ss. from a record book (of vaccinations) of a medical clinic [?], before 1939. (See Ring. II/228, II/230, II/232, II/234.).
According to E.R. (*Kronika*, p. 470), Icchak Giterman made additions to the lists of victims in his presence.

## 262. RING. II/232. Mf. ŻIH—798; USHMM—53.

- 12.1942, Warsaw Ghetto
- [Emanuel Ringelblum], "Vi azoy iz untergegangen di yidishe inteligents fun Varshe?" [How did the Jewish intelligentsia of Warsaw perish?] (12.1942)
- Fate of authors, poets, journalists, public activists during the first liquidation action of the Warsaw Ghetto.
- ***Description:*** original, handwritten manuscript (ER*), ink, Yiddish, 156×198, 214×265 mm, ss. 25, pp. 46.

Manuscript written on ss. from a recordbook (of vaccinations) of a medical clinic [?], before 1939. (See Ring. II/228, II/230, II/231, II/234.).
See *Archiwum Ringelbluma*, p. 242 (summary).
Published: *Kronika getta*, pp. 447–467.

## 263. RING. II/233. Mf. ŻIH—798; USHMM—53.

- Before 1.01.1943, Warsaw Ghetto
- [Emanuel Ringelblum], Notes entitled "O-Sh." [Oyneg Shabes]
- Genesis, organization of the group's work and development of the underground archive of the Warsaw Ghetto. Attached note of 1.01.1943 (inf. about an article from *Schwarze Korps*).
- ***Description:*** original, handwritten manuscript (ER*), notebook, ink, Yiddish, 155×198 mm, sewn, ss. 33, pp. 54.

See *Archiwum Ringelbluma*, p. 242 (summary).
Published: *Kronika getta*, pp. 469 (note of 1.01.1943), 470–494. *Selected Documents*, pp. 2–21.

## 264. RING. II/234. Mf. ŻIH—798; USHMM—53.

- After 18.01.1943, Warsaw Ghetto
- [Emanuel Ringelblum], Note entitled "Itskhak Giterman"
- Profile of the Director of the headquarters of the Joint in Poland, who was shot on 18.01.1943.
- ***Description:*** original, handwritten manuscript (ER*), ink, Yiddish, 157×198 mm, ss. 1, pp. 1.

Manuscript written on a sheet from a record notebook (of vaccinations) from a medical clinic [?], before1939. (See Ring. II/228, II/230, II/231, II/232.).
See *Archiwum Ringelbluma*, p. 156 (summary).
Published: *Kronika getta*, p. 470.

**265. RING. II/236/1. Mf. ŻIH—798; USHMM—53.**

- Date unknown, Warsaw Ghetto
- [Emanuel Ringelblum], Notes
- Miscellaneous notes, addresses and surnames, Polish–Jewish relations, outlines for planned projects. Attached letter to Żytnicki (request for registration card for Szmul Mittelberg).
- ***Description:*** original, handwritten manuscript (ER*), ink, pencil, Polish, Yiddish, 67×98, 223×174 mm, ss. 13, pp. 21.

**266. RING. II/107. Mf. ŻIH—794; USHMM—49.**

- 1940, Warsaw Ghetto
- NN., Account "A bezukh bay di umgliklikhe kinder" [A visit to the unfortunate children]
- Inspection of the orphanage ("Foundlings home" [Central Jewish Sheltering Home (Główny Dom Schronienia Starozakonnych)], ul. Leszno 127 and ul. Wolska 18); comparison of the situation before the war and after 09.1939—high mortality of children from hunger and cold since autumn 1939.
- ***Description:*** original or transcript, typescript (handwritten additions, ink), Yiddish, 213×280 mm, minor damages and losses of text, ss. 3, pp. 3.

  According to Ruta Sakowska, the account's author could be Menachem Mendel Kon; see *Kronika getta*, p. 123.

  Published: *Selected Documents*, pp. 396–401; *Kronika getta*, pp. 123–129.

  Index: Dr. [Mojżesz, Mieczysław] Mayzner, Dr. [Aleksander] Kirszbraum, Dr. [Róża] Frydmanówna, [Szewel] Epstein, administrator of the Central Jewish Sheltering Home in Warsaw [Głównego Domu Schronienia Starozakonnych w Warszawie]

**267. RING. II/129. Mf. ŻIH—795; USHMM—50.**

- After 25.01.1940, Warsaw
- NN., Memoir of the first months of the occupation in Warsaw (09.1939–01.1940).
- Author, a young person, an office worker of the Jewish Community. Description of the siege of Warsaw in 1939, of the situation of the Jewish population after the Germans' invasion, Jewish Council (list of members' names), occupier's policies toward Jews (oppressive measures, mass executions, forced contributions, theft of property, census of the Jewish population—28.10.1939).
- ***Description:*** original or transcript, typescript (handwritten additions, pencil), Polish, 202×290 mm, ss. 15 pp. 15.

  Published: *Selected Documents*, pp. 131–143.

  Index: Janusz Korczak; P. Szoszkies; W. Rippel; Rabbi Ch. Zylbersztein; Rabbi Sz. D. Kahane; Frydman, sentenced to death by the Germans in Warsaw (autumn 1939); Maurycy Mayzel; Adam Czerniaków; [Marek] Lichtenbaum, member of the Jewish Council in Warsaw; Ł[azarz] Łabędź, member of the Jewish Council in Warsaw; Herman Szwartz, member of the Jewish Council in Warsaw; Szylom [Meszulem (Szylim) Ber] Kaminer, member of the Jewish Council in Warsaw; Rafał Gutman; Hilary Tempel, attorney, member of the Jewish Council in Warsaw; A[polinary] M. Hartglas, attorney, member of the Jewish Council in Warsaw; M. Kerner [Mojżesz Koerner], member of the Jewish Council in Warsaw; M. Idelman, member of the Jewish Council in Warsaw; R. Szafar, member of the Jewish Council in Warsaw; I[zrael] Milejkowski, member of the Jewish Council in Warsaw; prof. M[ajer] Bałaban, member of the Jewish Council in Warsaw; A[braham] Weiss, member of the Jewish Council in Warsaw; Dr. [Chaim] Szoszkies, member of the Jewish Council in Warsaw; A. Zygelbojm, member of the Jewish Council in Warsaw; Icie Majer [Icchak Meir] Lewin, member of the Jewish Council in Warsaw; A.B. Ekierman [Ber Ajzyk Ekerman], member of the Jewish Council in Warsaw; A[braham] Gepner, member of the Jewish Council in Warsaw; Edward [Eliasz] Kobryner, member of the Jewish Council in Warsaw; J[ózef] Jaszuński, member of the Jewish Council in Warsaw; B.W. [Baruch Wolf] Rozental, member of the Jewish Council in Warsaw; B[ernard] Zundelewicz, attorney, member of the Jewish Council in Warsaw; Engineer St[anisław] Szereszewski, member of the Jewish Council in Warsaw; B[olesław] Rozensztat, attorney, member of the Jewish Council in Warsaw; B[eniamin] Zabłudowski, member of the Jewish Council in Warsaw; [Abraham (Adolf)] Sztolcman, member of the Jewish Council in Warsaw; T[adeusz] Bart, member of the Jewish Council in Warsaw; H. [Rachmil Henryk] Glücksberg, member of the Jewish Council in Warsaw; J[akub] Berman, member of the Jewish Council in Warsaw; H. [Chil, Hil] Rozen, member of the Jewish Council in Warsaw; A [braham] Wolfowicz, member of the Jewish Council in Warsaw; Jerzy Graff, L[eopold] Kupczykier, member of the Jewish Council in Warsaw; Błoch; Attorney Kahanowicz; Dr. Szalman; Gamarnik; D. Piżyc; Fial; [Karl] Brand, Gestapo agent; [Gerhard] Mende, Gestapo agent; W. Rippel, attorney; Pinkus Izrael Zylberyng (born 6.07.1919) of Warsaw; Abram Ajzner, member of the Jewish Community in Łódź [GŻ w Łodzi], arrested 9.11.1939, perished; Henryk Akawie, member of the Jewish Community in Łódź, arrested 9.11.1939, perished; Edward Babiański, member of the Jewish Community in Łódź, arrested 9.11.1939, perished; Dr. Juliusz Damm, member of the Jewish

Community in Łódź, arrested 9.11.1939, perished; Stefan Glatter, member of the Jewish Community in Łódź, arrested 9.11.1939, perished; Włodzimierz Glass, member of the Jewish Community in Łódź, arrested 9.11.1939, perished; Samuel Hochenberg, member of the Jewish Community in Łódź, arrested 9.11.1939, perished; Ignacy Jaszuński, member of the Jewish Community in Łódź, arrested 9.11.1939, perished; Lejb Liberman, member of the Jewish Community in Łódź, arrested 9.11.1939, perished; Juliusz Loewsztein, member of the Jewish Community in Łódź, arrested 9.11.1939, perished; Dr. Leon Rubin, member of the Jewish Community in Łódź, arrested 9.11.1939, perished; Jonas Rozen, member of the Jewish Community in Łódź, arrested 9.11.1939, perished; Paweł Rozenfeld, member of the Jewish Community in Łódź, arrested 9.11.1939, perished; Dawid Stahl, member of the Jewish Community in Łódź, arrested 9.11.1939, perished; Dr. Jakub Szloser, member of the Jewish Community in Łódź, arrested 9.11.1939, perished; Robert Szwitgal, member of the Jewish Community in Łódź, arrested 9.11.1939, perished; Izydor Wajnsztein, member of the Jewish Community in Łódź, arrested 9.11.1939, perished; Kazimierz Andrzej Kott, Azriel Bojko, attorney-intern [aplikant adwokacki] (ul. Grzybowska 23)

### 268. RING. II/214. Mf. ŻIH—798; USHMM—53.

- After 22.10.1941, Warsaw Ghetto
- NN., Account entitled "Di iberzidlung" [The Resettlement]
- Preparations for reduction of the ghetto (threat of liquidation of "the little ghetto"). Encl. notes
- ***Description:*** original, handwritten manuscript (ChW*), pencil Yiddish, 104×153, 113×160 mm, minor damages and losses of text, ss. 3, pp. 6.

Page 1 written on the reverse of circular no. 28 [1941] of the Jewish Council in Warsaw, addressed to the Designated Plenipotentiary of the [Board] for Secured [Property] (Pełnomocnika Ko[misarycznego Zarządu] Zabezpieczonych [Nieruchomości]), address recorded in ink: "Ogrodo[wa]." (fragment, printed matter, Polish).

Page 2 written on the reverse of a circular letter of the Council of Chairmen of District Committees at the Department of Payments for the Benefit of Hosp[itals] and Health Service (Date unknown, duplicated typescript, Polish).

Page 3 written on the reverse of an envelope (fragment) addressed (ink) to S. Gutgeld (ul. Mariańska 8/5), stamp of Jewish Council in Warsaw: 16.12.1941.

Published: *Selected Documents*, pp. 79–80.

### 269. RING. II/259. Mf. ŻIH—799; USHMM—54.

- After 08.1942, Warsaw Ghetto
- NN., "Notitsen fun a shop arbeter" [Notes of a workshop laborer]
- Author, employee of the tailoring workshop [of Walter Caspar] Többens (ul. Gęsia 6); liquidation action, increase in the number of workers, blockades, removal to the Umschlagplatz (27.07–14.08.1942).
- ***Description:*** original, handwritten manuscript, pencil, Yiddish, 149×193 mm, ss. 5, pp. 9.

See *Archiwum Ringelbluma*, p. 134 (summary).
Published: *Selected Documents*, pp. 284–287.
Index: Perelman of the workshop of W.C. Többens, Filc of the workshop of W.C. Többens

### 270. RING. II/206. Mf. ŻIH—798; USHMM—53.

- After 6.09.1942, Warsaw Ghetto
- NN., Account of the selection on 6.09.1942 in the Warsaw Ghetto
- Author (ul. Miła), employee of the workshop. Selection in neighboring streets: Miła, Lubecki, and Niska.
- ***Description:*** original, handwritten manuscript, pencil, Polish, 158×195 mm, ss. 4, pp. 8.

Published: *Archiwum Ringelbluma*, pp. 140–143; BŻIH, no. 62/1967, pp. 149–152 (fragments).
Index: Fels, foreman of the workshop; Bergazyn, director of the workshop; [Jakub] Lejkin

### 271. RING. II/284. Mf. ŻIH—800; USHMM—55.

- After 7.09.1942, Warsaw Ghetto
- NN., Account about the first liquidation action of the Warsaw Ghetto (missing ending)
- Author from the workshop of Herman Brauer [?], course of the action (behavior of the Order Service, fight for life, selections, situation in Brauer's workshop).
- ***Description:*** original, handwritten manuscript, ink, Yiddish, 207×275 mm, ss. 6, pp. 12.

See *Archiwum Ringelbluma*, p. 134 (summary).
Published: *Selected Documents*, pp. 276–283.
Index: Kowal, manager in the workshop of Herman Brauer; Baskind; Grochowiak, manager in the shop of Herman Brauer; Stefański of Herman Brauer's workshop; Paszwa[?] of Herman Brauer's workshop; Kohn of Herman Brauer's workshop

### 272. RING. II/197. Mf. ŻIH—797; USHMM—52.

- After 10.1942, Warsaw Ghetto
- NN., Account entitled "Last stage of resettlement is death" (missing ending)
- Beginning of the first liquidation action of the Warsaw Ghetto (events preceding the action, first days of the action—22–23.07.1942).

- ***Description:*** transcript, typescript, Polish, 204×292, 211×297 mm, ss. 13, pp. 13.

  Doc. written on several (4) typewriters and on miscellaneous ss. of paper.

  This text is ascribed to Gustawa Jarecka; see *Archiwum Ringelbluma*, p. 264; *Dwa etapy*, p. 160; *Kronika getta*, p. 579.

  Published: BŻIH, no. 62/1967, pp. 137–142; *Archiwum Ringelbluma*, pp. 264–275; *Dwa etapy*, pp. 160–173; *Selected Documents*, pp. 703–708.

### 273. RING. II/203. Mf. ŻIH—797; USHMM—52.

- 12.1942, Warsaw Ghetto
- NN., Account of the liquidation action in the Warsaw Ghetto (7–11.09.1942) (fragment, missing beginning)
- Employee of the Factory Guard (Werkschutz) of the OBW workshop describes a selection in the OBW workshop and the blockade of employee housing at ul. Miła 61–64 (7–11.09.1942).
- ***Description:*** original, handwritten manuscript, notebooks, ink, Polish, 145×196 mm, sewn, missing notebook no. I, ss. 32, pp. 58.

  On the covers notation (pencil): "Notebook II," "Notebook III."

  Published: *Archiwum Ringelbluma*, pp. 144–151.

  Index: Abram Bortensztajn [Borensztajn?], taken from Miła to the Umschlagplatz on 8.09.1942.

### 274. RING. II/200. Mf. ŻIH—797; USHMM—52.

- 1942, Warsaw Ghetto
- NN., Account of the Warsaw Ghetto (fragment)
- Description of events preceding the first liquidation action (July 1942)
- ***Description:*** original or transcript, handwritten manuscript (LEG*), ink, Yiddish, 150×195 mm, missing pages, only pp. 60–62 have been preserved, ss. 3, pp. 3.

  See *Archiwum Ringelbluma*, p. 105 (summary).

  Index: Kagan, merchant from ul. Grzybowska

### 275. RING. II/180. Mf. ŻIH—797; USHMM—52.

- Date unknown, Warsaw Ghetto
- NN., Diary (4–18.05.[. . .]) (fragment)
- Scenes of life in the Warsaw Ghetto.
- ***Description:*** original, handwritten manuscript, ink, Yiddish, Polish, 144×215 mm, damages and losses of text, ss. 1, pp. 2.

  On p. 2 text in Polish (different handwriting, child's hand, ink): notation about Stefanek and Pela of the point for refugees [?].

### 276. RING. II/161. Mf. ŻIH—795; USHMM—50.

- Date unknown, Warsaw Ghetto
- NN., Account entitled "Punkt Leshno 2" [Point Leszno 2]
- Sanitary conditions, high mortality, lack of medical care; situation in the bathhouse for refugees at ul. Solna 4 (unheated room, cold water).
- ***Description:*** original, handwritten manuscript, ink, Yiddish, 146×186 mm, ss. 2, pp. 2.

## *CORRESPONDENCE IN THE WARSAW GHETTO*

### 277. RING. II/131. Mf. ŻIH—795; USHMM—50.

- 10.08.1940, Warsaw
- A. Ajzenman (Warsaw, Miła 40/32), Letter of 10.08.1940 to Icek Liberman (Biała near Goryniewa, district of Stolin [Polesie province]). Questions about health, greetings.
- ***Description:*** original, handwritten manuscript on a postcard, ink, Polish, 145×100 mm, ss. 1, pp. 2.

  No postage stamp or postmark. Letter was not sent.

### 278. RING. II/149. Mf. ŻIH—795; USHMM—50.

- Date unknown, Warsaw Ghetto
- Bebe [prison on ul. Gęsia?], Letter ("gryps": secret message smuggled into or out of prison) to NN. and Pola Elster (ul. Miła 54, apt. 21)
- Young girl writes to family and asks for help.
- ***Description:*** original, handwritten manuscript, pencil, Polish, 144×187 mm, minor damages and losses of text, ss. 1, pp. 2.

  On p. 1 notation: "[Pinia] Rzomska, room 11"; see Ring. II/253.

  Index: Gitler of "Centos," Brzeziński.

### 279. RING. II/222. Mf. ŻIH—798; USHMM—53.

- [08.1942], Warsaw Ghetto
- NN. (Cesia), Letters (2) to NN.
- Author transmits information about immediate family, whom [Menachem Mendel (?)] Kohn twice rescued from being transported from the Umschlagplatz.
- ***Description:*** original, handwritten manuscript, ink, Yiddish, 225×245 mm, ss. 2, pp. 4.

  See *Archiwum Ringelbluma*, p. 168 (summary).

### 280. RING. II/221. Mf. ŻIH—798; USHMM—53.

- 29.07.1942, Warsaw Ghetto
- Dawid ("Chasyd"), Letter of 29.07.1942 to S. [Szmul] Winter. Request for help.
- ***Description:*** original, handwritten manuscript, ink, Yiddish, 222×162 mm, ss. 1, pp. 1.

### 281. RING. II/155. Mf. ŻIH—795; USHMM—50.

- After 08.1941, Warsaw Ghetto
- Josef Ehrlich (ul. Nowolipki 24, apt. 46), Correspondence

  1) Letter dated 27.05.1941 to Sicherheitspolizei in Warsaw with request for aid in obtaining

consent to import lemons[11] into the Warsaw Ghetto;
2) Letter dated 27.05.1941 to Sicherheitspolizei in Warsaw with request for help in obtaining a permit to operate a movie theater in the Warsaw Ghetto;
3) Letter dated 8.08.1941 to Hauptzollamt West in Warsaw with request for consent to deal in tobacco products in the Warsaw Ghetto.

- ***Description:*** transcript, typescript, German, 209×297 mm, ss. 3, pp. 3.
  On the margins office-use initials NN. (ink); compare Ring. II/157.
  About Ehrlich, a Gestapo agent, see *Kronika getta*, pp. 331–332.

### 282. RING. II/156. Mf. ŻIH—795; USHMM—50.

- After 5.08.1942, Warsaw Ghetto
- Joseph Ehrlich (Leiter II des Ordnungsdienstes [Order Service]), Letter dated 5.08.1942 to Ostdeutsche Bautischlerei-Werkstaetten[12] GmbH (ul. Gęsia 30) to [Dir. Aleksander Lejb] Landau
- Recommendation regarding hiring of Abram Bialer (ul. Nalewki 11).
- ***Description:*** transcript [?], typescript, German, 208×147 mm, ss. 1, pp. 1.
  See *Archiwum Ringelbluma*, p. 42 (summary).

### 283. RING. II/167/2. Mf. ŻIH—795; USHMM—50.

- 24.04.[1942], Warsaw Ghetto
- I. Fiszbin (ul. Lubeckiego 17/39), Letter of 24.04.[1942] to J. Liberman (13, Ch. de Waterloo, Brusseles [Belgium]).
- Inf. about the illness of Fela and father, death of Josek and Mendel's entire family, request to send clothing.
- ***Description:*** original, handwritten manuscript on a postcard (Belgian), ink, Polish, 138×189 mm ss. 1, pp. 2.
  Letter was not sent out of the Warsaw Ghetto.

### 284. RING. II/257. Mf. ŻIH—799; USHMM—54.

- 22.09.1942, Warsaw Ghetto
- Frenkel, Rabbi (ul. Nowolipie 33, apt. 13), Letter of 22.09.1942 to D. [Dawid] Guzik (Warsaw Ghetto)
- Request for aid through Zonensztajn.
- ***Description:*** original, handwritten manuscript, ink, Yiddish, 218×189 mm, ss. 1, pp. 1.
  See *Archiwum Ringelbluma*, p. 176 (summary).

### 285. RING. II/277. Mf. ŻIH—800; USHMM—55.

- 23.01.1943, Warsaw Ghetto
- Marysia Gilde (Warsaw Ghetto), Letter of 23.01.1943 to Róża Zylbermanowa or Saba Faktorowa
- Inf. about liquidation of workshop, request for apartment for several days.
- ***Description:*** original, handwritten manuscript, ink, Polish, 156×199 mm, ss. 1, pp. 2.
  See *Archiwum Ringelbluma*, p. 203 (summary).

### 286. RING. II/157. Mf. ŻIH—795; USHMM—50.

- 6.02.1942, Warsaw Ghetto
- N. Gutlas (Gutglass) (ul. Grzybowska 18, apt. 30), Letter dated 6.02.1942 to [SS] Untersturmführer [Karl Georg] Brandt
- Request for intervention with [Józef Andrzej] Szeryński in the matter of allocation of bread.
- ***Description:*** original [?], handwritten manuscript, ink, German, 208×298 mm, ss. 2, pp. 1.
  At bottom signature (ink) in another handwriting and another form of the surname: "N. Gutglass."
  At bottom are office reference initials (archival [?]) NN. (ink); compare Ring. II/155.
  Letter presumably was not sent.

### 287. RING. II/241. Mf. ŻIH—799; USHMM—54.

- 1.01.1943, Warsaw Ghetto
- Chaim Kubartowski [Lubartowski ?] (pseudonym Szmueli), Letter of 1.01.1943 to Emanuel Ringelblum
- Request for acceptance of deposit of materials (letters and documents) for use. Attached materials absent. Letter sent out in own name and of friends: Bencjon Lichtenbaum (pseudonym Ben Cijon [Ben Tsiyon]) and Joshua Szwarcberg (pseudonym Yehoshua).
- ***Description:*** original, handwritten manuscript, ink, Hebrew, 156×179 mm, ss. 1, pp. 1.
  According to Ruta Sakowska, the letter's author was named Kowartowski; see *Archiwum Ringelbluma*, p. 202 (summary).
  Index: Oksenberg (Tel Aviv, Hakishon 45)

### 288. RING. II/226. Mf. ŻIH—798; USHMM—53.

- 4.09.[1942], Warsaw Ghetto
- A. Landau, Letter of 4.09.[1942] to G.H. Rabinowicz. Demand for return of money.
- ***Description:*** original, handwritten manuscript, ink, Yiddish, 157×95 mm, ss. 1, pp. 2.
  On the reverse notation in Yiddish (pencil): "They won't get money by threat and blackmail."
  See *Archiwum Ringelbluma*, p. 173 (summary).

### 289. RING. II/274/7. Mf. ŻIH—799; USHMM—54.

- After 21.12.1942, Warsaw Ghetto
- M. Micner (workshop of F. Schultz, Warsaw, ul. Nowolipki 29), Letter of 21.12.1942 to Jewish Council in Turobin

11. The Polish word *cytryna* might also refer to the etrog, the citrus fruit employed in the rituals of the autumn holiday of Sukkot.
12. Abbreviated OBW.

- Request for information about son Izaak Micner.
- ***Description:*** transcript, handwritten manuscript (LP*), pencil, Polish, 110×145 mm, ss. 1, pp. 2.
  On p. 1 notation in German: "return"; as well as postscript: "Your son Izaak Micner departed into the bosom of Abraham, er ist schon kaput. Council of Elders." [sic] Letter returned to Warsaw.
  Published: *Archiwum Ringelbluma*, pp. 200–201.

### 290. RING. II/224. Mf. ŻIH—798; USHMM—53.

- 08.1942, Warsaw Ghetto
- Lonia [Wyszyńska] (Warsaw Ghetto), Letters (4) of 22, 24, 25 and 26.08.1942 to husband I. (Icek) [Icchak] Wyszyński (ul. Gęsia 35a, apt. 67 or Zamenhofa 11).
- Inf. about the health of young son Abuś, work in the workshop [?], thanks for letter, money, food, request for further help.
- ***Description:*** original, handwritten manuscript., pencil, Polish, Yiddish, 95×154, 147×215 mm, ss. 6, pp. 11.
  On letter dated 24.08.1942 notation in Polish and Yiddish (pencil): "Letter was not finished due to the blockade of [the workshop of] Többens"; "22.08.42, Miss Cygielman, works Leszno 58, Emergency Rescue Ser[vice]."
  See *Archiwum Ringelbluma*, p. 168 (summary of part of doc.).
  Index: [Abraham] Sztolcman of the Jewish Council in Warsaw, Cygielmanowa, Hechtszajn, Goldin

### 291. RING. II/219/2. Mf. ŻIH—798; USHMM—53.

- 08.1942, Warsaw Ghetto
- NN., Letter to [Aleksander Lejb] Landau ("Ostdeutsche" [OBW], ul. Gęsia 30)
- Request for rescue from Umschlagplatz of Rabbi [Jechiel Meir] Blumenfeld with family, employed in the workshop of OBW.
- ***Description:*** original, handwritten manuscript, pencil, Polish, 290×139 mm, ss. 1, pp. 2.
  On p. 1 at bottom notation (pencil): "11.14."
  On p. 2 at top notation (H*, pencil): "[August 1942]."
  Published: *Archiwum Ringelbluma*, pp. 162–163 (photocopy).

### 292. RING. II/219/3. Mf. ŻIH—798; USHMM—53.

- 1942, Warsaw Ghetto
- NN., Letter to Mr. Mall [?]
- Request for help. Attached surnames and notation: Bluma Waser [Wasser] of Ostdeutsche [OBW]) IV p. 11; Blima Luftig of "Ursus"; [Mundle?] Szyfryn [of "Ursus"?], Jarome [?] Recenberg [of "Ursus"?], Izrael Rycenberg [Recenberg of "Ursus"?], Eugeniusz Finkelbrau [of "Ursus"?], Kajla Fryndman [of "Ursus"?].
- ***Description:*** original, handwritten manuscript (two handwritings), pencil, Polish, 74×113 mm, ss. 1, pp. 1.
  On p. 1 notation in Yiddish (LEG*, pencil): "from Umschlagplatz."
  Note: Jewish workers were employed in the firm "Ursus"; see Ring. II/246.

### 293. RING. II/120. MISSING ORIGINAL

- 1942, place unknown
- Letters to rabbis.
- ***Description:*** original or transcript, handwritten manuscript, Hebrew, Yiddish, ss. 3, pp. 5.

## *STUDIES (DRAFTS AND OUTLINES OF ESSAYS, SCIENTIFIC PAPERS, COMPOSITIONS, TABLES, NOTES)*

### 294. RING. II/169. Mf. ŻIH—795; USHMM—50.

- Date unknown, Warsaw Ghetto
- NN., "Draft of study ('Situation of the Jewish district in Warsaw in 1941 in numbers')"
- Titles of chapters of the study. Encl. "Draft of informational talk with experts of a certain occupation."
- ***Description:*** transcript (2 copies), typescript, Polish, 200×293 mm, minor damages and losses of text, ss. 2, pp. 4.

### 295. RING. II/193. Mf. ŻIH—797; USHMM—52.

- After 09.1942, Warsaw Ghetto
- NN., Study entitled "Tezn tsum barikht" [Points for report]
- Outline of study about preparations for and course of the liquidation action in Warsaw Ghetto in 1942.
- ***Description:*** original or transcript, handwritten manuscript (LEG*), pencil, Yiddish, 191×257 mm, ss. 2, pp. 4.
  See *Archiwum Ringelbluma*, p. 264 (summary).

### 296. RING. II/194. Mf. ŻIH—797; USHMM—52.

- After 09.1942, Warsaw Ghetto
- NN., Draft of study about the liquidation action of the Warsaw Ghetto (07–09.1942)
- Titles of chapters; calendar written from 6 to 26.09.1942, with marking of Yom Kippur.
- ***Description:*** original, handwritten manuscript (H*, LEG*), Polish, Yiddish, 156×217 mm, ss. 1, pp. 1.
  Published: *Archiwum Ringelbluma*, pp. 260–261 (photocopy).

### 297. RING. II/243. Mf. ŻIH—799; USHMM—54.

- Date unknown, Warsaw Ghetto
- NN., Prospectus of a work on workshops in Warsaw Ghetto.
- ***Description:*** original, typescript (additions, ink), Yiddish, 210×295 mm, ss. 2, pp. 2.
  Published: BŻIH, no. 71–72/1969, pp. 156–160; *Archiwum Ringelbluma*, pp. 239–240.

298. RING. II/242. Mf. ŻIH—799; USHMM—54.
- Date unknown, Warsaw Ghetto
- NN., Study entitled "Verkshuts" [Factory Guard]
- Prospectus of a work about the Jewish factory guard in the workshops.
- *Description:* original or transcript, typescript (additions in pencil), Yiddish, 210×295 mm, ss. 1, pp. 2.
  Published: BŻIH, no. 71–72/1969, pp.159–160; *Archiwum Ringelbluma*, pp. 237–238.

299. RING. II/158. Mf. ŻIH—795; USHMM—50.
- After 18.04.1942, Warsaw Ghetto
- "List of persons shot on the night of the 17th to the 18th of Ap[ril 1942]" in Warsaw Ghetto
- Names and surnames of victims, ages, home address as well as places where the bodies were found.
- *Description:* transcript [?], typescript, Polish, 209×299 mm, damages and losses of text, ss. 1, pp. 1.
  At bottom notation (ink): "51 people."
  Index: Frydman Mojsze (born 21.02.1905), ul. Miła 52/40 (ul. Miła 49); Szklarski Peretz (age 30), ul. Gęsia 87; Finkielstein Pinkus Matys (born 14.07.1904), ul. Gęsia; Stołowy Srul, ul. Gęsia 39 (ul. Gęsia corner of ul. Smocza); Stołowy (brother of Srul), ul. Gęsia 39 (ul. Gęsia corner of ul. Smocza); Ubfal Mordka (age 30), ul. Muranowska 13/26 (injured); Blustein Gdala (age 45), ul. Muranowska 13/26; Blajman Faniel, (age 48), ul. Zamenhofa 24; Blajman (wife of Faniel) (age 40), ul. Zamenhofa 24; Leruch Josef (age 60), janitor of house, ul. Wołyńska 2; Leruch Naftal (age 23), janitor's son, ul. Wołyńska 2; Hinenfeld Abram (age 40), ul. Miła 45/48 (ul. Miła 49); Rozen Izaak (ul. Miła 5); Lindner Mendel (born 1911), ul. Leszno 52 (ul. Mylna 9); Szerman Abram (age 50), ul. Nowolipie 49 (ul. Nowolipie 41); Kamień Hersz (age 52), ul. Leszno 27 (Karmelicka 25); Miński Chil (born 1893), ul. Nowolipie 18 (ul. Nowolipie 18); Folman Michał (born 1921), ul. Nowolipie 18 (ul. Nowolipie 18); Myśliborski Dyonizy (born 1891), ul. Nowolipie 18 (ul. Nowolipie 18); Spät Artur (age 35), ul. Nowolipie 18 (ul. Nowolipie 18); Lindenfeld Ludwik (age 30), ul. Elektoralna 32 (ul. Nowolipie 18); Szon Abram (age 22), ul. Nowolipie 5 (ul. Mylna); Kahan Moszek Mordka (born 16.03.1880), ul. Nalewki 23 (ul. Gęsia 1); Kahan Eliasz (age 56), ul. Nalewki 3 (ul. Gęsia 1); Neuding Jerzy (born 1906), ul. Biała 8 (ul. Solna 19); Tałasowicz Mojsze Lejb (age 30), ul. Nalewki 11 (ul. Nalewki 15); Cukierman Pejsach (age 42), ul. Muranowska 13 (ul. Muranowska 19); Klajnweksler, printer, ul. Nowolipie 62/13 (ul. Nowolipie 52); Goldberg Moszek, ul. Nowolipki 36 (ul. Nowolipki 34); Goldberg (wife of Moszek), ul. Nowolipki 36 (ul. Nowolipki 34); Frumak Izrael (born 25.11.1884), ul. Muranowska 29/55 (ul. Muranowska 33); Tekel, ul. Twarda 20 (ul. Ciepła/Twarda); Wajnberg (father), ul. Sienna 30 (ul. Prosta 12); Wajnberg (son), (ul. Prosta 12); Szajnfeld Jankiel, ul. Grzybowska 30 (injured); Rurman Szmulek, ul. Leszno 45 (ul. Żelazna 78); Szulc Aron (age 40), ul. Dzielna 34 (ul. Dzielna 34); Szulc Józio (age 10), ul. Dzielna 34 (ul. Dzielna 34); Goldberg Moszek (born 27.05.1904), ul. Leszno 35 (ul. Dzielna 19); Wajsbaum Beniamin (ul. Dzielna 19); Brzeziński Pinchos (born 1889), ul. Pawia 44/7 (ul. Dzielna 19); Wicher Anszel (born 1897), ul. Dzielna 5/3 (ul. Dzielna 19); Włodawer Lejb (born 1918), ul. Nalewki 27/53 (ul. Dzielna 1); Klin Szlama Moszek (born 17.04.1904), ul. Pawia 50a (ul. Dzielna 19); Kamień Abram (born 6.02.1918), ul. Leszno 27 (ul. Dzielna 19); Kurman O., ul. Dzielna 25 (ul. Dzielna 34); Olsztejn Majer (born 1885)

300. RING. II/192. Mf. ŻIH—836; USHMM—67.
- 15.11.1942, Warsaw Ghetto
- Report entitled "Liquidation of Jewish Warsaw"
- Description of the first liquidation action in the Warsaw Ghetto (from 22.07.1942), extermination camp in Treblinka, ghetto population statistics in the period 07–11.1942, lists of names of selected victims of the liquidation action; situation of the Jewish population outside Warsaw. Attached transcripts of documents: "Map of the ghetto of Warsaw November 1942" and map of the camp in Treblinka. Report prepared by underground organizations of the Warsaw Ghetto addressed to the Government of the Republic of Poland in London and to governments of allied nations.
- *Description:* original or transcript (2 copies and p.13 in 4 copies, p. 20 in 6 copies [4 copies originate from another transcript], p. 33 in 3 copies, p. 36 in 3 copies; third copy has significant damages and losses of text), typescript, handwritten manuscript, pencil, Polish, 215×143, 219×289 mm, ss. 106, pp. 106.
  Published: *Archiwum Ringelbluma*, pp. 275–320; BFG, vol. IV, nr. 2/1951, pp.177–234; BŻIH, no. 1/1951, pp. 59–126; *Selected Documents*, pp. 34–54 (fragment).

301. RING. II/196. Mf. ŻIH—797; USHMM—52.
- After 20.11.1942, Warsaw Ghetto
- NN., Study on the first liquidation action in the Warsaw Ghetto (07–09.1942)
- Organization and successive stages of the liquidation action, participation of the Order Service, special German units.
- *Description:* original, handwritten manuscript, pencil, Polish, 209×295, 223×353 mm, ss. 32, pp. 33.
  Text divided into chapters: 1) "First day of the resettlement action at Dzika 3"; 2) "Most

important turning points of the resettlement action in W[arsaw]"; 3) "Blockades"; 4) "Legal enunciations and their results"; 5) "External appearance of the ghetto during the displacement action"; 6) "Lublin group."

Published (fragment): *Archiwum Ringelbluma*, pp. 131–133; *Selected Documents*, pp. 691–696.

Index: Spodkowski, district officer of the Order Service [obwodowy SP], conducted resettlement of the point at ul. Dzika 3; Kucberg, Połaniecki, Ruta Goldwasser from Aleksandrów, departed from Umschlagplatz 22.07.1942; E. Cukier (age 17), saved herself during the first action; Sz. Knecht, escaped from Treblinka 23.07.1942 and returned to the Warsaw Ghetto; Engineer Brzeziński, district officer of Order Service, conducted loading of people into wagons; Gutgeld, district officer of Order Service, supervised blockades in the ghetto during the action; Wartski, district officer of Order Service, supervised blockades in the ghetto during the action; Kac, district officer of Order Service, supervised blockades in the ghetto during the action; Blaupapier, Fürstenberg, district officers of Order Service, supervised blockades in the ghetto during the action; Berek, Frajda and Sala Alterman (ul. Zamenhofa 36), transported to Treblinka during the action of 1942.

### 302. RING. II/198. Mf. ŻIH—797; USHMM—52.

- 09.1942, Warsaw Ghetto
- [Jechiel Górny], Study entitled "Khurbn Varshe" [Destruction of Warsaw]
- Course of the first liquidation action and of events during 21.07.1942—1.09.1942 (missing ending). Encl. outline of the study, notes, and calculations.
- ***Description:*** original, handwritten manuscript (U*), notebook, ink, pencil, Polish, Yiddish, 63×99, 88×208, 150×210 mm, ss. 22, pp. 17.

See *Archiwum Ringelbluma*, p. 237 (summary).

Published: *Selected Documents*, pp. 701–702 (fragment).

### 303. RING. II/199. Mf. ŻIH—797; USHMM—52.

- 31.08–09.1942, Warsaw Ghetto
- [Jehoszua Perle?], Study entitled "Khurbn Varshe" [Destruction of Warsaw]
- Crimes of Gestapo, posture of the Jewish Council, activity of the Order Service, tragedy of the ghetto's residents, hiring and work in the workshops.
- ***Description:*** original, handwritten manuscript (JP*), ink, Yiddish, 110×177 mm, ss. 132, pp. 132.

Author of the text: Yehoshua Perle; see *Archiwum Ringelbluma*, p. 217 (summary).

Published: BFG, vol. IV, no. 3/1951, pp. 101–140; vol. V, no. 3/1952, pp. 53–62; *Tsvishn lebn un toyt* [Between life and death], ed. B. Mark, Warsaw 1955, pp. 142–149; *Ghetto. Berichte aus dem Warschauer Ghetto 1939–1945*, Berlin 1966, pp. 187–227.

### 304. RING. II/239/2. Mf. ŻIH—799; USHMM—54.

- After 07.1942, Warsaw Ghetto
- [Hersz Wasser], Notes
- About the first liquidation action in the Warsaw Ghetto (attempts at resistance, lack of postal service, confiscation of parcels, lists of names of victims).
- ***Description:*** original, handwritten manuscript (H.W.*), ink, Polish, Yiddish, 142×217, 145×218 mm, ss. 4, pp. 5.

Two ss. written on invoice forms of the Wholesale Store of Fashion Goods and Lace Merchandise "Freidkin and Lewit" in Warsaw (ul. Długa 50) (before 1915, printed matter, Polish, Russian).

See *Archiwum Ringelbluma*, p. 130 (summary).

### 305. RING. II/204. Mf. ŻIH—797; USHMM—52.

- 12.1941 or 01.1942, Warsaw Ghetto
- Perec Opoczyński, Report entitled "Ba-leil afel. Mi-marot ha-geto" [On a dark night. From scenes of the ghetto]
- Scenes of life of the Warsaw Ghetto
- ***Description:*** original or transcript, typescript (additions, handwritten manuscript, ink), Hebrew, 224×298 mm, ss. 2, pp. 2.

Published: *Selected Documents*, pp. 650–653.

### 306. RING. II/211. Mf. ŻIH—798; USHMM—53.

- [II half of 1942], Warsaw Ghetto
- NN., Note about authors and musicians murdered during the first liquidation action in the Warsaw Ghetto
- Kalman Lis; Jakub Preker [Preger]; Jechiel Mojżesz [Apelbaum], journalist of *Moment*; [Marysia] Ajzensztadt, daughter of [Dawid]; [Dawid] Ajzensztadt, composer; Izrael Gladsztajn, musician; Jakub Gladsztajn, musician; [Adam] Furmański, director; NN. [Szmuel Hirszhorn?], journalist of *Nasz Przegląd*.
- ***Description:*** original, handwritten manuscript, pencil, ink, Yiddish, 189×156 mm, ss. 1, pp. 1.

See *Archiwum Ringelbluma*, p. 130 (summary).

### 307. RING. II/195. Mf. ŻIH—797; USHMM—52.

- After 10.1942, Warsaw Ghetto
- NN., Population statistics of the Warsaw Ghetto for the period from 22.07.1942 to 10.1942
- Tables and charts regarding changes in the number of people in the ghetto, the number of those "resettled" (on individual days 22.07–21.09.1942), those murdered during the "action," those left in the ghetto and the workshops.
- ***Description:*** original, handwritten manuscript, ink, pencil, Polish, 207×295, 207×286 mm, ss. 6, pp. 9.

See *Archiwum Ringelbluma*, p. 237 (summary).

### 308. RING. II/285. Mf. ŻIH—800; USHMM—55.

- 15.12.1942, Warsaw Ghetto
- NN., Study entitled "Demographic structure of the Jewish population remaining in Warsaw (according to the situation from the end of October 1942)" (15.12.1942)
- Analysis of the number and distribution of the population after the first liquidation action, "rate of resettlement" for various age and gender groups (tables, graph).
- ***Description:*** original or transcript, typescript, Polish, 208×295 mm, ss. 14, pp. 14.

See *Archiwum Ringelbluma*, p. 241 (summary).
Published: BŻIH, no. 37/1961, pp. 98–105.

### 309. RING. II/286. Mf. ŻIH—800; USHMM—55.

- After 11.1942, Warsaw Ghetto
- NN., Study entitled "Social phenomena in November 1942"
- Statistics of the Warsaw Ghetto: number of dinners issued (with division into various groups of population and institutions), kitchens, foreign gifts, welfare institutions for children, Order Service, provisioning, mail, mortality, number of patients in hospital, population change, forced labor.
- ***Description:*** original or transcript, typescript, Polish, 207×286 mm, ss. 1, pp. 2.

See *Archiwum Ringelbluma*, p. 155 (summary).
Published: BŻIH, no. 71–72/1969, pp. 148–151; *Selected Documents*, pp. 163–166.

### 310. RING. II/368. Mf. ŻIH—803; USHMM—58.

- 20.09.1941, Warsaw Ghetto
- NN., Note entitled "Talk at celebration on 20.09.[19]41"
- Concerns fate of children in the Warsaw Ghetto.
- ***Description:*** original, handwritten manuscript, ink, Polish, 208×296 mm, ss. 1, pp. 1.

### 311. RING. II/283. Mf. ŻIH—800; USHMM—55.

- 12.1942, Warsaw Ghetto
- NN., Article entitled "Le-sakanat ha-shmad" [About the danger of apostasy]
- Warning against placement of Jewish children in Catholic institutions, since there is a danger of their conversion to Christianity. Text dedicated to daughter Miriam Sara, transported on 5.09.1942.
- ***Description:*** original, handwritten manuscript, ink, Hebrew, 158×183 mm, ss. 5, pp. 5.

Text is signed with initials (with Hebrew letters): alef, hei, and khaf.
See *Archiwum Ringelbluma*, p. 152 (summary).
Published: *Selected Documents*, pp. 407–409.

### 312. RING. II/210. Mf. ŻIH—798; USHMM—53.

- Date unknown, Warsaw Ghetto
- NN., List of names of rabbis residing in the Warsaw Ghetto
- Name and surname, functions, places of origin and other data.
- ***Description:*** original or transcript (handwritten manuscript—two handwritings, ink), transcript (typescript), Hebrew, 157×198, 223×265, 208×298 mm, ss. 7, pp. 9.

There are minor differences between the transcript and the original; the transcript contains data about 129 names, while the original has 126.
See *Archiwum Ringelbluma*, p. 122 (summary).
Index: Alter Mosze Becalel, Góra Kalwaria; Alter Mendel, Kalisz, chairman of the Association of Rabbis in Poland; Alter Meir, son of the rabbi of Góra Kalwaria, Warsaw; Alter Abraham Mordechaj, Żychlin, murdered together and his wife; Ajbeszyc[13] Jakub, Zgierz; Adalberg Icchak Hirsz, Maków; Ajbeszyc Jehonan, Warsaw; Albek Icchak, Warsaw; Ajger Szlomo, Lublin; Albersztajn Icchak, Bielsk; Beer Dawid, Ozorków, vice chairman of the Assoc. of Rabbis in Poland; Bornsztajn Israel, Płońsk; Blaksztajn Berisz, Sobota; Bornsztajn Abraham, Kutno; Blomberg Bencyjon, Dobrzyń; Biderman Lejb, Warsaw, member of the [official Communal] Rabbinate; Blumenfeld Jechiel Meir, Warsaw, teacher at the Tachkemoni yeshiva; Biderman Icchak Dawid, Warsaw; Biderman, Warsaw; Glikson Hirsz, director of the Yeshiva Torat Chaim, Warsaw; Gutbrot, Nowy Dwór, son-in-law of the Gaon Chaim [Soloveitchik] of Brześć [Brisk, Brest-Litovsk]; Grinberg Mosze, Ostrołęka; Gibersztajn Mosze, Łomianki; Gezundhajt Jakub, Warsaw, grandson of the rabbi of Warsaw, secretary of the Association of Rabbis in Poland; Dancygier Icchak Mendel, Aleksandrów; Dancygier Abraham Chaim, Aleksandrów; Dancygier Israel, son of the rabbi, Aleksandrów; Gelenter Josef, Skierniewice; Horwic Chaim Eliezer, Bełchatów; Horwic Zelman, Wieluń; Horwic Icchak, Sanok; Huberband Szymon, Warsaw, member of the Rabbinate; Hajman Meir, Warsaw; Hochglober Josef, Warsaw, Ćmielów; Hochglober Szlome, Warsaw; Herc Mendel, Nowogródek, Warsaw; Herc Melech Pinkas, Krzepice; Hoffer Mendel, director of yeshiva, Warsaw; Warszawiak Pinchas, Warsaw,

13. German spelling: Eibeschütz, but since the document is in Hebrew there is no way to know how the name was spelled in Roman characters. Yiddish transliteration in English would be Aybeshits.

member of the Rabbinate; Wajngarten Szlome, Warsaw; Wajnberg Abraham, Warsaw, member of the Rabbinate; Weltfroid Szlome, Tomaszów; Żychliński Sidi, Stryków; Zawłodawer Aaron Naftali, Warsaw, member of the Rabbinate; Ziemba Eliezer, Wołomin; Zamczyk Jakub, Warsaw, member of the Rabbinate; Tob (Tow) Menachem Dawid, Kazimierz, Praga, died on the way; Tob (Tow) Jakub Naftali, Nowy Dwór, Zwoleń; Tob (Tow) Szmuel Icchak, Zwoleń; Tob (Tow) Jakub, Legionowo; Tob (Tow) Dawid, Wołomin; Tob (Tow) Mosze Lejb, Kazimierz; Jakubowicz Jechiel Mosze, Warsaw; Kac Icchak, Warsaw; Morgensztern Jakub Arie, Radzymin; Morgensztern Josef, Serock; Morgensztern Elimelech, Mszczonów; Michelsohn Hersz Jechezkiel, Warsaw, member of the Rabbinate; Majmin Efraim, Warsaw, member of the Rabbinate; Merker Szlomo, Warsaw, member of the Rabbinate; Morgensztern Meir, Warsaw; Mendelsohn Jakir, Warsaw; Nutkowicz Natan Nata, Rypin; Nojfeld Reuwen Lejb, Nowy Dwór, secretary of the Association of Rabbis in Poland; Nojfeld Berisz, Raciąż; Natan Mosze, Nadarzyn; Nomberg Hirsz Dawid, Zacisze (?); Srebrnik Icchak, Zakroczym; Srebrnik Mosze, Brodnica; Srebrnik Josef Hirsz, Golub, Zakroczym, Association of Rabbis; Elberg Abraham Natan, Błaszki; Fisz Josef Aszer, Stryków, Rabbi of Kock; Frydman Szamaj, Kraków; Finkel Mosze, Mir, son of the director of the yeshiva; Frydling Hirsz, Bliskowice (?), Warsaw; Fettman Eli, Warsaw, member of the Rabbinate; Fajgenbojm Iser, Warsaw; Cukerkorn Jehoszua Mordechaj, Lipno; Cuker Jerucham Fiszel, Piątków; Celniker Aaron, Warsaw; Cukert Jakub Dawid, Warsaw; Kohn Szlomo Lejb, Zgierz; Kalisz Jeremiasz, Łowicz; Karlin Aaron, Stolin; Kalisz Jeremiasz, Opole; Klejn Mosze Perec, Koło; Król Mordechaj Nusyn, Łódź, member of the Rabbinate; Kanał Icchak Meir, Warsaw, Błaszki, member of the Association of Rabbis in Poland; Kolbe Abraham, Lubicz; Kolbe Efroim, Warsaw; Klejner Dawid, Warsaw; Kestenberg Chaim, Wawer; Kac Natan Dawid, Warsaw; Rotszyld Mosze, Bieżuń; Rabinowicz Mordechaj Samuel, Białobrzegi; Rubinsztejn Elimelech, Nasielsk; Rabinowicz Chanoch Hirsz, Radomsko, killed with his wife at home; Rabinowicz Dawid Mosze, Radomsko, killed with his wife at home, director of yeshiva; Rogoźnicki Noach, Warsaw, member of the Rabbinate; Rabinowicz Jakub, Węgrów; Rozenfeld Berisz, Warsaw; Rottenberg, Brody, Pabianice; Rotfeld Mordechaj, Kutno, Koło; Szpiro Izrael, Grodzisk; Szpiro Elimelech, Grodzisk; Szpiro Elimelech, Kozienice; Szpiro Fiszel, Błonie; Szmukler Mendel, Grójec; Szterling Jezajasz, Warsaw, murdered; Szpiro Natan, Błędów; Szpiro Szalom, Łódź; Szczedrowicki Icchak, Skierniewice; Szwergold Jakub, Warsaw; Kryszek Lipman Hirsz, Nowe Miasto, Kluboński (Klubownicki), Drobin; Rabinowicz Hirsz Mendel, Szydłowiec; Rabinowicz Mosze, Końskie; Różany Josef, Grochów; Różany Eliezer, Okuniew; Twerski Nahum, Złotopol, Turzysk; Morgensztern Icchak, Łomazy [Łomża ?]; Morgensztern Menachem Mendel, Łuków, son-in-law of the Gaon Józef; Dembiński Eliezer, Maków, grandson of the rabbi of Aleksandrów; Rozencwajg, Jeżowice; Lerner Szalom Mordechaj, Działoszyn; Aszkenazy Jakub, Kołokolin (?); Gelernter Josef, Skępe; Lewi Lipman, Iława; Morgensztern Jakub Arie, Radzymin, Wyszków; Michelsohn Jechezkiel Cwi, Turzysk; Kolbe Baruch, Lubicz; Frajdenrajch Alter Eliezer, Warsaw; Ekhojz Hirsz, Warsaw; Nisenbojm Icchak, Warsaw

### 313. RING. II/281. Mf. ŻIH—800; USHMM—55.

- Date unknown, Warsaw Ghetto
- NN., Biographic articles about some rabbis residing in the Warsaw Ghetto
- Icchak Mendel Dancygier of Aleksandrów, son of Rabbi Samuel Hirsz of Aleksandrów; Natan Note Nutkiewicz of Rypin; Mosze Becalel Alter of Góra Kalwaria and his youngest son Menachem Mendel Alter of Kalisz.
- ***Description:*** original, handwritten manuscript (two handwritings), ink, Yiddish, 158×198, 210×148 mm, ss. 4, pp. 5.

    See *Archiwum Ringelbluma*, p. 122 (summary).
    Published: *Selected Documents*, pp. 427–429.

### 314. RING. II/171. Mf. ŻIH—795; USHMM—50.

- After 11.1941, Warsaw Ghetto
- NN., Chart of the fluctuations of the dollar's exchange rate in the Warsaw Ghetto from 11.1940 to 12.1941
- Material for study about the trade in foreign currencies in the Warsaw Ghetto.
- ***Description:*** original, handwritten manuscript (LEG*), ink, Yiddish, 206×290 mm, ss. 2, pp. 2.

    Doc. contains information used in a study entitled "Czarna giełda" [Black market]; see Ring. I/61.
    Doc. written on the reverse of a proclamation of rabbis concerning fighting epidemics: "A ruf tsu der yidisher bafelkerung fun di hadmo"rim ve-rabonim" [A proclamation to the Jewish population from the Hasidic Rebbes and Rabbis] (1941, original—2 copies, duplicated typescript, Yiddish; published: *Selected Documents*, pp. 414–415).

### 315. RING. II/172. Mf. ŻIH—795; USHMM—50.

- After 1940, Warsaw Ghetto
- NN., Study entitled "Fiscal oppression of Jews of the ghet[t]o"
- Organization, structure and staff of the treasury [taxation] bureaus responsible for the Warsaw Ghetto, relations with Polish tax officials.
- ***Description:*** original, handwritten manuscript, ink, Polish, 221×355 mm, ss. 6, pp. 11.
  Index: Slufski; Kulik; Pecz; Wawrzyniak; Maślankiewicz; Bednarczyk; Kuchciński; Jan Dinces; Deńca; Józef Rozencwajg, son-in-law of Rabbi Poznański of Warsaw; Wanda Lichtensztajnowa; Urbas; Stanisław Tanenbaum; Wolf Monka [Morka?]; Wójcicki; Bełchatowski family (ul. Solna 16); Zelechowski, proprietor of mill (ul. Żelazna 62); Basiewicz; Wochna; Dąbrowski; Górzyński

### 316. RING. II/278. Mf. ŻIH—800; USHMM—55.

- After 15.09.1942, Warsaw Ghetto
- NN., "Rations for Jewish population for period of 1 month, starting from 15.09.1942"
- List of products with legend of weight or number of pieces going to each person.
- ***Description:*** original or transcript, handwritten manuscript (JW*), ink, Polish, 205×142 mm, minor damages and losses of text, ss. 1., pp. 1.
  See *Archiwum Ringelbluma*, p. 67 (summary).
  Published: BŻIH, no. 71/72/1969, p. 170.

### 317. RING. II/132. Mf. ŻIH—795; USHMM—50.

- Date unknown, Warsaw
- [Leon] Berenson, Study entitled "Organization of the Civ[il Committee] (Komitetu Obywatelskiego)"
- Proposal for an organization at the Jewish Council for collaboration with Labor Battalion.
- ***Description:*** original or transcript, typescript, Polish, 210×296 mm, minor damages and losses of text, ss. 1, pp. 1.
  See Ring. I/1220/52.

### 318. RING. II/57. Mf. ŻIH—793; USHMM—48.

- Date unknown, Warsaw Ghetto
- M[eir] Przedecz, "Organizational sketch of the Central Social Sector (Centralnego Sektora Społecznego)."
- Organizational chart, staff, principles of activity of an organization engaged in social work in the Warsaw Ghetto.
- ***Description:*** original or transcript, typescript, Polish, 210×295 mm, ss. 3, pp. 3.

### 319. RING. II/113. Mf. ŻIH—794; USHMM—49.

- 28.06.1941, Warsaw Ghetto
- Kazimierz Herszaft (ul. Chłodna 30), Study entitled "In the matter of reorganization of social welfare" (28.08.1941)
- Plan for creation of a new organization dealing with social work in the Warsaw Ghetto: Jewish League for Social Welfare (Żydowskiej Ligi Opieki Społecznej).
- ***Description:*** original or transcript, typescript, Polish, 210×296 mm, ss. 6, pp. 6.

### 320. RING. II/114. Mf. ŻIH—794; USHMM—49.

- After 16.09.1941, Warsaw Ghetto
- A. [Abraham] M. [Mordechaj] Rogowy (ul. Nowolipie 8, apt. 58), Open Letter "Vos denkn di mentshn fun tat un gutn viln?, 'Unzer sotsyale umger-ekhtikeyt—tsum mishpet'," [What do people of action and good will think? "Our social injustice—on trial"]
- Concerning social welfare activity in the Warsaw Ghetto (third letter by Rogowy—notation in encl. letter from Rogowy to NN.; missing p. 1). First letter, about which he writes in the cover letter: "Rational distribution of the shoe shipment."
- ***Description:*** original or transcript, typescript, Yiddish, 218×125, 218×350 mm, missing p. 1, ss. 3, pp. 3.
  For another transcript (complete) of this doc., see Ring. I/335.
  Index: Wielikowski

### 321. RING. II/115. Mf. ŻIH—794; USHMM—49.

- Date unknown, Warsaw Ghetto
- A. [Abraham] M. [Mordechaj] Rogowy, Article entitled "ŻOS czy S.O.S.?" [ŻOS or S.O.S.?]
- Proposals for changes in the organization of social welfare in the Warsaw Ghetto.
- ***Description:*** original, typescript (handwritten additions, ink), Polish, 220×350 mm, ss. 1, pp. 1.
  Published: *Selected Documents*, pp. 359–361.
  Index: Gepner, chairman

### 322. RING. II/118. Mf. ŻIH—794; USHMM—49.

- Date unknown, Warsaw Ghetto
- NN., "Di yudishe [sic] plog" [The Jewish Plague]
- Critical appraisal of the activity of ŻSS and Joint.
- ***Description:*** original or transcript, typescript, English, French, Yiddish, 223×284 mm, ss. 4, pp. 4.

### 323. RING. II/215. Mf. ŻIH—798; USHMM—53.

- After 07.1942, Warsaw Ghetto
- NN., Study entitled "Ha-doar ha-yehudi be-Varsha ve-ha-gerush" [The Jewish Postal Service in Warsaw and the Expulsion][14]

14. The Hebrew word *gerush* means "expulsion," as in the Spanish Expulsion of 1492. Use of the term "resettlement" is euphemistic and would not reflect the perception of the author of the document.

- Activity of the postal service in the Warsaw Ghetto in the period 22.07–1.08.1942. Statement of losses.
- ***Description:*** original, handwritten manuscript, ink, Hebrew, 96×176 mm, ss. 17, pp. 17.

  On p. 17 is a copy of a badge worn by postal employees of the Warsaw Ghetto.

  According to Ruta Sakowska, the author of the text is Perec Opoczyński; Józef Kermisz supports this claim. See *Archiwum Ringelbluma*, p. 222; *Selected Documents*, p. 157.

  See *Archiwum Ringelbluma*, p. 222 (summary).

  Published: *Selected Documents*, pp. 157–163.

### 324. RING. II/280. Mf. ŻIH—800; USHMM—55.

- 20.10.1942, Warsaw Ghetto
- NN., Studies entitled "Report [from] hospital" and "Post Office"
- Fate of the "Czyste" Jewish Infectious Diseases Hospital from 22.07.1942 to its liquidation on 12.09.1942; formation of infirmary (ul. Pawia 6) and hospital at Gęsia 6/8; statistics on the work of the post office in the Warsaw Ghetto, from 21.07.1942 to 20.10.1942.
- ***Description:*** original or transcript, handwritten manuscript, ink, Polish, 154×198 mm, ss. 4, pp. 8.

  Published: BŻIH, no. 71–72/1969, pp. 144–148.

  Index: Ignacy Sztabholz, administrative director of the "Czyste" hospital

### 325. RING. II/244. Mf. ŻIH—799; USHMM—54.

- 10.1942–11.1942, Warsaw Ghetto
- [Perec Opoczyński], Study entitled "Di shopn" [The Workshops]
- Genesis, organization, production, employees. The greatest attention is devoted to the shirt-making workshop [Bonifraterska 11 and 31, Leszno 74 and others].
- ***Description:*** original, handwritten manuscript (OP*), notebooks, ink, Yiddish, 150×195 mm, minor damages and losses of text, ss. 26, pp. 37.

  See *Archiwum Ringelbluma*, p. 222 (summary).

  Published: BFG, vol. VII, no. 4/1954, pp. 86–98.

### 326. RING. II/246. Mf. ŻIH—799; USHMM—54.

a)

- After 21.11.[1942], Warsaw Ghetto
- NN., List of German firms taking advantage of forced labor of Jewish workers
- Inf. about number of those employed and about payments made for the workers' labor in the period 1.09–21.11.[1942].
- ***Description:*** original or transcript, handwritten manuscript (Wink.*), ink, Polish, 205×296 mm, ss. 1, pp. 1.

  Doc. written on the back of a questionnaire of the Jewish Council in Warsaw filled out by Chaja Zygelberg (born 1877) (Warsaw, ul. Dzielna 5, apt. 20) (printed item, handwritten manuscript, ink, Polish); notation (pencil): "Wirchowski[?] Lejzor, 2,3,4 September, Nalewki 27."

  See *Archiwum Ringelbluma*, p. 83 (summary).

  Published: BŻIH, no. 71/72/1969, pp. 152–156.

b)

- Date unknown, Warsaw Ghetto
- NN., "List of apartment houses belonging to the Workshop blocks"
- Addresses of apartment houses within the Warsaw Ghetto occupied by workers of the firms: W.C. [Walter Caspar] Többens, B. [Bernhard] Hallmann, [Wilfried] Hoffmann, C.G. Schultz, [Oskar] Schilling, W.[Wilhelm] Döring, H.O.F., [Kurt] Röhrich, [Fritz] Schultz.
- ***Description:*** original or transcript, typescript, Polish, 208×298 mm, ss. 1, pp. 2.

  See *Archiwum Ringelbluma*, p. 83 (summary).

  Published: BŻIH, no. 71/72/1969, pp. 152–156.

c)

- Date unknown, Warsaw Ghetto
- NN., "Anerkannte Firmen im jüdischer Wohnbezirk" [Recognized firms in the Jewish residential district]
- Inf. about the number of employed Jewish workers of the Warsaw Ghetto.
- ***Description:*** original or transcript, handwritten manuscript (H.W.*), ink, German, 207×257 mm, minor damages and losses of text, ss. 1, pp. 1.

  See *Archiwum Ringelbluma*, p. 83 (summary).

  Published: BŻIH, no. 71/72/1969, pp. 152–156.

d)

- Date unknown, Warsaw Ghetto
- NN., List of German firms benefitting from forced labor of Jewish workers
- Firm's address, telephone number, and number of Jewish workers employed from the Warsaw Ghetto.
- ***Description:*** original or transcript, typescript, German, 208×300 mm, minor damages and losses of text, ss. 1, pages 2.

### 327. RING. II/475. Mf. ŻIH—808; USHMM—63.

- Date unknown, place unknown
- NN., "Artikln–reshime fun Sh. Vinter" [List of articles by Sz. Winter]
- List of texts (87) by Szmul Winter published in the years 1926–1938 in an unknown periodical [?].
- ***Description:*** original or transcript, typescript (additions, handwritten manuscript, ink), Yiddish, 218×285, 216×344 mm, ss. 2, pp. 2.

  Title: handwritten manuscript (LEG*), pencil.

### 328. RING. II/369. Mf. ŻIH—803; USHMM—58.

- 13.09.1941, Warsaw Ghetto
- NN., Lecture at a literary evening devoted to [Icchak Majer] Wajsenberg. (13.09.1941)
- Speech opening a series of meetings devoted to the intellectual life of Jews.

- *Description:* original or transcript, handwritten manuscript, ink, Yiddish, 218×278 mm, ss. 1, pp. 2.
  Published: *Selected Documents*, pp. 450–452 (according to J.K. the lecture's author was Abraham Lewin).

329. RING. II/300/2. Mf. ŻIH—800; USHMM—55.

- Second half of 1942, Warsaw Ghetto
- NN., Sketch for map of the remnants of the Warsaw Ghetto.
- *Description:* original, handwritten manuscript, pencil, 220×290 mm, ss. 1, pp. 1.
  The same person who made the sketch also produced the manuscript of Ring. II/300/1.

## IV. Materials on the History of Jewish Population Centers outside of Warsaw

330. RING. II/225. Mf. ŻIH—798; USHMM—53.

- 7.09.[1942], Berlin
- Lea (Berlin), Letter of 7.09.[1942] to NN. (Rand [?]) (Warsaw Ghetto, OBW, ul. Gęsia 30)
- Inf. concerning Henryk (Heini) and help for him.
- *Description:* original, handwritten manuscript, ink, German, 140×168 mm, ss. 2, pp. 3.
  Index: Landau, Modrow
  Published: *Listy o Zagładzie*, pp. 209–212.

331. RING. II/312. Mf. ŻIH—801; USHMM—56.

- 05–10.1941, Berne (Switzerland)
- Consulado de la República del Paraguay en Berna [Consulate of the Republic of Paraguay in Berne], Letters of 9.05.1941 and 12.10.1941 to Ozjasz Leon Weingort (Lwów, ul. Bernsteina 8)
- Concerning permission for departure of the addressee to Paraguay.
- *Description:* original, typescript, German, 209×295 mm, ss. 2, pp. 2.
  At bottom stamps and signatures of consul (illegible).

332. RING. II/275/6. Mf. ŻIH—799; USHMM—54.

- 28.10.1942, Bendsburg [Będzin].
- NN. (Szymon) (Bendsburg [Będzin]), Letter of 28.10.1942 to I.M. [Icchak Meir] Kramarz (Warsaw Ghetto, OBW, ul. Gęsia 30)
- Request for information about family: parents, uncle Auberman, Kalinowski (ul. Nalewki 36), Bekermans.
- *Description:* original, handwritten manuscript on a postcard, postmark and stamp of the Jewish Council in Warsaw, ink, Polish, 147×104 mm, ss. 1, pp. 2.
  On p. 1 notation (pencil): "Gęsia firm [. . . ?]; address of sender: "Hanna Sara Bornstein, Bendsburg [. . . ?], Alter Ring 11, apt. 11."
  Published: *Listy o Zagładzie*, pp. 273–275.

333. RING. II/275/3. Mf. ŻIH—799; USHMM—54.

- 30.09.1942, Bodzentyn.
- NN. (Rózia) (Bodzentyn), Letter of 30.09.1942 to Józek Frydman (Warsaw Ghetto, ul. Dzielna 31, apt. 45)
- Arrived in Bodzentyn, for 4 weeks, lack of news from Warsaw.
- *Description:* original, handwritten manuscript on a postcard, postmark and stamp of the Jewish Council in Warsaw, pencil, Polish, 147×104 mm, ss. 1, pp. 2.
  See *Archiwum Ringelbluma*, p. 177 (summary).
  Published: *Listy o Zagładzie*, pp. 220–222.

334. RING. II/275/5. Mf. ŻIH—799; USHMM—54.

- 19.10.1942, Breslau [Wrocław].
- NN. (Breslau [Wrocław]), Letter of 19.10.1942 to Roman Weinberg (Warsaw Ghetto, ul. Nowolipie 58)
- Request for letter and transmission of news to father-in-law; information about wife Adela and son Pucuś (remained at father-in-law's). Encl. address for correspondence: R. Hochberger, Breslau XIII, Victoriastr. 107).
- *Description:* original, handwritten manuscript, ink, Polish, 145×211 mm, ss. 2, pp. 2.
  Encl. envelope (handwritten manuscript, postmark and stamp of the Jewish Council in Warsaw, ink, German, 177×124 mm, ss. 1, pp. 2).
  See *Archiwum Ringelbluma*, p. 182 (summary).
  Published: *Listy o Zagładzie*, pp. 261–263.

335. RING. II/167/1. Mf. ŻIH—795; USHMM—50.

- 4.04.1942, Bruxelles (Brussels).
- NN. (Bernard) (Bruxelles), Letter of 4.04.1942 to I. Fiszbin (Warsaw Ghetto, ul. Lubeckiego 17, apt. 39)
- Letter to sister and brother-in-law. Lack of response to parcels sent.
- *Description:* original, handwritten manuscript on a postcard, ink, postmark and stamp of the Jewish Council in Warsaw, Polish, 138×189 mm, ss. 1, pp. 2.
  On p. 1 notation (pencil): "69" and "1949/86."

336. RING. II/301. Mf. ŻIH—801; USHMM—56.

- After 01.1941, Warsaw Ghetto
- NN., "Bydgoszcz. List of persons who, to the extent that it is not written otherwise, were arrested as a result of the major roundups organized in October 1939 and all traces of these unfortunates vanished"
- The following lost their lives in pogroms and raids: Bresler; Szachne and Szyja Szapiro; Aron Wołkowicz; Dr. Chaskiel; Libermanowa; Piotr Gerson and his sons Józek and Arek; Straszun; Zahler; Samuel

Rubinsztajn; Blau; Widrer; Zwoźniak and his son; Werthamus and his son; Kirsblum [Kirsablum?]; Zygmunt Rozental and his wife and sister Betty Rozental; Józef Smużyk; Iwanowicz; Michael Katowski; Israel and his wife; Abram Sojkow. Moreover, due to war operations, Join [Jonah?] Szapiro and his son lost their lives—buried in Ożarów.
- ***Description:*** original or transcript, handwritten manuscript (FLIG*), ink, Polish, 212×298 mm, ss. 2, pp. 2.

### 337. RING. II/223/1. Mf. ŻIH—798; USHMM—53.

- 26.07.1942, Częstochowa
- Rafał Zajdman (Częstochowa, ul. Warszawska 20), Letter of 26.07.1942 to A. Sandacz (Warsaw Ghetto, ul. Krochmalna 25, apt. 29)
- Lack of news from Warsaw.
- ***Description:*** original, handwritten manuscript on a postcard, ink, postmark and stamp of the Jewish Council in Warsaw, Polish, 148×104 mm, ss. 1, pp. 2.

On p. 1 notation (pencil): "premises closed."
See Ring. II/269.
Published: *Listy o Zagładzie*, pp. 197–198.

### 338. RING. II/269. Mf. ŻIH—799; USHMM—54.

- 21.08.1942, Częstochowa
- R. [Rafał] Zajdman (Częstochowa, ul. Warszawska 20), Letter of 21.08.1942 to A. Sandacz (Warsaw Ghetto, ul. Krochmalna 25, apt. 29)
- Lack of news from Warsaw.
- ***Description:*** original, handwritten manuscript on a postcard, ink, postmark and stamp of the Jewish Council in Warsaw, Polish, 148×104 mm, ss. 1, pp. 2.

See Ring. II/223/1.
Published: *Archiwum Ringelbluma*, pp. 166–167; *Listy o Zagładzie*, pp. 199–200.

### 339. RING. II/274/5. Mf. ŻIH—799; USHMM—54.

- [17.12.1942], Częstochowa
- Guta Fuks (from the transport passing through Częstochowa), Letter of [17.12.1942 postmark, Częstochowa] to Rotblat (Warsaw Ghetto, ul. Zamenhofa 19)
- They do not know where they are going.
- ***Description:*** original, handwritten manuscript on a postcard, postmark and stamp of the Jewish Council in Warsaw, pencil, Polish, 147×104 mm, ss. 1, pp. 2.

Letter addressed to the surname: "Rogozek."
See *Archiwum Ringelbluma*, p. 191 (summary).
Published: *Listy o Zagładzie*, p. 329.

### 340. RING. II/274/6. Mf. ŻIH—799; USHMM—54.

- [17.12.1942?], Częstochowa
- NN. (Marek [of Płońsk?]) (from the transport passing through Częstochowa), Letter of [17.12.1942 ?] [29.12.1942 postmark, Częstochowa] to A. Bogaty (Warsaw Ghetto, Többens workshop, ul. Leszno 70)
- Second day en route, they traveled via Warsaw (Praga); they are traveling to the labor camp at Tarnowskie Góry or Oświęcim.
- ***Description:*** original, handwritten manuscript on a postcard, postmark and stamp of the Jewish Council in Warsaw, ink, Polish, 147×104 mm, ss. 1, pp. 2.

Published: *Archiwum Ringelbluma*, p. 202; *Listy o Zagładzie*, pp. 329–331.

### 341. RING. II/176. Mf. ŻIH—797; USHMM—52.

- 8.07.1942, Danzig [Gdańsk]
- David Jonas (Danzig, Mausegasse 7), Letter of 8.07.1942 to Maximilian Jezierski (Brwinów)
- Situation of the Jewish population in Gdańsk, help for persons transported to the Warsaw Ghetto, drama of 512 refugees to Palestine on the ship "Pentcho." Encl.: 1) Statistics on Jewish population changes in major cities of the Reich (1940–1942); 2) Information about some residents of Gdańsk (list of names) collected on basis of questionnaire of 11.06.1942 (fragment [?]).
- ***Description:*** original, typescript, handwritten manuscript, ink, pencil, German, 210×214, 208×292 mm, ss. 7, pp. 9.

On p. 1 (letter) initials (pencil): of Maximilian Jezierski, with date (16.07.1942) and notation in German: "I received." On p. 3 (letter) signature (ink): of David Jonas.
Index: Estera Leibow of Gdańsk; Walter Eisenstädt of Gdańsk; Emil Beiker of Gdańsk; Bruno Beiker of Gdańsk; Szlamek Charlupski of Gdańsk; Isidor Eisenstädt of Gdańsk; Amalie Rosenbaum of Gdańsk; Anna Jakobsohn of Gdańsk; Max and Marttha Behrent of Gdańsk; Max Lewandowski of Gdańsk; Leopold and Sara Rosenbaum of Gdańsk; Marie Chose of Gdańsk (from Białystok) ; Ruth Samankiewitsch [?] of Gdańsk; J. Rosenbaum of Gdańsk; Margarette Borowska of Gdańsk; Albert Sachs of Gdańsk; Ewa Sachs of Gdańsk; Betty Nast of Gdańsk; Frieda Reach of Gdańsk; Bajla Kniżyńska of Gdańsk; Mayer Feuerberg of Gdańsk; Amalie Schwerherz [?] of Gdańsk; Hilda Friedländer with mother; Dr. Kerb, physician of the Jewish Community in Gdańsk; Berent; Dr. Itzig of Gdańsk; Dr. Falkenstein (age 67) of Berlin; Konrad Silberstein and his wife of Gdańsk; Brunno Damm of Gdańsk

### 342. RING. II/223/4. Mf. ŻIH—798; USHMM—53.

- [Before 23.10.1942], Firlej
- Symcha Guterman (Firlej), Letter of [23.10.1942—postmark, Lublin] to sister Frania (Warsaw, ul. Gęsia 30, apt. 2[0?])
- Lack of news from Warsaw.
- ***Description:*** original, handwritten manuscript on a postcard, postmark and stamp of the Jewish Council in Warsaw, ink, Polish, 148×104 mm, ss. 1, pp. 2.

Letter addressed to the surname: "Maria Ostrołęk."
See *Archiwum Ringelbluma*, p. 178 (summary).
Published: *Listy o Zagładzie*, pp. 214–215.

### 343. RING. II/164. Mf. ŻIH—795; USHMM—50.

- 5.09.1941, Geneva
- Komitee zur Hilfeleistung für die kriegsbetroffene jüdische Bevölkerung [Committee for provision of aid for the Jewish population caught up in the war] (Genève, 52, rue des Pâquis), Letter of 5.09.1941 to Chuna Cejtlin (Warsaw Ghetto, ul. Śliska 6, apt. 58[?])
- Notification about dispatch for the addressee of 2 parcels of food from Portugal.
- ***Description:*** original, printed on a postcard, postmark and stamp of the Jewish Council in Warsaw, German, 147×104 mm, postage stamp removed, ss. 1, pp. 2.

### 344. RING. II/398. Mf. ŻIH—804; USHMM—59.

- 25.10.1942, Hohensalza [Inowrocław]
- Staatlische Kriminalpolizei, Kriminalpolizeistelle Hohensalza [State Police Office, Inowrocław], Announcement dated 25.10.1942 about establishment of a reward for aid in uncovering the perpetrators of the attack on forester Heinrich Skade in Turzynów (district of Kutno)
- ***Description:*** original, printed matter, German, Polish, 580×399 mm, ss. 1, pp. 1.

### 345. RING. II/182. Mf. ŻIH—797; USHMM—52.

a)

- 22.02.1942, Izbica [Lubelska]
- Frajda Szniaursan [Shneyerson?] (Izbica), Letter of 22.02.1942 to NN. (cousin)
- Request for intervention at the Jewish Council in Staszów in matter of work. Encl. address for correspondence: Elisza [?] Tenenwurcel, Staszów, ul. Przejazdowa 2.
- ***Description:*** original, handwritten manuscript, ink, Yiddish, 122×202 mm, ss. 2, pp. 3.
  At top notation in Polish (ink): "Izbica, 22.02.42."

b)

- Date unknown, place unknown
- Frajda Szniaursan [Shneyerson?] [Izbica?], Letter to NN. (aunt and uncle)
- Difficult situation of family (father's illness, brother in camp). Request for aid and intervention with Giterman and Goldfarb. Encl. postscript by mother Frajda to sister and brother-in-law with request for help.
- ***Description:*** original, handwritten manuscript, ink, Yiddish, 128×210 mm, ss. 2, pp. 4.

### 346. RING. II/275/2. Mf. ŻIH—799; USHMM—54.

- [5.09.1942], Kałuszyn
- NN. (Chuma) (Kałuszyn), Letter of [5.09.1942 postmark date] to brother J. [Jankiel] Goldsztejn (ul. Gęsia 30, apt. 40)
- Is with her child in Kałuszyn; has no news from husband and sister.
- ***Description:*** original, handwritten manuscript on a postcard, postmark and stamp of the Jewish Council in Warsaw (11.11.1942 [sic]), ink, Polish, 147×104 mm, ss. 1, pp. 2.
  On p. 1 address of sender: "Srul Drylich, Kałuszyn, ul. Zielona" and notation (pencil): "1) marmolade kupi ewent." [Buy marmalade if need be. ?]
  See Ring. II/275/1.
  See *Archiwum Ringelbluma*, p. 189 (summary).
  Published: *Listy o Zagładzie*, pp. 207–208.

### 347. RING. II/303. Mf. ŻIH—801; USHMM—56.

- After 10.1940, Warsaw Ghetto
- Neuman, Account entitled "Koło (From the stories of a young Jew)"
- Oppressive measures after German entry into Koło, torching of synagogue, forced labor, Labor Bureau (Wrona, Neuman, Borkowski, Lissek, Borensztajn, Frenkiel), escape to Żychlin (24.11.1939) and Łowicz (15.12.1939), work in the Registration Commission (to 25.03.1940) and Order Service (from 25.03.1940 author was director of Order Service in Łowicz), return to Koło to wife and children (09.1940), participation in organization of resettlement of Jews from Koło to Nowiny Brdowskie and Bugaj, organization of colonies, work on the soil.
- ***Description:*** original (o), handwritten manuscript (FLIG*), ink, Polish, 210×297 mm, ss. 5, pp. 5.
  On p. 2 is a fragment interpolated into the text of the account by the copyist: "I will not describe the fortunes of Łowicz during the time when the narrator lived there; because he was the commandant of the Jewish Order Service in that town, I attempted to investigate him in relation to certain dark doings of that institution and behind-the-scenes machinations. My efforts remained ineffective, since my interlocutor furnished very skimpy information, and in addition strove indeed to exonerate the leadership of the Order Service, as well as the Łowicz Judenrat; therefore, this account will also be not only very incomplete, but also subjective."
  Index: Rozen (age 80), shot in 09.1939 in Koło; Salomon Bieżuński (age 37), shot in 09.1939 in Koło; Sywosz, shot in 11.1939 in Koło; Warnbrum, director of the colony in Bugaj; Weinsztok of the Order Service in Łowicz; Zylberger of Order Service in Łowicz

### 348. RING. II/291. Mf. ŻIH—800; USHMM—55.

a)

- After 28.10.1942, Warsaw Ghetto
- Der Höhere SS und Polizeiführer im Generalgouvernement. Der Staatssekretär für das Sicherheitswesen, [Higher SS and Police Leader in the Generalgou-

vernement. Secretary of State for Security Friedrich Wilhelm] Krüger, "Polizeiverordnung über die Bildung von Judenwohnbezirken in den Distrikten Warschau und Lublin vom 28.10.42" [Police decree on the formation of Jewish residential districts in the districts of Warsaw and Lublin] (Kraków, 28.10.1942)

- List of localities (ghettos) in which Jews are permitted to reside after 1.12.1942.
- ***Description:*** transcript, typescript, German, 205×294 mm, ss. 2, pp. 2.

b)

- After 11.11.1942, Warsaw Ghetto
- "List of localities, in which Jews are allowed to reside on the basis of the dec[ree] of 28.10.[19]42 (supplement of 10.11.[19]42)"
- Localities in the districts of Radomsko, Kraków, Galicia.
- ***Description:*** transcript, handwritten manuscript (two handwritings: JW* and supplements H.W.*), pencil, German, Polish, 215×300 mm, ss. 1, pp. 1

### 349. RING. II/80. Mf. ŻIH—794; USHMM—49.

- After 22.04.1942, place unknown
- Regierung des GG Hauptabteilung Innere Verwaltung Abt. Bevölkerungswesen und Fürsorge—Krakau (Government of Generalgouvernement Main Department of Internal Administration Department of Population and Welfare in Kraków), Letter dated 22.04.1942 to ŻSS in Kraków
- Concerns announcement by ŻSS of an internal loan for the needs of this organization. Letter signed by Dr. [Walther] Föhl. Encl. regulations for the aforementioned loan.
- ***Description:*** transcript (2 copies), typescript, German, 210×295, 223×288 mm, ss. 4, pp. 4.

### 350. RING. II/83. Mf. ŻIH—794; USHMM—49.

- After 11.06.1942, place unknown
- ŻSS—Kraków. Department of Labor Assistance [Wydział Pomocy Pracy], Circular no. 61 of 11.06.1942
- Concerns search for work for the Jewish population. Encl. "Instruction for organization of communities of labor."
- ***Description:*** transcript, typescript, Polish, 222×283 mm, minor damages and losses of text, ss. 2, pp. 4.

### 351. RING. II/305. Mf. ŻIH—801; USHMM—56.

- After 04.1942, Warsaw Ghetto
- NN., Account "Lublin"
- Fate of Jewish population from the Germans' entry (23.09.1939) to the liquidation action (forced labor camp Bełżec, Tyszowce, displacement into the province, camps on ul. Browarna and ul. Lipowa 7, searches, arrests, executions, hunger, "fur collection action," epidemics of typhus, description of the liquidation actions in 03–04.1942, resettlement into ghetto in Majdan Tatarski).
- ***Description:*** original (o), handwritten manuscript (FLIG*), ink, Polish, 210×297 mm, ss. 6 pp. 6.

  Published: *Selected Documents*, pp. 181–188.

  Index: Bolesław Tenenbaum of the "13," shot in Lublin; Dolps [Dolff], commandant of the labor camp in Bełżec; Kestenberg, chairman of the Jewish Council in Lublin, shot in 1942

### 352. RING. II/306. Mf. ŻIH—801; USHMM—56.

- After 11.1942, Warsaw Ghetto
- Finkelsztajns, Account entitled "Khurbn Lukov" [Destruction of Łuków]
- Brother and sister from Łuków (Warsaw, ul. Muranowska 36) describe the liquidation actions of the ghetto in Łuków (5.10–11.1942), their escape from the transport to Treblinka, behavior of the Polish population toward fleeing Jews.
- ***Description:*** transcript, handwritten manuscript (H.W.*), pencil, Yiddish, ink, 220×290 mm, ss. 5, pp. 5.

  Published: *Selected Documents*, pp. 210–213.

### 353. RING. II/307. Mf. ŻIH—801; USHMM—56.

- After 7.11.1942, Warsaw Ghetto
- NN., Account of escape from the ghetto in Majdan Tatarski near Lublin
- Author and his wife and 3 sons escaped during the liquidation action in Majdan Tatarski (7.11.1942, description of liquidation of ghetto) of transport to extermination camp; after numerous ordeals made it into the Warsaw Ghetto.
- ***Description:*** transcript, handwritten manuscript (Tr*), ink, Polish, 150×192 cm, ss. 6, pp. 11.

  On p. 1 at top notation (pencil): "Majdan."

### 354. RING. II/223/2. Mf. ŻIH—798; USHMM—53.

- [11.08.1942], Ostrowiec Kielecki
- Pela Okonowska (Ostrowiec Kielecki, ul. Szeroka 8), Letter of [11.08.1942 postmark date] to Grabska (Warsaw Ghetto, ul. Pawia 1)
- Request for news about Blima, Fiszel, and Beniamin.
- ***Description:*** original, handwritten manuscript on a postcard, postmark and stamp of the Jewish Council in Warsaw, ink, Polish, 148×104 mm, ss. 1, pp. 2.

  On p. 2 at top notation in Hebrew (ink): "With God's help."

  Letter addressed to the name: "S.R. Grabski."

  See *Archiwum Ringelbluma*, pp. 165–166 (photocopy, fragment, summary).

  Published: *Listy o Zagładzie*, pp. 193–195.

### 355. RING. II/308. Mf. ŻIH—801; USHMM—56.

- After 08.1942, Warsaw Ghetto
- NN., Account from Otwock
- Searches for surviving Jews in hiding after the liquidation action (19.08.1942) conducted by the chief of the Rembertów gendarmerie, 450 people shot in the police station, among them groups of Orthodox Jews (Nokhem Kohn, Isokher Fersztejn, Baruch Bin,

Mejer Sechekiem [?] and Buński; Lipser [?] carried out the execution).

- ***Description:*** original or transcript, handwritten manuscript (SJ*), ink, Yiddish, 104×267 mm, ss. 1, pp. 2.

## 356. RING. II/145. Mf. ŻIH—795; USHMM—50.

- 12.03.1942, Piotrków Trybunalski
- J. Krell (Piotrków Trybunalski, Plac Lipowy 4), Stub of payment of money order (50 zł).
- ***Description:*** original, printed matter, handwritten manuscript, ink, postmark, German, Polish, 41×105 mm, ss. 1, pp. 2.

  At top the date stamp: "14 Marz. 1942"; on reverse stamp: "(30 gr) Payment for the benefit of 'child care.'"

## 357. RING. II/238. Mf. ŻIH—799; USHMM—54.

- After 14.12.1942, Warsaw Ghetto
- NN. (Sala and Dyna) (Płońsk ghetto), Letters (2) of 13 and 14.12.1942 to sister NN. (Rózia) (Warsaw Ghetto)
- Farewell letters written before the approaching liquidation action (deportation from the ghetto in Płońsk).
- ***Description:*** transcript, handwritten manuscript (RA*) (underlinings with pencil), ink, Polish, 150×191 mm, ss. 2, pp. 4.

  Published: *Archiwum Ringelbluma*, p. 192 (letter of 14.12.1942 and description letter of 13.12.1942); *Listy o Zagładzie*, pp. 316–323.
  Index: Kirszenbaum

## 358. RING. II/274/1. Mf. ŻIH—799; USHMM—54.

- After 16.12.1942, Warsaw Ghetto
- NN. (Płońsk, railroad station), Letter of 16.12.1942 to NN. [Warsaw Ghetto]
- Letter written from transport departing from Płońsk, Request for passing on of news to the Bams (Warsaw Ghetto, ul. Niska 6).
- ***Description:*** transcript, handwritten manuscript (LP*), ink, Polish, 170×93 mm, ss. 1, pp. 2.

  Published: *Archiwum Ringelbluma*, pp. 196–197 (description, photocopy);
  *Listy o Zagładzie*, pp. 323–324.

## 359. RING. II/274/2. Mf. ŻIH—799; USHMM—54.

- [After 16.12.1942], Warsaw Ghetto
- NN. (Dawid [from Płońsk?]) (from transport passing through Legionowo), Letter of [16.12.1942] to NN. (Warsaw Ghetto, ul. Nalewki 47, apt. 19)
- Today they departed from Płońsk with the entire family and with the rest of the Jewish population.
- ***Description:*** transcript, handwritten manuscript (LP*), ink, Polish, 148×90 mm, ss. 1, pp. 2.

  See *Archiwum Ringelbluma*, p. 194 (description, photocopy).
  Published: *Listy o Zagładzie*, pp. 325–326.

## 360. RING. II/274/3. Mf. ŻIH—799; USHMM—54.

- After 16.12.1942, Warsaw Ghetto
- NN. (Laja [Łaja] [from Płońsk?]) (from transport passing through Praga [Warsaw]), Letter of 16.12.1942 to L. Przygoda (Warsaw Ghetto, ul. Miła 46)
- They don't know where they are going.
- ***Description:*** transcript, handwritten manuscript (LP*), ink, Polish, 216×76 mm, ss. 1, pp. 2.

  Published: *Archiwum Ringelbluma*, p. 197 (description, photocopy); *Listy o Zagładzie*, pp. 326–327.

## 361. RING. II/274/4. Mf. ŻIH—799; USHMM—54.

- After 17.12.1942, Warsaw Ghetto
- NN. (Gitla [from Płońsk?]) (from transport passing through Częstochowa), Letter of 17.12.1942 to NN. ([Warsaw Ghetto], ul. Muranowska 40, apt. 35)
- Second day en route, they passed through Warsaw; they are going to work.
- ***Description:*** transcript, handwritten manuscript (LP*), ink, Polish, 216×94 mm, ss. 1, pp. 2.

  On p. 2 notation H.W.* (ink): "In the space of" [(?) Na przestrzeni]
  See *Archiwum Ringelbluma*, pp. 198–199 (description, photocopy).
  Published: *Listy o Zagładzie*, pp. 327–328.

## 362. RING. II/302. Mf. ŻIH—801; USHMM—56.

- After 11.1942, Warsaw Ghetto
- NN., Notes on the situation of the Jewish population in the vicinity of Radzymin and in the Białystok region
- Activity of units of Jewish self-defense (e.g., in the vicinity of Jadów under the command of Mosze Zieleniec, age 25); liquidation action in Radzymin (1.10.1942); escapes from ghetto.
- ***Description:*** original, handwritten manuscript, ink, Yiddish, 222×340 mm, ss. 1, pp. 2.

  Published: *Selected Documents*, pp. 587–588.

## 363. RING. II/275/8. Mf. ŻIH—799; USHMM—54.

- 3.01.1943, Sandomierz
- Mosze Rozner and NN. (his niece Rachela) (Sandomierz ghetto), Letter of 3.01.1943 to NN. (Szulim) [Warsaw Ghetto]
- About voluntary registration for departure to Palestine. Increasing the isolation of the ghetto from 1.01.1943.
- ***Description:*** original, handwritten manuscript, pencil, Polish, Yiddish, 220×229 mm, ss. 1, pp. 2.

  See *Archiwum Ringelbluma*, p. 203 (summary).
  Published: *Listy o Zagładzie*, pp. 338–341.
  Index: Jechiel Topel Alter, Mojsze Szmukler

## 364. RING. II/310. Mf. ŻIH—801; USHMM—56.

- Date unknown, Warsaw Ghetto
- NN., "Słonim. (Notes of a young Jewess)"
- Author from Warsaw, escapes to the east (7.12.1939), robbed by wagon driver during attempt to make it

through to region occupied by the USSR (7.12.1939), reaches Białystok, and then Lwów. Describes the situation of the population (Soviet struggle against commerce, lack of food and work, speculation, passportization in June 1940, deportations).
- ***Description:*** original (o), handwritten manuscript (FLIG*), ink, Polish, 209×297, 222×287 mm, ss. 4, pp. 8.
  Subtitle "Notes of a young Jewess" written in a different handwriting.
  Published: *Relacje z Kresów*, pp. 188–201.

### 365. RING. II/309. Mf. ŻIH—801; USHMM—56.

- After 09.1942, Warsaw Ghetto
- Mosze Zalcman, Account entitled "Khurbn Subin" [Destruction of Sobienie(-Jeziory)]
- Author fled from Otwock to the ghetto in Sobienie, describes the liquidation action there 09/10.1942 (2,000 Jews, summary executions, transports to Treblinka).
- ***Description:*** transcript, handwritten manuscript (SJ*), ink, Yiddish, 154×199 mm, ss. 2, pp. 4.
  Account recorded by K.M.[H?] Band [Kalman Huberband?]; see Ring. I/218.
  Index: Mosze Klajnman, Kalkowicz family (18 persons), shot in Sobienie at the cemetery

### 366. RING. II/270/2. Mf. ŻIH—799; USHMM—54.

- 11.08.1942, Stanisławów
- Julius Gerner (Stanisławów, Bundgasse 26), Letter of 11.08.1942 to Izydor Gerner (Warsaw Ghetto, ul. Elektoralna 30)
- Lack of news from Warsaw.
- ***Description:*** original, handwritten manuscript on a postcard, postmark and stamp of the Jewish Council in Warsaw, ink, German, 147×105 mm, ss. 1, pp. 2.
  Published: *Listy o Zagładzie*, pp. 191–192.

### 367. RING. II/275/7. Mf. ŻIH—799; USHMM—54.

- 11.11.1942, Stanisławów
- Samuel Nelken (Jewish Hospital in Stanisławów), Letter of 11.11.1942 to Izydor Seret, pharmacist (Warsaw Ghetto). Request for help.
- ***Description:*** original, handwritten manuscript, ink, Polish, 153×194 mm, ss. 1, pp. 1.
  Attached envelope with the imprint of the L. Schleien firm (Stanisławów) (handwritten manuscript, postal stamps, ink, German, 177×110 mm, ss. 1, pp. 2). Letter was mailed to the address of the Jewish Council in Warsaw.
  See *Archiwum Ringelbluma*, p. 187 (summary).
  Published: *Listy o Zagładzie*, pp. 289–291.
  Index: Mina Igel (Uhersko), W. Sobel (Lwów, ul. Weissenhofa 10)

### 368. RING. II/223/3. Mf. ŻIH—798; USHMM—53.

- [12.08.1942], Starachowice
- NN. (Pela) (Starachowice), Letter of [12.08.1942 postmark date] to uncle J.J. Głowiński (Warsaw Ghetto, Nowolipki 16, apt. 19). Request for news.
- ***Description:*** original, handwritten manuscript on a postcard, postmark and stamp of the Jewish Council in Warsaw, ink, Polish, 148×104 mm, ss. 1, pp. 2.
  See *Archiwum Ringelbluma*, pp. 164–165 (photocopy, fragment, summary).
  Published: *Listy o Zagładzie*, pp. 195–196.

### 369. RING. II/275/1. Mf. ŻIH—799; USHMM—54.

- [4.09.1942], Stoczek near Węgrów
- Fela [Manyszewicz?] (Stoczek Węgrowski), Letter of [4.09.1942 postmark date] to brother Jankiel Goltsztejn [Goldsztejn?] (Warsaw Ghetto, ul. Gęsia 30, apt. 40)
- Lack of news from Warsaw.
- ***Description:*** original, handwritten manuscript on a postcard, postmark and stamp of the Jewish Council in Warsaw (11.11.1942 [s]), ink, Polish, 147×105 mm, ss. 1, pp. 2.
  On p. 1 addressee of the letter: "Hersz Manyszewicz, Stoczek Węgrowski" and sketch of map (pencil); according to Ruta Sakowska, it is a map of the extermination camp in Treblinka; see *Listy o Zagładzie*, p. 205.
  See Ring. II/275/2.
  Published: *Archiwum Ringelbluma*, pp. 170–171 (photocopy); *Listy o Zagładzie*, pp. 205–207.

### 370. RING. II/311. Mf. ŻIH—801; USHMM—56.

- After 05.1942, Warsaw Ghetto
- NN., Account entitled "Kidesh–Ha-shem" [Martyrdom]
- On the public executions of Jews in Zduńska Wola (10 persons) and in Sieradz (10 persons, including 4 members of the Jewish Council) (21.05.1942).
- ***Description:*** original or transcript, handwritten manuscript, ink, Yiddish, 210×293 mm, ss. 2, pp. 3.
  Published: *Selected Documents*, pp. 421–423.
  Index: Szlomo Żelechowski (age 36), rabbi, hanged in Zduńska Wola 21.05.1942; Beniamin Feiwel Rudol (age 54), hanged in Zduńska Wola 21.05.1942; Berl Walfisz (age 54), hanged in Zduńska Wola 21.05.1942; Mordechaj Morgensztern, hanged in Zduńska Wola 21.05.1942; Szlomo Gerszonowicz (age 38), hanged in Zduńska Wola on 21.05.1942; Nachum Eli Zilberberg, hanged in Zduńska Wola on 21.05.1942; [Eli] Laskowski (age 62), rabbi with son, hanged in Sieradz in 05.1942; Dawid Beer, rabbi

# V. Materials on Labor Camps, Transit Camps, and Extermination Camps (Centers)

### 371. RING. II/273/3. Mf. ŻIH—799; USHMM—54.

- 3.10.1942, [Warsaw] Bielany
- Berek Engel ([Warsaw] Bielany, ul. Kamedułów 71), Letter of 3.10.1942 to Hela and M. [Mietek] Engel (Warsaw Ghetto, ul. Nowolipki 36, apt. 24, ul. Dzielna 31, apt. 24). Request for help.
- ***Description:*** original, handwritten manuscript on a postcard, postmark and stamp of the Jewish Council in Warsaw, pencil, Polish, 148×105 mm, ss. 1, pp. 2.

  Name of street: "ul. Nowolipki 36–24" crossed out and "Dzielna 31, apt. 24" inscribed (pencil)

  See *Archiwum Ringelbluma*, p. 178 (summary).

  Published: *Listy o Zagładzie*, pp. 222–223.

### 372. RING. II/273/6. Mf. ŻIH—799; USHMM—54.

- 10.11.1942, Hohensalza [Inowrocław]
- S. Rudnik (Hohensalza [Inowrocław], Gemeinschafts-Lager DAF [Deutsche Arbeitsfront; German Labor Front Community Camp] no. 16, Pakoscherstr.), Letter of 10.11.1942 to A. Finkielstein (Warsaw Ghetto, ul. Pawia 1, apt. 4)
- Author and his wife were transported out of Płock Request for information about daughter.
- ***Description:*** original, handwritten manuscript on a postcard, postmark and stamp of the Jewish Council in Warsaw, ink, German, 148×105 mm, ss. 1, pp. 2.

  Published: *Listy o Zagładzie*, pp. 283–284.

### 373. RING. II/273/4. Mf. ŻIH—799; USHMM—54.

- [31.10.1942], Kawęczyn
- J.[?] Guterman (Kawęczyn 53, Judenlager [Jews camp]), Letter of [31.10.1942 postmark date] to H. [?] Jezioro [?] (Warsaw Ghetto, hairdressing shop, ul. Leszno 24).
- ***Description:*** original, handwritten manuscript on a postcard, postmark and stamp of the Jewish Council in Warsaw pencil, Polish, 147×105 mm, ss. 1, pp. 2.

### 374. RING. II/273/1. Mf. ŻIH—799; USHMM—54.

- 09–10.1942, Lautawerk Süd–Lager [labor camp]
- Schimon J. [Szymon Józef] Taube (Lautawerk Süd–Lager I, stube 7 [labor camp]), Letters (2) dated 6.09. and 10.10.1942 to brother Uszer Taube (Warsaw Ghetto, ul. Nowolipie 15, apt. 30)
- Inf. about friends and family, situation in camp, lack of news from Kłodawa.
- ***Description:*** original, handwritten manuscript on a postcard, handwritten manuscript, postmark and stamp of the Jewish Council in Warsaw (postcard), Yiddish in Roman transliteration, ink, 207×295, 148×105 mm, ss. 2, pp. 4.

  Published: *Listy o Zagładzie*, pp. 244–254.

  Index: M.M. Kibel from Szydłowiec; Welner; Toba and Libcia Pińczewski; W.D. Lewin; Szymon Josef Lissak, died in camp in Kostrzyń; M.L. Pińczewski; St. Pomykała (Lautawerk Süd–Lager 3); Jakub Pińczewski; Moniek Mazur; Wierzbicki, brothers; Abram Rzeszewski-Mały; Ab. Opoczyński; Icchak Kryszek

### 375. RING. II/167/3. Mf. ŻIH—795; USHMM—50.

- 11.10.1942, Lautawerk Süd–Lager [labor camp]
- Szymon Józef Taube (Lautawerk Süd–Lager I, stube 7 [labor camp]), Letter of 11.10.1942 to brother Uszer Taube (Warsaw Ghetto, ul. Franciszkańska 21, apt. 109. Brushmakers Workshop)
- Situation in camp, notation about acquaintances.
- ***Description:*** original, handwritten manuscript on a postcard, ink, postmark and stamp of the Jewish Council in Warsaw, Yiddish in Roman transliteration, 147×104 mm, ss. 1, pp. 2.

  Index: [Chaim] Rumkowski, Kołodziejski, M. Kantorski, Ida Herszkowicz.

  Published: *Listy o Zagładzie*, pp. 254–257; *Archiwum Ringelbluma*, p. 181 (summary).

### 376. RING. II/128. Mf. ŻIH—794; USHMM—49.

- Beginning of 1941, Warsaw Ghetto
- [Jewish Council], Memorandum concerning labor camps organized in the Lublin region for the Jewish population in autumn 1940
- Organization of camps, deployment, number of workers, conditions of work and of housing, in encl. statistical data, instruction ("Directions [for] delegates of the Jewish Council in Labor Camps" [fragment]), reports of inspection of individual camps, transcripts, lists of workers, documents.
- ***Description:*** transcript, typescript, German, Polish, 206×294, 224×295 mm, ss. 88, pp. 88.

  Other copies of this document: See Ring. I/3.

### 377. RING. II/273/5. Mf. ŻIH—799; USHMM—54.

- 25.10.1942, Lublin
- Abram Borowski (Lublin, ul. Lipowa 7 [labor camp]), Letter of 25.10.1942 to brother D. Borowski (Warsaw Ghetto, OBW, ul. Gęsia 30)
- Request for help, notation about acquaintances.
- ***Description:*** original, handwritten manuscript, pencil, Polish, 116×197 mm, ss. 2, pp. 4.

  Attached envelope (handwritten manuscript, postal stamp, stamp of camp censor and of the Jewish Council in Warsaw, ink, 155×125 mm, ss. 1, pp. 2.); on p. 1 (envelope) erroneously written street name, "Gęstrase," corrected (with pencil): "Gęsia"; on p. 2 (envelope) notation (pencil): "ul. Gęsia 30, there is no house, addressee unknown 29.10.[1942]."

  See *Archiwum Ringelbluma*, p. 184 (summary).

  Published: *Listy o Zagładzie*, pp. 266–271.

Index: Ms. Tympulper, P. Borowski, Berek Mangut, Lande [Landau?], Fela Borodowska, Bronka Borer (workshop of Kurt Röhrich, ul. Nowolipie 80), Szmul Zeldman, prisoner of labor camp in Lublin (ul. Lipowa 7), Aron Zeldman (ul. Miła 49, apt. 6)

### 378. RING. II/295. Mf. ŻIH—800; USHMM—55.

- After 09.1942, Warsaw Ghetto
- NN., Account of a fugitive from Treblinka, with attached map of the extermination camp in Treblinka (ending missing)
- Author, a worker in the "Palm" factory for artificial honey in the Warsaw Ghetto, on 25.08.1942 was transported to Treblinka. He evaded death by applying for work. After several weeks he escaped, stayed in the ghetto of Stoczek near Węgrów, returned to Warsaw. Encl. map of the extermination camp in Treblinka (with summary).
- ***Description:*** transcript, handwritten manuscript (two handwritings: Tr* and NN.), ink, Polish, 152×191, 196×310 mm, ss. 7, pp. 14.

  Initial part of the account (pp. 1–4) was recorded (or copied) by two persons, who alternated in the work. From the middle of page 4 text was written by only one female copyist (one male copyist [?]).

  According to Ruta Sakowska, the account's author was Jakub Krzepicki; see *Archiwum Ringelbluma*, p. 152 (summary).

  Published: BŻIH, no. 40/1961, pp. 78–85; *Selected Documents*, pp. 710–716; *Kronika getta*, pp. 636 (photocopy of encl.).

  See Ring. II/299.

### 379. RING. II/296. Mf. ŻIH—800; USHMM—55.

- 28.08.[1942], Warsaw Ghetto
- Dawid Nowodworski, Account of stay in the extermination camp in Treblinka (28.08.[1942])
- Author (age 26), 17.08.1942 transported from Umschlagplatz to Treblinka (journey, description of camp, escape, stay in Stoczek near Węgrów, return to Warsaw).
- ***Description:*** original (o), handwritten manuscript (LEG* i H*), notebook, pencil, Polish, Yiddish, 143×205 mm, ss. 11, pp. 10.

  Presumably the account was recorded at the dictation of the author; hence, the text is written carelessly and in places is difficult to read. Abraham Lewin also writes about the creation of this document (*Dziennik z warszawskiego getta*, BŻIH, no. 22/1957, pp. 95).

  See *Archiwum Ringelbluma*, p. 110 (summary).

### 380. RING. II/297. Mf. ŻIH—800; USHMM—55.

- After 09.1942, Warsaw Ghetto
- NN., Account by an escapee from Treblinka
- Author (born 1922), resident of Częstochowa (ul. Dreszera), transported to Treblinka 21.09.1942, worked in sorting of clothing (organization of camp servants [służb obozowych] and their treatment by Germans), escaped from the camp and found his way into the Warsaw Ghetto. Encl. 4 sketches of map of the camp in Treblinka (with explanations).
- ***Description:*** original or transcript, handwritten manuscript, ink, Polish, 150×197, 185×200 mm, ss. 10, pp. 18.

  Published: BŻIH, no. 40/1961, pp. 85–88 (without encl.); *Archiwum Ringelbluma*, pp. 124–125 (photocopy of maps, printed text of explanations).

### 381. RING. II/298. Mf. ŻIH—800; USHMM—55.

- 09.1942, Warsaw Ghetto
- NN., Account of the extermination camp in Treblinka (fragment)
- Arrival of successive transports with people; camp during preparations for a Soviet air raid.
- ***Description:*** transcript, handwritten manuscript (H*), ink, Polish, 224×316 mm, ss. 1, pp. 2.

  On p. 1 notation in Hebrew: "turn away."

  Author of the account was probably Jakub Rabinowicz, who escaped from Treblinka and returned to the ghetto in the second half of September 1942; see A. Lewin, *Dziennik z warszawskiego getta*, BŻIH, no. 22/1957, p. 105; *Kronika getta*, p. 416.

  Published: *Archiwum Ringelbluma*, p. 122–123; *Selected Documents*, pp. 709–710.

### 382. RING. II/299. Mf. ŻIH—800; USHMM—55.

- After 26.12.1942, Warsaw Ghetto
- [Jakub Krzepicki], Account entitled "A mentsh iz antlofn fun Treblinke . . . geshprekhn mit tsurikgekumene" [A person escaped from Treblinka . . . Conversations with returnees]
- Author seized and transported from Warsaw 25.08.1942, describes in detail the route to Treblinka, stay in the camp and forced labor, the extermination of successive transports of Jew, sorting of things left by those murdered, selections of workers in the camp, escape from Treblinka, and sneaking into the Warsaw Ghetto (10.1942). Account was recorded and preceded by general introduction by Rachela Auerbach. Encl. map of the camp
- ***Description:*** transcript, handwritten manuscript (RA*), notebooks, ink, pencil, German, Polish, Yiddish, 118×68, 59×85, 152×197, 160×197, 223×344 mm, photograph, ss. 286, pp. 323.

  On the reverse of photograph a stamp: "8154 Foto «Dager» [ul.] Zamenhofa 3"; notation (handwritten manuscript—RA*, ink): "Jakub Krzepicki." Photograph was initially clipped by a pin to the sheet with notation (two handwritings, pencil, Polish, ink, Yiddish): "Jakub Krzepicki, Gdańsk, Japengasse 27, born

14.08.1915 in Praszka in district of Wieluń; Roza Krzepicka, Palestine, Tel-Aviv, Michaelstrasse 4; Abram Krzepicki, Mauritius, Port Louis, POB 1000"; as well as notation in Yiddish: "In the event of my death, please notify about my fate."
- Encl. sketch of map of camp (handwritten manuscript, pencil, ss. 1, pp. 1.

Published: BFG, vol. IX, no. 1–2/1956, pp. 71–141; BŻIH, no. 43–44/1962, pp. 84–109 (fragment).

Index: Engineer Galewski of Łódź, kapo at Treblinka; Pozner, kapo at Treblinka; Berliner of Warsaw, mortally injured an SS-man in Treblinka, murdered by guards with shovels; Jakow Lichtensztajn, transported to Treblinka; Herszkowicz, father and son, escaped from Treblinka together with Krzepicki; Mosze Blanket, transported to Treblinka; Maks Bihler, SS-man in Treblinka, mortally wounded by one of the prisoners; Żelechower, transported to Treblinka; Samek Kapłan, transported to Treblinka; Winer, escaped from Treblinka; Mędrzycki, escaped from Treblinka

### 383. RING. II/273/2. Mf. ŻIH—799; USHMM—54.

- 5.10.1942, Treblinka
- Hersz Lepalk (Treblinka [camp]), Letter of 5.10.1942 to wife NN. [Warsaw Ghetto]
- Is in camp from 31.08.1942, works in workshop as a carpenter.
- ***Description:*** original, handwritten manuscript, ink, German, 148×210 mm, ss. 2, pp. 1.

See *Archiwum Ringelbluma*, p. 179 (summary). Published: *Listy o Zagładzie*, pp. 225–227.

### 384. RING. II/300/1. Mf. ŻIH—800; USHMM—55.

- II half 1942, Warsaw Ghetto
- NN., Sketch for map of extermination camp in Treblinka
- ***Description:*** original (4 copies), handwritten manuscript, pencil, 220×290 mm, ss. 4, pp. 5.

On reverse of fourth copy is an outline sketch of map of the extermination camp in Treblinka (another handwriting, pencil); similar sketches (one handwriting); see Ring. II/297. See also manuscript from Ring. II/300/2.

### 385. RING. II/488. Mf. ŻIH—809; USHMM—64.

- After 07.1942, Warsaw Ghetto
- NN., Map of the extermination camp in Treblinka
- ***Description:*** original, handwritten manuscript, pencil, ink, Polish, 440×352 mm, ss. 1, pp. 1.
- 386. Ring. II/293/4. Mf. ŻIH—800; USHMM—55.
- Date unknown, place unknown
- Labor camp NN., Armband of overseer [brygadzisty] from the labor camp.
- ***Description:*** original, cloth (ribbon) with imprint: "Vorarbeiter, Lager 1" [Foreman, Camp 1], German, 345×73 mm, minor damages and losses of text, ss. 1, pp. 1.

## VI. Literary Texts

### 387. RING. II/473. MISSING ORIGINAL

- Date unknown, place unknown
- Sholem Aleichem
- ***Description:*** original, handwritten manuscript, Yiddish

### 388. RING. II/364. Mf. ŻIH—803; USHMM—58.

- 9.01.1943, Warsaw Ghetto
- B. Bigielman, Poem entitled "Numery-numerki" [Numbers-checks] (9.01.1943)
- Satire of the OBW carpentry workshop.
- ***Description:*** original, handwritten manuscript, ink, Polish, 220×355 mm, ss. 1, pp. 2.

See *Archiwum Ringelbluma*, p. 234 (summary).

### 389. RING. II/476. Mf. ŻIH—808; USHMM—63.

- Before 1939, Łódź[?]
- Jochanan Hamwaksz [Yohanan Ha-Mevakesh, Yohanan the Seeker], Story entitled "Na ve-nad" [Wandering]
- Jewish wanderer goes from town to town and tells about life. Text translated into Yiddish and dedicated to the memory of Rabbi Simcha Eliezer, son of Rabbi Yosef Dan.
- ***Description:*** original, handwritten manuscript, ink, Hebrew,[15] 108×340 mm, sewn, ss. 14, pp. 26.

### 390. RING. II/355. Mf. ŻIH—802; USHMM—57.

- After 1.05.1941, Warsaw Ghetto
- [Icchak Kacenelson (Yitshak Katzenelson)], Poem entitled "Der bal" [The Ball] (1.05.1941)
- ***Description:*** original, typescript (additions, handwritten manuscript—IK*, pencil), Yiddish, 210×295 mm, ss. 2., pp. 2.

Published: BFG, vol. VII, no. 2–3/1954, pp. 206; Y. Katzenelson, *Yiddish Ghetto Writings. Warsaw 1940–1943*, edited by Y. Szeintuch, Ghetto Fighters' House and Hakibbutz Hameuchad Publishing House 1984, pp. 485–491.

15. The description states that it is translated into Yiddish.

**391. RING. II/346. Mf. ŻIH–802; USHMM–57.**

- 06.1941, Warsaw Ghetto
- Icchak Kacenelson [Yitzhak Katzenelson], Iyov—biblishe tragedie in dray aktn [Job—A Biblical Tragedy in Three Acts] [Warsaw 1941]
- Drama published by the Dror publishing house, on the title page an illustration by Salomon Nusbaum.
- ***Description:*** original, duplicated typescript, Yiddish, 200×266, 205×275 mm, ss. 50, pp. 100.

Published: BfG, vol. XX/1981, pp. 169–272; Y. Katzenelson, *Yiddish Ghetto Writings. Warsaw 1940–1943*, edited by Y. Szeintuch, Ghetto Fighters' House and Hakibbutz Hameuchad Publishing House 1984, pp. 500–609.

**392. RING. II/347. Mf. ŻIH–802; USHMM–57.**

- Date unknown, Warsaw Ghetto
- [Yitzhak Katzenelson], Poem entitled "Vegn Shloyme Zhelikhovski" [On Shloyme Zhelikhovski]
- ***Description:*** original or transcript, typescript (handwritten additions, ink), Yiddish, 210×294 mm, ss. 4, pp. 4

See I. Kacenelson, *Pieśń o zamordowanym żydowskim narodzie* [Song of the Murdered Jewish People], translated by Jerzy Ficowski, Warsaw 1986, p. 10.

Published: Y. Katzenelson, *Yiddish Ghetto Writings. Warsaw 1940–1943*, edited by Y. Szeintuch, Ghetto Fighters' House and Hakibbutz Hameuchad Publishing House 1984, pp. 642–648; D. Roskies, ed., *The Literature of Destruction* (1989), pp. 531–547.

**393. RING. II/348. Mf. ŻIH–802; USHMM–57.**

- After 05.1942, Warsaw Ghetto
- [Yitzhak Katzenelson], Poem entitled "Vey dir . . ." [Woe to you . . .]
- Composition written under the influence of news about the extermination of the Jews of Lublin.
- ***Description:*** transcript, typescript, Yiddish, 210×295 mm, ss. 3, pp. 3

See I. Kacenelson, *Pieśń o zamordowanym żydowskim narodzie*, translated by Jerzy Ficowski, Warsaw 1986, p. 10.

Published (photocopy and in translation into Polish): *Archiwum Ringelbluma*, pp. 213–216, 368–370; Y. Katzenelson, *Yiddish Ghetto Writings. Warsaw 1940–1943*, edited by Y. Szeintuch, Ghetto Fighters' House and Hakibbutz Hameuchad Publishing House 1984, pp. 634–639.

**394. RING. II/349. Mf. ŻIH–802; USHMM–57.**

- After 14.08.1942 and after 9.10.1942, Warsaw Ghetto
- [Yitzhak Katzenelson], "Der tog [14.08.1942] fun mayn groysn umglik" [The Day (14.08.1942) of my great misfortune]
- Poem written after loss of wife (Chana) and 2 sons (Ben-Tsiyon and Yomele-Binyomin) transported to Treblinka on 14.08.1942.
- ***Description:*** original (typescript with handwritten additions –IK*, ink, damages and losses of text), transcript (2 copies, various versions, typescript), Yiddish, 216×280, 208×293 mm, ss. 22, pp. 22.

On p. 7 (transcript, first copy) date: "8–9.10.42."

Published: BFG, vol. XIX/1980, pp. 15–26; BŻIH, no. 100/1978, pp. 7–17; (photocopy original and translation into Polish): *Archiwum Ringelbluma*, pp. 207–212, 348–367; Y. Katzenelson, *Yiddish Ghetto Writings. Warsaw 1940–1943*, edited by Y. Szeintuch, Ghetto Fighters' House and Hakibbutz Hameuchad Publishing House 1984, pp. 707–731.

**395. RING. II/350. Mf. ŻIH–802; USHMM–57.**

- 15.11.1942–7.01.1943, Warsaw Ghetto
- [Yitzhak Katzenelson], Poem entitled "Dos lid vegn radziner" [The Song about the Rebbe of Radzyń] (15.11.1942–7.01.1943)
- About Rabbi Szmuel Szlojme Lajner of Radzyń Podlaski, who perished in 05.1942 in Włodawa. Composition dedicated to the poet's wife, Chana.
- ***Description:*** original, handwritten manuscript (IK*), notebooks, ink, Yiddish, 155×195, 155×200 mm, sewn, ss. 13, pp. 20.

See *Archiwum Ringelbluma*, p. 234 (summary).

Published: Y. Katzenelson, *Yiddish Ghetto Writings. Warsaw 1940–1943*, edited by Y. Szeintuch, Ghetto Fighters' House and Hakibbutz Hameuchad Publishing House 1984, pp. 663–706.

**396. RING. II/351. Mf. ŻIH–802; USHMM–57.**

- 1942, Warsaw Ghetto
- [Josef Kirman], Poems (2): "Di oygn blaybn ofn" [The Eyes Remain Open] (1942); "Nokh der blokade. (A khronik)" [After the Blockade. (A Chronicle)] (1942).
- ***Description:*** original, handwritten manuscript, ink, Yiddish, 219×278, 220×286 mm, ss. 2, pp. 2.

At top notation in Yiddish (pencil): "Kirman."

Published (photocopy and in Polish translation): *Archiwum Ringelbluma*, pp. 217–219, 371–372.

**397. RING. II/352. Mf. ŻIH–802; USHMM–57.**

- 1942, Warsaw Ghetto
- Szmuel Marwil, Poems (2): "Dos lid tsu di herrn" [The Song to the Gentlemen]; "Di gas" [The Street]
- Encl. Letter of 13.04.1942 to I. [Icchak] Giterman with thanks for financial aid.
- ***Description:*** original, handwritten manuscript, ink, Yiddish, 120×204, 219×288, 200×322 mm, damages and losses of text, ss. 10, pp. 10.

Poem "Di gas" written on the reverse of printed items "Protest wekslu" [Protest of Promissory Note] (Before 09.1939, printed matter, Polish).

Index: Sz. I. Stupnicki, H. Cejtlin, I. [Icchak] Kacenelson, Dir. Guzik, Knaster, physician

**398. RING. II/361. Mf. ŻIH–803; USHMM–58.**

- After 07.1942, Warsaw Ghetto
- Rachela Ofenberg, Collection of poems: "Nad morzem" [At the sea], "Polesie," "Wojna" [War], "Szop szczotkarski" [Brushmaking Workshop], "Górnicy" [Miners] and a scene ("short comedy") entitled "Zima" [Winter].
- ***Description:*** original, handwritten manuscript, notebook, pencil, Polish, 144×206 mm, ss. 11, pp. 22 (11 written on [zapisanych]).

  On p. 1 notation (pencil): "Rokhelke"; on p. 20 notation in Yiddish (handwritten manuscript-LEG*[?], pencil): "lider" [poems]. On p. 10 notation (handwritten manuscript—RA*[?], pencil): "Written [by] Rokhelke Ofenberg, 11 years [old], in the brushmakers' boarding school. Parents brushmakers, Pawia 7. Taken during the first blockade in the Św. Jerska 32 workshop."

  Manuscript written in notebook of "J. Prużański school notebooks and paper products factory, Warsaw Rynkowa 1 (former Gnojna, at Grzybowska) . . ."; on p. 1 notation with symbol (in Hebrew and Polish): "Keren Hatora Agudas Isroel w Polsce" [Torah Fund of Agudas Israel in Poland] beneath in Hebrew and Yiddish: "Good words," collection of 8 dictums (precepts) of a good pupil; on p. 22 (p. 1 of notebook—cover) photo. of Rabbi Natan Birnbojm [Nathan Birnbaum].

  See *Archiwum Ringelbluma,* p. 234 (summary).

**399. RING. II/471. Mf. ŻIH–808; USHMM–63.**

- Date unknown, no date
- Avrom Sutskever, Poem entitled "O brider mayner" [O, My Brothers]
- ***Description:*** transcript, handwritten manuscript, ink, Yiddish, 189×109 mm, ss. 1, pp. 1.

  On reverse notations.

**400. RING. II/353. Mf. ŻIH–802; USHMM–57.**

- Date unknown, Warsaw Ghetto
- [Władysław Szlengel], Poems (5): 1) "Paszport" [Passport]; 2) "Mała stacja Treblinki" [Little Station of Treblinka]; 3) "Rzeczy" [Things]; 4) "Telefon" [Telephone]; 5) "Za pięść I dwunasta" [Five of Twelve].
- ***Description:*** transcript (poem "Rzeczy" in 2 copies, handwritten manuscript—JG*, pencil, and typescript, 218×290, 205×294 mm; poem "Telefon" in 2 copies, typescript, 208×297, 222×348 mm), typescript, handwritten manuscript, pencil, Polish, 223×289, 222×348 mm, ss. 9, pp. 10.

  There are minor differences between the handwritten copy and the typescript of the poem "Rzeczy."

  Published: Szlengel, pp. 61–64, 71, 74–75, 125–128, 131–133 ("Mała stacja Treblinki," "Paszport," "Rzeczy," "Za pięść I dwunasta," "Telefon"); *Archiwum Ringelbluma,* pp. 228–229, 232–233 ("Mała stacja Treblinki," "Za pięść I dwunasta"); *Pieśń ujdzie cało. Antologia wierszy o żydach pod okupacją niemiecką,* ed. M. Borwicz, Warsaw-Łódź-Kraków 1947, pp. 169–172, 172–175 ("Rzeczy," "Telefon").

**401. RING. II/354. Mf. ŻIH–802; USHMM–57.**

- 12.1942, Warsaw Ghetto
- [Władysław Szlengel], Poem entitled "Już czas! Czas!" [It's time! Time!] (12.1942)
- ***Description:*** transcript, typescript, Polish, 211×260 mm, ss. 1, pp. 1.

  Published: Szlengel, p. 129; *Archiwum Ringelbluma,* pp. 230–231.

**402. RING. II/474. Mf. ŻIH–808; USHMM–63.**

- 11.04.1935, place unknown
- NN., "A bletl geshikhte fun der mentshhayt" [A page from the history of humanity] (11.04.1934)
- Composition written on the basis of a poem [?] by Julian Tuwim.
- ***Description:*** original or transcript, handwritten manuscript, pencil, Yiddish, 146×207 mm, ss. 1, pp. 1.

**403. RING. II/359. Mf. ŻIH–802; USHMM–57.**

- After 07.1942, Warsaw Ghetto
- NN., Poem entitled "Vu iz got?" [Where is God?].
- ***Description:*** original or transcript, handwritten manuscript, ink, Yiddish 175×216 mm, ss. 1, pp. 2.

  Published (photocopy and Polish translation): *Archiwum Ringelbluma,* pp. 219–221, 373–374.

**404. RING. II/358. Mf. ŻIH–802; USHMM–57.**

- 09/10.1942, Warsaw Ghetto
- NN., Poem entitled "Ve-natati nikmati ba-edom" [And I inflicted my vengeance on Edom].
- ***Description:*** transcript, typescript, Hebrew, 210×295 mm, ss. 3, pp. 3.

  See *Archiwum Ringelbluma,* p. 221 (summary).

**405. RING. II/357. Mf. ŻIH–802; USHMM–57.**

- 1942, Warsaw Ghetto
- NN., Poem entitled "Heykhan at biti?" [Where are you, my daughter?].
- ***Description:*** transcript, typescript, Hebrew, 205×290 mm, minor damages and losses of text, ss. 2, pp. 2.

**406. RING. II/366. Mf. ŻIH–803; USHMM–58.**

- 27.01.[1943?], Warsaw Ghetto
- NN., Song entitled "Verk no. 5" [Work no. 5] (27.01.[1943?])
- Satire on life in a workshop in the Warsaw Ghetto.
- ***Description:*** original or transcript, handwritten manuscript (U*), pencil, Yiddish, 109×290 mm, ss. 2, pp. 4.

**407. RING. II/477. Mf. ŻIH—808; USHMM—63.**

- Date unknown, place unknown
- NN., Drama entitled "Statek na wodzie. Tagedia w 4 aktach (X obrazach)." [Ship on the water. Tragedy in 4 acts (X scenes)].
- ***Description:*** original or transcript, handwritten manuscript, notebook, ink, Polish, 146×205 mm, sewn, ss. 64, pp. 122.

  On p. 2 notation (handwritten manuscript, two handwritings): "Ms. [Ida] Kamińska, director [of the Warsaw] 'Nowości' Theater, assembled—member of the board—supposedly was v[ery] good play"; on p. 1: "T. Albert, Głowaczów, Kozienice district," crossed out: "Wajnberg, Warsaw, Ogrodowa 33/16."

**408. RING. II/356. Mf. ŻIH—802; USHMM—57.**

- Date unknown, Warsaw Ghetto
- NN., Poem entitled "Ba-yamim adumim" [In purple days (?)]
- ***Description:*** original or transcript, handwritten manuscript (LEG*), pencil, Hebrew, 55×88 mm, ss. 1, pp. 1.

  See *Archiwum Ringelbluma*, p. 234 (summary).

**409. RING. II/360. Mf. ŻIH—802; USHMM—57.**

- Date unknown, Warsaw Ghetto
- NN., Poem entitled "Das jüdische Kind" [The Jewish child].
- ***Description:*** original or transcript, handwritten manuscript, pencil, German, 104×148 mm, ss. 1, pp. 1.

**410. RING. II/362. Mf. ŻIH—803; USHMM—58.**

- Date unknown, Warsaw Ghetto
- NN., Satire by [Ha-]Shomer [Ha-Tsair] of the "Tel-Amal" brigade in the Warsaw Ghetto
- Monologues, dialogues, sketches, scenes entitled "Straszna niedziela" [Awful Sunday], "Reportaż z orkiestry" [Report from the orchestra].
- ***Description:*** original or transcript, handwritten manuscript (TA*), ink, Polish, 150×200, 150×195, 160×202 mm, ss. 18, pp. 25.

  Doc. was kept in a binder.

  See Ring. II/480, II/481.

**411. RING.II/363. Mf. ŻIH—803; USHMM—58.**

- Date unknown, Warsaw Ghetto
- NN., Humorous tale entitled "Sen nocy zimowej" [A Winter's Night's Dream]
- Satiric story of the life of Ha-Shomer Ha-Tsair members [szomrów].
- ***Description:*** original, handwritten manuscript, ink, pencil, Polish, 159×202 mm, ss. 4, pp. 8.

  Doc. was kept in a binder.

**412. RING. II/365. Mf. ŻIH—803; USHMM—58.**

- Date unknown, Warsaw Ghetto
- NN., Song entitled "Kuplety więzienne" [Prison couplets]
- Satire on the prison in the Warsaw Ghetto (ul. Gęsia).
- ***Description:*** original or transcript, typescript, Polish, Yiddish in Roman transcription, 206×297 mm, ss. 1, pp. 2.

**413. RING. II/371. Mf. ŻIH—836; USHMM—67.**

- Date unknown, Warsaw Ghetto
- NN., "Spetsyel farfaste tfile tsu der yetstiger tsayt" [Specially composed prayer for the present time]
- Text arranged in the Warsaw Ghetto [?].
- ***Description:*** original or transcript, typescript, Yiddish, 209×296 mm, minor damages and losses of text, ss. 1, pp. 1.

  Published: *Archiwum Ringelbluma*, pp. 332–333; *Selected Documents*, pp. 429–430.

## VII. Periodicals and Other Publications

### *JEWISH PRESS IN THE PERIOD OF THE SEPTEMBER CAMPAIGN OF 1939*

**414. RING. II/326. Mf. ŻIH—802; USHMM—57.**

- 09.1939, Warsaw
- *Naye folkstsaytung* [New People's Newspaper], no. 267 of 16.09.1939
- Daily, press organ of Bund.
- ***Description:*** original, printed matter, Yiddish, 366×504 mm, ss. 1, pp. 2.

  See Ring. I/679.

### *PRESS AND OFFICIAL PUBLICATIONS ISSUED IN GERMANY AND IN THE OCCUPIED TERRITORIES*

**415. RING. II/325. Mf. ŻIH—802; USHMM—57.**

- 11–12.1942, Berlin
- *Novoe Slovo* [New Word], no. 93 (475) of 22.11., no. 94 (476) of 25.11., no. 103 (485) of 27.12.1942
- German newspaper published in Russian.
- ***Description:*** original (no. 94 (476) in 2 copies), printed matter, Russian, 312×467 mm, ss. 16, pp. 32.

  See Ring. I/757.

**416. RING. II/345. Mf. ŻIH—802; USHMM—57.**

- 1940–01.1943, Warsaw, Kraków, Hamburg, Berlin
- Collection of press clippings (*Gazeta Żydowska*,

*Hamburger Fremdenblatt, Krakauer Zeitung, Nowy Kurier Warszawski, Deutsche Allgemeine Zeitung, Das Reich, Berliner Ilustrierte Zeitung, Warschauer Zeitung, Völkischer Beobachter*, and others)
- ***Description:*** original, printed matter, German, Polish, 76×60, 175×182, 383×575, damages and lossesof text, ss. 106, pp. 200.
  On some clippings handwritten notes—H.W.*, H* (ink, pencil). Clippings have original [?] numbering from 1 to 93 (red pencil) (missing 19, 24, 82).

### 417. RING. II/318. Mf. ŻIH—801; USHMM—56.

- 30.09.1941–7.08.1942, Kraków.
- *Gazeta Żydowska* [Jewish Newspaper], no. 92 of 30.09.1941, no. 77 of 1.07.1942, no. 83 of 15.07.1942, no. 93 of 7.08.1942
- Daily, official organ of the official Jewish communities [gmin Żydowskich] in the Generalgouvernement.
- ***Description:*** original, printed matter, Polish, 290×428 mm, ss. 9, pp. 18.
  See Ring. I/702.

### 418. RING. II/327. Mf. ŻIH—802; USHMM—57.

a)
- After 06.1941, place unknown
- Leaflet: Генерал зима тает . . . [General Winter is thawing . . .]
- German propaganda publication calling on soldiers of the Red Army to surrender and cross over to the German side.
- ***Description:*** original, printed matter, German, Russian, 148×215 mm, ss. 1, pp. 2.

b)
- After 12.1941, place unknown
- Leaflet: Бойцы и командиры Красной Армии! Народы Советского Союза! [Fighters and Commanders of the Red Army! Peoples of the Soviet Union!]
- German propaganda publication to the soldiers of the Red Army and the civilian population of the USSR.
- ***Description:*** original, printed matter, Russian, 149×204 mm, minor damages and losses of text, ss. 1, pp. 2.

c)
- After 06.1941, place unknown
- Leaflet: Советские партизаны—партийные и беспартийные! [Soviet Partisans—Party and Nonparty!]
- German propaganda publication calling on Soviet partisans to surrender.
- ***Description:*** original, printed matter, German, Russian, 143×214 mm, ss. 1, pp. 1.

## *UNDERGROUND PRESS OF THE WARSAW GHETTO*

### 419. RING. II/316/1. Mf. ŻIH—801; USHMM—56.

- 12.1942–02.1943, Warsaw [ghetto?]
- *Biuletyn Informacyjny Żagiew* [The Torch Information Bulletin], no. of 13–15.12.1942, no. 898 of 5.01.1943, no. 900 of 7.01., no. 904 of 12.01., no. 907 of 14.01., no. 908 of 15.01., no. 909 of 16.01., no. 912 of 27.01., no. 915 of 30.01., no. 916 of 31.01., no. 917 of 1.02., no. 917 of 1.02.1943 (special edition)
- Underground publication of the Żagiew [Torch] organization.
- ***Description:*** original, duplicated typescript, Polish, 219×350, 208×297, 207×293 mm, ss. 20, pp. 20.
  No. of 13–15.12.1942 bears the title: *Biuletyn Informacyjny Org. Żagiew. Komunikaty Wojenne* [Information Bulletin of the Torch Organization. War Announcements]; in: *Centralny katalog*, p. 268 (the publication is under the title: *Żagiew. Biuletyn Informacyjny* [Torch. Information Bulletin]).
  See Cukierman, p. 233.
  See Ring. I/730.

### 420. RING. II/316/2. Mf. ŻIH—801; USHMM—56.

- Date unknown, Warsaw [ghetto?]
- Chief Commandant of the Organization Żagiew [Torch], Proclamation
- Call for solidarity in struggle for freedom. Proclamation signed by T.L.
- ***Description:*** original, duplicated typescript, Polish, 207×293 mm, ss. 1, pp. 1.

### 421. RING. II/317. Mf. ŻIH—801; USHMM—56.

- 11.1942–01.1943, Warsaw Ghetto
- Announcements from radio intercepts (various), no. of 28.11., 11.12., 16–20.12., 21.12., 29–30.12.1942, 3–5.01.1943, and 11.01.1943.
- ***Description:*** original, typescript, handwritten manuscript (various handwritings: H* and others), pencil, Polish, 218×288, 144×185, 223×287, 223×142 mm, ss. 11, pp. 12.
  No. of 11.12.1942 bears title: *Biuletyn Radiowy* [Radio Bulletin]; no. of 30.12.1942: "Announcements and News" (See Ring. I/768).
  Part of the announcements numbered (red pencil): from no. "21" to "26."
  See *Archiwum Ringelbluma*, pp. 322, 327–328, 333–334 (summary).

### 422. RING. II/329. Mf. ŻIH—802; USHMM—57.

- 12.1942, Warsaw Ghetto
- *Oyf der Vakh* [On Guard], no. 2 of 4.12.1942 and no. 3 of 26.12.1942.
- Underground publication of Bund.
- ***Description:*** original (no. 3 in 2 copies), duplicated typescript, Yiddish, 219×350 mm, ss. 24, pp. 24.

On no. 2 notation (red pencil): "19"; on no. 3 notation (red pencil): "20"; on no. 3 (second copy) notation (red pencil): "20a"
See *Archiwum Ringelbluma*, pp. 324–326, 328 (description, published fragment of no. 2).
See *Centralny katalog*, p. 144.
Published: BFG, vol. IV, no. 1/1951, pp. 80–84 (fragment).

### 423. RING. II/338/1. Mf. ŻIH—836; USHMM—67.

- 11.1942–01.1943, Warsaw Ghetto
- *Wiadomości. ARG* [News. ARG], [No. 1] of 14–21.11., no. 2 of 22.11–5.12., no. 3 of 12.12.1942, no. 4 of 23–31.12.1942, no. 5 of 1–8.01.1943, and no. 6 of 9–15.01.1943
- Underground publication of the Jewish Coordinating Committee of the Jewish National Committee and the Bund [prepared by members of "Oyneg Shabes"?].
- ***Description:*** original (no. 1, 3 in 2 copies), no. 2 in 8 copies (including 1 incomplete copy, missing p. 1), no. 5 in 4 copies (including 1 incomplete copy, missing pp. 1, 4 and 7), no. 6 in 3 copies), typescript, Polish, 218×290 225×288 mm, minor damages and losses of text (no. 1), ss. 94, pp. 96.

At top (on all pages) on right side of page notation: "ARG."
On p. 1 (no. 1 in 1 copy) notation (handwritten manuscript—H*[?], red pencil): "Complete" [Pełny].
See *Archiwum Ringelbluma*, pp. 322, 326, 328, 334 (summary).
Published: BŻIH, no. 76/1970, pp. 49–79 (no. 1, 2, 3, 5, 6); no. 213/2005, pp. 30–50 (no. 4).

### 424. RING. II/334. Mf. ŻIH—802; USHMM—57.

- Date unknown, Warsaw Ghetto
- Underground newspaper (missing title, fragment)
- Article entitled "From conversation"; Proclamation: "To You" (plea for struggle against the occupier).
- ***Description:*** original, typescript, Polish, 210×295 mm, ss. 1, pp. 1.

At top notation (red pencil): "27."
Published: *Archiwum Ringelbluma*, pp. 320–321.

## *OTHER UNDERGROUND PUBLICATIONS OF THE WARSAW GHETTO*

### 425. RING. II/343. Mf. ŻIH—836; USHMM—67.

- 1942, Warsaw Ghetto
- *Z problematyki ruchu w chwili obecnej* [Of the Movement's Issues at the Present Moment] [Warsaw, 1942]
- Brochure issued by the High Command of "Gordonia," contains movement's political program and educational tasks, inter alia. "Tracking bankrupt phraseology," "Scouting education in the present time."
- ***Description:*** original, printed matter, duplicated typescript, Polish, 170×245 mm, ss. 37, pp. 74.

See Ring. I/739.
See *Bibliografia druków*, p. 262.

### 426. RING. II/333. Mf. ŻIH—802; USHMM—57.

a)

- 30.10.1942, Warsaw Ghetto
- Underground organization in the Warsaw Ghetto, Announcement dated 30.10.1942 about execution of death sentence on Jakub Lejkin (29.10.1942).
- ***Description:*** original, duplicated typescript, Polish, 208×295 mm, ss. 1, pp. 1.

Published: BŻIH, no. 5/1953, p. 15; *Archiwum Ringelbluma*, pp. 261–262; *Selected Documents*, p. 588; *Kronika getta*, p. 713 (photocopy).

b)

- [01.1943], Warsaw Ghetto
- [ŻOB?], Proclamation: "Jews! The occupier is beginning the second act of your extermination! . . ."
- Call for struggle against the occupier.
- ***Description:*** original, duplicated typescript, Polish, 220×140 mm, ss. 1, pp. 1.

Published: *Archiwum Ringelbluma*, p. 337; *Selected Documents*, p. 591; *Kronika getta*, p. 721 (photocopy).

c)

- [01.1943], Warsaw Ghetto
- [Jewish Military Union (Żydowski Związek Wojskowy)], Proclamation: "Prepare for action! Keep alert!!!"
- Call to fight the occupier.
- ***Description:*** original, duplicated typescript, Polish, 225×287 mm, ss. 1, pp. 1.

Published: B. Mark, *Powstanie w Warszawskim getcie na tle ruchu oporu w Polsce*, 2nd ed., Warsaw 1954, pp. 174–176; idem, *Powstanie w Warszawskim getcie. Nowe uzupełnione wydanie i zbiór dokumentów*, Warsaw 1963, pp. 209–211 (photograph after p. 354); *Archiwum Ringelbluma*, pp. 334–335; *Selected Documents*, pp. 590–591; *Kronika getta*, p. 715 (photocopy).

d)

- [Before 22.01.1943], Warsaw Ghetto
- "Varshe-geto" [Warsaw Ghetto], no. 1 of 01.1943
- Communiqué [ŻOB] containing proclamation calling for fight against the occupier.
- ***Description:*** original, typescript, Yiddish, 218×284 mm, ss. 1, pp. 1.

Published: BFG, vol. IV, no. 1/1951, pp.80–84; in Polish translation: BŻIH, no. 5/1953, pp. 15–16; B. Mark, *Powstanie w Warszawskim getcie na tle ruchu oporu w Polsce*, 2nd ed., Warsaw 1954, pp. 173–174; idem, *Powstanie w Warszawskim getcie. Nowe uzupełnione wydanie i zbiór dokumentów*, Warsaw 1963, pp. 207–209; *Archiwum Ringelbluma*, pp. 336–337; *Selected Documents*, p. 589.

**427. RING. II/316/3. Mf. ŻIH—801; USHMM—56.**

- 12.1942, Warsaw Ghetto
- Propaganda Department of POW [Polska Organizacja Wojskowa (Polish Military Organization)?], Proclamation entitled "To Jewish society in Warsaw" (12.1942)
- Summons to take up the fight for honor and national dignity.
- ***Description:*** transcript, handwritten manuscript (H.W.*), pencil, Polish, 222×355 mm, ss. 1, pp. 1.
  At bottom notation: "written on machine."

**428. RING. II/316/4. Mf. ŻIH—801; USHMM—56.**

- After 23.12.1942, Warsaw Ghetto
- POW [Polska Organizacja Wojskowa (Polish Military Organization) (?)]. Warsaw Ghetto Unit, Letter dated 23.12.1942 to Klara [sic] (Warsaw Ghetto)
- Concerns an order to contribute a payment in the amount of 20,000 [zł.?] for the benefit of the organization. Document signed Traugutt [sic].
- ***Description:*** transcript, handwritten manuscript (two handwritings: H.W.* i H*), pencil, Polish, 222×355 mm, ss. 1, pp. 1.

## *POLISH UNDERGROUND PRESS*

**429. RING. II/315/2. Mf. ŻIH—801; USHMM—56.**

- 01.1943, Warsaw
- *Agencja Radiowa* (Radio Agency), no. 13 (1109) of 13.01.1943
- Announcements from radio intercepts (Delegacy [Delegatura] of the [Polish] Government[-in-Exile]).
- ***Description:*** original, duplicated typescript, Polish, 206×291 mm, ss. 1, pp. 2.
  See Ring. I/769.
  See *Centralny katalog*, pp. 24–26.

**430. RING. II/313. Mf. ŻIH—801; USHMM—56.**

- 12.1942, Warsaw
- *Barykada Wolności* (Barricade of Freedom), no. of 6.12.1942
- Weekly of the Warsaw Workers Committee of the Polish Socialists [Tygodnik Warszawskiego Komitetu Robotniczego Polskich Socjalistów].
- ***Description:*** original, duplicated typescript, Polish, 208×293 mm, ss. 2, pp. 4.
  See *Centralny katalog*, p. 32.

**431. RING. II/314. Mf. ŻIH—801; USHMM—56.**

- 10.1941—01.1943, Warsaw
- *Biuletyn Informacyjny* (Information Bulletin), no. of 2.10., 9.10., 16.10., 23.10., 30.10. (missing original), 6.11., 13.11., 20.11., 27.11., 4.12., 11.12., [18.12.] [?], 23.12., 30.12.1941, no. 1(105) of 8.01., no. 2 (106) 15.01., no. 3 (107) 22.01., no. 4 (108) of 29.01., no. 5 (109) 5.02., no. 6 (110) 12.02., no. 7 (111) of 19.02., no. 8 (112) of 26.02., no. 9 (113) of 5.03., no. 10 (114) of 12.03., no. 11 (115) of 19.03., no. 12 (116) of 26.03., no. 15 (119) of 16.04., no. 16 (120) of 23.04., no. 17 (121) of 30.04., no. 15 (119) of 16.04., 18 (122) of 7.05., no. 19 (123) of 14.05., no. 20 (124) of 21.05., no. 45 (149) of 19.11., no. 46 (150) of 26.11., no. 48 (152) of 10.12., no. 50 (154) of 24.12., no. 51 (155) of 31.12.1942, no. 1 (156) of 7.01., and no. 2 (157) of 14.01.1943
- *Biuletyn Informacyjny, Edition "P"* [Powiat (District)], no. 53 of 20.11.1942
- Weekly of ZWZ-AK.
- ***Description:*** original (no. 2 (157) in 2 copies), printed matter, Polish, 125×175 mm, 149×221 mm, ss. 180, pp. 360.
  See Ring. I/719.
  See *Centralny katalog*, pp. 35–38.

**432. RING. II/319. Mf. ŻIH—801; USHMM—56.**

a)

- 01.1943–01.1943, Warsaw
- *Głos Warszawy* [Voice of Warsaw], no. 1 (10) of 1.01., no. 2 (11) of 5.01.1943
- Publication of the Warsaw Committee of the Polish Workers' Party (Komitetu Warszawskiego Polskiej Partii Robotniczej).
- ***Description:*** original (no. 1 (10) in 2 copies), printed matter, Polish, 158×215 mm, ss. 6, pp. 12.
  See *Centralny katalog*, pp. 79–80.

b)

- After 09.1942, Warsaw
- NN., Article "Obóz śmierci w Treblince" [Death Camp in Treblinka]
- Reprint from *Głos Warszawy.*
- ***Description:*** original, duplicated typescript, Polish, 207×294 mm, ss. 1, pp. 2.

**433. RING. II/320. Mf. ŻIH—801; USHMM—56.**

- 05.[1942], Warsaw
- *Gwardzista* [The Guardsman], no. [2 of 10.06.1942]
- Underground biweekly of the Gwardia Ludowa [People's Guard]. The issue contains call "To the units of the Gwardia Ludowa moving out into the field. Order of 15.05.[1942]."
- ***Description:*** original, duplicated typescript, Polish, 210×296 mm, ss. 8, pp. 8.
  In Ring. I/709 there is a printed version of this issue.
  See *Centralny katalog*, p. 85.

**434. RING. II/338/2. Mf. ŻIH—836; USHMM—67.**

- 12.1942, Warsaw Ghetto [?]
- *Informacja Bieżąca* [Current Information], no. 44 (69) of 2.12., no. 45 of 3.12., no. 47 (71) of 17.12.1942 (fragments)
- Underground publication of the ZWZ-AK.
- ***Description:*** transcript, typescript, Polish, 204×266 mm, ss. 8, pp. 8.
  Copies of fragments concerning Jewish matters. It seems that the document was included into the Oyneg Shabes/Ringelblum Archive collection after the war.

See *Archiwum Ringelbluma*, pp. 322, 327 (description no. 44 (69), 47 (71)).
See *Centralny katalog*, p. 88.

### 435. RING. II/321. Mf. ŻIH—801; USHMM—56.

- 04.1942–01.1943, Warsaw
- *Insurekcja* [Insurrection], 4 (16) of 04.1942, 1 (22) of 01.1943
- Underground monthly of ZWZ-AK.
- ***Description:*** original, printed matter, Polish, 125×177 mm, ss. 16, pp. 32.
  See *Centralny katalog*, pp. 92–93.

### 436. RING. II/322. Mf. ŻIH—801; USHMM—56.

- 12.1942, Warsaw
- *Jutro PN* [Tomorrow Independent Poland], no. 34 of 12.12.1942
- Underground weekly of the organization Polska Niepodległa [Independent Poland].
- ***Description:*** original, printed matter, Polish, 150×215 mm, minor damages and losses of text, ss. 4, pp. 8.
  See Ring. I/761.
  See *Centralny katalog*, pp. 96–97.

### 437. RING. II/315/1. Mf. ŻIH—801; USHMM—56.

- 12.1942, Warsaw
- *K.O.P. Biuletyn Informacyjny Grupy M* [?] [K.O.P. Information Bulletin of Group M], no. of 27.12.1942
- Underground publication of the Komenda Obrońców Polski [Central Command of the Defenders of Poland] (of the Polski Ruch Zjednoczenia Narodów [Polish Movement for the Union of Nations]).
- ***Description:*** original, duplicated typescript, Polish, 209×295 mm, ss. 1, pp. 2.

### 438. RING. II/324. Mf. ŻIH—801; USHMM—56.

- 11–12.1942, Warsaw
- *Myśl Państwowa* [State Thought], no. 31 of 27.11.1942 and no. 32 of 18.12.1942
- Underground biweekly of the Konwent Organizacji Niepodległościowych [Assembly of Organizations for Independence].
- ***Description:*** original, printed matter, Polish, 126×178 mm, minor damages and losses of text, ss. 20, pp. 40.
  On no. 31 note (red pencil): "9"; on no. 32 note (red pencil): "10."
  See Ring. I/721.
  See *Centralny katalog*, p. 125.

### 439. RING. II/328. Mf. ŻIH—802; USHMM—57.

- 12.1942–01.1943, Warsaw
- *Nowy Dzień* [New Day], no. 452 of 22.12., no. 455 of 29.12., no. 456 of 30.12.1942, no. 466 of 13.01.1943
- Underground daily of the organization Zbrojne Pogotowie Narodu [Armed Emergency Service of the Nation].
- ***Description:*** original, duplicated typescript, Polish, 209×295, 217×308 mm, ss. 10, pp. 20.
  *Centralny katalog*, p. 140.
  On no. 452 notation (red pencil): "1"

### 440. RING. II/330. Mf. ŻIH—802; USHMM—57.

- 12.1942, Warsaw
- *Polityka* [Politics], no. 1 of 12.1942
- Underground monthly of the organization Miecz i Pług [Sword and Plow].
- ***Description:*** original, printed matter, Polish, 183×244 mm, ss. 6, pp. 12.
  See *Centralny katalog*, p. 159.
  On p. 1 notation (red pencil): "17."

### 441. RING. II/331. Mf. ŻIH—802; USHMM—57.

- 05.1942, Warsaw
- *Prawda* [Truth], no. of 05.1942
- Underground monthly of the Front Odrodzenia Polski [Front for the Rebirth of Poland].
- ***Description:*** original, printed matter, Polish, 175×248 mm, ss. 4, pp. 8.
  See *Centralny katalog*, p. 172.

### 442. RING. II/335/1. Mf. ŻIH—802; USHMM—57.

- 11.1942, Warsaw
- *Trybuna Chłopska* [Peasant Tribune], no. 9 of 11.1942
- Underground monthly of the Polish Workers' Party [Polskiej Partii Robotniczej].
- ***Description:*** original, printed matter, Polish, 168×223, 153×216 mm, damages and losses of text, ss. 3, pp. 6.
  See *Centralny katalog*, pp. 219–220.

### 443. RING. II/335/2. Mf. ŻIH—802; USHMM—57.

- 01.1943, Warsaw
- *Trybuna Wolności* [Tribune of Freedom], no. 23 of 1.01.1943
- Underground biweekly Polish Workers' Party [Polskiej Partii Robotniczej].
- ***Description:*** original (2 copies), printed matter, Polish, 160×218, 158×201 mm, ss. 8, pp. 16.
  See *Centralny katalog*, p. 222.

### 444. RING. II/336. Mf. ŻIH—802; USHMM—57.

- 12.1942, Warsaw
- *Wiadomości Codzienne Miecza i Pługa* [Daily News of Sword and Plow], no. 243 of 23.12., no. 244 of 24.12.1942
- Underground publication of the organization Miecz i Pług [Sword and Plow].
- ***Description:*** original, printed matter, Polish, 158×238 mm, ss. 2, pp. 4.
  See Ring. I/725.
  *Centralny katalog*, pp. 239–240.

### 445. RING. II/339. Mf. ŻIH—802; USHMM—57.

- 01.1942–01.1943, Warsaw
- *Wiadomości Polskie* [Polish News], no. 1 (58) of 1.01.,

no. 2 (59) of 15.01., no. 3 (60) of 29.01. (encl. illustrated new year's supplement of 01/02.1942), no. 4 (61) of 12.02., no. 5 (62) of 1.04., no. 6 (63) of 15.04., no. 7 (64) of 29.04., no. 8 (65) of 13.05., no. 20 (77) of 4.11., no. 22 (79) of 2.12.1942, and no. 1 (81) of 13.01.1943
- Underground biweekly ZWZ-AK.
- ***Description:*** original (no. 22 (79) in 2 copies), printed matter, Polish, 152×215, 155×238 mm, ss. 46, pp. 92.

  See Ring. I/715.

  See *Centralny katalog*, pp. 241–242.

### 446. RING. II/400. Mf. ŻIH—804; USHMM—59.

- 01.1943, Warsaw
- *Wiadomości Polskie* [Polish News], illustrated supplement to no. 2 (82) ("Wojsko Polskie na obczyźnie" [Polish Armed Forces in Exile].
- ***Description:*** original, printed matter, Polish, 238×315 mm, ss. 1, pp. 2.

### 447. RING. II/337. Mf. ŻIH—802; USHMM—57.

- 12.1942, Warsaw
- *Wolność* [Freedom], no. 5 (21) of 12.1942. (fragment)
- Underground publication of the Polish Socialist Party (Freedom Equality Independence) [Polska Partia Socjalisticzna (Wolność Równość Niepodległość)].
- ***Description:*** original, printed matter, Polish, 124×170, 127×174 mm, missing pp. 7–10, ss. 6, pp. 12.

  See Ring. I/708.

  See *Centralny katalog*, pp. 255–256.

### 448. RING. II/340. Mf. ŻIH—802; USHMM—57.

- 12.1942, Warsaw
- *Załoga* [The Crew], no. 12 of 7.12.1942
- Underground publication of the Obóz Narodowo-Radykalny—Szaniec [National-Radical Camp—the Rampart].
- ***Description:*** original, printed matter, Polish, 175×249 mm, minor damages and losses of text, ss. 4, pp. 8.

  See *Centralny katalog*, p. 262.

### 449. RING. II/341. Mf. ŻIH—802; USHMM—57.

- 12.1942, Warsaw
- *Żołnierz Polski* [Polish Soldier], no. 9 (22) of 11.1942, no. 10 (23) of 12.1942
- Underground monthly of ZWZ-AK.
- ***Description:*** original (no. 10 in 2 copies), printed matter, Polish, 125×170, 123×179 mm, ss. 24, pp. 48.

  See *Centralny katalog*, pp. 269–270.

  On p. 1 (no. 9) notation (red pencil): "5."

## *OTHER UNDERGROUND PRINTED ITEMS*

### 450. RING. II/342. Mf. ŻIH—802; USHMM—57.

- 1942 [Warsaw]
- *Życie i śmierć dla Polski* [Life and Death for Poland], [Warsaw] 1942
- Programmatic brochure of Konfederacja Narodu [Confederacy of the Nation].
- ***Description:*** original, printed matter, Polish 118×156 mm, ss. 8, pp. 16.

  See *Bibliografia druków*, p. 277.

### 451. RING. II/332. Mf. ŻIH—802; USHMM—57.

- After 01.1942, Warsaw
- Leaflet entitled: "Do robotników, chłopów i inteligencji, do wszystkich patriotów polskich" [To workers, peasants and intelligentsia, to all Polish patriots]
- Programmatic proclamation of Polish Workers' Party [Polska Partia Robotnicza].
- ***Description:*** original (2 copies), (printed, 161×216 mm), transcript (typescript, 223×288 mm), ss. 3, pp. 6.

  See Ring. I/748.

  On p. 1 (original, first copy) notation (red pencil): "28."

  On p. 1 (transcript) notation (red pencil): "28a."

# VIII. Bequests[16]

## *DOCUMENTS OF RACHELA AUERBACH AND ICYK [ITSIK] MANGER*

### 452. RING. II/438. Mf. ŻIH—807; USHMM—62.

- 06.1926, place unknown
- [Rachela Auerbach], Fragments of chapters and notes for a work [entitled "The Individual and Individuality" (Indywiduum i indywidualność?)]
- Fragments of chapters V and VI: "Hipotezy i diagnozy psychognostyczne a ustalenie faktu rozwoju 'maski'," "Warunki i formy 'maski'" [Psychognostic Hypotheses and Diagnosis and Determination of the Fact of the Development of the "Mask," Conditions and Forms of the "Mask"].
- ***Description:*** original, handwritten manuscript (RA*), ink, pencil, Polish, 170×209, 209×339 mm, minor damages and losses of text, ss. 50, pp. 50.

  See Ring. II/439.

16. These records apparently consist of documents "bequeathed" to the Oyneg Shabes archive.

### 453. RING. II/439. Mf. ŻIH—807; USHMM—62.

- 1926, place unknown
- Rachela Auerbach, Study entitled "The Individual and Individuality. Objective Conditions of Individual Originality" [Indywiduum i indywidualność. Obiektywne warunki oryginalności indywidualnej] (25.06.1926)
- ***Description:*** original, typescript (supplements and corrections, two handwritings: RA* and NN., ink, pencil), handwritten manuscript, Polish, 211×340 mm, ss. 128, s.130.

  On the reverse of p. 128 stamp in Yiddish (illegible).

  Titles of chapters: I. "Inconsistency between psychic contents and external bearing" ; II. "Study of psychic contents on the basis of external bearing"; III. "Conditions and forms of the mask in the depiction of Elsa Voigtlander and Gustaw Ichheiser"; IV. "Function of disclosure and expression of the external bearing"; V. "Psychological contents of the individual and the psychological meaning of his external bearing"; VI. "Apperception of expression (perception) and supposition (inference) of psychological contents"; VII. "Causal analysis of conditions of the mask"; VIII. "Principal conditions of the 'mask' and the meaning of their establishment for psychognostic development."

### 454. RING. II/440. Mf. ŻIH—807; USHMM—62.

- Before 09.1939, Warsaw
- Rachela Auerbach, Article entitled "Duchowe przygody" [Spiritual adventures]
- About meeting and conversation with Stanisław Vincenz.
- ***Description:*** original or transcript, typescript, Polish, 224×355 mm, ss. 6, pp. 6.

### 455. RING. II/441. Mf. ŻIH—807; USHMM—62.

a)

- Date unknown, place unknown
- [Rachela Auerbach] Rokhel Oyerbakh, "A maysele mit a kultur-moral" [A story with a cultural moral]
- Response to criticism of a play by Itsik Manger (adaptation of Abraham Goldfaden's play, "The Witch").
- ***Description:*** original or transcript, typescript, Yiddish, 210×294 mm, ss. 4, pp. 4.

b)

- Before 09.1939, place unknown
- Rachela Auerbach, Article entitled "Warsaw produces a Yiddish sound movie"
- Concerns the "Kinor" company, involved in production of Yiddish films.
- ***Description:*** original or transcript, typescript, Polish, 222×354 mm, ss. 4, pp. 4.

c)

- Before 09.1939, place unknown
- [Rachela Auerbach], Article entitled "Dramat Buechnera Wocek w Teatrze 'Młoda Scena'" [Buechner's drama *Wocek* in the "Young Stage" Theater]
- Concerns staging in Warsaw of the play by Georg Büchner entitled *Wocek* in the translation by Itsik Manger.
- ***Description:*** original, typescript (supplements, handwritten manuscript—RA*, ink), Polish, 222×354 mm, ss. 2, pp. 2.

### 456. RING. II/442. Mf. ŻIH—807; USHMM—62.

- Before 09.1939, place unknown
- Rachela Auerbach, Article entitled "Dr. Klaftynowa tells"
- Interview with Dr. Cecylia Klaftynowa after her return from the United States, where she had been invited by the Galician Landsmanshaft [Ziomkostwo Galicyjskie].
- ***Description:*** original or transcript, typescript, Polish, 222×338, 222×291 mm, ss. 8, pp. 8.

### 457. RING. II/443. Mf. ŻIH—807; USHMM—62.

- Before 09.1939, place unknown
- Rachela Auerbach, Article entitled "Calea Dudesti sings in Yiddish. (From a journey through Romania)"
- About street art by Jews of Bucharest (e.g., Icek Goldenberg).
- ***Description:*** original or transcript, typescript, Polish, Yiddish in Roman transliteration, 222×352 mm, ss. 4, pp. 4.

### 458. RING. II/444. Mf. ŻIH—807; USHMM—62.

- Date unknown, place unknown
- [Rachela Auerbach], Notes from the lectures of Prof. F. Schneersohn: "Principles of study of the human being and the theory of nervous disorders" [Zasady nauki o człowieku i teoria nerwowości] and "Psychological exposition" [Ekspozycja psychologiczna].
- ***Description:*** original, typescript, handwritten manuscript, ink, Polish, 157×198, 218×173, 180×218 mm, ss. 35, pp. 46.

### 459. RING. II/458. Mf. ŻIH—807; USHMM—62.

- Before 12.1936, Lwów, Warsaw
- Abram (Abraham) Morewski [Menaker], Recollections entitled "Tam i z powrotem" [There and Back] (fragments)
- Childhood in Wilno, studies in St. Petersburg (theater) and in Dorpat (pharmacy), return to St. Petersburg (end of the 19th cent.–1908). Text translated from Yiddish (original title: "Ahin un tsurik" [There and back]) by Rachela Auerbach and intended for publication in *Chwila* (Lwów) and *Nasz Przegląd* (Warsaw). Encl. clippings from *Chwila* and *Nasz Przegląd* with fragments of Morewski's recollections.

- *Description:* original, printed matter, typescript (handwritten additions RA*, ink), Polish, 220×355, 318×470 mm, ss. 63, pp. 70.

  Fragments of recollections divided into chapters and subchapters: "There and Back. Fragments of the memoirs of Abraham Morewski" [Tam i z powrotem. Fragmenty pamiętników Abrahama Morewskiego] (attached introduction by Rachela Auerbach, "From the translator" and the author's introduction); "Fragments of the recollections of a Jewish actor" [Fragmenty wspomnień aktora-żyda] ("St. Petersburg," "Laurels and Shoes," "Sałtan Sałtanowicz" [?], "Left-handedness" [Sankt Petersburg, Wawrzyny i buty, Sałtan Sałtanowicz, Mańkuctwo] (Published: *Chwila*, no. 617 of 29.08.1936, p. 5); "Prawożitielstwo" [?] (Published: *Chwila*, no. 618 of 31.08.1936, p. 5); "Lies, or the story of how I became a pharmacist's assistant" [Kłamstwa, czyli historia o tem, jak stałem się pomocnikiem aptekarskim] (Published: *Chwila*, no. 619, 620 of 1, 2.09.1936, p. 5); "Only children" [Jedynacy (?)] (Published: *Chwila*, no. 621 of 3.09.1936, p. 5); "Cholera" and "Characters and episodes from the life of a Jewish actor" ("First impulses") [Postacie i epizody z życia aktora-żyda (Pierwsze porywy]) (Published: *Nasz Przegląd*, 1.11.1936, p. 11); "First Performance" [Pierwszy «występ»] (Published: *Nasz Przegląd*, 8.11.1936, p. 9); "Srul—Heinrich Gorpenko").

  Subchapter "Srul—Heinrich Gorpenko" (in 2 copies, first copy with handwritten additions—RA*, ink).

### 460. RING. II/276. Mf. ŻIH—799; USHMM—54.

- 10.10.1942, Warsaw Ghetto
- Rachela [Auerbach] (Warsaw Ghetto), Letter of 10.10.1942 to nephew Mundek (Lwów)
- Inf. about remittance of money, description of a typical day in the Warsaw Ghetto.
- *Description:* original, handwritten manuscript (RA*), ink, Polish, 175×216 mm, ss. 2, pp. 3.

  Letter was not sent or the author made a copy of the original.

  See *Archiwum Ringelbluma*, p. 180 (summary).

## Papers of Itsik Manger

### 461. RING. II/446. MISSING ORIGINAL

- Date unknown, place unknown
- Icyk [Itzik] Manger, Poems.
- *Description:* original or transcript, typescript, Polish, ss. 5, pp. 5.

  Note: Description of doc. on basis of inv.

### 462. RING. II/447. MISSING ORIGINAL

- Date unknown, place unknown
- Icyk [Itzik] Manger, Poem.
- *Description:* original or transcript, handwritten manuscript, Yiddish, ss. 1, pp. 1.

  Note: Description of doc. on basis of inv.

### 463. RING. II/448. MISSING ORIGINAL

- Date unknown, place unknown
- Icyk [Itzik] Manger, Poems.
- *Description:* original or transcript, typescript, Romanian, ss. 3, pp. 3.

  Note: Description of doc. on basis of inv.

### 464. RING. II/449. MISSING ORIGINAL

- Date unknown, place unknown
- Icyk Manger, Drama entitled *Di Kishuf-makhern* [The witch] pub. 1936] adapted from Abraham Goldfaden.
- *Description:* original or transcript, handwritten manuscript, Yiddish, ss. 56, pp. 56.

  Note: Description of doc. on basis of inv.

### 465. RING. II/450. MISSING ORIGINAL

- Date unknown, place unknown
- Icyk [Itzik] Manger, Józef Kamen [?].
- *Description:* original or transcript, typescript, handwritten manuscript, Polish, Yiddish, ss. 7, pp. 7.

  Note: Description of doc. on basis of inv.

### 466. RING. II/451. MISSING ORIGINAL

- Date unknown, place unknown
- Icyk [Itzik] Manger, [Shmuel Abervo][?]. [See *Dos Bukh fun gan-eydn*, 1939; *The Book of Paradise*, trans. L. Wolf, 1965]
- *Description:* original or transcript, handwritten manuscript, Yiddish, ss. 1, pp. 1.

  Note: Description of doc. on basis of inv.

### 467. RING. II/454. Mf. ŻIH—807; USHMM—62.

- Before 1939, place unknown
- I[cyk] [Itzik] Manger, Article entitled "S.J. [Samuel Jakub] Imber (Z okazji 30-letniego jubileuszu poety)." [S.J. Imber (On the occasion of the 30th anniversary of the poet)]
- Discussion of the poet's works.
- *Description:* transcript, typescript, Polish, 222×355 mm, ss. 4, pp. 4.

### 468. RING. II/452. Mf. ŻIH—807; USHMM—62.

- Before 09.1939, place unknown
- Georg Bikhner [Georg Büchner], Drama entitled *Woytsek* [*Wocek*]
- Trans. into Yiddish by Icyk [Itzik] Manger. Encl. Icyk [Itzik] Manger's synopsis of the play *Wocek*.
- *Description:* original, transcript (encl. in 3 copies), typescript, handwritten manuscript (two handwritings: NN. and additions—IM*[?]), ink, Polish, Yiddish, 223×253, 223×354 mm, ss. 37, pp. 38.

  First copy (encl.) with additions, handwritten manuscript-RA*, ink)

### 469. RING. II/453. Mf. ŻIH–807; USHMM–62.

- After 15.04.1929, place unknown
- Yankev Shternberg [Jakub Sternberg], "I. [Icyk] Manger—'Er iz shoyn do!'" [I. (Itsyk) Manger—"He's already here!"]
- Profile of Itzik Manger. Text published in the periodical *Unzer Veg* [Our Way] (Bucharest, no. of 15.04.1929).
- ***Description:*** transcript, typescript, Yiddish, 210×340 mm, ss. 1, pp. 1.
  On bottom notation in Yiddish (ink): critical observations by NN. on the subject of the article (signature illegible).

### 470. RING. II/445. Mf. ŻIH–807; USHMM–62.

- 1929, Warsaw
- Aron Cejtlin [Aron Tseytlin, Aharon Zeitlin], *Brener* [Brenner] (Warsaw, 1929) (fragment)
- Drama.
- ***Description:*** original, printed matter, Yiddish, 145×208 mm, missing pages, ss. 6, pp. 10.
  Book published by the Marek Rakowski Library. Printed by the Brothers Wójcikiewicz, Warsaw (ul. Pawia 10). On the title page author's dedication to Itzik Manger, dated 30.09.1929 (handwritten manuscript, ink, Yiddish).

### 471. RING. II/455. Mf. ŻIH–807; USHMM–62.

- 1902, Warsaw
- Abraham Goldfaden, *Shulamis oder bas-yerushalaim* [Shulamis or daughter of Jerusalem] (Warsaw, 1902)
- Drama.
- ***Description:*** original, printed matter, Russian, Yiddish, 157×236 mm, ss. 30, pp. 60.
  Printed at the Lewin-Epsztajn printworks, Warsaw (ul. Pawia 14).

### 472. RING. II/456. Mf. ŻIH–807; USHMM–62.

- 1902, Warsaw
- Abraham Goldfaden, *Di kishuf-makhern* [The Witch] (Warsaw 1902)
- Drama.
- ***Description:*** original, printed matter, Russian, Yiddish, 152×240 mm, ss. 33, pp. 65.
  Printed in the Lewin-Epsztajn printworks, Warsaw (ul. Pawia 14).

### 473. RING. II/457. Mf. ŻIH–807; USHMM–62.

- 04.1937, Łódź
- K. Kabaker, Polemical articles (3) regarding Avrom Morewski's review in *Literarishe Bleter* [Literary Pages], no. 14/1937 (3.04., 6.04., 7.04.1937).
- On the works of Itzik Manger (adaptation of Abraham Goldfaden's drama, *The Witch*).
- ***Description:*** original, typescript, German, 216×282, 197×277 mm, ss. 3, pp. 6.
  Article of 3.04.1937 carries title: "Ein Kultur-Skandal." Articles are signed by the author (ink).

### 474. RING. II/472. Mf. ŻIH–808; USHMM–63.

- 1934, Czerniowce [Czernowitz] (Romania)
- Simkhe Shvarts, Novel entitled *Podeloy* (about the life of a small town in Moldova) (fragment); Poem entitled "Soldatske" [Soldierly]
- Attached letter of 3.10.1934 to Itzik Manger with request for evaluation of fragments of the novel *Podeloy*.
- ***Description:*** original, typescript (handwritten additions, ink), Yiddish, 208×340 mm, ss. 15, pp. 15.

### 475. RING. II/493. Mf. ŻIH–811; USHMM–66.

- Before 05.1935, Wilno [?]
- NN., Poem entitled "Ver mit gantsn hartsn tsu unzern libn hern . . ." [Who wholeheartedly to our dear lord . . .]
- ***Description:*** original, handwritten manuscript, ink, Yiddish, 218×290, 218×230 mm, ss. 16, pp. 16.
  Attached envelope (imprint of the Society of Friends of the Jewish Scientific Institute [YIVO]), in which the poem was sent: M. Weinreich (Wilno, Wielka Pohulanka 14), Letter of [28.05.1935 postmark date] to I[tzik] Manger (Warsaw, ul. Nowolipki 6, apt. 2, at Dr. Jawic) (printed, handwritten manuscript, ink, Polish, Yiddish, 190×123 mm, ss. 2, pp. 2).
  M. Weinreich studied Yiddish dialects.

### 476. RING. II/436. Mf. ŻIH–807; USHMM–62.

- After 11.03.1938, Warsaw
- Dr. Mark Wischnitzer (Paris), "Memo für das Warschauer Büro." [Memo for the Warsaw Bureau]
- Letter of 11.03.1938 to NN. (editorial board of publication [?]) in the matter of the article "Das Dorfgewerbe in Polen" [Village industry in Poland] in: *Osteuropa*, October/1929, and development of handicrafts among the rural Jewish population in Poland.
- ***Description:*** transcript, typescript (additions, handwritten manuscript, ink), German, 209×268 mm, ss. 5, pp. 5.

### 477. RING. II/437. Mf. ŻIH–807; USHMM–62.

- After 1936, before 09.1939, Bucharest
- Meer Sternberg, Max Halm (Bucarest I, Calea Victoriei 5), Letter to the firm "Greenfilm" (Warsaw, ul. Jasna 24)
- Concerns the right to distribute the film entitled *Yidl mitn fidl* [Yidl with the fiddle]
- ***Description:*** transcript (2 copies), typescript, German, 224×355 mm, ss. 6, pp. 6.
  Film made in 1936

## *MATERIALS OF ICCHAK GITERMAN*

### 478. RING. II/372. Mf. ŻIH–803; USHMM–58.

a)

- 23.11.1940, Warsaw

- Warsaw Labor Office, Exemption dated 23.11.1940 of Mordchaj Giterman (ul. Śliska 6) from forced labor in camps until 31.12.1940
- Reason for deferment: official of the American Joint Distribution Committee.
- *Description:* original, printed matter, handwritten manuscript, ink, stamp, German, Polish, 148×114 mm, ss. 1, pp. 2.

b)

- 16.01.1941, Warsaw
- Der Chef des Distrikts Warschau [Chief of Warsaw District], Certificate dated 16.01.1941 for Icek Zusia[Zushe?] Giterman for travel to Kraków on 23–27.01.1941 (return by 20.02.1941)
    Doc. signed by Schubert.
- *Description:* original, typescript, handwritten manuscript, ink, stamp, German, 210×146 mm, ss. 1, pp. 1.
    On reverse inspection stamp of the Main Rail Station in Kraków (date illegible)

c)

- 23.07.1941, Warsaw Ghetto
- Mordechaj Giterman (ul. Śliska 6/8, apt. 9), Document (declaration) of 23.07.1941 to the Food Cooperative of Employees of the Jewish Council in Warsaw
- Request for assignment to distribution point no. 1 (ul. Pańska 36) and for registration of provisioning cards for his family (3 persons).
- *Description:* original, duplicated typescript, handwritten manuscript, ink, Polish, 211×167 mm, ss. 1, pp. 1.

d)

- 02.1942, Warsaw Ghetto
- ŻOS, Receipts (7) of 1.02., 3.02., 12.02., 16.02., 20.02., 25.02., and 27.02.1942 for [Icchak] Giterman, payments for the benefit of the "Winter Relief 1941/42" campaign
- Altogether Giterman paid in: 10,200 zł
- *Description:* original, printed matter, handwritten manuscript, pencil, stamp, Polish, 154×120 mm, ss. 7, pp. 7.
    Doc. signed by NN. (pencil).

e)

- 6.03.1942, Warsaw Ghetto
- Jewish Council in Warsaw. Health Department, Receipts (3) of 6.03.1942 for [Icchak] Giterman (ul. Żelazna 103, apt. 21) for bringing in payments for: "[Health?] Committee," disinfection and "sanitary materials from the storehouse"
- Attached Coupon no. 4646 of 6.03.1942 for Mordechaj Giterman to the Sanitary Storehouse of the Health Department of the Jewish Council in Warsaw (ul. Leszno 31) for disinfection materials.
- *Description:* original, printed matter, handwritten manuscript, pencil, stamps, Polish, 172×53, 90×83 mm, damages and losses of text, ss. 4, pp. 4.
    Stamp: "Przewodniczący Rady Żydowskiej w Warszawie. Zarząd Dzielnicy Żydowskiej w Warszawie. Wydział Zdrowia. Dział opłat i grzywien" [Chairman of the Jewish Council in Warsaw. Administration of the Jewish District in Warsaw. Health Department. Department of Fees and Fines]
    On the attached document, a stamp (Jewish Council in Warsaw. Health Department) and illegible signature.

f)

- Before 10.02.1942, Warsaw
- Municipality of Warsaw. Financial Department. Form for payment of tax from residents for the year 1941, filled out for Zusia Giterman (ul. Śliska 6/8, apt. 9).
- *Description:* original, printed matter, handwritten manuscript, pencil, German, Polish, 102×148 mm, ss. 3, pp. 6.

g)

- 7.05.1942, Warsaw Ghetto
- 18th Tax Bureau (Urząd Skarbowy) in Warsaw (ul. Leszno 53/55), Reminder dated 7.05.1942 for Izaak Giterman (ul. Żelazna 103, apt. 21) to pay the residence tax.
- *Description:* original, printed matter, handwritten manuscript, pencil, stamps, German, Polish, 209×204 mm, ss. 1, pp. 1.

## *MATERIALS OF ELIASZ GUTKOWSKI*

### 479. RING. II/373. Mf. ŻIH–803; USHMM–58.

a)

- 27.06.1921, Łódź
- Boys Gimnazjum of the Society of Jewish Secondary Schools in Łódź,[17] Certificate dated 27.06.1921 of completion of class VIII and failure of examination for diploma [i nie zdania egzaminu dojrzałości] by Eliasz Gutkowski, student of the school since 09.1914.
- *Description:* original, printed matter, handwritten manuscript, ink, stamp, Polish, 228×368 mm, ss. 2, pp. 2.

b)

- 9.09.1921, Łódź
- Boys Gimnazjum of the Jewish Society of Secondary

17. The Boys Gymnazjum, founded and headed by R. Dr. Mordecai Markus Braude, preacher at the progressive Synagoga in Łódź, was the flagship of a network of elite secondary schools whose students pursued intensive academic studies taught in both Polish and Hebrew. It was not an elementary school or grammar school, although by the 1930s each of the secondary schools operated an affiliated preparatory school for younger children.

Schools in Łódź, transcript (abridged) dated 9.09.1921 of the certificate of completion of class VIII by Eliasz Gutkowski.

- ***Description:*** original, typescript, Hebrew, 210×274 mm, ss. 1, pp. 2.

  On bottom, a notation in Polish and school's stamp (ink): "I certify the conformity of the present copy with the original I. Fajner, Łódź, 14.09.21."

c)

- 11.06.1912, Kalwaria (Suwalki gubernia)
- Certificate of Citizenship in Kalvaria, transcript of 11.06.1912, document no. 42/1900, of the birth [certificate] of Eliasz Gutkowski, born 1.06.1900 [according to Old Style; according to New Style: 14.06.1900] in the town of Kalwaria, son of Jankiel and Sara-Lea, daughter of Eliasz Witenberg.
- ***Description:*** original, printed matter, handwritten manuscript, ink, stamp, Russian, 206×167 mm, minor damages and losses of text, ss. 1, pp. 1.

d)

- 2.07.1924, Łódź
- School Inspector of the City of Łódź, Cz. Bagieński, Letter dated 28.10.1921 to Eliasz Gutkowski (Łódź, ul. Pomorska 44).
- Inf. about nomination to a provisional teaching position at the 7-grade public school no. 150 (Łódź, ul. Młynarska 2) from 1.11.1921
- ***Description:*** transcript, typescript, Polish, 210×339 mm, ss. 1, pp. 2.

  On pp. 1–2 certification dated 2.07.1924 about the conformity of the copy with the original, signed by Mikołaj Kulczycki, deputy notary public in Łódź Stefan Korn (Łódź, ul. Pomorska 23) (typescript, stamp, signature illegible).

e)

- 23.07.1925, Łódź
- School Inspector of the City of Łódź, Cz. Bagieński, Letter dated 5.08.1922 to Eliasz Gutkowski, provisional teacher at public school no. 150 in Łódź
- Inf. about transfer from 31.08.1922 to post of provisional teacher at the 7-grade public school no. 128 (Łódź, ul. Nowo-Zakrzewska 20).
- ***Description:*** transcript, typescript, Polish, 221×354 mm, ss. 1, pp. 1.

  On p. 1 at bottom certification dated 23.07.1925 about the conformity of the copy with the original, signed by Mikołaj Kulczycki, deputy notary public in Łódź Stefan Korn (Łódź, ul. Pomorska 23) (typescript, stamp, signature illegible).

f)

- 26.11.1924, Łódź
- State Examination Commission for active but nonqualified[18] elementary school teachers, Certificate of first teacher's examination (supplemental examination) of 26.11.1924 for Eliasz Gutkowski.
- ***Description:*** original, printed matter, handwritten manuscript, ink, stamp, Polish, 222×352 mm, ss. 1, pp. 1.

g)

- 21.09.1925, Warsaw
- State Training College for Teachers of the Mosaic Religion in Warsaw, Diploma dated 21.09.1925 for Eliasz Gutkowski.
- ***Description:*** original, printed matter, handwritten manuscript, ink, stamp, Polish, 220×353 mm, ss. 2, pp. 2.

h)

- 22.09.1925, Łódź
- School Superintendent's Office of the School District of Łódź (Kuratorium Okręgu Szkolnego Łódzkiego), Letter dated 22.09.1925 to Eliasz Gutkowski, teacher of public school no. 128 in Łódź
- Inf. about transfer from 1.10.1925 of teacher to public school no. 151 in Łódź.
- ***Description:*** original, printed matter, handwritten manuscript, ink, Polish, 210×171 mm, ss. 1, pp. 1.

i)

- 1.02.1926, Łódź
- 7-grade Community Elementary School no. 32 "Jesodej Hatora" [Yesodei Ha-Torah] no. 1 at the Association of Orthodox Jews [Zrzeszeniu Żydów Ortodoksów = Agudas Israel] (Łódź, ul. Południowa 11), Certificate dated 1.02.1926 for Eliasz Gutkowski, about fulfillment of teaching duties in school year 1923/24 and 1924/25.
- ***Description:*** original, typescript, stamps, Polish, 213×278 mm, ss. 1, pp. 1.

j)

- 21.10.1926, Warsaw
- State Advanced Teacher's Course (Państwowy Wyższy Kurs Nauczycielski) in Warsaw, Diploma dated 21.10.1926 for Eliasz Gutkowski.
- ***Description:*** original, printed matter, handwritten manuscript, ink, stamps, Polish, 209×339 mm, ss. 1, pp. 2.

k)

- 5.09.1928, Łódź
- Girls Secondary School (Gimnazjum) of Eugenia Jaszuńska-Zeligmanowa (Łódź, ul. Południowa 18). Eugenia Jaszuńska-Zeligman, director, Certificate dated 5.09.1928 for Eliasz Gutkowski, about fulfillment of teacher's duties in the years 1924/25–1927/28.

18. Not yet certified as qualified teachers.

- *Description:* original, handwritten manuscript, stamp, Polish, 206×332 mm, ss. 1, pp. 1.

l)

- 23.01.1929, Łódź
- School Superintendent's Office of the School District of Łódź (Kuratorium Okręgu Szkolnego Łódzkiego). Dr. A. Ryniewicz, superintendent of schools, Letter dated 23.01.1929 to Eliasz Gutkowski, teacher of public school no. 151 in Łódź
- Inf. about awarding of the Tenth Anniversary of Regained Independence Medal (Medalu Dziesięciolecia Odzyskanej Niepodległości).
- *Description:* original, printed matter, handwritten manuscript, ink, stamps, Polish, 226×299 mm, ss. 1, pp. 1.

ł)

- 17.06.1931, Łódź
- School Inspector of the City of Łódź, Letter dated 17.06.1931 to Eliasz Gutkowski, teacher of public school no. 151 in Łódź
- Inf. about appointment to position of permanent teacher; date of swearing in: 7.06.1931
- *Description:* original, printed matter, handwritten manuscript, ink, stamp, Polish, 206×289 mm, ss. 1, pp. 1.

m)

- 21.10.1926, Warsaw
- School Superintendent's Office of the Warsaw School District. National Examination Commission, Secondary school certificate dated 26.10.1934 for Eliasz Gutkowski.
- *Description:* original, printed matter, handwritten manuscript, ink, stamp, Polish, 216×347 mm, photograph, ss. 2, pp. 3.

n)

- 12.05.1938, Warsaw
- School Superintendent's Office of the Warsaw School District in Warsaw, Diploma of 12.05.1938 awarding to Eliasz Gutkowski a bronze medal for long-term service.
- *Description:* original, printed matter, typescript, stamp, Polish, 208×294 mm, ss. 1, pp. 1.

o)

- 27.06.1938, Warsaw
- Free University of Poland (Wolna Wszechnica Polska) in Warsaw. Humanities Department, Diploma dated 27.06.1938 awarding to Eliasz Gutkowski the degree of master of philosophy.
- *Description:* original (4 copies, including 1 copy on handmade paper), printed matter, Polish, 293×464 mm, ss. 5, pp. 8.

p)

- 27.06.1939, Warsaw
- State Examination Commission for teachers of Mosaic religion in secondary schools in Warsaw (ul. Tłomackie 5), Certificate dated 27.06.1939 about establishment of the examination for teachers of Mosaic religion
  Doc. signed by Prof. Dr. Mojżesz Schorr, chairman of the Commission.
- *Description:* original, typescript, handwritten manuscript, ink, stamp, Polish, 221×177 mm, ss. 1, pp. 1.

r)

- 2.12.1939, Łódź
- Private Girls Secondary School (Gimnazjum) and Private Girls Elementary School of Maria Hochsteinowa (Łódź, ul. Wólczańska 23, new address: ul. Narutowicza 17). Certificate dated 2.12.1939 of employment of Eliasz Gutkowski.
- *Description:* original, typescript, German, Polish, 208×111 mm, photograph, ss. 1, pp. 1.

## 480. RING. II/380. Mf. ŻIH—803; USHMM—58.

a)

- 25.06.1930, Łódź
- Boys Secondary School (Gimnazjum) of the Soc[iety] "Tora W'Derech Erec" [Hebrew: Torah ve-derekh-erets (Torah and Respect)] in Łódź (ul. Cegielniana 60), H. Finkielkraut, director, Certificate dated 25.06.1930 about employment of Luba Gutkowska, as secretary of the school in the years 1924/25–1929/30.
- *Description:* original, typescript, stamp, Polish, 213×278 mm, ss. 1, pp. 1.

b)

- 16.12.1938, Łódź
- [Municipal Administration] in Łódź. Registration Bureau Fr. Adamczewski, Confirmation dated 16.12.1938 of the registration of [Gabriel] Gutkowski on 18.11.1938 in Łódź (ul. [. . .] 67, apt. 37).
- *Description:* original (2 copies), printed matter, hand written manuscript, ink, stamp, Polish, 113×39 mm, ss. 2, pp. 4.

c)

- 12.06.1939, Łódź
- S. [Samuel] Halborn, Dr. med. (Łódź), Certificate dated 12.06.1939 about vaccination of Gabriel Gutkowki against smallpox.
- *Description:* original, handwritten manuscript, ink, Polish, 137×106 mm, ss. 1, pp. 1.

d)

- 04.1940, Warsaw
- "Higiena" Medical Analysis Laboratory (Warsaw, ul. Ogrodowa 5, apt. 2), Urinalysis dated 26.04.1940 [Eliasz] Gutkowski (ordered by Dr. Makower).
- *Description:* original, printed matter, handwritten manuscript, ink, Polish, 230×301 mm, ss. 1, pp. 2.

e)

- 6.11.1940, Warsaw
- Municipal Government in Warsaw, Confirmations (2) dated 6.11.1940 of registration of Luba Dyna and

Gabriel Zeew Gutkowski on 5.11.1940 in Warsaw (ul. Nowolipie 50, apt. 23) (newly arrived from Łódź).
- ***Description:*** original, printed matter, handwritten manuscript, ink, stamp, Polish, 114×40 mm, ss. 2, pp. 4.

f)
- 6.12.1940, Warsaw Ghetto
- [Jewish Council] in Warsaw, Confirmations (3) dated 6.12.1940 of registration of Eliasz, Luba Dyna and Gabriel Gutkowski on 2 (Luba Gutkowska) and 3.12.1940 in Warsaw (ul. Muranowska 7/9, apt. 5).
- ***Description:*** original, printed matter, handwritten manuscript, ink, stamp, Polish, 112×43 mm, ss. 3, pp. 6.

g)
- 3.12.[1940], Warsaw Ghetto
- [Jewish Council] in Warsaw, Confirmations of registration of Eliasz, Luba Dyna, and Gabriel Gutkowski on 3.12.[1940] in Warsaw (ul. Muranowska 7/9, apt. 5).
- ***Description:*** original, printed matter, handwritten manuscript, ink, stamp, German, Polish, 115×47 mm, ss. 3, pp. 3.

h)
- 12.01.1941, Warsaw Ghetto
- "Mikro" Analytic and Chemical-Bacteriological Laboratory (Warsaw, ul. Dzielna 51/53, apt. 1), Result of blood test of 12.01.1941 of Gabriel Gutkowski (ordered by Dr. [Jechiel Jerzy] Herszfinkel).
- ***Description:*** original, handwritten manuscript, ink, stamp, Polish, 222×295 mm, ss. 1, pp. 1.

  Attached envelope (handwritten manuscript, ink, stamp, 155×124 mm, ss. 2, pp. 1).

i)
- 15.07.1942, Warsaw Ghetto
- A.L. Bloch [?] [Lipe Lejzer Bloch?], Letter of 15.07.1942 to NN.
- Request for grant of aid to Gutkowski.
- ***Description:*** original, handwritten manuscript, ink, Hebrew, 144×106 mm, ss. 1, pp. 1.

j)
- Before 09.1939, Łódź[?]
- Gabriel Gutkowski (born 18.11.1938), son of Eliasz and Luba.
- ***Description:*** original, photograph, 135×87 mm, ss. 1, pp. 1.

  On reverse stamp: "Foto «Ira» Kolumna, Szosa no. 3."

k)
- Before 09.1939, Łódź[?]
- A demonstration.
- ***Description:*** original, photograph, 137×88 mm, ss. 1, pp. 1.

l)
- 19[?].03.1942, Warsaw Ghetto
- Jewish Council in Warsaw, Confirmation dated 19[?].03.1942 for Gabriel Zeew Gutkowski (ul. Nowolipki 31, apt. 31) of submission of questionnaire for residents of the Jewish District in Warsaw.
- ***Description:*** original, printed matter, handwritten manuscript, ink, stamp, Polish, 113×43 mm, ss. 1, pp. 1.

ł)
- Date unknown, place unknown
- NN., Sheet with address: "Gęsia 57a fr. [front], p. [ground floor], clinic."
- ***Description:*** original, handwritten manuscript, ink, Polish, 118×78 mm, ss. 1, pp. 1.

**481. RING. II/379. Mf. ŻIH—803; USHMM—58.**
- 24.08.1939, Tel Aviv
- Yaakov Gutkowski, Rabbi (Tel Aviv, Achad ha-Am 65), Letter of 24.08.1939 to Eliasz Gutkowski (Łódź, ul. 11 Listopada 57)
- Yaakov Gutkowski transfers authorial rights to the manuscript of the work entitled "Korot am olam" [History of the Eternal People] to his son Eliasz Gutkowski.
- ***Description:*** original, handwritten manuscript, ink, stamp, Hebrew, 206×194 mm, ss. 1, pp. 1.

  Encl. envelope with address of sender and addressee (handwritten manuscript, ink, postal stamp, Hebrew, Polish, 155×119 mm, ss. 2, pp. 2).

**482. RING. II/375. Mf. ŻIH—803; USHMM—58.**
- 10.1939, Łódź
- Financial Commission of the City of Łódź, Receipts dated 2.10. and 24.10.1939 for acceptance of securities from Eliasz Gutkowski (Łódź, ul. 11 Listopada 57) and receipts dated 6.10. and 26.10.1939 for the sums payed to Eliasz Gutkowski for the aforementioned securities.
- ***Description:*** original, printed matter, handwritten manuscript, ink, pencil, Polish, 227×170, 218×283 mm, ss. 4, pp. 4.

**483. RING. II/383/1. Mf. ŻIH—803; USHMM—58.**
- 1940, Warsaw
- Municipal Government in Warsaw, "Provisioning[19] Card no. 295185" made out for Eliasz Gutkowski (ul. Ogrodowa 67, apt. 25).
- ***Description:*** original, printed matter, handwritten manuscript, ink, German, Polish, 142×188 mm, some of the coupons cut out, ss. 1, pp. 1.

  On reverse stamps: "Toiletry Store of P. Muszko [Muszek?], ul. Ogrodowa 67"; "F. Osiński Coal

19. *Karta aprowizacyjna* was a ration card for food and other commodities, such as wood or coal for fuel. See the stamps on the back of the card for a toiletry store, a coal yard, and a food shop.

Yard, ul. Ogrodowa 67"; "F.S. Lachman Food Shop, Ogrodowa 69."

**484. RING. II/384. Mf. ŻIH—803; USHMM—58.**

a)

- 01.1940, Warsaw
- Coordinating Committee of Social and Welfare Organizations "TOZ," "Centos," and others (ul. Leszno 13), Certificates dated 10.01., 13.01.1940 about employment of Eliasz Gutkowski (ul. Ogrodowa 67, apt. 25).
- ***Description:*** original, typescript, stamps, German, Polish, 225×300, 222×297 mm, ss. 2, pp. 2.
  Both documents signed (handwritten manuscript, ink) by Emanuel Ringelblum [?].

b)

- 2.03.1940, Warsaw
- Coordinating Committee of Social and Welfare Organizations 'TOZ,' 'Centos,' and others (ul. Leszno 13), Certificate dated 2.03.1940 about employment of Eliasz Gutkowski as an instructor.
- ***Description:*** original, typescript, stamp, German, Polish, 225×299 mm, ss. 1, pp. 1.
  At bottom illegible signature (ink) and stamp: "Coordinating Committee of Social and Welfare Organizations 'TOZ,' 'Centos,' and others in Warsaw. Registration Department" [Komisja Koordynacyjna Organizacji Społecznych i Opiekuńczych "TOZ," "Centos" i in. w Warszawie. Wydział Rejestracyjny].

c)

- 4.04.1940, Warsaw
- Coordinating Committee of Social and Welfare Organizations "TOZ," "Centos," and others (ul. Leszno 13), Certificate dated 4.04.1940 commissioning Eliasz Gutkowski as a trainer for money collection.
- ***Description:*** original, typescript, German, Polish, 226×150 mm, ss. 1, pp. 1.
  At bottom illegible signature (ink).

d)

- 05–11.1940, Warsaw
- Coordinating Committee of ŻSS (ul. Leszno 13, Tłomackie 5), Certificates dated 1.05., 30.06., 30.07., 1.11.1940 of employment of Eliasz Gutkowski (ul. Ogrodowa 67; on the certificate dated 1.11.1940 ul. Nowolipie 50, apt. 23) and authorization to collect contributions for the benefit of fire victims, refugees, and public kitchens.
- ***Description:*** original, duplicated typescript, typescript, stamps, German, Polish, 215×277, 219×298 mm, ss. 4, pp. 4.
  At bottom illegible signatures (inter alia, of Emanuel Ringelblum [?]) (pencil, ink).

e)

- 25.11.1940, Warsaw Ghetto
- ŻTOS, District VI (ul. Nowolipki 29), Certificate dated 25.11.1940 authorizing Eliasz Gutkowski to collect contributions and donations to ŻTOS at ul. Smocza 1–31 (odd-numbered side).
- ***Description:*** original, duplicated typescript, typescript, Polish, 220×122 mm, ss. 1, pp. 1.
  At bottom illegible signature and signature of L. Waksberg, financial clerk (referenta finansowego) (ink).

f)

- Before 31.12.1940, Warsaw Ghetto
- ŻTOS (ul. Tłomackie 5), Certificate [before 31.12.1940] of employment of Eliasz Gutkowski (ul. Muranowska 7, apt. 9) and authorization to collect donations for the benefit of fire victims, refugees, and public kitchens.
- ***Description:*** original, duplicated typescript, typescript, Polish, 222×297 mm, ss. 1, pp. 1.
  At bottom illegible signature and signature of Emanuel Ringelblum [?] (ink).

g)

- 31.01.1941, Warsaw Ghetto
- Jewish Council in Warsaw, Certificate dated 31.01.1941 about employment of Eliasz Gutkowski (ul. Muranowska 7) as a collector.
  Doc. signed by Adam Czerniaków.
- ***Description:*** original, duplicated typescript, typescript, stamp, German, Polish, 210×193 mm, ss. 1, pp. 1.

h)

- 01–06.1941, Warsaw Ghetto
- Jewish Council in Warsaw. Department of Payments for the benefit of Hospital Management and the Health Service, Certificates (2) dated 31.01. and 29.06.1941 about employment of Eliasz Gutkowski (ul. Muranowska 7) as a collector of balances due for fees for the benefit of hospital management and the health service
  Doc. signed by Hilary Ekerman, director of the Department
- ***Description:*** original, typescript, stamps, Polish, 208×194, 210×194 mm, ss. 2, pp. 2.

i)

- 02–04.1941, Warsaw Ghetto
- ŻTOS, Certificates (2) dated 28.02.1941 (no. 2344) and 30.04.1941 (no. 4943) of employment of Eliasz Gutkowski (ul. Muranowska 7, apt. 9).
- ***Description:*** original, printed matter, handwritten manuscript, ink, stamps, German, Polish, 82×136, 86×140 mm, ss. 4, pp. 8.
  At bottom illegible signatures and signature of Emanuel Ringelblum [?] (ink).

j)

- 24[29?].06.1941, Warsaw Ghetto
- Jewish Council in Warsaw. Personnel Department, Letter dated 24 [29?].06.1941 to Eliasz Gutkowski
  Note of employment as collector for the

Department of Payments for the benefit of the Hospitals and Health Service from 1.05.1941 with remuneration of 60 zł. monthly. Doc. signed by Adam Czerniaków.
- *Description:* original, duplicated typescript, handwritten manuscript, ink, Polish, 209×156 mm, ss. 1, pp. 1.

k)
- 9.05.1941, Warsaw Ghetto
- ŻSS-KOM, Care for Children and Orphans "Centos" (ul. Leszno 2), Letter dated 9.05.1941 to Eliasz Gutkowski (ul. Nowolipki 31, apt. 31)
- Request for loan of typewriter Underwood model no. 357070.
- *Description:* original, typescript, stamp, German, Polish, 225×294 mm, ss. 1, pp. 1.
  Index: Abram Kancyger (ul. Muranowska 35).

l)
- 22.10.1941, Warsaw Ghetto
- Eliasz Gutkowski (ul. Nowolipki 31, apt. 31), Letter dated 22.10.1941 to the Sponsors' Committee of the Mina Werde Home for the Elderly and Orphans in Częstochowa
- Second request (first letter in this matter dated 16.10.1941) for employment as director of the Mina Werde Home for the Elderly and Orphans in Częstochowa. Information about qualifications possessed and encl. CV.
- *Description:* transcript, typescript, Polish, 225×290 mm, ss. 2, pp. 2.

ł)
- 04.1941 [?]-1942, Warsaw Ghetto
- ŻSS-KOM, "Temporary Identification Card Papers" of Eliasz Gutkowski (ul. Nowolipki 31, apt. 31) entitling him to benefit from dinners in a public kitchen.
- *Description:* original, printed matter, handwritten manuscript, ink, stamps, Polish, 122×84 mm, ss. 1, pp. 1.
  Numerous date stamps from 1941[?] and 1942 and stamp: "Kitchen Sb. [?] no. 28, Orla 13."

m)
- 1.10.1942, Warsaw Ghetto
- OBW, Pass dated 1.10.1942 for Eliasz Gutkowski and his wife to go in a family matter to ul. Leszno 74 (W.C. Többens).
- *Description:* original, typescript, handwritten manuscript, ink, stamp, German, 148×106 mm, ss. 1, pp. 1.

n)
- 5.01.1943, Warsaw Ghetto
- OBW, Pass dated 5.01.1943 for [Eliasz] Gutkowski and [Hersz] Wasser to go to ul. Franciszkańska and Leszno 50 to ZZ [?].
- *Description:* original, typescript, handwritten manuscript, ink, stamp, German, 150×104 mm, ss. 1, pp. 1.

## 485. RING. II/376. Mf. ŻIH—803; USHMM—58.

a)
- 18.03.1940, Warsaw
- Jewish Council in Warsaw. Department V. Schools, Receipt dated 18.03.1940 for Eliasz Gutkowski (ul. Ogrodowa 67) for money received (30 zł).
- *Description:* original, printed matter, handwritten manuscript, pencil, stamp, Polish, 200×95 mm, ss. 1, pp. 1.

b)
- 24.03.1940, Warsaw
- [Jewish Council in Warsaw. Labor Battalion], Receipt dated 24.03.1940 for Eliasz Gutkowski for money (5 zł) paid out for work in September.
- *Description:* original, printed matter, handwritten manuscript, pencil, Polish, 107×114 mm, ss. 1, pp. 1.
  On the statement is glued a stamp of 50 gr for "Aid for war victims. Jewish Social Self-Help Society" and the impression of a stamp.

c)
- 06.1940, Warsaw
- Labor Battalion at the Jewish Council in Warsaw. "Call-up Card" for the month of June 1940 to forced labor for Eliasz Gutkowski (ul. Ogrodowa 67, apt. 25) dated 2.06.1940
- *Description:* original, printed matter, handwritten manuscript, pencil, German, Polish, 95×159 mm, ss. 1, pp. 2.

d)
- 08.1940, Warsaw
- Labor Battalion at the Jewish Council in Warsaw. "Call-up Card for the month of August" 1940 to forced labor for Eliasz Gutkowski (ul. Ogrodowa 67, apt. 25) dated 2.08.1940
- *Description:* original, printed matter, handwritten manuscript, pencil, German, Polish, 160×95, 95×80 mm, ss. 11, pp. 12.
  On p. 1 notation (ink): "employee of ŻSS."

da)
- 09.1940, Warsaw
- Labor Battalion at the Jewish Council in Warsaw. "Call-up Card for the month of September" 1940 to forced labor for Eliasz Gutkowski (ul. Ogrodowa 67, apt. 25) dated 5.09.1940
- *Description:* original, printed matter, handwritten manuscript, ink, pencil, German, Polish, 84×162, 83×83 mm, ss. 9, pp. 10.
  On p. 1 notation (ink): "employee of ŻSS."

e)
- 29.12.1941, Warsaw Ghetto
- Jewish Council in Warsaw. Department III. Contributions and Levies, Payment Order dated 29.12.1941 for Eliasz Gutkowski (ul. Nowolipki 31, apt. 31) in the matter of payment of "housing levy" (aid for displaced persons).
- *Description:* original, printed matter, handwritten manuscript, pencil, Polish, 155×100 mm, ss. 1, pp. 2.

f)

- 25.02.1942, Warsaw Ghetto
- Kitchen Sb. [?] 28 (ul. Orla 13), Receipt dated 25.02.1942 for Eliasz Gutkowski for received sum (10 zł).
- ***Description:*** original, printed matter, handwritten manuscript, pencil, stamp, Polish, 106×116 mm, ss. 1, pp. 1.

g)

- 25.02.1942, Warsaw Ghetto
- NN., Receipt dated 25.02.1942 for Eliasz Gutkowski for money received for contributions for 04–05.1942 (1 zł).
- ***Description:*** original, printed matter, handwritten manuscript, pencil, Polish, 112×105 mm, ss. 1, pp. 1.

h)

- 17.03.1942, Warsaw Ghetto
- Cooperative of ŻTOS [?], Receipt dated 17.03.1942 for Eliasz Gutkowski for money received (21 zł).
- ***Description:*** original, printed matter, handwritten manuscript, pencil, Polish, 104×115 mm, ss. 1, pp. 1.
  At top notation (pencil): "Spółdz. ŻTOS."

i)

- 19.07.1942, Warsaw Ghetto
- Sponsors' Committee of ŻTOS Public Kitchen no. 118 (ul. Nowolipki 35), Receipt dated 19.07.1942 for Eliasz Gutkowski for money received (5 zł).
- ***Description:*** original, printed matter, handwritten manuscript, pencil, stamp, Polish, 73×97 mm, ss. 1, pp. 1.

j)

- 25.06.1942, Warsaw Ghetto
- NN., Receipt no. 3 dated 25.06.1942 for Eliasz Gutkowski.
- ***Description:*** original, printed matter, handwritten manuscript, ink, Polish, 75×58 mm, ss. 1, pp. 1.

## 486. RING. II/374. Mf. ŻIH—803; USHMM—58.

a)

- After 14.08.1940, place unknown
- Der Bevollmächtigte des Generalgouverneurs für die besetzten polnischen Gebiete in Berlin [Plenipotentiary of the General Governor for the Occupied Polish Territories in Berlin], Certificate dated 14.08.1940 for L. [Luba] Gutkowska (Łódź, Bleigasse 21, apt. 3) and her son Gabriel Gutkowski for one-time crossing of the border of Generalgouvernement in the period 21.08–4.09.1940
- ***Description:*** transcript, typescript, German, 209×145 mm, ss. 1, pp. 1.

b)

- 30.09.1940, Berlin
- Der Bevollmächtigte des Generalgouverneurs für die besetzten polnischen Gebiete in Berlin [Plenipotentiary of the General Governor for the Occupied Polish Territories, in Berlin], Certificate dated 30.09.1940 for L. [Luba] Gutkowska (Łódź, Bleigasse 21, apt. 3) and her son Gabriel Gutkowski for one-time crossing of the border of Generalgouvernement in the period 5.10–20.10.1940
- ***Description:*** original, typescript, stamp, German, 210×146 mm, ss. 1, pp. 1.

c)

- 24.10.1940, Łódź
- Städt. [Städtischer] Gesundheitsamt. Entlausungsanstalt [Municipal Health Bureau. Delousing Facility] (Litzmannstadt, Baluter Ring), Certificates of disinfection (2) dated 24.10.1940 for Luba [Liba (sic)] and Gabriel Gutowski.
- ***Description:*** original, typescript, German, 105×88 mm, ss. 2, pp. 2.

d)

- 23.10.1940, Łódź
- Chief of the Jewish Elders in Łódź [Przełożony Starszeństwa Żydów w Łodzi], Letter dated 23.10.1940 to Luba and Gabriel Gutkowski (Łódź, Bleigasse 21, apt. 3)
- Summons to the office of the Jewish Community (Łódź, Pl. Kościelny 4) in the matter of journey to Warsaw.
- ***Description:*** original, printed matter, handwritten manuscript, pencil, stamp, Polish, 125×86 mm, ss. 1, pp. 2.
  On p. 2 at top notation (pencil): "departure to W[arsa]w of 2 persons on 24.10.40 [. . .]."

e)

- After 31.12.1939, Warsaw
- Municipal Administration in Warsaw, Confirmation of registration on 31.12.1939 of Eliasz Gutkowski in the house at ul. Ogrodowa 67, apt. 25
- Previous address: Łódź, ul. 11 Listopada 57.
- ***Description:*** original, printed matter, handwritten manuscript, ink, stamp, Polish, 110×39 mm, ss. 1, pp. 2.

f)

- 13.11.1940, Warsaw
- Eliasz Gutkowski (Warsaw, ul. Nowolipie 50, apt. 23), Letter dated 13.11.1940 to Der Bevollmächtigte des Generalgouverneurs für die besetzten polnischen Gebiete in Berlin [Plenipotentiary of the General Governor for the Occupied Polish Territories, in Berlin]
- Request for consent for departure of his sister Rajzla Ajzner-Gutkowska from the Łódź ghetto (Bleigasse 21, apt. 3) to Warsaw.
- ***Description:*** transcript, typescript, German, 208×295 mm, ss. 1, pp. 1.

## 487. RING. II/377. Mf. ŻIH—803; USHMM—58.

a)

- 8.06.1941, Warsaw Ghetto
- Food Cooperative of Employees of the Jewish Council in Warsaw, Receipt dated 8.06.1941 for Eliasz Gutkowski for money received (5 zł).

- *Description:* original, printed matter, handwritten manuscript, ink, stamp, Polish, 180×101 mm, ss. 1, pp. 1.

b)

- 12.1941–02.1942, Warsaw Ghetto
- Jewish Council in Warsaw, Voucher dated 18.12.1941 for Eliasz Gutkowski for disbursement of relief grant (70 zł).
- *Description:* original, printed matter, handwritten manuscript, pencil, stamp, Polish, 178×189 mm, ss. 1, pp. 1.

  At bottom stamp of cashier with date stamp: "26.02.1942."

c)

- 29.12.1941, Warsaw Ghetto
- [ŻSS], Voucher dated 29.12.1941 for the Centos Distribution Point (ul. Tłomackie 5) for issuance to Eliasz Gutkowski (ul. Nowolipki 31) of 10 kg of potatoes.
- *Description:* original, typescript, handwritten manuscript (H.W.*), ink, Polish, 110×175 mm, ss. 1, pp. 1.

  At bottom two illegible signatures (in a different handwriting, ink).

d)

- 27.02.1942, Warsaw Ghetto
- Food Cooperative of Employees of the Jewish Council in Warsaw, "Share card" [Karta przydziału] no. 1405 issued 27.02.1942 for Eliasz Gutkowski (ul. Muranowska 7 [crossed out] ul. Nowolipki 31).
- *Description:* original, printed matter, typescript, handwritten manuscript, ink, stamp, Polish, 110×154 mm, some of the coupons cut out, ss. 1, pp. 1.

e)

- 21.05.1942, Warsaw Ghetto
- ZZ, "Order Card" no. 021929 dated 21.05.1942 for Eliasz Gutkowski (ul. Nowolipki 31, apt. 31) for purchase of one pair of shoes or leather for one pair of shoes.
- *Description:* original, printed matter, handwritten manuscript, ink, stamp, German, Polish, 199×148 mm, ss. 1, pp. 2.

  On reverse glued stamp: "Our children must live. Children's Month 1942 [?]"; date stamps: "21.05.1942" and circular stamp ZZ; alongside stamp: "Department of Individual Aid. Subcommission [. . .]" and illegible signature (ink).

f)

- 18.03.1942, Warsaw Ghetto
- Supply Card [?] no. 543 of [Eliasz] Gutkowski.
- *Description:* original, printed matter, handwritten manuscript, ink, stamp, Polish, 190×114 mm, ss. 1, pp. 2.

  On pp. 1 and 2 various notes and calculations (pencil, ink), stamp: "M. E.[. . .]"; date: 18.03.42; notation: "Gutkowski."

## 488. RING. II/378. Mf. ŻIH—803; USHMM—58.

a)

- After 18.11.1941, place unknown
- [Eliasz Gutkowski], Letter of (after 18.11.[1941]) to female cousin M.Wohlgelemter [Wohlgelernter?] (Detroit—Michigan, USA, 205 Gladstone). (fragment)
- Thanks for parcel dated 30.04.[1941], Request for further aid, their son Gabriel [Gutkowski] 18.11.[1941] turned 3 years old.
- *Description:* transcript, handwritten manuscript (H*), ink, pencil, German, 220×94 mm, damages and losses of text, ss. 1, pp. 2.

b)

- 12.07.1942, Bełchatów
- J. Lipschütz (Bełchatów, Litzmannstädterstr. 9), Letter of 12.07.1942 to E. [Eliasz] Gutkowski (Warsaw Ghetto, ul. Nowolipki 31, apt. 31)
- Question about registration for departure to Palestine. Information about family. Attached postcard with return address.
- *Description:* original, handwritten manuscript on a postcard, ink, postmark and stamp of the Jewish Council in Warsaw, Polish, 148×104 mm, ss. 2, pp. 3.

c)

- [29.09.1940], Date unknown, Działoszyce
- Józef Arkusz (Działoszyce, Rynek 11), Letters (2) dated [29.09.1940 postmark date] and no date to E. [Eliasz] Gutkowski (Warsaw, ul. Ogrodowa 67, apt. 25). (fragments)
- Only the envelopes were preserved.
- *Description:* original, handwritten manuscript, ink, postal stamps ("Działoszyce" and on the letter dated 29.09.1940: "Krakau 2"), Polish, 119×91 mm, ss. 4, pp. 4.

## 489. RING. II/383/5. Mf. ŻIH—803; USHMM—58.

- Date unknown, Warsaw Ghetto
- ZZ, "Supplemental Card for children of pre-school age no. 014183" made out for Gabriel Gutkowski (ul. Nowolipki 31, apt. 31).
- *Description:* original, printed matter, handwritten manuscript, ink, German, Polish, 142×154 mm, part of the coupons cut off, ss. 1, pp. 1.

  Card has inscription: "Remind Mom that each of us must help the poor child!"

  On reverse stamps: "Friendly Mutual Aid of Employees of Institutions of the Jewish District" [Samopomoc Koleżeńska Pracowników Instytucji Dzielnicy Żydowskiej].

## 490. RING. II/383/7. Mf. ŻIH—803; USHMM—58.

- 06–07.1942, Warsaw Ghetto
- [ZZ], "Food Card" no. 137372, 137373, 124517, 124518, 124519, dated 06–07.1942 for Gabriel, Eliasz, and Luba Gutkowski (ul. Nowolipki 31, apt. 31).
- *Description:* original printed matter, handwritten

manuscript, stamps, German, Polish, 204×189 mm, part of the coupons cut off, ss. 5, pp. 5.

On p. 1 and on reverse stamp (on all the cards): "Friendly Mutual Aid of Employees of Institutions of the Jewish District" [Samopomoc Koleżeńska Pracowników Instytucji Dzielnicy Żydowskiej].

On cards of 06.1942 inscription: "Tuberculosis decimates hungry children! The only rescue is organization of Social Welfare!" On cards of 07.1942 inscription: "Things are still very bad for our children! Remember that August is the 'Month of the Child'!"

## *MATERIALS OF SZYMON HUBERBAND*

### 491. RING. II/385. Mf. ŻIH–803; USHMM–58.

a)

- 09.1940–08.1942, Warsaw, Warsaw Ghetto
- Arbeitsamt Warschau Nebenstelle für den jüd.[ische] Wohnbezirk, "Meldekarte für Juden no. 21321" [Warsaw Labor Office Branch for the Jew. Residential District, "Registration Card for Jews no. 21321"] of Szymon Huberband (born 19.04.1909 in Chęciny)
- Inf. about employment in the period 1.09.1940–18.08.1942.
- ***Description:*** original, printed matter, typescript, handwritten manuscript, ink, stamps, German, Polish, Ukrainian, 103×190 mm, photograph, ss. 4, pp. 7.

See HWC, 34/3 (another copy of "Meldekarte . . . ," no. 63226; missing notation about origin).

Published: *Archiwum Ringelbluma*, pp. 255–258 (description, photocopy).

b)

- 10–11.1942, Siedlce
- R. Popower (Siedlce, ul. Sokołowska 12), Letters dated [24.10. and 11.11.1942 postmark date] to brother K. [Kalman] Huberband (Warsaw Ghetto, ul. Miła 9)
- Request for news and money.
- ***Description:*** original, handwritten manuscript on postcards, pencil, ink, postmark and stamp of the Jewish Council in Warsaw, Polish, 149×104 mm, ss. 2, pp. 4.

## *MATERIALS OF IZRAEL LICHTENSZTAJN AND GELA SEKSZTAJN*

### 492. RING. II/389. Mf. ŻIH–803; USHMM–58.

a)

- 30.06.1930, Warsaw
- 6-Grade Elementary School "Nasza Szkoła" [Our School] (ul. Nowolipki 68) of the Union of Jewish [Yiddish?] Schools in Warsaw, Certificate dated 30.06.1930 for Gela Seksztajn (born 1907) of completion of school in 1924.
- ***Description:*** original, printed matter, handwritten manuscript, ink, stamp, Polish, Yiddish, 220×352 mm, ss. 2, pp. 2.

Printed by: J. Kelter [Warsaw] ul. Rymarska 8.

b)

- 10.05.1941, Warsaw Ghetto
- Dr NN., Certificate dated 10.05.1941 of vaccination against Typhus of Genia [Gela] Seksztajn (ul. Pawia 81).
- ***Description:*** original, printed matter, handwritten manuscript, ink, German, Polish, 208×150 mm, damages and losses of text, ss. 1, pp. 2.

Published: *Kronika getta*, p. 287 (photocopy).

c)

- 15.06.1942, Warsaw Ghetto
- Der Kommissar für den Jüdischen Wohnbezirk in Warschau [Commissioner for the Jewish Residential District], Identification Card "J" no. 37799 dated 15.06.1942 of Estera Lichtensztejn (born 23.08.1917 in Warsaw) (ul. Ciepła 26).
- ***Description:*** original, printed matter, handwritten manuscript, ink, stamps, German, Polish, 98×142 mm, ss. 3, pp. 6.

### 493. RING. II/258. Mf. ŻIH–799; USHMM–54.

- 22.09.1942, Warsaw Ghetto
- Genia [Gela] Seksztajn-Lichtensztajn, Letter dated 22.09.1942 to Hirszel, director of workshop (Warsaw Ghetto)
- Request for registration in the workshop (allocation of number).
- ***Description:*** transcript, typescript, Yiddish, 223×288 mm, ss. 1, pp. 1.

On bottom inf. (handwritten manuscript—IL*, pencil): "Nothing came of this! Because . . . there is no understanding, Lichtensztajn."

Published (photocopy and in Polish translation): *Archiwum Ringelbluma*, pp. 175, 347. According to Ruta Sakowska, application to workshop of Hallmann.

## *MATERIALS OF PEREC OPOCZYŃSKI*

### 494. RING. II/459. Mf. ŻIH–807; USHMM–62.

- Date unknown, place unknown
- [Perec Opoczyński], Articles and stories
  1) "Be-shalshelot shel barzel. Tsiyur min ha-haim shel shvuyei ha-milhama" [In chains of iron. Sketch from the life of the war prisoners];
  2) "Rekhovot shel Lodzh" [Streets of Łódź];
  3) "Khanukah" [Hanukkah];
  4) "Lag ba-Omer";
  5) "Mishloah ha-manot" [Purim food gift parcels];
  6) "Dmaot ha-yatom" [The Orphan's Tears];
  7) "Ha-siyum" [(Celebration of) the completion (of a unit of Torah study)];
  8) "Namushot" [Cry (?)].

- ***Description:*** original, typescript (handwritten additions-OP*, ink), Hebrew, 115×390, 115×318, 120×350, 210×343 mm, ss. 23, pp. 23.

## 495. RING. II/460. Mf. ŻIH–808; USHMM–63.

a)

- Date unknown, 22.05.1942, place unknown, Warsaw Ghetto
- Perec Opoczyński, Hasidic Stories
  1) "Rav Khaim David ha-Rofeh mi-Piotrkov" [Rabbi Chaim David the Physician of Piotrków];
  2) "Ki lo nihesh be-Yaakov" [For a spell has no power over Jacob];
  3) "Din Torah" [Rabbinical Court Case];
  4) "Ha-tsadik megin al ha-makom" [The saintly man defends the place];
  5) "Taut haver" [A friend's error];
  6) "Ha-gaon mi-Vilna khazar bo" [The Vilna Gaon changed his mind];
  7) "Ha-maksheh le-yeled" [The boy's obstacle];
  8) "Yagata u-matsata—taamin" [You reached out and found—believe];
  9) "Hagurato shel ha-rabi rav Ber" [Rabbi Ber's Belt];
  10) "Nitskhani beni" [My son has vanquished me];
  11) "Kapdanuto shel khaver" [A friend's strictness];
  12) "Le-susati be-rikhvei Besht" [For my horse in the Besht's chariots];
  13) "Ha-sholeah pitka la-shamaim" [One who sends a note to Heaven];
  14) "Mida ke-neged mida" [Measure for measure];
  15) "Koho shel nigun" [A melody's power];
  16) "Orot" [Lights];
  17) "Kufsato shel rav Meir baal hanes" [Rabbi Meir the Wonder-worker's collection box];
  18) "Neshama yeteira" [Extra soul];
  19) "Ki-bitah zakuk la" [Because her daughter needs her];
  20). "Ptah lanu shaar" [Open a gate for us];
  21) "Simhat bet ha-shoeva" [Celebration of the Water-drawing];
  22) "Keitsad nitgale" [How revealed];
  23) "Itsele khata" [Itsele sinned];
  24) "Lo al ha-lekhem levado yihye ha-adam" [Man does not live by bread alone];
  25) "Onesh shel shalosh kosot" [Punishment of three cups];
  26) "Ashkenazi zuta" [Little Ashkenazi];
  27) "Mishnat hasidim" [Hasidic doctrine];
  28) "Ha-hoker mi-Kuznits" [The investigator of Kozienice];
  29) "Rakhmana liba bai" [The Merciful (God) requires one's heart];[20]
  30) "Ke-she-ha-yeitser notel min ha-adam et nekudat ha-emet . . ." [When the drive (to do good or evil) takes the point of truth from the man . . .];
  31) "Ha-maggid mi-Mezeritsh roe or be-moshvotav" [The Preacher of Mezeritsh sees light in his villages];
  32) "Ha-vikuah she-bein kneset Israel be-dmut ha-saba mi-Shpula . . ." [The controversy among the assembly of Israel in the figure of the Shpoler Zeyde (Grandfather of Shpola) . . .];
  33) "Kakh shama ha-rabi rav Bunem be-seudah ha-shlishit shel Shabbat be-heykhal ha-shvii" [Thus heard Rabbi Bunem during the Third Sabbath Meal in the seventh palace];
  34) "Hoy, hoy, shotim shel Hanipoli, be-zkhut mi atem nitsalim?" [Hey, Hey, silly men of Anapol, by whose merit are you saved?];

  Encl. Letter dated 22.05.1942 to Icchak Giterman with request for evaluation and perhaps publication of the attached stories.
- ***Description:*** original (Docs. 1, 2, 4, 5, 8, 9, 10, 11, 12, 25, 28, 29, and 31 in 2 copies), typescript (handwritten additions—OP*, ink), Hebrew, 95×135, 228×284, 218×340 mm, ss. 121, pp. 122.

  Two ss. written on the reverse of a list of names: "Ajenci –poczta" [Postal clerks] (2 copies, typescript).

b)

- Date unknown, place unknown
- [Perec Opoczyński], Story entitled "Sliha lah" [Pardon for her]
- ***Description:*** original, handwritten manuscript (OP*), notebook, ink, Hebrew, 145×206 mm, ss. 16, pp. 8.

## 496. RING. II/461. Mf. ŻIH–808; USHMM–63.

- Date unknown, place unknown
- P. [Perec] Opoczyński [?], Story about a Hasidic family (missing ending)
- Main character is seven-year-old Khane (Hannah)—fate of the child of a poor Jewish family.
- ***Description:*** original or transcript, handwritten manuscript, ink,Yiddish, 119×251, ss. 11, pp. 21.

  Fragment of this story ("Khanes heym." [Hannah's home]), see Ring. II/462.

20. An ancient rabbinic phrase cited by Isaac Abravanel in explicating Deuteronomy 4:29 (according to Nehama Leibowitz, *Studies in Devarim Deuteronomy*, trans. Aryeh Newman [Jerusalem, 1996], p. 54). For a similar phrase, see Babylonian Talmud, Sanhedrin 106b at bottom: "Merciful God requires one's innermost thoughts" (citation provided by Dr. Meir Katz of Baltimore).

**497. RING. II/462. Mf. ŻIH—808; USHMM—63.**

- Date unknown, place unknown
- Perec Opoczyński, Stories
  1) "Khanes heym" [Hannah's home] (fragment);
  2) "Der zeyde un di bobe" [Grandfather and grandmother];
  3) "Feldshers" [Barber-surgeons];
  4) "Dos kranke kind" [The sick child]; "Shenkt mir a shtikl fayer . . ." [Give me a bit of fire . . .];
  5) Story about a pogrom;
  6) ". . . Dovid Lelever hot milkhome gehaltn . . ." [. . . David Lelewer made war . . .];
  7) "A zoyne bbbukh . . . !" [A prostitute bbbook . . . !][21]
- *Description:* original, typescript, handwritten manuscript (two handwritings: OP* i NN.), ink, Yiddish, 134×221, 137×273, 178×300 mm, ss. 44, pp. 44.
  Story "Khanes heym" [Hannah's home], see Ring. II/461. Text of doc. 7 is in a different handwriting (copy [?]).
  Pages of individual stories written on the reverse of printed matter of the Bank for Commerce and Industry in Warsaw (before 1925, printed matter, Polish), Jewish calendar (1936) (printed item, Hebrew, German, Polish, Yiddish), inventory ledger (forest management) (before 09.1939, printed item, Polish), printed items concerning the 3 percent Bonus Investment Loan (23.05.1935, printed matter, Polish).

**498. RING. II/463. Mf. ŻIH—808; USHMM—63.**

- Date unknown, place unknown
- Perec Opoczyński, Stories
  1) "Ferd fleysh" [Horse meat];
  2) "Eyne fun draysik toyznt" [One of thirty thousand];
  3) "Groz" [Grass];
  4) "Di veynendike erd" [The Weeping earth];
  5) "Jip-jip-jip" [Cheep-cheep-cheep (?)];
  6) "Shvartse fligl" [Black wings];
  7) "Gehongen" [Hanged];
  8) "Di heym" [The Home];
  9) "Der monastir" [The Monastery];
  10) "Dos zuntog gebet" [Sunday prayer];
  11) "Di tikerin" [The Bathhouse attendant];
  12) "Sholem" [Peace];
  13) "In khazer shtal" [In a Pigsty];
  14) "Der toyt fun a Rumener" [Death of a Romanian];
  15) "Dos tsigele" [The Little goat];
  16) "Dos royte blimel" [The Red flower];
  17) "Shvomen" [Mushrooms];
  18) "Dem galekhs dinst" [The Priest's servant];
  19) "Di matseyve" [The Tombstone];
  20) "Likht" [Light];
  21) "Shulomis" [Shulamis];
  21)[22] "Arum Marushn" [Around Marusia];
  22) "Khaskil Fontshner (Fontdner) tsit ka Lodzh" [Ezekiel Fontshner (Fontdner) is moving to Łódź];
  23) "Royt Łódź" [Red Łódź];
  24) "Lodzher gasn . . ." [Łódź streets . . .];
  25) "Lodzher dires" [Łódź apartments].
- *Description:* original, typescript (handwritten additions—OP*, ink), Yiddish, 223×290, 218×340, 220×352 mm, ss. 140, pp. 140.

**499. RING. II/464. Mf. ŻIH—808; USHMM—63.**

- 09.1921–07.1922, Łódź
- [Perec Opoczyński?], Poems
  1) "Farvoglt" [Homeless] (Łódź, 3.09.1922);
  2) "Kerner" [Seeds] (missing ending);
  3) "In geruder fun shtot" [In the City's commotion] (Łódź, 10.1922);
  4) "Umru" [Disquiet] (Łódź, 2.05.1922);
  5) "On zere" [Without Seed] (Łódź, summer 192[. . . ?];
  6) "Degeneratsye" [Degeneration] (Łódź, 12.08.1921);
  "Ikh zing in der nakht . . ." [I sing in the night . . .] (Łódź, 16.08.1921);
  "Ikh mit zhabe shketelekh in di hent . . ." [I with frog caskets in my hands . . . (?)] (Łódź, 14.09.1921);
  "Likht" [Light].
- *Description:* original or transcript, handwritten manuscript, ink, Yiddish, 123×199 mm, ss. 20, pp. 22.

**500. RING. II/465. Mf. ŻIH—808; USHMM—63.**

- Date unknown, place unknown
- [Perec Opoczyński], Articles (4):
  1) "Ratsaanim" [Shoemakers];
  2) "Smartutim" [Rags];
  3) "Ha-sabal ve-ha-mekhona" [The porter and the machine];
  4) "Nahagim" [Drivers]
- Socioeconomic situation of small craftsmen before 1939.
- *Description:* original, typescript (handwritten additions—OP*, ink), Hebrew, 213×296, 222×299 227×295 mm, ss. 13, pp. 13.

**501. RING. II/466. Mf. ŻIH—808; USHMM—63.**

- Date unknown, place unknown
- [Perec Opoczyński], Story for children about return from vacation to the city (fragment).

21. It is difficult to decipher the Yiddish writing that is rendered as "bbbukh."
22. Sic numbering in Polish catalog.

- ***Description:*** original, handwritten manuscript (OP*), ink, Hebrew, 154×200 mm, ss. 3, pp. 5.
  Written on the reverse of a form: "Notification about change of wages" of the Fund for the Sick of the City of Łódź (before 09.1939, printed matter, Polish).
  On reverse of p. 1 notes in Yiddish; on reverse of p. 3 address in Yiddish (ink): "Zamenhofa 46 [40], apt. 15" [or 15, apt. 40 or 46?].

### 502. RING. II/467. Mf. ŻIH—808; USHMM—63.

- Date unknown, place unknown
- [Perec Opoczyński], Story about sales of hides and shoes (fragment)
- Encl. glossary with Hebrew vocabulary.
- ***Description:*** original, handwritten manuscript (OP*), ink, Yiddish, 110×283 mm, ss. 3, pp. 3.
  Manuscript written on ss. from a cashbook ledger (printed, German, Russian).

### 503. RING. II/435. Mf. ŻIH—807; USHMM—62.

- Date unknown, place unknown
- Perec Opoczyński, Article entitled "Lamah yigra helkam?" [Why should their portion be reduced?]
- Concerns emigration of youth to Palestine.
- ***Description:*** transcript, typescript, Hebrew, 216×340 mm, ss. 2, pp. 2.

### 504. RING. II/468. Mf. ŻIH—808; USHMM—63.

- 1922–1939, place unknown
- Collection of press clippings with texts by Perec Opoczyński or concerning him as well as others.
  1) P. Opoczyński, "Likht" [Light] (*Lodzher tageblat* [Łódź Daily], 1921);
  2) Yankev Shatski, "Di yidishe literatur in yor 1923" [Yiddish literature in 1923] (in *Fraynt* [The Friend], January–February 1924, p. 9, fragment);
  3) H. Lang, "Di amerikaner arbeter bavegung (a blik in yor 1923)" [The American labor movement (a glance at the year 1923) (in *Fraynt*, January–February 1924, p. 11, fragment);
  4) P. Opoczyński, "Asher Shvartsman (kharakteristik)" [Asher Shvartsman (profile)] (15.06.1923);
  5) P. Opoczyński, "Mi-bayit le-bayit" [From house to house] (in: *Nayer folksblat* [New People's Paper], 1925);
  6) P. Opoczyński, "A kind tsu ferkoyfn . . ." [A child for sale . . .] (in: *Lodzher tageblat*, no. 60, 10.03.1932);
  7) P. Opoczyński, "Shnorer" [Beggar] (15.08.1932);
  8) Clipping from the newspaper *Frayhayt* (New York) with article about literature (inf. about Perec Opoczyński); P. Opoczyński, Poems (4): "Di noyt" [Need], "Herbstiger ovnt" [Autumnal evening], "Ovent" [Evening], "Vinter" [Winter] (in: *Lodzher folksblat*);
  9) Clippings with good wishes on the occasion of birth of son (from Icchak Goldin) to Perec Opoczyński and condolences on the death of his mother (from Józef Turkow, Abram Czerchowski, and Mosze Chaim Tiger), daughter (Miriam) and son (Binus);
  10) P. Opoczyński, "Dikhter fun troyer un pashtes" [Poet of sadness and simplicity] (about Chaim Król);
  11) P. Opoczyński, "Di yubiley fayerung fun Sholem Ash" [The Jubilee celebration of Sholem Asch];
  12) P. Opoczyński, "A folk veynt . . ." [A people cries . . .] (about presentation of Abraham Goldfaden's play at the Habima Theater);
  13) [Perec Opoczyński], "Zayfenblozen" [Soap Bubbles] (*Frayhayt*, New York, 23.08.1927)
- ***Description:*** original, printed matter (handwritten additions, ink), Yiddish, 72×27, 183×329, 208×307 mm, ss. 22, pp. 42.

### 505. RING. II/386. Mf. ŻIH—803; USHMM—58.

a)

- 1.05.1923[?], Łódź.
- Editorial board of *Folksblat* [People's Paper] (Łódź), Identification dated 1.05.1923[?] for P. [Perec] Opoczyński, coworker of the editorial board.
- ***Description:*** original, printed matter, handwritten manuscript, ink, stamp, Polish, Yiddish, 136×89 mm, ss. 1, pp. 1.
  Stamp: "Wydawnictwo Folksblat" [Folksblat Publishing House].
  On reverse notes in Yiddish (ink) "Baruch Huliszdowski [?], 32, Zduńska Wola, [. . .] in Pabianice. He received the card near Mława, Ostrołęka."

b)

- 1.10.1925, Łódź
- Editorial board of *Unzer togblat* [Our Daily Paper] (Łódź), Identification no. 32 dated 1.10.1925 for P. [Perec] Opoczyński, permanent coworker of the publication.
- ***Description:*** original, printed matter, handwritten manuscript, ink, stamps, French., Polish, Yiddish, 93×136 mm, missing photograph, ss. 2, pp. 4.

c)

- 10.02.1926, Łódź
- Editorial board of *Lodzer tageblat* (Łódź), Identification card no. 3, dated 10.02.1926, of Perec Opoczyński (Łódź, ul. Piotrkowska 82), editorial board coworker (fragment).
- ***Description:*** original, printed matter, typescript, handwritten manuscript, ink, stamps, French, Polish, Yiddish, 80×110, 80×105 mm, ss. 2, pp. 3.

d)

- 10.02.1930, Łódź
- Editorial board of *Lodzer Tageblat* (Łódź), Identification card no. 3, dated 12.02.1930, of Perec Opoczyński, coworker of the publication.
- ***Description:*** original, printed matter, typescript, stamps, French, Polish, Yiddish, 80×105 mm, missing photograph, ss. 3, pp. 4.

e)

- Date unknown, place unknown
- Perec Opoczyński (Opoczyner), Visiting card.
- ***Description:*** original (2 copies), printed matter, 104×59 mm, ss. 2, pp. 2.
  On reverse of first copy notation in Hebrew [?]

f)

- Date unknown, place unknown
- Photograph of woman (mother of Perec Opoczyński [?]).
- ***Description:*** original, fragments of stamps, photograph, 54×84 mm, ss. 1, pp. 1.
  Photo. glued on cardboard.

### 506. RING. II/469. Mf. ŻIH—808; USHMM—63.

a)

- 29.03.1922, Warsaw
- Editorial board of Ringen [Rings], Letter of 29.03.1922 to [Perec] Opoczyński.
- Confirmation of receipt of materials.
- ***Description:*** original, handwritten manuscript, ink, stamp, Yiddish, 142×228 mm, ss. 1, pp. 1.

b)

- 8.07.1924, Warsaw
- Sztybel Publishing House (Warsaw, ul. Orla 11), Kohen, Letter of 8.07.1924 to Perec Opoczyński (Łódź, ul. Rokicińska 14)
- Concerns story entitled "Na ve-nad" [Wandering], which was to be published in no. 22 or 24 of the periodical *Ha-Tekufa* [The Era].
- ***Description:*** original, handwritten manuscript, ink, Hebrew, 220×287 mm, ss. 1, pp. 1.
  Encl. envelope (handwritten manuscript, ink, Hebrew, Polish, 157×126 mm, ss. 2, pp. 1).

c)

- 8.01.1925, Warsaw
- Sztybel Publishing House (Warsaw, ul. Orla 11), Kohen, Letter of 8.01.1925 to P. [Perec] Opoczyński (Łódź, ul. Piotrkowska 82)
- Concerns story entitled "Na ve-nad" [Wandering], which was to be published in no. 22 [of the periodical *Ha-Tekufa* [The Era].
- ***Description:*** original, handwritten manuscript on a postcard, Hebrew, 143×90 mm, ss. 1, pp. 2.

d)

- 9.07.1925, Warsaw
- Sztybel Publishing House (Warsaw, ul. Orla 11), Letter of 9.07.1925 to Perec Opoczyński (Łódź, ul. Piotrkowska 82)
- Concerns story entitled "Na ve-nad" [Wandering], which was to be published in no. 24 of the publication *Ha-Tekufa* [The Era], after the annual break in publication of the periodical.
- ***Description:*** original, typescript on a postcard, Hebrew, 142×92 mm, ss. 1, pp. 2.
  On bottom of p. 2 signature (ink).

e)

- [7.10.1933], Kalisz
- R. Jakubowicz (Kalisz, ul. Szkolna 4), Letter of [7.10.1933 postmark date] to P. [Perec] Opoczyński (Łódź, ul. Piotrkowska 69)
- Editorial remarks (proofreading).
- ***Description:*** original, handwritten manuscript on a postcard, ink, Yiddish, 148×104 mm, ss. 1, pp. 2.

f)

- 19.03.[no year], New York (USA).
- *Ha-Doar* [The Post] *Hebrew Weekly* (New York, 114 Fifth Avenue), Menachem Ribalow, Letter dated 19.03.[no year], to Perec Opoczyński (Łódź)
- Refusal to publish Opoczyński's text in the periodical *Ha-Doar.*
- ***Description:*** original, handwritten manuscript, ink, Hebrew, 114×216 mmk. 1, pp. 1.

g)

- [10.09.[no year], Bolesławiec
- Rozes [?] (Bolesławiec, Rynek), Letter of [10.09. [no year], postmark date] to P. [Perec] Opoczyński (Łódź, ul. Piotrkowska 69)
- New Year's greetings.
- ***Description:*** original, handwritten manuscript on a postcard (Keren Kayemet Le-Israel, Jewish National Fund]), Hebrew, 144×109 mm, ss. 1, pp. 2.

h)

- Before 09.1939, Wilno
- Zalman Rejzin (Wilno, Wielka Pohulanka 11, apt. 10), Letter to Perec Opoczyński (Łódź, ul. Piotrkowska 82)
- Request for dispatch of materials for the lexicon of Jewish literature, press, and philosophy.
- ***Description:*** original, printed matter, Polish, Yiddish, 132×292 mm, ss. 1, pp. 1.
  Name and surname written manually (ink).
  Printed at the print works of B. A. Kleckin's "Wydawnictwo Wileńskie" [Wilno Publishing House] (Warsaw, ul. Leszno 36, apt. 22).

i)

- Date unknown, place unknown
- Perec Opoczyński, Letter to Mitler
- Inf. concerning Opoczyński's article.
- ***Description:*** transcript, handwritten manuscript (OP*), ink, Yiddish, 92×358 mm, ss. 2, pp. 4.

j)

- Before 09.1939, Łódź[?]
- NN., Letter to Perec Opoczyński (Editorial board of [*Lodzher*] *Tageblat*, Łódź, ul. Piotrkowska 16). (fragment—only the envelope was preserved).
- ***Description:*** original, handwritten manuscript, ink, stamp, Polish, 148×97 mm, ss. 2, pp. 1.

### 507. RING. II/470. Mf. ŻIH—808; USHMM—63.

a)

- 09.1922–01.1923, Warsaw
- Z. Berger-Rawicz (Warsaw, ul. Nowolipki 41, apt. 6), Letters dated 14.09., 22.09., 15.10., 5.11.1922, and 14.01.1923 to Perec Opoczyński (Łódź, ul. Rokicińska 14)
- Concerning publication matters.
- ***Description:*** original, handwritten manuscript, ink, stamps, Yiddish, 218×278, 175×225 mm, ss. 5, pp. 6.
  On reverse of letter of 14.09.1922 address (ink): "Editor, *Freiheit*, 47 Chrystie St., New York, USA."
  At top stamp: "Z. Berger-Rawicz, Warsaw, Nowolipki 41, apt. 6"
  Attached are two envelopes (handwritten manuscript, ink, postal stamp and sender's stamp, 148×97 mm, ss. 4, pp. 4)

b)

- 30.04.1925, Warsaw
- Wydawnictwo Wileńskie B.A. Kleckina [B.A. Kleckin's Wilno Publishing House] (Warsaw, ul. Leszno 36, apt. 22). Editorial board of *Literarishe bleter* [Literary Pages], Letter of 30.04.1925 to Perec Opoczyński (Łódź, ul. Piotrkowska 82)
- Concerning publication matters.
- ***Description:*** original, typescript, stamp, Yiddish, 223×283 mm, ss. 1, pp. 1.
  On bottom signature of (ink): Z. Berger-Rawicz.
  Attached envelope with imprint of "Wydawnictwo Wileńskie" (printed, handwritten manuscript, ink, Polish, Yiddish, 155×125 mm, ss. 2, pp. 1).

## *MATERIALS OF HENRYK PIÓRNIK AND WACŁAW KĄCZKOWSKI*

### 508. RING. II/483. Mf. ŻIH—809; USHMM—64.

- 1929–1935, Warsaw
- Patents of Henryk Piórnik and Wacław Kączkowski issued by the Patent Office of the Republic of Poland
  1) H. Piórnik's Patent of 2.08.1929 on "Method of production of panels and objects with free forms from bakelite, wood and paper";
  2) H. Piórnik's Patent of 16.03.1933 on "Method of production of objects from one, two or a larger number of layers of combined materials";
  3) Patent of W. Kączkowski and H. Piórnik of 19.08.1933 on "Method of production of artificial plastic masses that can be hardened";
  4) Patent of H. Piórnik of 25.06.1934 on "Method of production of plywood" (attached supplemental patent of 25.06.1934 on "Method of production of plywood").
- ***Description:*** original, printed matter, typescript, payment stamps, Polish, 190×242, 192×249, 210×300 mm, ss. 20, pp. 39.
  See Ring. II/484.
  Docs. were preserved in binder.

### 509. RING. II/484. Mf. ŻIH—809; USHMM—64.

- 1930–1938, Berlin, Milan, Rome, London, Paris, Prague, Oslo, Stockholm, Vienna, Bern, Brussels, Ottawa, Washington, Calcutta
- Patents and Certificates for protection of the patent rights of Henryk Piórnik (Warsaw, ul. Ceglana 7) and Wacław Kączkowski issued by the patent offices of Germany, Italy, Great Britain, France, Czechoslovakia, Norway, Sweden, Austria, Switzerland, Belgium, Canada, USA.
- ***Description:*** original, printed matter, typescript, handwritten manuscript, ink, pencil, English, Czech, French, German, Swedish, Italian, 127×76, 145×228, 228×365 mm, ss. 58, pp. 70.
  See Ring. II/483.

## *MATERIALS OF CWI PRYŁUCKI [TSVI PRILUTSKI]*

### 510. RING. II/175. Mf. ŻIH—796; USHMM—51.

- Before 4.05.1940–11.06.1941, place unknown
- [Cwi Pryłucki?], Journal (missing beginning)
- Political situation in the period of the Revolution of 1905 in the Polish Kingdom and Russia, struggle for a Yiddish press, author's publishing activity (inter alia, *Der Moment*), Zionist movement.
- ***Description:*** original, handwritten manuscript, notebooks (12), ink, Polish, Yiddish, ink, 157×202 mm, sewn, missing notebooks 1–5 of part I, ss. 469, pp. 449.
  Part of the manuscript is written in notebooks with the imprint: "Prywatne Gimnazjum Żeńskie S. Pryłuckiej Długa 29. Zeszyt . . . , Uczenicy kl. . . . Rok szkolny 1936/37 [lub] 1938/39." [Private Girls Secondary School of S. Prylucka Długa 29. Notebook . . . , Of Student in class . . . School year 1936–37 [or] 1938/39.]
  Author was editor of the Yiddish daily, *Der Moment* (1910–1939).

## *MATERIALS OF EMANUEL RINGELBLUM*

### 511. RING. II/401. Mf. ŻIH—804; USHMM—59.

- Date unknown, place unknown
- [Emanuel Ringelblum], Study entitled "Dzieje Żydów [w Warszawie]" [History of the Jews (in Warsaw)] (fragment)
- Jewish population in Warsaw from 1527 until the end of the 18th century. Continuation of the work *Żydzi w Warszawie. Od czasów najdawniejszych do ostatniego wypędzenia w* 1527 [Jews in Warsaw. From the Most Ancient Times to the Last Expulsion in 1527] (Warsaw 1932). Rough draft of text with footnotes, with supplemental notes.

- *Description:* original, typescript, handwritten manuscript (ER*), ink, French, Latin, Polish, Yiddish, 178×220, 160×200 mm, ss. 258, pp. 269.

## 512. RING. II/402. Mf. ŻIH—804; USHMM—59.

- Date unknown, Warsaw
- [Emanuel Ringelblum], Study entitled ["Dzieje Żydów w Warszawie" ("History of the Jews of Warsaw")] (fragment)
- Titles of individual fragments: "Commerce," "Purveyors," "Credit," "Bankers, artisans, lease-holding and agriculture." Attached article entitled "Baytragn tsu der geshikhte fun yidishe doktoyrim in Poyln" [Contributions to the history of Jewish doctors in Poland], in: *Sotsyale Meditsin* [Social Medicine], no. 9–10, pp. 127–131 (text with handwritten corrections by the author).
- *Description:* original, printed matter, typescript, handwritten manuscript, notebooks, ink, French, Latin, Polish, Yiddish, 158×44, 160×200, 155×383, 215×299 mm, ss. 341, pp. 348.

## 513. RING. II/403. Mf. ŻIH—805; USHMM—60.

- Date unknown, place unknown
- [Emanuel Ringelblum], Study entitled ["Dzieje Żydów w Warszawie" (History of the Jews of Warsaw")] (fragment)
- "Di rekhtlekh gezelshaftlekhe lage fun di varshever yidn" [The legal-social situation of the Warsaw Jews].
- *Description:* original, handwritten manuscript (ER*), notebooks, ink, French, Yiddish, 215×279, 160×196 mm, sewn, ss. 96, pp. 103.

  According to notation of E.R. this text was printed.

## 514. RING. II/404. Mf. ŻIH—805; USHMM—36.

- Date unknown, place unknown
- [Emanuel Ringelblum], Study entitled ["Dzieje Żydów w Warszawie" ("History of the Jews of Warsaw")] (fragment)
- "Obtsoln fun gorkukhn" [Fees of canteens], XVIII cent.—contribution to the work *Dzieje Żydów w Warszawie*, volume II.
- *Description:* original, handwritten manuscript, ink, Polish, Yiddish, 165×200 mm, ss. 11, pp. 11.

## 515. RING. II/406/1. Mf. ŻIH—805; USHMM—60.

- Date unknown, place unknown
- [Emanuel Ringelblum], Study entitled ["Dzieje Żydów w Warszawie" ("History of the Jews of Warsaw")]
- (fragment)
- "Oysergevenlekhe shtayern. Shtayer oyf farendikn di kasern" [Extraordinary taxes. Tax for completing the barracks].
- *Description:* original, handwritten manuscript, notebook, ink, French, Polish, Yiddish, 160×198, 145×200, 40×180 mm, ss. 28, pp. 25.

## 516. RING. II/406/2. Mf. ŻIH—805; USHMM—60.

- 12.1936, Warsaw
- Emanuel Ringelblum, "Tsu der geshikhte fun 'laybtsol' in Poyln" [Contribution to the history of the "body tax" in Poland]
- Article appeared in the periodical *Landkentenish* [Tourism], no. 2 (22) of 12.1936.
- *Description:* original, printed (supplements, handwritten manuscript—ER*, ink), Yiddish, 193×267 mm, ss. 4, pp. 8.

## 517. RING. II/405. Mf. ŻIH—805; USHMM—60.

- Date unknown, place unknown
- [Emanuel Ringelblum], Study entitled "Dzieje Żydów w Warszawie" [History of the Jews of Warsaw]
- (fragment)
- Thematic index to source extracts.
- *Description:* original, handwritten manuscript, notebook, ink, Polish, 160×200 mm, ss. 69, pp. 95.

## 518. RING. II/407. Mf. ŻIH—805; USHMM—60.

- Before 09.1939, place unknown
- [Emanuel Ringelblum], Notes from archival documents and other sources for the history of Jews on Polish lands.
- *Description:* original, handwritten manuscript, ink, pencil, Hebrew, French, Latin, Polish, 85×105, 85×212, 178×128, 208×338 mm, k.18, pp. 25.

## 519. RING. II/408. Mf. ŻIH—805; USHMM—60.

- After 1935, place unknown
- Emanuel Ringelblum, "Di geshikhte fun di lodzher yidn" [History of the Łódź Jews]
- Review of Filip Friedman's book, *Dzieje Żydów w Łodzi. Od początków osadnictwa Żydów do roku 1863* [History of the Jews of Łódź. From the beginnings of Jewish Settlement until 1863], (Łódź 1935).
- *Description:* original, typescript, Yiddish, 214×278 mm, ss. 15, pp. 15.

## 520. RING. II/485. Mf. ŻIH—809; USHMM—64.

- Date unknown, place unknown
- [Emanuel Ringelblum], Study entitled "Umdirekte shtayern. Shkhite-gelt" [Indirect taxes. Ritual slaughter fees]
- Fragment of a larger historical study regarding the situation of the Jewish population in Warsaw in the 18th century, revenues of the Paving Commission (Komisji Brukowej) from taxes levied on Jews.
- *Description:* original, typescript (additions, handwritten manuscript-ER*, ink, pencil), Yiddish, 219×350 mm, only pp. 38–39 were preserved, ss. 2, pp. 2.

  Only pp. 38–39, chapter without ending and endnotes.

**521. RING. II/387. Mf. ŻIH—803; USHMM—58.**

- 23.03.1939, Warsaw
- Society of Supporters of the Main Judaic Library at the Great Synagogue (Towarzystwo Miłośników Głównej Biblioteki Judaistycznej przy Wielkiej Synagodze) (ul. Tłomackie 5), Letter dated 23.03.1939 to Dr. [Emanuel Ringelblum].
- Thanks for presenting on 22.03.1939 a lecture entitled "From the history of the struggle for the right of residence of Jews in Warsaw." Letter signed by Engineer Mojżesz Koerner, vice chairman.
- ***Description:*** original, typescript, stamp, Polish, Yiddish, 219×294 mm, ss. 1, pp. 1.

**522. RING. II/388. Mf. ŻIH—803, 836; USHMM—34, 67.**

a)

- 15.11.1928, Warsaw
- State Examination Commission in Warsaw for candidates to be secondary school teachers, Diploma of secondary school teacher, dated 15.11.1928, for Emanuel Ringelblum
- Contains Ringelblum's biography.
- ***Description:*** original, typescript, stamp, Polish, 242×377 mm, ss. 2, pp. 1.

b)

- 26.08.1938, Venice (Italy)
- Casino Municipale di Venezia, Ticket of admission dated 26.08.1938 for Emanuel Ringelblum.
- ***Description:*** original, printed matter, handwritten manuscript, ink, Italian, 92×64 mm, ss. 1, pp. 2.

c)

- 10.12.1940, Warsaw Ghetto
- Eldorado Theater (ul. Dzielna 1), Invitation to the premiere of a play entitled In reydl. [In the little circle] on 10.12.1940
- ***Description:*** original, printed matter, handwritten manuscript, ink, stamp, Polish, 120×90 mm, ss. 1, pp. 1.

  On reverse no.: "129."

  Published: *Kronika getta*, p. 540 (photocopy).

d)

- 08.1941, Warsaw Ghetto
- Sponsors' Committee of Kitchen no. 132 (ul. Nowolipki 22), Invitation for [Emanuel] Ringelblum to the kitchen's opening after repairs 17.08.1941.
- ***Description:*** original, printed matter, handwritten manuscript, ink, Hebrew, Yiddish, 110×89 mm, ss. 2, pp. 2.

e)

- 14.11.1941, Warsaw Ghetto
- Jewish Council in Warsaw. Department of Payments for the benefit of the Hospital Management and the Health Service (ul. Ceglana 7), Proof of payment dated 14.11.1941 of Em. [Emanuel] Ringelblum (ul. Leszno 18, apt. 31).
- ***Description:*** original, printed matter, handwritten manuscript, pencil, stamp, Polish, 136×75 mm, ss. 1, pp. 1.

  Attached card (Jewish Council in Warsaw. Department of Payments for the benefit of the Hospital Management and the Health Service (ul. Ceglana 7) with notation on reverse: "Ringelblum Em. from 09.41, after present payment 2 installments" (printed, handwritten manuscript, pencil, 103×42 mm, ss. 1, pp. 2.).

f)

- 01.1942, Warsaw Ghetto
- Sponsors' Committee of the "Dobra Wola" ("Good Will") Boarding School Orphanage [ul. Dzielna 61], Invitation for Dr. [Emanuel] Ringelblum to celebration of opening on 10.01.1942
- Program. Announces members of the orphanage's Sponsors' Committee: Z. Cederbaum, A. [Abraham] Gepner, E. [Edward Eliasz] Kobryner, D. Mauer, M. [Maria] Pinkiertowa, N. Rothnerowa, T. Rotsz-teinowa, S. [Stanisław] Szereszewski, K. and Wajsberżanka.
- ***Description:*** original, printed matter, Polish, 100×138 mm, ss. 2, pp. 3.

  On p. 1 address: "Dr. Ringenblum [sic] location ul. Leszno [number effaced, corrected (after 1946) with ballpoint pen to "18]" and stamp: "«Eildienst» Centr. Biuro Doręczeń" ["Rush Service" of the Centr. Bureau of Deliveries], below is stamp: "Paid delivery."

g)

- 4.08.1942, Warsaw Ghetto
- OBW, Certificate dated 4.08.1942 about transfer to SS of the registration card of Leon Ringelblum (ul. Dzika 25), employee of the workshop.
- ***Description:*** original, typescript, handwritten manuscript, ink, German, 208×56 mm, ss. 1, pp. 1.

h)

- 19.09.1942, Buczacz
- Jizia [Giza Eisenbach] (Buczacz), Telegram dated 19.09.1942 to Judyta Ringelblum (ul. Leszno 18, apt. 31)
- Request for information about family.
- ***Description:*** original, typescript postal form, German, Polish, 208×148 mm, ss. 1, pp. 1.

  At top notation (pencil): "Halman N-lipki" [carpentry workshop of Bernhard Hallmann, Nowolipki 59].

  Giza Eisenbach, wife of Artur Eisenbach, historian, was sister of Emanuel Ringelblum; see *Archiwum Ringelbluma*, p. 174

  Published: *Archiwum Ringelbluma*, p. 174 (photocopy).

i)

- 2.11.1942, Warsaw Ghetto
- Deutsche Textil-Verarbeitung W. [Wilfried] Hoffmann [Hoffman German Textile Manufactur-

ing], Pass dated 2.11.1942 for Emanuel Ringelblum, authorizing entry into the grounds of the workshop.
- *Description:* original, typescript, German, 208×148 mm, ss. 1, pp. 1.
  At bottom illegible signature (ink).
  See *Archiwum Ringelbluma*, pp. 262–263 (description, photocopy).

## *MATERIALS OF HERSZ WASSER*

### 523. RING. II/392. Mf. ŻIH—803; USHMM—58.

a)
- 05–08.1940, Warsaw
- Labor Battalion at the Jewish Council in Warsaw, "Call-up card for the month" June (dated 26.05.1940), July (dated 25.06.1940), August (dated [?]) and September (dated 26.08.1940) to forced labor for Hirsz or Herman [Hersz] Wasser (ul. Bielańska 15/17, apt. 26). Attached inspection stubs.
- ***Description:*** original, printed matter, handwritten manuscript, pencil, ink, stamps, German, Polish, 160×88, 94×155, 93×81 mm, ss. 22, pp. 26.

b)
- 8.12.1940, Warsaw Ghetto
- Labor Battalion at the Jewish Council in Warsaw, "Labor order" dated 8.12.1940 for forced labor for Hersz Wasser (ul. Muranowska 6, apt. 15).
- ***Description:*** original, printed matter, handwritten manuscript, ink, German, Polish, 83×160 mm, ss. 1, pp. 2.
  On reverse stamp and notation (ink): "Employees of ŻSS" and illegible signature.

### 524. RING. II/383/3. Mf. ŻIH—803; USHMM—58.

- 1940/41, Warsaw Ghetto
- ZZ, "Potato card for 1941 no. 180703" made out for Bluma Wasser (ul. Muranowska 6).
- ***Description:*** original, printed matter, handwritten manuscript (H.W.*), ink, German, Polish, 145×87 mm, some of the coupons torn out, ss. 1, pp. 2.
  On reverse stamp: "Distribution Point for Potatoes and Vegetables F. [Fiszel?] Fliderblum [?] Pawia 60."

### 525. RING. II/390. Mf. ŻIH—803; USHMM—58.

- 31.12.[1941], Warsaw Ghetto
- Jewish Council in Warsaw, Receipt no. 31536 dated 31.12.[1941] for delivery by Bluma Wasser (ul. Muranowska 6, apt. 15) of fur collar and muff in connection with the order of 25.12.1941 about the obligation of Jews to surrender furs and fur goods.
- ***Description:*** original, printed matter, handwritten manuscript, pencil, German, Polish, 127×188 mm, ss. 1, pp. 1.
  On bottom signatures (pencil): of Bluma Wasser and NN.

### 526. RING. II/391. Mf. ŻIH—803; USHMM—58.

a)
- 1.10.1940, Warsaw
- ŻSS. Coordinating Committee, Certificate dated 1.10.1940 about employment of Hirsz [Hersz] Wasser (ul. Bielańska 15/17, apt. 26).
- ***Description:*** original, duplicated typescript, typescript, stamps, German, Polish, 213×275 mm, ss. 1, pp. 2.
  At bottom signatures of NN. and Emanuel Ringelblum [?] (ink).
  On reverse stamps with notation about extension of validity until 30.11.1940 and stamp of ŻSS, of contribution to "Aid for victims of the war" 20 gr (printed, stamp, Polish, Yiddish).

b)
- 1941–1942, Warsaw Ghetto
- ŻSS-KOM, Identification cards (2) no. 136303 dated 16.07.1941 and no. 136303 dated 15.06.1942 for Hersz (Hirsz) Wasser, authorizing him to use kitchen (no. 32—identification no. 136303).
- ***Description:*** original, printed matter, handwritten manuscript, ink, stamps, Polish, Yiddish, 123×71 mm, ss. 2, pp. 4.
  On both docs. stamp: Jewish Council in Warsaw.

c)
- 3.03.1942, Warsaw Ghetto
- ŻOS (ul. Tłomackie 5), Receipt no. 40193 dated 3.03.1942 for Hersz Wasser (ul. Muranowska 6, apt. 15) of payment of 5 zł to "Winter Aid 1941/42."
- ***Description:*** original, printed matter, handwritten manuscript, ink, stamp, Polish, 126×97 mm, ss. 1, pp. 1.
  At bottom illegible signature (ink).

d)
- 23.08.1942, Warsaw Ghetto
- OBW, Pass dated 23.08.1942 for Hirsz Herman [Hersz] Wasser and Hersz Berliński, authorizing them to go to ul. Leszno.
- ***Description:*** original, typescript, stamp, German, 198×127 mm, ss. 1, pp. 1.
  At bottom illegible signature (ink).
  Published: *Kronika getta*, p. 691 (photocopy).

e)
- 2.09.1942, Warsaw Ghetto
- OBW, "Speiseausweis no. 393" [Food ID card no. 393] dated 2.09.1942 for Hersz or Herman Wasser, for September 1942
- Inf. about category of worker: office worker.
- ***Description:*** original, printed matter, handwritten manuscript, ink, German, 122×85 mm, ss. 1, pp. 2.
  At bottom illegible signatures (ink).
  See *Archiwum Ringelbluma*, p. 259 (description, photocopy).

f)
- 27.11.1942, Warsaw Ghetto

- OBW, Pass dated 27.11.1942 for Hirsz [Hersz] Wasser, authorizing him to go to the workshop of W.C. Többens (ul. Leszno, Franciszkańska 32, Świętojerska 32).
- ***Description:*** original, typescript, handwritten manuscript, ink, stamp, German, 148×104 mm, ss. 1, pp. 1.
  On bottom illegible signatures (ink).

g)

- 12.12.1942, Warsaw Ghetto
- OBW, Pass dated 12.12.1942 for H. [Hersz] Wasser and [Eliasz] Gutkowski, authorizing them to go to ZZ (ul. Franciszkańska 35).
- ***Description:*** original, typescript, handwritten manuscript, ink, stamp, German, 147×104 mm, ss. 1, pp. 1.
  At bottom illegible signature (ink).

### 527. RING. II/270/1. Mf. ŻIH—799; USHMM—54.

- [15.07.1942], Dubienka
- Genia Elbint (Dubienka, in care of Segał), Letter of [15.07.1942 postmark date] to Blumka and Heńiek Wasser (Warsaw Ghetto, Nowolipie 63, apt. 82, [formerly] Muranowska 6, apt. 15)
- Inf. about family and acquaintances.
- ***Description:*** original, handwritten manuscript on a postcard, postmark and stamp of the Jewish Council in Warsaw, ink, Polish, 148×104 mm, ss. 1, pp. 2.
  On p. 1 before the name of the street: "N-pie 63/82" [Nowolipie] date: "19VII"
  Index: Cesia Cukierman, Dora Rapoport, Basia Zylberblech (Borensztejn).

### 528. RING. II/419/2. Mf. ŻIH—806; USHMM—61.

- [27.07[?].1942], Warsaw Ghetto
- NN., Letter of [27.07[?].1942] to [Hersz] Wasser (ul. Nowolipki 29 m.16).
- Card from the Umschlagplatz [?]: "Ratujcie nas, nie jesteśmy nie załatwieni" [s] [Save us, we have not been dealt with yet].
- ***Description:*** original, handwritten manuscript, pencil, ss. 1, pp. 2.
  On p. 1 notation H.W.* (ink): "27.7.1942."
  Alongside illegible signature.

### 529. RING. II/393. Mf. ŻIH—803; USHMM—58.

a)

- [27.08.1942], Łódź ghetto
- Chaim Rumkowski (Łódź ghetto), Letter of [27.08.1942 postmark date] to Hirsz [Hersz] Wasser (Warsaw, ul. Muranowska 6, apt. 15).
- Official notification that Estera and Lejb Wasser are healthy and residing in the Łódź ghetto at ul. Hohensteiner 43/45, apt. 101.
- ***Description:*** original, printed matter, handwritten manuscript, ink, postmark and stamp of the Jewish Council in Warsaw, German, 147×104 mm, ss. 1, pp. 2.
  See Ring. I/544.
  Published: *Listy o Zagładzie*, pp. 201–202.

b)

- [27.08.1942], Łódź ghetto
- Chaim Rumkowski (Łódź ghetto), Letter of [27.08.1942 postmark date] to Bluma Kirszenfeld (Warsaw, ul. Muranowska 6, apt. 15)
- Official notifications that Dora and Sulamita Elbirt are healthy and residing in the Łódź ghetto at ul. Hohensteiner 43, apt. 101.
- ***Description:*** original, printed matter, handwritten manuscript, ink, postmark and stamp of the Jewish Council in Warsaw, German, 146×104 mm, ss. 1, pp. 2.
  See Ring. I/544.
  Published: *Listy o Zagładzie*, pp. 203–205.

c)

- 20.07.1942, Biłgoraj
- Josef Kirszenfeld (Biłgoraj, ul Nadstawna 42), Letter of 20.07.1942 to Hirsz [Hersz] [and Bluma] Wasser (Warsaw Ghetto, ul. Nowolipki 29, apt. 16)
- Thanks for money, request for further aid; notes hard labor and high food prices.
- ***Description:*** original, handwritten manuscript on a postcard, pencil, postmark and stamp of the Jewish Council in Warsaw, Polish, 148×104 mm, ss. 1, pp. 2.
  Index: Szaja Kesner

d)

- 6.10[?].[1942], Warsaw Ghetto
- NN. (Warsaw Ghetto), Letter of 6.10[?].[1942] to Heńiek [Wasser] (Warsaw Ghetto)
- Request for aid, notation about liquidation of the tailoring workshop.
- ***Description:*** original, handwritten manuscript, pencil, Polish, 105×65 mm, ss. 1, pp. 1.
  At bottom illegible signature.
  Published: *Kronika getta*, p. 693 (photocopy).

### 530. RING. II/252. Mf. ŻIH—799; USHMM—54.

- 7.12.1942, Warsaw Ghetto
- OBW, Pass dated 7.12.1942 for H. [Hersz] Waser [Wasser] for allocation of a cart to bring bread to the workshop.
- ***Description:*** original, typescript, handwritten manuscript, ink, stamp, German, 133×107 mm, ss. 1, pp. 1.
  At bottom two illegible signatures (ink, pencil).
  See *Archiwum Ringelbluma*, p. 326 (summary).

## *MATERIALS OF CHASKIEL WILCZYŃSKI*

### 531. RING. II/409. Mf. ŻIH—805; USHMM—60.

- Date unknown, place unknown
- [Chaskiel Wilczyński], Study entitled "Yidishe kolonizatsye in Poyln. Period fun Kongres-Poyln" [Jewish colonization in Poland. Period of Congress Poland (missing ending)

- ***Description:*** original, handwritten manuscript, pencil, Yiddish, 106×140, 119×244 mm, ss. 54, pp. 56.
    Manuscript written on printed receipts of the Jewish Community in Częstochowa (before 1930, printed matter, Polish).

## 532. RING. II/410. Mf. ŻIH—805; USHMM—60.

a)

- Date unknown, place unknown
- [Chaskiel Wilczyński], Notes for a study about the situation of the Jewish population in the period of the Polish Kingdom (1815–1830)
- Jews in agriculture
- Attached: Müntzen, mayor of Stara Częstochowa, Letter of 30.07.1815 to the Częstochowa kahal (Jewish Community) with request to provide [gun-]powder and vodka for church celebrations connected with the rise of the Polish Kingdom.
- ***Description:*** original, transcript (attached), handwritten manuscript (two handwritings: ChW* and NN.—attachment), pencil, ink, Polish, Yiddish, 90×119, 158×201, 120×178 mm, ss. 21, pp. 51.
    Notes contain fragments of study from Ring. II/409.
    Part of the manuscript written on printed matter: "Wykaz dokumentów złożonych Związkowej Centrali Inkasowej Sp. z odp. ogran. [List of documents supplied to the Central Trade Union Collection Co[mpany], L.L.C."[23] (before 09.1939, printed matter, Polish); one sheet of manuscript written on printed receipts of the Jewish Community in Częstochowa (before 1930, Polish).

b)

- 3.06.1935, Czarnocin
- NN. (Czarnocin), Letter of 3.06.1935 to Engineer M. [Chaskiel?] Wilczyński (Grodziec near Będzin, ul. Legionów 7)
- Inf. regarding rural Jewish colonies established in the 19th century (in the Pińczów district: colonies of Łabędź and Ksawerów near Działoszyce).
- ***Description:*** original, typescript (additions, handwritten manuscript, ink), Polish, 214×140, 214×277 mm, ss. 2, pp. 2.
    At bottom illegible signature (ink)

## 533. RING. II/411/1. Mf. ŻIH—805; USHMM—60.

- After 1941, Warsaw Ghetto
- [Chaskiel Wilczyński], Study entitled "Erd-arbet in Varshever Firshtntum" [Agriculture in the Warsaw Duchy] (fragment [?])
- Situation of Jews in agriculture in Polish lands at the turn of the 18th–19th cent.
- ***Description:*** original, handwritten manuscript (ChW*), Polish, Yiddish, 175×210 mm, ss. 14, pp. 15.
    For writing the manuscript, he made use of waste paper from his own correspondence; e.g., a circular letter of the ZZ, Jewish Council (letter dated 20.07.1941 concerning keeping property clean); circular no. 34 dated 16.05.1941 (stamps: "Kommissarische Verwaltung sichergestellter Grundstücke in Warschau «Jüdischer Wohnbezirk» L. Tyber der jüdischer Beauftragte"); circular no. 50; Letter of H. [Chaskiel] Wilczyński dated 1.12.1941 to the Jewish Council; Haskiel [s] Wilczyński, "List of persons registered by 26 October 1941 in the house at ul. Ogrodowa 43, for whom provisioning cards for the month of November were not purchased and not issued" (30.10.1941) (fragments) (duplicated typescript, handwritten manuscript—ChW*, ink).
    Index: Aron Klajnbajch (ul Ogrodowa 43, apt. 17, previously Żelazna 69), Frymeta Sura Miller (ul Ogrodowa 43, apt. 17, previously Żelazna 69), Balbina Gliksman (ul Ogrodowa 43, apt. 21/22, previously Sienna 45), Roman Kejlin and Halina (ul Ogrodowa 43, apt. 25, previously Sienna 43), Mindla and Mojżesz Rajndorf (ul Ogrodowa 43, apt. 38, previously Chłodna 30, apt. 1), Berek, Rajzla, Nison and Jakub Jonasz [?] (ul Ogrodowa 43, apt. 30, previously Wielka 1, apt. 1[?])

## 534. RING. II/411/2. Mf. ŻIH—805; USHMM—60.

- Date unknown, place unknown
- [Chaskiel Wilczyński], Study concerning the situation of Jews in the Polish Kingdom in the 1st half of the 19th cent. (fragments)
- Notes, source notes, biographies.
- ***Description:*** original, handwritten manuscript (ChW* and another handwriting), pencil, Polish, Yiddish, 56×176, 163×209, 174×221 mm, ss. 17, pp. 33.
    On the reverse of one sheet of printed matter is written (in Yiddish): "Information about t[r]ansactions for the year 193. . . ." (before 09.1939, printed matter, Polish).

## 535. RING. II/412. Mf. ŻIH—805; USHMM—60.

- Date unknown, place unknown
- Chaskiel Wilczyński, Study entitled "Di likvidatsye fun di kehiles mit zeyere farmegens un khoyves" [The liquidation of the Jewish communities with their possessions and debts]
- Situation of Jews in the Polish Kingdom. Appended table with list of objects taken from the Jewish population in Warsaw for payment of taxes.
- ***Description:*** original, handwritten manuscript

23. L.L.C. = limited liability company.

(ChW*), Yiddish, ink, 122×243 mm, ss. 14, pp. 14.
Manuscript written on printed receipts of the Jewish Community in Częstochowa (before 1930, Polish).

### 536. RING. II/413. Mf. ŻIH—805; USHMM—60.

- Date unknown, place unknown
- [Chaskiel Wilczyński], Study entitled "Di gsise fun der varshever kehile-reprezentants" [The death-agony of the Warsaw Jewish community representation]
- Situation of Jews in Warsaw in the period of the Polish Kingdom (1815–1830).
- ***Description:*** original, handwritten manuscript (ChW*), pencil, Yiddish, 122×243 mm, ss. 32, pp. 32
Manuscript written on printed receipts of the Jewish Community in Częstochowa (before 1930, Polish).

### 537. RING. II/414. Mf. ŻIH—805; USHMM—60.

- Date unknown, place unknown
- [Chaskiel Wilczyński], Study entitled "Di ershte dozores in der rezidents" [The first synagogue supervisors in (Warsaw, 1820–1824)]
- Inf. concerning the number of Jews in Warsaw (by street); about the budget of the first synagogue supervisory board (dozoru bóżniczego) in Warsaw.
- ***Description:*** original, handwritten manuscript (ChW*), pencil, Yiddish,122×243 mm, ss. 16, pp. 16.
Manuscript written on printed receipts of the Jewish Community in Częstochowa (before 1930, printed matter, Polish).

### 538. RING. II/415. Mf. ŻIH—805; USHMM—60.

- Date unknown, place unknown
- [Chaskiel Wilczyński], work entitled "Dos aynfirn fun di dozor-bozhnitses" [The introduction of the synagogue supervisory boards]
- Establishment of the synagogue supervisory boards (dozorów bóżniczych) in the Polish Kingdom in the years 1816–1820.
- ***Description:*** original, handwritten manuscript (ChW*), pencil, Yiddish, 122×240 mm, ss. 11, pp. 11
Manuscript written on printed receipts of the Jewish Community in Częstochowa (before 1930, printed matter, Polish).

### 539. RING. II/416. Mf. ŻIH—805; USHMM—60.

- Date unknown, place unknown
- [Chaskiel Wilczyński], Study entitled "Der kamf arum der likvidatsye fun di kehiles" [The struggle around the liquidation of the Jewish communities]
- Kahals in the Polish Kingdom.
- ***Description:*** original, handwritten manuscript, pencil, Yiddish, 122×243 mm, ss. 14, pp. 14.
Manuscript written on printed receipts of the the Jewish Community in Częstochowa (before 1930, printed matter, Polish).

### 540. RING. II/417. Mf. ŻIH—805; USHMM—60.

- Date unknown, place unknown
- [Chaskiel Wilczyński], Study entitled "Likvidatsye fun di khevres" [Liquidation of the societies]
- Concerning religious organizations (burial societies).
- ***Description:*** original, handwritten manuscript (ChW*), pencil, Yiddish, 122×243 mm, ss. 13, pp. 13.
Manuscript written on printed receipts of the the Jewish Community in Częstochowa (before 1930, printed matter, Polish).

### 541. RING. II/418. Mf. ŻIH—805; USHMM—60.

- Date unknown, place unknown
- [Chaskiel Wilczyński], Study entitled "Di yidishe tsushtelungen fun peltsn far poylisher armey beys november oyfshtand" [The Jewish deliveries of furs for the Polish army during the November Uprising]
- ***Description:*** original, handwritten manuscript (ChW*), pencil, Yiddish, 146×205, 128×202, 126×227, ss. 22, pp. 27.
Text in two versions (rough draft and clean copy with additions and corrections).
Rough draft written on waste paper of correspondence and documents of H. Wilczyński (e.g., on 3 vouchers of the "Tow. Kont. dla Handlu i Przemysłu S.A. Fabryka Armatur Łagiewniki" (22.06–8.07.1937); on an order form from the "Fabryki Wyrobów Metalowych Sz. Zelingier i H. Wilczyński, Częstochowa, [ul.] Warszawska 96" dated 22.04.1930; one sheet of the manuscript with notation written in a child's hand: "Halinka Wilczyńska, Gutka Cywiak, Gutka Groman, Sala Hajdenretyk, Reginka Kieniksman" (before 09.1939, printed matter, handwritten manuscript, typescript, ink, pencil, Polish).
Clean copy written on the reverse of questionnaires concerning housing matters (after 09.1939 [?], duplicated typescript, German, Polish).

### 542. RING. II/419/1. Mf. ŻIH—806; USHMM—61.

- Date unknown, place unknown
- [Chaskiel Wilczyński], Study entitled "Militer-shtayern fun yidn beys november oyfshtand" [Military taxes of Jews during the November Uprising]
- Fragment of a larger work about the military service and taxes for the benefit of the army from Polish Jews.
- ***Description:*** original, handwritten manuscript (ChW*), pencil, Polish, Yiddish, 79×244, 98×160, 140×208, 147×208 mm, ss. 74, pp. 80.
Text in two versions (rough draft and clean copy with additions and corrections). Rough draft written on waste paper of correspondence of Chaskiel Wilczyński, notes with texts of other works by Wilczyński, source transcripts, printed materials (e.g., receipts of the Jewish Community in Częstochowa; before 1930,

printed matter, Polish), on waste paper of other people's correspondence (before 1939, printed matter, handwritten manuscript, typescript, duplicated typescript, Polish, Yiddish). Clean copy written on reverse of questionnaires concerning housing matters (after 09.1939 [?], duplicated typescript, German, Polish).

### 543. RING. II/420. Mf. ŻIH—806; USHMM—61.

- Date unknown, place unknown
- [Chaskiel Wilczyński], Study entitled "Yidishe militer-dinst un rekrutn-obtsol in amulikn Poyln" [Jewish military service and recruit fees in former Poland]
- ***Description:*** original, handwritten manuscript (ChW*), Polish, Yiddish, 116×217, 123×293 mm, ss. 14, pp. 16.

  Manuscript written on printed receipts of the the Jewish Community in Częstochowa (before 1930, printed matter, Polish).

### 544. RING. II/421. Mf. ŻIH—806; USHMM—61.

- Date unknown, place unknown
- [Chaskiel Wilczyński], Study entitled "Rekrutn-shtayer, peryod Kongres Poyln" [Recruit tax, period of Congress Poland]
- Concerns the tax from Jewish recruits.
- ***Description:*** original, handwritten manuscript (ChW*), pencil, Polish, Yiddish, 117×217, 120×312 mm, ss. 42, pp. 42.

  Manuscript written on printed receipts of the the Jewish Community in Częstochowa (before 1930, printed matter, Polish) and on waste paper of correspondence and official documents concerning the administration of apartment houses on ul. Ogrodowa (inter alia fragments of lists of names of residents of the apartment house at ul. Ogrodowa no. 43).

### 545. RING. II/422. Mf. ŻIH—806; USHMM—61.

- Date unknown, Warsaw Ghetto
- [Chaskiel Wilczyński], Notes and references to sources, regarding military service of Jews in the 19th cent.
- ***Description:*** original, handwritten manuscript (ChW*), pencil, Polish, Yiddish, 80×115, 78×243, 126×200 mm, ss. 42, pp. 50.

  Manuscript written on printed receipts of the Jewish Community in Częstochowa (before 1930, printed matter, Polish) and on waste paper of correspondence and official documents regarding the administration of apartment houses on ul. Ogrodowa (filled out printed registration forms dated 11.11.1941: Dwojra Ajzenberg, born 22.03.1900; Krystyna Ajzenberg, born 16.06.1933; and Seweryn Ajzenberg, born 10.04.1930; children Dawid and Dwojra, moved on 26.10.1941 from ul. Ogrodowa 43, apt. 19 to ul. Pańska 31, apt. 9); official letters, e.g., Jewish Council in Warsaw, Social Welfare Department, Department of Relief Payments and Subventions, Letter dated 25.06.1942 to Karola Wilczyńska (ul. Przejazd 9, apt. 9) (summons to appear at the office).

### 546. RING. II/423. Mf. ŻIH—806; USHMM—61.

- Date unknown, place unknown
- [Chaskiel Wilczyński], Study entitled "Inyen Poyzner in y. 1831" [Posner matter in 1831]
- Concerning Zelman Posner.
- ***Description:*** original, handwritten manuscript (ChW*), Polish, Yiddish, 79×243 mm, ss. 19, pp. 19.

  Manuscript written on printed receipts of the the Jewish Community in Częstochowa (before 1930, printed matter, Polish).

### 547. RING. II/424, II/425. Mf. ŻIH—806; USHMM—61.

**a) Ring. II/424, II/425.**

- Date unknown, place unknown
- [Chaskiel Wilczyński], Study entitled "Bamiungen fun poylishe yidn arayntsubakumen zikh in fraye profesyes" [Efforts of Polish Jews to gain entry into free professions]
- ***Description:*** Ring. II/424—original, handwritten manuscript (ChW*), pencil, Polish, Yiddish, 135×185, 78×243 mm, minor damages and losses of text, ss. 27, pp. 30.; Ring. II/425—original, handwritten manuscript (ChW*), pencil, Polish, Yiddish, 145×208 mm, ss. 14, pp. 14.

  Text in two versions (rough draft—Ring. II/424, and clean copy with additions and corrections—Ring. II/425). In the rough copy, title in Polish: "Walka żydów o zdobycie dostępu do zawodów" [Struggle of Jews to gain access to professions]

  Rough draft written on printed receipts of the Jewish Community in Częstochowa (before 1930, printed matter, Polish); two ss. (pp. 1–2) on electoral leaflets of PPS (list 2, municipal elections): Obywatele! Towarzysze! [Citizens! Comrades!] (before 18.12.1938 [?], Warsaw, printed matter, Polish, 134×186 mm); clean copy written on the reverse of questionnaires regarding housing matters (after 09.1939 [?], duplicated typescript, German, Polish).

**b) Ring. II/424.**

- Date unknown, place unknown
- [Chaskiel Wilczyński], Notes, references, fragments of studies
- Regarding the situation of the Jewish population in the Duchy of Warsaw.
- ***Description:*** original, handwritten manuscript (ChW*), pencil, Polish, Yiddish, 88×118, 117×223, 162×204 mm, ss. 13, pp. 24.

One sheet written on the reverse of a circular of the Jewish Council in Warsaw (printed item, Polish).

### 548. RING. II/426. Mf. ŻIH—806; USHMM—61.

- Date unknown, Warsaw Ghetto
- [Chaskiel Wilczyński], Study entitled "Tsu der geshikhte fun di barditshever yidn" [Contribution to the history of the Berdyczów (Berditshever) Jews]
- Jewish population in Berdyczów at turn of the 18th and at the beginning of the 19th cent.
- ***Description:*** original, handwritten manuscript (ChW*), pencil, Polish, Yiddish, 97×134, 145×207 mm, minor damages and losses of text, ss. 28, pp. 38.

  Text in two versions (rough draft and clean copy with additions and corrections).

  Some ss. of the rough draft written on reverse of correspondence of Wilczyński; children's drawings; clean copy written on reverse of questionnaires regarding housing matters (after 09.1939 [?], duplicated typescript, German, Polish).

### 549. RING. II/427. Mf. ŻIH—806; USHMM—61.

- Date unknown, place unknown
- Chaskiel Wilczyński, engineer, Study entitled "Tsu der geshikhte funem khasidizm in Poylin" [Contribution to the history of Hasidism in Poland]
- ***Description:*** original, handwritten manuscript, ink, pencil, Yiddish, 146×223, 146×298 mm, ss. 44, pp. 47.

  Manuscript written on reverse of stationery of the "Society of Supporters of the History of the Jews in Częstochowa (Częstochowa, Nowy Rynek 14). Honorary Sponsors' Committee: Dr. L. Batawia, Attorney J. Glikson, Councilman M. Neufeld, Dr. Al. Wolberg. Presidium of Board: Dr. Al. Wolberg, chairman, Chairman J. Rosenberg, vice chairman, Dir. Z. Markowicz, treasurer, Engineer H. Wilczyński, secretary" (before 09.1939, printed matter, Polish, Yiddish).

### 550. RING. II/428. Mf. ŻIH—806; USHMM—61.

- After 1935, place unknown
- [Chaskiel Wilczyński], Study entitled "Żydzi a służba chrześcijańska" [Jews and the Christian servant]
- Legislation in Polish lands regarding employment of Christians by Jews (XVI–XIX cent.).
- ***Description:*** original, handwritten manuscript (ChW*), pencil, Polish, 104×183, 110×214 mm, ss. 9, pp. 10.

  Part of the manuscript written on printed material of the Social Insurance Administration (Ubezpieczalni Społecznej), bills sent to Henryk Wilczyński (Grodziec, ul. Legionów 7) (1935–1936, printed matter, handwritten manuscript, ink, stamps, Polish).

### 551. RING. II/381. Mf. ŻIH—803; USHMM—58.

a)

- 28.08.1941, Warsaw Ghetto
- ŻTOS. SPS. Department of Instruction and Inspection. Section of Annual Reports of Apartment House Committees, Letter dated 28.08.1941 to [Chaskiel] Wilczyński (ul. Ogrodowa 43)
- Request that he send in notebooks for the Annual Reports of Apartment House Committees.
- ***Description:*** original, typescript, stamp, Polish, 209×149 mm, ss. 1, pp. 1.

  On bottom two illegible signatures (ink). On reverse stamp: "Ogrodowa no. 43 hip. 364, Komisariat VII."

b)

- Before 7.[09.1941], Warsaw Ghetto
- ŻTOS. SPS. Department of Instruction and Inspection. Section for Annual Reports of Apartment House Committees, Letter preceding 7.[09.1941] to [Chaskiel] Wilczyński (ul. Ogrodowa 43).
- Request that he come to the office at ul. Tłomackie 5 on 7.[09.1941].
- ***Description:*** original, typescript, stamp, Polish, 224×141 mm, ss. 1, pp. 1.

  At bottom two illegible signatures (ink).

c)

- 10.09.1941, Warsaw Ghetto
- ŻTOS. SPS, Letter dated 10.09.1941 to [Chaskiel] Wilczyński (ul. Ogrodowa 43)
- Request for contact with Dr. Ringelblum.
- ***Description:*** original, typescript, stamp, Yiddish, 227×124 mm, ss. 1, pp. 1.

  On bottom illegible signature (ink).

  At top notation in Polish (pencil): "Wilczyński, Ogrodowa 43."

  On reverse calculations (ink, pencil).

d)

- 26.09.1941, Warsaw Ghetto
- ŻTOS. SPS. Department of Training and Inspection. Section for Annual Reports of Apartment House Committees, Letter of 26.09.1941 to [Chaskiel] Wilczyński (ul. Ogrodowa 43)
- Request that he come to the office at ul. Tłomackie 5 on 29.09.1941.
- ***Description:*** original, typescript, stamp, Polish, 209×149 mm, ss. 1, pp. 1.

  At bottom illegible signature (pencil).

  On reverse notation (pencil): "Ogr. [Ogrodowa] 43/21."

### 552. RING. II/394. Mf. ŻIH—803; USHMM—58.

a)

- 13.01.1941, Warsaw Ghetto
- Jewish Council in Warsaw, "Payment order" dated 13.01.1941 for Haskiel [sic] Wilczyński (ul. Ogrodowa

43, apt. 23), for payment of contribution for 1941 (36 zł) for the benefit of the Jewish hospital management.
Doc. signed by Adam Czerniaków.
- *Description:* original, printed material, handwritten manuscript, pencil, Polish, 164×198 mm, ss. 1, pp. 1.

b)
- 7.04.1941, Warsaw Ghetto
- Jewish Council in Warsaw. Department III of Communal Contribution, Notification dated 7.04.1941 for H. [Chaskiel] Wilczyński (ul. Ogrodowa 43, apt. 23), about abatement of communal contribution (79 zł).
- *Description:* original, printed matter, handwritten manuscript, pencil, stamps, Polish, 210×149 mm, ss. 1, pp. 1.

c)
- 17.04.[1941], Warsaw Ghetto
- ZZ. Fuel Department, Receipt dated 17.04.[1941] for Ch. [Chaskiel] Wilczyński (ul. Przejazd 9, apt. 9) for payment of 15 zł.
- *Description:* original, printed matter, handwritten manuscript, pencil, stamp, Polish, 156×122 mm, ss. 1, pp. 1.
At bottom illegible signature (pencil).

d)
- 3.06.1941, Warsaw Ghetto
- ZZ, Receipt dated 3.06.1941 for [Chaskiel] Wilczyński (ul. Ogrodowa 43) for payment of 1 zł. for provisioning cards picked up.
- *Description:* original, printed matter, handwritten manuscript, pencil, Polish, 133×98 mm, ss. 1, pp. 1.
At bottom illegible signature (pencil).

### 553. RING. II/395. Mf. ŻIH—803; USHMM—58.

- Chaskiel Wilczyński, Documents of administration of the apartment house at ul. Ogrodowa 43 as well as loose notes concerning the properties at ul. Ogrodowa from no. 40 to 55.

a)
- 2.04.1941, Warsaw Ghetto
- Jewish Council in Warsaw. Health Department. Health Center II, Dr. Zofia Ettinger, Certificate dated 2.04.1941 for Szlama Hepner (ul. Ogrodowa 43, apt. 25) about vaccination against typhoid fever.
- *Description:* original, printed matter, handwritten manuscript, ink, stamps, Polish, 140×102 mm, ss. 1, pp. 2.
On reverse stamp: "Stamped food card."

b)
- 1941, Warsaw
- Kommissarische Verwaltung sichergestellter Grundstücke in Warschau "Jüdischer Wohnbezirk" L. Tyber der jüdische Beaufragte [Commissioner Administration of Secured Real Estate in Warsaw "Jewish Residential District" L. Tyber appointee], Letters to H. Wilczyński, administrator of the apartment house at ul. Ogrodowa 43
- Circular letters and correspondence regarding the real estate board (zarządu nieruchomością) (06–11.1941).
- *Description:* original, duplicated typescript, typescript, handwritten manuscript, ink, pencil, stamps, Polish, 212×149, 210×145, 210×296 mm, ss. 11, pp. 15.
On reverse of some letters (08–09.1941) notes (handwritten manuscript—ChW*, pencil, Polish, Yiddish).

c)
- 11.1941, Warsaw Ghetto
- House administration at ul. Ogrodowa 43, H. Wilczyński, Forms dated 14 and 15.11.1941 for reporting change of address
- Concerning the following persons who reported a change of address on 26.10.1941: Gitla Rubinsztejn (born 1907), Szyndla Dwojra Zylbertrest (born 15.06.1924); Estera Rosa Zylbertrest (born 25.09.1922); Szyfra Gołda Zylbertrest (born 4.07.1904), daughter of Moszek Icek Zylbersztejn; Mendel Majer Zylbertrest (born 17.03.1898), husband of Szyfra Gołda; Lejzor Kamer (born 1896); Sura Ruchla Kamer (born 1891), daughter of Berek Blumberg; Gitla Kamer (born 1.09.1923); Chana Kamer (born 15.08.1925).
- *Description:* original, printed matter, handwritten manuscript (ChW*), ink, stamps, Polish, 133×160, 144×153 mm, ss. 17, pp. 17.

d)
- Before 26.10.1941, Warsaw Ghetto
- [Chaskiel Wilczyński], "List of tenants of the apartment house at Ogrodowa 43"
- List of names along with prior address within Warsaw.
- *Description:* original, handwritten manuscript (ChW*), ink, Polish, 209×340 mm, minor damages and losses of text, sheet torn, ss. 1, pp. 1.

e)
- Before 26.10.1941, Warsaw Ghetto
- [Chaskiel Wilczyński], "List of persons registered at ul. Ogrodowa 43, who appear in the list of residents of this building for the month of November, but have not yet received provisioning cards"
- List of names along with prior address within Warsaw.
- *Description:* original, handwritten manuscript (ChW*), ink, Polish, 177×223 mm, ss. 1, pp. 1.
On the right side of page a note in Yiddish (pencil).

f)
- Date unknown, 1941, Warsaw Ghetto
- [Chaskiel Wilczyński], Notes concerning administration of houses at ul. Ogrodowa 43, 47, 49, 55
- Appended list of names of residents, calculations, notes.
- *Description:* original, handwritten manuscript (ChW*), ink, pencil, Polish, 90×155, 210×274 mm, ss. 11, pp. 15.

g)

- Date unknown, 07.1939, place unknown
- [Chaskiel Wilczyński], Notes.
- ***Description:*** original, handwritten manuscript (various handwritings: ChW* and others), ink, stamp, Polish, 103×93, 155×194 mm, ss. 4, pp. 3.

h)

- Date unknown, Warsaw Ghetto
- NN., List of names of craftsmen in the Warsaw Ghetto (fragment)
- ***Description:*** original or transcript, typescript, German, 211×132 mm, ss. 1, pp. 2.

## IX. Miscellaneous

### 554. RING. II/479. Mf. ŻIH—809; USHMM—64.

- 1935, place unknown
- NN., "Seyfer shel shirim" [Book of Songs] (11.07.1935)
- Collection of songs sung by pioneers of the kibbutz "Verba" [?].
- ***Description:*** original, handwritten manuscript, notebook, ink, Hebrew, Polish, Yiddish, 148×206 mm, sewn, ss. 57, pp. 102.

### 555. RING. II/480. Mf. ŻIH—809; USHMM—64.

- Before 09.1939, place unknown
- NN., Texts of songs, dialogues, skits, little theater scenes of the [Ha-Shomer Ha-Tsair] pioneer battalion "Tel-Amal" [Hill of Labor] of Warsaw residing at colonies in the villa of "Oleksówka" near Zakopane.
- ***Description:*** original, handwritten manuscript (TA*), ink, Polish, 158×200 mm, ss. 59, pp. 68.

  See Ring. II/362.

  Doc. was kept in a binder.

### 556. RING. II/481. Mf. ŻIH—809; USHMM—64.

- 07.1939, place unknown
- *Iton hituli* [Diaper Newspaper, a satiric newspaper]
- Children's news-sheet of the Ha-Shomer Ha-Tsair camp "Tel-Amal" from Warsaw in "Oleksówka" near Zakopane
- Stories, dialogues, skits.
- ***Description:*** original, handwritten manuscript (TA*), notebook, ink, drawings (pencil), Polish, Yiddish, 169×202 mm, ss. 28, pp. 30.

### 557. RING. II/411/3. Mf. ŻIH—805; USHMM—60.

- Before 09.1939, Warsaw
- Printed advertisement: "Hemostyl. Dr. Roussel's hemopoietic preparation" (Warsaw, Grzybowska 88)
- ***Description:*** original, printed matter, Polish, 215×108 mm, ss. 1, pp. 1.

  Printed by: "Galewski and Bau, Warsaw."

### 558. RING. II/492. Mf. ŻIH—811; USHMM—66.

- After 07.1942, Warsaw Ghetto
- Card placed on entrance doors with information on how to ring particular tenants of an apartment in the Warsaw Ghetto
- List of tenants: Lurie, Rotsztajn, Rogozińskis, Koplewicz, [Władysław] Szlengel and [Michał] Brandsteter, Lunia and Wanda.
- ***Description:*** original, handwritten manuscript, ink, Polish, 75×218 mm, ss. 1, pp. 1.

# Concordance of Call Numbers in Ringelblum I: New Document Numbers to Old and Oldest Call Numbers

This concordance keys the consecutive new document numbers in the present catalog to the old and oldest call numbers of the documents. Old call numbers (e.g., I/121) were those used to identify the files between 1955 and 2006. Files that included multiple documents are indicated as follows: I/1152/2 or I/1220/56. Oldest call numbers, given here in parentheses, were those in use before 1955. Also in parentheses, preceded by the prefix Lb (abbreviation for "consecutive number" in Polish), are document numbers used in the first catalog of the Ringelblum Archive in 1946.

1. I/1152/2 (1471)
2. I/1176 (1495), I/675, I/1088 (1407)
3. I/ I/1147 (1466)
4. I/674/6. (Lb. 1688)
5. I/105
6. I/117. (Lb. 1043)
7. I/134. (Lb. 1086)
8. I/142. (Lb. 1598)
9. I/640. (Lb. 667)
10. I/127
11. I/507/4
12. I/155
13. I/45
14. I/507/3
15. I/126. (Lb. 1564)
16. I/131
17. I/132
18. I/42. (Lb. 271)
19. I/141. (Lb. 113)
20. I/339
21. I/137/3
22. I/492
23. I/259. (Lb. 1289)
24. I/262. (Lb. 1198)
25. I/473. (Lb. 273), I/937 (1256)
26. I/665
27. I/469, I/937 (1256)
28. I/1217
29. I/1062/1 (1381)
30. I/1062/2 (1381)
31. I/1062/3 (1381)
32. I/813 (1132)
33. I/261, II/486
34. I/317. (Lb. 470)
35. I/472, I/1063 (1382), II/487
36. I/471 (Lb. 273)
37. I/1220/38
38. I/1220/39
39. I/88. (Lb. 1574)
40. I/507/5
41. I/457
42. I/336
43. I/166/2
44. I/1220/37
45. I/144
46. I/167
47. I/448
48. I/166/1
49. I/1220/40
50. I/318
51. I/319. (Lb. 699)
52. I/1088 (1407)
53. I/1175 (1494). (Lb. 1215)
54. I/1089 (1408). (Lb. 1571)
55. I/113
56. I/120
57. I/122. (Lb. 494)
58. I/1220/3
59. I/452
60. I/108
61. I/150
62. I/121
63. I/48
64. I/146
65. I/34
66. I/147
67. I/148
68. I/173
69. I/1220/56
70. I/194
71. I/542. (Lb. 1702)
72. I/599/43
73. I/599/54
74. I/599/48
75. I/599/5
76. I/599/44
77. I/599/4
78. I/599/40
79. I/599/47
80. I/599/46
81. I/599/39
82. I/599/45
83. I/599/41
84. I/599/42
85. I/599/57
86. I/599/66
87. I/599/80
88. I/599/101
89. I/599/11
90. I/599/55
91. I/599/68
92. I/599/35
93. I/599/49
94. I/599/82
95. I/599/103
96. I/599/1
97. I/599/23
98. I/599/31
99. I/599/20a
100. I/599/20
101. I/599/22
102. I/599/38
103. I/599/21
104. I/599/34
105. I/599/62
106. I/599/114
107. I/599/71
108. I/599/104, I/595/3, I/595/5
109. I/599/107
110. I/595/2
111. I/595/4

112. I/595/6
113. I/599/53
114. I/599/97
115. I/599/92
116. I/599/98
117. I/599/63
118. I/599/65
119. I/599/91
120. I/599/26
121. I/599/73
122. I/599/60
123. I/599/72
124. I/599/2
125. I/1220/7
126. I/557/2
127. I/599/19
128. I/599/78
129. I/599/64
130. I/599/110
131. I/1220/6
132. I/599/36
133. I/599/27
134. I/599/6
135. I/599/95
136. I/599/70
137. I/599/51
138. I/599/32
139. I/599/59
140. I/599/33
141. I/599/69
142. I/599/25
143. I/599/24
144. I/599/37
145. I/599/30
146. I/599/58
147. I/599/50
148. I/595/4, I/595/7
149. I/1220/76
150. I/1220/77
151. I/1220/78
152. I/599/28
153. I/599/61
154. I/599/74
155. I/599/75
156. I/599/76
157. I/599/81
158. I/599/96
159. I/599/100
160. I/599/111
161. I/599/117
162. I/599/8
163. I/599/10
164. I/539
165. I/536
166. I/531
167. I/534
168. I/540/2
169. I/533
170. I/540/1, I/1220/11
171. I/532/1
172. I/538/2
173. I/532/2
174. I/535
175. I/541
176. I/537
177. I/538/3
178. I/538/1
179. I/781/7 (1100)
180. I/308. (Lb. 1515)
181. I/211/3. (Lb. 881)
182. I/208. (Lb. 1452)
183. I/781/5 (1100)
184. I/781/3 (1100)
185. I/1220/85
186. I/781/4 (1100)
187. I/1220/64
188. I/273. (Lb. 542, 834)
189. I/1087 (1406). (Lb. 760)
190. I/1102 (1421). (Lb. 1263)
191. I/1220/81
192. I/1103 (1422). (Lb. 1294)
193. I/278/1. (Lb. 766)
194. I/781/1 (1100)
195. I/1142 (1461). (Lb. 45), I/1199 (1518)
196. I/249
197. I/1112/3 (1431). (Lb. 1428)
198. I/1220/79
199. I/276. (Lb. 172)
200. I/656/1
201. I/656/2
202. I/274/1
203. I/1105/3 (1424)
204. I/1105/4 (1424)
205. I/656/3
206. I/274/2
207. I/300. (Lb. 714)
208. I/656/4
209. I/656/5
210. I/656/6
211. I/278/2. (Lb. 766)
212. I/1105/1 (1424)
213. I/310
214. I/299. (Lb. 597), I/778 (1099)
215. I/656/7
216. I/575/3
217. I/272. (Lb. 556)
218. I/1220/66
219. I/344. (Lb. 706)
220. I/285. (Lb. 917)
221. I/275. (Lb. 993, 134)
222. I/1220/80
223. I/1105/2 (1424)
224. I/213. (Lb. 868, 869)
225. I/279. (Lb. 557)
226. I/662, I/664/1
227. I/179. (Lb. 566)
228. I/295. (Lb. 563)
229. I/664/2
230. I/296. (Lb. 564), I/664/3
231. I/265. (Lb. 57)
232. I/778/1 (1099)
233. I/778/2 (1099)
234. I/775 (1099)
235. I/1082 (1401). (Lb. 601)
236. I/324. (Lb. 1632)
237. I/1113 (1432). (Lb. 1673)
238. I/357. (Lb. 524)
239. I/224
240. I/1201 (1520)
241. I/28
242. I/1123 (1442), I/97, I/1213
243. I/1220/52
244. I/778/3 (1099)
245. I/19. (Lb. 164)
246. I/247. (Lb. 870, 220)
247. I/1106/1 (1425). (Lb. 1716, 1717, 1718)
248. I/1084 (1403). (Lb. 592)
249. I/205
250. I/103
251. I/227
252. I/14
253. I/206. (Lb. 523)
254. I/229
255. I/1143 (1462)
256. I/1135 (1454). (Lb. 171)

257. I/246
258. I/338/1
259. I/777/4 (1099)
260. I/20. (Lb. 181)
261. I/777/3 (1099)
262. I/257. (Lb. 522)
263. I/230
264. I/244. (Lb. 204), I/664/4
265. I/333
266. I/1101 (1420). (Lb. 1536)
267. I/7
268. I/350
269. I/163. (Lb. 514, 514a), I/164
270. I/191
271. I/260. (Lb. 1189)
272. I/787/2 (1106)
273. I/180. (Lb. 1629)
274. I/364. (Lb. 1512)
275. I/1080 (1399). (Lb. 818)
276. I/ I/775 (1099), I/776/1 (1099), I/777/5 (1099), I/1220/86
277. I/777/2 (1099)
278. I/776/2 (1099)
279. I/82
280. I/1220/8
281. I/1220/17
282. I/575/1
283. I/575/2, I/502/a
284. I/779/3 (1099)
285. I/1158/3 (1477). (Lb. 1592)
286. I/1133 (1452)
287. I/1126 (1445). (Lb. 24)
288. I/1092 (1411). (Lb. 576)
289. I/1197 (1516)
290. I/1220/67
291. I/1220/69a
292. I/215. (Lb. 867, 867a), I/322
293. I/1125 (1444). (Lb. 23)
294. I/359. (Lb. 553)
295. I/1106/3 (1425). (Lb. 1716, 1717, 1718)
296. I/184. (Lb. 958, 52)
297. I/78. (Lb. 1443)
298. I/79. (Lb. 1057)
299. I/80/1
300. I/37/2
301. I/37/1
302. I/210. (Lb. 884)
303. I/1220/44
304. I/1114 (1433). (Lb. 520)
305. I/321. (Lb. 21)
306. I/1220/68
307. I/37/3
308. I/1220/9
309. I/1158/1 (1477). (Lb. 1592)
310. I/197
311. I/334. (Lb. 575)
312. I/1121 (1440). (Lb. 1674)
313. I/1220/10
314. I/657/3
315. I/222. (Lb. 704)
316. I/201. (Lb. 515), I/298
317. I/219. (Lb. 260, 759)
318. I/360/2
319. I/1119 (1438). (Lb. 1538)
320. I/355. (Lb. 1714)
321. I/231. (Lb. 694)
322. I/200
323. I/13
324. I/41
325. I/356. (Lb. 1712)
326. I/232. (Lb. 688)
327. I/290. (Lb. 1065)
328. I/182
329. I/923 (1242)
330. I/599/3
331. I/820 (1139). (Lb. 1506)
332. I/674/1. (Lb. 1688)
333. I/360/1
334. I/577
335. I/777/1 (1099)
336. I/779/2 (1099). (Lb. 28)
337. I/342. (Lb. 11)
338. I/343. (Lb. 15)
339. I/76
340. I/80/2
341. I/307/1. (Lb. 1676, 1677)
342. I/307/2. (Lb. 1676, 1677)
343. I/370. (Lb. 859)
344. I/366
345. I/780/3 (1099)
346. I/304
347. I/314. (Lb. 1669)
348. I/32. (Lb. 1671)
349. I/170
350. I/1096/2 (1415). (Lb. 654)
351. I/306. (Lb. 573)
352. I/178
353. I/303
354. I/217
355. I/1107 (1426). (Lb. 1463)
356. I/1110/2 (1429). (Lb. 1426)
357. I/1106/2 (1425). (Lb. 1716, 1717, 1718)
358. I/87. (Lb. 610)
359. I/460
360. I/89. (Lb. 1194)
361. I/1096/1 (1415). (Lb. 654)
362. I/1112/4 (1431). (Lb. 1429)
363. I/1187 (1506). (Lb. 669)
364. I/777/6 (1099)
365. I/657/2
366. I/269. (Lb. 18, 19, 19a)
367. I/777/7 (1099)
368. I/1205 (1524)
369. I/294
370. I/594/2
371. I/1098 (1417). (Lb. 655), I/1111 (1430)
372. I/777/9 (1099)
373. I/1220/25
374. I/1220/60
375. I/1220/69b
376. I/329
377. I/320. (Lb. 9)
378. I/1128 (1447). (Lb. 5)
379. I/601
380. I/1097 (1416). (Lb. 655)
381. I/1110/1 (1429). (Lb. 1426)
382. I/1108/3 (1427)
383. I/556. (Lb. 302)
384. I/27. (Lb. 4)
385. I/1207 (1526)
386. I/628
387. I/1193 (1512). (Lb. 205)
388. I/1192 (1511). (Lb. 124)
389. I/780/1 (1099)
390. I/780/2 (1099)
391. I/779/1 (1099)
392. I/1108/2 (1427)
393. I/1108/1 (1427)
394. I/777/10 (1099)
395. I/1158/2 (1477). (Lb. 1592)
396. I/1158/4 (1477). (Lb. 1592)
397. I/1158/5 (1477). (Lb. 1592)
398. I/1160 (1479), I/1199 (1518)
399. I/1127 (1446). (Lb. 3)

400. I/1220/59
401. I/1136 (1455). (Lb. 1535)
402. I/25. (Lb. 8)
403. I/1031 (1350)
404. I/1009 (1328). (Lb. 331)
405. I/641, I/654. (Lb. 640)
406. I/655
407. I/602
408. I/1145 (1464)
409. I/177
410. I/202
411. I/263
412. I/464
413. I/435
414. I/29, I/96, I/264, I/895 (1215), I/1060 (1379), I/1220/87
415. I/432. (Lb. 1720)
416. I/1018 (1337). (Lb. 386)
417. I/218
418. I/347
419. I/996 (1315). (Lb. 495)
420. I/96. (Lb. 443), I/365
421. I/446
422. = 420
423. I/251. (Lb. 1290)
424. I/235
425. I/189
426. I/168. (Lb. 1292)
427. I/95. (Lb. 444)
428. I/221
429. I/282
430. I/484
431. I/988 (1307)
432. I/209
433. I/1220/1
434. I/234
435. I/100
436. I/480
437. I/52
438. I/207
439. I/242
440. I/981 (1300)
441. I/990/2 (1309). (Lb. 416)
442. I/674/3. (Lb. 1688)
443. I/1051 (1370)
444. I/368
445. I/503/1
446. I/504
447. I/505
448. I/506
449. I/507/1, I/514
450. I/510
451. I/511/1
452. I/511/2
453. I/511/3
454. I/1039 (1358)
455. I/428. (Lb. 1468)
456. I/429
457. I/485. (Lb. 1591)
458. I/198. (Lb. 968), I/668. (Lb. 1158), I/1220/98
459. I/1071 (1390, 1393). (Lb. 913, 1640)
460. I/176. (Lb. 854, 880)
461. I/984 (1303)
462. I/1040 (1359)
463. I/248
464. I/270
465. I/195
466. I/196
467. I/302, I/490, I/853 (1172), I/1090 (1409)
468. I/491
469. I/116. (Lb. 1187)
470. I/1099 (1418). (Lb. 730)
471. I/489
472. I/1075 (1394). (Lb. 1412)
473. I/466. (Lb. 1432)
474. I/185
475. I/1011 (1330). (Lb. 314)
476. I/467. (Lb. 1188)
477. I/993 (1312). (Lb. 423)
478. I/1019 (1338). (Lb. 383)
479. I/674/4. (Lb. 1688)
480. I/1007 (1326). (Lb. 334)
481. I/1021 (1340). (Lb. 356)
482. I/995 (1314). (Lb. 401)
483. I/1026 (1345). (Lb. 345)
484. I/1059 (1378)
485. I/361
486. I/1012 (1331). (Lb. 380)
487. I/1025 (1344). (Lb. 346)
488. I/22
489. I/1069 (1388)
490. I/989 (1308). (Lb. 414)
491. I/1024 (1343). (Lb. 354)
492. I/1017 (1336). (Lb. 368)
493. I/1020 (1339). (Lb. 365)
494. I/1010 (1329). (Lb. 317)
495. I/1022 (1341). (Lb. 355)
496. I/1015 (1334). (Lb. 369)
497. I/1030 (1349). (Lb. 723)
498. I/107
499. I/1005 (1324). (Lb. 338)
500. I/362
501. I/326
502. I/93, I/291. (Lb. 1659)
503. I/449
504. I/212 (Lb. 876), I/239
505. I/240
506. I/158 (Lb. 971, 972)
507. I/1214
508. I/346
509. I/86
510. I/253
511. I/241
512. I/1052 (1371)
513. I/203. (Lb. 922, 891)
514. I/470
515. I/243. (Lb. 207)
516. I/434. (Lb. 208)
517. I/31. (Lb. 29)
518. I/461
519. I/1001 (1320). (Lb. 622)
520. I/289. (Lb. 1557, 561)
521. I/437
522. I/1036 (1355)
523. I/267
524. I/237
525. I/1032 (1351). (Lb 728)
526. I/768 (1093)
527. I/268
528. I/992 (1311)
529. I/442
530. I/439. (Lb. 1457)
531. I/1220/27
532. I/1220/34
533. I/426
534. I/1220/73
535. I/1220/74
536. I/674/2. (Lb. 1688)
537. I/1220/46
538. I/517
539. I/598/1
540. I/589. (Lb. 26)
541. I/543/3
542. I/1215
543. I/1220/45
544. I/325
545. I/507/6

546. I/1100 (1419). (Lb. 727)
547. I/594/1
548. I/1210
549. I/598/8
550. I/586/3
551. I/316
552. I/1220/26
553. I/598/3
554. I/98
555. I/130. (Lb. 112)
556. I/124
557. I/140
558. I/125
559. I/133. (Lb. 666)
560. I/128
561. I/138. (Lb. 540)
562. I/136. (Lb. 1087)
563. I/139. (Lb. 590)
564. I/137/1
565. I/137/2
566. I/129
567. I/135
568. I/1220/54
569. I/674/13. (Lb. 1688)
570. I/1150 (1469)
571. I/674/15. (Lb. 1688)
572. I/81
573. I/667. (Lb. 1456)
574. I/1153 (1472). (Lb. 1228)
575. I/1035 (1354). (Lb. 387)
576. I/175
577. I/154
578. I/512. (Lb. 1570)
579. I/335
580. I/990/1 (1309). (Lb. 416)
581. I/277. (Lb. 1151, 1152)
582. I/1220/83
583. I/112
584. I/293
585. I/114. (Lb. 114)
586. I/250
587. I/292. (Lb. 562)
588. I/143
589. I/309
590. I/220. (Lb. 602)
591. I/190
592. I/358. (Lb. 516)
593. I/47
594. I/994 (1313). (Lb. 418)
595. I/149
596. I/46
597. I/49
598. I/36
599. I/91. (Lb. 357)
600. I/1091 (1410). (Lb. 199)
601. I/508
602. I/349. (Lb. 1451)
603. I/313 (Lb. 1661)
604. I/1220/82
605. I/1211
606. I/204
607. I/83. (Lb. 337)
608. I/84, I/223. (Lb. 698)
609. I/85
610. I/214
611. I/363
612. I/102. (Lb. 1002)
613. I/64. (Lb. 347)
614. I/503/2. (Lb. 460)
615. I/53
616. I/99
617. I/1220/32
618. I/65
619. I/216
620. I/58
621. I/59. (Lb. 894)
622. I/101. (Lb. 536)
623. I/161
624. I/238
625. I/283. (Lb. 1157)
626. I/371. (Lb. 867a)
627. I/123. (Lb. 951)
628. I/256
629. I/62, I/284
630. I/55
631. I/56
632. I/57. (Lb. 1552), I/104. (Lb. 1003, 1061)
633. I/509
634. I/61. (Lb. 1224)
635. I/51. (Lb. 446)
636. I/226
637. I/323
638. I/187
639. I/157
640. I/18
641. I/54
642. I/192
643. I/315. (Lb. 687)
644. I/507/2
645. I/233
646. I/502
647. I/115
648. I/181
649. I/174
650. I/1152/1 (1471)
651. I/77. (Lb. 538)
652. I/66
653. I/297. (Lb. 569)
654. I/68
655. I/106
656. I/67
657. I/1220/63
658. I/40. (Lb. 923)
659. I/92
660. I/1048 (1367). (Lb. 909)
661. I/50
662. I/90
663. I/186
664. I/341
665. I/1220/75
666. I/345
667. I/70
668. I/71. (Lb. 896)
669. I/74
670. I/43, I/1220/89
671. I/604
672. I/38. (Lb.1562), I/69,I/72
673. I/1064 (1383)
674. I/332
675. I/1067 (1386)
676. I/39
677. I/1065 (1384)
678. I/44
679. I/1066 (1385)
680. I/305. (Lb. 572, 582)
681. I/1068 (1387)
682. I/603
683. I/1222. (Lb. 1297—1372)
684. I/789 (1108)
685. I/566, I/599/94
686. I/788 (1107). (Lb. 328)
687. I/436
688. I/258. (Lb. 1700)
689. I/1016 (1335). (Lb. 367)
690. I/1083 (1402). (Lb. 591)
691. I/1000 (1319)
692. I/1220/15
693. I/1046 (1365). (Lb. 496)
694. I/73

695. I/488
696. I/1070 (1389). (Lb. 1125)
697. I/791 (1110). (Lb. 1262)
698. I/792 (1111). (Lb. 440)
699. I/795 (1114). (Lb. 342)
700. I/972 (1291). (Lb. 344)
701. I/888 (1208)
702. I/1045 (1364). (Lb. 309)
703. I/1047 (1366). (Lb. 1474)
704. I/382. (Lb. 1070)
705. I/271
706. I/951 (1270)
707. I/817 (1137). (Lb. 717)
708. I/818 (1136). (Lb. 1615)
709. I/1006 (1325). (Lb. 335)
710. I/568/1
711. I/870 (1189). (Lb. 451)
712. I/796 (1115). (Lb. 315)
713. I/592/8
714. I/784 (1103). (Lb. 13)
715. I/183, I/245 (Lb. 594), I/1220/90
716. I/797 (1116)
717. I/867 (1186)
718. I/440
719. I/497
720. I/799 (1118). (Lb. 1233)
721. I/610
722. I/1095 (1414). (Lb. 287)
723. I/802 (1121). (Lb. 1146)
724. I/674/5. (Lb. 1688)
725. I/801 (1120). (Lb. 363)
726. I/803 (1122). (Lb. 1477)
727. I/568/2
728. I/581/1
729. I/463. (Lb. 1486)
730. I/1198 (1517). (Lb. 303)
731. I/986 (1305). (Lb 1281, 1649)
732. I/808 (1127). (Lb. 361)
733. I/1220/4
734. I/599/67
735. I/599/67a
736. I/599/67b
737. I/554
738. I/1014 (1333). (Lb. 370, 370a)
739. I/1023 (1342). (Lb. 353)
740. I/16. (Lb. 31)
741. I/447
742. I/804 (1123). (Lb. 428)
743. I/438
744. I/952 (1271)
745. I/570
746. I/809 (1128). (Lb. 1221)
747. I/547
748. I/549
749. I/934 (1253)
750. I/805 (1124). (Lb. 1587)
751. I/327
752. I/21/2
753. I/21/3
754. I/1086 (1405)
755. I/1078 (1397). (Lb. 752)
756. I/806 (1125). (Lb. 351)
757. I/8, I/9, I/15. (Lb. I/8–633, 925; I/15–845, 925, 844b, 829, 596)
758. I/10
759. I/21/1
760. I/881 (1201). (Lb. 174)
761. I/1054 (1373)
762. I/1173 (1492)
763. I/807 (1126). (Lb. 352)
764. I/816 (1135) (Lb. 955)
765. I/591
766. I/978 (1297)
767. I/1132 (1451). (Lb. 750)
768. I/810 (1129)
769. I/811 (1130). (Lb. 486)
770. I/814 (1133). (Lb. 206, 231, 526)
771. I/550
772. I/552/2
773. I/812 (1131), I/998 (1317)
774. I/815 (1134). (Lb. 143)
775. I/954 (1273)
776. I/819 (1138). (Lb. 382).
777. I/949 (1268)
778. I/599/109
779. I/578
780. I/821 (1140). (Lb. 1588)
781. I/980 (1299)
782. I/564/2
783. I/826 (1145). (Lb. 842); I/825 (1144). (Lb. 842), I/476, I/830 (1149). (Lb. 866), I/1218
784. I/441
785. I/827 (1146). (Lb. 1617)
786. I/828 (1147). (Lb. 324)
787. I/829 (1148)
788. I/444
789. I/255, I/1219
790. I/557/1
791. I/822 (1141). (Lb. 410)
792. I/823 (1142). (Lb. 434)
793. I/1220/12
794. I/211/4. (Lb. 881)
795. I/1220/20
796. I/1177 (1496). (Lb. 1215)
797. I/560
798. I/843 (1162). (Lb. 362)
799. I/844 (1163). (Lb. 860)
800. I/845 (1164). (Lb. 1508)
801. I/841 (1160). (Lb. 848)
802. I/842 (1161)
803. I/674/14. (Lb. 1688)
804. I/832 (1151). (Lb. 402)
805. I/835 (1154). (Lb. 893)
806. I/500
807. I/638
808. I/479
809. I/997 (1316)
810. I/846 (1165). (Lb. 1226)
811. I/785/1 (1104)
812. I/785/2 (1104)
813. I/785/3 (1104)
814. I/785/4 (1104)
815. I/1220/13
816. I/1220/14
817. I/351. (Lb. 1144)
818. I/1220/70
819. I/286. (Lb. 918)
820. I/211/1. (Lb. 881)
821. I/287/1. (Lb. 919)
822. I/211/5. (Lb. 881)
823. I/211/2. (Lb. 881)
824. I/287/2. (Lb. 919)
825. I/674/11. (Lb. 1688)
826. I/674/9. (Lb. 1688)
827. I/833 (1152). (Lb. 462)
828. I/573/1
829. I/573/2
830. I/573/3
831. I/573/4
832. I/573/5
833. I/573/7
834. I/836 (1155). (Lb. 312)
835. I/837 (1156). (Lb. 311)
836. I/838 (1157). (Lb. 312, 735, 1208, 1672)
837. I/839 (1158). (Lb. 865)
838. I/840 (1159). (Lb. 1138)
839. I/576
840. I/254. (Lb. 1563)

841. I/854 (1173)
842. I/974 (1293). (Lb. 1586)
843. I/495
844. I/494. (Lb. 1634)
845. I/487
846. I/864 (1183). (Lb. 847)
847. I/852 (1171). (Lb. 427)
848. I/855 (1174). (Lb. 1646)
849. I/948 (1267)
850. I/1172 (1491). (Lb. 1215)
851. I/1174 (1493). (Lb. 1215)
852. I/1212
853. I/598/2
854. I/599/85
855. I/552/3
856. I/552/4
857. I/552/5
858. I/23. (Lb. 27), I/468
859. I/483
860. I/499. (Lb. 1583), I/955 (1273)
861. I/1041 (1360). (Lb. 1278)
862. I/475
863. I/1042 (1361). (Lb. 1257)
864. I/420
865. I/481
866. I/450
867. I/1043 (1362)
868. I/459, I/75. (Lb. 1054)
869. I/427
870. I/431
871. I/443
872. I/851 (1170). (Lb. 424)
873. I/973 (1292). (Lb. 722)
874. I/847 (1166). (Lb. 360)
875. I/1149 (1468)
876. I/848 (1167). (Lb. 379)
877. I/849 (1168). (Lb. 381)
878. I/850 (1169). (Lb. 731, 958)
879. I/564/1
880. I/118, I/281
881. I/331
882. I/367
883. I/786 (1105)
884. I/856 (1175)
885. I/193
886. I/1144 (1144)
887. I/862 (1181). (Lb. 605)
888. I/857 (1176). (Lb. 326, 327)
889. I/858 (1177). (Lb. 404)
890. I/859 (1178)
891. I/991 (1310). (Lb. 307)
892. I/860 (1179). (Lb. 405)
893. I/1013 (1332). (Lb. 371)
894. I/30
895. I/957 (1276)
896. I/958 (1277). (Lb. 430)
897. I/959 (1278). (Lb. 433)
898. I/960 (1279)
899. I/961 (1280)
900. I/962 (1281)
901. I/963 (1282)
902. I/964 (1283). (Lb. 425)
903. I/1008 (1327). (Lb. 332)
904. I/1079 (1398)
905. I/1029 (1348). (Lb. 397)
906. I/1037 (1356). (Lb. 407)
907. I/965 (1284). (Lb. 415)
908. I/966 (1285)
909. I/967 (1286). (Lb. 384)
910. I/968 (1287). (Lb. 321, 413)
911. I/969 (1288). (Lb. 388)
912. I/970 (1289)
913. I/482
914. I/971 (1290)
915. I/1004 (1323). (Lb. 366)
916. I/999 (1318)
917. I/863 (1182). (Lb. 988)
918. I/674/10. (Lb. 1688), I/423
919. I/544/1
920. I/1220/47
921. I/1208 (1527)
922. I/63
923. I/987 (1306). (Lb. 308)
924. I/60. (Lb. 947)
925. I/1034 (1353). (Lb. 1573)
926. I/558
927. I/866 (1185). (Lb. 200)
928. I/1220/30
929. I/865 (1184). (Lb. 390)
930. I/580
931. I/790 (1109). (Lb. 364)
932. I/868 (1187). (Lb. 733)
933. I/873 (1193). (Lb. 939)
934. I/871 (1190). (Lb. 1063)
935. I/453
936. I/869 (1188). (Lb. 389, 389a)
937. I/872 (1191). (Lb. 1475)
938. I/501
939. I/875 (1195). (Lb. 1216)
940. I/354. (Lb. 56), I/97
941. I/199
942. I/567
943. I/587
944. I/1151 (1470)
945. I/553
946. I/782 (1101)
947. I/569
948. I/573/6
949. I/585
950. I/599/13
951. I/599/14
952. I/599/15
953. I/763 (1087)
954. I/659
955. I/787/1 (1106), I/876 (1196), I/882 (1202)
956. I/877 (1197). (Lb. 400, 660, 1057)
957. I/878 (1198). (Lb. 764)
958. I/340, I/97, I/288, I/369. (Lb. 836), I/879 (1199), I/880 (1200). (Lb. 593)
959. I/151
960. I/451
961. I/1220/33
962. I/884 (1204). (Lb. 392)
963. I/889 (1209). (Lb. 1625)
964. I/883 (1203). (Lb. 421)
965. I/886 (1206)
966. I/674/8. (Lb. 1688)
967. I/885 (1205). (Lb. 682)
968. I/1050 (1369), I/454
969. I/1072 (1391). (Lb. 739, 913)
970. I/892 (1212). (Lb. 452)
971. I/890 (1210)
972. I/891 (1211)
973. I/893 (1213)
974. I/898 (1218). (Lb. 1453)
975. I/1157 (1476)
976. I/1220/19
977. I/897 (1217). (Lb. 411)
978. I/236
979. I/900 (1220). (Lb. 1479, 1525)
980. I/561
981. I/513
982. I/1206 (1525)
983. I/901 (1221). (Lb. 1141)
984. I/794 (1113). (Lb. 1445)
985. I/598/7
986. I/328/3
987. I/328/4

988. I/559
989. I/899 (1219). (Lb. 1279)
990. I/896 (1216). (Lb. 732, 954)
991. I/953 (1272)
992. I/1056 (1375)
993. I/1104 (1423). (Lb. 1517)
994. I/905 (1224). (Lb. 394, 487)
995. I/907 (1226). (Lb. 313)
996. I/1168 (1487). (Lb. 1018)
997. I/1169 (1488). (Lb. 1207)
998. I/912 (1231). (Lb. 306)
999. I/917 (1236). (Lb. 874)
1000. I/902 (1222). (Lb. 450)
1001. I/1038 (1357)
1002. I/903 (1223)
1003. I/1220/18
1004. I/906 (1225)
1005. I/908 (1227). (Lb. 435)
1006. I/913 (1232). (Lb. 1238)
1007. I/465
1008. I/938 (1257)
1009. I/352. (Lb. 30)
1010. I/353
1011. I/1146 (1465)
1012. I/909 (1228). (Lb. 437)
1013. I/915 (1234). (Lb. 1557, 1696)
1014. I/914 (1233). (Lb. 1692)
1015. I/574
1016. I/5, I/11, I/12
1017. I/579
1018. I/1117 (1436)
1019. I/911 (1230)
1020. I/910 (1229). (Lb. 403)
1021. I/918 (1237). (Lb. 1647)
1022. I/545
1023. I/599/56
1024. I/920 (1239). (Lb. 724)
1025. I/921 (1240). (Lb. 377)
1026. I/919 (1238)
1027. I/922 (1241). (Lb. 489)
1028. I/925 (1244). (Lb. 1626)
1029. I/1003 (1322). (Lb. 1414)
1030. I/924 (1243). (Lb. 1269)
1031. I/1061 (1380). (Lb. 663)
1032. I/582
1033. I/939 (1258). (Lb. 1142)
1034. I/929 (1248). (Lb. 975)
1035. I/930 (1249)
1036. I/931 (1250)
1037. I/932 (1251)
1038. I/979 (1298). (Lb. 498)
1039. I/1209
1040. I/165
1041. I/433, I/935 (1254)
1042. I/1220/31
1043. I/1220/57
1044. I/1220/58
1045. I/551/2
1046. I/942 (1261)
1047. I/941 (1260). (Lb. 883)
1048. I/456
1049. I/940 (1259). (Lb. 1449)
1050. I/936 (1255). (Lb. 1178)
1051. I/927 (1246). (Lb. 378)
1052. I/674/12. (Lb. 1688)
1053. I/565
1054. I/563
1055. I/926 (1245). (Lb. 1704)
1056. I/928 (1247). (Lb. 1556)
1057. I/394
1058. I/943 (1262). (Lb. 319)
1059. I/946 (1265). (Lb. 719)
1060. I/1220/5
1061. I/950 (1269)
1062. I/571
1063. I/478
1064. I/474
1065. I/1220/29
1066. I/1220/53
1067. I/599/87
1068. I/153
1069. I/944 (1263). (Lb. 323)
1070. I/945 (1264). (Lb. 441)
1071. I/381
1072. I/572
1073. I/328/1
1074. I/328/2
1075. I/947 (1266)
1076. I/674/7. (Lb. 1688)
1077. I/543/2
1078. I/983/1 (1302). (Lb. 763)
1079. I/983/2 (1302). (Lb. 763)
1080. I/145
1081. I/24
1082. I/983/3 (1302). (Lb. 763)
1083. I/1027 (1346). (Lb. 343)
1084. I/982 (1301)
1085. I/462. (Lb. 1485)
1086. I/1073 (1392)
1087. I/422. (Lb. 1166)
1088. I/421
1089. I/252. (Lb. 1526), I/496
1090. I/458. (Lb. 1217)
1091. I/498
1092. I/337
1093. I/159
1094. I/188
1095. I/672
1096. I/985 (1304)
1097. I/1028 (1347). (Lb. 398)
1098. I/1076 (1395). (Lb. 1135)
1099. I/445
1100. I/486
1101. I/1220/50
1102. I/1220/51
1103. I/94. (Lb. 1715)
1104. I/377
1105. I/671
1106. I/169. (Lb. 274, 275)
1107. I/1220/41
1108. I/396
1109. I/423
1110. I/410
1111. I/599/113
1112. I/592/1
1113. I/592/9
1114. I/592/13
1115. I/412
1116. I/543/1
1117. I/413
1118. I/1055 (1374)
1119. I/670. (Lb. 173)
1120. I/1118 (1437). (Lb. 940)
1121. I/592/6
1122. I/592/5
1123. I/1/2. (Lb. 678)
1124. I/388
1125. I/228. (Lb. 230)
1126. I/397
1127. I/607
1128. I/385/7
1129. I/404
1130. I/171
1131. I/379
1132. I/425. (Lb. 920)
1133. I/390
1134. I/6
1135. I/402
1136. I/783 (1102)
1137. I/592/7. (Lb. 1489)

1138. I/392. (Lb. 1047)
1139. I/592/10
1140. I/592/11
1141. I/598/5
1142. I/384
1143. I/387. (Lb. 920)
1144. I/3, I/4, I/416
1145. I/1154 (1473)
1146. I/376
1147. I/411
1148. I/666. (Lb. 1124)
1149. I/372. (Lb. 886)
1150. I/419
1151. I/398, I/1220/91
1152. I/592/14
1153. I/389, I/375
1154. I/562, I/663
1155. I/555
1156. I/385/2
1157. I/385/3
1158. I/424
1159. I/401
1160. I/1085 (1404). (Lb. 768)
1161. I/395
1162. I/658. (Lb. 1137)
1163. I/374
1164. I/301, I/956
1165. I/956 (1275), I/374
1166. I/415
1167. I/887 (1207). (Lb. 1001), I/1057 (1376)
1168. I/417
1169. I/418
1170. I/1155 (1474)
1171. I/1216
1172. I/400
1173. I/669
1174. I/894 (1214). (Lb. 393)
1175. I/393
1176. I/916 (1235). (Lb. 1641)
1177. I/385/4
1178. I/385/5, I/385/6
1179. I/619. (Lb. 408)
1180. I/409. (Lb. 396)
1181. I/546, I/548.
1182. I/408
1183. I/1/1. (Lb. 53, 102, 103, 221, 222, 274, 275, 293)
1184. I/2
1185. I/592/12
1186. I/386
1187. I/592/3
1188. I/406
1189. I/373
1190. I/26
1191. I/391. (Lb. 949)
1192. I/405. (Lb. 322)
1193. I/407. (Lb. 305)
1194. I/592/4
1195. I/661
1196. I/592/15
1197. I/385/1
1198. I/592/16
1199. I/378
1200. I/380
1201. I/403. (Lb. 325)
1202. I/280
1203. I/399
1204. I/493. (Lb. 1052)
1205. I/592/2
1206. I/622. (Lb. 715)
1207. I/1171 (1490)
1208. I/1156 (1475)
1209. I/1137 (1456)
1210. I/600. (Lb. 585)
1211. I/1138 (1457). (Lb. 1596)
1212. I/522
1213. I/1164 (1483). (Lb. 589)
1214. I/527. (Lb. 1569)
1215. I/528. (Lb. 1568)
1216. I/521
1217. I/1162 (1481). (Lb. 508)
1218. I/1166 (1485). (Lb. 963)
1219. I/1167 (1486). (Lb. 1594)
1220. I/631. (Lb. 1734)
1221. I/519
1222. I/630. (Lb. 1735)
1223. I/618
1224. I/1139 (1458). (Lb. 634)
1225. I/520, I/621
1226. I/515
1227. I/1044 (1363)
1228. I/1140 (1459)
1229. I/33
1230. I/455
1231. I/430
1232. I/162
1233. I/605
1234. I/653. (Lb. 1656)
1235. I/639
1236. I/652
1237. I/530
1238. I/1170 (1489). (Lb. 1010)
1239. I/525. (Lb. 1711)
1240. I/526
1241. I/111. (Lb. 466)
1242. I/172
1243. I/1053 (1372)
1244. I/627
1245. I/612
1246. I/611
1247. I/523
1248. I/651. (Lb. 448)
1249. I/1165 (1484). (Lb. 532)
1250. I/650. (Lb. 503)
1251. I/606
1252. I/676
1253. I/17. (Lb. 127)
1254. I/648
1255. I/629
1256. I/524
1257. I/109. (Lb. 457, 992)
1258. I/1163 (1482). (Lb. 584)
1259. I/119. (Lb. 1693)
1260. I/516
1261. I/609
1262. I/617
1263. I/635
1264. I/643. (Lb. 534)
1265. I/644
1266. I/646. (Lb. 467)
1267. I/649. (Lb. 504)
1268. I/1093 (1412). (Lb. 1533)
1269. I/1131 (1450). (Lb. 269, 575)
1270. I/1220/22
1271. I/1220/71
1271a. I/616
1272. I/679 (1003)
1273. I/734 (1058)
1274. I/1182 (1501)
1275. I/1180 (1499)
1276. I/759 (1083)
1277. I/755 (1079). (Lb. 1543)
1278. I/766 (1090)
1279. I/1181 (1500)
1280. I/757 (1081). (Lb. 753)
1281. I/765 (1089). (Lb. 1707)
1282. I/785/5 (1104)
1283. I/266
1284. I/1134 (1453)

1285. I/1178 (1497)
1286. I/738 (1062). (Lb. 1460)
1287. I/746 (1070). (Lb. 129)
1288. I/747 (1071). (Lb. 110)
1289. I/1033 (1352). (Lb. 761)
1290. I/1202 (1521)
1291. I/861 (1180). (Lb. 1656)
1292. I/702 (1026)
1293. I/678 (1002)
1294. I/688 (1012). (Lb. 1090)
1295. I/741 (1065)
1296. I/686 (1010)
1297. I/697 (1021)
1298. I/695 (1019). (Lb. 1503)
1299. I/1058 (1377). (Lb. 1130)
1300. I/682 (1006)
1301. I/680 (1004). (Lb. 1284)
1302. I/716 (1040)
1303. I/705 (1029). (Lb. 679)
1304. I/706 (1030)
1305. I/701 (1025)
1306. I/737 (1061)
1307. I/740 (1064)
1308. I/690 (1014), I/975 (1293)
1309. I/684 (1008)
1310. I/685 (1009)
1311. I/687 (1011)
1312. I/731 (1055). (Lb. 944)
1313. I/769/1 (1093)
1314. I/769/2 (1093)
1315. I/769/3 (1093)
1316. I/744 (1068)
1317. I/692 (1016). (Lb. 1036)
1318. I/691 (1015). (Lb. 1036), I/933 (1252)
1319. I/699 (1023)
1320. I/698 (1022)
1321. I/477. (Lb. 518)
1322. I/704 (1028). (Lb. 546)
1323. I/689 (1013)
1324. I/754 (1078)
1325. I/751 (1075). (Lb. 1655)
1326. I/707 (1031)
1327. I/733 (1057)
1328. I/694 (1018)
1329. I/742 (1095, 1066). (Lb. 587, 1006)
1330. I/703 (1027). (Lb. 225, 226, 227, 228, 547)
1331. I/720 (1044)
1332. I/677 (1001)
1333. I/696 (1020)
1334. I/752 (1076). (Lb. 933)
1335. I/724 (1048)
1336. I/693 (1017). (Lb. 1113)
1337. I/683 (1007)
1338. I/681 (1005)
1339. I/768 (1092). (Lb. 604)
1340. I/700 (1024). (Lb. 1, 14)
1341. I/714 (1038). (Lb. 217)
1342. I/730 (1054)
1343. I/1220/35
1344. I/1220/36
1345. I/1220/72
1346. I/599/105
1347. I/1220/42
1348. I/160
1349. I/35
1350. I/739 (1063), I/1220/92
1351. I/743 (1067). (Lb. 911)
1352. I/1077 (1396). (Lb. 1266)
1353. I/769/5 (1093). (Lb. 25)
1354. I/712 (1036). (Lb. 10)
1355. I/719 (1042, 1043). (Lb. 22)
1356. I/769/4 (1093)
1357. I/769/7 (1093)
1358. I/727 (1051). (Lb. 1602, 1602a)
1359. I/717 (1041). (Lb. 193)
1360. I/710 (1034)
1361. I/711 (1035)
1362. I/709 (1033)
1363. I/760 (1084). (Lb. 182)
1364. I/773 (1097)
1365. I/761 (1085). (Lb. 104)
1366. I/769/6 (1093)
1367. I/726 (1050). (Lb. 250, 251)
1368. I/721 (1045). (Lb. 247, 248)
1369. I/728 (1052). (Lb. 950)
1370. I/735 (1059)
1371. I/718 (1042). (Lb. 1373)
1372. I/976 (1295)
1373. I/723 (1047). (Lb. 1377)
1374. I/762 (1086). (Lb. 107)
1375. I/736 (1060)
1376. I/725 (1049). (Lb. 253, 254)
1377. I/715 (1039)
1378. I/732 (1056). (Lb. 192)
1379. I/708 (1032)
1380. I/722 (1046). (Lb. 7, 1376)
1381. I/729 (1053). (Lb. 96)
1382. I/713 (1037)
1383. I/769/8 (1093)
1384. I/772 (1096). (Lb. 567)
1385. I/338/2
1386. I/977 (1296)
1387. I/748 (1072). (Lb. 1705)
1388. I/774 (1098)
1389. I/749 (1073). (Lb. 1572)
1390. I/767 (1091). (Lb. 1610)
1391. I/750 (1074). (Lb. 1577)
1392. I/753 (1077). (Lb. 1578)
1393. I/756 (1080). (Lb. 1509)
1394. I/764 (1088). (Lb. 1719)
1395. I/1220/43
1396. I/777/14 (1099)
1397. I/777/15 (1099)
1398. I/777/16 (1099)
1399. I/608. (Lb. 1723)
1400. I/613
1401. I/614
1402. I/615
1403. I/637
1404. I/626
1405. I/632. (Lb. 1736)
1406. I/633. (Lb. 1721)
1407. I/636
1408. I/623
1409. I/624
1410. I/518. (Lb. 1729)
1411. I/1183 (1502). (Lb. 1581, 1581a, 1581b, 1581c)
1412. I/1184 (1503). (Lb. 1652)
1413. I/1185 (1504)
1414. I/1186 (1505)
1415. I/634. (Lb. 1219)
1416. I/642. (Lb. 1651)
1417. I/645
1418. I/647
1419. I/1109 (1428). (Lb. 1500)
1420. I/1124 (1443). (Lb. 17)
1421. I/1189 (1508)
1422. I/281
1423. I/660
1424. I/593. (Lb. 659)
1425. I/156
1426. I/597/2. (Lb. 1116)
1427. I/597/3. (Lb. 1116)
1428. I/597/4. (Lb. 1116)
1429. I/597/12. (Lb. 1116)
1430. I/597/6. (Lb. 1116)

1431. I/597/7. (Lb. 1116)
1432. I/597/5. (Lb. 1116)
1433. I/1220/48
1434. I/597/10. (Lb. 1116)
1435. I/1220/49
1436. I/597/8. (Lb. 1116)
1437. I/597/9. (Lb. 1116)
1438. I/551/1
1439. I/597/1. (Lb. 1116)
1440. I/225
1441. I/1081/1 (1400), I/1115 (1434)
1442. I/1220/21
1443. I/1220/61
1444. I/1200 (1519)
1445. I/1204 (1523)
1446. I/1220/62
1447. I/1081/2 (1400)
1448. I/1094 (1413). (Lb. 16, 16a)
1449. I/597/11
1450. I/1190 (1509). (Lb. 670)
1451. I/552/1
1452. I/1195 (1514). (Lb. 674)
1453. I/777/12 (1099). (Lb. 673)
1454. I/777/13 (1099). (Lb. 673)
1455. I/1203 (1523)
1456. I/1196 (1515). (Lb. 672)
1457. I/1221
1458. I/777/8 (1099)
1459. I/657/1
1460. I/673
1461. I/1220/84
1462. I/1161 (1480)
1463. I/1188 (1507). (Lb. 608), I/288
1464. I/1129 (1448). (Lb. 1002), I/288
1465. I/834 (1153). (Lb. 673)
1466. I/1148 (1467)
1467. I/1112/2 (1431). (Lb. 1427)
1468. I/1130 (1449). (Lb. 20)
1469. I/1122 (1441). (Lb. 1494)
1470. I/1120 (1439). (Lb. 1675)
1471. I/1112/1 (1431)
1472. I/1116 (1435). (Lb. 1495)
1473. I/594/3
1474. I/529
1475. I/598/6
1476. I/588
1477. I/584
1478. I/599/102
1479. I/544/3
1480. I/581/2
1481. I/596
1482. I/583
1483. I/586/2
1484. I/586/1
1485. I/544/2
1486. I/594/4
1487. I/598/4
1488. I/586/4
1489. I/544/4
1490. I/1141 (1460)
1491. I/595/1
1492. I/1220/28
1493. I/1220/16
1494. I/770 (1094). (Lb. 261)
1495. I/110
1496. I/824 (1143). (Lb. 500)
1497. I/592/17
1498. I/1220/23
1499. I/1220/65
1500. I/599/86
1501. I/590
1502. I/620. (Lb. 718)
1503. I/781/6 (1100)
1504. I/1159 (1478). (Lb. 86)
1505. I/599/116

# Concordance of Call Numbers in Ringelblum I: Old and Oldest Call Numbers to New document Numbers

This concordance keys the old call numbers, which were created in 1955, the oldest call numbers, which were in use before 1955, and call numbers in the 1946 catalog of Ring. I to the consecutive document numbers in the present catalog. An equal sign (=) precedes the new document number. Oldest call numbers are in parentheses. Document numbers in the 1946 list, also in parentheses, are preceded by the prefix Lb. In the old call numbers, files that included multiple documents are indicated as follows: I/328/1, I/328/2, I/328/3, etc.

I/1/1 = 1183
I/1/2 = 1123
I/2 = 1184
I/3 = 1144
I/4 = 1144
I/5 = 1016
I/6 = 1134
I/7 = 267
I/8 = 757
I/9 = 757
I/10 = 758
I/11 = 1016
I/12 = 1016
I/13 = 323
I/14 = 252
I/15 = 757
I/16 = 740
I/17 = 1253
I/18 = 640
I/19 = 245
I/20 = 260
I/21/1 = 759
I/21/2 = 752
I/21/3 = 753
I/22 = 488
I/23 = 858
I/24 = 1081
I/25 = 402
I/26 = 1190
I/27 = 384
I/28 = 241
I/29 = 414
I/30 = 894
I/31 = 517
I/32 = 348
I/33 = 1229
I/34 = 65

I/35 = 1349
I/36 = 598
I/37/1 = 301
I/37/2 = 300
I/37/3 = 307
I/38 = 672
I/39 = 676
I/40 = 658
I/41 = 324
I/42 = 18
I/43 = 670
I/44 = 678
I/45 = 13
I/46 = 596
I/47 = 593
I/48 = 63
I/49 = 597
I/50 = 661
I/51= 635
I/52 = 437
I/53 = 615
I/54 = 641
I/55 = 630
I/56 = 631
I/57 = 632
I/58 = 620
I/59 = 621
I/60 = 924
I/61 = 634
I/62 = 629
I/63 = 922
I/64 = 613
I/65 = 618
I/66 = 652
I/67 = 656
I/68 = 654
I/69 = 672

I/70 = 667
I/71 = 668
I/72 = 672
I/73 = 694
I/74 = 669
I/75 = 868
I/76 = 339
I/77 = 651
I/78 = 297
I/79 = 298
I/80/1 = 299
I/80/2 = 340
I/81= 572
I/82 = 279
I/83 = 607
I/84 = 608
I/85 = 609
I/86 = 509
I/87 = 358
I/88 = 39
I/89 = 360
I/90 = 662
I/91 = 599
I/92 = 659
I/93 = 502
I/94 = 1103
I/95 = 427
I/96 = 414
I/96 = 420
I/97/1 = 242
I/97/2 = 940
I/97/3 = 958
I/98 = 554
I/99 = 616
I/100 = 435
I/101= 622
I/102 = 612

I/103 = 250
I/104 = 632
I/105 = 5
I/106 = 655
I/107 = 498
I/108 = 60
I/109 = 1257
I/110 = 1495
I/111 = 1241
I/112 = 583
I/113 = 55
I/114 = 585
I/115 = 647
I/116 = 469
I/117 = 6
I/118 = 880
I/119 = 1259
I/120 = 56
I/121 = 62
I/122 = 57
I/123 = 627
I/124 = 556
I/125 = 558
I/126 = 15
I/127 = 10
I/128 = 560
I/129 = 566
I/130 = 555
I/131 = 16
I/132 = 17
I/133 = 559
I/134 = 7
I/135 = 567
I/136 = 562
I/137/1 = 564
I/137/2 = 565
I/137/3 = 21

I/138 = 561
I/139 = 563
I/140 = 557
I/141 = 19
I/142 = 8
I/143 = 588
I/144 = 45
I/145 = 1080
I/146 = 64
I/147 = 66
I/148 = 67
I/149 = 595
I/150 = 61
I/151 = 959
I/153 = 1068
I/154 = 577
I/155 = 12
I/156 = 1425
I/157 = 639
I/158 = 506
I/159 = 1093
I/160 = 1348
I/161 = 623
I/162 = 1232
I/163 = 269
I/164 = 269
I/165 = 1040
I/166/1 = 48
I/166/2 = 43
I/167 = 46
I/168 = 426
I/169 = 1106
I/170 = 349
I/171 = 1130
I/172 = 1242
I/173 = 68
I/174 = 649
I/175 = 576
I/176 = 460
I/177 = 409
I/178 = 352
I/179 = 227
I/180 = 273
I/181 = 648
I/182 = 328
I/183 = 715
I/184 = 296
I/185 = 474
I/186 = 663
I/187 = 638
I/188 = 1094
I/189 = 425
I/190 = 591
I/191 = 270
I/192 = 642
I/193 = 885
I/194 = 70
I/195 = 465
I/196 = 466
I/197 = 310
I/198 = 458
I/199 = 941
I/200 = 322
I/201 = 316
I/202 = 410
I/203 = 513
I/204 = 606
I/205 = 249
I/206 = 253
I/207 = 438
I/208 = 182
I/209 = 432
I/210 = 302
I/211/1 = 820
I/211/2 = 823
I/211/3 = 181
I/211/4 = 794
I/211/5 = 822
I/212 = 504
I/213 = 224
I/214 = 610
I/215 = 292
I/216 = 619
I/217 = 354
I/218 = 417
I/219 = 317
I/220 = 590
I/221 = 428
I/222 = 315
I/223 = 608
I/224 = 239
I/225 = 1440
I/226 = 636
I/227 = 251
I/228 = 1125
I/229 = 254
I/230 = 263
I/231 = 321
I/232 = 326
I/233 = 645
I/234 = 434
I/235 = 424
I/236 = 978
I/237 = 524
I/238= 624
I/239 = 504
I/240 = 505
I/241 = 511
I/242 = 439
I/243 = 515
I/244 = 264
I/245 = 715
I/246 = 257
I/247 = 246
I/248 = 463
I/249 = 196
I/250 = 586
I/251 = 423
I/252 = 1089
I/253 = 510
I/254 = 840
I/255 = 789
I/256 = 628
I/257 = 262
I/258 = 688
I/259 = 23
I/260 = 271
I/261 = 33
I/262 = 24
I/263 = 411
I/264 = 414
I/265 = 231
I/266 = 1283
I/267 = 523
I/268 = 527
I/269 = 366
I/270 = 464
I/271 = 705
I/272 = 217
I/273 = 188
I/274/1 = 202
I/274/2 = 206
I/275 = 221
I/276 = 199
I/277 = 581
I/278/1 = 193
I/278/2 = 211
I/279 = 225
I/280 = 1202
I/281/1 = 1422
I/281/2 = 880
I/282 = 429
I/283 = 625
I/284 = 629
I/285 = 220
I/286 = 819
I/287/1 = 821
I/287/2 = 824
I/288/1 = 1463
I/288/2 = 1464
I/288/3 = 958
I/289 = 520
I/290 = 327
I/291 = 502
I/292 = 587
I/293 = 584
I/294 = 369
I/295 = 228
I/296 = 230
I/297 = 653
I/298 = 316
I/299 = 214
I/300 = 207
I/301 = 1164
I/302 = 467
I/303 = 353
I/304 = 346
I/305 = 680
I/306 = 351
I/307/1 = 341
I/307/2 = 342
I/308 = 180
I/309 = 589
I/310 = 213
I/313 = 603
I/314 = 347
I/315 = 643
I/316 = 551
I/317 = 34
I/318 = 50
I/319 = 51
I/320 = 377
I/321 = 305
I/322 = 292
I/323 = 637
I/324 = 236
I/325 = 544
I/326 = 501
I/327 = 751
I/328/1 = 1073

I/328/2 = 1074
I/328/3 = 986
I/328/4 = 987
I/329 = 376
I/331 = 881
I/332 = 674
I/333 = 265
I/334 = 311
I/335 = 579
I/336 = 42
I/337 = 1092
I/338/1 = 258
I/338/2 = 1385
I/339 = 20
I/340 = 958
I/341 = 664
I/342 = 337
I/343 = 338
I/344 = 219
I/345 = 666
I/346 = 508
I/347 = 418
I/349 = 602
I/350 = 268
I/351 = 817
I/352 = 1009
I/353 = 1010
I/354 = 940
I/355 = 320
I/356 = 325
I/357 = 238
I/358 = 592
I/359 = 294
I/360/1 = 333
I/360/2 = 318
I/361 = 485
I/362 = 500
I/363 = 611
I/364 (Lb. 1512) = 274
I/365 = 420
I/366 = 344
I/367 = 882
I/368 = 444
I/369 = 958
I/370 = 343
I/371 = 626
I/372 = 1149
I/373 = 1189
I/374/1 = 1163
I/374/2 = 1165

I/375 = 1153
I/376 = 1146
I/377 = 1004
I/378 = 1199
I/379 = 1131
I/380 = 1200
I/381 = 1071
I/382 = 704
I/384 = 1142
I/385/1 = 1197
I/385/2 = 1156
I/385/3 = 1157
I/385/4 = 1177
I/385/5 = 1178
I/385/6 = 1178
I/385/7 = 1128
I/386 = 1186
I/387 = 1143
I/388 = 1124
I/389 = 1153
I/390 = 1133
I/391 = 1191
I/392 = 1138
I/393 = 1175
I/394 = 1057
I/395 = 1161
I/396 = 1108
I/397 = 1126
I/398 = 1151
I/399 = 1203
I/400 = 1172
I/401 = 1159
I/402 = 1135
I/403 = 1201
I/404 = 1129
I/405 = 1192
I/406 = 1188
I/407 = 1193
I/408 = 1182
I/409 = 1180
I/410 = 1110
I/411= 1147
I/412 = 1115
I/413 = 1117
I/415 = 1166
I/416 = 1144
I/417 = 1168
I/418 = 1169
I/419 = 1150
I/420 = 864

I/421 = 1088
I/422 = 1087
I/423 = 918
I/423 = 1109
I/424 = 1158
I/425 = 1132
I/426 = 533
I/427 = 869
I/428 = 455
I/429 = 456
I/430 = 1231
I/431 = 870
I/432 = 415
I/433 = 1041
I/434 = 516
I/435 = 413
I/436 = 687
I/437 = 521
I/438 = 743
I/439 = 530
I/440 = 718
I/441 = 784
I/442 = 529
I/443 = 871
I/444 = 788
I/445 = 1099
I/446 = 421
I/447 = 741
I/448 = 47
I/449 = 503
I/450 = 866
I/451 = 960
I/452 = 59
I/453 = 935
I/454 = 968
I/455 = 1230
I/456 = 1048
I/457 = 41
I/458 = 1090
I/459 = 868
I/460 = 359
I/461 = 518
I/462 = 1085
I/463 = 729
I/464 = 412
I/465 = 1007
I/466 = 473
I/467 = 476
I/468 = 858
I/469 = 27

I/470 = 514
I/471 = 36
I/472 = 35
I/473 = 25
I/474 = 1064
I/475 = 862
I/476 = 783
I/477 = 1321
I/478 = 1063
I/479 = 808
I/480 = 436
I/481 = 865
I/482 = 913
I/483 = 859
I/484 = 430
I/485 = 457
I/486 = 1100
I/487 = 845
I/488 = 695
I/489 = 471
I/490 = 467
I/491 = 468
I/492 = 22
I/493 = 1204
I/494 = 844
I/495 = 843
I/496 = 1089
I/497 = 719
I/498 = 1091
I/499 = 860
I/500 = 806
I/501 = 938
I/502/1 = 646
I/502/2 = 283
I/503/1 = 445
I/503/2 = 614
I/504 = 446
I/505 = 447
I/506 = 448
I/507/1 = 449
I/507/2 = 644
I/507/3 = 14
I/507/4 = 11
I/507/5 = 40
I/508 = 601
I/509 = 633
I/510 = 450
I/511/1 = 451
I/511/2 = 452
I/511/3 = 453

I/512 = 578
I/513 = 981
I/514 = 449
I/515 = 1226
I/516 = 1260
I/517 = 538
I/518 = 1410
I/519 = 1221
I/520 = 1225
I/521 = 1216
I/522 = 1212
I/523 = 1247
I/524 = 1256
I/525 = 1239
I/526 = 1240
I/527 = 1214
I/528 = 1215
I/529 = 1474
I/530 = 1237
I/531 = 166
I/532/1 = 171
I/532/2 = 173
I/533 = 169
I/534 = 167
I/535 = 174
I/536 = 165
I/537 = 176
I/538/1 = 178
I/538/2 = 172
I/538/3 = 177
I/539 = 164
I/540/1 = 170
I/540/2 = 168
I/541 = 175
I/542 = 71
I/543/1 = 1116
I/543/2 = 1077
I/543/3 = 541
I/544/1 = 919
I/544/2 = 1485
I/544/3 = 1479
I/544/4 = 1489
I/545 = 1022
I/546 = 1181
I/547 = 747
I/548 = 1181
I/549 = 748
I/550 = 771
I/551/1 = 1438
I/551/2 = 1045

I/552/1 = 1451
I/552/2 = 772
I/552/3 = 855
I/552/4 = 856
I/552/5 = 857
I/553 = 945
I/554 = 737
I/555 = 1155
I/556 = 383
I/557/1 = 790
I/557/2 = 126
I/558 = 926
I/559 = 988
I/560 = 797
I/561 = 980
I/562 = 1154
I/563 = 1054
I/564/1 = 879
I/564/2 = 782
I/565 = 1053
I/566 = 685
I/567 = 942
I/568/1 = 710
I/568/2 = 727
I/569 = 947
I/570 = 745
I/571 = 1062
I/572 = 1072
I/573/1 = 828
I/573/2 = 829
I/573/3 = 830
I/573/4 = 831
I/573/5 = 832
I/573/6 = 948
I/573/7 = 833
I/574 = 1015
I/575/1 = 282
I/575/2 = 283
I/575/3 = 216
I/576 = 839
I/577 = 334
I/578 = 779
I/579 = 1017
I/580 = 930
I/581/1 = 728
I/581/2 = 1480
I/582 = 1032
I/583 = 1482
I/584 = 1477
I/585 = 949

I/586/1 = 1484
I/586/2 = 1483
I/586/3 = 550
I/586/4 = 1488
I/587 = 943
I/588 = 1476
I/589 = 540
I/590 = 1501
I/591 = 765
I/592/1 = 1112
I/592/2 = 1205
I/592/3 = 1187
I/592/4 = 1194
I/592/5 = 1122
I/592/6 = 1121
I/592/7 = 1137
I/592/8 = 713
I/592/9 = 1113
I/592/10 = 1139
I/592/11 = 1140
I/592/12 = 1185
I/592/13 = 1114
I/592/14 = 1152
I/592/15 = 1196
I/592/16 = 1198
I/592/17 = 1497
I/593 = 1424
I/594/1 = 547
I/594/2 = 370
I/594/3 = 1473
I/594/4 = 1486
I/595/1 = 1491
I/595/2 = 110
I/595/3 = 108
I/595/4 = 111
I/595/4 = 148
I/595/5 = 108
I/595/6 = 112
I/595/7 = 148
I/596 = 1481
I/597/1 = 1439
I/597/2 = 1426
I/597/3 = 1427
I/597/4 = 1428
I/597/5 = 1432
I/597/6 = 1430
I/597/6 = 545
I/597/7 = 1431
I/597/8 = 1436
I/597/9 = 1437

I/597/10 = 1434
I/597/11 = 1449
I/597/12 = 1429
I/598/1 = 539
I/598/2 = 853
I/598/3 = 553
I/598/4 = 1487
I/598/5 = 1141
I/598/6 = 1475
I/598/7 = 985
I/598/8 = 549
I/599/1 = 96
I/599/2 = 124
I/599/3 = 330
I/599/4 = 77
I/599/5 = 75
I/599/6 = 134
I/599/8 = 162
I/599/10 = 163
I/599/11 = 89
I/599/13 = 950
I/599/14 = 951
I/599/15 = 952
I/599/19 = 127
I/599/20 = 100
I/599/20a = 99
I/599/21 = 103
I/599/22 = 101
I/599/23 = 97
I/599/24 = 143
I/599/25 = 142
I/599/26 = 120
I/599/27 = 133
I/599/28 = 152
I/599/30 = 145
I/599/31 = 98
I/599/32 = 138
I/599/33 = 140
I/599/34 = 104
I/599/35 = 92
I/599/36 = 132
I/599/37 = 144
I/599/38 = 102
I/599/39 = 81
I/599/40 = 78
I/599/41 = 83
I/599/42 = 84
I/599/43 = 72
I/599/44 = 76
I/599/45 = 82

I/599/46 = 80
I/599/47 = 79
I/599/48 = 74
I/599/49 = 93
I/599/50 = 147
I/599/51 = 137
I/599/53 = 113
I/599/54 = 73
I/599/55 = 90
I/599/56 = 1023
I/599/57 = 85
I/599/58 = 146
I/599/59 = 139
I/599/60 = 122
I/599/61 = 153
I/599/62 = 105
I/599/63 = 117
I/599/64 = 129
I/599/65 = 118
I/599/66 = 86
I/599/67 = 734
I/599/67a = 735
I/599/67b = 736
I/599/68 = 91
I/599/69 = 141
I/599/70 = 136
I/599/71 = 107
I/599/72 = 123
I/599/73 = 121
I/599/74 = 154
I/599/75 = 155
I/599/76 = 156
I/599/78 = 128
I/599/80 = 87
I/599/81 = 157
I/599/82 = 94
I/599/85 = 854
I/599/86 = 1500
I/599/87 = 1067
I/599/91 = 119
I/599/92 = 115
I/599/94 = 685
I/599/95 = 135
I/599/96 = 158
I/599/97 = 114
I/599/98 = 116
I/599/100 = 159
I/599/101 = 88
I/599/102 = 1478
I/599/103 = 95

I/599/104 = 108
I/599/105 = 1346
I/599/107 = 109
I/599/109 = 778
I/599/110 = 130
I/599/111 = 160
I/599/113 = 1111
I/599/114 = 106
I/599/116 = 1505
I/599/117 = 161
I/600 = 1210
I/601 = 379
I/602 = 407
I/603 = 682
I/604 = 671
I/605 = 1233
I/606 = 1251
I/607 = 1127
I/608 = 1399
I/609 = 1261
I/610 = 721
I/611 = 1246
I/612 = 1245
I/613 = 1400
I/614 = 1401
I/615 = 1402
I/616 = 1271a
I/617 = 1262
I/618 = 1223
I/619 = 1179
I/620 = 1502
I/621 = 1225
I/622 = 1206
I/623 = 1408
I/624 = 1409
I/626 = 1404
I/627 = 1244
I/628 = 386
I/629 = 1255
I/630 = 1222
I/631 = 1220
I/632 = 1405
I/633 = 1406
I/634 = 1415
I/635 = 1263
I/636 = 1407
I/637 = 1403
I/638 = 807
I/639 = 1235
I/640 = 9

I/641 = 405
I/642 = 1416
I/643 = 1264
I/644 = 1265
I/645 = 1417
I/646 = 1266
I/647 = 1418
I/648 = 1254
I/649 = 1267
I/650 = 1250
I/651 = 1248
I/651a = 200
I/652 = 1236
I/653 = 1234
I/654 = 405
I/655 = 406
I/656/2 = 201
I/656/3 = 205
I/656/4 = 208
I/656/5 = 209
I/656/6 = 210
I/656/7 = 215
I/657/1 = 1459
I/657/2 = 365
I/657/3 = 314
I/658 = 1162
I/659 = 954
I/660 = 1423
I/661 = 1195
I/662 = 226
I/663 = 1154
I/664/1 = 226
I/664/2 = 229
I/664/3 = 230
I/664/4 = 264
I/665 = 26
I/666 = 1148
I/667 = 573
I/668 = 458
I/669 = 1173
I/670 = 1119
I/671 = 1105
I/672 = 1095
I/673 = 1460
I/674/1 = 332
I/674/2 = 536
I/674/3 = 442
I/674/4 = 479
I/674/5 = 724
I/674/6 = 4

I/674/7 = 1076
I/674/8 = 966
I/674/9 = 826
I/674/10 = 918
I/674/11 = 825
I/674/12 = 1052
I/674/13 = 569
I/674/14 = 803
I/674/15 = 571
I/675 = 2
I/676 = 1252
I/677 (1001) = 1332
I/678 (1002) = 1293
I/679 (1003) = 1272
I/680 (1004) = 1301
I/681 (1005) = 1338
I/682 (1006) = 1300
I/683 (1007) = 1337
I/684 (1008) = 1309
I/685 (1009) = 1310
I/686 (1010) = 1296
I/687 (1011) = 1311
I/688 (1012) = 1294
I/689 (1013) = 1323
I/690 (1014) = 1308
I/691 (1015) = 1318
I/692 (1016) = 1317
I/693 (1017) = 1336
I/694 (1018) = 1328
I/695 (1019) = 1298
I/696 (1020) = 1333
I/697 (1021) = 1297
I/698 (1022) = 1320
I/699 (1023) = 1319
I/700 (1024) = 1340
I/701 (1025) = 1305
I/702 (1026) = 1292
I/703 (1027) = 1330
I/704 (1028) = 1322
I/705 (1029) = 1303
I/706 (1030) = 1304
I/707 (1031) = 1326
I/708 (1032) = 1379
I/709 (1033) = 1362
I/710 (1034) = 1360
I/711 (1035) = 1361
I/712 (1036) = 1354
I/713 (1037) = 1382
I/714 (1038) = 1341
I/715 (1039) = 1377

I/716 (1040) = 1302
I/717 (1041) = 1359
I/718 (1042) = 1371
I/719 (1042, 1043) = 1355
I/720 (1044) = 1331
I/721 (1045) = 1368
I/722 (1046) = 1380
I/723 (1047) = 1373
I/724 (1048) = 1335
I/725 (1049) = 1376
I/726 (1050) = 1367
I/727 (1051) = 1358
I/728 (1052) = 1369
I/729 (1053) = 1381
I/730 (1054) = 1342
I/731 (1055) = 1312
I/732 (1056) = 1378
I/733 (1057) = 1327
I/734 (1058) = 1273
I/735 (1059) = 1370
I/736 (1060) = 1375
I/737 (1061) = 1306
I/738 (1062) = 1286
I/739 (1063) = 1350
I/740 (1064) = 1307
I/741 (1065) = 1295
I/742 (1095, 1066) = 1329
I/743 (1067) = 1351
I/744 (1068) = 1316
I/746 (1070) = 1287
I/747 (1071) = 1288
I/748 (1072) = 1387
I/749 (1073) = 1389
I/750 (1074) = 1391
I/751 (1075) = 1325
I/752 (1076) = 1334
I/753 (1077) = 1392
I/754 (1078) = 1324
I/755 (1079) = 1277
I/756 (1080) = 1393
I/757 (1081) = 1280
I/759 (1083) = 1276
I/760 (1084) = 1363
I/761 (1085) = 1365
I/762 (1086) = 1374
I/763 (1087) = 953
I/764 (1088) = 1394
I/765 (1089) = 1281
I/766 (1090) = 1278
I/767 (1091) = 1390
I/768/1 (1092) = 1339
I/768/2 (1093) = 526
I/769/1 (1093) = 1313
I/769/2 (1093)= 1314
I/769/3 (1093) = 1315
I/769/4 (1093) = 1356
I/769/5 (1093) = 1353
I/769/6 (1093) = 1366
I/769/7 (1093) = 1357
I/769/8 (1093) = 1383
I/770 (1094) = 1494
I/772 (1096) = 1384
I/773 (1097) = 1364
I/774 (1098) = 1388
I/775/1 (1099) = 234
I/775/2 (1099) = 276
I/776/1 (1099) = 276
I/776/2 (1099) = 278
I/777/1 (1099) = 335
I/777/2 (1099) = 277
I/777/3 (1099) = 261
I/777/4 (1099) = 259
I/777/5 (1099) = 276
I/777/6 (1099) = 364
I/777/7 (1099) = 367
I/777/8 (1099) = 1458
I/777/9 (1099) = 372
I/777/10 (1099) = 394
I/777/12 (1099) = 1453
I/777/13 (1099) = 1454
I/777/14 (1099) = 1396
I/777/15 (1099) = 1397
I/777/16 (1099) = 1398
I/778/1 (1099) = 214
I/778/2 (1099) = 232
I/778/3 (1099) = 233
I/778/4 (1099) = 244
I/779/1 (1099) = 391
I/779/2 (1099) = 336
I/779/3 (1099) = 284
I/780/1 (1099) = 389
I/780/2 (1099) = 390
I/780/3 (1099) = 345
I/781/1 (1100) = 194
I/781/3 (1100) = 184
I/781/4 (1100) = 186
I/781/5 (1100) = 183
I/781/6 (1100) = 1503
I/781/7 (1100) = 179
I/782 (1101) = 946
I/783 (1102) = 1136
I/784 (1103) = 714
I/785/1 (1104) = 811
I/785/2 (1104) = 812
I/785/3 (1104) = 813
I/785/4 (1104) = 814
I/785/5 (1104) = 1282
I/786 (1105) = 883
I/787/1 (1106) = 955
I/787/2 (1106) = 272
I/788 (1107) = 686
I/789 (1108) = 684
I/790 (1109) = 931
I/791 (1110) = 697
I/792 (1111) = 698
I/794 (1113) = 984
I/795 (1114) = 699
I/796 (1115) = 712
I/797 (1116) = 716
I/799 (1118) = 720
I/801 (1120) = 725
I/802 (1121) = 723
I/803 (1122) = 726
I/804 (1123) = 742
I/805 (1124) = 750
I/806 (1125) = 756
I/807 (1126) = 763
I/808 (1127) = 732
I/809 (1128) = 746
I/810 (1129) = 768
I/811 (1130) = 769
I/812 (1131) = 773
I/813 (1132) = 32
I/814 (1133) = 770
I/815 (1134) = 774
I/816 (1135) = 764
I/817 (1137) = 707
I/818 (1136) = 708
I/819 (1138) = 776
I/820 (1139) = 331
I/821 (1140) = 780
I/822 (1141) = 791
I/823 (1142) = 792
I/824 (1143) = 1496
I/825 (1144) = 783
I/826 (1145) = 783
I/827 (1146) = 785
I/828 (1147) = 786
I/829 (1148) = 787
I/830 (1149) = 783
I/832 (1151) = 804
I/833 (1152) = 827
I/834 (1153) = 1465
I/835 (1154) = 805
I/836 (1155) = 834
I/837 (1156) = 835
I/838 (1157) = 836
I/839 (1158) = 837
I/840 (1159) = 838
I/841 (1160) = 801
I/842 (1161) = 802
I/843 (1162) = 798
I/844 (1163) = 799
I/845 (1164) = 800
I/846 (1165) = 810
I/847 (1166) = 874
I/848 (1167) = 876
I/849 (1168) = 877
I/850 (1169) = 878
I/851 (1170) = 872
I/852 (1171) = 847
I/853 (1172) = 467
I/854 (1173) = 841
I/855 (1174) = 848
I/856 (1175) = 884
I/857 (1176) = 888
I/858 (1177) = 889
I/859 (1178) = 890
I/860 (1179) = 892
I/861 (1180) = 1291
I/862 (1181) = 887
I/863 (1182) = 917
I/864 (1183) = 846
I/865 (1184) = 929
I/866 (1185) = 927
I/867 (1186) = 717
I/868 (1187) = 932
I/869 (1188) = 936
I/870 (1189) = 711
I/871 (1190) = 934
I/872 (1191) = 937
I/873 (1193) = 933
I/875 (1195) = 939
I/876 (1196) = 955
I/877 (1197) = 956
I/878 (1198) = 957
I/879 (1199) = 958
I/880 (1200) = 958
I/881 (1201) = 760
I/882 (1202) = 955

I/883 (1203) = 964
I/884 (1204) = 962
I/885 (1205) = 967
I/886 (1206) = 965
I/887 (1207) = 1167
I/888 (1208) = 701
I/889 (1209) = 963
I/890 (1210) = 971
I/891 (1211) = 972
I/892 (1212) = 970
I/893 (1213) = 973
I/894 (1214) = 1174
I/895 (1215) = 414
I/896 (1216) = 990
I/897 (1217) = 977
I/898 (1218) = 974
I/899 (1219) = 989
I/900 (1220) = 979
I/901 (1221) = 983
I/902 (1222) = 1000
I/903 (1223) = 1002
I/905 (1224) = 994
I/906 (1225) = 1004
I/907 (1226) = 995
I/908 (1227) = 1005
I/909 (1228) = 1012
I/910 (1229) = 1020
I/911 (1230) = 1019
I/912 (1231) = 998
I/913 (1232) = 1006
I/914 (1233) = 1014
I/915 (1234) = 1013
I/916 (1235) = 1176
I/917 (1236) = 999
I/918 (1237) = 1021
I/919 (1238) = 1026
I/920 (1239) = 1024
I/921 (1240) = 1025
I/922 (1241) = 1027
I/923 (1242) = 329
I/924 (1243) = 1030
I/925 (1244) = 1028
I/926 (1245) = 1055
I/927 (1246) = 1051
I/928 (1247) = 1056
I/929 (1248) = 1034
I/930 (1249) = 1035
I/931 (1250) = 1036
I/932 (1251) = 1037
I/933 (1252) = 1318
I/934 (1253) = 749
I/935 (1254) = 1041
I/936 (1255) = 1050
I/937/1 (1256) = 25
I/937/2 (1256) = 27
I/938 (1257) = 1008
I/939 (1258) = 1033
I/940 (1259) = 1049
I/941 (1260) = 1047
I/942 (1261) = 1046
I/943 (1262) = 1058
I/944 (1263) = 1069
I/945 (1264) = 1070
I/946 (1265) = 1059
I/947 (1266) = 1075
I/948 (1267) = 849
I/949 (1268) = 777
I/950 (1269) = 1061
I/951 (1270) = 706
I/952 (1271) = 744
I/953 (1272) = 991
I/954 (1273) = 775
I/955 (1274) = 860
I/956/1 (1275) = 1164
I/956/2 (1275) = 1165
I/957 (1276) = 895
I/958 (1277) = 896
I/959 (1278) = 897
I/960 (1279) = 898
I/961 (1280) = 899
I/962 (1281) = 900
I/963 (1282) = 901
I/964 (1283) = 902
I/965 (1284) = 907
I/966 (1285) = 908
I/967 (1286) = 909
I/968 (1287) = 910
I/969 (1288) = 911
I/970 (1289) = 912
I/971 (1290) = 914
I/972 (1291) = 700
I/973 (1292) = 873
I/974 (1293) = 842
I/975 (1293) = 1308
I/976 (1295) = 1372
I/977 (1296) = 1386
I/978 (1297) = 766
I/979 (1298) = 1038
I/980 (1299) = 781
I/981 (1300) = 440
I/982 (1301) = 1084
I/983/1 (1302) = 1078
I/983/2 (1302) = 1079
I/983/3 (1302) = 1082
I/984 (1303) = 461
I/985 (1304) = 1096
I/986 (1305) = 731
I/987 (1306) = 923
I/988 (1307) = 431
I/989 (1308) = 490
I/990/1 (1309) = 580
I/990/2 (1309) = 441
I/991 (1310) = 891
I/992 (1311) = 528
I/993 (1312) = 477
I/994 (1313) = 594
I/995 (1314) = 482
I/996 (1315) = 419
I/997 (1316) = 809
I/998 (1317) = 773
I/999 (1318) = 916
I/1000 (1319) = 691
I/1001 (1320) = 519
I/1003 (1322) = 1029
I/1004 (1323) = 915
I/1005 (1324) = 499
I/1006 (1325) = 709
I/1007 (1326) = 480
I/1008 (1327) = 903
I/1009 (1328) = 404
I/1010 (1329) = 494
I/1011 (1330) = 475
I/1012 (1331) = 486
I/1013 (1332) = 893
I/1014 (1333) = 738
I/1015 (1334) = 496
I/1016 (1335) = 689
I/1017 (1336) = 492
I/1018 (1337) = 416
I/1019 (1338) = 478
I/1020 (1339) = 493
I/1021 (1340) = 481
I/1022 (1341) = 495
I/1023 (1342) = 739
I/1024 (1343) = 491
I/1025 (1344) = 487
I/1026 (1345) = 483
I/1027 (1346) = 1083
I/1028 (1347) = 1097
I/1029 (1348) = 905
I/1030 (1349) = 497
I/1031 (1350) = 403
I/1032 (1351) = 525
I/1033 (1352) = 1289
I/1034 (1353) = 925
I/1035 (1354) = 575
I/1036 (1355) = 522
I/1037 (1356) = 906
I/1038 (1357) = 1001
I/1039 (1358) = 454
I/1040 (1359) = 462
I/1041 (1360) = 861
I/1042 (1361) = 863
I/1043 (1362) = 867
I/1044 (1363) = 1227
I/1045 (1364) = 702
I/1046 (1365) = 693
I/1047 (1366) = 703
I/1048 (1367) = 660
I/1050 (1369) = 968
I/1051 (1370) = 443
I/1052 (1371) = 512
I/1053 (1372) = 1243
I/1054 (1373) = 761
I/1055 (1374) = 1118
I/1056 (1375) = 992
I/1057 (1376) = 1167
I/1058 (1377) = 1299
I/1059 (1378) = 484
I/1060 (1379) = 414
I/1061 (1380) = 1031
I/1062/1 (1381) = 29
I/1062/2 (1381) = 30
I/1062/3 (1381) = 31
I/1063 (1382) = 35
I/1064 (1383) = 673
I/1065 (1384) = 677
I/1066 (1385) = 679
I/1067 (1386) = 675
I/1068 (1387) = 681
I/1069 (1388) = 489
I/1070 (1389) = 696
I/1071 (1390, 1393) = 459
I/1072 (1391) = 969
I/1073 (1392) = 1086
I/1075 (1394) = 472
I/1076 (1395) = 1098
I/1077 (1396) = 1352
I/1078 (1397) = 755
I/1079 (1398) = 904

I/1080 (1399) = 275
I/1081/1 (1400) = 1441
I/1081/2 (1400) = 1447
I/1082 (1401) = 235
I/1083 (1402) = 690
I/1084 (1403) = 248
I/1085 (1404) = 1160
I/1086 (1405) = 754
I/1087 (1406) = 189
I/1088/1 (1407) = 52
I/1088/2 (1407) = 2
I/1089 (1408) = 54
I/1090 (1409) = 467
I/1091 (1410) = 600
I/1092 (1411) = 288
I/1093 (1412) = 1268
I/1094 (1413) = 1448
I/1095 (1414) = 722
I/1096/1 (1415) = 361
I/1096/2 (1415) = 350
I/1097 (1416) = 380
I/1098 (1417) = 371
I/1099 (1418) = 470
I/1100 (1419) = 546
I/1101 (1420) = 266
I/1102 (1421) = 190
I/1103 (1422) = 192
I/1104 (1423) = 993
I/1105/1 (1424) = 212
I/1105/2 (1424) = 223
I/1105/3 (1424) = 203
I/1105/4 (1424) = 204
I/1106/1 (1425) = 247
I/1106/2 (1425) = 357
I/1106/3 (1425) = 295
I/1107 (1426) = 355
I/1108/1 (1427) = 393
I/1108/2 (1427) = 392
I/1108/3 (1427) = 382
I/1109 (1428) = 1419
I/1110/1 (1429) = 381
I/1110/2 (1429) = 356
I/1111 (1430) = 371
I/1112/1 (1431) = 1471
I/1112/2 (1431) = 1467
I/1112/3 (1431) = 197
I/1112/4 (1431) = 362
I/1113 (1432) = 237
I/1114 (1433) = 304
I/1115 (1434) = 1441
I/1116 (1435) = 1472
I/1117 (1436) = 1018
I/1118 (1437) = 1120
I/1119 (1438) = 319
I/1120 (1439) = 1470
I/1121 (1440) = 312
I/1122 (1441) = 1469
I/1123 (1442) = 242
I/1124 (1443) = 1420
I/1125 (1444) = 293
I/1126 (1445) = 287
I/1127 (1446) = 399
I/1128 (1447) = 378
I/1129 (1448) = 1464
I/1130 (1449) = 1468
I/1131 (1450) = 1269
I/1132 (1451) = 767
I/1133 (1452) = 286
I/1134 (1453) = 1284
I/1135 (1454) = 256
I/1136 (1455) = 401
I/1137 (1456) = 1209
I/1138 (1457) = 1211
I/1139 (1458) = 1224
I/1140 (1459) = 1228
I/1141 (1460) = 1490
I/1142 (1461) = 195
I/1143 (1462) = 255
I/1144 (1144) = 886
I/1145 (1464) = 408
I/1146 (1465) = 1011
I/1147 (1466) = 3
I/1148 (1467) = 1466
I/1149 (1468) = 875
I/1150 (1469) = 570
I/1151 (1470) = 944
I/1152/1 (1471) = 650
I/1152/2 (1471) = 1
I/1153 (1472) = 574
I/1154 (1473) = 1145
I/1155 (1474) = 1170
I/1156 (1475) = 1208
I/1157 (1476) = 975
I/1158/1 (1477) = 309
I/1158/2 (1477) = 395
I/1158/3 (1477) = 285
I/1158/4 (1477) = 396
I/1158/5 (1477) = 397
I/1159 (1478) = 1504
I/1160 (1479) = 398
I/1161 (1480) = 1462
I/1162 (1481) = 1217
I/1163 (1482) = 1258
I/1164 (1483) = 1213
I/1165 (1484) = 1249
I/1166 (1485) = 1218
I/1167 (1486) = 1219
I/1168 (1487) = 996
I/1169 (1488) = 997
I/1170 (1489) = 1238
I/1171 (1490) = 1207
I/1172 (1491) = 850
I/1173 (1492) = 762
I/1174 (1493) = 851
I/1175 (1494) = 53
I/1176 (1495) = 2
I/1177 (1496) = 796
I/1178 (1497) = 1285
I/1180 (1499) = 1275
I/1181 (1500) = 1279
I/1182 (1501) = 1274
I/1183 (1502) = 1411
I/1184 (1503).
(Lb. 1652) = 1412
I/1185 (1504) = 1413
I/1186 (1505) = 1414
I/1187 (1506) = 363
I/1188 (1507) = 1463
I/1189 (1508) = 1421
I/1190 (1509) = 1450
I/1192 (1511) = 388
I/1193 (1512) = 387
I/1195 (1514) = 1452
I/1196 (1515) = 1456
I/1197 (1516) = 289
I/1198 (1517) = 730
I/1199/1 (1518) = 195
I/1199/2 (1518) = 398
I/1200 (1519) = 1444
I/1201 (1520) = 240
I/1202 (1521) = 1290
I/1203 (1523) = 1455
I/1204 (1523) = 1445
I/1205 (1524) = 368
I/1206 (1525) = 982
I/1207 (1526) = 385
I/1208 (1527) = 921
I/1209 = 1039
I/1210 = 548
I/1211 = 605
I/1212 = 852
I/1213 = 242
I/1214 = 507
I/1215 = 542
I/1216 = 1171
I/1217 = 28
I/1218 = 783
I/1219 = 789
I/1220/1 = 433
I/1220/3 = 58
I/1220/4 = 733
I/1220/5 = 1060
I/1220/6 = 131
I/1220/7 = 125
I/1220/8 = 280
I/1220/9 = 308
I/1220/10 = 313
I/1220/11 = 170
I/1220/12 = 793
I/1220/13 = 815
I/1220/14 = 816
I/1220/15 = 692
I/1220/16 = 1493
I/1220/17 = 281
I/1220/18 = 1003
I/1220/19 = 976
I/1220/20 = 795
I/1220/21 = 1442
I/1220/22 = 1270
I/1220/23 = 1498
I/1220/25 = 373
I/1220/26 = 552
I/1220/27 = 531
I/1220/28 = 1492
I/1220/29 = 1065
I/1220/30 = 928
I/1220/31 = 1042
I/1220/32 = 617
I/1220/33 = 961
I/1220/34 = 532
I/1220/35 = 1343
I/1220/36 = 1344
I/1220/37 = 44
I/1220/38 = 37
I/1220/39 = 38
I/1220/40 = 49
I/1220/41 = 1107
I/1220/42 = 1347
I/1220/43 = 1395
I/1220/44 = 303

I/1220/45 = 543
I/1220/46 = 537
I/1220/47 = 920
I/1220/48 = 1433
I/1220/49 = 1435
I/1220/50 = 1101
I/1220/51 = 1102
I/1220/52 = 243
I/1220/53 = 1066
I/1220/54 = 568
I/1220/56 = 69
I/1220/57 = 1043
I/1220/58 = 1044
I/1220/59 = 400
I/1220/60 = 374
I/1220/61 = 1443
I/1220/62 = 1446
I/1220/63 = 657
I/1220/64 = 187
I/1220/65 = 1499
I/1220/66 = 218
I/1220/67 = 290
I/1220/68 = 306
I/1220/69a = 291
I/1220/69b = 375
I/1220/70 = 818
I/1220/71 = 1271
I/1220/72 = 1345
I/1220/73 = 534
I/1220/74 = 535
I/1220/75 = 665
I/1220/76 = 149
I/1220/77 = 150
I/1220/78 = 151
I/1220/79 = 198
I/1220/80 = 222
I/1220/81 = 191
I/1220/82 = 604
I/1220/83 = 582
I/1220/84 = 1461
I/1220/85 = 185
I/1220/86 = 276
I/1220/87 = 414
I/1220/89 = 670
I/1220/90 = 715
I/1220/91 = 1151
I/1220/92 = 1350
I/1220/98 = 458
I/1221 = 1457
I/1222 = 683
II/486 = 33
II/487 = 35

# Concordance of Call Numbers in Ringelblum I: Oldest (pre-1955) Call Numbers to New Document Numbers

This concordance keys the oldest call numbers in Ring. I, which were in use before 1955, to the new document numbers used in the present catalog. An equal sign (=) precedes the new document number. In some cases the contents of a file bearing an oldest call number was divided among more than one new document number. This is indicated as follows: 1381/1 = 29, 1381/2 =30, 1381/3 = 31

1001 = 1332
1002 = 1293
1003 = 1272
1004 = 1301
1005 = 1338
1006 = 1300
1007 = 1337
1008 = 1309
1009 = 1310
1010 = 1296
1011 = 1311
1012 = 1294
1013 = 1323
1014 = 1308
1015 = 1318
1016 = 1317
1017 = 1336
1018 = 1328
1019 = 1298
1020 = 1333
1021 = 1297
1022 = 1320
1023 = 1319
1024 = 1340
1025 = 1305
1026 = 1292
1027 = 1330
1028 = 1322
1029 = 1303
1030 = 1304
1031 = 1326
1032 = 1379
1033 = 1362
1034 = 1360
1035 = 1361
1036 = 1354
1037 = 1382
1038 = 1341
1039 = 1377

1040 = 1302
1041 = 1359
1042/1 = 1355
1042/2 = 1371
1043 = 1355
1044 = 1331
1045 = 1368
1046 = 1380
1047 = 1373
1048 = 1335
1049 = 1376
1050 = 1367
1051 = 1358
1052 = 1369
1053 = 1381
1054 = 1342
1055 = 1312
1056 = 1378
1057 = 1327
1058 = 1273
1059 = 1370
1060 = 1375
1061 = 1306
1062 = 1286
1063 = 1350
1064 = 1307
1065 = 1295
1066 = 1329
1067 = 1351
1068 = 1316
1070 = 1287
1071 = 1288
1072 = 1387
1073 = 1389
1074 = 1391
1075 = 1325
1076 = 1334
1077 = 1392
1078 = 1324

1079 = 1277
1080 = 1393
1081 = 1280
1083 = 1276
1084 = 1363
1085 = 1365
1086 = 1374
1087 = 953
1088 = 1394
1089 = 1281
1090 = 1278
1091 = 1390
1092 = 1339
1093/1 = 1313
1093/2 = 1314
1093/3 = 1315
1093/4 = 1353
1093/5 = 1356
1093/6 = 1357
1093/7 = 1366
1093/8 = 1383
1093/9 = 526
1094 = 1494
1095 = 1329
1096 = 1384
1097 = 1364
1098 = 1388
1099/1 = 1396
1099/2 = 1397
1099/3 = 1398
1099/4 = 1453
1099/5 = 1454
1099/6 = 1458
1099/7 = 214
1099/8 = 232
1099/9 = 233
1099/10 = 234
1099/11 = 244
1099/12 = 259

1099/13 = 261
1099/14 = 276
1099/15 = 277
1099/16 = 278
1099/17 = 284
1099/18 = 335
1099/19 = 336
1099/20 = 345
1099/21 = 364
1099/22 = 367
1099/23 = 372
1099/24 = 389
1099/25 = 390
1099/26 = 391
1099/27 = 394
1100/1 = 184
1100/2 = 1503
1100/3 = 179
1100/4 = 183
1100/5 = 186
1100/6 = 194
1101 = 946
1102 = 1136
1103 = 714
1104/1 = 1282
1104/2 = 811
1104/3 = 812
1104/4 = 813
1104/5 = 814
1105 = 883
1106/1 = 272
1106/2 = 955
1107 = 686
1108 = 684
1109 = 931
1110 = 697
1111 = 698
1113 = 984
1114 = 699

1115 = 712
1116 = 716
1118 = 720
1120 = 725
1121 = 723
1122 = 726
1123 = 742
1124 = 750
1125 = 756
1126 = 763
1127 = 732
1128 = 746
1129 = 768
1130 = 769
1131 = 773
1132 = 32
1133 = 770
1134 = 774
1135 = 764
1136 = 708
1137 = 707
1138 = 776
1139 = 331
1140 = 780
1141 = 791
1142 = 792
1143 = 1496
1144/1 = 783
1144/2 = 886
1145 = 783
1146 = 785
1147 = 786
1148 = 787
1149 = 783
1151 = 804
1152 = 827
1153 = 1465
1154 = 805
1155 = 834
1156 = 835
1157 = 836
1158 = 837
1159 = 838
1160 = 801
1161 = 802
1162 = 798
1163 = 799
1164 = 800
1165 = 810
1166 = 874
1167 = 876
1168 = 877
1169 = 878
1170 = 872
1171 = 847
1172 = 467
1173 = 841
1174 = 848
1175 = 884
1176 = 888
1177 = 889
1178 = 890
1179 = 892
1180 = 1291
1181 = 887
1182 = 917
1183 = 846
1184 = 929
1185 = 927
1186 = 717
1187 = 932
1188 = 936
1189 = 711
1190 = 934
1191 = 937
1193 = 933
1195 = 939
1196 = 955
1197 = 956
1198 = 957
1199 = 958
1200 = 958
1201 = 760
1202 = 955
1203 = 964
1204 = 962
1205 = 967
1206 = 965
1207 = 1167
1208 = 701
1209 = 963
1210 = 971
1211 = 972
1212 = 970
1213 = 973
1214 = 1174
1215 = 414
1216 = 990
1217 = 977
1218 = 974
1219 = 989
1220 = 979
1221 = 983
1222 = 1000
1223 = 1002
1224 = 994
1225 = 1004
1226 = 995
1227 = 1005
1228 = 1012
1229 = 1020
1230 = 1019
1231 = 998
1232 = 1006
1233 = 1014
1234 = 1013
1235 = 1176
1236 = 999
1237 = 1021
1238 = 1026
1239 = 1024
1240 = 1025
1241 = 1027
1243 = 1030
1244 = 1028
1245 = 1055
1246 = 1051
1247 = 1056
1248 = 1034
1249 = 1035
1250 = 1036
1251 = 1037
1252 = 1318
1253 = 749
1254 = 1041
1255 = 1050
1256/1 = 25
1256/2 = 27
1257 = 1008
1258 = 1033
1259 = 1049
1260 = 1047
1261 = 1046
1262 = 1058
1263 = 1069
1264 = 1070
1265 = 1059
1266 = 1075
1267 = 849
1268 = 777
1269 = 1061
1270 = 706
1271 = 744
1272 = 991
1273/1 = 775
1273/2 = 860
1275/1 = 1164
1275/2 = 1165
1276 = 895
1277 = 896
1278 = 897
1279 = 898
1280 = 899
1281 = 900
1282 = 901
1283 = 902
1284 = 907
1285 = 908
1286 = 909
1287 = 910
1288 = 911
1289 = 912
1290 = 914
1291 = 700
1292 = 873
1293/1 = 1308
1293/2 = 842
1295 = 1372
1296 = 1386
1297 = 766
1298 = 1038
1299 = 781
1300 = 440
1301 = 1084
1302/1 = 1078
1302/2 = 1079
1302/3 = 1082
1303 = 461
1304 = 1096
1305 = 731
1306 = 923
1307 = 431
1308 = 490
1309/1 = 441
1309/2 = 580
1310 = 891
1311 = 528
1312 = 477
1313 = 594
1314 = 482

1316 = 809
1317 = 773
1318 = 916
1319 = 691
1320 = 519
1322 = 1029
1323 = 915
1324 = 499
1325/1 = 419
1325/2 = 709
1326 = 480
1327 = 903
1328 = 404
1329 = 494
1330 = 475
1331 = 486
1332 = 893
1333 = 738
1334 = 496
1335 = 689
1336 = 492
1337 = 416
1338 = 478
1339 = 493
1340 = 481
1341 = 495
1342 = 739
1343 = 491
1344 = 487
1345 = 483
1346 = 1083
1347 = 1097
1348 = 905
1349 = 497
1350 = 403
1351 = 525
1352 = 1289
1353 = 925
1354 = 575
1355 = 522
1356 = 906
1357 = 1001
1358 = 454
1359 = 462
1360 = 861
1361 = 863
1362 = 867
1363 = 1227
1364 = 702
1365 = 693
1366 = 703
1367 = 660
1369 = 968
1370 = 443
1371 = 512
1372 = 1243
1373 = 761
1374 = 1118
1375 = 992
1376 = 1167
1377 = 1299
1378 = 484
1379 = 414
1380 = 1031
1381/1 = 29
1381/2 = 30
1381/3 = 31
1382 = 35
1383 = 673
1384 = 677
1385 = 679
1386 = 675
1387 = 681
1388 = 489
1389 = 696
1390 = 459
1391 = 969
1392 = 1086
1393 = 459
1394 = 472
1395 = 1098
1396 = 1352
1397 = 755
1398 = 904
1399 = 275
1400/1 = 1441
1400/2 = 1447
1401 = 235
1402 = 690
1403 = 248
1404 = 1160
1405 = 754
1406 = 189
1407/1 = 2
1407/2 = 52
1408 = 54
1409 = 467
1410 = 600
1411 = 288
1412 = 1268
1413 = 1448
1414 = 722
1415/1 = 350
1415/2 = 361
1416 = 380
1417 = 371
1418 = 470
1419 = 546
1420 = 266
1421 = 190
1422 = 192
1423 = 993
1424/1 = 203
1424/2 = 204
1424/3 = 212
1424/4 = 223
1425/1 = 247
1425/2 = 295
1425/3 = 357
1426 = 355
1427/1 = 382
1427/2 = 392
1427/3 = 393
1428 = 1419
1429/1 = 356
1429/2 = 381
1430 = 371
1431/1 = 1467
1431/2 = 1471
1431/3 = 197
1431/4 = 362
1432 = 237
1433 = 304
1434 = 1441
1435 = 1472
1436 = 1018
1437 = 1120
1438 = 319
1439 = 1470
1440 = 312
1441 = 1469
1442 = 242
1443 = 1420
1444 = 293
1445 = 287
1446 = 399
1447 = 378
1448 = 1464
1449 = 1468
1450 = 1269
1451 = 767
1452 = 286
1453 = 1284
1454 = 256
1455 = 401
1456 = 1209
1457 = 1211
1458 = 1224
1459 = 1228
1460 = 1490
1461 = 195
1462 = 255
1464 = 408
1465 = 1011
1466 = 3
1467 = 1466
1468 = 875
1469 = 570
1470 = 944
1471/1 = 1
1471/2 = 650
1472 = 574
1473 = 1145
1474 = 1170
1475 = 1208
1476 = 975
1477/1 = 285
1477/2 = 309
1477/3 = 395
1477/4 = 396
1477/5 = 397
1478 = 1504
1479 = 398
1480 = 1462
1481 = 1217
1482 = 1258
1483 = 1213
1484 = 1249
1485 = 1218
1486 = 1219
1487 = 996
1488 = 997
1489 = 1238
1490 = 1207
1491 = 850
1492 = 762
1493 = 851
1494 = 53
1495 = 2
1496 = 796

1497 = 1285
1499 = 1275
1500 = 1279
1501 = 1274
1502 = 1411
1503 = 1412
1504 = 1413
1505 = 1414
1506 = 363
1507 = 1463
1508 = 1421
1509 = 1450
1511 = 388
1512 = 387
1514 = 1452
1515 = 1456
1516 = 289
1517 = 730
1518/1 = 195
1518/2 = 398
1519 = 1444
1520 = 240
1521 = 1290
1523/1 = 1445
1523/2 = 1455
1524 = 368
1525 = 982
1526 = 385
1527 = 921

# Concordance of Call Numbers in Ringelblum II: New Document Numbers to Old Call Numbers

This concordance keys the consecutive new document numbers in the present catalog to the old call numbers for Ring. II, which were in use between 1955 and 2006. In the old call numbers, files that included multiple documents are indicated as follows: II/236/2, II/239/1.

1. II/212
2. II/236/2
3. II/126
4. II/125
5. II/168
6. II/290
7. II/292
8. II/429
9. II/430
10. II/184
11. II/433
12. II/239/1
13. II/304
14. II/431
15. II/370
16. II/432
17. II/434
18. II/482
19. II/478
20. II/399
21. II/397
22. II/323
23. II/143
24. II/144
25. II/190
26. II/294
27. II/265
28. II/383/2
28a. II/13
29. II/240
30. II/247
31. II/253
32. II/254
33. II/235
34. II/255
35. II/293/5
36. II/216
37. II/248
38. II/249
39. II/250
40. II/256
41. II/260
42. II/134
43. II/139
44. II/140
45. II/138
46. II/127
47. II/29
48. II/135
49. II/136
50. II/152
51. II/141
52. II/186
53. II/189
54. II/187
55. II/266
56. II/262
57. II/263
58. II/191, II/189
59. II/124
60. II/147
61. II/148
62. II/151
63. II/150
64. II/382
65. II/264
66. II/153
67. II/116
68. II/188
69. II/293/3
70. II/36
71. II/396
72. II/220
73. II/261
74. II/142
75. II/133
76. II/28
77. II/137
78. II/146
79. II/383/4
80. II/383/8
81. II/383/6
82. II/154
83. II/130
84. II/272/2
85. II/271/2
86. II/270/7
87. II/269/2
88. II/275/4
89. II/272/1
90. II/163
91. II/268/4, II/268/5
92. II/269/1
93. II/271/3
94. II/268/1
95. II/271/1
96. II/270/5
97. II/268/2
98. II/223/5
99. II/272/5
100. II/272/3
101. II/270/4
102. II/270/3
103. II/269/4
104. II/269/3
105. II/268/6
106. II/271/4
107. II/268/3
108. II/268/7
109. II/162
110. II/268/8
111. II/270/6
112. II/166
113. II/267
114. II/272/4
115. II/268/9
116. II/293/2
117. II/1
118. II/2
119. II/3
120. II/16
121. II/7
122. II/14
123. II/8
124. II/10
125. II/17
126. II/22
127. II/20
128. II/23
129. II/21
130. II/25
131. II/18
132. II/19
133. II/24
134. II/26
135. II/122
136. II/15
137. II/31
138. II/117
139. II/32
140. II/35
141. II/34/2
142. II/33
143. II/34/1
144. II/90
145. II/30
146. II/99
147. II/37
148. II/91
149. II/84
150. II/38
151. II/39
152. II/40
153. II/41
154. II/98
155. II/66
156. II/58
157. II/42
158. II/43
159. II/44

160. II/59
161. II/105
162. II/45
163. II/60
164. II/46
165. II/61
166. II/92
167. II/47
168. II/67
169. II/48
170. II/74
171. II/93
172. II/94
173. II/95
174. II/63
175. II/56
176. II/96
177. II/62
178. II/75
179. II/64
180. II/71
181. II/65
182. II/82
183. II/97
184. II/108
185. II/50
186. II/88
187. II/49
188. II/77
189. II/69
190. II/70
191. II/68
192. II/85
193. II/87
194. II/185
195. II/79
196. II/78
197. II/72
198. II/89
199. II/86
200. II/73
201. II/55
202. II/76
203. II/112
204. II/123
205. II/160
206. II/217
207. II/218
208. II/251
209. II/165
210. II/106
211. II/181/7
212. II/219/1
213. II/103
214. II/181/6
215. II/181/8
216. II/104
217. II/119
218. II/181/4
219. II/181/3
220. II/181/1
221. II/181/2
222. II/181/5
223. II/101
224. II/100
225. II/102
226. II/121
227. II/159
228. II/110
229. II/111
230. II/51
231. II/54
232. II/52
233. II/53
234. II/109
235. II/367
236. II/177
237. II/27
238. II/293/1
239. II/179
240. II/178
241. II/279
242. II/170
243. II/494
244. II/205, II/207
245. II/209
246. II/237, II/287
247. II/288
248. II/183
249. II/208
250. II/282
251. II/174
252. II/202
253. II/173
254. II/245
255. II/201
256. II/289
257. II/227
258. II/228
259. II/229
260. II/230
261. II/231
262. II/232
263. II/233
264. II/234
265. II/236/1
266. II/107
267. II/129
268. II/214
269. II/259
270. II/206
271. II/284
272. II/197
273. II/203
274. II/200
275. II/180
276. II/161
277. II/131
278. II/149
279. II/222
280. II/221
281. II/155
282. II/156
283. II/167/2
284. II/257
285. II/277
286. II/157
287. II/241
288. II/226
289. II/274/7
290. II/224
291. II/219/2
292. II/219/3
293. II/120
294. II/169
295. II/193
296. II/194
297. II/243
298. II/242
299. II/158
300. II/192
301. II/196
302. II/198
303. II/199
304. II/239/2
305. II/204
306. II/211
307. II/195
308. II/285
309. II/286
310. II/368
311. II/283
312. II/210
313. II/281
314. II/171
315. II/172
316. II/278
317. II/132
318. II/57
319. II/113
320. II/114
321. II/115
322. II/118
323. II/215
324. II/280
325. II/244
326. II/246
327. II/475
328. II/369
329. II/300/2
330. II/225
331. II/312
332. II/275/6
333. II/275/3
334. II/275/5
335. II/167/1
336. II/301
337. II/223/1
338. II/269
339. II/274/5
340. II/274/6
341. II/176
342. II/223/4
343. II/164
344. II/398
345. II/182
346. II/275/2
347. II/303
348. II/291
349. II/80
350. II/83
351. II/305
352. II/306
353. II/307
354. II/223/2
355. II/308
356. II/145
357. II/238
358. II/274/1
359. II/274/2

360. II/274/3
361. II/274/4
362. II/302
363. II/275/8
364. II/310
365. II/309
366. II/270/2
367. II/275/7
368. II/223/3
369. II/275/1
370. II/311
371. II/273/3
372. II/273/6
373. II/273/4
374. II/273/1
375. II/167/3
376. II/128
377. II/273/5
378. II/295
379. II/296
380. II/297
381. II/298
382. II/299
383. II/273/2
384. II/300/1
385. II/488
386. II/293/4
387. II/473
388. II/364
389. II/476
390. II/355
391. II/346
392. II/347
393. II/348
394. II/349
395. II/350
396. II/351
397. II/352
398. II/361
399. II/471
400. II/353
401. II/354
402. II/474
403. II/359
404. II/358
405. II/357
406. II/366
407. II/477
408. II/356
409. II/360
410. II/362
411. II/363
412. II/365
413. II/371
414. II/326
415. II/325
416. II/345
417. II/318
418. II/327
419. II/316/1
420. II/316/2
421. II/317
422. II/329
423. II/338/1
424. II/334
425. II/343
426. II/333
427. II/316/3
428. II/316/4
429. II/315/2
430. II/313
431. II/314
432. II/319
433. II/320
434. II/338/2
435. II/321
436. II/322
437. II/315/1
438. II/324
439. II/328
440. II/330
441. II/331
442. II/335/1
443. II/335/2
444. II/336
445. II/339
446. II/400
447. II/337
448. II/340
449. II/341
450. II/342
451. II/332
452. II/438
453. II/439
454. II/440
455. II/441
456. II/442
457. II/443
458. II/444
459. II/458
460. II/276
461. II/446
462. II/447
463. II/448
464. II/449
465. II/450
466. II/451
467. II/454
468. II/452
469. II/453
470. II/445
471. II/455
472. II/456
473. II/457
474. II/472
475. II/493
476. II/436
477. II/437
478. II/372
479. II/373
480. II/380
481. II/379
482. II/375
483. II/383/1
484. II/384
485. II/376
486. II/374
487. II/377
488. II/378
489. II/383/5
490. II/383/7
491. II/385
492. II/389
493. II/258
494. II/459
495. II/460
496. II/461
497. II/462
498. II/463
499. II/464
500. II/465
501. II/466
502. II/467
503. II/435
504. II/468
505. II/386
506. II/469
507. II/470
508. II/483
509. II/484
510. II/175
511. II/401
512. II/402
513. II/403
514. II/404
515. II/406/1
516. II/406/2
517. II/405
518. II/407
519. II/408
520. II/485
521. II/387
522. II/388
523. II/392
524. II/383/3
525. II/390
526. II/391
527. II/270/1
528. II/419/2
529. II/393
530. II/252
531. II/409
532. II/410
533. II/411/1
534. II/411/2
535. II/412
536. II/413
537. II/414
538. II/415
539. II/416
540. II/417
541. II/418
542. II/419/1
543. II/420
544. II/421
545. II/422
546. II/423
547. II/424, II/425
548. II/426
549. II/427
550. II/428
551. II/381
552. II/394
553. II/395
554. II/479
555. II/480
556. II/481
557. II/411/3
558. II/492

# Concordance of Call Numbers in Ringelblum II: Old Call Numbers to New Document Numbers

This concordance keys the old call numbers, in use between 1955 and 2006, to the new document numbers in the present catalog. In the old call numbers, files that included multiple documents are indicated as follows: II/167/1, II/167/2, II/167/3.

II/1 = 117
II/2 = 118
II/3 = 119
II/7 = 121
II/8 = 123
II/10 = 124
II/13 = 28a
II/14 = 122
II/15 = 136
II/16 = 120
II/17 = 125
II/18 = 131
II/19 = 132
II/20 = 127
II/21 = 129
II/22 = 126
II/23 = 128
II/24 = 133
II/25 = 130
II/26 = 134
II/27 = 237
II/28 = 76
II/29 = 47
II/30 = 145
II/31 = 137
II/32 = 139
II/33 = 142
II/34/1 = 143
II/34/2 = 141
II/35 = 140
II/36 = 70
II/37 = 147
II/38 = 150
II/39 = 151
II/40 = 152
II/41 = 153
II/42 = 157
II/43 = 158
II/44 = 159
II/45 = 162
II/46 = 164
II/47 = 167
II/48 = 169
II/49 = 187
II/50 = 185
II/51 = 230
II/52 = 232
II/53 = 233
II/54 = 231
II/55 = 201
II/56 = 175
II/57 = 318
II/58 = 156
II/59 = 160
II/60 = 163
II/61 = 165
II/62 = 177
II/63 = 174
II/64 = 179
II/65 = 181
II/66 = 155
II/67 = 168
II/68 = 191
II/69 = 189
II/70 = 190
II/71 = 180
II/72 = 197
II/73 = 200
II/74 = 170
II/75 = 178
II/76 = 202
II/77 = 188
II/78 = 196
II/79 = 195
II/80 = 349
II/82 = 182
II/83 = 350
II/84 = 149
II/85 = 192
II/86 = 199
II/87 = 193
II/88 = 186
II/89 = 198
II/90 = 144
II/91 = 148
II/92 = 166
II/93 = 171
II/94 = 172
II/95 = 173
II/96 = 176
II/97 = 183
II/98 = 154
II/99 = 146
II/100 = 224
II/101 = 223
II/102 = 225
II/103 = 213
II/104 = 216
II/105 = 161
II/106 = 210
II/107 = 266
II/108 = 184
II/109 = 234
II/110 = 228
II/111 = 229
II/112 = 203
II/113 = 319
II/114 = 320
II/115 = 321
II/116 = 67
II/117 = 138
II/118 = 322
II/119 = 217
II/120 = 293
II/121 = 226
II/122 = 135
II/123 = 204
II/124 = 59
II/125 = 4
II/126 = 3
II/127 = 46
II/128 = 376
II/129 = 267
II/130 = 83
II/131 = 277
II/132 = 317
II/133 = 75
II/134 = 42
II/135 = 48
II/136 = 49
II/137 = 77
II/138 = 45
II/139 = 43
II/140 = 44
II/141 = 51
II/142 = 74
II/143 = 23
II/144 = 24
II/145 = 356
II/146 = 78
II/147 = 60
II/148 = 61
II/149 = 278
II/150 = 63
II/151 = 62
II/152 = 50
II/153 = 66
II/154 = 82
II/155 = 281
II/156 = 282
II/157 = 286
II/158 = 299
II/159 = 227
II/160 = 205
II/161 = 276
II/162 = 109
II/163 = 90
II/164 = 343
II/165 = 209
II/166 = 112
II/167/1 = 335
II/167/2 = 283
II/167/3 = 375
II/168 = 5
II/169 = 294
II/170 = 242
II/171 = 314
II/172 = 315
II/173 = 253
II/174 = 251
II/175 = 510
II/176 = 341
II/177 = 236
II/178 = 240
II/179 = 239
II/180 = 275
II/181/1 = 220
II/181/2 = 221
II/181/3 = 219
II/181/4 = 218
II/181/5 = 222
II/181/6 = 214
II/181/7 = 211
II/181/8 = 215
II/182 = 345
II/183 = 248
II/184 = 10
II/185 = 194
II/186 = 52
II/187 = 54
II/188 = 68
II/189/1 = 53
II/189/2 = 58
II/190 = 25
II/191 = 58
II/192 = 300
II/193 = 295
II/194 = 296
II/195 = 307
II/196 = 301

II/197 = 272
II/198 = 302
II/199 = 303
II/200 = 274
II/201 = 255
II/202 = 252
II/203 = 273
II/204 = 305
II/205 = 244
II/206 = 270
II/207 = 244
II/208 = 249
II/209 = 245
II/210 = 312
II/211 = 306
II/212 = 1
II/214 = 268
II/215 = 323
II/216 = 36
II/217 = 206
II/218 = 207
II/219/1 = 212
II/219/2 = 291
II/219/3 = 292
II/220 = 72
II/221 = 280
II/222 = 279
II/223/1 = 337
II/223/2 = 354
II/223/3 = 368
II/223/4 = 342
II/223/5 = 98
II/224 = 290
II/225 = 330
II/226 = 288
II/227 = 257
II/228 = 258
II/229 = 259
II/230 = 260
II/231 = 261
II/232 = 262
II/233 = 263
II/234 = 264
II/235 = 33
II/236/1 = 265
II/236/2 = 2
II/237 = 246
II/238 = 357
II/239/1 = 12
II/239/2 = 304
II/240 = 29
II/241 = 287
II/242 = 298
II/243 = 297
II/244 = 325
II/245 = 254
II/246 = 326
II/247 = 30
II/248 = 37
II/249 = 38
II/250 = 39
II/251 = 208
II/252 = 530
II/253 = 31
II/254 = 32
II/255 = 34
II/256 = 40
II/257 = 284
II/258 = 493
II/259 = 269
II/260 = 41
II/261 = 73
II/262 = 56
II/263 = 57
II/264 = 65
II/266 = 55
II/267 = 113
II/268/1 = 94
II/268/2 = 97
II/268/3 = 107
II/268/4 = 91
II/268/5 = 91
II/268/6 = 105
II/268/7 = 108
II/268/8 = 110
II/268/9 = 115
II/269 = 338
II/269/1 = 92
II/269/2 = 87
II/269/3 = 104
II/269/4 = 103
II/270/1 = 527
II/270/2 = 366
II/270/3 = 102
II/270/4 = 101
II/270/5 = 96
II/270/6 = 111
II/270/7 = 86
II/271/1 = 95
II/271/2 = 85
II/271/3 = 93
II/271/4 = 106
II/272/1 = 89
II/272/2 = 84
II/272/3 = 100
II/272/4 = 114
II/272/5 = 99
II/273/1 = 374
II/273/2 = 383
II/273/3 = 371
II/273/4 = 373
II/273/5 = 377
II/273/6 = 372
II/274/1 = 358
II/274/2 = 359
II/274/3 = 360
II/274/4 = 361
II/274/5 = 339
II/274/6 = 340
II/274/7 = 289
II/275/1 = 369
II/275/2 = 346
II/275/3 = 333
II/275/4 = 88
II/275/5 = 334
II/275/6 = 332
II/275/7 = 367
II/275/8 = 363
II/276 = 460
II/277 = 285
II/278 = 316
II/279 = 241
II/280 = 324
II/281 = 313
II/282 = 250
II/283 = 311
II/284 = 271
II/285 = 308
II/286 = 309
II/287 = 246
II/288 = 247
II/289 = 256
II/290 = 6
II/291 = 348
II/292 = 7
II/293/1 = 238
II/293/2 = 116
II/293/3 = 69
II/293/4 = 386
II/293/5 = 35
II/294 = 26
II/295/1 = 27
II/295/2 = 378
II/296 = 379
II/297 = 380
II/298 = 381
II/299 = 382
II/300/1 = 384
II/300/2 = 329
II/301 = 336
II/302 = 362
II/303 = 347
II/304 = 13
II/305 = 351
II/306 = 352
II/307 = 353
II/308 = 355
II/309 = 365
II/310 = 364
II/311 = 370
II/312 = 331
II/313 = 430
II/314 = 431
II/315/1 = 437
II/315/2 = 429
II/316/1 = 419
II/316/2 = 420
II/316/3 = 427
II/316/4 = 428
II/317 = 421
II/318 = 417
II/319 = 432
II/320 = 433
II/321 = 435
II/322 = 436
II/323 = 22
II/324 = 438
II/325 = 415
II/326 = 414
II/327 = 418
II/328 = 439
II/329 = 422
II/330 = 440
II/331 = 441
II/332 = 451
II/333 = 426
II/334 = 424
II/335/1 = 442
II/335/2 = 443
II/336 = 444
II/337 = 447
II/338/1 = 423
II/338/2 = 434
II/339 = 445
II/340 = 448
II/341 = 449
II/342 = 450
II/343 = 425
II/345 = 416
II/346 = 391
II/347 = 392
II/348 = 393
II/349 = 394
II/350 = 395
II/351 = 396
II/352 = 397
II/353 = 400
II/354 = 401
II/355 = 390
II/356 = 408
II/357 = 405
II/358 = 404
II/359 = 403
II/360 = 409
II/361 = 398
II/362 = 410
II/363 = 411
II/364 = 388
II/365 = 412
II/366 = 406
II/367 = 235
II/368 = 310
II/369 = 328
II/370 = 15
II/371 = 413
II/372 = 478
II/373 = 479
II/374 = 486
II/375 = 482
II/376 = 485
II/377 = 487
II/378 = 488
II/379 = 481
II/380 = 480
II/381 = 551

II/382 = 64
II/383/1 = 483
II/383/2 = 28
II/383/3 = 524
II/383/4 = 79
II/383/5 = 489
II/383/6 = 81
II/383/7 = 490
II/383/8 = 80
II/384 = 484
II/385 = 491
II/386 = 505
II/387 = 521
II/388 = 522
II/389 = 492
II/390 = 525
II/391 = 526
II/392 = 523
II/393 = 529
II/394 = 552
II/395 = 553
II/396 = 71
II/397 = 21
II/398 = 344
II/399 = 20
II/400 = 446
II/401 = 511
II/402 = 512
II/403 = 513
II/404 = 514
II/405 = 517
II/406/1 = 515
II/406/2 = 516
II/407 = 518
II/408 = 519
II/409 = 531
II/410 = 532
II/411/1 = 533
II/411/2 = 534
II/411/3 = 557
II/412 = 535
II/413 = 536
II/414 = 537
II/415 = 538
II/416 = 539
II/417 = 540
II/418 = 541
II/419/1 = 542
II/419/2 = 528
II/420 = 543
II/421 = 544
II/422 = 545
II/423 = 546
II/424 = 547
II/425 = 547
II/426 = 548
II/427 = 549
II/428 = 550
II/429 = 8
II/430 = 9
II/431 = 14
II/432 = 16
II/433 = 11
II/434 = 17
II/435 = 503
II/436 = 476
II/437 = 477
II/438 = 452
II/439 = 453
II/440 = 454
II/441 = 455
II/442 = 456
II/443 = 457
II/444 = 458
II/445 = 470
II/446 = 461
II/447 = 462
II/448 = 463
II/449 = 464
II/450 = 465
II/451 = 466
II/452 = 468
II/453 = 469
II/454 = 467
II/455 = 471
II/456 = 472
II/457 = 473
II/458 = 459
II/459 = 494
II/460 = 495
II/461 = 496
II/462 = 497
II/463 = 498
II/464 = 499
II/465 = 500
II/466 = 501
II/467 = 502
II/468 = 504
II/469 = 506
II/470 = 507
II/471 = 399
II/472 = 474
II/473 = 387
II/474 = 402
II/475 = 327
II/476 = 389
II/477 = 407
II/478 = 19
II/479 = 554
II/480 = 555
II/481 = 556
II/482 = 18
II/483 = 508
II/484 = 509
II/485 = 520
II/488 = 385
II/492 = 558
II/493 = 475
II/494 = 243

# List of Superseded Archival Units

This list includes archival units with Old Call Numbers from which some or all documents were transferred to other Old Call Numbers before the start of work on the new catalog numbering system.

**Ring. I**

I/4 => I/3
I/152 => I/150
I/239 => I/150
I/311 => I/228 and I/241
I/312 => I/277
I/330 => I/786
I/348 => I/171 and I/322
I/383 => I/440
I/414 => I/397
I/625 => I/1136
I/745 => I/740
I/758 => I/759
I/771 => I/742
I/793 => I/536
I/798 => I/440
I/800 => I/533
I/831 => I/479
I/895 => I/811
I/904 => I/903
I/1049 => I/1033
I/1074 => I/1071
I/1179 => I/1178
I/1191 => I/1080

**Ring. II**

II/4 => II/1
II/5 => II/1
II/6 => II/2
II/9 => II/2
II/11 => II/2
II/12 => II/3
II/81 => II/80
II/213 => II/239
II/486 => I/33
II/487 => I/35

# Index of Names Ringelblum I

The Name Index is organized alphabetically according to the Polish alphabet, which differs somewhat from English. The Name Index includes an estimated 70 percent of names appearing in the Oyneg Shabes–Ringelblum Archive. References are to the former document call numbers. The appropriate entry in the present new catalog can be found by consulting the concordance of old and new call numbers. Thus, Ring. I/450 is described in entry no. 866.

**Polish alphabet:**

A Ą B C Ć D E Ę F G H I J K L Ł M N O Ó P R S Ś T U V W X Y Z Ź Ż

a ą b c ć d e ę f g h i j k l ł m n o ó p r s ś t u v w x y z ź ż

# Index of Names Ringelblum II

The Index of Names is organized alphabetically according to the Polish alphabet, which differs somewhat from English. The Name Index includes an estimated 70 percent of names appearing in the Oyneg Shabes–Ringelblum Archive. References are to the former document call numbers. The appropriate entry in the present new catalog can be found by consulting the concordance of old and new call numbers. Thus, Ring. I/450 is described in entry no. 866.

**Polish alphabet:**

A Ą B C Ć D E Ę F G H I J K L Ł M N O Ó P R S Ś T U V W X Y Z Ź Ż

a ą b c ć d e ę f g h i j k l ł m n o ó p r s ś t u v w x y z ź ż

# Index of Places Ringelblum I

The Index of Places for Ringelblum I is organized alphabetically according to the Polish alphabet. References are to the Old Call Numbers, which were in use between 1955 and 2006. The appropriate entry in the present catalog can be found by consulting the Concordance of Old and Oldest Call Numbers to New Document Numbers for Ringelblum I. Thus, for example, a reference to Brussels, identified as located in Ring. I/599/103 in the Index of Places, can be found in Ring. I Document No. 95.

**Polish alphabet:**

A Ą B C Ć D E Ę F G H I J K L Ł M N O Ó P R S Ś T U V W X Y Z Ź Ż

a ą b c ć d e ę f g h i j k l ł m n o ó p r s ś t u v w x y z ź ż



1. The abbreviation "k." here means "in the vicinity of."

# Index of Places Ringelblum II

The Index of Places for Ringelblum II is organized alphabetically according to the Polish alphabet. References are to the Old Call Numbers, which were in use between 1955 and 2006. The appropriate entry in the present catalog can be found by consulting the Concordance of Old Call Numbers to New Document Numbers for Ringelblum II. Thus, for example, a reference to Augsburg, identified as located in Ring. II/269/1 in the Index of Places, can be found in Ring. II Document No. 92.

**Polish alphabet:**

A Ą B C Ć D E Ę F G H I J K L Ł M N O Ó P R S Ś T U V W X Y Z Ź Ż

a ą b c ć d e ę f g h i j k l ł m n o ó p r s ś t u v w x y z ź ż



1. The abbreviation "k." here means "in the vicinity of."

**Robert Moses Shapiro**
is Associate Professor of Judaic Studies, Brooklyn College, City University of New York. He is translator and editor of *Łódź Ghetto: A History* by Isaiah Trunk (Indiana University Press in association with the United States Holocaust Memorial Museum, 2006).

**Tadeusz Epsztein,**
a Polish historian, is an associate of the Institute of History of the Polish Academy of Sciences and the Emanuel Ringelblum Jewish Historical Institute in Warsaw.

**Samuel D. Kassow,**
Charles Northam Professor of History at Trinity College, is author of *Who Will Write Our History? Emanuel Ringelblum, the Warsaw Ghetto, and the Oyneg Shabes Archive* (Indiana University Press, 2007).

www.ingramcontent.com/pod-product-compliance
Lightning Source LLC
LaVergne TN
LVHW070406060826
844660LV00009B/301
* 9 7 8 0 2 5 3 3 5 3 2 7 6 *